Expert One-on-One™ Oracle

Thomas Kyte

apress™

Expert One-on-One™ Oracle

ISBN (pbk): 1-59059-243-3

Printed and bound in Canada 5678910

Distributed to the book trade in the United States by Springer-Verlag New York, Inc., 175 Fifth Avenue, New York, NY, 10010 and outside the United States by Springer-Verlag GmbH & Co. KG, Tiergartenstr. 17, 69112 Heidelberg, Germany.

In the United States: phone 1-800-SPRINGER, email orders@springer-ny.com, or visit http://www.springer-ny.com. Outside the United States: fax +49 6221 345229, email orders@springer.de, or visit http://www.springer.de.

For information on translations, please contact Apress directly at 2560 Ninth Street, Suite 219, Berkeley, CA 94710. Phone 510-549-5930, fax 510-549-5939, email info@apress.com, or visit http://www.apress.com.

The source code for this book is available to readers at http://www.apress.com in the Downloads section.

Credits

About the Author

I am Tom Kyte. I have been working for Oracle since version 7.0.9 (that's 1993 for people who don't mark time by Oracle versions). However, I've been working *with* Oracle since about version 5.1.5c ($99 single user version for DOS on 360 KB floppy disks). Before coming to work at Oracle, I worked for more than six years as a systems integrator, building large scale, heterogeneous databases and applications, mostly for military and government customers. These days, I spend a great deal of my time working with the Oracle database and, more specifically, helping people who are using the Oracle database. I work directly with customers, either in specifying and building their systems or, more frequently, helping them rebuild or tune them ('tuning' frequently being a synonym for rebuilding). In addition, I am the Tom behind 'AskTom' in Oracle Magazine, answering people's questions about the Oracle database and tools. On a typical day I receive and answer 30 to 40 questions at http://asktom.oracle.com. Every two months, I publish a 'best of' in the magazine (all of the questions asked are available on the Web – stored in an Oracle database of course). Basically, I spend a lot of my time helping people be successful with the Oracle database. Oh yes, in my spare time, I build applications and develop software within Oracle Corporation itself.

This book is a reflection of what I do everyday. The material within, covers topics and questions that I see people struggling with every day. These issues are covered from a perspective of 'When *I* use this, *I* do it this way'. It is the culmination of many years experience of using the product, in a myriad of situations.

Acknowledgments

I would like to thank many people for helping me complete this book. At Oracle, I work with the best and brightest people I have ever known, and they all have contributed in one way or another. Specifically, I would like to thank Joel Kallman for his help in developing the interMedia section of this book. When working on 'AskTom', I frequently go to Joel for help in this area – Joel is 'the man', when it comes to interMedia and related technologies. I would also like to thank David Knox for his help in developing the SSL-based examples in the UTL_HTTP section. Without his diligence and willingness to help me figure it all out, this section would not exist. Lastly, I would like to thank everyone I work with for their support during this book-writing ordeal. It took a lot more time and energy than I ever imagined, and I appreciate their flexibility in that regard. In particular, I would like to thank Tim Hoechst and Mike Hichwa, whom I've worked with and known for almost 10 years now – their constant questioning and pushing helped me to discover things that I would never have even thought of investigating on my own.

I would also like to acknowledge the people who use the Oracle software and ask so many good questions. Without them, I would never even have thought of writing this book. Much of what is found here is a direct result of someone asking me 'how' or 'why,' at one time or another.

Lastly, but most importantly, I would like to acknowledge the unceasing support I've received from my family. You know you must be important to someone when you hear 'but Dad, why are you still writing that book?' for about the hundredth time. Without the continual support of my wife Lori, son Alan, and daughter Megan I don't see how I could have finished this.

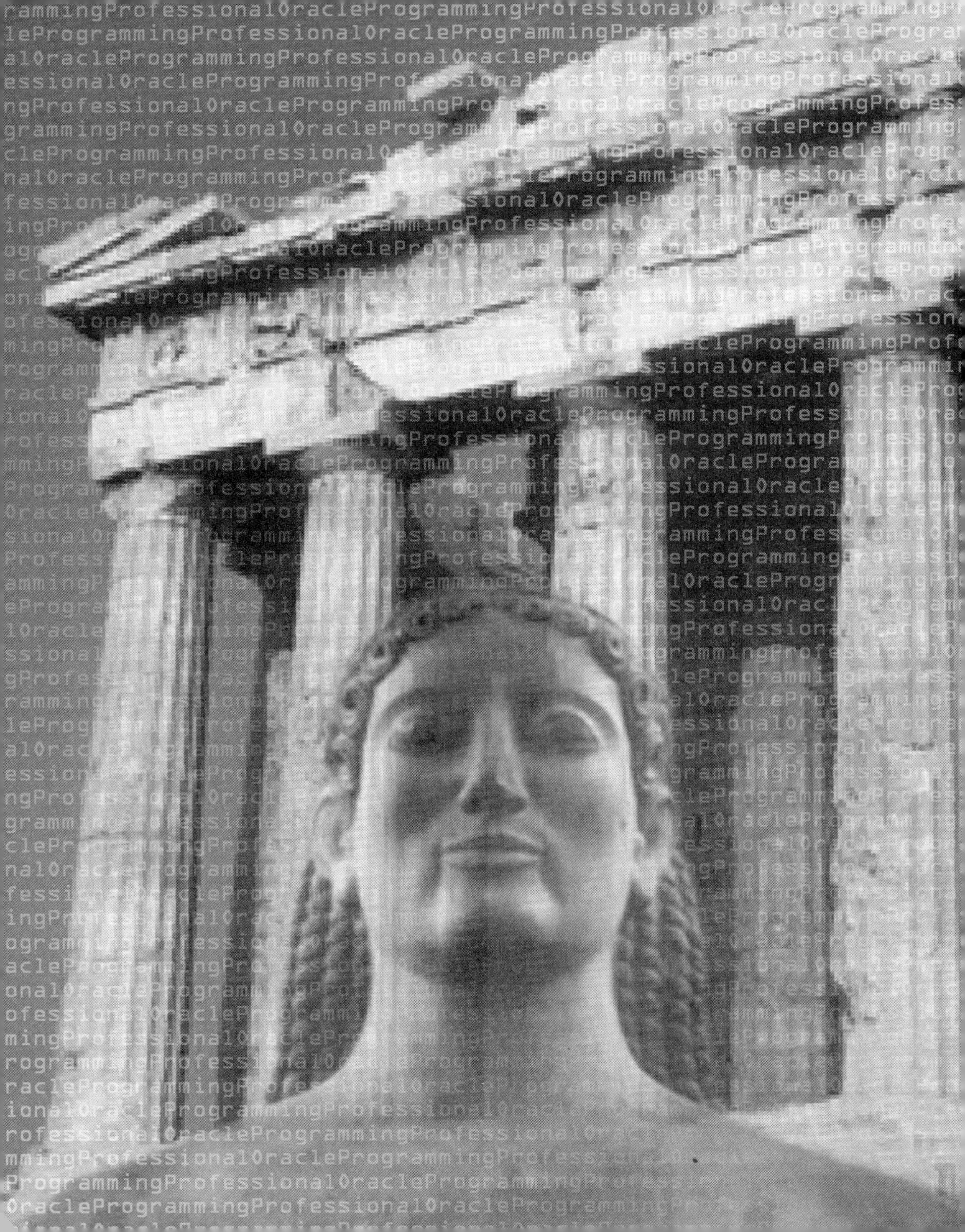

Table of Contents

Table of Contents

Table of Contents

Table of Contents

Table of Contents

Table of Contents

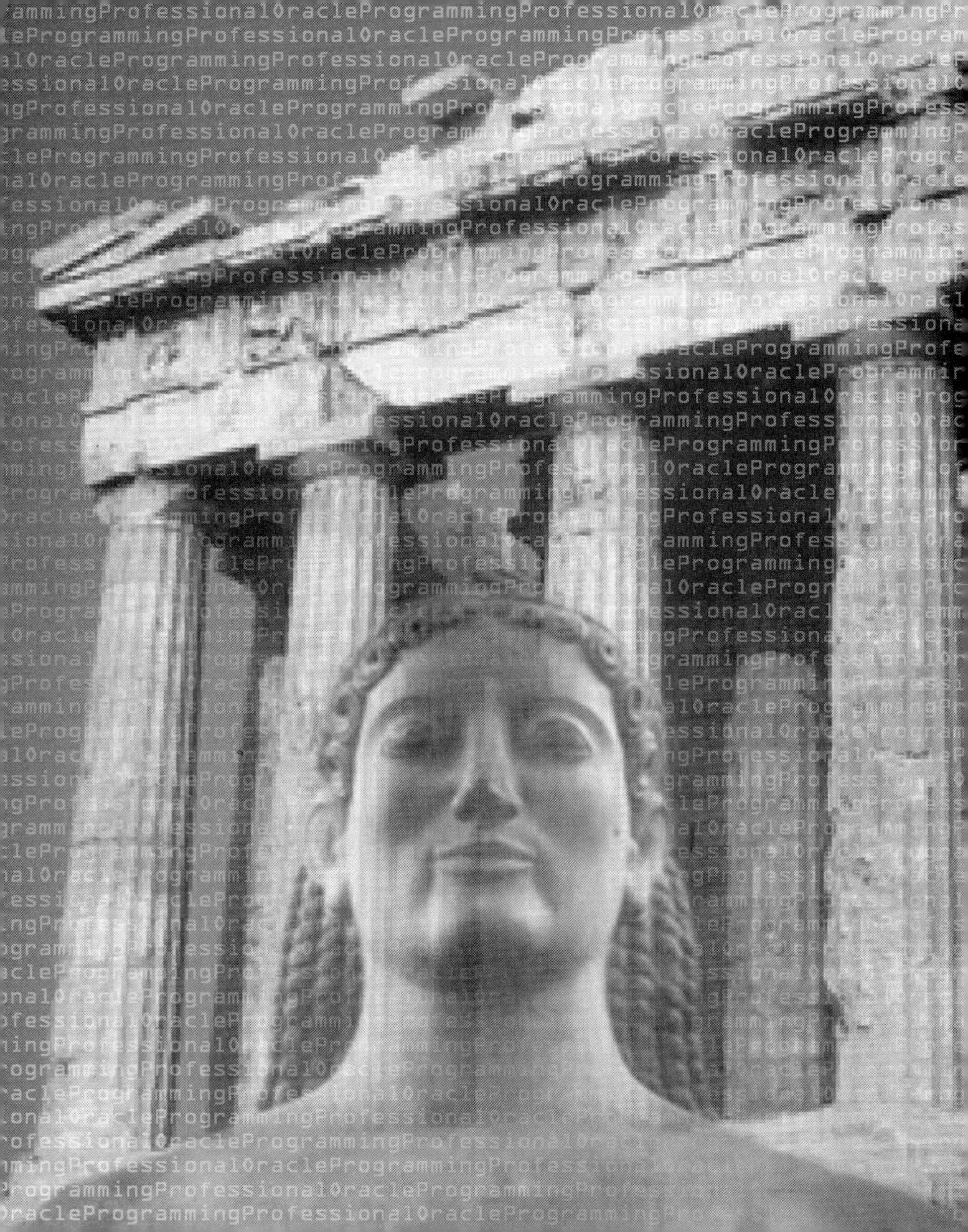

Introduction

The inspiration for the material contained in this book comes from my experiences developing Oracle software and working with fellow Oracle developers, helping them build reliable and robust applications based on the Oracle database. The book is basically a reflection of what I do everyday and of the issues I see people encountering each and every day.

I covered what I felt was most relevant – namely the Oracle database and its architecture. I could have written a similarly-titled book explaining how to develop an application using a specific language and architecture – for example, one using Java Server Pages that speak to Enterprise Java Beans, that use JDBC to communicate with Oracle. However, at the end of the day, you really do need to understand the topics covered here in order to build such an application successfully. This book deals with what I believe needs to be universally known to develop successfully with Oracle, whether you are a Visual Basic programmer using ODBC, a Java programmer using EJBs and JDBC, or a Perl programmer using DBI Perl. This book does not promote any specific application architecture; it does not compare 3-tier to client-server. Rather, it covers what the database can do and what you must understand about the way it works. Since the database is at the heart of any application architecture, the book should have a broad audience.

What This Book Is About

One of the problems with having plenty of development options is in trying to figure out which one might be the best choice for your particular needs. Everyone wants as much flexibility as possible (as many choices as they can possibly have) but they also want things to be very cut and dry; in other words, easy. Oracle presents the developer with almost unlimited choice. No one ever says 'you can't do that in Oracle'– they say 'how many different ways would you like to do that in Oracle?' I hope that this book will help you make the correct choice.

It is a book for those people who appreciate the choice but would also like some guidelines and practical implementation details on Oracle features and functions. For example, Oracle has a really neat feature called the **virtual private database**. Oracle documentation tells you how to use this feature and what it does. Oracle documentation does not, however, tell you *when* you should use this feature and, perhaps even more importantly, *when you should not* use this feature. It does not always tell you the implementation details of this feature, and if you're not aware of them, this can really come back to haunt you (I'm not referring to bugs, but really the way it is supposed to work and what the feature was really designed to do).

Who Should Use This Book?

The target audience for this book is anyone who develops applications with Oracle as the database backend. It is a book for professional Oracle developers who need to know how to get things done in the database. The practical nature of the book means that many sections should also be very interesting to the DBA. Most of the examples in the book use SQL*PLUS to demonstrate the key features, so you won't find out how to develop a really cool GUI – but you will find out how the Oracle database works, what its key features can do and when they should (and should not) be used.

It is a book for anyone who wants to get more out of Oracle with less work. It is for anyone who wants to see new ways to use existing features. It is for anyone who wants to see how these features can be applied in the real world (not just examples of how to use the feature but why the feature is relevant in the first place). Another category of people that would find this book of interest would be the technical manager in charge of the developers who work on Oracle projects. In some respects, it is just as important that they understand why knowing the database is crucial to success. This book can provide ammunition for the manager who would like to get their personnel trained in the correct technologies, or in ensuring that they already know what they need to know.

In order to get the most out of this book, the reader should have:

- ❑ **Knowledge of SQL.** You don't have to be the best SQL coder ever, but a good working knowledge would help.
- ❑ **An understanding of PL/SQL.** This is not a pre-requisite but will help you to 'absorb' the examples. This book will not, for example, teach you how to program a FOR loop or declare a record type – the Oracle documentation and numerous books cover this well. However, that's not to say that you won't learn a lot about PL/SQL by reading this book. You will. You'll become very intimate with many features of PL/SQL and you'll see new ways to do things, become aware of packages/features that perhaps you did not know existed.
- ❑ **Exposure to some 3GL language such as C or Java.** I believe that anyone who can read and write code in a 3GL language will be able to successfully read and understand the examples in this book.
- ❑ **Familiarity with the Oracle Server Concepts Manual.**

A few words on that last point: due to its vast size, many people find the Oracle documentation set to be somewhat intimidating. If you are just starting out or haven't read any of it as yet, I can tell you that the *Oracle8i Concepts* manual is exactly the right place to start. It is about 800 pages long and touches on many of the major Oracle concepts that you need to know about. It may not give you each, and every technical detail (this is what the other 10,000 to 20,000 pages of documentation are for) but it will educate you on all of the important concepts. This manual touches the following topics (to name a few):

- ❑ The structures in the database, how data is organized and stored.
- ❑ Distributed processing.
- ❑ Oracle's memory architecture.
- ❑ Oracle's process architecture.
- ❑ Schema objects you will be using (tables, indexes, clusters, and so on).
- ❑ Built-in data types and user-defined data types.
- ❑ SQL-stored procedures.
- ❑ How transactions work.
- ❑ The optimizer.
- ❑ Data integrity.
- ❑ Concurrency control.

I will come back to these topics myself time and time again. These are the fundamentals – without knowledge of them, your Oracle applications will be prone to failure. I encourage you to read through the manual and get an understanding of some of these topics.

How This Book Is Structured

To help you use this book, it is organized into six discrete sections (described below). These are not rigid divisions, but they will help you navigate quickly to the area you need most. This book has 23 chapters and each is like a 'mini-book'– a virtually standalone component. Occasionally, I refer to examples or features in other chapters (the *Security* section, in particular, relies a little more on examples and concepts that are built up over several chapters) but you could pretty much pick a chapter out of the book and read it standalone. You will not have to read Chapter 10 to understand or make use of Chapter 14, for example.

The format and style of each chapter is virtually identical:

❑ An introduction to the feature or capability.

❑ Why you might want to use it (or not). I outline the times you would consider using this feature and when you would not want to use it.

❑ How to use this feature. Not just a copy of the SQL reference here but rather step by step – here is what you need, here is what you have to do, these are the switches you need to go through to get started. Things covered in this section will be:

How to implement it

Examples, examples, and examples

Debugging this feature

Caveats of using this feature

Handling errors (proactively)

❑ A summary to bring it all together.

There will be lots of examples, and lots of code, all of which will be available for download at http://www.apress.com. Following is a detailed breakdown of the content of each section:

Understanding the Database

❑ **Chapter 1, Developing Successful Oracle Applications**. This chapter sets out my essential approach to database programming. All databases are *not* created equal and in order to develop database-driven applications successfully and on time, you need to understand exactly *what* your particular database can do and *how* it does it. If you do not know what your database can do, you run the risk of continually 're-inventing the wheel' – developing functionality that the database already provides. If you do not know how your database works you are likely to develop applications that perform poorly and do not behave in a predictable manner.

The chapter takes an empirical look at some applications where a lack of basic understanding of the database has lead to project failure. With this example-driven approach, the chapter discusses the basic features and functions of the database that you, the developer, need to understand. The bottom line is that you cannot afford to treat the database as a black box that will simply 'churn out the answers' and take care of scalability and performance by itself.

❏ **Chapter 2, Architecture**. The Oracle database is a highly complex tool. Every time you connect to a database or issue an UPDATE command, a whole host of processes occur in the background to make sure that you're application runs smoothly and that data integrity is maintained. For example, the database ensures that it has enough information to restore the data to its original state should it need to. It will cache program data and automatically re-use it where appropriate. And so on. Most of the time all of this is occurs transparently (to the developer, at least) but when problems occur, half the battle is knowing where to look to fix them.

This chapter covers the three major components of the Oracle architecture – its memory structures (specifically, the System Global Area), its physical processes, and its set of files (parameter files, redo log files...). Understanding the Oracle architecture is fundamental to understanding the unique way in which Oracle implements certain features and how this will affect your application.

❏ **Chapter 3, Locking and Concurrency**. Different databases have different ways of doing things (what works well in SQL Server may not work as well in Oracle) and understanding how Oracle implements locking and concurrency control is absolutely vital to the success of your application.

This chapter discussed Oracle's basic approach to these issues, the types of locks that can be applied (DML, DDL, latches...) and the problems that can arise if locking is not implemented carefully (deadlocking, blocking and escalation). The concurrency control section discusses the functions provided by Oracle that allow us to control how users can access and modify the database.

❏ **Chapter 4, Transactions**. Transactions are a fundamental feature of all databases – they are part of what distinguishes a database from a file system. And yet, they are often misunderstood and many developers do not even know that they are accidentally not using them. This chapter examines how transactions should be used in Oracle and also exposes some 'bad habits' that have been picked up when developing with other databases. In particular, we look at the implications of atomicity and how it affects statements in Oracle. We then move on to discuss transaction control statements (COMMIT, SAVEPOINT, ROLLBACK), integrity constraints and distributed transactions (the two-phase commit). Finally, we look at some real world issues surrounding use of transactions – how they are logged, and the role of redo and undo.

Database Structures and Utilities

❏ **Chapter 5, Redo and Rollback**. It can be said that the developer does not need to understand the detail of redo and rollback as much as the DBA, but developers do need to know the roles they play in the database. After first defining redo, we examine what exactly a COMMIT does. We also consider issues such as how much redo is being generated, turning off logging and also analyzing redo.

In the rollback section of the chapter we first look what generates the most and least undo, before looking at the set transaction SQL statement. This is generally used to pick a large rollback section for some very large operation. Then we focus on the infamous 'ORA-01555 snapshot too old' error, looking at causes and solutions.

❏ **Chapter 6, Tables**. Oracle now supports numerous types of table. This chapter looks at each different type – heap organized (the default, 'normal' table), index organized, index clustered, hash clustered, nested, temporary, and object – and discusses when, how, and why you should use them. Most of time the heap-organized table is sufficient, but you should be able to recognize when one of the other types might be more appropriate.

❏ **Chapter 7, Indexes**. Indexes are a crucial aspect of your application design. Correct implementation requires an in-depth knowledge of the data, how it is distributed, how it will be used. Too often, indexes are treated as an afterthought in application development, and performance suffers as a consequence.

This chapter we look in detail at the different types of indexes, including B*Tree, bitmap, function-based, and application domain indexes, and discuss where they should and should not be used. We'll also answer some of those common queries in the *Frequently Answered Questions* section, such as 'Do indexes work on views?' and 'Why isn't my index getting used?'

❑ **Chapter 8, Import and Export**. Import and export are two of the oldest tools supplied with Oracle, used to extract tables, schemas or entire database definitions from one Oracle instance to be imported into another instance or schema, yet many developers do not how to use them properly. We cover topics such as large exports, sub-setting and transporting data, and using them as backup or reorganization tools. The chapter finishes by highlighting some of the potential pitfalls and problems in the use of these tools.

❑ **Chapter 9, Data Loading**. This chapter focuses on SQLLDR and covers the various ways in which we can use this tool to load and modify data in the database. Issues covered include loading delimited data, updating existing rows and inserting new ones, unloading data, and how to call SQLLDR from a stored procedure. Again, SQLLDR it is a well-established and crucial tool but is the source of many questions with regard to its practical use.

Performance

❑ **Chapter 10, Tuning Strategies and Tools**. This is one of my 'specialist topics' and here I detail my approach to tuning Oracle applications and then embark on a highly practical guide to the tools and techniques that I use. The opening section concentrates on application tuning, covering topics such as bind variables and parsing, SQL_TRACE, TIMED_STATISTICS and TKPROF, the DBMS_PROFILER, and the importance of logging in your applications. With the application fully tuned, attention turns to the database and specifically to the StatsPack group of utilities and the V$ tables you will use in tuning efforts.

❑ **Chapter 11, Optimizer Plan Stability**. Developers using Oracle 8i (and later) now have the ability to save a set of 'hints to the server', known as an optimizer plan, detailing how best to execute a specific SQL statement in the database. This has obvious performance benefits and we take a detailed look at how you can generate these outlines and how to manage them.

Advanced SQL Features

❑ **Chapter 12, Analytic Functions**. Certain questions are asked of the database very regularly, but the queries that can answer them are difficult to write in straight SQL (and will not always perform quickly, anyway). Oracle 8.1.6 introduced analytic functions. These functions add extensions to the SQL language that make such queries easier to code, and dramatically increase performance over the equivalent straight SQL query. This chapter deals with the way in which analytical functions work, looking at the full syntax (including the function, partition and windowing clauses) and then gives full, practical examples of how these functions can be used.

❑ **Chapter 13, Materialized Views**. Certain 'aggregate' queries must process potentially terabytes of data to produce an answer. The performance implications are clear – especially if it is a common query, meaning that a vast amount of data has to be processed each and every time the question is asked. With this feature, we simply do some of the work beforehand – we summarize the data needed to answer a certain query in a materialized view and future queries are directed at this summary data. Furthermore, the database can recognize *similar* queries that make use of this summary data, and automatically re-writes the query to allow them to do so. This chapter discusses how all this works and how to set up materialized views, including use of constraints, dimensions, and the DBMS_OLAP package.

- ❏ **Chapter 14, Partitioning**. Partitioning is designed to facilitate the management of very large tables and indexes, by implementing a 'divide-and-conquer' logic – basically breaking up a table or index into many smaller, and more manageable, pieces. It is an area where the DBA and developer must work together to maximize application availability and performance. This chapter covers both table and index partitioning. We look at partitioning using local indexes (common in data warehouses) and global indexes (common in OLTP systems).

- ❏ **Chapter 15, Autonomous Transactions**. With this feature, we can create a sub-transaction that can commit or rollback changes independently of its parent transaction. We look at the situations when this might be desired, such as when auditing an 'illegal' attempt to modify secure information, to avoid mutating a table or as a way of performing DDL in triggers. The discussion will span issues such as transactional control, scope, ending an autonomous transaction, and savepoints.

- ❏ **Chapter 16, Dynamic SQL**. In this chapter, we compare two methods of using SQL statements in our programs: 'normal' static SQL and dynamic SQL. Dynamic SQL is the SQL executed at run-time, but was not known at compile time. We will look at two methods of using dynamic SQL in your programs, namely with the supplied built-in package DBMS_SQL and native dynamic SQL, a declarative method for use with PL/SQL. There are various reasons why you would choose one over the other, such as whether the bind variables are known at compile time, whether you know the outputs at compile time, and whether a given statement will be executed once, or many times in a session and we will explore these issues in detail.

Extensibility

- ❏ **Chapter 17, interMedia**. This chapter focuses on interMedia Text. Rather than a detailed 'how to use interMedia Text', we will cover what it is and what it provides, and the features of the database that enable this functionality. We look at how to search for text, manage a variety of documents, index text from many data sources, and search XML applications. The chapter finishes with a look at some of the caveats of interMedia, including the synchronization of indexes and indexing information outside of the database.

- ❏ **Chapter 18, C-Based External Procedures**. With Oracle 8.0 came the ability to implement procedures in the database server that were written in languages other than PL/SQL– for example, C or Java. These are referred to as *external* procedures. In this chapter, we will cover C-based procedures from an architectural perspective. We see how to configure your server to use these procedures, test the installation, and create an example procedure for passing and manipulating various types of variables. We also examine the LOB to File (LOB_IO) external procedure, which writes the CLOBs, BLOBs, and BFILEs to disk.

- ❏ **Chapter 19, Java Stored Procedures**. With judicious use of small amounts of Java, we can achieve a great deal of useful functionality that is beyond the reach of PL/SQL. In this chapter, we look at practical examples of where this ability is useful – such as when getting a directory listing or running an operating system command. Again, we round off the chapter with some of the errors that you may encounter when you try to use this feature, and some possible solutions.

- ❏ **Chapter 20, Using Object Relational Features**. The availability of object-relational features in the database (with Oracle 8i onwards) greatly extends the set of data types available to the developer – but when should they be used (and, equally, when shouldn't they be used)? In this chapter, we show how to add new data types to your system (we create a new PL/SQL data type) and look at the unique uses for collections. Finally we look at object relational views, which are for those of you who want to work with object relational features but still present a relational view of the data to the application.

Security

- ❏ **Chapter 21, Fine Grained Access Control**. This feature allows you to attach a predicate, at runtime, to all queries issued to a database. The fact that this feature is implemented on the server means that any application that can access the database can use the feature. Further reasons to use this feature include ease of maintenance and the ability to host an application as an ASP. You will also see how it works by testing a couple of examples, one based on implementing a security policy and one using application contexts. The chapter is rounded off with a section on caveats, which include referential integrity, import and export issues, and a section on errors.

- ❏ **Chapter 22, n-Tier Authentication**. In this chapter we will discuss the effects of the Web, which gives rise to situations where your client presents their credentials to a middle-tier application server, before actually accessing your database. We will see how this feature can be implemented and how it works. We will look at how you can grant privileges and audit proxy accounts.

- ❏ **Chapter 23, Invoker and Definer Rights**. Starting with Oracle 8i, we can now grant a different set of privileges to different users of a stored procedure. With invoker rights, we can now develop a stored procedure that executes with the privilege set of the invoker at run-time We examine why this feature might be useful, such as in the development of generic utilities and data dictionary applications and why, in the majority of cases, definer rights is still the correct choice. In the 'how it works' section, we look at what exactly happens when we compile definers and invokers rights procedures.

Appendices

- ❏ **Appendix A, Necessary Supplied Packages**. Many of these packages are overlooked in development efforts – or their intention not truly understood. Here I try to make sense of them, show you how to use them and extend them.

Conventions

We have used a number of different styles of text and layout in this book to help you differentiate between the different kinds of information. Here are examples of the styles we use and an explanation of what they mean:

Code has several fonts. If it's a word that we're talking about in the text, for example when discussing a PL/SQL SELECT query, it's in this font. If it's a block of code that you can type as a program and run, then it is in a gray box:

```
tkyte@DEV816> create or replace procedure StaticEmpProc(p_job in varchar2)
  2  as
  3    begin
  4      for x in (select ename from emp where job = p_job)
  5        loop
  6          dbms_output.put_line( x.ename );
  7        end loop;
  8  end;
  9  /

Procedure created.
```

In this book we have also shown line numbers directly from the SQL*PLUS session, for ease of reference.

Advice, hints, and background information comes in this type of font.

> **Important pieces of information come in boxes like this.**

Bullets appear indented, with each new bullet marked as follows:

- ❑ **Important Words** are in a bold type font
- ❑ Words that appear on the screen in menus like File or Window, are in a similar font to that you would see on a Windows desktop
- ❑ Keys that you press on the keyboard like *Ctrl* and *Enter*, are in italics

Source Code and Updates

As you work through the examples in this book, you may decide that you prefer to type in all the code by hand. Many readers prefer this because it is a good way to get familiar with the coding techniques that are being used.

Whether you want to type the code in or not, we have made all the source code for this book available in the Downloads section of our web site at the following address:

http://www.apress.com/

If you're one of those readers who likes to type in the code, you can use our files to check the results you should be getting - they should be your first stop if you think you might have typed in an error. If you're one of those readers who does not like typing, then downloading the source code from our web site is a must!

Also, errata sheets are available for all our books at http://www.apress.com on on each book's page. If you find an error that hasn't already been reported, please let us know.

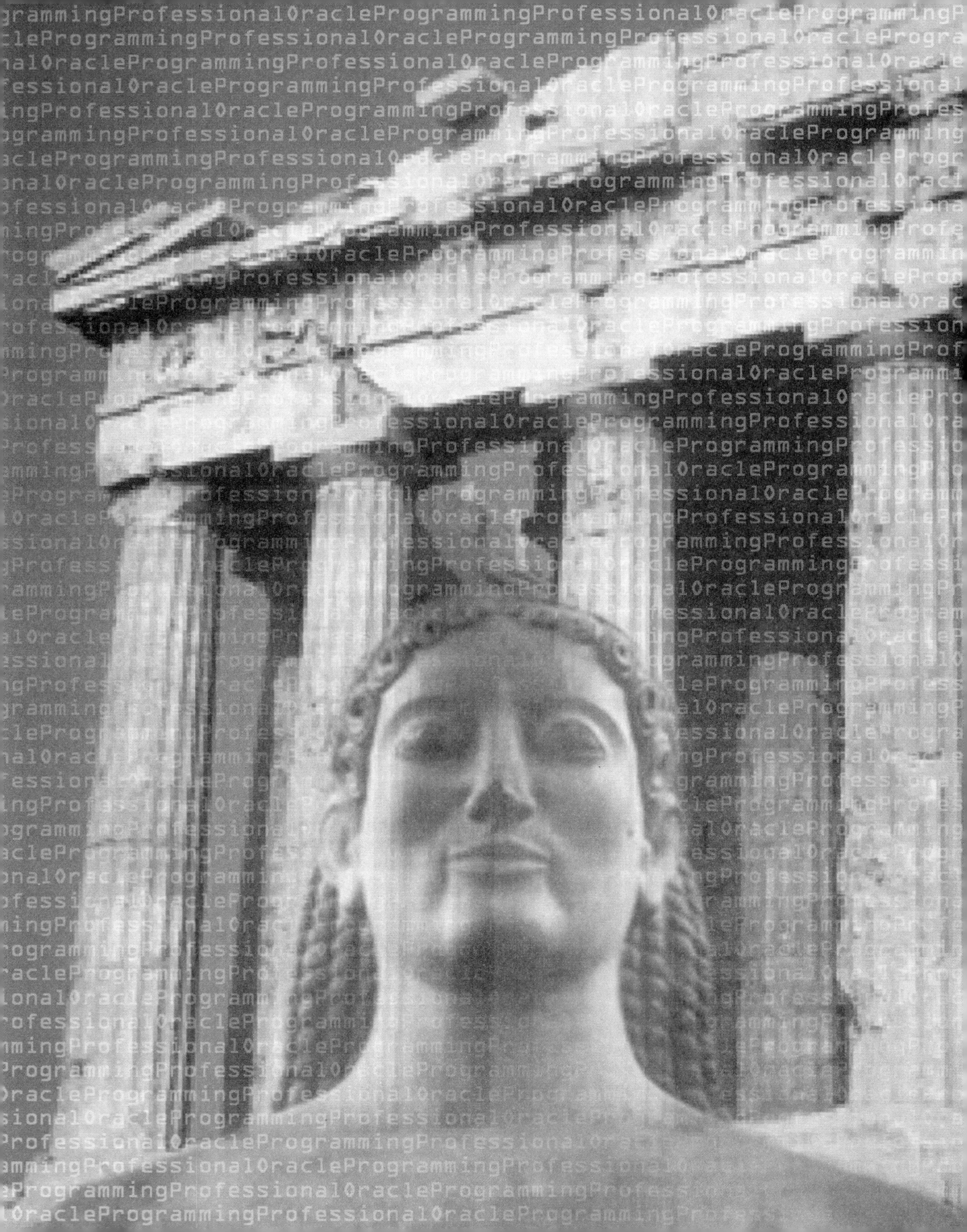
OracleProgrammingProfessional

Setting Up

In this section I will describe how to set up an environment capable of executing the examples in this book. I will cover:

- ❑ How to set up the SCOTT/TIGER demonstration schema
- ❑ The environment you need to have up and running
- ❑ How to configure AUTOTRACE, a SQL*PLUS facility
- ❑ The C compiler set up
- ❑ The coding conventions I use in this book

Setting up the SCOTT/TIGER Schema

The SCOTT/TIGER schema may already exist many times in your database. It is generally included during a typical installation, but it is not a mandatory component of the database. You may install the SCOTT example schema into any database account – there is nothing magic about using the SCOTT account. You could install the EMP/DEPT tables directly into your own database account if you wish.

Many of my examples in this book draw on the tables in the SCOTT schema. If you would like to be able to work along with them, you will need these tables as well. If you were working on a shared database, it would be advisable to install your own copy of these tables in some account other than SCOTT to avoid side effects caused by other users using and modifying the same data.

In order to create the SCOTT demonstration tables, you will simply:

- ❑ cd [ORACLE_HOME]/sqlplus/demo
- ❑ run demobld.sql when connected as any user

The demobld.sql script will create and populate five tables for us. When it is complete, it exits SQL*PLUS automatically, so don't be surprised when SQL*PLUS disappears after running the script – it is supposed to do that.

The standard demo tables do include the standard constraints that impose referential integrity. Some of my examples count on them having referential integrity. After you run the demobld.sql script, it is recommended you also execute the following:

```
alter table emp add constraint emp_pk primary key(empno);
alter table dept add constraint dept_pk primary key(deptno);
alter table emp add constraint emp_fk_dept
                            foreign key(deptno) references dept;
alter table emp add constraint emp_fk_emp foreign key(mgr) references emp;
```

This finishes off the installation of the demonstration schema. If you would like to drop this schema at any time to clean up, you can simply execute [ORACLE_HOME]/sqlplus/demo/demodrop.sql. This will drop the five tables, and exit SQL*PLUS.

The SQL*PLUS Environment

Most of the examples in this book are designed to run 100 percent in the SQL*PLUS environment. The notable exceptions are the C-based examples where, of course, you require a C compiler, separate from Oracle (see the *C Compilers* section a little later). Other than that, SQL*PLUS is the only thing that you need to set up and configure. SQL*PLUS provides many useful options and commands that we'll make fequent use of throughout this book. For example, almost all of the examples in this book use DBMS_OUTPUT in some fashion. In order for DBMS_OUTPUT to work, the following SQL*PLUS command must be issued:

```
SQL> set serveroutput on
```

If you are like me, you will soon get tired of typing this in each and every time. Fortunately, SQL*PLUS allows us to set up a login.sql file, a script that is executed each and every time we start a SQL*PLUS session. Further, it allows us to set an environment variable, SQLPATH, so that it can find this start-up script, regardless of the directory in which it is stored.

The login.sql script that I used for all examples in this book is as follows:

```
define _editor=vi

set serveroutput on size 1000000

set trimspool on
set long 5000
set linesize 100
set pagesize 9999
```

```
column plan_plus_exp format a80

column global_name new_value gname
set termout off
select lower(user) || '@' ||
decode(global_name, 'ORACLE8.WORLD', '8.0', 'ORA8I.WORLD',
'8i', global_name ) global_name from global_name;
set sqlprompt '&gname> '
set termout on
```

Where:

- ❑ DEFINE EDITOR=VI sets the default editor for SQL*PLUS. You may set this to be your favorite text editor (not a word processor) such as Notepad or EMACs.

- ❑ SET SERVEROUTPUT ON SIZE 1000000 enables DBMS_OUTPUT to be on by default (hence we don't have to type it in each and every time). Also set the default buffer size to be as large as possible.

- ❑ SET TRIMSPOOL ON ensures that, when spooling text, lines will be blank-trimmed and not fixed width. If this is set to off (the default setting), spooled lines will be as wide as your linesize setting

- ❑ SET LONG 5000 sets the default number of bytes displayed when selecting LONG and CLOB columns.

- ❑ SET LINESIZE 100 sets the width of the lines displayed by SQL*PLUS to be 100 characters.

- ❑ SET PAGESIZE 9999 sets the pagesize, which controls how frequently SQL*PLUS prints out headings, to a big number (we get one set of headings per page).

- ❑ COLUMN PLAN_PLUS_EXP FORMAT A80 sets the default width of the EXPLAIN PLAN output we receive with AUTOTRACE. A width of a80 is generally enough to hold the full plan.

The next section of the login.sql sets up my SQL*PLUS prompt, starting with the line:

```
column global_name new_value gname
```

This directive tells SQL*PLUS to take the last value it retrieves for any column named GLOBAL_NAME, and place it into the substitution variable GNAME. We then have the following query:

```
select lower(user) || '@' ||
decode(global_name, 'ORACLE8.WORLD', '8.0', 'ORA8I.WORLD',
'8i', global_name ) global_name from global_name;
```

This selects the GLOBAL_NAME from the database, using the DECODE function to assign familiar names to some of my more common database instances, and concatenates it with the username with which I am currently logged in. Finally, we reflect this information in the SQL*PLUS prompt:

```
set sqlprompt '&gname> '
```

Thus my prompt will look something like this:

```
tkyte@TKYTE816>
```

In this manner, I know *who* I am, as well as *where* I am. Another very handy script to have in the same directory as login.sql is this connect.sql script:

```
set termout off
connect &1
@login
set termout on
```

SQL*PLUS will only execute the login.sql script when it initially starts up. Generally, we want it to execute every time we connect. I have just trained myself to use:

```
tkyte@TKYTE816> @connect scott/tiger
```

instead of just CONNECT SCOTT/TIGER. This way, my prompt is always set properly, as are all other settings, such as SERVEROUTPUT.

Setting up AUTOTRACE in SQL*PLUS

Throughout the book it will be useful for us to monitor the performance of the queries we execute by getting a report of the execution plan used by the SQL optimizer, along with other useful execution statistics. Oracle provides a tool called EXPLAIN PLAN that, with use of the EXPLAIN PLAN command, allows us to generate this execution plan output.

> *For information about interpreting the output of EXPLAIN PLAN, see the Oracle8i Designing and Tuning for Performance guide.*

However, SQL*PLUS provides an AUTOTRACE facility that allows us to see the execution plans of the queries we've executed, and the resources they used, without having to use the EXPLAIN PLAN command. The report is generated after successful SQL DML (that is, SELECT, DELETE, UPDATE, and INSERT) statements. This book makes extensive use of this facility. There is more than one way to to configure the AUTOTRACE facility. These are the steps that I use:

- ❏ cd [ORACLE_HOME]/rdbms/admin
- ❏ log into SQL*PLUS as SYSTEM
- ❏ run @utlxplan
- ❏ run CREATE PUBLIC SYNONYM PLAN_TABLE FOR PLAN_TABLE;
- ❏ run GRANT ALL ON PLAN_TABLE TO PUBLIC;

If you wish, you can replace the GRANT...TO PUBLIC with a GRANT to a specific user. By granting the privelege to the PUBLIC role, you are effectively letting anyone trace using SQL*PLUS. This is not a bad thing in my opinion as it prevents each and every user from having to install their own plan table. The alternative is for you to run @UTLXPLAN in every schema where you want to use the AUTOTRACE facility.

The next step is to create and grant the PLUSTRACE role:

- ❏ cd [ORACLE_HOME]/sqlplus/admin
- ❏ log into SQL*PLUS as SYS
- ❏ run @plustrce
- ❏ run GRANT PLUSTRACE TO PUBLIC;

Again, if you wish, you can replace PUBLIC in the GRANT with a specific user.

Controlling the Execution Plan Report

You can control the information displayed in the execution plan report by setting the AUTOTRACE system variable.

SET AUTOTRACE OFF	No AUTOTRACE report is generated. This is the default.
SET AUTOTRACE ON EXPLAIN	The AUTOTRACE report shows only the optimizer execution path.
SET AUTOTRACE ON STATISTICS	The AUTOTRACE report shows only the SQL statement execution statistics.
SET AUTOTRACE ON	The AUTOTRACE report includes both the optimizer execution path, and the SQL statement execution statistics.
SET AUTOTRACE TRACEONLY	Like SET AUTOTRACE ON, but suppresses the printing of the user's query output, if any.

Interpreting the Execution Plan

The execution plan shows the SQL optimizer's query execution path. Each line of the Execution Plan has a sequential line number. SQL*PLUS also displays the line number of the parent operation.

The execution plan consists of four columns displayed in the following order:

Column Name	Description
ID_PLUS_EXP	Shows the line number of each execution step.
PARENT_ID_PLUS_EXP	Shows the relationship between each step, and its parent. This column is useful for large reports.
PLAN_PLUS_EXP	Shows each step of the report.
OBJECT_NODE_PLUS_EXP	Shows the database links or parallel query servers used.

The format of the columns may be altered with the COLUMN command. For example, to stop the PARENT_ID_PLUS_EXP column being displayed, enter:

```
SQL> column parent_id_plus_exp noprint
```

C Compilers

The Oracle-supported compiler varies by operating system. On Microsoft Windows, I used Microsoft Visual C/C++. I used only the command line portion of this tool (nmake and cl). None of my examples use the GUI development environment. However, they may also be developed in this environment if you wish. It would be up to you to configure the appropriate include files, and link in the proper libraries. Each makefile contained in this book are very small and simple – it is obvious what include files and libraries are necessary.

On Sun Solaris, the supported C compiler is the Sun SparcsWorks compiler. Again, I've used only the command line tools, `make` and `cc`, in order to compile the scripts.

Coding Conventions

The only coding convention used in this book that I would like to explicitly point out, is how I name variables in PL/SQL code. For example, consider a package body like this:

```
create or replace package body my_pkg
as
    g_variable varchar2(25);

    procedure p( p_variable in varchar2 )
    is
        l_variable varchar2(25);
    begin
        null;
    end;
end;
/
```

Here I have three variables, a global package variable G_VARIABLE, a formal parameter to the procedure, P_VARIABLE, and finally a local variable, L_VARIABLE. I name my variables according to their scope – all globals begin with G_, parameters with P_, and local variables with L_. The main reason for this is to distinguish PL/SQL variables from columns in a database table. For example, a procedure such as:

```
create procedure p( ENAME in varchar2 )
as
begin
    for x in ( select * from emp where ename = ENAME ) loop
        Dbms_output.put_line( x.empno );
    end loop;
end;
```

would always print out every row in the EMP table. SQL sees ename = ENAME, and compares the ename column to itself (of course). We could use ename = P.ENAME – that is, qualify the reference to the PL/SQL variable with the procedure name, but this is too easy to forget, leading to errors.

I always name my variables after the scope. That way, I can easily distinguish parameters from local variables and globals, in addition to removing any ambiguity with respect to column names and variable names.

Other Issues

Each chapter in this book is fairly self-contained. At the beginning of each chapter, I dropped my testing account, and recreated it. That is, each chapter started with a clean schema – no objects. If you work the examples from start to finish in each chapter, you will want to do the same. When I query the data dictionary and such, to see what objects have been created as a side effect of some command or another, it might get confusing if you have left over objects from other examples. Also, I tended to reuse table names (especially the table T), so if you don't clean up the schema between chapters, you may hit a conflict there.

Additionally, if you attempt to manually drop the objects created by the example (as opposed to just dropping the user via drop user USERNAME cascade, and recreating it), you must be aware that the Java objects are all in mixed case. So, if you run the example in Chapter 19, *Java Stored Procedures*:

```
tkyte@TKYTE816> create or replace and compile
  2  java source named "demo"
  3  as
  4  import java.sql.SQLException;
...
```

you will find that in order to drop it, you need to:

```
tkyte@TKYTE816> drop java source "demo";

Java dropped.
```

Remember to use the double quotes around the identifier for Java objects as they are created and stored in mixed case.

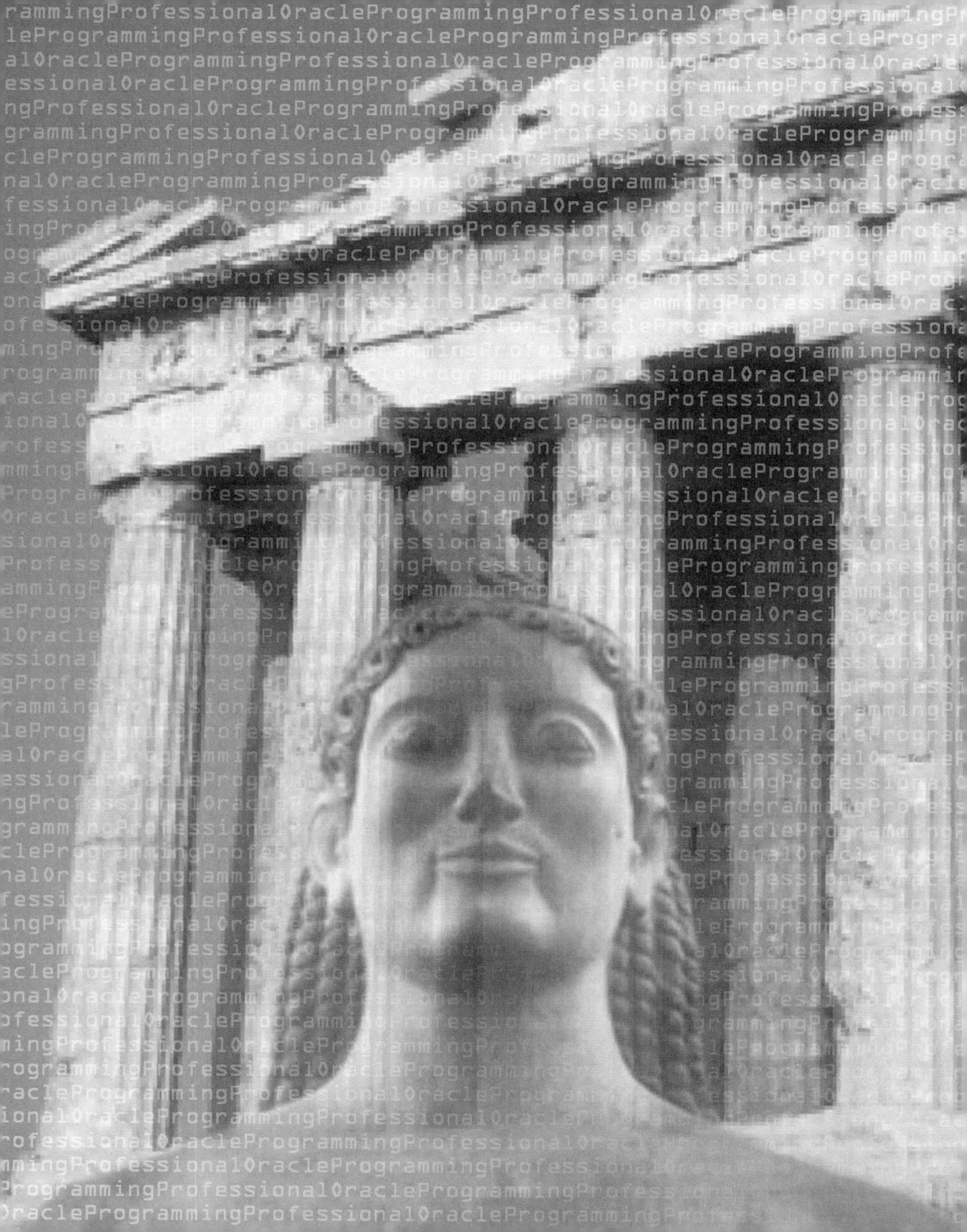

Developing Successful Oracle Applications

I spend the bulk of my time working with Oracle database software and, more to the point, with people who use this software. Over the last twelve years, I've worked on many projects – successful ones as well as failures, and if I were to encapsulate my experiences into a few broad statements, they would be:

❑ An application built around the database – dependent on the database – will succeed or fail based on how it uses the database.

❑ A development team needs at its heart a core of 'database savvy' coders who are responsible for ensuring the database logic is sound and the system is tuned.

These may seem like surprisingly obvious statements, but in my experience, I have found that too many people approach the database as if it were a 'black box' – something that they don't need to know about. Maybe they have a SQL generator that will save them from the hardship of having to learn SQL. Maybe they figure they will just use it like a flat file and do 'keyed reads'. Whatever they figure, I can tell you that thinking along these lines is most certainly misguided; you simply cannot get away with not understanding the database. This chapter will discuss *why* you need to know about the database, specifically why you need to understand:

❑ The database architecture, how it works, and what it looks like.

❑ What concurrency controls are, and what they mean to you.

❑ How to tune your application from day one.

❑ How some things are implemented in the database, which is not necessary the same as how you think they should be implemented.

❑ What features your database already provides for you and why it is generally better to use a provided feature then to build your own.

❑ Why you might want more than a cursory knowledge of SQL.

Now this may seem like a long list of things to learn before you start, but consider this analogy for a second: if you were developing a highly scalable, enterprise application on a brand new operating system (OS), what would be the first thing you would do? Hopefully, you answered, 'find out how this new OS works, how things will run on it, and so on'. If you did not, you would fail.

Consider, for example, one of the early versions of Windows (Windows 3.x, say). Now this, like UNIX, was a 'multi-tasking' operating system. However, it certainly didn't multi-task like UNIX did – it used a non-preemptive multi-tasking model (meaning that if the running application didn't give up control, nothing else could run – including the operating system). In fact, compared to UNIX, Windows 3.x was not really a multi-tasking OS at all. Developers had to understand exactly how the Windows 'multi-tasking' feature was implemented in order to develop effectively. If you sit down to develop an application that will run natively on an OS, then understanding that OS is very important.

What is true of applications running natively on operating systems is true of applications that will run on a database: understanding that database is crucial to your success. If you do not understand what your particular database does or how it does it, your application will fail. If you assume that because your application ran fine on SQL Server, it will necessarily run fine on Oracle then, again, your application is likely to fail.

My Approach

Before we begin, I feel it is only fair that you understand my approach to development. I tend to take a database-centric approach to problems. If I can do it in the database, I will. There are a couple of reasons for this – the first and foremost being that I know that if I build functionality in the database, I can *deploy* it anywhere. I am not aware of a server operating system on which Oracle is not available – from Windows to dozens of UNIX systems to the OS/390 mainframe, the same exact Oracle software and options are available. I frequently build test solutions on my laptop, running Oracle8*i* on Windows NT. I deploy them on a variety of UNIX servers running the same database software. When I have to implement a feature outside of the database, I find it extremely hard to deploy that feature anywhere I want. One of the main features that makes Java appealing to many people – the fact that their programs are always compiled in the same virtual environment, the **J**ava **V**irtual **M**achine (**JVM**), and so are highly portable – is the exact same feature that make the database appealing to me. The database is *my* Virtual Machine. It is *my* 'virtual operating system'.

My approach is to do everything I can in the database. If my requirements go beyond what the database environment can offer, I do it in Java outside of the database. In this way, almost every operating system intricacy will be hidden from me. I still have to understand how *my* 'virtual machines' work (Oracle, and occasionally a JVM) – you need to know the tools you are using – but they, in turn, worry about how best to do things on a given OS for me.

Thus, simply knowing the intricacies of this one 'virtual OS' allows you to build applications that will perform and scale well on many operating systems. I do not intend to imply that you can be totally ignorant of your underlying OS – just that as a software developer building database applications you can be fairly well insulated from it, and you will not have to deal with many of its nuances. Your DBA, responsible for running the Oracle software, will be infinitely more in tune with the OS (if he or she is not, please get a new DBA!). If you develop client-server software and the bulk of your code is outside of the database and outside of a VM (Java Virtual Machines perhaps being the most popular VM), you will have to be concerned about your OS once again.

I have a pretty simple mantra when it comes to developing database software:

❏   You should do it in a single SQL statement if at all possible.

❏   If you cannot do it in a single SQL Statement, then do it in PL/SQL.

❏   If you cannot do it in PL/SQL, try a Java Stored Procedure.

❏   If you cannot do it in Java, do it in a C external procedure.

❏   If you cannot do it in a C external routine, you might want to seriously think about why it is you need to do it...

Throughout this book, you will see the above philosophy implemented. We'll use PL/SQL and Object Types in PL/SQL to do things that SQL itself cannot do. PL/SQL has been around for a very long time, over thirteen years of tuning has gone into it, and you will find no other language so tightly coupled with SQL, nor any as optimized to interact with SQL. When PL/SQL runs out of steam – for example, when we want to access the network, send e-mails' and so on – we'll use Java. Occasionally, we'll do something in C, but typically only when C is the only choice, or when the raw speed offered by C is required. In many cases today this last reason goes away with native compilation of Java – the ability to convert your Java bytecode into operating system specific object code on your platform. This lets Java run just as fast as C.

The Black Box Approach

I have an idea, borne out by first-hand experience, as to why database-backed software development efforts so frequently fail. Let me be clear that I'm including here those projects that may not be documented as failures, but take much longer to roll out and deploy than originally planned because of the need to perform a major 're-write', 're-architecture', or 'tuning' effort. Personally, I call these delayed projects 'failures': more often than not they could have been completed on schedule (or even faster).

The single most common reason for failure is a lack of practical knowledge of the database – a basic lack of understanding of the fundamental tool that is being used. The 'blackbox' approach involves a conscious decision to protect the developers from the database. They are actually encouraged not to learn anything about it! In many cases, they are prevented from exploiting it. The reasons for this approach appear to be FUD-related (**F**ear, **U**ncertainty, and **D**oubt). They have heard that databases are 'hard', that SQL, transactions and data integrity are 'hard'. The solution – don't make anyone do anything 'hard'. They treat the database as a black box and have some software tool generate all of the code. They try to insulate themselves with many layers of protection so that they do not have to touch this 'hard' database.

This is an approach to database development that I've never been able to understand. One of the reasons I have difficulty understanding this approach is that, for me, learning Java and C was a lot harder then learning the concepts behind the database. I'm now pretty good at Java and C but it took a lot more hands-on experience for me to become competent using them than it did to become competent using the database. With the database, you need to be aware of how it works but you don't have to know everything inside and out. When programming in C or Java, you do need to know everything inside and out and these are *huge* languages.

Another reason is that if you are building a database application, then *the most important piece of software is the database*. A successful development team will appreciate this and will want its people to know about it, to concentrate on it. Many times I've walked into a project where almost the opposite was true.

A typical scenario would be as follows:

❑ The developers were fully trained in the GUI tool or the language they were using to build the front end (such as Java). In many cases, they had had weeks if not months of training in it.

❑ The team had zero hours of Oracle training and zero hours of Oracle experience. Most had no database experience whatsoever.

❑ They had massive performance problems, data integrity problems, hanging issues and the like (but very pretty screens).

As a result of the inevitable performance problems, I would be called in to help solve the difficulties. I can recall one particular occasion when I could not fully remember the syntax of a new command that we needed to use. I asked for the *SQL Reference* manual, and I was handed an Oracle 6.0 document. The development was taking place on version 7.3, five years after the release of version.6.0! It was all they had to work with, but this did not seem to concern them at all. Never mind the fact that the tool they really needed to know about for tracing and tuning didn't really exist back then. Never mind the fact that features such as triggers, stored procedures, and many hundreds of others, had been added in the five years since the documentation to which they had access was written. It was very easy to determine why they needed help– fixing their problems was another issue all together.

The idea that developers building a **database application** should be shielded from the database is amazing to me but still the attitude persists. Many people still take the attitude that developers should be shielded from the database, they cannot take the time to get trained in the database – basically, they should not have to know anything about the database. Why? Well, more than once I've heard '... but Oracle is the most scalable database in the world, my people don't have to learn about it, it'll just do that'. It is true; Oracle is the most scalable database in the world. However, I can write bad code that does not scale in Oracle easier then I can write good, scaleable code in Oracle. You can replace Oracle with any technology and the same will be true. This is a fact – it is easier to write applications that perform poorly than it is to write applications that perform well. It is sometimes too easy to build a single-user system in the world's most scalable database if you don't know what you are doing. The database is a tool and the improper use of any tool can lead to disaster. Would you take a nutcracker and smash walnuts with it as if it were a hammer? You could but it would not be a proper use of that tool and the result would be a mess. Similar effects can be achieved by remaining ignorant of your database.

I was recently working on a project where the system architects had designed a very elegant architecture. A web browser client would talk over HTTP to an application server running Java Server Pages (JSP). The application logic would be 100 percent generated by a tool and implemented as EJBs (using container managed persistence) and would be physically located on another application server. The database would hold tables and indexes and nothing else.

So, we start with a technically complex architecture: we have four entities that must talk to each other in order to get the job done: web browser to a JSP in the Application Server to an EJB to the database. It would take technically competent people to develop, test, tune, and deploy this application. I was asked to help benchmark this application post-development. The first thing I wanted to know about was their approach to the database:

❑ What did they feel would be the major choke points, areas of contention?

❑ What did they view as the major obstacles to overcome?

They had no idea. When asked, 'OK, when we need to tune a generated query, who can help me rewrite the code in the EJB?' The answer was, 'Oh, you cannot tune that code, you have to do it all in the database'. The application was to remain untouched. At that point, I was ready to walk away from the project – it was already clear to me that there was no way this application would work:

❑ The application was built without a single consideration for scaling the database level.

❑ The application itself could not be tuned or touched.

❑ Experience shows that 80 to 90 percent of *all* tuning is done at the application level, not at the database level.

❑ The developers had no idea what the beans did in the database or where to look for potential problems.

That was shown to be the case in the first hour of testing. As it turns out, the first thing the application did was a:

```
select * from t for update;
```

What this did was to force a serialization of *all* work. The model implemented in the database was such that before any significant work could proceed, you had to lock an extremely scarce resource. That immediately turned this application into a very large single user system. The developers did not believe me (in another database, employing a shared read lock, the observed behavior was different). After spending ten minutes with a tool called TKPROF (you'll hear a lot more about this in *Tuning Strategies and Tools*, Chapter 10) I was able to show them that, yes, in fact this was the SQL executed by the application (they had no idea – they had never seen the SQL). Not only was it the SQL executed by the application but by using two SQL*PLUS sessions I was able to show them that session two will wait for session one to completely finish its work before proceeding.

So, instead of spending a week benchmarking the application, I spent the time teaching them about tuning, database locking, concurrency control mechanisms, how it worked in Oracle versus Informix versus SQL Server versus DB2 and so on (it is different in each case). What I had to understand first, though, was the *reason* for the SELECT FOR UPDATE. It turned out the developers wanted a repeatable read.

> *Repeatable read is a database term that says if I read a row once in my transaction and I read the row again later in the same transaction, the row will not have changed – the read is repeatable.*

Why did they want this? They had heard it was a 'good thing'. OK, fair enough, you want repeatable read. The way to do that in Oracle is to set the isolation level to **serializable** (which not only gives you a repeatable read for any row of data, it gives you a repeatable read for a query – if you execute the same query two times in a transaction, you'll get the same results). To get a repeatable read in Oracle, you do not want to use SELECT FOR UPDATE, which you only do when you want to physically serialize access to data. Unfortunately, the tool they utilized did not know about that – it was developed primarily for use with another database where this *was* the way to get a repeatable read.

So, what we had to do in this case, in order to achieve serializable transactions, was to create a logon trigger in the database that altered the session for these applications and set the isolation level to serializable. We went back to the tool they were using and turned off the switches for repeatable reads and re-ran the application. Now, with the FOR UPDATE clause removed, we got some actual concurrent work done in the database.

That was hardly the end of the problems on this project. We had to figure out:

❑ How to tune SQL without changing the SQL (that's hard, we'll look at some methods in Chapter 11 on *Optimizer Plan Stability*).

❑ How to measure performance.

❑ How to see where the bottlenecks were.

❑ How and what to index. And so on.

At the end of the week the developers, who had been insulated from the database, were amazed at what the database could actually provide for them, how easy it was to get that information and, most importantly, how big a difference it could make to the performance of their application. We didn't do the benchmark that week (they had some reworking to do!) but in the end they were successful – just behind schedule by a couple of weeks.

This is not a criticism of tools or technologies like EJBs and container managed persistence. This is a criticism of purposely remaining ignorant of the database and how it works and how to use it. The technologies used in this case worked well – after the developers got some insight into the database itself.

The bottom line is that the database is typically the cornerstone of your application. If it does not work well, nothing else really matters. If you have a black box and it does not work well – what are you going to do about it? About the only thing you can do is look at it and wonder why it is not doing so well. You cannot fix it, you cannot tune it, you quite simply do not understand how it works – and you made the decision to be in this position. The alternative is the approach that I advocate: understand your database, know how it works, know what it can do for you, and use it to its fullest potential.

How (and how not) to Develop Database Applications

That's enough hypothesizing, for now at least. In the remainder of this chapter, I will take a more empirical approach, discussing why knowledge of the database and its workings will definitely go a long way towards a successful implementation (without having to write the application twice!). Some problems are simple to fix as long as you understand how to find them. Others require drastic rewrites. One of the goals of this book is to help you avoid the problems in the first place.

In the following sections, I discuss certain core Oracle features without delving into exactly what these features are and all of the ramifications of using them. For example, I discuss just one of the implications of using Multi-Threaded Server (MTS) architecture– a mode in which you can (and sometimes have to) configure Oracle in order to support multiple database connections. I will not, however, go fully into what MTS is, how it works and so on. Those facts are covered in detail in the Oracle Server Concepts Manual (with more information to be found in the Net8 Administrators Guide).

Understanding Oracle Architecture

I was working on a project recently where they decided to use only the latest, greatest technologies: everything was coded in Java with EJBs. The client application would talk to the database server using beans – no Net8. They would not be passing SQL back and forth between client and server, just EJB calls using Remote Method Invocation (RMI) over Internet Inter-Orb Protocol (IIOP).

> *If you are interested in the details of RMI over IIOP you can refer to* http://java.sun.com/products/rmi-iiop/.

This is a perfectly valid approach. This functionality works and can be extremely scalable. The people responsible for the architecture understood Java, EJBs, the protocols involved – all of that stuff. They felt they were in a strong position to successfully build such a project. When their application would not scale beyond a couple of users they decided that the database was at fault and severely doubted Oracle's claim to be the 'most scaleable database ever'.

The problem was not the database but a lack of knowledge of how the database worked – a lack of knowledge that meant that certain key decisions were made at design time that doomed this particular application to failure. In order to deploy EJBs in the database Oracle must be configured to run in MTS mode rather than dedicated server mode. What the team did not understand, crucially, was how using MTS with EJBs in the database would affect them. Without this understanding, and without a general knowledge of how Oracle worked, two key decisions were made:

❏ We will run some stored procedures that take 45 seconds or longer (much longer at times) in our beans.

❏ We will not support the use of bind variables. All of our queries will hard code the constant values in the predicate. All inputs to stored procedures will use strings. This is 'easier' than coding bind variables.

These two seemingly minor decisions guaranteed that the project would fail – utterly guaranteed it. They made it so that a highly scalable database would literally fall over and fail with a very small user load. A lack of knowledge of how the database worked more then overwhelmed their intricate knowledge of Java beans and distributed processing. If they had taken time to learn a bit more about the way Oracle worked, and consequently followed the following two simple guidelines, then their project would have had a much better chance of success the first time out.

Do not run Long Transactions Under MTS

The decision to run 45+ second transactions under MTS betrayed a lack of understanding of what MTS was designed to do and how it works in Oracle. Briefly, MTS works by having a shared pool of server processes that service a larger pool of end users. It is very much like connection pooling – since process creation and management are some of the most expensive operations you can ask an operating system to perform, MTS is very beneficial in a large-scale system. So, I might have 100 users but only five or ten shared servers.

When a shared server gets a request to run an update, or execute a stored procedure, then that shared server is dedicated to that task until completion. No one else will use that shared server until that update completes or that stored procedure finishes execution. Thus, when using MTS your goal must be to have very short statements. MTS is designed to scale up **O**n-**L**ine **T**ransaction **P**rocessing (**OLTP**) systems – a system characterized by statements that execute with sub-second response times. You'll have a single row update, insert a couple of line items, and query records by primary key. You won't (or shouldn't) run a batch process that takes many seconds or minutes to complete.

If all of our statements execute very rapidly, then MTS works well. We can effectively share a number of processes amongst a larger community of users. If, on the other hand, we have sessions that monopolize a shared server for extended periods of time then we will see apparent database 'hangs'. Say we configured ten shared servers for 100 people. If, at some point, ten people simultaneously execute the process that takes 45 seconds or longer then every other transaction (including new connections) will have to wait. If some of the queued sessions want to run that same long process, then we have a *big* problem – the apparent 'hang' won't last 45 seconds, it will appear to last much longer for most people. Even if we only have a few people wanting to execute this process simultaneously rather than ten, we will still observe what appears to be a large degradation in performance from the server. We are taking away, for an extended period of time, a shared resource and this is not a good thing. Instead of having ten shared servers processing quick requests on a queue, we now have five or six (or less). Eventually the system will be running at some fraction of its capability, solely due to this resource being consumed.

The 'quick and dirty' solution was to start up more shared servers, but the logical conclusion to this is that you need a shared server per user and this is not a reasonable conclusion for a system with thousands of users (as this system was). Not only would that introduce bottlenecks into the system itself (the more servers you have to manage – the more processing time spent managing), but also it is simply not the way MTS was designed to work.

The real solution to this problem was simple: do not execute long running transactions under MTS. Implementing this solution was not. There was more then one way to implement this and they all required fundamental architectural changes. The most appropriate way to fix this issue, requiring the least amount of change, was to use **A**dvanced **Q**ueues (**AQ**).

> *AQ is a message-oriented middleware hosted in the Oracle database. It provides the ability for a client session to enqueue a message into a database queue table. This message is later, typically immediately after committing, 'dequeued' by another session and the content of the message is inspected. This message contains information for the other session to process. It can be used to give the appearance of lightening fast response times by decoupling the long running process from the interactive client.*

So, rather than execute a 45-second process, the bean would place the request, along with all its inputs, on a queue and execute it in a loosely coupled (asynchronous) rather than tightly coupled (synchronous) fashion. In this way, the end user would not have to wait 45 seconds for a response – the system would apparently be much more responsive

While this approach sounds easy – just drop in 'AQ' and the problem is fixed – there was more to it than that. This 45-second process generated a transaction ID that was required by the next step in the interface in order to join to other tables – as designed, the interface would not work without it. By implementing AQ, we were not waiting for this transaction ID to be generated here – we were just asking the system to do it for us at some point. So, the application was stuck. On the one hand, we could not wait 45 seconds for the process to complete, but on the other hand, we needed the generated ID in order to proceed to the next screen and we could only get that after waiting 45 seconds. To solve this problem, what we had to do was to synthesize a pseudo-transaction ID, modify the long running process to accept this generated pseudo ID and have it update a table when it was done, by which mechanism the real transaction ID was associated with the pseudo id. That is, instead of the transaction ID being an output of the long running process, it would be an input to it. Further, all 'downstream' tables would have to use this pseudo-transaction ID – not the real one (since the real one would not be generated for a while). We also had to review the usage of this transaction ID in order to see what impact this change might have on other modules and so on.

Another consideration was the fact that, while we were running synchronously, if the 45-second process failed then the end user was alerted right away. They would fix the error condition (fix the inputs, typically) and resubmit the request. Now, with the transaction being processed asynchronously under AQ, we don't have that ability. New functionality had to be added in order to support this delayed response. Specifically, we needed some workflow mechanism to route any failed transaction to the appropriate person.

The upshot of all this is that we had to undertake major changes in the database structure. New software had to be added (AQ). New processes had to be developed (workflows and such). On the plus side, the removal of 45 seconds of lag time from an interactive process not only solved the MTS architecture issue, it enhanced the user experience – it meant that the end user got much faster 'apparent' response times. On the down side, all of this delayed the project considerably because none of it was detected until immediately before deployment, during scalability testing. It is just too bad that it was not designed the right way from the beginning. With knowledge of how MTS worked physically, it would have been clear that the original design would not scale very well.

Use Bind Variables

If I were to write a book about how to build *non-scalable* Oracle applications, then *Don't use Bind Variables* would be the first and last chapter. This is a major cause of performance issues and a major inhibitor of scalability. The way the Oracle shared pool (a very important shared memory data structure) operates is predicated on developers using bind variables. If you want to make Oracle run slowly, even grind to a total halt – just refuse to use them.

Bind variable is a placeholder in a query. For example, to retrieve the record for employee 123, I can query:

```
select * from emp where empno = 123;
```

Alternatively, I can query:

```
select * from emp where empno = :empno;
```

In a typical system, you would query up employee 123 maybe once and then never again. Later, you would query up employee 456, then 789, and so on. If you use literals (constants) in the query then each and every query is a brand new query, never before seen by the database. It will have to be parsed, qualified (names resolved), security checked, optimized, and so on – in short, each and every unique statement you execute will have to be compiled every time it is executed.

The second query uses a bind variable, :empno, the value of which is supplied at query execution time. This query is compiled once and then the query plan is stored in a shared pool (the library cache), from which it can be retrieved and reused. The difference between the two in terms of performance and scalability is huge, dramatic even.

From the above description it should be fairly obvious that parsing a statement with hard-coded variables (called a **hard** parse) will take longer and consume many more resources than reusing an already parsed query plan (called a **soft** parse). What may not be so obvious is the extent to which the former will reduce the number of users your system can support. Obviously, this is due in part to the increased resource consumption, but an even larger factor arises due to the latching mechanisms for the library cache. When you hard parse a query, the database will spend more time holding certain low-level serialization devices called **latches** (see Chapter 3, *Locking and Concurrency*, for more details). These latches protect the data structures in the shared memory of Oracle from concurrent modifications by two sessions (else Oracle would end up with corrupt data structures) and from someone reading a data structure while it is being modified. The longer and more frequently we have to latch these data structures, the longer the queue to get these latches will become. In a similar fashion to having long transactions running under MTS, we will start to monopolize scarce resources. Your machine may appear to be under-utilized at times – and yet everything in the database is running very slowly. The likelihood is that someone is holding one of these serialization mechanisms and a line is forming – you are not able to run at top speed.It only takes one ill behaved application in your database to dramatically affect the performance of every other application. A single, small application that does not use bind variable will cause the relevant SQL of other well tuned applications to get discarded from the shared pool over time. You only need one bad apple to spoil the entire barrel.

If you use bind variables, then everyone who submits the same exact query that references the same object will use the compiled plan from the pool. You will compile your subroutine once and use it over and over again. This is very efficient and is the way the database intends you to work. Not only will you use fewer resources (a soft parse is much less resource intensive), but also you will hold latches for less time and need them less frequently. This increases your performance and greatly increases your scalability.

Just to give you a tiny idea of how huge a difference this can make performance-wise, you only need to run a very small test:

```
tkyte@TKYTE816> alter system flush shared_pool;

System altered.
```

Here I am starting with an 'empty' shared pool. If I was to run this test more than one time, I would need to flush the shared pool every time, or else the non-bind variable SQL below would, in fact, be cached and appear to run very fast.

```
tkyte@TKYTE816> set timing on
tkyte@TKYTE816> declare
    2       type rc is ref cursor;
    3       l_rc rc;
    4       l_dummy all_objects.object_name%type;
    5       l_start number default dbms_utility.get_time;
    6   begin
    7       for i in 1 .. 1000
    8       loop
    9           open l_rc for
   10           'select object_name
   11             from all_objects
   12           where object_id = ' || i;
   13           fetch l_rc into l_dummy;
   14           close l_rc;
   15       end loop;
   16       dbms_output.put_line
   17       ( round( (dbms_utility.get_time-l_start)/100, 2 ) ||
   18       ' seconds...' );
   19   end;
   20   /
14.86 seconds...

PL/SQL procedure successfully completed.
```

The above code uses dynamic SQL to query out a single row from the ALL_OBJECTS table. It generates 1000 unique queries with the values 1, 2, 3, ... and so on 'hard-coded' into the WHERE clause. On my 350MHz Pentium laptop, this took about 15 seconds (the speed may vary on different machines).

Next, we do it using bind variables:

```
tkyte@TKYTE816> declare
    2       type rc is ref cursor;
    3       l_rc rc;
    4       l_dummy all_objects.object_name%type;
    5       l_start number default dbms_utility.get_time;
    6  begin
    7       for i in 1 .. 1000
    8       loop
    9           open l_rc for
   10           'select object_name
   11             from all_objects
   12             where object_id = :x'
   13           using i;
   14           fetch l_rc into l_dummy;
   15           close l_rc;
   16       end loop;
   17       dbms_output.put_line
   18       ( round( (dbms_utility.get_time-l_start)/100, 2 ) ||
   19         ' seconds...' );
   20  end;
   21  /
1.27 seconds...

PL/SQL procedure successfully completed.
```

We use the same logic here – the only thing that has changed is the fact that we are not hard coding the values 1, 2, 3... and so on into the query – we are using bind variables instead. The results are pretty dramatic. The fact is that not only does this execute much faster (we spent more time *parsing* our queries then actually *executing* them!) it will let more users use your system simultaneously.

Executing SQL statements without bind variables is very much like compiling a subroutine before each and every method call. Imagine shipping Java source code to your customers where, before calling a method in a class, they had to invoke the Java compiler, compile the class, run the method, and then throw away the byte code. Next time they wanted to execute the exact same method, they would do the same thing; compile it, run it, and throw it away. You would never consider doing this in your application – you should never consider doing this in your database either.

> In Chapter10, Tuning Strategies and Tools, we will look at ways to identify whether or not you are using bind variables, different ways to use them, an 'auto binder' feature in the database and so on. We will also discuss a specialized case where you don't want to use bind variables.

As it was, on this particular project, rewriting the existing code to use bind variables was the only possible course of action. The resulting code ran orders of magnitude faster and increased many times the number of simultaneous users that the system could support. However, it came at a high price in terms of time and effort. It is not that using bind variables is hard, or error prone, it's just that they did not do it initially and thus were forced to go back and revisit virtually *all* of the code and change it. They would not have paid this price if they had understood that it was vital to use bind variables in their application from day one.

Understanding Concurrency Control

Concurrency control is one area where databases differentiate themselves. It is an area that sets a database apart from a file system and that sets databases apart from each other. As a programmer, it is vital that your database application works correctly under concurrent access conditions, and yet this is something people fail to test time and time again. Techniques that work well if everything happens consecutively do not work so well when everyone does them simultaneously. If you don't have a good grasp of how your particular database implements concurrency control mechanisms, then you will:

❑ Corrupt the integrity of your data.

❑ Run slower than you should with a small number of users.

❑ Decrease your ability to scale to a large number of users.

Notice I don't say, 'you might...' or 'you run the risk of...' but rather that invariably you *will* do these things. You will do these things without even realizing it. Without correct concurrency control, you will corrupt the integrity of your database because something that works in isolation will not work as you expect in a multi-user situation. You will run slower than you should because you'll end up waiting for data. You'll lose your ability to scale because of locking and contention issues. As the queues to access a resource get longer, the wait gets longer and longer. An analogy here would be a backup at a tollbooth. If cars arrive in an orderly, predictable fashion, one after the other, we never have a backup. If many cars arrive simultaneously, queues start to form. Furthermore, the waiting time does not increase in line with the number of cars at the booth. After a certain point we are spending considerable additional time 'managing' the people that are waiting in line, as well as servicing them (in the database, we would talk about context switching).

Concurrency issues are the hardest to track down – the problem is similar to debugging a multi-threaded program. The program may work fine in the controlled, artificial environment of the debugger but crashes horribly in the 'real world'. For example, under 'race conditions' you find that two threads can end up modifying the same data structure simultaneously. These kinds of bugs are terribly hard to track down and fix. If you only test your application in isolation and then deploy it to dozens of concurrent users, you are likely to be (painfully) exposed to an undetected concurrency issue.

Over the next two sections, I'll relate two small examples of how the lack of understanding concurrency control can ruin your data or inhibit performance and scalability.

Implementing Locking

The database uses locks to ensure that, at most, one transaction is modifying a given piece of data at any given time. Basically, they are the mechanism that allows for concurrency – without some locking model to prevent concurrent updates to the same row, for example, multi-user access would not be possible in a database. However, if overused or used improperly, locks can actually inhibit concurrency. If you or the database itself locks data unnecessarily, then fewer people will be able to concurrently perform operations. Thus, understanding what locking is and how it works in your database is vital if you are to develop a scalable, correct application.

What is also vital is that you understand that each database implements locking differently. Some have page-level locking, others row level; some implementations escalate locks from row-level to page-level, some do not; some use read locks, others do not; some implement serializable transactions via locking and others via read-consistent views of data (no locks). These small differences can balloon into huge performance issues or downright bugs in your application if you do not understand how they work.

The following points sum up Oracle's locking policy:

❏ Oracle locks data at the row level on modification only. There is no lock escalation to a block or table level, ever.

❏ Oracle never locks data just to read it. There are no locks placed on rows of data by simple reads.

❏ A writer of data does not block a reader of data. Let me repeat – *reads* are not blocked by *writes*. This is fundamentally different from almost every other database, where reads are blocked by writes.

❏ A writer of data is blocked only when another writer of data has already locked the row it was going after. A reader of data never blocks a writer of data.

These facts must be taken into consideration when developing your application and you must also realize that this policy is unique to Oracle. A developer who does not understand how his or her database handles concurrency will certainly encounter data integrity issues (this is particularly common when a developer moves from another database to Oracle, or vice versa, and neglects to take the differing concurrency mechanisms into account in their application.

One of the side-effects of Oracle's 'non-blocking' approach is that if you actually want to ensure that no more than one user has access to a row at once, then you, the developer, need to do a little work yourself. Consider the following example. A developer was demonstrating to me a resource-scheduling program (for conference rooms, projectors, etc.) that he had just developed and was in the process of deploying. The application implemented a business rule to prevent the allocation of a resource to more than one person, for any given period of time. That is, the application contained code that specifically checked that no other user had previously allocated the time slot (as least the developer thought it did). This code queried the schedules table and, if no rows existed that overlapped that time slot, inserted the new row. So, the developer was basically concerned with two tables:

```
create table resources ( resource_name varchar2(25) primary key, ... );
create table schedules( resource_name varchar2(25) references resources,
                        start_time    date,
                        end_time      date );
```

And, before making, say, a room reservation, the application would query:

```
select count(*)
  from schedules
 where resource_name = :room_name
   and (start_time between :new_start_time and :new_end_time
        or
        end_time between :new_start_time and :new_end_time)
```

It looked simple and bullet-proof (to the developer anyway); if the count came back zero, the room was yours. If it came back non-zero, you could not reserve it for that period. Once I knew what his logic was, I set up a very simple test to show him the error that would occur when the application went live. An error that would be incredibly hard to track down and diagnose after the fact – one would be convinced it *must* be a database bug.

All I did was get someone else to use the terminal next to him. They both navigated to the same screen and, on the count of three, each hit the Go button and tried to reserve the same room for the exact same time. Both people got the reservation – the logic, which worked perfectly in isolation, failed in a multi-user environment. The problem in this case was caused by Oracle's non-blocking reads. Neither session ever blocked the other session. Both sessions simply ran the above query and then performed the logic to schedule the room. They could both run the query to look for a reservation, even if the other session had already started to modify the `schedules` table (the change wouldn't be visible to the other session until commit, by which time it was too late). Since they were never attempting to modify the same row in the `schedules` table, they would never block each other and, thus, the business rule could not enforce what it was intended to enforce.

The developer needed a method of enforcing the business rule in a multi-user environment, a way to ensure that exactly one person at a time made a reservation on a given resource. In this case, the solution was to impose a little serialization of his own – in addition to performing the count(*) above, the developer must first:

```
select * from resources where resource_name = :room_name FOR UPDATE;
```

A little earlier in the chapter, we discussed an example where use of the FOR UPDATE clause caused problems, but here it is what makes this business rule work in the way intended. What we did here was to lock the resource (the room) to be scheduled immediately *before* scheduling it, in other words before we query the `Schedules` table for that resource. By locking the resource we are trying to schedule, we have ensured that no one else is modifying the schedule for this resource simultaneously. They must wait until we commit our transaction – at which point, they would be able to see our schedule. The chance of overlapping schedules is removed. The developer must understand that, in the multi-user environment, they must at times employ techniques similar to those used in multi-threaded programming. The FOR UPDATE clause is working like a semaphore in this case. It serializes access to the `resources` tables for that particular row – ensuring no two people can schedule it simultaneously.

This is still highly concurrent as there are potentially thousands of resources to be reserved – what we have done is ensure that only one person modifies a resource at any time. This is a rare case where the manual locking of data you are not going to actually update is called for. You need to be able to recognize where you need to do this and, perhaps as importantly, where not to (I have an example of when not to below). Additionally, this does not lock the resource from other people reading the data as it might in other databases, hence this will scale very well.

Issues such as the above have massive implications when attempting to port an application from database to database (I return to this theme a little later in the chapter), and this trips people up time and time again. For example, if you are experienced in other databases, where writers block readers and vice versa then you may have grown reliant on that fact to protect you from data integrity issues. The *lack* of concurrency is one way to protect yourself from this – that is how it works in many non-Oracle databases. In Oracle, concurrency rules supreme and you must be aware that, as a result, things will happen differently (or suffer the consequences).

For 99 percent of the time, locking is totally transparent and you need not concern yourself with it. It is that other 1 percent that you must be trained to recognize. There is no simple checklist of 'if you do this, you need to do this' for this issue. This is a matter of understanding how your application will behave in a multi-user environment and how it will behave in your database.

Multi-Versioning

This is a topic very closely related to concurrency control, as it forms the foundation for Oracle's concurrency control mechanism – Oracle operates a multi-version read-consistent concurrency model. In Chapter 3, *Locking and Concurrency*, we'll cover the technical aspects of this in more detail but, essentially, it is the mechanism by which Oracle provides for:

- ❑ **Read-consistent queries**: Queries that produce consistent results with respect to a point in time.

- ❑ **Non-blocking queries**: Queries are never blocked by writers of data, as they would be in other databases.

These are two very important concepts in the Oracle database. The term multi-versioning basically comes from the fact that Oracle is able to simultaneously maintain multiple versions of the data in the database. If you understand how multi-versioning works, you will always understand the answers you get from the database. Before we explore in a little more detail how Oracle does this, here is the simplest way I know to *demonstrate* multi-versioning in Oracle:

```
tkyte@TKYTE816> create table t
  2  as
  3  select * from all_users;
Table created.

tkyte@TKYTE816> variable x refcursor

tkyte@TKYTE816> begin
  2          open :x for select * from t;
  3  end;
  4  /

PL/SQL procedure successfully completed.

tkyte@TKYTE816> delete from t;

18 rows deleted.

tkyte@TKYTE816> commit;

Commit complete.

tkyte@TKYTE816> print x

USERNAME                          USER_ID CREATED
------------------------------- --------- ---------
SYS                                     0 04-NOV-00
SYSTEM                                  5 04-NOV-00
DBSNMP                                 16 04-NOV-00
AURORA$ORB$UNAUTHENTICATED             24 04-NOV-00
ORDSYS                                 25 04-NOV-00
ORDPLUGINS                             26 04-NOV-00
MDSYS                                  27 04-NOV-00
CTXSYS                                 30 04-NOV-00
...
DEMO                                   57 07-FEB-01

18 rows selected.
```

In the above example, we created a test table, T, and loaded it with some data from the ALL_USERS table. We opened a cursor on that table. We fetched *no data* from that cursor: we just opened it.

> *Bear in mind that Oracle and does not 'answer' the query, does not copy the data anywhere when you open a cursor – imagine how long it would take to open a cursor on a one billion row table if it did. The cursor opens instantly and it answers the query as it goes along. In other words, it would just read data from the table as you fetched from it.*

In the same session (or maybe another session would do this), we then proceeded to delete all data from that table. We even went as far as to COMMIT work on that delete. The rows are gone – but are they? In fact, they are retrievable via the cursor. The fact is that the resultset returned to us by the OPEN command was pre-ordained at the point in time we opened it. We had touched not a single block of data in that table during the open, but the answer was already fixed in stone. We have no way of knowing what the answer will be until we fetch the data – however the result is immutable from our cursor's perspective. It is not that Oracle copied all of the data above to some other location when we opened the cursor; it was actually the delete command that preserved our data for us by placing it into a data area called a **rollback segment**.

This is what read-consistency is all about and if you do not understand how Oracle's multi-versioning scheme works and what it implies, you will not be able to take full advantage of Oracle nor will you be able to write correct applications in Oracle (ones that will ensure data integrity).

Let's look at the implications of multi-versioning, read-consistent queries and non-blocking reads. If you are not familiar with multi-versioning, what you see below might be surprising. For the sake of simplicity, we will assume that the table we are reading stores one row per database block (the smallest unit of storage in the database), and that we are fullscanning the table in this example.

The table we will query is a simple accounts table. It holds balances in accounts for a bank. It has a very simple structure:

```
create table accounts
( account_number number primary key,
  account_balance number
);
```

In reality the accounts table would have hundreds of thousands of rows in it, but for simplicity we're just going to consider a table with four rows (we will visit this example in more detail in Chapter 3, *Locking and Concurrency*):

Row	Account Number	Account Balance
1	123	$500.00
2	234	$250.00
3	345	$400.00
4	456	$100.00

What we would like to do is to run the end-of-day report that tells us how much money is in the bank. That is an extremely simple query:

```
select sum(account_balance) from accounts;
```

And, of course, in this example the answer is obvious: $1250. However, what happens if we read row 1, and while we're reading rows 2 and 3, an Automated Teller Machine (ATM) generates transactions against this table, and moves $400 from account 123 to account 456? Our query counts $500 in row 4 and comes up with the answer of $1650, doesn't it? Well, of course, this is to be avoided, as it would be an error – at no time did this sum of money exist in the account balance column. It is the way in which Oracle avoids such occurrences, and how Oracle's methods differ from every other database, that you need to understand.

In practically every other database, if you wanted to get a 'consistent' and 'correct' answer to this query, you would either have to lock the whole table while the sum was calculated *or* you would have to lock the rows as you read them. This would prevent people from changing the answer as you are getting it. If you lock the table up-front, you'll get the answer that was in the database at the time the query began. If you lock the data as you read it (commonly referred to as a shared read lock, which prevents updates but not other readers from accessing the data), you'll get the answer that was in the database at the point the query finished. Both of these methods inhibit concurrency a great deal. The table lock would prevent any updates from taking place against the entire table for the duration of your query (for a table of four rows, this would only be a very short period – but for tables with hundred of thousands of rows, this could be several minutes). The 'lock as you go' method would prevent updates on data you have read and already processed and could actually cause deadlocks between your query and other updates.

Now, I said earlier that you would not be able to take full advantage of Oracle if you did not understand the concept of multi-versioning. Here is one reason why that is true. Oracle uses multi-versioning to get the answer, as it existed at the point in time the query began, and the query will take place *without locking a single thing* (while our account transfer transaction updates rows 1 and 4, these rows will be locked to other writers – but not locked to other readers, such as our SELECT SUM...query). In fact, Oracle doesn't have a 'shared read' lock common in other databases – it does not need it. Everything inhibiting concurrency that can be removed, has been removed.

So, how does Oracle get the correct, consistent answer ($1250) during a read without locking any data– in other words, without decreasing concurrency? The secret lies in the transactional mechanisms that Oracle uses. Whenever you modify data, Oracle creates entries in two different locations. One entry goes to the redo logs where Oracle stores enough information to **redo** or 'roll forward' the transaction. For an insert this would be the row inserted. For a delete, it is a message to delete the row in file X, block Y, row slot Z. And so on. The other entry is an **undo** entry, written to a rollback segment. If your transaction fails and needs to be undone, Oracle will read the 'before' image from the rollback segment and restore the data. In addition to using this rollback segment data to undo transactions, Oracle uses it to undo changes to blocks as it is reading them – to restore the block to the point in time your query began. This gives you the ability to read right through a lock and to get consistent, correct answers without locking any data yourself.

So, as far as our example is concerned, Oracle arrives at its answer as follows:

Time	Query	Account transfer transaction
T1	Reads row 1, sum = $500 so far	
T2		Updates row 1, puts an exclusive lock on row 1 preventing other updates. Row 1 now has $100
T3	Reads row 2, sum = $750 so far	
T4	Reads row 3, sum = $1150 so far	
T5		Updates row 4, puts an exclusive lock on block 4 preventing other updates (but not reads). Row 4 now has $500.
T6	Reads row 4, discovers that row 4 has been modified. It will actually rollback the block to make it appear as it did at time = T1. The query will read the value $100 from this block	
T7		Commits transaction
T8	Presents $1250 as the answer	

At time T6, Oracle is effectively 'reading through' the lock placed on row 4 by our transaction. This is how non-blocking reads are implemented – Oracle only looks to see if the data changed, it does not care if the data is currently locked (which implies that it has changed). It will simply retrieve the old value from the rollback segment and proceed onto the next block of data.

This is another clear demonstration of multi-versioning – there are multiple versions of the same piece of information, all at different points in time, available in the database. Oracle is able to make use of these 'snapshots' of data at different points in time to provide us with read-consistent queries and non-blocking queries.

This read-consistent view of data is always performed at the SQL statement level, the results of any single SQL statement are consistent with respect to the point in time they began. This quality is what makes a statement like the following insert a predictable set of data:

```
for x in (select * from t)
loop
    insert into t values (x.username, x.user_id, x.created);
end loop;
```

The result of the SELECT * FROM T is preordained when the query begins execution. The SELECT will not see any of the new data generated by the INSERT. Imagine if it did – this statement might be a never-ending loop. If, as the INSERT generated more rows in CUSTOMER, the SELECT could 'see' those newly inserted rows – the above piece of code would create some unknown number of rows. If the table

T started out with 10 rows, we might end up with 20, 21, 23, or an infinite number of rows in T when we finished. It would be totally unpredictable. This consistent read is provided to all statements so that an INSERT such as the following is predicable as well:

```
insert into t select * from t;
```

The INSERT statement will with be provided a read-consistent view of T – it will not see the rows that it itself just inserted, it will only insert the rows that existed at the time the INSERT began. Many databases won't even permit recursive statements such as the above due to the fact that they cannot tell how many rows might actually be inserted.

So, if you are used to the way other databases work with respect to query consistency and concurrency, or you have never had to grapple with such concepts (no real database experience), you can now see how understanding how this works will be important to you. In order to maximize Oracle's potential, you need to understand these issues as they pertain to Oracle – not how they are implemented in other databases.

Database Independence?

By now, you might be able to see where I'm going in this section. I have made references above to other databases and how features are implemented differently in each. With the exception of some read-only applications, it is my contention that building a wholly database-independent application that is highly scalable is extremely hard – and is in fact quite impossible unless you know exactly how each database works in great detail.

For example, let's revisit our initial resource scheduler example (prior to adding the FOR UPDATE clause). Let's say this application had been developed on a database with an entirely different locking/concurrency model from Oracle. What I'll show here is that if you migrate your application from one database to another database you will have to verify that it still works correctly in these different environments.

Let's assume that we had deployed the initial resource scheduler application in a database that employed page-level locking with blocking reads (reads are blocked by writes) and there was an index on the SCHEDULES table:

```
create index schedules_idx on schedules( resource_name, start_time );
```

Also consider that the business rule was implemented via a database trigger (*after* the INSERT had occurred but before the transaction committed we would verify that only our row existed in the table for that time slot). In a page-locking system, due to the update of the index page by RESOURCE_NAME and START_TIME it is very likely that we would have serialized these transactions. The system would have processed these inserts sequentially due to the index page being locked (all of the RESOURCE_NAMEs with START_TIMEs near each other would be on the same page). In that page level locking database our application would be apparently well behaved – our checks on overlapping resource allocations would have happened one after the other, not concurrently.

If we migrated this application to Oracle and simply assumed that it would behave in the same way, we would be in for a shock. On Oracle, which does row level locking and supplies non-blocking reads, it appears to be ill behaved. As we saw previously, we had to use the FOR UPDATE clause to serialize access. Without this clause, two users could schedule the same resource for the same times. This is a direct consequence of not understanding how the database we have works in a multi-user environment.

I have encountered issues such as this many times when an application is being moved from database A to database B. When an application that worked flawlessly in database A does not work, or works in an apparently bizarre fashion, on database B, the first thought is that database B is a 'bad database'. The simple truth is that database B just does it *differently* – neither database is wrong or 'bad', they are just different. Knowing and understanding how they work will help you immensely in dealing with these issues.

For example, very recently I was helping to convert some Transact SQL (the stored procedure language for SQL Server) into PL/SQL. The developer doing the conversion was complaining that the SQL queries in Oracle returned the 'wrong' answer. The queries looked like this:

```
declare
    l_some_variable    varchar2(25);
begin
    if ( some_condition )
    then
        l_some_variable := f( ... );
    end if;

    for x in ( select * from T where x = l_some_variable )
    loop
        ...
```

The goal here was to find all of the rows in T where X was Null if some condition was not met or where x equaled a specific value if some condition was met.

The complaint was that, in Oracle, this query would return no data when L_SOME_VARIABLE was not set to a specific value (when it was left as Null). In Sybase or SQL Server, this was not the case – the query would find the rows where X was set to a Null value. I see this on almost every conversion from Sybase or SQL Server to Oracle. SQL is supposed to operate under tri-valued logic and Oracle implements Null values the way ANSI SQL requires them to be implemented. Under those rules, comparing X to a Null is neither True or False – it is, in fact, *unknown*. The following snippet shows what I mean:

```
ops$tkyte@ORA8I.WORLD> select * from dual;

D
-
X

ops$tkyte@ORA8I.WORLD> select * from dual where null=null;

no rows selected

ops$tkyte@ORA8I.WORLD> select * from dual where null<>null;

no rows selected
```

This can be confusing the first time you see it – it proves that, in Oracle, Null is neither equal to nor not equal to Null. SQL Server, by default, does not do it that way: in SQL Server and sybase, Null is equal to Null. Neither Oracle's, sybase nor SQL Server's SQL processing is *wrong* – they are just *different*. Both databases are in fact ANSI compliant databases but they still work differently. There are ambiguities, backward compatibility issues, and so on, to be overcome. For example, SQL Server supports the ANSI method of

Null comparison, just not by default (it would break thousands of existing legacy applications built on that database).

In this case, one solution to the problem was to write the query like this instead:

```
select *
  from t
 where ( x = l_some_variable OR (x is null and l_some_variable is NULL ))
```

However, this leads to another problem. In SQL Server, this query would have used an index on x. This is not the case in Oracle since a B*Tree index (more on indexing techniques in Chapter 7) will not index an entirely Null entry. Hence, if you need to find Null values, B*Tree indexes are not very useful.

What we did in this case, in order to minimize impact on the code, was to assign X some value that it could never in reality assume. Here, X, by definition, was a positive number – so we chose the number –1. Thus, the query became:

```
select * from t where nvl(x,-1) = nvl(l_some_variable,-1)
```

And we created a function-based index:

```
create index t_idx on t( nvl(x,-1) );
```

With minimal change, we achieved the same end result. The important points to recognize from this are that:

- ❑ Databases are different. Experience in one will in part carry over to another but you must be ready for some *fundamental* differences as well as some very minor differences.

- ❑ Minor differences (such as treatment of Nulls) can have as big an impact as fundamental differences (such as concurrency control mechanism).

- ❑ Being aware of the database and how it works and how its features are implemented is the only way to overcome these issues.

Developers frequently ask me (usually more than once a day) how to do something specific in the database. For example, they will ask the question 'How do I create a temporary table in a stored procedure?' I do not answer such questions with a direct answer – I always respond with a question: 'Why do you want to do that?. Many times, the answer will come back: 'In SQL Server we created temporary tables in our stored procedures and we need to do this in Oracle.' That is what I expected to hear. My response, then, is easy – 'you do not want to create temporary tables in a stored procedure in Oracle (you only think you do).' That would, in fact, be a very bad thing to do in Oracle. If you created the tables in a stored procedure in Oracle you would find that:

- ❑ Doing DDL is a scalability inhibitor.
- ❑ Doing DDL constantly is not fast.
- ❑ Doing DDL commits your transaction.
- ❑ You would have to use Dynamic SQL in all of your stored procedures in order to access this table – no static SQL.
- ❑ Dynamic SQL in PL/SQL is not as fast or as optimized as static SQL.

The bottom line is that you don't want to do it exactly as you did it in SQL Server (if you even need the temporary table in Oracle at all). You want to do things as they are best done in Oracle. Just as if you were going the other way from Oracle to SQL Server, you would not want to create a single table for all users to share for temporary data (that is how Oracle does it). That would limit scalability and concurrency in those other databases. All databases are not created equal – they are all very different.

The Impact of Standards

If all databases are SQL92-compliant, then they must be the same. At least that is the assumption made many times. In this section I would like to dispel that myth.

SQL92 is an ANSI/ISO standard for databases. It is the successor to the SQL89 ANSI/ISO standard. It defines a language (SQL) and behavior (transactions, isolation levels, and so on) that tell you how a database will behave. Did you know that many commercially available databases are SQL92-compliant? Did you know that it means very little as far as query and application portability goes?

Starting with the standard, we will find that the SQL92 standard has four levels:

❑ **Entry-level** – This is the level to which most vendors have complied. This level is a minor enhancement of the predecessor standard, SQL89. No database vendors have been certified higher and in fact the National Institute of Standards and Technology (NIST), the agency that used to certify for SQL-compliance, does not even certify anymore. I was part of the team that got Oracle 7.0 NIST-certified for SQL92 entry-level compliance in 1993. An entry level compliant database has the feature set of Oracle 7.0.

❑ **Transitional** – This is approximately 'halfway' between entry-level and intermediate-level as far as a feature set goes.

❑ **Intermediate** – this adds many features including (not by any means an exhaustive list):

Dynamic SQL

Cascade DELETE for referential integrity

DATE and TIME data types

Domains

Variable length character strings

A CASE expression

CAST functions between data types

❑ **Full** – Adds provisions for (again, not exhaustive):

Connection management

A BIT string data type

Deferrable integrity constraints

Derived tables in the FROM clause

Subqueries in CHECK clauses

Temporary tables

The entry-level standard does not include features such as outer joins, the new inner join syntax, and so on. Transitional does specify outer join syntax and inner join syntax. Intermediate adds more, and Full is, of course all of SQL92. Most books on SQL92 do not differentiate between the various levels leading to confusion on the subject. They demonstrate what a theoretical database implementing SQL92 FULL would look like. It makes it impossible to pick up a SQL92 book, and apply what you see in the book to just any SQL92 database. For example, in SQL Server the 'inner join' syntax is supported in SQL statements, whereas in Oracle it is not. But, they are both SQL92-compliant databases. You can do inner joins and outer joins in Oracle, you will just do it differently than in SQL Server. The bottom line is that SQL92 will not go very far at the entry-level and, if you use any of the features of intermediate or higher, you risk not being able to 'port' your application.

You should not be afraid to make use of vendor-specific features – after all, you are paying a lot of money for them. Every database has its own bag of tricks, and we can always find a way to perform the operation in each database. Use what is best for your current database, and re-implement components as you go to other databases. Use good programming techniques to isolate yourself from these changes. The same techniques are employed by people writing OS-portable applications. The goal is to fully utilize the facilities available to you, but ensure you can change the implementation on a case-by-case basis.

For example, a common function of many database applications is the generation of a unique key for each row. When you insert the row, the system should automatically generate a key for you. Oracle has implemented the database object called a SEQUENCE for this. Informix has a SERIAL data type. Sybase and SQL Server have an IDENTITY type. Each database has a way to do this. However, the methods are different, both in how you do it, and the possible outcomes. So, to the knowledgeable developer, there are two paths that can be pursued:

- ❑ Develop a totally database-independent method of generating a unique key.

- ❑ Accommodate the different implementations and use different techniques when implementing keys in each database.

The theoretical advantage of the first approach is that to move from database to database you need not change anything. I call it a 'theoretical' advantage because the 'con' side of this implementation is so huge that it makes this solution totally infeasible. What you would have to do to develop a totally database-independent process is to create a table such as:

```
create table id_table ( id_name varchar(30), id_value number );
insert into id_table values ( 'MY_KEY', 0 );
```

Then, in order to get a new key, you would have to execute the following code:

```
update id_table set id_value = id_value + 1 where id_name = 'MY_KEY';
select id_value from id_table where id_name = 'MY_KEY';
```

Looks simple enough, but the outcome is that only one user at a time may process a transaction now. We need to update that row to increment a counter, and this will cause our program to serialize on that operation. At best, one person at a time will generate a new value for this key. This issue is compounded by the fact that our transaction is much larger then we have outlined above. The UPDATE and SELECT we have in the example are only two statements of potentially many other statements that make up our transaction. We have yet to insert the row into the table with this key we just generated, and do whatever other work it takes to complete this transaction. This serialization will be a huge limiting factor in scaling. Think of the ramifications if this technique was used on web sites that processed orders, and this was how we generated order numbers. There would be no multi-user concurrency, so we would be forced to do everything sequentially.

The correct approach to this problem would be to use the best code for each database. In Oracle this would be (assuming the table that needs the generated primary key is T):

```
create table t ( pk number primary key, ... );
create sequence t_seq;
create trigger t_trigger before insert on t for each row
begin
    select t_seq.nextval into :new.pk from dual;
end;
```

This will have the effect of automatically, and transparently, assigning a unique key to each row inserted. The same effect can be achieved in the other databases using their types – the create tables syntax will be different, the net results will be the same. Here, we have gone out of our way to use each databases feature to generate a *non-blocking*, highly concurrent unique key, and have introduced no real changes to the application code – all of the logic is contained in this case in the DDL.

Another example of defensive programming to allow for portability is, once you understand that each database *will implement features in a different way*, to layer your access to the database when necessary. Let's say you are programming using JDBC. If all you use is straight SQL SELECTs, INSERTs, UPDATEs, and DELETEs, you probably do not need a layer of abstraction. You may very well be able to code the SQL directly in your application, as long as you limit the constructs you use to those constructs supported by each of the databases you intend to support. Another approach that is both more portable and offers better performance, would be to use stored procedures to return resultsets. You will discover that every vendor's database can return resultsets from stored procedures but how they are returned is different. The actual source code you must write is different for different databases.

Your two choices here would be to either not use stored procedures to return resultsets, or to implement different code for different databases. I would definitely follow the 'different code for different vendors' method, and use stored procedures heavily. This apparently seems to increase the amount of time it would take to implement on a different database. However, you will find it is actually easier to implement on multiple databases with this approach. Instead of having to find the perfect SQL that works on *all* databases (perhaps better on some than on others), you will implement the SQL that works best on that database. You can do this outside of the application itself, giving you more flexibility in tuning the application. We can fix a poorly performing query in the database itself, and deploy that fix immediately, without having to patch the application. Additionally, you can take advantage of vendor extensions to SQL using this method freely. For example, Oracle supports hierarchical queries via the CONNECT BY operation in its SQL. This unique feature is great for resolving recursive queries. In Oracle you are free to utilize this extension to SQL since it is 'outside' of the application (hidden in the database). In other databases, you would use a temporary table and procedural code in a stored procedure to achieve the same results, perhaps. You paid for these features so you might as well use them.

These are the same techniques developers who implement multi-platform code utilize. Oracle Corporation for example uses this technique in the development of its own database. There is a large amount of code (a small percentage of the database code overall) called **OSD** (**O**perating **S**ystem **D**ependent) code that is implemented specifically for each platform. Using this layer of abstraction, Oracle is able to make use of many native OS features for performance and integration, without having to rewrite the large majority of the database itself. The fact that Oracle can run as a multi-threaded application on Windows and a multi-process application on UNIX attests to this feature. The mechanisms for inter-process communication are abstracted to such a level that they can be re-implemented on an OS-by-OS basis, allowing for radically different implementations that perform as well as an application written directly, and specifically, for that platform.

In addition to SQL syntactic differences, implementation differences, and differences in performance of the same query in different databases outlined above, there are the issues of concurrency controls, isolation levels, query consistency, and so on. We cover these items in some detail in Chapter 3, *Locking and Concurrency*, and Chapter 4, *Transactions* of this book, and see how their differences may affect you. SQL92 attempted to give a straightforward definition of how a transaction should work, how isolation levels are to be implemented, but in the end, you'll get different results from different databases. It is all due to the implementation. In one database an application will deadlock and block all over the place. In another database, the same exact application will not – it will run smoothly. In one database, the fact that you did block (physically serialize) was used to your advantage and when you go to deploy on another database, and it does not block, you get the wrong answer. Picking an application up and dropping it on another database takes a lot of hard work and effort, even if you followed the standard 100 percent.

Features and Functions

A natural extension of the argument that you shouldn't necessarily strive for 'database independence' is the idea that you should understand exactly what your specific database has to offer and make full use of it. This is not a section on all of the features that Oracle 8i has to offer. That would be an extremely large book in itself. The new features of Oracle 8i themselves fill a book in the Oracle documentation set. With about 10,000 pages of documentation provided by Oracle, covering each and every feature and function would be quite an undertaking. Rather, this is a section on why it would benefit you to get at least a cursory knowledge of what is provided.

As I've said before, I answer questions about Oracle on the web. I'd say that 80 percent of my answers are simply URLs to the documentation. People are asking how they might go about writing some complex piece of functionality in the database (or outside of it). I just point them to the place in the documentation that tells them how Oracle has already implemented it, and how to use it. Replication comes up this way frequently. I'll receive the question 'I would like to keep a copy of my data elsewhere. I would like this to be a read-only copy. I need it to update only once a day at midnight. How can I write the code to do that?' The answer is as simple as a `CREATE SNAPSHOT` command. This is what built-in functionality in the database.

It is true you can write your own replication, it might even be fun to do so, but at the end of the day, it would not be the smartest thing to do. The database does a lot of stuff. In general, it can do it better then we can ourselves. Replication for example is internalized in the kernel, written in C. It's fast, it's fairly easy, and it is robust. It works across versions, across platforms. It is supported, so if you hit a problem, Oracle's support team will be glad to help. If you upgrade, replication will be supported there as well, probably with some new features. Now, consider if you had developed your own. You would have to provide support for all of the versions you wanted to support. Inter-operability between 7.3 and 8.0 and 8.1 and 9.0, and so on – this would be your job. If it 'broke', you won't be calling support. At least, not until you can get a test case that is small enough to demonstrate your basic issue. When the new release of Oracle comes out, it will be up to you to migrate your replication code to that release.

Not having a full understanding of what is available to you can come back to haunt you in the long run. I was recently talking with some developers and their management. They were demonstrating a 'very cool' piece of software they had developed. It was a message-based system that solved the database queue problem. You see this normally in a database if you wanted many people to use a table as a 'queue'. You would like many people to be able to lock the next record in the queue, skipping over any previously locked records (these queue records are being processed already). The problem you encounter is that there is no documented syntax in the database for skipping locked rows. So, if you didn't know anything about Oracle's features, you would assume that if you wanted queuing software on top of the database, you would have to build it (or buy it).

That is what these developers did. They built a series of processes, and developed APIs for doing message queuing on top of the database. They spent quite a bit of time on it, and used quite a few man-hours to achieve it. The developers were quite sure it was unique. Immediately after seeing it, and hearing of its functionality, I had one thing to say – Advanced Queues. This is a native feature of the database. It solves the 'get the first unlocked record in the queue table and lock it for me' problem. It was right there all along. Their developers, not knowing that this feature existed, spent a lot of time and energy writing their own. In addition to spending lots of time in the past on it, they would be spending lots of time maintaining it in the future. Their manager was less than impressed upon discovering the unique piece of software in effect emulated a native database feature.

I have seen people in an Oracle 8i database set up daemon processes that reads messages off of pipes (a database IPC mechanism). These daemon processes execute the SQL contained within the pipe message, and commit the work. They did this so that they could execute auditing in a transaction that would not get rolled back if the bigger transaction did. Usually, if a trigger or something were used to audit an access to some data, but a statement failed later on, all of the work would be rolled back (see Chapter 4 on *Transactions*, we discuss this statement level atomicity in some detail). So, by sending a message to another process, they could have a separate transaction do the work and commit it. The audit record would stay around, even if the parent transaction rolled back. In versions of Oracle before Oracle 8I, this was an appropriate (and pretty much the only) way to implement this functionality. When I told them of the database feature called autonomous transactions (we will take a detailed look at these in Chapter 15), they were quite upset with themselves. Autonomous transactions, implemented with a single line of code, do exactly what they were doing. On the bright side, this meant they could discard a lot of code and not have to maintain it. In addition, the system ran faster overall, and was easier to understand. Still, they were upset at the amount of time they had wasted reinventing the wheel. In particular the developer who wrote the daemon processes was quite upset at having just written a bunch of 'shelf-ware'.

The above list of examples is something I see repeated time, and time again – large complex solutions to problems that are already solved by the database itself. Unless you take the time to learn what is available, you are doomed to do the same thing at some point. In the second section of this book, *Database Structures and Utilities*, we are going to take an in-depth look at a *handful* of functionality provided by the database. I picked and chose the features and functions that I see people using frequently, or in other cases, functionality that should be used more often but is not. It is only the tip of the iceberg however. There is so much more to Oracle than can be presented in a single book.

Solving Problems Simply

There are always two ways to solve everything: the easy way and the hard way. Time and time again, I see people choosing the hard way. It is not always done consciously. More usually, it is done out of ignorance. They never expected the database to be able to do 'that'. I, on the other hand, expect the database to be capable of anything and only do it the 'hard' way (by writing it myself) when I discover it cannot do something.

For example, I am frequently asked 'How can I make sure the end user has only one session in the database?' (There are hundreds of other examples I could have used here). This must be a requirement of many applications but none that I've ever worked on – I've not found a good reason for limiting people in this way. However, people want to do it and when they do, they usually do it the hard way. For example, they will have a batch job run by the operating system that will look at the V$SESSION table and arbitrarily kill sessions of users who have more then one session. Alternatively, they will create their own tables and have the application insert a row when a user logs in, and remove the row when they log out. This implementation invariably leads to lots of calls to the help desk because when the application 'crashes', the row never gets removed. I've seen lots of other 'creative' ways to do this, but none is as easy as:

```
ops$tkyte@ORA8I.WORLD> create profile one_session limit sessions_per_user 1;
Profile created.

ops$tkyte@ORA8I.WORLD> alter user scott profile one_session;
User altered.

ops$tkyte@ORA8I.WORLD> alter system set resource_limit=true;
System altered.
```

That's it – now any user with the ONE_SESSION profile can log on only once. When I bring up this solution, I can usually hear the smacking of a hand on the forehead followed by the statement 'I never knew it could do that'. Taking the time to familiarize yourself with what the tools you have to work with are capable of doing can save you lots of time and energy in your development efforts.

The same 'keep in simple' argument applies at the broader architecture level. I would urge people to think carefully before adopting very complex implementations. The more moving parts you have in your system, the more things you have that can go wrong and tracking down exactly where that error is occurring in an overly complex architecture is not easy. It may be really 'cool' to implement using umpteen tiers, but it is not the right choice if a simple stored procedure can do it better, faster and with less resources.

I've worked on a project where the application development had been on going for over a year. This was a web application, to be rolled out to the entire company. The HTML client talked to JSPs in the middle tier, which talked to CORBA objects, which talked to the database. The CORBA objects would maintain 'state' and a connection to the database in order to maintain a session. During the testing of this system we found that they would need many front end application servers and a very large database machine to support the estimated 10,000 concurrent users. Not only that, but stability was an issue at times given the complex nature of the interaction between the various components (just exactly where in that stack is the error coming from and why? – that was a hard question to answer). The system would scale, it would just take a lot of horsepower to do it. Additionally, since the implementation used a lot of complex technologies – it would require experienced developers to not only to develop it but to maintain it. We took a look at that system and what it was trying to do and realized that the architecture was a little more complex than it needed to be in order to do the job. We saw that simply by using the PL/SQL module of Oracle iAS and some stored procedures, we could implement the exact system on a fraction of the hardware, and using less 'experienced' developers. No EJBs, no complex interaction between JSPs and EJBs – just the simple translation of a URL into a stored procedure call. This new system is still up and running today, exceeding the estimated user count and with response times that people do not believe. It uses the most basic of architectures, has the fewest moving pieces, runs on an inexpensive 4-CPU workgroup server and never breaks (well a tablespace filled up once, but that's another issue).

I will always go with the simplest architecture that solves the problem completely over a complex one any day. The payback can be enormous. Every technology has its place – not every problem is a nail, we can use more than a hammer in our toolbox.

Openness

There is another reason that I frequently see people doing things the hard way and again it relates to the idea that one should strive for 'openness' and 'database independence' at all costs. The developers wish to avoid using 'closed', 'proprietary' database features – even something as simple as 'stored procedures' or 'sequences' because that will lock them into a database system. Well, let me put forth the idea that the instant you develop a read/write application you are already somewhat locked in. You will find subtle (and sometimes not so subtle) differences between the databases as soon as you start running queries and modifications. For example, in one database you might find that your SELECT COUNT(*) FROM T deadlocks with a simple update of two rows. In Oracle, you'll find that the SELECT COUNT(*) never blocks for a writer. We've seen the case where a business rule appears to get enforced on one database, due to side effects of the database's
s locking model, and does not get enforced in another database. You'll find that, given the same exact transaction mix, reports come out with different answers in different databases – all because of fundamental implementation differences. You will find that it is a very rare application that can simply be picked up and moved from one database to another. Differences in the way the SQL is interpreted (for example, the NULL=NULL example) and processed will always be there.

On a recent project, the developers were building a web-based product using Visual Basic, ActiveX Controls, IIS Server, and the Oracle 8i database. I was told that the development folks had expressed concern that since the business logic had been written in PL/SQL, the product had become database dependent and was asked: 'How can we correct this?'

I was a little taken aback by this question. In looking at the list of chosen technologies I could not figure out how being database dependent was a 'bad' thing:

❑ They had chosen a language that locked them into a single operating system and is supplied by a single vendor (they could have opted for Java).

❑ They had chosen a component technology that locked them into a single operating system and vendor (they could have opted for EJB or CORBA).

❑ They had chosen a web server that locked them in to a single vendor and single platform (why not Apache?).

Every other technology choice they had made locked them into a very specific configuration – in fact the only technology that offered them any choice as far as operating systems go was in fact the database.

Regardless of this – they must have had good reasons to choose the technologies they did – we still have a group of developers making a conscious decision to not utilize the functionality of a critical component in their architecture, and doing it in the name of 'openness'. It is my belief that you pick your technologies carefully and then you exploit them to the fullest possible extent. You have paid a lot for these technologies – would it not be in your best interest to exploit them fully? I had to assume that they were looking forward to utilizing the full potential of the other technologies – so why was the database an exception? An even harder question to answer in light of the fact that it was crucial to their success.

We can put a slightly different spin on this argument if we consider it from the perspective of 'openness'. You put all of your data into the database. The database is a very open tool. It supports data access via SQL, EJBs, HTTP, FTP, SMB, and many other protocols and access mechanisms. Sounds great so far, the most open thing in the world.

Then, you put all of your application logic and more importantly, your *security* outside of the database. Perhaps in your beans that access the data. Perhaps in the JSPs that access the data. Perhaps in your Visual Basic code running under Microsoft's Transaction Server (MTS). The end result is that you have just closed off your database – you have made it 'non-open'. No longer can people hook in existing technologies to make use of this data – they *must* use your access methods (or bypass security altogether). This sounds all well and fine today, but what you must remember is that the 'whiz bang' technology of today, EJBs for example, yesterday's concept, and tomorrow's old, tired technology. What has persevered for over 20 years in the relational world (and probably most of the object implementations as well) is the database itself. The front ends to the data change almost yearly, and as they do, the applications that have all of the security built inside themselves, not in the database, become obstacles, roadblocks to future progress.

The Oracle database provides a feature called **Fine Grained Access Control** (Chapter 21 is dedicated to it). In a nutshell, this technology allows the developer to embed procedures in the database that can modify queries as they are submitted to the database. This query modification is used to restrict the rows the client will receive or modify. The procedure can look at who is running the query, when they are running the query, what terminal they are running the query from, and so on, and can constrain access to the data as appropriate. With FGAC, we can enforce security such that, for example:

❑ Any query executed outside of normal business hours by a certain class of users returned zero records.

❑ Any data could be returned to a terminal in a secure facility but only non-sensitive information to a 'remote' client terminal.

Basically, it allows us to locate access control in the database, *right next to the data*. It no longer matters if the user comes at the data from a Bean, a JSP, a VB application using ODBC, or SQL*PLUS, the same security protocols will be enforced. You are well situated for the next technology that comes along.

Now, I ask you – which implementation is more 'open'? The one that makes all access to the data possible only through calls to the VB code and ActiveX controls (replace VB with Java and ActiveX with EJB if you like – I'm not picking on a particular technology but an implementation here) or the solution that allows access from anything that can talk to the database, over protocols as diverse as SSL, HTTP and Net8 (and others) or using APIs such as ODBC, JDBC, OCI, and so on? I have yet to see an ad-hoc reporting tool that will 'query' your VB code. I know of dozens that can do SQL, though.

The decision to strive for database independence and total 'openness' is one that people are absolutely free to take, and many try, but I believe that it is the wrong decision. No matter what database you are using, you should exploit it fully, squeezing every last bit of functionality you can out of that product. You'll find yourself doing that in the tuning phase (which again always seems to happen right after deployment) anyway. It is amazing how quickly the database independence requirement can be dropped when you can make the application run five times faster just by exploiting the software's capabilities.

How Do I Make it Run Faster?

The question in the heading is one I get asked all the time. Everyone is looking for the fast = true switch, assuming 'database tuning' means that you tune the database. In fact, it is my experience that more than 80 percent (frequently much more, 100 percent) of all performance gains are to be realized at the application level – not the database level. You cannot tune a database until you have tuned the applications that run on the data.

As time goes on there are some switches we can 'throw' at the database level to help lessen the impact of egregious programming blunders. For example, Oracle 8.1.6 adds a new parameter, CURSOR_SHARING=FORCE. This feature implements an 'auto binder' if you will. It will silently take a query written as SELECT * FROM EMP WHERE EMPNO = 1234 and rewrite it for us as SELECT * FROM EMP WHERE EMPNO = :x. This *can* dramatically decrease the number of hard parses, and decrease the library latch waits we discussed in the Architecture sections – *but* (there is always a but) it can have some side effects. You may hit an issue (a.k.a. 'bug') with regards to this feature, for example in the first release:

```
ops$tkyte@ORA8I.WORLD> alter session set cursor_sharing=force;
Session altered.

ops$tkyte@ORA8I.WORLD> select * from dual where dummy='X'and 1=0;
select * from dual where dummy='X'and 1=0
                                        *
ERROR at line 1:
ORA-00933: SQL command not properly ended

ops$tkyte@ORA8I.WORLD> alter session set cursor_sharing=exact;
Session altered.

ops$tkyte@ORA8I.WORLD> select * from dual where dummy='X'and 1=0;
no rows selected
```

The way they rewrote the query (because of the lack of whitespace between 'X' and the word AND) didn't work in 8.1.6. The query ended up being:

```
select * from dual where dummy=:SYS_B_0and :SYS_B_1=:SYS_B_2;
```

The key word AND became part of the bind variable :SYS_B_0. In 8.1.7, however, this query is rewritten as:

```
select * from dual where dummy=:"SYS_B_0"and :"SYS_B_1"=:"SYS_B_2";
```

This works *syntactically* but might negatively affect your program's performance. For example, in the above, notice how 1=0 (also False) is rewritten to be :"SYS_B_1" = :"SYS_B_2". The optimizer no longer has all of the information at parse time, it can no longer see that this query returns zero rows (before it even executes it). While I don't expect you to have lots of queries with 1=0 in them, I would expect you to have some queries that do use literals in them *on purpose*. You may have a column with very skewed values in it, for example 90 percent of the values of the column are greater than 100, 10 percent are less then 100. Further, 1 percent is less then 50. You would want the query:

```
select * from t where x < 50;
```

to use an index, and the query:

```
select * from t where x > 100;
```

to *not* use an index. If you use CURSOR_SHARING = FORCE, the optimizer will not have the 50 or 100 values to consider when optimizing – hence it will come up with a generic plan that probably does not use the index (even if 99.9 percent of your queries are of the type WHERE x < 50).

Additionally, I have found that while CURSOR_SHARING = FORCE runs much faster than parsing and optimizing lots of unique queries, I have also found it to be slower than using queries where the developer did the binding. This arises not from any inefficiency in the cursor sharing code, but rather in inefficiencies in the program itself. In Chapter 10, *Tuning Strategies and Tools*, we'll discover how parsing of SQL queries can affect our performance. In many cases, an application that does not use bind variables is not efficiently parsing and reusing cursors either. Since the application believes each query is unique (it built them as unique statements) it will never use a cursor more than once. The fact is that if the programmer had used bind variables in the first place, they could have parsed a query once and reused it many times. It is this overhead of parsing that decreases the overall potential performance you could see.

Basically, it is important to keep in mind that simply turning on CURSOR_SHARING = FORCE will not necessarily fix your problems. It may very well introduce new ones. CURSOR_SHARING is, in some cases, a very useful tool, but it is not a silver bullet. A well-developed application would never need it. In the long term, using bind variables where appropriate, and constants when needed, is the correct approach.

Even if there are some switches that can be thrown at the database level, and they are truly few and far between, problems relating to concurrency issues and poorly executing queries (due to poorly written queries or poorly structured data) cannot be fixed with a switch. These situations require rewrites (and frequently a re-architecture). Moving datafiles around, changing the multi-block read count, and other 'database' level switches frequently have a minor impact on the overall performance of an application. Definitely not anywhere near the 2, 3, ... N times increase in performance you need to achieve to make the application acceptable. How many times has your application been 10 percent too slow? 10 percent too slow, no one complains about. Five times too slow, people get upset. I repeat: you will not get a 5-times increase in performance by moving datafiles around. You will only achieve this by fixing the application – perhaps by making it do significantly less I/O.

Performance is something you have to design for, to build to, and to test for continuously throughout the development phase. It should never be something to be considered after the fact. I am amazed at how many times people wait until the application has been shipped to their customer, put in place and is actually running before they even start to tune it. I've seen implementations where applications are shipped with nothing more than primary keys – no other indexes whatsoever. The queries have never been tuned or stress tested. The application has never been tried out with more than a handful of users. Tuning is considered to be part of the installation of the product. To me, that is an unacceptable approach. Your end users should be presented with a responsive, fully tuned system from day one. There will be enough 'product issues' to deal with without having poor performance be the first thing they experience. Users are expecting a few 'bugs' from a new application, but at least don't make them wait a painfully long time for them to appear on screen.

The DBA-Developer Relationship

The back cover of this book talks of the importance of a DBA knowing what the developers are trying to accomplish and of developers knowing how to exploit the DBA's data management strategies. It's certainly true that the most successful information systems are based on a symbiotic relationship between the DBA and the application developer. In this section I just want to give a developer's perspective on the division of work between developer and DBA (assuming that every serious development effort has a DBA team).

As a developer, you should not necessarily have to know how to install and configure the software. That should be the role of the DBA and perhaps the SA (System Administrator). Setting up Net8, getting the listener going, configuring MTS, enabling connection pooling, installing the database, creating the database, and so on – these are functions I place in the hands of the DBA/SA.

In general, a developer should not have to know how to tune the operating system. I myself generally leave this task to the SAs for the system. As a software developer for database applications you will need to be competent in use of your operating system of choice, but you shouldn't expect to have to tune it.

Perhaps one of the biggest concerns of the DBA is how to back up and restore a database, and I would say that this is the sole responsibility of the DBA. Understanding how rollback and redo work – yes, that is something a developer has to know. Knowing how to perform a tablespace point in time recovery is something a developer can skip over. Knowing that you can do it might come in handy, but actually having to do it – no.

Tuning at the database instance level, figuring out what the optimum SORT_AREA_SIZE should be – that's typically the job of the DBA. There are exceptional cases where a developer might need to change some setting for a session, but at the database level, the DBA is responsible for that. A typical database supports more than just a single developer's application. Only the DBA who supports all of the applications can make the right decision.

Allocating space and managing the files is the job of the DBA. Developers will contribute their estimations for space (how much they feel they will need) but the DBA/SA will take care of the rest.

Basically, developers do not need to know how to run the database. They need to know how to run *in* the database. The developer and the DBA will work together on different pieces of the same puzzle. The DBA will be visiting you, the developer, when your queries are consuming too many resources, and you will be visiting them when you cannot figure out how to make the system go any faster (that's when instance tuning can be done, when the application is fully tuned).

This will all vary by environment, but I would like to think that there is a division. A good developer is usually a very bad DBA, and vice versa. They are two different skillsets, two different mindsets, and two different personalities in my opinion.

Summary

Here we have taken a somewhat anecdotal look at why you need to know the database. The examples I have given are not isolated – they happen every day, day in and day out. I observe a continuous cycle of this happening over and over again and again. Let's quickly recap the key points. If you are developing with Oracle:

❑ You need to understand the Oracle architecture. You don't have to know it so well that you are able to rewrite the server if you wanted but you should know it well enough that you are aware of the implications of using a particular feature.

❑ You need to understand locking and concurrency control and that every database implements this differently. If you don't, your database will give 'wrong' answers and you will have large contention issues – leading to poor performance.

❑ Do not treat the database as a black box, something you need not understand. The database is the most critical piece of most applications. To try to ignore it would be fatal.

❑ Do not re-invent the wheel. I've seen more then one development team get in trouble, not only technically but on a personal level, due to a lack of awareness what Oracle provides for free. This will happen when it is pointed out that the feature they just spent the last couple of months implementing was actually a core feature of the database all along.

❑ Solve problems as simply as possible, using as much of Oracle's built-in functionality as possible. You paid a lot for it.

❑ Software projects come and go, programming languages and frameworks come and go. We developers are expected to have systems up and running in weeks, maybe months, and then move on to the next problem. If we re-invent the wheel over and over, we will never come close to keeping up with the frantic pace of development. Just as you would never build your own hash table class in Java – since it comes with one – you should use the database functionality you have at your disposal. The first step to being able to do that, of course, is to understand what it is you have at your disposal. Read on.

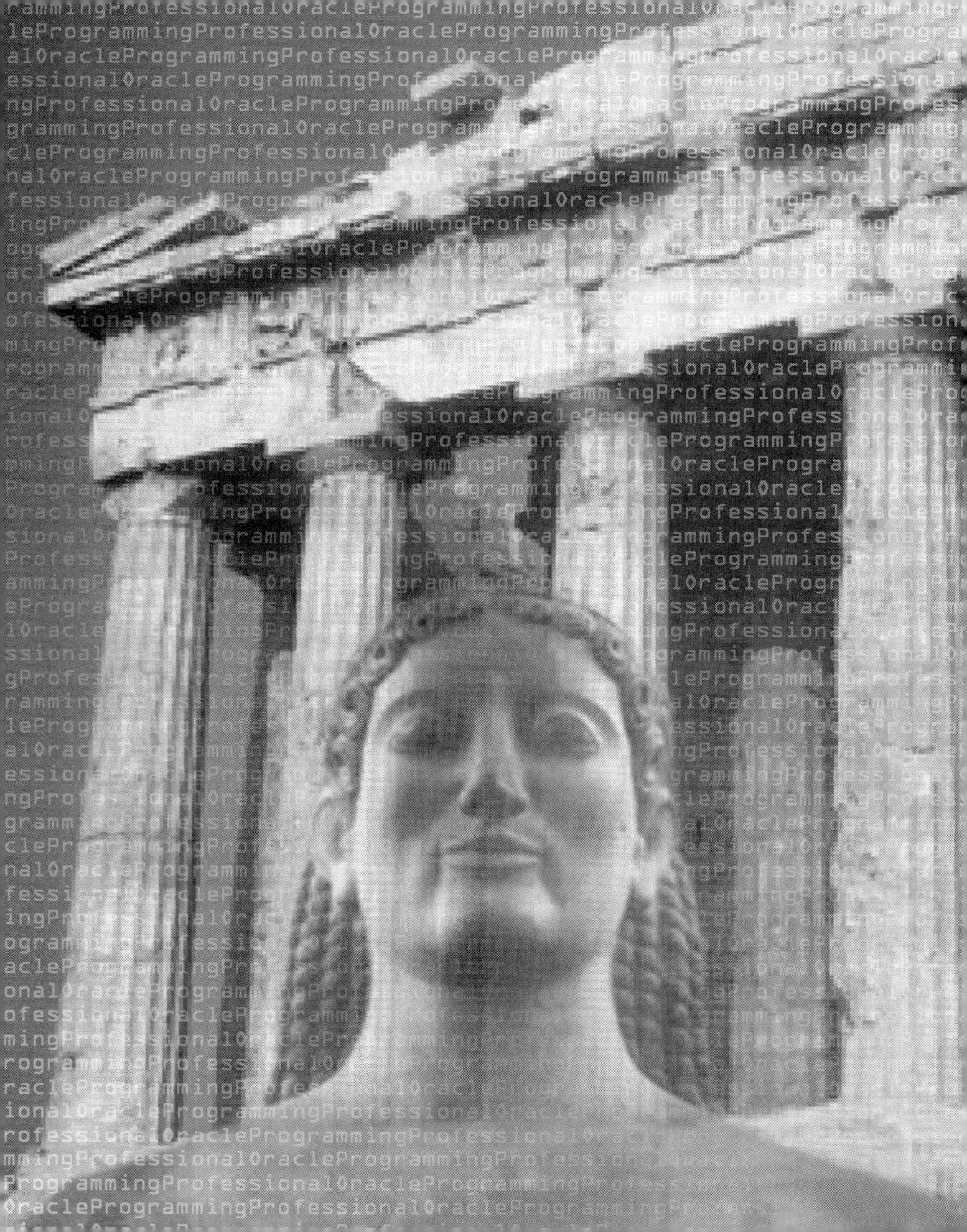

2

Architecture

Oracle is designed to be a very portable database – it is available on every platform of relevance. For this reason, the physical architecture of Oracle looks different on different operating systems. For example, on a UNIX operating system, you will see Oracle implemented as many different operating system processes, virtually a process per major function. On UNIX, this is the correct implementation, as it works on a multi-process foundation. On Windows however, this architecture would be inappropriate and would not work very well (it would be slow and non-scaleable). On this platform, Oracle is implemented as a single, threaded process, which is the appropriate implementation mechanism on this platform. On IBM mainframe systems running OS/390 and zOS, the Oracle operating system-specific architecture exploits multiple OS/390 address spaces, all operating as a single Oracle instance. Up to 255 address spaces can be configured for a single database instance. Moreover, Oracle works together with OS/390 **W**ork**L**oad **M**anager (**WLM**) to establish execution priority of specific Oracle workloads relative to each other, and relative to all other work in the OS/390 system. On Netware we are back to a threaded model again. Even though the physical mechanisms used to implement Oracle from platform to platform vary, the architecture is sufficiently generalized enough that you can get a good understanding of how Oracle works on all platforms.

In this chapter, we will look at the three major components of the Oracle architecture:

- ❑ Files – we will go through the set of five files that make up the database and the instance. These are the **parameter**, **data**, **temp**, and **redo log** Files.

- ❑ Memory structures, referred to as the **S**ystem **G**lobal **A**rea (**SGA**) – we will go through the relationships between the SGA, PGA, and UGA. Here we also go through the Java pool, shared pool, and large pool parts of the SGA.

- ❑ Physical processes or threads – we will go through the three different types of processes that will be running on the database: **server** processes, **background** processes, and **slave** processes.

The Server

It is hard to decide which of these components to cover first. The processes use the SGA, so discussing the SGA before the processes might not make sense. On the other hand, by discussing the processes and what they do, I'll be making references to the SGA. The two are very tied together. The files are acted on by the processes and would not make sense without understanding what the processes do. What I will do is define some terms and give a general overview of what Oracle looks like (if you were to draw it on a whiteboard) and then we'll get into some of the details.

There are two terms that, when used in an Oracle context, seem to cause a great deal of confusion. These terms are 'instance' and 'database'. In Oracle terminology, the definitions would be:

❑   **Database** – A collection of physical operating system files

❑   **Instance** – A set of Oracle processes and an SGA

The two are sometimes used interchangeably, but they embrace very different concepts. The relationship between the two is that a database may be **mounted** and **opened** by many instances. An instance may mount and open a single database at any point in time. The database that an instance opens and mounts does not have to be the same every time it is started.

Confused even more? Here are some examples that should help clear it up. An instance is simply a set of operating system processes and some memory. They can operate on a database, a database just being a collection of files (data files, temporary files, redo log files, control files). At any time, an instance will have only one set of files associated with it. In most cases, the opposite is true as well; a database will have only one instance working on it. In the special case of **O**racle **P**arallel **S**erver (**OPS**), an option of Oracle that allows it to function on many computers in a clustered environment, we may have many instances simultaneously mounting and opening this one database. This gives us access to this single database from many different computers at the same time. Oracle Parallel Server provides for extremely highly available systems and, when implemented correctly, extremely scalable solutions. In general, OPS will be considered out of scope for this book, as it would take an entire book to describe how to implement it.

So, in most cases, there is a one-to-one relationship between an instance and a database. This is how the confusion surrounding the terms probably arises. In most peoples' experience, a database is an instance, and an instance is a database.

In many test environments, however, this is not the case. On my disk, I might have, five separate databases. On the test machine, I have Oracle installed once. At any point in time there is only one instance running, but the database it is accessing may be different from day to day or hour to hour, depending on my needs. By simply having many different configuration files, I can mount and open any one of these databases. Here, I have one 'instance' but many databases, only one of which is accessible at any point in time.

So now when someone talks of the instance, you know they mean the processes and memory of Oracle. When they mention the database, they are talking of the physical files that hold the data. A database may be accessible from many instances, but an instance will provide access to exactly one database at a time.

Now we might be ready for an abstract picture of what Oracle looks like:

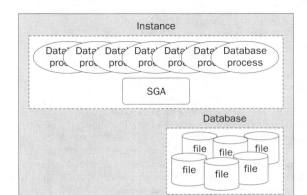

In its simplest form, this is it. Oracle has a large chunk of memory call the SGA where it will: store many internal data structures that all processes need access to; cache data from disk; cache redo data before writing it to disk; hold parsed SQL plans, and so on. Oracle has a set of processes that are 'attached' to this SGA and the mechanism by which they attach differs by operating system. In a UNIX environment, they will physically attach to a large shared memory segment – a chunk of memory allocated in the OS that may be accessed by many processes concurrently. Under Windows, they simply use the C call `malloc()` to allocate the memory, since they are really threads in one big process. Oracle will also have a set of files that the database processes/threads read and write (and Oracle processes are the only ones allowed to read or write these files). These files will hold all of our table data, indexes, temporary space, redo logs, and so on.

If you were to start up Oracle on a UNIX-based system and execute a `ps` (process status) command, you would see that many physical processes are running, with various names. For example:

```
$ /bin/ps -aef | grep ora816
  ora816 20827    1  0  Feb 09  ?         0:00 ora_d000_ora816dev
  ora816 20821    1  0  Feb 09  ?         0:06 ora_smon_ora816dev
  ora816 20817    1  0  Feb 09  ?         0:57 ora_lgwr_ora816dev
  ora816 20813    1  0  Feb 09  ?         0:00 ora_pmon_ora816dev
  ora816 20819    1  0  Feb 09  ?         0:45 ora_ckpt_ora816dev
  ora816 20815    1  0  Feb 09  ?         0:27 ora_dbw0_ora816dev
  ora816 20825    1  0  Feb 09  ?         0:00 ora_s000_ora816dev
  ora816 20823    1  0  Feb 09  ?         0:00 ora_reco_ora816dev
```

I will cover what each of these processes are, but they are commonly referred to as the **Oracle background processes**. They are persistent processes that make up the instance and you will see them from the time you start the database, until the time you shut it down. It is interesting to note that these are processes, not programs. There is only one Oracle program on UNIX; it has many personalities. The same 'program' that was run to get `ora_lgwr_ora816dev`, was used to get the process `ora_ckpt_ora816dev`. There is only one binary, named simply `oracle`. It is just executed many times with different names. On Windows, using the `tlist` tool from the Windows resource toolkit, I will find only one process, `Oracle.exe`. Again, on NT there is only one binary program. Within this process, we'll find many threads representing the Oracle background processes. Using `tlist` (or any of a number of tools) we can see these threads:

```
C:\Documents and Settings\Thomas Kyte\Desktop>tlist 1072
1072 ORACLE.EXE
   CWD:      C:\oracle\DATABASE\
   CmdLine: c:\oracle\bin\ORACLE.EXE TKYTE816
   VirtualSize:    144780 KB   PeakVirtualSize:    154616 KB
   WorkingSetSize: 69424 KB    PeakWorkingSetSize: 71208 KB
   NumberOfThreads: 11
      0 Win32StartAddr:0x00000000 LastErr:0x00000000 State:Initialized
      5 Win32StartAddr:0x00000000 LastErr:0x00000000 State:Initialized
      5 Win32StartAddr:0x00000000 LastErr:0x00000000 State:Initialized
      5 Win32StartAddr:0x00000000 LastErr:0x00000000 State:Initialized
      5 Win32StartAddr:0x00000000 LastErr:0x00000000 State:Initialized
      5 Win32StartAddr:0x00000000 LastErr:0x00000000 State:Initialized
      5 Win32StartAddr:0x00000000 LastErr:0x00000000 State:Initialized
      5 Win32StartAddr:0x00000000 LastErr:0x00000000 State:Initialized
      5 Win32StartAddr:0x00000000 LastErr:0x00000000 State:Initialized
      5 Win32StartAddr:0x00000000 LastErr:0x00000000 State:Initialized
      5 Win32StartAddr:0x00000000 LastErr:0x00000000 State:Initialized
      0.0.0.0 shp  0x00400000   ORACLE.EXE
   5.0.2163.1 shp  0x77f80000   ntdll.dll
      0.0.0.0 shp  0x60400000   oraclient8.dll
      0.0.0.0 shp  0x60600000   oracore8.dll
      0.0.0.0 shp  0x60800000   oranls8.dll
...
```

Here, there are eleven threads executing inside the single process `Oracle`. If I were to log into this database, I would see the thread count jump to twelve. On UNIX, I would probably see another process get added to the list of oracle processes running. This brings us to the next iteration of the diagram. The previous diagram gave a conceptual depiction of what Oracle would look like immediately after starting. Now, if we were to connect to Oracle in its most commonly used configuration, we would see something like:

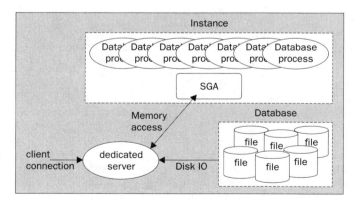

Typically, Oracle will create a new process for me when I log in. This is commonly referred to as the **dedicated server** configuration, since a server process will be dedicated to me for the life of my session. For each session, a new dedicated server will appear in a one-to-one mapping. My client process (whatever program is trying to connect to the database) will be in direct contact with this dedicated server over some networking conduit, such as a TCP/IP socket. It is this server that will receive my SQL and execute it for me. It will read data files, it will look in the database's cache for my data. It will perform my update statements. It will run my PL/SQL code. Its only goal is to respond to the SQL calls that I submit to it.

Oracle may also be executing in a mode called multi-threaded server (MTS) in which we would not see an additional thread created, or a new UNIX process appear. In MTS mode, Oracle uses a pool of 'shared servers' for a large community of users. Shared servers are simply a connection pooling mechanism. Instead of having 10000 dedicated servers (that's a lot of processes or threads) for 10000 database sessions, MTS would allow me to have a small percentage of this number of shared servers, which would be (as their name implies) shared by all sessions. This allows Oracle to connect many more users to the database than would otherwise be possible. Our machine might crumble under the load of managing 10000 processes, but managing 100 or 1000 processes would be doable. In MTS mode, the shared server processes are generally started up with the database, and would just appear in the `ps` list (in fact in my previous `ps` list, the process `ora_s000_ora816dev` is a shared server process).

A big difference between MTS mode and dedicated server mode is that the client process connected to the database never talks directly to a shared server, as it would to a dedicated server. It cannot talk to a shared server since that process is in fact shared. In order to share these processes we need another mechanism through which to 'talk'. Oracle employs a process (or set of processes) called **dispatchers** for this purpose. The client process will talk to a dispatcher process over the network. The dispatcher process will put the client's request into a request queue in the SGA (one of the many things the SGA is used for). The first shared server that is not busy will pick up this request, and process it (for example, the request could be UPDATE T SET X = X+5 WHERE Y = 2. Upon completion of this command, the shared server will place the response in a response queue. The dispatcher process is monitoring this queue and upon seeing a result, will transmit it to the client. Conceptually, the flow of an MTS request looks like this:

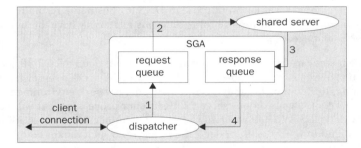

The client connection will send a request to the dispatcher. The dispatcher will first place this request onto the request queue in the SGA (1). The first available shared server will dequeue this request (2) and process it. When the shared server completes, the response (return codes, data, and so on) is placed into the response queue (3) and subsequently picked up by the dispatcher (4), and transmitted back to the client.

As far as the developer is concerned, there is no difference between a MTS connection and a dedicated server connection. So, now that we understand what dedicated server and shared server connections are, this begs the questions, 'How do we get connected in the first place?' and 'What is it that would start this dedicated server?' and 'How might we get in touch with a dispatcher?' The answers depend on our specific platform, but in general, it happens as described below.

We will investigate the most common case – a network based connection request over a TCP/IP connection. In this case, the client is situated on one machine, and the server resides on another machine, the two being connected on a TCP/IP network. It all starts with the client. It makes a request to the Oracle client software to connect to database. For example, you issue:

```
C:\> sqlplus scott/tiger@ora816.us.oracle.com
```

Here the client is the program SQL*PLUS, scott/tiger is my username and password, and ora816.us.oracle.com is a TNS service name. TNS stands for **T**ransparent **N**etwork **S**ubstrate and is 'foundation' software built into the Oracle client that handles our remote connections – allowing for peer-to-peer communication. The TNS connection string tells the Oracle software how to connect to the remote database. Generally, the client software running on your machine will read a file called TNSNAMES.ORA. This is a plain text configuration file commonly found in the [ORACLE_HOME]\network\admin directory that will have entries that look like:

```
ORA816.US.ORACLE.COM =
  (DESCRIPTION =
    (ADDRESS_LIST =
      (ADDRESS = (PROTOCOL = TCP)(HOST = aria.us.oracle.com)(PORT = 1521))
    )
    (CONNECT_DATA =
      (ORACLE_SID = ora816)
    )
  )
```

It is this configuration information that allows the Oracle client software to turn ora816.us.oracle.com into something useful – a hostname, a port on that host that a 'listener' process will accept connections on, the **SID** (**S**ite **ID**entifier) of the database on the host to which we wish to connect, and so on. There are other ways that this string, ora816.us.oracle.com, could have been resolved. For example it could have been resolved using Oracle Names, which is a distributed name server for the database, similar in purpose to DNS for hostname resolution. However, use of the TNSNAMES.ORA is common in most small to medium installations where the number of copies of such a configuration file is manageable.

Now that the client software knows where to connect to, it will open a TCP/IP socket connection to the machine aria.us.oracle.com on the port 1521. If the DBA for our server has setup Net8, and has the listener running, this connection may be accepted. In a network environment, we will be running a process called the **TNS Listener** on our server. This listener process is what will get us physically connected to our database. When it receives the inbound connection request, it inspects the request and, using its own configuration files, either rejects the request (no such database for example, or perhaps our IP address has been disallowed connections to this host) or accepts it and goes about getting us connected.

If we are making a dedicated server connection, the listener process will create a dedicated server for us. On UNIX, this is achieved via a fork() and exec() system call (the only way to create a new process after initialization in UNIX is fork()). We are now physically connected to the database. On Windows, the listener process requests the database process to create a new thread for a connection. Once this thread is created, the client is 'redirected' to it, and we are physically connected. Diagrammatically in UNIX, it would look like this:

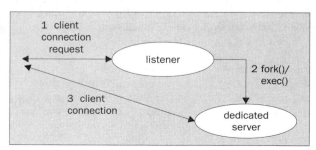

On the other hand, if we are making a MTS connection request, the listener will behave differently. This listener process knows the dispatcher(s) we have running on the database. As connection requests are received, the listener will choose a dispatcher process from the pool of available dispatchers. The listener will send back to the client the connection information describing how the client can connect to the dispatcher process. This must be done because the listener is running on a well-known hostname and port on that host, but the dispatchers will be accepting connections on 'randomly assigned' ports on that server. The listener is aware of these random port assignments and picks a dispatcher for us. The client then disconnects from the listener and connects directly to the dispatcher. We now have a physical connection to the database. Graphically this would look like this:

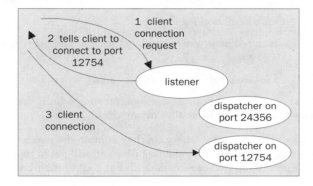

So, that is an overview of the Oracle architecture. Here, we have looked at what an Oracle instance is, what a database is, and how you can get connected to the database either through a dedicated server, or a shared server. The following diagram sums up what we've seen so far; showing the interaction between the a client using a shared server (MTS) connection and a client using a dedicated server connection. It also shows that an Oracle instance may use both connection types simultaneously:

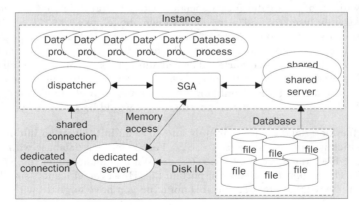

Now we are ready to take a more in-depth look at the processes behind the server, what they do, and how they interact with each other. We are also ready to look inside the SGA to see what is in there, and what its purpose it. We will start by looking at the types of files Oracle uses to manage the data and the role of each file type.

The Files

We will start with the five types of file that make up a database and instance. The files associated with an instance are simply:

❑ **Parameter files** – These files tell the Oracle instance where to find the control files. For example, how big certain memory structures are, and so on.

The files that make up the database are:

❑ **Data files** – For the database (these hold your tables, indexes and all other segments).

❑ **Redo log files** – Our transaction logs.

❑ **Control files** – Which tell us where these data files are, and other relevant information about their state.

❑ **Temp files** – Used for disk-based sorts and temporary storage.

❑ **Password files –** Used to authenticate users performing administrative activities over the network. We will not discuss these files in any detail.

The most important files are the first two, because they contain the data you worked so hard to accumulate. I can lose any and all of the remaining files and still get to my data. If I lose my redo log files, I may start to lose *some* data. If I lose my data files and all of their backups, I've *definitely* lost that data forever.

We will now take a look at the types of files and what we might expect to find in them.

Parameter Files

There are many different parameter files associated with an Oracle database, from a TNSNAMES.ORA file on a client workstation (used to 'find' a server as shown above), to a LISTENER.ORA file on the server (for the Net8 listener startup), to the SQLNET.ORA, PROTOCOL.ORA, NAMES.ORA, CMAN.ORA, and LDAP.ORA files. The most important parameter file however, is the databases parameter file for without this, we cannot even get a database started. The remaining files are important; all of them are related to networking and getting connected to the database. However, they are out of the scope for our discussion. For information on their configuration and setup, I would refer you to the *Oracle Net8 Administrators Guide.* Typically as a developer, these files would be set up for you, not by you.

The parameter file for a database is commonly known as an **init file**, or an **init.ora** file. This is due to its default name, which is init<ORACLE_SID>.ora. For example, a database with a SID of tkyte816 will have an init file named, inittkyte816.ora. Without a parameter file, you cannot start an Oracle database. This makes this a fairly important file. However, since it is simply a plain text file, which you can create with any text editor, it is not a file you have to guard with your life.

For those of you unfamiliar with the term SID or ORACLE_SID, a full definition is called for. The SID is a site identifier. It and ORACLE_HOME (where the Oracle software is installed) are hashed together in UNIX to create a unique key name for attaching an SGA. If your ORACLE_SID or ORACLE_HOME is not set correctly, you'll get ORACLE NOT AVAILABLE error, since we cannot attach to a shared memory segment that is identified by magic key. On Windows, we don't use shared memory in the same fashion as UNIX, but the SID is still important. We can have more than one database on the same ORACLE_HOME, so we need a way to uniquely identify each one, along with their configuration files.

The Oracle `init.ora` file is a very simple file in its construction. It is a series of variable name/value pairs. A sample `init.ora` file might look like this:

```
db_name = "tkyte816"

db_block_size = 8192

control_files = ("C:\oradata\control01.ctl", "C:\oradata\control02.ctl")
```

In fact, this is pretty close to the minimum `init.ora` file you could get away with. If I had a block size that was the default on my platform (the default block size varies by platform), I could remove that. The parameter file is used at the very least to get the name of the database, and the location of the control files. The control files tell Oracle the location every other file, so they are very important to the 'bootstrap' process of starting the instance.

The parameter file typically has many other configuration settings in it. The number of parameters and their names vary from release to release. For example in Oracle 8.1.5, there was a parameter `plsql_load_without_compile`. It was not in any prior release, and is not to be found in any subsequent release. On my 8.1.5, 8.1.6, and 8.1.7 databases I have 199, 201, and 203 different parameters, respectively, that I may set. Most parameters like `db_block_size`, are very long lived (they won't go away from release to release) but over time many other parameters become obsolete as implementations change. If you would like to review these parameters and get a feeling for what is available and what they do, you should refer to the *Oracle8i Reference* manual. In the first chapter of this document, it goes over each and every documented parameter in detail.

Notice I said 'documented' in the preceding paragraph. There are undocumented parameters as well. You can tell an undocumented parameter from a documented one in that all undocumented parameters begin with an underscore. There is a great deal of speculation about these parameters – since they are undocumented, they must be 'magic'. Many people feel that these undocumented parameters are well known and used by Oracle insiders. I find the opposite to be true. They are not well known and are hardly ever used. Most of these undocumented parameters are rather boring actually, representing deprecated functionality and backwards compatibility flags. Others help in the recovery of data, not of the database itself, they enable the database to start up in certain extreme circumstances, but only long enough to get data *out*, you have to rebuild after that. Unless directed to by support, there is no reason to have an undocumented `init.ora` parameter in your configuration. Many have side effects that could be devastating. In my development database, I use only one undocumented setting:

```
_TRACE_FILES_PUBLIC = TRUE
```

This makes trace files readable by all, not just the DBA group. On my development database, I want my developers to use `SQL_TRACE`, `TIMED_STATISTICS`, and the `TKPROF` utility frequently (well, I demand it actually); hence they need to be able to read the trace files. In my real database, I don't use any undocumented settings.

In general, you will only use these undocumented parameters at the request of Oracle Support. The use of them can be damaging to a database and their implementation can, and will, change from release to release.

Now that we know what database parameter files are and where to get more details about the valid parameters that we can set, the last thing we need to know is where to find them on disk. The naming convention for this file by default is:

```
init$ORACLE_SID.ora      (Unix environment variable)
init%ORACLE_SID%.ora     (Windows environment variable)
```

And by default they will be found in

```
$ORACLE_HOME/dbs         (Unix)
%ORACLE_HOME%\DATABASE   (Windows)
```

It is interesting to note that, in many cases, you will find the entire contents of this parameter file to be something like:

```
IFILE='C:\oracle\admin\tkyte816\pfile\init.ora'
```

The IFILE directive works in a fashion similar to a #include in C. It includes in the current file, the contents of the named file. The above includes an init.ora file from a non-default location.

It should be noted that the parameter file does not have to be in any particular location. When starting an instance, you may use the startup pfile = filename. This is most useful when you would like to try out different init.ora parameters on your database to see the effects of having different settings.

Data Files

Data files, along with redo log files, are the most important set of files in the database. This is where all of your data will ultimately be stored. Every database has at least one data file associated with it, and typically will have many more than one. Only the most simple 'test' database will have one file. Any real database will have at *least* two – one for the SYSTEM data, and one for USER data. What we will discuss in this section is how Oracle organizes these files, and how data is organized within them. In order to understand this we will have to understand what a tablespace, segment, extent, and block are. These are the units of allocation that Oracle uses to hold objects in the database.

We will start with segments. Segments are simply your database objects that consume storage – objects such as tables, indexes, rollback segments, and so on. When you create a table, you are creating a table segment. When you create a partitioned table – you create a segment per partition. When you create an index, you create an index segment, and so on. Every object that consumes storage is ultimately stored in a single segment. There are rollback segments, temporary segments, cluster segments, index segments, and so on.

Segments themselves consist of one or more **extent**. An extent is a contiguous allocation of space in a file. Every segment starts with at least one extent and some objects may require at least two (rollback segments are an example of a segment that require at least two extents). In order for an object to grow beyond its initial extent, it will request another extent be allocated to it. This second extent will not necessarily be right next to the first extent on disk, it may very well not even be allocated in the same file as the first extent. It may be located very far away from it, but the space within an extent is always contiguous in a file. Extents vary in size from one block to 2 GB in size.

Extents, in turn, consist of blocks. A block is the smallest unit of space allocation in Oracle. Blocks are where your rows of data, or index entries, or temporary sort results will be stored. A block is what Oracle generally reads and writes from and to disk. Blocks in Oracle are generally one of three common sizes – 2 KB, 4 KB, or 8 KB (although 16 KB and 32 KB are also permissible). The relationship between segments, extents, and blocks looks like this:

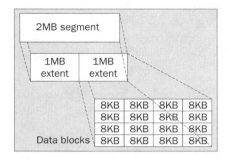

A segment is made up of one or more extents – an extent is a contiguous allocation of blocks.

The block size for a database is a constant once the database is created – each and every block in the database will be the same size. All blocks have the same general format, which looks something like this:

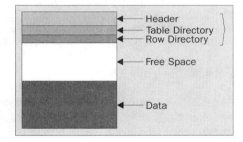

The **block header** contains information about the type of block (a table block, index block, and so on), transaction information regarding active and past transactions on the block, and the address (location) of the block on the disk. The **table directory**, if present, contains information about the tables that store rows in this block (data from more than one table may be stored on the same block). The **row directory** contains information describing the rows that are to be found on the block. This is an array of pointers to where the rows are to be found in the data portion of the block. These three pieces of the block are collectively known as the **block overhead** – space used on the block that is not available for your data, but rather is used by Oracle to manage the block itself. The remaining two pieces of the block are rather straightforward – there will possibly be *free* space on a block and then there will generally be *used* space that is currently storing data.

Now that we have a cursory understanding of segments, which consist of extents, which consist of blocks, we are ready to see what a tablespace is, and then how files fit into the picture. A tablespace is a container – it holds segments. Each and every segment belongs to exactly one tablespace. A tablespace may have many segments within it. All of the extents for a given segment will be found in the tablespace associated with that segment. Segments never cross tablespace boundaries. A tablespace itself has one or more data files associated with it. An extent for any given segment in a tablespace will be contained entirely within one data file. However, a segment may have extents from many different data files. Graphically it might look like this:

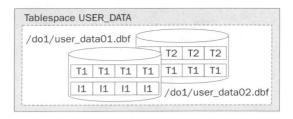

So, here we see tablespace named USER_DATA. It consists of two data files, user_data01, and user_data02. It has three segments allocated it, T1, T2, and I1 (probably two tables and an index). The tablespace has four extents allocated in it and each extent is depicted as a contiguous set of database blocks. Segment T1 consists of two extents, one extent in each file. Segment T2 and I1 each have one extent depicted. If we needed more space in this tablespace, we could either resize the data files already allocated to the tablespace, or we could add a third data file to it.

Tablespaces are a logical storage container in Oracle. As developers we will create segments in tablespaces. We will never get down to the raw 'file level' – we do not specify that we want our extents to be allocated in a specific file. Rather, we create objects in tablespaces and Oracle takes care of the rest. If at some point in the future, the DBA decides to move our data files around on disk to more evenly distribute I/O – that is OK with us. It will not affect our processing at all.

In summary, the hierarchy of storage in Oracle is as follows:

1. A database is made up of one or more tablespaces.

2. A tablespace is made up of one or more data files. A tablespace contains segments.

3. A segment (TABLE, INDEX, and so on) is made up of one or more extents. A segment exists in a tablespace, but may have data in many data files within that tablespace.

4. An extent is a contiguous set of blocks on disk. An extent is in a single tablespace and furthermore, is always in a single file within that tablespace.

5. A block is the smallest unit of allocation in the database. A block is the smallest unit of I/O used by a database.

Before we leave this topic of data files, we will look at one more topic to do with tablespaces. We will look at how extents are managed in a tablespace. Prior to Oracle 8.1.5, there was only one method to manage the allocation of extents within a tablespace. This method is called a **dictionary-managed tablespace**. That is, the space within a tablespace was managed in data dictionary tables, much in the same way you would manage accounting data, perhaps with a DEBIT and CREDIT table. On the debit side, we have all of the extents allocated to objects. On the credit side, we have all of the free extents available for use. When an object needed another extent, it would ask the system to get one. Oracle would then go to its data dictionary tables, run some queries, find the space (or not), and then update a row in one table (or remove it all together), and insert a row into another. Oracle managed space in very much the same way you will write your applications by modifying data, and moving it around.

This SQL, executed on your behalf in the background to get the additional space, is referred to as **recursive SQL**. Your SQL INSERT statement caused other recursive SQL to be executed to get more space. This recursive SQL could be quite expensive, if it is done frequently. Such updates to the data dictionary must be serialized; they cannot be done simultaneously. They are something to be avoided.

In earlier releases of Oracle, we would see this space management issue, this recursive SQL overhead, most often occurred in temporary tablespaces (this is before the introduction of 'real' temporary tablespaces). Space would frequently be allocated (we have to delete from one dictionary table and insert into another) and de-allocated (put the rows we just moved back where they were initially). These operations would tend to serialize, dramatically decreasing concurrency, and increasing wait times. In version 7.3, Oracle introduced the concept of a temporary tablespace to help alleviate this issue. A temporary tablespace was one in which you could create no permanent objects of your own. This was fundamentally the only difference; the space was still managed in the data dictionary tables. However, once an extent was allocated in a temporary tablespace, the system would hold onto it (would not give the space back). The next time someone requested space in the temporary tablespace for any purpose, Oracle would look for an already allocated extent in its memory set of allocated extents. If it found one there, it would simply reuse it, else it would allocate one the old fashioned way. In this fashion, once the database had been up and running for a while, the temporary segment would appear full but would actually just be 'allocated'. The free extents were all there; they were just being managed differently. When someone needed temporary space, Oracle would just look for that space in an in-memory data structure, instead of executing expensive, recursive SQL.

In Oracle 8.1.5 and later, Oracle goes a step further in reducing this space management overhead. They introduced the concept of a locally managed tablespace as opposed to a dictionary managed one. This effectively does for all tablespaces, what Oracle7.3 did for temporary tablespaces – it removes the need to use the data dictionary to manage space in a tablespace. With a locally managed tablespace, a bitmap stored in each data file is used to manage the extents. Now, to get an extent all the system needs to do is set a bit to 1 in the bitmap. To free space – set it back to 0. Compared to using dictionary-managed tablespaces, this is incredibly fast. We no longer serialize for a long running operation at the database level for space requests across all tablespaces. Rather, we serialize at the tablespace level for a very fast operation. Locally managed tablespaces have other nice attributes as well, such as the enforcement of a uniform extent size, but that is starting to get heavily into the role of the DBA.

Temp Files

Temporary data files (temp files) in Oracle are a special type of data file. Oracle will use temporary files to store the intermediate results of a large sort operation, or result set, when there is insufficient memory to hold it all in RAM. Permanent data objects, such as a table or an index, will never be stored in a temporary file, but the contents of a temporary table or index would be. So, you'll never create your application tables in a temporary data file, but you might store data there when you use a temporary table.

Temporary files are treated in a special way by Oracle. Normally, each and every change you make to an object will be recorded in the redo logs – these transaction logs can be replayed at a later date in order to 'redo a transaction'. We might do this during recovery from failure for example. Temporary files are excluded from this process. Temporary files never have redo generated for them, although they do have UNDO generated, when used for global temporary tables, in the event you decide to rollback some work you have done in your session. Your DBA never needs to back up a temporary data file, and in fact if they do they are only wasting their time, as you can never restore a temporary data file.

It is recommended that your database be configured with locally managed temporary tablespaces. You'll want to make sure your DBA uses a CREATE TEMPORARY TABLESPACE command. You do not want them to just alter a permanent tablespace to a temporary one, as you do not get the benefits of temp files that way. Additionally, you'll want them to use a locally managed tablespace with uniform extent sizes that reflect your sort_area_size setting. Something such as:

```
tkyte@TKYTE816> create temporary tablespace temp
  2  tempfile 'c:\oracle\oradata\tkyte816\temp.dbf'
  3  size 5m
  4  extent management local
  5  uniform size 64k;

Tablespace created.
```

As we are starting to get deep into DBA-related activities once again, we'll move onto the next topic.

Control Files

The control file is a fairly small file (it can grow up to 64 MB or so in extreme cases) that contains a directory of the other files Oracle needs. The parameter file (init.ora file) tells the instance where the control files are, the control files tell the instance where the database and online redo log files are. The control files also tell Oracle other things, such as information about checkpoints that have taken place, the name of the database (which should match the db_name init.ora parameter), the timestamp of the database as it was created, an archive redo log history (this can make a control file large in some cases), and so on.

Control files should be multiplexed either by hardware (RAID) or by Oracle when RAID or mirroring is not available – more than one copy of them should exist and they should be stored on separate disks, to avoid losing them in the event you have a disk failure. It is not fatal to lose your control files, it just makes recovery that much harder.

Control files are something a developer will probably never have to actually deal with. To a DBA they are an important part of the database, but to a software developer they are not extremely relevant.

Redo Log Files

Redo log files are extremely crucial to the Oracle database. These are the transaction logs for the database. They are used only for recovery purposes – their only purpose in life is to be used in the event of an instance or media failure, or as a method of maintaining a standby database for failover. If the power goes off on your database machine, causing an instance failure, Oracle will use the online redo logs in order to restore the system to exactly the point it was at immediately prior to the power outage. If your disk drive containing your datafile fails permanently, Oracle will utilize archived redo logs, as well as online redo logs, in order to recover a backup of that drive to the correct point in time. Additionally, if you 'accidentally' drop a table or remove some critical information and commit that operation, you can restore a backup and have Oracle restore it to the point immediately prior to the 'accident' using these online and archive redo log files.

Virtually every operation you perform in Oracle generates some amount of redo to be written to the online redo log files. When you insert a row into a table, the end result of that insert is written to the redo logs. When you delete a row, the fact that you deleted that row is written. When you drop a table, the effects of that drop are written to the redo log. The data from the table you dropped is not written; however the recursive SQL that Oracle performs to drop the table, does generate redo. For example, Oracle will delete a row from the SYS.OBJ$ table and this will generate redo.

Some operations may be performed in a mode that generates as little redo as possible. For example, I can create an index with the NOLOGGING attribute. This means that the initial creation of that index will not be logged, but any recursive SQL Oracle performs on my behalf will be. For example the insert of a row into SYS.OBJ$ representing the existence of the index will not be logged. All subsequent modifications of the index using SQL inserts, updates and deletes will however, be logged.

There are two types of redo log files that I've referred to – online and archived. We will take a look at each. In Chapter 5, *Redo and Rollback*, we will take another look at redo in conjunction with rollback segments, to see what impact they have on you the developer. For now, we will just concentrate on what they are and what purpose they provide.

Online Redo Log

Every Oracle database has at least two online redo log files. These online redo log files are fixed in size and are used in a circular fashion. Oracle will write to log file 1, and when it gets to the end of this file, it will switch to log file 2, and rewrite the contents of that file from start to end. When it has filled log file 2, it will switch back to log file 1 (assuming we have only two redo log files, if you have three, it would of course proceed onto the third file):

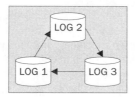

The act of switching from one log file to the other is called a **log switch**. It is important to note that a log switch may cause a temporary 'hang' in a poorly tuned database. Since the redo logs are used to recover transactions in the event of a failure, we must assure ourselves that we won't need the contents of a redo log file in the event of a failure before we reuse it. If Oracle is not sure that it won't need the contents of a log file, it will suspend operations in the database momentarily, and make sure that the data this redo 'protects' is safely on disk itself. Once it is sure of that, processing will resume and the redo file will be reused. What we've just started to talk about here is a key database concept – **checkpointing**. In order to understand how online redo logs are used, we'll need to know something about checkpointing, how the database buffer cache works, and what a process called **Database Block Writer** (DBWn) does. The database buffer cache and DBWn are covered in more detail a little later on, but we will skip ahead a little anyway and touch on them now.

The database buffer cache is where database blocks are stored temporarily. This is a structure in the SGA of Oracle. As blocks are read, they are stored in this cache – hopefully to allow us to not have to physically re-read them later. The buffer cache is first and foremost a performance-tuning device, it exists solely to make the very slow process of physical I/O appear to be much faster then it is. When we modify a block by updating a row on it, these modifications are done in memory, to the blocks in the buffer cache. Enough information to redo this modification is stored in the redo log buffer, another SGA data structure. When you COMMIT your modifications, making them permanent, Oracle does not go to all of the blocks you modified in the SGA and write them to disk. Rather, it just writes the contents of the redo log buffer out to the online redo logs. As long as that modified block is in the buffer cache and is not on disk, we need the contents of that online redo log in the event the database fails. If at the instant after we committed, the power was turned off, the database buffer cache would be wiped out.

If this happens, the only record of our change is in that redo log file. Upon restart of the database, Oracle will actually replay our transaction, modifying the block again in the same way we did, and committing it for us. So, as long as that modified block is cached and not written to disk, we cannot reuse that redo log file.

This is where DBWn comes into play. It is the Oracle background process that is responsible for making space in the buffer cache when it fills up and, more importantly, for performing **checkpoints**. A checkpoint is the flushing of dirty (modified) blocks from the buffer cache to disk. Oracle does this in the background for us. Many things can cause a checkpoint to occur, the most common event being a redo log switch. As we filled up log file 1 and switched to log file 2, Oracle initiated a checkpoint. At this point in time, DBWn started flushing to disk all of the dirty blocks that are protected by log file 1. Until DBWn flushes all of these blocks protected by that log file, Oracle cannot reuse it. If we attempt to use it before DBWn has finished its checkpoint, we will get a message like this:

```
...
Thread 1 cannot allocate new log, sequence 66
Checkpoint not complete
  Current log# 2 seq# 65 mem# 0: C:\ORACLE\ORADATA\TKYTE816\REDO02.LOG
...
```

In our databases ALERT log (the alert log is a file on the server that contains informative messages from the server such as startup and shutdown messages, and exceptional events, such as an incomplete checkpoint). So, at this point in time, when this message appeared, processing was suspended in the database while DBWn hurriedly finished its checkpoint. Oracle gave all the processing power it could, to DBWn at that point in the hope it would finish faster.

This is a message you never want to see in a nicely tuned database instance. If you do see it, you know for a fact that you have introduced artificial, unnecessary waits for your end users. This can always be avoided. The goal (and this is for the DBA, not the developer necessarily) is to have enough online redo log files allocated so that you never attempt to reuse a log file before the checkpoint initiated by it completes. If you see this message frequently, it means your DBA has not allocated sufficient online redo logs for your application, or that DBWn needs to be tuned to work more efficiently. Different applications will generate different amounts of redo log. A **DSS** (**D**ecision **S**upport **S**ystem, query only) system will naturally generate significantly less online redo log then an OLTP (transaction processing) system would. A system that does a lot of image manipulation in **BLOB**s (**B**inary **L**arge **OB**jects) in the database may generate radically more redo then a simple order entry system. An order entry system with 100 users will probably generate a tenth the amount of redo 1,000 users would generate. There is no 'right' size for your redo logs, although you do want to ensure they are large enough.

There are many things you must take into consideration when setting both the size of, and the number of, online redo logs. Many of them are out of the scope of this particular book, but I'll list some of them to give you an idea:

❑ **Standby database** – If you are utilizing the standby database feature, whereby redo logs are sent to another machine after they are filled and applied to a copy of your database, you will most likely want lots of small redo log files. This will help ensure the standby database is never too far out of sync with the primary database.

❑ **Lots of users modifying the same blocks** – Here you might want large redo log files. Since everyone is modifying the same blocks, we would like to update them as many times as possible before writing them out to disk. Each log switch will fire a checkpoint so we would like to switch logs infrequently. This may, however, affect your recovery time.

❏ **Mean time to recover** – If you must ensure that a recovery takes as little time as possible, you may be swayed towards smaller redo log files, even if the previous point is true. It will take less time to process one or two small redo log files than one gargantuan one upon recovery. The overall system will run slower than it absolutely could day-to-day perhaps (due to excessive checkpointing), but the amount of time spent in recovery will be smaller. There are other database parameters that may also be used to reduce this recovery time, as an alternative to the use of small redo log files.

Archived Redo Log

The Oracle database can run in one of two modes – NOARCHIVELOG mode and ARCHIVELOG mode. I believe that a system is not a production system unless it is in ARCHIVELOG mode. A database that is not in ARCHIVELOG mode will, some day, *lose data*. It is inevitable; you will lose data if you are not in ARCHIVELOG mode. Only a test or development system should execute in NOARCHIVELOG mode.

The difference between these two modes is simply what happens to a redo log file when Oracle goes to reuse it. 'Will we keep a copy of that redo or should Oracle just overwrite it, losing it forever?' It is an important question to answer. Unless you keep this file, we cannot recover data from a backup to the current point in time. Say you take a backup once a week on Saturday. Now, on Friday afternoon, after you have generated hundreds of redo logs over the week, your hard disk fails. If you have not been running in ARCHIVELOG mode, the only choices you have right now are:

❏ Drop the tablespace(s) associated with the failed disk. Any tablespace that had a file on that disk must be dropped, including the contents of that tablespace. If the SYSTEM tablespace (Oracle's data dictionary) is affected, you cannot do this.

❏ Restore last Saturday's data and lose all of the work you did that week.

Neither option is very appealing. Both imply that you lose data. If you had been executing in ARCHIVELOG mode on the other hand, you simply would have found another disk. You would have restored the affected files from Saturday's backup onto it. Lastly, you would have applied the archived redo logs, and ultimately, the online redo logs to them (in effect replay the weeks worth of transactions in fast forward mode). You lose nothing. The data is restored to the point in time of the failure.

People frequently tell me they don't need ARCHIVELOG mode for their production systems. I have yet to meet anyone who was correct in that statement.Unless they are willing to lose data some day, they must be in ARCHIVELOG mode. 'We are using RAID-5, we are totally protected' is a common excuse. I've seen cases where, due to a manufacturing error, all five disks in a raid set froze, all at the same time. I've seen cases where the hardware controller introduced corruption into the data files, so they safely protected corrupt data. If we had the backups from before the hardware failure, and the archives were not affected, we could have recovered. The bottom line is that there is no excuse for not being in ARCHIVELOG mode on a system where the data is of any value. Performance is no excuse – properly configured archiving adds little overhead. This and the fact that a 'fast system' that 'loses data' is useless, would make it so that even if archiving added 100 percent overhead, you would need to do it.

Don't let anyone talk you out of being in ARCHIVELOG mode. You spent a long time developing your application, so you want people to trust it. Losing their data will not instill confidence in them.

Files Wrap-Up

Here we have explored the important types of files used by the Oracle database, from lowly parameter files (without which you won't even be able to get started), to the all important redo log and data files. We have explored the storage structures of Oracle from tablespaces to segments, and then extents, and finally down to database blocks, the smallest unit of storage. We have reviewed how checkpointing works in the database, and even started to look ahead at what some of the physical processes or threads of Oracle do. In later components of this chapter, we'll take a much more in depth look at these processes and memory structures.

The Memory Structures

Now we are ready to look at Oracle's major memory structures. There are three major memory structures to be considered:

❑ **SGA, System Global Area** – This is a large, shared memory segment that virtually all Oracle processes will access at one point or another.

❑ **PGA, Process Global Area** – This is memory, which is private to a single process or thread, and is not accessible from other processes/threads.

❑ **UGA, User Global Area** – This is memory associated with your session. It will be found either in the SGA or the PGA depending on whether you are running in MTS mode (then it'll be in the SGA), or dedicated server (it'll be in the PGA).

We will briefly discuss the PGA and UGA, and then move onto the really big structure, the SGA.

PGA and UGA

As stated earlier, the PGA is a process piece of memory. This is memory specific to a single operating system process or thread. This memory is not accessible by any other process/thread in the system. It is typically allocated via the C run-time call `malloc()`, and may grow (and shrink even) at run-time. The PGA is never allocated out of Oracle's SGA – it is always allocated locally by the process or thread.

The UGA is in effect, your session's state. It is memory that your session must always be able to get to. The location of the UGA is wholly dependent on how Oracle has been configured to accept connections. If you have configured MTS, then the UGA must be stored in a memory structure that everyone has access to – and that would be the SGA. In this way, your session can use any one of the shared servers, since any one of them can read and write your sessions data. On the other hand, if you are using a dedicated server connection, this need for universal access to your session state goes away, and the UGA becomes virtually synonymous with the PGA – it will in fact be contained in the PGA. When you look at the system statistics, you'll find the UGA reported in the PGA in dedicated server mode (the PGA will be greater than, or equal to, the UGA memory used; the PGA memory size will include the UGA size as well).

One of the largest impacts on the size of your PGA/UGA will be the `init.ora` or session-level parameters, `SORT_AREA_SIZE` and `SORT_AREA_RETAINED_SIZE`. These two parameters control the amount of space Oracle will use to sort data before writing it to disk, and how much of that memory segment will be retained after the sort is done. The `SORT_AREA_SIZE` is generally allocated out of your PGA and the `SORT_AREA_RETAINED_SIZE` will be in your UGA. We can monitor the size of the

UGA/PGA by querying a special Oracle V$ table, also referred to as a dynamic performance table. We'll find out more about these V$ tables in Chapter 10, *Tuning Strategies and Tools*. Using these V$ tables, we can discover our current usage of PGA and UGA memory. For example, I'll run a small test that will involve sorting lots of data. We'll look at the first couple of rows and then discard the result set. We can look at the 'before' and 'after' memory usage:

```
tkyte@TKYTE816> select a.name, b.value
  2  from v$statname a, v$mystat b
  3  where a.statistic# = b.statistic#
  4  and a.name like '%ga %'
  5  /

NAME                                VALUE
-----------------------------       ----------
session uga memory                  67532
session uga memory max              71972
session pga memory                  144688
session pga memory max              144688

4 rows selected.
```

So, before we begin we can see that we have about 70 KB of data in the UGA and 140 KB of data in the PGA. The first question is, how much memory are we using between the PGA and UGA? It is a trick question, and one that you cannot answer unless you know if we are connected via a dedicated server or a shared server over MTS, and even then it might be hard to figure out. In dedicated server mode, the UGA is totally contained within the PGA. There, we would be consuming 140 KB of memory in our process or thread. In MTS mode, the UGA is allocated from the SGA, and the PGA is in the shared server. So, in MTS mode, by the time we get the last row from the above query, our process may be in use by someone else. That PGA isn't 'ours', so technically we are using 70 KB of memory (except when we are actually running the query at which point we are using 210 KB of memory between the combined PGA and UGA).

Now we will do a little bit of work and see what happens with our PGA/UGA:

```
tkyte@TKYTE816> show parameter sort_area

NAME                                TYPE      VALUE
-----------------------------       -------   -----------------------------
sort_area_retained_size             integer   65536
sort_area_size                      integer   65536

tkyte@TKYTE816> set pagesize 10
tkyte@TKYTE816> set pause on
tkyte@TKYTE816> select * from all_objects order by 1, 2, 3, 4;


...(control C after first page of data) ...

tkyte@TKYTE816> set pause off

tkyte@TKYTE816> select a.name, b.value
  2  from v$statname a, v$mystat b
  3  where a.statistic# = b.statistic#
  4  and a.name like '%ga %'
```

```
    5  /

NAME                                  VALUE
------------------------------   ----------
session uga memory                    67524
session uga memory max               174968
session pga memory                   291336
session pga memory max               291336

4 rows selected.
```

As you can see, our memory usage went up – we've done some sorting of data. Our UGA temporarily increased by about the size of SORT_AREA_RETAINED_SIZE while our PGA went up a little more. In order to perform the query and the sort (and so on), Oracle allocated some additional structures that our session will keep around for other queries. Now, let's retry that operation but play around with the size of our SORT_AREA:

```
tkyte@TKYTE816> alter session set sort_area_size=1000000;

Session altered.

tkyte@TKYTE816> select a.name, b.value
  2  from v$statname a, v$mystat b
  3  where a.statistic# = b.statistic#
  4  and a.name like '%ga %'
  5  /

NAME                                  VALUE
------------------------------   ----------
session uga memory                    63288
session uga memory max               174968
session pga memory                   291336
session pga memory max               291336

4 rows selected.

tkyte@TKYTE816> show parameter sort_area

NAME                                  TYPE      VALUE
-----------------------------------   -------   ------------------------------
sort_area_retained_size               integer   65536
sort_area_size                        integer   1000000

tkyte@TKYTE816> select * from all_objects order by 1, 2, 3, 4;

...(control C after first page of data) ...

tkyte@TKYTE816> set pause off

tkyte@TKYTE816> select a.name, b.value
  2  from v$statname a, v$mystat b
  3  where a.statistic# = b.statistic#
  4  and a.name like '%ga %'
  5  /
```

```
NAME                            VALUE
------------------------------  ----------
session uga memory                   67528
session uga memory max              174968
session pga memory                 1307580
session pga memory max             1307580

4 rows selected.
```

As you can see, our PGA has grown considerably this time. By about the 1,000,000 bytes of SORT_AREA_SIZE we are using. It is interesting to note that the UGA did not move at all in this case. We can change that by altering the SORT_AREA_RETAINED_SIZE as follows:

```
tkyte@TKYTE816> alter session set sort_area_retained_size=1000000;
Session altered.

tkyte@TKYTE816> select a.name, b.value
  2  from v$statname a, v$mystat b
  3  where a.statistic# = b.statistic#
  4  and a.name like '%ga %'
  5  /

NAME                            VALUE
------------------------------  ----------
session uga memory                   63288
session uga memory max              174968
session pga memory                 1307580
session pga memory max             1307580

4 rows selected.

tkyte@TKYTE816> show parameter sort_area

NAME                                 TYPE     VALUE
------------------------------------ -------  ------------------------------
sort_area_retained_size              integer  1000000
sort_area_size                       integer  1000000

tkyte@TKYTE816> select * from all_objects order by 1, 2, 3, 4;

...(control C after first page of data) ...

tkyte@TKYTE816> select a.name, b.value
  2  from v$statname a, v$mystat b
  3  where a.statistic# = b.statistic#
  4  and a.name like '%ga %'
  5  /

NAME                            VALUE
------------------------------  ----------
session uga memory                   66344
session uga memory max             1086120
session pga memory                 1469192
session pga memory max             1469192

4 rows selected.
```

Here, we see that our UGA memory max shot way up – to include the SORT_AREA_RETAINED_SIZE amount of data, in fact. During the processing of our query, we had a 1 MB of sort data 'in memory cache'. The rest of the data was on disk in a temporary segment somewhere. After our query completed execution, this memory was given back for use elsewhere. Notice how PGA memory does not shrink back. This is to be expected as the PGA is managed as a heap and is created via malloc()'ed memory. Some processes within Oracle will explicitly free PGA memory – others allow it to remain in the heap (sort space for example stays in the heap). The shrinking of a heap like this typically does nothing (processes tend to grow in size, not to shrink). Since the UGA is a 'sub-heap' (the 'parent' heap being either the PGA or SGA) it is made to shrink. If we wish, we can force the PGA to shrink:

```
tkyte@TKYTE816> exec dbms_session.free_unused_user_memory;

PL/SQL procedure successfully completed.


tkyte@TKYTE816> select a.name, b.value
  2  from v$statname a, v$mystat b
  3  where a.statistic# = b.statistic#
  4  and a.name like '%ga %'
  5  /

NAME                              VALUE
------------------------------  ----------
session uga memory                73748
session uga memory max          1086120
session pga memory               183360
session pga memory max          1469192
```

However, you should be aware that on most systems, this is somewhat a waste of time. You may have shrunk the size of the PGA heap as far as Oracle is concerned, but you haven't really given the OS any memory back in most cases. In fact, depending on the OS method of managing memory, you may actually be using more memory in total according to the OS. It will all depend on how malloc(), free(), realloc(), brk(), and sbrk() (the C memory management routines) are implemented on your platform.

So, here we have looked at the two memory structures, the PGA and the UGA. We understand now that the PGA is private to a process. It is the set of variables that an Oracle dedicated or shared server needs to have independent of a session. The PGA is a 'heap' of memory in which other structures may be allocated. The UGA on the other hand, is also a heap of memory in which various session-specific structures may be defined. The UGA is allocated from the PGA when you use the dedicated server mode to connect to Oracle, and from the SGA in MTS mode. This implies that when using MTS, you must size your SGA to have enough UGA space in it to cater for every possible user that will ever connect to your database concurrently. So, the SGA of a database running MTS is generally much larger than the SGA for a similarly configured, dedicated server mode only, database.

SGA

Every Oracle instance has one big memory structure collectively referred to as the **SGA**, the **S**ystem **G**lobal **A**rea. This is a large, shared memory structure that every Oracle process will access at one point or another. It will vary from a couple of MBs on small test systems to hundreds of MBs on medium to large systems, and into many GBs in size for really big systems.

On a UNIX operating system, the SGA is a physical entity that you can 'see' from the operating system command line. It is physically implemented as a shared memory segment – a standalone piece of memory that processes may attach to. It is possible to have an SGA on a system without having any Oracle processes; the memory stands alone. It should be noted however that if you have an SGA without any Oracle processes, it indicates that the database crashed in some fashion. It is not a normal situation but it can happen. This is what an SGA 'looks' like on UNIX:

```
$ ipcs -mb
IPC status from <running system> as of Mon Feb 19 14:48:26 EST 2001
T        ID      KEY          MODE        OWNER      GROUP      SEGSZ
Shared Memory:
m        105     0xf223dfc8  --rw-r-----   ora816      dba    186802176
```

On Windows, you really cannot see the SGA as you can in UNIX. Since Oracle executes as a single process with a single address space on that platform, the SGA is allocated as private memory to the ORACLE.EXE process. If you use the Windows Task Manager or some other performance tool, you can see how much memory ORACLE.EXE has allocated, but you cannot see what is the SGA versus any other piece of allocated memory.

Within Oracle itself we can see the SGA regardless of platform. There is another magic V$ table called V$SGASTAT. It might look like this:

```
tkyte@TKYTE816> compute sum of bytes on pool
tkyte@TKYTE816> break on pool skip 1
tkyte@TKYTE816> select pool, name, bytes
  2    from v$sgastat
  3    order by pool, name;

POOL        NAME                                   BYTES
----------- ------------------------------- ----------
java pool   free memory                         18366464
            memory in use                        2605056
*********** -----------
sum                                             20971520

large pool  free memory                          6079520
            session heap                           64480
*********** -----------
sum                                              6144000

shared pool Checkpoint queue                       73764
            KGFF heap                               5900
            KGK heap                               17556
            KQLS heap                             554560
            PL/SQL DIANA                          364292
            PL/SQL MPCODE                         138396
            PLS non-lib hp                          2096
            SYSTEM PARAMETERS                      61856
            State objects                         125464
            VIRTUAL CIRCUITS                       97752
            character set object                   58936
            db_block_buffers                      408000
            db_block_hash_buckets                 179128
            db_files                              370988
```

```
           dictionary cache                319604
           distributed_transactions-       180152
           dlo fib struct                   40980
           enqueue_resources                94176
           event statistics per sess       201600
           file # translation table         65572
           fixed allocation callback          320
           free memory                    9973964
           joxlod: in ehe                   52556
           joxlod: in phe                    4144
           joxs heap init                     356
           library cache                  1403012
           message pool freequeue          231152
           miscellaneous                   562744
           processes                        40000
           sessions                        127920
           sql area                       2115092
           table columns                    19812
           transaction_branches            368000
           transactions                     58872
           trigger defini                    2792
           trigger inform                     520
***********                           ----------
sum                                     18322028

           db_block_buffers              24576000
           fixed_sga                        70924
           log_buffer                       66560
***********                           ----------
sum                                     24713484


43 rows selected.
```

The SGA is broken up into various **pools**. They are:

❑ **Java pool** – The Java pool is a fixed amount of memory allocated for the JVM running in the database.

❑ **Large pool** – The large pool is used by the MTS for session memory, by Parallel Execution for message buffers, and by RMAN Backup for disk I/O buffers.

❑ **Shared pool** – The shared pool contains shared cursors, stored procedures, state objects, dictionary caches, and many dozens of other bits of data.

❑ **The 'Null' pool** – This one doesn't really have a name. It is the memory dedicated to block buffers (cached database blocks), the redo log buffer and a 'fixed SGA' area.

So, an SGA might look like this:

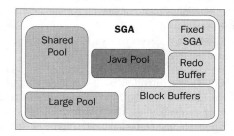

The `init.ora` parameters that have the most effect on the overall size of the SGA are:

- ❑   JAVA_POOL_SIZE – controls the size of the Java pool.
- ❑   SHARED_POOL_SIZE – controls the size of the shared pool, to some degree.
- ❑   LARGE_POOL_SIZE – controls the size of the large pool.
- ❑   DB_BLOCK_BUFFERS – controls the size of the block buffer cache.
- ❑   LOG_BUFFER – controls the size of the redo buffer to some degree.

With the exception of the SHARED_POOL_SIZE and LOG_BUFFER, there is a one-to-one correspondence between the `init.ora` parameters, and the amount of memory allocated in the SGA. For example, if you multiply DB_BLOCK_BUFFERS by your databases block size, you'll typically get the size of the DB_BLOCK_BUFFERS row from the NULL pool in V$SGASTAT (there is some overhead added for latches). If you look at the sum of the bytes from V$SGASTAT for the large pool, this will be the same as the LARGE_POOL_SIZE parameter.

Fixed SGA

The **fixed SGA** is a component of the SGA that varies in size from platform to platform and release to release. It is 'compiled' into the Oracle binary itself at installation time (hence the name 'fixed'). The fixed SGA contains a set of variables that point to the other components of the SGA, and variables that contain the values of various parameters. The size of the fixed SGA is something over which we have no control, and it is generally very small. Think of this area as a 'bootstrap' section of the SGA, something Oracle uses internally to find the other bits and pieces of the SGA.

Redo Buffer

The redo buffer is where data that needs to be written to the online redo logs will be cached temporarily before it is written to disk. Since a memory-to-memory transfer is much faster then a memory to disk transfer, use of the redo log buffer can speed up operation of the database. The data will not reside in the redo buffer for a very long time. In fact, the contents of this area are flushed:

- ❑   Every three seconds, or
- ❑   Whenever someone commits, or
- ❑   When it gets one third full or contains 1 MB of cached redo log data.

For these reasons, having a redo buffer in the order of many tens of MB in size is typically just a waste of good memory. In order to use a redo buffer cache of 6 MB for example, you would have to have very long running transactions that generate 2 MB of redo log every three seconds or less. If anyone in your system commits during that three-second period of time, you will never use the 2MB of redo log space; it'll continuously be flushed. It will be a very rare system that will benefit from a redo buffer of more than a couple of megabytes in size.

The default size of the redo buffer, as controlled by the LOG_BUFFER init.ora parameter, is the greater of 512 KB and (128 * number of CPUs) KB. The minimum size of this area is four times the size of the largest database block size supported on that platform. If you would like to find out what that is, just set your LOG_BUFFERS to 1 byte and restart your database. For example, on my Windows 2000 instance I see:

```
SVRMGR> show parameter log_buffer
NAME                                        TYPE     VALUE
----------------------------------------- ------- ---------------------------
log_buffer                                  integer 1

SVRMGR> select * from v$sgastat where name = 'log_buffer';
POOL        NAME                            BYTES
----------- ------------------------------- ----------
            log_buffer                      66560
```

The smallest log buffer I can really have, regardless of my init.ora settings, is going to be 65 KB. In actuality – it is a little larger then that:

```
tkyte@TKYTE816> select * from v$sga where name = 'Redo Buffers';

NAME                             VALUE
------------------------------- ----------
Redo Buffers                     77824
```

It is 76 KB in size. This extra space is allocated as a safety device – as 'guard' pages to protect the redo log buffer pages themselves.

Block Buffer Cache

So far, we have looked at relatively small components of the SGA. Now we are going to look at one that is possibly huge in size. The block buffer cache is where Oracle will store database blocks before writing them to disk, and after reading them in from disk. This is a crucial area of the SGA for us. Make it too small and our queries will take forever to run. Make it too big and we'll starve other processes (for example, you will not leave enough room for a dedicated server to create its PGA and you won't even get started).

The blocks in the buffer cache are basically managed in two different lists. There is a 'dirty' list of blocks that need to be written by the database block writer (DBWn – we'll be taking a look at that process a little later). Then there is a list of 'not dirty' blocks. This used to be a **LRU** (**L**east **R**ecently **U**sed) list in Oracle 8.0 and before. Blocks were listed in order of use. The algorithm has been modified slightly in Oracle 8i and in later versions. Instead of maintaining the list of blocks in some physical order, Oracle employs a 'touch count' schema. This effectively increments a counter associated with a block every time you hit it in the cache. We can see this in one of the truly magic tables, the X$ tables. These X$ tables are wholly undocumented by Oracle, but information about them leaks out from time to time.

The X$BH table shows information about the blocks in the block buffer cache. Here, we can see the 'touch count' get incremented as we hit blocks. First, we need to find a block. We'll use the one in the DUAL table, a special table with one row and one column that is found in all Oracle databases. We need to know the file number and block number for that block:

```
tkyte@TKYTE816> select file_id, block_id
  2  from dba_extents
  3  where segment_name = 'DUAL' and owner = 'SYS';

   FILE_ID    BLOCK_ID
---------- ----------
         1         465
```

Now we can use that information to see the 'touch count' on that block:

```
sys@TKYTE816> select tch from x$bh where file# = 1 and dbablk = 465;

       TCH
----------
        10

sys@TKYTE816> select * from dual;

D
-
X

sys@TKYTE816> select tch from x$bh where file# = 1 and dbablk = 465;

       TCH
----------
        11

sys@TKYTE816> select * from dual;

D
-
X

sys@TKYTE816> select tch from x$bh where file# = 1 and dbablk = 465;

       TCH
----------
        12
```

Every time I touch that block, the counter goes up. A buffer no longer moves to the head of the list as it is used, rather it stays where it is in the list, and has its 'touch count' incremented. Blocks will naturally tend to move in the list over time however, because blocks are taken out of the list and put into the dirty list (to be written to disk by DBWn). Also, as they are reused, when the buffer cache is effectively full, and some block with a small 'touch count' is taken out of the list, it will be placed back into approximately the middle of the list with the new data. The whole algorithm used to manage these lists is fairly complex and changes subtly from release to release of Oracle as improvements are made. The actual full details are not relevant to us as developers, beyond the fact that heavily used blocks will be cached and blocks that are not used heavily will not be cached for long.

The block buffer cache, in versions prior to Oracle 8.0, was one big buffer cache. Every block was cached alongside every other block – there was no way to segment or divide up the space in the block buffer cache. Oracle 8.0 added a feature called multiple buffer pools to give us this ability. Using the multiple buffer pool feature, we can set aside a given amount of space in the block buffer cache for a specific segment or segments (segments as you recall, are indexes, tables, and so on). Now, we could carve out a space, a buffer pool, large enough to hold our 'lookup' tables in memory, for example. When Oracle reads blocks from these tables, they always get cached in this special pool. They will compete for space in this pool only with other segments targeted towards this pool. The rest of the segments in the system will compete for space in the default buffer pool. This will increase the likelihood of their staying in the cache and not getting aged out by other unrelated blocks. A buffer pool that is set up to cache blocks like this is known as a KEEP pool. The blocks in the KEEP pool are managed much like blocks in the generic block buffer cache described above – if you use a block frequently, it'll stay cached. If you do not touch a block for a while, and the buffer pool runs out of room, that block will be aged out of the pool.

We also have the ability to carve out a space for segments in the buffer pool. This space is called a RECYCLE pool. Here, the aging of blocks is done differently to the KEEP pool. In the KEEP pool, the goal is to keep 'warm' and 'hot' blocks cached for as long as possible. In the recycle pool, the goal is to age out a block as soon as it is no longer needed. This is advantageous for 'large' tables (remember, large is always relative, there is no absolute size we can put on 'large') that are read in a very random fashion. If the probability that a block will ever be re-read in a reasonable amount of time, there is no use in keeping this block cached for very long. Therefore, in a RECYCLE pool, things move in and out on a more regular basis.

So, taking the diagram of the SGA a step further, we can break it down to:

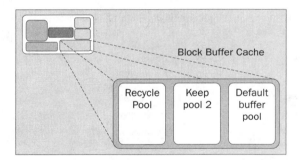

Shared Pool

The shared pool is one of the most critical pieces of memory in the SGA, especially in regards to performance and scalability. A shared pool that is too small can kill performance to the point where the system appears to hang. A shared pool that is too large can do the same thing. A shared pool that is used incorrectly will be a disaster as well.

So, what exactly is the shared pool? The shared pool is where Oracle caches many bits of 'program' data. When we parse a query, the results of that are cached here. Before we go through the job of parsing an entire query, Oracle searches here to see if the work has already been done. PL/SQL code that you run is cached here, so the next time you run it, Oracle doesn't have to read it in from disk again. PL/SQL code is not only cached here, it is shared here as well. If you have 1000 sessions all executing the same code, only one copy of the code is loaded and shared amongst all sessions. Oracle stores the system parameters in the shared pool. The data dictionary cache, cached information about database objects, is stored here. In short, everything but the kitchen sink is stored in the shared pool.

The shared pool is characterized by lots of small (4 KB or thereabouts) chunks of memory. The memory in the shared pool is managed on a LRU basis. It is similar to the buffer cache in that respect – if you don't use it, you'll lose it. There is a supplied package, DBMS_SHARED_POOL, which may be used to change this behavior – to forcibly pin objects in the shared pool. You can use this procedure to load up your frequently used procedures and packages at database startup time, and make it so they are not subject to aging out. Normally though, if over time a piece of memory in the shared pool is not reused, it will become subject to aging out. Even PL/SQL code, which can be rather large, is managed in a paging mechanism so that when you execute code in a very large package, only the code that is needed is loaded into the shared pool in small chunks. If you don't use it for an extended period of time, it will be aged out if the shared pool fills up and space is needed for other objects.

The easiest way to break Oracle's shared pool is to not use bind variables. As we saw in Chapter 1 on *Developing Successful Oracle Applications*, not using bind variables can bring a system to its knees for two reasons:

❏ The system spends an exorbitant amount of CPU time parsing queries.

❏ The system expends an extremely large amount of resources managing the objects in the shared pool as a result of never reusing queries.

If every query submitted to Oracle is a unique query with the values hard-coded, the concept of the shared pool is substantially defeated. The shared pool was designed so that query plans would be used over and over again. If every query is a brand new, never before seen query, then caching only adds overhead. The shared pool becomes something that *inhibits performance*. A common, misguided technique that many try in order to solve this issue is to add more space to the shared pool, but this typically only makes things worse than before. As the shared pool inevitably fills up once again, it gets to be even *more* of an overhead than the smaller shared pool, for the simple reason that managing a big, full-shared pool takes more work than managing a smaller full-shared pool.

The only true solution to this problem is to utilize shared SQL – to reuse queries. Later, in Chapter 10 on *Tuning Strategies and Tools*, we will take a look at the init.ora parameter CURSOR_SHARING that can work as a short term 'crutch' in this area, but the only real way to solve this issue is to use reusable SQL in the first place. Even on the largest of large systems, I find that there are at most 10,000 to 20,000 unique SQL statements. Most systems execute only a few hundred unique queries.

The following real-world example demonstrates just how bad things can get if you use of the shared pool poorly. I was asked to work on a system where the standard operating procedure was to shut down the database each and every night, in order to wipe out the SGA, and restart it clean. The reason for doing this was that the system was having issues during the day whereby it was totally CPU-bound and, if the database were left to run for more than a day, performance would really start to decline. This was solely due to the fact that, in the time period from 9am to 5pm, they would fill a 1 GB shared pool inside of a 1.1 GB SGA. This is true – 0.1 GB dedicated to block buffer cache and other elements, and 1 GB dedicated to caching unique queries that would never be executed again. The reason for the cold start was that if they left the system running for more than a day, they would run out of free memory in the shared pool. At that point, the overhead of aging structures out (especially from a structure so large) was such that it overwhelmed the system and performance was massively degraded (not that performance was that great anyway, since they were managing a 1 GB shared pool). Additionally, the people working on this system constantly wanted to add more and more CPUs to the machine, due to the fact that hard parsing SQL is so CPU-intensive. By correcting the application, allowing it to use bind variables, not only did the physical machine requirements drop (they then had many times more CPU power then they needed), the memory utilization was reversed. Instead of a 1 GB shared pool, they had less then 100 MB allocated – and never used it all over many weeks of continuous uptime.

One last comment about the shared pool and the `init.ora` parameter, `SHARED_POOL_SIZE`. There is no relationship between the outcome of the query:

```
sys@TKYTE816> select sum(bytes) from v$sgastat where pool = 'shared pool';
SUM(BYTES)
----------
  18322028
1 row selected.
```

and the `SHARED_POOL_SIZE init.ora` parameter:

```
sys@TKYTE816> show parameter shared_pool_size
NAME                                 TYPE     VALUE
------------------------------------ -------- ----------------------------------
shared_pool_size                     string   15360000
SVRMGR>
```

other than the fact that the `SUM(BYTES) FROM V$SGASTAT` will always be larger than the `SHARED_POOL_SIZE`. The shared pool holds many other structures that are outside the scope of the corresponding `init.ora` parameter. The `SHARED_POOL_SIZE` is typically the largest contributor to the shared pool as reported by the `SUM(BYTES)`, but it is not the only contributor. For example, the `init.ora` parameter, `CONTROL_FILES`, contributes 264 bytes per file to the 'miscellaneous' section of the shared pool. It is unfortunate that the 'shared pool' in `V$SGASTAT` and the `init.ora` parameter `SHARED_POOL_SIZE` are named as they are, since the `init.ora` parameter contributes to the size of the shared pool, but it is not the *only* contributor.

Large Pool

The large pool is not so named because it is a 'large' structure (although it may very well be large in size). It is so named because it is used for allocations of large pieces of memory, bigger than the shared pool is designed to handle. Prior to its introduction in Oracle 8.0, all memory allocation took place in the shared pool. This was unfortunate if you were using features that made use of 'large' memory allocations such as MTS. This issue was further confounded by the fact that processing, which tended to need a lot of memory allocation, would use the memory in a different manner to the way in which the shared pool managed it. The shared pool manages memory in a LRU basis, which is perfect for caching and reusing data. Large memory allocations, however, tended to get a chunk of memory, use it, and then were done with it – there was no need to cache this memory.

What Oracle needed was something similar to the `RECYCLE` and `KEEP` buffer pools implemented for the block buffer cache. This is exactly what the large pool and shared pool are now. The large pool is a `RECYCLE`-style memory space whereas the shared pool is more like the `KEEP` buffer pool – if people appear to be using something frequently, then you keep it cached.

Memory allocated in the large pool is managed in a heap, much in the way C manages memory via `malloc()` and `free()`. As soon as you 'free' a chunk of memory, it can be used by other processes. In the shared pool, there really was no concept of 'freeing' a chunk of memory. You would allocate memory, use it, and then stop using it. After a while, if that memory needed to be reused, Oracle would age out your chunk of memory. The problem with using just a shared pool is that one size doesn't always fit all.

The large pool is used specifically by:

- ❑ **MTS** – to allocate the UGA region in the SGA.

- ❑ **Parallel Execution of statements** – to allow for the allocation of inter-process message buffers, used to coordinate the parallel query servers.

- ❑ **Backup** – for RMAN disk I/O buffers.

As you can see, none of the above memory allocations should be managed in an LRU buffer pool designed to manage small chunks of memory. With MTS memory, for example, once a session logs out, this memory is never going to be reused so it should be immediately returned to the pool. Also, MTS memory tends to be 'large'. If you review our earlier examples, with the SORT_AREA_RETAINED_SIZE, the UGA can grow very large, and is definitely bigger than 4 KB chunks. Putting MTS memory into the shared pool causes it to fragment into odd sized pieces of memory and, furthermore you will find that large pieces of memory that will never be reused will age out memory that could be reused. This forces the database to do more work to rebuild that memory structure later.

The same is true for parallel query message buffers. Once they have delivered their message, they are no longer needed. Backup buffers, even more so – they are large, and once Oracle is done using them, they should just 'disappear'.

The large pool is not mandatory when using MTS, but it is highly recommended. If you do not have a large pool and use MTS, the allocations come out of the shared pool as they always did in Oracle 7.3 and before. This will definitely lead to degraded performance over some period of time, and should be avoided. The large pool will default to some size if either one of two init.ora parameters, DBWn_IO_SLAVES or PARALLEL_AUTOMATIC_TUNING are set. It is recommended that you set the size of the large pool manually yourself. The default mechanism is typically not the appropriate value for your situation.

Java Pool

The Java pool is the newest pool in the Oracle 8i database. It was added in version 8.1.5 to support the running of Java in the database. If you code a stored procedure in Java or put an EJB (Enterprise JavaBean) into the database, Oracle will make use of this chunk of memory when processing that code. An early quirk of the Java pool, in Oracle 8.1.5, was that it did not show up in the SHOW SGA command, and was not visible in V$SGASTAT view. This was particularly confusing at the time, since the JAVA_POOL_SIZE init.ora parameter that controls the size of this structure defaults to 20 MB. This oversight had people wondering why their SGA was taking an extra 20 MB of RAM for the database.

As of version 8.1.6, however, the Java pool is visible in the V$SGASTAT view, as well as the variable size in the SHOW SGA command. The init.ora parameter JAVA_POOL_SIZE is used to fix the amount of memory allocated to the Java pool for all session-specific Java code and data. In Oracle 8.1.5, this parameter could take values from 1 MB to 1 GB. In Oracle 8.1.6 and later versions, the valid range of values is 32 KB to 1 GB in size. This is contrary to the documentation, which stills refers to the old minimum of 1 MB.

The Java pool is used in different ways, depending on the mode in which the Oracle server is running. In dedicated server mode, the Java pool includes the shared part of each Java class, which is actually used per session. These are basically the read-only parts (execution vectors, methods, and so on) and are about 4 to 8 KB per class.

Thus, in dedicated server mode (which will most likely be the case for applications using purely Java stored procedures), the total memory required for the Java pool is quite modest and can be determined based on the number of Java classes you will be using. It should be noted that none of the per-session state is stored in the SGA in dedicated server mode, as this information is stored in the UGA and, as you will recall, the UGA is included in the PGA in dedicated server mode.

When executing in MTS mode, the Java pool includes:

❑   The shared part of each Java class, *and*

❑   Some of the UGA used for per-session state of each session, which is allocated from the `java_pool` within the SGA. The remainder of the UGA will be located as normal in the shared pool, or if the large pool is configured it will be allocated there instead.

As the total size of the Java pool is fixed, application developers will need to estimate the total requirement of their applications, and multiply this by the number of concurrent sessions they need to support. This number will dictate the overall size of the Java pool. Each Java UGA will grow or shrink as needed, but bear in mind that the pool must be sized such that all UGAs combined must be able to fit in at the same time.

In MTS mode, which will be the case for applications using CORBA or EJBs (as pointed out in Chapter 1 on *Developing Successful Oracle applications*), the Java pool may need to be very large. Instead of being a function of the number of classes you use in your applications, it will be a function of the number of concurrent users. Just as the large pool could become very large under MTS, the Java pool may also become very large.

Memory Structures Wrap-Up

In this section, we have taken a look at the Oracle memory structure. We started at the process and session level, taking a look at the PGA (Process Global Area) and UGA (User Global Area), and their relationship to each other. We have seen how the mode in which you connect to Oracle will dictate how memory is organized. A dedicated server connection implies more memory used in the server process than under MTS, but that MTS implies there will be the need for a significantly larger SGA. Then, we discussed the components of the SGA itself, looking at its six main structures. We discovered the differences between the shared pool and the large pool, and looked at why you might want a large pool in order to 'save' your shared pool. We covered the Java pool and how it is used under various conditions. We looked at the block buffer cache and how that can be subdivided into smaller, more focused pools.

Now we are ready to move onto the physical processes that make up the rest of an Oracle instance.

The Processes

We have reached the last piece of the puzzle. We've investigated the database and the set of physical files that constitute a database. In covering the memory used by Oracle, we have looked at one half of an instance. The last remaining architectural issue is the set of processes that constitute the other half of the instance. Some of these processes, such as the database block writer (DBWn), and the log writer (LGWR) have cropped up already. Here, we will take a closer look at the function of each, what they do and why they do it. When we talk of 'process' here, it will be synonymous with 'thread' on operating systems where Oracle is implemented with threads. So, for example, when we talk about the DBWn process, the equivalent on windows is the DBWn thread.

There are three classes of processes in an Oracle instance:

❑ **Server Processes** – These perform work based on a client's request. We have already looked at dedicated, and shared servers to some degree. These are the server processes.

❑ **Background Processes** – These are the processes that start up with the database, and perform various maintenance tasks, such as writing blocks to disk, maintaining the online redo log, cleaning up aborted processes, and so on.

❑ **Slave Processes** – These are similar to background processes but they are processes that perform extra work on behalf of either a background or a server process.

We will take a look at the processes in each of these three classes to see how they fit into the picture.

Server Processes

We briefly touched on these processes earlier in this section when we discussed dedicated and shared servers. Here, we will revisit the two server processes and review their architectures in more detail.

Both dedicated and shared servers have the same jobs – they process all of the SQL you give to them. When you submit a SELECT * FROM EMP query to the database, it is an Oracle dedicated/shared server that will parse the query, and place it into the shared pool (or find it in the shared pool already, hopefully). It is this process that will come up with the query plan. It is this process that will execute the query plan, perhaps finding the necessary data in the buffer cache, or reading the data from disk into the buffer cache. These server processes are the 'work horse' processes. Many times, you will find these processes to be the highest consumers of CPU time on your system, as they are the ones that do your sorting, your summing, your joining – pretty much everything.

In dedicated server mode, there will be a one-to-one mapping between a client session and a server process (or thread, as the case may be). If you have 100 sessions on a UNIX machine, there will be 100 processes executing on their behalf. Graphically it would look like this:

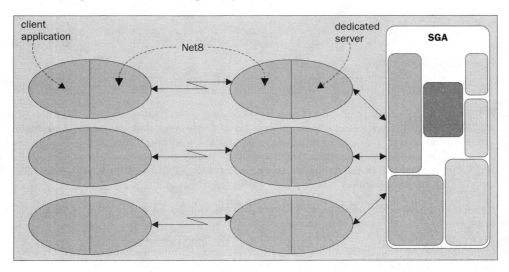

Your client application will have Oracle libraries linked into it. These libraries provide the **A**pplication **P**rogram **I**nterface (API) that you need in order to talk to the database. These APIs know how to submit a query to the database, and process the cursor that is returned. They know how to bundle your requests into network calls that the dedicated server will know how to un-bundle. This piece of the picture is called **Net8**. This is the networking software/protocol that Oracle employs to allow for client server processing (even in a n-tier architecture, there is a client server program lurking). Oracle employs this same architecture even if Net8 is not technically involved in the picture. That is, when the client and server are on the same machine this two-process (also known as two-task) architecture is employed. This architecture provides two benefits:

❑ **Remote Execution** – It is very natural for the client application to be executing on a machine other than the database itself.

❑ **Address Space Isolation** – The server process has read-write access to the SGA. An errant pointer in a client process could easily corrupt data structures in the SGA, if the client process and server process were physically linked together.

Earlier in this chapter we saw how these dedicated servers are 'spawned' or created by the Oracle Net8 Listener process. We won't cover that process again, but rather we'll quickly look at what happens when the listener is not involved. The mechanism is much the same as it was with the listener, but instead of the listener creating the dedicated server via a `fork()`/`exec()` in UNIX and an **IPC** (**I**nter **P**rocess **C**ommunication) call in Windows, it is the client process itself that creates it. We can see this clearly on UNIX:

```
ops$tkyte@ORA8I.WORLD> select a.spid dedicated_server,
  2                            b.process clientpid
  3      from v$process a, v$session b
  4     where a.addr = b.paddr
  5       and b.audsid = userenv('sessionid')
  6  /

DEDICATED CLIENTPID
--------- ---------
7055      7054

ops$tkyte@ORA8I.WORLD> !/bin/ps -lp 7055
 F S   UID   PID  PPID  C PRI NI     ADDR      SZ    WCHAN TTY    TIME CMD
 8 S 30174  7055  7054  0  41 20 61ac4230   36815 639b1998 ?     0:00 oracle

ops$tkyte@ORA8I.WORLD> !/bin/ps -lp 7054
 F S   UID   PID  PPID  C PRI NI     ADDR      SZ    WCHAN TTY    TIME CMD
 8 S 12997  7054  6783  0  51 20 63eece30    1087 63eecea0 pts/7 0:00 sqlplus
```

Here, I used a query to discover the **Process ID** (PID) associated with my dedicated server (the SPID from V$PROCESS is the operating system process ID of the process that was being used during the execution of that query). Also, by looking at the PROCESS column in V$SESSION, I discovered the process ID of the client accessing the database. Using a simple ps command, I can clearly see that the PPID (**P**arent **P**rocess **ID**) of my dedicated server is in fact SQL*PLUS. In this case, it was SQL*PLUS that created my dedicated server, via `fork()` / `exec()` commands.

Let's now take a look at the other type of Server process, the shared server process, in more detail. These types of connections mandate the use of Net8 even if the client and server are on the same machine – you cannot use MTS without using the Net8 listener. As we described earlier in this section, the client application will connect to the Net8 listener and will be redirected to a dispatcher. The dispatcher will act as the conduit between the client application and the shared server process. Following is a diagram of the architecture of a shared server connection to the database:

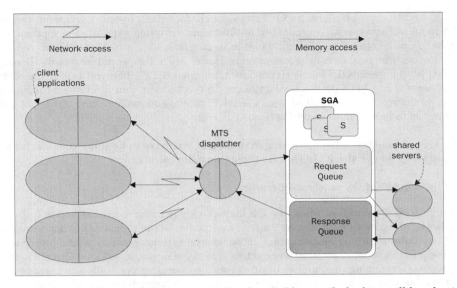

Here, we can see that the client applications, with the Oracle libraries linked in, will be physically connected to a MTS dispatcher. We may have many MTS dispatchers configured for any given instance but it is not uncommon to have just one dispatcher for many hundreds, to thousands, of users. The dispatcher is simply responsible for receiving inbound requests from the client applications, and putting them into the SGA in a request queue. The first available shared server process, which is basically the same as a dedicated server process, will pick up the request from the queue, and attach the UGA of the associated session (the 'S' boxes depicted in the above diagram). The shared server will process that request and place any output from it into the response queue. The dispatcher is constantly monitoring the response queue for results, and transmits them back to the client application. As far as the client is concerned, it cannot really tell if it is connected via a dedicated server, or a MTS connection – they appear to be the same. Only at the database level is the difference apparent.

Dedicated Server versus Shared Server

Before we continue onto the rest of the processes, we'll discuss why there are two modes of connections, and when one might be more appropriate over the other. Dedicated server mode is by far the most common method of connection to the Oracle database for all SQL-based applications. It is the easiest to set up and provides the easiest way to establish connections. It requires little to no configuration. MTS setup and configuration, while not difficult, is an extra step. The main difference between the two is not, however, in their set up. It is in their mode of operation. With dedicated server, there is a one-to-one mapping between client session, and server process. With MTS there is a many-to-one relationship – many clients to a shared server. As the name implies, shared server is a shared resource, whereas the dedicated server is not. When using a shared resource, you must be careful not to monopolize it for long periods of time. As we saw in Chapter 1, *Developing Successful Oracle Applications*, with the EJB example running a long running stored procedure, monopolizing this resource can lead to a system that appears to be hanging. In the above picture, I have two shared servers. If I have three clients, and all of them attempt to run a 45-second process more or less at the same time, two of them will get their response in 45 seconds; the third will get its response in 90 seconds. This is rule number one for MTS – make sure your transactions are short in duration. They can be frequent, but they should be short (as characterized by OLTP systems). If they are not, you will get what appears to be a total system slowdown due to shared resources being monopolized by a few processes. In extreme cases, if all of the shared servers are busy, the system will appear to be hang.

So, MTS is highly appropriate for an OLTP system characterized by short, frequent transactions. In an OLTP system, transactions are executed in milliseconds – nothing ever takes more then a fraction of a second. MTS on the other hand is highly inappropriate for a data warehouse. Here, you might execute a query that takes one, two, five, or more minutes. Under MTS, this would be deadly. If you have a system that is 90 percent OLTP and 10 percent 'not quite OLTP', then you can mix and match dedicated servers and MTS on the same instance. In this fashion, you can reduce the number of processes on the machine dramatically for the OLTP users, and make it so that the 'not quite OLTP' users do not monopolize their shared servers.

So, what are the benefits of MTS, bearing in mind that you have to be somewhat careful about the transaction types you let use it? MTS does three things for us, mainly:

Reduces the number of OS processes/threads:

On a system with thousands of users, the OS may quickly become overwhelmed in trying to manage thousands of processes. In a typical system, only a fraction of the thousands of users are concurrently active at any point in time. For example, I've worked on systems recently with 5000 concurrent users. At any one point in time, at most 50 were active. This system would work effectively with 50 shared server processes, reducing the number of processes the operating system has to manage by two orders of magnitude (100 times). The operating system can now, to a large degree, avoid context switching.

Allows you to artificially limit the degree of concurrency:

As a person who has been involved in lots of benchmarks, the benefits of this are obvious to me. When running benchmarks, people frequently ask to run as many users as possible until the system breaks. One of the outputs of these benchmarks is always a chart that shows the number of concurrent users versus number of transactions:

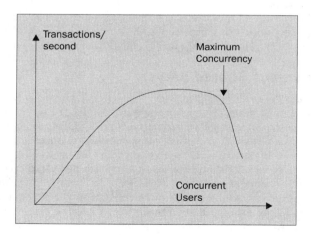

Initially, as you add concurrent users, the number of transactions goes up. At some point however, adding additional users does not increase the number of transactions you can perform per second – it tends to go flat. The throughput has peaked and now response time starts to go up (we are doing the same number of TPS, but the end users are observing slower response times). As you continue adding users, you will find that the throughput will actually start to decline. The concurrent user count before this drop off is the maximum degree of concurrency you want to allow on the system. Beyond this point, the system is becoming flooded and the queues are forming to perform work. Much like a backup at a tollbooth, the system can no longer keep up. Not only does response time rise dramatically at this point, but throughput from the system falls as well. If we limit the maximum concurrency to the point right before this drop, we can sustain maximum throughput, and minimize the increase in the response time for most users. MTS allows us to limit the maximum degree of concurrency on our system to this number.

Reduces the memory needed on the system:

This is one of the most highly touted reasons for using MTS – it reduces the amount of required memory. It does, but not as significantly as you might think. Remember that when we use MTS, the UGA is located in the SGA. This means that when switching over to MTS, you must be able to accurately determine your expected UGA memory needs, and allocate appropriately in the SGA, via the LARGE_POOL. So, the SGA requirements for the MTS configuration are typically very large. This memory must be pre-allocated and thus, can only be used by the database. Contrast this with dedicated server, where anyone can use any memory not allocated to the SGA. So, if the SGA is much larger due to the UGA being located in it, where does the memory savings come from? It comes from having that many less PGAs allocated. Each dedicated/shared server has a PGA. This is process information. It is sort areas, hash areas, and other process related structures. It is this memory need that you are removing from the system by using MTS. If you go from using 5000 dedicated servers to 100 shared servers, it is the cumulative sizes of the 4900 PGAs you no longer need, that you are saving with MTS.

Of course, the final reason to use MTS is when you have no choice. If you want to talk to an EJB in the database, you must use MTS. There are many other advanced connection features that require the use of MTS. If you want to use database link concentration between databases, for example, then you must be using MTS for those connections.

A Recommendation

Unless your system is overloaded, or you need to use MTS for a specific feature, a dedicated server will probably serve you best. A dedicated server is simple to set up, and makes tuning easier. There are certain operations that must be done in a dedicated server mode so every database will have either both, or just a dedicated server set up.

On the other hand, if you have a very large user community and *know* that you will be deploying with MTS, I would urge you to *develop and test* with MTS. It will increase your likelihood of failure if you develop under just a dedicated server and never test on MTS. Stress the system, benchmark it, make sure that your application is well behaved under MTS. That is, make sure it does not monopolize shared servers for too long. If you find that it does so during development, it is much easier to fix than during deployment. You can utilize features such as the **A**dvanced **Q**ueues (**AQ**) to turn a long running process into an apparently short one, but you have to *design* that into your application. These sorts of things are best done when you are developing.

> *If you are already using a connection-pooling feature in your application (for example, you are using the J2EE connection pool), and you have sized your connection pool appropriately, using MTS will only be a performance inhibitor. You already sized your connection pool to cater for the number of concurrent connections that you will get at any point in time – you want each of those connections to be a direct dedicated server connection. Otherwise, you just have a connection pooling feature connecting to yet another connection pooling feature.*

Background Processes

The Oracle instance is made up of two things: the SGA and a set of background processes. The background processes perform the mundane maintenance tasks needed to keep the database running. For example, there is a process that maintains the block buffer cache for us, writing blocks out to the data files as needed. There is another process that is responsible for copying an online redo log file to an archive destination as it fills up. There is another process responsible for cleaning up after aborted processes, and so on. Each of these processes is pretty focused on its job, but works in concert with all of the others. For example, when the process responsible for writing to the log files fills one log and goes to the next, it will notify the process responsible for archiving that full log file that there is work to be done.

There are two classes of background processes: those that have a focused job to do (as we have just described), and those that do a variety of other jobs. For example, there is a background process for the internal job queues in Oracle. This process monitors the job queues and runs whatever is inside of them. In many respects, it resembles a dedicated server process, but without a client connection. We will look at each of these background processes now, starting with the ones that have a focused job, and then going into the 'all-purpose' processes.

Focused Background Processes

The following diagram depicts the Oracle background processes that have a focused purpose:

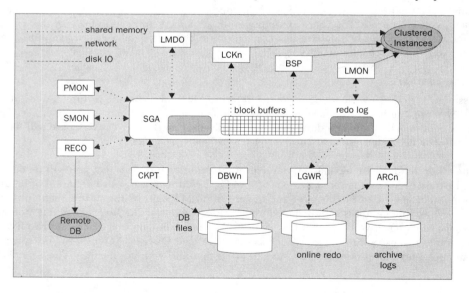

You may not see all of these processes when you start your instance, but the majority of them will be present. You will only see ARCn (the archiver) if you are in Archive Log Mode and have enabled automatic archiving. You will only see the LMD0, LCKn, LMON, and BSP (more details on those processes below) processes if you are running Oracle Parallel Server (a configuration of Oracle that allows many instances on different machines in a cluster mount), and open the same physical database. For the sake of clarity, missing from the above picture are the MTS dispatcher (Dnnn) and shared server (Snnn) processes. As we just covered them in some detail, I left them out in order to make the diagram a little more readable. The previous figure depicts what you might 'see' if you started an Oracle instance, and mounted and opened a database. For example, on my UNIX system, after starting the instance up, I have the following processes:

```
$ /bin/ps -aef | grep 'ora_.*_ora8i$'
  ora816 20642    1  0   Jan 17 ?          5:02 ora_arc0_ora8i
  ora816 20636    1  0   Jan 17 ?        265:44 ora_snp0_ora8i
  ora816 20628    1  0   Jan 17 ?         92:17 ora_lgwr_ora8i
  ora816 20626    1  0   Jan 17 ?          9:23 ora_dbw0_ora8i
  ora816 20638    1  0   Jan 17 ?          0:00 ora_s000_ora8i
  ora816 20634    1  0   Jan 17 ?          0:04 ora_reco_ora8i
  ora816 20630    1  0   Jan 17 ?          6:56 ora_ckpt_ora8i
  ora816 20632    1  0   Jan 17 ?        186:44 ora_smon_ora8i
  ora816 20640    1  0   Jan 17 ?          0:00 ora_d000_ora8i
  ora816 20624    1  0   Jan 17 ?          0:05 ora_pmon_ora8i
```

They correspond to the processes depicted above, with the exception of the SNPn process listed (which we will cover shortly; it is not a 'focused' background process). It is interesting to note the naming convention used by these processes. The process name starts with ora_. It is followed by four characters representing the actual name of the process, and then by _ora8i. As it happens, my ORACLE_SID (site identifier) is ora8i. On UNIX, this makes it very easy to identify the Oracle background processes and associate them with a particular instance (on Windows, there is no easy way to do this, as the backgrounds are threads in a larger, single process). What is perhaps most interesting, but not readily apparent from the above, is that *they are all really the same exact binary*. Search as hard as you like but you will not find the arc0 binary executable on disk anywhere. You will not find LGWR or DBW0. These processes are all really oracle (that's the name of the binary executable that is run). They just alias themselves upon start-up in order to make it easier to identify which process is which. This enables a great deal of object code to be efficiently shared on the UNIX platform. On Windows, this is not nearly as interesting, as they are just threads within the process – so of course they are one big binary.

let's now take a look at the function performed by each process.

PMON – The Process Monitor

This process is responsible for cleaning up after abnormally terminated connections. For example, if your dedicated server 'fails' or is killed for some reason, PMON is the process responsible for releasing your resources. PMON will rollback uncommitted work, release locks, and free SGA resources allocated to the failed process.

In addition to cleaning up after aborted connections, PMON is responsible for monitoring the other Oracle background processes and restarting them if necessary (and if possible). If a shared server or a dispatcher fails (crashes) PMON will step in, and restart another one (after cleaning up for the failed process). PMON will watch all of the Oracle processes, and either restart them or terminate the instance as appropriate. For example, it is appropriate to restart the instance in the event the database log writer process, LGWR (), fails. This is a serious error and the safest path of action is to terminate the instance immediately and let normal recovery fix up the data. This is a very rare occurrence and should be reported to Oracle support immediately.

The other thing PMON does for the instance, in Oracle 8i, is to register it with the Net8 listener. When an instance starts up, the PMON process polls the well-known port address (unless directed otherwise) to see whether or not a listener is up and running. The well-known/default port used by Oracle is 1521. Now, what happens if the listener is started on some different port? In this case the mechanism is the same, except that the listener address needs to be explicitly mentioned in the init.ora parameter via the LOCAL_LISTENER setting. If the listener is started, PMON communicates with the listener and passes to it relevant parameters, such as the service name.

SMON – The System Monitor

SMON is the process that gets to do all of the jobs no one else wants to do. It is a sort of 'garbage collector' for the database. Some of the jobs it is responsible for include:

❑ **Temporary space clean up** – With the advent of 'true' temporary tablespaces, this job has lessened, but has not gone away. For example, when building an index, the extents allocated for the index during the creation are marked as TEMPORARY. If the CREATE INDEX session is aborted for some reason, SMON is responsible for cleaning them up. There are other operations that create temporary extents that SMON would be responsible for as well.

❑ **Crash recovery** – SMON is responsible for performing crash recovery of a failed instance, upon restart.

❑ **Coalescing free space** – If you are using dictionary-managed tablespaces, SMON is responsible for taking extents that are free in a tablespace and contiguous with respect to each other, and coalescing them into one 'bigger' free extent. This occurs only on dictionary managed tablespace with a default storage clause that has pctincrease set to a non-zero value.

❑ **Recovering transactions active against unavailable files** – This is similar to its role during database startup. Here SMON recovers failed transactions that were skipped during instance/crash recovery due to a file(s) not being available to recover. For example, the file may have been on a disk that was unavailable or not mounted. When the file does become available, SMON will recover it.

❑ **Instance recovery of failed node in OPS** – In an Oracle Parallel Server configuration, when a node in the cluster goes down (the machine fails), some other node in the instance will open that failed node's redo log files, and perform a recovery of all data for that failed node.

❑ **Cleans up OBJ$** – OBJ$ is a low-level data dictionary table that contains an entry for almost every object (table, index, trigger, view, and so on) in the database. There are many times entries in here that represent deleted objects, or objects that represent 'not there' objects, used in Oracle's dependency mechanism. SMON is the process that removes these no longer needed rows.

❑ **Shrinks rollback segments** – SMON is the process that will perform the automatic shrinking of a rollback segment to its optimal size, if it is set.

❑ **'Offlines' rollback segments** – It is possible for the DBA to 'offline' or make unavailable, a rollback segment that has active transactions. It may be possible that active transactions are using this off lined rollback segment. In this case, the rollback is not really off lined; it is marked as 'pending offline'. SMON will periodically try to 'really' offline it in the background until it can.

That should give you a flavor of what SMON does. As evidenced by the ps listing of processes I introduced above, SMON can accumulate quite a lot of CPU over time (the instance from which ps was taken was an active instance that had been up for well over a month). SMON periodically wakes up (or is woken up by the other backgrounds) to perform these housekeeping chores.

RECO – Distributed Database Recovery

RECO has a very focused job; it recovers transactions that are left in a prepared state because of a crash or loss of connection during a two-phase commit (2PC). A 2PC is a distributed protocol that allows for a modification that affects many disparate databases to be committed atomically. It attempts to close the window for distributed failure as much as possible before committing. In a 2PC between N databases, one of the databases, typically (but not always) the one the client logged in to initially, will be the coordinator. This one site will ask the other N-1 sites if they are ready to commit. In effect, this one site will go to the N-1 sites, and ask them to be prepared to commit. Each of the N-1 sites reports back their 'prepared state' as YES or NO. If any one of the sites votes NO, the entire transaction is rolled back. If all sites vote YES, then the site coordinator broadcasts a message to make the commit permanent on each of the N-1 sites.

If after some site votes YES, they are prepared to commit, but before they get the directive from the coordinator to actually commit, the network fails or some other error occurs, the transaction becomes an **in-doubt distributed transaction**. The 2PC tries to limit the window of time in which this can occur, but cannot remove it. If we have a failure right then and there, the transaction will become the responsibility of RECO. RECO will try to contact the coordinator of the transaction to discover its outcome. Until it does that, the transaction will remain in its uncommitted state. When the transaction coordinator can be reached again, RECO will either commit the transaction or roll it back.

It should be noted that if the outage is to persist for an extended period of time, and you have some outstanding transactions, you can commit/roll them back manually yourself. You might want to do this since an in doubt distributed transaction can cause **writers to block readers** – this is the one time this can happen in Oracle. Your DBA could call the DBA of the other database and ask them to query up the status of those in-doubt transactions. Your DBA can then commit or roll them back, relieving RECO of this task.

CKPT – Checkpoint Process

The checkpoint process doesn't, as its name implies, do a checkpoint (that's mostly the job of DBWn). It simply assists with the checkpointing process by updating the file headers of the data files. It used to be that CKPT was an optional process, but starting with version 8.0 of the database it is always started, so if you do a ps on UNIX, you'll always see it there. The job of updating data files' headers with checkpoint information used to belong to the LGWR (Log Writer) however, as the number of files increased along with the size of a database over time, this additional task for LGWR became too much of a burden. If LGWR had to update dozens, or hundreds, or even thousands of files, there would be a good chance sessions waiting to commit these transactions would have to wait far too long. CKPT removes this responsibility from LGWR.

DBWn – Database Block Writer

The Database Block Writer (DBWn) is the background process responsible for writing dirty blocks to disk. DBWn will write dirty blocks from the buffer cache, usually in order to make more room in the cache (to free buffers for reads of other data), or to advance a checkpoint (to move forward the position in an online redo log file from which Oracle would have to start reading, in order to recover the instance in the event of failure). As we discussed previously, when Oracle switches log files, a checkpoint is signaled. Oracle needs to advance the checkpoint so that it no longer needs the online redo log file it just filled up. If it hasn't been able to do that by the time we need to reuse that redo log file, we get the 'checkpoint not complete' message and we must wait.

As you can see, the performance of DBWn can be crucial. If it does not write out blocks fast enough to free buffers for us, we will see waits for FREE_BUFFER_WAITS and 'Write Complete Waits' start to grow.

We can configure more then one DBWn, up to ten in fact (DBW0 ... DBW9). Most systems run with one database block writer but larger, multi-CPU systems can make use of more than one. If you do configure more then one DBWn, be sure to also increase the init.ora parameter, DB_BLOCK_LRU_LATCHES. This controls the number of LRU list latches (now called **touch lists** in 8i) – in effect, you want each DBWn to have their own list. If each DBWn shares the same list of blocks to write out to disk then they would only end up contending with other in order to access this list.

Normally, the DBWn uses asynchronous I/O to write blocks to disk. With asynchronous I/O, DBWn gathers up a batch of blocks to be written, and gives them to the operating system. DBWn does not wait for the OS to actually write the blocks out, rather it goes back and collects the next batch to be written. As the OS completes the writes, it asynchronously notifies DBWn that it completed the write. This allows DBWn to work much faster than if it had to do everything serially. We'll see later, in the *Slave Processes* section, how we can use I/O slaves to simulate asynchronous I/O on platforms or configurations that do not support it.

I would like to make one final point about DBWn. It will, almost by definition, write out blocks scattered all over disk – DBWn does lots of scattered writes. When you do an update, you'll be modifying index blocks that are stored here and there and data blocks that are randomly distributed on disk as well. LGWR, on the other hand, does lots of sequential writes to the redo log. This is an important distinction, and one of the reasons that Oracle has a redo log *and* a LGWR process. Scattered writes are significantly slower then sequential writes. By having the SGA buffer dirty blocks and the LGWR process do large sequential writes that can recreate these dirty buffers, we achieve an increase in performance. The fact that DBWn does its slow job in the background while LGWR does its faster job while the user waits, gives us overall better performance. This is true even though Oracle may technically be doing more I/O then it needs to (writes to the log and to the datafile) – the writes to the online redo log could be skipped if, during a commit, Oracle physically wrote the modified blocks out to disk instead.

LGWR – Log Writer

The LGWR process is responsible for flushing to disk the contents of the redo log buffer, located in the SGA. It does this:

- ❑ Every three seconds, or
- ❑ Whenever you commit, or
- ❑ When the redo log buffer is a third full or contains 1 MB of buffered data.

For these reasons, having an enormous redo log buffer is not practical – Oracle will never be able to use it all. The logs are written to with sequential writes as compared to the scattered I/O DBWn must perform. Doing large batch writes like this is much more efficient than doing many scattered writes to various parts of a file. This is one of the main reasons for having a LGWR and redo logs in the first place. The efficiency in just writing out the changed bytes using sequential I/O outweighs the additional I/O incurred. Oracle could just write database blocks directly to disk when you commit but that would entail a lot of scattered I/O of full blocks – this would be significantly slower than letting LGWR write the changes out sequentially.

ARCn – Archive Process

The job of the ARCn process is to copy an online redo log file to another location when LGWR fills it up. These archived redo log files can then be used to perform media recovery. Whereas online redo log is used to 'fix' the data files in the event of a power failure (when the instance is terminated), archive redo logs are used to 'fix' data files in the event of a hard disk failure. If you lose the disk drive containing the data file, /d01/oradata/ora8i/system.dbf, we can go to our backups from last week, restore that old copy of the file, and ask the database to apply all of the archived and online redo log generated since that backup took place. This will 'catch up' that file with the rest of the data files in our database, and we can continue processing with no loss of data.

ARCn typically copies online redo log files to at least two other locations (redundancy being a key to not losing data!). These other locations may be disks on the local machine or, more appropriately, at least one will be located on another machine altogether, in the event of a catastrophic failure. In many cases, these archived redo log files are copied off by some other process to some tertiary storage device, such as tape. They may also be sent to another machine to be applied to a 'standby database', a failover option offered by Oracle.

BSP – Block Server Process

This process is used exclusively in an Oracle Parallel Server (OPS) environment. An OPS is a configuration of Oracle whereby more then one instance mounts and opens the same database. Each instance of Oracle in this case is running on a different machine in a cluster, and they all access in a read-write fashion the same exact set of database files.

In order to achieve this, the SGA block buffer caches must be kept consistent with respect to each other. This is the main goal of the BSP. In earlier releases of OPS this was accomplished via a 'ping'. That is, if a node in the cluster needed a read consistent view of a block that was locked in exclusive mode by another node, the exchange of data was done via a disk flush (the block was pinged). This was a very expensive operation just to read data. Now, with the BSP, this exchange is done via very fast cache-to-cache exchange over the clusters high-speed connection.

LMON – Lock Monitor Process

This process is used exclusively in an OPS environment. The LMON process monitors all instances in a cluster to detect the failure of an instance. It then facilitates the recovery of the global locks held by the failed instance, in conjunction with the distributed lock manager (DLM) employed by the cluster hardware.

LMD – Lock Manager Daemon

This process is used exclusively in an OPS environment. The LMD process controls the global locks and global resources for the block buffer cache in a clustered environment. Other instances will make requests to the local LMD, in order to request it to release a lock or help find out who has a lock. The LMD also handles global deadlock detection and resolution.

LCKn – Lock Process

The LCKn process is used exclusively in an OPS environment. This process is very similar in functionality to the LMD described above, but handles requests for all global resources other than database block buffers.

Utility Background Processes

These background processes are totally optional, based on your need for them. They provide facilities not necessary to run the database day-to-day, unless you are using them yourself, or are making use of a feature that uses them.

There are two of these utilitarian background processes. One deals with the running of submitted jobs. Oracle has a batch job queue built into the database that allows you to schedule either one-off or recurring jobs to be executed. The other process manages and processes the queue tables associated with the Advanced Queuing (AQ) software. The AQ software provides a message-oriented middle-ware solution built into the database.

They will be visible in UNIX as any other background process would be – if you do a `ps` you will see them. In my `ps` listing above, you can see that I am running one job queue process (`ora_snp0_ora8I`) and no queue processes on my instance.

SNPn – Snapshot Processes (Job Queues)

The `SNPn` process is poorly named these days. In the first 7.0 release, Oracle provided replication. This was done in the form of a database object known as a **snapshot**. The internal mechanism for refreshing, or making current, these snapshots was the `SNPn` process, the snapshot process. This process monitored a job table that told it when it needed to refresh various snapshots in the system. In Oracle 7.1, Oracle Corporation exposed this facility for all to use via a database package called `DBMS_JOB`. What was solely the domain of the snapshot in 7.0 become the 'job queue' in 7.1 and later versions. Over time, the parameters for controlling the behavior of the queue (how frequently it should be checked and how many queue processes there should be) changed their name from `SNAPSHOT_REFRESH_INTERVAL` and `SNAPSHOT_REFRESH_PROCESSES` to `JOB_QUEUE_INTERVAL` and `JOB_QUEUE_PROCESSES`. The name of the operating system process however was not changed.

You may have up to 36 job queue processes. Their names will be `SNP0`, `SNP1`, ... , `SNP9`, `SNPA`, ... , `SNPZ`. These job queues' processes are used heavily in replication as part of the snapshot or materialized view refresh process. Developers also frequently use them in order to schedule one-off (background) jobs or recurring jobs. For example, later in this book we will show how to use the job queues to make things 'apparently faster' – by doing a little extra work in one place, we can make the end-user experience much more pleasant (similar to what Oracle does with `LGWR` and `DBWn`).

The `SNPn` processes are very much like a shared server, but with aspects of a dedicated server. They are shared – they process one job after the other, but they manage memory more like a dedicated server would (UGA in the PGA issue). Each job queue process will run exactly one job at a time, one after the other, to completion. That is why we may need multiple processes if we wish to run jobs at the same time. There is no threading or pre-empting of a job. Once it is running, it will run to completion (or failure). Later on in Appendix A on *Necessary Supplied Packages*, we will be taking a more in-depth look at the `DBMS_JOB` package and creative uses of this job queue.

QMNn – Queue Monitor Processes

The `QMNn` process is to the AQ tables what the `SNPn` process is to the job table. They monitor the Advanced Queues and alert waiting 'dequeuers' of messages, that a message has become available. They are also responsible for queue propagation – the ability of a message enqueued (added) in one database to be moved to a queue in another database for dequeueing.

The queue monitor is an optional background process. The `init.ora` parameter `AQ_TM_PROCESS` specifies creation of up to ten of these processes named `QMN0`, ... , `QMN9`. By default, there will be no QMNn processes.

EMNn – Event Monitor Processes

The EMNn is part of the Advanced Queue architecture. It is a process that is used to notify queue subscribers of messages they would be interested in. This notification is performed asynchronously. There are Oracle Call Interface (OCI) functions available to register a callback for message notification. The callback is a function in the OCI program that will be invoked automatically whenever a message of interest is available in the queue. The EMNn background process is used to notify the subscriber. The EMNn process is started automatically when the first notification is issued for the instance. The application may then issue an explicit `message_receive(dequeue)` to retrieve the message.

Slave Processes

Now we are ready to look at the last class of Oracle processes, the 'slave' processes. There are two types of slave processes with Oracle – I/O slaves and Parallel Query slaves.

I/O Slaves

I/O slaves are used to emulate asynchronous I/O for systems, or devices, that do not support it. For example, tape devices (notoriously slow) do not support asynchronous I/O. By utilizing I/O slaves, we can mimic for tape drives what the OS normally provides for disk drives. Just as with true asynchronous I/O, the process writing to the device, batches up a large amount of data and hands it off to be written. When it is successfully written, the writer (our I/O slave this time, *not* the OS) signals the original invoker, who removes this batch of data from their list of data that needs to be written. In this fashion, we can achieve a much higher throughput, since the I/O slaves are the ones spent waiting for the slow device, while their caller is off doing other important work getting the data together for the next write.

I/O slaves are used in a couple of places in Oracle 8i –DBWn and LGWR can make use of them to simulate asynchronous I/O and the RMAN (**R**ecovery **MAN**ager) will make use of them when writing to tape.

There are two init.ora parameters controlling the use of I/O slaves:

- ❑ BACKUP_TAPE_IO_SLAVES – This specifies whether I/O slaves are used by the RMAN to backup, copy, or restore data to tape. Since this is designed for *tape* devices, and tape devices may be accessed by only one process at any time, this parameter is a Boolean, not a number of slaves to use as you would expect. RMAN will start up as many slaves as is necessary for the number of physical devices being used. When BACKUP_TAPE_IO_SLAVES = TRUE, an I/O slave process is used to write to, or read from a tape device. If this parameter is FALSE (the default), then I/O slaves are not used for backups. Instead, the shadow process engaged in the backup will access the tape device.

- ❑ DBWn_IO_SLAVES – This specifies the number of I/O slaves used by the DBWn process. The DBWn process and its slaves always perform the writing to disk of dirty blocks in the buffer cache. By default, the value is 0 and I/O slaves are not used.

Parallel Query Slaves

Oracle 7.1 introduced parallel query capabilities into the database. This is the ability to take a SQL statement such as a SELECT, CREATE TABLE, CREATE INDEX, UPDATE, and so on and create an execution plan that consists of *many* execution plans that can be done simultaneously. The outputs of each of these plans are merged together into one larger result. The goal is to do an operation in a fraction of the time it would take if you did it serially. For example, if you have a really large table spread across ten different files, 16 CPUs at your disposal, and you needed to execute an ad-hoc query on this table, it might be advantageous to break the query plan into 32 little pieces, and really make use of that machine. This is as opposed to just using one process to read and process all of that data serially.

Summary

That's it – the three pieces to Oracle. We've covered the files used by Oracle, from the lowly, but important, init.ora, to data files, redo log files and so on. We've taken a look inside the memory structures used by Oracle, both in the server processes and the SGA. We've seen how different server configurations such as MTS versus dedicated server mode for connections will have a dramatic impact on how memory is used by the system. Lastly we looked at the processes (or threads depending on the operating system) that make Oracle do what it does. Now we are ready to look at the implementation of some other features in Oracle such as *Locking and Concurrency* controls, and *Transactions* in the following chapters.

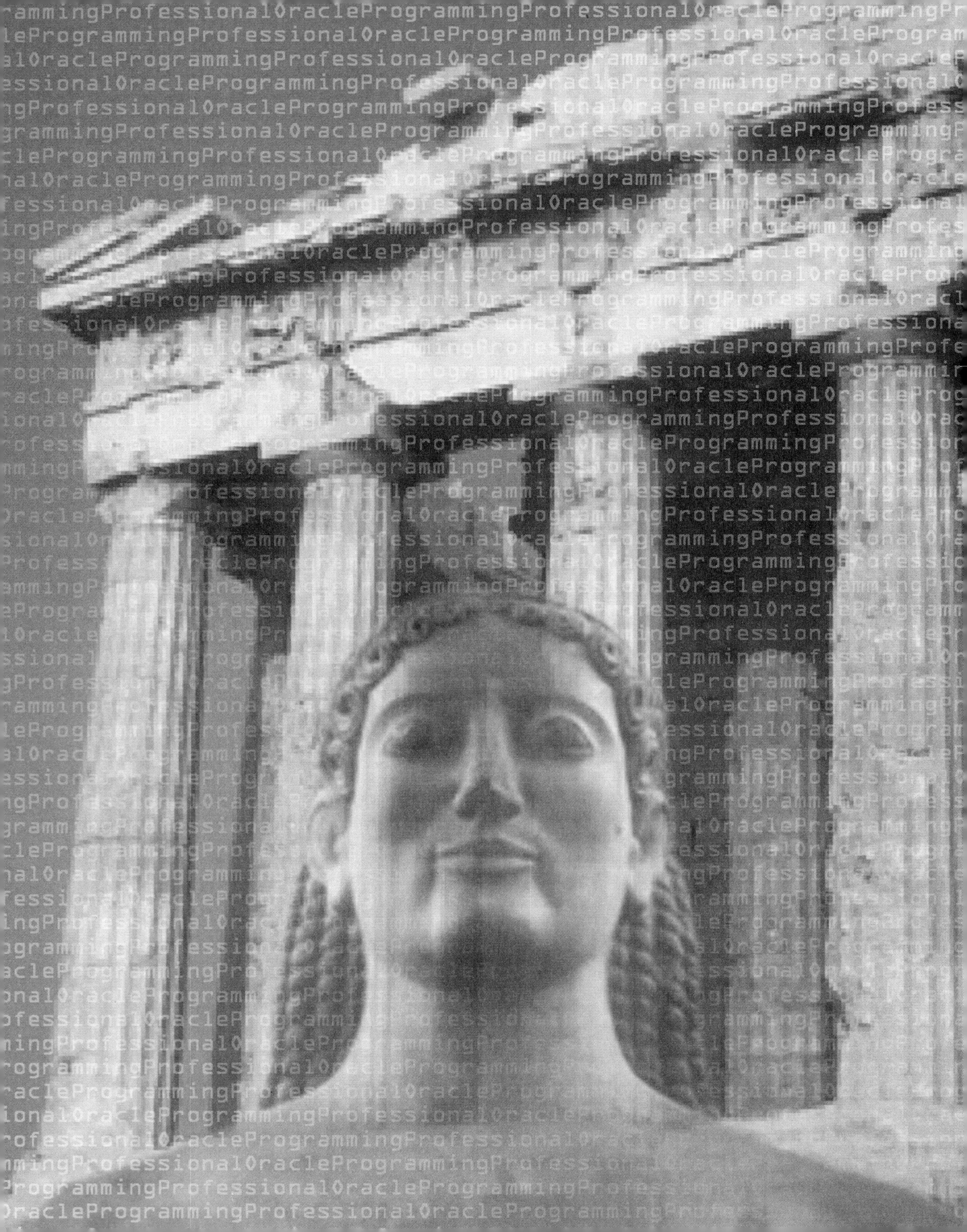
ProfessionalOracleProgramming

3

Locking and Concurrency

One of the key challenges in developing multi-user, database-driven applications is to maximize concurrent access but, at the same time, to ensure that each user is able to read and modify the data in a consistent fashion. The **locking** and **concurrency** controls that allow this to happen are key features of any database, and Oracle excels in providing them. However, Oracle's implementation of these features is unique and it is up to you, the application developer, to ensure that when your application performs data manipulation, it uses these mechanisms correctly. If you fail to do so, your application will behave in an unexpected way and, inevitably, the integrity of your data will be compromised (as was demonstrated in Chapter 1 on *Developing successful Oracle Applications*).

In this chapter we're going to take a detailed look at how Oracle locks data, and the implications of this model for writing multi-user applications. We will investigate the granularity to which Oracle locks data, how Oracle achieves 'multi-version read consistency', and what that all means to you, the developer. When appropriate, I'll contrast Oracle's locking scheme with other popular implementations, mostly to dispel the myth that 'row level locking adds overhead'. It only adds overhead if the implementation adds overhead.

What are Locks?

A **lock** is a mechanism used to regulate concurrent access to a shared resource. Note how I used the term 'shared resource', not 'database row'. It is true that Oracle locks table data at the row level, but it also uses locks at many other levels to provide concurrent access to various resources. For example, while a stored procedure is executing, the procedure itself is locked in a mode that allows others to execute it, but will not permit another user to alter it in any way. Locks are used in the database to permit concurrent access to these shared resources, while at the same time providing data integrity and consistency.

In a single-user database, locks are not necessary. There is, by definition, only one user modifying the information. However, when multiple users are accessing and modifying data or data structures, it is crucial to have a mechanism in place to prevent concurrent modifications to the same piece of information. This is what locking is all about.

It is very important to understand that there are as many ways to implement locking in a database as there are databases. Just because you are experienced with the locking model of one particular RDBMS does not mean you know everything about locking. For example, before I got heavily involved with Oracle, I used other databases such as Sybase and Informix. All three of these databases provide locking mechanisms for concurrency control, but there are deep and fundamental differences in the way locking is implemented in each one. In order to demonstrate this, I'll outline my progression from a Sybase developer to an Informix user and finally an Oracle developer. This happened many years ago, and the Sybase fans out there will tell me 'but we have row-level locking now'. It is true: Sybase now uses row-level locking, but the way in which it is implemented is *totally different* to the way in which it is done in Oracle. It is a comparison between apples and oranges, and that is the key point.

As a Sybase programmer, I would hardly ever consider the possibility of multiple users inserting data into a table concurrently – it was something that just didn't often happen in that database. At that time, Sybase provided only for page-level locking and, since all the data tended to be inserted into the last page of non-clustered tables, concurrent inserts by two users was simply not going to happen. Exactly the same issue affected concurrent updates (since an UPDATE is really a DELETE followed by an INSERT). Perhaps this is why Sybase, by default, commits or rolls back immediately after execution of each and every statement.

Compounding the fact that, in most cases, multiple users could not simultaneously modify the same table, was the fact that while a table modification was in progress, many queries were also effectively blocked against that table. If I tried to query a table and needed a page that was locked by an update, I waited (and waited and waited). The locking mechanism was so poor that providing support for transactions that took more than a microsecond was deadly – the entire database would appear to 'freeze' if you did. I learned a lot of bad habits here. I learned that transactions were 'bad', that you ought to commit rapidly and never hold locks on data. Concurrency came at the expense of consistency. You either wanted to get it right or get it fast. I came to believe that you couldn't have both.

When I moved on to Informix, things were better, but not by much. As long as I remembered to create a table with row-level locking enabled, then I could actually have two people simultaneously insert data into that table. Unfortunately, this concurrency came at a high price. Row-level locks in the Informix implementation were expensive, both in terms of time and memory. It took time to acquire and 'unacquire' or release them, and each lock consumed real memory. Also, the total number of locks available to the system had to be computed prior to starting the database. If you exceeded that number then you were just out of luck. Consequently, most tables were created with page-level locking anyway, and, as with Sybase, both row and page-level locks would stop a query in its tracks. As a result of all this, I found that once again I would want to commit as fast as I could. The bad habits I picked up using

Sybase were simply re-enforced and, furthermore, I learned to treat a lock as a very scarce resource, something to be coveted. I learned that you should manually escalate locks from row-level to table-level to try to avoid acquiring too many of them and bringing the system down.

When I started using Oracle I didn't really bother reading the manuals to find out how locking worked here. After all, I had been using databases for quite a while and was considered something of an expert in this field (in addition to Sybase and Informix, I had used Ingress, DB2, Gupta SQLBase, and a variety of other databases). I had fallen into the trap of believing that I knew how things *should* work, so of course they *will* work in that way. I was wrong in a big way.

It was during a benchmark that I discovered just how wrong I was. In the early days of these databases, it was common for the vendors to 'benchmark' for really large procurements – to see who could do the work the fastest, the easiest, with the most features. It was set up between Informix, Sybase and Oracle. Oracle was first. Their technical people came on-site, read through the benchmark specs, and started setting it up. The first thing I noticed was that they were going to use a database table to record their timings, even though we were going to have many dozens of connections doing work, each of which would frequently need to insert and update data in this log table. Not only that, but they were going to *read* the log table during the benchmark as well! I, being a nice guy, pulled one of them aside to ask him if he was crazy – why would they purposely introduce another point of contention into the system? Wouldn't the benchmark processes all tend to serialize around their operations on this single table? Would we jam up the benchmark by trying to read from this table as others were heavily modifying it? Why would you want to introduce all of these extra locks you need to manage? I had dozens of 'why would you even consider that' - type of questions. The technical folks from Oracle thought I was a little daft at that point. That is until I pulled up a window into Sybase or Informix, and showed them the effects of two people inserting into a table, or someone trying to query a table with others inserting rows (the query returns zero rows per second). The differences between the way Oracle does it, and the way almost every other database does it, are phenomenal – they are night and day. Needless to say, neither Informix nor Sybase were too keen on the database log table approach during their attempts. They preferred to record their timings to flat files in the operating system.

The moral to this story is twofold; *all databases are fundamentally different* and, when designing your application, *you must approach each as if you never used a database before.* Things you would do in one database are either not necessary, or simply won't work in another database.

In Oracle you will learn that:

- ❑ Transactions are what databases are all about; they are good.
- ❑ You should defer committing as long as you have to. You should not do it quickly to avoid stressing the system, as it does not stress the system to have long or large transactions. The rule is *commit when you must, and not before.* Your transactions should only be as small or large as your business logic dictates.
- ❑ You should hold locks on data as long as you need to. They are tools for you to use, not things to be avoided. Locks are not a scarce resource.
- ❑ There is no overhead involved with row level locking in Oracle, none.
- ❑ You should never escalate a lock (for example, use a table lock instead of row locks) because it would be 'better on the system'. In Oracle it won't be better for the system – it will save no resources.
- ❑ Concurrency and consistency can be achieved. You can get it fast and correct, every time.

As we go through the remaining components in this chapter, we'll be reinforcing the above points.

Locking Issues

Before we discuss the various types of locks that Oracle uses, it is useful to look at some locking issues – many of which arise from badly designed applications that do not make correct use (or make no use) of the database's locking mechanisms.

Lost Updates

A lost update is a classic database problem. Simply put, a lost update occurs when the following events occur, in the order presented:

1. User 1 retrieves (queries) a row of data.

2. User 2 retrieves that same row.

3. User 1 modifies that row, updates the database and commits.

4. User 2 modifies that row, updates the database and commits.

This is called a lost update because all of the changes made in step three above will be lost. Consider, for example, an employee update screen – one that allows a user to change an address, work number and so on. The application itself is very simple – a small search screen to generate a list of employees and then the ability to drill down into the details of each employee. This should be a piece of cake. So, we write the application with no locking on our part, just simple SELECT and UPDATE commands.

So, an end user (user 1) navigates to the details screen, changes an address on the screen, hits **Save**, and receives confirmation that the update was successful. Fine, except that when user 1 checks the record the next day, in order to send out a tax form, the old address is still listed. How could that have happened? Unfortunately it can happen all too easily. In this case another end user (USER2) had queried the same record about 5 minutes before user 1 and still had the old data displayed on their screen. User 1 came along, queried up the data on his terminal, performed his update, received confirmation, and even re-queried to see the change for himself. However, user 2 then updated the work telephone number field and hit save – blissfully unaware of the fact that he has just overwritten user 1's changes to the address field with the old data! The reason this can happen is that the application developer, finding it easier to update all columns instead of figuring out exactly which columns changed, wrote the program such that when one particular field is updated, all fields for that record are 'refreshed'.

Notice that for this to happen, user 1 and user 2 didn't even need to be working on the record at the exact same time. All it needed was for them to be working on the record at **about** the same time

This is a database issue that I've seen crop up time and time again when GUI programmers, with little or no database training, are given the task of writing a database application. They get a working knowledge of SELECT, INSERT, UPDATE and DELETE and then set about writing the application. When the resulting application behaves in the manner described above, it completely destroys people's confidence in it, especially since it seems so random, so sporadic, and is totally irreproducible in a controlled environment (leading the developer to believe it must be user error).

Many tools, such as Oracle Forms, transparently protect you from this behavior by ensuring the record is unchanged from when you queried it and locked before you make any changes to it – but many others (such as a handwritten VB or Java program) do not. What the tools that protect you do behind the scenes, or what the developers must do themselves, is to use one of two types of locking.

Pessimistic Locking

This locking method would be put into action in the instant before we modify a value on screen – for example when the user selects a specific row and indicates their intention to perform an update (by hitting a button on the screen, say). So, a user queries the data out without locking:

```
scott@TKYTE816> SELECT EMPNO, ENAME, SAL FROM EMP WHERE DEPTNO = 10;

    EMPNO ENAME            SAL
---------- ---------- ----------
     7782 CLARK           2450
     7839 KING            5000
     7934 MILLER          1300
```

Eventually, the user picks a row they would like to update. Let's say in this case, they choose to update the MILLER row. Our application will at that point in time (before they make any changes on screen) issue the following command:

```
scott@TKYTE816> SELECT EMPNO, ENAME, SAL
  2    FROM EMP
  3    WHERE EMPNO = :EMPNO
  4      AND ENAME = :ENAME
  5      AND SAL = :SAL
  6    FOR UPDATE NOWAIT
  7  /

    EMPNO ENAME            SAL
---------- ---------- ----------
     7934 MILLER          1300
```

What the application does is supply values for the bind variables from the data on the screen (in this case 7934, MILLER and 1300) and re-queries up this same row from the database – this time locking the row against updates by other sessions. This is why this approach is called **pessimistic** locking. We lock the row before we attempt to update because we doubt that the row will remain unchanged otherwise.

Since all tables have a primary key (the above SELECT will retrieve at most one record since it includes the primary key, EMPNO) and primary keys should be immutable (we should never update them) we'll get one of three outcomes from this statement:

❑   If the underlying data has not changed, we will get our MILLER row back and this row will be locked from updates by others (but not read).

❑   If another user is in the process of modifying that row, we will get an ORA-00054 Resource Busy error. We are blocked and must wait for the other user to finish with it.

❑   If, in the time between selecting the data and indicating our intention to update, someone has already changed the row then we will get zero rows back. The data on our screen is stale. The application needs to **requery** and lock the data before allowing the end user to modify any of the data in order to avoid the lost update scenario described above. In this case, with pessimistic locking in place, when user 2 attempts to update the telephone field the application would now recognize that the address field had been changed and would re-query the data. Thus user 2 would not overwrite user 1's change with the old data in that field.

Once we have locked the row successfully, the application will issue some update and commit the changes:

```
scott@TKYTE816> UPDATE EMP
   2   SET ENAME = :ENAME, SAL = :SAL
   3   WHERE EMPNO = :EMPNO;
1 row updated.

scott@TKYTE816> commit;
Commit complete.
```

We have now very safely changed that row. It is not possible for us to overwrite someone else's changes as we verified the data did not change between the time we initially read it out and when we locked it.

Optimistic Locking

The second method, referred to as **optimistic** locking, is to keep the old and new values in the application and upon updating the data use an update like this:

```
Update table
   Set column1 = :new_column1, column2 = :new_column2, ….
Where column1 = :old_column1
  And column2 = :old_column2
   …
```

Here, we are optimistically hoping that the data doesn't get changed. In this case, if our update updates **one** row – we got lucky, the data didn't change between the time we read it out and the time we got around to submitting the update. If we update **zero** rows, we lose – someone else changed the data and now we must figure out what we want to do in order to avoid the lost update. Should we make the end user re-key the transaction after querying up the new values for the row (potentially frustrating them no end as there is a chance the row will change yet again on them)? Should we try to merge the values of the two updates, performing update conflict resolution based on business rules (lots of code)? Of course, for disconnected users, the last option is the only one available.

It should be noted that you can use a SELECT FOR UPDATE NOWAIT here as well. The UPDATE above will in fact avoid a lost update, but it does stand a chance of blocking – hanging while it waits for an UPDATE of that row by another session to complete. If all of your applications use optimistic locking then using a straight UPDATE is generally OK, rows are locked for a very short duration as updates are applied and committed. If some of your applications use pessimistic locking, however, which will hold locks on rows for relatively long periods, then you would want to consider using a SELECT FOR UPDATE NOWAIT immediately prior to the UPDATE to avoid getting blocked by another session.

So, which method is best? In my experience, pessimistic locking works very well in Oracle (but perhaps not other databases) and has many advantages over optimistic locking.

With pessimistic locking the user can have confidence that the data they are modifying on the screen is currently 'owned' by them – they in effect have the record checked out and nobody else can modify it. Some would argue that if you lock the row before changes are made, other users would be locked out from that row and the scalability of the application would be decreased. The fact is that, however you do it, only one user will ultimately be able to update the row (if we want to avoid the lost update). If you lock the row first, and then update it, your end user has a better experience. If you don't lock it and try to update it later your end user may put time and energy into making changes only to be told 'sorry, the data has changed, please try again'. To limit the time that a row is locked before updating, you could have the application release the lock if the user walks away and doesn't actually use the record for some period of time or use Resource Profiles in the database to time out idle sessions.

Furthermore, locking the row in Oracle does not prevent reads of that record as in other databases; the locking of the row does not prevent any normal activity from taking place. This is due 100% to Oracle's concurrency and locking implementation. In other databases, the converse is true. If I tried to do pessimistic locking in them, no application would work. The fact that a locked row in those databases block queries prevents this approach from even being considered. So, it may be necessary to unlearn 'rules' you have learned in one database in order to be successful in a different database.

Blocking

Blocking occurs when one session holds a lock on a resource that another session is requesting. As a result, the requesting session will be blocked, it will 'hang' until the holding session gives up the locked resource. In almost every case, blocking is avoidable. In fact, if you do find yourself blocking in an interactive application you are most likely suffering from the lost update bug described above (your logic is flawed and that is the cause of the blocking).

There are four common DML statements that will block in the database – INSERT, UPDATE, DELETE, and SELECT FOR UPDATE. The solution to a blocked SELECT FOR UPDATE is trivial: simply add the NOWAIT clause and it will no longer block. Instead, your application would report back to the end user that the row is already locked. The interesting cases are the remaining three DML statements. We'll look at each of them and see why they should not block, and when they do – how to correct that.

Blocked Inserts

The only time an INSERT will block is when you have a table with a primary key or unique constraint placed on it and two sessions simultaneously attempt to insert a row with the same value. One of the sessions will block until the other session either commits (in which case the blocked session will receive an error about a duplicate value) or rolls back (in which case the blocked session succeeds). This typically happens with applications that allow the end user to generate the primary key/unique column value. It is most easily avoided via the use of Oracle sequences in the generation of primary keys as they are a highly concurrent method of generating unique keys in a multi-user environment. In the event that you cannot use a sequence, you can use the technique outlined in Appendix A, on the DBMS_LOCK package, where I demonstrate how to use manual locks to avoid this issue.

Blocked Updates and Deletes

In an interactive application – one where you query some data out of the database, allow an end user to manipulate it and then 'put it back' into the database, a blocked UPDATE or DELETE indicates that you probably have a lost update problem in your code. You are attempting to UPDATE a row that someone else is already updating, in other words that someone else already has locked. You can avoid the blocking issue by using the SELECT FOR UPDATE NOWAIT query to:

❑ Verify the data has not changed since you queried it out (lost update prevention)

❑ Lock the row (prevents the update or delete from blocking)

As discussed earlier, you can do this regardless of the locking approach you take – both pessimistic and optimistic locking may employ the SELECT FOR UPDATE NOWAIT to verify the row has not changed. Pessimistic locking would use that statement the instant the user indicated their intention to modify the data. Optimistic locking would use that statement immediately prior to updating the data in the database. Not only will this resolve the blocking issue in your application, it will also correct the data integrity issue.

Deadlocks

Deadlocks occur when two people hold a resource that the other wants. For example, if I have two tables, A and B in my database, and each has a single row in it, I can demonstrate a deadlock easily. All I need to do is open two sessions (two SQL*PLUS sessions, for example), and in Session A, I update table A. In session B, I update table B. Now, if I attempt to update table A in session B, I will become blocked. Session A has this row locked already. This is not a deadlock, this is just blocking. We have not yet deadlocked since there is a chance that the session A will commit or rollback, and session B will simply continue at that point.

If we go back to session A, and then try to update table B, we will cause a deadlock. One of the two sessions will be chosen as a 'victim', and will have its statement rolled back. For example, the attempt by session B to update table A may be rolled back, with an error such as:

```
update a set x = x+1
       *
ERROR at line 1:
ORA-00060: deadlock detected while waiting for resource
```

Session A's attempt to update table B will remain blocked – Oracle will not rollback the entire transaction. Only one of the statements that contributed to the deadlock is rolled back. Session B still has the row in table B locked, and session A is patiently waiting for the row to become available. After receiving the deadlock message, session B must decide whether to commit the outstanding work on table B, roll it back, or continue down an alternate path and commit later. As soon as this session does commit or rollback, the other blocked session will continue on as if nothing ever happened.

Oracle considers deadlocks to be so rare, so unusual, that it creates a trace file on the server each and every time one does occur. The contents of the trace file will look something like this:

```
*** 2001-02-23 14:03:35.041
*** SESSION ID:(8.82) 2001-02-23 14:03:35.001
DEADLOCK DETECTED
Current SQL statement for this session:
update a set x = x+1
The following deadlock is not an ORACLE error. It is a
deadlock due to user error in the design of an application
or from issuing incorrect ad-hoc SQL. The following...
```

Obviously, Oracle considers deadlocks a self-induced error on part of the application and, for the most part, they are correct. Unlike in many other RDBMSs, deadlocks are so rare in Oracle they can be considered almost non-existent. Typically, you must come up with artificial conditions to get one.

The number one cause of deadlocks in the Oracle database, in my experience, is un-indexed foreign keys. There are two cases where Oracle will place a full table lock on a child table after modification of the parent table:

❑ If I update the parent table's primary key (a very rare occurrence if you follow the rules of relational databases that primary keys should be immutable), the child table will be locked in the absence of an index.

❑ If I delete a parent table row, the entire child table will be locked (in the absence of an index) as well.

So, as a demonstration of the first point, if I have a pair of tables set up such as:

```
tkyte@TKYTE816> create table p ( x int primary key );
Table created.

tkyte@TKYTE816> create table c ( y references p );
Table created.

tkyte@TKYTE816> insert into p values ( 1 );
tkyte@TKYTE816> insert into p values ( 2 );

tkyte@TKYTE816> commit;
```

And then I execute:

```
tkyte@TKYTE816> update p set x = 3 where x = 1;
1 row updated.
```

I will find that my session has locked the table C. No other session can delete, insert or update any rows in C. Again, updating a primary key is a huge 'no-no' in a relational database, so this is generally not really an issue. Where I have seen this updating of the primary key become a serious issue is when you use tools that generate your SQL for you and those tools update every single column – regardless of whether the end user actually modified that column or not. For example, if you use Oracle Forms and create a default layout on any table Oracle Forms by default will generate an update that modifies every single column in the table you choose to display. If you build a default layout on the DEPT table and include all three fields Oracle Forms will execute the following command whenever you modify *any* of the columns of the DEPT table:

```
update dept set deptno=:1,dname=:2,loc=:3 where rowid=:4
```

In this case, if the EMP table has a foreign key to DEPT and there is no index on the DEPTNO column in the EMP table – the entire EMP table will be locked after an update to DEPT. This is something to watch out for carefully if you are using any tools that generate SQL for you. Even though the value of the primary key does not change, the child table EMP will be locked after the execution of the above SQL statement. In the case of Oracle Forms, the solution is to mark that table's property update changed columns only to Yes. Oracle Forms will generate an update statement that includes only the changed columns (not the primary key).

Problems arising from deletion of a row in a parent table are far more common. If I delete a row in table P, then the child table, C, will become locked – preventing other updates against C from taking place for the duration of my transaction (assuming no one else was modifying C, of course; in which case my delete will wait). This is where the blocking and deadlock issues come in. By locking the entire table C, I have seriously decreased the concurrency in my database – no one will be able to modify anything in C. In addition, I have increased the probability of a deadlock, since I now 'own' lots of data until I commit. The probability that some other session will become blocked on C is now much higher; any session that tries to modify C will get blocked. Therefore, I'll start seeing lots of sessions that hold some pre-existing locks getting blocked in the database. If any of these blocked sessions are, in fact, holding a lock that my session needs – we will have a deadlock. The deadlock in this case is caused by my session obtaining many more locks then it ever needed. When someone complains of deadlocks in the database, I have them run a script that finds un-indexed foreign keys and ninety-nine percent of the time we locate an offending table. By simply indexing that foreign key, the deadlocks, and lots of other contention issues, go away. Here is an example of how to automatically find these un-indexed foreign keys:

```
tkyte@TKYTE816> column columns format a30 word_wrapped
tkyte@TKYTE816> column tablename format a15 word_wrapped
tkyte@TKYTE816> column constraint_name format a15 word_wrapped

tkyte@TKYTE816> select table_name, constraint_name,
  2         cname1 || nvl2(cname2,',''||cname2,null) ||
  3         nvl2(cname3,',''||cname3,null) || nvl2(cname4,',''||cname4,null) ||
  4         nvl2(cname5,',''||cname5,null) || nvl2(cname6,',''||cname6,null) ||
  5         nvl2(cname7,',''||cname7,null) || nvl2(cname8,',''||cname8,null)
  6               columns
  7    from ( select b.table_name,
  8                   b.constraint_name,
  9                   max(decode( position, 1, column_name, null )) cname1,
 10                   max(decode( position, 2, column_name, null )) cname2,
 11                   max(decode( position, 3, column_name, null )) cname3,
 12                   max(decode( position, 4, column_name, null )) cname4,
 13                   max(decode( position, 5, column_name, null )) cname5,
 14                   max(decode( position, 6, column_name, null )) cname6,
 15                   max(decode( position, 7, column_name, null )) cname7,
 16                   max(decode( position, 8, column_name, null )) cname8,
 17                   count(*) col_cnt
 18             from (select substr(table_name,1,30) table_name,
 19                          substr(constraint_name,1,30) constraint_name,
 20                          substr(column_name,1,30) column_name,
 21                          position
 22                     from user_cons_columns ) a,
 23                  user_constraints b
 24           where a.constraint_name = b.constraint_name
 25             and b.constraint_type = 'R'
 26           group by b.table_name, b.constraint_name
 27         ) cons
 28   where col_cnt > ALL
 29         ( select count(*)
 30             from user_ind_columns i
 31            where i.table_name = cons.table_name
 32              and i.column_name in (cname1, cname2, cname3, cname4,
 33                                    cname5, cname6, cname7, cname8 )
 34              and i.column_position <= cons.col_cnt
 35            group by i.index_name
 36         )
 37  /
```

TABLE_NAME	CONSTRAINT_NAME	COLUMNS
C	SYS_C004710	Y

This script works on foreign key constraints that have up to 8 columns in them (if you have more than that, you probably want to rethink your design). It starts by building an inline view, named CONS in the above query. This inline view transposes the appropriate column names in the constraint from rows into columns, the result being a row per constraint and up to 8 columns that have the names of the columns in the constraint. Additionally there is a column, COL_CNT, which contains the number of columns in the foreign key constraint itself. For each row returned from the inline view we execute a correlated subquery that checks all of the indexes on the table currently being processed. It counts the columns in that index that match columns in the foreign key constraint and then groups them by index name. So, it generates a set of numbers, each of which is a count of matching columns in some index on that table. If the original COL_CNT is greater than *all* of these numbers then there is no index on that table that supports that constraint. If COL_CNT is less than all of these numbers then there is at least one index that supports that constraint. Note the use of the NVL2 function (new to Oracle 8.15), which we used to 'glue' the list of column names into a comma-separated list. This function takes three arguments A, B, C. If argument A is not null then it returns argument B, else it returns argument C. This query assumes that the owner of the constraint is the owner of the table and index as well. If another user indexed the table, or the table is in another schema, it will not work correctly (both rare events).

So, this script shows us that table C has a foreign key on the column Y, but no index. By indexing Y, we can remove this locking issue all together. In addition to this table lock, an un-indexed foreign key can also be problematic in the following cases:

- ❑ When you have an ON DELETE CASCADE and have not indexed the child table. For example, EMP is child of DEPT. DELETE DEPTNO = 10 should CASCADE to EMP. If DEPTNO in EMP is not indexed, you will get a full table scan of EMP. This full scan is probably undesirable, and if you delete many rows from the parent table, the child table will be scanned once for each parent row deleted.

- ❑ When you query from the parent to the child. Consider the EMP/DEPT example again. It is very common to query the EMP table in the context of a DEPTNO. If you frequently run the following query, say to generate a report, you'll find that not having the index in place will slow down the queries:

```
select * from dept, emp
where emp.deptno = dept.deptno and dept.deptno = :X;
```

So, when do you *not* need to index a foreign key? The answer is, in general, when the following conditions are met:

- ❑ You do *not* delete from the parent table.

- ❑ You do *not* update the parent table's unique/primary key value (watch for unintended updates to the primary key by tools!)

- ❑ You do *not* join from the parent to the child (like DEPT to EMP)

If you satisfy all three above, feel free to skip the index – it is not needed. If you do any of the above, be aware of the consequences. This is the one very rare time when Oracle tends to 'over-lock' data.

Lock Escalation

When lock escalation occurs, the system is decreasing the granularity of your locks. An example would be the database system turning your 100 row-level locks against a table into a single table-level lock. You are now using 'one lock to lock everything' and, typically, you are also locking a whole lot more data than you were before. Lock escalation is used frequently in databases that consider a lock to be a scarce resource, overhead to be avoided.

> **Oracle will never escalate a lock. *Never.***

Oracle never escalates locks, but it does practice **lock conversion**, or **lock promotion** – terms that are often confused with lock escalation.

The terms 'lock conversion' and 'lock promotion' are synonymous – Oracle typically refers to the process as conversion.

It will take a lock at the lowest level possible (the least restrictive lock possible) and will convert that lock to a more restrictive level. For example, if you select a row from a table with the FOR UPDATE clause, two locks will be created. One lock is placed on the row(s) you selected (and this will be an exclusive lock, no one else can lock that specific row in exclusive mode). The other lock, a ROW SHARE TABLE lock, is placed on the table itself. This will prevent other sessions from placing an exclusive lock on the table and thus will prevent them from altering the structure of the table, for example. All other statements against the table are permitted. Another session can even come in and make the table read-only using LOCK TABLE X IN SHARE MODE, preventing modifications. In reality, however, this other session cannot be allowed to prevent the modification that is already taking place. So, as soon as the command to actually update that row is issued, Oracle will convert the ROW SHARE TABLE lock into the more restrictive ROW EXCLUSIVE TABLE lock and the modification will proceed. This lock conversion happens transparently.

Lock escalation is not a database 'feature'. It is not a desired attribute. The fact that a database supports lock escalation implies there is some inherent overhead in its locking mechanism, that there is significant work performed to managed hundreds of locks. In Oracle the overhead to have one lock or a million locks is the same – none.

Types of Lock

The five general classes of locks in Oracle are listed below. The first three are common (used in every Oracle database) and the last two are unique to OPS (Oracle Parallel Server). We will introduce the OPS-specific locks, but will concentrate on the common locks:

❑ **DML locks** – DML stands for **D**ata **M**anipulation **L**anguage, in general SELECT, INSERT, UPDATE, and DELETE. DML locks will be, for example, locks on a specific row of data, or a lock at the table level, which locks every row in the table.

❑ **DDL locks** – DDL stands for **D**ata **D**efinition **L**anguage, in general CREATE, ALTER, and so on. DDL locks protect the definition of the structure of objects.

❑ **Internal locks and latches** – These are the locks Oracle uses to protect its internal data structures. For example, when Oracle parses a query and generates an optimized query plan, it will 'latch' the library cache in order to put that plan in there for other sessions to use. A latch is a lightweight low-level serialization device employed by Oracle – similar in function to a lock.

❑ **Distributed locks** – These are used by OPS to ensure that resources on the various nodes remain consistent with respect to each other. Distributed locks are held by a database instance, not by individual transactions.

❑ **PCM (Parallel Cache Management) Locks** – These are locks that protect one or more cached data blocks in the buffer cache across multiple instances.

We will now take a more detailed look at the specific types of locks within each of these general classes and implications of their use. There are more lock types than I can cover here. The ones I am covering are the most common ones and are the ones that are held for a long duration. The other types of lock are generally held for very short periods of time.

DML Locks

DML locks are used to ensure only one person at a time modifies a row, and that no one can drop a table upon which you are working. Oracle will place these locks for you, more or less transparently, as you do work.

TX – (Transaction) Locks

A TX lock is acquired when a transaction initiates its first change, and is held until the transaction performs a COMMIT or ROLLBACK. It is used as a queueing mechanism so that other sessions can wait for the transaction to complete. Each and every row you modify or SELECT FOR UPDATE will 'point' to an associated TX lock. While this sounds expensive, it is not. To understand why, we need a conceptual understanding of where locks 'live' and how they are managed. In Oracle, locks are stored as an attribute of the data (see Chapter 2, *Architecture*, for an overview of the Oracle block format). Oracle does not have a traditional lock manager that keeps a big long list of every row that is locked in the system. Many other databases do it that way because, for them, locks are a scarce resource the use of which needs to be monitored. The more locks in use, the more they have to manage so it is a concern in these systems if 'too many' locks are being used.

If Oracle had a traditional lock manager, the act of locking a row would resemble:

1. Find the address of the row you want to lock.

2. Get in line at the lock manager (must be serialized, it is a common in-memory structure.)

3. Lock the list.

4. Search through the list to see if anyone else has locked this row.

5. Create a new entry in the list to establish the fact that you have locked the row.

6. Unlock the list.

Now that you have the row locked, you can modify it. Later, as you commit your changes you must:

7. Get in line again.

8. Lock the list of locks.

9. Search through it and release all of your locks.

10. Unlock the list.

As you can see, the more locks acquired, the more time spent on this operation, both before and after modifying the data. Oracle does not do it that way. Oracle does it more like this:

1. Find the address of the row you want to lock.
2. Go to the row.
3. Lock it (waiting for it if it is already locked, unless we are using the NOWAIT option).

That's it, period. Since the lock is stored as an attribute of the data, Oracle does not need a traditional lock manager. Our transaction will simply go to the data and lock it (if it is not locked already). The interesting thing is that the data may appear locked when we get to it, even if it is not. When we lock rows of data in Oracle a transaction ID is associated with the bock containing the data and when the lock is released, that transaction ID is left behind. This transaction ID is unique to our transaction, and represents the rollback segment number, slot, and sequence number. We leave that on the block that contains our row to tell other sessions that 'we own this data' (not all of the data on the block, just the one row we are modifying). When another session comes along, it sees the lock ID and, using the fact that it represents a transaction, it can quickly see if the transaction holding the lock is still active. If it is not active, the data is theirs. If it is still active, that session will ask to be notified as soon as it finishes. Hence, we have a queueing mechanism: the session requesting the lock will be queued up waiting for that transaction to complete and then it will get the data.

Here is a small example showing how this happens. We will use three V$ tables in order to see how this works:

- ❑ V$TRANSACTION, which contains an entry for every active transaction/
- ❑ V$SESSION, which shows us the sessions logged in.
- ❑ V$LOCK, which contains an entry for all locks being held as well as for sessions that are waiting on locks.

First, let's start a transaction:

```
tkyte@TKYTE816> update dept set deptno = deptno+10;
4 rows updated.
```

Now, let's look at the state of the system at this point:

```
tkyte@TKYTE816> select username,
  2            v$lock.sid,
  3            trunc(id1/power(2,16)) rbs,
  4            bitand(id1,to_number('ffff','xxxx'))+0 slot,
  5            id2 seq,
  6            lmode,
  7            request
  8   from v$lock, v$session
  9   where v$lock.type = 'TX'
 10     and v$lock.sid = v$session.sid
 11     and v$session.username = USER
 12   /
```

USERNAME	SID	RBS	SLOT	SEQ	LMODE	REQUEST
TKYTE	8	2	46	160	6	0

```
tkyte@TKYTE816> select XIDUSN, XIDSLOT, XIDSQN
  2    from v$transaction
  3   /
```

XIDUSN	XIDSLOT	XIDSQN
2	46	160

The interesting points to note here are:

❑ The `LMODE` is 6 in the `V$LOCK` table and the request is 0. If you refer to the definition of the `V$LOCK` table in the *Oracle Server Reference Manual*, you will find that `LMODE=6` is an exclusive lock. A value of 0 in the request means we are not making a request – we have the lock.

❑ There is only one row in this table. This `V$LOCK` table is more of a queueing table than a lock table. Many people expect there would be four rows in `V$LOCK` since we have four rows locked. What you must remember however is that Oracle does not store a master list of every row locked anywhere. To find out if a row is locked, we must go to that row.

❑ I took the `ID1` and `ID2` columns, and performed some manipulation on them. Oracle needed to save three 16 bit numbers, but only had two columns in order to do it. So, the first column `ID1` holds two of these numbers. By dividing by 2^{16} with `trunc(id1/power(2,16))` rbs and by masking out the high bits with `bitand(id1,to_number('ffff','xxxx'))+0` slot, I am able to get the two numbers that are hiding in that one number back out.

❑ The `RBS`, `SLOT`, and `SEQ` values match the `V$TRANSACTION` information. This is my transaction ID.

Now I'll start another session using the same user name, update some rows in `EMP`, and then try to update `DEPT`:

```
tkyte@TKYTE816> update emp set ename = upper(ename);
14 rows updated.

tkyte@TKYTE816> update dept set deptno = deptno-10;
```

I am now blocked in this session. If we run the `V$` queries again, we see:

```
tkyte@TKYTE816> select username,
  2           v$lock.sid,
  3              trunc(id1/power(2,16)) rbs,
  4              bitand(id1,to_number('ffff','xxxx'))+0 slot,
  5              id2 seq,
  6           lmode,
  7              request
  8  from v$lock, v$session
  9  where v$lock.type = 'TX'
 10    and v$lock.sid = v$session.sid
 11    and v$session.username = USER
 12  /

USERNAME         SID         RBS        SLOT         SEQ       LMODE     REQUEST
--------  ----------  ----------  ----------  ----------  ----------  ----------
TKYTE              8           2          46         160           6           0
TKYTE              9           2          46         160           0           6
TKYTE              9           3          82         163           6           0

tkyte@TKYTE816> select XIDUSN, XIDSLOT, XIDSQN
  2     from v$transaction
  3  /

    XIDUSN     XIDSLOT      XIDSQN
----------  ----------  ----------
         3          82         163
         2          46         160
```

What we see here is that a new transaction has begun, with a transaction ID of (3,82,163). Our new session, SID=9, has two rows in V$LOCK this time. One row represents the locks that it owns (where LMODE=6). It also has a row in there that shows a REQUEST with a value of 6. This is a request for an exclusive lock. The interesting thing to note here is that the RBS/SLOT/SEQ values of this request row are the transaction ID of the *holder* of the lock. The transaction with SID=8 is blocking the transaction with SID=9. We can see this more explicitly simply by doing a self-join of V$LOCK:

```
tkyte@TKYTE816> select
          (select username from v$session where sid=a.sid) blocker,
    2           a.sid,
    3         ' is blocking ',
    4           (select username from v$session where sid=b.sid) blockee,
    5             b.sid
    6    from v$lock a, v$lock b
    7   where a.block = 1
    8     and b.request > 0
    9     and a.id1 = b.id1
   10     and a.id2 = b.id2
   11  /

BLOCKER            SID 'ISBLOCKING'  BLOCKEE        SID
--------    ----------  -------------  --------  ----------
TKYTE                8  is blocking  TKYTE            9
```

Now, if we commit our original transaction, SID=8, and rerun our query, we find that the request row has gone:

```
tkyte@TKYTE816> select username,
    2             v$lock.sid,
    3               trunc(id1/power(2,16)) rbs,
    4               bitand(id1,to_number('ffff','xxxx'))+0 slot,
    5             id2 seq,
    6           lmode,
    7               request, block
    8    from v$lock, v$session
    9   where v$lock.type = 'TX'
   10     and v$lock.sid = v$session.sid
   11     and v$session.username = USER
   12  /

USERNAME          SID         RBS         SLOT          SEQ       LMODE     REQUEST
--------   ----------  ----------  ----------  ----------  ----------  ----------
TKYTE               9           3          82          163           6           0

tkyte@TKYTE816> select XIDUSN, XIDSLOT, XIDSQN
    2      from v$transaction
    3  /

    XIDUSN     XIDSLOT      XIDSQN
----------  ----------  ----------
         3          82          163
```

The request row disappeared the instant the other session gave up its lock. That request row was the queuing mechanism. The database is able to wake up the blocked sessions the instant the transaction is completed.

There are infinitely more 'pretty' displays with various GUI tools, but in a pinch, having knowledge of the tables you need to look at is very useful.

However, before we can say that we have a good understanding of how the row locking in Oracle works we must look at one last piece, that is, how the locking and transaction information is managed with the data itself. It is part of the block overhead. In Chapter 2, *Architecture*, we discussed how the basic format of a block included some leading 'overhead' space in which to store a transaction table for that block. This transaction table contains an entry for each 'real' transaction that has locked some data in that block. The size of this structure is controlled by two physical attribute parameters on the CREATE statement for an object:

- ❑ INITRANS – the initial, pre-allocated size of this structure. This defaults to 2 for indexes and 1 for tables.

- ❑ MAXTRANS – the maximum size to which this structure may grow. It defaults to 255.

So, each block starts life with, by default, one or two transaction slots. The number of simultaneous active transactions that a block can ever have is constrained by the value of MAXTRANS, and by the availability of space on the block. You may not be able to achieve 255 concurrent transactions on the block if there is not sufficient space to grow this structure.

We can artificially demonstrate how this works by creating a table with a constrained MAXTRANS. For example:

```
tkyte@TKYTE816> create table t ( x int ) maxtrans 1;
Table created.

tkyte@TKYTE816> insert into t values ( 1 );
1 row created.

tkyte@TKYTE816> insert into t values ( 2 );
1 row created.

tkyte@TKYTE816> commit;
Commit complete.
```

Now, in one session we issue:

```
tkyte@TKYTE816> update t set x = 3 where x = 1;
1 row updated.
```

and in another:

```
tkyte@TKYTE816> update t set x = 4 where x = 2;
```

Now, since those two rows are undoubtedly on the same database block and we set MAXTRANS (the maximum degree of concurrency for that block) to one, the second session will be blocked. This demonstrates what happens when more than MAXTRANS transactions attempt to access the same block simultaneously. Similarly, blocking may also occur if the INITRANS is set low and there is not enough space on a block to dynamically expand the transaction. In most cases the defaults of 1 and 2 for INITRANS is sufficient as the transaction table will dynamically grow (space permitting), but in some environments you may need to increase this setting to increase concurrency and decrease waits. An example of when you might need to do this would be a table, or even more frequently, on an index (since index blocks can get many more rows on them than a table can typically hold) that is frequently modified. We may need to increase INITRANS to set aside ahead of time sufficient space on the block for the number of expected concurrent transactions. This is especially true if the blocks are expected to be nearly full to begin with, meaning there is no room for the dynamic expansion of the transaction structure on the block.

TM – (DML Enqueue) Locks

These locks are used to ensure that the structure of a table is not altered while you are modifying its contents. For example, if you have updated a table, you will acquire a TM lock on that table. This will prevent another user from executing DROP or ALTER commands on that table. If they attempt to perform DDL on the table while you have a TM lock on it, they will receive the following error message:

```
drop table dept
       *
ERROR at line 1:
ORA-00054: resource busy and acquire with NOWAIT specified
```

This is a confusing messag, at first, since there is no method to specify NOWAIT or WAIT on a DROP TABLE at all. It is just the generic message you get when you attempt to perform an operation that would be blocked, but the operation does not permit blocking. As we've seen before, it is the same message that you get if you issue a SELECT FOR UPDATE NOWAIT against a locked row.

Below, we see how these locks would appear to us in the V$LOCK table:

```
tkyte@TKYTE816> create table t1 ( x int );
Table created.

tkyte@TKYTE816> create table t2 ( x int );
Table created.

tkyte@TKYTE816> insert into t1 values ( 1 );
1 row created.

tkyte@TKYTE816> insert into t2 values ( 1 );
1 row created.

tkyte@TKYTE816> select username,
  2          v$lock.sid,
  3              id1, id2,
  4          lmode,
  5            request, block, v$lock.type
  6   from v$lock, v$session
  7   where v$lock.sid = v$session.sid
  8     and v$session.username = USER
  9   /

USERNAME           SID         ID1        ID2    LMODE    REQUEST      BLOCK TY
---------   ----------  ----------  ---------  -------  ----------  ---------- --
TKYTE                8       24055          0        3          0          0 TM
TKYTE                8       24054          0        3          0          0 TM
TKYTE                8      327697        165        6          0          0 TX

tkyte@TKYTE816> select object_name, object_id from user_objects;

OBJECT_NAME                         OBJECT_ID
-------------------------------   ----------
T1                                     24054
T2                                     24055
```

Whereas we only get one TX lock per transaction, we can get as many TM locks as the objects we modify. Here, the interesting thing is that the `ID1` column for the TM lock is the object ID of the DML-locked object so it easy to find the object on which the lock is being held.

An interesting aside to the TM lock: the total number of TM locks allowed in the system is configurable by you (for details, see the `DML_LOCKS init.ora` parameter definition in the *Oracle8i Server Reference* manual). It may in fact be set to zero. This does not mean that your database becomes a read-only database (no locks), but rather that DDL is not permitted. This is useful in very specialized applications, such as OPS, to reduce the amount of intra-instance coordination that would otherwise take place. You can also remove the ability to gain TM locks on an objectbyobject basis, using the `ALTER TABLE TABLENAME DISABLE TABLE LOCK` command.

DDL Locks

DDL locks are automatically placed against objects during a DDL operation to protect them from changes by other sessions. For example, if I perform the DDL operation `ALTERTABLE T`, the table `T` will have an exclusive DDL lock placed against it, preventing other sessions from getting DDL locks and TM locks on this table. DDL locks are held for the duration of the DDL statement, and are released immediately afterwards. This is done, in effect, by always wrapping DDL statements in implicit commits (or a commit/rollback pair). It is for this reason that DDL always commits in Oracle. Every `CREATE`, `ALTER`, and so on, statement is really executed as shown in this pseudo-code:

```
Begin
    Commit;
    DDL-STATEMENT
    Commit;
Exception
    When others then rollback;
End;
```

So, DDL will always commit, even if it is unsuccessful. DDL starts by committing – be aware of this. It commits first so that if it has to rollback, it will not roll back your transaction. If you execute DDL, it'll make permanent any outstanding work you have performed, even if the DDL is not successful. If you need to execute DDL, but do not want it to commit your existing transaction, you may use an autonomous transaction (see Chapter 15, *Autonomous Transactions*, for further details).

There are three types of DDL locks:

❑ **Exclusive DDL locks** – These prevent other sessions from gaining a DDL lock or TM (DML) lock themselves. This means that you may query a table during a DDL operation but may not modify it in any way.

❑ **Share DDL locks** – This protects the structure of the referenced object against modification by other sessions, but allows modifications to the data.

❑ **Breakable Parse locks** – This allows an object, such as a query plan cached in the shared pool, to register its reliance on some other object. If you perform DDL against that object, Oracle will review the list of objects that have registered their dependence, and invalidate them. Hence, these 'locks' are 'breakable'; they do not prevent the DDL from occurring.

Most DDL takes an **exclusive** DDL lock. If you issue a statement such as:

```
Alter table t add new_column date;
```

the table T will be unavailable for modifications during the execution of that statement. The table may be queried using SELECT during this time, but most other operations will be prevented, including all DDL statements. In Oracle 8i, some DDL operations may now take place without DDL locks. For example, I can issue:

```
create index t_idx on t(x) ONLINE;
```

The ONLINE keyword modifies the method by which the index is actually built. Instead of taking an exclusive DDL lock, preventing modifications of data, Oracle will only attempt to acquire a low-level (mode 2) TM lock on the table. This will effectively prevent other DDL from taking place, but will allow DML to occur normally. Oracle accomplishes this feat by keeping a record of modifications made to the table during the DDL statement, and applying these changes to the new index as it finishes the CREATE. This greatly increases the availability of data.

Other types of DDL take **share** DDL locks. These are taken out against dependent objects when you create stored, compiled objects, such as procedures and views. For example, if you execute:

```
Create view MyView
as
select *
  from emp, dept
 where emp.deptno = dept.deptno;
```

Share DDL locks will be placed against both EMP and DEPT, while the CREATE VIEW command is being processed. We can modify the contents of these tables, but we cannot modify their structure.

The last type of DDL lock is a **breakable parse** lock. When our session parses a statement, a parse lock is taken against every object referenced by that statement. These locks are taken in order to allow the parsed, cached statement to be invalidated (flushed) in the shared pool if a referenced object is dropped or altered in some way.

A view that is invaluable for looking at this information is the DBA_DDL_LOCKS view. There is no V$ view for us to look at. The DBA_DDL_LOCKS view is built on the more mysterious X$ tables and, by default, it will not be installed in your database. You can install this and other locking views by running the CATBLOCK.SQL script found in the directory [ORACLE_HOME]/rdbms/admin. This script must be executed as the user SYS in order to succeed. Once you have executed this script, you can run a query against the view. For example in a single user database I see:

```
tkyte@TKYTE816> select * from dba_ddl_locks;

session                                                          mode mode
    id OWNER  NAME                          TYPE                 held reqe
------- ------ ----------------------------- -------------------- ---- ----
      8 SYS    DBMS_APPLICATION_INFO         Body                 Null None
      8 SYS    DBMS_APPLICATION_INFO         Table/Procedure/Type Null None
      8 SYS    DBMS_OUTPUT                   Table/Procedure/Type Null None
      8 SYS    DBMS_OUTPUT                   Body                 Null None
      8 TKYTE  TKYTE                         18                   Null None
      8 SYS    DATABASE                      18                   Null None

6 rows selected.
```

These are all the objects that my session is 'locking'. I have breakable parse locks on a couple of the `DBMS_*` packages. These are a side effect of using SQL*PLUS; it calls `DBMS_APPLICATION_INFO`, for example. I may see more than one copy of various objects here – this is normal, and just means I have more than one thing I'm using in the shared pool that references these objects. It is interesting to note that in the view, the `OWNER` column is not the owner of the lock; rather it is the owner of the object being locked. This is why you see many `SYS` rows with – `SYS` owns these packages, but they all belong to my session.

To see a breakable parse lock in action, we will first create and run a stored procedure, P:

```
tkyte@TKYTE816> create or replace procedure p as begin null; end;
  2  /
Procedure created.

tkyte@TKYTE816> exec p

PL/SQL procedure successfully completed.
```

The procedure, P, will now show up in the `DBA_DDL_LOCKS` view. We have a parse lock on it:

```
tkyte@TKYTE816> select * from dba_ddl_locks;
```

session id	OWNER	NAME	TYPE	mode held	mode reqe
8	TKYTE	P	Table/Procedure/Type	Null	None
8	SYS	DBMS_APPLICATION_INFO	Body	Null	None
8	SYS	DBMS_APPLICATION_INFO	Table/Procedure/Type	Null	None
8	SYS	DBMS_OUTPUT	Table/Procedure/Type	Null	None
8	SYS	DBMS_OUTPUT	Body	Null	None
8	TKYTE	TKYTE	18	Null	None
8	SYS	DATABASE	18	Null	None

```
7 rows selected.
```

We then recompile our procedure, and query the view again:

```
tkyte@TKYTE816> alter procedure p compile;

Procedure altered.

tkyte@TKYTE816> select * from dba_ddl_locks;
```

session id	OWNER	NAME	TYPE	mode held	mode reqe
8	SYS	DBMS_APPLICATION_INFO	Body	Null	None
8	SYS	DBMS_APPLICATION_INFO	Table/Procedure/Type	Null	None
8	SYS	DBMS_OUTPUT	Table/Procedure/Type	Null	None
8	SYS	DBMS_OUTPUT	Body	Null	None
8	TKYTE	TKYTE	18	Null	None
8	SYS	DATABASE	18	Null	None

```
6 rows selected.
```

We find that P is now missing from the view – our parse lock has been broken.

This view is useful to you, as a developer, when it is found that some piece of code won't compile in the test or development system – it hangs and eventually times out. This indicates that someone else is using it (actually running it) and you can use this view to see who that might be. The same will happen with GRANTS and other types of DDL against the object. You cannot grant EXECUTE on a procedure that is running, for example. You can use the same method as above to discover the potential blockers and waiters.

Latches and Internal Locks (Enqueues)

Latches and enqueues are lightweight serialization devices used to coordinate multi-user access to shared data structures, objects and files.

Latches are locks that are held for extremely short periods of time, for example the time it takes to modify an in-memory data structure. They are used to protect certain memory structures, such as the database block buffer cache or the library cache in the shared pool (as described in Chapter 2, *Architecture*). Latches are typically requested internally in a 'willing to wait' mode. This means that if the latch is not available, the requesting session will sleep for a short period of time and retry the operation later. Other latches may be requested in an 'immediate' mode, meaning that the process will go do something else rather than sit and wait for the latch to become available. Since many requestors may be waiting for a latch at the same time, you may see some processes waiting longer than others. Latches are assigned rather randomly, based on the 'luck of the draw', if you will. Whichever session asks for a latch right after it was released will get it. There is no line of latch waiters, just a 'mob' of waiters constantly retrying.

Oracle uses atomic instructions like 'test and set' for operating on latches. Since the instructions to set and free latches are atomic, the operating system itself guarantees that only one process gets it. Since it is only one instruction, it can be quite fast. Latches are held for short periods of time and provide a mechanism for clean-up in case a latch holder 'dies' abnormally while holding it. This cleaning up process would be performed by PMON.

Enqueues are another, more sophisticated, serialization device, used when updating rows in a database table, fro example. They differ from latches in that they allow the requestor to 'queue up' and wait for the resource. With a latch request, the requestor is told right away whether they got the latch or not. With an enqueue, the requestor will be blocked until they actually attain it. As such, they are not as fast as a latch can be, but they do provided functionality over and above that which a latch can offer. Enqueues may be obtained at various levels, so you can have many 'share' locks and locks with various degrees of 'shareability'.

Manual Locking and User-Defined Locks

So far we have looked mostly at locks that Oracle places for us transparently. When we update a table, Oracle places a TM lock on it to prevent other sessions from dropping that table (or perform most DDL in fact). We have TX locks that are left on the various blocks we modify so others can tell what data we 'own'. The database employs DDL locks to protect objects from change while we are ourselves changing them. It uses latches and locks internally to protect its own structure. Now, let's take a look at how we can get involved in some of this locking action. Our options are:

- ❑   Manually locking data via a SQL statement.
- ❑   Creating our own locks via the DBMS_LOCK package.

We will briefly discuss why you might want to do each of these.

Manual Locking

We have, in fact, already seen a couple of cases where we might want to use manual locking. The SELECT...FOR UPDATE statement is the predominant method of manually locking data. We used it in previous examples in order to avoid the lost update issue, whereby one session would overwrite another session's changes. We've seen it used as a method to serialize access to detail records in order to enforce business rules (the resource scheduler example from Chapter 1, *Developing Successful Oracle Applications*).

We can also manually lock data using the LOCK TABLE statement. This is actually only used rarely, because of the coarseness of the lock. It simply locks the table, not the rows in the table. If you start modifying the rows they will be 'locked' as normal. So, it is not a method to save on resources (as it might be in other RDBMSs). You might use the LOCK TABLE IN EXCLUSIVE MODE statement if you were writing a large batch update that would affect most of the rows in a given table, and you wanted to be sure that no one would 'block' you. By locking the table in this manner, you can be assured that your update will be able to do all of its work without getting blocked by other transactions. It would be the rare application however that has a LOCK TABLE statement in it.

Creating your own Locks

Oracle actually exposes to developers the enqueue lock mechanism that it uses internally, via the DBMS_LOCK package (which we will cover in much more detail in Appendix A). You might be wondering why you would want to create your own locks. The answer is typically application-specific. For example, you might use this package to serialize access to some resource external to Oracle. Say you are using the UTL_FILE routine that allows you to write to a file on the server's file system. You might have developed a common message routine that every application calls to record messages. Since the file is external, Oracle won't coordinate the many users trying to modify it simultaneously. In comes the DBMS_LOCK package. Now, before you open, write, and close the file, you will request a lock named after the file in exclusive mode and after you close the file, you will manually release the lock. In this fashion, only one person at a time will be able to write a message to this file. Everyone else will queue up. The DBMS_LOCK package allows you to manually release a lock when you are done with it, or to give it up automatically when you commit, or even to keep it as long as you are logged in.

What is Concurrency Control?

Concurrency controls are the collection of functions that the database provides in order to allow many people to access and modify data simultaneously. The implementation of locking in the database is perhaps the most crucial factor in determining the degree of concurrency that your application can support (basically, how well it will scale). As we discussed previously, there are many different types of locks – from TX transaction locks, which are extremely scalable both in terms of performance and cardinality (whether you have one or one billion of them), to TM and DDL locks (applied in the least restrictive mode whenever possible), to the internal locks that Oracle employs to mediate access to its shared data structures, from the very lightweight and fast latching mechanism to the heavier, but feature-rich, enqueue.

But concurrency control goes beyond locks. There are other things that the database can do to provide controlled, yet highly concurrent, access to data. For example, there is a feature of Oracle called multi-versioning (introduced in Chapter 1). Since Oracle uses multi-versioning to provide read-consistent views of data, we get the rather pleasant side effect that a reader of data will never be blocked by a writer of data; – writes do not block reads. This is one of the fundamental differences between Oracle and the rest of the databases out there. A read query in Oracle will never be blocked, it will never deadlock with another session, and it will never get an answer that didn't exist in the database.

Oracle's multi-versioning model for read consistency is always applied at the statement level (for each and every query) and can also be applied at the transaction level. What I would like to do in this section is to demonstrate how multi-versioning ties in with the various transaction isolation levels defined in the SQL92 standard.

Transaction Isolation Levels

The ANSI/ISO SQL92 standard defines four levels of transaction isolation, with different possible outcomes for the same transaction scenario. That is, the same work performed in the same fashion with the same inputs, may result in different answers, depending on your isolation level. These isolation levels are defined in terms of three 'phenomena' that are either permitted or not at a given isolation level:

❑ **Dirty read** – The meaning of this is as bad as it sounds. You are permitted to read uncommitted, or 'dirty', data. This is the effect you would achieve by just opening an OS file that someone else is writing, and reading whatever data happened to be there. Data integrity is compromised, foreign keys violated, unique constraints ignored.

❑ **Non-REPEATABLE READ** – This simply means that if you read a row at time T1, and attempt to re-read that row at time T2, the row may have changed. It may have disappeared, it may have been updated, and so on.

❑ **Phantom read** – This means that if you execute a query at time T1, and re-execute it at time T2, additional rows may have been added to the database, which will affect your results. This differs from the non-repeatable read in that in this case, data you already read has not been changed but rather that *more* data satisfies your query criteria than before.

The SQL92 isolation levels are defined based on whether or not they allow each of the above phenomena:

Isolation Level	Dirty Read	Non-REPEATABLE READ	Phantom Read
READ UNCOMMITTED	Permitted	Permitted	Permitted
READ COMMITTED		Permitted	Permitted
REPEATABLE READ			Permitted
SERIALIZABLE			

Oracle explicitly supports the READ COMMITTED and SERIALIZABLE isolation levels, as they are defined in the standard. However, this doesn't tell the whole story. The SQL92 standard was attempting to set up isolation levels that would permit various degrees of consistency for queries performed in each level. REPEATABLE READ is the isolation level that they claim will guarantee a read consistent result from a query. In their definition, READ COMMITTED does not give you consistent results and READ UNCOMMITTED is the level to use to get non-blocking reads.

In Oracle, READ COMMITTED has all of the attributes required to achieve Read-consistent queries. In other databases, READ COMMITTED queries can and will return answers that never existed in the database at any point in time. Moreover, Oracle also supports the *spirit* of READ UNCOMMITTED. The goal of providing a dirty read is to supply a non-blocking read, whereby queries are not blocked by, and do not block, updates of the same data. However, Oracle does not need dirty reads to achieve this goal, nor does it support them. Dirty reads are an implementation other databases must use in order to provide non-blocking reads.

In addition to the four defined SQL92 isolation levels, Oracle provides another level, read only. A read-only transaction is equivalent to a read-only REPEATABLE READ or SERIALIZABLE in SQL92. It only sees those changes that were committed at the time the transaction began, but inserts, updates and deletes are not permitted in this mode (other sessions may update data, but not the read-only transaction). Using this mode you can achieve REPEATABLE READ and SERIALIZABLE READ, without phantoms.

Let's now move on to discuss exactly how multi-versioning and read consistency fits into the above isolation schemes, and how other databases that do not support multi-versioning would achieve the same results. This is instructive for anyone who has used another database and believes they understand how the isolation levels must work. It is also interesting to see how a standard that was supposed to remove the differences from the databases, SQL92, actually allows for it. The standard, while very detailed, can be implemented in very different ways.

READ UNCOMMITTED

The READ UNCOMMITTED isolation level permits for dirty reads. Oracle does not make use of dirty reads, nor does it even allow for them. The basic goal of a READ UNCOMMITTED isolation level is to provide a standards-based definition that caters for non-blocking reads. As we have seen, Oracle provides for non-blocking reads by default. You would be hard-pressed to make a SELECT query block in the database (there is the special case of a distributed in-doubt transaction, which we discuss in Chapter 4). Every single query, be it a SELECT, INSERT, UPDATE, or DELETE, executes in a read-consistent fashion.

In Chapter 1, *Developing building Successful Oracle Applications*, Oracle's method of obtaining read-consistency was demonstrated by way of an accounts example. We're now going to revisit that example to discuss in more detail what happens in Oracle, using multi-versioning, and what would happen in any number of other databases. Again, we are assuming one database row per block.

We will start with the same basic table and query:

```
create table accounts
( account_number number primary key,
  account_balance number
);

select sum(account_balance) from accounts;
```

Before the query begins, we have the following data:

Row	Account Number	Account Balance
1	123	$500.00
2	456	$240.25
...	...	...
342,023	987	$100.00

Now, our select statement starts executing and reads row 1, row 2, and so on. At some point while we are in the middle of the query, a transaction moves $400.00 from account 123 to account 987. This transaction does the two updates, but does not commit. The table now looks like this:

Row	Account Number	Account Balance	LOCKED
1	123	($500.00) changed to $100.00	X
2	456	$240.25	
...	...	...	
342,023	987	($100.00) changed to $500.00	X

So, two of those rows are locked – if anyone tried to update them they would be blocked. So far the behavior we are seeing is more or less consistent across all databases. The difference will be in what happens when the query gets to the locked data.

When the query we are executing gets to the locked block, it will notice that the data on it has changed since the beginning of its execution. In order to provide a consistent (correct) answer, Oracle will at this point recreate the block with the locked data as it existed when the query began. That is, Oracle takes a detour around the lock – it reads around it, reconstructing it from the rollback segment. A consistent and correct answer comes back without waiting for the transaction to commit.

Now, a database that allowed a dirty read would simply return the value it saw in account 987 at the time it read it, in this case $500. The query would count the transferred $400 twice and would present a total that never existed in the accounts table at any point in time. In a multi-user database, a dirty read can be a dangerous feature and, personally, I have never seen the usefulness of it. It not only returns the wrong answer, but it may see data that will never actually exist in the database at any point in time. Say that, rather than transferring, the transaction was actually just depositing $400 in account 987. The dirty read would count the $400 and get the 'right' answer, wouldn't it? Well, suppose the uncommitted transaction was rolled back. We have just counted $400 that was never actually in the database.

The point here is that dirty read is not a feature – rather it is a liability. In Oracle, it is just not needed. You get all of the advantages of a dirty read (no blocking) without any of the incorrect results.

READ COMMITTED

The READ COMMITTED isolation level states that a transaction may only read data that was committed before the transaction began. There are no dirty reads. There may be non- REPEATABLE READ s (re-reads of the same row return a different answer) and phantom reads (newly inserted rows become visible to a query that were not visible earlier in the transaction). READ COMMITTED is perhaps the most commonly used isolation level in database applications everywhere. It is rare to see a different isolation level used.

READ COMMITTED isolation is not as cut and dry as it sounds. If you look at the matrix above, it looks straightforward. Obviously, given the rules above, a query executed in any database using READ COMMITTED isolation would behave in the same way, would it not? It will not. If you query multiple rows in a single statement then, in almost every other database, READ COMMITTED isolation can be as bad as a dirty read, depending on the implementation.

In Oracle, using multi-versioning and read consistent queries, the answer we get from the accounts query is the same in READ COMMITTED as it was in the READ UNCOMMITTED example. Oracle will reconstruct the modified data as it appeared when the query began, returning the answer that was in the database when the query started.

Let's now take a look at how our above example might work in READ COMMITTED mode in other databases – you might find the answer surprising. We'll pick up our example at the point described in the previous table:

❑   We are in the middle of the table. We have read and summed the first N rows.

❑   The other transaction has moved $400 from account 123 to 987.

❑   It has not yet committed, so rows 123 and 987 are locked.

We know what happens in Oracle when it gets to account 987 – it will read around the modified data, find out it should be $100.00 and complete. Let's see how another database, running in some default READ COMMITTED mode, might arrive at the answer:

Time	Query	Account transfer transaction
T1	Reads row 1, sum = $500 so far.	
T2	Reads row 2, sum = $740.25 so far.	
T3		Updates row 1, puts an exclusive lock on block 1 preventing other updates and reads. Row 1 now has $100.
T4	Reads row N, sum = ...	
T5		Updates row 342023, puts an exclusive lock on this block. Row now has $500.
T6	Reads row 342023, discovers that it has been modified. This session will block and wait for this block to become available. All processing on this query stops.	
T7		Commits transaction.
T8	Reads row 342,023, sees $500 and presents final answer.	

The first thing to notice is that this other database, upon getting to account 987, will block our query. This session must wait on that row until the transaction holding the exclusive lock commits. This is one reason why many people have a bad habit of committing in the middle of their transactions. Updates interfere with reads in most other databases. The really bad news in this scenario is that we are making the end user wait for the *wrong* answer. You still receive an answer that never existed in the database at any point in time, as with the dirty read, but this time we made them wait for the wrong answer.

The important lesson here is that various databases executing in the same, apparently safe isolation level, can, and will, return very different answers under the exact same circumstances. It is important to understand that, in Oracle, non-blocking reads are not had at the expense of correct answers. You can have your cake and eat it too, sometimes.

REPEATABLE READ

The goal of REPEATABLE READ in SQL92 is to provide an isolation level that gives consistent, correct answers, and prevents lost updates. We'll take a look at both examples, and see what we have to do in Oracle to achieve this, and what happens in other systems.

Getting a Consistent Answer

If I have a REPEATABLE READ isolation, the results from a given query must be consistent with respect to some point in time. Most databases (not Oracle) achieve REPEATABLE READs via the use of row-level, shared read locks. A shared read lock prevents other sessions from modifying data that you have read. This of course decreases concurrency. Oracle opted for the more concurrent, multi-versioning model to provide read consistent answers.

In Oracle, using multi-versioning, you get an answer that is consistent with respect to the point in time the query began execution. In other databases, using shared read locks, you get an answer that is consistent with respect to the point in time the query completes – that is, when you can get the answer at all (more on this in a moment).

In a system that employs a shared read lock to provide REPEATABLE READs, you would observe rows in a table getting locked as the query processed them. So, using the example from above, as our query reads the accounts table, it would leave shared read locks on each row:

Time	Query	Account transfer transaction
T1	Reads row 1, sum = $500 so far. Block 1 has a shared read lock on it.	
T2	Reads row 2, sum = $740.25 so far. Block 2 has a shared read lock on it.	
T3		Attempts to update row 1 but is blocked. Transaction is suspended until it can obtain an exclusive lock.
T4	Reads row N, sum = ...	
T5	Reads row 342023, sees $100 and presents final answer.	
T6	Commits transaction.	
T7		Updates row 1, puts an exclusive lock on this block. Row now has $100.
T8		Updates row 342023, puts an exclusive lock on this block. Row now has $500. Commits.

This table shows that we now get the correct answer, but at the cost of physically serializing the two transactions. This is one of the side effects of shared read locks for consistent answers: *readers of data will block writers of data*. This is in addition to the fact that, in these systems, writers of data will block readers of data.

So, you can see how shared read locks would inhibit concurrency, but they can also cause spurious errors to occur. In this example we start with our original table but this time with the goal of transferring $50.00 from account 987, to account 123:

Time	Query	Account transfer transaction
T1	Reads row 1, sum = $500 so far. Block 1 has a shared read lock on it.	
T2	Reads row 2, sum = $740.25 so far. Block 2 has a shared read lock on it.	
T3		Updates row 342023, puts an exclusive lock on block 342023 preventing other updates and shared read locks. This row now has $50.
T4	Reads row N, sum = ...	
T5		Attempts to update row 1 but is blocked. Transaction is suspended until it can obtain an exclusive lock.
T6	Attempts to read row 342023 but cannot as an exclusive lock is already in place.	

We have just reached the classic deadlock condition. Our query holds resources the update needs, and vice versa. Our query has just deadlocked with our update transaction. One of them will be chosen as the victim and will be killed. We just spent a long time and a lot of resources only to fail, and get rolled back at the end. This is the second side effect of shared read locks: *readers and writers of data can and frequently will deadlock each other*.

As we have seen in Oracle, we have statement level read consistency without reads blocking writes or deadlocks. Oracle never uses shared read locks – *ever*. Oracle has chosen the harder to implement, but infinitely more concurrent multi-versioning scheme.

Lost Update Prevention

A common use of REPEATABLE READ would be for lost update prevention. If we have REPEATABLE READ enabled, this cannot happen. By definition, a re-read of that row in the same session will result in the same exact data being returned.

In databases other than Oracle, a REPEATABLE READ may be implemented using SELECT FOR UPDATE and shared read locks. If two users select the same row for update, both will place a shared read lock on that data. When the first user attempts to update they will be blocked. When the second user attempts to update, a deadlock will occur. This is not ideal but it does prevent the lost update.

In Oracle, if we want REPEATABLE READ, but do not actually want to physically serialize access to a table with SELECT FOR UPDATE NOWAIT (as demonstrated earlier in the chapter), we actually need to set the isolation level to SERIALIZABLE.

SERIALIZABLE encompasses the lower levels of isolation so if you can do SERIALIZABLE, you can do REPEATABLE READ

In Oracle, a SERIALIZABLE transaction is implemented so that the read-consistency we normally get at the statement level is extended to the transaction. That is, the answers to every query we will execute in our transaction is fixed at the point in time our transaction began. In this mode if we:

```
Select * from T;
Begin dbms_lock.sleep( 60*60*24 ); end;
Select * from T;
```

The answers returned from T would be the same, even though we just slept for 24 hours (or we might get an ORA-1555, snapshot too old error). The isolation level would assure us these two queries would always returns the same results. Oracle does this in the same way it provided a read consistent query. It uses the rollback segments to reconstruct the data as it existed when our transaction began, instead of just when our statement began. In a SERIALIZABLE mode transaction however, if we attempt to update data and discover at that point in time the data has changed since our transaction began, we will receive an error about not being able to serialize access. We will cover this in more detail shortly.

It is clear that this is not the optimum approach for our HR application. What would happen in that application is that both users would query the data; both users would update the data on screen. The first user would save their changes, and would succeed. The second user however, would receive an error when they attempted to save their changes. They just wasted a lot of time for nothing. They must restart the transaction, receive our changes, and do it all over again. It prevented the lost update, but at the price of an annoyed end-user. However, if a situation arises where REPEATABLE READ is required, and you do not expect transactions to attempt to update the same rows, then use of the SERIALIZABLE mode is a possible solution.

SERIALIZABLE

This is generally considered the most restrictive level of transaction isolation, but provides the highest degree of isolation. A SERIALIZABLE transaction operates in an environment that makes it appear as if there are no other users modifying data in the database, the database will be 'frozen' at the point in time your query began. Your transaction sees the database consistently, at a single point in time. Side effects (changes) made by other transactions are not visible to it, regardless of how long it has been running. SERIALIZABLE **does not** mean that all transactions executed by the users are the same as if they were executed one right after another in a serial fashion. It does not imply that there is some serial ordering of the transactions that would result in the same outcome. This last point is a frequently misunderstood concept and a small demonstration will clear it up. The following table represents two sessions performing work over time. The database tables A and B start out empty and are created as follows:

```
tkyte@TKYTE816> create table a ( x int );
Table created.

tkyte@TKYTE816> create table b ( x int );
Table created.
```

Now, we have the following series of events:

Time	Session 1 Executes	Session 2 Executes
0:00	Alter session set isolation_level=serializable;	
0:01		Alter session set isolation_level=serializable;
0:02	Insert into a select count(*) from b;	
0:03		Insert into b select count(*) from a;
0:04	Commit;	
0:05		Commit;

Now, when this is all said and done – tables A and B will each have a row with the value of zero in it. If there was some 'serial' ordering of the transactions we could not possibly have both tables containing the value zero in them. If Session 1 executed before Session 2 – then table B would have a count of 1. If Session 2 executed before Session 1 – then table A would have a count of 1. As executed above, however, both tables will have a count of *zero*. They just executed as if they were the only transaction in the database at that point in time. No matter how many times Session 1 queried table B, the count will be the count that was committed in the database at time 0:00. Likewise, no matter how many times Session 2 queries table A, it will be the same as it was at time 0:01.

In Oracle, serializability is achieved by extending the read consistency we get at the statement level to the transaction level. Instead of results being consistent with respect to the start of a statement, they are pre-ordained at the time you begin the transaction. Pretty deep thought there – the database already knows the answer to any question you might ask it, before you ask it.

This degree of isolation comes with a price – that price is the error:

```
ERROR at line 1:
ORA-08177: can't serialize access for this transaction
```

You will get this message whenever you attempt to update a row that has changed since your transaction began. Oracle takes an optimistic approach to serialization; it gambles on the fact that the data your transaction wants to update won't be updated by any other transaction. This is typically the way it happens and the then gamble pays off, especially in OLTP type systems. If no one else updates your data during your transaction, this isolation level, which will generally decrease concurrency in other systems, will provide the same degree of concurrency as it would without SERIALIZABLE transactions. The downside to this is that you may get the ORA-08177 error if the gamble doesn't pay off. If you think about it, however, the gamble is worth the risk. If you're using SERIALIZABLE transaction, you should not be expecting to update the same information as other transactions. If you do, you should use the SELECT ... FOR UPDATE as shown above, and this will serialize the access. So, if you

- ❑ Have a high probability of no one else modifying the same data;
- ❑ Need transaction level read consistency;
- ❑ Will be doing short transactions (in order to help make the first bullet point a reality);

then using an isolation level of SERIALIZABLE will be achievable and effective. Oracle finds this method scalable enough to run all of their TPC-Cs (an industry standard OLTP benchmark, see http://www.tpc.org for details). In many other implementations, you would find this being achieved with shared read locks and their corresponding deadlocks, and blocking. Here in Oracle, we do not get any blocking but we will get the ORA-08177 if other sessions change the data we want to change as well. However, we will not get it as frequently as you will get deadlocks and blocks in the other systems.

Read-Only Transactions

Read-only transactions are very similar to SERIALIZABLE transactions, the only difference being that they do not allow modifications so are not susceptible to the ORA-08177 error. Read-only transactions are intended to support reporting needs, where the contents of the report needs to be consistent with respect to a single point in time. In other systems, you would use the REPEATABLE READ, and suffer the associated affects of the shared read lock. In Oracle you will use the read-only transaction. In this mode, the output you produce in a report that uses 50 SELECT statements to gather the data, will be consistent with respect to a single point in time – the time the transaction began. You will be able to do this without locking a single piece of data anywhere.

This is achieved by using the same multi-versioning as used for individual statements. The data is reconstructed as needed from the rollback segments and presented to you as it existed when the report began. Read-only transactions are not trouble-free however. Whereas we might see an ORA-08177 in a SERIALIZABLE transaction, we might expect to see an ORA-1555 snapshot too old error with read-only transactions. This will happen on a system where other people are actively modifying the information we are reading. Their changes (undo) are recorded in the rollback segments. But rollback segments are used in a circular fashion in much the same manner as redo logs. The longer the report takes to run, the larger the chance that some undo we need to reconstruct our data won't be there anymore. The rollback segment will have wrapped around, and portion of it we need has been reused by some other transaction. At this point, you will receive the ORA-1555, and will have to start over again. The only solution to this sticky issue is to have rollback segments that are sized correctly for your system. Time and time again, I see people trying to save a few MBs of disk space by having the smallest possible rollback segments (why 'waste' space on something I don't really need?). The problem is that the rollback segments are a key component of the way the database works, and unless they are sized correctly, you will hit this error. In 12 years of using Oracle 6, 7 and 8, I can say I have never hit an ORA-1555 outside of a testing or development system. If you hit them there, you know you have not sized the rollback segments correctly and you fix it. We will revisit this issue in Chapter 5, *Redo and Rollback*.

Summary

In this section, we covered a lot of material that, at times, makes you scratch your head. While locking is rather straightforward, some of the side effects are not. However, it is vital that you understand these issues. For example, if you were not aware of the table lock Oracle uses to enforce a foreign key relationship when the foreign key is not indexed, then your application would suffer from poor performance. If you did not understand how to review the data dictionary to see who was locking whom, you might never figure that one out. You would just assume that the database 'hangs' sometimes. I sometimes wish I had a dollar for every time I was able to solve the 'insolvable' hanging issue by simply running the query to detect un-indexed foreign keys, and suggesting that we index the one causing the problem – I would be very rich.

We took a look at the meaning of the isolation levels set out in the SQL92 standard, and at how other databases implement their meaning, compared to Oracle. We saw that in other implementations, ones that employ read locks to provide consistent data, there is a huge trade-off between concurrency and consistency. In order to get highly concurrent access to data you would have to decrease your needs for consistent answers. In order to get consistent, correct answers – you would need to live with decreased concurrency. We saw how in Oracle that is not the case – all to multi-versioning. This short table sums up what you might expect in a database that employs read locking versus Oracles multi-versioning:

Isolation Level	Implementation	Writes block reads	Reads block writes	Deadlock sensitive reads	Incorrect query results	Lost updates	Lock escalation or limits
READ UNCOMMITTED	Read locking	No	No	No	Yes	Yes	Yes
READ COMMITTED	(Other databases)	Yes	No	No	Yes	Yes	Yes
REPEATABLE READ		Yes	Yes	Yes	No	No	Yes
SERIALIZABLE		Yes	Yes	Yes	No	No	Yes
READ COMMITTED	Multi-versioning	No	No	No	No	No*	No
SERIALIZABLE	(Oracle)	No	No	No	No	No	No

* With `select for update nowait`

Concurrency controls, and how the database implements them, are definitely things you want to have a good grasp of. I've been singing the praises of multi-versioning and read-consistency, but like everything else in the world, it is a double-edged sword. If you don't understand that it is there and how it works, you will make errors in application design. Consider the resource scheduler example from Chapter 1. In a database without multi-versioning, and its associated non-blocking reads, the original logic employed by the program may very well have worked. However, this logic would fall apart when implemented in Oracle – it would allow data integrity to be compromised. Unless you know how it works, you will write programs that corrupt data. It is that simple.

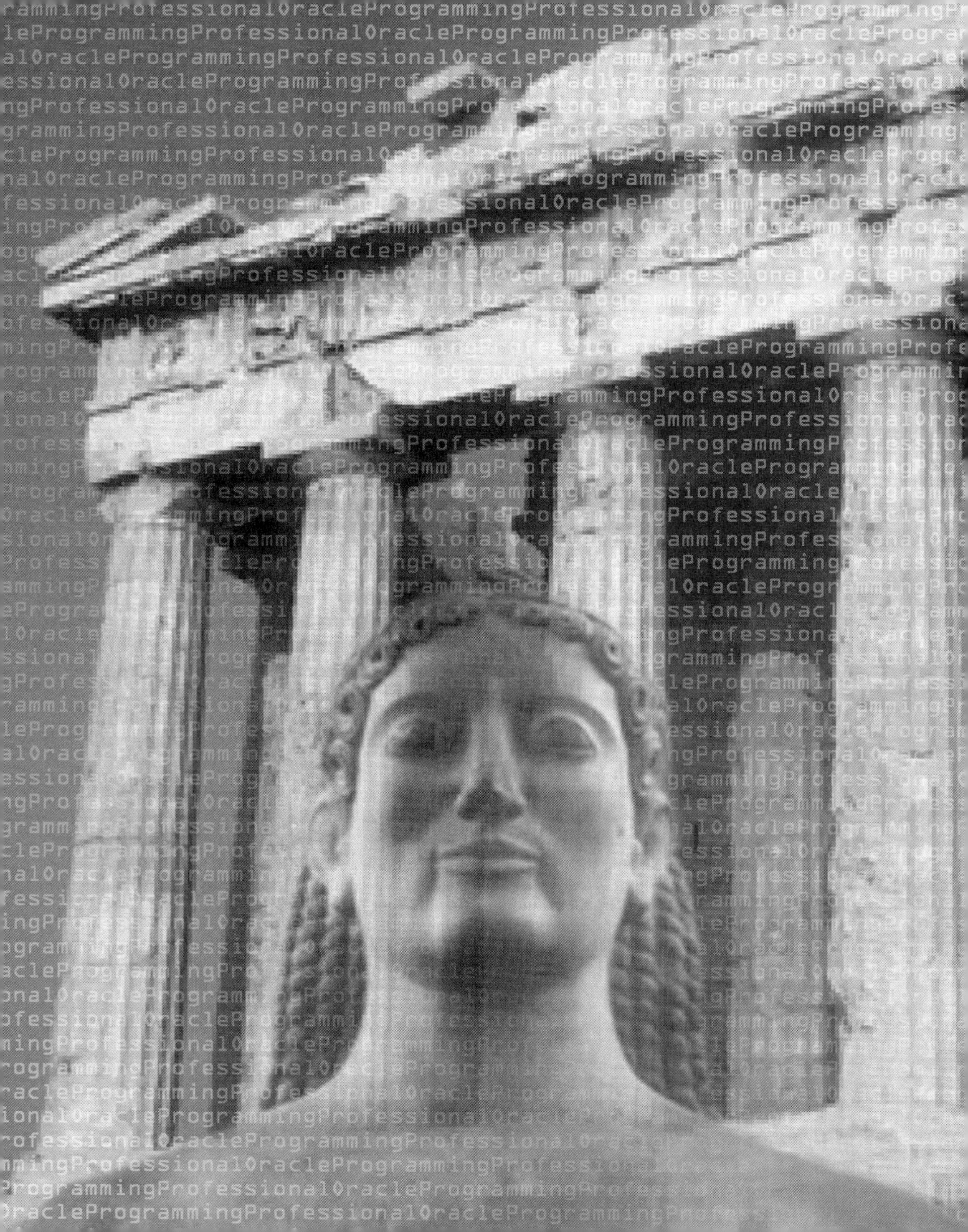

Transactions

4

Transactions are one of the features that set a database apart from a file system. In a file system, if you are in the middle of writing a file and the operating system crashes, this file is likely to be corrupted. It is true there are 'journaled' file systems, and the like, which may be able to recover your file to some point in time. However, if you need to keep two files synchronized, it won't help you there – if you update one file, and the system fails before you finish updating the second then you will have out-of-sync files.

This is the main purpose of transactions in the database – they take the database from one consistent state to the next. That is their job. When you commit work in the database, you are assured that either all of your changes have been saved, or none of them are saved. Furthermore, you are assured that your various rules and checks that implement data integrity are carried out.

Database transactions should exhibit attributes described by the **ACID properties**. ACID is an acronym for:

- ❑ **Atomicity** – A transaction either happens completely, or none of it happens.
- ❑ **Consistency** – A transaction takes the database from one consistent state to the next.
- ❑ **Isolation** – The effects of a transaction may not be visible to other transactions until the transaction has committed.
- ❑ **Durability** – Once the transaction is committed, it is permanent.

Transactions in Oracle exhibit all of the above characteristics. In this chapter, we'll discuss the implications of atomicity, and how it affects statements in Oracle. We'll cover transaction control statements such as COMMIT, SAVEPOINT, and ROLLBACK and discuss how integrity constraints and such are enforced in a transaction. We will also look at why you may have some bad transaction habits if you have been developing in other databases. We will look at distributed transactions and the **two-phase commit**. Lastly, we will look at some real-world issues with regards to transactions, how they are logged, and what role rollback segments might play.

Transaction Control Statements

There is no 'begin transaction' statement in Oracle. A transaction implicitly begins with the first statement that modifies data (the first statement that gets a TX lock). Issuing either a COMMIT or ROLLBACK statement explicitly ends transactions. You should always explicitly terminate your transactions with a COMMIT or ROLLBACK – otherwise the tool/environment you are using will pick one or the other for you. If you exit your SQL*PLUS session normally without committing or rolling back, SQL*PLUS will assume you wish you commit your work, and will do so for you. If you terminate a Pro*C program on the other hand, a rollback will take place.

Transactions are atomic in Oracle – either every statement that comprises the transaction is committed (made permanent), or all of the statements are rolled back. This protection is extended to individual statements as well. A statement either entirely succeeds, or it is entirely rolled back. Note that I said the *statement* is rolled back. The failure of one statement does not cause previously executed statements to be automatically rolled back. Their work is preserved and must either be committed or rolled back by you. Before we get into the details of exactly what it means for a statement and transaction to be 'atomic', we will take a look at the various transaction control statements available to us. They are:

❑   COMMIT – In its simplest form, you would just issue COMMIT. You could be more verbose and say COMMIT WORK, but the two are equivalent. A COMMIT ends your transaction and makes any changes permanent (durable). There are extensions to the COMMIT statement used in distributed transactions. These extensions allow you to label a COMMIT (label a transaction) with some meaningful comment, and to force the commit of an in-doubt distributed transaction.

❑   ROLLBACK – In its simplest form, you would just issue ROLLBACK. Again, you could be more verbose and say ROLLBACK WORK, but the two are equivalent. A rollback ends your transaction and undoes any uncommitted changes you have outstanding. It does this by reading information stored in the rollback segments, and restoring the database blocks to the state they were in prior to your transaction beginning.

❑   SAVEPOINT – A SAVEPOINT allows you to create a 'marked point' within a transaction. You may have multiple SAVEPOINTs within a single transaction.

❑   ROLLBACK TO <SAVEPOINT> – This is used with the SAVEPOINT command above. You may roll back your transaction to that marked point without rolling back any of the work that preceded it. So, you could issue two UPDATE statements, followed by a SAVEPOINT and then two DELETE statements. If an error, or some sort or exceptional condition, occurs during execution of the DELETE statements, the transaction will rollback to the named SAVEPOINT, undoing the DELETEs but not the UPDATE statements.

❑   SET TRANSACTION – This statement allows you to set various transaction attributes, such as its isolation level and whether it is read-only or readwrite. You can also use this statement to instruct the transaction to use a specific rollback segment.

That's it – there are no more. The most frequently used control statements are COMMIT and ROLLBACK. The SAVEPOINT statement has a somewhat special purpose. Internally, Oracle uses it frequently, and you may find some use for it in your application as well.

Now that we've had a brief overview of the transaction control statements, we are ready to see what is meant by statement and transaction atomicity. Consider the following statement:

```
Insert into t values ( 1 );
```

It seems fairly clear that if it fails due to a constraint violation, our row will not be inserted. However, consider the following example, where an insert or delete on table T fires a trigger that adjusts the cnt column in table T2, appropriately:

```
tkyte@TKYTE816> create table t2 ( cnt int );
Table created.

tkyte@TKYTE816> insert into t2 values ( 0 );
1 row created.

tkyte@TKYTE816> create table t ( x int check ( x>0 ) );
Table created.

tkyte@TKYTE816> create trigger t_trigger
  2  before insert or delete on t for each row
  3  begin
  4      if ( inserting ) then
  5          update t2 set cnt = cnt +1;
  6      else
  7          update t2 set cnt = cnt -1;
  8      end if;
  9      dbms_output.put_line( 'I fired and updated ' ||
                              sql%rowcount || ' rows' );
 10  end;
 11  /
Trigger created.
```

In this situation it is less clear what should happen. If the error occurs *after* the trigger has fired, should the effects of the trigger be there or not? That is, if the trigger fired and updated T2, but the row was not inserted into T, what should the outcome be? Clearly the answer is that we would not like the cnt column in T2 to be incremented if a row is not actually inserted into T. Fortunately, in Oracle, the original statement from the client, the INSERT INTO T in this case, either entirely succeeds, or entirely fails. This statement is atomic. We can confirm this, as follows:

```
tkyte@TKYTE816> set serveroutput on

tkyte@TKYTE816> insert into t values ( 1 );
I fired and updated 1 rows

1 row created.

tkyte@TKYTE816> insert into t values (-1 );
insert into t values (-1 )
*
ERROR at line 1:
ORA-02290: check constraint (TKYTE.SYS_C001570) violated


tkyte@TKYTE816> exec null  /* this is needed to retrieve the dbms_output */
I fired and updated 1 rows

PL/SQL procedure successfully completed.

tkyte@TKYTE816> select * from t2;

       CNT
----------
         1
```

We successfully inserted one row into T, duly receiving the message, I fired and updated 1 rows. The next INSERT statement violates the integrity constraint we have on T. I needed to exec NULL, to run a Null statement, and get SQL*PLUS to show me the DBMS_OUTPUT information, (since SQL*PLUS will not print out the DBMS_OUTPUT buffer after a SELECT), but this shows that again, the trigger fired and updated one row. We would maybe expect T2 to have a value of 2 now, but we see it has a value of 1. Oracle made the original insert atomic.

It does this by silently wrapping a SAVEPOINT around each of our calls. The above two inserts were really treated like this:

```
Savepoint statement1;
   Insert into t values ( 1 );
If error then rollback to statement1;
Savepoint statement2;
   Insert into t values ( -1 );
If error then rollback to statement2;
```

For programmers used to Sybase or SQLServer, this may be confusing at first. In those databases *exactly the opposite is true.* The triggers in those systems execute independently of the firing statement. If they encounter an error, the triggers must explicitly roll back their own work, and then raise another error to roll back the triggering statement. Otherwise, the work done by a trigger could persist even if the triggering statement, or some other part of the statement, ultimately fails.

In Oracle, this statement level atomicity extends as deep as it needs to. If in the above example, the INSERT INTO T fired a trigger that updates another table, and that table has a trigger that deletes from another table (and so on, and so on) either *all* of the work succeeds, or *none* does. You do not need to code anything special to ensure this – it is the way it works.

It is interesting to note that Oracle considers PL/SQL anonymous blocks to be statements as well. Consider the following stored procedure:

```
tkyte@TKYTE816> create or replace procedure p
  2  as
  3  begin
  4          insert into t values ( 1 );
  5          insert into t values (-1 );
  6  end;
  7  /
Procedure created.

tkyte@TKYTE816> select * from t;
no rows selected

tkyte@TKYTE816> select * from t2;

        CNT
----------
          0
```

So, we have a procedure we know will fail. The second insert will always fail in this case. Let's see what happens if we just run that stored procedure:

```
tkyte@TKYTE816> begin
  2      p;
  3   end;
  4   /
I fired and updated 1 rows
I fired and updated 1 rows
begin
*
ERROR at line 1:
ORA-02290: check constraint (TKYTE.SYS_C001570) violated
ORA-06512: at "TKYTE.P", line 5
ORA-06512: at line 2


tkyte@TKYTE816> select * from t;

no rows selected

tkyte@TKYTE816> select * from t2;

       CNT
----------
         0
```

As you can see, Oracle treated the stored procedure call as an atomic statement. The client submitted a block of code, BEGIN P; END;, and Oracle wrapped a SAVEPOINT around it. Since P failed, Oracle restored the database back to the point right before it was called. Now, if we submit a slightly different block, we will get entirely different results:

```
tkyte@TKYTE816> begin
  2           p;
  3   exception
  4           when others then null;
  5   end;
  6   /
I fired and updated 1 rows
I fired and updated 1 rows

PL/SQL procedure successfully completed.

tkyte@TKYTE816> select * from t;

         X
----------
         1

tkyte@TKYTE816> select * from t2;

       CNT
----------
         1
```

Here, we ran a block of code that ignored any, and all, errors and the difference in outcome here is huge. Whereas the first call to P effected no changes, here the first INSERT succeeds and the cnt column in T2 is incremented accordingly. Oracle considered the 'statement' to be the block that the client submitted. This statement succeeded, by catching and ignoring the error itself, so the 'If error then rollback...' didn't come into effect and Oracle did not roll back to the SAVEPOINT after execution. Hence, the partial work performed by P was preserved. The reason that this partial work was preserved in the first place is that we have statement level atomicity within P – each statement in P is atomic. P becomes the client of Oracle when it submits its two INSERT statements. Each INSERT either entirely succeeds, or fails. This is evidenced by the fact that we can see the trigger on T fired twice and updated T2 twice, yet the count in T2 only reflects one update. The second INSERT executed in P had an implicit SAVEPOINT wrapped around it.

The difference between the two blocks of code is subtle, and something you must consider in your applications. Adding an exception handler to a block of PL/SQL code can radically change its behaviour. A more correct way to code this, one that restores the statement level atomicity to the entire PL/SQL block would be:

```
tkyte@TKYTE816> begin
  2          savepoint sp;
  3          p;
  4   exception
  5          when others then
  6                  rollback to sp;
  7   end;
  8   /
I fired and updated 1 rows
I fired and updated 1 rows

PL/SQL procedure successfully completed.

tkyte@TKYTE816>
tkyte@TKYTE816> select * from t;

no rows selected

tkyte@TKYTE816> select * from t2;

       CNT
----------
         0
```

Here, by mimicking the work Oracle normally does for us with the SAVEPOINT, we are able to restore the original behavior while still catching and 'ignoring' the error.

Integrity Constraints and Transactions

It is interesting to note exactly when integrity constraints are checked. By default, integrity constraints are checked after the entire SQL statement has been processed. Note I said 'SQL statement' and not just 'statement'. If I have many SQL statements in a PL/SQL stored procedure, then each SQL statement will have its integrity constraints validated immediately after their individual execution, not after the stored procedure completes. Integrity constraint checking can be programmatically postponed until the transaction commits, or until you the developer want to validate them.

So, why are constraints validated *after* the SQL statement executes, why not during? This is because it is very natural for a single statement to make individual rows in a table momentarily 'inconsistent'. Taking a look at the partial work of a statement would result in Oracle rejecting the results, even if the end result would be OK. For example, suppose you have a table like this:

```
tkyte@TKYTE816> create table t  ( x int unique );
Table created.

tkyte@TKYTE816> insert into t values ( 1 );
1 row created.

tkyte@TKYTE816> insert into t values ( 2 );
1 row created.
```

And now we want to execute a multiple-row update:

```
tkyte@TKYTE816> update t set x = x+1;
2 rows updated.
```

If Oracle checked the constraint after each row was updated then on any given day you would stand a 50/50 chance of having the update fail. The rows in T are accessed in some order, and if Oracle updated the X=1 row first, then we would momentarily have a duplicate value for X and it would reject the update. Since Oracle waits patiently to the end of the statement, the statement succeeds because by the time it is done, there are no duplicates.

Starting with Oracle 8.0, we also have the ability to **defer** constraint checking. This ability can be quite advantageous for various operations. The one that immediately jumps to mind is the requirement to cascade an update of a primary key to the child keys. There are many that will say you should never need to do this, that primary keys are immutable (I am one of those people), but many people persist in their desire to have a cascading update. Deferrable constraints make this possible.

In prior releases, it was actually possible to do a cascade update, but it involved a tremendous amount of work, and had certain limitations. With deferrable constraints, it becomes almost trivial. It could look like this:

```
tkyte@TKYTE816> create table p
  2  ( pk  int primary key )
  3  /
Table created.

tkyte@TKYTE816>
tkyte@TKYTE816> create table c
  2  ( fk  int constraint c_fk
  3           references p(pk)
  4           deferrable
  5           initially immediate
  6  )
  7  /
Table created.

tkyte@TKYTE816> insert into p values ( 1 );
1 row created.

tkyte@TKYTE816> insert into c values ( 1 );
1 row created.
```

So, I have a parent table P, and a child table C. Table C references table P, and the constraint used to enforce that rule is called C_FK (child foreign key). This constraint was created as DEFERRABLE, but it is set to INITIALLY IMMEDIATE. This means I can defer that constraint until commit or to some other time. By default, however, it will be validated at the statement level. This is the most common use of the deferrable constraints. Most existing applications won't be checking for constraint violations on a COMMIT statement, it is best not to surprise them with that. As defined, our table C behaves in the fashion tables always have, but it gives us the ability to explicitly change its behaviour. Now, lets try some DML on the tables and see what happens:

```
tkyte@TKYTE816> update p set pk = 2;
update p set pk = 2
         *
ERROR at line 1:
ORA-02292: integrity constraint (TKYTE.C_FK) violated - child record found
```

Since the constraint is in IMMEDIATE mode, this update fails. We will change the mode and try again:

```
tkyte@TKYTE816> set constraint c_fk deferred;
Constraint set.

tkyte@TKYTE816> update p set pk = 2;
1 row updated.
```

Now it succeeds. For illustration purposes, I am going to show how to check a DEFERRED constraint procedurally, to see if the modifications you made are in agreement with the business rules (in other words, that the constraint hasn't been violated). It is a good idea to do this before committing or releasing control to some other part of the program (which may not be expecting the DEFERRED constraints):

```
tkyte@TKYTE816> set constraint c_fk immediate;
set constraint c_fk immediate
         *
ERROR at line 1:
ORA-02291: integrity constraint (TKYTE.C_FK) violated - parent key not found
```

It fails and returns an error immediately, as expected since we knew that the constraint had been violated. The update to P was not rolled back (that would violate the statement level atomicity). It is still outstanding. You should also note that our transaction is still working with the C_FK constraint DEFERRED since the SET CONSTRAINT command failed. We'll continue on now by cascading the update to C:

```
tkyte@TKYTE816> update c set fk = 2;
1 row updated.

tkyte@TKYTE816> set constraint c_fk immediate;
Constraint set.

tkyte@TKYTE816> commit;
Commit complete.
```

And that is the way it works.

Bad Transaction Habits

Many developers have some bad habits when it comes to transactions. I see this frequently with developers who have worked with a database that 'supports' but does not 'promote' the use of transactions. For example, in Informix (by default), Sybase and SQLServer you must explicitly BEGIN a transaction, otherwise each individual statement is a transaction all by itself. In a similar manner to the way in which Oracle wraps a SAVEPOINT around discrete statements, they wrap a BEGIN WORK/COMMIT or ROLLBACK around each statement. This is because, in these databases, locks are a precious resource and readers block writers, and writers block readers. In an attempt to increase concurrency, they would like you to make the transaction as short as possible – sometimes at the expense of data integrity.

Oracle takes the opposite approach. Transactions are always implicit and there is no way to have an 'autocommit' unless an application implements it (see the discussion of the JDBC API, at the end of this section). In Oracle, every transaction should be committed when you must and never before. Transactions should be as large as they need to be. Issues such as locks, blocking, and so on should not really be considered – data integrity is the driving force behind the size of your transaction. Locks are not a scarce resource, and there are no contention issues between concurrent readers and writers of data. This allows you to have robust transactions in the database. These transactions do not have to be short in duration – they should be exactly as long as they need to be. Transactions are not for the convenience of the computer and its software, they are to protect your data.

Faced with the task of updating many rows, most programmers will try to figure out some procedural way to do it in a loop, so that they can commit every so many rows. There are two main reasons that I hear for doing it this way:

❑   It is faster and more efficient to frequently commit lots of small transactions than it is to process and commit one big one.

❑   We don't have enough rollback space.

Both of these conclusions are misguided. It is generally not faster to commit frequently – it is almost always faster to do the work in a single SQL statement. By way of a small example, let's say we have a table T with lots of rows, and we want to update a column value for every row in that table. We could simply do it in a single update like this:

```
tkyte@TKYTE816> create table t as select * from all_objects;
Table created.

tkyte@TKYTE816> set timing on
tkyte@TKYTE816> update t set object_name = lower(object_name);

21946 rows updated.

Elapsed: 00:00:01.12
```

Many people however, for whatever reason, feel compelled to do it like this:

```
tkyte@TKYTE816> begin
  2      for x in ( select rowid rid, object_name, rownum r
  3                    from t )
  4      loop
  5          update t
  6             set object_name = lower(x.object_name)
  7           where rowid = x.rid;
  8          if ( mod(x.r,100) = 0 ) then
  9              commit;
 10          end if;
 11      end loop;
 12      commit;
 13  end;
 14  /
PL/SQL procedure successfully completed.

Elapsed: 00:00:05.99
```

In this simple example, it is about five times *slower* to commit frequently in a loop. If you can do it in a *single* SQL statement, do it that way, as it is almost certainly faster.

Let's now look at the second reason, which arises from developers using a 'limited resource' (rollback segments) sparingly. This is a configuration issue; you *need* to ensure that you have enough rollback space to size your transactions correctly. Committing in a loop, apart from generally being slower, is also the most common cause of the dreaded ORA-01555 error. Let's look at this in more detail.

As you will appreciate after reading the *Locking and Concurrency* and *Developing Successful Oracle Applications* chapters, Oracle's multi-versioning model uses rollback segment data to reconstruct blocks as they appeared at the beginning of your statement or transaction (depending on the isolation mode). If the necessary rollback information no longer exists, you will receive an ORA-01555 snapshot too old error message, and your query will not complete. So, if you are modifying the table that you are reading (as in the above procedure), you are generating rollback information required for your query. Your update generates undo information that your query will probably be making use of in order to get the read consistent view of the data it needs to update. If you commit, you are allowing the system to reuse the rollback segment space you just filled up. If it does reuse the rollback, wiping out old rollback data that your query subsequently needs, you are in big trouble. Your SELECT will fail and your update will stop part of the way through. You have a part-finished transaction, and probably no good way to restart it (more about this in a moment). Let's see this in action with a small demonstration. In a small test database I had setup a table:

```
tkyte@TKYTE816> create table t as select * from all_objects;
Table created.

tkyte@TKYTE816> create index t_idx on t(object_name);
Index created.
```

I then offlined all of my rollback segments and created a small one:

```
tkyte@TKYTE816> create rollback segment rbs_small storage (initial 64k
  2  next 64k minextents 2 maxextents 4 ) tablespace tools;

Rollback segment created.
```

Now, with only the small rollback segment online, I ran this block of code to do the update:

```
tkyte@TKYTE816> begin
  2      for x in ( select rowid rid, object_name, rownum r
  3                   from t
  4                  where object_name > chr(0) )
  5      loop
  6          update t
  7              set object_name = lower(x.object_name)
  8           where rowid = x.rid;
  9          if ( mod(x.r,100) = 0 ) then
 10              commit;
 11          end if;
 12      end loop;
 13      commit;
 14  end;
 15  /
begin
*
ERROR at line 1:
ORA-01555: snapshot too old: rollback segment number 10 with name "RBS_SMALL" too
small
ORA-06512: at line 2
```

I get the error. I should point out that I added an index and a WHERE clause. I wanted to make sure that I was reading the table randomly. The WHERE clause will use the index (I used the rule-based optimizer for this). When we process a table via an index, we will tend to read a block for a single row and then the next row we want will be on a different block. We will process all of the rows on block 1, just not concurrently. Block 1 might hold, say, rows A, M, N, Q, and Z. So we would hit the block four times with long time intervals between each hit. Since we are committing frequently and reusing rollback space, we eventually revisit a block we can simply no longer reproduce and get the error.

This was a very artificial example just to show how it happens, in a reliable manner. Our UPDATE statement was generating rollback. We had four 64K extents of rollback to play with, for a total of 256K. We wrapped around in our rollback segment many times, since they are used in a circular fashion. Every time we committed we allowed Oracle to overwrite the rollback data we generated. Eventually, we needed some piece of data that we had generated, but it no longer existed and we received the ORA-01555 error.

You would be right to point out that, in this case, if we had not committed we would get the following error:

```
begin
*
ERROR at line 1:
ORA-01562: failed to extend rollback segment number 10
ORA-01628: max # extents (4) reached for rollback segment RBS_SMALL
ORA-06512: at line 6
```

The major differences between the two errors, however, are:

- ❑ The ORA-01555 example *left our update in a totally unknown state*. Some of the work had been done, some had not.

- ❑ There is absolutely *nothing we can do to avoid the* ORA-01555, given that we committed in the cursor FOR loop.

- ❑ *We can always avoid the* ORA-01562, by allocating appropriate resources in our system. The second error is avoidable by right sizing; the first error is not.

The bottom line here is that you cannot 'save' on rollback space by committing frequently – you need that rollback (I was in a single user system when I received the ORA-01555. It only takes one session to get that). Developers and DBAs need to work together to size these objects adequately for the jobs that need to be done. There can be no short-changing here. You must discover, through analysis of your system, what your biggest transactions are, and size appropriately for them. Given the above example, this might be a one-time update. In that case, I might have created a *huge* rollback segment somewhere on my system for the sole purpose of doing this update. I would then use the SET TRANSACTION statement to tell my transaction to use this really large rollback segment. I would then drop that rollback segment, and release the space. If this is not a one-time thing but is run frequently, then you need to size that into your system, and have the space readily available. Many people consider things like temp, rollback, and redo as 'overhead' – things to allocate as little storage to as possible. This is reminiscent of a problem the computer industry had on January 1, 2000 – all caused by trying to save 2 bytes in a date field. These components of the database are not overhead, but rather are key components of the system – they must be sized appropriately (not too big, not too small, just right).

Of course, the most serious problem with the 'commit before the transaction is over' approach, is the fact that it frequently leaves your database in an unknown state, if the update fails half way through. Unless you planned for this ahead of time, it is very hard to restart the failed transaction, allowing it to pick up where it left off. For example, say we were not applying the LOWER() function to the column, but rather some other function of the column such as:

```
last_ddl_time = last_ddl_time + 1;
```

If we halted the update loop partway through, how would we restart it? We could not just rerun it, as we would end up adding 2 to some dates, and one to others. If we fail again, we would add 3 to some 2 to others, and 1 to the rest, and so on. We need yet more complex logic – some way to 'partition' the data. For example, we could process all of the object_names that start with A, and then B, and so on:

```
tkyte@TKYTE816> create table to_do
  2  as
  3  select distinct substr( object_name, 1,1 ) first_char
  4    from T
  5  /
```

```
    Table created.
tkyte@TKYTE816> begin
    2           for x in ( select * from to_do )
    3           loop
    4                 update t set last_ddl_time = last_ddl_time+1
    5                   where object_name like x.first_char || '%';
    6
    7                 dbms_output.put_line( sql%rowcount || ' rows updated' );
    8                 delete from to_do where first_char = x.first_char;
    9
    10               commit;
    11          end loop;
    12   end;
    13   /
11654 rows updated
21759 rows updated
309 rows updated
6 rows updated
270 rows updated
830 rows updated
412 rows updated
7 rows updated
378 rows updated
95 rows updated
203 rows updated
2482 rows updated
13 rows updated
318 rows updated
83 rows updated
14 rows updated
1408 rows updated
86 rows updated
2 rows updated
35 rows updated
2409 rows updated
57 rows updated
306 rows updated
379 rows updated
1 rows updated
1 rows updated

PL/SQL procedure successfully completed.
```

Now, we could restart this process if it fails, since we would not process any object name that had already been processed successfully. The problem with this approach, however, is that unless you have some attribute that evenly partitions the data, you will end up having a very wide distribution of rows. The second update did more work than all of the others combined. Additionally, if other sessions are accessing this table and modifying the data, they might update the object_name field as well. Suppose that some other session updates the object named Z to be A, *after* you already processed the A's – you would miss that record. Furthermore, this is a very inefficient process compared to update t set last_ddl_time = last_ddl_time+1. We are probably using an index to read every row in the table, or we are full scanning it n-times – both of which are undesirable. There are so many bad things to be said about this approach.

The best approach here is the one I advocated in the opening section of Chapter 1: do it simply. If it can be done in SQL, do it in SQL. What can't be done in SQL, do in PL/SQL. Do it using the least amount of code you can. Have sufficient resources allocated. Always think about what happens in the event of an error. So many times, I've seen people code update loops that worked great on the test data but then failed halfway through when applied to the real data. Now they are really stuck, as they have no idea where it stopped processing. It is a lot easier to size rollback correctly than it is to write a restartable transaction. If you have truly large tables that need to be updated, you should be using partitions (more on that in Chapter 14, *Partitioning*), allowing you to update each partition individually. You can even use parallel DML to perform the update.

My final word on bad transaction habits concerns the one that arises from use of the popular programming APIs ODBC and JDBC. These APIs 'autocommit' by default. Consider the following statements, transferring $1000 from a checking to a savings account:

```
update accounts set balance = balance - 1000 where account_id = 123;
update accounts set balance = balance + 1000 where account_id = 456;
```

If your program is using JDBC when you submit these statements, JDBC will (silently) inject a commit after *each* update. Consider the impact of this if the system fails after the first update, and before the second. You've just lost $1000!

I can understand why ODBC does this. The developers of SQLServer designed ODBC and this database demands that you use very short transactions due to its concurrency model (writes block reads, reads block writes, and locks are a scarce resource). What I cannot understand is how this got carried over into JDBC, an API that is supposed to be in support of the 'Enterprise'. It is my belief that the very next line of code after opening a connection in JDBC should always be:

```
connection conn81 = DriverManager.getConnection
            ("jdbc:oracle:oci8:@ora8idev","scott","tiger");

conn81.setAutoCommit (false);
```

This will return control over the transaction back to you, the developer, which is where it belongs. You can then safely code your account transfer transaction, and commit it after both statements have succeeded. Lack of knowledge of your API can be deadly in this case. I've seen more than one developer, unaware of this autocommit 'feature', get into big trouble with their application when an error occurred.

Distributed Transactions

One of the really nice features of Oracle is its ability to transparently handle distributed transactions for us. I can update data in many different databases in the scope of a single transaction. When I commit, I either commit the updates in all of the instances, or I commit none of them (they will all be rolled back). I need no extra code to achieve this, I simply 'commit'.

A key to distributed transactions in Oracle is the **database link**. A database link is a database object that describes how to log into another instance from your instance. However, the purpose of this section is not to cover the syntax of the database link command (it is fully documented). Once you have the database link set up, accessing remote objects is as easy as:

```
select * from T@another_database;
```

This would select from the table T in the database instance defined by the database link ANOTHER_DATABASE. Typically, you would 'hide' the fact that T is a remote table by creating a view of it, or a synonym. For example, I can:

```
create synonym T for T@another_database;
```

and then access T as if it were a local table. Now that we have this database link set up and can read some tables, we are also able to modify them (given that we have the appropriate privileges, of course). Performing a distributed transaction is now no different from a local transaction. All we would do is:

```
update local_table set x = 5;
update remote_table@another_database set y = 10;
commit;
```

That is it. Oracle will either commit in both databases or in neither. It uses a two-phase distributed commit (2PC) protocol to do this. The 2PC is a distributed protocol that allows for a modification that affects many disparate databases to be committed atomically. It attempts to close the window for distributed failure as much as possible before committing. In a 2PC between many databases, one of the databases, typically the one the client is logged into initially, will be the coordinator for the distributed transaction. This one site will ask the other sites if they are ready to commit. In effect, this one site will go to the other sites, and ask them to be prepared to commit. Each of the other sites reports back their 'prepared state' as YES or NO. If any one of the sites votes NO, the entire transaction is rolled back. If all sites vote YES, the site coordinator broadcasts a message to make the commit permanent on each of the sites.

This limits the window in which a serious error could occur. Prior to the 'voting' on the two-phase commit, any distributed error would result in all of the sites rolling back. There would be no doubt as to the outcome of the transaction. After the order to commit or rollback, there again is no doubt as to the outcome of the distributed transaction. It is only during the very short window when the coordinator is collecting the votes that the outcome might be in doubt, after a failure. Assume for example, we have three sites participating in the transaction with Site 1 being the coordinator. Site 1 has asked Site 2 to prepare to commit, and Site 2 has done so. Site 1 then asks Site 3 to prepare to commit, and it does so. At this point in time, Site 1 is the only site that knows the outcome of the transaction and it is now responsible for broadcasting the outcome to the other sites. If an error occurs right now – the network fails, Site 1 loses power, whatever – Site 2 and Site 3 will be left 'hanging'. They will have what is known as an in-doubt distributed transaction. The two-phase commit protocol attempts to close the window of error as much as possible, but it cannot close it entirely. Sites 2 and 3 must keep that transaction open, awaiting notification from Site 1 of the outcome. If you recall from the architecture discussion in Chapter 2, it is the function of the RECO process to resolve this issue. This is also where the COMMIT and ROLLBACK with the FORCE option come into play. If the cause of the problem was a network failure between Sites 1, 2, and 3, then the DBAs at Sites 2 and 3 could actually call the DBA at Site 1, ask them for the outcome, and apply the commit or rollback manually, as appropriate.

There are some limits to what you can do in a distributed transaction. Not many though, and they are reasonable (to me they seem reasonable anyway). The big ones are:

❑ You cannot issue a COMMIT over a database link. You may only commit from the site that initiated the transaction.

❑ You cannot do DDL over a database link. This is a direct result of the first issue above. DDL commits. You cannot commit from any other site other then the initiating site, hence we cannot do DDL over a database link.

149

❑ You cannot issue a SAVEPOINT over a database link. In short, you cannot issue any transaction control statements over a database link.

The lack of transaction control over a database link is reasonable, since the initiating site is the only one that has a list of everyone involved in the transaction. If in our three-site configuration above, Site 2 attempted to commit, it would have no way of knowing that Site 3 was involved. In Oracle, only Site 1 can issue the commit command. At that point it is then permissible for Site 1 to delegate responsibility for distributed transaction control to another site.

We can influence which site will be the actual commit site by setting the commit point strength (an init.ora parameter) of the site. A commit point strength associates a relative level of importance to a server in a distributed transaction – the more important the server (the more available the data needs to be), the more probable that it will coordinate the distributed transaction. You might want to do this in the event that you need to perform a distributed transaction between your production machine and a test machine. Since the transaction coordinator is *never* in doubt as to the outcome of a transaction, it would be best if the production machine coordinated the distributed transaction. You do not care so much if your test machine has some open transactions and locked resources. You certainly do care if your production machine does.

The inability to do DDL over a database link is actually not so bad at all. First off, DDL is 'rare'. You do it once at installation, or after an upgrade. Production systems don't do DDL (well, they *shouldn't* do DDL). Secondly, there is a method to do DDL over a database link, in a fashion, using the job queue facility, DBMS_JOB (covered in the *Necessary Supplied Packages* appendix). Instead of trying to do DDL over the link, we use the link to schedule a job to be executed as soon as we commit. In that fashion, the job runs on the remote machine, is not a distributed transaction, and can do the DDL. In fact, this is the method by which the Oracle Replication services perform distributed DDL to do schema replication.

Redo and Rollback

I would like to finish up this chapter on transactions with a description of how redo and rollback (undo) are generated, and how they fit into transactions, recovery, and so on. This is a question I am asked frequently. A good conceptual understanding of how redo and undo work, and what takes place, will help you understand the database in general. It is important for developers as well as DBA's to have a good working knowledge of what really happens when an update takes place. You need to understand the ramifications of your actions. What I am presenting below is the pseudo-code for these mechanisms in Oracle. What actually takes place is a little more involved, but having a good understanding of the flow of how it works is valuable.

As an example, we will investigate what might happen with a transaction like this:

```
insert into t (x,y) values (1,1);
update t set x = x+1 where x = 1;
delete from t where x = 2;
```

We will follow this transaction down different paths and discover:

❑ What happens if the system fails after the update?

❑ What happens if we succeed and commit?

❑ What happens if we rollback?

The initial INSERT INTO T will generate both redo and undo. The undo generated will be enough information to make the insert 'go away'. The redo generated will be enough information to make the insert 'happen again'. The undo may consist of many pieces of information. There may be indexes on the columns X and Y for example, and their changes must also be undone upon a rollback as well Undo is stored in a rollback segment. A rollback segment is stored in a tablespace, and (this is the important part) is protected by the redo log just like any other segment. In other words, rollback data is treated just like table data or index data – changes to rollback segments generate some redo, which is logged. (why this is so will become clear in a moment when we discuss what happens when the system crashes). Undo data is added to the rollback segment, and is cached in the buffer cache just like any other piece of data would be. Like the undo generated, redo may consist of many pieces of information as well.

So, at this point in time, after the insert has occurred we have:

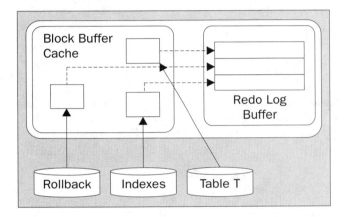

There are some cached, modified rollback blocks, index blocks and table data blocks. Each of these modified blocks is protected by entries in the redo log buffer. All of this information is cached right now.

Hypothetical scenario: *the system crashes right now*. Everything is OK. The SGA is wiped out but we don't need anything that was in the SGA. It will be as if this transaction never happened when we restart. None of the blocks with changes got flushed, and none of the redo got flushed.

Hypothetical scenario: *the buffer cache fills up right now*. DBWR must make room and must flush the blocks we just modified. In this case, DBWR will start by asking LGWR to flush the redo blocks that protect the database blocks. Before DBWR can write any of the blocks that are changed to disk, LGWR must flush the redo information related to these blocks. This makes sense, for if we flush the modified blocks for table T, and did not flush the redo for the associated undo blocks, and the system failed, we would have a modified table T block with no undo information associated with it. We need to flush the redo log buffers before writing these blocks out so that we can redo all of these changes necessary to get the SGA back into the state it is in right now, so that a rollback can take place.

This second scenario should show some of the foresight that has gone into all of this. The set of conditions 'if we flushed table T blocks *and* did not flush the redo for the undo blocks *and* the system failed' is starting to get complex. It only gets more complex as you add users, and more objects, and concurrent processing, and so on.

So, at this point, we have the situation depicted on the previous page. We have generated some modified table and index blocks. These have created some new rollback segment blocks, and all three types of blocks have generated redo to protect them. If you recall from our earlier discussion on the redo log buffer, it is flushed every three seconds, when a third full, and whenever a commit takes place. It is very likely that at some point during our processing, the redo log buffer will be flushed, and some of our changes will go to disk as well. In that case the picture becomes this:

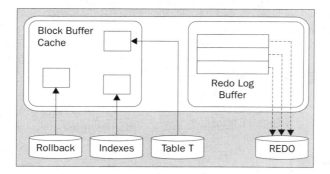

Now, the blocks themselves may end up on disk, but probably not in this case. Next, we do the update. Much the same sort of things take place. This time, the amount of undo will be larger (we now have some 'before' images to save as a result of the update). Now, we have the following picture:

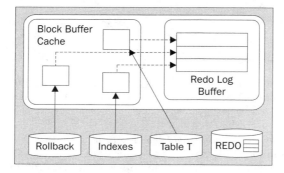

We have more new rollback segment blocks in the block buffer cache. In order to undo the update, if necessary, we have modified database table and index blocks in the cache. We have also generated more redo log buffer entries. Some of our generated redo log is on disk, some is in cache.

Hypothetical scenario: *the system crashes right now.* Upon startup, Oracle would read the redo logs, and find some redo log entries for our transaction. Given the state in which we left the system, with the redo entries for the insert in the redo log files, and the redo for the update still in the buffer, Oracle would 'roll forward' the insert. We would end up with a picture much like the first, with some rollback segment undo blocks (to undo the insert), modified table blocks (right after the insert), and modified index blocks (right after the insert). Now Oracle will discover that our transaction never committed and will roll it back since the system is doing crash recovery and, of course, our session is no longer connected. It will take the undo it just rolled forward in the buffer cache, and apply it to the data and index blocks, making them look as they did before the insert took place. Now everything is back the way it was. The blocks that are on disk may, or may not, reflect the INSERT (it depends on whether or not our blocks got flushed before the crash). If they do, then the insert has been, in effect, undone and when the blocks are flushed from the buffer cache, the data file will reflect that. If they do not reflect the insert – so be it, they will be overwritten later anyway.

Hypothetical scenario: *the application rolls back the transaction.* At this point, Oracle will find the undo information for this transaction, either in the cached rollback segment blocks (most likely), or on disk if they have been flushed (more likely for very large transactions). It will apply the undo information to the data and index blocks in the buffer cache, or if they are no longer in the cache request, they are read from disk into the cache to have the UNDO applied to them. These blocks will later be flushed to the data files in the original form.

The first scenario covers the rudimentary details of a crash recovery. The system performs this as a two-step process. First it rolls forward, bringing the system right to the point of failure, and then it proceeds to rollback everything that had not yet committed. This action will resynchronize the data files. It replays the work that was in progress, and undoes anything that had not yet completed.

The second scenario is one that is played out much more often. It is useful to note that during the rollback process, the redo logs are never involved. The only time redo logs are read is during recovery and archival. This is a key tuning concept – redo logs are written to. Oracle does not read them during normal processing. As long as you have sufficient devices so that when ARCH is reading a file, LGWR is writing to a different device, then there is no contention for redo logs. Many other databases treat the log files as 'transaction logs'. They do not have this separation of redo and undo – they keep both in the same file. For those systems, the act of rolling back can be disastrous – the rollback process must read the logs their log writer is trying to write to. They introduce contention into the part of the system that can least stand it. Oracle's goal is to make it so that logs are written sequentially, and no one ever reads them while they are being written – ever.

Now, onto the DELETE statement. Again, undo is generated, blocks are modified, and redo is sent over to the redo log buffer. This is not very different from before. In fact, it is so similar to the UPDATE that we are going to go right onto the COMMIT. We've looked at various failure scenarios and different paths, and now we finally made it to the COMMIT. Here, Oracle will flush the redo log buffer to disk and the picture will look like this:

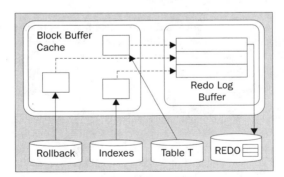

The modified blocks are in the buffer cache; maybe some of them have been flushed to disk. All of the redo necessary to replay this transaction is safely on disk and the changes are now permanent. If we were to read the data directly from the data files, we probably would see the blocks as they existed *before* the transaction took place, as DBWR most likely has not yet written them. That is OK – the redo log files can be used to restore those blocks in the event of a failure. The undo information will hang around until the rollback segment wraps around and reuses those blocks. Oracle will use that undo to provide for consistent reads of the affected objects for any session that needs it.

Summary

In this section we looked at many aspects of transaction management in Oracle. Transactions are one of the major features that set a database apart from a file system. Understanding how they work how to use them is necessary and in order to implement applications correctly in any database. Understanding that, in Oracle, all statements are atomic (including their side effects) and that this atomicity is extended to stored procedures is crucial. We saw how the placement of a WHEN OTHERS exception handler in a PL/SQL block could radically affect what changes took place in the database. As database developers, having a good understanding of how transactions work is crucial.

We took a look at the somewhat complex interaction between integrity constraints (unique keys, check constraints and the like) and transactions in Oracle. We discussed how Oracle typically processes integrity constraints immediately after a statement executes, but that we can defer this constraint validation until the end of the transaction if we wish. This feature is key in implementing complex multi-table updates when the tables being modified are all dependent on each other – the cascading update was an example of that.

We moved on to consider some of the bad transaction habits that people tend to pick up from working with databases that 'support' rather than 'promote' the use of transactions. We looked at the cardinal rule of transactions: they should be as sort as they can be but as long as they need to be. Data integrity drives the transaction size – that is a key concept to take away from this chapter. The only things that should drive the size of your transactions are the business rules that govern your system, not rollback space, not locks – business rules.

We covered distributed transactions and how they differ from single database transactions. We explored the limitations imposed upon us in a distributed transaction and discussed why they are there. Before you build a distributed system, you need to understand these limitations. What works in a single instance might not work in a distributed database.

We closed with a look at redo and undo, the architectural features that serve to enforce the ACID transaction properties discussed at the start of this chapter. We looked at what happens when we modify data in a transaction with regards to redo and undo (rollback data). This last topic will be considered in much more detail in the next chapter.

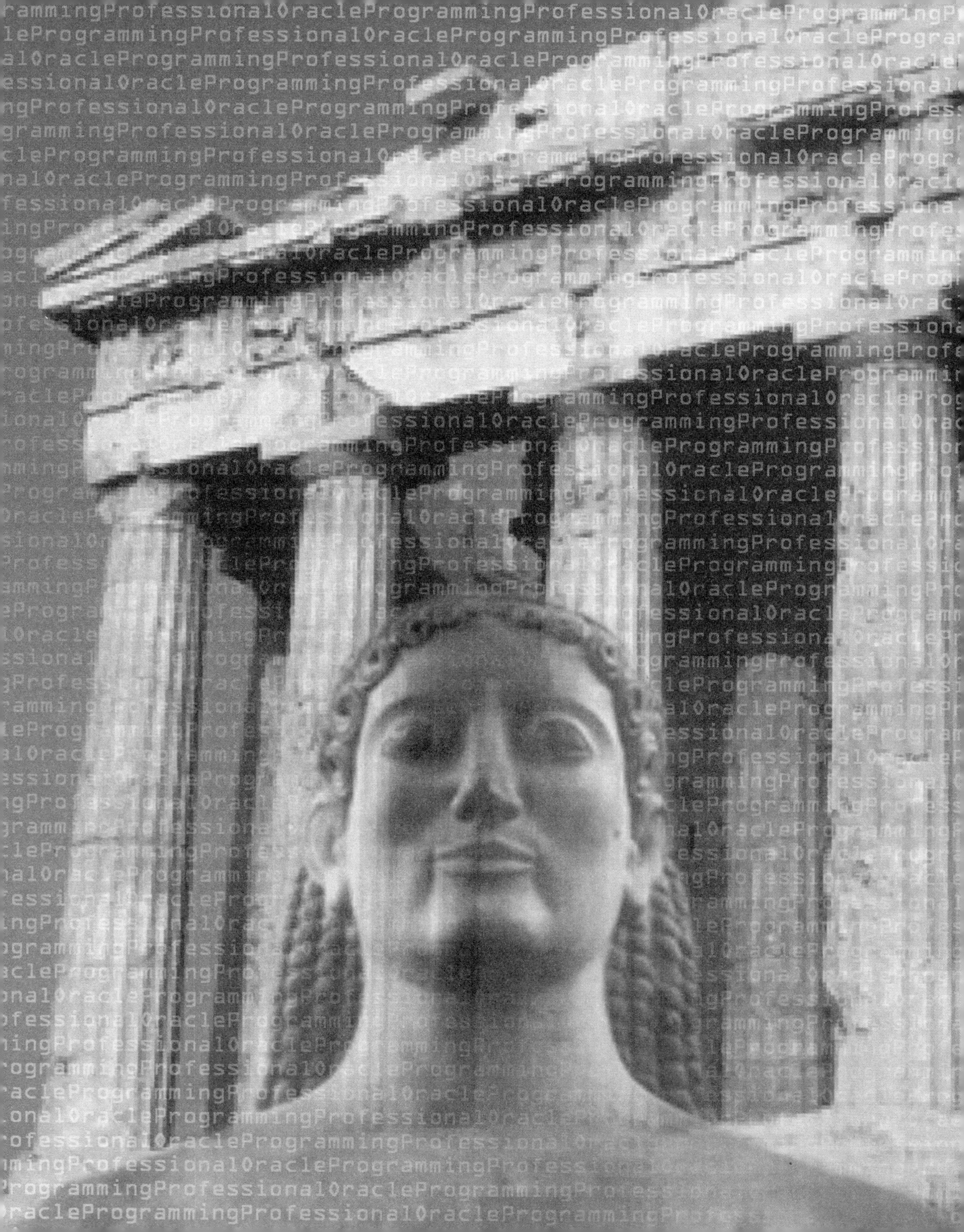

5

Redo and Rollback

In Chapter 4 on *Transactions*, we covered the basic mechanics of **redo** and **rollback** (also known as **undo**). There we covered what redo is. Simply put, it is the information Oracle records in the online redo log files in order to replay your transaction in the event of a failure. It allows Oracle to, in effect, 'redo' your transaction(s). We also covered undo, or rollback, the information Oracle records in the rollback segments in order to undo or roll back your transaction. Additionally, we touched on a couple of issues, such as why you might get an `ORA-01555: snapshot too old` error, and why you might see `checkpoint not complete, cannot allocate new log`. What I would like to do in this chapter, is go over in more depth the concepts behind redo and rollback, and what you, the developer, need to know about them.

Redo and rollback is a topic that bridges the DBA and developer roles. Both need a good fundamental understanding of their purpose, how they work, and how to avoid issues with regards to them. We'll be covering this information here. What we will not cover are the things your DBA should be exclusively in charge of figuring out and tuning. For example, how to find the optimum setting for `RECOVERY_PARALLELISM` or the `FAST_START_IO_TARGET init.ora` parameters are topics we will not cover. Instead, we will concentrate on the things that a database developer should be concerned with, and how they will impact your application.

Redo

Redo log files are extremely crucial to the Oracle database. These are the transaction logs for the database. They are used only for recovery purposes; their only purpose in life is to be used in the event of an instance or media failure. If the power goes off on your database machine, causing an instance failure, Oracle will use the online redo logs in order to restore the system to exactly the point it was at, immediately prior to the power outage. If your disk drive fails, Oracle will utilize archived redo logs as well as online redo logs in order to restore a backup of that drive to the correct point in time. Additionally, if you 'accidentally' drop a table, or remove some critical information and commit this operation, you can restore a backup of the affected data and restore it to the point in time immediately prior to the 'accident', using these online and archive redo log files.

Oracle maintains two types of redo log files, **online** and **archived**. Every Oracle database has at least two online redo log files. These online redo log files are used in a circular fashion. Oracle will write to log file 1, and when it gets to the end of that file, it will switch to log file 2, and begin writing to this one. When it has filled log file 2, it will switch back to log file 1 (assuming we have only two redo log files, if you have three, it would of course proceed onto the third file). Archived redo log files are simply copies of old, full online redo log files. As the system fills up log files, the ARCH process will make a copy of the online redo log file in another location. These archived redo log files are used to perform media recovery, when a failure is caused by a disk drive going bad, or some other physical fault. Oracle can take these archived redo log files, and apply them to backups of the data files to catch them up to the rest of the database. They are the transaction history of the database.

Redo, or transaction logs, are one of the major features that make a database a database. They are perhaps its most important recovery structure, although without the other pieces such as rollback segments, distributed transaction recovery, and so on, nothing works. They are major components of what sets a database apart from a file system. The online redo logs allow us to effectively recover from a power outage – one that happens while Oracle might be in the middle of a write. The archived redo logs allow us to recover from media failures, when for instance, the hard disk goes bad. Without them, the database would not offer any more protection than a file system.

It is important for us to understand how these log files might impact on us as developers. We will look at how the different ways we can write our code affect their utilization. We will look at why some database errors (specifically the `ORA-01555: snapshot too old`) happen, and how to avoid them. We've already seen the mechanics of redo in Chapter 4, and now we'll look at some specific issues. Many of these scenarios might be detected by you, but would be fixed by the DBA as they affect the database instance as a whole. We'll start with what happens during a `COMMIT`, and then get into commonly asked questions and issues surrounding the online redo logs.

What Does a COMMIT Do?

Sometimes, people want to understand exactly what happens during a `COMMIT`, and as a developer you should have an understanding of what goes on. A `COMMIT` is a very fast operation, regardless of the transaction size. One might think that the bigger a transaction is (in other words, the more data it affects) the longer a `COMMIT` will take. This is not true. The response time of a `COMMIT` is generally 'flat', regardless of the transaction size. This is because a `COMMIT` does not really have too much work to do, but what it does do is vital.

One of the reasons this is an important fact to understand and embrace, is that it will lead you down the path of letting your transactions be as big as they should be. Many developers artificially constrain the size of their transactions, committing every so many rows, instead of committing when a logical unit of work has been performed. They do this in the mistaken belief that they are lessening the resources on the system, when in fact they are increasing them. If a `COMMIT` of one row takes X units of time, and the `COMMIT` of one thousand rows takes the same X units of time, then performing work in a manner that does 1000 one-row `COMMIT`s will not take an additional 1000*X units of time to perform. By only committing when you have to (when the transaction is complete), you will not only increase performance, but also reduce contention for shared resources (the log files, various internal latches, and the like). A simple example demonstrates that it necessarily takes longer:

```
tkyte@TKYTE816> create table t ( x int );
tkyte@TKYTE816> set serveroutput on
tkyte@TKYTE816> declare
```

```
  2             l_start number default dbms_utility.get_time;
  3             begin
  4             for i in 1 .. 1000
  5             loop
  6                     insert into t values ( 1 );
  7             end loop;
  8             commit;
  9             dbms_output.put_line
 10             ( dbms_utility.get_time-l_start || ' hsecs' );
 11    end;
 12    /
7 hsecs

PL/SQL procedure successfully completed.

tkyte@TKYTE816> declare
  2             l_start number default dbms_utility.get_time;
  3    begin
  4             for i in 1 .. 1000
  5             loop
  6                     insert into t values ( 1 );
  7                     commit;
  8             end loop;
  9             dbms_output.put_line
 10             ( dbms_utility.get_time-l_start || ' hsecs' );
 11    end;
 12    /
21 hsecs

PL/SQL procedure successfully completed.
```

In this case, it is three times longer – your mileage will vary on this. When you compound the above example with multiple users doing the same work, all committing too frequently, the numbers will go up rapidly. We've seen this, time and time again with other similar situations. For example, we've seen how not using bind variables and performing hard parses frequently severely reduces concurrency due to library cache contention, and excessive CPU utilization. Even when we switch to using bind variables, soft parsing too frequently incurs massive overhead. You must only perform operations when you need to – a COMMIT is just another operation like a parse. It is best to size your transactions based on business need, not based on misguided attempts to lessen resource usage on the database.

So, why is a COMMIT's response time fairly flat, regardless of the transaction size? Before we even go to COMMIT in the database, we have already done the really hard work. We've already modified the data in the database, so we've already done 99.9 percent of the work. For example, operations such as the following have already taken place:

- Rollback segment records have been generated in the SGA.
- Modified data blocks have been generated in the SGA.
- Buffered redo for the above two items has been generated in the SGA.
- Depending on the size of the above three, and the amount of time spent, some combination of the above data may be flushed onto disk already.
- All locks have been acquired.

When we COMMIT, all that is left to happen is the following:

❑ Generate a **SCN** (**S**ystem **C**hange **N**umber) for our transaction.

❑ LGWR writes all of our *remaining* buffered redo log entries to disk, and records the SCN in the online redo log files as well. This step is actually the COMMIT. If this step occurs, we have committed. Our transaction entry is removed, this shows that we have committed. Our record in the V$TRANSACTION view will 'disappear'.

❑ All locks held by our session are released, and everyone who was enqueued waiting on locks we held will be released.

❑ Many of the blocks our transaction modified will be visited and 'cleaned out' in a fast mode if they are still in the buffer cache.

As you can see, there is very little to do in order to process a COMMIT. The lengthiest operation is, and always will be, the activity performed by LGWR, as this is physical disk I/O. The amount of time spent by LGWR here will be gated (limited) by the fact that it has already been flushing the contents of the redo log buffer on a recurring basis. LGWR will not buffer all of the work you do for as long as you do it. Rather, it will incrementally flush the contents of the redo log buffer in the background as we are going along. This is to avoid having a COMMIT wait for a very long time in order to flush all of your redo at once. LGRW does this flushing continuously as we are processing at least:

❑ Every three seconds.
❑ When one third or one MB full.
❑ Upon any transaction COMMIT.

So, even if we have a long running transaction, much of the buffered redo log it generates will have been flushed to disk, prior to committing. On the flip side of this however, is the fact that when we COMMIT, we must wait until *all* buffered redo we've generated that has not been written yet, is safely on disk. That is, our call to LGWR is a **synchronous** one. While LGWR may use asynchronous I/O to write in parallel to our log files, our transaction will wait for LGWR to complete all writes, and receive confirmation that the data exists on disk before returning.

In case you are not familiar with it, the SCN I refer to above is a simple timing mechanism Oracle uses to guarantee the ordering of transactions, and to enable recovery from failure. It is also used to guarantee read-consistency, and checkpointing in the database. Think of the SCN as a ticker; every time someone COMMITs, the SCN is incremented by one.

The last point to clarify from the above list, is what is meant by 'cleaned out' as related to database blocks. I said that we would revisit some of the blocks our transaction modified during the COMMIT process, and clean them out. This refers to the lock-related information we store in the database block header. In the section on *Block Cleanout* below, we will discuss this in more detail. Briefly, we are cleaning out our transaction information on the block, so the next person who visits the block won't have to. We are doing this in a way that need not generate redo log information, saving considerable work later.

In order to demonstrate that a COMMIT is a 'flat response time' operation, I'll generate varying amounts of redo, and time the INSERTs and COMMITs. In order to do this, we'll need a couple of GRANTs on some V$ tables (see Chapter 10, *Tuning Strategies and Tools*, for more information on these tables). Once we get those GRANTs, we'll set up a fairly large table to test with. In this example, I use the ALL_OBJECTS view to generate rows of data, and INSERT enough copies of these rows to give me about 100,000 rows to work with (your INSERTs may need to be executed more or less times to achieve the same row counts):

```
tkyte@TKYTE816> connect sys/change_on_install

sys@TKYTE816> grant select on v_$mystat to tkyte;

Grant succeeded.

sys@TKYTE816> grant select on v_$statname to tkyte;

Grant succeeded.

sys@TKYTE816> connect tkyte/tkyte

tkyte@TKYTE816> drop table t;

Table dropped.

tkyte@TKYTE816> create table t
  2  as
  3  select * from all_objects
  4  /

Table created.

tkyte@TKYTE816> insert into t select * from t;

21979 rows created.

tkyte@TKYTE816> insert into t select * from t;

43958 rows created.

tkyte@TKYTE816> insert into t select * from t where rownum < 12000;

11999 rows created.

tkyte@TKYTE816> commit;

Commit complete.

tkyte@TKYTE816> create or replace procedure do_commit( p_rows in number )
  2  as
  3      l_start         number;
  4      l_after_redo    number;
  5      l_before_redo   number;
  6  begin
  7      select v$mystat.value into l_before_redo
  8        from v$mystat, v$statname
  9       where v$mystat.statistic# = v$statname.statistic#
 10         and v$statname.name = 'redo size';
 11
 12      l_start := dbms_utility.get_time;
 13      insert into t select * from t where rownum < p_rows;
 14      dbms_output.put_line
 15      ( sql%rowcount || ' rows created' );
 16      dbms_output.put_line
 17      ( 'Time to INSERT: ' ||
 18         to_char( round( (dbms_utility.get_time-l_start)/100, 5 ),
 19                   '999.99') ||
 20       ' seconds' );
 21
```

```
22        l_start := dbms_utility.get_time;
23        commit;
24        dbms_output.put_line
25        ( 'Time to COMMIT: ' ||
26           to_char( round( (dbms_utility.get_time-l_start)/100, 5 ),
27                     '999.99') ||
28          ' seconds' );
29
30        select v$mystat.value into l_after_redo
31          from v$mystat, v$statname
32         where v$mystat.statistic# = v$statname.statistic#
33           and v$statname.name = 'redo size';
34
35        dbms_output.put_line
36        ( 'Generated ' ||
37           to_char(l_after_redo-l_before_redo,'999,999,999,999') ||
38          ' bytes of redo' );
39        dbms_output.new_line;
40  end;
41  /

Procedure created.
```

Now we are ready to see the effects of committing various sizes of transactions. We will call the above procedure, ask it to create new rows in varying sizes, and then report the results:

```
tkyte@TKYTE816> set serveroutput on format wrapped
tkyte@TKYTE816> begin
  2        for i in 1 .. 5
  3        loop
  4            do_commit( power(10,i) );
  5        end loop;
  6  end;
  7  /
9 rows created
Time to INSERT:      .06 seconds
Time to COMMIT:      .00 seconds
Generated            1,512 bytes of redo

99 rows created
Time to INSERT:      .06 seconds
Time to COMMIT:      .00 seconds
Generated            11,908 bytes of redo

999 rows created
Time to INSERT:      .05 seconds
Time to COMMIT:      .00 seconds
Generated            115,924 bytes of redo

9999 rows created
Time to INSERT:      .46 seconds
Time to COMMIT:      .00 seconds
Generated            1,103,524 bytes of redo

99999 rows created
Time to INSERT:     16.36 seconds
Time to COMMIT:      .00 seconds
```

```
     Generated        11,220,656 bytes of redo


PL/SQL procedure successfully completed.

tkyte@TKYTE816> show parameter log_buffer

NAME                                 TYPE    VALUE
------------------------------------ ------- ------------------------------
log_buffer                           integer 512000
```

As you can see, as we generate varying amount of redo from 1,512 bytes to 11,220,656 bytes, the time to COMMIT is not measurable using a timer with a one hundredth of a second resolution. I timed the INSERTs specifically to demonstrate that the timer logic actually 'works'. If you do something that takes a measurable amount of time, it'll report it – the COMMITs just happened too fast. As we were processing, and generating the redo log, LGWR was constantly flushing our buffered redo information to disk in the background as we went along. So, when we generated eleven MB of redo log information, LGWR was busy flushing every 170 KB or so (a third of 512,000 bytes). When it came to the COMMIT, there wasn't much left to do – not much more than when we created nine rows of data. You should expect to see similar (but not exactly the same) results, regardless of the amount of redo generated.

What Does a ROLLBACK Do?

Now, if we change the COMMIT to ROLLBACK, we can expect a totally different result. The time to roll back will definitely be a function of the amount of data modified. I changed the DO_COMMIT routine we developed in the *What Does a COMMIT Do?* section to perform a ROLLBACK instead (simply change the COMMIT on line 23 to ROLLBACK) and the timings are very different. For example:

```
9 rows created
Time to INSERT:     .06 seconds
Time to ROLLBACK:   .02 seconds
Generated         1,648 bytes of redo

99 rows created
Time to INSERT:     .04 seconds
Time to ROLLBACK:   .00 seconds
Generated        12,728 bytes of redo

999 rows created
Time to INSERT:     .04 seconds
Time to ROLLBACK:   .01 seconds
Generated       122,852 bytes of redo

9999 rows created
Time to INSERT:     .94 seconds
Time to ROLLBACK:   .08 seconds
Generated     1,170,112 bytes of redo

99999 rows created
Time to INSERT:     8.08 seconds
Time to ROLLBACK:   4.81 seconds
Generated    11,842,168 bytes of redo


PL/SQL procedure successfully completed.
```

This is to be expected, as a ROLLBACK has to physically undo the work we've done. Similar to a COMMIT, there is a series of operations that must be performed. Before we even get to the ROLLBACK, the database has already done a lot of work. To recap, the following would have happened:

❑ Rollback segment records have been generated in the SGA.

❑ Modified data blocks have been generated in the SGA.

❑ Buffered Redo log for the above two items has been generated in the SGA.

❑ Depending on the size of the above three, and the amount of time spent, some combination of the above data may be flushed onto disk already.

❑ All locks have been acquired.

When we ROLLBACK:

❑ We undo all of the changes made. This is accomplished by reading the data back from the ROLLBACK (undo) segment, and in effect, reversing our operation. If we inserted a row, a ROLLBACK will delete it. If we updated a row, a rollback will reverse the update. If we deleted a row, a rollback will re-insert it again.

❑ All locks held by our session are released, and everyone who was enqueued waiting on locks we held will be released.

A COMMIT on the other hand just flushes any remaining data in the redo log buffers. It does very little work compared to a ROLLBACK. The point here is that you don't want to roll back unless you have to. It is expensive since you spend a lot of time doing the work, and you'll also spend a lot of time undoing the work. Don't do work unless you are sure you are going to want to COMMIT it. This sounds like common sense; of course, I wouldn't do all of the work unless I wanted to COMMIT it. I have seen many times however, where a developer will utilize a 'real' table as a temporary table, fill it up with data, and then roll back. Below, we'll talk about true temporary tables, and how to avoid this issue.

How Much Redo Am I Generating?

As a developer, you will find that it can be relevant to be able to measure how much redo your operations generate. The more redo you generate, the longer your operations will take, and the slower the entire system will be. You are not just affecting *your* session, but *every* session. Redo management is a point of serialization within the database – eventually all transactions end up at LGWR, asking it to manage their redo and COMMIT their transaction. The more it has to do, the slower the system will be. By seeing how much redo an operation tends to generate, and testing more than one approach to a problem, you can find the best way to do things.

It is pretty straightforward to see how much redo I am generating, as shown above. I used the dynamic performance view V$MYSTAT, which has just my session's statistics in it, joined to V$STATNAME. I retrieved the value of statistic named redo size. I didn't have to guess at this name, because I used the view V$STATNAME to find it:

```
ops$tkyte@DEV816> select * from v$statname
  2  where name like 'redo%';

STATISTIC# NAME                               CLASS
---------- ---------------------------------- ----------
```

```
  61 redo synch writes                            8
  62 redo synch time                              8
  98 redo entries                                 2
  99 redo size                                    2
 100 redo buffer allocation retries               2
 101 redo wastage                                 2
 102 redo writer latching time                    2
 103 redo writes                                  2
 104 redo blocks written                          2
 105 redo write time                              2
 106 redo log space requests                      2
 107 redo log space wait time                     2
 108 redo log switch interrupts                   2
 109 redo ordering marks                          2

14 rows selected.
```

Now we are ready to investigate how we might go about determining the amount of redo a given transaction would generate. It is straightforward to estimate how much redo will be generated if you know how much data you will be modifying. Below, I will create a table whose row size is about 2010 bytes, plus or minus a couple of bytes. Since the CHAR data type always consumes the maximum amount of storage, this row is 2000 bytes for the CHAR, seven bytes for the DATE, and three bytes for the number – about 2010 bytes, plus some row overhead:

```
tkyte@TKYTE816> create table t ( x int, y char(2000), z date );

Table created.
```

We'll take a look at what it takes to INSERT, then UPDATE, and then DELETE one, ten, and lots of these rows. We will also see if there is any measurable difference between updating a set of rows in bulk, versus updating each row one by one, based on the amount of redo generated. We already know that updating row by row is slower than using a single UPDATE statement.

To measure the redo generated, we will use either the SQL*PLUS AUTOTRACE facility, or a direct query against a view of V$MYSTAT/V$STATNAME that shows our session's redo size:

```
tkyte@TKYTE816> create or replace view redo_size
  2  as
  3  select value
  4    from v$mystat, v$statname
  5   where v$mystat.statistic# = v$statname.statistic#
  6     and v$statname.name = 'redo size';

View created.
```

For the statements that AUTOTRACE will trace (INSERTs, UPDATEs, and DELETEs), we'll use it. For our PL/SQL blocks, we'll resort to V$MYSTAT/V$STATNAME instead, since AUTOTRACE will not generate information for these statements.

Now, for the process to exercise redo generation, we will use the table T above which has a fairly fixed row size of 2010 bytes if all of the columns are not Null. We will do various operations and measure the redo generated for each. What we will do is INSERT a single row, then ten rows with a single statement, then 200 rows with a single statement, and then 200 rows one at a time. We will do similar operations for UPDATE and DELETE as well.

The code for this example follows. Instead of the usual cut and paste directly from SQL*PLUS, we'll just look at the statements that were used, and then look at a table that summarizes the results:

```
set autotrace traceonly statistics
insert into t values ( 1, user, sysdate );

insert into t
select object_id, object_name, created
  from all_objects
 where rownum <= 10;

insert into t
select object_id, object_name, created
  from all_objects
 where rownum <= 200
/

declare
   l_redo_size number;
   l_cnt        number := 0;
begin
   select value into l_redo_size from redo_size;
   for x in ( select * from all_objects where rownum <= 200 )
   loop
       insert into t values
       ( x.object_id, x.object_name, x.created );
       l_cnt := l_cnt+1;
   end loop;
   select value-l_redo_size into l_redo_size from redo_size;
   dbms_output.put_line( 'redo size = ' || l_redo_size ||
                         ' rows = ' || l_cnt );
end;
/
```

The above code fragment does our INSERTs as described – 1, 10, 200 at a time, and then 200 individual INSERTs. Next, we'll do the UPDATEs:

```
update t set y=lower(y) where rownum = 1;

update t set y=lower(y) where rownum <= 10;

update t set y=lower(y) where rownum <= 200;

declare
  l_redo_size number;
  l_cnt        number := 0;
begin
  select value into l_redo_size from redo_size;
  for x in ( select rowid r from t where rownum <= 200 )
  loop
     update t set y=lower(y) where rowid = x.r;
     l_cnt := l_cnt+1;
  end loop;
  select value-l_redo_size into l_redo_size from redo_size;
  dbms_output.put_line( 'redo size = ' || l_redo_size ||
                        ' rows = ' || l_cnt );
end;
/
```

and then the DELETEs:

```
delete from t where rownum = 1;

delete from t where rownum <= 10;

delete from t where rownum <= 200;

declare
  l_redo_size number;
  l_cnt       number := 0;
begin
  select value into l_redo_size from redo_size;
  for x in ( select rowid r from t ) loop
     delete from t where rowid = x.r;
     l_cnt := l_cnt+1;
  end loop;
  select value-l_redo_size into l_redo_size from redo_size;
  dbms_output.put_line( 'redo size = ' || l_redo_size ||
                        ' rows = ' || l_cnt );
end;
/
```

Here are the end results:

Operation	Rows Affected	Total Redo	Average per Row
INSERT one row	1	2,679	2,679
INSERT 10 rows in one statement	10	22,260	2,226
INSERT 200 rows in one statement	200	442,784	2,213
INSERT 200 rows, one at a time	200	464,224	2,321
UPDATE one row	1	4,228	4,228
UPDATE 10 rows in one statement	10	42,520	4,252
UPDATE 200 rows in one statement	200	849,600	4,248
UPDATE 200 rows individually	200	849,700	4,248
DELETE one row	1	2,236	2,236
DELETE 10 rows in bulk	10	23,688	2,369
DELETE 200 rows in bulk	200	469,152	2,345
DELETE 200 rows one at a time	200	469,212	2,346

The interesting thing to note is that, in general, whether you UPDATE 200 rows with one statement or 200 statements, the same amount of redo is generated. The same is true for the DELETEs – one statement or 200 statements, the result is pretty much the same. An INSERT behaves a little differently. It generates slightly more redo for single row inserts which is reasonable, given that it must organize data on the block differently when inserting one at a time, versus many at a time (it does slightly more work).

As you can see, the redo generated is a function of the amount of data modified. If we INSERT 2000 byte rows, we generate a little more than 2000 bytes per row. When we UPDATE, we generate double the amount of redo (we log the data and rollback as you recall, so that makes sense). A DELETE is similar to an INSERT in size. The entire row is recorded in the rollback segment and this is logged, as well as the block changes themselves, accounting for the small disparity. So, as long as you understand the amount of data you will be modifying, and to some extent, *how* you modify it, determining the amount of redo is straightforward.

This is not a case study that proves that single row processing is as efficient as set processing. It only shows that the amount of redo generated is the same. We have seen in other sections that procedurally processing a row at a time is never as efficient as doing the set operation itself. Additionally, if you are tempted to throw a COMMIT in the loop, as many people do in the mistaken belief it will conserve some resource, you'll only compound the problem. Now that we know how to measure the redo we generate, we can see the effect of this bad idea clearly. We'll use the same example schema from above and measure what happens when we throw a COMMIT in the loop:

```
tkyte@TKYTE816> declare
  2      l_redo_size number;
  3      l_cnt       number := 200;
  4      procedure report
  5      is
  6      begin
  7          select value-l_redo_size into l_redo_size from redo_size;
  8          dbms_output.put_line( 'redo size = ' || l_redo_size ||
  9                              ' rows = ' || l_cnt || ' ' ||
 10                              to_char(l_redo_size/l_cnt,'99,999.9') ||
 11                              ' bytes/row' );
 12      end;
 13  begin
 14      select value into l_redo_size from redo_size;
 15      for x in ( select object_id, object_name, created
 16                   from all_objects
 17                  where rownum <= l_cnt )
 18      loop
 19          insert into t values
 20          ( x.object_id, x.object_name, x.created );
 21          commit;
 22      end loop;
 23      report;
 24
 25      select value into l_redo_size from redo_size;
 26      for x in ( select rowid rid from t )
 27      loop
 28          update t set y = lower(y) where rowid = x.rid;
 29          commit;
 30          end loop;
```

```
31      report;
32
33      select value into l_redo_size from redo_size;
34      for x in ( select rowid rid from t )
35      loop
36          delete from t where rowid = x.rid;
37          commit;
38      end loop;
39      report;
40   end;
41   /
redo size = 530396 rows = 200    2,652.0 bytes/row
redo size = 956660 rows = 200    4,783.3 bytes/row
redo size = 537132 rows = 200    2,685.7 bytes/row

PL/SQL procedure successfully completed.
```

As you can see, committing each row increased the amount of redo generated measurably, (the table below summarizes this). There are other performance-related issues as to why you should not COMMIT every row (or possibly even groups of rows). We saw concrete proof of this above, where a COMMIT for each row took three times as long as committing when the transaction was complete. There is the overhead of calling into the database kernel with each individual statement, there is unnecessary latching and contention for shared resources for each individual statement. The bottom line is that if you can do it in a single SQL statement – do it. Additionally make sure you COMMIT when the transaction is *complete*, never before.

Operation	Rows affected	Total redo (no COMMITs)	Total redo (with COMMITs)	% increase
INSERT 200 rows	200	442,784	530,396	20%
UPDATE 200 rows	200	849,600	956,660	13%
DELETE 200 rows	200	469,152	537,132	14%

The method we outline above is useful in general for seeing the side effects of various other options. One question that comes up frequently is, other than the fact that you can modify the values of a row in a BEFORE trigger, are there any other differences? Well, as it turns out, yes there is. A BEFORE trigger tends to add additional redo information, even if it does not modify any of the values in the row. In fact, this is an interesting case study and using the techniques above we'll discover that:

❑ A BEFORE or AFTER trigger does not affect DELETEs.

❑ An INSERT generates extra redo in the same volume for either a BEFORE or AFTER trigger.

❑ An UPDATE is affected only by the existence of a BEFORE trigger – the AFTER trigger adds no additional redo.

❑ The size of the row affects the amount of additional redo generated for INSERTs, but not for the UPDATE.

In order to perform this test, we'll use the table T from above:

```
create table t ( x int, y char(N), z date );
```

but we'll create it with varying sizes for N. In this example, we'll use N = 30, 100, 500, 1000, and 2000 to achieve rows of varying widths. I used a simple log table to capture the results of my many runs:

```
create table log ( what varchar2(15),    -- will be no trigger, after or before
                   op varchar2(10),       -- will be insert/update or delete
                   rowsize int,           -- will be the size of Y
                   redo_size int,         -- will be the redo generated
                   rowcnt int );          -- will be the count of rows affected
```

After we run our test for various sized Y columns, we'll analyze the results. I used this stored procedure to generate my transactions, and record the redo generated. The subprocedure REPORT is a local procedure (only visible in the DO_WORK procedure), and it simply reports out on screen what happened, and captures the findings into our LOG table. The main body of the procedure does the real transactions we are monitoring. They all start by capturing our session's current redo size, performing some work, committing, and then generating the report:

```
tkyte@TKYTE816> create or replace procedure do_work( p_what in varchar2 )
  2  as
  3      l_redo_size number;
  4      l_cnt       number := 200;
  5
  6      procedure report( l_op in varchar2 )
  7      is
  8      begin
  9         select value-l_redo_size into l_redo_size from redo_size;
 10         dbms_output.put_line(l_op || ' redo size = ' || l_redo_size ||
 11                              ' rows = ' || l_cnt || ' ' ||
 12                              to_char(l_redo_size/l_cnt,'99,999.9') ||
 13                              ' bytes/row' );
 14      insert into log
 15      select p_what, l_op, data_length, l_redo_size, l_cnt
 16        from user_tab_columns
 17       where table_name = 'T'
 18         and column_name = 'Y';
 19      end;
 20  begin
 21      select value into l_redo_size from redo_size;
 22      insert into t
 23      select object_id, object_name, created
 24        from all_objects
 25       where rownum <= l_cnt;
 26      l_cnt := sql%rowcount;
 27      commit;
 28      report('insert');
 29
 30      select value into l_redo_size from redo_size;
 31      update t set y=lower(y);
 32      l_cnt := sql%rowcount;
 33      commit;
```

```
34      report('update');
35
36      select value into l_redo_size from redo_size;
37      delete from t;
38      l_cnt := sql%rowcount;
39      commit;
40      report('delete');
41  end;
42  /

Procedure created.
```

Now, once I have this in place, I drop and create the table T, changing the size of the column Y. I then run the following script to test the various scenarios (no TRIGGER, before TRIGGER, and after TRIGGER):

```
tkyte@TKYTE816> truncate table t;

Table truncated.

tkyte@TKYTE816> exec do_work( 'no trigger' );
insert redo size = 443280 rows = 200    2,216.4 bytes/row
update redo size = 853968 rows = 200    4,269.8 bytes/row
delete redo size = 473620 rows = 200    2,368.1 bytes/row

PL/SQL procedure successfully completed.

tkyte@TKYTE816> create or replace trigger before_insert_update_delete
  2  before insert or update or delete on T for each row
  3  begin
  4          null;
  5  end;
  6  /

Trigger created.

tkyte@TKYTE816> truncate table t;

Table truncated.

tkyte@TKYTE816> exec do_work( 'before trigger' );
insert redo size = 465640 rows = 200    2,328.2 bytes/row
update redo size = 891628 rows = 200    4,458.1 bytes/row
delete redo size = 473520 rows = 200    2,367.6 bytes/row

PL/SQL procedure successfully completed.

tkyte@TKYTE816> drop trigger before_insert_update_delete;

Trigger dropped.

tkyte@TKYTE816> create or replace trigger after_insert_update_delete
  2  after insert or update or delete on T
  3  for each row
  4  begin
```

```
   5              null;
   6    end;
   7    /

Trigger created.

tkyte@TKYTE816> truncate table t;

Table truncated.

tkyte@TKYTE816> exec do_work( 'after trigger' );
insert redo size = 465600 rows = 200    2,328.0 bytes/row
update redo size = 854028 rows = 200    4,270.1 bytes/row
delete redo size = 473580 rows = 200    2,367.9 bytes/row

PL/SQL procedure successfully completed.
```

The above output was from a run where the size of Y was 2000 bytes. After all of the runs were complete, I was able to query the log table and see:

```
tkyte@TKYTE816> break on op skip 1
tkyte@TKYTE816> set numformat 999,999

tkyte@TKYTE816> select op, rowsize, no_trig, before_trig-no_trig, after_trig-
no_trig
  2    from ( select op, rowsize,
  3                sum(decode( what, 'no trigger', redo_size/rowcnt, 0 ) )
                                                                  no_trig,
  4                sum(decode( what, 'before trigger', redo_size/rowcnt, 0 ) )
                                                                  before_trig,
  5                sum(decode( what, 'after trigger', redo_size/rowcnt, 0 ) )
                                                                  after_trig
  6            from log
  7            group by op, rowsize
  8          )
  9    order by op, rowsize
 10    /

OP           ROWSIZE   NO_TRIG BEFORE_TRIG-NO_TRIG AFTER_TRIG-NO_TRIG
---------- --------- --------- ------------------- -------------------
delete            30       272                   0                   0
                 100       344                  -0                  -0
                 500       765                  -0                  -0
               1,000     1,293                  -1                  -0
               2,000     2,368                  -1                  -0

insert            30        60                 213                 213
                 100       136                 208                 208
                 500       574                 184                 184
               1,000     1,113                 162                 162
               2,000     2,216                 112                 112

update            30       294                 189                   0
                 100       431                 188                   0
                 500     1,238                 188                  -0
               1,000     2,246                 188                  -0
               2,000     4,270                 188                   0

15 rows selected.
```

If you are curious about this query and how I pivoted the result set, see Chapter 12 on Analytic Functions where I discuss pivoting of result sets in detail.

What the inner most query generated was a resultset that computed the average redo bytes generated per row for each of the three test cases. The outer query simply displays the average bytes per row for the case where no trigger was in place, and then the subsequent two columns show the difference between the other cases, and the case with no trigger in place. So, we can see that for the DELETE cases, there was no measurable difference in the amount of redo generated per row at any time. Looking at the INSERT case however, we can see that there was an overhead of 213 to 112 bytes per row, regardless of the trigger type used (before or after). The bigger the row, the less the overhead for some reason (I did not investigate *why* this is so, but just that this is the case). Lastly, for the UPDATE case we see two things. First, the amount of redo generated is constant regardless of the redo size – the overhead for UPDATEs is fixed. Secondly, we can see that an AFTER trigger is much more efficient for UPDATEs, as it does not affect the redo generation at all. For this reason, you can develop a rule of thumb; use AFTER triggers whenever possible for UPDATEs. If, and only if, you need functionality available in the BEFORE trigger should you actually use one.

So, now you know how to estimate the amount of redo, which every developer should be able to do. You can:

- ❏ Estimate your 'transaction' size – how much data you modify.
- ❏ Add 10 to 20 percent overhead depending on the number of rows you will be modifying – the more rows, the less overhead.
- ❏ Double this value for UPDATEs.

In most cases, this will be a good estimate. The doubling on the UPDATEs is a guess – it really depends on how you modify the data. The doubling assumes you take a row of X bytes, and UPDATE it to be a row of X bytes. If you take a small row and make it big, you will not double the value (it will behave more like an INSERT). If you take a big row and make it small, you will not double the value (it will behave like a DELETE). The doubling is a 'worst case' number, as there are various options and features that will impact this, for example the existence of indexes (or lack thereof as in my case) will contribute to the bottom line. The amount of work that must be done in order to maintain the index structure may vary from UPDATE to UPDATE, and so on. Side effects from triggers have to be taken into consideration (in addition to the fixed overhead described above). Implicit operations performed on your behalf, such as an ON DELETE CASCADE setting on a foreign key, must be considered as well. This will allow you to estimate the amount of redo for sizing/performance purposes. Only real-world testing will tell you for sure. Given the above script, you can see how to measure this for yourself, given any of your objects and transactions.

Can I Turn Off Redo Log Generation?

This question is often asked. The simple short answer is 'no', since redo logging is crucial for the database; it is not overhead, it is not a waste. You do need it, regardless of whether you believe you do or not. It is a fact of life, and it is the way the database works. However, that said, there are some operations that can be done without generating redo log in some cases.

Some SQL statements and operations support the use of a NOLOGGING clause. This does not mean that all operations against the object will be performed without generating redo log, just that some very specific operations will generate *significantly less* redo then normal. Note that I said 'significantly less', not 'none'. All operations will generate some redo – all data dictionary operations will be logged regardless of the logging mode. The amount of redo generated can be significantly less. For example, I ran the following in a database running in ARCHIVELOG mode. If you test on a NOARCHIVELOG mode database, you will not see any differences. The CREATE TABLE will not be logged, with the exception of the data dictionary modifications in a NOARCHIVELOG mode database. Oracle 7.3 users however, will see the difference, as this optimization was not present in that database. They will have to use UNRECOVERABLE instead of the NOLOGGING keyword as well (NOLOGGING used to be UNRECOVERABLE in prior releases of Oracle). If you would like to see the difference on a NOARCHIVELOG mode database, you can replace the DROP TABLE and CREATE TABLE with a DROP INDEX and CREATE INDEX statement on some table. These operations are logged by default, regardless of the mode in which the database is running. This also points out a valuable tip – test your system in the mode it will be run in production, as the behavior may be different. Your production system will be running in ARCHIVELOG mode; if you perform lots of operations that generate redo in this mode, but not in NOARCHIVELOG mode, you'll want to discover this during testing, not during rollout to the users! Now for the example of the NOLOGGING clause:

```
tkyte@TKYTE816> column value new_value old_value
tkyte@TKYTE816> select value from redo_size;

     VALUE
----------
   5195512

tkyte@TKYTE816> create table t
  2   as
  3   select * from all_objects
  4   /

Table created.

tkyte@TKYTE816> select value-&old_value REDO_GENERATED from redo_size;
old   1: select value-&old_value REDO_GENERATED from redo_size
new   1: select value-  5195512 REDO_GENERATED from redo_size

REDO_GENERATED
--------------
       2515860
```

Here, over 2.5 MB of redo is generated in my database.

```
tkyte@TKYTE816> drop table t;

Table dropped.

tkyte@TKYTE816> select value from redo_size;

     VALUE
----------
   7741248

tkyte@TKYTE816> create table t
  2   NOLOGGING
  3   as
  4   select * from all_objects
  5   /

Table created.

tkyte@TKYTE816> select value-&old_value REDO_GENERATED from redo_size;
old   1: select value-&old_value REDO_GENERATED from redo_size
new   1: select value-  7741248 REDO_GENERATED from redo_size

REDO_GENERATED
--------------
         43264
```

This time, there is only 50 KB of redo generated.

As you can see, this makes a tremendous difference; 2.5 MB of redo versus 50 KB. The 2.5 MB is the actual table data itself – it was written directly to disk, with no redo log generated for it. Of course, it is now obvious that we will do everything we can with NOLOGGING, right? In fact the answer is a resounding *no*. You must use this very carefully, and only after discussing the issues with the person in charge of backup and recovery. Let's say you create this table and it is now part of your application (for example, you used a CREATE TABLE AS SELECT NOLOGGING as part of an upgrade script). Your users modify this table over the course of the day. That night, the disk that the table is on fails. No problem the DBA says – we are running in ARCHIVELOG mode, we can perform media recovery. The problem is however, that the initially created table, since it was not logged, is not recoverable from the archived redo log. This table is unrecoverable and this brings out the very most important point about NOLOGGING operations – they must be coordinated with your DBA and the system as a whole. If you use them, and others are not aware of the fact, you may compromise the ability of your DBA to recover your database fully after a media failure. They must be used judiciously and carefully.

The important things to note with NOLOGGING operations are:

❑   Some amount of redo will be generated, as a matter of fact. This redo is to protect the data dictionary. There is no avoiding this at all. It will be of a significantly less amount than before, but there will be some.

❑   NOLOGGING does not prevent redo from being generated by all subsequent operations. In the above example, I did not create a table that is never logged. Only the single, individual operation of creating the table was not logged. All subsequent 'normal' operations such as INSERTs, UPDATEs, and DELETEs will be logged. Other special operations such as a direct path load using SQLLDR, or a direct path insert using the INSERT /*+ APPEND */ syntax will not be logged. In general however, the operations your application performs against this table will be logged.

❑   After performing NOLOGGING operations in an ARCHIVELOG mode database, you must take a new baseline backup of the affected data files as soon as possible. This is in order to avoid losing subsequent changes to these objects due to media failure. We wouldn't actually lose the changes, as these are in the redo log. What we've actually lost is the data to apply the changes to.

There are two ways to use the NOLOGGING option. You have already seen one method, by embedding the keyword NOLOGGING in the SQL command itself at the appropriate location. The other method allows operations to be performed implicitly in a NOLOGGING mode. For example, I can alter an index to be NOLOGGING by default. This means that subsequent direct path loads and direct path inserts performed which affect this index, will not be logged (the index will not generate redo – other indexes and the table itself might but this index will not).

The operations that may be performed in a NOLOGGING mode are:

❑   Index creations and ALTERs (rebuilds).

❑   Bulk INSERTs using a 'direct path insert' via the /*+ APPEND */ hint.

❑   LOB operations (updates to large objects do not have to be logged).

❑   Table creations via the CREATE TABLE AS SELECT.

❑   Various ALTER TABLE operations such as MOVE and SPLIT.

❑   TRUNCATE (but it does not need a NOLOGGING clause, as it is always in NOLOGGING mode).

Used appropriately on an ARCHIVELOG mode database, NOLOGGING can speed up many operations by dramatically reducing the amount of redo log generated. Suppose you have a table you need to move from one tablespace to another. You can schedule this operation to take place immediately before a backup occurs – you would ALTER the table to be NOLOGGING, move it, rebuild the indexes (without logging as well), and then ALTER the table back to logging mode. Now, an operation that might have take X hours can happen in X/2 hours perhaps. The appropriate use of this feature includes involvement of the DBA, or whoever is responsible for database backup and recovery. If they are not aware of the use of this feature and a media failure occurs, you may lose data. This is something to seriously consider.

Cannot Allocate a New Log?

I see this happen all of the time, though not on my database of course! You are getting warning messages to this effect (this will be found in your alert.log on your server):

```
Sun Feb 25 10:59:55 2001
Thread 1 cannot allocate new log, sequence 326
Checkpoint not complete
```

It might say Archival required instead of Checkpoint not complete, but the effect is pretty much the same. This is really something the DBA should be looking out for however. In the event that they do not do this, it is something you need to look for yourself. This message will be written to the alert.log on the server whenever the database attempts to reuse an online redo log file, and finds that it cannot. This will happen when DBWR has not yet finished checkpointing the data protected by the redo log, or ARCH has not finished copying the redo log file to the archive destination. If DBWR or ARCH do not mean anything to you, please review Chapter 2 on *Architecture*, for more information. At this point in time, the database effectively *halts* as far as the end user is concerned. It stops cold. DBWR or ARCH will be given priority to flush the blocks to disk. Upon completion of the checkpoint or archival, everything goes back to normal.The reason the database suspends user activity is that there is simply no place to record the changes they are making. Oracle is attempting to reuse an online redo log file, but because either the file is needed to recover the database in the event of a failure (Checkpoint not complete), or the archiver has not yet finished copying it (Archival required). Oracle must wait (and our end users will wait) until the redo log file can safely be reused.

If you see that your sessions spend a lot of time waiting on a 'log file switch', 'log buffer space', or 'log file switch checkpoint or archival incomplete', then you are most likely hitting this (refer to Chapter 10, *Tuning Strategies and Tools*, for how to see what wait events your session is suffering from). You will notice it during prolonged periods of database modifications if your log files are sized incorrectly, or because DBWR and ARCH need to be tuned by the DBA or System Administrator. I frequently see this with the 'starter' database that has not been customized. The 'starter' database typically sizes the redo logs far too small for any sizable amount of work (including the initial database build of the data dictionary itself). As soon as you start loading up the database, you will notice that the first 1000 rows go fast, and then things start going in spurts; 1000 go fast, then hang, then fast, then hang, and so on. These are the indications you are hitting this condition.

There are a couple of things you can do to solve this:

❑ Make DBWR faster. Have your DBA tune DBWR by enabling ASYNC I/O, using DBWR I/O slaves, or using multiple DBWR processes. Look at the I/O on the system and see if one disk, or a set of disks, is 'hot' so we need to, therefore, spread it out. The same general advice applies for ARCH as well. The pros of this are that you get 'something for nothing' here – increased performance without really changing any logic/structures/code. There really are no downsides to this approach.

❑ Add more redo log files. This will postpone the `Checkpoint not complete` in some cases and, after a while, will postpone it so long that it perhaps doesn't happen (we gave DBWR enough breathing room to checkpoint). The same applies to the `Archival required` message. The benefit to this approach is the removal of the 'pauses' in your system. The downside is it consumes more disk, but the benefit far outweighs any downside here.

❑ Recreate the log files with a larger size. This will extend the amount of time between the time we fill the online redo log, and the time we need to reuse it. The same applies to the `Archival required` message, if the redo log file usage is 'bursty'. If you have a period of massive log generation (nightly loads, batch processes) followed by periods of relative calm, then having larger online redo logs can buy enough time for ARCH to catch up during the calm periods. The pros and cons are identical to the above approach of adding more files. Additionally, it may postpone a checkpoint from happening until later, since checkpoints happen at each log switch (at least), and the log switches will now be further apart.

❑ Cause checkpointing to happen more frequently, and more continuously. Use a smaller block buffer cache (not entirely desirable), or various `init.ora` settings such as `FAST_START_IO_TARGET`, `DB_BLOCK_MAX_DIRTY_TARGET`, `LOG_CHECKPOINT_INTERVAL`, and `LOG_CHECKPOINT_TIMEOUT`. This will force DBWR to flush dirty blocks more frequently. The pros to this approach is that recovery time from a failure is reduced. There will always be less work in the online redo logs to be applied. The downside is that blocks will be written to disk more frequently. The buffer cache will not be as effective as it could be, and can defeat the block cleanout mechanism discussed below.

❑ The approach you take will depend on your circumstances. This is something that must be fixed at the database level, taking the entire instance into consideration.

Block Cleanout

If you recall earlier, Chapter 3 on *Locking and Concurrency*, when we talked about data locks and how they were managed, I described how they are actually attributes of the data, stored on the block header. A side effect of this is that the next time that block is accessed, we may have to 'clean it out', in other words, remove the transaction information. This action generates redo and causes the block to become 'dirty' if it wasn't already. What this means is that a simple SELECT may generate redo, and may cause lots of blocks to be written to disk with the next checkpoint. Under most normal circumstances however, this will not happen. If you have mostly small to medium-sized transactions (OLTP), or you are a data warehouse that analyzes tables after bulk operations, you'll find the blocks are generally 'cleaned' for you. If you recall from the earlier section *What Does a COMMIT Do?* one of the steps of COMMIT-time processing is to revisit our blocks if they are still in the SGA, if they are accessible (no one else is modifying them), and then clean them out. This activity is known as a **commit clean out**. Our transaction cleans out the block enough so that a SELECT (read) will not have to clean it out. Only an UPDATE of this block would truly clean out our residual transaction information, and since this is already generating redo, the cleanout is not noticeable.

We can force a cleanout to happen to see the side effects by understanding how the commit cleanout functions. Oracle will allocate lists of blocks we have modified in a commit list associated with our transaction. Each of these lists is 20 blocks long, and Oracle will allocate as many of these lists as it needs up to a point. If the sum of the blocks we modify exceeds 10 percent of the block buffer cache size, Oracle will stop allocating new lists for us. For example, if our block buffer cache is set to 3,000, Oracle will maintain a list of up to 300 blocks (10 percent of 3,000) for us. Upon COMMIT, Oracle will process each of these lists of 20 block pointers, and if the block is still available, it will perform a fast cleanout. So, as long as the number of blocks we modify does not exceed 10 percent of the number of blocks in the cache *and* our blocks are still in the cache and available to us, Oracle will clean them out upon COMMIT. Otherwise, it just skips them (does not clean them out). Given this understanding, we can set up artificial conditions to see how this works. I set my DB_BLOCK_BUFFERS to a low value of 300. Then, I created a table such that a row fits on exactly one block – we'll never have two rows per block. Then, I fill this table up with 499 rows and COMMIT. We'll measure the amount of redo I have generated so far, run a SELECT that will visit each block, and then measure the amount of redo that SELECT generated.

Surprising to many people, the SELECT will have generated redo. Not only that, but it will also have 'dirtied' these modified blocks, causing DBWR to write them again. This is due to the block cleanout. Next, I'll run the SELECT once again and we'll see that no redo is generated. This is expected as the blocks are all 'clean' at this point.

```
tkyte@TKYTE816> create table t
  2  ( x char(2000) default 'x',
  3    y char(2000) default 'y',
  4    z char(2000) default 'z' )
  5  /

Table created.

tkyte@TKYTE816> insert into t
  2  select 'x','y','z'
  3  from all_objects where rownum < 500
  4  /

499 rows created.

tkyte@TKYTE816> commit;

Commit complete.
```

So, this is our table with one row per block (in my 8 KB block size database). Now we will measure the amount of redo generated during the read of the data:

```
tkyte@TKYTE816> column value new_value old_value
tkyte@TKYTE816> select * from redo_size;

     VALUE
----------
   3250592

tkyte@TKYTE816> select *
  2      from t
  3    where x = y;

no rows selected

tkyte@TKYTE816> select value-&old_value  REDO_GENERATED from redo_size;
old   1: select value-&old_value  REDO_GENERATED from redo_size
new   1: select value-  3250592   REDO_GENERATED from redo_size

REDO_GENERATED
--------------
         29940

tkyte@TKYTE816> commit;

Commit complete.
```

So, this SELECT generated about 30 KB of redo during it's processing. This represents the block headers it modified during the full scan of T. DBWR will be writing these modified blocks back out to disk at some point in the future. Now, if we run the query again:

```
tkyte@TKYTE816> select value from redo_size;

     VALUE
----------
   3280532

tkyte@TKYTE816> select *
  2    from t
  3    where x = y;

no rows selected

tkyte@TKYTE816>
tkyte@TKYTE816> select value-&old_value  REDO_GENERATED from redo_size;
old   1: select value-&old_value  REDO_GENERATED from redo_size
new   1: select value-  3280532  REDO_GENERATED from redo_size

REDO_GENERATED
--------------
             0

Commit complete.
```

we see that no redo is generated – the blocks are all clean.

If we were to re-run the above example with block buffers set to 6,000 instead of 300, we'll find that we generate no redo on any of the SELECTs – we will have dirtied no blocks during either of our SELECT statements. This is because the 499 blocks we modified fit comfortably into 10 percent of our block buffer cache, and we are the only user. There is no one else is mucking around with the data, and no one else is causing our data to be flushed to disk or accessing those blocks. In a live system, it will be normal for at least some of the blocks to not be cleaned out sometimes.

Where this behavior will most affect you, is after a large INSERT (as demonstrated above), UPDATE, or DELETE – one that affects many blocks in the database (anything more than 10 percent of the size of the cache will definitely do it). You will notice that the first query to touch the block after this will generate a little redo and dirty the block, possibly causing it to be rewritten if DBWR had already flushed it, or the instance had been shutdown, clearing out the buffer cache all together. There is not too much you can do about it. It is normal and to be expected. If Oracle did not do this deferred cleanout of a block, a COMMIT could take as long to process as the transaction itself. The COMMIT would have to revisit each and every block, possibly reading them in from disk again (they could have been flushed). If you are not aware of block cleanouts and how they work, it will be one of those mysterious things that just seem to happen for no reason. For example, you UPDATE a lot of data and COMMIT. Now you run a query against that data to verify the results. The query appears to generate tons of write I/O and redo. Seems impossible if you are unaware of this – it was to me the first time I saw it. You go and get someone to observe this with you but it is not reproducible, as the blocks are now 'clean' on the second query. You simply write it off as one of those 'mysteries'.

In an OLTP system, you will probably never see this happening. All of the transactions are short and sweet. Modify a couple of blocks and they all get cleaned out. In a warehouse where you make massive UPDATEs to the data after a load, block cleanouts may be a factor in your design. Some operations will create data on 'clean' blocks. For example, CREATE TABLE AS SELECT, direct path loaded data, direct path inserted data; they will all create 'clean' blocks. An UPDATE, normal INSERT, or DELETE, may create blocks that need to be cleaned with the first read. This could really affect you if your processing consists of:

❑ Bulk loading lots of new data into the data warehouse.

❑ Running UPDATEs on all of the data you just loaded (producing blocks that need to be cleaned out).

❑ Letting people query the data.

You will have to realize that the first query to touch the data will incur some additional processing if the block needs to be cleaned. Realizing this, you yourself should 'touch' the data after the UPDATE. You just loaded or modified a ton of data, you need to analyze it at the very least. Perhaps you need to run some reports yourself to validate the load. This will clean the block out, and make it so the next query doesn't have to do this. Better yet, since you just bulk loaded the data, you now need to refresh the statistics anyway. Running the ANALYZE command to update statistics will clean out all of the blocks as well.

Log Contention

This, like the Cannot Allocate New Log message, is something the DBA must fix, typically in conjunction with the system administrator. However, it is something you might detect if they aren't watching close enough. When we discuss the important V$ dynamic performance views in Chapter 10 on *Tuning Strategies and Tools*, we will look at how to see what exactly we are waiting on. Many times, the biggest wait event will be 'log file sync'. If it is, you are experiencing contention on the redo logs; they are not going fast enough. This can happen for many reasons. One application reason (one that the DBA cannot fix, but which the developer must fix) is that you are committing too frequently – committing inside of a loop doing INSERTs for example. Here, you have introduced the COMMIT in the misguided hope of reducing your need for resources. Committing too frequently, aside from being a bad programming practice, is a surefire way to introduce lots of log file waits, as we must wait for LGWR to flush our redo log buffers to disk. Normally, LGWR can do this in the background and we don't have to wait. When we COMMIT more often than we should (or have to), we wait more than we should. Assuming all of your transactions are correctly sized (you are not committing more frequently than your business rules dictate), the most common causes for log file waits that I've seen are:

❑ Putting redo on a slow device. The disks are just poor performing disks. It is time to buy faster disks.

❑ Putting redo on the same device as other files. Redo is designed to be written with large sequential writes and to be on dedicated devices. If other components of your system, even other Oracle components, are attempting to read and write to this device at the same time as LGWR, you will experience some degree of contention. Here, you want to ensure LGWR has exclusive access to them.

❑ Mounting the devices in a buffered manner. Here, you are using a 'cooked' file system (not RAW disks). The operating system is buffering the data, the database is also buffering the data (redo log buffer). Double buffering slows things down. If possible, mount the devices in a 'direct' fashion. How to do this varies by operating system and device, but it is usually possible.

❑ Putting redo on a slow technology, such as RAID-5. RAID-5 is great for reads, but it is terrible for writes. As we saw earlier on what happens during a COMMIT, we must wait for LGWR to ensure the data is on disk. Using any technology that slows this down will not be a good idea.

If at all possible, you really want at least five dedicated devices for logging, and optimally six in order to mirror your archives as well. In the days of 9, 20, 36 GB, and larger disks, this is getting harder, but if you can set aside four of the smallest, fastest disks you can find and one or two big ones, you can affect LGWR and ARCH in a positive fashion. To lay out the disks, we would break them into three groups:

- ❑ Redo Group 1 – Disks 1 and 3

- ❑ Redo Group 2 – Disks 2 and 4

- ❑ Archive – Disk 5 and optionally disk 6 (the big disk)

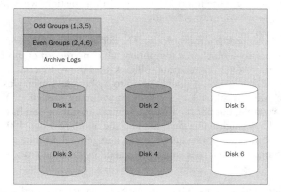

You would place redo log group 1 with members A and B onto Group 1. You would place redo log group 2 with members C and D onto Group 2. If you have groups 3, 4, and so on, they'll go onto the odd and even groups of disks. The effect of this is that LGWR, when using group 1, will write to disk 1 and disk 3 simultaneously. When this group fills up, LGWR will move to disks 2 and 4. When they fill up it will go back to disks 1 and 3. Meanwhile, ARCH will be processing the full online redo logs, and writing them to Group 3, the big disk. The net effect is neither ARCH nor LGWR is ever reading a disk being written to, or writing to a disk being read from – there is no contention:

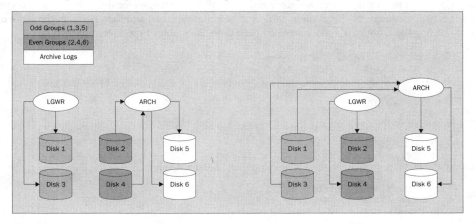

So, when LGWR is writing Group 1, ARCH is reading Group 2, and writing to the archive disks. When LGWR is writing Group 2, ARCH is reading Group 1, and writing to the archive disks. In this fashion, each of LGWR and ARCH will have their own dedicated devices, and will not be contending with anyone, not even each other.

Log files are the one set of Oracle files that benefit the most from the use of RAW disks. If there is one set of files you might consider for RAW, log files would be the ones. There is much back and forth discussion on the pros and cons of using RAW versus cooked file systems. As this is not a book on DBA/SA tasks, we won't get into them. I'll just mention that if you are going to use them anywhere, log files would be the best candidates. You never backup online redo log files, so the fact that they are on RAW partitions versus a cooked file system won't impact any backup scripts you might have. ARCH will always turn the RAW logs into cooked file system files (you cannot use a RAW device to archive to), hence the 'mystique' of RAW devices is very much minimized in this case.

Temporary Tables and Redo/Rollback

Temporary tables are a new feature of Oracle 8.1.5. As such, there is an amount of confusion surrounding them, in particular in the area of logging. In Chapter 6 on the different types of database *Tables* available to you, we will cover how and why you might use temporary tables. In this section, we will cover only the question of, 'How do temporary tables work with respect to logging?'

Temporary tables generate no redo for their blocks. Therefore, an operation on a temporary table is not 'recoverable'. When you modify a block in a temporary table, no record of this change will be made in the redo log files. However, temporary tables do generate rollback, and the rollback is logged. Hence, temporary tables will generate some redo. At first glance, it doesn't seem to make total sense: why would they need to generate rollback? This is because you can rollback to a savepoint within a transaction. You might erase the last 50 INSERTs into a temporary table, but not the first 50. Temporary tables can have constraints and everything else a normal table can have. They might fail a statement on the 500th row of a 500 row INSERT, necessitating a rollback of that statement. Since temporary tables behave in general just like a 'normal' table, temporary tables must generate rollback. Since rollback data must be logged, they will generate some redo log for the rollback they generate.

This is not nearly as ominous as it seems. The primary SQL statements used against temporary tables are INSERTs and SELECTs. Fortunately, INSERTs generate very little rollback (you need to restore the block to 'nothing', and it doesn't take very much room to store 'nothing'), and SELECTs generate no rollback. Hence, if you use temporary tables for INSERTs and SELECTs exclusively, this section means nothing to you. It is only if you UPDATE or DELETE you might be concerned about this.

I set up a small test to demonstrate the amount of redo generated, an indication therefore, of the amount of rollback generated for temporary tables, since only the rollback is logged for them. In order to do this we will take an identically configured 'permanent' table and 'temporary' table, and then perform the same operations on them, measuring the amount of redo generated each time. The tables I used were simply:

```
tkyte@TKYTE816> create table perm
  2  ( x char(2000) default 'x',
  3    y char(2000) default 'y',
  4    z char(2000) default 'z' )
  5  /

Table created.

tkyte@TKYTE816>
tkyte@TKYTE816>
tkyte@TKYTE816> create global temporary table temp
  2  ( x char(2000) default 'x',
  3    y char(2000) default 'y',
  4    z char(2000) default 'z' )
  5  on commit preserve rows
  6  /

Table created.
```

I set up a small stored procedure to do some SQL on the table, and report the results:

```
tkyte@TKYTE816> create or replace procedure do_sql( p_sql in varchar2 )
  2  as
  3       l_start_redo    number;
  4       l_redo          number;
  5  begin
  6  select value into l_start_redo from redo_size;
  7
  8       execute immediate p_sql;
```

```
 9         commit;
10
11         select value-l_start_redo into l_redo from redo_size;
12
13         dbms_output.put_line
14         ( to_char(l_redo,'9,999,999') ||' bytes of redo generated for "' ||
15           substr( replace( p_sql, chr(10), ' '), 1, 25 ) || '"...' );
16   end;
17   /

Procedure created.
```

Then, I ran equivalent INSERTs, UPDATEs, and DELETEs against them:

```
tkyte@TKYTE816> set serveroutput on format wrapped
tkyte@TKYTE816> begin
  2         do_sql( 'insert into perm
  3                   select 1,1,1
  4                     from all_objects
  5                    where rownum <= 500' );
  6
  7         do_sql( 'insert into temp
  8                   select 1,1,1
  9                     from all_objects
 10                    where rownum <= 500' );
 11
 12         do_sql( 'update perm set x = 2' );
 13         do_sql( 'update temp set x = 2' );
 14
 15         do_sql( 'delete from perm' );
 16         do_sql( 'delete from temp' );
 17   end;
 18   /
3,238,688 bytes of redo generated for "insert into perm"...
   72,572 bytes of redo generated for "insert into temp"...
2,166,376 bytes of redo generated for "update perm set x = 2"...
1,090,336 bytes of redo generated for "update temp set x = 2"...
3,320,244 bytes of redo generated for "delete from perm"...
3,198,236 bytes of redo generated for "delete from temp"...

PL/SQL procedure successfully completed.
```

As you can see:

❑ The INSERT into the 'real' table generated a lot of redo. Almost no redo was generated for the temporary table. This makes sense – there is very little rollback data generated for INSERTs and only rollback data is logged for temporary tables.

❑ The UPDATE of the real table generated about twice the amount of redo as the temporary table. Again, this makes sense. About half of that UPDATE, the 'before image', had to be saved. The 'after image' (redo) for the temporary table did not have to be saved.

❑ The DELETEs took about the same amount of redo space. This makes sense as the rollback for a DELETE is big, but the redo for the modified blocks is very small. Hence, a DELETE against a temporary table takes place very much in the same fashion as a DELETE against a permanent table.

The rules of thumb therefore are the following:

❑ An INSERT will generate little to no rollback/redo activity.

❑ A DELETE will generate the same amount of redo as a normal table.

❑ An UPDATE of a temporary table will generate about half the redo of an UPDATE of a normal table.

There are notable exceptions to the last rule of thumb. For example, if I UPDATE a column that is entirely Null with 2000 bytes of data, there will be very little rollback data generated. This UPDATE will behave like the INSERT. On the other hand, if I UPDATE a column with 2000 bytes of data to be Null, it will behave like the DELETE as far as redo generation is concerned. On average, you can expect an UPDATE against a temporary table to produce about 50 percent of the rollback/redo you would experience with a real table.

In general, common sense prevails on the amount of redo created. If the operation you perform causes rollback data to be created, then determine how easy or hard it will be to reverse (undo) the effect of your operation. If you INSERT 2000 bytes, the reverse of this is easy. You simply go back to no bytes. If you DELETE 2000 bytes, the reverse is INSERTing 2000 bytes. In this case, the redo is substantial.

Armed with this knowledge, you will avoid deleting from temporary tables. You can use TRUNCATE, or just let them empty themselves automatically after a COMMIT or when your session terminated. All of these methods generate no rollback and therefore, no redo. You will try to avoid updating a temporary table unless you really have to for the same reason. You will use temporary tables mostly as something to be INSERTed into and SELECTed from. In this fashion, you'll make optimum use of their unique ability to not generate redo.

Analyzing Redo

Lastly in the area of redo log, is a question that is asked frequently, 'How do you analyze these files?' In the past, prior to Oracle 8i, it was very difficult. You could call Oracle Support and get the magic command to 'dump' a redo log file. This would create a textual report that you could read and, if you really understood lots of internal, undocumented stuff about Oracle, you might be able to make sense of them. Practically speaking, this was not feasible, especially if you want to analyze the redo log files to find out when a table was dropped, or what transaction set the SALARY column to a negative value, and so on.

Enter **LogMiner**; which is a new package, DBMS_LOGMNR, supplied with Oracle 8i that allows you to load your redo log files into a database V$ table, and query them using SQL. You can see the before and after values of each column affected by a DML statement. You can see the SQL that would effectively 'replay' your transaction or 'undo' your transaction. You can look in there to find the DELETE against OBJ$ (a SYS-owned data dictionary table) to see when your table was dropped 'accidentally', in the hopes that your DBA can reverse to a point in time right before this DROP TABLE and recover it.

For now, I'm just going to mention Log Miner. In *Appendix A* on *Necessary Supplied Packages*, I go into some depth on the DBMS_LOGMNR package. Refer to the section at the back of this book for more details in this area.

Rollback

We've already discussed a lot of rollback segment topics. We've seen how they are used during recovery, how they interact with the redo logs, and that they are used for consistent, non-blocking reads of data. In this section, I would like to cover the most frequently raised issues with rollback segments. The bulk of our time will be spent on the infamous ORA-01555: snapshot too old error as this single issue causes more confusion than any other topic in the entire database set of topics. Before we do this, we'll investigate two other rollback-related issues. First, we will address the question of what generates the most/least undo (you might already be able to answer that yourself given the preceding examples with temporary tables). Then, we will look at using the SET TRANSACTION statement to pick a rollback segment, and discuss why we might want to use it. Then, we'll finish up with a detailed look at the mysterious ORA-01555.

What Generates the Most/Least Undo?

This is a frequently asked, but easily answered question. An INSERT will generate the least amount of undo, since all Oracle needs to record for this is a row ID to 'delete'. An UPDATE is typically second in the race (in most cases). All that needs to be recorded are the changed bytes. It is most common that you UPDATE some small fraction of the entire row's data. Therefore, a small fraction of the row must be remembered in the undo. Many of my examples above run counter to this rule of thumb, but that is because they update large, fixed sized rows, and update the entire row. It is much more common to UPDATE a row and change a small percentage of the total row. A DELETE will in general, generate the most undo. For a DELETE, Oracle must record the entire row's before image into the undo segment. The temporary table example, with regards to redo generation above, is a classic example of this. The INSERT generated very little undo that needed to be logged. The UPDATE generated an amount equal to the before image of the data that was changed, and the DELETE generates the entire set of data written into the rollback segment.

SET TRANSACTION

The SET TRANSACTION SQL statement may be used to 'pick' the rollback segment you would like your transaction to use. This is generally used in order to have a really big rollback segment for some large operation. I am generally *not* a big fan of this practice, especially when it is overused. For some infrequent mass updates, this might be an OK thing to do on a one-time basis. It is my opinion however, that you should have equi-sized rollback segments (all rollback segments are the same size), and you let the system pick and choose the one you are going to use for a given transaction. If you use rollback segments that can grow (MAXEXTENTS is high enough) and, if need be, have an optimal setting so they shrink back to some size after extending a large amount, you do not need to have a special 'big one'.

One of the problems with one big rollback segment, is that there is nothing to stop any other transaction from using it. There is nothing that you can realistically do to make a rollback segment belong to a single transaction. You are going to have others working in your space. It is just much more straightforward to let the system pick a rollback segment and let it grow. It also gets to be an issue if the tool you are using does not allow you to choose a rollback segment, for example IMP (import) does not, a snapshot refresh on the other hand does, SQLLDR does not, and so on. I believe strongly that your rollback segments should be sized for the transactions your system performs, and any rollback segment should be big enough.

That being said, there are infrequent, one-time uses for this statement. If you have to perform some sort of mass update of lots of information, this might be a good use of the feature. You would create a temporary rollback segment on some scratch disks and do your update. After the update is done, you would offline, and drop the rollback segment. Perhaps a better alternative to this even, would be to have the really large table partitioned in the first place, and perform a parallel update. In this case, each of the parallel query slaves will be assigned to their own rollback segment, making it possible for your transaction to, in effect, use all of the available rollback segments simultaneously. This is something you cannot do with a serially executed update.

'ORA-01555: snapshot too old'

The ORA-01555 is one of those errors that confound people. It is the foundation for many myths, inaccuracies, and suppositions. The error is actually straightforward and has only two real causes, but since there is a special case of one of them that happens so frequently, I'll say that there are three. They are:

- ❑ The rollback segments are too small for the work you perform on your system.
- ❑ Your programs fetch across COMMITs (actually a variation on the above).
- ❑ Block cleanout.

Points one and two above are directly related to Oracle's read consistency model. As you recall from Chapter 2, *Architecture*, the results of your query are 'pre-ordained' – they are well-defined before Oracle goes to retrieve even the first row. Oracle provides this consistent point in time 'snapshot' of the database by using the rollback segments to roll back blocks that have changed since your query began. Every statement you execute such as:

```
update t set x = 5 where x = 2;

insert into t select * from t where x = 2;

delete from t where x = 2;

select * from t where x = 2;
```

will see a read consistent view of T and the set of rows where x=2, regardless of any other concurrent activity in the database. All statements that 'read' the table take advantage of this read consistency. In the above, the UPDATE reads the table to find rows where x=2 (and then UPDATEs them). The INSERT reads the table to find where x=2, and then INSERTs them, and so on. It is this dual use of the rollback segments, both to roll back failed transactions, and to provide for read consistency that results in the ORA-01555.

The third item above is a more insidious cause of the ORA-01555, in that it can happen in a database where there is a single session, and this session is not modifying the table that raises the error! This doesn't seem possible; why would we need rollback data for a table we can guarantee is not being modified? We'll find out below.

Before we take a look at all three cases with illustrations, I'd like to share with you the solutions to the ORA-1555. In general they are:

- ❑ Analyze related objects. This will help avoid the third bullet point above. Since the block cleanout is the result of a very large mass UPDATE or INSERT, this needs to be done anyway after a mass UPDATE or large load.

- ❑ Increase or add more rollback segments. This decreases the likelihood of rollback data being overwritten during the course of your long running query. This goes towards solving all three of the above points.

- ❑ Reduce the run time of your query (tune it). This is always a good thing if possible, so it might be the first thing you try. This will reduce the need for larger rollback segments. This goes towards solving all three of the above points.

We'll come back to these again below, as they are important facts to know. It seemed appropriate to display them prominently before we begin.

Rollback Segments Are in Fact Too Small

The scenario is this: you have a system where the transactions are small. As a result of this, you need very little rollback segment space allocated. Say, for example, the following is true:

- ❑ Each transaction generates 1 KB of undo on average.

- ❑ You do five of these transactions per second on average (5 KB of undo per second, 300 KB per minute).

- ❑ You have a transaction that generates 1 MB of undo that occurs once per minute on average. In total, you generate about 1.3 MB of undo per minute.

- ❑ You have 5 MB of rollback configured for the system.

That is more than sufficient undo for this database when processing transactions. The rollback segments will wrap around, and reuse space about every three to four minutes or so, on average. If we were to size rollback segments based on our transactions that do modifications, we did alright.

In this same environment however, you have some reporting needs. Some of these queries take a really long time to run – five minutes, perhaps. Here is where the problem comes in. If these queries take five minutes to execute *and* they need a view of the data as it existed when the query began, we have a very good probability of the ORA-01555 error occurring. Since our rollback segments will wrap during this query execution, we know that some rollback information generated since our query began is gone – it has been overwritten. If we hit a block that was modified near the time we started our query, the undo information for this block will be missing, and we will receive the ORA-01555.

Here is a small example. Let's say we have a table with blocks 1, 2, 3, ... 1,000,000 in it. The following is a serial list of events that could occur:

Time(min:secs)	Action
0:00	Our query begins.
0:01	Another session UPDATEs block 1,000,000. Rollback information for this is recorded into some rollback segment.
0:01	This UPDATE session COMMITs. The rollback data it generated is still there, but is now subject to being overwritten if we need the space.
1:00	Our query is still chugging along. It is at block 200,000.
1:01	Lots of activity going on, we have generated a little over 1.3 MB of rollback by now.
3:00	Our query is still going strong. We are at block 600,000 or so by now.
4:00	Our rollback segments start to wrap around and reuse the space that was active when our query began at time 0:00. Specifically, we have just reused the rollback segment space that the UPDATE to block 1,000,000 used back at time 0:01.
5:00	Our query finally gets to block 1,000,000. It finds it has been modified since the query began. It goes to the rollback segment and attempts to find the undo for that block to get a consistent read on it. At this point, it discovers the information it needs no longer exists. ORA-01555 is raised and the query fails.

This is all it takes. If your rollback segments are sized such that they have a good chance of wrapping around during the execution of your queries, and your queries access data that will probably be modified, you stand a very good chance of hitting the ORA-01555 on a recurring basis. It is at this point you must resize your rollback segments and make them larger (or have more of them). You need enough rollback configured to last as long as your long running queries. The system was sized for the transactions that modify data – and we forgot to size for the other components of the system. This is where one of the points of confusion comes into play. People will say, 'Well, we have X MB of rollback configured but they can grow – we have MAXEXTENTS set at 500 and each extent is 1 MB, so the rollback can get quite large.' The problem is that the rollback segments will never grow due to a query, only due to INSERTs, UPDATEs, and DELETEs. The fact that a long running query is executing does not cause Oracle to grow a rollback segment to retain the data in case it might need it. Only a long running UPDATE transaction would do this. In the above example, even if the rollback segments had the potential to grow, they will not. What you need to do for this system is have rollback segments that are already big. You need to permanently allocate space to the rollback segments, not give them the opportunity to grow on their own.

The only solutions to the above problem are to either make it so that the rollback segments are sized so they do not wrap but every six to ten minutes, or make it so your queries never take more than two to three minutes to execute. The first suggestion is based on the fact that we have queries that take five minutes to execute. In this case, the DBA needs to make the amount of permanently allocated rollback two to three times larger. The second suggestion, a perfectly valid suggestion, is equally appropriate. Any time you can make the queries go faster, you should. If the rollback generated since the time your query began is never overwritten, you will avoid the ORA-01555.

The important thing to remember is that the probability of an ORA-01555 is dictated by the *smallest* rollback segment in your system, not the largest, not the average. Adding one 'big' rollback segment will not make this problem go away. All it takes is for the smallest rollback segment to wrap around while a query is processing, and then this query stands a chance of an ORA-01555. This is why I am a big fan of equi-sized rollback segments. In this fashion, each rollback segment is both the smallest and the largest. This is also why I avoid using 'optimally' sized rollback segments. If you shrink a rollback segment that was forced to grow, you are throwing away a lot of undo that may be needed right after that. It discards the oldest rollback data when it does this, minimizing the risk but still, the risk is there. I prefer to manually shrink rollback segments during off peak time if at all. I am getting a little too deep into the DBA role at this point, so we'll be moving on to the next case. It is just important that you understand the ORA-01555 in this case, is due to the system not being sized correctly for your workload. The only solutions are to size correctly for your workload. It is not your fault, but it is your problem since you hit it. It is the same as if you run out of temporary space during a query. You either configure sufficient temporary space for the system, or you rewrite the queries so they use a plan that does not require temporary space.

In order to see this effect for yourself, we can set up a small, but somewhat artificial test. What I will do below is create a very small rollback segment. We'll have one session that will use only this rollback segment, virtually assuring us that it will wrap around and reuse its allocated space many times. The session that uses this rollback segment will be modifying a table T. It will use a full scan of T, and read it from 'top' to 'bottom'. In another session, we will execute a query that will read the table T via an index. In this fashion, it will read the table somewhat randomly. It will read row 1, then row 1000, then row 500, then row 20,001, and so on. In this way, we will tend to visit blocks very randomly, and perhaps many times during the processing of our query. The odds of getting an ORA-01555 in this case are virtually 100 percent. So, in one session we start with:

```
tkyte@TKYTE816> create rollback segment rbs_small
  2   storage
  3   ( initial 8k next 8k
  4     minextents 2 maxextents 3 )
  5   tablespace rbs_test
  6   /

Rollback segment created.

tkyte@TKYTE816> alter rollback segment rbs_small online;

Rollback segment altered.

tkyte@TKYTE816> create table t
  2   as
  3   select *
  4     from all_objects
  5   /

Table created.

tkyte@TKYTE816> create index t_idx on t(object_id)
  2   /
```

```
Index created.

tkyte@TKYTE816> begin
  2          for x in ( select rowid rid from t )
  3          loop
  4                  commit;
  5                  set transaction use rollback segment rbs_small;
  6                  update t
  7                     set object_name = lower(object_name)
  8                   where rowid = x.rid;
  9          end loop;
 10      commit;
 11  end;
 12  /
```

Now, in another session, while this PL/SQL block is executing, we issue:

```
tkyte@TKYTE816> select object_name from t where object_id > 0 order by object_id;

OBJECT_NAME
------------------------------
i_obj#
tab$
...
/91196853_activationactivation
/91196853_activationactivation
ERROR:
ORA-01555: snapshot too old: rollback segment number 10 with name "RBS_SMALL" too
small

3150 rows selected.

tkyte@TKYTE816> select count(*) from t;

  COUNT(*)
----------
     21773
```

As you can see, it took a little while, but after reading about three thousand rows (about one seventh of the data) randomly, we eventually hit the ORA-01555. In this case, it was purely due to the fact that we read the table T via the index, and performed random reads all over the table. If we had full scanned the table instead, there is a good chance we would not get the ORA-01555 *in this particular case*. (Try it: change the SELECT query to be SELECT /*+ FULL(T) */ ... and see what happens. On my system, this query did not get the ORA-1555 in repeated runs). This is because both the SELECT and UPDATE would have been full scanning T, and the SELECT would most likely race ahead of the UPDATE during its scan (the SELECT just has to read, the UPDATE must read and update, therefore it'll go slower). By doing the random reads, we increase the probability that the SELECT will need to read a block, which the UPDATE modified and committed many rows ago. This just demonstrates the somewhat insidious nature of the ORA-01555. It's occurrence depends on how concurrent sessions access, and manipulate the underlying tables.

You Fetch Across COMMITs

This is simply a variation on the theme. It is the same case as above, but you are doing it to yourself. You need no help from another session. We've already investigated this in Chapter 4 on *Transactions*, and will briefly review it again. The bottom line is this; fetching across COMMITs is a surefire way to get the ORA-01555. My observation is that most occurrences of the ORA-01555 are because of this operation. The amusing thing is that people sometimes react to this error by committing even more frequently since the message says rollback segment too small. The thinking is that this will help the problem (that our modification must be using too much rollback is the incorrect conclusion here), when in fact it will only ensure that it happens even faster.

The scenario is that you have to update lots of information. You are hesitant to configure the system with sufficient rollback space for whatever reasons. So, you decide to COMMIT every X rows to 'save' on rollback. Never mind that this is both probably slower, and in the end, generates more undo and redo, it is also the surefire way to get into the ORA-01555. Continuing with the above example, I can easily demonstrate this. Using the same table T from above, simply execute:

```
tkyte@TKYTE816> declare
    2           l_cnt number default 0;
    3   begin
    4           for x in ( select rowid rid, t.* from t where object_id > 0 )
    5           loop
    6                   if ( mod(l_cnt,100) = 0 )
    7                   then
    8                           commit;
    9                           set transaction use rollback segment rbs_small;
   10                   end if;
   11                   update t
   12                      set object_name = lower(object_name)
   13                    where rowid = x.rid;
   14                   l_cnt := l_cnt + 1;
   15           end loop;
   16       commit;
   17   end;
   18   /
declare
*
ERROR at line 1:
ORA-01555: snapshot too old: rollback segment number 10 with name "RBS_SMALL" too
small
ORA-06512: at line 4
```

Here, we are performing a random read on the table T via the index. We UPDATE a single row at a time in the loop. Every 100 rows of UPDATEs, we COMMIT. At some point in time, we will revisit a block with our *query* that we modified with our UPDATE, and that block will no longer be recoverable from the rollback segments (since we overwrote that data long ago). Now we are in the uncomfortable position of having our UPDATE process fail partway through.

We could, as outlined in Chapter 4 on *Transactions*, come up with a more sophisticated method of updating the data. For example, we could find the minimum OBJECT_ID and the maximum. We could divide this up into ranges of 100 and do the UPDATEs, recording in another table what we had successfully updated so far. This makes the process, which *should* be a single statement and a single transaction, many individual transactions implemented in complex procedural code that could be restarted from a failure. For example:

```
tkyte@TKYTE816> create table done( object_id int );

Table created.

tkyte@TKYTE816> insert into done values ( 0 );

1 row created.

tkyte@TKYTE816> declare
  2          l_cnt number;
  3          l_max number;
  4  begin
  5          select object_id into l_cnt from done;
  6          select max(object_id) into l_max from t;
  7
  8          while ( l_cnt < l_max )
  9          loop
 10              update t
 11                 set object_name = lower(object_name)
 12               where object_id > l_cnt
 13                 and object_id <= l_cnt+100;
 14
 15              update done set object_id = object_id+100;
 16
 17              commit;
 18              set transaction use rollback segment rbs_small;
 19              l_cnt := l_cnt + 100;
 20          end loop;
 21  end;
 22  /

PL/SQL procedure successfully completed.
```

What we did here mostly, was to come up with a complex solution that has to be tested and reviewed for accuracy, and will run much slower than the simple:

```
update t set object_name = lower(object_name) where object_id > 0;
```

The simple, and in my opinion correct, solution to this dilemma, is to configure an appropriate amount of rollback space for your system, and use the single UPDATE statement. If you have the very occasional large update, use a 'scratch' rollback segment that you create just for the large process, and drop it afterwards. It is so much easier and less error-prone than coming up with a complex solution that might fail, simply due to its complexity (programming error). It is so much easier to let the system do what it needs to do rather than try to come up with complex workarounds to 'save space'.

Delayed Block Cleanout

This cause of the ORA-01555 is harder to eliminate entirely, but is rare, as the circumstances under which it occurs do not happen frequently (at least not in Oracle 8i anymore). We have already discussed the block cleanout mechanism, but to summarize, it is the process whereby the next session to access a block after it has been modified, may have to check to see if the transaction that last modified the block is still active. Once it determines that it is not active, it cleans out the block so that the next session to access it does not have to go through the same process again. In order to clean out the block, Oracle determines the rollback segment used for the previous transaction (from the block's header), and then determines whether the rollback header indicates whether it has been committed or not. This confirmation is accomplished in one of two ways. One way is that Oracle can determine that the transaction committed a long time ago, even though it's transaction slot has been overwritten in the rollback segment transaction table. The other way is that the COMMIT SCN is still in the transaction table of the rollback segment, meaning the transaction committed a short period of time ago, and it's transaction slot hasn't been overwritten.

In order to receive the ORA-01555 from a delayed block cleanout, all of the following conditions must be met:

❑   A modification is made and COMMITed, and the blocks are not cleaned out automatically (for example, it modified more blocks than can be fitted in 10 percent of the SGA block buffer cache).

❑   These blocks are not touched by another session, and will not be touched until our unfortunate query below hits it.

❑   A 'long running' query begins. This query will ultimately read some of those blocks from above. This query starts at SCN t1. This is the read consistent SCN it must roll data back to, in order to achieve read consistency. The transaction entry for the modification transaction is still in the rollback segment transaction table when we began.

❑   During the query, many commits are made in the system. These transactions do not touch the blocks in question (if they did, then we wouldn't have the impending problem).

❑   The transaction tables in the rollback segments roll around and reuse slots due to the high degree of COMMITs. Most importantly, the transaction entry for the original modification transaction is cycled over and reused. In addition, the system has reused rollback segment extents, so as to prevent a consistent read on the rollback segment header block itself.

❑   Additionally, the lowest SCN recorded in the rollback segment now exceeds t1 (it is higher than the read consistent SCN of the query), due to the large amount of commits.

Now, when our query gets to the block that was modified and committed before it began, it is in trouble. Normally, it would go to the rollback segment pointed to by the block and find the status of the transaction that modified it (in other words, find the COMMIT SCN of that transaction). If the COMMIT SCN is less than t1, our query can use this block. If the COMMIT SCN is greater tha t1, our query must roll back that block. The problem is however, that our query is unable to determine in this particular case if the COMMIT SCN of the block is greater than or less than t1. It is unsure as to whether it can use it or not. The ORA-01555 then results.

We can force this error to occur artificially with a single session, but it is more impressive if we use two sessions, as that will drive home the point that this error is not caused by fetching across COMMITs. We'll show both examples as they are both small, and very similar.

What we will do is create many blocks in a table that need to be cleaned out. We will then open a cursor on that table and, inside of a tight loop, initiate many transactions. I am making all modifications to go into the same rollback segment to cause this error to occur in a predicable fashion. Eventually, the ORA-01555 will occur as the outer query in the loop (SELECT * FROM T) hits this block cleanout issue, due to the small UPDATE inside the innermost loop modifying and committing frequently:

```
tkyte@TKYTE816> create table small( x int );

Table created.

tkyte@TKYTE816> insert into small values ( 0 );

1 row created.

tkyte@TKYTE816> begin
  2      commit;
  3      set transaction use rollback segment rbs_small;
  4      update t
  5         set object_type = lower(object_type);
  6      commit;
```

```
7
8                  for x in ( select * from t )
9                  loop
10                     for i in 1 .. 20
11                     loop
12                         update small set x = x+1;
13                         commit;
14                         set transaction use rollback segment rbs_small;
15                     end loop;
16                 end loop;
17   end;
18   /
begin
*
ERROR at line 1:
ORA-01555: snapshot too old: rollback segment number 10 with name "RBS_SMALL" too
small
ORA-06512: at line 8

tkyte@TKYTE816> select * from small;

         X
----------
    196900
```

In order to 'achieve' the above error, I used the same table T as before with some 22,000 rows in it (about 300 blocks on my system). I had a block buffer cache of 300 blocks (10 percent of that is 30). The UPDATE on line 4 should have left about 270 blocks in need of a block cleanout. We then proceeded to SELECT * from this table, where lots of blocks were in need of cleanout. For every row we fetched, we performed 20 transactions, and I made sure that these transactions were directed to the same rollback segment that did the UPDATE in the first place (the goal after all is to overwrite that transaction slot). After processing about 10,000 rows in our query from T (as evidenced by the value in SMALL), we hit the ORA-01555.

Now, to show this is not caused by the fetch across COMMIT (it looks like it could be since we are fetching across a COMMIT), we'll use two sessions. The first session we'll start by creating a table called STOP_OTHER_SESSION. We'll use this table to notify the other session that generates lots of transactions, that it is time to stop. Then, it will dirty lots of blocks in the table again like the above did, and start a long running query on this table. The DBMS_LOCK.SLEEP is used to put a wait between each row fetched to make this simple query a long running one. It simulates the think time that the work would be performing on each row:

```
tkyte@TKYTE816> create table stop_other_session ( x int );

Table created.

tkyte@TKYTE816> declare
2           l_cnt number := 0;
3   begin
4       commit;
5       set transaction use rollback segment rbs_small;
6       update t
7          set object_type = lower(object_type);
8       commit;
9
10      for x in ( select * from t )
11      loop
12          dbms_lock.sleep(1);
13      end loop;
14   end;
.15  /
```

Now, while the above code is executing, you would run the following in another session:

```
tkyte@TKYTE816> create table small( x int );

Table created.

tkyte@TKYTE816> insert into small values ( 0 );

1 row created.

tkyte@TKYTE816> begin
  2          commit;
  3          set transaction use rollback segment rbs_small;
  4          for i in 1 .. 500000
  5          loop
  6                  update small set x = x+1;
  7          commit;
  8          set transaction use rollback segment rbs_small;
  9          for x in ( select * from stop_other_session )
 10          loop
 11                  return; -- stop when the other session tells us to
 12          end loop;
 13      end loop;
 14  end;
 15  /

PL/SQL procedure successfully completed.
```

After a while, the first session will report back with:

```
declare
*
ERROR at line 1:
ORA-01555: snapshot too old: rollback segment number 10 with name "RBS_SMALL" too
small
ORA-06512: at line 10
```

This is the same error, but this time we did not fetch across a COMMIT. In fact, no one was modifying any of the data we were reading.

As I said, the above is a rare case. It took a lot of conditions, that all must exist simultaneously to occur. We needed blocks that were in need of a cleanout to exist and these blocks are rare in Oracle8i (they used to occur more frequently in version 7.x and 8.0 releases, but are relatively rare in 8.1). An ANALYZE statement to collect statistics, gets rid of them so the most common causes, large mass updates and bulk loads, should not be a concern, since the tables need to be analyzed after such operations anyway. Most transactions tend to touch less then 10 percent of the block the buffer cache and hence, do not generate blocks that need to be cleaned out. In the event that you believe this issue is encountered, whereby a SELECT against a table that has no other DML applied to it is raising the ORA-01555, the things to try are:

- ❑ Ensure you are using 'right sized' transactions in the first place. Make sure you are not committing more frequently than you should.

- ❑ `ANALYZE` related objects. Since the block cleanout is the result of a very large mass `UPDATE` or `INSERT`, this needs to be done anyway.

- ❑ Increase or add more rollback segments. This decreases the likelihood of a rollback segment transaction table slot being overwritten during the course of your long running query. This is the same as the solution for the other cause of an `ORA-01555` (in fact, the two are very much related; you are experiencing rollback segment reuse during the processing of your query).

- ❑ Reduce the run-time of your query (tune it). This is always a good thing if possible, so it might be the first thing you try.

Summary

In this chapter, we have taken a look at redo and rollback, and what they mean to the developer. What I have presented here is mostly things for you to be on the look out for, since it is actually the DBAs or SAs who must correct these issues. The most important things to take away from this chapter are the importance of redo and rollback, and the fact that they are not overhead – they are in fact integral components of the database, they are necessary and mandatory. Once you have a good understanding of how they work, and what they do, you'll be able to make better use of them. Understanding that you are not 'saving' anything by committing more frequently than you should (you are actually wasting resources, it takes more CPU, more disk, and more programming), is probably the most important point. Understand what the database needs to do, and then let the database do it.

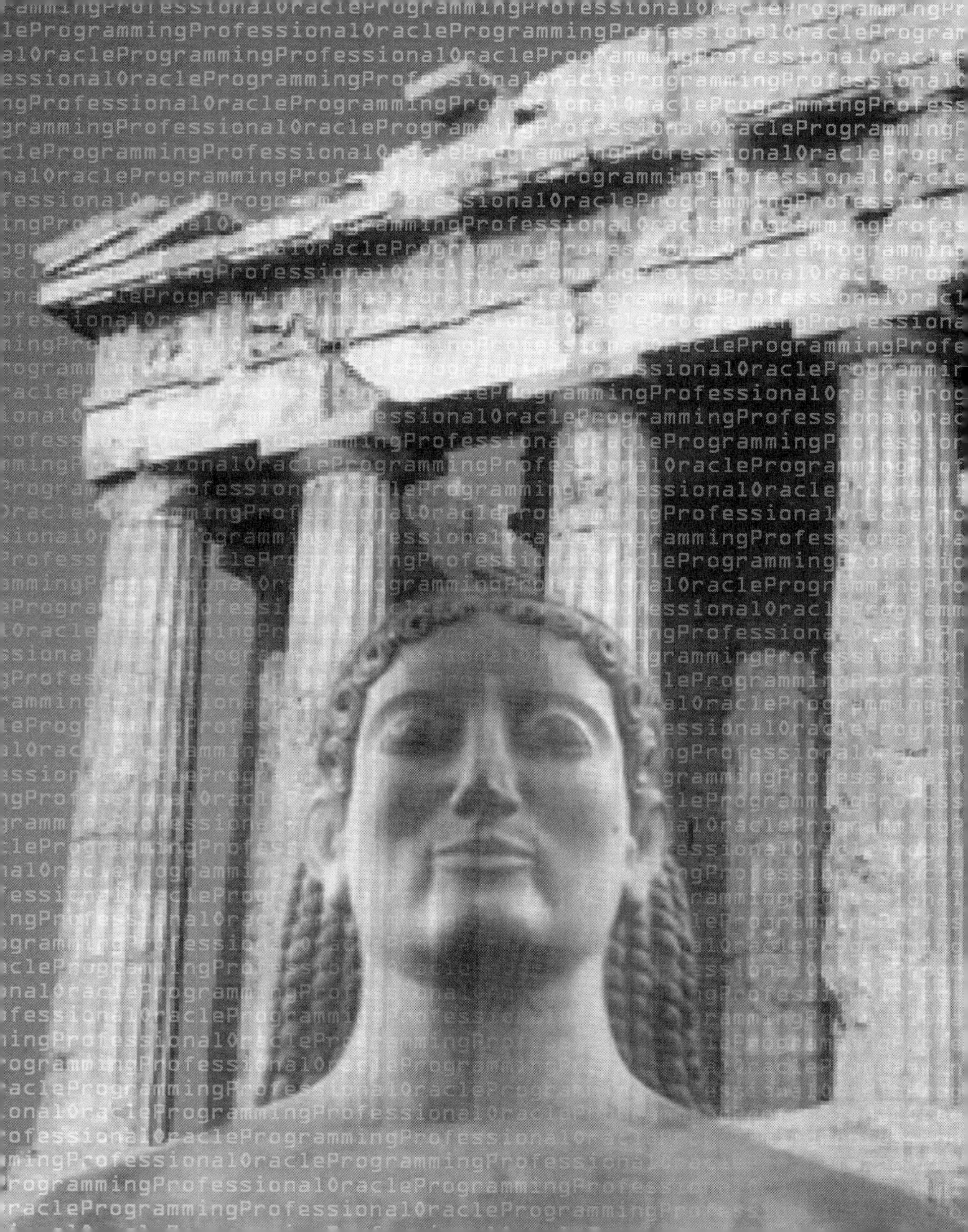

6

Database Tables

In this chapter, we will discuss database tables. We will look at the various types of tables and see when you might want to use each type; when one type of table is more appropriate than another. We will be concentrating on the physical storage characteristics of the tables; how the data is organized and stored.

Once upon a time, there was only one type of table really; a 'normal' table. It was managed in the same way a 'heap' is managed (the definition of which is below). Over time, Oracle added more sophisticated types of tables. There are clustered tables (two types of those), index organized tables, nested tables, temporary tables, and object tables in addition to the heap organized table. Each type of table has different characteristics that make it suitable for use in different application areas.

Types of Tables

We will define each type of table before getting into the details. There are seven major types of tables in Oracle 8i. They are:

❑ **Heap Organized Tables** – This is a 'normal', standard database table. Data is managed in a heap-like fashion. As data is added, the first free space found in the segment that can fit the data will be used. As data is removed from the table, it allows space to become available for reuse by subsequent INSERTs and UPDATEs. This is the origin of the name heap as it refers to tables like this. A heap is a bunch of space and it is used in a somewhat random fashion.

❑ **Index Organized Tables** – Here, a table is stored in an index structure. This imposes physical order on the rows themselves. Whereas in a heap, the data is stuffed wherever it might fit, in an index organized table the data is stored in sorted order, according to the primary key.

- ❑ **Clustered Tables** – Two things are achieved with these. First, many tables may be stored physically joined together. Normally, one would expect data from only one table to be found on a database block. With clustered tables, data from many tables may be stored together on the same block. Secondly, all data that contains the same cluster key value will be physically stored together. The data is 'clustered' around the cluster key value. A cluster key is built using a B*Tree index.

- ❑ **Hash Clustered Tables** – Similar to the clustered table above, but instead of using a B*Tree index to locate the data by cluster key, the hash cluster hashes the key to the cluster, to arrive at the database block the data should be on. In a hash cluster the data is the index (metaphorically speaking). This would be appropriate for data that is read frequently via an equality comparison on the key.

- ❑ **Nested Tables** – These are part of the Object Relational extensions to Oracle. They are simply system generated and maintained child tables in a parent/child relationship. They work much in the same way as EMP and DEPT in the SCOTT schema. EMP is considered to be a child of the DEPT table, since the EMP table has a foreign key, DEPTNO, that points to DEPT. The main difference is that they are not 'standalone' tables like EMP.

- ❑ **Temporary Tables** – These tables store scratch data for the life of a transaction or the life of a session. These tables allocate temporary extents as needed from the users temporary tablespace. Each session will only see the extents it allocates and never sees any of the data created in any other session.

- ❑ **Object Tables** – These are tables that are created based on an object type. They are have special attributes not associated with non-object tables, such as a system generated REF (object identifier) for each row. Object tables are really special cases of heap, index organized, and temporary tables, and may include nested tables as part of their structure as well.

In general, there are a couple of facts about tables, regardless of their type. Some of these are:

- ❑ A table can have up to 1,000 columns, although I would recommend against a design that does, unless there was some pressing need. Tables are most efficient with far fewer than 1,000 columns.

- ❑ A table can have a virtually unlimited number of rows. Although you will hit other limits that prevent this from happening. For example, a tablespace can have at most 1,022 files typically. Say you have 32 GB files, that is to say 32,704 GB per tablespace. This would be 2,143,289,344 blocks, each of which are 16 KB in size. You might be able to fit 160 rows of between 80 to 100 bytes per block. This would give you 342,926,295,040 rows. If we partition the table though, we can easily multiply this by ten times or more. There are limits, but you'll hit other practical limitations before even coming close to these figures.

- ❑ A table can have as many indexes as there are permutations of columns, taken 32 at a time (and permutations of functions on those columns), although once again practical restrictions will limit the actual number of indexes you will create and maintain.

- ❑ There is no limit to the number of tables you may have. Yet again, practical limits will keep this number within reasonable bounds. You will not have millions of tables (impracticable to create and manage), but thousands of tables, yes.

We will start with a look at some of the parameters and terminology relevant to tables and define them. After that we'll jump into a discussion of the basic 'heap organized' table and then move onto the other types.

Terminology

In this section, we will cover the various storage parameters and terminology associated with tables. Not all parameters are used for every table type. For example, the PCTUSED parameter is not meaningful in the context of an index organized table. We will mention in the discussion of each table type below which parameters are relevant. The goal is to introduce the terms and define them. As appropriate, more information on using specific parameters will be covered in subsequent sections.

High Water Mark

This is a term used with objects stored in the database. If you envision a table for example as a 'flat' structure, as a series of blocks laid one after the other in a line from left to right, the **high water mark** would be the right most block that ever contained data. For example:

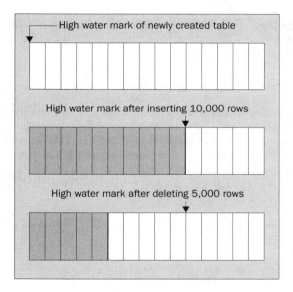

This shows that the high water mark starts at the first block of a newly created table. As data is placed into the table over time and more blocks get used, the high water mark rises. If we delete some (or even *all*) of the rows in the table, we might have many blocks that no longer contain data, but they are still *under* the high water mark and will remain under the high water mark until the object is rebuilt or truncated.

The high water mark is relevant since Oracle will scan all blocks under the high water mark, even when they contain *no* data, during a full scan. This will impact the performance of a full scan – especially if most of the blocks under the high water mark are empty. To see this, just create a table with 1,000,000 rows (or create any table with a large number of rows). Do a SELECT COUNT(*) from this table. Now, DELETE every row in it and you will find that the SELECT COUNT(*) takes just as long to count *zero* rows as it did to count 1,000,000. This is because Oracle is busy reading all of the blocks below the high water mark to see if they contain data. You should compare this to what happens if you used TRUNCATE on the table instead of deleting each individual row. TRUNCATE will reset the high water mark of a table back to 'zero'. If you plan on deleting every row in a table, TRUNCATE would be the method of my choice for this reason.

FREELISTS

The **FREELIST** is where Oracle keeps tracks of blocks under the high water mark for objects that have free space on them. Each object will have at least one FREELIST associated with it and as blocks are used, they will be placed on or taken off of the FREELIST as needed. It is important to note that only blocks under the high water mark of an object will be found on the FREELIST. The blocks that remain above the high water mark, will be used only when the FREELISTs are empty, at which point Oracle advances the high water mark and adds these blocks to the FREELIST. In this fashion, Oracle postpones increasing the high water mark for an object until it has to.

An object may have more than one FREELIST. If you anticipate heavy INSERT or UPDATE activity on an object by many concurrent users, configuring more then one FREELIST can make a major positive impact on performance (at the cost of possible additional storage). As we will see later, having sufficient FREELISTs for your needs is crucial.

Freelists can be a huge positive performance influence (or inhibitor) in an environment with many concurrent inserts and updates. An extremely simple test can show the benefits of setting this correctly. Take the simplest table in the world:

```
tkyte@TKYTE816> create table t ( x int );
```

and using two sessions, start inserting into it like wild. If you measure the system-wide wait events for block related waits before and after, you will find huge waits, especially on data blocks (trying to insert data). This is frequently caused by insufficient FREELISTs on tables (and on indexes but we'll cover that again in Chapter 7, *Indexes*). For example, I set up a temporary table:

```
tkyte@TKYTE816> create global temporary table waitstat_before
  2   on commit preserve rows
  3   as
  4   select * from v$waitstat
  5   where 1=0
  6   /

Table created.
```

to hold the before picture of waits on blocks. Then, in two sessions, I simultaneously ran:

```
tkyte@TKYTE816> truncate table waitstat_before;

Table truncated.

tkyte@TKYTE816> insert into waitstat_before
  2   select * from v$waitstat
  3   /

14 rows created.

tkyte@TKYTE816> begin
  2           for i in 1 .. 100000
  3           loop
  4                   insert into t values ( i );
  5                   commit;
```

```
    6          end loop;
    7  end;
    8 /


PL/SQL procedure successfully completed.
```

Now, this is a very simple block of code, and we are the only users in the database here. We should get as good performance as you can get. I've plenty of buffer cache configured, my redo logs are sized appropriately, indexes won't be slowing things down; this should run fast. What I discover afterwards however, is that:

```
tkyte@TKYTE816> select a.class, b.count-a.count count, b.time-a.time time
    2    from waitstat_before a, v$waitstat b
    3    where a.class = b.class
    4  /

CLASS                    COUNT        TIME
-------------------- ---------- ----------
bitmap block                 0           0
bitmap index block           0           0
data block                4226        3239
extent map                   0           0
free list                    0           0
save undo block              0           0
save undo header             0           0
segment header               2           0
sort block                   0           0
system undo block            0           0
system undo header           0           0
undo block                   0           0
undo header                649          36
unused                       0           0
```

I waited over 32 seconds during these concurrent runs. This is entirely due to not having enough FREELISTs configured on my tables for the type of concurrent activity I am expecting to do. I can remove all of that wait time easily, just by creating the table with multiple FREELISTs:

```
tkyte@TKYTE816> create table t ( x int ) storage ( FREELISTS 2 );

Table created.
```

or by altering the object:

```
tkyte@TKYTE816> alter table t storage ( FREELISTS 2 );

Table altered.
```

You will find that both wait events above go to zero; it is that easy. What you want to do for a table is try to determine the maximum number of concurrent (truly concurrent) inserts or updates that will require more space. What I mean by truly concurrent, is how often do you expect two people at exactly the same instant, to request a free block for that table. This is not a measure of overlapping transactions, it is a measure of sessions doing an insert at the same time, regardless of transaction boundaries. You want to have about as many FREELISTs as concurrent inserts into the table to increase concurrency.

You should just set FREELISTs really high and then not worry about it, right? Wrong – of course, that would be too easy. Each process will use a single FREELIST. It will not go from FREELIST to FREELIST to find space. What this means is that if you have ten FREELISTs on a table and the one your process is using exhausts the free buffers on its list, it will not go to another list for space. It will cause the table to advance the high water mark, or if the tables high water cannot be advanced (all space is used), to extend, to get another extent. It will then continue to use the space on its FREELIST only (which is empty now). There is a tradeoff to be made with multiple FREELISTs. On one hand, multiple FREELISTs is a huge performance booster. On the other hand, it will probably cause the table to use more disk space then absolutely necessary. You will have to decide which is less bothersome in your environment.

Do not underestimate the usefulness of this parameter, especially since we can alter it up and down at will with Oracle 8.1.6 and up. What you might do is alter it to a large number to perform some load of data in parallel with the conventional path mode of SQLLDR. You will achieve a high degree of concurrency for the load with minimum waits. After the load, you can alter the FREELISTs back down to some, more day-to-day, reasonable number, the blocks on the many existing FREELISTs will be merged into the one master FREELIST when you alter the space down.

PCTFREE and PCTUSED

These two settings control when blocks will be put on and taken off the FREELISTs. When used with a table (but not an Index Organized Table as we'll see), **PCTFREE** tells Oracle how much space should be reserved on a block for future updates. By default, this is 10 percent. What this means is that if we use an 8 KB block size, as soon as the addition of a new row onto a block would cause the free space on the block to drop below about 800 bytes, Oracle will use a new block instead of the existing block. This 10 percent of the data space on the block is set aside for updates to the rows on that block. If we were to update them – the block would still be able to hold the updated row.

Now, whereas PCTFREE tells Oracle when to take a block off the FREELIST making it no longer a candidate for insertion, **PCTUSED** tells Oracle when to put a block *on* the FREELIST again. If the PCTUSED is set to 40 percent (the default), and the block hit the PCTFREE level (it is not on the FREELIST currently), then 61 percent of the block must be free space before Oracle will put the block back on the FREELIST. If we are using the default values for PCTFREE (10) and PCTUSED (40) then a block will remain on the FREELIST until it is 90 percent full (10 percent free space). Once it hits 90 percent, it will be taken off of the FREELIST and remain off the FREELIST, until the free space on the block exceeds 60 percent of the block.

Pctfree and PCTUSED are implemented differently for different table types as will be noted below when we discuss each type. Some table types employ both, others only use PCTFREE and even then only when the object is created.

There are three settings for PCTFREE, too high, too low, and just about right. If you set PCTFREE for blocks too high, you will waste space. If you set PCTFREE to 50 percent and you never update the data, you have just wasted 50 percent of every block. On another table however, 50 percent may be very reasonable. If the rows start out small and tend to double in size, a large setting for PCTFREE will avoid row migration.

Row Migration

So, that poses the question; what exactly is row migration? Row migration is when a row is forced to leave the block it was created on, because it grew too large to fit on that block with the rest of the rows. I'll illustrate a row migration below. We start with a block that looks like this:

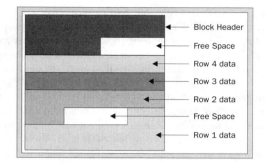

Approximately one seventh of the block is free space. However, we would like to more than double the amount of space used by row 4 via an UPDATE (it currently consumes a seventh of the block). In this case, even if Oracle coalesced the space on the block like this:

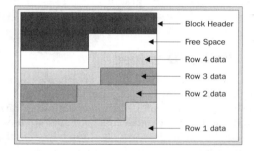

there is still insufficient room to grow row 4 by more than two times its current size, because the size of the free space is less than the size of row 4. If the row could have fitted in the coalesced space, then this would have happened. This time however, Oracle will not perform this coalescing and the block will remain as it is. Since row 4 would have to span more than one block if it stayed on this block, Oracle will move, or migrate, the row. However, it cannot just move it; it must leave behind a 'forwarding address'. There may be indexes that physically point to this address for row 4. A simple update will not modify the indexes as well (note that there is a special case with partitioned tables that a row ID, the address of a row, will change. We will look at this case in the Chapter 14 on *Partitioning*,). Therefore, when Oracle migrates the row, it will leave behind a pointer to where the row really is. After the update, the blocks might look like the following:

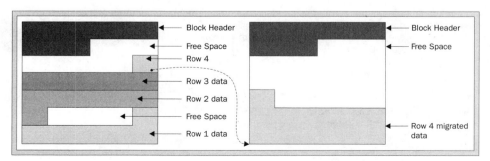

So, this is what a migrated row is; it is a row that had to move from the block it was inserted into, onto some other block. Why is this an issue? Your application will never know, the SQL you use is no different. It only matters for performance reasons. If we go to read this row via an index, the index will point to the original block. That block will point to the new block. Instead of doing the two or so I/Os to read the index plus one I/O to read the table, we'll need to do yet one more I/O to get to the actual row data. In isolation, this is no 'big deal'; you won't even notice this. However, when you have a sizable percentage of your rows in this state with lots of users you will begin to notice this side effect. Access to this data will start to slow down (additional I/Os add to the access time), your buffer cache efficiency goes down (you need to buffer twice the amount of blocks you would if they were not migrated), and your table grows in size and complexity. It is for these reasons that you do not want migrated rows. It is interesting to note what Oracle will do if the row that was migrated from the block on the left to the block on the right, in the diagram above, was to have to migrate *again* at some future point in time. This would be due to other rows being added to the block it was migrated to and then updating this row to make it even larger. Oracle will actually migrate the row *back* to the original block and if there is sufficient space leave it there (the row might become 'un-migrated'). If there isn't sufficient space, Oracle will migrate the row to another block all together and change the forwarding address on the *original* block. As such, row migrations will always involve one level of indirection. So, now we are back to PCTFREE and what it is used for; it is the setting that will help you to minimize row chaining when set properly.

Setting PCTFREE and PCTUSED values

Setting PCTFREE and PCTUSED is an important, and a greatly overlooked, topic, I would like to show you how you can measure the behavior of your objects, to see how space is being used. I will use a stored procedure that will show the effects of inserts on a table with various PCTFREE/PCTUSED settings followed by a series of updates to the same data. This will illustrate how these settings can affect the number of blocks available on the FREELIST (which ultimately will affect how space is used, how many rows are migrated and so on). These scripts are illustrative; they don't tell you what to set the values to, they can be used by you to figure out how Oracle is treating your blocks given various types of updates. They are templates that you will have to modify in order to effectively use them.

I started by creating a test table:

```
tkyte@TKYTE816> create table t ( x int, y char(1000) default 'x' );

Table created.
```

It is a very simple table but for illustrative purposes will serve nicely. By using the CHAR type, I've ensured every row with a non-null value for Y will be 1,000 bytes long. I should be able to 'guess' how things will work given a specific block size. Now for the routine to measure FREELIST and block usage:

```
tkyte@TKYTE816> create or replace procedure measure_usage
  2  as
  3      l_free_blks            number;
  4      l_total_blocks         number;
  5      l_total_bytes          number;
  6      l_unused_blocks        number;
  7      l_unused_bytes         number;
  8      l_LastUsedExtFileId    number;
  9      l_LastUsedExtBlockId   number;
 10      l_LAST_USED_BLOCK      number;
 11
 12      procedure get_data
 13      is
```

```
14          begin
15              dbms_space.free_blocks
16                ( segment_owner       =>  USER,
17                  segment_name        =>  'T',
18                  segment_type        =>  'TABLE',
19                  FREELIST_group_id   =>  0,
20                  free_blks           =>  l_free_blks );
21
22              dbms_space.unused_space
23                ( segment_owner       =>  USER,
24                  segment_name        =>  'T',
25                  segment_type        =>  'TABLE',
26                  total_blocks        =>  l_total_blocks,
27                  total_bytes         =>  l_total_bytes,
28                  unused_blocks       =>  l_unused_blocks,
29                  unused_bytes        =>  l_unused_bytes,
30                  LAST_USED_EXTENT_FILE_ID => l_LastUsedExtFileId,
31                  LAST_USED_EXTENT_BLOCK_ID => l_LastUsedExtBlockId,
32                  LAST_USED_BLOCK => l_last_used_block ) ;
33
34
35              dbms_output.put_line( L_free_blks || ' on FREELIST, ' ||
36                              to_number(l_total_blocks-l_unused_blocks-1 ) ||
37                              ' used by table' );
38          end;
39  begin
40          for i in 0 .. 10
41          loop
42              dbms_output.put( 'insert ' || to_char(i,'00') || ' ' );
43              get_data;
44              insert into t (x) values ( i );
45              commit ;
46          end loop;
47
48
49          for i in 0 .. 10
50          loop
51              dbms_output.put( 'update ' || to_char(i,'00') || ' ' );
52              get_data;
53              update t set y = null where x = i;
54              commit;
55          end loop;
56  end;
57  /

Procedure created.
```

Here we use two routines in the DBMS_SPACE package that tell us how many blocks are on a segment's FREELIST, how many blocks are allocated to the table, unused blocks and so on. We can use this information to tell ourselves how many of the blocks that have been used by the table (below the high water mark of the table) are on the FREELIST. I then insert 10 rows into the table with a non-Null Y. Then I come back and update Y to Null row by row. Given that I have an 8 KB block size, with a default PCTFREE of 10 and a default PCTUSED of 40, I would expect that seven rows should fit nicely on the block (the calculation below is done without considering the block/row overhead):

```
(2+1)bytes for X + (1000+2)bytes for Y = 1005
1005 bytes/row * 7 rows = 7035
```

```
8192 - 7035 bytes (blocksize) = 1157 bytes

1157 bytes are leftover, insufficient for another row plus 800+ bytes (10% of the
block)
```

Now, since 10 percent of the 8 KB block is about 800 + bytes, we know we cannot fit another row onto that block. If we wanted to, we could calculate the block header exactly, here we will just guess that it is less then 350 + bytes (1157 − 800 = 357). That gives us room for seven rows per block.

Next estimate how many updates it will take to put a block back on the FREELIST. Here, we know the block must be less than 40 percent used – that is only a maximum of 3,275 bytes can be in use to get back onto the free list. We would expect then that if each UPDATE gives back 1,000 bytes, it would take about four UPDATEs to put a block back on the FREELIST. Well, lets see how well I did:

```
tkyte@TKYTE816> exec measure_usage;
insert  00 0 on FREELIST, 0 used by table
insert  01 1 on FREELIST, 1 used by table
insert  02 1 on FREELIST, 1 used by table
insert  03 1 on FREELIST, 1 used by table
insert  04 1 on FREELIST, 1 used by table
insert  05 1 on FREELIST, 1 used by table
insert  06 1 on FREELIST, 1 used by table
insert  07 1 on FREELIST, 1 used by table  -- between the 7th and 8th rows
insert  08 1 on FREELIST, 2 used by table     we added another block 'in use'
insert  09 1 on FREELIST, 2 used by table
insert  10 1 on FREELIST, 2 used by table
update  00 1 on FREELIST, 2 used by table
update  01 1 on FREELIST, 2 used by table
update  02 1 on FREELIST, 2 used by table
update  03 1 on FREELIST, 2 used by table
update  04 2 on FREELIST, 2 used by table  -- the 4th update put another
update  05 2 on FREELIST, 2 used by table     block back on the free list
update  06 2 on FREELIST, 2 used by table
update  07 2 on FREELIST, 2 used by table
update  08 2 on FREELIST, 2 used by table
update  09 2 on FREELIST, 2 used by table
update  10 2 on FREELIST, 2 used by table

PL/SQL procedure successfully completed.
```

Sure enough, after seven INSERTs, another block is added to the table. Likewise, after four UPDATEs, the blocks on the FREELIST increase from 1 to 2 (both blocks are back on the FREELIST, available for INSERTs). If we drop and recreate the table T with different settings and then measure it again, we get the following:

```
tkyte@TKYTE816> create table t ( x int, y char(1000) default 'x' ) pctfree 10
  2    pctused 80;

Table created.

tkyte@TKYTE816> exec measure_usage;
insert  00 0 on FREELIST, 0 used by table
insert  01 1 on FREELIST, 1 used by table
```

```
insert   02 1 on FREELIST, 1 used by table
insert   03 1 on FREELIST, 1 used by table
insert   04 1 on FREELIST, 1 used by table
insert   05 1 on FREELIST, 1 used by table
insert   06 1 on FREELIST, 1 used by table
insert   07 1 on FREELIST, 1 used by table
insert   08 1 on FREELIST, 2 used by table
insert   09 1 on FREELIST, 2 used by table
insert   10 1 on FREELIST, 2 used by table
update   00 1 on FREELIST, 2 used by table
update   01 2 on FREELIST, 2 used by table    -- first update put a block
update   02 2 on FREELIST, 2 used by table       back on the free list due to the
update   03 2 on FREELIST, 2 used by table       much higher pctused
update   04 2 on FREELIST, 2 used by table
update   05 2 on FREELIST, 2 used by table
update   06 2 on FREELIST, 2 used by table
update   07 2 on FREELIST, 2 used by table
update   08 2 on FREELIST, 2 used by table
update   09 2 on FREELIST, 2 used by table
update   10 2 on FREELIST, 2 used by table

PL/SQL procedure successfully completed.
```

We can see the effect of increasing PCTUSED here. The very first UPDATE had the effect of putting the block back on the FREELIST. That block can be used by another INSERT again that much faster.

Does that mean you should increase your PCTUSED? No, not necessarily. It depends on how your data behaves over time. If your application goes through cycles of:

1. Adding data (lots of INSERTs) followed by,

2. UPDATEs – Updating the data causing the rows to grow and shrink.

3. Go back to adding data.

I might *never* want a block to get put onto the FREELIST as a result of an update. Here we would want a very low PCTUSED, causing a block to go onto a FREELIST only after all of the row data has been deleted. Otherwise, some of the blocks that have rows that are temporarily 'shrunken' would get newly inserted rows if PCTUSED was set high. Then, when we go to update the old and new rows on these blocks; there won't be enough room for them to grow and they migrate.

In summary, PCTUSED and PCTFREE are *crucial*. On one hand you need to use them to avoid too many rows from migrating, on the other hand you use them to avoid wasting too much space. You need to look at your objects, describe how they will be used, and then you can come up with a logical plan for setting these values. Rules of thumb may very well fail us on these settings; they really need to be set based on how you use it. You might consider (and remember high and low are *relative* terms):

❑ High PCTFREE, Low PCTUSED – For when you insert lots of data that will be updated and the updates will increase the size of the rows frequently. This reserves a lot of space on the block after inserts (high PCTFREE) and makes it so that the block must almost be empty before getting back onto the free list (low PCTUSED).

❑ Low PCTFREE, High PCTUSED – If you tend to only ever INSERT or DELETE from the table or if you do UPDATE, the UPDATE tends to shrink the row in size.

INITIAL, NEXT, and PCTINCREASE

These are storage parameters that define the size of the **INITIAL** and subsequent extents allocated to a table and the percentage by which the **NEXT** extent should grow. For example, if you use an INITIAL extent of 1 MB, a NEXT extent of 2 MB, and a **PCTINCREASE** of 50 – your extents would be:

1. 1 MB.

2. 2 MB.

3. 3 MB (150 percent of 2).

4. 4.5 MB (150 percent of 3).

and so on. I consider these parameters to be *obsolete*. The database should be using locally managed tablespaces with uniform extent sizes exclusively. In this fashion the INITIAL extent is always equal to the NEXT extent size and there is no such thing as PCTINCREASE – a setting that only causes fragmentation in a tablespace.

In the event you are not using locally managed tablespaces, my recommendation is to always set INITIAL = NEXT and PCTINCREASE to ZERO. This mimics the allocations you would get in a locally managed tablespace. All objects in a tablespace should use the same extent allocation strategy to avoid fragmentation.

MINEXTENTS and MAXEXTENTS

These settings control the number of extents an object may allocate for itself. The setting for **MINEXTENTS** tells Oracle how many extents to allocate to the table initially. For example, in a locally managed tablespace with uniform extent sizes of 1 MB, a MINEXTENTS setting of 10 would cause the table to have 10 MB of storage allocated to it.

MAXEXTENTS is simply an upper bound on the possible number of extents this object may acquire. If you set MAXEXTENTS to 255 in that same tablespace, the largest the table would ever get to would be 255 MB in size. Of course, if there is not sufficient space in the tablespace to grow that large, the table will not be able to allocate these extents.

LOGGING and NOLOGGING

Normally objects are created in a **LOGGING** fashion, meaning all operations performed against them that can generate redo will generate it. **NOLOGGING** allows certain operations to be performed against that object without the generation of redo. NOLOGGING only affects only a few specific operations such as the initial creation of the object, or direct path loads using SQLLDR, or rebuilds (see the *SQL Language Reference Manual* for the database object you are working with to see which operations apply).

This option does not disable redo log generation for the object in general; only for very specific operations. For example, if I create a table as SELECT NOLOGGING and then, INSERT INTO THAT_TABLE VALUES (1), the INSERT will be logged, but the table creation would not have been.

INITRANS and MAXTRANS

Each block in an object has a block header. Part of this block header is a transaction table, entries will be made in the transaction table to describe which transactions have what rows/elements on the block locked. The initial size of this transaction table is specified by the **INITRANS** setting for the object. For tables this defaults to 1 (indexes default to 2). This transaction table will grow dynamically as needed up to **MAXTRANS** entries in size (given sufficient free space on the block that is). Each allocated transaction entry consumes 23 bytes of storage in the block header.

Heap Organized Table

A heap organized table is probably used 99 percent (or more) of the time in applications, although that might change over time with the advent of index organized tables, now that index organized tables can themselves be indexed. A heap organized table is the type of table you get by default when you issue the CREATE TABLE statement. If you want any other type of table structure, you would need to specify that in the CREATE statement itself.

A heap is a classic data structure studied in computer science. It is basically, a big area of space, disk, or memory (disk in the case of a database table, of course), which is managed in an apparently random fashion. Data will be placed where it fits best, not in any specific sort of order. Many people expect data to come back out of a table in the same order it was put into it, but with a heap, this is definitely not assured. In fact, rather the opposite is guaranteed; the rows will come out in a wholly unpredictable order. This is quite easy to demonstrate. I will set up a table, such that in my database I can fit one full row per block (I am using an 8 KB block size). You do not need to have the case where you only have one row per block I am just taking advantage of that to demonstrate a predictable sequence of events. The following behavior will be observed on tables of all sizes, in databases with any blocksize:

```
tkyte@TKYTE816> create table t
  2  ( a int,
  3    b varchar2(4000) default rpad('*',4000,'*'),
  4    c varchar2(3000) default rpad('*',3000,'*')
  5  )
  6  /

Table created.

tkyte@TKYTE816> insert into t (a) values ( 1);
1 row created.

tkyte@TKYTE816> insert into t (a) values ( 2);

1 row created.

tkyte@TKYTE816> insert into t (a) values ( 3);

1 row created.

tkyte@TKYTE816> delete from t where a = 2 ;

1 row deleted.

tkyte@TKYTE816> insert into t (a) values ( 4);

1 row created.
```

```
tkyte@TKYTE816> select a from t;

         A
----------
         1
         4
         3
```

Adjust columns B and C to be appropriate for your block size if you would like to reproduce this. For example, if you have a 2 KB block size, you do not need column C, and column B should be a VARCHAR2(1500) with a default of 1500 asterisks. Since data is managed in a heap in a table like this, as space becomes available, it will be reused. A full scan of the table will retrieve the data as it hits it, never in the order of insertion. This is a key concept to understand about database tables; in general, they are inherently unordered collections of data. You should also note that we do not need to use a DELETE in order to observe the above – I could achieve the same results using *only* INSERTs. If I insert a small row, followed by a very large row that will not fit on the block with the small row, and then a small row again, I may very well observe that the rows come out by default in the order 'small row, small row, large row'. They will not be retrieved in the order of insertion. Oracle will place the data where it fits, not in any order by date or transaction.

If your query needs to retrieve data in order of insertion, we must add a column to that table that we can use to order the data when retrieving it. That column could be a number column for example that was maintained with an increasing sequence (using the Oracle SEQUENCE object). We could then approximate the insertion order using 'select by ordering' on this column. It will be an approximation because the row with sequence number 55 may very well have committed before the row with sequence 54, therefore it was officially 'first' in the database.

So, you should just think of a heap organized table as a big, unordered collection of rows. These rows will come out in a seemingly random order and depending on other options being used (parallel query, different optimizer modes and so on), may come out in a different order with the same query. Do not ever count on the order of rows from a query unless you have an ORDER BY statement on your query!

That aside, what is important to know about heap tables? Well, the CREATE TABLE syntax spans almost 40 pages in the SQL reference manual provided by Oracle so there are lots of options that go along with them. There are so many options that getting a hold on all of them is pretty difficult. The 'wire diagrams' (or 'train track' diagrams) alone take eight pages to cover. One trick I use to see most of the options available to me in the create table statement for a given table, is to create the table as simply as possible, for example:

```
tkyte@TKYTE816> create table t
  2  ( x int primary key ,
  3    y date,
  4    z clob )
  5  /

Table created.
```

Then using the standard export and import utilities (see Chapter 8 on *Import and Export*), we'll export the definition of it and have import show us the verbose syntax:

```
exp userid=tkyte/tkyte tables=t
imp userid=tkyte/tkyte full=y indexfile=t.sql
```

I'll now find that T.SQL contains my CREATE table statement in its most verbose form, I've formatted it a bit for easier reading but otherwise it is straight from the DMP file generated by export:

```
CREATE TABLE "TKYTE"."T"
("X" NUMBER(*,0), "Y" DATE, "Z" CLOB)
PCTFREE 10 PCTUSED 40
INITRANS 1 MAXTRANS 255
LOGGING STORAGE(INITIAL 32768 NEXT 32768
            MINEXTENTS 1 MAXEXTENTS 4096
            PCTINCREASE 0 FREELISTS 1 FREELIST GROUPS 1
            BUFFER_POOL DEFAULT
            )
TABLESPACE "TOOLS"
LOB ("Z") STORE AS (TABLESPACE "TOOLS"
            ENABLE STORAGE IN ROW CHUNK 8192
            PCTVERSION 10 NOCACHE
            STORAGE(INITIAL 32768 NEXT 32768
                MINEXTENTS 1 MAXEXTENTS 4096
                PCTINCREASE 0
                FREELISTS 1 FREELIST GROUPS 1
                BUFFER_POOL DEFAULT)) ;

ALTER TABLE "TKYTE"."T"
ADD PRIMARY KEY ("X")
USING INDEX
PCTFREE 10 INITRANS 2 MAXTRANS 255
STORAGE(INITIAL 32768 NEXT 32768
        MINEXTENTS 1 MAXEXTENTS 4096
        PCTINCREASE 0
        FREELISTS 1 FREELIST GROUPS 1
        BUFFER_POOL DEFAULT)
TABLESPACE "TOOLS" ENABLE ;
```

The nice thing about the above is that it shows many of the options for my CREATE TABLE statement. I just have to pick data types and such; Oracle will produce the verbose version for me. I can now customize this verbose version, perhaps changing the ENABLE STORAGE IN ROW to DISABLE STORAGE IN ROW – this would disable the stored of the LOB data in the row with the structured data, causing it to be stored in another segment. I use this trick myself all of the time to save the couple minutes of confusion I would otherwise have if I tried to figure this all out from the huge wire diagrams. I can also use this to learn what options are available to me on the CREATE TABLE statement under different circumstances.

This is how I figure out what is available to me as far as the syntax of the CREATE TABLE goes – in fact I use this trick on many objects. I'll have a small testing schema, create 'bare bones' objects in that schema, export using OWNER = THAT_SCHEMA, and do the import. A review of the generated SQL file shows me what is available.

Now that we know how to see most of the options available to us on a given CREATE TABLE statement, what are the important ones we need to be aware of for *heap* tables? In my opinion they are:

❑ **FREELISTS** – every table manages the blocks it has allocated in the heap on a FREELIST. A table may have more then one FREELIST. If you anticipate heavy insertion into a table by many users, configuring more then one FREELIST can make a major positive impact on performance (at the cost of possible additional storage). Refer to the previous discussion and example above (in the section *FREELISTS*) for the sort of impact this setting can have on performance.

❑ **PCTFREE** – a measure of how full a block can be made during the INSERT process. Once a block has less then the 'PCTFREE' space left on it, it will no longer be a candidate for insertion of new rows. This will be used to control row migrations caused by subsequent updates and needs to be set based on how you use the table.

❑ **PCTUSED** – a measure of how empty a block must become, before it can be a candidate for insertion again. A block that has less then PCTUSED space used is a candidate for insertion of new rows. Again, like PCTFREE, you must consider how you will be using your table in order to set this appropriately.

❑ **INITRANS** – the number of transaction slots initially allocated to a block. If set too low (defaults to 1) this can cause concurrency issues in a block that is accessed by many users. If a database block is nearly full and the transaction list cannot be dynamically expanded – sessions will queue up waiting for this block as each concurrent transaction needs a transaction slot. If you believe you will be having many concurrent updates to the same blocks, you should consider increasing this value

Note: LOB data that is stored out of line in the LOB segment does not make use of the PCTFREE/PCTUSED parameters set for the table. These LOB blocks are managed differently. They are always filled to capacity and returned to the FREELIST only when completely empty.

These are the parameters you want to pay particularly close attention to. I find that the rest of the storage parameters are simply not relevant any more. As I mentioned earlier in the chapter, we should use locally managed tablespaces, and these do not utilize the parameters PCTINCREASE, NEXT, and so on.

Index Organized Tables

Index organized tables (IOTs) are quite simply a table stored in an index structure. Whereas a table stored in a heap is randomly organized, data goes wherever there is available space, data in an IOT is stored and sorted by primary key. IOTs behave just like a 'regular' table does as far as your application is concerned; you use SQL to access it as normal. They are especially useful for information retrieval (IR), spatial, and OLAP applications.

What is the point of an IOT? One might ask the converse actually; what is the point of a heap-organized table? Since all tables in a relational database are supposed to have a primary key anyway, isn't a heap organized table just a waste of space? We have to make room for both the table and the index on the primary key of the table when using a heap organized table. With an IOT, the space overhead of the primary key index is removed, as the index is the data, the data is the index. Well, the fact is that an index is a complex data structure that requires a lot of work to manage and maintain. A heap on the other hand is trivial to manage by comparison. There are efficiencies in a heap-organized table over an IOT. That said, there are some definite advantages to IOTs over their counterpart the heap. For example, I remember once building an inverted list index on some textual data (this predated the introduction of interMedia and related technologies). I had a table full of documents. I would parse the documents and find words within the document. I had a table that then looked like this:

```
create table keywords
( word  varchar2(50),
  position  int,
  doc_id int,
  primary key(word,position,doc_id)
);
```

Here I had a table that consisted solely of columns of the primary key. I had over 100 percent overhead; the size of my table and primary key index were comparable (actually the primary key index was larger since it physically stored the row ID of the row it pointed to whereas a row ID is not stored in the table – it is inferred). I only used this table with a WHERE clause on the WORD or WORD and POSITION columns. That is, I never used the table; I only used the index on the table. The table itself was no more then overhead. I wanted to find all documents containing a given word (or 'near' another word and so on). The table was useless, it just slowed down the application during maintenance of the KEYWORDS table and doubled the storage requirements. This is a perfect application for an IOT.

Another implementation that begs for an IOT is a code lookup table. Here you might have ZIP_CODE to STATE lookup for example. You can now do away with the table and just use the IOT itself. Anytime you have a table, which you access via its primary key frequently it is a candidate for an IOT.

Another implementation that makes good use of IOTs is when you want to build your own indexing structure. For example, you may want to provide a case insensitive search for your application. You could use function-based indexes (see Chapter 7 on *Indexes* for details on what this is). However, this feature is available with Enterprise and Personal Editions of Oracle only. Suppose you have the Standard Edition, one way to provide a case insensitive, keyword search would be to 'roll your own' function-based index. For example, suppose you wanted to provide a case-insensitive search on the ENAME column of the EMP table. One approach would be to create another column, ENAME_UPPER, in the EMP table and index that column. This shadow column would be maintained via a trigger. If you didn't like the idea of having the extra column in the table, you can just create your own function-based index, with the following:

```
tkyte@TKYTE816> create table emp as select * from scott.emp;

Table created.

tkyte@TKYTE816> create table upper_ename
  2  ( x$ename, x$rid,
  3    primary key (x$ename,x$rid)
  4  )
  5  organization index
  6  as
  7  select upper(ename), rowid from emp
  8  /
Table created.

tkyte@TKYTE816> create or replace trigger upper_ename
  2  after insert or update or delete on emp
  3  for each row
  4  begin
  5      if (updating and (:old.ename||'x' <> :new.ename||'x'))
  6      then
  7          delete from upper_ename
  8            where x$ename = upper(:old.ename)
  9              and x$rid = :old.rowid;
 10
 11          insert into upper_ename
 12          (x$ename,x$rid) values
 13          ( upper(:new.ename), :new.rowid );
 14      elsif (inserting)
 15      then
 16          insert into upper_ename
```

```
17              (x$ename,x$rid) values
18            ( upper(:new.ename), :new.rowid );
19        elsif (deleting)
20        then
21            delete from upper_ename
22             where x$ename = upper(:old.ename)
23               and x$rid = :old.rowid;
24        end if;
25   end;
26   /

Trigger created.

tkyte@TKYTE816> update emp set ename = initcap(ename);

14 rows updated.

tkyte@TKYTE816> commit;

Commit complete.
```

Now, the table UPPER_ENAME is in effect our case-insensitive index, much like a function-based index would be. We must explicitly use this 'index', Oracle doesn't know about it. The following shows how you might use this 'index' to UPDATE, SELECT, and DELETE data from the table:

```
tkyte@TKYTE816> update
  2  (
  3  select ename, sal
  4    from emp
  5   where emp.rowid in ( select upper_ename.x$rid
  6                          from upper_ename
  7                         where x$ename = 'KING' )
  8  )
  9  set sal = 1234
 10  /

1 row updated.
tkyte@TKYTE816> select ename, empno, sal
  2    from emp, upper_ename
  3   where emp.rowid = upper_ename.x$rid
  4     and upper_ename.x$ename = 'KING'
  5  /

ENAME          EMPNO      SAL
---------- ---------- ----------
King            7839     1234

tkyte@TKYTE816> delete from
  2  (
  3  select ename, empno
  4    from emp
  5   where emp.rowid in ( select upper_ename.x$rid
  6                          from upper_ename
  7                         where x$ename = 'KING' )
  8  )
  9  /

1 row deleted.
```

We can either use an IN or a JOIN when selecting. Due to 'key preservation' rules, we must use the IN when updating or deleting. A side note on this method, since it involves storing a row ID: our index organized table, as would any index, must be rebuilt if we do something that causes the row IDs of the EMP table to change – such as exporting and importing EMP or using the ALTER TABLE MOVE command on it.

Finally, when you want to enforce co-location of data or you want data to be physically stored in a specific order, the IOT is the structure for you. For users of Sybase and SQL Server, this is when you would have used a clustered index, but it goes one better. A clustered index in those databases may have up to a 110 percent overhead (similar to my KEYWORDS table example above). Here, we have a 0 percent overhead since the data is stored only once. A classic example of when you might want this physically co-located data would be in a parent/child relationship. Let's say the EMP table had a child table:

```
tkyte@TKYTE816> create table addresses
  2  ( empno      number(4) references emp(empno) on delete cascade,
  3    addr_type  varchar2(10),
  4    street     varchar2(20),
  5    city       varchar2(20),
  6    state      varchar2(2),
  7    zip        number,
  8    primary key (empno,addr_type)
  9  )
 10  ORGANIZATION INDEX
 11  /

Table created.
```

Having all of the addresses for an employee (their home address, work address, school address, previous address, and so on) physically located near each other will reduce the amount of I/O you might other wise have to perform when joining EMP to ADDRESSES. The logical I/O would be the same, the physical I/O could be significantly less. In a heap organized table, each employee address might be in a physically different database block from any other address for that employee. By storing the addresses organized by EMPNO and ADDR_TYPE – we've ensured that all addresses for a given employee are 'near' each other.

The same would be true if you frequently use BETWEEN queries on a primary or unique key. Having the data stored physically sorted will increase the performance of those queries as well. For example, I maintain a table of stock quotes in my database. Every day we gather together the stock ticker, date, closing price, days high, days low, volume, and other related information. We do this for hundreds of stocks. This table looks like:

```
tkyte@TKYTE816> create table stocks
  2  ( ticker     varchar2(10),
  3    day        date,
  4    value      number,
  5    change     number,
  6    high       number,
  7    low        number,
  8    vol        number,
  9    primary key(ticker,day)
 10  )
 11  organization index
 12  /

Table created.
```

We frequently look at one stock at a time – for some range of days (computing a moving average for example). If we were to use a heap organized table, the probability of two rows for the stock ticker ORCL existing on the same database block are almost zero. This is because every night, we insert the records for the day for all of the stocks. That fills up at least one database block (actually many of them). Therefore, every day we add a new ORCL record but it is on a block different from every other ORCL record already in the table. If we query:

```
Select * from stocks
  where ticker = 'ORCL'
    and day between sysdate and sysdate - 100;
```

Oracle would read the index and then perform table access by row ID to get the rest of the row data. Each of the 100 rows we retrieve would be on a different database block due to the way we load the table – each would probably be a physical I/O. Now consider that we have this in an IOT. That same query only needs to read the relevant index blocks and it already has all of the data. Not only is the table access removed but all of the rows for ORCL in a given range of dates are physically stored 'near' each other as well. Less logical I/O and less physical I/O is incurred.

Now we understand when we might want to use index organized tables and how to use them. What we need to understand next is what are the options with these tables? What are the caveats? The options are very similar to the options for a heap-organized table. Once again, we'll use EXP/IMP to show us the details. If we start with the three basic variations of the index organized table:

```
tkyte@TKYTE816> create table t1
  2  (  x int primary key,
  3     y varchar2(25),
  4     z date
  5  )
  6  organization index;

Table created.

tkyte@TKYTE816> create table t2
  2  (  x int primary key,
  3     y varchar2(25),
  4     z date
  5  )
  6  organization index
  7  OVERFLOW;

Table created.

tkyte@TKYTE816> create table t3
  2  (  x int primary key,
  3     y varchar2(25),
  4     z date
  5  )
  6  organization index
  7  overflow INCLUDING y;

Table created.
```

We'll get into what OVERFLOW and INCLUDING do for us but first, let's look at the detailed SQL required for the first table above:

```
CREATE TABLE "TKYTE"."T1"
("X" NUMBER(*,0),
 "Y" VARCHAR2(25),
 "Z" DATE,
 PRIMARY KEY ("X") ENABLE
)
ORGANIZATION INDEX
NOCOMPRESS
PCTFREE 10
INITRANS 2 MAXTRANS 255
LOGGING
STORAGE ( INITIAL 32768
          NEXT 32768
          MINEXTENTS 1 MAXEXTENTS 4096
          PCTINCREASE 0
          FREELISTS 1
          FREELIST GROUPS 1
          BUFFER_POOL DEFAULT
        )
TABLESPACE "TOOLS"
PCTTHRESHOLD 50 ;
```

It introduces two new options, NOCOMPRESS and PCTTHRESHOLD, we'll take a look at those in a moment. You might have noticed that something is missing from the above CREATE TABLE syntax; there is no PCTUSED clause but there is a PCTFREE. This is because an index is a complex data structure, not randomly organized like a heap; data must go where it 'belongs'. Unlike a heap where blocks are sometimes available for inserts, blocks are always available for new entries in an index. If the data belongs on a given block because of its values, it will go there regardless of how full or empty the block is. Additionally, PCTFREE is used only when the object is created and populated with data in an index structure. It is not used like it is used in the heap-organized table. PCTFREE will reserve space on a newly created index, but not for subsequent operations on it for much the same reason as why PCTUSED is not used at all. The same considerations for FREELISTs we had on heap organized tables apply in whole to IOTs.

Now, onto the newly discovered option NOCOMPRESS. This is an option available to indexes in general. It tells Oracle to store each and every value in an index entry (do not compress). If the primary key of the object was on columns A, B, and C, every combination of A, B, and C would physically be stored. The converse to NOCOMPRESS is COMPRESS N where N is an integer, which represents the number of columns to compress. What this does is remove repeating values, factors them out at the block level, so that the values of A and perhaps B that repeat over and over are no longer physically stored. Consider for example a table created like this:

```
tkyte@TKYTE816> create table iot
  2  ( owner, object_type, object_name,
  3    primary key(owner,object_type,object_name)
  4  )
  5  organization index
  6  NOCOMPRESS
  7  as
  8  select owner, object_type, object_name from all_objects
  9  /

Table created.
```

It you think about it, the value of OWNER is repeated many hundreds of times. Each schema (OWNER) tends to own lots of objects. Even the value pair of OWNER, OBJECT_TYPE repeats many times; a given schema will have dozens of tables, dozens of packages, and so on. Only all three columns together do not repeat. We can have Oracle suppress these repeating values. Instead of having an index block with values:

Sys,table,t1	Sys,table,t2	Sys,table,t3	Sys,table,t4
Sys,table,t5	Sys,table,t6	Sys,table,t7	Sys,table,t8
…	…	…	…
Sys,table,t100	Sys,table,t101	Sys,table,t102	Sys,table,t103

We could use COMPRESS 2 (factor out the leading two columns) and have a block with:

Sys,table	t1	t2	t3
t4	t5	…	…
…	t103	t104	…
t300	t301	t302	t303

That is, the values SYS and TABLE appear once and then the third column is stored. In this fashion, we can get many more entries per index block than we could otherwise. This does not decrease concurrency or functionality at all. It takes slightly more CPU horsepower, Oracle has to do more work to put together the keys again. On the other hand, it may significantly reduce I/O and allows more data to be cached in the buffer cache – since we get more data per block. That is a pretty good trade off. We'll demonstrate the savings by doing a quick test of the above CREATE TABLE as SELECT with NOCOMPRESS, COMPRESS 1, and COMPRESS 2. We'll start with a procedure that shows us the space utilization of an IOT easily:

```
tkyte@TKYTE816> create or replace
  2  procedure show_iot_space
  3  ( p_segname in varchar2 )
  4  as
  5      l_segname              varchar2(30);
  6      l_total_blocks         number;
  7      l_total_bytes          number;
  8      l_unused_blocks        number;
  9      l_unused_bytes         number;
 10      l_LastUsedExtFileId    number;
 11      l_LastUsedExtBlockId   number;
 12      l_last_used_block      number;
 13  begin
 14      select 'SYS_IOT_TOP_' || object_id
 15        into l_segname
 16        from user_objects
 17       where object_name = upper(p_segname);
 18
 19      dbms_space.unused_space
 20      ( segment_owner      => user,
 21        segment_name       => l_segname,
```

```
22          segment_type        => 'INDEX',
23          total_blocks        => l_total_blocks,
24          total_bytes         => l_total_bytes,
25          unused_blocks       => l_unused_blocks,
26          unused_bytes        => l_unused_bytes,
27          LAST_USED_EXTENT_FILE_ID => l_LastUsedExtFileId,
28          LAST_USED_EXTENT_BLOCK_ID => l_LastUsedExtBlockId,
29          LAST_USED_BLOCK => l_last_used_block );
30
31      dbms_output.put_line
32      ( 'IOT used ' || to_char(l_total_blocks-l_unused_blocks) );
33  end;
34  /

Procedure created.
```

And now we'll create our IOT without compression:

```
tkyte@TKYTE816> create table iot
  2  ( owner, object_type, object_name,
  3    primary key(owner,object_type,object_name)
  4  )
  5  organization index
  6  NOCOMPRESS
  7  as
  8  select owner, object_type, object_name from all_objects
  9  order by owner, object_type, object_name
 10  /

Table created.

tkyte@TKYTE816> set serveroutput on
tkyte@TKYTE816> exec show_iot_space( 'iot' );
IOT used 135

PL/SQL procedure successfully completed.
```

If you are working these examples as we go along, I would expect that you see a different number, something other than 135. It will be dependent on your block size and the number of objects in your data dictionary. We would expect this number to decrease however in the next example:

```
tkyte@TKYTE816> create table iot
  2  ( owner, object_type, object_name,
  3    primary key(owner,object_type,object_name)
  4  )
  5  organization index
  6  compress 1
  7  as
  8  select owner, object_type, object_name from all_objects
  9  order by owner, object_type, object_name
 10  /

Table created.
```

```
tkyte@TKYTE816> exec show_iot_space( 'iot' );
IOT used 119

PL/SQL procedure successfully completed.
```

So that IOT is about 12 percent smaller then the first one; we can do better by compressing it even more:

```
tkyte@TKYTE816> create table iot
  2  ( owner, object_type, object_name,
  3    primary key(owner,object_type,object_name)
  4  )
  5  organization index
  6  compress 2
  7  as
  8  select owner, object_type, object_name from all_objects
  9  order by owner, object_type, object_name
 10  /

Table created.

tkyte@TKYTE816> exec show_iot_space( 'iot' );
IOT used 91

PL/SQL procedure successfully completed.
```

The COMPRESS 2 index is about a third smaller then the uncompressed IOT. Your mileage will vary but the results can be fantastic.

The above example points out an interesting fact with IOTs. They are tables, but only in name. Their segment is truly an index segment. In order to show the space utilization I had to convert the IOT table name into its underlying index name. In these examples, I allowed the underlying index name be generated for me; it defaults to SYS_IOT_TOP_<object_id> where OBJECT_ID is the internal object id assigned to the table. If I did not want these generated names cluttering my data dictionary, I can easily name them:

```
tkyte@TKYTE816> create table iot
  2  ( owner, object_type, object_name,
  3    constraint iot_pk primary key(owner,object_type,object_name)
  4  )
  5  organization index
  6  compress 2
  7  as
  8  select owner, object_type, object_name from all_objects
  9  /

Table created.
```

Normally, it is considered a good practice to name your objects explicitly like this. It typically provides more meaning to the actual use of the object than a name like SYS_IOT_TOP_1234 does.

I am going to defer discussion of the PCTTHRESHOLD option at this point as it is related to the next two options for IOTs; OVERFLOW and INCLUDING. If we look at the full SQL for the next two sets of tables T2 and T3, we see the following:

```
CREATE TABLE "TKYTE"."T2"
("X" NUMBER(*,0),
 "Y" VARCHAR2(25),
 "Z" DATE,
 PRIMARY KEY ("X") ENABLE
)
ORGANIZATION INDEX
NOCOMPRESS
PCTFREE 10
INITRANS 2 MAXTRANS 255
LOGGING
STORAGE ( INITIAL 32768 NEXT 32768 MINEXTENTS 1 MAXEXTENTS 4096
         PCTINCREASE 0 FREELISTS 1 FREELIST GROUPS 1 BUFFER_POOL DEFAULT )
TABLESPACE "TOOLS"
PCTTHRESHOLD 50
OVERFLOW
        PCTFREE 10
                   PCTUSED 40
        INITRANS 1
        MAXTRANS 255
        LOGGING
        STORAGE ( INITIAL 32768 NEXT 32768 MINEXTENTS 1 MAXEXTENTS 4096
                 PCTINCREASE 0 FREELISTS 1 FREELIST GROUPS 1
                 BUFFER_POOL DEFAULT )
TABLESPACE "TOOLS" ;
CREATE TABLE
"TKYTE"."T3"
("X" NUMBER(*,0),
 "Y" VARCHAR2(25),
 "Z" DATE,
 PRIMARY KEY ("X") ENABLE
)
ORGANIZATION INDEX
NOCOMPRESS
PCTFREE 10
INITRANS 2
MAXTRANS 255
LOGGING
STORAGE(INITIAL 32768 NEXT 32768 MINEXTENTS 1 MAXEXTENTS 4096
        PCTINCREASE 0 FREELISTS 1 FREELIST GROUPS 1 BUFFER_POOL DEFAULT )
TABLESPACE "TOOLS"
PCTTHRESHOLD 50
INCLUDING "Y"
OVERFLOW PCTFREE 10 PCTUSED 40 INITRANS 1 MAXTRANS 255 LOGGING
        STORAGE ( INITIAL 32768 NEXT 32768 MINEXTENTS 1 MAXEXTENTS 4096
                 PCTINCREASE 0 FREELISTS 1 FREELIST GROUPS 1
                 BUFFER_POOL DEFAULT )
TABLESPACE "TOOLS" ;
```

So, now we have PCTTHRESHOLD, OVERFLOW, and INCLUDING left to discuss. These three items are intertwined with each other and their goal is to make the index leaf blocks (the blocks that hold the actual index data) able to efficiently store data. An index typically is on a subset of columns. You will generally find many more times the number of rows on an index block than you would on a heap table block. An index counts on being able to get many rows per block, Oracle would spend large amounts of time maintaining an index otherwise, as each INSERT or UPDATE would probably cause an index block to split in order to accommodate the new data.

The OVERFLOW clause allows you to setup another segment where the row data for the IOT can overflow onto when it gets too large. Notice that an OVERFLOW reintroduces the PCTUSED clause to an IOT. PCTFREE and PCTUSED have the same meanings for an OVERFLOW segment as they did for a heap table. The conditions for using an overflow segment can be specified in one of two ways:

- ❑ PCTTHRESHOLD – When the amount of data in the row exceeds that percentage of the block, the trailing columns of that row will be stored in the overflow. So, if PCTTHRESHOLD was 10 percent and your block size was 8 KB, any row that was greater then about 800 bytes in length would have part of it stored elsewhere – off the index block.

- ❑ INCLUDING – All of the columns in the row up to and including the one specified in the INCLUDING clause, are stored on the index block, the remaining columns are stored in the overflow.

Given the following table with a 2 KB block size:

```
ops$tkyte@ORA8I.WORLD> create table iot
  2  ( x      int,
  3    y      date,
  4    z      varchar2(2000),
  5    constraint iot_pk primary key (x)
  6  )
  7  organization index
  8  pctthreshold 10
  9  overflow
 10  /

Table created.
```

Graphically, it could look like this:

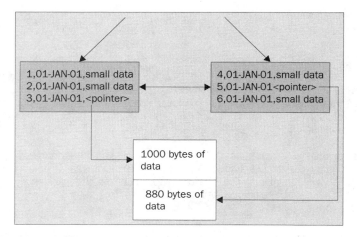

The gray boxes are the index entries, part of a larger index structure (in the Chapter 7 on *Indexes*, you'll see a larger picture of what an index looks like). Briefly, the index structure is a tree, and the leaf blocks (where the data is stored), are in effect a doubly-linked list to make it easier to traverse the nodes in order once you have found where you want to start at in the index. The white box represents an OVERFLOW segment. This is where data that exceeds our PCTTHRESHOLD setting will be stored. Oracle will work backwards from the last column up to but not including the last column of the primary key to find out what columns need to be stored in the overflow segment. In this example, the number column X and the date column Y will always fit in the index block. The last column, Z, is of varying length. When it is less than about 190 bytes or so (10 percent of a 2 KB block is about 200 bytes, add in 7 bytes for the date and 3 to 5 for the number), it will be stored on the index block. When it exceeds 190 bytes, Oracle will store the data for Z in the overflow segment and set up a pointer to it.

The other option is to use the INCLUDING clause. Here you are stating explicitly what columns you want stored on the index block and which should be stored in the overflow. Given a create table like this:

```
ops$tkyte@ORA8I.WORLD> create table iot
  2  ( x       int,
  3    y       date,
  4    z       varchar2(2000),
  5    constraint iot_pk primary key (x)
  6  )
  7  organization index
  8  including y
  9  overflow
 10  /

Table created.
```

We can expect to find:

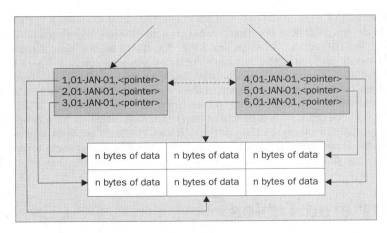

In this situation, regardless of the size of the data stored in it, Z will be stored 'out of line' in the overflow segment.

Which is better then, PCTTHRESHOLD, INCLUDING, or some combination of both? It depends on your needs. If you have an application that always, or almost always, uses the first four columns of a table, and rarely accesses the last five columns, this sounds like an application for using INCLUDING. You would include up to the fourth column and let the other five be stored out of line. At runtime, if you need them, they will be retrieved in much the same way as a migrated or chained row would be. Oracle will read the 'head' of the row, find the pointer to the rest of the row, and then read that. If on the other hand, you cannot say that you almost always access these columns and hardly ever access those columns, you would be giving some consideration to PCTTHRESHOLD. Setting the PCTTHRESHOLD is easy once you determine the number of rows you would like to store per index block on average. Suppose you wanted 20 rows per index block. Well, that means each row should be 1/20th (5 percent) then. Your PCTTHRESHOLD would be five; each chunk of the row that stays on the index leaf block should consume no more then 5 percent of the block.

The last thing to consider with IOTs is indexing. You can have an index *on* an index, as long as the primary index is an IOT. These are called **secondary indexes**. Normally an index contains the physical address of the row it points to, the row ID. An IOT secondary index cannot do this; it must use some other way to address the row. This is because a row in an IOT can move around a lot and it does not 'migrate' in the way a row in a heap organized table would. A row in an IOT is expected to be at some position in the index structure, based on its primary key; it will only be moving because the size and shape of the index itself is changing. In order to accommodate this, Oracle introduced a logical row ID. These logical row IDs are based on the IOT's primary key. They may also contain a 'guess' as to the current location of the row (although this guess is almost always wrong after a short while, data in an IOT tends to move). An index on an IOT is slightly less efficient then an index on a regular table. On a regular table, an index access typically requires the I/O to scan the index structure and then a single read to read the table data. With an IOT there are typically two scans performed, one on the secondary structure and the other on the IOT itself. That aside, indexes on IOTs provide fast and efficient access to the data in the IOT using columns other then the primary key.

Index Organized Tables Wrap-up

Getting the right mix of data on the index block versus data in the overflow segment is the most critical part of the IOT set up. Benchmark various scenarios with different overflow conditions. See how it will affect your INSERTs, UPDATEs, DELETEs, and SELECTs. If you have a structure that is built once and read frequently, stuff as much of the data onto the index block as you can. If you frequently modify the structure, you will have to come to some balance between having all of the data on the index block (great for retrieval) versus reorganizing data in the index frequently (bad for modifications). The FREELIST consideration you had for heap tables applies to IOTs as well. PCTFREE and PCTUSED play two roles in an IOT. PCTFREE is not nearly as important for an IOT as for a heap table and PCTUSED doesn't come into play normally. When considering an OVERFLOW segment however, PCTFREE and PCTUSED have the same interpretation as they did for a heap table; set them for an overflow segment using the same logic you would for a heap table.

Index Clustered Tables

I generally find peoples understanding of what a cluster is in Oracle to be inaccurate. Many people tend to confuse this with a SQL Server or Sybase 'clustered index'. They are not. A cluster is a way to store a group of tables that share some common column(s) in the same database blocks and to store related data together on the same block. A clustered index in SQL Server forces the rows to be stored in sorted order according to the index key, they are similar to an IOT described above. With a cluster, a single block of data may contain data from many tables. Conceptually, you are storing the data 'pre-joined'. It can also be used with single tables. Now you are storing data together grouped by some column. For example, all of the employees in department 10 will be stored on the same block (or as few blocks as possible, if they all don't fit). It is not storing the data sorted – that is the role of the IOT. It is storing the data clustered by some key, but in a heap. So, department 100 might be right next to department 1, and very far away (physically on disk) from departments 101 and 99.

Graphically, you might think of it as I have depicted below. On the left-hand side we are using conventional tables. EMP will be stored in its segment. DEPT will be stored on its own. They may be in different files, different tablespaces, and are definitely in separate extents. On the right-hand side, we see what would happen if we clustered these two tables together. The square boxes represent database blocks. We now have the value 10 factored out and stored once. Then, all of the data from all of the tables in the cluster for department 10 is stored in that block. If all of the data for department 10 does not fit on the block, then additional blocks will be chained to the original block to contain the overflow, very much in the same fashion as the overflow blocks for an IOT:

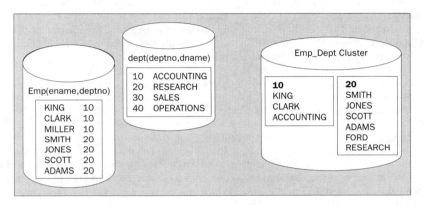

So, let's look at how you might go about creating a clustered object. Creating a cluster of tables in it is straightforward. The definition of the storage of the object (PCTFREE, PCTUSED, INITIAL, and so on) is associated with the CLUSTER, not the tables. This makes sense since there will be many tables in the cluster, and they each will be on the same block. Having different PCTFREEs would not make sense. Therefore, a CREATE CLUSTER looks a lot like a CREATE TABLE with a small number of columns (just the cluster key columns):

```
tkyte@TKYTE816> create cluster emp_dept_cluster
  2  ( deptno number(2) )
  3  size 1024
  4  /

Cluster created.
```

Here we have created an index cluster (the other type being a hash cluster; we'll look at that below). The clustering column for this cluster will be the DEPTNO column, the columns in the tables do not have to be called DEPTNO, but they *must* be a NUMBER(2), to match this definition. I have, on the cluster definition, a SIZE 1024 option. This is used to tell Oracle that we expect about 1,024 bytes of data to be associated with each cluster key value. Oracle will use that to compute the *maximum* number of cluster keys that could fit per block. Given that I have an 8 KB block size, Oracle will fit up to seven cluster keys (but maybe less if the data is larger then expected) per database block. This is, the data for the departments 10, 20, 30, 40, 50, 60, 70 would tend to go onto one block, as soon as you insert department 80 a new block will be used. That does not mean that the data is stored in a sorted manner, it just means that if you inserted the departments in that order, they would naturally tend to be put together. If you inserted the departments in the following order: 10, 80, 20, 30, 40, 50, 60, and then 70, the final department, 70, would tend to be on the newly added block. As we'll see below, both the size of the data and the order in which the data is inserted will affect the number of keys we can store per block.

The size parameter therefore controls the maximum number of cluster keys per block. It is the single largest influence on the space utilization of your cluster. Set the size too high and you'll get very few keys per block and you'll use more space then you need. Set the size too low and you'll get excessive chaining of data, which offsets the purpose of the cluster to store all of the data together on a single block. It is the important parameter for a cluster.

Now, for the cluster index on our cluster. We need to index the cluster before we can put data in it. We could create tables in the cluster right now, but I am going to create and populate the tables simultaneously and we need a cluster index *before* we can have any data. The cluster index's job is to take a cluster key value and return the block address of the block that contains that key. It is a primary key in effect where each cluster key value points to a single block in the cluster itself. So, when you ask for the data in department 10, Oracle will read the cluster key, determine the block address for that and then read the data. The cluster key index is created as follows:

```
tkyte@TKYTE816> create index emp_dept_cluster_idx
  2  on cluster emp_dept_cluster
  3  /

Index created.
```

It can have all of the normal storage parameters of an index and can be stored in another tablespace. It is just a regular index, one that happens to index into a cluster and can also include an entry for a completely null value (see Chapter 7 on *Indexes* for the reason why this is interesting to note). Now we are ready to create our tables in the cluster:

```
tkyte@TKYTE816> create table dept
  2  ( deptno number(2) primary key,
  3    dname  varchar2(14),
  4    loc       varchar2(13)
  5  )
  6  cluster emp_dept_cluster(deptno)
  7  /

Table created.

tkyte@TKYTE816> create table emp
  2  ( empno number primary key,
  3    ename varchar2(10),
  4    job       varchar2(9),
  5    mgr       number,
  6    hiredate date,
  7    sal       number,
  8    comm      number,
  9    deptno number(2) references dept(deptno)
 10  )
 11  cluster emp_dept_cluster(deptno)
 12  /

Table created.
```

Here the only difference from a 'normal' table is that I used the CLUSTER keyword and told Oracle which column of the base table will map to the cluster key in the cluster itself. We can now load them up with the initial set of data:

```
tkyte@TKYTE816> begin
  2          for x in ( select * from scott.dept )
  3          loop
  4                  insert into dept
  5                  values ( x.deptno, x.dname, x.loc );
  6                  insert into emp
  7                  select *
  8                     from scott.emp
  9                    where deptno = x.deptno;
 10          end loop;
 11  end;
 12  /

PL/SQL procedure successfully completed.
```

You might be asking yourself 'Why didn't we just insert all of the DEPT data and then all of the EMP data or vice-versa, why did we load the data DEPTNO by DEPTNO like that?' The reason is in the design of the cluster. I was simulating a large, initial bulk load of a cluster. If I had loaded all of the DEPT rows first – we definitely would have gotten our 7 keys per block (based on the SIZE 1024 setting we made) since the DEPT rows are very small, just a couple of bytes. When it came time to load up the EMP rows, we might have found that some of the departments had many more than 1,024 bytes of data. This would cause excessive chaining on those cluster key blocks. By loading all of the data for a given cluster key at the same time, we pack the blocks as tightly as possible and start a new block when we run out of room. Instead of Oracle putting up to seven cluster key values per block, it will put as many as can fit. A quick example will show the difference between the two approaches. What I will do is add a large column to the EMP table; a CHAR(1000). This column will be used to make the EMP rows much larger then they are now. We will load the cluster tables in two ways – once we'll load up DEPT and then load up EMP. The second time we'll load by department number – a DEPT row and then all the EMP rows that go with it and then the next DEPT. We'll look at the blocks each row ends up on, in the given case, to see which one best achieves the goal of co-locating the data by DEPTNO. In this example, our EMP table looks like:

```
create table emp
( empno number primary key,
  ename varchar2(10),
  job   varchar2(9),
  mgr   number,
  hiredate date,
  sal   number,
  comm  number,
  deptno number(2) references dept(deptno),
  data   char(1000) default '*'
)
cluster emp_dept_cluster(deptno)
/
```

When we load the data into the DEPT and the EMP tables we see that many of the EMP rows are not on the same block as the DEPT row anymore (DBMS_ROWID is a supplied package useful for peeking at the contents of a row ID):

```
tkyte@TKYTE816> insert into dept
  2  select * from scott.dept
  3  /

4 rows created.
```

```
tkyte@TKYTE816> insert into emp
  2  select emp.*, '*' from scott.emp
  3  /

14 rows created.

tkyte@TKYTE816> select dbms_rowid.rowid_block_number(dept.rowid) dept_rid,
  2            dbms_rowid.rowid_block_number(emp.rowid) emp_rid,
  3                dept.deptno
  4    from emp, dept
  5    where emp.deptno = dept.deptno
  6  /

  DEPT_RID    EMP_RID DEPTNO
---------- ---------- ------
        10         12     10
        10         11     10
        10         11     10
        10         10     20
        10         10     20
        10         12     20
        10         11     20
        10         11     20
        10         10     30
        10         10     30
        10         10     30
        10         10     30
        10         11     30
        10         11     30

14 rows selected.
```

More then half of the EMP rows are not on the block with the DEPT row. Loading the data using the cluster key instead of the table key, we get:

```
tkyte@TKYTE816> begin
  2      for x in ( select * from scott.dept )
  3      loop
  4          insert into dept
  5          values ( x.deptno, x.dname, x.loc );
  6          insert into emp
  7          select emp.*, 'x'
  8            from scott.emp
  9           where deptno = x.deptno;
 10      end loop;
 11  end;
 12  /

PL/SQL procedure successfully completed.

tkyte@TKYTE816> select dbms_rowid.rowid_block_number(dept.rowid) dept_rid,
  2            dbms_rowid.rowid_block_number(emp.rowid) emp_rid,
  3                dept.deptno
```

```
4    from emp, dept
5    where emp.deptno = dept.deptno
6    /

DEPT_RID     EMP_RID DEPTNO
---------- ---------- ------
        11         11     30
        11         11     30
        11         11     30
        11         11     30
        11         11     30
        11         11     30
        12         12     10
        12         12     10
        12         12     10
        12         12     20
        12         12     20
        12         12     20
        12         10     20
        12         10     20

14 rows selected.
```

Most of the EMP rows are on the same block as the DEPT rows are. This example was somewhat contrived in that I woefully undersized the SIZE parameter on the cluster to make a point, but the approach suggested is correct for an initial load of a cluster. It will ensure that if for some of the cluster keys you exceed the estimated SIZE, you will still end up with most of the data clustered on the same block. If you load a table at a time, you will not.

This only applies to the initial load of a cluster – after that, you would use it as your transactions deem necessary, you will not adapt you application to work specifically with a cluster.

Here is a bit of puzzle to amaze and astound your friends with. Many people mistakenly believe a row ID uniquely identifies a row in a database, that given a row ID I can tell you what table the row came from. In fact, *you cannot.* You can and will get duplicate row IDs from a cluster. For example, after executing the above you should find:

```
tkyte@TKYTE816> select rowid from emp
  2  intersect
  3  select rowid from dept;

ROWID
------------------
AAAGB0AAFAAAAJyAAA
AAAGB0AAFAAAAJyAAB
AAAGB0AAFAAAAJyAAC
AAAGB0AAFAAAAJyAAD
```

Every row ID assigned to the rows in DEPT has been assigned to the rows in EMP as well. That is because it takes a table *and* row ID to uniquely identify a row. The row ID pseudo column is unique only within a table.

I also find that many people believe the cluster object to be an esoteric object that no one really uses. Everyone just uses normal tables. The fact is, that you use clusters every time you use Oracle. Much of the data dictionary is stored in various clusters. For example:

```
sys@TKYTE816> select cluster_name, table_name from user_tables
  2  where cluster_name is not null
  3  order by 1
  4  /

CLUSTER_NAME                     TABLE_NAME
------------------------------   ------------------------------
C_COBJ#                          CCOL$
                                 CDEF$
C_FILE#_BLOCK#                   SEG$
                                 UET$
C_MLOG#                          MLOG$
                                 SLOG$
C_OBJ#                           ATTRCOL$
                                 COL$
                                 COLTYPE$
                                 CLU$
                                 ICOLDEP$
                                 LIBRARY$
                                 LOB$
                                 VIEWTRCOL$
                                 TYPE_MISC$
                                 TAB$
                                 REFCON$
                                 NTAB$
                                 IND$
                                 ICOL$
C_OBJ#_INTCOL#                   HISTGRM$
C_RG#                            RGCHILD$
                                 RGROUP$
C_TOID_VERSION#                  ATTRIBUTE$
                                 COLLECTION$
                                 METHOD$
                                 RESULT$
                                 TYPE$
                                 PARAMETER$
C_TS#                            FET$
                                 TS$
C_USER#                          TSQ$
                                 USER$

33 rows selected.
```

As can be seen, most of the object related data is stored in a single cluster (the C_OBJ# cluster), 14 tables all together sharing the same block. It is mostly column-related information stored there, so all of the information about the set of columns of a table or index is stored physically on the same block. This makes sense; when Oracle parses a query, it wants to have access to the data for all of the columns in the referenced table. If this data was spread all over the place, it would take a while to get it together. Here it is on a single block typically, and readily available.

When would you use a cluster? It is easier perhaps to describe when not to use them:

❑ Clusters may negatively impact the performance of DML – If you anticipate the tables in the cluster to be modified heavily, you must be aware that an index cluster will have certain negative performance side effects. It takes more work to manage the data in a cluster.

- ❑ Full scans of tables in clusters are affected – Instead of just having to full scan the data in your table, you have to full scan the data for (possibly) many tables. There is more data to scan through. Full scans will take longer.

- ❑ If you believe you will frequently need to TRUNCATE and load the table – Tables in clusters cannot be truncated, that is obvious since the cluster stores more then one table on a block, we must delete the rows in a cluster table.

So, if you have data that is mostly read (that does *not* mean 'never written', it is perfectly OK to modify cluster tables) and read via indexes, either the cluster key index or other indexes you put on the tables in the cluster, and join this information together frequently, a cluster would be appropriate. Look for tables that are logically related and always used together, like the people who designed the Oracle data dictionary when they clustered all column-related information together.

Index Clustered Tables Wrap-up

Clustered tables give you the ability to physically 'pre-join' data together. You use clusters to store related data from many tables on the same database block. Clusters can help read intensive operations that always join data together or access related sets of data (for example, everyone in department 10). They will reduce the number of blocks that Oracle must cache; instead of keeping 10 blocks for 10 employees in the same department, they will be put in one block and therefore would increase the efficiency of your buffer cache. On the downside, unless you can calculate your SIZE parameter setting correctly, clusters may be inefficient with their space utilization and can tend to slow down DML heavy operations.

Hash Cluster Tables

Hash clustered tables are very similar in concept to the index cluster described above with one main exception. The cluster key index is replaced with a hash function. The data in the table is the index, there is no physical index. Oracle will take the key value for a row, hash it using either an internal function or one you supply, and use that to figure out where the data should be on disk. One side effect of using a hashing algorithm to locate data however, is that you cannot range scan a table in a hash cluster without adding a conventional index to the table. In an index cluster above, the query:

```
select * from emp where deptno between 10 and 20
```

would be able to make use of the cluster key index to find these rows. In a hash cluster, this query would result in a full table scan unless you had an index on the DEPTNO column. Only exact equality searches may be made on the hash key without using an index that supports range scans.

In a perfect world, with little to no collisions in the hashing algorithm, a hash cluster will mean we can go straight from a query to the data with one I/O. In the real world, there will most likely be collisions and row chaining periodically, meaning we'll need more then one I/O to retrieve some of the data.

Like a hash table in a programming language, hash tables in the database have a fixed 'size'. When you create the table, you must determine the number of hash keys your table will have, forever. That does not limit the amount of rows you can put in there.

Below, we can see a graphical representation of a hash cluster with table EMP created in it. When the client issues a query that uses the hash cluster key in the predicate, Oracle will apply the hash function to determine which block the data should be in. It will then read that one block to find the data. If there have been many collisions or the SIZE parameter to the CREATE CLUSTER was underestimated, Oracle will have allocated overflow blocks that are chained off of the original block.

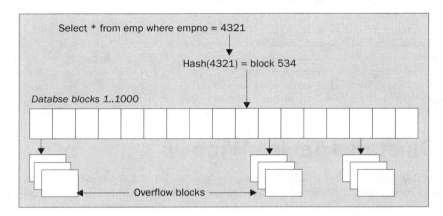

When you create a hash cluster, you will use the same CREATE CLUSTER statement you used to create the index cluster with different options. We'll just be adding a HASHKEYs option to it to specify the size of the hash table. Oracle will take your HASHKEYS values and round it up to the nearest prime number, the number of hash keys will always be a prime. Oracle will then compute a value based on the SIZE parameter multiplied by the modified HASHKEYS value. It will then allocate at least that much space in bytes for the cluster. This is a big difference from the index cluster above, which dynamically allocates space, as it needs it. A hash cluster pre-allocates enough space to hold (HASHKEYS/trunc(blocksize/SIZE)) bytes of data. So for example, if you set your SIZE to 1,500 bytes and you have a 4 KB block size, Oracle will expect to store 2 keys per block. If you plan on having 1,000 HASHKEYs, Oracle will allocate 500 blocks.

It is interesting to note that unlike a conventional hash table in a computer language, it is OK to have hash collisions, in fact, it is desirable in many cases. If you take the same DEPT/EMP example from above, you could set up a hash cluster based on the DEPTNO column. Obviously, many rows will hash to the same value – you expect them to (they have the same DEPTNO), this is what the cluster is about in some respects, clustering like data together. This is why Oracle asks you to specify the HASHKEYs (how many department numbers do you anticipate over time) and SIZE (what is the size of the data that will be associated with each department number). It allocates a hash table to hold HASHKEY number of departments of SIZE bytes each. What you do want to avoid is unintended hash collisions. It is obvious that if you set the size of the hash table to 1,000 (really 1,009 since the hash table size is always a prime number and Oracle rounds up for us) and put 1,010 departments in the table, there will be at least one collision (two different departments hashing to the same value). Unintended hash collisions are to be avoided as they add overhead and increase the probability of row chaining occurring.

In order to see what sort of space hash clusters take, we'll write a small utility stored procedure SHOW_SPACE that we'll use in this chapter and in the next chapter on *Indexes*. This routine just uses the DBMS_SPACE routines we've seen in part above to display space used by objects in the database:

```
tkyte@TKYTE816> create or replace
  2  procedure show_space
  3  ( p_segname in varchar2,
```

```
 4      p_owner    in varchar2 default user,
 5      p_type     in varchar2 default 'TABLE',
 6      p_partition in varchar2 default NULL )
 7  as
 8          l_free_blks                 number;
 9
10          l_total_blocks              number;
11          l_total_bytes               number;
12          l_unused_blocks             number;
13          l_unused_bytes              number;
14          l_LastUsedExtFileId         number;
15          l_LastUsedExtBlockId        number;
16          l_last_used_block           number;
17          procedure p( p_label in varchar2, p_num in number )
18          is
19          begin
20              dbms_output.put_line( rpad(p_label,40,'.') ||
21                                    p_num );
22          end;
23  begin
24          dbms_space.free_blocks
25          ( segment_owner      => p_owner,
26            segment_name       => p_segname,
27            segment_type       => p_type,
28              partition_name     => p_partition,
29            freelist_group_id => 0,
30            free_blks          => l_free_blks );
31
32          dbms_space.unused_space
33          ( segment_owner      => p_owner,
34            segment_name       => p_segname,
35            segment_type       => p_type,
36              partition_name     => p_partition,
37            total_blocks       => l_total_blocks,
38            total_bytes        => l_total_bytes,
39            unused_blocks      => l_unused_blocks,
40            unused_bytes       => l_unused_bytes,
41            last_used_extent_file_id => l_LastUsedExtFileId,
42            last_used_extent_block_id => l_LastUsedExtBlockId,
43            last_used_block => l_last_used_block );
44
45      p( 'Free Blocks', l_free_blks );
46      p( 'Total Blocks', l_total_blocks );
47      p( 'Total Bytes', l_total_bytes );
48      p( 'Unused Blocks', l_unused_blocks );
49      p( 'Unused Bytes', l_unused_bytes );
50      p( 'Last Used Ext FileId', l_LastUsedExtFileId );
51      p( 'Last Used Ext BlockId', l_LastUsedExtBlockId );
52      p( 'Last Used Block', l_last_used_block );
53  end;
54  /

Procedure created.
```

Now if I issue a CREATE CLUSTER statement, such as the following, we can see the storage it allocated:

```
tkyte@TKYTE816> create cluster hash_cluster
  2  ( hash_key number )
  3  hashkeys 1000
  4  size 8192
  5  /

Cluster created.

tkyte@TKYTE816> exec show_space( 'HASH_CLUSTER', user, 'CLUSTER' )
Free Blocks.............................0
Total Blocks...........................1016
Total Bytes............................8323072
Unused Blocks..........................6
Unused Bytes...........................49152
Last Used Ext FileId...................5
Last Used Ext BlockId..................889
Last Used Block........................2

PL/SQL procedure successfully completed.
```

I can see that the total number of blocks allocated to the table is 1,016. Six of these blocks are unused (free). One block goes to table overhead, to manage the extents. Therefore, there are 1,009 blocks under the high water mark of this object, and these are used by the cluster. 1,009 just happens to be the next largest prime over 1,000 and since my block size is 8 KB we can see that Oracle did in fact allocate (8192 * 1009) blocks. This figure is a little higher than this, due to the way extents are rounded and/or by using locally managed tablespaces with uniformly-sized extents.

This points out one of the issues with hash clusters you need to be aware of. Normally, if I create an empty table, the number of blocks under the high water mark for that table is 0. If I full scan it, it reaches the high water mark and stops. With a hash cluster, the tables will start out big and will take longer to create as Oracle must initialize each block, an action that normally takes place as data is added to the table. They have the potential to have data in their first block and their last block, with nothing in between. Full scanning a virtually empty hash cluster will take as long as full scanning a full hash cluster. This is not necessarily a bad thing; you built the hash cluster to have very fast access to the data by a hash key lookup. You did not build it to full scan it frequently.

Now I can start placing tables into the hash cluster in the same fashion I did with index clusters. For example:

```
tkyte@TKYTE816> create table hashed_table
  2  ( x number, data1 varchar2(4000), data2 varchar2(4000) )
  3  cluster hash_cluster(x);

Table created.
```

To see the difference a hash cluster can make, I set up a small test. I created a hash cluster, loaded some data up in it, copied this data to a 'regular' table with a conventional index on it and then I did 100,000 random reads on each table (the same 'random' reads on each). Using SQL_TRACE and TKPROF (more on these tools in Chapter 10 on *Tuning Strategies and Tools*), I was able to determine the performance characteristics of each. Below is the set up I performed followed by the analysis of it:

```
tkyte@TKYTE816> create cluster hash_cluster
  2  ( hash_key number )
  3  hashkeys 50000
```

```
     4  size 45
     5  /

Cluster created.

tkyte@TKYTE816> create table emp
     2  cluster hash_cluster(empno)
     3  as
     4  select rownum empno, ename, job, mgr, hiredate, sal, comm, deptno
     5    from scott.emp
     6   where 1=0
     7  /

Table created.
```

I created the hash cluster with a SIZE of 45 bytes. This is because I determined the average row size for a row in my table would be about 45 bytes (I analyzed the SCOTT.EMP table to determine this). I then created an empty table in that cluster that resembles the SCOTT.EMP table. The one modification was to select ROWNUM instead of EMPNO so the table I created was made with a NUMBER instead of NUMBER(4) column. I wanted more than 9,999 rows in this table; I was going for about 50,000.

Next I filled up the table and created the 'conventional clone' of it:

```
tkyte@TKYTE816> declare
     2          l_cnt    number;
     3          l_empno number default 1;
     4  begin
     5          select count(*) into l_cnt from scott.emp;
     6
     7          for x in ( select * from scott.emp )
     8          loop
     9             for i in 1 .. trunc(50000/l_cnt)+1
    10             loop
    11                   insert into emp values
    12                   ( l_empno, x.ename, x.job, x.mgr, x.hiredate, x.sal,
    13                     x.comm, x.deptno );
    14                   l_empno := l_empno+1;
    15             end loop;
    16          end loop;
    17          commit;
    18  end;
    19  /

PL/SQL procedure successfully completed.

tkyte@TKYTE816> create table emp_reg
     2  as
     3  select * from emp;

Table created.

tkyte@TKYTE816> alter table emp_reg add constraint emp_pk primary key(empno);

Table altered.
```

Now, all I needed was some 'random' data to pick rows from each of the tables with:

```
tkyte@TKYTE816> create table random ( x int );

Table created.

tkyte@TKYTE816> begin
  2             for i in 1 .. 100000
  3             loop
  4                     insert into random values
  5                     ( mod(abs(dbms_random.random),50000)+1 );
  6             end loop;
  7  end;
  8  /

PL/SQL procedure successfully completed.
```

Now we are ready to do a test:

```
tkyte@TKYTE816> alter session set sql_trace=true;

Session altered.

tkyte@TKYTE816> select count(ename)
  2      from emp, random
  3      where emp.empno = random.x;

COUNT(ENAME)
------------
      100000

tkyte@TKYTE816> select count(ename)
  2      from emp_reg, random
  3      where emp_reg.empno = random.x;

COUNT(ENAME)
------------
      100000
```

I knew the optimizer would FULL SCAN random in both cases since there is no other access method available for that table. I was counting on it doing a nested loops join to the EMP and EMP_REG table (which it did). This did 100,000 random reads into the two tables. The TKPROF report shows me:

```
select count(ename)
  from emp, random
 where emp.empno = random.x

call     count       cpu    elapsed    disk      query    current       rows
-------  ------  --------  ---------  ------  ---------  ----------  ----------
Parse        1      0.00       0.00       0          0           2           0
Execute      1      0.00       0.00       0          0           0           0
Fetch        2      3.44       3.57      13     177348           4           1
-------  ------  --------  ---------  ------  ---------  ----------  ----------
total        4      3.44       3.57      13     177348           6           1
```

```
Misses in library cache during parse: 1
Optimizer goal: CHOOSE
Parsing user id: 66


Rows      Row Source Operation
-------   --------------------------------------------------
      1   SORT AGGREGATE
 100000    NESTED LOOPS
 100001     TABLE ACCESS FULL RANDOM
 100000     TABLE ACCESS HASH EMP


*************************************************************************

select count(ename)
  from emp_reg, random
 where emp_reg.empno = random.x
```

call	count	cpu	elapsed	disk	query	current	rows
Parse	1	0.01	0.01	0	1	3	0
Execute	1	0.00	0.00	0	0	0	0
Fetch	2	1.80	6.26	410	300153	4	1
total	4	1.81	6.27	410	300154	7	1

```
Misses in library cache during parse: 1
Optimizer goal: CHOOSE
Parsing user id: 66


Rows      Row Source Operation
-------   --------------------------------------------------
      1   SORT AGGREGATE
 100000    NESTED LOOPS
 100001     TABLE ACCESS FULL RANDOM
 100000     TABLE ACCESS BY INDEX ROWID EMP_REG
 200000      INDEX UNIQUE SCAN (object id 24743)
```

The points of interest here are:

❏   The hash cluster did significantly less I/O (query column). This is what we had anticipated. The query simply took the random numbers, performed the hash on them, and went to the block. The hash cluster has to do at least one I/O to get the data. The conventional table with an index had to perform index scans followed by a table access by row ID to get the same answer. The indexed table has to do at least two I/Os to get the data.

❏   The hash cluster query took significantly more CPU. This too could be anticipated. The act of performing a hash is very CPU-intensive. The act of performing an index lookup is I/O-intensive.

❏   The hash cluster query had a better elapsed time. This will vary. On my system (a single user laptop for this test; slow disks but I own the CPU), I was not CPU-bound – I was disk-bound. Since I had exclusive access to the CPU, the elapsed time for the hash cluster query was very close to the CPU time. On the other hand, the disks on my laptop were not the fastest. I spent a lot of time waiting for I/O.

This last point is the important one. When working with computers, it is all about resources and their utilization. If you are I/O bound and perform queries that do lots of keyed reads like I did above, a hash cluster may improve performance. If you are already CPU-bound, a hash cluster will possibly decrease performance since it needs more CPU horsepower. This is one of the major reasons why rules of thumb do not work on real world systems – what works for you might not work for others in similar but different conditions.

There is a special case of a hash cluster and that is a 'single table' hash cluster. This is an optimized version of the general hash cluster we've already looked at. It supports only one table in the cluster at a time (you have to DROP the existing table in a single table hash cluster before you can create another). Additionally, if there is a one to one mapping between hash keys and data rows, the access to the rows is somewhat faster as well. These hash clusters are designed for those occasions when you want to access a table by primary key and do not care to cluster other tables with it. If you need fast access to an employee record by EMPNO – a single table hash cluster might be called for. I did the above test on a single table hash cluster as well and found the performance to be even better than just a hash cluster. I went a step further with this example however and took advantage of the fact that Oracle will allow me to write my own specialized hash function (instead of using the default one provided by Oracle). You are limited to using only the columns available in the table and may only use the Oracle built-in functions (no PL/SQL code for example) when writing these hash functions. By taking advantage of the fact that EMPNO is a number between 1 and 50,000 in the above example – I made my 'hash function' simply be the EMPNO column itself. In this fashion, I am guaranteed to never have a hash collision. Putting it all together, we'll create a single table hash cluster with my own hash function via:

```
tkyte@TKYTE816> create cluster single_table_hash_cluster
  2  ( hash_key INT )
  3  hashkeys 50000
  4  size 45
  5  single table
  6  hash is HASH_KEY
  7  /

Cluster created.
```

We've simply added the key words SINGLE TABLE to make it a single table hash cluster. Our HASH IS function is simply the HASH_KEY cluster key in this case. This is a SQL function, we could have used trunc(mod(hash_key/324+278,555)/abs(hash_key+1)) if we wanted (not that this is a good hash function, it just demonstrates that you can use a complex function there if you wish). Then, we create our table in that cluster:

```
tkyte@TKYTE816> create table single_table_emp
  2  ( empno   INT ,
  3    ename   varchar2(10),
  4    job     varchar2(9),
  5    mgr     number,
  6    hiredate date,
  7    sal     number,
  8    comm    number,
  9    deptno number(2)
 10  )
 11  cluster single_table_hash_cluster(empno)
 12  /

Table created.
```

and load it up with the EMP data from before:

```
tkyte@TKYTE816> insert into single_table_emp
  2  select * from emp;

50008 rows created.
```

After running the same query we did for the other two tables, we discover from the TKPROF report that:

```
select count(ename)
  from single_table_emp, random
 where single_table_emp.empno = random.x
call     count     cpu    elapsed  disk       query    current        rows
------- ------  -------- ----------  -----  ----------  ----------  ----------
Parse        1    0.00     0.00       0           0           0           0
Execute      1    0.00     0.00       0           0           0           0
Fetch        2    3.29     3.44     127      135406           4           1
------- ------  -------- ----------  -----  ----------  ----------  ----------
total        4    3.29     3.44     127      135406           4           1

Misses in library cache during parse: 0
Optimizer goal: CHOOSE
Parsing user id: 264

Rows     Row Source Operation
-------  ---------------------------------------------------
      1  SORT AGGREGATE
 100000   NESTED LOOPS
 100001    TABLE ACCESS FULL RANDOM
 100000    TABLE ACCESS HASH SINGLE_TABLE_EMP
```

This query processed three quarters of the number of blocks that the other hash cluster did. This is due to some combination of using our own hash function that assured us of no collisions and using a single table hash cluster.

Hash Clusters Wrap-up

That is the 'nuts and bolts' of a hash cluster. They are similar in concept to the index cluster above with the exception that a cluster index is not used. The data is the index in this case. The cluster key is hashed into a block address and the data is expected to be there. The important things to really understand are that:

❑ The hash cluster is allocated right from the beginning. Oracle will take your HASHKEYS/trunc(blocksize/SIZE) and will allocate that space right away. As soon as the first table is put in that cluster, any full scan will hit every allocated block. This is different from every other table in this respect.

❑ The number of HASHKEYs in a hash cluster is a fixed size. You cannot change the size of the hash table without a rebuild of the cluster. This does not in any way limit the amount of data you can store in this cluster, it simply limits the number of unique hash keys that can be generated for this cluster. That may affect performance due to unintended hash collisions if it was set too low.

❑ Range scanning on the cluster key is not available. Predicates such as WHERE cluster_key BETWEEN 50 AND 60 cannot use the hashing algorithm. There are an infinite number of possible values between 50 and 60 – the server would have to generate them all in order to hash each one and see if there was any data there. This is not possible. The cluster will be full scanned if you use a range on a cluster key and have not indexed it using a conventional index.

Hash clusters are suitable when:

❑ You know with a good degree of accuracy how many rows the table will have over its life, or if you have some reasonable upper bound. Getting the size of the HASHKEYs and SIZE parameters right is crucial to avoid a rebuild. If the life of the table is short (for example, a data mart/data warehouse), this is easy.

❑ DML, especially inserts, is light. Updates do not introduce significant overhead, unless you update the HASHKEY, which would not be a good idea. That would cause the row to migrate.

❑ You access the data by the HASHKEY value constantly. For example, you have a table of parts, and part number accesses these parts. Lookup tables are especially appropriate for hash clusters.

Nested Tables

Nested tables are part of the **O**bject **R**elational **E**xtensions to Oracle. A nested table, one of the two collection types in Oracle, is very similar to a child table in a traditional parent/child table pair in the relational model. It is an unordered set of data elements, all of the same data type, which could either be a built-in data type or an object data type. It goes one step further however, since it is designed to give the illusion that each row in the parent table has its *own* child table. If there are 100 rows in the parent table, then there are *virtually* 100 nested tables. Physically, there is only the single parent and the single child table. There are large syntactic and semantic differences between nested tables and parent/child tables as well, and we'll look at those in this section.

There are two ways to use nested tables. One is in your PL/SQL code as a way to extend the PL/SQL language. We cover this technique in Chapter 20 *Using Object Relational Features*. The other is as a physical storage mechanism, for persistent storage of collections. I personally use them in PL/SQL all of the time but very infrequently as a permanent storage mechanism.

What I am going to do in this section is briefly introduce the syntax to create, query, and modify nested tables. Then we will look at some of the implementation details, what is important to know about how Oracle really stores them.

Nested Tables Syntax

The creation of a table with a nested table is fairly straightforward, it is the syntax for manipulating them that gets a little complex. I will use the simple EMP and DEPT tables to demonstrate. We are familiar with that little data model which is implemented relationally as:

```
tkyte@TKYTE816> create table dept
  2  (deptno  number(2) primary key,
  3   dname      varchar2(14),
  4   loc        varchar2(13)
  5  );
```

```
Table created.

tkyte@TKYTE816> create table emp
  2   (empno        number(4) primary key,
  3    ename        varchar2(10),
  4    job          varchar2(9),
  5    mgr          number(4) references emp,
  6    hiredate     date,
  7    sal          number(7, 2),
  8    comm         number(7, 2),
  9    deptno       number(2) references dept
 10   );

Table created.
```

with primary and foreign keys. We will do the equivalent implementation using a nested table for the EMP table:

```
tkyte@TKYTE816> create or replace type emp_type
  2   as object
  3   (empno        number(4),
  4    ename        varchar2(10),
  5    job          varchar2(9),
  6    mgr          number(4),
  7    hiredate     date,
  8    sal          number(7, 2),
  9    comm         number(7, 2)
 10   );
 11   /

Type created.

tkyte@TKYTE816> create or replace type emp_tab_type
  2   as table of emp_type
  3   /

Type created.
```

In order to create a table with a nested table, we need a nested table type. The above code creates a complex object type EMP_TYPE and a nested table type of that called EMP_TAB_TYPE. In PL/SQL, this will be treated much like an array would. In SQL, it will cause a physical nested table to be created. Here is the simple CREATE TABLE statement that uses it:

```
tkyte@TKYTE816> create table dept_and_emp
  2   (deptno number(2) primary key,
  3    dname       varchar2(14),
  4    loc         varchar2(13),
  5    emps        emp_tab_type
  6   )
  7   nested table emps store as emps_nt;

Table created.

tkyte@TKYTE816> alter table emps_nt add constraint emps_empno_unique
  2               unique(empno)
  3   /

Table altered.
```

The important part of this create table is the inclusion of the column EMPS of EMP_TAB_TYPE and the corresponding NESTED TABLE EMPS STORE AS EMPS_NT. This created a real physical table EMPS_NT separate from, and in addition to, the table DEPT_AND_EMP. I added a constraint on the EMPNO column directly on the nested table in order to make the EMPNO unique as it was in our original relational model. I cannot implement our full data model. However, there is the self-referencing constraint:

```
tkyte@TKYTE816> alter table emps_nt add constraint mgr_fk
  2  foreign key(mgr) references emps_nt(empno);
alter table emps_nt add constraint mgr_fk
*
ERROR at line 1:
ORA-30730: referential constraint not allowed on nested table column
```

This will simply not work. Nested tables do not support referential integrity constraints as they cannot reference any other table, even itself. So, we'll just skip that for now. Now, let's populate this table with the existing EMP and DEPT data:

```
tkyte@TKYTE816> insert into dept_and_emp
  2  select dept.*,
  3     CAST( multiset( select empno, ename, job, mgr, hiredate, sal, comm
  4                       from SCOTT.EMP
  5                      where emp.deptno = dept.deptno ) AS emp_tab_type )
  6    from SCOTT.DEPT
  7  /

4 rows created.
```

There are two things to notice here:

❑   Only 'four' rows were created. There are really only four rows in the DEPT_AND_EMP table. The 14 EMP rows don't really exist independently.

❑   The syntax is getting pretty exotic. CAST and MULTISET – syntax most people have never used. You will find lots of exotic syntax when dealing with object relational components in the database. The MULTISET keyword is used to tell Oracle the subquery is expected to return more then one row (subqueries in a SELECT list have previously been limited to returning 1 row). The CAST is used to instruct Oracle to treat the returned set as a collection type – in this case we CAST the MULTISET to be a EMP_TAB_TYPE. CAST is a general purpose routine not limited in use to collections – for example if you wanted to fetch the EMPNO column from EMP as a VARCHAR2(20) instead of a NUMBER(4) type, you may query: select cast(empno as VARCHAR2(20)) e from emp;

We are now ready to query the data. Let's see what one row might look like:

```
tkyte@TKYTE816> select deptno, dname, loc, d.emps AS employees
  2  from dept_and_emp d
  3  where deptno = 10
  4  /


    DEPTNO DNAME         LOC           EMPLOYEES(EMPNO, ENAME, JOB, M
---------- ------------- ------------- ------------------------------
        10 ACCOUNTING    NEW YORK      EMP_TAB_TYPE(EMP_TYPE(7782,
                                       'CLARK', 'MANAGER', 7839,
                                       '09-JUN-81', 2450, NULL),
```

```
                                        EMP_TYPE(7839, 'KING',
                                        'PRESIDENT', NULL,
                                        '17-NOV-81', 5000, NULL),
                                        EMP_TYPE(7934, 'MILLER',
                                        'CLERK', 7782, '23-JAN-82',
                                        1300, NULL))
```

All of the data is there, in a single column. Most applications, unless they are specifically written for the object relational features, will not be able to deal with this particular column. For example, ODBC doesn't have a way to deal with a nested table (JDBC, OCI, Pro*C, PL/SQL, and most other APIs, and languages do). For those cases, Oracle provides a way to un-nest a collection and treats it much like a relational table. For example:

```
tkyte@TKYTE816> select d.deptno, d.dname, emp.*
  2   from dept_and_emp D, table(d.emps) emp
  3   /

DEPTNO DNAME         EMPNO ENAME        JOB          MGR HIREDATE     SAL  COMM
------ ------------ ------ ------------ ---------- ----- --------- ----- -----
    10 ACCOUNTING    7782 CLARK        MANAGER     7839 09-JUN-81  2450
    10 ACCOUNTING    7839 KING         PRESIDENT        17-NOV-81  5000
    10 ACCOUNTING    7934 MILLER       CLERK       7782 23-JAN-82  1300
    20 RESEARCH      7369 SMITH        CLERK       7902 17-DEC-80   800
    20 RESEARCH      7566 JONES        MANAGER     7839 02-APR-81  2975
    20 RESEARCH      7788 SCOTT        ANALYST     7566 09-DEC-82  3000
    20 RESEARCH      7876 ADAMS        CLERK       7788 12-JAN-83  1100
    20 RESEARCH      7902 FORD         ANALYST     7566 03-DEC-81  3000
    30 SALES         7499 ALLEN        SALESMAN    7698 20-FEB-81  1600   300
    30 SALES         7521 WARD         SALESMAN    7698 22-FEB-81  1250   500
    30 SALES         7654 MARTIN       SALESMAN    7698 28-SEP-81  1250  1400
    30 SALES         7698 BLAKE        MANAGER     7839 01-MAY-81  2850
    30 SALES         7844 TURNER       SALESMAN    7698 08-SEP-81  1500     0
    30 SALES         7900 JAMES        CLERK       7698 03-DEC-81   950

14 rows selected.
```

We are able to cast the EMPS column as a table and it naturally did the join for us – no join conditions were needed. In fact, since our EMP type doesn't have the DEPTNO column, there is nothing for us apparently to join on. Oracle takes care of that nuance for us.

So, how can we update the data? Let's say you want to give department 10 a $100 bonus. You would code the following:

```
tkyte@TKYTE816> update
  2     table( select emps
  3               from dept_and_emp
  4                   where deptno = 10
  5             )
  6   set comm = 100
  7   /

3 rows updated.
```

Here is where the 'virtually a table for every row' comes into play. In the SELECT predicate shown earlier, it may not have been obvious that there was a table per row, especially since the joins and such aren't there, it looks a little like 'magic'. The UPDATE statement however shows that there is a table per row. We selected a discrete table to UPDATE; this table has no name, only a query to identify it. If we use a query that does not SELECT *exactly* one table, we will receive:

```
tkyte@TKYTE816> update
  2      table( select emps
  3              from dept_and_emp
  4              where deptno = 1
  5          )
  6  set comm = 100
  7  /
update
*
ERROR at line 1:
ORA-22908: reference to NULL table value


tkyte@TKYTE816> update
  2      table( select emps
  3              from dept_and_emp
  4              where deptno > 1
  5          )
  6   set comm = 100
  7  /
  table( select emps
            *
ERROR at line 2:
ORA-01427: single-row subquery returns more than one row
```

If you return less then one row (one nested table instance), the update fails. Normally an update of zero rows is OK but not in this case, it returns an error the same as if you left the table name off of the update. If you return more then one row (more then one nested table instance), the update fails. Normally an update of many rows is perfectly OK. This shows that Oracle considers each row in the DEPT_AND_EMP table to point to another table, not just another set of rows as the relational model does. This is the semantic difference between a nested table and a parent/child relational table. In the nested table model, there is one table per parent row. In the relational model, there is one set of rows per parent row. This difference can make nested tables somewhat cumbersome to use at times. Consider this model we are using, which provides a very nice view of the data from the perspective of single department. It is a terrible model if you want to ask questions like 'what department does KING work for?', 'how many accountants do I have working for me?', and so on. These questions are best asked of the EMP relational table but in this nested table model we can only access the EMP data via the DEPT data. We must always join, we cannot query the EMP data alone. Well, we can't do it in a supported, documented method – we can use a trick (more on this trick later). If we needed to update every row in the EMPS_NT, we would have to do 4 updates; once each for the rows in DEPT_AND_EMP to update the virtual table associated with each row.

Another thing to consider is that when we updated the employee data for department 10, we were semantically updating the EMPS column in the DEPT_AND_EMP table. Physically, we understand there are two tables involved but semantically there is only one. Even though we updated no data in the department table, the row that contains the nested table we did modify is locked from update by other sessions. In a traditional parent/child table relationship, this would not be the case.

These are the reasons why I tend to stay away from nested tables as a persistent storage mechanism. It is the *rare* child table that is not queried standalone. In the above, the EMP table should be a strong entity. It stands alone, and so, it needs to be queried alone. I find this to be the case almost all of the time. I tend to use nested tables via views on relational tables. We'll investigate this in Chapter 20 on *Using Object Relational Features*.

So, now that we have seen how to update a nested table instance, inserting and deleting are pretty straightforward. Let's add a row to the nested table instance department 10 and remove a row from department 20:

```
tkyte@TKYTE816> insert into table
  2  ( select emps from dept_and_emp where deptno = 10 )
  3  values
  4  ( 1234, 'NewEmp', 'CLERK', 7782, sysdate, 1200, null );

1 row created.

tkyte@TKYTE816> delete from table
  2  ( select emps from dept_and_emp where deptno = 20 )
  3  where ename = 'SCOTT';

1 row deleted.

tkyte@TKYTE816> select d.dname, e.empno, ename
  2  from dept_and_emp d, table(d.emps) e
  3  where d.deptno in ( 10, 20 );

DNAME              EMPNO ENAME
-------------- ---------- ----------
RESEARCH            7369 SMITH
RESEARCH            7566 JONES
RESEARCH            7876 ADAMS
RESEARCH            7902 FORD
ACCOUNTING          7782 CLARK
ACCOUNTING          7839 KING
ACCOUNTING          7934 MILLER
ACCOUNTING          1234 NewEmp

8 rows selected.
```

So, that is the basic syntax of how to query and modify nested tables. You will find many times that you must un-nest these tables as I have above, especially in queries, to make use of them. Once you conceptually visualize the 'virtual table per row' concept, working with nested tables becomes much easier.

Previously I stated: 'We must always join, we cannot query the EMP data alone' but then followed that up with a caveat: 'you can if you really need to'. It is undocumented and not supported, so use it *only* as a last ditch method. Where it will come in most handy is if you ever need to mass update the nested table (remember, we would have to do that through the DEPT table with a join). There is an undocumented hint, NESTED_TABLE_GET_REFS, used by EXP and IMP to deal with nested tables. It will also be a way to see a little more about the physical structure of the nested tables. This magic hint is easy to discover after you export a table with a nested table. I exported the table above, in order to get its 'larger' definition from IMP. After doing the export, I found the following SQL in my shared pool (V$SQL table):

```
SELECT /*+NESTED_TABLE_GET_REFS+*/ NESTED_TABLE_ID,SYS_NC_ROWINFO$ FROM
"TKYTE"."EMPS_NT"
```

A simple query like `SELECT SQL_TEXT FROM V$SQL WHERE UPPER(SQL_TEXT) LIKE '%EMP%` found it for me. If you run this, you'll get some 'magic' results:

```
tkyte@TKYTE816> SELECT /*+NESTED_TABLE_GET_REFS+*/
  2            NESTED_TABLE_ID,SYS_NC_ROWINFO$
  3    FROM "TKYTE"."EMPS_NT"
  4    /

NESTED_TABLE_ID                  SYS_NC_ROWINFO$(EMPNO, ENAME,
-------------------------------- ------------------------------
9A39835005B149859735617476C9A80E EMP_TYPE(7782, 'CLARK',
                                 'MANAGER', 7839, '09-JUN-81',
                                 2450, 100)

9A39835005B149859735617476C9A80E EMP_TYPE(7839, 'KING',
                                 'PRESIDENT', NULL,
                                 '17-NOV-81', 5000, 100)
```

Well, this is somewhat surprising, if you describe this table:

```
tkyte@TKYTE816> desc emps_nt
 Name                                      Null?    Type
 ----------------------------------------- -------- -----------------------
 EMPNO                                              NUMBER(4)
 ENAME                                              VARCHAR2(10)
 JOB                                                VARCHAR2(9)
 MGR                                                NUMBER(4)
 HIREDATE                                           DATE
 SAL                                                NUMBER(7,2)
 COMM                                               NUMBER(7,2)
```

These two columns don't even show up. They are part of the hidden implementation of nested tables. The NESTED_TABLE_ID is really a foreign key to the parent table DEPT_AND_EMP. DEPT_AND_EMP which actually has a hidden column in it that is used to join to EMPS_NT. The SYS_NC_ROWINF$ 'column' is a magic column, it is more of a function than a column. The nested table here is really an object table (it is made of an object type) and SYS_NC_INFO$ is the internal way Oracle references the row as an object, instead of referencing each of the scalar columns. Under the covers, all Oracle has done for us is to implement a parent/child table with system generated primary and foreign keys. If we dig a little further, we can query the 'real' data dictionary to see all of the columns in the DEPT_AND_EMP table:

```
tkyte@TKYTE816> select name
  2    from sys.col$
  3    where obj# = ( select object_id
  4                     from user_objects
  5                     where object_name = 'DEPT_AND_EMP' )
  6    /

NAME
------------------------------
DEPTNO
```

```
DNAME
LOC
EMPS
SYS_NC0000400005$


tkyte@TKYTE816> select SYS_NC0000400005$ from dept_and_emp;

SYS_NC0000400005$
--------------------------------
9A39835005B149859735617476C9A80E
A7140089B1954B39B73347EC20190D68
20D4AA0839FB49B0975FBDE367842E16
56350C866BA24ADE8CF9E47073C52296
```

The weird looking column name, SYS_NC0000400005$, is the system-generated key placed into the DEPT_AND_EMP table. If you dig even further you will find that Oracle has placed a unique index on this column. Unfortunately however, it neglected to index the NESTED_TABLE_ID in EMPS_NT. This column really needs to be indexed, as we are always joining *from* DEPT_AND_EMP to EMPS_NT. This is an important thing to remember about nested tables if you use them with all of the defaults as I did above, always index the NESTED_TABLE_ID in the nested tables!

I've gotten off of the track though at this point. I was talking about how to treat the nested table as if it were a real table. The NESTED_TABLE_GET_REFS hint does that for us. We can use that like this:

```
tkyte@TKYTE816> select /*+ nested_table_get_refs */ empno, ename
  2  from emps_nt where ename like '%A%';

    EMPNO ENAME
---------- ----------
     7782 CLARK
     7876 ADAMS
     7499 ALLEN
     7521 WARD
     7654 MARTIN
     7698 BLAKE
     7900 JAMES
7 rows selected.

tkyte@TKYTE816> update /*+ nested_table_get_refs */ emps_nt
  2  set ename = initcap(ename);

14 rows updated.

tkyte@TKYTE816> select /*+ nested_table_get_refs */ empno, ename
  2  from emps_nt where ename like '%a%';

    EMPNO ENAME
---------- ----------
     7782 Clark
     7876 Adams
     7521 Ward
     7654 Martin
     7698 Blake
     7900 James
6 rows selected.
```

Again, this is not a documented supported feature. It may not work in all environments. It has a specific functionality – for EXP and IMP to work. This is the only environment it is assured to work in. Use it at your own risk. Use it with caution though, and do not put it into production code. Use it for one-off fixes of data or to see what is in the nested table out of curiosity. The supported way to report on the data is to un-nest it like this:

```
tkyte@TKYTE816> select d.deptno, d.dname, emp.*
  2  from dept_and_emp D, table(d.emps) emp
  3  /
```

This is what you should use in queries and production code.

Nested Table Storage

We have already seen some of the storage of the nested table structure. We'll take a more in-depth look at the structure created by Oracle by default, and what sort of control over that we have. Working with the same create statement from above:

```
tkyte@TKYTE816> create table dept_and_emp
  2  (deptno number(2) primary key,
  3   dname     varchar2(14),
  4   loc       varchar2(13),
  5   emps      emp_tab_type
  6  )
  7  nested table emps store as emps_nt;

Table created.

tkyte@TKYTE816> alter table emps_nt add constraint emps_empno_unique
  2            unique(empno)
  3  /

Table altered.
```

We know that Oracle really creates a structure like this:

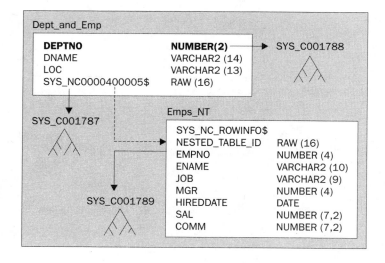

The code created two real tables. The table we asked to have is there but it has an extra hidden column (we'll have one extra hidden column by default for *each* nested table column in a table). It also created a *unique* constraint on this hidden column. Oracle created the nested table for us – EMPS_NT. This table has two hidden columns, one that is not really a column, SYS_NC_ROWINFO$, but really a virtual column that returns all of the scalar elements as an object. The other is the foreign key, called NESTED_TABLE_ID, which can be joined back to the parent table. Notice the *lack* of an index on this column! Finally, Oracle added an index on the DEPTNO column in the DEPT_AND_EMP table in order to enforce the primary key. So, we asked for a table and got a lot more then we bargained for. If you look at it, it is a lot like what you might create for a parent/child relationship, but we would have used the existing primary key on DEPTNO as the foreign key in EMPS_NT instead of generating a surrogate RAW(16) key.

If we look at the EXP/IMP dump of our nested table example, we see the following:

```
CREATE TABLE "TKYTE"."DEPT_AND_EMP"
("DEPTNO" NUMBER(2, 0),
 "DNAME"  VARCHAR2(14),
 "LOC"    VARCHAR2(13),
 "EMPS" "EMP_TAB_TYPE")
PCTFREE 10 PCTUSED 40 INITRANS 1 MAXTRANS 255 LOGGING
STORAGE(INITIAL 131072 NEXT 131072
        MINEXTENTS 1 MAXEXTENTS 4096
        PCTINCREASE 0 FREELISTS 1 FREELIST GROUPS 1
        BUFFER_POOL DEFAULT)
TABLESPACE "USERS"
NESTED TABLE "EMPS"
    STORE AS "EMPS_NT"
    RETURN AS VALUE
```

The only new thing we notice here so far is the RETURN AS VALUE. It is used to describe how the nested table is returned to a client application. By default, Oracle will return the nested table by value to the client – the actual data will be transmitted with each row. This can also be set to RETURN AS LOCATOR meaning the client will get a pointer to the data, not the data itself. If, and only if, the client de-references this pointer will the data be transmitted to it. So, if you believe the client will typically not look at the rows of a nested table for each parent row, you can return a locator instead of the values, saving on the network round trips. For example, if you have a client application that displays the lists of departments and when the user double clicks on a department it shows the employee information, you may consider using the locator. This is because the details are usually not looked at – it is the exception, not the rule.

So, what else can we do with the nested table? Firstly, the NESTED_TABLE_ID column must be indexed. Since we always access the nested table *from* the parent *to* the child, we really need that index. We can index that column using the create index but a better solution is to use an index organized table to store the nested table. The nested table is another perfect example of what an IOT is excellent for. It will physically store the child rows co-located by NESTED_TABLE_ID (so retrieving the table is done with less physical I/O). It will remove the need for the redundant index on the RAW(16) column. Going one step further, since the NESTED_TABLE_ID will be the leading column in the IOT's primary key, we should also incorporate index key compression to suppress the redundant NESTED_TABLE_ID s that would be there otherwise. In addition, we can incorporate our UNIQUE and NOT NULL constraint on the EMPNO column into the CREATE TABLE command. Therefore, if I take the above CREATE TABLE and modify it slightly:

```
CREATE TABLE "TKYTE"."DEPT_AND_EMP"
("DEPTNO" NUMBER(2, 0),
 "DNAME"  VARCHAR2(14),
 "LOC"    VARCHAR2(13),
```

```
    "EMPS"  "EMP_TAB_TYPE")
  PCTFREE 10 PCTUSED 40 INITRANS 1 MAXTRANS 255 LOGGING
  STORAGE(INITIAL 131072 NEXT 131072
          MINEXTENTS 1 MAXEXTENTS 4096
          PCTINCREASE 0 FREELISTS 1 FREELIST GROUPS 1
          BUFFER_POOL DEFAULT)
  TABLESPACE "USERS"
  NESTED TABLE "EMPS"
      STORE AS "EMPS_NT"
      ( (empno NOT NULL, unique (empno), primary key(nested_table_id,empno))
        organization index compress 1 )
      RETURN AS VALUE
/
```

and now we get the following set of objects. Instead of having a conventional table EMP_NT, we now have an IOT EMPS_NT as signified by the index structure overlaid on the table below:

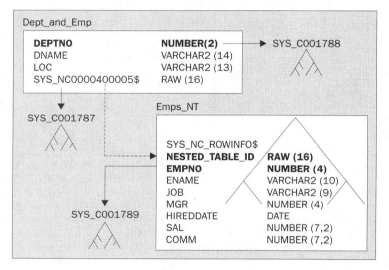

Where the EMPS_NT is an IOT using compression, this should take less storage than the original default nested table *and* it has the index we badly need.

Nested Tables Wrap-up

I do not use nested tables as a permanent storage mechanism myself, and this is for the following reasons:

❑ The overhead of the RAW(16) columns that are added. Both the parent and child table will have this extra column. The parent table will have an extra 16 byte RAW for each nested table column it has. Since the parent table typically already has a primary key (DEPTNO in my examples) it would make sense to use this in the child tables, not a system generated key.

❑ The overhead of the unique constraint on the parent table, when it already typically has a unique constraint.

❑ The nested table is not easily used by itself, without using unsupported constructs (NESTED_TABLE_GET_REFS). It can be un-nested for queries but not mass updates.

I do use nested tables heavily as a programming construct and in views. This is where I believe they are in their element and in Chapter 20 on *Using Object Relational Features* we see how to exploit them in this fashion. As a storage mechanism, I would much prefer creating the parent/child tables myself. After creating the parent/child tables we can in fact create a view that makes it appear as if we had a real nested table. That is, we can achieve all of the advantages of the nested table construct without incurring the overhead. Again in Chapter 20 *Using Object Relational Features* we'll take a detailed look at how to accomplish this.

If you do use them as a storage mechanism, be sure to make the nested table an index organized table to avoid the overhead of an index on the NESTED_TABLE_ID and the nested table itself. See the section above on IOTs for advice on setting them up with overflow segments and other options. If you do not use an IOT, make sure then to create an index on the NESTED_TABLE_ID column in the nested table to avoid full scanning it to find the child rows.

Temporary Tables

Temporary tables are used to hold intermediate resultsets, either for the duration of a transaction or a session. The data held in a temporary table is only ever visible to the current session – no other session will ever see any other session's data, even if the current session COMMITs the data. Multi-user concurrency is not an issue with regards to temporary tables either, one session can never block another session by using a temporary table. Even if we 'lock' the temporary table, it will not prevent other sessions using their temporary table As we observed in Chapter 3 on *Redo and Rollback*, temporary tables generate significantly less REDO then regular tables would. However, since they must generate UNDO information for the data they contain, they will generate some amount of REDO Log. UPDATEs and DELETEs will generate the largest amount; INSERTs and SELECTs the least amount.

Temporary tables will allocate storage from the currently logged in users temporary tablespace, or if they are accessed from a definers rights procedure, the temporary tablespace of the owner of that procedure will be used. A global temporary table is really just a template for the table itself. The act of creating a temporary table involves no storage allocation; no INITIAL extent is allocated, as it would be for a non-temporary table. Rather, at runtime when a session first puts data into the temporary table a temporary segment for that session will be created at that time. Since each session gets its own temporary segment, (not just an extent of an existing segment) every user might be allocating space for their temporary table in different tablespaces. USER1 might have their temporary tablespace set to TEMP1 – their temporary tables will be allocated from this space. USER2 might have TEMP2 as their temporary tablespace and their temporary tables will be allocated there.

Oracle's temporary tables are similar to temporary tables in other relational databases with the main exception being that they are 'statically' defined. You create them once per database, not once per stored procedure in the database. They always exist – they will be in the data dictionary as objects, but will always appear empty until your session puts data into them. The fact that they are statically defined allows us to create views that reference temporary tables, to create stored procedures that use static SQL to reference them, and so on.

Temporary tables may be *session*-based (data survives in the table across commits but not a disconnect/reconnect). They may also be *transaction*-based (data disappears after a commit). Here is an example showing the behavior of both. I used the SCOTT.EMP table as a template:

```
tkyte@TKYTE816> create global temporary table temp_table_session
  2  on commit preserve rows
  3  as
  4  select * from scott.emp where 1=0
  5  /

Table created.
```

The ON COMMIT PRESERVE ROWS clause makes this a session-based temporary table. Rows will stay in this table until my session disconnects or I physically remove them via a DELETE or TRUNCATE. Only my session can see these rows; no other session will ever see 'my' rows even after I COMMIT:

```
tkyte@TKYTE816> create global temporary table temp_table_transaction
  2  on commit delete rows
  3  as
  4  select * from scott.emp where 1=0
  5  /

Table created.
```

The ON COMMIT DELETE ROWS makes this a transaction-based temporary table. When your session commits, the rows disappear. The rows will disappear by simply giving back the temporary extents allocated to our table – there is no overhead involved in the automatic clearing of temporary tables. Now, let's look at the differences between the two types:

```
tkyte@TKYTE816> insert into temp_table_session select * from scott.emp;

14 rows created.

tkyte@TKYTE816> insert into temp_table_transaction select * from scott.emp;

14 rows created.
```

We've just put 14 rows into each temp table and this shows we can 'see' them:

```
tkyte@TKYTE816> select session_cnt, transaction_cnt
  2    from ( select count(*) session_cnt from temp_table_session ),
  3         ( select count(*) transaction_cnt from temp_table_transaction );

SESSION_CNT TRANSACTION_CNT
----------- ---------------
         14              14

tkyte@TKYTE816> commit;
```

Since we've committed, we'll see the session-based rows but not the transaction-based rows:

```
tkyte@TKYTE816> select session_cnt, transaction_cnt
  2    from ( select count(*) session_cnt from temp_table_session ),
  3         ( select count(*) transaction_cnt from temp_table_transaction );

SESSION_CNT TRANSACTION_CNT
```

```
----------- ----------------
         14               0

tkyte@TKYTE816> disconnect
Disconnected from Oracle8i Enterprise Edition Release 8.1.6.0.0 - Production
With the Partitioning option
JServer Release 8.1.6.0.0 - Production
tkyte@TKYTE816> connect tkyte/tkyte
Connected.
```

Since we've started a new session, we'll see no rows in either table:

```
tkyte@TKYTE816> select session_cnt, transaction_cnt
  2     from ( select count(*) session_cnt from temp_table_session ),
  3          ( select count(*) transaction_cnt from temp_table_transaction );

SESSION_CNT TRANSACTION_CNT
----------- ----------------
          0                0
```

If you have experience of temporary tables in SQL Server and/or Sybase, the major consideration for you is that instead of executing select x, y, z into #temp from some_table to dynamically create and populate a temporary table, you will:

❑   Once per database, create all of your TEMP tables as a global temporary table. This will be done as part of the application install, just like creating your permanent tables.

❑   In your procedures simply insert into temp (x,y,z) select x,y,y from some_table.

Just to drive home the point, the goal here is to not create tables in your stored procedures at runtime. That is not the proper way to do this in Oracle. DDL is an expensive operation, we want to avoid doing that at runtime. The temporary tables for an application should be created during the application installation *never* at run-time.

Temporary tables can have many of the attributes of a permanent table. They may have triggers, check constraints, indexes, and so on. Features of permanent tables that they do not support include:

❑   They cannot have referential integrity constraints – they can neither be the *target* of a foreign key, nor may they have a foreign key defined on them.

❑   They cannot have VARRAY or NESTED TABLE type columns.

❑   They cannot be indexed organized tables.

❑   They cannot be in an index or hash cluster.

❑   They cannot be partitioned.

❑   They cannot have statistics generated via the ANALYZE table command.

One of the drawbacks of a temporary table in any database, is the fact that the optimizer has no real statistics on it. When using the **Cost-Based Optimizer** (CBO), valid statistics are vital to the optimizer's success (or failure). In the absence of statistics, the optimizer will make guesses as to the distribution of data, the amount of data, the selectivity of an index. When these guesses are wrong, the query plans generated for queries that make heavy use of temporary tables could be less than optimal. In many cases, the correct solution is to not use a temporary table at all, but rather to use an INLINE VIEW (for an example of an INLINE VIEW refer to the last SELECT we ran above – it has two of them) in its place. In this fashion, Oracle will have access to all of the relevant statistics for a table and can come up with an optimal plan.

I find many times people use temporary tables because they learned in other databases that joining too many tables in a single query is a 'bad thing'. This is a practice that must be unlearned for Oracle development. Rather then trying to out-smart the optimizer and breaking what should be a single query into three or four queries that store their sub results into temporary tables and then joining the temporary tables, you should just code a single query that answers the original question. Referencing many tables in a single query is OK; the temporary table crutch is not needed in Oracle for this purpose.

In other cases however, the use of a temporary table in a process is the correct approach. For example, I recently wrote a Palm Sync application to synchronize the date book on a Palm Pilot with calendar information stored in Oracle. The Palm gives me a list of all records that have been modified since the last hot synchronization. I must take these records and compare them against the live data in the database, update the database records and then generate a list of changes to be applied to the Palm. This is a perfect example of when a temporary table is very useful. I used a temporary table to store the changes from the Palm in the database. I then ran a stored procedure that bumps the palm generated changes against the live (and very large) permanent tables to discover what changes need to be made to the Oracle data and then to find the changes that need to come from Oracle back down to the Palm. I have to make a couple of passes on this data, first I find all records that were modified only on the Palm and make the corresponding changes in Oracle. I then find all records that were modified on both the Palm and my database since the last synchronization and rectify them. Then I find all records that were modified only on the database and place their changes into the temporary table. Lastly, the Palm sync application pulls the changes from the temporary table and applies them to the Palm device itself. Upon disconnection, the temporary data goes away.

The issue I encountered however is that because the permanent tables were analyzed, the CBO was being used. The temporary table had no statistics on it (you can analyze the temporary table but no statistics are gathered) and the CBO would 'guess' many things about it. I, as the developer, knew the average number of rows you might expect, the distribution of the data, the selectivity of the indexes and so on. I needed a way to inform the optimizer of these *better* guesses. The DBMS_STATS package is a great way to do this.

Since the ANALYZE command does not collect statistics on a temporary table, we must use a manual process to populate the data dictionary with representative statistics for our temporary tables. For example, if on average the number of rows in the temporary table will be 500, the average row size will be 100 bytes and the number of blocks will be 7, we could simply use:

```
tkyte@TKYTE816> begin
  2      dbms_stats.set_table_stats( ownname => USER,
  3                                  tabname => 'T',
  4                                  numrows => 500,
  5                                  numblks => 7,
  6                                  avgrlen => 100 );
  7  end;
  8  /

PL/SQL procedure successfully completed.
```

```
tkyte@TKYTE816> select table_name, num_rows, blocks, avg_row_len
  2              from user_tables
  3              where table_name = 'T';

TABLE_NAME                       NUM_ROWS     BLOCKS AVG_ROW_LEN
------------------------------ ---------- ---------- -----------
T                                     500          7         100
```

Now, the optimizer won't use its best guess, it will use *our* best guess for this information. Going a step further, we can use Oracle to set the statistics to an even greater level of detail. The following example shows the use of a temporary table with the CBO. The query plan generated without statistics is suboptimal; the CBO chose to use an index when it should not have. It did that because it assumed default information about index selectivity, number of rows in the table and number of rows to be returned and such. What I did to correct this was to drop the temporary table for a moment, create a permanent table of the same name and structure and populated it with representative data. I then analyzed this table as thoroughly as I wanted to (I could generate histograms and so on as well) and used DBMS_STATS to export the statistics for this permanent table. I then dropped the permanent table and recreated my temporary table. All I needed to do then was import my representative statistics and the optimizer did the right thing:

```
tkyte@TKYTE816> create global temporary table temp_all_objects
  2  as
  3  select * from all_objects where 1=0
  4  /

Table created.

tkyte@TKYTE816> create index temp_all_objects_idx on temp_all_objects(object_id)
  2  /

Index created.

tkyte@TKYTE816> insert into temp_all_objects
  2  select * from all_objects where rownum < 51
  3  /

50 rows created.

tkyte@TKYTE816> set autotrace on explain
tkyte@TKYTE816> select /*+ ALL_ROWS */ object_type, count(*)
  2     FROM temp_all_objects
  3   where object_id < 50000
  4     group by object_type
  5  /

OBJECT_TYPE          COUNT(*)
------------------- ----------
JAVA CLASS                 50


Execution Plan
----------------------------------------------------------
   0      SELECT STATEMENT Optimizer=HINT: ALL_ROWS (Cost=13 Card=409
   1    0   SORT (GROUP BY) (Cost=13 Card=409 Bytes=9816)
```

```
     2    1       TABLE ACCESS (BY INDEX ROWID) OF 'TEMP_ALL_OBJECTS' (Cost=10
     3    2          INDEX (RANGE SCAN) OF 'TEMP_ALL_OBJECTS_IDX' (NON-UNIQUE)

tkyte@TKYTE816> set autotrace off
```

This shows that the CBO did the wrong thing. Any time you access more than 10-20 percent of the table, you should not use an index. Here, we accessed 100 percent of the table; in fact the table is so small that using the index in this case is not buying us anything at all. Here is how to give the optimizer the information it needs to develop the correct plan:

```
tkyte@TKYTE816> drop table temp_all_objects;

Table dropped.

tkyte@TKYTE816> create table temp_all_objects
  2  as
  3  select * from all_objects where 1=0
  4  /

Table created.

tkyte@TKYTE816> create index temp_all_objects_idx on temp_all_objects(object_id)
  2  /

Index created.

tkyte@TKYTE816> insert into temp_all_objects
  2  select * from all_objects where rownum < 51;

50 rows created.

tkyte@TKYTE816> analyze table temp_all_objects compute statistics;

Table analyzed.

tkyte@TKYTE816> analyze table temp_all_objects compute statistics for all
  2  indexes;

Table analyzed.
```

What I have done is created a permanent table that looks just like the temporary table. I populated it with representative data. That is the tricky part here; you must carefully consider what you put into this table when you analyze it. You will be overriding the optimizer's best guess with this data so you had better be giving it better data than it can make up itself. In some cases, it might be enough to just set the table or index statistics manually, as I did above to inform the CBO as the to the cardinality, and range of values. In other cases, you may need to add many pieces of information to the data dictionary in order to give the CBO the data it needs. Instead of manually adding this data, we can let Oracle do the work for us. The method below gets all of the information that you can set easily:

```
tkyte@TKYTE816> begin
  2          dbms_stats.create_stat_table( ownname => USER,
  3                                        stattab => 'STATS' );
  4
  5          dbms_stats.export_table_stats( ownname => USER,
```

```
    6                                          tabname => 'TEMP_ALL_OBJECTS',
    7                                          stattab => 'STATS' );
    8        dbms_stats.export_index_stats( ownname => USER,
    9                                          indname => 'TEMP_ALL_OBJECTS_IDX',
   10                                          stattab => 'STATS' );
   11  end;
   12  /

PL/SQL procedure successfully completed.

tkyte@TKYTE816> drop table temp_all_objects;
Table dropped.

tkyte@TKYTE816> create global temporary table temp_all_objects
    2  as
    3  select * from all_objects where 1=0
    4  /

Table created.

tkyte@TKYTE816> create index temp_all_objects_idx on temp_all_objects(object_id)
    2  /

Index created.

tkyte@TKYTE816> begin
    2        dbms_stats.import_table_stats( ownname => USER,
    3                                          tabname => 'TEMP_ALL_OBJECTS',
    4     .                                    stattab => 'STATS' );
    5        dbms_stats.import_index_stats( ownname => USER,
    6                                          indname => 'TEMP_ALL_OBJECTS_IDX',
    7                                          stattab => 'STATS' );
    8  end;
    9  /

PL/SQL procedure successfully completed.
```

We've just put statistics in our temporary table, based on our representative result set. The CBO will now use this to make decisions about the plans based on that table as evidenced by the next query:

```
tkyte@TKYTE816> insert into temp_all_objects
    2  select * from all_objects where rownum < 51
    3  /

50 rows created.

tkyte@TKYTE816> set autotrace on
tkyte@TKYTE816> select /*+ ALL_ROWS */ object_type, count(*)
    2     FROM temp_all_objects
    3    where object_id < 50000
    4     group by object_type
    5  /

OBJECT_TYPE              COUNT(*)
------------------      -----------
JAVA CLASS                     50
```

```
Execution Plan
----------------------------------------------------------
     0      SELECT STATEMENT Optimizer=HINT: ALL_ROWS (Cost=3 Card=1 Bytes=14)
     1    0   SORT (GROUP BY) (Cost=3 Card=1 Bytes=14)
     2    1    TABLE ACCESS (FULL) OF 'TEMP_ALL_OBJECTS' (Cost=1 Card=50
```

Temporary Table Wrap-up

Temporary tables can be useful in an application where you need to temporarily store a set of rows to be processed against other tables, either for a session or a transaction. They are not meant to be used as a means to take a single larger query and 'break it up' into smaller result sets that would be joined back together (which seems to be the most popular use of temporary tables in other databases). In fact, you will find in almost all cases that a single query broken up into smaller temporary table queries, performs more slowly in Oracle than the single query would have. I've seen this behavior time and time again, when given the opportunity to write the series of INSERTs into temporary tables as SELECTs in the form of one large query, it goes much faster.

Temporary tables generate a minimum amount of REDO, however, they still generate some REDO and there is no way to disable that. The REDO is generated for the rollback data and in most typical uses will be negligible. If you only INSERT and SELECT from temporary tables, the amount of REDO generated will not be noticeable. Only if you DELETE or UPDATE a temporary table heavily will you see large amounts of redo generated.

Statistics used by the CBO cannot be generated on a temporary table, however, a better guess set of statistics may be set on a temporary table using the DBMS_STATS package. You may either set a few of the relevant statistics such as the number of rows, average row length, and so on, or you may use a permanent table populated with representative data to generate a complete set. One word of caution, make sure your guess is better than the default guess, otherwise the query plans that the CBO generates will be even worse than before.

Object Tables

We have already seen a partial example of an object table above with nested tables. An object table is a table that is created based on a TYPE, not as a collection of columns. Normally, a CREATE TABLE would look like this:

```
create table t ( x int, y date, z varchar2(25);
```

An object table creation statement looks more like this:

```
create table t of Some_Type;
```

The attributes (columns) of t are derived from the definition of SOME_TYPE. Let's look at a quick example involving a couple of types and review the resulting data structures:

```
tkyte@TKYTE816> create or replace type address_type
  2  as object
  3  ( city    varchar2(30),
  4    street  varchar2(30),
  5    state   varchar2(2),
  6    zip     number
  7  )
  8  /

Type created.

tkyte@TKYTE816> create or replace type person_type
  2  as object
  3  ( name            varchar2(30),
  4    dob             date,
  5    home_address    address_type,
  6    work_address    address_type
  7  )
  8  /

Type created.

tkyte@TKYTE816> create table people of person_type
  2  /

Table created.

tkyte@TKYTE816> desc people
 Name               Null?    Type
 ------------------ -------- ------------
 NAME                        VARCHAR2(30)
 DOB                         DATE
 HOME_ADDRESS                ADDRESS_TYPE
 WORK_ADDRESS                ADDRESS_TYPE
```

So, in a nutshell that's all there is to it. You create some type definitions and then you can create tables of that type. The table appears to have four columns representing the four attributes of the PERSON_TYPE we created. We are at the point where we can now perform DML on the object table to create and query data:

```
tkyte@TKYTE816> insert into people values ( 'Tom', '15-mar-1965',
  2  address_type( 'Reston', '123 Main Street', 'Va', '45678' ),
  3  address_type( 'Redwood', '1 Oracle Way', 'Ca', '23456' ) );

1 row created.

tkyte@TKYTE816> select * from people;

NAME DOB        HOME_ADDRESS(CITY, S WORK_ADDRESS(CI
---- ---------  -------------------- ---------------
Tom  15-MAR-65 ADDRESS_TYPE('Reston  ADDRESS_TYPE('R
               ', '123 Main          edwood', '1
               Street', 'Va',        Oracle Way',
               45678)                'Ca', 23456)
```

```
tkyte@TKYTE816> select name, p.home_address.city from people p;

NAME HOME_ADDRESS.CITY
---- -----------------------------
Tom  Reston
```

You are starting to see some of the object syntax necessary to deal with object types. For example, in the INSERT statement we had to wrap the HOME_ADDRESS and WORK_ADDRESS with a CAST. We cast the scalar values to be of an ADDRESS_TYPE. Another way of saying this is that we create an ADDRESS_TYPE instance for that row by using the default constructor for the ADDRESS_TYPE object.

Now, as far as the external face of the table is concerned, there are four columns in our table. By now, after seeing the hidden magic that took place for the nested tables, we can probably guess that there is something else going on. Oracle stores all object relational data in plain old relational tables – at the end of the day it is all in rows and columns. If we dig into the 'real' data dictionary, we can see what this table really looks like:

```
tkyte@TKYTE816> select name, segcollength
  2     from sys.col$
  3   where obj# = ( select object_id
  4                     from user_objects
  5                    where object_name = 'PEOPLE' )
  6  /

NAME                 SEGCOLLENGTH
-------------------- ------------
SYS_NC_OID$                    16
SYS_NC_ROWINFO$                 1
NAME                           30
DOB                             7
HOME_ADDRESS                    1
SYS_NC00006$                   30
SYS_NC00007$                   30
SYS_NC00008$                    2
SYS_NC00009$                   22
WORK_ADDRESS                    1
SYS_NC00011$                   30
SYS_NC00012$                   30
SYS_NC00013$                    2
SYS_NC00014$                   22

14 rows selected.
```

This looks quite different from what describe tells us. Apparently, there are 14 columns in this table, not 4. In this case they are:

❑ SYS_NC_OID$ – This is the system-generated object ID of the table. It is a unique RAW(16) column. It has a unique constraint on it – there is a corresponding unique index created on it as well.

❑ SYS_NC_ROWINFO – This is the same 'magic' function as we observed with the nested table. If we select that from the table it returns the entire row as a single column.:

```
tkyte@TKYTE816> select sys_nc_rowinfo$ from people;

SYS_NC_ROWINFO$(NAME, DOB, HOME_ADDRESS(CITY, STREET, STATE, ZIP),…
----------------------------------------------------------------------
PERSON_TYPE('Tom', '15-MAR-65', ADDRESS_TYPE('Leesburg', '1234 Main Street', 'Va',
20175), ADDRESS_TYPE('Reston', '1910 Oracle Way', 'Va', 20190))
```

❏ NAME, DOB – These are the scalar attributes of our object table. They are stored much as you would expect, as regular columns

❏ HOME_ADDRESS, WORK_ADDRESS – These are 'magic' functions as well, they return the collection of columns they represent as a single object. These consume no real space except to signify NULL or NOT NULL for the entity.

❏ SYS_NCnnnnn$ – These are the scalar implementations of our embedded object types. Since the PERSON_TYPE had the ADDRESS_TYPE embedded in it, Oracle needed to make room to store them in the appropriate type of columns. The system-generated names are necessary since a column name must be unique and there is nothing stopping us from using the same object type more then once as we did here. If the names were not generated, we would have ended up with the ZIP column twice.

So, just like with the nested table, there is lots going on here. A pseudo primary key of 16 bytes was added, there are virtual columns, and an index created for us. We can change the default behavior with regards to the value of the object identifier assigned to an object, as we'll see in a moment. First, let's look at the full verbose SQL that would generate our table for us, again this was generated using EXP/IMP:

```
CREATE TABLE "TKYTE"."PEOPLE"
OF "PERSON_TYPE" OID '36101E4C6B7E4F7E96A8A6662518965C'
OIDINDEX (PCTFREE 10 INITRANS 2 MAXTRANS 255
        STORAGE(INITIAL 131072 NEXT 131072
            MINEXTENTS 1 MAXEXTENTS 4096
            PCTINCREASE 0 FREELISTS 1 FREELIST GROUPS 1
            BUFFER_POOL DEFAULT)
TABLESPACE "USERS")
PCTFREE 10 PCTUSED 40
INITRANS 1 MAXTRANS 255
LOGGING STORAGE(INITIAL 131072 NEXT 131072
            MINEXTENTS 1 MAXEXTENTS 4096
            PCTINCREASE 0 FREELISTS 1 FREELIST GROUPS 1
            BUFFER_POOL DEFAULT) TABLESPACE "USERS"
/

ALTER TABLE "TKYTE"."PEOPLE" MODIFY
("SYS_NC_OID$" DEFAULT SYS_OP_GUID())
/
```

This gives us a little more insight into what is actually taking place here. We see the OIDINDEX clause clearly now and we see a reference to the SYS_NC_OID$ column. This is the hidden primary key of the table. The function SYS_OP_GUID, is the same as the function SYS_GUID. They both return a globally unique identifier that is a 16 byte RAW field.

The `OID '<big hex number>'` syntax is not documented in the Oracle documentation. All this is doing is ensuring that during an EXP and subsequent IMP, the underlying type `PERSON_TYPE` is in fact the *same* type. This will prevent an error that would occur if you:

1. Created the `PEOPLE` table.

2. Exported it.

3. Dropped it and the underlying `PERSON_TYPE`.

4. Created a new `PERSON_TYPE` with different attributes.

5. Imported the old `PEOPLE` data.

Obviously, this export cannot be imported into the new structure – it will not fit. This check prevents that from occurring. You can refer to the Chapter 8 on *Import and Export* later on for guidelines regarding import and export and more details on object tables.

If you remember, I mentioned that we can change the behavior of the object identifier assigned to an object instance. Instead of having the system generate a pseudo primary key for us, we can use the natural key of an object. At first, this might appear self defeating – the `SYS_NC_OID$` will still appear in the table definition in `SYS.COL$`, and in fact it, will appear to consume massive amounts of storage as compared to the system generated column. Once again however, there is 'magic' at work here. The `SYS_NC_OID$` column for an object table that is based on a *primary key* and not *system* generated, is a virtual column and consumes no real storage on disk. Here is an example that shows what happens in the data dictionary and shows that there is no physical storage consume for the `SYS_NC_OID$`. We'll start with an analysis of the system generated `OID` table:

```
tkyte@TKYTE816> CREATE TABLE "TKYTE"."PEOPLE"
  2  OF "PERSON_TYPE"
  3  /

Table created.

tkyte@TKYTE816> select name, type#, segcollength
  2     from sys.col$
  3   where obj# = ( select object_id
  4                    from user_objects
  5                   where object_name = 'PEOPLE' )
  6     and name like 'SYS\_NC\_%' escape '\'
  7  /

NAME                             TYPE# SEGCOLLENGTH
------------------------------ --------- ------------
SYS_NC_OID$                         23           16
SYS_NC_ROWINFO$                    121            1

tkyte@TKYTE816> insert into people(name)
  2  select rownum from all_objects;

21765 rows created.
```

```
tkyte@TKYTE816> analyze table people compute statistics;
Table analyzed.

tkyte@TKYTE816> select table_name, avg_row_len from user_object_tables;

TABLE_NAME                      AVG_ROW_LEN
------------------------------- -----------
PEOPLE                                   25
```

So, we see here that the average row length is 25 bytes, 16 bytes for the SYS_NC_OID$ and 9 bytes for the NAME. Now, let's do the same thing, but use a primary key on the NAME column as the object identifier:

```
tkyte@TKYTE816> CREATE TABLE "TKYTE"."PEOPLE"
  2  OF "PERSON_TYPE"
  3  ( constraint people_pk primary key(name) )
  4  object identifier is PRIMARY KEY
  5  /

Table created.

tkyte@TKYTE816> select name, type#, segcollength
  2     from sys.col$
  3   where obj# = ( select object_id
  4                    from user_objects
  5                   where object_name = 'PEOPLE' )
  6     and name like 'SYS\_NC\_%' escape '\'
  7  /

NAME                            TYPE# SEGCOLLENGTH
------------------------------- ----- ------------
SYS_NC_OID$                        23           81
SYS_NC_ROWINFO$                   121            1
```

According to this, instead of a small 16 byte column, we have a large 81 byte column! In reality, there is no data stored in there. It will be Null. The system will generate a unique ID based on the object table, its underlying type and the value in the row itself. We can see this in the following:

```
tkyte@TKYTE816> insert into people (name)
  2  values ( 'Hello World!' );

1 row created.

tkyte@TKYTE816> select sys_nc_oid$ from people p;

SYS_NC_OID$
----------------------------------------------------------------
7129B0A94D3B49258CAC926D8FDD6EEB00000017260100010001002900000
0000000C07001E0100002A00078401FE000000140C48656C6C6F20576F72
6C642100000000000000000000000000000000000000000

tkyte@TKYTE816> select utl_raw.cast_to_raw( 'Hello World!' ) data
  2  from dual;
```

```
DATA
------------------------------------------------------------
48656C6C6F20576F726C6421

tkyte@TKYTE816> select utl_raw.cast_to_varchar2(sys_nc_oid$) data
  2  from people;

DATA
------------------------------------------------------------
<garbage data..........>Hello World!
```

If we select out the SYS_NC_OID$ column and inspect the HEX dump of the string we inserted, we see that the row data itself is embedded in the object ID. Converting the object id into a VARCHAR2, we can just confirm that visually. Does that mean our data is stored twice with a lot of overhead with it? Actually it can not:

```
tkyte@TKYTE816> insert into people(name)
  2  select rownum from all_objects;

21766 rows created.

tkyte@TKYTE816> analyze table people compute statistics;

Table analyzed.

tkyte@TKYTE816> select table_name, avg_row_len from user_object_tables;

TABLE_NAME                     AVG_ROW_LEN
------------------------------ -----------
PEOPLE                                   8
```

The average row length is only 8 bytes now. The overhead of storing the system-generated key is gone and the 81 bytes you might think we are going to have isn't really there. Oracle synthesizes the data upon selecting from the table.

Now for an opinion. The object relational components (nested tables, object tables) are primarily what I call 'syntactic sugar'. They are always translated into 'good old' relational rows and columns. I prefer not to use them as physical storage mechanisms personally. There are too many bits of 'magic' happening – side effects that are not clear. You get hidden columns, extra indexes, surprise pseudo columns, and so on. *This does not mean that the object relational components are a waste of time*, on the contrary really. I use them in PL/SQL constantly. I use them with object views. I can achieve the benefits of a nested table construct (less data returned over the network for a master detail relationship, conceptually easier to work with, and so on) without any of the physical storage concerns. That is because I can use object views to synthesize my objects from my relational data. This solves most all of my concerns with object tables/nested tables in that the physical storage is dictated by me, the join conditions are setup by me, and the tables are available as relational tables (which is what many third party tools and applications will demand) naturally. The people who require an object view of relational data can have it and the people who need the relational view have it. Since object tables are really relational tables in disguise, we are doing the same thing Oracle does for us behind the scenes, only we can do it more efficiently, since we don't have to do it generically as they do. For example, using the types defined above I could just as easily use the following:

```
tkyte@TKYTE816> create table people_tab
  2  ( name          varchar2(30) primary key,
  3    dob           date,
  4    home_city     varchar2(30),
  5    home_street   varchar2(30),
  6    home_state    varchar2(2),
  7    home_zip      number,
  8    work_city     varchar2(30),
  9    work_street   varchar2(30),
 10    work_state    varchar2(2),
 11    work_zip      number
 12  )
 13  /

Table created.

tkyte@TKYTE816> create view people of person_type
  2  with object identifier (name)
  3  as
  4  select name, dob,
  5    address_type(home_city,home_street,home_state,home_zip) home_adress,
  6    address_type(work_city,work_street,work_state,work_zip) work_adress
  7    from people_tab
  8  /

View created.

tkyte@TKYTE816> insert into people values ( 'Tom', '15-mar-1965',
  2  address_type( 'Reston', '123 Main Street', 'Va', '45678' ),
  3  address_type( 'Redwood', '1 Oracle Way', 'Ca', '23456' ) );

1 row created.
```

However I achieve very much the same effect, I know exactly what is stored, how it is stored, and where it is stored. For more complex objects we may have to code INSTEAD OF triggers on the Object Views to allow for modifications through the view.

Object Table Wrap-up

Object tables are used to implement an object relational model in Oracle. A single object table will create many physical database objects typically, and add additional columns to your schema to manage everything. There is some amount of 'magic' associated with object tables. Object Views allow you to take advantage of the syntax and semantics of 'objects' while at the same time retaining complete control over the physical storage of the data and allowing for relational access to the underlying data. In that fashion, you can achieve the best of both the relational and object relational worlds.

Summary

Hopefully, after reading this chapter you have come to the conclusion that not all tables are created equal. Oracle provides a rich variety of table types that you can exploit. In this chapter, we have covered many of the salient aspects of tables in general and the many different table types Oracle provides for us to use.

We began by looking at some terminology and storage parameters associated with tables. We looked at the usefulness of FREELISTs in a multi-user environment where a table is frequently inserted/updated by many people simultaneously. We investigated the meaning of PCTFREE and PCTUSED, and developed some guidelines for setting them correctly.

Then we got into the different types of tables starting with the common heap. The heap organized table is by far the most commonly used table in most Oracle applications and is the default table type. We moved onto index organized tables, the ability store your table data in an index. We saw how these are applicable for various uses such as lookup tables and inverted lists where a heap table would just be a redundant copy of the data. Later, we saw how they can really be useful when mixed with other table types, specifically the nested table type.

We looked at cluster objects of which Oracle has two kinds; Index and Hash. The goals of the cluster are twofold:

❑ To give us the ability to store data from many tables together – on the same database block(s); and

❑ To give us the ability to force like data to be stored physically 'together' based on some cluster key – in this fashion all of the data for department 10 (from many tables) may be stored together.

These features allow us to access this related data very quickly, with minimal physical I/O that might otherwise be needed to pull together all of the data. We observed the main differences between index clusters and hash clusters and discussed when each would be appropriate (and when they would not).

Next, we moved onto Nested Tables. We reviewed the syntax, semantics, and usage of these types of tables. We saw how they are in a fact a system generated and maintained parent/child pair of tables and discovered how Oracle physically does this for us. We looked at using different table types for Nested tables which by default use a heap based table. We found that there would probably never be a reason not to use an IOT instead of a heap table for nested tables.

Then we looked into the ins and outs of Temporary tables; looking at how to create them, where they get their storage from, and the fact that they introduce no concurrency related issues at runtime. We explored the differences between session level and transaction level temporary table. We discussed the appropriate method for using temporary tables in an Oracle database.

This section closed up with a look into the workings of object tables. Like nested tables, we discovered there is a lot going on under the covers with object tables in Oracle. We discussed how object views on top of relational tables can give us the functionality of an object table while at the same time giving us access to the underlying relational data easily; a topic we will look at in more detail in Chapter 20 on *Using Object Relational Features*.

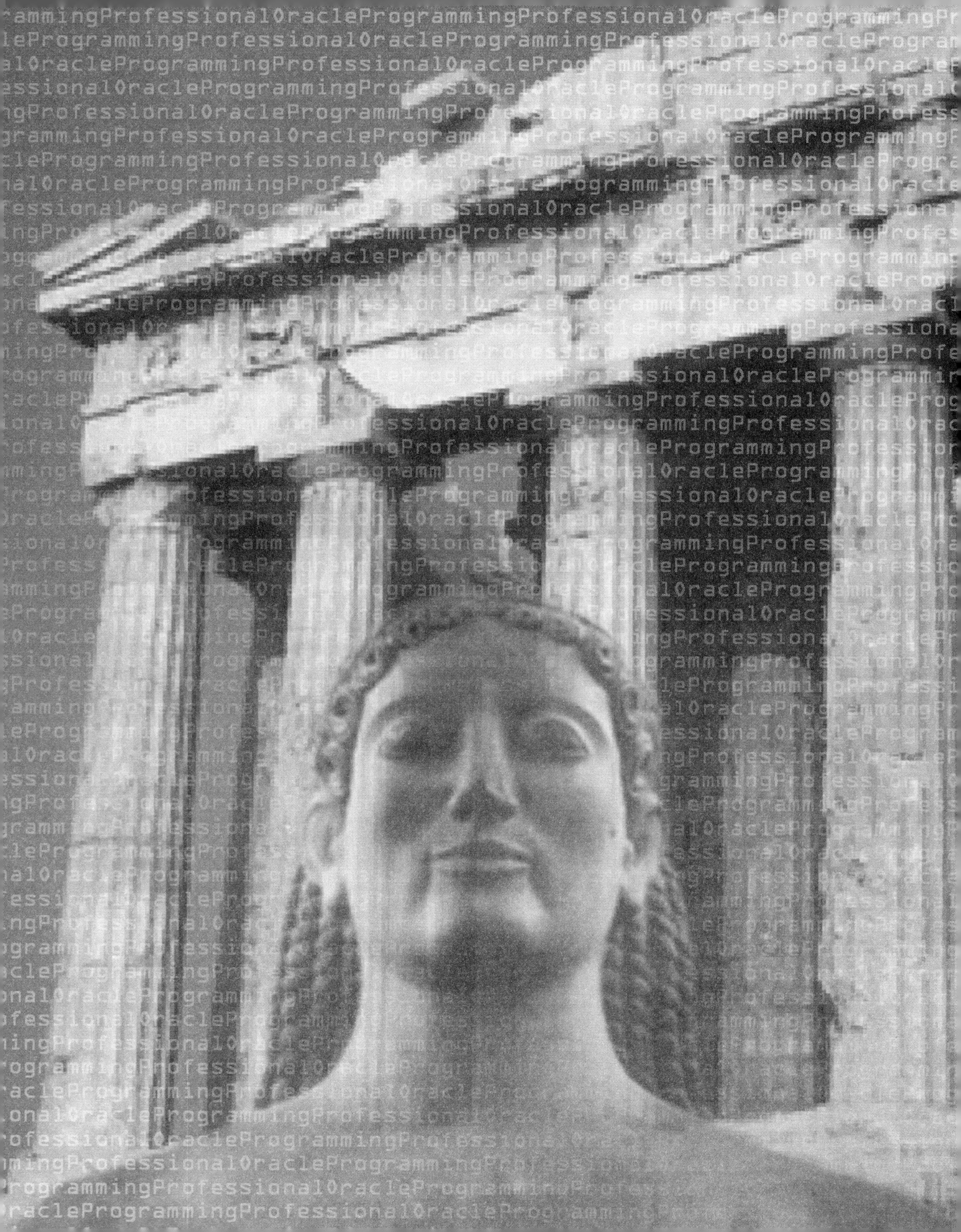

7

Indexes

Indexing is a crucial aspect of your application design and development. Too many indexes and the performance of DML will suffer. Too few indexes and the performance of queries (including inserts, updates and deletes) will suffer. Finding the right mix is critical to your application performance.

I find frequently that indexes are an afterthought in application development. I believe that this is the wrong approach. From the very beginning, if you understand how the data will be used, you should be able to come up with the representative set of indexes you will use in your application. Too many times the approach seems to be to throw the application out there and then see where indexes are needed. This implies you have not taken the time to understand how the data will be used and how many rows you will ultimately be dealing with. You'll be adding indexes to this system forever as the volume of data grows over time (reactive tuning). You'll have indexes that are redundant, never used, and this wastes not only space but also computing resources. A few hours at the start, spent properly considering when and how to index your data will save you many hours of 'tuning' further down the road (note that I said 'it will', not 'it might').

The basic remit of this chapter is to give an overview of the indexes available for use in Oracle and discuss when and where you might use them. This chapter will differ from others in this book in terms of its style and format. Indexing is a huge topic – you could write an entire book on the subject. Part of the reason for this is that it bridges the developer and DBA roles. The developer must be aware of them, how they apply to their applications, when to use them (and when not to use them), and so on. The DBA is concerned with the growth of an index, the degree of fragmentation within an index and other physical properties. We will be tackling indexes mainly from the standpoint of their practical use in applications (we will not deal specifically with index fragmentation, and so on). The first half of this chapter represents the basic knowledge I believe you need in order to make intelligent choices about when to index and what type of index to use. The second answers some of the most frequently asked questions about indexes.

The various examples in this book require different base releases of Oracle. When a specific feature requires Oracle 8i Enterprise or Personal Edition I'll specify that. Many of the B*Tree indexing examples require Oracle 7.0 and later versions. The bitmap indexing examples require Oracle 7.3.3 or later versions (Enterprise or Personal edition). Function-based indexes and application domain indexes require Oracle 8i Enterprise or Personal Editions. The section *Frequently Asked Questions* applies to all releases of Oracle.

An Overview of Oracle Indexes

Oracle provides many different types of indexes for us to use. Briefly they are as follows:

❑   **B*Tree Indexes** – These are what I refer to as 'conventional' indexes. They are by far the most common indexes in use in Oracle, and most other databases. Similar in construct to a binary tree, they provide fast access, by key, to an individual row or range of rows, normally requiring few reads to find the correct row. The B*Tree index has several 'subtypes':

Index Organized Tables – A table stored in a B*Tree structure. We discussed these in some detail Chapter 4, *Tables*. That section also covered the physical storage of B*Tree structures, so we will not cover that again here.

B*Tree Cluster Indexes – These are a slight variation of the above index. They are used to index the cluster keys (see *Index Clustered Tables* in Chapter 4) and will not be discussed again in this chapter. They are used not to go from a key to a row, but rather from a cluster key to the block that contains the rows related to that cluster key.

Reverse Key Indexes – These are B*Tree indexes where the bytes in the key are 'reversed'. This is used to more evenly distribute index entries throughout an index that is populated with increasing values. For example, if I am using a sequence to generate a primary key, the sequence will generate values like 987500, 987501, 987502, and so on. Since these values are sequential, they would all tend to go the same block in the index, increasing contention for that block. With a reverse key index, Oracle would be indexing: 205789, 105789, 005789 instead. These values will tend to be 'far away' from each other in the index and would spread out the inserts into the index over many blocks.

Descending Indexes – In the future, descending indexes will not be notable as a special type of index. However, since they are brand new with Oracle 8i they deserve a special look. Descending indexes allow for data to be sorted from 'big' to 'small' (descending) instead of small to big (ascending) in the index structure. We'll take a look at why that might be important and how they work.

❑   **Bitmap Indexes** – Normally in a B*Tree, there is a one-to-one relationship between an index entry and a row – an index entry points to a row. With a bitmap index, a single index entry uses a bitmap to point to many rows simultaneously. They are appropriate for low cardinality data (data with few distinct values) that is mostly read-only. A column that takes on three values: Y, N, and NULL, in a table of one million rows might be a good candidate for a bitmap index. Bitmap indexes should never be considered in an OLTP database for concurrency related issues (which we'll discuss in due course).

❑   **Function-based indexes** – These are B*Tree or Bitmap indexes that store the computed result of a function on a rows column(s) – not the column data itself. These may be used to speed up queries of the form: SELECT * FROM T WHERE FUNCTION(DATABASE_COLUMN) = SOME_VALUE since the value FUNCTION(DATABASE_COLUMN) has already been computed and stored in the index.

❑   **Application Domain Indexes** – These are indexes you build and store yourself, either in Oracle or perhaps even outside of Oracle. You will tell the optimizer how selective your index is, how costly it is to execute and the optimizer will decide whether or not to use your index, based on that information. The interMedia text index is an example of an application domain index; it is built using the same tools you may use to build your own index.

❑   **interMedia Text Indexes** – This is a specialized index built into Oracle to allow for keyword searching of large bodies of text. We'll defer a discussion of these until the Chapter 17 on *interMedia*.

As you can see, there are many types of indexes to choose from. What I would like to do in the following sections is to present some technical details on how they work and when they should be used. I would like to stress again that we will not be covering certain DBA-related topics. For example, we will not cover the mechanics of an online rebuild, but rather will concentrate on practical application-related details.

B*Tree Indexes

B*Tree, or what I call 'conventional', indexes are the most commonly used type of indexing structure in the database. They are similar in implementation to a binary search tree. Their goal is to minimize the amount of time Oracle spends searching for data. Loosely speaking, if you have an index on a number column then the structure might look like this:

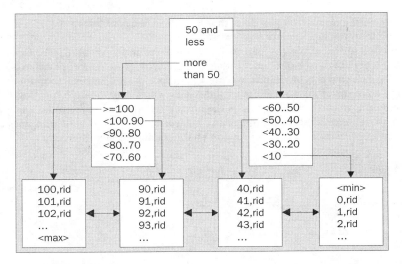

The lowest level blocks in the tree, called **leaf nodes**, contain every indexed key and a row ID (`rid` in the picture) that points to the row it is indexing. The interior blocks, above the leaf nodes, are known as **branch blocks**. They are used to navigate through the structure. For example, if we wanted to find the value 42 in the index, we would start at the top of the tree and go to the right. We would inspect that block and discover we needed to go to the block in the range 'less than 50 to 40'. This block would be the leaf block and would point us to the rows that contained the number 42. It is interesting to note that the leaf nodes of the index are actually a doubly linked list. Once we find out where to 'start' in the leaf nodes – once we have found that first value– doing an ordered scan of values (also known as an **index range scan**) is very easy. We don't have to navigate the structure any more; we just go forward through the leaf nodes. That makes solving a predicate, such as the following, pretty simple:

```
where x between 20 and 30
```

Oracle finds the first index block that contains 20 and then just walks horizontally, through the linked list of leaf nodes until, it finally hits a value that is greater than 30.

There really is no such thing as a non-unique index in a B*Tree. In a non-unique index, Oracle simply adds the row's row ID to the index key to make it unique. In a unique index, as defined by you, Oracle does not add the row ID to the index key. In a non-unique index, we will find that the data is sorted first by index key values (in the order of the index key), and then by row ID. In a unique index, the data is sorted by the index key values only.

One of the properties of a B*Tree is that all leaf blocks should be at the same level in the tree, although technically, the difference in height across the tree may vary by one. This level is also known as the **height** of the index, meaning that all the nodes above the leaf nodes only point to lower, more specific nodes, while entries in the leaf nodes point to specific row IDs, or a range of row IDs. Most B*Tree indexes will have a height of 2 or 3, even for millions of records. This means that it will take, in general, 2 or 3 reads to find your key in the index – which is not too bad. Another property is that the leaves, are self-balanced, in other words, all are at the same level, and this is mostly true. There are some opportunities for the index to have less than perfect balance, due to updates and deletes. Oracle will try to keep every block in the index from about three-quarters to completely full although, again, DELETEs and UPDATEs can skew this as well. In general, the B*Tree is an excellent general purpose indexing mechanism that works well for large and small tables and experiences little, if any, degradation as the size of the underlying table grows, as long as the tree does not get skewed.

One of the interesting things you can do with a B*Tree index is to 'compress' it. This is not compression in the same manner that zip files are compressed; rather this is compression that removes redundancies from concatenated indexes. We covered this in some detail in the section *Index Organized Tables* in Chapter 6, but we will take a brief look at it again here. The basic concept behind a key compressed index is that every entry is broken into two pieces – a 'prefix' and 'suffix' component. The prefix is built on the leading columns of the concatenated index and would have many repeating values. The suffix is the trailing columns in the index key and is the unique component of the index entry within the prefix. For example, we'll create a table and index and measure it's space without compression – then, we'll recreate the index with index key compression enabled and see the difference:

This example calls on the show_space procedure given in Chapter 6 on Tables

```
tkyte@TKYTE816> create table t
  2  as
  3  select * from all_objects
  4  /

Table created.

tkyte@TKYTE816> create index t_idx on
  2  t(owner,object_type,object_name);

Index created.

tkyte@TKYTE816>
tkyte@TKYTE816> exec show_space('T_IDX',user,'INDEX')
```

```
Free Blocks..............................0
Total Blocks..............................192
Total Bytes..............................1572864
Unused Blocks.............................35
Unused Bytes.............................286720
Last Used Ext FileId.....................6
Last Used Ext BlockId....................649
Last Used Block..........................29

PL/SQL procedure successfully completed.
```

The index allocated 192 blocks and has 35 that contain no data (157 blocks in total use). We could realize that the OWNER component is repeated many times. A single index block will have dozens of entries like this:

```
Sys,Package,Dbms_Alert
Sys,Package,Dbms_Application_Info
Sys,Package,Dbms_Aq
Sys,Package,Dbms_Aqadm
Sys,Package,Dbms_Aqadm_Sys
Sys,Package,Dbms_Aqadm_Syscalls
Sys,Package,Dbms_Aqin
Sys,Package,Dbms_Aqjms
....
```

We could factor the repeated OWNER column out of this, resulting in a block that looks more like this:

```
Sys
Package,Dbms_Alert
Package,Dbms_Application_Info
Package,Dbms_Aq
Package,Dbms_Aqadm
Package,Dbms_Aqadm_Sys
Package,Dbms_Aqadm_Syscalls
Package,Dbms_Aqin
Package,Dbms_Aqjms
....
```

Here the owner name appears once on the leaf blocks – not once per repeated entry. If we recreate that index using compression with the leading column:

```
tkyte@TKYTE816> drop index t_idx;
Index dropped.

tkyte@TKYTE816> create index t_idx on
  2    t(owner,object_type,object_name)
  3    compress 1;
Index created.

tkyte@TKYTE816> exec show_space('T_IDX',user,'INDEX')
Free Blocks..............................0
Total Blocks..............................192
Total Bytes..............................1572864
Unused Blocks.............................52
```

```
Unused Bytes........................425984
Last Used Ext FileId..................6
Last Used Ext BlockId.................649
Last Used Block.......................12


PL/SQL procedure successfully completed.
```

We can see this reduced the size of the overall index structure from 157 used blocks to 140, a reduction of about 10 percent. We can go further, compressing the leading two columns. This will result in blocks where both the OWNER and the OBJECT_TYPE are factored out to the block level:

> **Sys,Package**
> Dbms_Application_Info
> Dbms_Aq
> Dbms_Aqadm
> Dbms_Aqadm_Sys
> Dbms_Aqadm_Syscalls
> Dbms_Aqin
> Dbms_Aqjms
> ....

Now, when we use compression on the leading two columns:

```
tkyte@TKYTE816> drop index t_idx;
Index dropped.

tkyte@TKYTE816> create index t_idx on
  2  t(owner,object_type,object_name)
  3  compress 2;
Index created.

tkyte@TKYTE816>
tkyte@TKYTE816> exec show_space('T_IDX',user,'INDEX')
Free Blocks...........................0
Total Blocks..........................128
Total Bytes...........................1048576
Unused Blocks.........................15
Unused Bytes..........................122880
Last Used Ext FileId..................6
Last Used Ext BlockId.................585
Last Used Block.......................49


PL/SQL procedure successfully completed.
```

This index is 113 blocks, about thirty percent smaller then the original index. Depending on how repetitious your data is, this could really add up. Now, you do not get this compression for free. The compressed index structure is now more complex then it used to be. Oracle will spend more time processing the data in this structure, both while maintaining the index during modifications as well as when you search the index during a query. What we are doing here is trading off increased CPU time for reduced I/O time. Our block buffer cache will be able to hold more index entries than before, our cache-hit ratio might go up, our physical I/Os should go down but it will take a little more CPU horse power to process the index and also increases the chance of block contention. Just as in our discussion of the hash cluster, where it took more CPU to retrieve a million random rows but half the I/O, we must be aware of the trade-off. If you are currently CPU-bound, adding compressed key indexes may slow down your processing. On the other hand, if you are I/O bound, using them may speed things up.

Reverse Key Indexes

Another feature of a B*Tree index is the ability to 'reverse' their keys. At first, you might ask yourself, 'Why would I want to do that?' They were designed for a specific environment, for a specific issue. They were implemented to reduce contention on index leaf blocks in an Oracle Parallel Server (OPS) environment.

We discussed OPS in Chapter 2, Architecture.

It is a configuration of Oracle where multiple instances can mount and open the same database. If two instances need to modify the same block of data simultaneously, they will share the block by flushing it to disk so that the other instance can read it. This activity is known as 'pinging'. Pinging is something to be avoided when using OPS but will be virtually unavoidable if you have a conventional B*Tree index, this is on a column whose values are generated by a sequence number. Everyone will be trying to modify the left hand side of the index structure as they insert new values (see the figure at start of the section on *B*Tree Indexes* that shows 'higher values' in the index go to the left, lower values to the right). In an OPS environment, modifications to indexes on columns populated by sequences are focused on a small set of leaf blocks. Reversing the keys of the index allows insertions to be distributed across all the leaf keys in the index, though it tends to make the index much less efficiently packed.

A reverse key index will simply reverse the bytes of each column in an index key. If we consider the numbers 90101, 90102, 90103,and look at their internal representation using the Oracle DUMP function, we will find they are represented as:

```
tkyte@TKYTE816> select 90101, dump(90101,16) from dual
  2  union all
  3  select 90102, dump(90102,16) from dual
  4  union all
  5  select 90103, dump(90103,16) from dual
  6  /

     90101 DUMP(90101,16)
---------- --------------------
     90101 Typ=2 Len=4: c3,a,2,2
     90102 Typ=2 Len=4: c3,a,2,3
     90103 Typ=2 Len=4: c3,a,2,4
```

Each one is four bytes in length and only the last byte is different. These numbers would end up right next to each other in an index structure. If we reverse their bytes however, Oracle will insert:

```
tkyte@TKYTE816> select 90101, dump(reverse(90101),16) from dual
  2  union all
  3  select 90102, dump(reverse(90102),16) from dual
  4  union all
  5  select 90103, dump(reverse(90103),16) from dual
  6  /
```

```
       90101 DUMP(REVERSE(90101),1
---------- ----------------------
       90101 Typ=2 Len=4: 2,2,a,c3
       90102 Typ=2 Len=4: 3,2,a,c3
       90103 Typ=2 Len=4: 4,2,a,c3
```

The numbers will end up 'far away' from each other. This reduces the number of instances going after the same block (the leftmost block) and reduces the amount of pinging going on. One of the drawbacks to a reverse key index is that you cannot utilize it in all of the cases where a regular index can be applied. For example, in answering the following predicate, a reverse key index on x would not be useful:

```
where x > 5
```

The data in the index is not sorted before it is stored, hence the range scan will not work. On the other hand, some range scans can be done on a reverse key index. If I have a concatenated index on X, Y, the following predicate will be able to make use of the reverse key index and will 'range scan' it:

```
where x = 5
```

This is because the bytes for X are reversed and then the bytes for Y are reversed. Oracle does not reverse the bytes of X || Y, but rather stores reverse(X) || reverse(Y). This means all of the values for X = 5 will be stored together, so Oracle can range scan that index to find them all.

Descending Indexes

Descending Indexes are a new feature of Oracle 8i that extend the functionality of a B*Tree index. They allow for a column to be stored sorted from 'big' to 'small' in the index instead of ascending. Prior releases of Oracle have always supported the DESC (descending) keyword, but basically ignored it – it had no effect on how the data was stored or used in the index. In Oracle 8i however, it changes the way the index is created and used.

Oracle has had the ability to read an index backwards for quite a while, so you may be wondering why this feature is relevant. For example, if we used the table T from above and queried:

```
tkyte@TKYTE816> select owner, object_type
  2  from t
  3  where owner between 'T' and 'Z'
  4  and object_type is not null
  5  order by owner DESC, object_type DESC
  6  /
46 rows selected.


Execution Plan
----------------------------------------------------------
   0      SELECT STATEMENT Optimizer=CHOOSE (Cost=2 Card=46 Bytes=644)
   1    0    INDEX (RANGE SCAN DESCENDING) OF 'T_IDX' (NON-UNIQUE)...
```

It is shown that Oracle will just read the index backwards, there is no final sort step in this plan, the data is sorted. Where this descending index feature comes into play however, is when you have a mixture of columns and some are sorted ASC (ascending) and some DESC (descending). For example:

```
tkyte@TKYTE816> select owner, object_type
  2  from t
  3  where owner between 'T' and 'Z'
  4  and object_type is not null
  5  order by owner DESC, object_type ASC
  6  /
46 rows selected.


Execution Plan
----------------------------------------------------------
   0      SELECT STATEMENT Optimizer=CHOOSE (Cost=4 Card=46 Bytes=644)
   1    0   SORT (ORDER BY) (Cost=4 Card=46 Bytes=644)
   2    1     INDEX (RANGE SCAN) OF 'T_IDX' (NON-UNIQUE) (Cost=2 Card=
```

Oracle isn't able to use the index we have in place on (OWNER, OBJECT_TYPE, OBJECT_NAME) anymore to *sort* the data. It could have read it backwards to get the data sorted by OWNER DESC but it needs to read it 'forwards' to get OBJECT_TYPE sorted ASC. Instead, it collected together all of the rows and then sorted. Enter the DESC index:

```
tkyte@TKYTE816> create index desc_t_idx on t(owner DESC, object_type ASC )
  2  /
Index created.

tkyte@TKYTE816> select owner, object_type
  2  from t
  3  where owner between 'T' and 'Z'
  4  and object_type is not null
  5  order by owner DESC, object_type ASC
  6  /
46 rows selected.

Execution Plan
----------------------------------------------------------
   0      SELECT STATEMENT Optimizer=CHOOSE (Cost=4 Card=46 Bytes=644)
   1    0   INDEX (RANGE SCAN) OF 'DESC_T_IDX' (NON-UNIQUE)...
```

Now, once more, we are able to read the data sorted, there is no extra sort step at the end of the plan. It should be noted that unless your *compatible* init.ora parameter is set to 8.1.0 or higher, the DESC option on the create index will be silently ignored – no warning or error will be produced as this was the default behavior in prior releases.

When should you use a B*Tree Index?

Not being a big believer in 'rules of thumb' (there are exceptions to every rule), I don't have any rules of thumb for when to use (or not to use) a B*Tree index. To demonstrate why I don't have any rules of thumb for this case, I'll present two equally valid ones:

❑ Only use B*Tree to index columns if you are going to access a very small percentage of the rows in the table via the index

❑ Use a B*Tree index if you are going to process many rows of a table and the index can be used *instead of* the table.

These rules seem to offer conflicting advice, but in reality, they do not – they just cover two extremely different cases. There are two ways to use an index:

1. As the means to access rows in a table. You will read the index to get to a row in the table. Here you want to access a very small percentage of the rows in the table.

2. As the means to answer a query. The index contains enough information to answer the entire query – we will not have to go to the table at all. The index will be used as a 'thinner' version of the table.

The first case above says if you have a table T (using the same table T from above) and you have a query plan looks like this:

```
tkyte@TKYTE816> set autotrace traceonly explain

tkyte@TKYTE816> select owner, status
  2    from T
  3    where owner = USER;

Execution Plan
----------------------------------------------------------
   0      SELECT STATEMENT Optimizer=CHOOSE
   1    0   TABLE ACCESS (BY INDEX ROWID) OF 'T'
   2    1     INDEX (RANGE SCAN) OF 'T_IDX' (NON-UNIQUE)
```

You should be accessing a very small percentage of this table. The issue to look at here is the INDEX (RANGE SCAN) followed by the TABLE ACCESS BY INDEX ROWID. What this means is that Oracle will read the index and then, for each index entry, it will perform a database block read (logical or physical I/O) to get the row data. This is not the most efficient method if you are going to have to access a large percentage of the rows in T via the index (below we will define what a large percentage might be).

On the other hand, if the index can be used *instead* of the table, you can process 100 percent (or any percentage in fact) of the rows via the index. This is rule of thumb number two. You might use an index just to create a 'thinner' version of a table (in sorted order to boot).

The following query demonstrates this concept:

```
tkyte@TKYTE816> select count(*)
  2    from T
  3    where owner = USER;

Execution Plan
----------------------------------------------------------
   0      SELECT STATEMENT Optimizer=CHOOSE
   1    0   SORT (AGGREGATE)
   2    1     INDEX (RANGE SCAN) OF 'T_IDX' (NON-UNIQUE)
```

Here, only the index was used to answer the query – it would not matter now what percentage of rows we were accessing, we used the index only. We can see from the plan that the underlying table was never accessed; we simply scanned the index structure itself.

It is important to understand the difference between the two concepts. When we have to do a TABLE ACCESS BY INDEX ROWID, we must ensure we are accessing only a small percentage of the total rows in the table. If we access too high a percentage of the rows (larger then somewhere between 1 and 20 percent of the rows), it will take longer than just full scanning the table. With the second type of query above, where the answer is found entirely in the index, we have a different story. We read an index block and pick up many 'rows' to process, we then go onto the next index block, and so on – we never go to the table. There is also a **fast full scan** we can perform on indexes to make this even faster in certain cases. A fast full scan is when the database reads the index blocks in no particular order – it just starts reading them. It is no longer using the index as an index, but even more like a table at that point. Rows do not come out ordered by index entries from a fast full scan.

In general, a B*Tree index would be placed on columns that I use frequently in the predicate of a query, and expect some small fraction of the data from the table to be returned. On a 'thin' table, a table with few or small columns, this fraction may be very small. A query that uses this index should expect to retrieve 2 to 3 percent or less of the rows to be accessed in the table. On a 'fat' table, a table with many columns or a table with very wide columns, this fraction *might* go all of the way up to 20-25 percent of the table. This advice doesn't always seem to make sense to everyone immediately; it is not intuitive, but it is accurate. An index is stored sorted by index key. The index will be accessed in sorted order by key. The blocks that are pointed to are stored randomly in a heap. Therefore, as we read through an index to access the table, we will perform lots of **scattered**, random I/O. By scattered, I mean that the index will tell us to read block 1, block 1000, block 205, block 321, block 1, block 1032, block 1, and so on – it won't ask us to read block 1, then 2, then 3 in a consecutive manner. We will tend to read and re-read blocks in a very haphazard fashion. Doing this, single block I/O can be very slow.

As a simplistic example of this, let's say we are reading that 'thin' table via an index and we are going to read 20 percent of the rows. Assume we have 100,000 rows in the table. Twenty percent of that is 20,000 rows. If the rows are about 80 bytes apiece in size, on a database with an 8 KB block size, we will find about 100 rows per block. That means the table has approximately 1000 blocks. From here, the math is very easy. We are going to read 20,000 rows via the index; this will mean 20,000 TABLE ACCESS BY ROWID operations. We will process 20,000 table blocks in order to execute this query. There are only about 1000 blocks in the entire table however! We would end up reading and processing each block in the table on average 20 times! Even if we increased the size of the row by an order of magnitude to 800 bytes per row, 10 rows per block, we now have 10,000 blocks in the table. Index accesses for 20,000 rows would cause us to still read each block on average two times. In this case, a full table scan will be much more efficient than using an index, as it only has to touch each block once. Any query that used this index to access the data, would not be very efficient until it accesses on average less then 5 percent of the data for the 800 byte column (then we access about 5000 blocks) and even less for the 80 byte column (about 0.5 percent or less).

Of course, there are factors that change these calculations. Suppose you have a table where the rows have a primary key populated by a sequence. As data is added to the table, rows with sequential sequence numbers are in general 'next' to each other. The table is naturally clustered, in order, by the primary key, (since the data is added in more or less that order). It will not be strictly clustered in order by the key of course (we would have to use an IOT to achieve that), but in general rows with primary keys that are close in value will be 'close' together in physical proximity. Now when you issue the query:

```
select * from T where primary_key between :x and :y
```

The rows you want are typically located on the same blocks. In this case an index range scan may be useful even if it accesses a large percentage of rows, simply because the database blocks that we need to read and re-read will most likely be cached, since the data is co-located. On the other hand, if the rows are not co-located, using that same index may be disastrous for performance. A small demonstration will drive this fact home. We'll start with a table that is pretty much ordered by its primary key:

```
tkyte@TKYTE816> create table colocated ( x int, y varchar2(2000) ) pctfree 0;
Table created.

tkyte@TKYTE816> begin
  2      for i in 1 .. 100000
  3      loop
  4              insert into colocated values ( i, rpad(dbms_random.random,75,'*') );
  5      end loop;
  6   end;
  7   /
PL/SQL procedure successfully completed.

tkyte@TKYTE816> alter table colocated
  2    add constraint colocated_pk primary key(x);
Table altered.
```

This is a table fitting the description we laid out above – about 100 rows/block in my 8 KB database. In this table there is a very good chance that the rows with x = 1, 2, 3 are on the same block. Now, we'll take this table and purposely 'disorganize' it. In the COLOCATED table above, we created the Y column with a leading random number – we'll use that fact to 'disorganize' the data – so it will definitely not be ordered by primary key anymore:

```
tkyte@TKYTE816> create table disorganized nologging pctfree 0
  2    as
  3    select x, y from colocated ORDER BY y
  4    /
Table created.

tkyte@TKYTE816> alter table disorganized
  2   add constraint disorganized_pk primary key(x);
Table altered.
```

Arguably, these are the same tables – it is a relational database, physical organization plays no bearing on how things work (at least that's what they teach in theoretical database courses). In fact, the performance characteristics of these two tables are different as 'night and day'. Given the same exact query:

```
tkyte@TKYTE816> select * from COLOCATED where x between 20000 and 40000;
20001 rows selected.
Elapsed: 00:00:01.02

Execution Plan
----------------------------------------------------------
    0      SELECT STATEMENT Optimizer=CHOOSE
    1    0    TABLE ACCESS (BY INDEX ROWID) OF 'COLOCATED'
    2    1      INDEX (RANGE SCAN) OF 'COLOCATED_PK' (UNIQUE)
```

```
Statistics
----------------------------------------------------------
          0  recursive calls
          0  db block gets
       2909  consistent gets
        258  physical reads
          0  redo size
    1991367  bytes sent via SQL*Net to client
     148387  bytes received via SQL*Net from client
       1335  SQL*Net roundtrips to/from client
          0  sorts (memory)
          0  sorts (disk)
      20001  rows processed

tkyte@TKYTE816> select * from DISORGANIZED where x between 20000 and 40000;
20001 rows selected.
```
Elapsed: 00:00:23.34

```
Execution Plan
----------------------------------------------------------
     0       SELECT STATEMENT Optimizer=CHOOSE
     1    0    TABLE ACCESS (BY INDEX ROWID) OF 'DISORGANIZED'
     2    1      INDEX (RANGE SCAN) OF 'DISORGANIZED_PK' (UNIQUE)

Statistics
----------------------------------------------------------
          0  recursive calls
          0  db block gets
      21361  consistent gets
       1684  physical reads
          0  redo size
    1991367  bytes sent via SQL*Net to client
     148387  bytes received via SQL*Net from client
       1335  SQL*Net roundtrips to/from client
          0  sorts (memory)
          0  sorts (disk)
      20001  rows processed
```

I think this is pretty incredible. What a difference physical data layout can make! To summarize the results:

Table	Elapsed Time	Logical I/O
Colocated	1.02 seconds	2,909
Disorganized	23.34 seconds	21,361

In my database using an 8 KB block size – these tables had 1,088 total blocks apiece. The query against disorganized table bears out the simple math we did above – we did 20,000 plus logical I/Os. We processed each and every block 20 times!! On the other hand, the physically COLOCATED data took the logical I/Os way down. Here is the perfect example of why rules of thumb are so hard to provide – in one case, using the index works great, in the other – it stinks. Consider this the next time you dump data from your production system and load it into development – it may very well be part of the answer to the question that typically comes up of 'why is it running differently on this machine – they are identical?' They are not identical.

Just to wrap up this example – let's look at what happens when we full scan the disorganized table:

```
tkyte@TKYTE816> select /*+ FULL(DISORGANIZED) */ *
  2  from DISORGANIZED
  3  where x between 20000 and 40000;

20001 rows selected.

Elapsed: 00:00:01.42

Execution Plan
----------------------------------------------------------
   0      SELECT STATEMENT Optimizer=CHOOSE (Cost=162 Card=218 Bytes=2
   1    0   TABLE ACCESS (FULL) OF 'DISORGANIZED' (Cost=162 Card=218 B

Statistics
----------------------------------------------------------
         0  recursive calls
        15  db block gets
      2385  consistent gets
       404  physical reads
         0  redo size
   1991367  bytes sent via SQL*Net to client
    148387  bytes received via SQL*Net from client
      1335  SQL*Net roundtrips to/from client
         0  sorts (memory)
         0  sorts (disk)
     20001  rows processed
```

That shows that in this particular case – due to the way the data is physically stored on disk, the full scan is very appropriate. This begs the question – so how can I accommodate for this? The answer is – use the cost based optimizer (CBO) and it will do it for you. The above case so far has been executed in RULE mode since we never gathered any statistics. The only time we used the cost based optimizer was when we hinted the full table scan above and asked the cost based optimizer to do something specific for us. If we analyze the tables, we can take a peek at some of the information Oracle will use to optimize the above queries:

```
tkyte@TKYTE816> analyze table colocated
  2  compute statistics
  3  for table
  4  for all indexes
  5  for all indexed columns
  6  /
Table analyzed.

tkyte@TKYTE816> analyze table disorganized
  2  compute statistics
  3  for table
  4  for all indexes
  5  for all indexed columns
  6  /
Table analyzed.
```

Now, we'll look at some of the information Oracle will use. We are specifically going to look at the CLUSTERING_FACTOR column found in the USER_INDEXES view. The *Oracle Reference Manual* tells us this column has the following meaning, it:

Indicates the amount of order of the rows in the table based on the values of the index:

❑ If the value is near the number of blocks, then the table is very well ordered. In this case, the index entries in a single leaf block tend to point to rows in the same data blocks.

❑ If the value is near the number of rows, then the table is very randomly ordered. In this case, it is unlikely that index entries in the same leaf block point to rows in the same data blocks.

The CLUSTERING_FACTOR is an indication of how ordered the table is with respect to the index itself, when we look at these indexes we find:

```
tkyte@TKYTE816> select a.index_name,
  2              b.num_rows,
  3              b.blocks,
  4              a.clustering_factor
  5    from user_indexes a, user_tables b
  6   where index_name in ('COLOCATED_PK', 'DISORGANIZED_PK' )
  7     and a.table_name = b.table_name
  8  /

INDEX_NAME                          NUM_ROWS     BLOCKS CLUSTERING_FACTOR
------------------------------    ----------   --------- ------------------
COLOCATED_PK                         100000       1063               1063
DISORGANIZED_PK                      100000       1064              99908
```

The COLOCATED_PK is a classic 'the table is well ordered' example, whereas the DISORGANIZE_PK is the classic 'the table is very randomly ordered' example. It is interesting to see how this affects the optimizer now. If we attempted to retrieve 20,000 rows, Oracle will now choose a full table scan for both queries (retrieving 20 percent of the rows via an index is not the optimal plan even for the very ordered table). However, if we drop down to 10 percent of the table data:

```
tkyte@TKYTE816> select * from COLOCATED where x between 20000 and 30000;
10001 rows selected.

Elapsed: 00:00:00.11

Execution Plan
----------------------------------------------------------
   0      SELECT STATEMENT Optimizer=CHOOSE (Cost=129 Card=9996 Bytes=839664)
   1    0   TABLE ACCESS (BY INDEX ROWID) OF 'COLOCATED' (Cost=129 Card=9996
   2    1     INDEX (RANGE SCAN) OF 'COLOCATED_PK' (UNIQUE) (Cost=22 Card=9996)

Statistics
----------------------------------------------------------
         0  recursive calls
         0  db block gets
      1478  consistent gets
       107  physical reads
```

```
         0   redo size
    996087   bytes sent via SQL*Net to client
     74350   bytes received via SQL*Net from client
       668   SQL*Net roundtrips to/from client
         1   sorts (memory)
         0   sorts (disk)
     10001   rows processed
```

```
tkyte@TKYTE816> select * from DISORGANIZED where x between 20000 and 30000;
10001 rows selected.
```

```
Elapsed: 00:00:00.42
```

```
Execution Plan
----------------------------------------------------------
   0      SELECT STATEMENT Optimizer=CHOOSE (Cost=162 Card=9996 Bytes=839664)
   1    0   TABLE ACCESS (FULL) OF 'DISORGANIZED' (Cost=162 Card=9996
```

```
Statistics
----------------------------------------------------------
         0   recursive calls
        15   db block gets
      1725   consistent gets
       707   physical reads
         0   redo size
    996087   bytes sent via SQL*Net to client
     74350   bytes received via SQL*Net from client
       668   SQL*Net roundtrips to/from client
         1   sorts (memory)
         0   sorts (disk)
     10001   rows processed
```

Here we have the same table structures – same indexes, but different clustering factors. The optimizer in this case chose an index access plan for the COLOCATED table and a full scan access plan for the DISORGANIZED table.

The key point to this discussion is that indexes are not always the appropriate access method. The optimizer may very well be correct in choosing to not use an index, as the above example demonstrates. There are many factors that influence the use of an index by the optimizer – *including* physical data layout. You might run out and try to rebuild all of your tables now to make all indexes have a good clustering factor but that most likely would be a waste of time in most cases. It will affect cases where you do index range scans of a large percentage of a table – not a common case in my experience. Additionally, you must keep in mind that in general the table will only have *one* index with a good clustering factor! The data can only be sorted in one way. In the above example – if I had another index on the column Y – it would be very poorly clustered in the COLOCATED table, but very nicely clustered in the DISORGANIZED table. If having the data physically clustered is important to you – consider the use of an IOT over a table rebuild.

B*Trees Wrap-up

B*Tree indexes are by far the most common and well-understood indexing structures in the Oracle database. They are an excellent general purpose indexing mechanism. They provide very scalable access times, returning data from a 1,000 row index in about the same amount of time as a 100,000 row index structure.

When to index, and what columns to index, is something you need to pay attention to in your design. An index does not always mean faster access; in fact, you will find that indexes will decrease performance in many cases if Oracle uses them. It is purely a function of how large of a percentage of the table you will need to access via the index and how the data happens to be laid out. If you can use the index to 'answer the question', accessing a large percentage of the rows makes sense, since you are avoiding the extra scattered I/O to read the table. If you use the index to access the table, you will need to ensure you are processing a small percentage of the total table.

You should consider the design and implementation of indexes *during* the design of your application, not as an afterthought (as I so often see). With careful planning and due consideration of how you are going to access the data, the indexes you need will be apparent in most all cases.

Bitmap Indexes

Bitmap Indexes were added to Oracle in version 7.3 of the database. They are currently available with the Oracle 8i Enterprise and Personal Editions, but not the Standard Edition. Bitmap indexes are designed for data warehousing/ad-hoc query environments where the full set of queries that may be asked of the data is not totally known at system implementation time. They are specifically **not** designed for OLTP systems or systems where data is frequently updated by many concurrent sessions.

Bitmap indexes are structures that store pointers to many rows with a single index key entry, as compared to a B*Tree structure where there is parity between the index keys and the rows in a table. In a bitmap index, there will be a very small number of index entries, each of which point to many rows. In a B*Tree, it is one-to-one – an index entry points to a single row.

Let's say you were creating a bitmap index on the JOB column in the EMP table as follows:

```
scott@TKYTE816> create BITMAP index job_idx on emp(job);
Index created.
```

Oracle will store something like the following in the index:

Value/Row	1	2	3	4	5	6	7	8	9	10	11	12	13	14
ANALYST	0	0	0	0	0	0	0	1	0	1	0	0	1	0
CLERK	1	0	0	0	0	0	0	0	0	0	1	1	0	1
MANAGER	0	0	0	1	0	1	1	0	0	0	0	0	0	0
PRESIDENT	0	0	0	0	0	0	0	0	1	0	0	0	0	0
SALESMAN	0	1	1	0	1	0	0	0	0	0	0	0	0	0

This shows that rows 8, 10, and 13 have the value ANALYST whereas the rows 4, 6, and 7 have the value MANAGER. It also shows me that no rows are null (Bitmap indexes store null entries – the lack of a null entry in the index implies there are no null rows). If I wanted to count the rows that have the value MANAGER, the bitmap index would do this very rapidly. If I wanted to find all the rows such that the JOB was CLERK or MANAGER, I could simply combine their bitmaps from the index as follows:

Value/Row	1	2	3	4	5	6	7	8	9	10	11	12	13	14
CLERK	1	0	0	0	0	0	0	0	0	0	1	1	0	1
MANAGER	0	0	0	1	0	1	1	0	0	0	0	0	0	0
CLERK or MANAGER	1	0	0	1	0	1	1	0	0	0	1	1	0	1

This rapidly shows me that rows 1, 4, 6, 7, 11, 12, and 14 satisfy my criteria. The bitmap Oracle stores with each key value is set up so that each position represents a row ID in the underlying table, if we need to actually retrieve the row for further processing. Queries such as:

```
select count(*) from emp where job = 'CLERK' or job = 'MANAGER'
```

will be answered directly from the bitmap index. A query such as:

```
select * from emp where job = 'CLERK' or job = 'MANAGER'
```

on the other hand will need to get to the table. Here Oracle will apply a function to turn the fact that the i'th bit is on in a bitmap, into a row ID that can be used to access the table.

When Should you use a Bitmap Index?

Bitmap indexes are most appropriate on low cardinality data. This is data where the number of distinct items in the set of rows divided by the number of rows is a small number (near zero). For example, a GENDER column might take on the values M, F, and NULL. If you have a table with 20000 employee records in it then you would find that $3/20000 = 0.00015$. This column would be a candidate for a bitmap index. It would definitely *not* be a candidate for a B*Tree index as each of the values would tend to retrieve an extremely large percentage of the table. B*Tree indexes should be selective in general as outlined above. Bitmap indexes should not be selective, on the contrary they should be very 'unselective'.

Bitmap indexes are extremely useful in environments where you have lots of ad-hoc queries, especially queries that reference many columns in an ad-hoc fashion or produce aggregations such as COUNT. For example, suppose you have a table with three columns GENDER, LOCATION, and AGE_GROUP. In this table GENDER has a value of M or F, and LOCATION can take on the values 1 through 50 and AGE_GROUP is a code representing 18 and under, 19-25, 26-30, 31-40, 41 and over. You have to support a large number of ad-hoc queries that take the form:

```
Select count(*)
  from T
 where gender = 'M'
   and location in ( 1, 10, 30 )
```

```
      and age_group = '41 and over';

  select *
    from t
   where (    ( gender = 'M' and location = 20 )
          or ( gender = 'F' and location = 22 ))
      and age_group = '18 and under';

  select count(*) from t where location in (11,20,30);

  select count(*) from t where age_group = '41 and over' and gender = 'F';
```

You would find that a conventional B*Tree indexing scheme would fail you. If you wanted to use an index to get the answer, you would need at least three and up to six combinations of possible B*Tree indexes in order to access the data. Since any of the three columns or any subset of the three columns may appear, you would need large concatenated B*Tree indexes on:

❑   GENDER, LOCATION, AGE_GROUP – For queries that used all three, or GENDER with LOCATION, or GENDER alone.

❑   LOCATION, AGE_GROUP – For queries that used LOCATION and AGE_GROUP or LOCATION alone.

❑   AGE_GROUP, GENDER – For queries that used AGE_GROUP with GENDER or AGE_GROUP alone.

In order to reduce the amount of data being searched, other permutations might be reasonable as well, to reduce the size of the index structure being scanned. This is ignoring the fact that a B*Tree index on such low cardinality data is not a good idea.

Here the bitmap index comes into play. With three small bitmap indexes, one on each of the individual columns, you will be able to satisfy all of the above predicates efficiently. Oracle will simply use the functions AND, OR, and XOR with the bitmaps of the three indexes together, to find the solution set for any predicate that references any set of these three columns. It will take the resulting merged bitmap, convert the 1s into row IDs if necessary, and access the data (if we are just counting rows that match the criteria, Oracle will just count the 1 bits).

There are times when bitmaps are *not* appropriate as well. They work well in a read intensive environment, but they are extremely ill-suited for a write intensive environment. The reason is that a single bitmap index key entry points to *many* rows. If a session modifies the indexed data, then all of the rows that index entry points to are effectively locked. Oracle cannot lock an individual bit in a bitmap index entry; it locks the entire bitmap. Any other modifications that need to update that same bitmap will be locked out. This will seriously inhibit concurrency – each update will appear to lock potentially hundreds of rows preventing their bitmap columns from being concurrently updated. It will not lock *every* row as you might think, just many of them. Bitmaps are stored in chunks, using the EMP example from above we might find that the index key ANALYST appears in the index many times, each time pointing to hundreds of rows. An update to a row that modifies the JOB column will need to get exclusive access to two of these index key entries; the index key entry for the *old* value and the index key entry for the *new* value. The hundreds of rows these two entries point to, will be unavailable for modification by other sessions until that UPDATE commits.

Bitmap Indexes Wrap-up

'When in doubt – try it out'. It is trivial to add a bitmap index to a table (or a bunch of them) and see what they do for you. Also you can usually create bitmap indexes much faster than B*Tree indexes. Experimentation is the best way to see if they are suited for your environment. I am frequently asked 'What defines low cardinality?' There is no cut-and-dry answer for this. Sometimes it is 3 values out of 100,000. Sometimes it is 10,000 values out of 1,000,000. Low cardinality doesn't imply single digit counts of distinct values. Experimentation will be the way to discover if a bitmap is a good idea for your application. In general, if you have a large, mostly read-only environment with lots of ad-hoc queries, a set of bitmap indexes may be exactly what you need.

Function-Based Indexes

Function-based indexes were added to Oracle 8.1.5 of the database. They are currently available with the Oracle8i Enterprise and Personal Editions, but not the Standard Edition.

Function-based indexes give us the ability to index computed columns and use these indexes in a query. In a nutshell, this capability allows you to have case insensitive searches or sorts, search on complex equations, and extend the SQL language efficiently by implementing your own functions and operators and then searching on them.

There are many reasons why you would want to use a function-based index. Leading among them are:

❑ They are easy to implement and provide immediate value.

❑ They can be used to speed up existing applications without changing any of their logic or queries.

Important Implementation Details

In order to make use of function-based Indexes, we must perform some setup work. Unlike B*Tree and Bitmap indexes above, function-based indexes require some initial setup before we can create and then use them. There are some init.ora or session settings you must use and to be able to create them, a privilege you must have. The following is a list of what needs to be done to use function-based indexes:

❑ You must have the system privilege QUERY REWRITE to create function-based indexes on tables in your own schema.

❑ You must have the system privilege GLOBAL QUERY REWRITE to create function-based indexes on tables in other schemas.

❑ Use the Cost Based Optimizer. Function-based indexes are only visible to the Cost Based Optimizer and will not be used by the Rule Based Optimizer ever.

❑ Use SUBSTR to constrain return values from user written functions that return VARCHAR2 or RAW types. Optionally hide the SUBSTR in a view (recommended). See below for examples of this.

❑ For the optimizer to use function-based indexes, the following session or system variables must be set:

```
QUERY_REWRITE_ENABLED=TRUE
QUERY_REWRITE_INTEGRITY=TRUSTED
```

You may enable these at either the session level with ALTER SESSION, or at the system level via ALTER SYSTEM, or by setting them in the init.ora parameter file. The meaning of QUERY_REWRITE_ENABLED is to allow the optimizer to rewrite the query to use the function-based index. The meaning of QUERY_REWRITE_INTEGRITY is to tell the optimizer to 'trust' that the code marked deterministic by the programmer is in fact deterministic (see below for examples of deterministic code and its meaning). If the code is in fact not deterministic (that is, it returns different output given the same inputs), the resulting rows retrieve via the index may be incorrect. That is something you must take care to ensure.

Once the above list has been satisfied, function-based indexes are as easy to use as the CREATE INDEX command. The optimizer will find and use your indexes at runtime for you.

Function-Based Index Example

Consider the following example. We want to perform a case insensitive search on the ENAME column of the EMP table. Prior to function-based indexes, we would have approached this in a very different manner. We would have added an extra column to the EMP table – called UPPER_ENAME, for example. This column would have been maintained by a database trigger on INSERT and UPDATE – that trigger would simply have set :NEW.UPPER_NAME := UPPER(:NEW.ENAME). This extra column would have been indexed. Now with function-based indexes, we remove the need for the extra column.

We'll begin by creating a copy of the demo EMP table in the SCOTT schema and add lots of data to it.

```
tkyte@TKYTE816> create table emp
  2  as
  3  select * from scott.emp;
Table created.

tkyte@TKYTE816> set timing on
tkyte@TKYTE816> insert into emp
  2  select -rownum EMPNO,
  3         substr(object_name,1,10) ENAME,
  4         substr(object_type,1,9) JOB,
  5            -rownum MGR,
  6            created hiredate,
  7         rownum SAL,
  8         rownum COMM,
  9         (mod(rownum,4)+1)*10 DEPTNO
 10    from all_objects
 11   where rownum < 10000
 12   /

9999 rows created.

Elapsed: 00:00:01.02
tkyte@TKYTE816> set timing off

tkyte@TKYTE816> commit;
Commit complete.
```

Now, we will change the data in the employee name column to be in mixed case. Then we will create an index on the UPPER of the ENAME column, effectively creating a case insensitive index:

```
tkyte@TKYTE816> update emp set ename = initcap(ename);
10013 rows updated.

tkyte@TKYTE816> create index emp_upper_idx on emp(upper(ename));
Index created.
```

Finally, we'll analyze the table since, as noted above, we need to make use of the cost based optimizer in order to utilize function-based indexes:

```
tkyte@TKYTE816> analyze table emp compute statistics
  2  for table
  3  for all indexed columns
  4  for all indexes;

Table analyzed.
```

We now have an index on the UPPER of a column. Any application that already issues 'case insensitive' queries (and has the requisite SYSTEM or SESSION settings), like this:

```
tkyte@TKYTE816> alter session set QUERY_REWRITE_ENABLED=TRUE;
Session altered.

tkyte@TKYTE816> alter session set QUERY_REWRITE_INTEGRITY=TRUSTED;
Session altered.

tkyte@TKYTE816> set autotrace on explain
tkyte@TKYTE816> select ename, empno, sal from emp where upper(ename)='KING';

ENAME          EMPNO        SAL
----------  ----------  ----------
King             7839       5000


Execution Plan
----------------------------------------------------------
   0        SELECT STATEMENT Optimizer=CHOOSE (Cost=2 Card=9 Bytes=297)
   1     0    TABLE ACCESS (BY INDEX ROWID) OF 'EMP' (Cost=2 Card=9 Bytes=297)
   2     1      INDEX (RANGE SCAN) OF 'EMP_UPPER_IDX' (NON-UNIQUE) (Cost=1 Card=9)
```

will make use of this index, gaining the performance boost an index can deliver. Before this feature was available, every row in the EMP table would have been scanned, uppercased, and compared. In contrast, with the index on UPPER(ENAME), the query takes the constant KING to the index, range scans a little data and accesses the table by row ID to get the data. This is very fast.

This performance boost is most visible when indexing user written functions on columns. Oracle 7.1 added the ability to use user-written functions in SQL so that you could do something like this:

```
SQL> select my_function(ename)
  2  from emp
  3  where some_other_function(empno) > 10
  4  /
```

This was great because you could now effectively extend the SQL language to include application-specific functions. Unfortunately, however, the performance of the above query was a bit disappointing at times. Say the EMP table had 1,000 rows in it, the function SOME_OTHER_FUNCTION would be executed 1,000 times during the query, once per row. In addition, assuming the function took one hundredth of a second to execute. This relatively simple query now takes at least 10 seconds.

Here is a real example. I've implemented a modified SOUNDEX routine in PL/SQL. Additionally, we'll use a package global variable as a counter in our procedure – this will allow us to execute queries that make use of the MY_SOUNDEX function and see exactly how many times it was called:

```
tkyte@TKYTE816> create or replace package stats
  2  as
  3          cnt number default 0;
  4  end;
  5  /
Package created.

tkyte@TKYTE816> create or replace
  2  function my_soundex( p_string in varchar2 ) return varchar2
  3  deterministic
  4  as
  5      l_return_string varchar2(6) default substr( p_string, 1, 1 );
  6      l_char          varchar2(1);
  7      l_last_digit    number default 0;
  8
  9      type vcArray is table of varchar2(10) index by binary_integer;
 10      l_code_table    vcArray;
 11
 12  begin
 13      stats.cnt := stats.cnt+1;
 14
 15      l_code_table(1) := 'BPFV';
 16      l_code_table(2) := 'CSKGJQXZ';
 17      l_code_table(3) := 'DT';
 18      l_code_table(4) := 'L';
 19      l_code_table(5) := 'MN';
 20      l_code_table(6) := 'R';
 21
 22
 23      for i in 1 .. length(p_string)
 24      loop
 25          exit when (length(l_return_string) = 6);
 26          l_char := upper(substr( p_string, i, 1 ) );
 27
 28          for j in 1 .. l_code_table.count
 29          loop
 30          if (instr(l_code_table(j), l_char ) > 0 AND j <> l_last_digit)
 31          then
 32                  l_return_string := l_return_string || to_char(j,'fm9');
 33                  l_last_digit := j;
 34          end if;
 35          end loop;
 36      end loop;
 37
 38      return rpad( l_return_string, 6, '0' );
 39  end;
 40  /

Function created.
```

Notice in this function, I am using a new keyword DETERMINISTIC. This declares that the above function – when given the same inputs – will always return the exact same output. It is needed in order to create an index on a user written function. You must tell Oracle that the function is DETERMINISTIC and will return a consistent result given the same inputs. This keyword goes hand in hand with the system/session setting of QUERY_REWRITE_INTEGRITY=TRUSTED. We are telling Oracle that this function should be trusted to return the same value – call after call – given the same inputs. If this was not the case, we would receive different answers when accessing the data via the index versus a full table scan. This deterministic setting implies, for example, that you cannot create an index on the function DBMS_RANDOM.RANDOM, the random number generator. Its results are not deterministic – given the same inputs you'll get random output. The built-in SQL function UPPER we used in the first example, on the other hand, is deterministic so you can create an index on the UPPER of a column.

Now that we have the function MY_SOUNDEX, lets see how it performs without an index. This uses the EMP table we created above with about 10,000 rows in it:

```
tkyte@TKYTE816> REM reset our counter
tkyte@TKYTE816> exec stats.cnt := 0

PL/SQL procedure successfully completed.

tkyte@TKYTE816> set timing on
tkyte@TKYTE816> set autotrace on explain
tkyte@TKYTE816> select ename, hiredate
  2    from emp
  3   where my_soundex(ename) = my_soundex('Kings')
  4  /

ENAME      HIREDATE
---------- ---------
King       17-NOV-81

Elapsed: 00:00:04.57

Execution Plan
----------------------------------------------------------
   0      SELECT STATEMENT Optimizer=CHOOSE (Cost=12 Card=101 Bytes=16
   1    0   TABLE ACCESS (FULL) OF 'EMP' (Cost=12 Card=101 Bytes=1616)

tkyte@TKYTE816> set autotrace off
tkyte@TKYTE816> set timing off

tkyte@TKYTE816> set serveroutput on
tkyte@TKYTE816> exec dbms_output.put_line( stats.cnt );
20026

PL/SQL procedure successfully completed.
```

So, we can see this query took over four seconds to execute and had to do a full scan on the table. The function MY_SOUNDEX was invoked over 20,000 times (according to our counter), twice for each row. Lets see how indexing the function can be used to speed things up.

The first thing we will do is create the index as follows:

```
tkyte@TKYTE816> create index emp_soundex_idx on
  2  emp( substr(my_soundex(ename),1,6) )
  3  /
Index created.
```

the interesting thing to note in this create index command is the use of the SUBSTR function. This is because we are indexing a function that returns a string. If we were indexing a function that returned a number or date this SUBSTR would not be necessary. The reason we must SUBSTR the user-written function that returns a string is that they return VARCHAR2(4000) types. That is too big to be indexed – index entries must fit within a third the size of the block. If we tried, we would receive (in a database with an 8 KB blocksize) the following:

```
tkyte@TKYTE816> create index emp_soundex_idx on emp( my_soundex(ename) );
create index emp_soundex_idx on emp( my_soundex(ename) )
                                                       *
ERROR at line 1:
ORA-01450: maximum key length (3218) exceeded
```

In databases with different block sizes, the number 3218 would vary, but unless you are using a 16 KB or larger block size, you will not be able to index a VARCHAR2(4000).

So, in order to index a user written function that returns a string, we must constrain the return type in the CREATE INDEX statement. In the above, knowing that MY_SOUNDEX returns at most 6 characters, we are sub-stringing the first six characters.

We are now ready to test the performance of the table with the index on it. We would like to monitor the effect of the index on INSERTs as well as the speedup for SELECTs to see the effect on each. In the un-indexed test case, our queries took over four seconds and the insert of 10000 records took about one second. Looking at the new test case we see:

```
tkyte@TKYTE816> REM reset counter
tkyte@TKYTE816> exec stats.cnt := 0
PL/SQL procedure successfully completed.

tkyte@TKYTE816> set timing on
tkyte@TKYTE816> truncate table emp;
Table truncated.

tkyte@TKYTE816> insert into emp
  2  select -rownum EMPNO,
  3         initcap( substr(object_name,1,10)) ENAME,
  4         substr(object_type,1,9) JOB,
  5         -rownum MGR,
  6         created hiredate,
  7         rownum SAL,
  8         rownum COMM,
  9         (mod(rownum,4)+1)*10 DEPTNO
 10    from all_objects
 11   where rownum < 10000
 12   union all
 13  select empno, initcap(ename), job, mgr, hiredate,
 14         sal, comm, deptno
 15    from scott.emp
 16  /
```

```
10013
rows created.

Elapsed: 00:00:05.07
tkyte@TKYTE816> set timing off

tkyte@TKYTE816> exec dbms_output.put_line( stats.cnt );
10013

PL/SQL procedure successfully completed.
```

This shows our INSERTs took about 5 seconds this time. This was the overhead introduced in the management of the new index on the MY_SOUNDEX function – both in the performance overhead of simply having an index (any type of index will affect insert performance) and the fact that this index had to call a stored procedure 10,013 times, as shown by the stats.cnt variable.

Now, to test the query, we'll start by analyzing the table and making sure our session settings are appropriate:

```
tkyte@TKYTE816> analyze table emp compute statistics
  2  for table
  3  for all indexed columns
  4  for all indexes;
Table analyzed.

tkyte@TKYTE816> alter session set QUERY_REWRITE_ENABLED=TRUE;
Session altered.

tkyte@TKYTE816> alter session set QUERY_REWRITE_INTEGRITY=TRUSTED;
Session altered.
```

and then actually run the query:

```
tkyte@TKYTE816> REM reset our counter
tkyte@TKYTE816> exec stats.cnt := 0
PL/SQL procedure successfully completed.

tkyte@TKYTE816> set timing on

tkyte@TKYTE816> select ename, hiredate
  2    from emp
  3   where substr(my_soundex(ename),1,6) = my_soundex('Kings')
  4  /

ENAME      HIREDATE
---------- ---------
King       17-NOV-81

Elapsed: 00:00:00.10

tkyte@TKYTE816> set timing off
```

```
tkyte@TKYTE816> set serveroutput on
tkyte@TKYTE816> exec dbms_output.put_line( stats.cnt );
2 /

PL/SQL procedure successfully completed.
```

If we compare the two examples (unindexed versus indexed) we find:

Operation	Unindexed	Indexed	Difference	Response
Insert	1.02	5.07	4.05	~5 times slower
Select	4.57	0.10	4.47	~46 times faster

The important things to note here are:

❑   The insert of 10,000 records took approximately five times longer. Indexing a user written function will necessarily affect the performance of inserts and some updates. You should realize that any index will impact performance of course – I did a simple test without the MY_SOUNDEX function, just indexing the ENAME column itself. That causes the INSERT to take about 2 seconds to execute – the PL/SQL function is not responsible for the entire overhead. Since most applications insert and update singleton entries, and each row took less then 5/10,000 of a second to insert, you probably won't even notice this in a typical application. Since we only insert a row once, we pay the price of executing the function on the column once, not the thousands of times we query the data.

❑   While the insert ran five times slower, the query ran something like 47 times faster. It evaluated the MY_SOUNDEX function two times instead of 20000. There is no comparison in the performance of this indexed query to the non-indexed query. Also, as the size of our table grows, the full scan query will take longer and longer to execute. The index-based query will always execute with nearly the same performance characteristics as the table gets larger.

❑   We had to use SUBSTR in our query. This is not as nice as just coding WHERE MY_SOUNDEX(ename)=MY_SOUNDEX('King'), but we can easily get around that, as we will show below.

So, the insert was affected but the query ran incredibly fast. The payoff for a small reduction in insert/update performance is huge. Additionally, if you never update the columns involved in the MY_SOUNDEX function call, the updates are not penalized at all (MY_SOUNDEX is invoked only if the ENAME column is updated).

We would now like to see how to make it so the query does not have use the SUBSTR function call. The use of the SUBSTR call could be error prone – your end users have to know to SUBSTR from 1 for 6 characters. If they used a different size, the index would not be used. Also, you want to control in the server the number of bytes to index. This will allow you to re-implement the MY_SOUNDEX function later with 7 bytes instead of 6 if you want to. We can do this – hiding the SUBSTR – with a view quite easily as follows:

```
tkyte@TKYTE816> create or replace view emp_v
  2  as
  3  select ename, substr(my_soundex(ename),1,6) ename_soundex, hiredate
  4    from emp
  5  /
View created.
```

Now when we query the view:

```
tkyte@TKYTE816> exec stats.cnt := 0;
PL/SQL procedure successfully completed.

tkyte@TKYTE816> set timing on

tkyte@TKYTE816> select ename, hiredate
  2     from emp_v
  3    where ename_soundex = my_soundex('Kings')
  4   /

ENAME      HIREDATE
---------- ---------
King       17-NOV-81

Elapsed: 00:00:00.10

tkyte@TKYTE816> set timing off

tkyte@TKYTE816> exec dbms_output.put_line( stats.cnt )
2

PL/SQL procedure successfully completed.
```

We see the same sort of query plan we did with the base table. All we have done here is hidden the SUBSTR(F(X), 1, 6) in the view itself. The optimizer still recognizes that this virtual column is, in fact, the indexed column and does the 'right thing'. We see the same performance improvement and the same query plan. Using this view is as good as using the base table, better even because it hides the complexity and allows you to change the size of the SUBSTR later.

Caveat

One quirk I have noticed with function-based indexes is that if you create one on the built-in function TO_DATE, it will not create. For example:

```
ops$tkyte@ORA8I.WORLD> create index t2 on t(to_date(y,'yyyy'));
create index t2 on t(to_date(y,'yyyy'))
                                      *
ERROR at line 1:
ORA-01743: only pure functions can be indexed
```

This is a filed bug and will be fixed in a later release of Oracle (after 8.1.7). Until that time, the solution is to create your own interface to TO_DATE and index that:

```
ops$tkyte@ORA8I.WORLD> create or replace
  2  function my_to_date( p_str in varchar2,
  3                       p_fmt in varchar2 ) return date
  4  DETERMINISTIC
  5  is
  6  begin
  7         return to_date( p_str, p_fmt );
```

```
   8  end;
   9  /
Function created.

ops$tkyte@ORA8I.WORLD> create index t2 on t(my_to_date(y,'yyyy'));
Index created.
```

Function-Based Index Wrap-up

Function-based indexes are easy to use, implement, and provide immediate value. They can be used to speed up existing applications without changing any of their logic or queries. Many orders of magnitude improvement may be observed. You can use them to pre-compute complex values without using a trigger. Additionally, the optimizer can estimate selectivity more accurately if the expressions are materialized in a function-based index.

On the downside, you cannot direct path load the table with a function-based index if that function was a user-written function and requires the SQL engine. That means you cannot direct path load into a table that was indexed using MY_SOUNDEX(X), but you could if it had indexed UPPER(x).

Function-based indexes will affect the performance of inserts and updates. Whether that warning is relevant or not to you, is something you must decide – if you insert and very infrequently query the data, this might not be an appropriate feature for you. On the other hand, keep in mind that you typically insert a row once, and you query it thousands of times. The performance hit on the insert (which your individual end user will probably never notice) may be offset many thousands of times by the speeding up of the queries.

In general, the pros heavily outweigh any of the cons in this case.

Application Domain Indexes

Application domain indexes are what Oracle calls 'extensible indexing'. It allows us to create our own index structure that works just like an index supplied by Oracle. When someone issues a CREATE INDEX statement using your index type, Oracle will run your code to generate the index. If someone analyzes the index to compute statistics on it, Oracle will execute your code to generate statistics in whatever format you care to store them in. When Oracle parses a query and develops a query plan that may make use of your index, Oracle will ask you 'how costly is this function to perform?' as it is evaluating the different plans. Application domain indexes, in short, give you the ability to implement a new index type that does not exist in the database as yet. For example, if you developed software that analyzed images stored in the database and produced information about the images – such as the colors found in them – you could create your own **image** index. As images were added to the database, your code would be invoked to extract the colors from the images and store them somewhere (where ever you wanted to store them). At query time, when the user asked for all 'blue images' – Oracle would ask you to provide the answer from your index when appropriate.

The best example of this is Oracles own interMedia text index. This index is used to provide keyword searching on large text items. interMedia introduces its own index type:

```
ops$tkyte@ORA8I.WORLD> create index myindex on mytable(docs)
  2  indextype is ctxsys.context
  3  /
Index created.
```

and its own operators into the SQL language:

```
select * from mytable where contains( docs, 'some words' ) > 0;
```

It will even respond to commands such as:

```
ops$tkyte@ORA8I.WORLD> analyze index myindex compute statistics;
Index analyzed.
```

It will participate with the optimizer at run-time to determine the relative cost of using a text index over some other index or a full scan. The interesting thing about all of this is that you or I could have developed this index. The implementation of the interMedia text index was done without 'inside kernel knowledge'. It was done using the documented and exposed API for doing these sorts of things. The Oracle database kernel is not aware of how the interMedia text index is stored (they store it in many physical database tables per index created). Oracle is not aware of the processing that takes place when a new row is inserted. interMedia is really an application built on top of the database, but in a wholly integrated fashion. To you and me, it looks just like any other Oracle database kernel function, but it is not.

I personally have not found the need to go and build a new exotic type of index structure. I see this particular feature as being of use mostly to third party solution providers that have innovative indexing techniques. For example, a company by the name of Virage, Inc. has used this same API to implement an index inside of Oracle. This index takes pictures you load into the database, and indexes them. You can then find pictures that 'look like' other pictures based on the texture, colors, lighting, and so on. Another use someone might find for this, would be to create an index, such that if we inserted a fingerprint into the database via a BLOB type, some external software would be invoked to index this, such as fingerprints that are indexed. It would store the point data related to the fingerprint either in database tables, clusters, or perhaps externally in flat files – wherever made the most sense. You would now be able to input a fingerprint into the database and find other fingerprints that matched it – just as easily as you SELECT * FROM T WHERE X BETWEEN 1 AND 2 using SQL.

Application Domain Indexes Wrap-up

I think the most interesting thing about application domain indexes is that it allows others to supply new indexing technology I can use in my applications. Most people will never make use of this particular API to build a new index type, but most of us will use the end results. Virtually every application I work on seems to have some *text* associated with it, *XML* to be dealt with, or *images* to be stored, and categorized. The interMedia set of functionality, implemented using the Application Domain Indexing feature, provides these capabilities. As time goes on, the set of available index types grows. For example, Oracle 8.1.7 added Rtree indexes to the database using this capability (Rtree indexing is useful for indexing spatial data).

Frequently Asked Questions About Indexes

As I said in the introduction to this book, I field lots of questions about Oracle. I am the Tom behind 'AskTom' in Oracle Magazine at http://asktom.oracle.com where I answer people's questions about the Oracle database and tools. In my experience, indexes is the topic that attract the most questions of all. In this section, I have answered some of the most frequently and repeatedly asked questions. Some of the answers may seem like common sense, other answers might surprise you. Suffice it to say, there are lots of myths and misunderstandings surrounding indexes.

Do Indexes Work On Views?

Or the related question, 'how can I index a view?' Well, the fact is that a view is nothing more then a stored query. Oracle will replace the text of the query that accesses the view with the view definition itself. Views are for the convenience of the end user – the optimizer works with the query against the base tables. Any, and all indexes that could have been used if the query had been written against the base tables, will be considered when you use the view. In order to 'index a view', you simply index the base tables.

Indexes and Nulls

B*Tree indexes, except in the special case of cluster B*Tree indexes, do not store completely Null entries, but bitmap and cluster indexes do. This side effect can be a point of confusion, but can actually be used to your advantage when you understand what this means.

To see the effect of the fact that Null values are *not* stored, consider this example:

```
ops$tkyte@ORA8I.WORLD> create table t ( x int, y int );
Table created.

ops$tkyte@ORA8I.WORLD> create unique index t_idx on t(x,y);
Index created.

ops$tkyte@ORA8I.WORLD> insert into t values ( 1, 1 );
1 row created.

ops$tkyte@ORA8I.WORLD> insert into t values ( 1, NULL );
1 row created.

ops$tkyte@ORA8I.WORLD> insert into t values ( NULL, 1 );
1 row created.

ops$tkyte@ORA8I.WORLD> insert into t values ( NULL, NULL );
1 row created.

ops$tkyte@ORA8I.WORLD> analyze index t_idx validate structure;
Index analyzed.

ops$tkyte@ORA8I.WORLD> select name, lf_rows from index_stats;

NAME                             LF_ROWS
------------------------------   ----------
T_IDX                                    3
```

The table has four rows, whereas the index only has three. The first three rows, where at least *one* of the index key elements was not Null, are in the index. The last row, with (NULL, NULL) is not in the index. One of the areas of confusion surrounding this is when the index is a unique index as above. Consider the effect of the following three INSERT statements:

```
ops$tkyte@ORA8I.WORLD> insert into t values ( NULL, NULL );
1 row created.

ops$tkyte@ORA8I.WORLD> insert into t values ( NULL, 1 );
insert into t values ( NULL, 1 )
*
ERROR at line 1:
ORA-00001: unique constraint (OPS$TKYTE.T_IDX) violated

ops$tkyte@ORA8I.WORLD> insert into t values ( 1, NULL );
insert into t values ( 1, NULL )
*
ERROR at line 1:
ORA-00001: unique constraint (OPS$TKYTE.T_IDX) violated
```

The new (NULL, NULL) row is not considered to be the same as the old row with (NULL, NULL):

```
ops$tkyte@ORA8I.WORLD> select x, y, count(*)
  2  from t
  3  group by x,y
  4  having count(*) > 1;

         X          Y   COUNT(*)
---------- ---------- ----------
                              2
```

This seems impossible – our unique key isn't unique if you consider all Null entries. The fact is that, in Oracle, (NULL, NULL) <> (NULL, NULL). The two are unique for comparisons but are the same as far as the GROUP BY clause is concerned. That is something to consider: each *unique* constraint should have at least one NOT NULL column in order to be truly unique.

The other issue that comes up with regards to indexes and Null values is the question 'why isn't my query using the index?' The query in question is something like:

```
select * from T where x is null;
```

This query cannot use the above index we created – the row (NULL, NULL) simply is not in the index, hence, the use of the index would in fact return the wrong answer. Only if at least *one* of the columns is defined as NOT NULL can the query use an index. For example, this shows Oracle will use an index for an X IS NULL predicate if there is an index with X on the leading edge and at least one other column in the index is NOT NULL:

```
ops$tkyte@ORA8I.WORLD> create table t ( x int, y int NOT NULL );
Table created.

ops$tkyte@ORA8I.WORLD> create unique index t_idx on t(x,y);
```

```
Index created.

ops$tkyte@ORA8I.WORLD> insert into t values ( 1, 1 );
1 row created.

ops$tkyte@ORA8I.WORLD> insert into t values ( NULL, 1 );
1 row created.

ops$tkyte@ORA8I.WORLD> analyze table t compute statistics;
Table analyzed.

ops$tkyte@ORA8I.WORLD> set autotrace on
ops$tkyte@ORA8I.WORLD> select * from t where x is null;

         X          Y
---------- ----------
                    1


Execution Plan
----------------------------------------------------------
   0      SELECT STATEMENT Optimizer=CHOOSE (Cost=1 Card=1 Bytes=8)
   1    0   INDEX (RANGE SCAN) OF 'T_IDX' (UNIQUE) (Cost=1 Card=1 Bytes=8)
```

Previously, I said that you can use to your advantage the fact that totally Null entries are not stored in a B*Tree index – here is how. Say you have a table with a column that takes exactly two values. The values are very skewed – say 90 percent or more of the rows take on one value and 10 percent or less take on the other value. We can index this column efficiently to gain quick access to the minority rows. This comes in handy when you would like to use an index to get to the minority rows but want to full scan to get to the majority rows and you want to conserve space. The solution is to use, a Null for majority rows and whatever value you want for minority rows.

For example, say the table was a 'queue' table of sorts. People inserted rows that would be worked on by another process. The vast majority of the rows in this table are in the processed state, very few in the unprocessed state. I might set up the table like this:

```
create table t ( ... other columns ..., timestamp DATE default SYSDATE);
create index t_idx on t(timestamp);
```

Now, when a new row is inserted, it will be 'stamped' with the current time. Our process that queries the data will use a query such as the following, using a date very far in the *past* to get all of the current records:

```
select * from T where timestamp > to_date('01010001','ddmmyyyyy') order by
timestamp;
```

And as it processes these records, it will update the timestamp column to NULL – effectively, removing it from the index. Thus, the index on this table stays very small, regardless of the number of rows in the table. If there is a chance that some records will not get processed over time – meaning that there could be some long-lived records in this particular index, you may want to physically reclaim space and compact this special index. This is accomplished using the ALTER INDEX COALESCE command. Otherwise, the index will tend to be much larger (less dense) over time than it should be. If the rows are always processed and removed from the index, this step is not necessary.

Now that you know how a B*Tree will treat Null values, you can use that to your advantage and take precautions with unique constraints on sets of columns that all allow Nulls (be prepared to have more than one row that is all Null as a possibility in this case).

Indexes on Foreign Keys

The question of whether or not foreign keys should be indexed comes up frequently. We touched on this subject in Chapter 3 on *Locking and Concurrency*, when discussing deadlocks. There, I pointed out that un-indexed foreign keys were the biggest single cause of deadlocks that I encounter, due to the fact that an update to a parent table's primary key or the removal of a parent record will place a full table lock on the child table (no modifications to the child table will be allowed until the transaction commits). This locks many more rows then it should, and decreases concurrency. I see it frequently when people are using tools that generate the SQL to modify a table. The tool generates an UPDATE statement that updates every column in the table, regardless of whether the value was modified or not. This in effect updates the primary key (even though you never change the value). For example, Oracle Forms will do this by default, unless you tell it to just send modified columns over to the database. In addition to the table lock issue that might hit you, an un-indexed foreign key is bad in the following cases as well:

❑ When you have an ON DELETE CASCADE and have not indexed the child table. For example EMP is child of DEPT. DELETE FROM DEPT WHERE DEPTNO = 10 should cascade to EMP. If DEPTNO in EMP is not indexed, you will get a full table scan of EMP. This full scan is probably undesirable and if you delete many rows from the parent table, the child table will be scanned once for each parent row deleted.

❑ When you query from the parent to the child. Consider the EMP/DEPT example again. It is very common to query the EMP table in the context of a DEPTNO. If you frequently query:

```
select *
  from dept, emp
  where emp.deptno = dept.deptno
  and dept.dname = :X;
```

to generate a report or something, you'll find not having the index in place will slow down the queries. This is the same argument I gave for indexing the NESTED_COLUMN_ID of a nested table in the chapter on tables. The hidden NESTED_COLUMN_ID of a nested table is nothing more then a foreign key.

So, when do you *not* need to index a foreign key? In general, when the following conditions are met:

❑ You do *not* delete from the parent table.

❑ You do *not* update the parent tables unique/primary key value, either purposely or by accident (via a tool).

❑ You do *not* join from the parent table to the child table, of more generally – the foreign key columns do not support an important access path to the child table. (like DEPT to EMP).

If you satisfy all three above, feel free to skip the index – it is not needed and will slow down DML on the child table. If you do any of the above, be aware of the consequences.

As a side note, if you believe that a child table is getting locked via an un-indexed foreign key and would like to prove it (or just prevent it in general), you can issue:

```
ALTER TABLE <child table name> DISABLE TABLE LOCK;
```

Now, any UPDATE or DELETE to the parent table that would cause the table lock will receive:

```
ERROR at line 1:
ORA-00069: cannot acquire lock -- table locks disabled for <child table name>
```

This is useful in tracking down the piece of code that is doing what you believe should not be done (no UPDATEs or DELETEs of the parent primary key) as the end users will immediately report this error back to you.

Why isn't my Index Getting Used?

There are many possible causes of this – we'll take a look at some of the most common.

Case 1

You are using a B*Tree index and your predicate does not use the leading edge of an index. In this case, you might have a table T with an index on T(x, y). You query SELECT * FROM T WHERE Y = 5. The optimizer will tend not to use the index since your predicate did not involve the column X – it must inspect each and every index entry in this case. It will typically opt for a full table scan of T instead. That does not preclude the index from being used. If the query was SELECT X, Y FROM T WHERE Y = 5, the optimizer would notice that it did not have to go to the table in order to get either X or Y (they are in the index) and may very well opt for a Fast Full Scan of the index itself, as the index is typically much smaller than the underlying table. Note also that this access path is only available with the Cost Based Optimizer (CBO).

Case 2

Your are using a SELECT COUNT(*) FROM T query (or something similar) and you have a B*Tree index on table T. However, the optimizer is full scanning the table, rather than counting the (much smaller) index entries. In this case, the index is probably on a set of columns that can contain Nulls. Since a totally Null index entry would never be made, the count of rows in the index will not be the count of rows in the table. Here the optimizer is doing the right thing – it would get the wrong answer if it used the index to count rows.

Case 3

For an indexed column, you query using:

```
select * from t where f(indexed_column) = value
```

and find that the index on INDEX_COLUMN is not used. This is due to the use of the function on the column. You indexed the values of INDEX_COLUMN – not the value of F(INDEXED_COLUMN). The index is nullified here. You can index the function if you choose to do it.

Case 4

You have indexed a character column. This column contains only numeric data. You query using the following syntax:

```
select * from t where indexed_column = 5
```

Note that the number five in the query is the constant *number* five (not a character string). The index on INDEXED_COLUMN is not used. This is because the above query is the same as:

```
select * from t where to_number(indexed_column) = 5
```

You have implicitly applied a function to the column and, as case 3 noted, this will nullify the use of the index. This is very easy to see with a small example:

```
ops$tkyte@ORA8I.WORLD> create table t ( x char(1) primary key );
Table created.

ops$tkyte@ORA8I.WORLD> insert into t values ( '5' );
1 row created.

ops$tkyte@ORA8I.WORLD> set autotrace on explain

ops$tkyte@ORA8I.WORLD> select * from t where x = 5;

X
-
5


Execution Plan
----------------------------------------------------------
    0      SELECT STATEMENT Optimizer=CHOOSE
    1    0    TABLE ACCESS (FULL) OF 'T'


ops$tkyte@ORA8I.WORLD> select * from t where x = '5';

X
-
5


Execution Plan
----------------------------------------------------------
    0      SELECT STATEMENT Optimizer=CHOOSE
    1    0    INDEX (UNIQUE SCAN) OF 'SYS_C0038216' (UNIQUE)
```

You should *always* avoid implicit conversions anyway. Always compare apples to apples and oranges to oranges. Another case where this comes up frequently is with dates. You try to query:

```
-- find all records for today
select * from t where trunc(date_col) = trunc(sysdate);
```

You discover that the index on DATE_COL will not be used. You can either index the TRUNC(DATE_COL) or, perhaps more easily, query using the BETWEEN comparison operator. The following demonstrates the use of BETWEEN on a date. Once you realize that the condition:

```
TRUNC(DATE_COL) = TRUNC(SYSDATE)
```

is the same as the condition:

```
DATE_COL BETWEEN TRUNC(SYSDATE)AND TRUNC (SYSDATE) PLUS ONE DAY MINUS ONE SECOND,
```

Then using BETWEEN clause is straightforward.

```
select *
  from t
  where date_col between trunc(sysdate) and trunc(sysdate)+1-1/(1*24*60*60)
```

> *Note: the expression 1/(1*24*60*60) is the fraction of one day that equals one second.*
> *Subtracting 1 would take away one day, 1/24 – one hour, and 1/(24*60) – one minute.*

This moves all of the functions to the right hand side of the equation, allowing us to use the index on DATE_COL (and has the same exact effect as WHERE TRUNC(DATE_COL) = TRUNC(SYSDATE)). **If possible, you should always remove the functions from database columns when they are in the predicate.** Not only will it allow for more indexes to be considered for use, it will reduce the amount of processing the database needs to do. In the above case, when we used:

```
between trunc(sysdate) and trunc(sydate)+1/(1*24*60*60)
```

the values are computed once for the query and then an index could be used to find just the qualifying values. When we used TRUNC(DATE_COL) = TRUNC(SYSDATE), the TRUNC(DATE_COL) had to be evaluated once *per row* for every row in the entire table (no indexes).

Case 5

The index, if used, would actually be slower. I see this a lot – people assume that, of course, an index will always make a query go faster. So, they set up a small table, analyze it, and find that the optimizer doesn't use the index. The optimizer is doing the exactly the right thing in this case. Oracle (under the CBO) will use an index only when it makes sense to do so. Consider this example:

```
ops$tkyte@ORA8I.WORLD> create table t
  2  ( x, y null, primary key (x) )
  3  as
  4  select rownum x, username
  5    from all_users
  6   where rownum <= 100
  7  /
Table created.

ops$tkyte@ORA8I.WORLD> analyze table t compute statistics;
Table analyzed.

ops$tkyte@ORA8I.WORLD> analyze table t compute statistics for all indexes;
Table analyzed.

ops$tkyte@ORA8I.WORLD> set autotrace on explain
ops$tkyte@ORA8I.WORLD> select count(y) from t where x < 50;
```

```
   COUNT(Y)
----------
        49


Execution Plan
----------------------------------------------------------
   0      SELECT STATEMENT Optimizer=CHOOSE (Cost=1 Card=1 Bytes=18)
   1    0   SORT (AGGREGATE)
   2    1     TABLE ACCESS (FULL) OF 'T' (Cost=1 Card=50 Bytes=900)
```

The CBO looked at this table and figured out that it would retrieve 50 percent of the rows. Doing this via an index would be slow; I would have to read an index block and then process each of the rows on it – and for every other row, I would be doing a database block get, to get the row data. It would be much more efficient just to read every row in the block and find the 50 percent of the rows we are going to process. Now, if we change the situation a little:

```
ops$tkyte@ORA8I.WORLD> set autotrace off
ops$tkyte@ORA8I.WORLD> insert into t
  2  select rownum+100, username
  3    from all_users
  4  /
41231 rows created.

ops$tkyte@ORA8I.WORLD> analyze table t compute statistics;
Table analyzed.

ops$tkyte@ORA8I.WORLD> analyze table t compute statistics for all indexes;
Table analyzed.

ops$tkyte@ORA8I.WORLD> set autotrace on explain
ops$tkyte@ORA8I.WORLD> select count(y) from t where x < 50;

   COUNT(Y)
----------
        49


Execution Plan
----------------------------------------------------------
   0      SELECT STATEMENT Optimizer=CHOOSE (Cost=3 Card=1 Bytes=21)
   1    0   SORT (AGGREGATE)
   2    1     TABLE ACCESS (BY INDEX ROWID) OF 'T' (Cost=3 Card=50
   3    2       INDEX (RANGE SCAN) OF 'SYS_C0038226' (UNIQUE) (Cost=2
```

The optimizer sees that the predicate will now retrieve about 0.1 percent of the rows – the index makes great sense.

This example shows two things actually. Firstly, indexes should *not* always be used. Before you jump to conclusions, prove that an index would actually be faster. Secondly, up-to-date statistics are very important. If I had not analyzed the tables after loading in lots of data, the optimizer would have made the wrong decision, which leads me to case 6.

Case 6

You haven't analyzed your tables in a while and they used to be small, but now when you look at them they have grown quite large. An index will now make sense, whereas it didn't originally. If you analyze the table, it will use the index. Reusing the above example, but running the query before and after the insert, we can see this clearly:

```
ops$tkyte@ORA8I.WORLD> insert into t
  2  select rownum+100, username
  3    from all_users
  4  /
41231 rows created.

ops$tkyte@ORA8I.WORLD> set autotrace on explain
ops$tkyte@ORA8I.WORLD> select count(y) from t where x < 50;

  COUNT(Y)
----------
        49


Execution Plan
----------------------------------------------------------
   0      SELECT STATEMENT Optimizer=CHOOSE (Cost=1 Card=1 Bytes=18)
   1    0   SORT (AGGREGATE)
   2    1     TABLE ACCESS (FULL) OF 'T' (Cost=1 Card=50 Bytes=900)

ops$tkyte@ORA8I.WORLD> set autotrace off

ops$tkyte@ORA8I.WORLD> analyze table t compute statistics;
Table analyzed.

ops$tkyte@ORA8I.WORLD> analyze table t compute statistics for all indexes;
Table analyzed.

ops$tkyte@ORA8I.WORLD> set autotrace on explain
ops$tkyte@ORA8I.WORLD> select count(y) from t where x < 50;

  COUNT(Y)
----------
        49


Execution Plan
----------------------------------------------------------
   0      SELECT STATEMENT Optimizer=CHOOSE (Cost=3 Card=1 Bytes=21)
   1    0   SORT (AGGREGATE)
   2    1     TABLE ACCESS (BY INDEX ROWID) OF 'T' (Cost=3 Card=50 Bytes=1050)
   3    2       INDEX (RANGE SCAN) OF 'SYS_C0038227' (UNIQUE) (Cost=2 Card=50)
```

Without up-to-date statistics, the CBO *cannot* make the correct decisions.

In my experience, these six cases are the *main* reasons I find that indexes are not being used. It usually boils down to a case of 'they cannot be used, using them would return incorrect results' or 'they should not be used, if they were used performance would be terrible'.

Are my Indexes Being Used?

This is a hard question to answer. Oracle does not audit accesses to indexes, so we cannot count rows in an audit trail table or anything as simple as that. There is no truly simple way to solve this problem. Two approaches are available however in Oracle 8i.

In Chapter 11 on *Optimizer Plan Stability*, I describe how stored query outlines, a feature whereby Oracle saves the hints for a query plan into a database table, might be used to find out what indexes are being used. You could enable the storage (but not use) of these plans. In that fashion, you can capture the plans for all of the queries executed without affecting the application in any other way. You could then query the outline tables to see which index access methods have been used, and even tie that back to the queries that use them.

Another method is to place each index into its own tablespace, or into its own file within a tablespace. Oracle will monitor I/O by file (via the V$FILESTAT dynamic performance view). If you see an index tablespace, such that the reads and writes are fairly equal, then you know you have an index that is not used for accessing the data. It is read *only* when it is being written (you are seeing Oracle maintain the index after INSERTs, UPDATEs, and DELETEs). If there are *no* reads on the tablespace, of course, the index is not being used and the table is not modified frequently. If the reads *outweigh* the writes, this would be a good indication that the index is currently being used.

The downside to all of this is that even if you find the indexes that are used versus not used, you still don't know if you have the *right* set of indexes on your data. These methods will not tell you that if you simply added column X to index Y; a table access by row ID could be avoided and efficiency would go way up. It is a common optimization technique to add columns to the end of an index to so that the index itself can answer the queries being asked, instead of having to use the table at all. It will not tell you if you have redundant indexes. For example, if you have indexes on T(X) and T(X, Y) and T(X, Y, Z) you could probably drop the first two without any loss of query performance and get an increase in update performance – there are cases, of course, where this is not true. The point is that a well designed, documented system would not have to ask itself frequently 'am I using my indexes?' as each index would be carefully thought out ahead of time for the system as a whole, not on a query-by-query basis. In a rapidly changing system with lots of developers that come and go, this typically is not the case however.

Myth: Space is Never Reused in an Index

This is a myth that I would like to dispel once and for all: space *is* reused in an index
The myth goes like this, you have a table T in which there is a column X. At some point you put the value X = 5 in the table. Later you delete it. The myth is that the space used by X = 5 will not be reused unless you put X = 5 back into the index later. The myth states that once an index slot is used, it will be there forever and can only be reused by the same value. A corollary to this is the myth that free space is never returned to the index structure, a block will never be reused. Again, this is simply not true.

The first part of the myth is trivial to disprove. All we need to do is to create a table like this:

```
tkyte@ORA8I.WORLD> create table t ( x int, constraint t_pk primary key(x) );
Table created.

tkyte@ORA8I.WORLD> insert into t values (1);
1 row created.
```

```
tkyte@ORA8I.WORLD> insert into t values (2);
1 row created.

tkyte@ORA8I.WORLD> insert into t values (9999999999);
1 row created.

tkyte@ORA8I.WORLD> exec show_space( 'T_PK', user, 'INDEX' );
Free Blocks.............................0
Total Blocks............................64
Unused Blocks...........................62

PL/SQL procedure successfully completed.
```

So, according to the myth, if I delete from T where x = 2, that space will never be reused unless I reinsert the number 2. Currently, this index is using two blocks of space, one for the extent map and one for the index data. If the index entries are never reused upon deletes and I keep inserting and deleting and never reuse a value, this index should grow like crazy. Let's see:

```
ops$tkyte@ORA8I.WORLD> begin
  2            for i in 2 .. 999999
  3            loop
  4                    delete from t where x = i;
  5                    commit;
  6                    insert into t values (i+1);
  7                    commit;
  8            end loop;
  9   end;
 10   /

PL/SQL procedure successfully completed.

ops$tkyte@ORA8I.WORLD> exec show_space( 'T_PK', user, 'INDEX' );
Free Blocks.............................0
Total Blocks............................64
Unused Blocks...........................62

PL/SQL procedure successfully completed.
```

So, this shows the space in the index was reused. As with most myths however, there is a nugget of truth in there. The truth is that the space used by that initial number 2 – in between 1 and 9,999,999,999 – would remain on that index block forever. The index will not 'coalesce' itself. What this means, is that if I load up a table with values 1 to 500,000 and then delete every other row (all of the even numbers) there will be 250,000 'holes' in the index on that column. Only if we reinsert data that will fit onto a block where there is a hole will the space be reused. Oracle will make no attempt to 'shrink' or compact the index. This can be done via an ALTER INDEX REBUILD or COALESCE command. On the other hand, if I loaded up a table with values 1 to 500,000 and then deleted from it every row where the value was 250,000 or less, I would find the blocks that were cleaned out of the index were put back onto the FREELIST for the index. This space can be totally reused. If you recall, this was the second myth. The myth was that index space is never 'reclaimed'. It states that once an index block is used, it will be stuck in that place in the index structure forever and will only be reused if you insert data that would go into that place in the index anyway. We can show that this is false as well. First we need to build a table with about 500,000 rows in it:

```
ops$tkyte@ORA8I.WORLD> create table t
  2  ( x int );
Table created.

ops$tkyte@ORA8I.WORLD> insert /*+ APPEND */ into t select rownum from all_objects;
30402 rows created.

ops$tkyte@ORA8I.WORLD> commit;
Commit complete.

ops$tkyte@ORA8I.WORLD> insert /*+ APPEND */ into t
  2  select rownum+cnt from t, (select count(*) cnt from t);
30402 rows created.

ops$tkyte@ORA8I.WORLD> commit;
Commit complete.

ops$tkyte@ORA8I.WORLD> insert /*+ APPEND */ into t
  2  select rownum+cnt from t, (select count(*) cnt from t);
60804 rows created.

ops$tkyte@ORA8I.WORLD> commit;
Commit complete.

ops$tkyte@ORA8I.WORLD> insert /*+ APPEND */ into t
  2  select rownum+cnt from t, (select count(*) cnt from t);
121608 rows created.

ops$tkyte@ORA8I.WORLD> commit;
Commit complete.

ops$tkyte@ORA8I.WORLD> insert /*+ APPEND */ into t
  2  select rownum+cnt from t, (select count(*) cnt from t);
243216 rows created.

ops$tkyte@ORA8I.WORLD> commit;
Commit complete.

ops$tkyte@ORA8I.WORLD> alter table t add constraint t_pk primary key(x)
  2  /
Table altered.
```

Now, we just measure its utilization before and after a mass deletion:

```
ops$tkyte@ORA8I.WORLD> exec show_space( 'T_PK', user, 'INDEX' );
Free Blocks.............................0
Total Blocks............................1024
Unused Blocks...........................5

PL/SQL procedure successfully completed.

ops$tkyte@ORA8I.WORLD> delete from t where x < 250000;
249999 rows deleted.

ops$tkyte@ORA8I.WORLD> commit;
Commit complete.
```

```
ops$tkyte@ORA8I.WORLD> exec show_space( 'T_PK', user, 'INDEX' );
Free Blocks.............................520
Total Blocks..........................1024
Unused Blocks...........................5

PL/SQL procedure successfully completed.
```

As you can see, over half of the index is on the FREELIST now. This means the block is totally empty (blocks on the FREELIST for an index must be empty, unlike blocks on the FREELIST for a heap organized table).

This demonstration highlights two points:

❏ Space is reused on index blocks as soon as a row comes along that can reuse it.

❏ When an index block is emptied, it is taken out of the index structure and may be reused later. This is probably the genesis of this myth in the first place – that blocks are not visible as having 'free space' on them in an index structure as they are in a table. In a table, you can see blocks on the free space, even if they have data on them. In an index, you will only see completely empty blocks on the FREELISTs; blocks that have at least one index entry (and remaining free space) will not be as clearly visible.

Myth: Most Discriminating Elements Should be First

This seems like common sense. If you are going to create an index on the columns C1, C2 in a table with 100,000 rows and you find the C1 has 100,000 unique values and the column C2 has 25,000 unique values, you would want to create the index on T(C1,C2). This means that C1 should be first, which is the 'common sense' approach. The fact is, when comparing vectors of data (consider C1, C2 to be a vector), it doesn't matter which you put first. Consider the following example. We will create a table based on all objects and an index on the OWNER, OBJECT_TYPE, and OBJECT_NAME columns (least discriminating to most discriminating) and also on OBJECT_NAME, OBJECT_TYPE, and OWNER:

```
tkyte@TKYTE816> create table t
  2  nologging
  3  as
  4  select * from all_objects;
Table created.

tkyte@TKYTE816> create index t_idx_1 on t(owner,object_type,object_name)
  2  nologging pctfree 0;
Index created.

tkyte@TKYTE816> create index t_idx_2 on t(object_name,object_type,owner)
  2  nologging pctfree 0;
Index created.

tkyte@TKYTE816> select count(distinct owner), count(distinct object_type),
  2     count(distinct object_name ), count(*)
  3     from t;
```

(DISTINCTOWNER)	(DISTINCTOBJECT_TYPE)	(DISTINCTOBJECT_NAME)	COUNT(*)
24	23	12265	21975

Now, to show that neither is more efficient space-wise, we'll measure their space utilization:

```
tkyte@TKYTE816> exec show_space( 'T_IDX_1', user, 'INDEX' );
Free Blocks.............................0
Total Blocks...........................192
Total Bytes............................1572864
Unused Blocks..........................51
Unused Bytes...........................417792
Last Used Ext FileId...................6
Last Used Ext BlockId..................4745
Last Used Block........................13

PL/SQL procedure successfully completed.

tkyte@TKYTE816> exec show_space( 'T_IDX_2', user, 'INDEX' );
Free Blocks.............................0
Total Blocks...........................192
Total Bytes............................1572864
Unused Blocks..........................51
Unused Bytes...........................417792
Last Used Ext FileId...................6
Last Used Ext BlockId..................4937
Last Used Block........................13

PL/SQL procedure successfully completed.
```

They use exactly the same amount of space – there are no differences there. However, the first index is a lot more *compressible* if we use index key compression! There is an argument for going from least discriminating to most discriminating. Now, lets see how they perform – see if either index is generally more efficient than the other. In order to test that, I used a PL/SQL block with hinted queries (so as to use one index or the other) like this:

```
tkyte@TKYTE816> alter session set sql_trace=true;
Session altered.

tkyte@TKYTE816> declare
  2          cnt int;
  3  begin
  4          for x in ( select owner, object_type, object_name from t )
  5          loop
  6                  select /*+ INDEX( t t_idx_1 ) */ count(*) into cnt
  7                    from t
  8                   where object_name = x.object_name
  9                     and object_type = x.object_type
 10                     and owner = x.owner;
 11
 12                  select /*+ INDEX( t t_idx_2 ) */ count(*) into cnt
 13                    from t
 14                   where object_name = x.object_name
 15                     and object_type = x.object_type
```

```
16                           and owner = x.owner;
17            end loop;
18   end;
19   /

PL/SQL procedure successfully completed.
```

These queries read every single row in the table by means of the index. The TKPROF report shows us:

```
SELECT /*+ INDEX( t t_idx_1 )  */COUNT(*)
FROM
 T  WHERE OBJECT_NAME = :b1  AND OBJECT_TYPE = :b2  AND OWNER = :b3


call      count       cpu    elapsed  disk      query    current       rows
-------  ------  --------  ---------- -----  ---------- ---------- ----------
Parse         1      0.00        0.00     0           0          0          0
Execute   21975      2.35        2.55     0           0          0          0
Fetch     21975      1.40        1.57     0       44088          0      21975
-------  ------  --------  ---------- -----  ---------- ---------- ----------
total     43951      3.75        4.12     0       44088          0      21975

Rows     Execution Plan
-------  ---------------------------------------------------
      0  SELECT STATEMENT   GOAL: CHOOSE
  21975   SORT (AGGREGATE)
  21975    INDEX (RANGE SCAN) OF 'T_IDX_1' (NON-UNIQUE)


********************************************************************************

SELECT /*+ INDEX( t t_idx_2 )  */COUNT(*)
FROM
 T  WHERE OBJECT_NAME = :b1  AND OBJECT_TYPE = :b2  AND OWNER = :b3


call      count       cpu    elapsed  disk      query    current       rows
-------  ------  --------  ---------- -----  ---------- ---------- ----------
Parse         1      0.00        0.00     0           0          0          0
Execute   21975      2.10        2.44     0           0          0          0
Fetch     21975      1.65        1.60     0       44088          0      21975
-------  ------  --------  ---------- -----  ---------- ---------- ----------
total     43951      3.75        4.04     0       44088          0      21975

Rows     Execution Plan
-------  ---------------------------------------------------
      0  SELECT STATEMENT   GOAL: CHOOSE
  21975   SORT (AGGREGATE)
  21975    INDEX (RANGE SCAN) OF 'T_IDX_2' (NON-UNIQUE)
```

They processed the same exact number of rows, blocks, used equivalent amounts of CPU time, and ran in about the same elapsed time (run this same test again and the CPU and ELAPSED numbers will be a little different but on average they will be the same). There are no inherent efficiencies to be gained by placing the columns in order of how discriminating they are.

In fact, the decision to put a column C1 before C2 *must* be driven by how the index is used. If you have lots of queries like:

```
select * from t where c1 = :x and c2 = :y;
select * from t where c2 = :y;
```

it will make more sense to place the index on T(C2,C1) – this single index could be used by either of the above queries. Additionally, using index key compression, (which we looked at with regards to index-organized tables and will look at again later), we can build a smaller index if C2 is first. This is because C2 repeats itself on average four times in the index. If C1 and C2 are both, on average, 10 bytes in length, the index entries for this index would nominally be 2,000,000 bytes (100,000 * 20). Using index key compression on (C2, C1) we could shrink this index to 1,250,000 (100,000 * 12.5) since 3 out of 4 repetitions of C2 could be suppressed.

In Oracle 5 (yes, version 5!), there was an argument for placing the most selective columns first in an index. It had to do with the way version 5 implemented index compression (not the same as index key compression). This feature was removed in version 6 with the addition of row-level locking. Since then, it is not true that putting the most discriminating entries first in the index would make the index smaller or more efficient. It seems like it would, but it will not. With index key compression, there is a compelling argument to go the other way since it can make the index smaller. However, it should be driven by *how* you use the index as stated above.

Summary

In this chapter, we covered the different types of indexes Oracle has to offer. We started with the basic B*Tree index and looked at various sub types of this index such as the reverse key index, designed for Oracle Parallel Server, and descending indexes – for retrieving data sorted in a mix of descending and ascending order. We spent some time looking at when you should use an index and why an index may not be useful in various circumstances.

We then looked at bitmap indexes, an excellent method for indexing low to medium cardinality data in a data warehouse (read intensive, non-OLTP) environment. We covered the times it would be appropriate to use a bitmapped index and why you would never consider them for use in an OLTP environment – or any environment where multiple users must concurrently update the same column.

We moved on to function-based indexes, which are actually special cases of B*Tree and Bitmapped indexes. A function-based index allows us to create an index on a function of column(s) which means that we can pre-compute and store the results of complex calculations and user-written functions, for blazing fast index retrieval later. We looked at some important implementation details surrounding function-based indexes, such as the necessary system and session level settings that must be in place for them to be used. We followed that with examples of function-based indexes both on built-in Oracle functions and user written ones. Lastly, we looked at a caveat with regards to function-based indexes based on the internal Oracle TO_DATE function and how to work around that issue.

We then looked at a very specialized index type – the Application Domain index. Rather than go into how to build one of those from scratch (a long, complex sequence of events) we looked at an example one that had already been implemented, the interMedia Text index. We will come back to this very important index in a chapter all to its own which is Chapter 17 on *interMedia*.

We closed with some of the most frequently asked questions on indexes that I receive. These range from the simple 'do indexes work with views' (yes) to the more complex and sublime 'space is never reused in an index' (a myth). We answered these questions mostly by example, demonstrating the concepts as we went along.

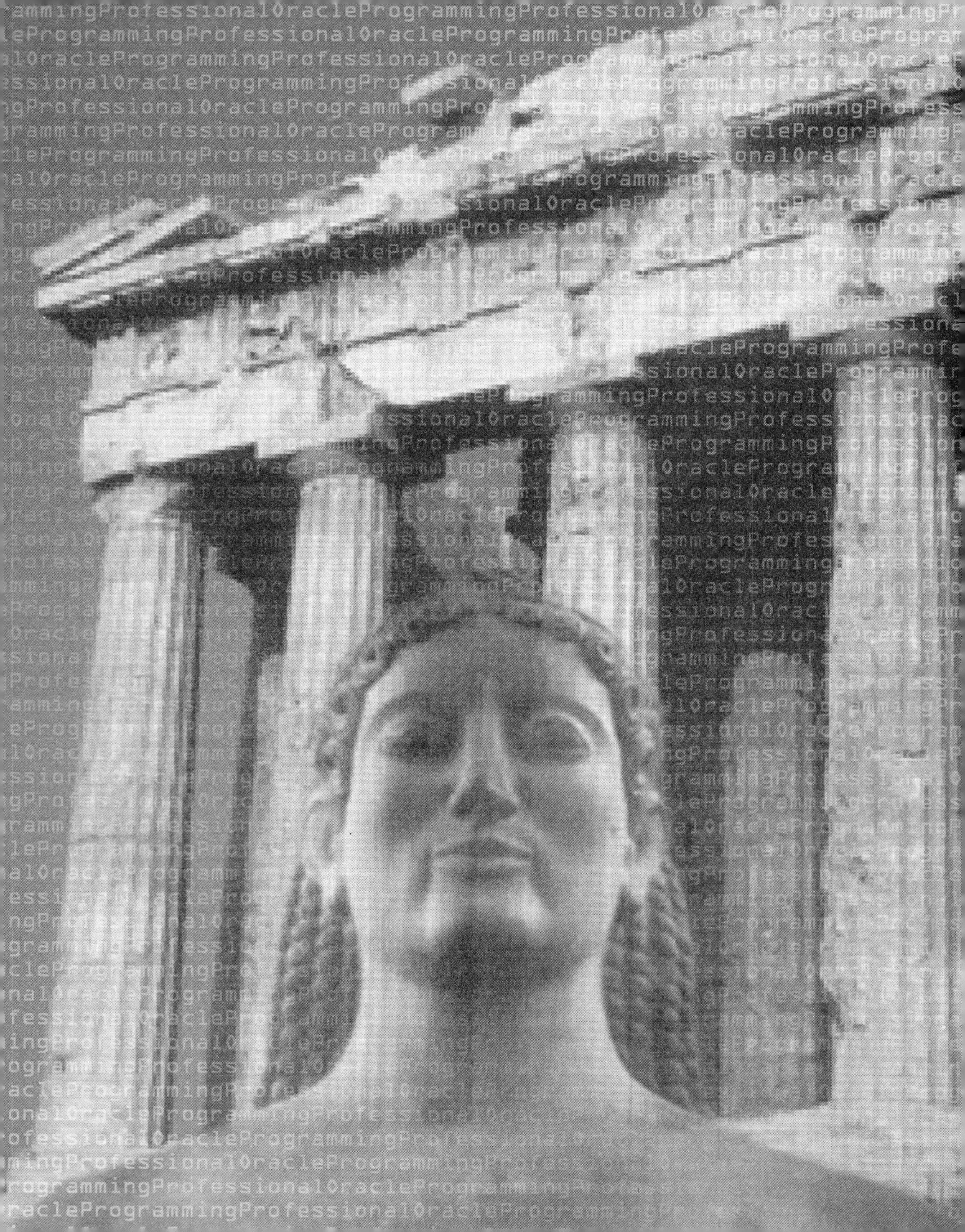
ProfessionalOracleProgramming

8

Import and Export

Import (IMP) and Export (EXP) are among the oldest surviving Oracle tools. They are command line tools used to extract tables, schemas, or entire database definitions from one Oracle instance, to be imported into another instance or schema.

Traditionally, Import and Export have been considered to be in the domain of the DBA. I actually find them to be more useful to the individual developer than as a DBA tool. As databases have grown, both in size and importance, the tools needed to manage them have grown as well. In days gone by, it would not have been unreasonable to use import and export to rebuild your database (perhaps to change the block size or to move your database to another platform) or as your backup method. With 'small' databases today starting in the gigabytes range, simple tools that process everything serially (such as import and export), just do not scale. While not useless to the DBA, they are definitely not as useful as they once were. Other tools and methods have come along to take their place. For example, we would now use Recovery Manager (RMAN) to perform an incremental backup of very large databases, not EXP. They still have many other uses such to detect logical and physical corruption, to transport datafiles from database to data, and so on.

EXP and IMP are tools you will probably use at some point or another. If you wish to copy a schema from one user to another, the easiest method will be to use EXP and IMP. If you wish to extract the DDL for a schema, EXP and IMP will be the tools you use. If you wish to partition an existing table into many physical partitions (which requires a rebuild of the table), EXP and IMP might be a valid approach for you. In this chapter, we will look how to:

- ❏ Subset data.

- ❏ Get our DDL back out of the database.

- ❏ Import small to medium amounts of data into different structures (structures different from those they were exported from).

- ❏ Clone a schema in the database – this looks easy with this tool but there are various 'gotchas' of which you must be aware.

We will tackle EXP and IMP mainly from the developer's perspective. I am going to cover many of the frequently asked about issues regarding the practical use of EXP and IMP. I use these tools myself and have either encountered these issues, or have been asked to provide a solution for them.

A Quick Example

To demonstrate the value of IMP and EXP, and their ease-of-use, we'll use them to extract the DDL of a table in the SCOTT/TIGER schema. I've seen many people search around for utilities to do this, or attempt to write their own DDL extractors – never realizing that there is one supplied with the database. It is as easy as this:

```
C:\ImpExp>exp userid=scott/tiger tables=emp

C:\ImpExp>imp userid=scott/tiger full=y indexfile=emp.sql

C:\ImpExp>type emp.sql

REM   CREATE TABLE "SCOTT"."EMP" ("EMPNO" NUMBER(4, 0) NOT NULL ENABLE,
REM   "ENAME" VARCHAR2(10), "JOB" VARCHAR2(9), "MGR" NUMBER(4, 0),
REM   "HIREDATE" DATE, "SAL" NUMBER(7, 2), "COMM" NUMBER(7, 2), "DEPTNO"
REM   NUMBER(2, 0)) PCTFREE 10 PCTUSED 40 INITRANS 1 MAXTRANS 255 LOGGING
REM   STORAGE(INITIAL 32768 NEXT 32768 MINEXTENTS 1 MAXEXTENTS 4096
REM   PCTINCREASE 0 FREELISTS 1 FREELIST GROUPS 1 BUFFER_POOL DEFAULT)
REM   TABLESPACE "TOOLS" ;
REM   ... 14 rows
CONNECT SCOTT;
CREATE UNIQUE INDEX "SCOTT"."EMP_PK" ON "EMP" ("EMPNO" ) PCTFREE 10
INITRANS 2 MAXTRANS 255 STORAGE(INITIAL 32768 NEXT 32768 MINEXTENTS 1
MAXEXTENTS 4096 PCTINCREASE 0 FREELISTS 1 FREELIST GROUPS 1 BUFFER_POOL
DEFAULT) TABLESPACE "TOOLS" LOGGING ;
REM   ALTER TABLE "SCOTT"."EMP" ADD CONSTRAINT "EMP_PK" PRIMARY KEY
REM   ("EMPNO") USING INDEX PCTFREE 10 INITRANS 2 MAXTRANS 255
REM   STORAGE(INITIAL 32768 NEXT 32768 MINEXTENTS 1 MAXEXTENTS 4096
REM   PCTINCREASE 0 FREELISTS 1 FREELIST GROUPS 1 BUFFER_POOL DEFAULT)
REM   TABLESPACE "TOOLS" ENABLE ;
REM   ALTER TABLE "SCOTT"."EMP" ADD CONSTRAINT "EMP_FK_DEPT" FOREIGN KEY
REM   ("DEPTNO") REFERENCES "DEPT" ("DEPTNO") ENABLE NOVALIDATE ;
REM   ALTER TABLE "SCOTT"."EMP" ADD CONSTRAINT "EMP_FK_EMP" FOREIGN KEY
REM   ("MGR") REFERENCES "EMP" ("EMPNO") ENABLE NOVALIDATE ;
REM   ALTER TABLE "SCOTT"."EMP" ENABLE CONSTRAINT "EMP_PK" ;
REM   ALTER TABLE "SCOTT"."EMP" ENABLE CONSTRAINT "EMP_FK_DEPT" ;
REM   ALTER TABLE "SCOTT"."EMP" ENABLE CONSTRAINT "EMP_FK_EMP" ;
```

There it is in all of its glorious verbosity (yours will probably look a little different – you are seeing some of the many 'enhancements' I've made to the SCOTT.EMP table during the writing of this book). That is the DDL you need to recreate the EMP table, as it currently exists. A little later, we'll take a look in some detail at using IMP and EXP to successfully extract DDL from the database (and at some scripts that are useful when IMP/EXP fall short).

> *Full documentation on EXP and IMP is available in the Oracle Server Utilities Guide. Rather than repeat much of what is there, I would encourage you to read through it as a supplement to this chapter.*

EXP creates a proprietary binary file, known as a dump file (often abbreviated to DMP), which is transportable across operating systems – you can transfer it from Windows 2000 to Sun Solaris, from Sun to MVS and it will still work.

What this means is that you will not use EXP to unload data from Oracle to be imported into SQLServer – it is not the appropriate tool for that. If you wish to do this, you could use the SQL*PLUS copy command in conjunction with either the Transparent Gateway to SQLServer or, even more simply, with the ODBC Net8 drivers provided with Oracle Developer/2000 (the latter allow SQL*PLUS to connect to an ODBC data source). You will not be editing the DMP file using your text editor (or any editor in fact). A DMP file has one use, and one use only – to be read and processed by the IMP tool.

Why You Might Use IMP and EXP

EXP has many uses, some are briefly mentioned above. Here I will list some of the situations where I find them most useful.

Detecting Corruption

I use EXP as a tool to proactively detect corruption, physical or logical, in my database. If you use EXP to perform a *full* database export, it will completely exercise the data dictionary, finding almost any logical dictionary corruption for us. Additionally, it will full scan every table in your database, reading out all of the rows. If there is a table somewhere with a bad block, this is bound to find it. It won't find certain types of logical corruption, such as an index that points to non-existent rows, since it simply full scans the tables, but it will find the most important types of error (we can always rebuild an index, rebuilding a table may not be possible).

Since EXP reads every table fully, it also takes care of any blocks that need cleaning out. This gives us the added bonus of preventing the occurrence of a spurious ORA-01555 (see the Chapter 5 on *Redo and Rollback* for more details on this). After I export the full database and verify the results (look for errors in the logs), I do a full import in SHOW mode. This has the nice side effect of creating a large log file with all of the DDL, the text of all procedures, triggers, views, and so on. On more than one occasion, I have used this to rescue a missing piece of code in an emergency. Additionally, if a table is 'accidentally' dropped, I may be able to quickly restore it from the DMP file, rather than going to my real backups to restore an object. If you have the space to store the DMP files (they are very compressible), I would encourage you to suggest exporting be done on your system during 'off peak' time. In the section on *Large Exports* below, I'll supply a script for UNIX systems that exports directly into compressed files saving considerably on space.

Extracting DDL

EXP is an excellent tool for extracting DDL from the database (as demonstrated in Chapter 6, *Tables*), providing an very easy way to see the verbose CREATE statement for many objects. In the section below on *Getting the DDL*, we'll revisit this idea and explore it further.

Cloning Schemas

EXP and IMP can be used to clone a schema for testing. Using the FROMUSER and TOUSER options of the IMP command, we can easily export data from one user account to another. This is also a supported method for 'renaming' a user – you would perform a user-level export, import into the new user account and then, upon verification of success, you would drop the old user.

Transporting Tablespaces

EXP and IMP can be used to 'transport' a tablespace or set of tablespaces. Only available in Oracle 8i, this allows us to take the formatted datafiles from one instance and 'plug' them into another instance. Consider the case where you have an online web site and wish to publish a large catalog. You can build the catalog on your side of the firewall, refining and testing it. Then upon publication of that catalog, you can simply EXP that tablespace, and all related tablespaces (with all supporting structures like indexes and such), and copy those datafiles to the various servers you have outside the firewall. No more 'dump and load' to publish data – the switchover from the old catalog to the new takes place very quickly. The uses in a data warehousing environment are obvious – instead of ETL (Extract, Transform, Load) we can just L (Load) by attaching the datafiles of our operational system to the data warehouse and using SQL to reformat the data. I've also used this feature heavily in my testing and development. In order to test software, we always need a way to 'reset' the database. Using transportable tablespaces, we are able to do this quickly without having to restore the entire database, thus allowing many different projects to share the same database (we won't be resetting each others data). In this fashion, we can use one database instance, instead of one database instance per project.

Rebuilding Instances

Using EXP and IMP is a good way to rebuild a modestly sized instance. If you would like to change your database block size for example, EXP and IMP might be the right tool for you. On a large instance, it may be prohibitive time-wise to use EXP and IMP but for systems up to a couple of gigabytes, this is an option. I would not use this on my terabyte instance (or anything over 15 or so gigabytes)!

Copying Data between Platforms

EXP and IMP provide a good way to copy data from one platform to another, or even as a way to 'email' some data to someone else. If we create a DMP file on one platform, we can import that on any other platform – the data is platform-independent, even though the DMP file is a binary file.

There are other creative uses of these tools, but the above covers their main uses. What I will do now is answer the frequently ask questions concerned with the practical use of EXP and IMP, and how to use them to solve common problems.

How They Work

In this section, we'll cover many of the frequently asked 'how do I' questions about IMP and EXP. Before we begin, we'll go over the important options for each and what they are used for.

The Options

The inputs for EXP and IMP are all name-value pairs. You will either use:

```
exp parameter_name = value
```

or:

```
exp parameter_name = (value1,value2,value3...)
```

The second method is useful for certain operations, such as for table level export and for exporting more then one table at a time. You can save your IMP and EXP options in a parameter file, saving yourself the chore of typing in the same options over and over again.

Both EXP and IMP support a HELP = Y option, which will display brief usage information on screen. This is very handy when you can't remember the exact name of a specific parameter. If you just type EXP or IMP on the command line and hit *Enter*, they will go into 'interactive' mode and you will be prompted for the values of each parameter one by one.

EXP Parameters

The following is what EXP will display if you pass only the HELP = Y parameter:

```
C:\exp>exp help=y

Export: Release 8.1.6.0.0 - Production on Mon Mar 19 14:11:23 2001

(c) Copyright 1999 Oracle Corporation.  All rights reserved.

You can let Export prompt you for parameters by entering the EXP
command followed by your username/password:

     Example: EXP SCOTT/TIGER

Or, you can control how Export runs by entering the EXP command followed
by various arguments. To specify parameters, you use keywords:

     Format:  EXP KEYWORD=value or KEYWORD=(value1,value2,...,valueN)
     Example: EXP SCOTT/TIGER GRANTS=Y TABLES=(EMP,DEPT,MGR)
              or TABLES=(T1:P1,T1:P2), if T1 is partitioned table

USERID must be the first parameter on the command line.

Keyword  Description (Default)        Keyword      Description (Default)
--------------------------------------------------------------------------
USERID    username/password           FULL         export entire file (N)
BUFFER    size of data buffer         OWNER        list of owner usernames
FILE      output files (EXPDAT.DMP)   TABLES       list of table names
COMPRESS  import into one extent (Y)  RECORDLENGTH length of IO record
GRANTS    export grants (Y)           INCTYPE      incremental export type
INDEXES   export indexes (Y)          RECORD       track incr. export (Y)
ROWS      export data rows (Y)        PARFILE      parameter filename
CONSTRAINTS export constraints (Y)    CONSISTENT   cross-table consistency
LOG       log file of screen output   STATISTICS   analyze objects (ESTIMATe)
DIRECT    direct path (N)             TRIGGERS     export triggers (Y)
FEEDBACK  display progress every x rows (0)
FILESIZE  maximum size of each dump file
QUERY     select clause used to export a subset of a table


The following keywords only apply to transportable tablespaces
TRANSPORT_TABLESPACE export transportable tablespace metadata (N)
TABLESPACES list of tablespaces to transport
Export terminated successfully without warnings.
```

We'll take a look at the most important parameters and those that require clarification, in detail. Parameters that are obvious, such as USERID, will not be covered. Parameters that I consider obsolete, such as INCTYPE, will not be covered either:

Parameter Name	Default Value	Meaning/Notes
BUFFER	OS dependent	This setting sizes the array fetch buffer used by EXP. If you divide the BUFFER parameter by the maximum row size for a given table, this will tell you how many rows EXP will fetch at a time from that table. Larger array sizes improve performance. I have found 100 rows to be an all around 'good' array size.
		Note that some tables, in particular tables with LONG or LOB columns, are fetched one row at a time regardless of the buffer setting. You should ensure the buffer is set large enough for your largest LONG column.
COMPRESS	Y	This parameter *does not compress the contents of the exported data*. It controls how the STORAGE clause for exported objects will be generated. If left as Y, the storage clause for objects will have an initial extent that is equal to the sum of its current extents. That is, EXP will generate a CREATE statement that attempts to fit the object into one single extent.
		I recommend compress = N and the use of locally managed tablespaces.
ROWS	Y	Tells EXP whether to export the rows of data within exported tables or just the structure. I use this frequently with a setting of N just to do structural exports.
FILESIZE	0	If set to a positive value, sets the maximum size of DMP file that export will create. Used when exporting more then two gigabytes of data. See *Large Exports* later for details.
QUERY	N/A	Allows you to associate a WHERE clause to the tables being exported. This WHERE clause will be applied to the rows during a table level export, and only rows that satisfy the WHERE clause will be exported. This lets you export a 'slice' of a table. See the section *Subsetting Data* for an example.
FULL	N	If set to Y, export would perform a full database export. This will extract all users, tablespace definitions, system grants, and everything from the database.
OWNER	N/A	This lets you specify a list of schemas to export. Useful for cloning a schema or to 'rename' a user.
TABLES	N/A	Allows you to specify a list of tables to be exported.

Parameter Name	Default Value	Meaning/Notes
PARFILE	N/A	Specifies the name of a parameter file that contains the `parameter_name = values`. Can be used in place of specifying the parameters on the command line. Most useful with long lists of tables to export or when specifying a query.
CONSISTENT	N	Specifies if the export should be done in a read-only transaction. This would ensure cross table consistency. If you recall from Chapter 3 on *Locking and Concurrency* in, each individual query is executed in a read consistent fashion. A read-only transaction (or an isolation level of serializable) extends that read consistency to the transaction level. If you are exporting tables that are linked via declarative RI (Referential Integrity), or nested table objects and need to be able to import them together later, using `consistent = Y` would be advised. This is especially true if the tables are likely to be modified as the export takes place.
TRANSPORT_ TABLESPACE	N	Specifies whether EXP will be used to export the meta data for a transportable tablespace set or not. See the section on *Transporting Data* for details.
TABLESPACES	NA	Used with `Transport_tablespace` to list the tablespaces being transported.

IMP Parameters

The following is the IMP output when passed the HELP = Y parameter:

```
C:\exp>imp help=y

Import: Release 8.1.6.0.0 - Production on Mon Mar 19 16:10:14 2001

(c) Copyright 1999 Oracle Corporation.  All rights reserved.

You can let Import prompt you for parameters by entering the IMP
command followed by your username/password:

     Example: IMP SCOTT/TIGER

Or, you can control how Import runs by entering the IMP command followed
by various arguments. To specify parameters, you use keywords:

     Format:  IMP KEYWORD=value or KEYWORD=(value1,value2,...,valueN)
     Example: IMP SCOTT/TIGER IGNORE=Y TABLES=(EMP,DEPT) FULL=N
              or TABLES=(T1:P1,T1:P2), if T1 is partitioned table

USERID must be the first parameter on the command line.

Keyword  Description (Default)          Keyword     Description (Default)
--------------------------------------------------------------------------
USERID   username/password             FULL        import entire file (N)
```

```
FILE       input files (EXPDAT.DMP)    TOUSER        list of usernames
SHOW       just list file contents (N) TABLES        list of table names
IGNORE     ignore create errors (N)    RECORDLENGTH length of IO record
GRANTS     import grants (Y)           INCTYPE       incremental import type
INDEXES    import indexes (Y)          COMMIT        commit array insert (N)
ROWS       import data rows (Y)        PARFILE       parameter filename
LOG        log file of screen output   CONSTRAINTS  import constraints (Y)
DESTROY    overwrite tablespace data file (N)
INDEXFILE write table/index info to specified file
SKIP_UNUSABLE_INDEXES  skip maintenance of unusable indexes (N)
ANALYZE   execute ANALYZE statements in dump file (Y)
FEEDBACK display progress every x rows(0)
TOID_NOVALIDATE  skip validation of specified type ids
FILESIZE maximum size of each dump file
RECALCULATE_STATISTICS recalculate statistics (N)

The following keywords only apply to transportable tablespaces
TRANSPORT_TABLESPACE import transportable tablespace metadata (N)
TABLESPACES tablespaces to be transported into database
DATAFILES datafiles to be transported into database
TTS_OWNERS users that own data in the transportable tablespace set

Import terminated successfully without warnings.
```

We'll take a look at the important parameters that were not already discussed for EXP:

PARAMETER NAME	Default Value	Meaning/Notes
SHOW	N	If set to Y, import will SHOW you what it would have done; it will not actually do it. With SHOW = Y, no data will be added and no objects created.
IGNORE	N	When set to Y, IMP will ignore *most* object creation errors. Useful when you have pre-created the objects in the database and wish to use IMP just to populate the tables with data.
INDEXFILE	N/A	If specified, IMP will import all CREATE INDEX commands, and many other DDL statements, to the specified file (with REMs – comments – in front of them). *No other* objects are processed in the DMP file, only the index file is created.
FROMUSER	N/A	If set, this specifies a list of users to import from the DMP file. You can use this to restore a single schema from a full database export.
TOUSER	N/A	If set, this will import the objects from the user specified in the FROMUSER parameter, into the user specified by the TOUSER parameter. This allows you to 'clone' a user.

PARAMETER NAME	Default Value	Meaning/Notes
COMMIT	N	Specifies whether IMP will commit after each array insert. This is controlled by the BUFFER parameter. Normally, IMP will COMMIT after it loads a table fully. Since an insert generates the least amount of rollback possible, and because COMMITting frequently will slow down the insertion of data, as well as it causing generation of more redo logs, an IMP cannot be restarted after a failure. I recommend a setting of N for this parameter.
TTS_OWNERS	N/A	Used with TRANSPORTABLE_TABLESPACES, this will list the owners of objects in the transportable tablespace.

Large Exports

When EXP is used to write to a device that supports 'seeking', as a normal file does, it is limited in the size of the file it can generate. EXP uses the normal OS file APIs, which, on a 32-bit OS, limits the size of the file to 2GB. I know four solutions to this issue (although there are probably others), and we'll take a look at each of these.

Use the FILESIZE Parameter

This option first became available with Oracle 8i. Using the FILESIZE parameter we can set the maximum size (in bytes) of the DMP files that constitute our export, and EXP will create as many DMP files as necessary in order to export the data. For example, in order to export to a series of files that should be no larger then 500 MB apiece we can use:

```
exp userid=tkyte/tkyte file = f1,f2,f3,f4,f5 filesize = 500m owner = scott
```

This would create DMP files f1.dmp, f2.dmp, and so on, each of which would be up to 500 MB in size. If the total size of the export were less then 2GB, EXP would not need to create the f5.dmp file.

The downside to this feature however, is that unless you know approximately how big the export will be, the export will be interactive and hard to automate. Consider this export session. It should export about 2.3 MB of data into 500 KB DMP files:

```
C:\exp>exp userid=tkyte/tkyte tables=t file=(t1,t2,t3) filesize=500k

Export: Release 8.1.6.0.0 - Production on Mon Mar 19 14:54:12 2001

(c) Copyright 1999 Oracle Corporation.  All rights reserved.


Connected to: Oracle8i Enterprise Edition Release 8.1.6.0.0 - Production
With the Partitioning option
JServer Release 8.1.6.0.0 - Production
Export done in WE8ISO8859P1 character set and WE8ISO8859P1 NCHAR character set
```

```
About to export specified tables via Conventional Path ...
. . exporting table                               T
continuing export into file t2.DMP

continuing export into file t3.DMP

Export file: EXPDAT.DMP > t4

continuing export into file t4.DMP

Export file: EXPDAT.DMP > t5

continuing export into file t5.DMP
      21899 rows exported
Export terminated successfully without warnings.
```

The text Export file: EXPDAT.DMP> was an interactive prompt. After EXP used the filenames provided on the command line (t1, t2, t3), it started interactively prompting for the next file names to use. If this had been part of a background script, running late at night, EXP would have just waited for a response or, depending on the circumstances, it might have just failed since it would never get an answer. This feature may be acceptable in many cases – if you know the export will not go over 100 GB (a reasonable assumption on a 50 GB database for example), you could use a FILESIZE of two GB and generate a list of 50 filenames into a parameter file, (PARFILE) using a script. Then you could just use PARFILE = thatlist.par instead of FILE = (a very long list).

To import this data, we simply use IMP and list the files *in the order they should be applied.* IMP will not verify they are in the correct order and will fail miserably if you list them out of sequence. Fortunately, you can list more files then it needs, so if you use the PARFILE suggestion above, it can list files that do not exist and IMP will not complain. Here is an example:

```
C:\exp>imp userid=tkyte/tkyte full=y file=(t1,t2,t3,t4,t5,t6)

Import: Release 8.1.6.0.0 - Production on Mon Mar 19 15:49:24 2001

(c) Copyright 1999 Oracle Corporation.  All rights reserved.


Connected to: Oracle8i Enterprise Edition Release 8.1.6.0.0 - Production
With the Partitioning option
JServer Release 8.1.6.0.0 - Production

Export file created by EXPORT:V08.01.06 via conventional path
import done in WE8ISO8859P1 character set and WE8ISO8859P1 NCHAR character set
IMP-00046: using FILESIZE value from export file of 512000
. importing TKYTE's objects into TKYTE
. . importing table                          "T"      21899 rows imported
Import terminated successfully with warnings.
```

Export Smaller Pieces

This solves the problem by avoiding it altogether. If you have a 10 GB database with 50 application schemas, and each schema is under 2 GB in size, you can use user-level exports. You'll end up with 50 export files, each of which contain an application schema.

Export to an OS Pipe

This is a solution that works very well on UNIX. To date, I have not found a way to do this in the Windows environment. In this case I use the command mknod to create a named pipe. A named pipe is device by which one process can write into the pipe and another process can read out from the other end. EXP can write an unlimited amount of data to pipes, since they do not support 'seeking'. Further, the process that reads off of the other end of the pipe could be a compression routine. Using this, we can simultaneously export the data and compress it. In the event that the compressed file is still larger than 2 GB in size, we can use the split utility to break the file up into smaller pieces. Below is the commented script I use to do this on Unix. This script also shows how to import this compressed split data as well, since immediately after doing an export I run a full import with SHOW = Y to test the integrity of the DMP file I've just created:

```
#!/bin/csh -f

# Set this to the userid you want to perform the export as I always use OPS$ (os
# authenticated) accounts for all jobs that will be run in the background. In that
# way a password never appears in a script file or in the ps output.
setenv UID /

# This is the name of the export file. SPLIT will use this to name the pieces of
# the compressed DMP file.
setenv FN   exp.`date +%j_%Y`.dmp

# This is the name of the named pipe we will use.
setenv PIPE /tmp/exp_tmp_ora8i.dmp

# Here I limit the size of the compressed files to 500 MG each. Anything less
# than 2 GB would be fine.
setenv MAXSIZE 500m

# This is what we are going to export. By default I am doing a full database
# export.
setenv EXPORT_WHAT "full=y COMPRESS=n"


# This is where the export will go to.
cd /nfs/atc-netapp1/expbkup_ora8i

# Clear out the last export.
rm expbkup.log export.test exp.*.dmp* $PIPE

# Create the named pipe.
mknod $PIPE p

# Write the datetime to the log file.
date > expbkup.log

# Start a gzip process in the background. Gzip will read the pipe and put the
# compressed data out to split.  Split will then create 500 MB files out of the
# input data adding .aa, .ab, .ac, .ad, ... file extensions to the template name
# found in $FN.
( gzip < $PIPE ) | split -b $MAXSIZE - $FN. &

# Now, start up export. The Gzip above is waiting for export to start filling the
```

```
# pipe up.
exp userid=$UID buffer=20000000 file=$PIPE $EXPORT_WHAT >>& expbkup.log
date >> expbkup.log

# Now the export is done, this is how to IMP. We need to sort the filenames and
# then simply cat their contents into gunzip. We write that into the pipe. IMP
# will then read that pipe and write what it would do to stderr.  The >>& in the
# csh redirects both stdout and stderr for us.

date > export.test
cat `echo $FN.* | sort` | gunzip > $PIPE &
imp userid=$UID file=$PIPE show=y full=y >>& export.test
date >> export.test

# Clean up the pipe, we don't need it anymore.
rm -f $PIPE
```

If you are using UNIX, I personally feel that the above is a better approach than using FILESIZE = with multiple file names specified on the command line for two reasons. Firstly, it allows us to compress the data before storing it and secondly, it will not prompt us for a filename as EXP might.

Export to a Device that does not Support Seeking

This again is a UNIX-only solution. You can export directly to a tape device just by specifying the name of the device. For example:

```
exp userid=tkyte/tkyte file=/dev/rmt/0 volsize = 6000m full = y
```

This will export directly to tape, stopping every 6000 MB to let us change the tapes if needed.

Subsetting Data

Oracle 8i introduced the ability for EXP to export only selected rows from a table. Prior to this release, EXP was an all or nothing event; either every row was exported or no rows were. We can now use the QUERY= parameter to supply a WHERE clause that will be applied to each exported table. It should be noted that when using a WHERE clause (the QUERY parameter) that the direct mode of export is not allowed; if you want a subset of data, you will be using the conventional path mode of EXP.

The method by which you specify the QUERY = parameter depends on the operating system. A WHERE clause will generally contain many special characters, such as =, > ,<, and spaces. The shell command prompt in UNIX and Windows is not going to like those characters very much. They will have to be escaped and the way to do this is dependent on the OS. What I prefer to do is to always use a PARFILE with the QUERY option. In this way, I can use the same exact methods regardless of platform.

As an example of this, I have created a table T as SELECT * FROM ALL_OBJECTS. I want to export all rows such that the object_id is less than 5000. On Windows, I would have to execute:

```
C:\exp>exp userid=tkyte/tkyte tables=t query="""where object_id < 5000"""
```

Note that, in Windows, we need three double quotes on either side of the WHERE clause. Now, the equivalent command on UNIX is:

```
$ exp userid=tkyte/tkyte tables=t query=\"where object_id \< 5000\"
```

However, if I simply use a parameter file, `exp.par` containing the following argument:

```
query="where object_id < 5000"
```

I can now use the single command on both systems without change:

```
exp userid=tkyte/tkyte tables=t parfile=exp.par
```

I find this to be much easier than trying to properly escape the QUERY strings on each platform.

Transporting Data

A transportable tablespace is a mechanism for taking the formatted datafiles of one database, and attaching them to another. Instead of unloading the data from one database to a flat file, or a DMP file, and then inserting that data into the other database, transporting a tablespace lets you move the data as fast as you can copy files.

There are some restrictions on transporting tablespaces, namely:

❑ **The source and target databases must be running on the same hardware platforms** – You cannot take the datafiles from Windows NT and transfer them to HP/UX, for example. A DMP file can be copied from OS to OS – the **DATAFILES** of a database cannot be; the datafiles are not OS independent like a DMP file is.

❑ **The source and target databases must be using the same character set** – You cannot take a set of files from a database with a WE8ISO8859P1 character set and attach them to a UTF8 instance, for example.

❑ **The source database must not have a tablespace by the same name** – The tablespace name from the originating database will be used. If the source database already has a tablespace by that name, Oracle cannot attach another with that name.

❑ **The source and target database must have the same block sizes** – You cannot attach the files from a 4 KB blocksize database to an 8 KB blocksize database.

❑ **You must transport a self-contained set of objects** – For example, you cannot transport a tablespace that contains an index without also transporting the tablespace that contains the table, which the index is on.

❑ **There are some objects that cannot be transported** – These include snapshots/materialized views, function-based indexes, domain indexes (such as those produced by interMedia), scoped refs, and advanced queues with more then one recipient.

❑ **The source database must set the tablespace to be transported in READ ONLY mode for a short period of time** – This is the period of time it takes to export the tablespace meta data and copy the datafiles elsewhere.

❑ **SYS owned objects cannot be transported** – If a tablespace contains any object own by SYS, the transport will fail. This means that objects like rollback segments, the system tablespace, and so on cannot be transported (which is reasonable, as there would be no reason to transport those objects in any case).

The following example works through all of the steps involved in transporting a tablespace. Just to make it interesting, I'm using two tablespaces. I'll begin by setting up the tablespaces, tables, and creating a new user for the example:

```
SQL> create tablespace tts_ex1
  2  datafile 'c:\oracle\oradata\tkyte816\tts_ex1.dbf' size 1m
  3  extent management local uniform size 64k;
Tablespace created.

SQL> create tablespace tts_ex2
  2  datafile 'c:\oracle\oradata\tkyte816\tts_ex2.dbf' size 1m
  3  extent management local uniform size 64k;
Tablespace created.

SQL> create user tts_user identified by tts_user
  2  default tablespace tts_ex1
  3  temporary tablespace temp;
User created.

SQL> grant dba to tts_user;
Grant succeeded.

SQL> connect tts_user/tts_user
Connected.

SQL> create table emp as select * from scott.emp;
Table created.

SQL> create table dept as select * from scott.dept;
Table created.

SQL> create index emp_idx on emp(empno) tablespace tts_ex2;
Index created.

SQL> create index dept_idx on dept(deptno) tablespace tts_ex2;
Index created.

SQL> select object_type, object_name,
  2                  decode(status,'INVALID','*','') status,
  3                  tablespace_name
  4  from user_objects a, user_segments b
  5  where a.object_name = b.segment_name (+)
  6  order by object_type, object_name
  7  /

OBJECT_TYPE  OBJECT_NAME                     S TABLESPACE_NAME
-----------  ------------------------------  - ------------------------------
INDEX        DEPT_IDX                          TTS_EX2
             EMP_IDX                           TTS_EX2

TABLE        DEPT                              TTS_EX1
             EMP                               TTS_EX1
```

Prior to attempting to export, we need to ensure we have a self-contained set of objects for transport. We can transport a table without its indexes, but we cannot transport an index without its tables. The following shows the routine that we should use to check if a tablespace, or set of tablespaces, are self-contained:

```
SQL> exec sys.dbms_tts.transport_set_check( 'tts_ex1', TRUE );
PL/SQL procedure successfully completed.

SQL> select * from sys.transport_set_violations;
no rows selected

SQL> exec sys.dbms_tts.transport_set_check( 'tts_ex2', TRUE );
PL/SQL procedure successfully completed.

SQL> select * from sys.transport_set_violations;

VIOLATIONS
-----------------------------------------------------------------------
Index TTS_USER.EMP_IDX in tablespace TTS_EX2 points to table TTS_USER.EMP in
tablespace TTS_EX1
Index TTS_USER.DEPT_IDX in tablespace TTS_EX2 points to table TTS_USER.DEPT in
tablespace TTS_EX1

SQL> exec sys.dbms_tts.transport_set_check( 'tts_ex1, tts_ex2', TRUE );
PL/SQL procedure successfully completed.

SQL> select * from sys.transport_set_violations;
no rows selected
```

This shows that we can transport `TTS_EX1`, because it only contains table data and is self-contained. Any attempt to transport `TTS_EX2`, however, would fail since it contains indexes, but not the tables on which they are based. Lastly, both the tablespaces, `TTS_EX1` and `TTS_EX2` may be transported together, as we would be transporting both the tables and the indexes.

`SYS.DBMS_TTS` is executable by any DBA (they have `EXECUTE ANY PROCEDURE`) or any user with the `EXECUTE_CATALOG_ROLE`. It populates a dynamic table with any errors that would occur if we attempted to transport the tablespace(s). Now we are ready to 'detach' or transport these tablespace. We begin by making them `READ ONLY`:

```
SQL> alter tablespace tts_ex1 read only;
Tablespace altered.

SQL> alter tablespace tts_ex2 read only;
Tablespace altered.
```

We then issue the EXP command:

```
SQL> host exp userid="""sys/change_on_install as sysdba"""
             transport_tablespace=y  tablespaces=(tts_ex1,tts_ex2)

Export: Release 8.1.6.0.0 - Production on Mon Mar 19 19:26:26 2001

(c) Copyright 1999 Oracle Corporation.  All rights reserved.

Production
With the Partitioning option
JServer Release 8.1.6.0.0 - Production
Export done in WE8ISO8859P1 character set and WE8ISO8859P1 NCHAR character set
```

331

```
Note: table data (rows) will not be exported
About to export transportable tablespace metadata...
For tablespace TTS_EX1 ...
. exporting cluster definitions
. exporting table definitions
. . exporting table                              EMP
. . exporting table                              DEPT
For tablespace TTS_EX2 ...
. exporting cluster definitions
. exporting table definitions
. exporting referential integrity constraints
. exporting triggers
. end transportable tablespace metadata export
Export terminated successfully without warnings.
```

Note the need for the triple, double quotes in order to specify the userid on the command line. On UNIX, we would have to escape the / as well. If we want to avoid that, we can just let EXP prompt us for the username. Also, note that we used as SYSDBA. Only a SYSDBA (internal) account may perform a transport in Oracle 8.1.6 and later versions. In Oracle 8.1.5 the DBA role was sufficient. (Note that this command has to be put into SQL*PLUS on one line. However, it is shown on two lines in the example below.)

Now all we need to do is copy the datafiles to another location. This could have been done in parallel with the export above to reduce the amount of time spent in read-only mode:

```
SQL> host XCOPY c:\oracle\oradata\tkyte816\tts_ex?.dbf c:\temp
C:\oracle\oradata\tkyte816\TTS_EX1.DBF
C:\oracle\oradata\tkyte816\TTS_EX2.DBF
2 File(s) copied

SQL> alter tablespace tts_ex1 read write;
Tablespace altered.

SQL> alter tablespace tts_ex2 read write;
Tablespace altered.
```

The tablespace is available for READs and WRITEs. Now, we can take this set of files to another database and attach them:

```
C:\exp> imp file=expdat.dmp userid="""sys/manager as sysdba"""
    transport_tablespace=y
    "datafiles=(c:\temp\tts_ex1.dbf,c:\temp\tts_ex2.dbf)"

Import: Release 8.1.6.0.0 - Production on Mon Mar 19 19:26:39 2001

(c) Copyright 1999 Oracle Corporation.  All rights reserved.


Connected to: Oracle8i Enterprise Edition Release 8.1.6.0.0 - Production
With the Partitioning option
JServer Release 8.1.6.0.0 - Production

Export file created by EXPORT:V08.01.06 via conventional path
About to import transportable tablespace(s) metadata...
```

```
import done in WE8ISO8859P1 character set and WE8ISO8859P1 NCHAR character set
. importing SYS's objects into SYS
. importing TTS_USER's objects into TTS_USER
. . importing table                        "EMP"
. . importing table                        "DEPT"
Import terminated successfully without warnings.

SQL> update emp set ename=lower(ename);
update emp set ename=lower(ename)
       *
ERROR at line 1:
ORA-00372: file 9 cannot be modified at this time
ORA-01110: data file 9: 'C:\TEMP\TTS_EX1.DBF'

SQL> alter tablespace tts_ex1 read write;
Tablespace altered.

SQL> alter tablespace tts_ex2 read write;
Tablespace altered.

SQL>  update emp set ename=lower(ename);
14 rows updated.
```

And that's it; the files are attached to the database. The final step shows they get attached in a READ ONLY mode (this makes sense, as they were read-only when we transported them). We might need to alter them after attachment. If you would like to test this out on a single database, you could execute these commands, or their equivalent, on your database, after you make the tablespace READ WRITE again, but before you perform the IMP:

```
SQL> drop tablespace tts_ex1 including contents;
Tablespace dropped.

SQL> drop tablespace tts_ex2 including contents;
Tablespace dropped.

SQL> host erase c:\oracle\oradata\tkyte816\tts_ex?.dbf
```

This is how I 'reset' a database for testing purposes. I transport the 'seed' database before testing and then, when I need to reset, simply drop the existing tablespaces and reattach the 'seed' database.

Transportable tablespaces may also be used to manually perform a tablespace point-in-time recovery. Suppose that you have 'accidentally' dropped a table. You can perform a restore of this database's SYSTEM, ROLLBACK and the affected tablespace on another machine. You would recover this mini-database to the point in time immediately prior to the errant drop table. Now you can transport the tablespace containing this table to the other database and re-attach it. This is in effect what the Recovery Manager (**RMAN**) does when it performs a point-in-time recovery of a tablespace. If you are not using RMAN, you can perform this operation easily yourself.

Another interesting use of this feature could be to share a large amount of read-only (or mostly read-only) data between two instances on the same machine. You could build a large tablespace, set it read-only, export the metadata and then import it to the other instance. You now have two databases that have read-only access to the same set of files. If you ever needed to modify the information, you would:

- ❏   Drop the tablespace, including contents on the database to which you attached the datafiles
- ❏   Alter the tablespace to be read-write in the source

❑ Make the modifications

❑ Alter the tablespace to be read-only

❑ Export the metadata and re-import it to the other database.

The tablespace must be read-only whenever it is used by more than one database.

Getting the DDL

This is a nice side effect of EXP. We can use it to generate much of the DDL from our database. We've seen how this works in Chapter 6, *Tables*, where I used EXP and IMP to see a more verbose CREATE TABLE statement.

There are two ways to get the DDL: SHOW = Y and INDEXFILE = filename. I always recommend using the INDEXFILE option and never the SHOW = Y option. The latter is designed to show us what EXP would do if it was actually executed. The format of the output it produces is unusable as it is – it tends to wrap the DDL statements at awkward places and adds double quotes. Additionally, there is no clear delineation between the individual commands themselves. SHOW = Y is OK as a last ditch effort to extract some DDL, if that is all you have. We'll compare the results of the two options below and you'll see why INDEXFILE is the way to go.

Using the INDEXFILE option, we can reconstruct most of the DDL for a schema into a script file. For example, suppose I started with:

```
tkyte@TKYTE816> create table t1 ( x int primary key, y int );
Table created.

tkyte@TKYTE816> create table t2 (col1 int references t1, col2 int check (col2>0));
Table created.

tkyte@TKYTE816> create index t2_idx on t2(col2,col1);
Index created.

tkyte@TKYTE816> create trigger t2_trigger before insert or update of col1, col2
                                                     on t2 for each row
  2  begin
  3      if ( :new.col1 < :new.col2 ) then
  4          raise_application_error(-20001,
  5                      'Invalid Operation Col1 cannot be less then Col2');
  6      end if;
  7  end;
  8  /
Trigger created.

tkyte@TKYTE816> create view v
  2  as
  3  select t1.y t1_y, t2.col2 t2_col2 from t1, t2 where t1.x = t2.col1
  4  /
View created.
```

I can now run EXP and IMP as follows:

```
C:\>exp userid=tkyte/tkyte owner=tkyte
C:\>imp userid=tkyte/tkyte full=y indexfile=tkyte.sql
```

Inspecting `tkyte.sql` shows:

```
REM  CREATE TABLE "TKYTE"."T1" ("X" NUMBER(*,0), "Y" NUMBER(*,0)) PCTFREE
REM  10 PCTUSED 40 INITRANS 1 MAXTRANS 255 LOGGING STORAGE(INITIAL 524288)
REM  TABLESPACE "DATA" ;
REM  ... 0 rows
REM  ALTER TABLE "TKYTE"."T1" ADD PRIMARY KEY ("X") USING INDEX PCTFREE 10
REM  INITRANS 2 MAXTRANS 255 STORAGE(INITIAL 524288) TABLESPACE "DATA"
REM  ENABLE ;
REM  CREATE TABLE "TKYTE"."T2" ("COL1" NUMBER(*,0), "COL2" NUMBER(*,0))
REM  PCTFREE 10 PCTUSED 40 INITRANS 1 MAXTRANS 255 LOGGING STORAGE(INITIAL
REM  524288) TABLESPACE "DATA" ;
REM  ... 0 rows
CONNECT TKYTE;
CREATE INDEX "TKYTE"."T2_IDX" ON "T2" ("COL2" , "COL1" ) PCTFREE 10
INITRANS 2 MAXTRANS 255 STORAGE(INITIAL 524288) TABLESPACE "DATA" LOGGING ;
REM  ALTER TABLE "TKYTE"."T2" ADD CHECK (col2>0) ENABLE ;
REM  ALTER TABLE "TKYTE"."T2" ADD FOREIGN KEY ("COL1") REFERENCES "T1"
REM  ("X") ENABLE ;
```

If I remove the REM statements, I have the DDL for objects that consume space, but not my trigger or view (procedures and such would be missing as well). EXP exports these objects, but IMP does not show them to me in the INDEXFILE option. The one way we can get IMP to show us these objects is via the SHOW option:

```
C:\ImpExp> imp userid=tkyte/tkyte show=y full=y
Import: Release 8.1.6.0.0 - Production on Mon Apr 23 15:48:43 2001
(c) Copyright 1999 Oracle Corporation.  All rights reserved.
Connected to: Oracle8i Enterprise Edition Release 8.1.6.0.0 - Production
With the Partitioning option
JServer Release 8.1.6.0.0 - Production

Export file created by EXPORT:V08.01.06 via conventional path
import done in WE8ISO8859P1 character set and WE8ISO8859P1 NCHAR character set
. importing TKYTE's objects into TKYTE
 "CREATE TABLE "T1" ("X" NUMBER(*,0), "Y" NUMBER(*,0))  PCTFREE 10 PCTUSED 40"
 " INITRANS 1 MAXTRANS 255 LOGGING STORAGE(INITIAL 524288) TABLESPACE "DATA""
. . skipping table "T1"

 "CREATE TABLE "T2" ("COL1" NUMBER(*,0), "COL2" NUMBER(*,0))  PCTFREE 10 PCTU"
 "SED 40 INITRANS 1 MAXTRANS 255 LOGGING STORAGE(INITIAL 524288) TABLESPACE ""
 "DATA""
. . skipping table "T2"

 "CREATE INDEX "T2_IDX" ON "T2" ("COL2" , "COL1" )  PCTFREE 10 INITRANS 2 MAX"
 "TRANS 255 STORAGE(INITIAL 524288) TABLESPACE "DATA" LOGGING"
 "CREATE FORCE VIEW "TKYTE"."V"                              ("T1_Y","T2_COL2") "
 "AS "
 "select t1.y t1_y, t2.col2 t2_col2 from t1, t2 where t1.x = t2.col1"
```

```
"CREATE TRIGGER "TKYTE".t2_trigger before insert or update of col1, col2 on "
"t2 for each row"
""
"begin"
"    if ( :new.col1 < :new.col2 ) then"
"       raise_application_error(-20001,'Invalid Operation Col1 cannot be le"
"ss then Col2');"
"    end if;"
"end;"
"ALTER TRIGGER "T2_TRIGGER"  ENABLE"
Import terminated successfully without warnings.
```

You should note that this output is wholly unsuitable for general-purpose use. For example, consider:

```
"CREATE TABLE "T2" ("COL1" NUMBER(*,0), "COL2" NUMBER(*,0))  PCTFREE 10 PCTU"
"SED 40 INITRANS 1 MAXTRANS 255 LOGGING STORAGE(INITIAL 524288) TABLESPACE ""
```

IMP breaks lines at arbitrary places – the word PCTUSED is broken in half. Additionally each line begins and ends with a double quote. Simply removing these quotes will not make this script file usable because the commands are broken at inappropriate points. Not only that, but our source code is 'damaged' as well:

```
"    if ( :new.col1 < :new.col2 ) then"
"       raise_application_error(-20001,'Invalid Operation Col1 cannot be le"
"ss then Col2');"
"    end if;"
```

IMP stuck a newline right into the middle of our line of code. Lastly, the commands themselves are not separated by anything:

```
"CREATE INDEX "T2_IDX" ON "T2" ("COL2" , "COL1" )  PCTFREE 10 INITRANS 2 MAX"
"TRANS 255 STORAGE(INITIAL 524288) TABLESPACE "DATA" LOGGING"
"CREATE FORCE VIEW "TKYTE"."V"                      ("T1_Y","T2_COL2") "
"AS "
"select t1.y t1_y, t2.col2 t2_col2 from t1, t2 where t1.x = t2.col1"
"CREATE TRIGGER "TKYTE".t2_trigger before insert or update of col1, col2 on "
"t2 for each row"
```

The CREATE INDEX command runs into the CREATE VIEW, which runs into the CREATE TRIGGER, and so on (you get the point!). This file would need some serious editing to be useful. The things we were missing are here now – they are not in a format that is ready to run but they are salvageable. I find this useful in a pinch, when someone has accidentally dropped their last month's work (their code) and needs to retrieve it. That is why I export my database twice a week and do the IMP...SHOW = Y on it (as demonstrated in the section on *Large Exports*). More then once, I was able to resurrect a relatively recent copy of the code for them from the output of that command. This removed the need to do a database point-in-time recovery to get their code back (that would be the other alternative – the data is never lost in a database!).

Getting around the limitations with scripts

If I have to move PL/SQL code from one schema to another, I prefer to use scripts. I have scripts to retrieve a package, procedure, or function. Another script extracts views. Yet another does triggers. Moving these types of objects is not something EXP/IMP is adept at. Ask EXP/IMP for a table and it is great. Ask EXP/IMP to give your view definition back and it is not so good.

Since they are so useful, I'll include the scripts for extracting the above objects here in the EXP section. You probably came to this section trying to find out how to get IMP to give you back your code anyway. Now, you know that IMP is not going to give it to you in a format that is usable.

So, here is a script that will retrieve any package (including the package body), function, or procedure, and write it to a SQL file of that same name. If you execute SQL> @getcode my_procedure, this script will create a file my_procedure.sql that contains that PL/SQL routine:

```
REM getcode.sql - extract any procedure, function or package
set feedback off
set heading off
set termout off
set linesize 1000
set trimspool on
set verify off
spool &1..sql
prompt set define off
select decode( type||'-'||to_char(line,'fm99999'),
               'PACKAGE BODY-1', '/'||chr(10),
                null) ||
       decode(line,1,'create or replace ', '' ) ||
       text text
  from user_source
 where name = upper('&&1')
 order by type, line;
prompt /
prompt set define on
spool off
set feedback on
set heading on
set termout on
set linesize 100
```

For those of you who want to extract *all* code from a schema, I have a script called getallcode.sql. This will create a script file per PL/SQL object in the current working directory, and then create a script getallcode_INSTALL that will install the code in another schema for you:

```
set termout off
set heading off
set feedback off
set linesize 50
spool xtmpx.sql
select '@getcode ' || object_name
from user_objects
where object_type in ( 'PROCEDURE', 'FUNCTION', 'PACKAGE' )
/
spool off
```

```
spool getallcode_INSTALL.sql
select '@' || object_name
from user_objects
where object_type in ( 'PROCEDURE', 'FUNCTION', 'PACKAGE' )
/
spool off
set heading on
set feedback on
set linesize 130
set termout on
@xtmpx.sql
```

Now, the following script is used to extract a single view. If you execute SQL> @getaview view_name, it will create a file view_name.sql in the current directory with the CREATE VIEW statement in it:

```
REM getaview.sql
set heading off
set long 99999999
set feedback off
set linesize 1000
set trimspool on
set verify off
set termout off
set embedded on

column column_name format a1000
column text format a1000

spool &1..sql
prompt create or replace view &1 (
select decode(column_id,1,'',',') || column_name   column_name
  from user_tab_columns
 where table_name = upper('&1')
 order by column_id
/
prompt ) as
select text
  from user_views
 where view_name = upper('&1')
/
prompt /
spool off

set termout on
set heading on
set feedback on
set verify on
```

Of course, if you want *all* views, there is the script getallviews:

```
set heading off
set feedback off
set linesize 1000
```

```
set trimspool on
set verify off
set termout off
set embedded on

spool tmp.sql
select '@getaview ' || view_name
from user_views
/
spool off

set termout on
set heading on
set feedback on
set verify on
@tmp
```

Lastly, there is `gettrig.sql`. This does not handle every case of triggers. For example, I do not retrieve the `referencing OLD as ...` statement as I've never used it. The concept is the same as above and would be easy enough to modify if you find the trigger construct useful:

```
set echo off
set verify off
set feedback off
set termout off
set heading off
set pagesize 0
set long 99999999
spool &1..sql

select
'create or replace trigger "' ||
        trigger_name || '"' || chr(10)||
  decode( substr( trigger_type, 1, 1 ),
          'A', 'AFTER', 'B', 'BEFORE', 'I', 'INSTEAD OF' ) ||
              chr(10) ||
  triggering_event || chr(10) ||
  'ON "' || table_owner || '"."' ||
        table_name || '"' || chr(10) ||
  decode( instr( trigger_type, 'EACH ROW' ), 0, null,
             'FOR EACH ROW' ) || chr(10) ,
  trigger_body
from user_triggers
where trigger_name = upper('&1')
/
prompt /

spool off
set verify on
set feedback on
set termout on
set heading on
```

So, this shows how we can use EXP/IMP to get our DDL; our tables and indexes, things that consume space. For things that do not really consume space including, but not limited to, triggers, procedures, views, sequences, synonyms, and the like, simple SQL*PLUS scripts are the best approach. IMP with the SHOW = Y can be used in a pinch, but if you have an ongoing need to extract these objects, a script is what you want.

Backup and Recovery

EXP and IMP should *not* be considered backup tools. They are not appropriate to be your backup and recovery mechanism. RMAN and operating system backups are the only true backups. The reasons EXP/IMP should not be considered as your backup tools are:

❑ They present at best, a point-in-time picture of the database. Using CONSISTENT = Y will allow you to extract a point in time picture of the database (perhaps, remember the chance for the ORA-01555 snapshot too old increases with the length of your transaction), but it is just that – a single point-in-time. If you use this export to recover, you will lose *all* work that happened after the start of the EXP. Also, archived redo logs cannot be applied to an IMP.

❑ Restoring a database of any significant size using IMP is a slow process; all data will have to be inserted (through the SQL engine, generating rollback and redo), all indexes will have to be rebuilt, all constraints must be validated, all code must be compiled, and so on. What might take a few minutes with a real backup will take hours or days using IMP.

❑ Incremental EXP/IMP will soon no longer be a supported feature. The use of the INCTYPE = parameter will be removed. The quote from Oracle is 'Important: Incremental, cumulative, and complete Exports are obsolete features that will be phased out in a subsequent release. You should begin now to migrate to Oracle's Backup and Recovery Manager for database backups'. See *Oracle8i Operating System Backup and Recovery Guide* for more information.

Does this mean that EXP/IMP utilities are not useful as part of a larger backup and recovery plan? Well, I believe they *can* play an important role as part of a larger backup and recovery plan. Your production database must be running in archive log mode to allow you to perform 'point in time' and media recovery (recovery from a failed disk). This is crucial and there is no substitute for it. In addition to this, some proactive fault detection is a good idea as part of a well-rounded backup/recovery plan. As part of this, I use EXP as mentioned above. This fully exercises the data dictionary, using almost all of its indexes and objects, ensuring it is OK. It also scans all table data, ensuring that it is safe (if an index goes bad it is easily recreated so I'm not as worried about testing those). The resulting DMP file can also be useful to extract that lost piece of code, or that accidentally dropped table at times as well, saving us from having to perform a point in time recovery in many cases.

Other tools such as DBV (the database verifier), may be run against the datafiles periodically as well to ensure the physical integrity of the data, checking out those index structures that EXP might not get to.

IMP/EXP is not a Reorganization Tool (Any More)

This used to be one of the major uses of EXP/IMP. In order to 'defragment' a fragmented tablespace, DBAs would spend time exporting a set of objects, dropping them, and then importing them back in. Many DBAs spent a considerable amount of time doing this on a recurring basis. The fact is, they should never have had to do this more then once and, in most cases, never really needed to do it at all. They should never have had to do it more than once because if the tablespace really was fragmented, one would hope they would use more appropriate planning for storage during the export/import process; one that would avoid fragmentation. In most cases however, they did not, so history was doomed to repeat itself. In other cases, they were doing it because they heard it was a 'good thing', something that needed to be done, when in fact they probably did not need to do it at all.

That aside, using EXP/IMP in this manner was fraught with danger. You were taking all of the data *out* of the database, dropping it, and bringing it back in. There would be a period of time where the data was no longer protected by the database. There was the chance the IMP wouldn't work (it is just a program after all). There is a chance that someone would change the data as you were exporting it (you wouldn't see these changes in the export) and you would *lose* their changes. You could lose grants on objects and so on. It required a lot of planning and downtime to carry this out.

In Oracle8i, you never need to use EXP/IMP to reorganize data. If you truly believe you need to (and I am a firm believer that you should never need to more than *once* to correct a bad implementation), then you can use the ALTER TABLE MOVE command to move tables from tablespace to tablespace, change their storage characteristics, and so on. The table will be available for querying during this period of reorganization, but not for updates. Immediately after the move, the indexes will become unusable and will need to be rebuilt, so queries will be affected at that point in time. The downtime is *considerably* less than the corresponding downtime using EXP/IMP and none of the issues listed above come into play; there is never any time where the data is not protected by the database, there is no chance of losing an update to the data, grants are not touched by this process, and so on.

In short, the days of EXP/IMP as a reorganization tool are over. Do not even consider them for this job.

Importing into Different Structures

This is an issue that comes up frequently; you have an export of some data and need to import it into a slightly different structure. Is there any way to do that? I've seen this when exporting data from version 1 of a software package into a database that has version 2 of the software (or vice versa). The answer is *yes*, but we might need some help in doing so. There are 3 cases to consider here:

❑ You have *added* a column (no work required on your part, Oracle will put a Null or whatever default you have set in it)

❑ You have *dropped* a column (some work on your part)

❑ You have changed the data type of a column (again, some work on your part)

For the additional column case, we need to do nothing. Oracle will insert into the table normally using null values, or whatever default value that we have specified. For the dropped and modified columns, we will need to import into a view, using an INSTEAD OF trigger to perform whatever data mapping we need. Note that the use of an INSTEAD OF trigger will obviously add overhead – this is a fine solution for medium sets of data, but you would not want to load tens of millions of rows in this fashion! Here are the tables:

```
tkyte@TKYTE816> create table added_a_column ( x int );
Table created.

tkyte@TKYTE816> create table dropped_a_column ( x int, y int );
Table created.

tkyte@TKYTE816> create table modified_a_column( x int, y int );
Table created.

tkyte@TKYTE816> insert into added_a_column values ( 1 );
1 row created.

tkyte@TKYTE816> insert into dropped_a_column values ( 1, 1 );
```

```
1 row created.

tkyte@TKYTE816> insert into modified_a_column values ( 1, 1 );
1 row created.

tkyte@TKYTE816> commit;
Commit complete.
```

We will start by exporting the three tables (this command should be in one line, otherwise you will export the whole schema):

```
tkyte@TKYTE816> host exp userid=tkyte/tkyte
                    tables=(added_a_column,dropped_a_column,modified_a_column)

Export: Release 8.1.6.0.0 - Production on Tue Mar 20 09:02:34 2001
(c) Copyright 1999 Oracle Corporation.  All rights reserved.

Connected to: Oracle8i Enterprise Edition Release 8.1.6.0.0 - Production
With the Partitioning option
JServer Release 8.1.6.0.0 - Production
Export done in WE8ISO8859P1 character set and WE8ISO8859P1 NCHAR character set

About to export specified tables via Conventional Path ...
. . exporting table                ADDED_A_COLUMN          1 rows exported
. . exporting table              DROPPED_A_COLUMN          1 rows exported
. . exporting table             MODIFIED_A_COLUMN          1 rows exported
Export terminated successfully without warnings.
```

So, that constitutes our test case. We have exported the three tables 'as is'. Now, let's modify them:

```
tkyte@TKYTE816> alter table added_a_column add ( y int );
Table altered.

tkyte@TKYTE816> alter table dropped_a_column drop column y;
Table altered.

tkyte@TKYTE816> delete from modified_a_column;
1 row deleted.

tkyte@TKYTE816> alter table modified_a_column modify y date;
Table altered.
```

Now, if we attempt to import, we will find that ADDED_A_COLUMN works OK, but the rest fail:

```
tkyte@TKYTE816> host imp userid=tkyte/tkyte full=y ignore=y

Import: Release 8.1.6.0.0 - Production on Tue Mar 20 09:02:34 2001
(c) Copyright 1999 Oracle Corporation.  All rights reserved.

Connected to: Oracle8i Enterprise Edition Release 8.1.6.0.0 - Production
With the Partitioning option
JServer Release 8.1.6.0.0 - Production

Export file created by EXPORT:V08.01.06 via conventional path
```

```
import done in WE8ISO8859P1 character set and WE8ISO8859P1 NCHAR character set
. importing TKYTE's objects into TKYTE
. . importing table              "ADDED_A_COLUMN"           1 rows imported
. . importing table              "DROPPED_A_COLUMN"
IMP-00058: ORACLE error 904 encountered
ORA-00904: invalid column name
. . importing table              "MODIFIED_A_COLUMN"
IMP-00058: ORACLE error 932 encountered
ORA-00932: inconsistent datatypes
Import terminated successfully with warnings.
```

The next step is to create views in the database– views that look like the original tables. To accomplish this we will:

❑   Rename the tables for the duration of the import

❑   Create a view that selects constants of the correct type – for example, select 1 for a number, SELECT SYSDATE for a date, SELECT RPAD('*', 30, '*') for a VARCHAR2(30), and so on

❑   Create an INSTEAD OF trigger that 'does the right thing' for us, performing any data conversion/mapping we need

Here is the code to do this:

```
tkyte@TKYTE816> rename modified_a_column to modified_a_column_TEMP;
Table renamed.

tkyte@TKYTE816> create or replace view modified_a_column
  2  as
  3  select 1 x, 1 y from modified_a_column_TEMP;
View created.

tkyte@TKYTE816> create or replace trigger modified_a_column_IOI
  2  instead of insert on modified_a_column
  3  begin
  4          insert into modified_a_column_TEMP
  5          ( x, y )
  6          values
  7          ( :new.x, to_date('01012001','ddmmyyyy')+:new.y );
  8  end;
  9  /
Trigger created.
```

Here, we are converting the NUMBER that was stored in Y, into an offset from January 1, 2001. You would perform whatever conversion you required: from STRING to DATE, DATE to NUMBER, NUMBER to STRING, and so on. Now we take care of the dropped column:

```
tkyte@TKYTE816> rename dropped_a_column  to dropped_a_column_TEMP;
Table renamed.

tkyte@TKYTE816> create or replace view dropped_a_column
  2  as
  3  select 1 x, 1 y from dropped_a_column_TEMP;
View created.
```

```
tkyte@TKYTE816> create or replace trigger dropped_a_column_IOI
  2  instead of insert on dropped_a_column
  3  begin
  4          insert into dropped_a_column_TEMP
  5          ( x )
  6          values
  7          ( :new.x );
  8  end;
  9  /
Trigger created.
```

Here, we are just getting rid of :new.y. We do not do anything with it – we just ignore it. It needs to be in the view so IMP has something to insert into. Now we are ready to import again:

```
tkyte@TKYTE816> host imp userid=tkyte/tkyte full=y ignore=y

Import: Release 8.1.6.0.0 - Production on Tue Mar 20 09:21:41 2001
(c) Copyright 1999 Oracle Corporation.  All rights reserved.

Connected to: Oracle8i Enterprise Edition Release 8.1.6.0.0 - Production
With the Partitioning option
JServer Release 8.1.6.0.0 - Production

Export file created by EXPORT:V08.01.06 via conventional path
import done in WE8ISO8859P1 character set and WE8ISO8859P1 NCHAR character set
. importing TKYTE's objects into TKYTE
. . importing table              "ADDED_A_COLUMN"          1 rows imported
. . importing table            "DROPPED_A_COLUMN"          1 rows imported
. . importing table           "MODIFIED_A_COLUMN"          1 rows imported
Import terminated successfully without warnings.
```

The import runs cleanly. Next, we need to go into the database, drop our views, and rename our tables:

```
tkyte@TKYTE816> drop view modified_a_column;
View dropped.

tkyte@TKYTE816> drop view dropped_a_column;
View dropped.

tkyte@TKYTE816> rename dropped_a_column_TEMP to dropped_a_column;
Table renamed.

tkyte@TKYTE816> rename modified_a_column_TEMP to modified_a_column;
Table renamed.
```

When we look at the data, we expect to see the following:

❑ Three rows in added_a_column from the original insert and two imports

❑ Two rows in dropped_a_column from the original insert and one import that worked on it

❑ One row in modified_a_column since we had to empty this table prior to altering the column type

And that is what we get:

```
tkyte@TKYTE816> select * from added_a_column;

         X          Y
---------- ----------
         1
         1
         1

tkyte@TKYTE816> select * from dropped_a_column;

         X
----------
         1
         1

tkyte@TKYTE816> select * from modified_a_column;

         X Y
---------- ----------
         1 02-JAN-01
```

Direct Path Exports

A direct path export should not be considered the converse of a direct path load using SQLLDR (see Chapter 9). A direct path export does not read directly from the datafiles and write to the DMP file. SQLLDR does write directly to the datafiles from the DAT files. Export in direct path mode simply bypasses the SQL evaluation buffer (WHERE clause processing, column formatting and such). Ninety percent of the path is the same. EXP is still reading buffers into the buffer cache, doing the same consistent read processing, and so on.

The speedup obtained using the direct path export can be large, however. The ten percent of the processing that it cuts out, accounts for a much larger percentage of the run-time. For example, I have just exported about 100MB of data, and 1.2 million records. The direct path export took about one minute. The conventional path export on the other hand took three minutes. There is unfortunately, no corresponding 'direct path import'. Import uses conventional SQL to insert the data back into tables. SQLLDR is still the tool to use for high performance data loads.

It should be noted that in direct path mode, you cannot use the QUERY = parameter to select a subset of rows. This makes sense given that DIRECT = Y is simply a way to bypass the SQL evaluation buffer and that is where the where clause processing would normally take place.

Caveats and Errors

In this section, I would like to cover some of the issues and problems with EXP/IMP that people frequently encounter. Here, we will look into issues surrounding:

❑   Using EXP/IMP to 'clone' a schema

❑   Using EXP/IMP across heterogeneous versions of Oracle

- ❑ The case of the 'disappearing' Index
- ❑ The impact of constraints that have system-assigned names
- ❑ Issues with regards to NLS (National Language Support)
- ❑ Issues with regards to objects that may have multiple tablespace name references, such as tables with LOBs

Cloning

This is a common use of EXP/IMP; you want to copy an entire application schema. You need to copy all of the tables, triggers, views, procedures, and so on. In general, this works great, I simply use the following:

```
Exp userid=tkyte/tkyte owner=old_user
Imp userid=tkyte/tkyte fromuser=old_user touser=new_user
```

A potentially nasty issue arises, however, when the application schema you are copying from uses schema-qualified references to its own objects. What I mean is that, given a user A, they code something like:

```
create trigger MY_trigger
before insert on A.table_name
begin
    ...;
end;
/
```

This creates a trigger that is *explicitly* on the table A.TABLE_NAME. If we export that and import it into another schema, this trigger will *still* be on A.TABLE_NAME, it will not be on the table named TABLE_NAME in the other schema. EXP/IMP are a little inconsistent in the way they handle this condition, however. Consider the following schema:

```
tkyte@TKYTE816> create table t1
  2  ( x int primary key );
Table created.

tkyte@TKYTE816> create table t4 ( y int references TKYTE.t1 );
Table created.

tkyte@TKYTE816> create trigger t2_trigger
  2  before insert on TKYTE.t4
  3  begin
  4    null;
  5  end;
  6  /
Trigger created.

tkyte@TKYTE816> create or replace view v
  2  as
  3  select * from TKYTE.t1;
View created.
```

We have a referential integrity constraint that explicitly references TKYTE.T1, a trigger explicitly on TKYTE.T4, and a view that explicitly references TKYTE.T1. I'll export this schema and create a user to import it into and perform the import (note that the user performing the import with the FROMUSER and TOUSER options must have the role IMP_FULL_DATABASE granted to them):

```
tkyte@TKYTE816> host exp userid=tkyte/tkyte owner=tkyte
...
tkyte@TKYTE816> grant connect,resource to a identified by a;
Grant succeeded.

tkyte@TKYTE816> host imp userid=system/change_on_install fromuser=tkyte touser=a

Import: Release 8.1.6.0.0 - Production on Tue Mar 20 09:56:17 2001

(c) Copyright 1999 Oracle Corporation.  All rights reserved.


Connected to: Oracle8i Enterprise Edition Release 8.1.6.0.0 - Production
With the Partitioning option
JServer Release 8.1.6.0.0 - Production

Export file created by EXPORT:V08.01.06 via conventional path

Warning: the objects were exported by TKYTE, not by you

import done in WE8ISO8859P1 character set and WE8ISO8859P1 NCHAR character set
. importing TKYTE's objects into A
. . importing table                         "T1"          0 rows imported
. . importing table                         "T4"          0 rows imported
IMP-00041: Warning: object created with compilation warnings
 "CREATE FORCE VIEW "A"."V"                                ("X") AS "
 "select "X" from TKYTE.t1"
Import terminated successfully with warnings.
```

Now, we can see already that the view is a problem – it explicitly references TKYTE.T1 and the user A cannot create a view on that object, due to insufficient privileges. Fortunately, IMP makes it clear that the view created with an error. What is not so clear is what happened with the declarative RI and the trigger. Inspection of the data dictionary when logged in as A shows us:

```
a@TKYTE816> select table_name, constraint_name,
  2     constraint_type, r_constraint_name
  3     from user_constraints
  4  /

TABLE_NAME            CONSTRAINT_NAME               C R_CONSTRAINT_NAME
--------------------  ----------------------------  - --------------------
T1                    SYS_C002465                   P
T4                    SYS_C002466                   R SYS_C002465

a@TKYTE816> select trigger_name, table_owner, table_name
  2     from user_triggers
  3  /

TRIGGER_NAME         TABLE_OWNER           TABLE_NAME
----------------     --------------------  --------------------------------
T2_TRIGGER           TKYTE                 T4
```

Surprisingly, our referential integrity constraint points to user A's table. The R constraint is the reference and the constraint it points to, SYS_C002465, is the primary key constraint on table T1 – user A's table T1. If you continue further in this train of thought, if the schema TKYTE had a qualified RI constraint that pointed to a table B.T (a table T owned by B), this RI constraint would be imported into A's schema as pointing to B.T as well. If the qualified schema name on the referenced table in the constraint is the same as the owner of the table at export time, EXP will not preserve the name.

Consider this in comparison to the trigger. The trigger T2_TRIGGER is not on user A's table – it is actually on user TKYTE's table! This is a side effect that is potentially disastrous. Consider that the trigger is duplicated on TKYTE.T4 – its logic will execute two times alongside the fact that the trigger is not on A.T4 at all.

I would urge you to consider these issues when using EXP/IMP to clone a user. Be aware that they exist and look for them. If you execute the following, you'll be able to review all of the DDL, triggers, procedures, and so on, before running them in the database:

```
Imp userid=sys/manager fromuser=tkyte touser=a INDEXFILE=foo.sql
Imp userid=sys/manager fromuser=tkyte touser=a SHOW=Y
```

At the very least, consider doing the import into a database that does not have the FROMUSER account. For example, here I do the above import into a database where A exists, but TKYTE does not:

```
C:\exp>imp userid=sys/manager fromuser=tkyte touser=a

Import: Release 8.1.6.0.0 - Production on Tue Mar 20 10:29:37 2001
(c) Copyright 1999 Oracle Corporation.  All rights reserved.

Connected to: Oracle8i Enterprise Edition Release 8.1.6.0.0 - Production
With the Partitioning option
JServer Release 8.1.6.0.0 - Production

Export file created by EXPORT:V08.01.06 via conventional path

Warning: the objects were exported by TKYTE, not by you

import done in WE8ISO8859P1 character set and WE8ISO8859P1 NCHAR character set
. importing TKYTE's objects into A
. . importing table                          "T1"          0 rows imported
. . importing table                          "T4"          0 rows imported
. . importing table                          "T5"          0 rows imported
IMP-00041: Warning: object created with compilation warnings
 "CREATE FORCE VIEW "A"."V"                              ("X") AS "
 "select "X" from TKYTE.t1"
IMP-00017: following statement failed with ORACLE error 942:
 "CREATE TRIGGER "A".t2_trigger"
 "before insert on TKYTE.t4"
 ""
 "begin"
 "  null;"
 "end;"
IMP-00003: ORACLE error 942 encountered
ORA-00942: table or view does not exist
Import terminated successfully with warnings.
```

I will be able to discover these nuances immediately. I would highly recommend this approach to discovering the objects that have qualified schema names in them, and determining whether or not they are correct.

A similar, but slightly different issue occurs with Oracle's object types. Oracle allows you to create new datatypes in the database. In the same manner that they provide you with the NUMBER, DATE, VARCHAR2... types, you can add types to the database. You can then create tables of that type or create tables with columns, which are of that type. A common course of action is therefore, to create a schema and set about creating types in the schema and objects that rely on those types – everything in one user account. If you ever want to 'clone' that schema, you'll run into a serious problem. I'll demonstrate the problem first, and then describe why it happens and how to partially solve it.

First, we'll start with a schema like this:

```
tkyte@TKYTE816> create type my_type
  2  as object
  3  ( x int,
  4    y date,
  5    z varchar2(20)
  6  )
  7  /
Type created.

tkyte@TKYTE816> create table t1 of my_type
  2  /
Table created.

tkyte@TKYTE816> create table t2 ( a int, b my_type );
Table created.

tkyte@TKYTE816> insert into t1 values ( 1, sysdate, 'hello' );
1 row created.

tkyte@TKYTE816> insert into t2 values ( 55, my_type( 1, sysdate, 'hello') );
1 row created.

tkyte@TKYTE816> commit;
Commit complete.

tkyte@TKYTE816> host exp userid=tkyte/tkyte owner=tkyte
```

This gives us a copy of this schema. When we try to use the FROMUSER/TOUSER option however, we quickly discover this:

```
tkyte@TKYTE816> host imp userid=sys/manager fromuser=tkyte touser=a;

Import: Release 8.1.6.0.0 - Production on Tue Mar 20 12:44:26 2001

(c) Copyright 1999 Oracle Corporation.  All rights reserved.


Connected to: Oracle8i Enterprise Edition Release 8.1.6.0.0 - Production
With the Partitioning option
JServer Release 8.1.6.0.0 - Production
```

```
Export file created by EXPORT:V08.01.06 via conventional path

Warning: the objects were exported by TKYTE, not by you

import done in WE8ISO8859P1 character set and WE8ISO8859P1 NCHAR character set
. importing TKYTE's objects into A
IMP-00017: following statement failed with ORACLE error 2304:
 "CREATE TYPE "MY_TYPE" TIMESTAMP '2001-03-20:12:44:21' OID '4A301F5AABF04A46"
 "88552E4AF5793176'  "
 "as object"
 "( x int,"
 "  y date,"
 "  z varchar2(20)"
 ")"
IMP-00003: ORACLE error 2304 encountered
ORA-02304: invalid object identifier literal
IMP-00063: Warning: Skipping table "A"."T1" because object type "A"."MY_TYPE"
cannot be created or has different identifier
IMP-00063: Warning: Skipping table "A"."T2" because object type "A"."MY_TYPE"
cannot be created or has different identifier
Import terminated successfully with warnings.
```

We are basically stuck at this point. We cannot create the type in A's schema, and even if we could, it would be a *different* type and the import would still not be happy. It would be like having two different NUMBER types in the database – they would be different from each other. In the above, we were trying to create two different MY_TYPE types, but treat them as one.

The issue, and this is not clear in the documentation, is that we should not create a schema that has both types and objects, *especially* if we want to import/export the schema in this fashion. In a similar manner to the way in which CTXSYS and ORDSYS are setup for Oracle's interMedia, we should setup a schema to contain our types. If we wish to use interMedia Text, we use the types available from CTXSYS. If we wish to use interMedia image capabilities, we use ORDSYS types. We should do the same here. What we do is set up a schema that will hold our types – any and all of our types:

```
our_types@TKYTE816> connect OUR_TYPES

our_types@TKYTE816> create type my_type
  2   as object
  3   ( x int,
  4     y date,
  5     z varchar2(20)
  6   )
  7   /
Type created.

our_types@TKYTE816> grant all on my_type to public;
Grant succeeded.
```

All schemas will use *these* types, never their own personal types, which will become strongly tied to their account. Now, we will redo our example from above:

```
tkyte@TKYTE816> connect tkyte
```

```
tkyte@TKYTE816> create table t1 of our_types.my_type
  2  /
Table created.

tkyte@TKYTE816> create table t2 ( a int, b our_types.my_type );
Table created.

tkyte@TKYTE816> insert into t1 values ( 1, sysdate, 'hello' );
1 row created.

tkyte@TKYTE816> insert into t2 values ( 55,
  2  our_types.my_type( 1, sysdate, 'hello') );
1 row created.

tkyte@TKYTE816> commit;
Commit complete.

tkyte@TKYTE816> host exp userid=tkyte/tkyte owner=tkyte
```

So, the only difference here is that we are using OUR_TYPES.MY_TYPE, not just MY_TYPE. Since we can never create synonyms for types, this schema qualification is mandatory – we must fully qualify the object name with the schema name that owns them. This is the way we must do it when using interMedia types (CTXSYS, ORDSYS objects for example) and indexes as well– we always fully qualify them. Pick the schema name of your type holder with care for this reason, you will be living with it for a while!

Now, let's see how the import goes this time:

```
tkyte@TKYTE816> host imp userid=sys/manager fromuser=tkyte touser=a;

Import: Release 8.1.6.0.0 - Production on Tue Mar 20 12:49:33 2001
(c) Copyright 1999 Oracle Corporation.  All rights reserved.

Connected to: Oracle8i Enterprise Edition Release 8.1.6.0.0 - Production
With the Partitioning option
JServer Release 8.1.6.0.0 - Production

Export file created by EXPORT:V08.01.06 via conventional path

Warning: the objects were exported by TKYTE, not by you

import done in WE8ISO8859P1 character set and WE8ISO8859P1 NCHAR character set
. importing TKYTE's objects into A
IMP-00017: following statement failed with ORACLE error 2304:
 "CREATE TABLE "T1" OF "OUR_TYPES"."MY_TYPE" OID 'AC60D4D90ED1428B84D245357AD"
 "F2DF3' OIDINDEX (PCTFREE 10 INITRANS 2 MAXTRANS 255 STORAGE(INITIAL 524288)"
 " TABLESPACE "DATA") PCTFREE 10 PCTUSED 40 INITRANS 1 MAXTRANS 255 LOGGING S"
 "TORAGE(INITIAL 524288) TABLESPACE "DATA""
IMP-00003: ORACLE error 2304 encountered
ORA-02304: invalid object identifier literal
. . importing table                      "T2"          1 rows imported
Import terminated successfully with warnings.
```

We fared better, but it is still not perfect yet. The pure OBJECT table failed, but the relational table with the object type succeeded. This is to be expected. The object table is not the same object table, technically, and objects are very picky about that. We can work around this particular issue however, since these two tables are in fact to be constructed on the same type. What we must do is pre-create the object table in A's schema. We can use the IMP INDEXFILE= option to get the DDL:

```
a@TKYTE816> host imp userid=a/a tables=t1 indexfile=t1.sql
```

If we edit the resulting T1.SQL we'll find:

```
REM   CREATE TABLE "A"."T1" OF "OUR_TYPES"."MY_TYPE" OID
REM   'AC60D4D90ED1428B84D245357ADF2DF3' OIDINDEX (PCTFREE 10 INITRANS 2
REM   MAXTRANS 255 STORAGE(INITIAL 524288) TABLESPACE "DATA") PCTFREE 10
REM   PCTUSED 40 INITRANS 1 MAXTRANS 255 LOGGING STORAGE(INITIAL 524288)
REM   TABLESPACE "DATA" ;
REM   ALTER TABLE "A"."T1" MODIFY ("SYS_NC_OID$" DEFAULT SYS_OP_GUID()) ;
REM   ... 1 rows
```

We need to remove the REM characters as well as the OID xxxxx clause, and then execute:

```
a@TKYTE816> CREATE TABLE "A"."T1" OF "OUR_TYPES"."MY_TYPE"
  2   OIDINDEX (PCTFREE 10 INITRANS 2
  3   MAXTRANS 255 STORAGE(INITIAL 524288) TABLESPACE "DATA") PCTFREE 10
  4   PCTUSED 40 INITRANS 1 MAXTRANS 255 LOGGING STORAGE(INITIAL 524288)
  5   TABLESPACE "DATA" ;

Table created.

a@TKYTE816> ALTER TABLE "A"."T1" MODIFY ("SYS_NC_OID$" DEFAULT SYS_OP_GUID()) ;

Table altered.
```

Now we can execute:

```
a@TKYTE816> host imp userid=a/a tables=t1 ignore=y

Import: Release 8.1.6.0.0 - Production on Tue Mar 20 13:01:24 2001

(c) Copyright 1999 Oracle Corporation.  All rights reserved.


Connected to: Oracle8i Enterprise Edition Release 8.1.6.0.0 - Production
With the Partitioning option
JServer Release 8.1.6.0.0 - Production

Export file created by EXPORT:V08.01.06 via conventional path

Warning: the objects were exported by TKYTE, not by you

import done in WE8ISO8859P1 character set and WE8ISO8859P1 NCHAR character set
. importing TKYTE's objects into A
. . importing table                          "T1"          1 rows imported
Import terminated successfully without warnings.
```

```
a@TKYTE816> select * from t1;

        X Y           Z
---------- --------- --------------------
        1 20-MAR-01 hello
```

and we have our data back.

Using IMP/EXP Across Versions

You can easily IMP and EXP across different versions of Oracle. You can even EXP and IMP to and from version 7 databases and version 8 databases. However, you have to use the proper version of EXP and IMP when doing so. The rules for picking the version of IMP and EXP are:

❏   Always use the version of IMP that matches the version of the database. If you are going to import into version 8.1.6, use the 8.1.6 import tool.

❏   Always use the version of EXP that matches the lowest of the two versions of the database. If you were exporting from version 8.1.6 to 8.1.5, you would use the version 8.1.5 EXP tool, over Net8, against the version 8.1.6 database. If you were exporting from version 8.1.5 to 8.1.6, you would use the version 8.1.5 EXP tool directly against the 8.1.5 database.

This is crucial – if you attempt to export from 8.1.6 to 8.0.5, for example, and you use the version 8.1.6 EXP tool, you'll find that the 8.0.5 IMP tool cannot read the DMP file. Furthermore, you cannot use the version 8.1.6 IMP tool against version 8.0.5; it will not work. There are things in the 8.1.6 database that simply did not exist in 8.0.5.

If you bear this rule in mind – that the database into which you are importing dictates the version of IMP that should be used and the version of EXP to use is the lower of the two versions, then you'll be able to EXP/IMP across versions easily.

One last note: if you still have some Oracle 7 databases kicking around, you will need to run a script in your Oracle 8 databases to allow the version 7 EXP tool to work. This script is cat7exp.sql and is found in [ORACLE_HOME]/rdbms/admin. This script should be run by the user SYS when connected via the SVRMGRL command line tool. This will set up the version 7 compatible export scripts in the version 8 database. It will not replace the version 8 export views – they will remain intact. This script will simply add the additional version 7 views to your database allowing the version 7 EXP tool to function.

Where did my Indexes go?

You might expect that if you exported a schema, dropped all of the objects in that database schema, and then re-imported your exported schema, then you would end up with the same set of objects. Well, you might be surprised. Consider this simple schema:

```
tkyte@TKYTE816> create table t
  2  ( x int,
  3    y int,
  4    constraint t_pk primary key(x)
  5  )
  6  /
```

```
Table created.

tkyte@TKYTE816> create index t_idx on t(x,y)
  2  /
Index created.

tkyte@TKYTE816> create table t2
  2  ( x int primary key,
  3     y int
  4  )
  5  /
Table created.

tkyte@TKYTE816> create index t2_idx on t2(x,y)
  2  /
Index created.
```

Two very similar tables, the only difference being that one used a named primary key and the other let the system generate one. Let's take a look at the objects created in the database:

```
tkyte@TKYTE816> select object_type, object_name,
  2                  decode(status,'INVALID','*','') status,
  3                  tablespace_name
  4  from user_objects a, user_segments b
  5  where a.object_name = b.segment_name (+)
  6  order by object_type, object_name
  7  /

OBJECT_TYPE  OBJECT_NAME                        S TABLESPACE_NAME
------------ ------------------------------- - -------------------
INDEX        SYS_C002559                         DATA
             T2_IDX                              DATA
             T_IDX                               DATA
             T_PK                                DATA

TABLE        T                                   DATA
             T2                                  DATA


6 rows selected.
```

We see that each of our primary keys had an index generated for them – these are SYS_C002559 and T_PK. We also see the two extra indexes we created as well. After I dropped tables T and T2, I ran a full IMP. To my surprise, I discovered the following:

```
tkyte@TKYTE816> select object_type, object_name,
  2                  decode(status,'INVALID','*','') status,
  3                  tablespace_name
  4  from user_objects a, user_segments b
  5  where a.object_name = b.segment_name (+)
  6  order by object_type, object_name
  7  /

OBJECT_TYPE  OBJECT_NAME                        S TABLESPACE_NAME
------------ ------------------------------- - -------------------
```

```
INDEX         T2_IDX                          DATA
              T_IDX                           DATA
              T_PK                            DATA

TABLE         T                               DATA
              T2                              DATA
```

One of my indexes is 'missing'. What happened here is that Oracle used the index T2_IDX on (X,Y) to enforce the primary key. This is perfectly valid. We can reproduce this behavior ourselves just by running the CREATE commands in a slightly different order (run in a 'clean' schema with no other objects created):

```
tkyte@TKYTE816> create table t ( x int, y int );
Table created.

tkyte@TKYTE816> create index t_idx on t(x,y);
Index created.

tkyte@TKYTE816> alter table t add constraint t_pk primary key(x);
Table altered.

tkyte@TKYTE816> select object_type, object_name,
  2                    decode(status,'INVALID','*','') status,
  3                    tablespace_name
  4  from user_objects a, user_segments b
  5  where a.object_name = b.segment_name (+)
  6  order by object_type, object_name
  7  /

OBJECT_TYPE  OBJECT_NAME                    S TABLESPACE_NAME
-----------  ------------------------------ - --------------------
INDEX        T_IDX                            DATA

TABLE        T                                DATA
```

Here, Oracle will use the index T_IDX to enforce the primary key. We can see this clearly if we try to drop it:

```
tkyte@TKYTE816> drop index t_idx;
drop index t_idx
           *
ERROR at line 1:
ORA-02429: cannot drop index used for enforcement of unique/primary key
```

Well, a similar event is occurring with EXP/IMP. It does not export the index definition for indexes that have system-generated names. There would be an error if it did. EXP/IMP relies on the fact that the index is created implicitly upon object creation (if at all). If it did actually export our index SYS_C002559, and attempted to create it upon import, one of two errors might occur. First, the generated name SYS_C002559 may very well conflict with an *already* existing generated name in the database (for a check constraint, say). Second, the object creation itself may have already created the index – making this index redundant (and in error). So here, EXP and IMP are doing the right thing – you are just seeing a side effect of the fact that a constraint does *not* have to create an index.

By naming the primary key, we created an index that has a constant name; every time we create that object, the name of the index is immutable. EXP exports the definition of this index and IMP will import it.

The moral to this story is that default names for objects should be avoided, not only for the reason above, but also for the reason below. This, of course is apart from the fact that the name SYS_C002559 does not mean anything to anyone, whereas the name T_PK might mean 'primary key for table T' to someone.

Named versus Default-Named Constraints

Another issue with regards to system-generated named constraints is the fact that the import may cause a redundant constraint to be added to a table (I could have called this section *Where Did All of These Constraints Come From?*). Let's take a look at an example. We start with a table T:

```
tkyte@TKYTE816> create table t
  2  ( x int check ( x > 5 ),
  3    y int constraint my_rule check ( y > 10 ),
  4    z int not null ,
  5    a int unique,
  6    b int references t,
  7    c int primary key
  8  );
Table created.

tkyte@TKYTE816> select constraint_name name, constraint_type type,
search_condition
  2      from user_constraints where table_name = 'T';

NAME                                 T SEARCH_CONDITION
------------------------------------ - ------------------------
SYS_C002674                          C "Z" IS NOT NULL
SYS_C002675                          C x > 5
MY_RULE                              C y > 10
SYS_C002677                          P
SYS_C002678                          U
SYS_C002679                          R

6 rows selected.
```

It has lots of constraints on it – six all together. I'll export it, drop the table and import it again:

```
tkyte@TKYTE816> host exp userid=tkyte/tkyte owner=tkyte

tkyte@tkyte816> drop table T;
Table dropped.

tkyte@TKYTE816> host imp userid=tkyte/tkyte full=y ignore=y rows=n

tkyte@TKYTE816> select constraint_name name, constraint_type type,
search_condition
  2      from user_constraints where table_name = 'T';
```

```
NAME                              T SEARCH_CONDITION
------------------------------    - ------------------------
SYS_C002680                       C "Z" IS NOT NULL
SYS_C002681                       C x > 5
MY_RULE                           C y > 10
SYS_C002683                       P
SYS_C002684                       U
SYS_C002685                       R

6 rows selected.
```

Looks normal so far. Let's say, however, that we rerun the import for whatever reason (it failed part way through for example). What we'll then discover is:

```
tkyte@TKYTE816> host imp userid=tkyte/tkyte full=y ignore=y

Import: Release 8.1.6.0.0 - Production on Tue Mar 20 15:42:26 2001

(c) Copyright 1999 Oracle Corporation.  All rights reserved.


Connected to: Oracle8i Enterprise Edition Release 8.1.6.0.0 - Production
With the Partitioning option
JServer Release 8.1.6.0.0 - Production

Export file created by EXPORT:V08.01.06 via conventional path
import done in WE8ISO8859P1 character set and WE8ISO8859P1 NCHAR character set
. importing TKYTE's objects into TKYTE
. . importing table                           "T"            0 rows imported
IMP-00017: following statement failed with ORACLE error 2264:
 "ALTER TABLE "T" ADD  CONSTRAINT "MY_RULE" CHECK ( y > 10 ) ENABLE NOVALIDAT"
 "E"
IMP-00003: ORACLE error 2264 encountered
ORA-02264: name already used by an existing constraint
IMP-00017: following statement failed with ORACLE error 2261:
 "ALTER TABLE "T" ADD  UNIQUE ("A") USING INDEX PCTFREE 10 INITRANS 2 MAXTRAN"
 "S 255 STORAGE(INITIAL 524288) TABLESPACE "DATA" ENABLE"
IMP-00003: ORACLE error 2261 encountered
ORA-02261: such unique or primary key already exists in the table
About to enable constraints...
Import terminated successfully with warnings.

tkyte@TKYTE816> select constraint_name name, constraint_type type,
search_condition
  2      from user_constraints where table_name = 'T';

NAME                              T SEARCH_CONDITION
------------------------------    - ------------------------
SYS_C002680                       C "Z" IS NOT NULL
SYS_C002681                       C x > 5
MY_RULE                           C y > 10
SYS_C002683                       P
SYS_C002684                       U
SYS_C002685                       R
SYS_C002686                       C x > 5

7 rows selected.
```

We have an extra constraint. In fact, every time we run this, we'll have an extra constraint added. My named constraint however, generates a warning on screen – you cannot have the same named constraint twice. The unnamed constraint for x > 5 on the other hand – gets created again. This is because the database just generated a new name for it.

I've seen cases where people have been using EXP on one database, truncating the data on another, and using IMP to put the data back in. Over time, they had accumulated hundreds of check constraints on many columns. Performance was starting to go downhill and they wanted to know why. This is the reason why: every time they copied the data, they added yet another bunch of check constraints, all doing the same work. Lets see the effect that just one hundred redundant check constraints can have:

```
tkyte@TKYTE816> create table t
  2  ( x int check ( x > 5 )
  3  )
  4  /
Table created.

tkyte@TKYTE816> declare
  2      l_start number default dbms_utility.get_time;
  3  begin
  4      for i in 1 .. 1000
  5      loop
  6          insert into t values ( 10 );
  7      end loop;
  8      dbms_output.put_line
  9      ( round((dbms_utility.get_time-l_start)/100,2) || ' seconds' );
 10  end;
 11  /
.08 seconds

PL/SQL procedure successfully completed.

tkyte@TKYTE816> begin
  2      for i in 1 .. 100
  3      loop
  4          execute immediate
  5          'ALTER TABLE "TKYTE"."T" ADD CHECK ( x > 5 ) ENABLE ';
  6      end loop;
  7  end;
  8  /
PL/SQL procedure successfully completed.

tkyte@TKYTE816> declare
  2      l_start number default dbms_utility.get_time;
  3  begin
  4      for i in 1 .. 1000
  5      loop
  6          insert into t values ( 10 );
  7      end loop;
  8      dbms_output.put_line
  9      ( round((dbms_utility.get_time-l_start)/100,2) || ' seconds' );
 10  end;
 11  /
.17 seconds

PL/SQL procedure successfully completed.
```

Yet another good reason to name your constraints!

National Language Support (NLS) Issues

NLS stands for National Language Support. It allows us to store, process, and retrieve data in native languages. It ensures that database utilities and error messages, sort order, date, time, monetary, numeric, and calendar conventions automatically adapt to the native language and locale – for example so that numbers are displayed with commas and periods in the correct place. In some countries a number should be displayed as 999.999.999,99, in others 999,999,999.00. There are issues you should consider when using EXP/IMP to move data around in an environment with different character sets. Of particular importance are the character sets of:

❑ The EXP client versus the database being exported *from*

❑ The IMP client versus the EXP clients

❑ The IMP client versus the database being imported *into*

If *any* of them differ, you could end up unintentionally damaging your data. Consider this very trivial example (trivial, but common):

```
ops$tkyte@DEV816> create table t ( c varchar2(1) );
Table created.

ops$tkyte@DEV816> insert into t values ( chr(235) );
1 row created.

ops$tkyte@DEV816> select dump(c) from t;

DUMP(C)
-------------------------------------------------------------
Typ=1 Len=1: 235

ops$tkyte@DEV816> commit;
Commit complete.
```

So far, so good. Now lets export:

```
ops$tkyte@DEV816> host exp userid=tkyte/tkyte tables=t

Export: Release 8.1.6.2.0 - Production on Tue Mar 20 16:04:55 2001

(c) Copyright 1999 Oracle Corporation.  All rights reserved.


Connected to: Oracle8i Enterprise Edition Release 8.1.6.2.0 - Production
With the Partitioning option
JServer Release 8.1.6.2.0 - Production
Export done in US7ASCII character set and US7ASCII NCHAR character set
server uses WE8ISO8859P1 character set (possible charset conversion)

About to export specified tables via Conventional Path ...
. . exporting table                              T          1 rows exported
Export terminated successfully without warnings.
```

This message (possible charset conversion) needs to be noticed! We have just taken 8-bit data and exported it into a 7-bit character set. Let's now import this data back in:

```
ops$tkyte@DEV816> host imp userid=tkyte/tkyte full=y ignore=y

Import: Release 8.1.6.2.0 - Production on Tue Mar 20 16:05:07 2001

(c) Copyright 1999 Oracle Corporation.  All rights reserved.


Connected to: Oracle8i Enterprise Edition Release 8.1.6.2.0 - Production
With the Partitioning option
JServer Release 8.1.6.2.0 - Production

Export file created by EXPORT:V08.01.06 via conventional path
import done in US7ASCII character set and US7ASCII NCHAR character set
import server uses WE8ISO8859P1 character set (possible charset conversion)
. importing OPS$TKYTE's objects into OPS$TKYTE
. . importing table                              "T"          1 rows imported
Import terminated successfully without warnings.

ops$tkyte@DEV816> select dump(c) from t;

DUMP(C)
--------------------------
Typ=1 Len=1: 235
Typ=1 Len=1: 101
```

The SQL DUMP command shows us the data we took out and put back in is different. It is clearer if we look at the numbers in binary:

```
235 decimal = 11101011 binary
101 decimal = 01100101 binary
```

Our data has been mapped from one character set to another – it has been changed. It would be terrible to discover this *after* you dropped the table.

If you see this warning message, stop and think about the consequences. In my case, the solution is easy. On UNIX or NT, I just set the NLS_LANG environment variable to match the database:

```
$ echo $NLS_LANG
AMERICAN_AMERICA.WE8ISO8859P1
```

Now, neither EXP and IMP will perform any character set conversions. They will run much faster as well. On Windows NT/2000, the NLS_LANG may also be set in the registry.

Tables Spanning Multiple Tablespaces

In the beginning, CREATE TABLE statements were relatively simple. Over the years, they have gotten progressively more and more complex. The 'train tracks' or 'wire diagram' for the simple CREATE TABLE now spans eight pages. One of the newer features of tables is the ability for bits and pieces of them to exist in various tablespaces. For example, a table with a CLOB column will have a table segment, CLOB index segment, and CLOB data segment. We can specify the location of the table and the locations of the CLOB data. An index-organized table (IOT) can have the index segment, and an overflow segment. Partitioned tables of course may have many partitions, each in a separately specified tablespace.

With this complexity comes some confusion for EXP/IMP. It used to be that if you tried to import an object and it failed due to the tablespace either *not* existing, or because you exceeded your quota on that tablespace, IMP would rewrite the SQL for you to create the object in your DEFAULT tablespace. IMP will not do this with multi-tablespace objects, as it will with single tablespace object, even if all of the tablespaces specified in the CREATE command are the same. An example will demonstrate the problem, and then I'll describe how we can work around the situation.

First, we'll start with a schema that has a couple of multi-tablespace objects and a simple single tablespace table in a tablespace:

```
tkyte@TKYTE816> create tablespace exp_test
   2   datafile 'c:\oracle\oradata\tkyte816\exp_test.dbf'
   3   size 1m
   4   extent management local
   5   uniform size 64k
   6   /
Tablespace created.

tkyte@TKYTE816> alter user tkyte default tablespace exp_test
   2   /
User altered.

tkyte@TKYTE816> create table t1
   2   ( x int primary key, y varchar2(25) )
   3   organization index
   4   overflow tablespace exp_test
   5   /
Table created.

tkyte@TKYTE816> create table t2
   2   ( x int, y clob )
   3   /
Table created.

tkyte@TKYTE816> create table t3
   2   ( x int,
   3     a int default to_char(sysdate,'d')
   4   )
   5   PARTITION BY RANGE (a)
   6   (
   7   PARTITION part_1 VALUES LESS THAN(2),
   8   PARTITION part_2 VALUES LESS THAN(3),
   9   PARTITION part_3 VALUES LESS THAN(4),
  10   PARTITION part_4 VALUES LESS THAN(5),
  11   PARTITION part_5 VALUES LESS THAN(6),
  12   PARTITION part_6 VALUES LESS THAN(7),
  13   PARTITION part_7 VALUES LESS THAN(8)
  14   )
  15   /
```

```
Table created.

tkyte@TKYTE816> create table t4 ( x int )
  2  /
Table created.
```

So, we started by creating a tablespace and making this our *default* tablespace. We then created an IOT with two segments – the index and overflow. We created a table with a CLOB that has three segments. Then we have a partitioned table with seven segments. Lastly, we have the normal, simple 'table'. We export this schema:

```
tkyte@TKYTE816> host exp userid=tkyte/tkyte owner=tkyte
```

and proceed to drop that tablespace:

```
tkyte@TKYTE816> drop tablespace exp_test including contents;
Tablespace dropped.

tkyte@TKYTE816> alter user tkyte default tablespace data;
User altered.
```

When we import the schema, we discover most of the tables won't come back in:

```
tkyte@TKYTE816> host imp userid=tkyte/tkyte full=y

Import: Release 8.1.6.0.0 - Production on Tue Mar 20 19:03:18 2001

(c) Copyright 1999 Oracle Corporation.  All rights reserved.


Connected to: Oracle8i Enterprise Edition Release 8.1.6.0.0 - Production
With the Partitioning option
JServer Release 8.1.6.0.0 - Production

Export file created by EXPORT:V08.01.06 via conventional path
import done in WE8ISO8859P1 character set and WE8ISO8859P1 NCHAR character set
. importing TKYTE's objects into TKYTE
IMP-00017: following statement failed with ORACLE error 959:
 "CREATE TABLE "T2" ("X" NUMBER(*,0), "Y" CLOB)  PCTFREE 10 PCTUSED 40 INITRA"
 "NS 1 MAXTRANS 255 LOGGING STORAGE(INITIAL 65536) TABLESPACE "EXP_TEST" LOB "
 "("Y") STORE AS  (TABLESPACE "EXP_TEST" ENABLE STORAGE IN ROW CHUNK 8192 PCT"
 "VERSION 10 NOCACHE  STORAGE(INITIAL 65536))"
IMP-00003: ORACLE error 959 encountered
ORA-00959: tablespace 'EXP_TEST' does not exist
IMP-00017: following statement failed with ORACLE error 959:
 "CREATE TABLE "T3" ("X" NUMBER(*,0), "A" NUMBER(*,0))  PCTFREE 10 PCTUSED 40"
 " INITRANS 1 MAXTRANS 255 LOGGING TABLESPACE "EXP_TEST" PARTITION BY RANGE ("
 ""A" )  (PARTITION "PART_1" VALUES LESS THAN (2)  PCTFREE 10 PCTUSED 40 INIT"
 "RANS 1 MAXTRANS 255 STORAGE(INITIAL 65536) TABLESPACE "EXP_TEST" LOGGING, P"
 "ARTITION "PART_2" VALUES LESS THAN (3)  PCTFREE 10 PCTUSED 40 INITRANS 1 MA"
 "XTRANS 255 STORAGE(INITIAL 65536) TABLESPACE "EXP_TEST" LOGGING, PARTITION "
 ""PART_3" VALUES LESS THAN (4)  PCTFREE 10 PCTUSED 40 INITRANS 1 MAXTRANS 25"
 "5 STORAGE(INITIAL 65536) TABLESPACE "EXP_TEST" LOGGING, PARTITION "PART_4" "
```

```
       "VALUES LESS THAN (5)  PCTFREE 10 PCTUSED 40 INITRANS 1 MAXTRANS 255 STORAGE"
       "(INITIAL 65536) TABLESPACE "EXP_TEST" LOGGING, PARTITION "PART_5" VALUES LE"
       "SS THAN (6)  PCTFREE 10 PCTUSED 40 INITRANS 1 MAXTRANS 255 STORAGE(INITIAL "
       "65536) TABLESPACE "EXP_TEST" LOGGING, PARTITION "PART_6" VALUES LESS THAN ("
       "7)  PCTFREE 10 PCTUSED 40 INITRANS 1 MAXTRANS 255 STORAGE(INITIAL 65536) TA"
       "BLESPACE "EXP_TEST" LOGGING, PARTITION "PART_7" VALUES LESS THAN (8)  PCTFR"
       "EE 10 PCTUSED 40 INITRANS 1 MAXTRANS 255 STORAGE(INITIAL 65536) TABLESPACE "
       ""EXP_TEST" LOGGING )"
  IMP-00003: ORACLE error 959 encountered
  ORA-00959: tablespace 'EXP_TEST' does not exist
  . . importing table                            "T4"           0 rows imported
  IMP-00017: following statement failed with ORACLE error 959:
       "CREATE TABLE "T1" ("X" NUMBER(*,0), "Y" VARCHAR2(25),  PRIMARY KEY ("X") EN"
       "ABLE) ORGANIZATION INDEX  NOCOMPRESS PCTFREE 10 INITRANS 2 MAXTRANS 255 LOG"
       "GING STORAGE(INITIAL 65536) TABLESPACE "EXP_TEST" PCTTHRESHOLD 50 OVERFLOW "
       "PCTFREE 10 PCTUSED 40 INITRANS 1 MAXTRANS 255 LOGGING  STORAGE(INITIAL 6553"
       "6) TABLESPACE "EXP_TEST""
  IMP-00003: ORACLE error 959 encountered
  ORA-00959: tablespace 'EXP_TEST' does not exist
  Import terminated successfully with warnings.
```

Specifically, the *only* table that came back in without an error was the simple 'normal' table. For this table, IMP rewrote the SQL. It blanked out the first TABLESPACE EXP_TEST that it came across and retried the CREATE. This rewritten CREATE succeeded. The other CREATE commands, when similarly rewritten, did not succeed. The only solution to this is to create the tables beforehand, and then import with IGNORE=Y. If you do not have the DDL for the CREATE TABLE commands, you can retrieve it, of course, from the DMP file with INDEXFILE=Y. That will allow you to modify the DDL, supplying the correct tablespace information yourself. In this case, since I had the DDL to hand, I just created the three tables with new tablespaces specified, where necessary:

```
tkyte@TKYTE816> create table t1
  2  ( x int primary key, y varchar2(25) )
  3  organization index
  4  overflow tablespace data
  5  /
Table created.

tkyte@TKYTE816> create table t2
  2  ( x int, y clob )
  3  /
Table created.

tkyte@TKYTE816> create table t3
  2  ( x int,
  3    a int default to_char(sysdate,'d')
  4  )
  5  PARTITION BY RANGE (a)
  6  (
  7  PARTITION part_1 VALUES LESS THAN(2),
  8  PARTITION part_2 VALUES LESS THAN(3),
  9  PARTITION part_3 VALUES LESS THAN(4),
 10  PARTITION part_4 VALUES LESS THAN(5),
 11  PARTITION part_5 VALUES LESS THAN(6),
 12  PARTITION part_6 VALUES LESS THAN(7),
 13  PARTITION part_7 VALUES LESS THAN(8)
```

```
 14  )
 15  /
Table created.
```

and was able to import cleanly:

```
tkyte@TKYTE816> host imp userid=tkyte/tkyte full=y ignore=y

Import: Release 8.1.6.0.0 - Production on Tue Mar 20 19:03:20 2001

(c) Copyright 1999 Oracle Corporation.  All rights reserved.


Connected to: Oracle8i Enterprise Edition Release 8.1.6.0.0 - Production
With the Partitioning option
JServer Release 8.1.6.0.0 - Production

Export file created by EXPORT:V08.01.06 via conventional path
import done in WE8ISO8859P1 character set and WE8ISO8859P1 NCHAR character set
. importing TKYTE's objects into TKYTE
. . importing table                        "T2"          0 rows imported
. . importing partition            "T3":"PART_1"            0 rows imported
. . importing partition            "T3":"PART_2"            0 rows imported
. . importing partition            "T3":"PART_3"            0 rows imported
. . importing partition            "T3":"PART_4"            0 rows imported
. . importing partition            "T3":"PART_5"            0 rows imported
. . importing partition            "T3":"PART_6"            0 rows imported
. . importing partition            "T3":"PART_7"            0 rows imported
. . importing table                        "T4"          0 rows imported
. . importing table                        "T1"          0 rows imported
Import terminated successfully without warnings.
```

Now, I have seen an issue with some objects whereby the above workaround does not work. IMP still raises the ORA-00959 tablespace 'name' does not exist. The only way temporary work around I have found for this is to pre-create the object (as above) and then create very small tablespaces with the names that IMP demands. You would create these tablespaces with a file too small to actually create anything. Now the IMP will work and you can drop the tablespaces afterwards.

Summary

In this chapter, we have covered many uses of the tools Import and Export. I have presented the common solutions to the problems and questions I hear most frequently regarding these tools. EXP and IMP are extremely powerful once you get a trick or two under your belt. Given the complexity of objects in the database today, I am sometimes surprised that it works as seamlessly as it does.

The roles of IMP and EXP are changing over time. In the Oracle version 5 and 6 days, it was considered a viable backup tool. Databases were small (a 100MB database might have been considered large) and 24x7 was just beginning to be a requirement. Over time, the usefulness of IMP/EXP in the area of backup and recovery has severely diminished, to the point where I would say outright that it is not a backup and recovery tool at all. Today EXP and IMP are relatively simple tools that should be used to move a modest amount of data back and forth between instances, or, by using transportable tablespaces, to move massive amounts of data. To use it to backup a 500GB database would be ludicrous. To use it to transport 100GB of that database would be perfectly valid.

It still has many of its conventional uses, such as the ability to 'clone' a schema (given that you understand the potential 'gotchas') or to extract the DDL for a schema to a file. Mixed with other database features like INSTEAD OF triggers on views, you can even teach it some new tricks. Interesting uses, such as the ability for two databases to share a set of read-only files, are still waiting to be discovered with this tool, I'm sure.

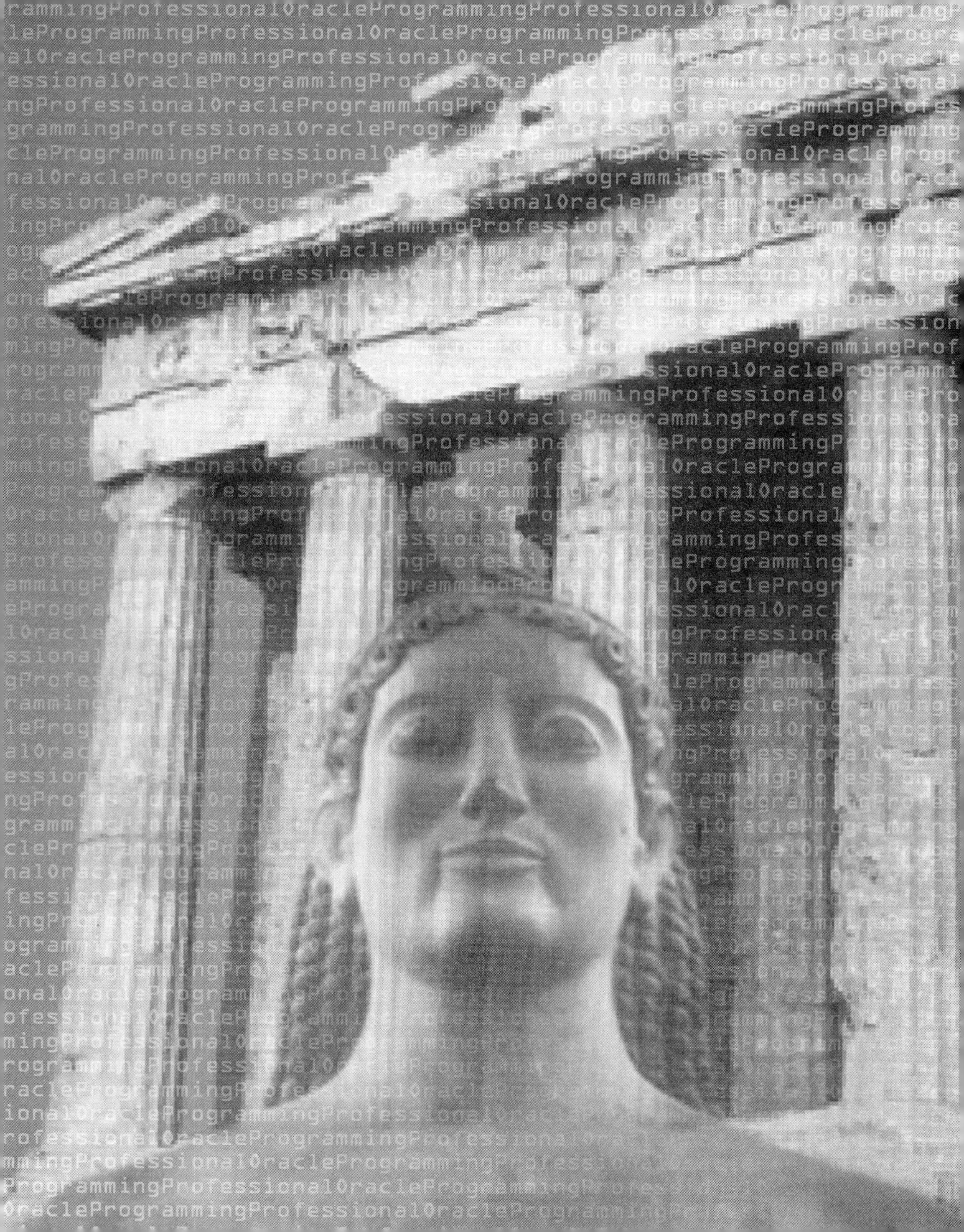

9

Data Loading

In this chapter, we will discuss data loading – in other words, how to get data *into* an Oracle database. The main focus of the chapter will be the SQL*LOADER tool (or SQLLDR, pronounced 'sequel loader'), as it is still the predominant method for loading data. However, we will look at a few other options along the way and will also briefly explore how to get data *out* of the database.

SQLLDR has been around for as long as I can remember, with various minor enhancements over time, but is still the subject of some confusion. My remit in this chapter is not to be comprehensive, but rather to tackle the issues that I see people encounter every day when using this tool. The chapter has a 'question and answer' format. I will present a frequently encountered requirement or issue, and explore possible solutions. In the process we'll cover many of the practicalities of using the SQLLDR tool and of data loading in general:

- ❑ Loading delimited and fixed format data.

- ❑ Loading dates.

- ❑ Loading data using sequences, in which we take a look at the addition of the CASE statement in SQL, added in Oracle 8.1.6.

- ❑ How to do an **upsert** (update if data exists, insert otherwise).

- ❑ Loading data with embedded newlines, where we rely on the use of some new features and options, such as the FIX, VAR, and STR attributes, added in Oracle 8.1.6.

- ❑ Loading LOBs using the new data types, BLOB and CLOB, introduced in Oracle8.0, which support a much deeper functionality than the legacy LONG and LONG RAW types.

We will *not* cover the direct path loader mode in any detail and nor will we cover topics such as using SQLLDR for data warehousing, parallel loads, and so on. These topics could fill an entire book by themselves.

An Introduction to SQL*LOADER

SQL*LOADER (SQLLDR) is Oracle's high speed, bulk data loader. It is an extremely useful tool, used to get data into an Oracle database from a variety of flat file formats. SQLLDR can be used to load enormous amounts of data in an amazingly short period of time. It has two modes of operation:

❏ **Conventional path** – SQLLDR will employ SQL inserts on our behalf to load data.

❏ **Direct path** – Does not use SQL. Formats database blocks directly.

The direct path load allows you to read data from a flat file, and write it directly to formatted database blocks, bypassing the entire SQL engine (and rollback and redo at the same time). When used in parallel, direct path load is the fastest way from no data to a fully loaded database, and can't be beaten.

We will not cover every single aspect of SQLLDR. For all of the details, the *Oracle Server Utilities Guide* dedicates six chapters to SQLLDR. The fact that it is six chapters is notable, since every other utility gets one chapter or less. For complete syntax and all of the options, I will point you to this reference guide – this chapter is intended to answer the 'How do I?' questions that a reference guide does not address.

It should be noted that the **OCI** (**O**racle **C**all **I**nterface for C) allows you to write your own direct path loader using C, with Oracle8.1.6 release 1 and onwards as well. This is useful when the operation you want to perform is not feasible in SQLLDR, or when seamless integration with your application is desired. SQLLDR is a command line tool – a separate program. It is not an API or anything that can be 'called from PL/SQL', for example.

If you execute SQLLDR from the command line with no inputs, it gives you the following help:

```
$ sqlldr

SQLLDR: Release 8.1.6.1.0 - Production on Sun Sep 17 12:02:59 2000
(c) Copyright 1999 Oracle Corporation.  All rights reserved.

Usage: SQLLOAD keyword=value [,keyword=value,...]

Valid Keywords:

    userid -- ORACLE username/password
   control -- Control file name
       log -- Log file name
       bad -- Bad file name
      data -- Data file name
   discard -- Discard file name
discardmax -- Number of discards to allow      (Default all)
      skip -- Number of logical records to skip (Default 0)
      load -- Number of logical records to load (Default all)
    errors -- Number of errors to allow         (Default 50)
      rows -- Number of rows in conventional path bind array or between
              direct path data saves
                 (Default: Conventional path 64, Direct path all)
  bindsize -- Size of conventional path bind array in bytes  (Default 65536)
    silent -- Suppress messages during run (header, feedback, errors,
              discards, partitions)
```

```
      direct -- use direct path                    (Default FALSE)
     parfile -- parameter file: name of file that contains parameter
                specifications
    parallel -- do parallel load                   (Default FALSE)
        file -- File to allocate extents from
skip_unusable_indexes -- disallow/allow unusable indexes or index partitions
                (Default FALSE)
skip_index_maintenance -- do not maintain indexes, mark affected indexes as
                unusable   (Default FALSE)
commit_discontinued -- commit loaded rows when load is discontinued
                (Default FALSE)
     readsize -- Size of Read buffer               (Default 1048576)
```

We will quickly go over the meaning of these parameters in the following table:

Parameter	Meaning
BAD	The name of a file that will contain rejected records at the end of the load. If you do not specify a name for this, the BAD file will be named after the CONTROL file (see later in the chapter for more details on control files), we use to load with. For example, if you use a CONTROL file named foo.ctl, the BAD file will default to foo.bad, which SQLLDR will write to (or overwrite if it already exists).
BINDSIZE	The size in bytes of the buffer used by SQLLDR to insert data in the conventional path loader. It is not used in a direct path load. It is used to size the array with which SQLLDR will insert data.
CONTROL	The name of a CONTROL file, which describes to SQLLDR how the input data is formatted, and how to load it into a table. You need a CONTROL file for every SQLLDR execution.
DATA	The name of the input file from which to read the data.
DIRECT	Valid values are True and False, with the default being False. By default, SQLLDR will use the conventional path load method.
DISCARD	The name of a file to write records that are not to be loaded. SQLLDR can be used to filter input records, allowing you to specify that only records meeting a specified criteria are loaded.
DISCARDMAX	Specifies the maximum number of discarded records permitted in a load. If you exceed this value, the load will terminate. By default, all records may be discarded without terminating a load.

Table continued on following page

Parameter	Meaning
ERRORS	The maximum number of errors encountered by SQLLDR that are permitted before the load terminates. These errors can be caused by many things, such as conversion errors (by trying to load ABC into a number field for example), duplicate records in a unique index, and so on. By default, 50 errors are permitted, and then the load will terminate. In order to allow all valid records to be loaded in that particular session (with the rejected records going to the BAD file), specify a large number such as 999999999.
FILE	When using the direct path load option in parallel, you may use this to tell SQLLDR exactly which database data file to load into. You would use this to reduce contention for the database data files during a parallel load, to ensure each loader session is writing to a separate device.
LOAD	The maximum number of records to load. Typically used to load a sample of a large data file, or used in conjunction with SKIP to load a specific range of records from an input file.
LOG	Used to name the LOG file. By default, SQLLDR will create a LOG file named after the CONTROL file in the same fashion as the BAD file.
PARALLEL	Will be TRUE or FALSE. When TRUE, it signifies you are doing a parallel direct path load. This is not necessary when using a conventional path load – they may be done in parallel without setting this parameter.
PARFILE	Can be used to specify the name of a file that contains all of these KEYWORD=VALUE pairs. This is used instead of specifying them all on the command line.
READSIZE	Specifies the size of the buffer used to read input data.
ROWS	The number of rows SQLLDR should insert between commits in a conventional path load. In a direct path load, this is the number of rows to be loaded before performing a data save (similar to a commit). In a conventional path load, the default is 64 rows. In a direct path load, the default is to not perform a data save until the load is complete.
SILENT	Suppresses various informational messages at run-time.
SKIP	Used to tell SQLLDR to skip x number of records in the input file. Most commonly used to resume an aborted load (skipping the records that have been already loaded), or to only load one part of an input file.

Parameter	Meaning
USERID	The USERNAME/PASSWORD@DATABASE connect string. Used to authenticate to the database.
SKIP_INDEX_MAINTENANCE	Does not apply to conventional path loads – all indexes are always maintained in this mode. In a direct path load, this tells Oracle not to maintain indexes by marking them as unusable. These indexes must be rebuilt after the load.
SKIP_UNUSABLE_INDEXES	Tells SQLLDR to allow rows to be loaded into a table that has unusable indexes, as long as the indexes are not unique indexes.

In order to use SQLLDR, you will need a **control file**. A control file simply contains information describing the input data – its layout, datatypes, and so on, as well as information about what table(s) it should be loaded into. The control file can even contain the data to load. In the following example, we build up a simple control file in a step-by-step fashion, with an explanation of the commands at each stage:

```
LOAD DATA
```

LOAD DATA – This tells SQLLDR what to do, in this case load data. The other thing SQLLDR can do is CONTINUE_LOAD, to resume a load. We would use this option only when continuing a multi-table direct path load.

```
INFILE *
```

INFILE * – This tells SQLLDR the data to be loaded is actually contained within the control file itself (see below). Alternatively you could specify the name of another file that contains the data. We can override this INFILE statement using a command line parameter if we wish. Be aware that *command line options override control file settings*, as we shall see in the *Caveats* section.

```
INTO TABLE DEPT
```

INTO TABLE DEPT – This tells SQLLDR to which table we are loading data, in this case the DEPT table.

```
FIELDS TERMINATED BY ','
```

FIELDS TERMINATED BY ',' – This tells SQLLDR that the data will be in the form of comma-separated values. There are dozens of ways to describe the input data to SQLLDR, this is just one of the more common methods.

```
(DEPTNO,
  DNAME,
  LOC
)
```

(DEPTNO, DNAME, LOC) – This tells SQLLDR what columns we are loading, their order in the input data, and their data types. The data types are of the data in the *input* stream, not the data types in the database. In this case, they are defaulting to CHAR(255), which is sufficient.

```
BEGINDATA
```

BEGINDATA – This tells SQLLDR we have finished describing the input data, and that the very next line will be the actual data to be loaded into the DEPT table:

```
10,Sales,Virginia
20,Accounting,Virginia
30,Consulting,Virginia
40,Finance,Virginia
```

So, this is a control file in one of its most simple and common formats – to load delimited data into a table. We will take a look at some much complex examples in this chapter, but this a good one to get our feet wet with. To use this control file, all we need to do is create an empty DEPT table:

```
tkyte@TKYTE816> create table dept
  2  ( deptno  number(2) constraint emp_pk primary key,
  3    dname   varchar2(14),
  4    loc         varchar2(13)
  5  )
  6  /

Table created.
```

and run the following command:

```
C:\sqlldr>sqlldr userid=tkyte/tkyte control=demo1.ctl

SQLLDR: Release 8.1.6.0.0 - Production on Sat Apr 14 10:54:56 2001
(c) Copyright 1999 Oracle Corporation.  All rights reserved.
Commit point reached - logical record count 4
```

If the table is not empty, you will receive an error message to the following effect:

```
SQLLDR-601: For INSERT option, table must be empty.  Error on table DEPT
```

This is because we allowed almost everything in the control file to default, and the default load option is INSERT (as opposed to APPEND, TRUNCATE, or REPLACE). In order to INSERT, SQLLDR assumes the table is empty. If we wanted to **add** records to the DEPT table, we could have specified APPEND, or to replace the data in the DEPT table, we could have used REPLACE or TRUNCATE.

Every load will generate a log file. The log file from our simple load looks like this:

```
SQLLDR: Release 8.1.6.0.0 - Production on Sat Apr 14 10:58:02 2001

(c) Copyright 1999 Oracle Corporation.  All rights reserved.

Control File:   demo1.ctl
```

```
    Data File:       demo1.ctl
     Bad File:       demo1.bad
     Discard File: none specified

    (Allow all discards)

    Number to load: ALL
    Number to skip: 0
    Errors allowed: 50
    Bind array:      64 rows, maximum of 65536 bytes
    Continuation:    none specified
    Path used:       Conventional

    Table DEPT, loaded from every logical record.
    Insert option in effect for this table: INSERT

       Column Name                   Position   Len  Term Encl Datatype
    -------------------------------- ---------- ----- ---- ---- --------------------
    DEPTNO                           FIRST       *    ,         CHARACTER
    DNAME                            NEXT        *    ,         CHARACTER
    LOC                              NEXT        *    ,         CHARACTER

    Table DEPT:
       4 Rows successfully loaded.
       0 Rows not loaded due to data errors.
       0 Rows not loaded because all WHEN clauses were failed.
       0 Rows not loaded because all fields were null.


    Space allocated for bind array:                  49536 bytes(64 rows)
    Space allocated for memory besides bind array:       0 bytes

    Total logical records skipped:          0
    Total logical records read:             4
    Total logical records rejected:         0
    Total logical records discarded:        0

    Run began on Sat Apr 14 10:58:02 2001
    Run ended on Sat Apr 14 10:58:02 2001

    Elapsed time was:      00:00:00.11
    CPU time was:          00:00:00.04
```

These log files tell us about many of the aspects of our load. We can see the options we used (defaulted or otherwise). We can see how many records were read, how many loaded, and so on. It specifies the locations of all BAD and DISCARD files. It even tells us how long it took. These log files are crucial for verifying that the load was successful, as well as for diagnosing errors. If the loaded data resulted in SQL errors (the input data was 'bad', and created records in the BAD file), these errors would be recorded here. The information in the log file is largely self-explanatory, so we will not spend any more time on it.

How to ...

We will now cover what I have found to be the most frequently asked questions with regards to loading and unloading data in an Oracle database, using SQLLDR.

Load Delimited Data

Delimited data, data that is separated by some special character, and perhaps enclosed in quotes, is the most popular data format for flat files today. On a mainframe, a fixed length, fixed format file would probably be the most recognized file format, but on UNIX and NT, delimited files are the norm. In this section, we will investigate the popular options used to load delimited data.

The most popular format for delimited data is the **CSV** format where CSV stands for **c**omma-**s**eparated **v**alues. In this file format, where each field of data is separated from the next by a comma, text strings can be enclosed within quotes, thus allowing for the string itself to contain a comma. If the string must contain a quotation mark as well, the convention is to double up the quotation mark (in the following code we use "" in place of just a ").

A typical control file to load delimited data will look much like this:

```
LOAD DATA
INFILE *
INTO TABLE DEPT
REPLACE
FIELDS TERMINATED BY ',' OPTIONALLY ENCLOSED BY '"'
(DEPTNO,
DNAME,
LOC
)
BEGINDATA
10,Sales,"""USA"""
20,Accounting,"Virginia,USA"
30,Consulting,Virginia
40,Finance,Virginia
50,"Finance","",Virginia
60,"Finance",,Virginia
```

The following line performs the bulk of the work:

```
FIELDS TERMINATED BY ',' OPTIONALLY ENCLOSED BY '"'
```

It specifies that a comma separates the data fields, and that each field *might* be enclosed in double quotes. When we run SQLLDR using this control file, the results will be:

```
tkyte@TKYTE816> select * from dept;

    DEPTNO DNAME          LOC
---------- -------------- -------------
        10 Sales          "USA"
        20 Accounting     Virginia,USA
        30 Consulting     Virginia
        40 Finance        Virginia
```

```
            50 Finance
            60 Finance

    6 rows selected.
```

Notice the following in particular:

- ❏ "USA" – This resulted from input data that was """USA""". SQLLDR counted the double occurrence of " as a single occurrence within the enclosed string. In order to load a string that contains the optional enclosure character, you must ensure they are doubled up.

- ❏ Virginia,USA in department 20 – This results from input data that was "Virginia,USA". This input data field had to be enclosed in quotes to retain the comma as part of the data. Otherwise, the comma would have been treated as the end of field marker, and Virginia would have been loaded without the USA text.

- ❏ Departments 50 and 60 were loaded with Null location fields. When data is missing, you can choose to enclose it or not, the effect is the same.

Another popular format is **tab-delimited data**: data that is separated by tabs rather than commas. There are two ways to load this data using the TERMINATED BY clause:

- ❏ TERMINATED BY X'09', which is the tab character using hexadecimal format (ASCII 9 is a tab character), or you might use

- ❏ TERMINATED BY WHITESPACE

The two are very different in implementation however, as the following shows. Using the DEPT table from above we'll load using this control file:

```
LOAD DATA
INFILE *
INTO TABLE DEPT
REPLACE
FIELDS TERMINATED BY WHITESPACE
(DEPTNO,
DNAME,
LOC)
BEGINDATA
10          Sales       Virginia
```

It is not readily visible on the page, but there are *two* tabs between each piece of data in the above. The data line is really:

```
10\t\tSales\t\tVirginia
```

Where the \t is the universally recognized tab escape sequence. When you use this control file with the TERMINATED BY WHITESPACE clause as above, the resulting data in the table DEPT is:

```
tkyte@TKYTE816> select * from dept;

    DEPTNO DNAME          LOC
---------- -------------- -------------
        10 Sales          Virginia
```

TERMINATED BY WHITESPACE parses the string by looking for the first occurrence of whitespace (tab, blank or newline) and then continues until it finds the next *non*-whitespace character. Hence, when it parsed the data, DEPTNO had 10 assigned to it, the two subsequent tabs were considered as whitespace, and then Sales was assigned to DNAME, and so on.

On the other hand, if you were to use FIELDS TERMINATED BY X'09', as the following control file does:

```
LOAD DATA
INFILE *
INTO TABLE DEPT
REPLACE
FIELDS TERMINATED BY X'09'
(DEPTNO,
DNAME,
LOC
)
BEGINDATA
10		Sales		Virginia
```

You would find DEPT loaded with the following data:

```
tkyte@TKYTE816> select * from dept;

    DEPTNO DNAME          LOC
---------- -------------- -------------
        10                Sales
```

Here, once SQLLDR encountered a tab, it output a value. Hence, 10 is assigned to DEPTNO, and DNAME gets Null since there is no data between the first tab, and the next occurrence of a tab. Sales gets assigned to LOC.

This is the intended behavior of TERMINATED BY WHITESPACE, and TERMINATED BY <character>. Which is more appropriate to use will be dictated by the input data, and how you need it to be interpreted.

Lastly, when loading delimited data such as this, it is very common to want to skip over various columns in the input record. For example, you might want to load columns 1, 3, and 5, skipping columns 2 and 4. In order to do this, SQLLDR provides the FILLER keyword. This allows us to map a column in an input record, but not put it into the database. For example, given the DEPT table from above, the following control file contains 4 delimited fields but will not load the second field into the database:

```
LOAD DATA
INFILE *
INTO TABLE DEPT
REPLACE
FIELDS TERMINATED BY ',' OPTIONALLY ENCLOSED BY '"'
( DEPTNO,
  FILLER_1 FILLER,
  DNAME,
  LOC
)
BEGINDATA
20,Something Not To Be Loaded,Accounting,"Virginia,USA"
```

The resulting DEPT table is:

```
tkyte@TKYTE816> select * from dept;

    DEPTNO DNAME          LOC
---------- -------------- -------------
        20 Accounting     Virginia,USA
```

Load Fixed Format Data

Often, you have a flat file generated from some external system, and this file is a fixed length file with positional data. For example, the NAME field is in bytes 1 to 10, the ADDRESS field is in bytes 11 to 35, and so on. We will look at how SQLLDR can import this kind of data for us.

This fixed width, positional data is the optimal data for SQLLDR to load. It will be the fastest for it to process as the input data stream is somewhat trivial to parse. SQLLDR will have stored fixed byte offsets and lengths into data records, and extracting a given field is very simple. If you have an extremely large volume of data to load, converting it to a fixed position format is generally the best approach. The downside to a fixed width file is, of course, that it can be much larger than a simple, delimited file format.

To load fixed position data, you will use the POSITION keyword in the control file. For example:

```
LOAD DATA
INFILE *
INTO TABLE DEPT
REPLACE
( DEPTNO position(1:2),
  DNAME   position(3:16),
  LOC     position(17:29)
)
BEGINDATA
10Accounting     Virginia,USA
```

This control file does not employ the FIELDS TERMINATED BY clause, rather it uses POSITION to tell SQLLDR where fields begin and end. Of interest to note with the POSITION clause is that we could use overlapping positions, and go back and forth in the record. For example if we were to alter the DEPT table as follows:

```
tkyte@TKYTE816> alter table dept add entire_line varchar(29);

Table altered.
```

And then use the following control file:

```
LOAD DATA
INFILE *
INTO TABLE DEPT
REPLACE
( DEPTNO          position(1:2),
  DNAME           position(3:16),
```

```
   LOC            position(17:29),
   ENTIRE_LINE position(1:29)
)
BEGINDATA
10Accounting      Virginia,USA
```

The field `ENTIRE_LINE` is defined as `position(1:29)` – it extracts its data from all 29 bytes of input data, whereas the other fields are substrings of the input data. The outcome of the above control file will be:

```
tkyte@TKYTE816> select * from dept;

    DEPTNO DNAME          LOC           ENTIRE_LINE
---------- -------------- ------------- ----------------------------
        10 Accounting     Virginia,USA  10Accounting     Virginia,USA
```

When using `POSITION`, we can use relative or absolute offsets. In the above, I used absolute offsets. I specifically denoted where fields begin, and where they end. I could have written the above control file as:

```
LOAD DATA
INFILE *
INTO TABLE DEPT
REPLACE
( DEPTNO        position(1:2),
  DNAME         position(*:16),
  LOC           position(*:29),
  ENTIRE_LINE position(1:29)
)
BEGINDATA
10Accounting      Virginia,USA
```

The * instructs the control file to pick up where the last field left off. Therefore `(*:16)` is just the same as `(3:16)` in this case. Notice that you can mix relative, and absolute positions in the control file. Additionally, when using the * notation, you can add to the offset. For example, if `DNAME` started 2 bytes *after* the end of `DEPTNO`, I could have used `(*+2:16)`. In this example the effect would be identical to using `(5:16)`.

The ending position in the `POSITION` clause must be the absolute column position where the data ends. At times, it can be easier to specify just the length of each field, especially if they are contiguous, as in the above example. In this fashion we would just have to tell SQLLDR the record starts at byte 1, and then specify the length of each field. This will save us from having to compute start and stop byte offsets into the record, which can be hard at times. In order to do this, we'll leave off the ending position, and instead, specify the *length* of each field in the fixed length record as follows:

```
LOAD DATA
INFILE *
INTO TABLE DEPT
REPLACE
( DEPTNO        position(1) char(2),
  DNAME         position(*) char(14),
  LOC           position(*) char(13),
```

```
    ENTIRE_LINE position(1) char(29)
)
BEGINDATA
10Accounting    Virginia,USA
```

Here we only had to tell SQLLDR where the first field begins, and its length. Each subsequent field starts where the last one left off, and continues for a specified length. It is not until the last field that we have to specify a position again, since this field goes back to the beginning of the record.

Load Dates

Loading dates using SQLLDR is fairly straightforward, but seems to be a common point of confusion. You simply need to use the DATE data type in the control file, and specify the date mask to be used. This date mask is the same mask you use with TO_CHAR and TO_DATE in the database. SQLLDR will apply this date mask to your data and load it for you.

For example, if we alter our DEPT table again:

```
tkyte@TKYTE816> alter table dept add last_updated date;

Table altered.
```

We can load it with the following control file:

```
LOAD DATA
INFILE *
INTO TABLE DEPT
REPLACE
FIELDS TERMINATED BY ','
(DEPTNO,
 DNAME,
 LOC,
 LAST_UPDATED date 'dd/mm/yyyy'
)
BEGINDATA
10,Sales,Virginia,1/5/2000
20,Accounting,Virginia,21/6/1999
30,Consulting,Virginia,5/1/2000
40,Finance,Virginia,15/3/2001
```

The resulting DEPT table will look like this:

```
tkyte@TKYTE816> select * from dept;

    DEPTNO DNAME          LOC           LAST_UPDA
---------- -------------- ------------- ---------
        10 Sales          Virginia      01-MAY-00
        20 Accounting     Virginia      21-JUN-99
        30 Consulting     Virginia      05-JAN-00
        40 Finance        Virginia      15-MAR-01
```

It is that easy. Just supply the format in the control file and SQLLDR will convert the date for us. In some cases, it might be appropriate to us a more powerful SQL function. For example, if your input file contains dates in many different formats: sometimes with the time component, sometimes without, sometimes in DD-MON-YYYY format, sometime in DD/MM/YYYY format, and so on. We'll see in the next section how we can use functions in SQLLDR to overcome these challenges.

Load Data Using Sequences and Other Functions

In this section we will see how to refer to sequences and other functions whilst loading data. Bear in mind however, that the use of database sequences and other functions require the SQL engine, and hence will not work in a direct path load.

Using functions in SQLLDR is very easy once you understand how SQLLDR builds its INSERT statement. To have a function applied to a field in a SQLLDR script, we simply add it to the control file in double quotes. For example, say you have the DEPT table from above, and would like to make sure the data being loaded is in uppercase. You could use the following control file to load it:

```
LOAD DATA
INFILE *
INTO TABLE DEPT
REPLACE
FIELDS TERMINATED BY ','
(DEPTNO,
  DNAME         "upper(:dname)",
  LOC           "upper(:loc)",
  LAST_UPDATED  date 'dd/mm/yyyy'
)
BEGINDATA
10,Sales,Virginia,1/5/2000
20,Accounting,Virginia,21/6/1999
30,Consulting,Virginia,5/1/2000
40,Finance,Virginia,15/3/2001
```

The resulting data in the database will be:

```
tkyte@TKYTE816> select * from dept;

DEPTNO DNAME           LOC            ENTIRE_LINE                    LAST_UPDA
------ --------------- -------------- ------------------------------ ---------
    10 SALES           VIRGINIA                                      01-MAY-00
    20 ACCOUNTING      VIRGINIA                                      21-JUN-99
    30 CONSULTING      VIRGINIA                                      05-JAN-00
    40 FINANCE         VIRGINIA                                      15-MAR-01
```

Notice how we are able to easily uppercase the data just by applying the UPPER function to a bind variable. It should be noted that the SQL functions could refer to any of the columns, regardless of the column the function is actually applied to. This means that a column can be the result of a function on two or more of the other columns. For example, if we wanted to load the column ENTIRE_LINE, we could use the SQL concatenation operator. It is a little more involved than that though in this case. Right now, the input data set has four data elements in it. If we were to simply add ENTIRE_LINE to the control file like this:

```
LOAD DATA
INFILE *
INTO TABLE DEPT
REPLACE
FIELDS TERMINATED BY ','
(DEPTNO,
  DNAME         "upper(:dname)",
  LOC           "upper(:loc)",
  LAST_UPDATED  date 'dd/mm/yyyy',
  ENTIRE_LINE   ":deptno||:dname||:loc||:last_updated"
)
BEGINDATA
10,Sales,Virginia,1/5/2000
20,Accounting,Virginia,21/6/1999
30,Consulting,Virginia,5/1/2000
40,Finance,Virginia,15/3/2001
```

We would find this error in our LOG file, for each input record:

```
Record 1: Rejected - Error on table DEPT, column ENTIRE_LINE.
Column not found before end of logical record (use TRAILING NULLCOLS)
```

Here, SQLLDR is telling us that it ran out of data in the record before it ran out of columns. The solution is easy in this case, and in fact SQLLDR even tells us what to do – USE TRAILING NULLCOLS. This will have SQLLDR bind a Null value in for that column if no data exists in the input record. In this case, adding TRAILING NULLCOLS will cause the bind variable :ENTIRE_LINE to be Null. So, we retry with this control file:

```
LOAD DATA
INFILE *
INTO TABLE DEPT
REPLACE
FIELDS TERMINATED BY ','
TRAILING NULLCOLS
(DEPTNO,
  DNAME         "upper(:dname)",
  LOC           "upper(:loc)",
  LAST_UPDATED  date 'dd/mm/yyyy',
  ENTIRE_LINE   ":deptno||:dname||:loc||:last_updated"
)
BEGINDATA
10,Sales,Virginia,1/5/2000
20,Accounting,Virginia,21/6/1999
30,Consulting,Virginia,5/1/2000
40,Finance,Virginia,15/3/2001
```

Now the data in the table is as follows:

```
tkyte@TKYTE816> select * from dept;

DEPTNO DNAME          LOC           ENTIRE_LINE                      LAST_UPDA
------ -------------- ------------- -------------------------------- ---------
    10 SALES          VIRGINIA      10SalesVirginia1/5/2000          01-MAY-00
    20 ACCOUNTING     VIRGINIA      20AccountingVirginia21/6/1999    21-JUN-99
```

```
    30 CONSULTING      VIRGINIA      30ConsultingVirginia5/1/2000   05-JAN-00
    40 FINANCE         VIRGINIA      40FinanceVirginia15/3/2001     15-MAR-01
```

What makes this feat possible is the way SQLLDR builds its INSERT statement. SQLLDR will look at the above, and see the DEPTNO, DNAME, LOC, LAST_UPDATED, and ENTIRE_LINE columns in the control file. It will set up five bind variables named after these columns. Normally, in the absence of any functions, the INSERT statement it builds is simply:

```
INSERT INTO DEPT ( DEPTNO, DNAME, LOC, LAST_UPDATED, ENTIRE_LINE )
VALUES ( :DEPTNO, :DNAME, :LOC, :LAST_UPDATED, :ENTIRE_LINE );
```

It would then parse the input stream, assigning the values to its bind variables, and then execute the statement. When we begin to use functions, SQLLDR incorporates them into its INSERT statement. In our example above, the INSERT statement SQLLDR builds will look like this:

```
INSERT INTO T (DEPTNO, DNAME, LOC, LAST_UPDATED, ENTIRE_LINE)
VALUES ( :DEPTNO, upper(:dname), upper(:loc), :last_updated,
         :deptno||:dname||:loc||:last_updated );
```

It then prepares, and binds, the inputs to this statement, and executes it. So, pretty much anything you can think of doing in SQL, you can incorporate into you SQLLDR scripts. With the addition of the CASE statement in SQL (added in Oracle), this can be extremely powerful and easy. For example, let's say sometimes our dates contained time components, and sometimes they did not. We could use a control file like this:

```
LOAD DATA
INFILE *
INTO TABLE DEPT
REPLACE
FIELDS TERMINATED BY ','
TRAILING NULLCOLS
(DEPTNO,
  DNAME         "upper(:dname)",
  LOC           "upper(:loc)",
  LAST_UPDATED "case when length(:last_updated) <= 10
                   then to_date(:last_updated,'dd/mm/yyyy')
                   else to_date(:last_updated,'dd/mm/yyyy hh24:mi:ss')
               end"
)
BEGINDATA
10,Sales,Virginia,1/5/2000 12:03:03
20,Accounting,Virginia,21/6/1999
30,Consulting,Virginia,5/1/2000 01:23:00
40,Finance,Virginia,15/3/2001
```

which results in:

```
tkyte@TKYTE816> alter session
  2              set nls_date_format = 'dd-mon-yyyy hh24:mi:ss';

Session altered.
```

```
tkyte@TKYTE816> select * from dept;

DEPTNO DNAME         LOC            ENTIRE_LINE        LAST_UPDATED
------ ------------- -------------- ------------------ --------------------
    10 SALES         VIRGINIA                          01-may-2000 12:03:03
    20 ACCOUNTING    VIRGINIA                          21-jun-1999 00:00:00
    30 CONSULTING    VIRGINIA                          05-jan-2000 01:23:00
    40 FINANCE       VIRGINIA                          15-mar-2001 00:00:00
```

Now, one of two date formats will be applied to the input character string (notice that we are *not* loading a DATE anymore, we are just loading a string). The CASE function will look at the length of the string to determine which of the two masks it should use.

It is interesting to note that we can write our *own* functions to be called from SQLLDR. This is a straightforward application of the fact that PL/SQL can be called from SQL. For example, suppose your dates are supplied in the input file in one of the following formats (I am surprised how frequently this comes up, apparently it is common to mix and match your date formats in input files for some reason):

```
dd-mon-yyyy
dd-month-yyyy
dd/mm/yyyy
dd/mm/yyyy hh24:mi:ss
number of seconds since January 1st 1970 GMT (aka "UNIX time")
```

Now, using the CASE statement would be very hard, since the length of the string does not imply the format to use. What we can do instead, is to create a function that tries date formats until it finds the one that works. The following routine loops over an array of formats trying them one by one until one of them succeeds. If, after looping, we still haven't converted the date, we assume it is a UNIX date, and perform the appropriate conversion. If this fails, the failure is simply allowed to propagate back to SQLLDR, which will place the record in the BAD file. The routine looks like this:

```
tkyte@TKYTE816> create or replace
  2  function my_to_date( p_string in varchar2 ) return date
  3  as
  4      type fmtArray is table of varchar2(25);
  5
  6      l_fmts  fmtArray := fmtArray( 'dd-mon-yyyy', 'dd-month-yyyy',
  7                                    'dd/mm/yyyy',
  8                                    'dd/mm/yyyy hh24:mi:ss' );
  9      l_return date;
 10  begin
 11      for i in 1 .. l_fmts.count
 12      loop
 13          begin
 14              l_return := to_date( p_string, l_fmts(i) );
 15          exception
 16              when others then null;
 17          end;
 18          EXIT when l_return is not null;
 19      end loop;
 20
 21      if ( l_return is null )
 22      then
```

```
23              l_return :=
24                new_time( to_date('01011970','ddmmyyyy') + 1/24/60/60 *
25                          p_string, 'GMT', 'EST' );
26      end if;
27
28      return l_return;
29  end;
30  /

Function created.
```

Then, we could use a control file such as:

```
LOAD DATA
INFILE *
INTO TABLE DEPT
REPLACE
FIELDS TERMINATED BY ','
(DEPTNO,
  DNAME            "upper(:dname)",
  LOC              "upper(:loc)",
  LAST_UPDATED "my_to_date( :last_updated )"
)
BEGINDATA
10,Sales,Virginia,01-april-2001
20,Accounting,Virginia,13/04/2001
30,Consulting,Virginia,14/04/2001 12:02:02
40,Finance,Virginia,987268297
50,Finance,Virginia,02-apr-2001
60,Finance,Virginia,Not a date
```

After loading, we would find the error message:

```
Record 6: Rejected - Error on table DEPT, column LAST_UPDATED.
ORA-06502: PL/SQL: numeric or value error: character to number conversion error
ORA-06512: at "TKYTE.MY_TO_DATE", line 30
ORA-06512: at line 1
```

indicating that the last record failed, but all the others were in fact loaded. This failed record will be in our BAD file. We can fix it and reload it later. Inspecting the data that did get loaded we see:

```
tkyte@TKYTE816> alter session
  2               set nls_date_format = 'dd-mon-yyyy hh24:mi:ss';

Session altered.

tkyte@TKYTE816> select deptno, dname, loc, last_updated from dept;

DEPTNO DNAME          LOC           LAST_UPDATED
------ -------------- ------------- --------------------
    10 SALES          VIRGINIA      01-apr-2001 00:00:00
    20 ACCOUNTING     VIRGINIA      13-apr-2001 00:00:00
    30 CONSULTING     VIRGINIA      14-apr-2001 12:02:02
    40 FINANCE        VIRGINIA      14-apr-2001 12:11:37
    50 FINANCE        VIRGINIA      02-apr-2001 00:00:00
```

Update Existing Rows and Insert New Rows

Frequently, you will receive a file of records for an existing table. You would like to use this data to update rows that already exist, by some primary key, or insert rows that do not yet exist. This is not really possible in one step, but can be accomplished in three easy steps. I'll first outline what we need to do, and then show you step-by-step what the code might look like. You would:

1. Load all of the data with the APPEND option and specifying ERRORS=99999999. Using a large number for errors lets all of the 'good' records get loaded. The records that would be used for UPDATES will get rejected based on a primary key or unique constraint violation. They will be written to a BAD file. We will get all of the new records loaded this way.

2. Load the BAD file into a working table with the TRUNCATE option. This table is structurally the same as the 'real' table – it should have the same set of constraints and such. This will make it so that only the duplicate records are loaded. Records that were rejected for other data validation reasons will be rejected again from this table.

3. Update the join of the real table and the working table.

Using the DEPT table from earlier, with the last set of data (departments 10, 20, 30, 40 and 50), we'll load the following data:

```
10, Sales,New York,14-april-2001
60,Finance,Virginia,14-april-2001
```

This should UPDATE one record and INSERT one record. Assume this data is in the file new.dat and you have the control file load.ctl as follows:

```
LOAD DATA
INTO TABLE DEPT
APPEND
FIELDS TERMINATED BY ','
(DEPTNO,
  DNAME        "upper(:dname)",
  LOC          "upper(:loc)",
  LAST_UPDATED "my_to_date( :last_updated )"
)
```

This is very similar to our last control file, with the exception that the INFILE * and BEGINDATA statements have been removed, and REPLACE was changed to APPEND. We will specify the data file to load on the command line, hence the INFILE is not needed and since the data is in an external file, the BEGINDATA is no longer needed. Since we want to INSERT new records and UPDATE existing ones, we will use the APPEND mode, not REPLACE as before. So, now we can load our data using:

```
C:\>sqlldr userid=tkyte/tkyte control=load.ctl data=new.dat errors=9999999
```

When we execute this, a BAD file will be generated with one record in it. The record for department 10 will be found in the new.bad file since it violated the primary key. We can verify that by reviewing the log file load.log:

```
Record 1: Rejected - Error on table DEPT.
ORA-00001: unique constraint (TKYTE.EMP_PK) violated
```

We will now take that BAD file and using virtually the same control file, load it. The only changes we'll make to the control file will be the name of the table being loaded into, DEPT_WORKING instead of DEPT, and to use the REPLACE option for the working table instead of APPEND. The table we load into is created like this:

```
tkyte@TKYTE816> create table dept_working
  2  as
  3  select * from dept
  4   where 1=0
  5  /

Table created.

tkyte@TKYTE816> alter table dept_working
  2   add constraint dept_working_pk
  3   primary key(deptno)
  4  /

Table altered.
```

When you load the data, make sure to use the BAD=<SOME FILENAME> option on the command line to avoid reading and writing the same file in during the load!

```
C:\sqlldr>sqlldr userid=tkyte/tkyte control=load_working.ctl bad=working.bad
data=new.bad
```

After we load this, we would find the one row loaded into the DEPT_WORKING table. If there are any records in WORKING.BAD, they would be *really* bad records, records that violated some other constraint, and must be reviewed. Now, once this is loaded, we can update the existing rows in DEPT via this single update statement:

```
tkyte@TKYTE816> set autotrace on explain
tkyte@TKYTE816> update ( select /*+ ORDERED USE_NL(dept) */
  2              dept.dname          dept_dname,
  3              dept.loc            dept_loc,
  4              dept.last_updated dept_last_updated,
  5              w.dname             w_dname,
  6              w.loc               w_loc,
  7              w.last_updated      w_last_updated
  8            from dept_working W, dept
  9           where dept.deptno = w.deptno )
 10     set dept_dname = w_dname,
 11         dept_loc   = w_loc,
 12         dept_last_updated = w_last_updated
 13  /

1 row updated.

Execution Plan
----------------------------------------------------------
```

```
  0        UPDATE STATEMENT Optimizer=CHOOSE (Cost=83 Card=67 Bytes=5226)
     1    0    UPDATE OF 'DEPT'
     2    1      NESTED LOOPS (Cost=83 Card=67 Bytes=5226)
     3    2        TABLE ACCESS (FULL) OF 'DEPT_WORKING' (Cost=1 Card=82
     4    2        TABLE ACCESS (BY INDEX ROWID) OF 'DEPT' (Cost=1 Card=8
     5    4          INDEX (UNIQUE SCAN) OF 'EMP_PK' (UNIQUE)

tkyte@TKYTE816> select deptno, dname, loc, last_updated from dept;

DEPTNO DNAME            LOC            LAST_UPDA
------ ------------     ------------   ---------
    10 SALES            NEW YORK       14-APR-01
    20 ACCOUNTING       VIRGINIA       13-APR-01
    30 CONSULTING       VIRGINIA       14-APR-01
    40 FINANCE          VIRGINIA       14-APR-01
    50 FINANCE          VIRGINIA       02-APR-01
    60 FINANCE          VIRGINIA       14-APR-01

6 rows selected.
```

Since DEPT_WORKING typically won't be analyzed, we'll use hints to tell the optimizer to use DEPT_WORKING as the driving table. We want it to full scan the DEPT_WORKING table. We will be updating a row for every row in there, and then do an indexed read into DEPT to update that row (this is the NESTED LOOPS). In most cases, this should be the most efficient approach.

Load Report-Style Input Data

Frequently, you have a TEXT report that contains data you would like to load. This data is in a formatted style, but the data you need comes from all over the report. For example, I was given the task of taking a report that looked like this:

```
3205679761 - Detailed Report

  July 01, 2000 21:24
    Location : location data 1
    Status   : status 1

  July 01, 2000 22:18
    Location : location data 2
    Status   : status 2

...

3205679783 - Detailed Report

  July 01, 2000 21:24
    Location : location data 3
    Status   : status data 3
...
```

which needed to be loaded into a table that looked like this:

```
tkyte@TKYTE816> create table t
```

```
    2  ( serial_no varchar2(20),
    3     date_time varchar2(50),
    4     location  varchar2(100),
    5     status    varchar2(100)
    6  )
    7  /

Table created.
```

Now, it is possible that by using some obtuse triggers, a PL/SQL package to maintain state, and some SQLLDR tricks, we could load this report directly. In fact, the *Oracle Server Utilities Guide* has an example of doing just such a thing. However, I find this approach, to be incredibly complex and obscure, not to mention that you would need to put triggers on a table in support of a load. What if the tables were used for other things? The triggers should not fire for them, but there is no way to create a trigger that only fires for SQLLDR. So, I set about to find an easier way.

Frequently, when the data is as complex as this, it is faster, cheaper, and easier to load the data into a 'scratch' table, and then use a small stored procedure to manipulate it. This is exactly what I did with the above report. I used a control file:

```
LOAD DATA
INTO TABLE TEMP
REPLACE
( seqno RECNUM,
  text Position(1:1024))
```

to load the data into a table that was created via:

```
tkyte@TKYTE816> create table temp
    2  ( seqno int primary key,
    3     text varchar2(4000) )
    4  organization index
    5  overflow tablespace data;

Table created.
```

The RECNUM clause in the control file directs SQLLDR to supply the current record number for that column as it loads the data. This will assign the number 1 to the first record, 100 to the 100th record, and so on. Then, I used a very small stored procedure to reformat the data as I wanted it. The logic of this routine is to read each line of input from the table in order. It then looks at the line, and if the line contains:

❑ Detailed Report, it extracts the number out of the line, placing it into the L_SERIAL_NO variable.

❑ Location, it extracts the location data into the L_LOCATION variable.

❑ Status, it extracts the status data into the L_STATUS variable *and* inserts the record. We are at the point in the report where we have collected all of the necessary fields by now. We have the serial number, the date and time (see next bullet point), and the location already.

❑ With anything else, we see if the field can be converted into a date. If it cannot, we skip this line of input totally. The exception block below does this for us.

Here is the routine:

```
tkyte@TKYTE816> create or replace procedure reformat
  2  as
  3      l_serial_no t.serial_no%type;
  4      l_date_time t.date_time%type;
  5      l_location  t.location%type;
  6      l_status    t.status%type;
  7      l_temp_date date;
  8  begin
  9      for x in ( select * from temp order by seqno )
 10      loop
 11          if ( x.text like '%Detailed Report%' ) then
 12              l_serial_no := substr( x.text, 1, instr(x.text,'-')-1 );
 13          elsif ( x.text like '%Location : %' ) then
 14              l_location := substr( x.text, instr(x.text,':')+2 );
 15          elsif ( x.text like '%Status %:%' ) then
 16              l_status := substr( x.text, instr(x.text,':')+2 );
 17              insert into t ( serial_no, date_time, location, status )
 18              values ( l_serial_no, l_date_time, l_location, l_status );
 19          else
 20              begin
 21                  l_temp_date := to_date( ltrim(rtrim(x.text)),
 22                                          'Month dd, yyyy hh24:mi');
 23                  l_date_time := x.text;
 24              exception
 25                  when others then null;
 26              end;
 27          end if;
 28      end loop;
 29  end;
 30  /

Procedure created.
```

When you compare this amount of work, to the amount of effort it would have taken to develop the extremely complex triggers to maintain a state between inserts, and to coordinate those triggers with other applications that access the table, there is no comparison. Loading directly into the table itself might have saved a couple of I/Os on the system, but the code to do so would have been unreliable, due to its complexity and level of trickery.

The moral of this example is that if you have to solve a complex task, try to minimize the complexity wherever possible. One way to do it is by using the appropriate tools. In this case, we used PL/SQL to write some procedural logic to help us re-format the data once it was loaded. It was the easiest way to do this. Trying to make SQLLDR do everything is not always the right approach. In other cases, we find that SQLLDR is a better tool than PL/SQL. Use the appropriate tool for the job.

Load a File into a LONG RAW or LONG Field

Even though the LONG RAW type is a deprecated type in Oracle8i, we will still find it from time to time in legacy applications, and still have to deal with it. Occasionally you might need to load a file, or files, into a long RAW and rather than write a custom program to do it, you *would* like to use SQLLDR. The good news is you can, but the bad news is that it is not very easy, and is not very adept at loading large amounts of files.

In order to load a long RAW using SQLLDR, we will in general need to have a control file per file (per row) to be loaded (unless the files are all the same size). There is a trick involved in getting SQLLDR to do this for us. We have to work with a series of 64KB or less buffers, and find some number of fixed sized records to concatenate together, to load with. For example, let's say you wanted to load a file that was 1075200 bytes long. The control file could look like this:

*The numbers in parentheses and **bold** on the right, are not actually part of the file. They are for our reference:*

```
options(bindsize=1075700, rows=1)              (1)
Load Data                                      (2)
Infile mydata.dat "fix 53760"                  (3)
concatenate 20                                 (4)
Preserve Blanks                                (5)
Into Table foo                                 (6)
Append                                         (7)
(id constant 1,bigdata raw(1075200))           (8)
```

The trick here is that $53760 * 20 = 1075200$ and 53760 is the largest number that is a factor of 1075200, less than 64k. We needed to find the largest integer less than 64KB to use as a 'fix' size, and then concatenate 20 of them together to reconstruct our physical record.

So, on line (3) above, we used the 53760 number to specify a fixed size input record. This disables the normal SQLLDR interpretation of a line feed as an end of line. SQLLDR now considers 53760 bytes to be a line – regardless of the data in it. Line (4) tells SQLLDR that a logical record (what gets loaded) will be 20 of these physical records concatenated together. We used bindsize=1075700 on line (1) in order to set up a bind buffer that is big enough to accommodate our input file, plus some extra (for the other column). Lastly, on line (8) we specify how big to make the raw column buffer for that column (default would be 255 bytes).

This control file will load the file MYDATA.DAT into the table FOO assigning the column ID the constant value of 1, and the BIGDATA column the contents of the file itself. Since this is such a tricky thing to do (find the largest integer less than 64KB and so on), I've set up a small portable C program, which I use to do this for me. I find I frequently need to load a LONG or LONG RAW column with the contents of a file, and at the same time, need to fill in one other column, some primary key column. So, I use this C program to write a control file just like the above. Its usage is the following:

```
genctl filename tablename lr_column_name pk_column_name pk_value RAW|CHAR
```

and I ran it like this to generate the above control file:

```
genctl mydata.dat foo bigdata id 1 RAW > test.ctl
```

The program looked at MYDATA.DAT, got its size, did the math, and generated the control file for me. You can find the source code for GENCTL on the Apress web site at http://www.apress.com.

Load Data with Embedded Newlines

This is something that has been problematic for SQLLDR historically – how to load free form data that may include a newline in it. The newline character is the default 'end of line' character to SQLLDR, and the ways around this did not offer much flexibility in the past. Fortunately, in Oracle 81.6 and later versions we have some new options.

The options for loading data with embedded newlines are now as follows:

❑ Load the data with some other character in the data that represents a newline (for example, put the string \n in the text where a newline should appear) and use a SQL function to replace that text with a CHR(10) during load time.

❑ Use the FIX attribute on the INFILE directive, and load a fixed length flat file.

❑ Use the VAR attribute on the INFILE directive, and load a varying width file that uses a format such that the first few bytes of each line is the length of the line to follow.

❑ Use the STR attribute on the INFILE directive to load a varying width file with some sequence of characters that represent the end of line, as opposed to just the newline character representing this.

We will demonstrate each in turn.

Use a Character Other than a Newline

This is an easy method if you have control over how the input data is produced. If it is easy enough to convert the data when creating the data file, this will work fine. The idea is to apply a SQL function to the data on the way into the database, replacing some string of characters with a newline. Lets add another column to our DEPT table:

```
tkyte@TKYTE816> alter table dept add comments varchar2(4000);

Table altered.
```

We'll use this column to load text into. An example control file with inline data could be:

```
LOAD DATA
INFILE *
INTO TABLE DEPT
REPLACE
FIELDS TERMINATED BY ','
TRAILING NULLCOLS
(DEPTNO,
    DNAME          "upper(:dname)",
    LOC            "upper(:loc)",
    LAST_UPDATED   "my_to_date( :last_updated )",
    COMMENTS       "replace(:comments,'\n',chr(10))"
)
BEGINDATA
10,Sales,Virginia,01-april-2001,This is the Sales\nOffice in Virginia
20,Accounting,Virginia,13/04/2001,This is the Accounting\nOffice in Virginia
30,Consulting,Virginia,14/04/2001,This is the Consulting\nOffice in Virginia
40,Finance,Virginia,987268297,This is the Finance\nOffice in Virginia
```

Now, there is something important to point out here. The above control file will only work on DOS-based platforms, such as Windows NT. On a UNIX platform, we must use:

```
COMMENTS       "replace(:comments,'\\n',chr(10))"
```

Notice how in the call to replace we had to use \\n not just \n. This is because \n is recognized by SQLLDR as a newline, and it would have converted it into a newline, not a two character string. We used \\n to get the character string constant \n into the control file in SQLLDR on UNIX. When we execute SQLLDR with the above control file (adjusted for UNIX if you are on that platform), the table DEPT is loaded with:

```
tkyte@TKYTE816> select deptno, dname, comments from dept;

DEPTNO DNAME          COMMENTS
------ -------------- ----------------------------------------
    10 SALES          This is the Sales
                      Office in Virginia

    20 ACCOUNTING     This is the Accounting
                      Office in Virginia

    30 CONSULTING     This is the Consulting
                      Office in Virginia

    40 FINANCE        This is the Finance
                      Office in Virginia
```

Use the FIX Attribute

The FIX attribute is another method available to us. If you use this, the input data must appear in fixed length records. Each record will be exactly the same number of bytes as any other record in the input data set. When using **positional** data, this is especially valid. These files are typically fixed length input files to begin with. When using 'free form' delimited data, it is less likely that you will have a fixed length file as these files are generally of varying length (this is the entire point of delimited files – to make each line only as big as it needs to be).

When using the FIX attribute, we must use an INFILE clause, as this is an option to INFILE. Additionally, the data must be stored externally, not in the control file itself using this option. So, assuming we have fixed length input records, we can use a control file such as this:

```
LOAD DATA
INFILE demo17.dat "fix 101"
INTO TABLE DEPT
REPLACE
FIELDS TERMINATED BY ','
TRAILING NULLCOLS
(DEPTNO,
  DNAME          "upper(:dname)",
  LOC            "upper(:loc)",
  LAST_UPDATED "my_to_date(:last_updated)",
  COMMENTS
)
```

This specifies an input data file that will have records that are 101 bytes each. *This includes the trailing newline* that may or may not be there. In this case, the newline is nothing special in the input data file. It is just another character to be loaded or not. This is the thing to understand – the newline at the end of the record (if present) will become part of the record. In order to fully understand this, we need a utility to dump the contents of a file on screen so we can see what is really in there. To do this in a totally portable fashion so that we have something that works on all platforms, we'll use the database. We can write a routine that uses a BFILE to read a file from the operating system, and dump it character by character on screen, showing us where carriage returns (ASCII 13), line feeds (ASCII 10), tabs (ASCII 9), and other special characters are in the file. Using PL/SQL it might look like this:

```
tkyte@TKYTE816> create or replace
  2  procedure file_dump( p_directory in varchar2,
  3                        p_filename  in varchar2 )
  4  as
  5      type array is table of varchar2(5) index by binary_integer;
  6
  7      l_chars   array;
  8      l_bfile   bfile;
  9      l_buffsize number default 15;
 10      l_data    varchar2(30);
 11      l_len     number;
 12      l_offset  number default 1;
 13      l_char    char(1);
 14  begin
 15      -- special cases, print out "escapes" for readability
 16      l_chars(0)  := '\0';
 17      l_chars(13) := '\r';
 18      l_chars(10) := '\n';
 19      l_chars(9)  := '\t';
 20
 21      l_bfile := bfilename( p_directory, p_filename );
 22      dbms_lob.fileopen( l_bfile );
 23
 24      l_len := dbms_lob.getlength( l_bfile );
 25      while( l_offset < l_len )
 26      loop
 27          -- first show the BYTE offsets into the file
 28          dbms_output.put( to_char(l_offset,'fm000000') || '-'||
 29                          to_char(l_offset+l_buffsize-1,'fm000000') );
 30
 31          -- now get BUFFSIZE bytes from the file to dump
 32          l_data := utl_raw.cast_to_varchar2
 33                      (dbms_lob.substr( l_bfile, l_buffsize, l_offset ));
 34
 35          -- for each character
 36          for i in 1 .. length(l_data)
 37          loop
 38              l_char := substr(l_data,i,1);
 39
 40              -- if the character is printable, just print it
 41              if ascii( l_char ) between 32 and 126
 42              then
 43                  dbms_output.put( lpad(l_char,3) );
 44              -- if it is one of the SPECIAL characters above, print
 45              -- it in using the text provided
```

```
46                  elsif ( l_chars.exists( ascii(l_char) ) )
47                  then
48                      dbms_output.put( lpad( l_chars(ascii(l_char)), 3 ) );
49                  -- else it is just binary data, display it in HEX
50                  else
51                      dbms_output.put( to_char(ascii(l_char),'0X') );
52                  end if;
53              end loop;
54              dbms_output.new_line;
55
56              l_offset := l_offset + l_buffsize;
57          end loop;
58          dbms_lob.close( l_bfile );
59  end;
60  /

Procedure created.
```

For more information on DBMS_LOB and BFILES see the Appendix A at the back of this book.

So, if you take a data file such as:

```
tkyte@TKYTE816> host type demo17.dat
10,Sales,Virginia,01-april-2001,This is the Sales
Office in Virginia
20,Accounting,Virginia,13/04/2001,This is the Accounting
Office in Virginia
30,Consulting,Virginia,14/04/2001 12:02:02,This is the Consulting
Office in Virginia
40,Finance,Virginia,987268297,This is the Finance
Office in Virginia

tkyte@TKYTE816> exec file_dump( 'MY_FILES', 'demo17.dat' );
000001-000015  1  0  ,  S  a  l  e  s  ,  V  i  r  g  i  n
000016-000030  i  a  ,  0  1  -  a  p  r  i  l  -  2  0  0
000031-000045  1  ,  T  h  i  s     i  s     t  h  e     S
000046-000060  a  l  e  s \r \n  O  f  f  i  c  e     i  n
000061-000075     V  i  r  g  i  n  i  a
000076-000090
000091-000105                          \r \n  2  0  ,  A
000106-000120  c  c  o  u  n  t  i  n  g  ,  V  i  r  g  i
000121-000135  n  i  a  ,  1  3  /  0  4  /  2  0  0  1  ,
000136-000150  T  h  i  s     i  s     t  h  e     A  c  c
000151-000165  o  u  n  t  i  n  g \r \n  O  f  f  i  c  e
000166-000180     i  n     V  i  r  g  i  n  i  a
000181-000195
000196-000210                          \r \n  3  0  ,  C  o  n  s  u
000211-000225  l  t  i  n  g  ,  V  i  r  g  i  n  i  a  ,
000226-000240  1  4  /  0  4  /  2  0  0  1     1  2  :  0
000241-000255  2  :  0  2  ,  T  h  i  s     i  s     t  h
000256-000270  e     C  o  n  s  u  l  t  i  n  g \r \n  O
000271-000285  f  f  i  c  e     i  n     V  i  r  g  i  n
000286-000300  i  a
000301-000315  \r \n  4  0  ,  F  i  n  a  n  c  e  ,  V
```

```
000316-000330   i  r  g  i  n  i  a  ,  9  8  7  2  6  8  2
000331-000345   9  7  ,  T  h  i  s        i  s        t  h  e
000346-000360   F  i  n  a  n  c  e \r \n  O  f  f  i  c  e
000361-000375      i  n     V  i  r  g  i  n  i  a
000376-000390
000391-000405                                          \r \n


PL/SQL procedure successfully completed.
```

So, using this utility we can see that every record is 101 bytes long. If you look at the line of data that starts with `000091-000105` we can see the end of line (`\r\n`). Since we know the last character on this display line is at byte 105 in the file, we can count backwards to see that the `\n` is at byte 101. Looking forwards to the line that begins with `000196-000210`, we see at offset 202 in the file, another end of line representing the end of that record.

Now that we know each and every record is 101 bytes long, we are ready to load it using the control file we listed above with the `FIX 101` clause. When we do so, we can see:

```
tkyte@TKYTE816> select '"' || comments || '"' comments from dept;

COMMENTS
--------------------------------
"This is the Sales
Office in Virginia

"

"This is the Accounting
Office in Virginia

"

"This is the Consulting
Office in Virginia

"

"This is the Finance
Office in Virginia

"
```

Notice how each row loaded ends with a newline, as evidenced by that the fact the ending quote we added is at the beginning of a line (the last character of the COMMENTS field is a newline, and causes the quote to be on a new line). This is because my input data always had a newline in the 101st byte, and SQLLDR did not count this as a record separator of any sort. If this is not desired, you should enclose your data in quotes, and use the OPTIONALLY ENCLOSED BY clause to have SQLLDR load just the enclosed data, minus the newline (and don't forget to account for that additional space on each line in the FIX attribute). In this fashion, the trailing newline will not be loaded as part of the input data. So, if you change the control file to:

```
LOAD DATA
INFILE demo18.dat "fix 101"
```

```
INTO TABLE DEPT
REPLACE
FIELDS TERMINATED BY ',' OPTIONALLY ENCLOSED BY '"'
TRAILING NULLCOLS
(DEPTNO,
  DNAME        "upper(:dname)",
  LOC          "upper(:loc)",
  LAST_UPDATED "my_to_date( :last_updated )",
  COMMENTS
)
```

and change the data file to:

```
C:\sqlldr>TYPE demo18.dat
10,Sales,Virginia,01-april-2001,"This is the Sales
Office in Virginia"
20,Accounting,Virginia,13/04/2001,"This is the Accounting
Office in Virginia"
30,Consulting,Virginia,14/04/2001 12:02:02,"This is the Consulting
Office in Virginia"
40,Finance,Virginia,987268297,"This is the Finance
Office in Virginia"
```

with quotes around the text, it will get loaded like this instead:

```
tkyte@TKYTE816> select '"' || comments || '"' comments from dept;

COMMENTS
------------------------------
"This is the Sales
Office in Virginia"

"This is the Accounting
Office in Virginia"

"This is the Consulting
Office in Virginia"

"This is the Finance
Office in Virginia"
```

A word of caution for those of you lucky enough to work on both Windows NT and UNIX. The end of line marker is different on these platforms. On UNIX it is simply \n. On Windows NT is it \r\n. Let's say we took the above example and simply ftp'ed (file transferred) the files to a UNIX machine. Doing the same FILE_DUMP as above will show us the problem you will encounter:

```
ops$tkyte@ORA8I.WORLD> EXEC file_dump( 'MY_FILES', 'demo17.dat' );
000001-000015  1 0 ,  S  a  l  e  s  ,  V  i  r  g  i  n
000016-000030  i a ,  0  1  -  a  p  r  i  l  -  2  0  0
000031-000045  1 ,  T  h  i  s     i  s     t  h  e     S
000046-000060  a l e s \n O  f  f  i  c  e     i  n
000061-000075  V i r  g  i  n  i  a
000076-000090
000091-000105                          \n 2 0 , A c c
```

```
000106-000120    o    u    n    t    i    n    g    ,    V    i    r    g    i    n    i
000121-000135    a    ,    1    3    /    0    4    /    2    0    0    1    ,    T    h
000136-000150    i    s         i    s         t    h    e         A    c    c    o    u
000151-000165    n    t    i    n    g   \n    O    f    f    i    c    e         i    n
000166-000180    V    i    r    g    i    n    i    a
000181-000195
000196-000210             \n    3    0    ,    C    o    n    s    u    l    t    i    n
000211-000225    g    ,    V    i    r    g    i    n    i    a    ,    1    4    /    0
000226-000240    4    /    2    0    0    1         1    2    :    0    2    :    0    2
000241-000255    ,    T    h    i    s         i    s         t    h    e         C    o
000256-000270    n    s    u    l    t    i    n    g   \n    O    f    f    i    c    e
000271-000285    i    n         V    i    r    g    i    n    i    a
000286-000300                                            \n    4    0    ,
000301-000315    F    i    n    a    n    c    e    ,    V    i    r    g    i    n    i
000316-000330    a    ,    9    8    7    2    6    8    2    9    7    ,    T    h    i
000331-000345    s         i    s         t    h    e         F    i    n    a    n    c
000346-000360    e   \n    O    f    f    i    c    e         i    n         V    i    r
000361-000375    g    i    n    i    a
000376-000390
000391-000405                        \n

PL/SQL procedure successfully completed.
```

This file is a totally different size, as are each of the records. Each \r\n pair is now just a \n sequence. In this particular example, we can simply adjust the FIX from 101 to 99, but this is *only* because I had the same exact number of newlines in each record! Each record's length was reduced by 2 bytes. If some of the records had three newlines, their length would have been reduced by three bytes not two. This would change the file in such a way that the records were no longer fixed length. In general, if you use the FIX approach, make sure to *create and load* the file on a homogenous platform (UNIX and UNIX, or Windows and Windows). Transferring the files from one system to the other will almost certainly render them unloadable.

Use the VAR Attribute

Another method of loading data with embedded newline characters is to use the VAR attribute. When using this format, each record will begin with some fixed number of bytes that represent the total length of the incoming record. Using this format, I can load varying length records that contain embedded newlines, but only if I have a **record length field** at the beginning of *each and every* record. So, if I use a control file such as:

```
LOAD DATA
INFILE demo19.dat "var 3"
INTO TABLE DEPT
REPLACE
FIELDS TERMINATED BY ','
TRAILING NULLCOLS
(DEPTNO,
    DNAME        "upper(:dname)",
    LOC          "upper(:loc)",
    LAST_UPDATED "my_to_date(:last_updated)",
    COMMENTS
)
```

then the vear 3 says that the first three bytes of each input record will be the length of that input record. If I take a data file such as:

```
C:\sqlldr>type demo19.dat
07110,Sales,Virginia,01-april-2001,This is the Sales
Office in Virginia
07820,Accounting,Virginia,13/04/2001,This is the Accounting
Office in Virginia
08730,Consulting,Virginia,14/04/2001 12:02:02,This is the Consulting
Office in Virginia
07140,Finance,Virginia,987268297,This is the Finance
Office in Virginia
```

I can load it using that control file. In my input data file, I have four rows of data. The first row starts with 071, meaning that the next 71 bytes represent the first input record. This 71 bytes includes the terminated newline after the word Virginia. The next row starts with 078. It has 78 bytes of text, and so on. Using this format data file, we can easily load our data with embedded newlines.

Again, if you are using UNIX and NT (the above example was NT where a newline is two characters long), you would have to adjust the length field for each record. On UNIX the above .DAT file would have to have 69, 76, 85, and 69 as the length fields in this particular example.

Use the STR Attribute

This is perhaps the most flexible method of loading data with embedded newlines. Using the STR attribute, I can specify a new end of line character (or sequence of characters). This allows you to create an input data file that has some special character at the end of each line – the newline is no longer 'special'.

I prefer to use a sequence of characters, typically some special 'marker', and then a newline. This makes it easy to see the end of line character when viewing the input data in a text editor or some utility, as each record still has a newline at the end of it. The STR attribute is specified in hexadecimal, and perhaps the easiest way to get the exact hexadecimal string you need is to use SQL and UTL_RAW (see the *Necessary Supplied Packages* appendix at the end of this book for details on UTL_RAW) to produce the hexadecimal string for us. For example, assuming you are on Windows NT where the end of line marker is CHR(13) || CHR(10) (carriage return/line feed) and your special marker character is a pipe |, we can write this:

```
tkyte@TKYTE816> select utl_raw.cast_to_raw( '|'||chr(13)||chr(10) ) from
                                                                   dual;


UTL_RAW.CAST_TO_RAW('|'||CHR(13)||CHR(10))
-----------------------------------------------------------
7C0D0A
```

which shows us that the STR we need to use is X'7C0D0A'. To use this, we might have a control file like this:

```
LOAD DATA
INFILE demo20.dat "str X'7C0D0A'"
INTO TABLE DEPT
REPLACE
```

```
FIELDS TERMINATED BY ',`
TRAILING NULLCOLS
(DEPTNO,
  DNAME          "upper(:dname)",
  LOC            "upper(:loc)",
  LAST_UPDATED "my_to_date( :last_updated )",
  COMMENTS
)
```

So, if your input data looks like this:

```
C:\sqlldr>type demo20.dat
10,Sales,Virginia,01-april-2001,This is the Sales
Office in Virginia|
20,Accounting,Virginia,13/04/2001,This is the Accounting
Office in Virginia|
30,Consulting,Virginia,14/04/2001 12:02:02,This is the Consulting
Office in Virginia|
40,Finance,Virginia,987268297,This is the Finance
Office in Virginia|
```

where each record in the data file ended with a |\r\n, the above control file will load it correctly.

Embedded Newlines Wrap-Up

So, we have explored at least four ways to load data with embedded newlines. In the very next section, we will use one of these, the STR attribute, in a generic unload utility to avoid issues with regards to newlines in text.

Additionally, one thing to be very aware of, and I've mentioned it above a couple of times, is that on Windows (all flavors), text files may end in \r\n (ASCII 13 + ASCII 10, carriage return/line feed). Your control file will have to accommodate this – that \r is part of the record. The byte counts in the FIX and VAR, and the string used with STR must accommodate this. For example, if you took any of the above .DAT files that currently contain just \n in them and ftp'ed them to Windows NT 4.0 using an ASCII transfer (the default), every \n would turn into \r\n. The same control file that just worked in UNIX would not be able to load the data anymore. This is something you must be aware of, and take into consideration when setting up the control file.

Unload Data

One thing SQLLDR does not do, and that Oracle supplies no tools for, is the unloading of data in a format understandable by SQLLDR. This would be useful for moving data from system to system without using EXP/IMP. Using EXP/IMP to move data from system to system works fine for moderate amounts of data. Since IMP does not support a direct path import, and would not build indexes in parallel, moving the data via SQLLDR, and then creating the indexes using a parallel, unrecoverable, index build may be many orders of magnitude faster.

We will develop a small PL/SQL utility that may be used to unload data on a server in a SQLLDR-friendly format. Also, equivalent tools for doing so in Pro*C and SQL*PLUS are provided on the Wrox web site. The PL/SQL utility will work fine in most cases, but better performance will be had using Pro*C, and if you need the files to be generated on the client (not the server which is where PL/SQL will generate and so on

The specification of the package we will create is:

```
tkyte@TKYTE816> create or replace package unloader
  2    as
  3      function run( p_query in varchar2,
  4                    p_tname in varchar2,
  5                    p_mode in varchar2 default 'REPLACE',
  6                    p_dir in varchar2,
  7                    p_filename in varchar2,
  8                    p_separator in varchar2 default ',',
  9                    p_enclosure in varchar2 default '"',
 10                    p_terminator in varchar2 default '|' )
 11      return number;
 12    end;
 13  /

Package created.
```

with the following meanings:

```
/* Function run  - Unloads data from any query into a file, and creates a
                   control file to reload this data into another table

     p_query    = SQL query to 'unload'. May be virtually any query.
     p_tname    = Table to load into. Will be put into control file.
     p_mode     = REPLACE|APPEND|TRUNCATE - how to reload the data
     p_dir      = Directory we will write the .ctl and .dat file to.
     p_filename = Name of file to write to. I will add .ctl and .dat to
                  this name
     p_separator = Field delimiter. I default this to a comma.
     p_enclosure = What each field will be wrapped in.
     p_terminator = End of line character. We use this so we can unload and
                   reload data with newlines in it. I default to '|\n' (a
                   pipe and a newline together), '|\r\n' on NT. You need
                   only to override this if you believe your data will
                   have this sequence in it. I ALWAYS add the OS 'end of
                   line' marker to this sequence, you should not.
*/
```

The package body follows. We use UTL_FILE to write a control file and a data file. Make sure to refer to UTL_FILE in the Appendix A on *Necessary Supplied Packages* at the back of this book for details on setting up UTL_FILE. Without the proper init.ora parameter settings, UTL_FILE will not work. DBMS_SQL is used to dynamically process any query (see the section in the appendix on DBMS_SQL for details on this package). We utilize one data type in our queries – a VARCHAR2(4000). This implies we cannot use this method to unload LOBS, and that is true if the LOB is greater than 4000 bytes. We can however, use this to unload up to 4000 bytes of any LOB using DBMS_LOB.SUBSTR. Additionally, since we are using a VARCHAR2 as the only output data type, we can handle RAWS up to 2000 bytes in length (4000 hexadecimal characters), which is sufficient for everything except LONG RAWS, and LOBS. The following solution is a 90 percent solution – it solves the problem 90 percent of the time. With a little

more work , and by using other tools described in this book, for example, the LOB_IO package
described in Chapter 18 on *C-Based External Procedures*, we could expand this easily to handle all data
types, including LOBS.

```
tkyte@TKYTE816> create or replace package body unloader
  2  as
  3
  4
  5  g_theCursor          integer default dbms_sql.open_cursor;
  6  g_descTbl            dbms_sql.desc_tab;
  7  g_nl                 varchar2(2) default chr(10);
  8
```

These are some global variables we use in this package. The global cursor is opened once, the first time
we reference this package, and will stay open until we log out. This avoids the overhead of getting a new
cursor every time you call this package. The G_DESCTBL is a PL/SQL table that will hold the output of a
DBMS_SQL.DESCRIBE call. G_NL is a newline character. We use this in strings that need to have
newlines embedded in them. We do not need to adjust this for Windows – UTL_FILE will see the
CHR(10) in the string of characters, and automatically turn that into a carriage return/line feed for us.

Next we have a small convenience function used to convert a character to hexadecimal. It uses the built-
in functions to do this:

```
  9
 10  function to_hex( p_str in varchar2 ) return varchar2
 11  is
 12  begin
 13      return to_char( ascii(p_str), 'fm0x' );
 14  end;
 15
```

The following is a procedure to create a control file to reload the unloaded data. It uses the DESCRIBE
table generated by dbms_sql.describe_columns to do this. It takes care of the OS specifics for us,
such as whether the OS uses a carriage return/line feed (used for the STR attribute), and whether the
directory separator is \ or /. It does this by looking at the directory name passed into it. If the directory
contains a \, we are on Windows, else we are on UNIX:

```
 16  /*
 17  */
 18
 19  procedure  dump_ctl( p_dir        in varchar2,
 20                       p_filename   in varchar2,
 21                       p_tname      in varchar2,
 22                       p_mode       in varchar2,
 23                       p_separator  in varchar2,
 24                       p_enclosure  in varchar2,
 25                       p_terminator in varchar2 )
 26  is
 27      l_output         utl_file.file_type;
 28      l_sep            varchar2(5);
 29      l_str            varchar2(5);
 30      l_path           varchar2(5);
 31  begin
 32      if ( p_dir like '%\%' )
```

```
33         then
34             -- Windows platforms --
35             l_str := chr(13) || chr(10);
36             if ( p_dir not like '%\' AND p_filename not like '\%' )
37             then
38                 l_path := '\';
39             end if;
40         else
41             l_str := chr(10);
42             if ( p_dir not like '%/' AND p_filename not like '/%' )
43             then
44                 l_path := '/';
45             end if;
46         end if;
47
48         l_output := utl_file.fopen( p_dir, p_filename || '.ctl', 'w' );
49
50         utl_file.put_line( l_output, 'load data' );
51         utl_file.put_line( l_output, 'infile ''' || p_dir || l_path ||
52                                      p_filename || '.dat'' "str x''' ||
53                                      utl_raw.cast_to_raw( p_terminator ||
54                                      l_str ) || '''"' );
55         utl_file.put_line( l_output, 'into table ' || p_tname );
56         utl_file.put_line( l_output, p_mode );
57         utl_file.put_line( l_output, 'fields terminated by X''' ||
58                                      to_hex(p_separator) ||
59                                      ''' enclosed by X''' ||
60                                      to_hex(p_enclosure) || ''' ' );
61         utl_file.put_line( l_output, '(' );
62
63         for i in 1 .. g_descTbl.count
64         loop
65             if ( g_descTbl(i).col_type = 12 )
66             then
67                 utl_file.put( l_output, l_sep || g_descTbl(i).col_name ||
68                                 ' date ''ddmmyyyyhh24miss'' ');
69             else
70                 utl_file.put( l_output, l_sep || g_descTbl(i).col_name ||
71                                 ' char(' ||
72                                 to_char(g_descTbl(i).col_max_len*2) ||' )' );
73             end if;
74             l_sep := ','||g_nl ;
75         end loop;
76         utl_file.put_line( l_output, g_nl || ')' );
77         utl_file.fclose( l_output );
78    end;
```

Here is a simple function to return a quoted string using the chosen enclosure character. Notice how it not only encloses the character, but also doubles them up if they exist in the string as well, so that they are preserved:

```
79
80    function quote(p_str in varchar2, p_enclosure in varchar2)
81         return varchar2
82    is
```

```
83  begin
84      return p_enclosure ||
85              replace( p_str, p_enclosure, p_enclosure||p_enclosure ) ||
86              p_enclosure;
87  end;
```

Next we have the main function, RUN. As it is fairly large, we'll comment on it as we go along:

```
88
89  function run( p_query        in varchar2,
90                p_tname       in varchar2,
91                p_mode        in varchar2 default 'REPLACE',
92                p_dir         in varchar2,
93                p_filename    in varchar2,
94                p_separator   in varchar2 default ',',
95                p_enclosure   in varchar2 default '"',
96                p_terminator  in varchar2 default '|' ) return number
97  is
98      l_output       utl_file.file_type;
99      l_columnValue  varchar2(4000);
100     l_colCnt       number default 0;
101     l_separator    varchar2(10) default '';
102     l_cnt          number default 0;
103     l_line         long;
104     l_datefmt      varchar2(255);
105     l_descTbl      dbms_sql.desc_tab;
106  begin
```

We will save the NLS DATE format into a variable so we can change it to a format that preserves the date and time when dumping the data to disk. In this fashion, we will preserve the time component of a date. We then set up an exception block so that we can reset the NLS_DATE_FORMAT upon any error:

```
107      select value
108        into l_datefmt
109        from nls_session_parameters
110       where parameter = 'NLS_DATE_FORMAT';
111
112      /*
113         Set the date format to a big numeric string. Avoids
114         all NLS issues and saves both the time and date.
115      */
116      execute immediate
117         'alter session set nls_date_format=''ddmmyyyyhh24miss'' ';
118
119      /*
120         Set up an exception block so that in the event of any
121         error, we can at least reset the date format.
122      */
123      begin
```

Next we will parse and describe the query. The setting of G_DESCTBL to L_DESCTBL is done to 'reset' the global table, otherwise it might contain data from a previous DESCRIBE, in addition to data for the current query. Once we have done that, we call DUMP_CTL to actually create the control file:

```
124        /*
125            Parse and describe the query. We reset the
126            descTbl to an empty table so .count on it
127            will be reliable.
128        */
129        dbms_sql.parse( g_theCursor, p_query, dbms_sql.native );
130        g_descTbl := l_descTbl;
131        dbms_sql.describe_columns( g_theCursor, l_colCnt, g_descTbl );
132
133        /*
134            Create a control file to reload this data
135            into the desired table.
136        */
137        dump_ctl( p_dir, p_filename, p_tname, p_mode, p_separator,
138                           p_enclosure, p_terminator );
139
140        /*
141            Bind every single column to a varchar2(4000). We don't care
142            if we are fetching a number or a date or whatever.
143            Everything can be a string.
144        */
```

Now we are ready to dump the actual data out to disk. We begin by defining every column to be a VARCHAR2(4000) for fetching into. All NUMBERs, DATEs, RAWs – every type will be converted into VARCHAR2, immediately after this we execute the query to prepare for the fetching phase:

```
145        for i in 1 .. l_colCnt loop
146            dbms_sql.define_column( g_theCursor, i, l_columnValue, 4000 );
147        end loop;
148
149        /*
150            Run the query - ignore the output of execute. It is only
151            valid when the DML is an insert/update or delete.
152        */
```

Now we open the data file for writing, fetch all of the rows from the query, and print it out to the data file:

```
153        l_cnt := dbms_sql.execute(g_theCursor);
154
155        /*
156            Open the file to write output to and then write the
157            delimited data to it.
158        */
159        l_output := utl_file.fopen( p_dir, p_filename || '.dat', 'w',
160                                          32760 );
161        loop
162            exit when ( dbms_sql.fetch_rows(g_theCursor) <= 0 );
163            l_separator := '';
164            l_line := null;
165            for i in 1 .. l_colCnt loop
166                dbms_sql.column_value( g_theCursor, i,
167                                          l_columnValue );
168                l_line := l_line || l_separator ||
```

```
169                             quote( l_columnValue, p_enclosure );
170                     l_separator := p_separator;
171                 end loop;
172                 l_line := l_line || p_terminator;
173                 utl_file.put_line( l_output, l_line );
174                 l_cnt := l_cnt+1;
175             end loop;
176             utl_file.fclose( l_output );
```

Lastly, we set the date format back (and the exception block will do the same if any of the above code fails for any reason) to what it was and return:

```
177
178             /*
179                 Now reset the date format and return the number of rows
180                 written to the output file.
181             */
182             execute immediate
183                 'alter session set nls_date_format=''' || l_datefmt || ''';
184             return l_cnt;
185         exception
186             /*
187                 In the event of ANY error, reset the data format and
188                 re-raise the error.
189             */
190             when others then
191                 execute immediate
192                 'alter session set nls_date_format=''' || l_datefmt || ''';
193                 RAISE;
194         end;
195     end run;
196
197
198 end unloader;
199 /

Package body created.
```

Now, to run this, we can simply use:

The following will of course, require that you have SELECT on SCOTT.EMP granted to your role.

```
tkyte@TKYTE816> drop table emp;

Table dropped.

tkyte@TKYTE816> create table emp as select * from scott.emp;

Table created.

tkyte@TKYTE816> alter table emp add resume raw(2000);
```

```
   Table altered.

tkyte@TKYTE816> update emp
   2      set resume = rpad( '02', 4000, '02' );

14 rows updated.

tkyte@TKYTE816> update emp
   2      set ename = substr( ename, 1, 2 ) || '"' ||
   3                    chr(10) || '"' || substr(ename,3);

14 rows updated.

tkyte@TKYTE816> set serveroutput on

tkyte@TKYTE816> declare
   2      l_rows    number;
   3  begin
   4      l_rows := unloader.run
   5              ( p_query      => 'select * from emp order by empno',
   6                p_tname      => 'emp',
   7                p_mode       => 'replace',
   8                p_dir        => 'c:\temp',
   9                p_filename   => 'emp',
  10                p_separator  => ',',
  11                p_enclosure  => '"',
  12                p_terminator => '~' );
  13
  14      dbms_output.put_line( to_char(l_rows) ||
  15                        ' rows extracted to ascii file' );
  16  end;
  17  /
14 rows extracted to ascii file

PL/SQL procedure successfully completed.
```

The control file that was generated by this shows:

*The numbers in parentheses and **bold** on the right are not actually in the file. They are for our reference below:*

```
load data                                          (1)
infile 'c:\temp\emp.dat' "str x'7E0D0A'"           (2)
into table emp                                     (3)
replace                                            (4)
fields terminated by X'2c' enclosed by X'22'       (5)
(                                                  (6)
EMPNO char(44 ),                                   (7)
ENAME char(20 ),                                   (8)
JOB char(18 ),                                     (9)
MGR char(44 ),                                     (10)
HIREDATE date 'ddmmyyyyhh24miss' ,                 (11)
SAL char(44 ),                                     (12)
```

```
COMM char(44 ),                                        (13)
DEPTNO char(44 ),                                      (14)
RESUME char(4000 )                                     (15)
)                                                      (16)
```

The things to note about this control file are:

- Line (2) – We use the new feature in Oracle 8.1.6, of STR. We can specify what character or string is used to terminate a record. This allows us to load data with embedded newlines easily. The above string of x'7E0D0A' is simply a tilde followed by a newline.

- Line (5) – We use our separator character and enclosure character. I do not use OPTIONALLY ENCLOSED BY, since I will be enclosing every single field, after doubling any occurrence of the enclosure character in the raw data.

- Line (11) – We use a large 'numeric' date format. This does two things. Firstly, it avoids any NLS issues with regards to the data, and secondly, it preserves the time component of the date field.

- Line (15) – We use char(4000). By default, SQLLDR will use a char(255) for fields. I doubled up the length of each and every field in the control file. This ensures SQLLDR will be able to read the data without truncating any fields. I chose to double the length in order to support RAW types, we will extract in VARCHAR2 format (in hexadecimal). That is, twice as long as the original source data.

The RAW data (the .dat) file generated from the above code will look like this:

```
"7369","SM""
""ITH","CLERK","7902","17121980000000","800","","20","0202020202020202020202020202
02020202020202020...<many occurrences removed> ...0202020202020202"~
"7499","AL""
""LEN","SALESMAN","7698","20021981000000","1600","300","30","0202020202020202020202
02020202020202020202...<many occurrences removed> ...0202020202020202"~
```

Things to note in the .dat file are:

- Each field is enclosed in our enclosure character.

- The ENAME field, into which we placed quotes and a \n character via an update, has a newline in it. Also, the quotation marks are doubled up to preserve them in the raw data.

- The DATES are unloaded as large numbers.

- The RAW field we added is preserved, and is dumped in hexadecimal format.

- Each line of data in this file ends with a~as requested.

We can now reload this data easily using SQLLDR. You may add options to the SQLLDR command line as you see fit.

You can use this functionality to do things that are otherwise hard, or impossible to do, via other methods. For example, if you wanted to rename the ENAME column of the EMP table to EMP_NAME, you could do the following. What I do here is unload the data for SQLLDR to reload. Notice how we 'rename' the column on the way out using the EMP_NAME alias in the SELECT list after ENAME. This will cause the control file to be created with a column name of EMP_NAME instead of ENAME. I truncate the table, drop the inappropriately named column, and add the new name. We then reload the table. I might choose this approach over a more simple 'add column, update new column to old column, and drop old column' if I wanted to reorganize the table anyway, or was concerned about the amount of rollback and redo I might generate by doing such an operation. I could use SQLLDR with the direct path mode to avoid all rollback and redo generation on the subsequent reload as well. Here are the steps:

```
tkyte@TKYTE816> declare
  2      l_rows    number;
  3  begin
  4      l_rows := unloader.run
  5              ( p_query     => 'select EMPNO, ENAME EMP_NAME,
  6                                       JOB , MGR, HIREDATE,
  7                                       SAL, COMM, DEPTNO
  8                                  from emp
  9                                 order by empno',
 10                p_tname     => 'emp',
 11                p_mode      => 'TRUNCATE',
 12                p_dir       => 'c:\temp',
 13                p_filename  => 'emp',
 14                p_separator => ',',
 15                p_enclosure => '"',
 16                p_terminator => '~' );
 17
 18      dbms_output.put_line( to_char(l_rows) ||
 19                            ' rows extracted to ascii file' );
 20  end;
 21  /

PL/SQL procedure successfully completed.

tkyte@TKYTE816> truncate table emp;

Table truncated.

tkyte@TKYTE816> alter table emp drop column ename;

Table altered.

tkyte@TKYTE816> alter table emp add emp_name varchar2(10);

Table altered.

tkyte@TKYTE816> host sqlldr userid=tkyte/tkyte control=c:\temp\emp.ctl
SQLLDR: Release 8.1.6.0.0 - Production on Sat Apr 14 20:40:01 2001
(c) Copyright 1999 Oracle Corporation.  All rights reserved.
Commit point reached - logical record count 14

tkyte@TKYTE816> desc emp
```

Name	Null?	Type
EMPNO	NOT NULL	NUMBER(4)
JOB		VARCHAR2(9)
MGR		NUMBER(4)
HIREDATE		DATE
SAL		NUMBER(7,2)

```
     COMM                                    NUMBER(7,2)
     DEPTNO                                  NUMBER(2)
     RESUME                                  RAW(2000)
     EMP_NAME                                VARCHAR2(10)

tkyte@TKYTE816> select emp_name from emp;

EMP_NAME
----------
SM"
"ITH
...
MI"
"LLER

14 rows selected.
```

You can use this method to perform other operations as well, such as modifying a data type, denormalize data (unload a JOIN for example), and so on.

As stated previously, the above logic of the unload package may be implemented in a variety of languages and tools. On the Apress web site, you will find this implemented not only in PL/SQL as above, but also in Pro*C and SQL*PLUS scripts. Pro*C will be the fastest implementation, and will always write to the client workstation file system. PL/SQL will be a good all around implementation (no need to compile and install on client workstations), but always writes to the server file system. SQL*PLUS will be a good middle ground, offering fair performance, and the ability to write to the client file system.

Load LOBs

We will now consider some methods for loading into LOBS. This is not a LONG, or LONG RAW field, but rather the preferred data types of BLOB and CLOB. These data types were introduced in Oracle 8.0 and upward, and support a much richer interface/set of functionality than the legacy LONG and LONG RAW types.

We will investigate two methods for loading these fields – SQLLDR and PL/SQL. Others exist, such as Java streams, Pro*C, and OCI. In fact, if you look at Chapter 18 on *C-Based External Procedures*, we review how to unload a LOB using Pro*C. Loading a LOB would be very similar except that instead of using EXEC SQL READ, we would use EXEC SQL WRITE.

We will begin working with the PL/SQL method of loading LOBs, and then look at using SQLLDR to load them as well.

Load a LOB via PL/SQL

The DBMS_LOB package has an entry point called LOADFROMFILE. This procedure allows us to utilize a BFILE (which can read OS files) to populate a BLOB or CLOB in the database. In order to use this procedure, we will need to create a DIRECTORY object in the database. This object will allow us to create BFILES (and open them) that point to a file existing on the file system, which the database server has access to. This last point '... the database server has access to' is a key point when using PL/SQL to load LOBS. The DBMS_LOB package executes entirely in the server. It can only see file systems the server can see. It cannot, in particular, see your local file system if you are accessing Oracle over the network.

Using PL/SQL to load a LOB is not appropriate, as the data to be loaded is not on the server machine.

So we need to begin by creating a DIRECTORY object in the database. This is straightforward to do. I will create two directories for this example (examples executed in a UNIX environment this time):

```
ops$tkyte@DEV816> create or replace directory dir1   as '/tmp/';

Directory created.

ops$tkyte@DEV816> create or replace directory "dir2" as '/tmp/';

Directory created.
```

The user that performs this operation needs to have the CREATE ANY DIRECTORY privilege. The reason I created two directories is to demonstrate a common case-related issue with regards to directory objects. When Oracle created the first directory DIR1 above it stored the object name in *uppercase* as it is the default. In the second example with DIR2, it will have created the directory object preserving the case I used in the name. Why this is important will be demonstrated below when we use the BFILE object.

Now, we want to load some data into either a BLOB or a CLOB. The method for doing so is rather easy, for example:

```
ops$tkyte@DEV816> create table demo
  2  ( id        int primary key,
  3    theClob   clob
  4  )
  5  /

Table created.

ops$tkyte@DEV816> host echo 'Hello World\!' > /tmp/test.txt

ops$tkyte@DEV816> declare
  2      l_clob    clob;
  3      l_bfile   bfile;
  4  begin
  5      insert into demo values ( 1, empty_clob() )
  6      returning theclob into l_clob;
  7
  8      l_bfile := bfilename( 'DIR1', 'test.txt' );
  9      dbms_lob.fileopen( l_bfile );
 10
 11      dbms_lob.loadfromfile( l_clob, l_bfile,
 12                             dbms_lob.getlength( l_bfile ) );
 13
 14      dbms_lob.fileclose( l_bfile );
 15  end;
 16  /

PL/SQL procedure successfully completed.

ops$tkyte@DEV816> select dbms_lob.getlength(theClob), theClob from demo
  2  /
```

```
DBMS_LOB.GETLENGTH(THECLOB) THECLOB
-------------------------- ---------------
                        13 Hello World!
```

It might be interesting to note that if you run the example as is on Windows (changing /tmp/ to an appropriate directory for that OS of course) the output will be:

```
tkyte@TKYTE816> select dbms_lob.getlength(theClob), theClob from demo
  2  /

DBMS_LOB.GETLENGTH(THECLOB) THECLOB
-------------------------- --------------------
                        18 'Hello World\!'
```

The length is larger due to the fact that the Windows shell does not treat quotes and escapes (\) in the same fashion as UNIX, and the end of line character is longer.

Walking through the code above we see:

❑   On lines 5, 6, 7, and 8, we created a row in our table, set the CLOB to an EMPTY_CLOB(), and retrieved its value in one call. With the exception of temporary LOBs, LOBs 'live' in the database – we cannot write to a LOB variable without having a point to either a temporary LOB, or a LOB that is already in the database. An EMPTY_CLOB() is not a Null CLOB – it is a valid non-Null pointer to an empty structure. The other thing this did for us was to get a LOB locator, which points to data in a row that is locked. If we were to have selected this value out without locking the underlying row, our attempts to write to it would fail because LOBs must be locked prior to writing (unlike other structured data). By inserting the row, we have of course locked the row. If this were coming from an existing row, we would have selected FOR UPDATE to lock it.

❑   On line 10, we create a BFILE object. Note how we use DIR1 in uppercase – this is key, as we will see in a moment. This is because we are passing to BFILENAME the *name* of an object, not the object itself. Therefore, we must ensure the name matches the case Oracle has stored for this object.

❑   On line 11, we open the LOB. This will allow us to read it.

❑   On line 12, we load the entire contents of the operating system file /tmp/test.txt into the LOB locator we just inserted. We use DBMS_LOB.GETLENGTH to tell the LOADFROMFILE routine how many bytes of the BFILE to load (all of them).

❑   Lastly, on line 13, we close the BFILE we opened, and the CLOB is loaded.

If we had attempted to use dir1 instead of DIR1 in the above example, we would have encountered the following error:

```
ops$tkyte@DEV816> declare
  2      l_clob    clob;
  3      l_bfile   bfile;
  4  begin
  5      insert into demo values ( 1, empty_clob() )
  6      returning theclob into l_clob;
  7
```

```
    8          l_bfile := bfilename( 'DIR1', 'test.txt' );
    9          dbms_lob.fileopen( l_bfile );
   10
   11          dbms_lob.loadfromfile( l_clob, l_bfile,
   12                                 dbms_lob.getlength( l_bfile ) );
   13
   14          dbms_lob.fileclose( l_bfile );
   15   end;
   16   /
declare
*
ERROR at line 1:
ORA-22285: non-existent directory or file for FILEOPEN operation
ORA-06512: at "SYS.DBMS_LOB", line 475
ORA-06512: at line 9
```

This is because the directory `dir1` does not exist – DIR1 does. If you prefer to use directory names in mixed case, you would use quoted identifiers when creating them as I did above for `dir2`. This will allow you to write code as shown here:

```
ops$tkyte@DEV816> declare
    2          l_clob     clob;
    3          l_bfile    bfile;
    4   begin
    5        insert into demo values ( 2, empty_clob() )
    6        returning theclob into l_clob;
    7
    8        l_bfile := bfilename( 'dir2', 'test.txt' );
    9        dbms_lob.fileopen( l_bfile );
   10
   11        dbms_lob.loadfromfile( l_clob, l_bfile,
   12                               dbms_lob.getlength( l_bfile ) );
   13
   14        dbms_lob.fileclose( l_bfile );
   15   end;
   16   /

PL/SQL procedure successfully completed.
```

There are methods other than LOADFROMFILE by which you can populate a LOB using PL/SQL. LOADFROMFILE is by far the easiest if you are going to load the entire file. If you need to process the contents of the file while loading it, you may also use DBMS_LOB.READ on the BFILE to read the data. The use of UTL_RAW.CAST_TO_VARCHAR2 is handy here if the data you are reading is in fact text, not RAW. See the appendix on *Necessary Supplied Packages* for more info on UTL_RAW. You may then use DBMS_LOB.WRITE or WRITEAPPEND to place the data into a CLOB or BLOB.

Load LOB Data via SQLLDR

We will now investigate how to load data into a LOB via SQLLDR. There is more than one method for doing this, but we will investigate the two most common:

❑   When the data is 'inline' with the rest of the data.

❑   When the data is stored out of line, and the input data contains a filename to be loaded with the row. This is also known as **secondary data files** (**SDF**s) in SQLLDR terminology.

We will start with data that is inline.

Load LOB Data that is Inline

These LOBS will typically have newlines and other special characters embedded in them. Therefore, you will almost always be using one of the four methods detailed above in the *Load Data with Embedded Newlines* section to load this data. Lets begin by modifying the DEPT table to have a CLOB instead of a big VARCHAR2 field for the COMMENTS column:

```
tkyte@TKYTE816> truncate table dept;

Table truncated.

tkyte@TKYTE816> alter table dept drop column comments;

Table altered.

tkyte@TKYTE816> alter table dept add comments clob;

Table altered.
```

For example, I have a data file (demo21.dat) that has the following contents:

```
10, Sales,Virginia,01-april-2001,This is the Sales
Office in Virginia|
20,Accounting,Virginia,13/04/2001,This is the Accounting
Office in Virginia|
30,Consulting,Virginia,14/04/2001 12:02:02,This is the Consulting
Office in Virginia|
40,Finance,Virginia,987268297,"This is the Finance
Office in Virginia, it has embedded commas and is
much longer than the other comments field. If you
feel the need to add double quoted text in here like
this: ""You will need to double up those quotes!"" to
preserve them in the string. This field keeps going for up to
1000000 bytes or until we hit the magic end of record marker,
the | followed by a end of line - it is right here ->"|
```

Each record ends with a pipe (|), followed by the end of line marker. If read, the text for department 40 is much longer than the rest, with many newlines, embedded quotes, and commas. Given this data file, I can create a control file such as this:

```
LOAD DATA
INFILE demo21.dat "str X'7C0D0A'"
INTO TABLE DEPT
REPLACE
FIELDS TERMINATED BY ',' OPTIONALLY ENCLOSED BY '"'
TRAILING NULLCOLS
(DEPTNO,
   DNAME         "upper(:dname)",
   LOC           "upper(:loc)",
   LAST_UPDATED  "my_to_date( :last_updated )",
   COMMENTS      char(1000000)
)
```

This example is from Windows where the end of line marker is two bytes, hence the STR setting in the above control file. On UNIX it would just be `'7C0A'`.

To load the datafile I specified CHAR(1000000) on column COMMENTS since SQLLDR defaults to CHAR(255) for any input field. The CHAR(1000000) will allow SQLLDR to handle up to 1000000 bytes of input text. You must set this to a value which is larger than any expected chunk of text in the input file. Reviewing the loaded data we see:

```
tkyte@TKYTE816> select comments from dept;

COMMENTS
--------------------------------------------------------------------
This is the Accounting
Office in Virginia

This is the Consulting
Office in Virginia

This is the Finance
Office in Virginia, it has embedded commas and is
much longer then the other comments field.  If you
feel the need to add double quoted text in here like
this: "You will need to double up those quotes!" to
preserve them in the string.  This field keeps going for upto
1,000,000 bytes or until we hit the magic end of record marker,
the | followed by a end of line -- it is right here ->

This is the Sales
Office in Virginia
```

The one thing to observe here is that the doubled up quotes are no longer doubled up. SQLLDR removed the extra quotes we placed there.

Load LOB Data that is Out of Line

A common scenario is to have a data file that contains the names of files to load into the LOBs, instead of having the LOB data mixed in with the structured data. This offers a greater degree of flexibility, as the data file given to SQLLDR does not have to use one of the four methods to get around having embedded newlines in the input data, as would frequently happen with large amounts of text or binary data. SQLLDR calls this type of additional data file a LOBFILE.

SQLLDR can also support the loading of a structured data file that points to another, single data file. We can tell SQLLDR how to parse LOB data from this other file, so that each row in the structured data gets loaded with a piece of it. I find this mode to be of limited use (I've never found a use for it myself to date) and will not be discussing it here. SQLLDR refers to these externally referenced files as complex secondary data files.

LOBFILES are relatively simple data files aimed at facilitating LOB loading. The attribute that distinguishes LOBFILEs from the main data files, is that in LOBFILEs, there is no concept of a record, hence newlines never get in the way. In LOBFILEs, the data is in any of the following formats:

❑ Fixed length fields (for example, load bytes 100 through 1000 from the LOBFILE).

❑ Delimited fields (terminated by something or enclosed by something).

❑ Length-value pairs, a varying length field.

The most common of these types will be the delimited fields, ones that are terminated by EOF (end of file) in fact. Typically, you have a directory full of files you would like to load into LOB columns – each file in its entirety will go into a BLOB. The LOBFILE statement with TERMINATED BY EOF is what you will use.

So, lets say you have a directory full of files you would like to load into the database. You would like to load the OWNER of the file, the TIMESTAMP of the file, the NAME of the file, and the file itself. Our table we would load into would be:

```
tkyte@TKYTE816> create table lob_demo
  2  ( owner      varchar2(255),
  3    timestamp  date,
  4    filename   varchar2(255),
  5    text       clob
  6  )
  7  /

Table created.
```

Using a simple ls -l on Unix, and dir /q /n on Windows, we can generate our input file, and load it using a control file such as this on Unix:

```
LOAD DATA
INFILE *
REPLACE
INTO TABLE LOB_DEMO
( owner      position(16:24),
  timestamp  position(34:45) date "Mon DD HH24:MI",
  filename   position(47:100),
  text       LOBFILE(filename) TERMINATED BY EOF
)
BEGINDATA
-rw-r--r--   1 tkyte        1785 Sep 27 12:56 demo10.log
-rw-r--r--   1 tkyte        1674 Sep 19 15:57 demo2.log
-rw-r--r--   1 tkyte        1637 Sep 17 14:43 demo3.log
-rw-r--r--   1 tkyte        2385 Sep 17 15:05 demo4.log
-rw-r--r--   1 tkyte        2048 Sep 17 15:32 demo5.log
-rw-r--r--   1 tkyte        1801 Sep 17 15:56 demo6.log
-rw-r--r--   1 tkyte        1753 Sep 17 16:03 demo7.log
-rw-r--r--   1 tkyte        1759 Sep 17 16:41 demo8.log
-rw-r--r--   1 tkyte        1694 Sep 17 16:27 demo8a.log
-rw-r--r--   1 tkyte        1640 Sep 24 16:17 demo9.log
```

or on Windows, it would be:

```
LOAD DATA
INFILE *
REPLACE
INTO TABLE LOB_DEMO
( owner      position(40:61),
  timestamp  position(1:18)
             "to_date(:timestamp||'m','mm/dd/yyyy  hh:miam')",
  filename   position(63:80),
```

```
     text LOBFILE(filename) TERMINATED BY EOF
)
BEGINDATA
04/14/2001   12:36p              1,697 BUILTIN\Administrators demo10.log
04/14/2001   12:42p              1,785 BUILTIN\Administrators demo11.log
04/14/2001   12:47p              2,470 BUILTIN\Administrators demo12.log
04/14/2001   12:56p              2,062 BUILTIN\Administrators demo13.log
04/14/2001   12:58p              2,022 BUILTIN\Administrators demo14.log
04/14/2001   01:38p              2,091 BUILTIN\Administrators demo15.log
04/14/2001   04:29p              2,024 BUILTIN\Administrators demo16.log
04/14/2001   05:31p              2,005 BUILTIN\Administrators demo17.log
04/14/2001   05:40p              2,005 BUILTIN\Administrators demo18.log
04/14/2001   07:19p              2,003 BUILTIN\Administrators demo19.log
04/14/2001   07:29p              2,011 BUILTIN\Administrators demo20.log
04/15/2001   11:26a              2,047 BUILTIN\Administrators demo21.log
04/14/2001   11:17a              1,612 BUILTIN\Administrators demo4.log
```

Notice we did not load a DATE into the timestamp column, we needed to use a SQL function to massage the Windows date format into one that the database could use. Now, if we inspect the contents of the LOB_DEMO table after running SQLLDR, well discover:

```
tkyte@TKYTE816> select owner, timestamp, filename, dbms_lob.getlength(text)
  2  from lob_demo;

OWNER                   TIMESTAMP FILENAME   DBMS_LOB.GETLENGTH(TEXT)
----------------------- --------- ---------- ------------------------
BUILTIN\Administrators  14-APR-01 demo10.log                     1697
BUILTIN\Administrators  14-APR-01 demo11.log                     1785
BUILTIN\Administrators  14-APR-01 demo12.log                     2470
BUILTIN\Administrators  14-APR-01 demo4.log                      1612
BUILTIN\Administrators  14-APR-01 demo13.log                     2062
BUILTIN\Administrators  14-APR-01 demo14.log                     2022
BUILTIN\Administrators  14-APR-01 demo15.log                     2091
BUILTIN\Administrators  14-APR-01 demo16.log                     2024
BUILTIN\Administrators  14-APR-01 demo17.log                     2005
BUILTIN\Administrators  14-APR-01 demo18.log                     2005
BUILTIN\Administrators  14-APR-01 demo19.log                     2003
BUILTIN\Administrators  14-APR-01 demo20.log                     2011
BUILTIN\Administrators  15-APR-01 demo21.log                     2047

13 rows selected.
```

This works with BLOBs as well as LOBs. Loading a directory of images using SQLLDR in this fashion is easy.

Load LOB Data into Object Columns

Now that we know how to load into a simple table we have created ourselves, we might also find the need to load into a table that has a complex object type with a LOB in it. This happens most frequently when using the interMedia image capabilities or the Virage Image Cartridge (VIR) with the database. Both use a complex object type ORDSYS.ORDIMAGE as a database column. We need to be able to tell SQLLDR how to load into this. In order to load a LOB into an ORDIMAGE type column, we must understand a little more of the structure of the ORDIMAGE type. Using a table we want to load into, and a DESCRIBE on that table in SQL*PLUS, we can discover that we have a column called IMAGE of type

ORDSYS.ORDIMAGE, which we want to ultimately load into IMAGE.SOURCE.LOCALDATA. The following examples will only work if you have interMedia, or the Virage Image Cartridge installed and configured, otherwise the data type ORDSYS.ORDIMAGE will be an unknown type:

```
ops$tkyte@ORA8I.WORLD> create table image_load(
  2      id number,
  3      name varchar2(255),
  4      image ordsys.ordimage
  5  )
  6  /

Table created.

ops$tkyte@ORA8I.WORLD> desc image_load
 Name                                     Null?    Type
 ---------------------------------------- -------- ----------------------------
 ID                                                NUMBER
 NAME                                              VARCHAR2(255)
 IMAGE                                             ORDSYS.ORDIMAGE

ops$tkyte@ORA8I.WORLD> desc ordsys.ordimage
 Name                                     Null?    Type
 ---------------------------------------- -------- ----------------------------
 SOURCE                                            ORDSOURCE
 HEIGHT                                            NUMBER(38)
 WIDTH                                             NUMBER(38)
 CONTENTLENGTH                                     NUMBER(38)
 ...

ops$tkyte@ORA8I.WORLD> desc ordsys.ordsource
 Name                                     Null?    Type
 ---------------------------------------- -------- ----------------------------
 LOCALDATA                                         BLOB
 SRCTYPE                                           VARCHAR2(4000)
 SRCLOCATION                                       VARCHAR2(4000)
 ...
```

so, a control file to load this might look like this:

```
LOAD DATA
INFILE *
INTO TABLE image_load
REPLACE
FIELDS TERMINATED BY ','
( ID,
  NAME,
  file_name FILLER,
  IMAGE column object
  (
    SOURCE column object
    (
      LOCALDATA LOBFILE (file_name) TERMINATED BY EOF
             NULLIF file_name = 'NONE'
    )
  )
```

```
    )
    BEGINDATA
    1,icons,icons.gif
```

In the above, I have introduced two new constructs:

❑ COLUMN OBJECT – This tells SQLLDR that this is not a column name, but rather part of a column name. It is not mapped to a field in the input file, but is rather used to build the correct object column reference to be used during the load. In the above, we have two column object tag's one nested in the other. Therefore, the column name that will be used its IMAGE.SOURCE.LOCALDATA, as we need it to be. Note that we are not loading any of the other attributes of these two object types. For example, IMAGE.HEIGHT, IMAGE.CONTENTLENGTH, IMAGE.SOURCE.SRCTYPE. Below, we'll see how to get those populated.

❑ NULLIF FILE_NAME = 'NONE' – This tells SQLLDR to load a Null into the object column in the event that the field FILE_NAME contains the word NONE in it.

Once you have loaded an interMedia type, you will typically need to post-process the loaded data using PL/SQL to have interMedia operate on it. For example, with the above, you would probably want to run the following to have the properties for the image set up correctly:

```
begin
    for c in ( select * from image_load ) loop
        c.image.setproperties;
    end loop;
end;
/
```

SETPROPERTIES is an object method provided by the ORDSYS.ORDIMAGE type, which processes the image itself, and updates the remaining attributes of the object with appropriate values. See Chapter 17 on *interMedia* for more information regarding image manipulation.

Load VARRAYS/Nested Tables with SQLLDR

We will now look at how to load VARRAYS and nested table types with SQLLDR. Basically, VARRAYS and nested table types (just called arrays from now on) will typically be encoded into the input file as follows:

❑ A field will be included in the data file. This field will contain the number of array elements to expect in the data file. This field will not be loaded, but will be used by SQLLDR to figure out how many array elements are coming in the file.

❑ Followed by a (set of) field(s) representing the elements of the array.

So, we expect arrays of a varying length to be encoded in the input data file with a field that tells us how many elements are coming, and then the elements themselves. We can also load array data when there are a fixed number of array elements in each record (for example, each input record will have five array elements). We will look at both methods using the types below:

```
tkyte@TKYTE816> create type myArrayType
  2  as varray(10) of number(12,2)
  3  /
```

```
Type created.

tkyte@TKYTE816> create table t
  2  ( x int primary key, y myArrayType )
  3  /

Table created.
```

This is the schema that we want to load our data into. Now, here is a sample control/data file we can use to load it. This demonstrates the varying number of array elements. Each input record will be in the format:

- Value of `x`.

- Number of elements in `y`.

- Repeating field representing the individual elements of `y`.

```
LOAD DATA
INFILE *
INTO TABLE t
replace
fields terminated by ","
(
  x,
  y_cnt                FILLER,
  y                    varray count (y_cnt)
  (
    y
  )
)

BEGINDATA
1,2,3,4
2,10,1,2,3,4,5,6,7,8,9,10
3,5,5,4,3,2,1
```

Note that in the above, we used the keyword FILLER to allow us to map a variable Y_CNT in the input file but not load this field. We also used the keywords VARRAY COUNT (Y_CNT) to tell SQLLDR that y is a VARRAY. If Y was a nested table, we would have used NESTED TABLE COUNT(Y_CNT) instead. Also note that these are SQLLDR keywords, not SQL functions, so we do not use quotes or colons for bind variables as we would with a SQL function.

The key thing to note in the input data is the inclusion of the COUNT. It tells SQLLDR how to size the array we are loading. For example, given the input line:

```
1,2,3,4
```

we will get:

- 1 – mapped to x, the primary key.

- 2 – mapped to y_cnt, the count of array elements.

- 3,4 – mapped to y, the array elements themselves.

After running SQLLDR, we find:

```
tkyte@TKYTE816> select * from t;

        X Y
---------- -----------------------------------------------
        1 MYARRAYTYPE(3, 4)
        2 MYARRAYTYPE(1, 2, 3, 4, 5, 6, 7, 8, 9, 10)
        3 MYARRAYTYPE(5, 4, 3, 2, 1)
```

This is exactly what we wanted. Now, lets say you wanted to load an input file where there are a fixed number of array elements. For example, you have an ID, and five observations to go along with this ID. We can use a type/table combination such as:

```
tkyte@TKYTE816> create or replace type myTableType
  2  as table of number(12,2)
  3  /

Type created.

tkyte@TKYTE816> create table t
  2  ( x int primary key, y myTableType )
  3  nested table y store as y_tab
  4  /

Table created.
```

The control file will look like this. Note the use of CONSTANT 5 in the nested table count construct. This is what tells SQLLDR how many elements to expect for each record now:

```
LOAD DATA
INFILE *
INTO TABLE t
replace
fields terminated by ","
(
  x,
  y                       nested table count (CONSTANT 5)
  (
    y
  )
)

BEGINDATA
1,100,200,300,400,500
2,123,243,542,123,432
3,432,232,542,765,543
```

and after executing SQLLDR, we find:

```
tkyte@TKYTE816> select * from t;

    X Y
--------- -------------------------------------------
        1 MYTABLETYPE(100, 200, 300, 400, 500)
        2 MYTABLETYPE(123, 243, 542, 123, 432)
        3 MYTABLETYPE(432, 232, 542, 765, 543)
```

This shows the data loaded up into our nested table. As a side note (getting away from SQLLDR for a moment), we can observe one of the properties of a nested table. I discovered by accident, that if we *reload* the table using SQLLDR and this sample data, we get a slightly different end result:

```
tkyte@TKYTE816> host sqlldr userid=tkyte/tkyte control=demo24.ctl
SQLLDR: Release 8.1.6.0.0 - Production on Sun Apr 15 12:06:56 2001

(c) Copyright 1999 Oracle Corporation.  All rights reserved.

Commit point reached - logical record count 3

tkyte@TKYTE816> select * from t;

    X Y
--------- -------------------------------------------
        1 MYTABLETYPE(200, 300, 400, 500, 100)
        2 MYTABLETYPE(123, 243, 542, 123, 432)
        3 MYTABLETYPE(432, 232, 542, 765, 543)
```

Notice how the number 100 is *last* in the first nested table. This is just a side effect of the way space happened to be reused in the table during the second load. It may (or may not) reproduce on all systems with all block sizes, it just happened that for me, it did. Nested tables do not preserve order, so do not be surprised when the nested table data comes out in an order different from the way you loaded it!

Call SQLLDR from a Stored Procedure

The short answer is that you cannot do this. SQLLDR is not an API, it is not something that is callable. SQLLDR is a command line program. You can definitely write an external procedure in Java or C that runs SQLLDR (see Chapter 19 on *Java Stored Procedures* for running a command at the OS level), but that won't be the same as 'calling' SQLLDR. The load will happen in another session, and will not be subject to your transaction control. Additionally, you will have to parse the resulting log file to determine if the load was successful or not, and how successful (how many rows got loaded before an error terminated the load) it may have been. Invoking SQLLDR from a stored procedure is not something I would recommend.

So, lets say you have a requirement to load data via a stored procedure. What are your options? The ones that come to mind are:

❑ Write a mini-SQLLDR in PL/SQL. It can either use BFILES to read binary data, or UTL_FILE to read text data to parse and load. We will demonstrate this here.

❑ Write a mini-SQLLDR in Java. This can be a little more sophisticated than a PL/SQL-based loader, and can make use of the many available Java routines.

❑ Write a SQLLDR in C, and call it as an external procedure.

I've put these in order of complexity and performance. As the complexity increases, so will the performance in many cases. It will be the case that PL/SQL and Java will be comparable in performance, and C will be faster (but less portable and harder to construct and install). I am a fan of simplicity and portability so I will demonstrate the idea using PL/SQL. It will be surprising how easy it is to write our own mini-SQLLDR. For example:

```
ops$tkyte@DEV816> create table badlog( errm varchar2(4000),
  2                             data varchar2(4000) );

Table created.
```

is a table we will use to place the records we could not load. Next, we have the function we will build:

```
ops$tkyte@DEV816> create or replace
  2  function  load_data( p_table       in varchar2,
  3                        p_cnames      in varchar2,
  4                        p_dir         in varchar2,
  5                        p_filename    in varchar2,
  6                        p_delimiter   in varchar2 default '|' )
  7  return number
```

It takes as input the name of the table to load into, the list of column names in the order they appear in the input file, the directory, the name of the file to load, and the delimiter, in other words, what separates the data files in the input file. The return value from this routine is the number of successfully loaded records. Next we have the local variables for this small routine:

```
  8  is
  9      l_input        utl_file.file_type;
 10      l_theCursor    integer default dbms_sql.open_cursor;
 11      l_buffer       varchar2(4000);
 12      l_lastLine     varchar2(4000);
 13      l_status       integer;
 14      l_colCnt       number default 0;
 15      l_cnt          number default 0;
 16      l_sep          char(1) default NULL;
 17      l_errmsg       varchar2(4000);
 18  begin
```

Next, we open the input file. We are expecting simple delimited data, and lines that are no larger than 4000 bytes. This limit could be raised to 32 KB (the maximum supported by UTL_FILE). To go larger, you would need to use a BFILE, and the DBMS_LOB package:

```
 19          /*
 20           * This will be the file we read the data from.
 21           * We are expecting simple delimited data.
 22           */
 23          l_input := utl_file.fopen( p_dir, p_filename, 'r', 4000 );
```

Now we build an INSERT TABLE that looks like INSERT INTO TABLE (COLUMNS) VALUES (BINDS). We determine the number of columns we are inserting by counting commas. This is done by taking the current length of the list of column names, subtracting the length of the same string with commas removed, and adding 1 (a generic way to count the number of a specific character in a string):

```
24
25        l_buffer := 'insert into ' || p_table ||
26                    '(' || p_cnames || ') values ( ';
27            /*
28             * This counts commas by taking the current length
29             * of the list of column names, subtracting the
30             * length of the same string with commas removed, and
31             * adding 1.
32             */
33        l_colCnt := length(p_cnames)-
34                        length(replace(p_cnames,',',''))+1;
35
36        for i in 1 .. l_colCnt
37        loop
38            l_buffer := l_buffer || l_sep || ':b'||i;
39            l_sep      := ',';
40        end loop;
41        l_buffer := l_buffer || ')';
42
43            /*
44             * We now have a string that looks like:
45             * insert into T ( c1,c2,... ) values ( :b1, :b2, ... )
46             */
```

Now that we have the string that is our INSERT statement, we parse it:

```
47        dbms_sql.parse(  l_theCursor, l_buffer, dbms_sql.native );
```

and then read each line of the input file, and break it into the individual columns:

```
48
49        loop
50            /*
51             * Read data and exit there is when no more.
52             */
53            begin
54                utl_file.get_line( l_input, l_lastLine );
55            exception
56                when NO_DATA_FOUND then
57                    exit;
58            end;
59            /*
60             * It makes it easy to parse when the line ends
61             * with a delimiter.
62             */
63            l_buffer := l_lastLine || p_delimiter;
64
65
66            for i in 1 .. l_colCnt
67            loop
68                dbms_sql.bind_variable( l_theCursor, ':b'||i,
69                            substr( l_buffer, 1,
70                                instr(l_buffer,p_delimiter)-1 ) );
71                l_buffer := substr( l_buffer,
```

```
72                              instr(l_buffer,p_delimiter)+1 );
73          end loop;
74
75          /*
76           * Execute the insert statement. In the event of an error
77           * put it into the "bad" file.
78           */
79          begin
80              l_status := dbms_sql.execute(l_theCursor);
81              l_cnt := l_cnt + 1;
82          exception
83              when others then
84                  l_errmsg := sqlerrm;
85                  insert into badlog ( errm, data )
86                  values ( l_errmsg, l_lastLine );
87          end;
88      end loop;
```

Now that we have loaded every record possible, and placing any we could not back into the BAD table, we clean up and return:

```
89
90      /*
91       * close up and commit
92       */
93      dbms_sql.close_cursor(l_theCursor);
94      utl_file.fclose( l_input );
95      commit;
96
97      return l_cnt;
98  exception
99          when others then
100         dbms_sql.close_cursor(l_theCursor);
101                 if ( utl_file.is_open( l_input ) ) then
102                         utl_file.fclose(l_input);
103                 end if;
104                 RAISE;
105 end load_data;
106 /

Function created.
```

We can use the above as follows:

```
ops$tkyte@DEV816> create table t1 ( x int, y int, z int );

Table created.

ops$tkyte@DEV816> host echo 1,2,3 > /tmp/t1.dat
ops$tkyte@DEV816> host echo 4,5,6 >> /tmp/t1.dat
ops$tkyte@DEV816> host echo 7,8,9 >> /tmp/t1.dat
ops$tkyte@DEV816> host echo 7,NotANumber,9 >> /tmp/t1.dat

ops$tkyte@DEV816> begin
```

```
   2     dbms_output.put_line(
   3         load_data( 'T1',
   4                    'x,y,z',
   5                    'c:\temp',
   6                    't1.dat',
   7                    ',' ) || ' rows loaded' );
   8  end;
   9  /
3 rows loaded

PL/SQL procedure successfully completed.

ops$tkyte@DEV816> SELECT *
   2    FROM BADLOG;

ERRM                                     DATA
-------------------------------- --------------------
ORA-01722: invalid number          7,NotANumber,9

ops$tkyte@DEV816> select * from badlog;

         X          Y          Z
---------- ---------- ----------
         1          2          3
         4          5          6
         7          8          9
```

Now, this is not as powerful as SQLLDR, since we didn't have a way to specify the maximum number of errors, or where to put the bad records, or what might be a field enclosure, and so on, but you can see how easy it would be to add such features. For example, to add a field enclosure would be as easy as adding a parameter P_ENCLOSED_BY and change the DBMS_SQL.BIND call to be:

```
loop
    dbms_sql.bind_variable( l_theCursor, ':b'||i,
    trim( nvl(p_enclosed_by,chr(0)) FROM
                    substr( l_buffer, 1,
                        instr(l_buffer,p_delimiter)-1 ) );
    l_buffer := substr( l_buffer,
                    instr(l_buffer,p_delimiter)+1 );
end loop;
```

You now have the OPTIONALLY ENCLOSED BY option of SQLLDR. The above routine is adequate for loading small amounts of data, as noted in Chapter 16 on *Dynamic SQL*, though we should employ array processing in this routine if we need to scale it up. Refer to this chapter for examples of using array processing for inserts.

At the Apress web site you will find an additional mini-SQLLDR written in PL/SQL. This one was developed to facilitate the loading of dBASE format files. It employs BFILES as the input source (dBASE files contain 1, 2, and 4 byte binary integers that UTL_FILE cannot handle) and can either describe what is in a dBASE file, or load the contents of the dBASE file into the database.

Caveats

Here we will look at some things that you have to watch out for when using SQLLDR.

You Cannot Pick a Rollback Segment to Use

Often, you will use SQLLDR with the option REPLACE, when loading. What this does is issue a DELETE, prior loading the data. The data may generate an enormous amount of rollback. You might want to use a specific rollback segment to use in order to perform this operation. SQLLDR has no facility to permit that. You must ensure any rollback segment is large enough to accommodate the DELETE, or use the TRUNCATE option instead. Since an INSERT does not generate much rollback, and SQLLDR commits frequently, this issue really only applies to the REPLACE option.

TRUNCATE Appears to Work Differently

The TRUNCATE option of SQLLDR might appear to work differently than TRUNCATE does in SQL*PLUS, or any other tool. SQLLDR, working on the assumption you will be reloading the table with a similar amount of data, uses the extended form of TRUNCATE. Specifically, it issues:

```
truncate table t reuse storage
```

The REUSE STORAGE option does not release allocated extents – it just marks them as 'free space'. If this were not the desired outcome, you would truncate the table prior to executing SQLLDR.

SQLLDR Defaults to CHAR(255)

The default length of input fields is 255 characters. If your field is longer than this, you will receive an error message:

```
Record N: Rejected - Error on table T, column C.
Field in data file exceeds maximum length
```

This does not mean the data will not fit into the database column, but rather SQLLDR was expecting 255 bytes or less of input data, and received somewhat more than that. The solution is to simply use CHAR(N) in the control file, where N is big enough to accommodate the largest field length in the input file.

Command Line Overrides Control File

Many of the SQLLDR options may be placed in either the control file, or used on the command line. For example, I can use INFILE filename as well as SQLLDR ... DATA=FILENAME. The command line overrides any options in the control file. You cannot count on the options in a control file actually being used, as the person executing SQLLDR can override them.

Summary

In this chapter, we explored many areas of loading data. We covered the typical day to day things we will encounter – the loading of delimited files, loading fixed length files, the loading of a directory full of image files, using functions on input data to transform them, unloading data, and so on. We did not cover massive data loads using the direct path loader in any detail. Rather, we touched lightly on that subject. Our goal was to answer the questions that arise frequently with the use of SQLLDR and affect the broadest audience.

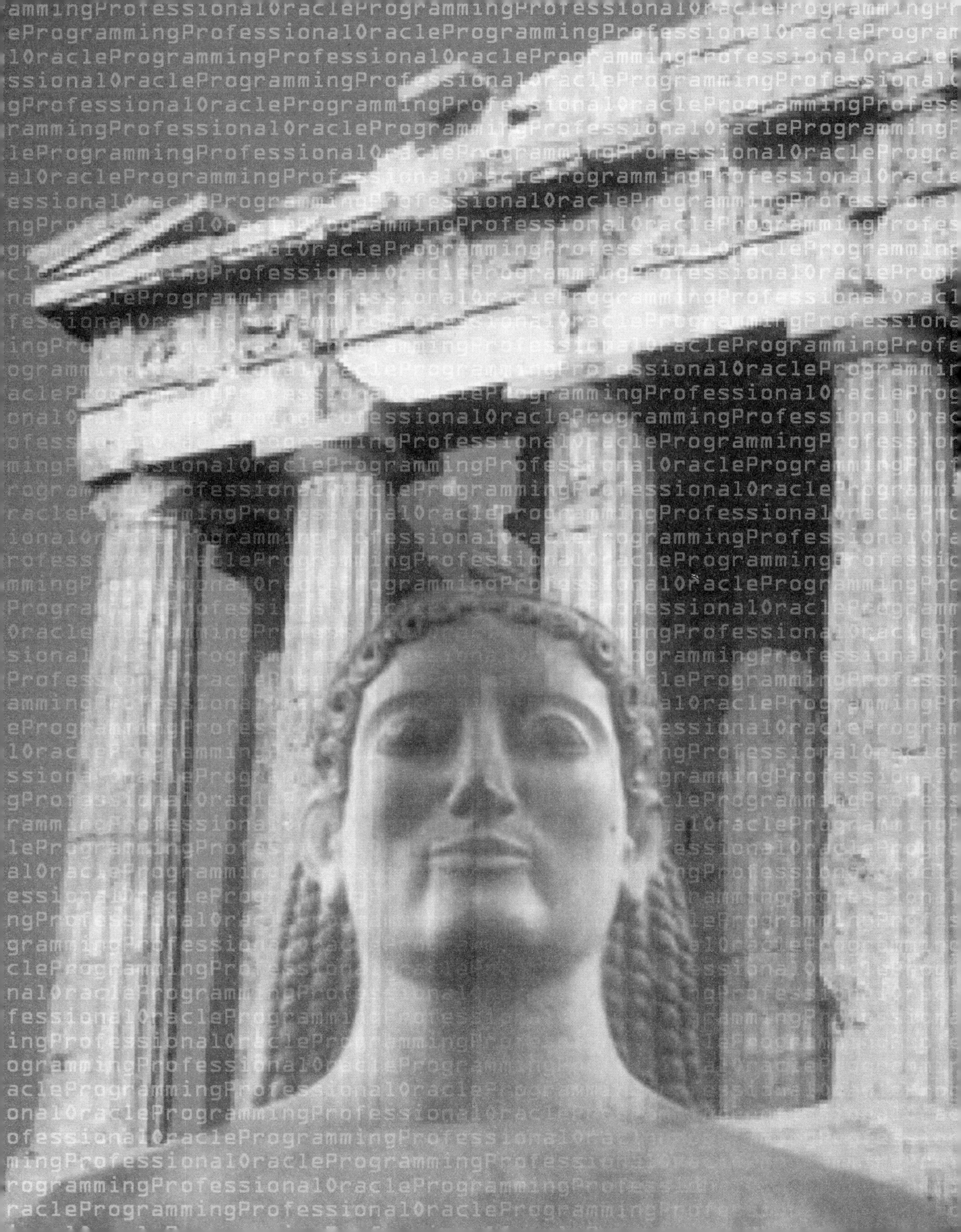

10

Tuning Strategies and Tools

I am extremely familiar with tuning. I spend a lot of time tuning systems, in particular systems that I did not architect or code. This leaves me at a distinct disadvantage; it might take me a while to figure out not only where to look, but also where not to look. Tuning in this way is a very tricky thing, and is usually done under extreme pressure. No one tunes when everything is going OK – they only seem to want to tune, when it is all falling apart.

This chapter describes my approach to tuning and the tools I use. You will see that I adopt a 'defensive' approach – I try to make it so that I never have to tune at all; not after a rollout of an application anyway. Tuning is part of development that starts before the first line of code is ever written and ends the day before deployment; it is not a post deployment activity. Unfortunately, most of the tuning I am called in to do affects production systems that are already developed. This means we are tuning in a somewhat hostile environment (angry end users) and have many undesirable constraints applied to us (it is a production system, they don't like you to shut them down to change something). The best time to tune is well before you get to that point.

Specifically, this chapter will cover:

- ❑ Bind variables and performance.

- ❑ How to trace applications using SQL_TRACE and TIMED_STATISTICS and interpret the results using TKPROF.

- ❑ How to set up and use Statspack to tune the database instance.

- ❑ Some of the V$ tables that I use regularly and how I use them.

Identifying the Problem

Tuning an application can be a very interesting thing indeed. Not only can figuring out where the application is falling apart be difficult, but also implementing the fixes can be even more painful. In some cases, the overall architecture must change. In Chapter 1 on *Developing Successful Oracle Applications*, I described a system that used Oracle's multi-threaded server to execute long running stored procedures. This system needed an architectural overhaul to fix. In other cases, simply finding the worst performing SQL queries and tuning them, is all that it takes.

Not all tuning is database-related. I remember one particularly difficult tuning session where the client was using a commercially available time and attendance application built on top of Oracle. This particular application had quite a few installations at various locations and all was going well elsewhere. At this one location however, the biggest install to date, it was totally falling apart. Most of the time, it ran perfectly, as expected. At peak times, such as shift change and mealtime, a problem would arise – the entire system would periodically appear to hang. There seemed to be no reason why. I knew by observation that it was a locking/contention issue – I could see that clearly. Figuring out why we had locking and contention was the hard part. After spending two days kicking around in the database, looking at all of the V$ tables, reviewing code, and observing the problem, I asked to see the application in action. I understood conceptually what it did, but I didn't know how it did it. The clients took me to the warehouse floor where the end users (the factory workers) used the application. I saw how they actually used it. They would pass in a single file past one of the many terminals and swipe a bar code to clock in. The next person in line would hit the *Enter* key and swipe their card and on this goes. Eventually, as I was standing there, the application hung. No one could swipe their cards anymore. Then, someone walked up to an empty terminal, hit *Enter* and swiped their card – the system was back! Looking closer at the application, it was clear what was happening. It turned out to not be a database tuning issue at all – it was purely a human computer interface issue. The application interface was the cause of the hang. It turns out the system was designed to process a transaction like this:

1. Swipe the card that locked a user row in a table and inserted a row into another table.

2. See the message on screen that said row inserted, please hit enter.

3. You would hit *Enter* and then the application would COMMIT (until then, it would not have COMMITted).

4. Next person swipes the card.

As it turned out, people were doing the following:

1. Swipe the card, and leave the terminal.

2. Next person hits *Enter* for the last person, committing their work, swipes their card and leaves.

When the last person swiped their card, they were leaving a transaction open, which had locked resources. A background process that was running every couple of minutes locked a resource and then tried to lock the same resource that this 'open' transaction had. The background process would halt, but not before it locked some of the resources needed by the interactive application. This would block all of the terminals and the system would 'hang' in this fashion until someone walked by and noticed the Please hit enter to continue message, and hit the *Enter* key. Then everything worked OK. A simple fix in the user interface to commit the transaction solved this issue.

In another case, on my last tuning foray, I was looking at a very large application implementation. There were literally hundreds of people involved in the development, implementation, and deployment of this application. The situation was reaching crisis point (they always are when you are tuning). The complaint: 'The Oracle application is slow.' After taking a look at the application, the environment, and the database, it was not at all obvious where the problem was. After many walkthroughs and application overviews, a couple of possible choke points in the system began to become clear. As it turned out, it wasn't the Oracle application at all – it was an interface to an existing system. The new application was using the existing system in a way no one envisioned. The additional load on the existing system put it over the edge. The new application was killing the old application. It was very difficult to track this down because the code wasn't instrumented heavily (instrumentation meaning something as simple as 'debug' messages or application logs with timings, so you can see what is going on). We had to add a lot of 'after the fact' instrumentation to determine the cause of the slowdown (and eventual shutdown) of the system.

The moral of these stories is that tuning is tricky, and the solutions are not always intuitive. No two tuning exercises are going to be the same; the problems are not always in the database, they are not always in the application, and they are not always in the architecture. Finding them, especially if you do not understand how the application is to be used or how it works, is sometimes 'pure luck'. That's why tuning is considered 'black magic' by some. It is extremely hard to figure out how to tell someone to tune a system if the approach is to tune after the fact. Tuning after the fact requires the investigative skills of a detective, you are unraveling a mystery. It takes a fine mix of technical skills and people skills (no one ever wants to have the finger pointed at them, you have to be careful in this respect). There is no hard and fast roadmap to follow in after the fact tuning. I can tell you, however, how to tune *as* you develop; it is a strategy I will encourage. System tuning to me is a design time activity, something you build into the entire system. Tuning a system after the fact is not really tuning – that is recoding, re-architecting.

My Approach

In this section, I am going to introduce some of the general ideas I have about tuning. If there's one thing considered somewhat as a 'black art' in Oracle, it would be tuning. Anything you do not understand looks like magic. Database tuning is something a lot of people do not understand. I find the art of tuning rather straightforward. I believe there are three levels of tuning we all need to be aware of and follow:

- ❑ **Application tuning part 1** – Tuning your application in isolation. Getting it to run as fast as possible in single user mode.

- ❑ **Application tuning part 2** – Tuning your application in multi-user mode. Getting it to run as concurrently as possible with lots of users.

- ❑ **Database instance/server tuning.**

Application tuning parts 1 and 2 constitute a good *90 percent or more* of the effort. That's right; before we even get the DBA's involved, we the developers have done 90 percent of the work. This is why I think most people do not understand database tuning. They are constantly asking me to come in and tune their database, without touching the applications! Except in the rarest of cases, this is physically impossible. Everyone is in search of what I call the `fast=true init.ora` parameter. This magic parameter will make their database go faster. The sooner you accept the fact that it does not exist, the better off you'll be. It is extremely unlikely that we can make your queries go magically faster by flipping a switch in a parameter file. We may have to reorganize your data, and I'm not talking about moving data files around to speed up I/O, I'm talking about physically rearranging the columns in your tables, the number of tables you have, and what they contain. That is application redesign.

431

There are some issues that have to be tuned at the database level, but experience shows that most of the work is done by us in the applications themselves. It is most likely that only you will be able to take your query that does 1,000,000 logical I/Os to get its answer, and figure out a better query or alternate method to getting that answer. If you have architectural issues, only you will be able to correct or, work around, them.

Tuning is a Constant thing

Once you realize that most tuning is done at the application level, the next step is to determine that tuning is something done continuously. It doesn't have a start point and a stop point. It is part of the design phase, it is part of development, it is part of testing, and it is part of deployment and beyond.

Design for Performance

A database system is not something that can be approached with the 'build it now and tune it later approach'. Far too many decisions will be made in the 'build it' part that will directly impact the ability of the system to perform, and more importantly to scale. Remember I said earlier, 'it is far easier to build a non-scalable system than it is to build a scalable system in Oracle'. Building a non-scalable application is trivial – anyone can do that. It takes work to build one that performs *and* scales well. It must be designed this way from day one.

True story: a group of people developed an application. It was an extension to an existing system. It came with its own set of tables, and used some of the existing tables. The new application is deployed, and immediately, the existing system becomes unusable – the entire system is just too slow to use. It turns out the developers of the new application decided that they would figure out what indexes they needed 'in the field'. Short of primary keys, there wasn't a single index to be found. Virtually every query consisted of multiple full scans. Their question was 'how do we fix this quickly?' The only answer at that point was 'drop your tables and get out of your database.' To this group, tuning was an activity to be undertaken post-development. You get it working, and then you get it working faster. Needless to say, this project was a total failure. The database structures they had developed could not efficiently answer the questions they wanted to ask of it. It was back to square one, and they had to start over.

My approach starts from the very beginning of the application design phase and I would now like to relate a small story that illustrates my approach very well. There was once an internal system where I work called 'phone'. You could telnet into any e-mail machine (back when e-mail was character mode), and on the command line type phone <search string>. It would return data like this:

```
$ phone tkyte
TKYTE    Kyte, Tom           703/555 4567  Managing Technologies RESTON:
```

When the Web exploded in about 1995/1996, our group wrote a small web system that loaded this phone data into a table, and let people search it. Now that it was in a database and had a little GUI to go with it, it started becoming the de-facto standard within the company for looking up people. Over time, we started adding more data to it, and more fields. It really started to catch on. At some point, we decided to add a lot more fields to it, and rebuild the system with more features.

Our goal at this stage was to develop it from the very beginning to perform. We knew it would be a limiting factor in our total system performance. It might have been small in size (application-wise) but it would generate the most traffic on our site. The first thing we did, the very first, based on our knowledge and thoughts of how people would use this simple little system, was to design the tables to hold this data. We specifically designed these tables for what they were going to be used for. We had a little, read-only repository of data that people would be searching, and it needed to be fast. This system was growing in popularity every day, and was threatening to consume our machine with its resources. We had a single 67-column, 75000-row table upon which we wanted to perform a simple string search against various fields. So, if I put in ABC, it would find ABC in the e-mail address, or the first name, or the last name, or the middle name, and so on. Even worse, it was to be interpreted as %ABC%, and the data was in mixed case.

There wasn't an index in the world that could help us here – so we built our own. Every night as we refreshed the data from our HR system (a complete refresh of data), we would also issue:

```
CREATE TABLE FAST_EMPS
PCTFREE 0
CACHE
AS
SELECT upper(last_name)||'/'||upper(first_name)||'/' …. || '/' ||
                substr( phone, length(phone)-4) SEARCH_STRING,
       rowid row_id
  FROM EMPLOYEES
/
```

after we were done. In effect, we build the most dense, compact table possible (pctfree 0), and asked that it be cached if possible. Now, we would query:

```
select *
  from employees
 where rowid in ( select row_id
                    from fast_emp
                   where search_string like :bv
                   and rownum <= 500 )
```

This query would always *full scan* the FAST_EMP table, but we wanted it to. That was, given the types of questions we were using, the only choice. There is no indexing scheme we could use to answer this. Our goal from the outset was to minimize the amount of data that would be scanned, to limit the amount of data people would get back, and to make it as fast as possible. The above accomplishes all three goals. The FAST_EMP table is typically always in the buffer cache. It is small (less than 8 percent the size of the original table), and scans very fast. It has already done the work of the case-insensitive searching for us once (instead of once per query) by storing the data in uppercase. It limits the number of hits to 500 (if your search is broader than that, refine it – you'll *never* look at 500 hits anyway). In effect, that table works a lot like an index for us, since it stores the row ID in employees. There are no indexes employed on this system in order to do this search – just two tables.

This is a perfect example of an application with very particular design considerations – and of how taking these into account at the very beginning can lead to optimum performance.

Try many Approaches

It is crucial to test, to experiment, to try different implementations. 'Theory' is great – but often wrong, implemented tests are much more accurate. Try out your ideas. See what the real world performance is. The database has literally thousands of features. There is no single 'best solution' (if that was the case, then a database vendor would only need to supply this one solution). Sometimes partitioning data will increase performance, at other times it is not. Sometimes interMedia Text can speed up your searches, sometimes not. Sometimes a hash cluster is the best thing in the world, sometimes not. There are *no* 'evil' features (features to be avoided at all costs). Likewise, there are no 'silver bullet' features that solve all problems.

Before settling on this design for the above application, we tried a couple of alternative approaches. We tried using a *fast full scan* on a function-based index (close, but not as fast), we tried interMedia Text (not useful due to the %ABC% requirement), we tried having just an extra field in the base EMPLOYEES table (wiped out the buffer cache, too big to full scan). It seems funny to have spent so much time on this one detail. However, this one query is executed between 150,000 and 250,000 times a day. This is two to three times a second, every second, all day long, assuming a constant flow of traffic. That is not something we can assume – we frequently have spikes in activity as most systems do. If this single query performed poorly, our entire system would fall apart – and it is just one of thousands of queries we have to do. By determining where our weak points would be, the lowest hanging fruit so to say, and concentrating on them, we were able to build an application that scales very well. If we had tried the 'tuning after the fact' principle, we would have really found ourselves re-writing after the fact.

Program Defensively

Instrument your code, and leave it instrumented in production. Instrumentation is the practice of having a way to trace your application from the 'outside'. SQL_TRACE (covered in detail later in the chapter) is an instrumentation tool. The EVENT system within Oracle is an instrumentation tool (an example of EVENTs in Oracle is given below). The Oracle database is heavily instrumented so the Oracle kernel developers can diagnose performance issues without ever having to go onsite. You need this capability in your application as well. The only way to make things go faster is to understand where they are going slow. If you just point at a process and say 'it is going slow', you'll have a hard time tuning it. If the process is heavily instrumented and has the ability to log itself on demand, you'll be able to figure out where things are going slow.

Benchmark

Benchmarking periodically throughout the implementation is critical. Something that works fine with 10 users falls apart with 100 or 1000. Benchmarking is the only way to ensure you can meet your goals.

The first point to note here is that you should have **identified performance metrics from day one**. This is my nightmare: someone wants to do a benchmark and the goal is simply 'go as fast as you can'. This is an open invitation to benchmark for the rest of your life. Everything can always go a little faster. With the 'as fast as you can' goal, you are never done. You need to know what your constraints are, and develop to them. Additionally, if you are constrained to 'go as fast as you can', you also have license to 'go as slow as you want'. You have nothing to measure towards, so whatever you develop is fast enough. That last point should raise some eyebrows – 'as fast as you can' is the same as 'as slow as you want'. Metrics are the only thing that will prevent that from happening.

The first step is to **benchmark in isolation**. If you cannot get it to run fast in single user mode, it will only run slower in real life. Record these benchmarks, compare them to past and future tests. You'll find that a module that used to take 1 second, and now takes 1 minute, much easier this way.

The next step is to **benchmark to scale** and test your application (or your ideas) under your expected load to ensure what you are building scales up. In testing, many people test functionality. When I test, I test for scalability. Now we have all of the modules for our application together for the first time, we need to take the time and the energy to scale it up, and see if it will fly or not. It is at this point that you will discover the queries that do not use bind variables, the locking and contention introduced by the application, the architectural flaws. In a scalability test, these things become obvious – painfully obvious. If you want to be successful when you deploy your application, you will test it for scale before deployment

One thing I hear time and time again is 'we developed against a subset of the data and it ran fine. When we deployed the system in production, everything ran really slow. Help us quick!' In this case, the only thing you can do quickly is to un-deploy the system, and go back to the drawing board. You need to develop the system against the full set of data upon which it will be used. That full scan of 100 rows was no problem for your development machine. Now that it is 100,000 rows, and you have 100 people doing it simultaneously, it is something of a performance issue. You must develop with the real stuff, the real tables, the real security, everything. This is the only way to head off the really bad queries in the beginning. Again, record these benchmarks – you'll quickly discover the implementation that causes performance to nosedive by comparing current results to history. You'll also be able to justify that new piece of hardware/software down the road (it increased throughput by X) – you won't have to guess.

For example, the following sequence of statements work great in isolation:

```
declare
    l_rec t%rowtype;
begin
    select * from T into l_rec from T where rownum = 1 FOR UPDATE;
    process( l_rec );
    delete from t where t.pk = l_rec.pk;
    commit;
end;
```

It processes the first record in a table very quickly. You might time this in isolation and say 'I can do 5 transactions per second (TPS).' You then proceed to 'extrapolate' that number upwards and say 'if we run 10 of these processes, we can do 50 TPS.' The problem is that you will still only do 5 TPS (if that) with 10 processes, as they will all serialize; they all try to lock the first record and only one of them can do this at any one time. Getting something to run fast in isolation is great; getting it to run fast in an environment with many users is another thing all together.

Even if you have a read-only system, in other words, no possibility of a locking issue as above, you must benchmark to scale. Queries need resources – block buffers, I/O from disk, CPU to sort data with, and so on; anything that needs resources must be tested. The row lock from the example above is just a type of resource, there are hundreds of resources to contend for, regardless of the type of system you are building.

And finally, the *last component in the tuning loop* should be the database **instance tuning**. Most people are looking for what I like to call the FAST=TRUE setting in the init.ora file; some simple setting they can make in their database initialization file to make things go faster. *This setting does not exist.* In fact, database instance tuning in my experience will return the least amount of performance increase on a database that has *reasonable* settings already. There are extremely rare instances where the database setup is so bad that instance tuning will materially affect performance, but they are rare indeed (you might have 300 block buffers configured on a data warehouse, and you really needed between 30,000 and 300,000, for example). Application tuning, such as changing the database structures, and implementing better performing algorithms, is where the low hanging fruit is, where the opportunity to really tune lies. Often, there is little to nothing that can be done at the database instance level to fix things.

Now, back to the real world again where applications are built, never tested to scale, never held up to metrics during development, and aren't instrumented at all. What can we do with these (besides run away and hide)? In some cases, we'll be able to use some tools, to diagnose and correct their issues. In many other cases, instrumentation of the code itself will be necessary, particularly in large applications with many interacting modules. In order to diagnose large application issues, just finding out where to start may be difficult. If you have a Java client taking to an application server, that makes a call to a CORBA object, that ultimately updates the database – finding out where things are taking time is going to be tedious (unless you've instrumented). Even after you find it, fixing it will be hard as well. Many times the simple solution is the correct answer. The fewer moving parts to consider, the easier it is to tune.

Bind Variables and Parsing (Again)

We have covered bind variables a couple of times already, from various perspectives. We have seen for example that by not using bind variables, you might spend 90 percent of your execution time parsing queries instead of actually running them. We have seen how this can affect the shared pool, a precious resource in Oracle. By now, you understand that they are critical to a system's performance. Don't use them and you will run many times slower then you should, and you will reduce the number of users that can ultimately supported. Use them and your life will be much easier. At least you won't have to go back and fix your programs to use them.

Bind variables are important because one of the design features of the Oracle database is to reuse optimizer plans whenever possible. When you submit any SQL or PL/SQL to the database, Oracle will first search the shared pool to see if it already exists. For example, in the case of a SQL query, Oracle will look to see if that query has already been parsed and optimized. If it finds the query and it can be reused, you are ready to go. If it cannot find it, Oracle must go through the arduous process of parsing the query fully, optimizing the plan, performing the security checks, and so on. This not only consumes a lot of CPU power (typically many more times the CPU processing time than is used in executing the query itself), it tends to lock portions of the library cache for relatively long periods. The more people you have parsing queries, the longer the wait for the latch on the library cache and the system slowly grinds to a halt.

Bind variables and their uses are a good example of why you have to test to scale. In a single user system, one user parsing queries that do not use bind variables may not be noticeable. This single session will run slower than it could, but it will probably run 'fast enough'. It is when you start 10 or 100 of these sessions simultaneously that you discover the system grinds to a halt. You have a scarce resource (CPU, Library Cache, Library Cache Latches) and you are overusing them all. By simply using bind variables, you reduce the needs for these resources many times.

I am going to demonstrate the power that bind variables have over the performance of your application once again. In Chapter 1 on *Developing Successful Oracle Applications*, I showed this for a single session – not using bind variables would make an application run slower. In that section, we saw that a block of code using bind variables would take 15 seconds to execute. The same exact code written with bind variables ran in 1.5 seconds. Here, I will show you the effect of not using bind variables in a multi-user situation. We already understand that our code will definitely run slower without bind variables – now let's measure what it will do to our scalability.

For this test, I will use the following tables. Note that access to the V$SESSION_EVENT table must be available for this example to work – you may need to have SELECT on V$SESSION_EVENT granted to you. Additionally, the SESSION or SYSTEM parameter TIMED_STATISTICS must be enabled for the numbers to be meaningful (the times will be zero otherwise). This may be accomplished via the command ALTER SESSION SET TIMED_STATISTICS=TRUE. We'll start by creating a global temporary table SESS_EVENT that our session will use to hold 'before values' of the events our session has waited on. This SESS_EVENT table will be used to measure our sessions wait events (what it waited on), how many times it waited for an event, and how long it waited in hundredths of seconds.

```
tkyte@TKYTE816> create global temporary table sess_event
  2  on commit preserve rows
  3  as
  4  select * from v$session_event where 1=0;

Table created.
```

Now, we'll create the 'application' table to test with:

```
tkyte@TKYTE816> create table t
  2  ( c1 int, c2 int, c3 int, c4 int )
  3  storage ( freelists 10 );

Table created
```

I want to test the effects of multiple users inserting into this table concurrently. We saw in Chapter 6 on *Tables* the effect that multiple freelists can have on concurrent inserts so we've already incorporated this into our design. Now we'll measure what sorts of wait events our 'application' experiences. We do this by making a copy of our session's current wait events, running the block of code we wish to analyze, and then computing the waits that occurred during that block of code:

```
tkyte@TKYTE816> truncate table sess_event;

Table truncated.

tkyte@TKYTE816> insert into sess_event
  2  select * from v$session_event
  4  where sid = (select sid from v$mystat where rownum = 1);

3 rows created.

tkyte@TKYTE816> declare
  2      l_number number;
  3  begin
  4      for i in 1 .. 10000
  5      loop
  6          l_number := dbms_random.random;
  7
  8          execute immediate
  9          'insert into t values ( ' || l_number || ',' ||
 10                                       l_number || ',' ||
 11                                       l_number || ',' ||
 12                                       l_number || ')';
 13      end loop;
 14      commit;
 15  end;
 16  /

PL/SQL procedure successfully completed

tkyte@TKYTE816> select a.event,
  2          (a.total_waits-nvl(b.total_waits,0)) total_waits,
  3          (a.time_waited-nvl(b.time_waited,0)) time_waited
  4      from ( select *
```

```
  5              from v$session_event
  6           where sid = (select sid from v$mystat where rownum = 1 )) a,
  7        sess_event b
  8   where a.event = b.event(+)
  9     and (a.total_waits-nvl(b.total_waits,0)) > 0
 10  /


EVENT                           TOTAL_WAITS TIME_WAITED
------------------------------- ----------- -----------
SQL*Net message from client               4          14
SQL*Net message to client                 5           0
log file sync                             5           2
```

In this small test, we are building a *unique* INSERT statement that will look something like this:

```
insert into t values (12323, 12323, 12323, 12323);
insert into t values (632425, 632425, 632425, 632425);
...
```

The above results are from a single user run. When we run two of these at the same time, we'll see a wait report that looks more like this:

```
EVENT                                    TOTAL_WAITS TIME_WAITED
---------------------------------------- ----------- -----------
SQL*Net message from client                        4          18
SQL*Net message to client                          5           0
enqueue                                            2           0
latch free                                       142         235
log file sync                                      2           2
```

As you can see, this session waited many times for a latch free (and waited a long cumulative time). The other observed waits in this case were:

❑ SQL*Net message from client – the server was waiting for the client to send it a message, the client being SQL*PLUS in this case. In most cases, this wait event can be ignored, if the application has lots of think-time in it, this number will necessarily be high. In our case, the SQL*PLUS session should have been continuously been feeding statements to the database during the time we measured therefore we expect a low number there. If the number was high, it would have implied a client issue in this case (that the client was a bottleneck, not able to feed the database questions fast enough).

❑ SQL*Net message to client – The amount of time it took to send messages to the client (SQL*PLUS) from the server.

❑ Enqueue – A wait on a lock of some sort.

❑ Log file sync – Time spent waiting for LGWR to flush our buffered redo log to disk upon commit.

All wait events are documented in the Oracle8i Reference Manual in the Appendix 'Oracle Wait Events'. See this guide for details on any wait events you see in V$SESSION_EVENT

The **latch free** event is the one we need to focus in on in this case. This latch free is actually a latch on the shared SQL area. This is something I happen to know given the characteristics of the above transaction we executed. Further sleuthing in the V$ tables would confirm this (later in this section, we will discuss these V$ views in more detail). Since we had two sessions now doing 'hard parses' (parses of a query that has never been parsed yet), contention for the shared SQL area is introduced. They both needed to modify a shared data structure, and only one session at a time can do this. The following chart shows the latch free wait event for 1, 2, 3, 4, and 5 sessions executing the above transaction simultaneously:

	1 user	2 users	3 users	4 users	5 users
Waits	0	102	267	385	542
Time (seconds)	0	1.56	5.92	10.72	16.67

You have to remember that the above information is by session – each of the sessions had that many waits and waited that long. With two users we had about three seconds of wait time, with three users about 18, with four about 40, and so on. At some point, as we add more users, we will spend more time *waiting* than actually processing. The more users we add, the more time we spend waiting, and eventually the waits become so long that adding more users will decrease not only our response times, but also our overall throughput. How to fix this? If we simply rewrite the block of code to use bind variables like this:

```
tkyte@TKYTE816> declare
  2          l_number number;
  3  begin
  4          for i in 1 .. 10000
  5          loop
  6              l_number := dbms_random.random;
  7
  8              execute immediate
  9              'insert into t values ( :x1, :x2, :x3, :x4 )'
 10                      using l_number, l_number, l_number, l_number;
 11          end loop;
 12          commit;
 13  end;
 14  /

PL/SQL procedure successfully completed.
```

To run this example on Oracle 8.1.5 please see the errata at the Apress web site, http://www.apress.com

Using this, we notice a marked improvement:

	1 user	2 users	3 users	4 users	5 users
Waits	0	47 (46%)	65 (25%)	89 (23%)	113 (20%)
Time (seconds)	0	0.74 (47%)	1.29 (21%)	2.12 (19%)	3.0 (17%)

This is a dramatic improvement, but we can do *better*. With two users, the total number of waits for latch frees on the shared SQL area is down to 46 percent of the original count, as is the time waited. As we add more users, it gets even better. With five users, we are experiencing only 20 percent of the waits we had without bind variables and waiting only 17 percent of the time.

However, I said, we could go one step better. In the above example, while we are avoiding the hard parse, we are still experiencing 'soft parses'. Each iteration through the loop must find the INSERT statement in the shared pool and verify we can use it. The EXECUTE IMMEDIATE approach above is equivalent to coding:

```
loop
   parse
   bind
   execute
close
end;
```

We would much prefer to code:

```
parse
loop
   bind
   execute
end;
close;
```

In the above example, we could either use static SQL in PL/SQL or use DBMS_SQL and procedurally do the dynamic SQL (see Chapter 16 on *Dynamic SQL* later for examples and all of the details on DBMS_SQL). I will use static SQL with bind variables as follows:

```
tkyte@TKYTE816> declare
  2      l_number number;
  3  begin
  4      for i in 1 .. 10000
  5      loop
  6          l_number := dbms_random.random;
  7
  8          insert into t
  9                  values( l_number, l_number, l_number, l_number );
 10      end loop;
 11      commit;
 12  end;
 13  /

PL/SQL procedure successfully completed.
```

I know that PL/SQL will cache my cursor for me – that is one of the major advantages of PL/SQL. This insert will typically be soft parsed once per session for me if it was in a procedure. It will be soft parsed once per block in an anonymous block. Now, if we re-run the tests:

	1 user	2 users	3 users	4 users	5 users
Waits	0	1	1	7	7
Time (seconds)	0	0	0.01	0.10	0.08

For all intents and purposes, the latching is totally gone; it is barely measurable. The above demonstrates why:

❑ Using bind variables is crucial to the performance.

❑ Avoiding the soft parse of a query is equally as important.

Avoiding the soft parse of a SQL statement pays back even more than using bind variables in some cases, as demonstrated above. Don't be so fast to close a cursor – the overhead of having it remain open during your program execution if you might reuse it, is overshadowed by the performance increase you will receive by keeping it open.

In Oracle 8.1.6, a new feature was introduced called CURSOR_SHARING. Cursor sharing is an 'auto binder' of sorts. It causes the database to rewrite your query using bind variables before parsing it. This feature will take a query such as:

```
scott@TKYTE816> select * from emp where ename = 'KING';
```

and will automatically rewrite it as:

```
select * from emp where ename =:SYS_B_0
```

or in 8.1.6 and in 8.1.7

```
select * from emp where ename =:"SYS_B_0"
```

This is a step in the right direction, but should not be the final solution to the problem and should not be used long term. There are side effects from CURSOR_SHARING that you must aware of as well. A poorly written program may experience a large gain in performance by setting the CURSOR_SHARING=FORCE parameter, but it will still be running slower than it should, and it will still be limited in the degree to which it can scale. As we observed above, we were able to reduce by a large percentage many of the waits and the time spent waiting by simply using bind variables. We could achieve the same exact results using CURSOR_SHARING=FORCE. It was not until we avoided the soft parses however, that we were able to avoid 100 percent of the waits. Cursor sharing will *not* avoid these soft parses for us. It is a fact that if you can benefit greatly from CURSOR_SHARING, you are causing Oracle to parse many queries too frequently. If you are frequently causing many queries to be parsed, then adding CURSOR_SHARING will fix the bind variable issue, but you will still be left with the soft parse overhead. While not as egregious as the overhead of bind variables, high soft parse counts will limit your performance and scalability as well. The only correct solution is to use bind variables in the first place and to reuse your cursors whenever possible. For example, if I were coding a Java application I would never code a routine like this:

```
...
String getWordb(int ID, int IDLang, Connection conn) throws SQLException {
  CallableStatement stmt = null;

  stmt = conn.prepareCall("{ call get.wordb (?,?,?)}");
  stmt.setInt(1,ID);
  stmt.setInt(2,IDLang);
  stmt.registerOutParameter (3, java.sql.Types.VARCHAR);
  stmt.execute();
  String word = stmt.getString (3);
  stmt.close();
  return word;
}
...
```

I would code it like this:

```
...
CallableStatement stmt = null;

String getWordb(int ID, int IDLang, Connection conn)
throws SQLException {
  if ( stmt == null ) {
    stmt = conn.prepareCall("{call get.wordb (?,?,?)}");
    stmt.registerOutParameter (3, java.sql.Types.VARCHAR);
  }
  stmt.setInt(1,ID);
  stmt.setInt(2,IDLang);
  stmt.execute();
  return stmt.getString (3);
}
...
```

Here, I am ensuring the use of bind variables by using the placeholders in the statement. Additionally, I am parsing this statement *at most* once per program execution. This will make a huge difference in performance. In one test, I called the 'bad' and 'good' implementations 1000 times each. The bad implementation, with the soft parses for each call, took two and a half seconds to execute. The good implementation took one second. That was in single user mode. We know by now that adding additional users, each doing thousands of soft parses, will just slow each other down with latch waits during the soft parse. This is overhead we can, and must, avoid in our applications.

Now back to CURSOR_SHARING for a moment. I also said above that there are some side effects of CURSOR_SHARING that you must be aware of. They fall into the following categories:

❑ **Optimizer related issues** – CURSOR_SHARING will remove *all* character string and numeric constants from the query; the optimizer will have less information to work with. This may very well result in different query plans.

❑ **Query output related issues** – The lengths of columns that your query fetches will unexpectedly change. Queries that used to return a VARCHAR2(5) and a NUMBER(2), might start returning a VARCHAR2(30) and a NUMBER(5). The actual size of the data returned won't change, but the application will be told the potential for a 30 byte column is there – reports and other related applications may be affected.

❑ **Query plans are harder to evaluate** – This is due to the fact that EXPLAIN PLAN will 'see' a different query than the database does. This makes query tuning more difficult. Features like AUTOTRACE in SQL*PLUS are unreliable with CURSOR_SHARING.

We'll take a look at each of these issues in detail, but first let's take a closer look at the optimizer related issues. These will have direct performance related effects on your application. Consider the following simple example in which we will execute a query that uses a mixture of bind variables and character string constants. The performance of this query before CURSOR_SHARING is excellent. The performance after turning on CURSOR_SHARING is terrible. The reason for the performance hit is due to the fact that the optimizer has less information to work with. The optimizer, when it could see the character string constants, was able to determine that one index would be much more selective than another. When all of the constants were removed, the optimizer didn't have this foresight. This will be a common issue in many applications; it will not be a 'rare' occurrence. Most applications use a mixture of bind variables and constants in their SQL. Just as never using a bind variable is terrible, *always* using a bind variable can be just as bad. Here is the table setup for the example:

```
tkyte@TKYTE816> create table t as
  2  select * from all_objects;

Table created.

tkyte@TKYTE816> create index t_idx1 on t(OBJECT_NAME);

Index created.

tkyte@TKYTE816> create index t_idx2 on t(OBJECT_TYPE);

Index created.

tkyte@TKYTE816> analyze table t compute statistics
  2  for all indexed columns
  3  for table;

Table analyzed.
```

We have two indexes on this table. The index on OBJECT TYPE is used for our query below. The index on OBJECT NAME is used heavily by another application. We need to have both indexes in place. The query we will execute against this table is going to be:

```
select *
  from t
 where object_name like :search_str
   and object_type in( 'FUNCTION','PROCEDURE', 'TRIGGER' );
```

This query is designed to fill in a pop-up list in our application. From this list we would click on the procedure, function, or trigger we want to edit. This query is executed thousands of times a day.

If we take a look at the raw data in the table:

```
tkyte@TKYTE816> compute sum of cnt on report
tkyte@TKYTE816> break on report
tkyte@TKYTE816> select object_type, count(*) cnt from t group by
  2  object_type;
```

```
OBJECT_TYPE                CNT
-----------------  ----------
CONSUMER GROUP              2
CONTEXT                    4
DIRECTORY                  1
FUNCTION                  27
INDEX                    301
INDEXTYPE                  3
JAVA CLASS              8926
JAVA DATA                288
JAVA RESOURCE             69
JAVA SOURCE                4
LIBRARY                   33
LOB                        3
OPERATOR                  15
PACKAGE                  229
PACKAGE BODY             212
PROCEDURE                 24
SEQUENCE                  35
SYNONYM                 9817
TABLE                    292
TRIGGER                    7
TYPE                     137
TYPE BODY                 12
UNDEFINED                  1
VIEW                    1340
                  ----------
sum                    21782

24 rows selected.
```

we can see that 58 rows would be retrieved by the IN clause, and an indeterminate amount would be retrieved by the LIKE clause (anywhere from 0 to 21,782). If we run the query in SQL*PLUS like this:

```
tkyte@TKYTE816> variable search_str varchar2(25)
tkyte@TKYTE816> exec :search_str := '%';

PL/SQL procedure successfully completed.

tkyte@TKYTE816> set autotrace traceonly
tkyte@TKYTE816> select * from t t1 where object_name like :search_str
  2  and object_type in( 'FUNCTION','PROCEDURE', 'TRIGGER' );

58 rows selected.


Execution Plan
----------------------------------------------------------
   0      SELECT STATEMENT Optimizer=CHOOSE (Cost=5 Card=3 Bytes=291)
   1    0   INLIST ITERATOR
   2    1     TABLE ACCESS (BY INDEX ROWID) OF 'T' (Cost=5 Card=3 Bytes=291)
   3    2       INDEX (RANGE SCAN) OF 'T_IDX2' (NON-UNIQUE) (Cost=2 Card=3)

Statistics
----------------------------------------------------------
      222  recursive calls
        0  db block gets
       45  consistent gets
```

```
        3   physical reads
        0   redo size
     6930   bytes sent via SQL*Net to client
      762   bytes received via SQL*Net from client
        5   SQL*Net roundtrips to/from client
        1   sorts (memory)
        0   sorts (disk)
       58   rows processed
```

it is obvious with our knowledge of the data, that the optimizer should definitely use the index on OBJECT_TYPE to find the 58 rows out of the 21,000 and apply the LIKE clause to them. It also shows there are times when using a constant is relevant. In this particular case, we would rather not use a bind variable – we would rather use a constant. The optimizer can ascertain that this query will benefit from one index over the other greatly. If we do this:

```
tkyte@TKYTE816> alter session set cursor_sharing = force;

Session altered.

tkyte@TKYTE816> select * from t t2 where object_name like :search_str
  2  and object_type in( 'FUNCTION','PROCEDURE', 'TRIGGER' );

58 rows selected.


Execution Plan
----------------------------------------------------------
   0      SELECT STATEMENT Optimizer=CHOOSE (Cost=5 Card=3 Bytes=291)
   1    0   INLIST ITERATOR
   2    1     TABLE ACCESS (BY INDEX ROWID) OF 'T' (Cost=5 Card=3 Bytes=291)
   3    2       INDEX (RANGE SCAN) OF 'T_IDX2' (NON-UNIQUE) (Cost=2 Card=3)

Statistics
----------------------------------------------------------
        0   recursive calls
        0   db block gets
    19256   consistent gets
      169   physical reads
        0   redo size
     7480   bytes sent via SQL*Net to client
      762   bytes received via SQL*Net from client
        5   SQL*Net roundtrips to/from client
        2   sorts (memory)
        0   sorts (disk)
       58   rows processed
```

Although the optimizer plan does not appear to have changed (AUTOTRACE is showing the same exact plan) the difference in consistent GETS (logical reads) is significant – indicating that something changed. In fact, the database really ran the query:

```
select *
  from t t2
 where object_name like :search_str
   and object_type in( :SYS_B_0,:SYS_B_1, :SYS_B_2 )
```

and it was no longer able to determine the amount of rows it would access via the index on OBJECT_TYPE. The above example also demonstrates how CURSOR_SHARING can be harder to tune with. The explain plan SQL*PLUS printed out leads me to believe we performed an index read on T_IDX2, but if you look at the consistent gets (logical reads), we see 19,256 of them. The first query that really did do an index scan on T_IDX2 processed 45 blocks. Here, explain plan used by autotrace is tricked into giving us the wrong plan. It is not aware of the true query being executed. I turned on SQL_TRACE instead (more on that in the next section), and for the two queries we can then clearly see:

```
select * from t t1 where object_name like :search_str
and object_type in( 'FUNCTION','PROCEDURE', 'TRIGGER' )

call     count      cpu    elapsed  disk       query   current        rows
-------  ------  -------  --------- -----  ----------  ---------  ----------
Parse        1     0.00      0.00      0           0          0           0
Execute      1     0.00      0.00      0           0          0           0
Fetch        5     0.01      0.09     14          34          0          58
-------  ------  -------  --------- -----  ----------  ---------  ----------
total        7     0.01      0.09     14          34          0          58

Rows     Row Source Operation
-------  ---------------------------------------------------------
     58  INLIST ITERATOR
     58   TABLE ACCESS BY INDEX ROWID T
     61    INDEX RANGE SCAN (object id 25244)

select * from t t2 where object_name like :search_str
and object_type in( :SYS_B_0,:SYS_B_1, :SYS_B_2 )

call     count      cpu    elapsed  disk       query   current        rows
-------  ------  -------  --------- -----  ----------  ---------  ----------
Parse        1     0.00      0.00      0           0          0           0
Execute      1     0.00      0.00      0           0          0           0
Fetch        5     0.15      1.77    255       19256          0          58
-------  ------  -------  --------- -----  ----------  ---------  ----------
total        7     0.15      1.77    255       19256          0          58

Rows     Row Source Operation
-------  ---------------------------------------------------------
     58  TABLE ACCESS BY INDEX ROWID T
  21783   INDEX RANGE SCAN (object id 25243)
```

SQL_TRACE and TKPROF are able to show us what really happened here. The second query was executed using the other index (as evidenced by the differing object IDs), which in this case was the wrong plan. Our query takes 15 to 20 times longer to execute and accesses an incredible amount of data. This problem of **over binding** will show up in many applications that use a mixture of constants and bind variables. Without the additional information provided by the constants in the query, the optimizer may make the wrong decision. Only by correctly using bind variables where we intend to, and using constants when we must, will we achieve a fine balance. CURSOR_SHARING is a temporary crutch that may get you started, but should not be relied on long term for this reason.

In addition to the optimizer being tricked as above, the use of CURSOR_SHARING may affect other Oracle features. For example, if you refer back to Chapter 7 on *Indexes*, there is a feature called *Function-Based Indexes*. I can effectively create an index on a function. Well, Using the same example we used in that chapter where we created an index like this:

```
tkyte@TKYTE816> create index test_soundex_idx on
  2              test_soundex( substr(my_soundex(name),1,6) )
  3  /

Index created.
```

We would find that CURSOR_SHARING would remove the ability of this query:

```
tkyte@TKYTE816> select name
  2    from test_soundex C
  3   where substr(my_soundex(name),1,6) = my_soundex( 'FILE$' )
  4  /
```

To use the index, since the literal values 1 and 6 would be replaced by bind variables. Here, we can overcome the issue by 'hiding' the constants in a view, but it is an issue to consider none the less. What other 'surprise' incompatibilities will be out there?

Another side effect of CURSOR_SHARING is the possible unexpected change in the size of columns returned by a query. Consider the following example where I display the size of columns returned by a query before and after CURSOR_SHARING. This example uses DBMS_SQL to dynamically parse and describe a query. It will print out the sizes of the columns as reported to the application by Oracle:

```
tkyte@TKYTE816> declare
  2      l_theCursor     integer default dbms_sql.open_cursor;
  3      l_descTbl       dbms_sql.desc_tab;
  4      l_colCnt        number;
  5  begin
  6      execute immediate 'alter session set cursor_sharing=exact';
  7      dbms_output.put_line( 'Without Cursor Sharing:' );
  8      for i in 1 .. 2
  9      loop
 10          dbms_sql.parse(  l_theCursor,
 11                          'select substr( object_name, 1, 5 ) c1,
 12                                  55 c2,
 13                                  ''Hello'' c3
 14                            from all_objects t'||i,
 15                          dbms_sql.native );
 16
 17          dbms_sql.describe_columns( l_theCursor,
 18                                      l_colCnt, l_descTbl );
 19
 20          for i in 1 .. l_colCnt loop
 21              dbms_output.put_line( 'Column ' ||
 22                                    l_descTbl(i).col_name ||
 23                                    ' has a length of ' ||
 24                                    l_descTbl(i).col_max_len ) ;
 25          end loop;
 26          execute immediate 'alter session set cursor_sharing=force';
 27          dbms_output.put_line( 'With Cursor Sharing:' );
 28      end loop;
 29
 30      dbms_sql.close_cursor(l_theCursor);
 31      execute immediate 'alter session set cursor_sharing=exact';
 32  end;
```

```
  33   /
Without Cursor Sharing:
Column C1 has a length of 5
Column C2 has a length of 2
Column C3 has a length of 5
With Cursor Sharing:
Column C1 has a length of 30
Column C2 has a length of 22
Column C3 has a length of 32

PL/SQL procedure successfully completed.
```

The reason column one went from a length of 5 to a length of 30 is because the function
SUBSTR(OBJECT_NAME, 1, 5) was rewritten as SUBSTR(OBJECT_NAME, :SYS_B_0, :SYS_B_1). The
database no longer knew that the maximum length this function could possibly return was 5, it was now
30 (the length of OBJECT_NAME). The length of column two went from 2 to 22 because the database no
longer knew the number 55 would be returned – only that a *number* would be returned and numbers can
be up to 22 bytes in length. The last column just defaulted to a value – if HELLO had been larger, the
default would have been larger as well (for example, if you use a 35 byte string, the default would be
128 bytes).

You might say 'so what, the size of the returned data won't be different, just the reported length?' Well,
the problem will come in with any SQL*PLUS scripts that you have, any reports you run using various
tools, anything that relies on the database to tell it the length of the column for formatting will be
adversely affected. The output from these applications will be different than it was without
CURSOR_SHARING; your finely laid out reports will have their formatting destroyed in many cases. Just
consider what impact this might have on an existing suite of applications! The side effect is very easy to
observe:

```
tkyte@TKYTE816> > select substr(object_name,1,2)
  2      from all_objects t1
  3    where rownum = 1
  4    /

SU
--
/1

tkyte@TKYTE816> alter session set cursor_sharing = force;

Session altered.

tkyte@TKYTE816> select substr(object_name,1,2)
  2      from all_objects t2
  3    where rownum = 1
  4    /

SUBSTR(OBJECT_NAME,1,2)
-------------------------------
/1
```

SQL*PLUS went from 2 characters per column to 30 characters per column. This would adversely affect
reports that have been running successfully.

Am I Using Bind Variables?

One question I get, usually right after I ask 'are you using bind variables?', is 'how can I tell if I am?' Fortunately, figuring this out is pretty straightforward; all of the information we need is in the shared pool.

I've set up a script that I use (and pass around) frequently, which points out statements that look like they could be the same, only if they used bind variables. In order to show you how this script works, I'll artificially fill up my shared pool with 'bad' SQL that doesn't use bind variables:

```
tkyte@TKYTE816> create table t ( x int );

Table created.

tkyte@TKYTE816> begin
  2      for i in 1 .. 100
  3      loop
  4          execute immediate 'insert into t values ( ' || i || ')';
  5      end loop;
  6  end;
  7  /

PL/SQL procedure successfully completed.
```

Now, I'm ready for the script. It starts by creating a function that removes constants from strings. It will take SQL statements such as:

```
insert into t values ( 'hello', 55 );
insert into t values ( 'world', 66 );
```

And turn them into:

```
insert into t values ( '#', @ );
```

All statements that could look the same if they used bind variables will be clearly visible to us – both of the above unique inserts will become the same insert statement after substitution. The function to do this transformation for us then is the following:

```
tkyte@TKYTE816> create or replace
  2  function remove_constants( p_query in varchar2 )
  3  return varchar2
  4  as
  5      l_query long;
  6      l_char  varchar2(1);
  7      l_in_quotes boolean default FALSE;
  8  begin
  9      for i in 1 .. length( p_query )
 10      loop
 11          l_char := substr(p_query,i,1);
 12          if ( l_char = '''' and l_in_quotes )
 13          then
 14              l_in_quotes := FALSE;
```

```
15              elsif ( l_char = '''' and NOT l_in_quotes )
16              then
17                      l_in_quotes := TRUE;
18                      l_query := l_query || '''#';
19              end if;
20              if ( NOT l_in_quotes ) then
21                      l_query := l_query || l_char;
22              end if;
23          end loop;
24          l_query := translate( l_query, '0123456789', '@@@@@@@@@@' );
25          for i in 0 .. 8 loop
26              l_query := replace( l_query, lpad('@',10-i,'@'), '@' );
27              l_query := replace( l_query, lpad(' ',10-i,' '), ' ' );
28          end loop;
29          return upper(l_query);
30  end;
31  /

Function created.
```

For the main body of the script, we'll make a copy of the V$SQLAREA table – this view is expensive to query and we only want to query it once. We copy it into the temporary table, so we can work on its contents:

```
tkyte@TKYTE816> create global temporary table sql_area_tmp
  2  on commit preserve rows
  3  as
  4  select sql_text, sql_text sql_text_wo_constants
  5    from v$sqlarea
  6   where 1=0
  7  /

Table created.

tkyte@TKYTE816> insert into sql_area_tmp (sql_text)
  2  select sql_text from v$sqlarea
  3  /

436 rows created.
```

We go through and update each and every row in this table to compute the transformed SQL_TEXT, removing the constants:

```
tkyte@TKYTE816> update sql_area_tmp
  2      set sql_text_wo_constants = remove_constants(sql_text);
  3  /

436 rows updated.
```

and now we are readying to find the 'bad' SQL:

```
tkyte@TKYTE816> select sql_text_wo_constants, count(*)
  2     from sql_area_tmp
  3     group by sql_text_wo_constants
  4   having count(*) > 10
  5     order by 2
  6   /

SQL_TEXT_WO_CONSTANTS                    COUNT(*)
-----------------------------------   ----------
INSERT INTO T VALUES ( @)                    100
```

This clearly shows that there are 100 INSERT statements in my shared pool that differ only in one numeric field in the values clause. This would *most likely* indicate someone forgot to use bind variables. There are some legitimate cases where you might have a reasonable number of copies of a SQL statement in the shared pool – for example, there might be five tables named T in the database. Once we determine there is no legitimate cause, we must track down that person, teach them the proper way, and make them fix it. I count this as a *bug* in the program, not as something we have to live with – it must be corrected.

Bind Variables and Parsing Wrap-Up

In this section, we discussed the importance of using bind variables in your application, as well as the desire to minimize the number of times you parse a query as well. We looked at a feature, CURSOR_SHARING, which would appear to be a panacea to these issues, only to discover this is not entirely the case. CURSOR_SHARING may be used as a temporary stop-gap solution to particular application performance issues but ultimately, the only way to achieve all of the performance and scalability you can, you must implement your applications correctly.

I cannot stress this point enough. I have personally seen many more than one system fail due to not taking heed of the above facts. As I said in the very beginning of this book, if I were to write a book on how to build a non-scalable, non-performant Oracle application, it would have one chapter that simply said 'don't use bind variables.' Using bind variables and good parsing techniques in your applications won't guarantee scalability, but not using them however, will assure the opposite.

SQL_TRACE, TIMED_STATISTICS, and TKPROF

SQL_TRACE, TIMED_STATISTICS, and TKPROF are some of my favorite tools. I have used them countless times to determine where the performance issue in a system lies. Given that many times, one is tuning a system they did not write, knowing where to look is difficult. These settings and tool are a great place to start.

In a nutshell, SQL_TRACE enables the logging of all the SQL your application performs, performance statistics regarding the execution of that SQL, and the query plans your SQL actually used. As demonstrated in the previous section on CURSOR_SHARING, AUTOTRACE shows the wrong plan, SQL_TRACE and TKPROF got it right. TIMED_STATISTICS is a parameter that enables the server to tell us how long each step takes. Finally, TKPROF is a simple program used to format the raw trace file into something more readable. What I will do in this section is show you how to use SQL_TRACE and TKPROF, and to explain the meaning of what is included in the files used by these facilities. I will not be describing how you might take a particular query and tune it so much, as show how to use these tools to find the queries to tune. For more information on tuning individual queries – I recommend the *Oracle8i Designing and Tuning for Performance Manual*. It covers the various access plans queries may use, how to use hints to tune queries, and so on.

The parameter TIMED_STATISTICS controls whether Oracle will collect timing information for various activities in the database. It has two settings, TRUE and FALSE. This feature is so useful, I generally leave it on TRUE even when not tuning – it's performance impact on a database is negligible in general (there is an issue in Oracle 8.1.5 where by shared SQL might be defeated if TIMED_STATISTICS is set to TRUE). It may be set at either the SYSTEM or the SESSION level and may be 'globally' set in the initialization file for the database. If you put it in the INIT.ORA file for your instance, you will simply add:

```
timed_statistics=true
```

In the init.ora and the next time you restart the database, it will be enabled. Alternatively, to enable it for your session, you may issue:

```
tkyte@TKYTE816> alter session set timed_statistics=true;

Session altered.
```

And to turn this on for the entire system:

```
tkyte@TKYTE816> alter system set timed_statistics=true;

System altered.
```

As I said, this is so useful to have, that I just leave it on all of the time by setting it to TRUE in my init.ora parameter file. The performance overhead due to this is not measurable and the effect of not having this information is that you cannot monitor performance at all.

Setting Up Tracing

SQL_TRACE may also be enabled at the system or session level. It generates so much output and is such a performance impact that you will almost always selectively enable it – you will rarely, if ever, enable it for the system in the init.ora file. SQL_TRACE has two settings as well, TRUE and FALSE. If set to TRUE, it will generate trace files to the directory specified by the init.ora parameter USER_DUMP_DEST, when using dedicated servers to connect to Oracle and BACKGROUND_DUMP_DEST when using a multi-threaded server (MTS) connection. I would recommend never attempting to use SQL_TRACE with MTS however, as the output from your sessions queries will be written to many various trace files, as your session migrates from shared server to shared server. Under MTS, interpreting SQL_TRACE results is nearly impossible. Another important init.ora parameter is MAX_DUMP_FILE_SIZE. This limits the maximum size of a trace file Oracle will generate. If you discover that your trace files are truncated, you will increase this setting. It may be changed via an alter system or session command. MAX_DUMP_FILE_SIZE may be specified in one of three ways:

❑ A numerical value for MAX_DUMP_FILE_SIZE specifies the maximum size in operating system blocks.

❑ A number followed by a K or M suffix specifies the file size in kilobytes or megabytes.

❑ The string UNLIMITED. This means that there is no upper limit on trace file size. Thus, dump files can be as large as the operating system permits.

I do not recommend UNLIMITED – it is far too easy to completely fill up a file system in this manner; a setting of 50 to 100 MB should be more then sufficient.

What are the various ways to enable SQL_TRACE? There are quite a few, but the ones I use mostly are:

❑ ALTER SESSION SET SQL_TRACE=TRUE|FALSE – Executing this SQL will enable the default mode of SQL_TRACE in the current session. This is most useful in an interactive environment such as SQL*PLUS or embedded in an application so that the application, may turn SQL_TRACE on and off at will. It is a nice feature in all applications, as it would allow you to turn SQL_TRACE on and off for the application via a command line switch, menu selection, parameter, and so on, easily.

❑ SYS.DBMS_SYSTEM.SET_SQL_TRACE_IN_SESSION – This packaged procedure allows us to set SQL_TRACE on and off for any existing session in the database. All we need to do is identify the SID and SERIAL# for the session, this is available in the dynamic performance view V$SESSION.

❑ ALTER SESSION SET EVENTS – We can set an event to enable tracing with more information than is normally available via ALTER SESSION SET SQL_TRACE=TRUE. The SET EVENTS approach is not documented or supported by Oracle Corporation, however its existence is generally available knowledge (go to http://www.google.com/ and search for **alter session set events 10046** to see the many web sites that document this feature). Using this event we can not only get everything that SQL_TRACE tells us but we can also see the values of bind variables used by our SQL as well as the wait events (what slowed us down) for our SQL as well.

There are other methods as well, however, the above three are the ones I use and see used most often. The ALTER SESSION SET SQL_TRACE and SYS.DBMS_SYSTEM methods of setting SQL_TRACE on are very straightforward and they are self-explanatory. The EVENT method however, is a little more obscure. It uses an internal (and undocumented) event facility within Oracle. In short, the command you would use will look like this:

```
alter session set events '10046 trace name context forever, level <n>';
alter session set events '10046 trace name context off';
```

Where N is one of the following values:

❑ N=1 – Enable the standard SQL_TRACE facility. This is no different than setting SQL_TRACE=true.

❑ N=4 – Enable standard SQL_TRACE but also capture bind variable values in the trace file.

❑ N=8 – Enable standard SQL_TRACE but also capture wait events at the query level into the trace file.

❑ N=12 – Enable standard SQL_TRACE and include both bind variables and waits.

Using the DBMS_SUPPORT package is another method of setting SQL_TRACE with bind variable and wait event support. In order to get DBMS_SUPPORT however, you must contact Oracle Support, as it is not delivered as part of the normal installation, because it is simply an interface on top of the ALTER SYTEM SET EVENTS command above, using the ALTER command is perhaps easier.

Now we know how to turn SQL_TRACE on, the question becomes' how can we best make use of it? I myself, like to have a switch I can send to my applications on the command line or via a URL (if they are on the web) that tells them to turn tracing on. This lets me easily capture SQL_TRACE information for a single session. Many Oracle tools allow you to do this as well. For example, if you use Oracle forms, you can execute:

```
C:\> ifrun60 module=myform userid=scott/tiger statistics=yes
```

The STATISTICS=YES is a flag to forms to tell it to issue ALTER SESSION SET SQL_TRACE=TRUE. If all of your applications do the same, you will find that tuning that application is easier. You can ask the single user, who is having a performance issue, to run with tracing enabled. Then ask them to reproduce the performance issue. You'll have all of the information you need to figure out why it is running slow. You won't have to ask them for the steps to reproduce the slowdown – you'll ask them to reproduce the slowdown and just analyze the results of it. If you trace with bind variables and wait events, you'll have more than enough information to figure out what is going wrong.

If you have an application provided by a third party, or you have existing applications that are not SQL_TRACE-enabled, what can you do to trace them? There are two approaches that I take. One approach, if the application is a client-server application and stays connected to the database, is to have the session you want to trace start up the application and log into the database. Then, by querying V$SESSION, you would determine that session's SID and SERIAL#. Now you can call SYS.DBMS_SYSTEM.SET_SQL_TRACE_IN_SESSION to enable tracing in that single session. Today however, many applications are web-based and this trick does not work as well. The sessions are very short and they come and go frequently. What we need is an ability to set SQL_TRACE on for a 'user' – whenever this user is in the database, we need to have set SQL_TRACE on for them. Fortunately, we can do that via the LOGON DDL trigger in the database. For example, a trigger I frequently use in Oracle 8i (database event triggers such AFTER LOGON are a new feature of Oracle 8.1.5 and up) is:

```
create or replace trigger logon_trigger
after logon on database
begin
  if ( user = 'TKYTE' ) then
    execute immediate
    'ALTER SESSION SET EVENTS ''10046 TRACE NAME CONTEXT FOREVER, LEVEL 4''';
  end if;
end;/
```

This will enable tracing any time I logon to the database. The application does not have to participate in the setting of SQL_TRACE – we'll do this ourselves.

Using and Interpreting TKPROF Output

TKPROF is nothing more than a simple command line tool to format a raw trace file into something we can read easily. It is an excellent utility that is not used enough. I believe this is mostly due to ignorance of its existence. Now that you know it exists, I would expect you would use it constantly.

What I'll do in this section is to run a query with tracing enabled. We'll take a detailed look at the TKPROF report and learn what we need to look for in these reports:

```
tkyte@TKYTE816> show parameter timed_statistics;

NAME                                   TYPE     VALUE
------------------------------------   -------  ----------------------------
timed_statistics                       boolean  TRUE

tkyte@TKYTE816> alter session set sql_trace=true;

Session altered.

tkyte@TKYTE816> > select owner, count(*)
  2   from all_objects
  3   group by owner;

OWNER                           COUNT(*)
-----------------------------   ----------
CTXSYS                               185
DBSNMP                                 4
DEMO                                   5
DEMO11                                 3
MDSYS                                176
MV_USER                                5
ORDPLUGINS                            26
ORDSYS                               206
PUBLIC                              9796
SCOTT                                 18
SEAPARK                                3
SYS                                11279
SYSTEM                                51
TKYTE                                 32
TYPES                                  3

15 rows selected.

tkyte@TKYTE816> select a.spid
  2      from v$process a, v$session b
  3    where a.addr = b.paddr
  4       and b.audsid = userenv('sessionid')
  5   /

SPID
---------
1124
```

Here I verified that timed statistics was enabled (it is almost useless to execute SQL_TRACE without it) and then enabled SQL_TRACE. I then ran a query I wanted to analyze. Finally I ran a query to get my SPID, (server process ID) – this is very useful in identifying my trace file. After I executed this query, I exited SQL*PLUS and went to the directory on the database server specified by the USER_DUMP_DEST init.ora parameter. You can retrieve the value of this parameter online by querying the V$PARAMETER view or using DBMS_UTILITY, (which does not require access to the V$PARAMETER view):

```
tkyte@TKYTE816> declare
  2  l_intval number;
  3  l_strval varchar2(2000);
  4  l_type   number;
  5  begin
  6      l_type := dbms_utility.get_parameter_value
  7                      ('user_dump_dest', l_intval, l_strval);
  8      dbms_output.put_line(l_strval );
  9  end;
 10  /
C:\oracle\admin\tkyte816\udump

PL/SQL procedure successfully completed.
```

In this directory, I found:

```
C:\oracle\ADMIN\tkyte816\udump>dir
 Volume in drive C has no label.
 Volume Serial Number is F455-B3C3

 Directory of C:\oracle\ADMIN\tkyte816\udump

03/16/2001  02:55p      <DIR>           .
03/16/2001  02:55p      <DIR>           ..
03/16/2001  08:45a               5,114 ORA00860.TRC
03/16/2001  02:52p               3,630 ORA01112.TRC
03/16/2001  02:53p               6,183 ORA01124.TRC
               3 File(s)        14,927 bytes
               2 Dir(s)  13,383,999,488 bytes free
```

A few trace files – this is where the SPID will come in handy. My trace file is ORA01124.TRC. I know that because the SPID is part of the filename. On UNIX a similar naming convention is used that also incorporates the SPID. One issue with trace files is that the files in this directory may not be readable by you, if you are not in the administrative group for Oracle (for example, the DBA group in UNIX). If not, you should ask your DBA to set:

```
_trace_files_public = true
```

In the init.ora file of your test and development machines. This will allow all users to read trace files on the server. You should *not* use this setting on a production machine as these files can contain sensitive information. On a test or development platform, it should be safe to use. Notice that this init.ora parameter starts with an underscore. It is undocumented and unsupported by Oracle corporation. Again, like the EVENTS command we will use later, it is general knowledge and widely used – search Google or any other search engine for _trace_files_public, and you'll find many references to this parameter.

Now that we have identified our trace file, we need to format it. We can (and will, further on in this section) read the raw trace file. About 90 percent of the information we need is easily retrieved from a nicely formatted report however. The remaining 10 percent of the information is typically not needed, and when it is, we'll have to read it from the trace file itself. In order to format the trace file, we will use the TKPROF command line utility. In its simplest form we will just execute:

```
C:\oracle\ADMIN\tkyte816\udump>tkprof ora01124.trc report.txt

TKPROF: Release 8.1.6.0.0 - Production on Fri Mar 16 15:04:33 2001

(c) Copyright 1999 Oracle Corporation.  All rights reserved.
```

The parameters to the TKPROF command are the input file name and the output file name. Now, we just need to edit REPORT.TXT, and we will find the following information:

```
select owner, count(*)
from all_objects
group by owner

call     count       cpu    elapsed    disk       query     current        rows
-------  ------  --------  ---------- -----  ----------  ----------  ----------
Parse        1      0.00        0.00      0           0           0           0
Execute      1      0.00        0.00      0           0           0           0
Fetch        2      1.20        1.21      0       86091           4          15
-------  ------  --------  ---------- -----  ----------  ----------  ----------
total        4      1.20        1.21      0       86091           4          15

Misses in library cache during parse: 0
Optimizer goal: CHOOSE
Parsing user id: 69

Rows     Row Source Operation
-------  -------------------------------------------------------
     15  SORT GROUP BY
  21792   FILTER
  21932    NESTED LOOPS
     46     TABLE ACCESS FULL USER$
  21976     TABLE ACCESS BY INDEX ROWID OBJ$
  21976      INDEX RANGE SCAN (object id 34)
      1   FIXED TABLE FULL X$KZSPR
      1   FIXED TABLE FULL X$KZSPR
      0   FIXED TABLE FULL X$KZSPR
      0   FIXED TABLE FULL X$KZSPR
      1   FIXED TABLE FULL X$KZSPR
      1   FIXED TABLE FULL X$KZSPR
      1   FIXED TABLE FULL X$KZSPR
      1   FIXED TABLE FULL X$KZSPR
      1   FIXED TABLE FULL X$KZSPR
      1   FIXED TABLE FULL X$KZSPR
      1   FIXED TABLE FULL X$KZSPR
      1   FIXED TABLE FULL X$KZSPR
      1   FIXED TABLE FULL X$KZSPR
  11777   NESTED LOOPS
  30159    FIXED TABLE FULL X$KZSRO
  28971    TABLE ACCESS BY INDEX ROWID OBJAUTH$
  28973     INDEX RANGE SCAN (object id 101)
    631    TABLE ACCESS BY INDEX ROWID IND$
    654     INDEX UNIQUE SCAN (object id 36)
```

TKPROF is showing us a lot of information here. We'll take it piece by piece:

```
select owner, count(*)
from all_objects
group by owner
```

First, we see the original query as the server received it. We should be able to recognize our queries easily in here. In this case, it is exactly as I had typed it in. Next comes the overall execution report for this query:

call	count	cpu	elapsed	disk	query	current	rows
Parse	1	0.00	0.00	0	0	0	0
Execute	1	0.00	0.00	0	0	0	0
Fetch	2	1.20	1.21	0	86091	4	15
total	4	1.20	1.21	0	86091	4	15

Here we see the three main phases of the query:

❑ The PARSE phase – where Oracle finds the query in the shared pool (soft parse) or creates a new plan for the query (hard parse).

❑ The EXECUTE phase.This is the work done by Oracle upon the OPEN or EXECUTE of the query. For a SELECT, this will be many times 'empty' whereas for an UPDATE, this will be where all of the work is done.

❑ Then, there is the FETCH phase. For a SELECT, this will be where most of the work is done and visible, but a statement like an UPDATE will show no work (you don't 'FETCH' from an UPDATE).

The column headings in this section have the following meanings:

❑ CALL – Will be one of PARSE, EXECUTE, FETCH, or TOTAL. Simply denotes which phase of query processing we are looking at.

❑ COUNT – How many times the event occurred. This can be a very important number. Below, we will take a look at how to interpret the values.

❑ CPU – In CPU seconds, how much time was spent on this phase of the query execution. This is only filled in if TIMED_STATISTICS was enabled.

❑ ELAPSED – As measured by the wall clock; how long this phase of query execution took. This is only filled in if TIMED_STATISTICS is enabled.

❑ DISK – How many physical I/Os to the disk our query performed.

❑ QUERY – How many blocks we processed in consistent-read mode. This will include counts of blocks read from the rollback segment in order to 'rollback' a block.

❑ CURRENT – How many blocks were read in 'CURRENT' mode. CURRENT mode blocks are retrieved, as they exist right now, not in a consistent read fashion. Normally, blocks are retrieved for a query as they existed when the query *began*. Current mode blocks are retrieved, as they exist right now, not from a previous point in time. During a SELECT, we might see CURRENT mode retrievals due to reading the data dictionary to find the extent information for a table to do a full scan (we need the 'right now' information on that, not the consistent-read). During a modification, we will access the blocks in CURRENT mode in order to write to them.

❑ ROWS – How many rows were affected by that phase of processing. A SELECT will show them in the FETCH phase. An UPDATE would show how many rows were updated in the EXECUTE phase.

The important threads or facts to look for in this section of the report are as follows:

A high (near 100 percent) parse count to execute count ratio when the execute count is greater than one – Here, you take the number of times you parsed this statement and divide by the number of times you executed it. If this ratio is 1 – then you parsed this query each and every time you executed it and that needs to be corrected. We would like this ratio to approach zero. Ideally, the parse count would be one and the execute count would be higher than one. If we see a high parse count, this implies we are performing many soft parses of this query. If you recall from the previous section, this can drastically reduce your scalability, and will impact your run-time performance even in a single user session. You should ensure that you parse a query once per session and execute it repeatedly – you never want to have to parse your SQL for each execution.

Execute count of one for all or nearly all SQL – If you have a TKPROF report in which all SQL statements are executed one time only, you are probably not using bind variables (they queries all look alike except for some constant in them). In a real application trace, we would expect very little 'unique' SQL; the same SQL should be executed more than once. Too much unique SQL typically implies you are not using bind variables correctly.

A large disparity between CPU time and elapsed time – This would indicate that you spent a lot of time waiting for something. If you see that you took one CPU second to execute, but it required ten seconds by the wall clock, it means you spent 90 percent of your run-time waiting for a resource. We'll see later on in this section how we can use the raw trace file to determine the cause of the wait. This wait could be for any number of reasons. For example, an update that was blocked by another session would have a very large elapsed time versus CPU time. A SQL query that performs lots of physical disk I/O might have lots of wait time for I/O to complete.

A large CPU or elapsed time number – These are your queries that represent the 'lowest hanging fruit'. If you can make them go faster, your program will go faster. Many times, there is one monster query gumming up the works; fix this and the application works just fine.

A high (FETCH COUNT)/(rows fetched) ratio – Here we take the number of FETCH calls (two in our example) and the rows fetched count (15 in our example). If this number is near one and the rows fetched is greater than one, our application is not performing bulk fetches. Every language/API has the ability to do this – to fetch many rows at a time in a single call. If you do not utilize this ability to bulk fetch, you will spend much more time performing round trips from the client to the server than you should. This excessive switching back and forth, in addition to generating a very 'chatty' network situation, is much slower than fetching many rows in one call. How you direct your application to bulk fetch is 'language/API' dependent. For example, in Pro*C you would pre-compile with prefetch=NN, in Java/JDBC you would call the SETROWPREFETCH method, in PL/SQL you would use the BULK COLLECT directive in a SELECT INTO, and so on. The above example shows that SQL*PLUS (the client we used), called fetch twice in order to retrieve 15 rows. This shows that SQL*PLUS used an array size of at least eight rows. In fact, SQL*PLUS uses by default, an array size of 15 rows – the second fetch it made returned zero records, it just got the end-of file.

An excessively high disk count – This is harder to evaluate as a rule of thumb, however if the DISK COUNT = QUERY + CURRENT MODE BLOCK COUNT, then all blocks, were read from disk. We would hope that if the same query were executed again, some of the blocks would be found in the SGA. You should consider a high disk count value to be a red flag, something to investigate. You might have to do some SGA resizing or work on the query to develop one that requires less block reads.

An excessively high query or current count – This indicates your query does a lot of work. Whether this is an issue or not is subjective. Some queries just hit a lot of data, as our example above does. A query that is executed frequently however, should have relatively small counts. If you add query and current mode blocks from the total line and divide that by the count column from the execute line, you would expect a small number.

Lets go, onto the next part of the report:

```
Misses in library cache during parse: 0
Optimizer goal: CHOOSE
Parsing user id: 69
```

This is telling us that the query we executed was found in the shared pool – we did not generate a miss on the library cache during this parse. It indicates that we performed a soft parse of the query. The very first time a query is executed, we would expect this count to be one. If almost every query you execute has a one for this value, it would indicate you are not using bind variables (and you need to fix that). You are not reusing SQL.

The second line there, informs us of the optimizer mode that was in place during the execution of this query. This is informational only – the query plan developed and used would be affected by this setting.

Finally, the USERID used to parse the query is presented. This can be resolved into a USERNAME via:

```
tkyte@TKYTE816> select * from all_users where user_id = 69;

USERNAME                            USER_ID CREATED
-------------------------------- ---------- ---------
TKYTE                                    69 10-MAR-01
```

showing that I ran it. The last section of the TKPROF report for this query is the query plan. The query plan that appears by default is shown below:

```
Rows       Row Source Operation
-------    --------------------------------------------------
     15    SORT GROUP BY
  21792     FILTER
  21932      NESTED LOOPS
     46       TABLE ACCESS FULL USER$
  21976       TABLE ACCESS BY INDEX ROWID OBJ$
  21976        INDEX RANGE SCAN (object id 34)
      1     FIXED TABLE FULL X$KZSPR
      1     FIXED TABLE FULL X$KZSPR
      0     FIXED TABLE FULL X$KZSPR
      0     FIXED TABLE FULL X$KZSPR
      1     FIXED TABLE FULL X$KZSPR
      1     FIXED TABLE FULL X$KZSPR
      1     FIXED TABLE FULL X$KZSPR
      1     FIXED TABLE FULL X$KZSPR
```

```
       1    FIXED TABLE FULL X$KZSPR
       1    FIXED TABLE FULL X$KZSPR
       1    FIXED TABLE FULL X$KZSPR
       1    FIXED TABLE FULL X$KZSPR
       1    FIXED TABLE FULL X$KZSPR
       1    FIXED TABLE FULL X$KZSPR
   11777    NESTED LOOPS
   30159     FIXED TABLE FULL X$KZSRO
   28971     TABLE ACCESS BY INDEX ROWID OBJAUTH$
   28973      INDEX RANGE SCAN (object id 101)
     631     TABLE ACCESS BY INDEX ROWID IND$
     654      INDEX UNIQUE SCAN (object id 36)
```

This is the actual query plan that was used by Oracle at run-time. The interesting thing about this plan is that the rows that flow through each step of the plan are visible. We can see for example that 28971 rows were fetched from OBJAUTH$. These counts are the row counts of the rows flowing out of that step of the execution plan (after any predicates that could be applied where applied to OBJAUTH$, it sent 28971 onto the next step in the plan). In Oracle 8.0 and before, this count was the count of rows inspected by that phase of the execution plan (the number of rows flowing into this step). For example, if 50000 rows were considered in OBJAUTH$, but some WHERE clause was used to exclude them, a TKPROF report from Oracle 8.0 would have reported 50,000 instead. Using this sort of information, you can see what steps you might want to avoid in a query, and either record the query, or use HINTS to come up with a more desirable plan.

You'll notice that there are a mixture of object names (for example, TABLE ACCESS BY INDEX ROWID IND$) and object IDs (for example, INDEX UNIQUE SCAN (object id 36)). This is because the raw trace file does not record all of the object names, only the object IDs for some objects. Also, TKPROF will not connect to the database to turn the object IDs into object names by default. We can easily turn this object ID into an object name via the query:

```
tkyte@TKYTE816> select owner, object_type, object_name
  2  from all_objects
  3  where object_id = 36;

OWNER                           OBJECT_TYPE         OBJECT_NAME
------------------------------- ------------------- --------------
SYS                             INDEX               I_IND1
```

Alternatively, we could add the EXPLAIN= parameter to TKPROF as follows:

```
C:\oracle\ADMIN\tkyte816\udump>tkprof ora01124.trc x.txt explain=tkyte/tkyte
```

in this case, we would receive the following error in the output file:

```
error during parse of EXPLAIN PLAN statement
ORA-01039: insufficient privileges on underlying objects of the view
```

While we can run the query, the base table that the view accesses are not visible to us. In order to get the explain plan for this query we would use the SYS account, or some other account, that does have access to the underlying objects.

I prefer to never use the EXPLAIN= however and would recommend the same for you.

The reason is that the explain plan query may differ radically from the actual query used at run-time. The only plan that can be trusted is the plan saved in the trace file itself. Here is a simple example using TKPROF with the explain=userid/password that demonstrates this:

```
select count(object_type)
from
 t where object_id > 0

call     count       cpu    elapsed  disk       query     current       rows
------- ------  --------  ---------- -----  ----------  ----------  ----------
Parse        1      0.00        0.00     0           0           0           0
Execute      1      0.00        0.00     0           0           0           0
Fetch        2      0.19        2.07   337       20498           0           1
------- ------  --------  ---------- -----  ----------  ----------  ----------
total        4      0.19        2.07   337       20498           0           1

Misses in library cache during parse: 1
Optimizer goal: CHOOSE
Parsing user id: 69   (TKYTE)

Rows      Row Source Operation
-------  ---------------------------------------------------
      1   SORT AGGREGATE
  21790     TABLE ACCESS BY INDEX ROWID T
  21791       INDEX RANGE SCAN (object id 25291)


Rows      Execution Plan
-------  ---------------------------------------------------
      0   SELECT STATEMENT    GOAL: CHOOSE
      1     SORT (AGGREGATE)
  21790       TABLE ACCESS    GOAL: ANALYZED (FULL) OF 'T'
```

Obviously, one of the plans is incorrect; one shows an index range scan and table access by row ID, the other a simple full scan. Unless you knew *that I analyzed the table after you executed your query, but before you ran* TKPROF, you would be unable to explain this disparity. After I analyzed the table, the default plan for that query changed dramatically. TKPROF just uses the explain plan facility in Oracle. This will return the query plan that would be used at this point in time; *not* the plan that was actually used. Many features can impact the plan visible in the trace file versus the plan returned by explain plan. For example, the application could have been used stored query outlines (see Chapter 11 on *Optimizer Plan Stability* for more details on this feature). The query plan would have been based on a stored outline at run-time whereas the query plan returned by explain plan would be some other plan. In general, if you do use the EXPLAIN= parameter to TKPROF, you must verify that the two plans agree with each other step by step.

TKPROF has many command line options and if you just type TKPROF on the command line, you'll get to see them all:

```
C:\Documents and Settings\Thomas Kyte\Desktop>tkprof

Usage: tkprof tracefile outputfile [explain= ] [table= ]
              [print= ] [insert= ] [sys= ] [sort= ]
  table=schema.tablename   Use 'schema.tablename' with 'explain=' option.
```

```
explain=user/password    Connect to ORACLE and issue EXPLAIN PLAIN.
print=integer      List only the first 'integer' SQL statements.
aggregate=yes|no
insert=filename  List SQL statements and data inside INSERT statements.
sys=no             TKPROF does not list SQL statements run as user SYS.
record=filename  Record non-recursive statements found in the trace file.
sort=option        Set of zero or more of the following sort options:
  prscnt  number of times parse was called
  prscpu  cpu time parsing
  prsela  elapsed time parsing
  prsdsk  number of disk reads during parse
  prsqry  number of buffers for consistent read during parse
  prscu   number of buffers for current read during parse
  prsmis  number of misses in library cache during parse
  execnt  number of execute was called
  execpu  cpu time spent executing
  exeela  elapsed time executing
  exedsk  number of disk reads during execute
  exeqry  number of buffers for consistent read during execute
  execu   number of buffers for current read during execute
  exerow  number of rows processed during execute
  exemis  number of library cache misses during execute
  fchcnt  number of times fetch was called
  fchcpu  cpu time spent fetching
  fchela  elapsed time fetching
  fchdsk  number of disk reads during fetch
  fchqry  number of buffers for consistent read during fetch
  fchcu   number of buffers for current read during fetch
  fchrow  number of rows fetched
  userid  userid of user that parsed the cursor
```

The most useful option in my opinion is the `sort=` option. I like to sort by the various CPU and elapsed time metrics to get the 'worst' queries to pop up to the top of the trace file. You can also use this to find the queries that do too much I/O and so on. The remaining options are self-explanatory. 99.9 percent of the time I simply use `tkprof tracefilename reportfilename` and nothing else. This shows the SQL more or less in the order it was executed at run-time. I might use a tool such as `grep` in UNIX or `find` in windows to extract all of the `total` lines so I know what queries to zoom in on. For example, using our `report.txt`:

```
C:\oracle\ADMIN\tkyte816\udump>find "total" report.txt

---------- REPORT.TXT
total      2     0.00    0.00    0        0        0          0
total      4     0.01    0.02    1        1        4          1
total      4     1.20    1.21    0    86091        4         15
total      6     0.01    0.01    0        4        0          2
total      4     0.00    0.00    0        0        0          1
total     14     1.21    1.23    1    86092        8         17
total      6     0.01    0.01    0        4        0          2
```

shows me I should edit `report.txt` and search for `1.21` if I want to speed up this process. There are other statements in there but obviously; this is the one I need to focus on if I want this to go faster.

Using and Interpreting Raw Trace Files

There are two types of trace files in Oracle; those generated by SQL_TRACE (these are useful to us) and those generated as a result of a failed session (a bug in the database software). The second type, from a failed session, is not useful to us directly; they are only useful for sending to Oracle Support for analysis. The first type of trace file *is* very useful to us, especially if we know how to read and interpret them.

Most of the time, we will use TKPROF to format the trace files for use, however from time to time we need to dig into the trace file to understand more about what happened than TKPROF will tell us. For example, suppose someone gives you a TKPROF report with:

```
UPDATE EMP SET ENAME=LOWER(ENAME)
WHERE
 EMPNO = :b1


call     count       cpu    elapsed  disk      query    current       rows
-------  ------  --------  ---------- -----  ---------- ----------  ----------
Parse        1      0.00       0.00      0          0          0           0
Execute      1      0.00      54.25      0         17          8           1
Fetch        0      0.00       0.00      0          0          0           0
-------  ------  --------  ---------- -----  ---------- ----------  ----------
total        2      0.00      54.25      0         17          8           1
```

It is obvious we have a problem here – it took almost a minute to do an update of a single row, even though it took no measurable CPU time. The problem is that we had some massive wait event on something, but TKPROF won't tell us what we were waiting on. Additionally, it would be nice if we knew which row it was that we were going after (such as what the EMPNO value in :b1 was). Information like that might help us track down how we go into this situation. Fortunately, the application was traced with the following command:

```
alter session set events '10046 trace name context forever, level 12';
```

so the trace file has both wait events and bind variables in it. Let's take a look at the raw trace file from top to bottom. The piece of code that I traced was:

```
scott@TKYTE816> alter session set events
  2  '10046 trace name context forever, level 12';

Session altered.

scott@TKYTE816> declare
  2  l_empno number default 7698;
  3  begin
  4      update emp set ename = lower(ename) where empno = l_empno;
  5  end;
  6  /

PL/SQL procedure successfully completed.

scott@TKYTE816> exit
```

We do know the EMPNO being used in this simple example but in general, you would not. Here are the contents of the trace file interspersed with comments:

```
Dump file C:\oracle\admin\tkyte816\udump\ORA01156.TRC
Sat Mar 17 12:16:38 2001
ORACLE V8.1.6.0.0 - Production vsnsta=0
vsnsql=e vsnxtr=3
Windows 2000 Version 5.0 , CPU type 586
Oracle8i Enterprise Edition Release 8.1.6.0.0 - Production
With the Partitioning option
JServer Release 8.1.6.0.0 - Production
Windows 2000 Version 5.0 , CPU type 586
Instance name: tkyte816

Redo thread mounted by this instance: 1

Oracle process number: 11

Windows thread id: 1156, image: ORACLE.EXE
```

This is a standard trace file header. It is useful to identify the exact system version and database version you are executing on. It also has the Oracle SID in it (Instance Name), which is useful for confirming you are looking at the right trace file in the first place.

```
*** 2001-03-17 12:16:38.407
*** SESSION ID:(7.74) 2001-03-17 12:16:38.407
APPNAME mod='SQL*PLUS' mh=3669949024 act='' ah=4029777240
====================
```

The above APPNAME record was made by a call to the DBMS_APPLICATION_INFO package (see Appendix A on *Necessary Supplied Packages* for details on this package). Applications use this package to register themselves in the database, so that a query on V$SESSION can see 'who' they are. SQL*PLUS in particular makes use of this package. You may or may not see an APPNAME record in your trace file depending on the environment. It is an *excellent* idea for you to have all of your applications register themselves, so hopefully you will see this record with your own module name. The meaning of this record is:

```
APPNAME mod='%s' mh=%lu act='%s' ah=%lu
```

Field	Meaning
mod	Module name as passed to DBMS_APPLICATION_INFO
mh	Module hash value
act	Action as passed to DBMS_APPLICATION_INFO
ah	Action hash value

If you are a C programmer, you'll recognize the C printf format string. This can be used to tell us the data types we can expect to find in the APPNAME record; a %s is a string, the %lu is a long unsigned integer (a number). Continuing on, the next thing I see in my trace file is:

465

```
PARSING IN CURSOR #3 len=70 dep=0 uid=54 oct=42 lid=54 tim=6184206 hv=347037164
   ad='31883a4'
alter session set events '10046 trace name context forever, level 12'
END OF STMT
EXEC #3:c=0,e=0,p=0,cr=0,cu=0,mis=1,r=0,dep=0,og=4,tim=6184206
WAIT #3: nam='SQL*Net message to client' ela= 0 p1=1111838976 p2=1 p3=0
WAIT #3: nam='SQL*Net message from client' ela= 818 p1=1111838976 p2=1 p3=0
=====================
```

Here we can see the actual statement used to enable tracing. It is preceded by a CURSOR record, which will always be the case (all SQL in the trace file will be preceded by a cursor record). The meaning of the fields in the cursor record is:

```
Parsing in Cursor #%d len=%d dep=%d uid=%ld oct=%d lid=%ld tim=%ld hv=%ld ad='%s'
```

Field	Meaning
Cursor #	The cursor number. You can use this to find the maximum number of open cursors in your application as well since this number is incremented and decremented each time you open a new cursor and close an existing one.
len	Length of the SQL statement to follow.
dep	The recursive depth of a SQL statement. Recursive SQL is SQL performed on behalf of some other SQL. Typically, this is SQL executed by Oracle in order to parse a query or perform space management. It can also be caused by PL/SQL (which is SQL) running SQL. So, you may find your own SQL is 'recursive'.
uid	User ID of the current schema. Note, this may be different than the lid below, especially if you use alter session set current_schema to change the parsing schema.
oct	Oracle Command Type. Numeric code indicating the type of SQL command being parsed.
lid	The user ID used to security-check the access privileges against.
tim	A timer. Its resolution is hundredths of seconds. You can subtract these times from each other as you encounter them in the trace file to see how far apart they occurred.
ha	Hash ID of the SQL statement.
ad	ADDR column of V$SQLAREA that refers to this SQL statement.

Next in the trace file, we can see the statement was actually executed right after parsing. The meanings of the values found in the EXEC record are:

```
EXEC Cursor#:c=%d,e=%d,p=%d,cr=%d,cu=%d,mis=%d,r=%d,dep=%d,og=%d,tim=%d
```

Field	Meaning
Cursor #	The cursor number.
c	CPU time in hundredths of seconds.
e	Elapsed time in hundredths of seconds.
p	Number of physical reads performed.
cr	Consistent (query mode) reads (logical I/O).
cu	Current mode reads (logical I/O).
mis	Cursor miss in the library cache, indicates we had to parse the statement due to its being aged out of the shared pool, never having been in the shared pool, or it was otherwise invalidated.
r	Number of rows processed.
dep	Recursive depth of the SQL statement.
og	Optimizer goal, 1= all rows, 2 = first rows, 3 = rule, 4 = choose
tim	A timer.

There are other variations of the EXEC, record. Instead of the keyword EXEC we might also find:

Field	Meaning
PARSE	Parsing a statement.
FETCH	When fetching rows from a cursor.
UNMAP	Used to show freeing of temporary segments from intermediate results when they are no longer needed.
SORT UNMAP	Same as unmap but for sort segments.

The records for each of PARSE, FETCH, UNMAP, and SORT UNMAP contain the same information as an EXEC record does in the same order.

The last part of this section has our first reports of wait events. In this case they were:

```
WAIT #3: nam='SQL*Net message to client' ela= 0 p1=1111838976 p2=1 p3=0
WAIT #3: nam='SQL*Net message from client' ela= 818 p1=1111838976 p2=1 p3=0
```

These are typical 'busy' wait events that we discussed earlier in this chapter. The message to client is the server sending the client a message and waiting for a response. The message from client is the server waiting for the client to send a request over. In this case, the elapsed time (ela) on that event was 8.18 seconds. This just means I waited 8.18 seconds after sending the ALTER SESSION command to the database to send the next command in this example. Unless you are feeding a constant and continuous stream of requests to the server, 'message from client' waits will be unavoidable and normal. The wait record includes these fields:

```
WAIT Cursor#: nam='%s' ela=%d p1=%ul p2=%ul p3=%ul
```

Field	Meaning
Cursor #	The cursor number.
nam	The name of the wait event. The Oracle Server Reference has a complete list of wait events and details on each one.
ela	Elapsed time in hundredths of seconds for the event.
p1, p2, p3	The parameters specific to the wait event. Each event has its own set of parameters. Refer to the Oracle Server Reference for the meaning of p1, p2, p3 for a specific wait event.

Now we are ready to look at our first real statement in our trace file:

```
PARSING IN CURSOR #3 len=110 dep=0 uid=54 oct=47 lid=54 tim=6185026 hv=2018962105
   ad='31991c8'
declare
l_empno number default 7698;
begin
    update emp set ename = lower(ename) where empno = l_empno;
end;
END OF STMT
PARSE #3:c=0,e=0,p=0,cr=0,cu=0,mis=1,r=0,dep=0,og=4,tim=6185026
BINDS #3:
=====================
```

Here we see our PL/SQL block of code as we submitted it. We can see from the PARSE record that it parsed very quickly, even though it was not in the library cache yet (MIS=1). We see a BINDS record with nothing after it. That's because this particular block of code has no bind variables. We will revisit this bind record further on down. We'll continue onto the next statement in the trace file where things get really interesting:

```
PARSING IN CURSOR #4 len=51 dep=1 uid=54 oct=6 lid=54 tim=6185026 hv=2518517322
   ad='318e29c'
UPDATE EMP SET ENAME=LOWER(ENAME) WHERE EMPNO = :b1
END OF STMT
PARSE #4:c=0,e=0,p=0,cr=0,cu=0,mis=1,r=0,dep=1,og=0,tim=6185026
BINDS #4:
 bind 0: dty=2 mxl=22(21) mal=00 scl=00 pre=00 oacflg=03 oacfl2=1 size=24 offset=0
   bfp=07425360 bln=22 avl=03 flg=05
    value=7698
WAIT #4: nam='enqueue' ela= 308 p1=1415053318 p2=393290 p3=2947
WAIT #4: nam='enqueue' ela= 307 p1=1415053318 p2=393290 p3=2947
WAIT #4: nam='enqueue' ela= 307 p1=1415053318 p2=393290 p3=2947
WAIT #4: nam='enqueue' ela= 308 p1=1415053318 p2=393290 p3=2947
WAIT #4: nam='enqueue' ela= 307 p1=1415053318 p2=393290 p3=2947
WAIT #4: nam='enqueue' ela= 308 p1=1415053318 p2=393290 p3=2947
WAIT #4: nam='enqueue' ela= 307 p1=1415053318 p2=393290 p3=2947
WAIT #4: nam='enqueue' ela= 308 p1=1415053318 p2=393290 p3=2947
WAIT #4: nam='enqueue' ela= 307 p1=1415053318 p2=393290 p3=2947
WAIT #4: nam='enqueue' ela= 308 p1=1415053318 p2=393290 p3=2947
WAIT #4: nam='enqueue' ela= 307 p1=1415053318 p2=393290 p3=2947
```

```
WAIT #4: nam='enqueue' ela= 307 p1=1415053318 p2=393290 p3=2947
WAIT #4: nam='enqueue' ela= 308 p1=1415053318 p2=393290 p3=2947
WAIT #4: nam='enqueue' ela= 307 p1=1415053318 p2=393290 p3=2947
WAIT #4: nam='enqueue' ela= 308 p1=1415053318 p2=393290 p3=2947
WAIT #4: nam='enqueue' ela= 307 p1=1415053318 p2=393290 p3=2947
WAIT #4: nam='enqueue' ela= 308 p1=1415053318 p2=393290 p3=2947
WAIT #4: nam='enqueue' ela= 198 p1=1415053318 p2=393290 p3=2947
EXEC #4:c=0,e=5425,p=0,cr=17,cu=8,mis=0,r=1,dep=1,og=4,tim=6190451
EXEC #3:c=0,e=5425,p=0,cr=17,cu=8,mis=0,r=1,dep=0,og=4,tim=6190451
WAIT #3: nam='SQL*Net message to client' ela= 0 p1=1111838976 p2=1 p3=0
WAIT #3: nam='SQL*Net message from client' ela= 0 p1=1111838976 p2=1 p3=0
=====================
```

Here, we see our UPDATE statement as Oracle sees it. It is different than it was in the PL/SQL block of code; specifically our reference to 1_empno (a variable) is replaced with a bind variable. PL/SQL replaces all references to local variables with bind variables before executing the statement. We can also see from the PARSING IN CURSOR record that the recursive depth (dep) is now one, not zero as it was in the original PL/SQL block. We can tell that this is SQL executed by some *other* SQL (or PL/SQL); it was not submitted by the client application to the database. This is a flag we can use to tell us where to look for this SQL. If the dep is not zero, we know the SQL 'lives' in the database, not in a client application. We can use this to our advantage when tuning. SQL that lives in the database can be changed *easily* without affecting the application. SQL that lives in the client application requires us to find the client, change the code, recompile it, and re-deploy it. The more SQL I can get to live in my database, the better. I can fix it without touching the application itself.

We see a BINDS record in here again, this time with more information. This update statement has a bind value and we can clearly see what it is – the value of the first bind variable is 7,698. Now, if this were a problem query we were looking at (a poorly performing query), we would have most all of information we needed to tune it. We have the text of the query exactly. We have the values of all bind variables (so we can run it with the same inputs). We even have the wait events that slowed us down during the execution. The only thing missing is the query plan, but that is only because we haven't paged down far enough.

The BIND record in the trace file contains this information:

Field	Meaning
cursor #	The cursor number.
bind N	The bind position starting from 0 (0 being the first bind variable).
dty	Datatype (see below).
mxl	Maximum length of the bind variable.
mal	Maximum array length (when using array binds or bulk operations).
scl	Scale.
pre	Precision.

Table continued on following page

Field	Meaning
oacflg	Internal flags. If this number is odd, the bind variable might be null (allows nulls).
oacfl2	Continuation of internal flags.
size	Size of buffer.
offset	Used in piecewise binds.
bfp	Bind Address.
bln	Bind buffer length.
avl	Actual value length.
flag	Internal Flags.
value	The character string representation (if possible, might be a 'hex' dump) of the bind value – this is what we really want!

The dty (data type) number may be decoded using information from the USER_TAB_COLUMNS view. If you select text from all_views where view_name = 'USER_VIEWS', you'll see a decode function call that will map the dty numbers to their character string representations.

The really interesting information, what we were after ultimately, is right here now; the wait information. We can clearly see why the update took almost one minutes wall clock time to complete even though it took no CPU time. The resource we were waiting on was a lock – if you recall from Chapters 3 and 4 where we discussed *Locking and Concurrency* and *Transactions*, an enqueue is one of two locking mechanisms Oracle employs internally to serialize access to shared resources. The trace file shows us we were waiting on a lock, we were not waiting on I/O, we were not waiting on a log file sync, we were not waiting for buffers to become free – we were enqueued on some resource. Going further, we can take the p1 parameter, and decode it to see what type of lock we were waiting on. The process for doing that:

```
tkyte@TKYTE816> create or replace
  2  function enqueue_decode( l_p1 in number ) return varchar2
  3  as
  4      l_str varchar2(25);
  5  begin
  6      select chr(bitand(l_p1,-16777216)/16777215)||
  7             chr(bitand(l_p1, 16711680)/65535)  || ' ' ||
  8             decode( bitand(l_p1, 65535),
  9                         0, 'No lock',
 10                         1, 'No lock',
 11                         2, 'Row-Share',
 12                         3, 'Row-Exclusive',
 13                         4, 'Share',
 14                         5, 'Share Row-Excl',
 15                         6, 'Exclusive' )
 16          into l_str
 17          from dual;
 18
 19      return l_str;
```

```
 20  end;
 21  /

Function created.

tkyte@TKYTE816>
tkyte@TKYTE816> select enqueue_decode( 1415053318  ) from dual;

ENQUEUE_DECODE(1415053318)
-----------------------------------------------------------------------

TX Exclusive
```

This shows that we were waiting on an exclusive row level lock. The answer to why it took one minute to update this row is clear now. There was another session holding a lock on the row we wanted, and they held it for one minute while we waited for it. What we do about this is application-specific. For example, in the above application, I am doing a 'blind update'. If I do not want the application to block on the update, I might process it as:

```
select ename from emp where empno = :bv for update NOWAIT;
update emp set ename = lower(ename) where empno = :bv;
```

This would avoid the locking issue. At least now we are able to absolutely determine what caused this update to take so long and we are able to diagnose it in a post-mortem fashion. We don't have to 'be there' in order to diagnose this, we just need the relevant trace information.

Finishing up the trace file we see:

```
PARSING IN CURSOR #5 len=52 dep=0 uid=54 oct=47 lid=54 tim=6190451 hv=1697159799
  ad='3532750'
BEGIN DBMS_OUTPUT.GET_LINES(:LINES, :NUMLINES); END;
END OF STMT
PARSE #5:c=0,e=0,p=0,cr=0,cu=0,mis=0,r=0,dep=0,og=4,tim=6190451
BINDS #5:
 bind 0: dty=1 mxl=2000(255) mal=25 scl=00 pre=00 oacflg=43 oacfl2=10 size=2000
 offset=0
   bfp=07448dd4 bln=255 avl=00 flg=05
 bind 1: dty=2 mxl=22(02) mal=00 scl=00 pre=00 oacflg=01 oacfl2=0 size=24 offset=0
   bfp=0741c7e8 bln=22 avl=02 flg=05
   value=25
WAIT #5: nam='SQL*Net message to client' ela= 0 p1=1111838976 p2=1 p3=0
EXEC #5:c=0,e=0,p=0,cr=0,cu=0,mis=0,r=1,dep=0,og=4,tim=6190451
WAIT #5: nam='SQL*Net message from client' ela= 273 p1=1111838976 p2=1 p3=0
```

Now, this statement is a surprise. We never executed it ourselves and it isn't recursive SQL (dep=0). It came from the client application. This actually gives us insight into how SQL*PLUS and DBMS_OUTPUT work. I have set serveroutput on set in my login.sql file so whenever I log into SQL*PLUS, DBMS_OUTPUT is enabled by default. After every statement we execute that can generate DBMS_OUTPUT data, SQL*PLUS must call the GET_LINES procedure to get the data, and dump it to the screen (see the section on DBMS_OUTPUT in Appendix A on *Necessary Supplied Packages* for many more details on DBMS_OUTPUT). Here, we can see SQL*PLUS making that call. Further, we can see that the first parameter, :LINES is in fact an array with 25 slots (mal=25). So, now we know that SQL*PLUS will retrieve the DBMS_OUTPUT buffer 25 lines at a time and dump it to the screen. The fact that we can trace the behavior of SQL*PLUS is interesting; in fact, we can trace the behavior of any piece of software that executes against Oracle, to see what it does and how it does it.

Lastly, at the bottom of our trace file we see:

```
XCTEND rlbk=0, rd_only=0
WAIT #0: nam='log file sync' ela= 0 p1=988 p2=0 p3=0
STAT #4 id=1 cnt=1 pid=0 pos=0 obj=0 op='UPDATE EMP '
STAT #4 id=2 cnt=2 pid=1 pos=1 obj=24767 op='TABLE ACCESS FULL EMP '
```

The XCTEND (transaction boundary) record is a record of our commit, but once again, we didn't commit. SQL*PLUS did that for us silently when we exited. The values of the XCTEND record are:

Field	Meaning
rlbk	Rollack flag. If 0 we committed. If 1 we rolled back.
rd_Only	Read only flag. If 1 the transaction was read-only. If 0, changes were made and committed (or rolled back).

Immediately after the XCTEND record, we can see we had another wait event – this time for a log file sync. If we refer to the Oracle Server Reference and look up that wait event, we'll discover that the 988 for the p1 value represents the fact that buffer 988 in the redo log buffer had to be written out, and that's what we were waiting on. The wait was less than a hundredth of a second, as evidenced by ela=0.

The last records we observe in this trace file are the STAT records. These are the actual query plans used at run-time by our SQL. This is the plan we can trust. Not only that, but this plan will have the row counts correctly associated with each step of the plan. These records are only produced *after* the cursor they represent is closed. Generally, this means the client application must *exit* in order to see these records, simply executing an ALTER SESSION SET SQL_TRACE=FALSE will not necessarily produce these records in the trace file. The values in this record are:

Field	Meaning
cursor #	The cursor number.
id	The line of the explain plan from 1 to number of lines in the plan.
cnt	The number of rows flowing through this phase of the query plan.
pid	Parent ID of this step in the plan. Used to correctly reflect the hierarchy of the plan with indention.
pos	Position in the explain plan.
obj	Object ID of the referenced object if applicable.
op	The textual description of the operation performed.

There are only two other record types that we should find in a SQL_TRACE trace file. They represent errors encountered during the execution of a query. The errors will either be:

❑ PARSE Errors – The SQL statement was not valid SQL.

❑ Run-time errors – such as duplicate value on index, out of space, and so on.

I have used the fact that these errors are recorded to the trace file many times in problem solving. If you are using some off-the-shelf application, a third party tool, or even many Oracle commands and you get back a less than helpful error message, it may be very useful to run the command with SQL_TRACE enabled and see what happens. In many cases, the root cause of the error can be gleaned from the trace file since all of the SQL performed on your behalf is recorded there.

In order to demonstrate what these records look like, I executed the following SQL:

```
tkyte@TKYTE816> create table t ( x int primary key );

Table created.

tkyte@TKYTE816> alter session set sql_trace=true;

Session altered.

tkyte@TKYTE816> select * from;
select * from
             *
ERROR at line 1:
ORA-00903: invalid table name


tkyte@TKYTE816> insert into t values ( 1 );

1 row created.

tkyte@TKYTE816> insert into t values ( 1 );
insert into t values ( 1 )
*
ERROR at line 1:
ORA-00001: unique constraint (TKYTE.SYS_C002207) violated

tkyte@TKYTE816> exit
```

Upon reviewing the trace file I discovered:

```
=====================
PARSE ERROR #3:len=15 dep=0 uid=69 oct=3 lid=69 tim=7160573 err=903
select * from
=====================
PARSING IN CURSOR #3 len=27 dep=0 uid=69 oct=2 lid=69 tim=7161010 hv=1601248092
    ad='32306c0'
insert into t values ( 1 )
END OF STMT
PARSE #3:c=0,e=0,p=0,cr=0,cu=0,mis=0,r=0,dep=0,og=4,tim=7161010
=====================
...
EXEC #3:c=1,e=9,p=0,cr=9,cu=7,mis=0,r=0,dep=0,og=4,tim=7161019
ERROR #3:err=1 tim=7161019
```

As you can see, finding the problem SQL (the root cause of the error) is trivial with this method; we can clearly see what went wrong. This is extremely useful if you are debugging an error that is happening deep inside of a stored procedure, for example. I've seen more than one case where an error occurs in a deeply nested stored procedure, and someone has a WHEN OTHERS exception handler that catches and *ignores* all exceptions. It is my opinion that the WHEN OTHERS exception handler should never be used and all applications that use it, and do not re-raise the error immediately, should be erased immediately – they are bugs waiting to happen. In any case, the error happens, but is caught and ignored, and no one is ever notified of it. The procedure appears to have worked, but it did not actually work. Here, a simple SQL_TRACE will show us what the procedure actually does and we can see that there was an error. Then all we need do is figure out why in the world it is being ignored. I also use this when commands return less than useful error messages. For example, if a snapshot (materialized view) refresh returns ORA-00942: table or view does not exist, using SQL_TRACE will be extremely useful. You might not be aware of all of the SQL that is executed on your behalf to refresh a materialized view, and the number of tables that are 'touched'. Using SQL_TRACE you'll actually be able to figure out *which* table or view does not exist, and put the correct permissions in place.

The format of the PARSE ERROR record is:

Field	Meaning
len	Length of the SQL statement
dep	Recursive depth of the SQL statement
uid	Parsing schema (may be different from the privilege schema)
oct	Oracle command type
lid	Privilege schema ID, whose privilege set the statement is actually executing under
tim	A timer
err	The ORA error code. If you execute:

```
tkyte@TKYTE816> EXEC DBMS_OUTPUT.PUT_LINE(SQLERRM(-903));
ORA-00903: invalid table name
```

You can get the text of the error.

the contents of the ERROR record is simply:

Field	Meaning
cursor #	The cursor number
err	The ORA error code
tim	A timer

SQL_TRACE, TIMED_STATISTICS, and TKPROF Wrap-Up

In this section we took a fairly in depth look at a set of tools – a set of invaluable tools that work in all environments, and are always available to us. SQL_TRACE and the result reports available via TKPROF is one of the most powerful tuning and debugging tools you have available. I have used them to successfully debug and tune applications on countless occasions. Their ubiquity (there is no Oracle installation anywhere that does not have these tools) coupled with their power makes them second to none when it comes to tuning.

If you understand how to trace your application and how to interpret the results, you'll be halfway done with the tuning of your application. The other half is left to you – that is where you figure out why your query needs to access a million block buffers, or why it is waiting five minutes on enqueue waits. SQL_TRACE will tell you what to look at – fixing the problem is typically easier than finding it, especially if you are unfamiliar with the application in the first place.

DBMS_PROFILER

If you are a heavy PL/SQL user, you'll welcome the addition of a source code profiler in the database. With Oracle 8i, we have a full-blown source code profiler for PL/SQL integrated into the database. This package, DBMS_PROFILER, allows us to zero in on the routines and packages where we spend the largest amount of our execution time. Not only that, but it provides code coverage analysis, allowing us to tell if we have exercised 10 percent or 99 percent of our code with a given test run.

In Appendix A on *Necessary Supplied Packages*, I go into some detail on how to use the DBMS_PROFILER package and how to interpret the resulting reports and data. It is very straightforward to use and is nicely integrated in with PL/SQL itself. During the course of a PL/SQL stored procedure you can turn profiling on and off as you narrow down the section of code you would like to tune.

My stages of tuning an application would have me using SQL_TRACE and TKPROF first to identify and correct poorly tuned SQL in an application. After all of the SQL was executing as fast as it possibly could, I would start in with the source code profiler if need be to tune further. With the exception of a really bad algorithm, the biggest bang for the buck, performance-wise will come from tuning SQL. I find only moderate increases in tuning PL/SQL source code; worthy of the effort, but not as large as fixing a bad query. Of course, if the algorithm was terrible to begin with, this might not be true.

The other use of the profiler is to provide code coverage reports. This can be extremely useful during the testing phase of your application. Utilizing this feature, you can set up test cases and show that 100 percent of your code has been exercised during the test runs. While this does not guarantee bug free code, it does make sure nothing is obviously wrong.

Instrumentation

This is crucial to do, especially in a large application with many moving pieces. As applications get more complex, and have more interacting pieces, finding where the performance issue actually is has become more difficult then actually fixing the issue. By way of definition, instrumentation is including, in your code, enough logging capabilities that can selectively be enabled at will to figure out a) what the program is doing, and b) how long it takes it to do it. Everything from the simplest process to the most complex algorithm should be instrumented thoroughly. Yes, instrumentation adds overhead, even when you are not logging the messages, however the inability to determine where an issue is without it far outweighs any trivial performance overhead of having it.

In the beginning of this chapter, I related a story of my last tuning expedition. The architecture was complex to say the least. There was a browser front-end coming into a web server farm, across a very restrictive firewall. The web servers were executing Java Server Pages (JSPs). The JSPs used a connection pooling mechanism to get to the database to run some SQL and PL/SQL. They also made CORBA callouts to yet another application server, to interface with the legacy system. They were just a piece of a much larger application all together. There were batch jobs, background processes, queue processing, other off-the-shelf software, and so on. I came into that environment without knowing anything about the application, and unfortunately, not too many people there knew something about everything – they all knew their bits and pieces. Getting the big picture is always hard.

Since nothing was instrumented, not even a little, we had to use the tools listed above to try and isolate the issue. SQL_TRACE didn't show anything obvious (in fact it showed the SQL was executing OK). The profiler didn't supply any information beyond the fact that the PL/SQL was running OK. The V$ dynamic performance tables in the database showed us that it was OK. We could only use these tools to prove that it was not the database causing the slow down. We could not use them this time to find the problem. It was outside the database, somewhere between the browser and the database. Unfortunately, this was a maze of JSPs, EJBs, Connection Pools, and CORBA callouts. The only thing we could do is instrument the code to find out where the slow part was. It wasn't like we had a single program we could run in a debugger like the 'old days'. We had dozens of bits and pieces of code here and there glued together with a network – those bits and pieces of code had to tell us which one of them was slow.

We finally discovered it – it was a callout over CORBA to a legacy system that had to be done on almost every page. Only by creating log files with timestamps were we able to isolate this issue. It turned out to not even be a database problem, let alone an application problem, but we still looked pretty bad in the eyes of the end user. They really didn't care *whose* code was slow; they were just really upset that it took weeks to figure it all out.

How you instrument will vary based upon the language you choose. For example, in PL/SQL I use a custom developed package DEBUG. It uses a standardized logging mechanism to create a log file for any PL/SQL routine. We 'litter' our code with calls to debug.f like this:

```
create function foo ...
as
    ...
begin
    debug.f( 'Enter procedure foo' );
    if ( some_condition ) then
        l_predicate := 'x=1';
    end if;

    debug.f( 'Going to return the predicate "%s"', l_predicate );
    return l_predicate;
end;
```

and it created log entries like this for us:

```
011101 145055 ( FOO,  6) Enter procedure foo
011101 145056 ( FOO, 11) Going to return the predicate "x=1"
```

It automatically added the date (01/11/2001) and time (14:50:55), as well as what procedure/package called it and the line number to the log. We have the ability to turn tracing on and off for any given module or set of modules. Not only is this a useful debugging tool, but we also can look at the trace files and see right away what is taking a long time. We'll take another look at this DEBUG utility in Chapter 21 on *Fine Grained Access Control* where we use it heavily.

If every application, and every piece of every application, had such a facility, finding where to start looking for performance-related issues would be easier to say the least. In a non-instrumented system, it is very much like looking for a needle in a haystack. It might even be worse; at least with the needle in a haystack, you don't have lots of people with pre-conceived notions of where the problem is guiding you down the wrong paths initially.

In short, all application components, even the non-database ones, need to be instrumented, especially in today's environment where you don't have a single client application talking to a single server. With the explosion of web-based applications, particularly ones that use complex, distributed architectures, determining *where* the problems are, is infinitely harder than fixing them. By instrumenting your code from the very beginning, you'll be practicing a good defensive technique for problems that will come up down the road. I can guarantee you that you will never be sorry you instrumented; you'll only be sorry if you don't.

I encourage you to leave this instrumented code as is for production. *Do not remove it for production.* That is where it is most useful! My approach has been to implement an empty DEBUG package body (one where the functions all just immediately return). In this fashion, if I need to generate a trace – I just put the real DEBUG package body in, trace what I need to and then put back the empty one later. Removing the code from production 'for performance reasons' will obviate its usefulness. Consider the database itself – by setting a myriad of *events*, Oracle support can elicit a large amount of diagnostic data from your production database – the kernel developers recognize that the cost of *not* having the trace code in the production code far outweighs any perceived overhead.

StatsPack

So far, we have looked at tools that are useful to tune an application. SQL_TRACE, DBMS_PROFILER, instrumenting code – these are all application-level tuning tools. Once we believe we have an application working as well as it can, we should also look at the entire database instance and see how well is it doing. This is where the job duties between the DBA and the developer start to overlap and blur a little. The DBA might find the cause of the slowdown, but it will be the developer who has to fix it in many cases. Working together at this point is mandatory.

In the beginning, the tools one might use were called UTLBSTAT and UTLESTAT (begin statistics and end statistics). The UTLBSTAT script would take a snapshot of many V$ performance tables. At a later date, UTLESTAT would create a report based on the 'before' and 'after' values in the V$ tables. The statistics would then be 'wiped out' and you would be left with a simple textual report to review. Starting with Oracle8i, BSTAT/ESTAT have been formally replaced with the **StatsPack** set of utilities. This is a much more robust set of tools then BSTAT/ESTAT ever was. The most important new piece of functionality is the ability to have a history of the V$ tables stored for you. That is, instead of wiping out the statistics upon the generation of a report, StatsPack allows you to save the data and generate the reports at will, at a later date. With BSTAT/ESTAT for example, it would be impossible to generate a report every day during the week *and* a report that covered each hour of each day during the week. With StatsPack, I can simply set it up to collect statistics every hour (with hardly any measurable impact on my system), and then generate reports that compare any two of the 'snapshots'. In that fashion, I can create a report to cover any hour, as well as any day.

In addition to the reporting flexibility, StatsPack is more comprehensive in the data it displays. In this section, what I would like to do is cover how to install StatsPack, how to collect data, and then most importantly, how to read the resulting report.

Setting up StatsPack

StatsPack is designed to be installed when connected as INTERNAL or more appropriately, as SYSDBA (CONNECT SYS/CHANGE_ON_INSTALL AS SYSDBA), although it will execute a CONNECT INTERNAL. In order to install, you must be able to perform that operation. In many installations, this will be a task that you must ask the DBA or administrators to perform.

Once you have the ability to connect INTERNAl, installing StatsPack is trivial. You simply run statscre.sql in 8.1.6 or spcreate.sql in 8.1.7. These will be found in [ORACLE_HOME]\rdbms\admin when connected as INTERNAL via SQL*PLUS. It would look something like this:

```
C:\oracle\RDBMS\ADMIN>sqlplus internal

SQL*PLUS: Release 8.1.6.0.0 - Production on Sun Mar 18 11:52:32 2001

(c) Copyright 1999 Oracle Corporation.  All rights reserved.


Connected to:
Oracle8i Enterprise Edition Release 8.1.6.0.0 - Production
With the Partitioning option
JServer Release 8.1.6.0.0 - Production

sys@TKYTE816> @statscre
... Installing Required Packages
```

You'll need to know three pieces of information before running the statscre.sql script. They are:

❑ The default tablespace for the user PERFSTAT that will be created.

❑ The temporary tablespace for that user.

❑ The name of the tablespace you would like the StatsPack objects created in. You will not be prompted for this in 8.1.7, only in 8.1.6. This tablespace needs to have sufficient space for about 60 extents (so the size you need depends on your default initial extent size)

The script will prompt you for this information as it executes. In the event you make a typo or inadvertently cancel the installation, you should use spdrop.sql (8.1.7 and up) or statsdrp.sql (8.1.6 and before) to remove the user and installed views prior to attempting another install of StatsPack. The StatsPack installation will create three .lis files (the names of which will be displayed to you during the installation). You should review these for any possible errors that might have occurred. They should install cleanly however, as long as you supplied valid tablespace names (and didn't already have a user PERFSTAT).

Now that StatsPack is installed, all we need to do is collect at least two points of data. The simplest way to do this is to use the STATSPACK package now owned by PERFSTAT as follows:

```
perfstat@DEV2.THINK.COM> exec statspack.snap

PL/SQL procedure successfully completed.
```

Now, we just need to wait a while, let the system run 'normally', and then take another snapshot. Once we have two data points collected, running a report is just as easy. The script statsrep.sql (8.1.6) or spreport.sql (8.1.7) is available to be run for this purpose. It is a SQL*PLUS script designed to be run when connected as PERFSTAT (whose password by default is PERFSTAT – this should be immediately changed after installation!). The report format between version 8.1.6 and 8.1.7 changed slightly, and as I prefer the 8.1.7 format to the 8.1.6 format, this is the report we will run. To run it, we will simply execute:

```
perfstat@ORA8I.WORLD> @spreport


   DB Id      DB Name        Inst Num Instance
 ----------- ------------- -------- ------------
  4080044148 ORA8I                1 ora8i


Completed Snapshots

                            Snap                      Snap
Instance      DB Name        Id   Snap Started       Level Comment
------------ ------------- ----- ----------------- ----- -----------------------
ora8i         ORA8I           1 18 Mar 2001 12:44    10
                              2 18 Mar 2001 12:47    10



Specify the Begin and End Snapshot Ids
~~~~~~~~~~~~~~~~~~~~~~~~~~~~~~~~~~~~~~~
Enter value for begin_snap:
```

We are presented with a list of data points that we have collected, and will be asked to pick any two to compare. Then a default report name will be generated and we are prompted to accept it or to supply a new name. The report is then generated. The following is the 8.1.7 version of a StatsPack report section-by-section with comments describing what to look for, and how to interpret the results.

```
STATSPACK report for
DB Name          DB Id      Instance      Inst Num Release      OPS Host
------------ ----------- ------------ -------- ----------- --- ------------
ORA8I          4080044148 ora8i              1 8.1.6.2.0   NO  aria

                 Snap Id      Snap Time        Sessions
                 ------- ------------------- --------
   Begin Snap:        1 18-Mar-01 12:44:41      22
     End Snap:        3 18-Mar-01 12:57:23      22
       Elapsed:                 12.70 (mins)

Cache Sizes
~~~~~~~~~~~
             db_block_buffers:      16384        log_buffer:       512000
             db_block_size:          8192   shared_pool_size:   102400000
```

The first part of the report is purely informational. It shows what database this report was generated against, including the DB Name and DB Id. These should be unique in your environment. The Instance variable is the Oracle SID of the database. These three bits of data should help you identify exactly which database this report was generated from. That was one of the issues with the old BSTAT/ESTAT reports – they did not show this identifying information. More than once, I was given a report to critique, but it turned out the report wasn't run on the server with the problem. This should never happen again. The other information here is the timing information; when were these data points collected and how far apart they were. It is surprising to many that the data points do not have to be far apart from each other – the above report covers a 13 minute window. They only have to span a normal range of activity. A StatsPack report generated with a 15 minute window is as valid as one with a one-hour window (or an even larger timeframe). In fact, as the window gets larger, it may be more difficult to come to definitive conclusions given the raw numeric data. Lastly, in this section, we see some high-level configuration information for the server. The main components of the SGA are visible for review:

```
Load Profile
~~~~~~~~~~~~                                  Per Second      Per Transaction
                                              ---------------   ---------------
                           Redo size:          5,982.09          13,446.47
                        Logical reads:         1,664.37           3,741.15
                        Block changes:            17.83              40.09
                       Physical reads:            15.25              34.29
                      Physical writes:             5.66              12.73
                           User calls:             3.28               7.37
                              Parses:             16.44              36.96
                         Hard parses:              0.17               0.37
                               Sorts:              2.95               6.64
                              Logons:              0.14               0.32
                            Executes:             30.23              67.95
                        Transactions:             0.44
```

This section shows a great deal of information, in a very small amount of space. We can see how much REDO is generated on average every second and for every transaction. Here, I can see that I generate about 5 to 6 KB of redo per second. My average transaction generates just 13 KB of redo. The next bit of information has to do with logical and physical I/O. I can see here that about 1 percent of my logical reads resulted in physical I/O – that is pretty good. I can also see that on average, my transactions perform almost 4,000 logical reads. Whether that is high or not depends on the type of system you have. In my case, there were some large background jobs executing, so a high read count is acceptable.

Now for the really important information: my parse-related statistics. Here I can see that I do about 16 parses per second and about 0.17 of those are hard parses (SQL that never existed before). Every six seconds or so, my system is parsing some bit of SQL for the very first time. That is not bad. However, I would prefer a count of zero in this column in a finely tuned system that has been running for a couple of days. All SQL should be in the shared pool after some point in time.

```
    % Blocks changed per Read:    1.07    Recursive Call %:    97.39
    Rollback per transaction %:   0.29    Rows per Sort:      151.30
```

The next section in the above shows us some interesting numbers. The % Blocks Changed per Read shows us that in this case, 99 percent of the logical reads we do are for blocks that are only *read*, not updated. This system updates only about 1 percent of the blocks retrieved. The Recursive Call % is very high – over 97 percent. This does not mean that 97 percent of the SQL executed on my system is due to 'space management' or parsing. If you recall from our analysis of the raw trace file earlier from SQL_TRACE, SQL executed from PL/SQL is considered 'recursive SQL'. On my system, virtually all work is performed using PL/SQL, other than mod_plsql (an Apache web server module) and an occasional background job, everything is written in PL/SQL on my system. I would be surprised if the Recursive Call % were low in this case.

The percentage of transactions that rolled back (Rollback per transaction %) is very low, and that is a good thing. Rolling back is extremely expensive. First, we did the work, which was expensive. Then, we undid the work and again, this is expensive. We did a lot of work for nothing. If you find that most of your transactions roll back, you are spending too much time doing work and then immediately undoing it. You should investigate *why* you roll back so much, and how you can rework your application to avoid that. On the system reported on, one out of every 345 transactions resulted in a rollback – this is acceptable.

```
Instance Efficiency Percentages (Target 100%)
~~~~~~~~~~~~~~~~~~~~~~~~~~~~~~~~~~~~~~~~~~~~~~~~~
            Buffer Nowait %:  100.00      Redo NoWait %:  100.00
            Buffer  Hit  %:   99.08    In-memory Sort %:   99.60
            Library Hit  %:   99.46         Soft Parse %:   98.99
          Execute to Parse %:  45.61         Latch Hit %:  100.00
    Parse CPU to Parse Elapsd %:  87.88     % Non-Parse CPU:  100.00
```

Next, we have the `Instance Efficiency Percentages`. Here, they state the target is 100 percent, and this is mostly true. I think the one exception to that is the `Execute to Parse` ratio. This is a measure of how many times a statement was executed as opposed to being parsed. In a system where we parse, and then execute the statement, and never execute it again in the same session, this ratio will be zero. The above shows that for every one parse, I had about 1.8 executes (almost a two to one ratio). It will depend on the nature of the system as to whether this is good or bad. On my particular system, we use `mod_plsql` to do all of our applications. A session is created, a stored procedure is executed, a web page is formed, and the session is destroyed. Unless we execute the same exact SQL many times in a single stored procedure, our execute to parse ratio will be low. On the other hand, if I had a client server or a stateful connection to the database (perhaps via a servlet interface), I would expect this ratio to be much closer to the target of 100 percent. I understand however, that given the architecture I am using, achieving an extremely high execute to parse ratio is not something I can do.

In my mind, the most important ratios are the parse ratios – they get my attention immediately. The soft parse ratio is the ratio of how many *soft* versus *hard* parses we do. 99 percent of the parses on this system are *soft* parses (reused from the shared pool). That is good. If we see a low soft parse ratio, this would be indicative of a system that did not use bind variables. I would expect to see a very high ratio in this field regardless of tools or techniques used. A low number means you are wasting resources and introducing contention. The next number to look at is the `Parse CPU to Parse Elapsd`. Here, I show about 88 percent. This is a little low; I should work on that. In this case for every CPU second spent parsing we spent about 1.13 seconds wall clock time. This means we spent some time waiting for a resource – if the ratio was 100 percent, it would imply CPU time was equal to elapsed time and we processed without any waits. Lastly, when we look at `Non-Parse CPU`, this is a comparison of time spent doing real work versus time spent parsing queries. The report computes this ratio with `round(100*(1-PARSE_CPU/TOT_CPU),2)`. If the `TOT_CPU` is very high compared to the `PARSE_CPU` (as it should be), this ratio will be very near 100 percent, as mine is. This is good, and indicates most of the work performed by the computer was work done to *execute* the queries, and not to *parse* them.

All in all, in looking at the above section, my recommendation would be to reduce the hard parses even further. There obviously are a couple of statements still not using bind variables somewhere in the system (every six seconds a new query is introduced). This in turn would reduce the overall number of parses done because a *hard* parse has to perform a lot of recursive SQL itself. By simply removing a single hard parse call, we'll reduce the number of soft parses we perform as well. Everything else in that section looked acceptable. This first section we just reviewed is my favorite part of the StatsPack report, at a glance it gives a good overview of the relative 'health' of your system. Now, onto the rest of the report:

```
Shared Pool Statistics        Begin   End
                              ------  ------
            Memory Usage %:    75.03   75.26
    % SQL with executions>1:   79.18   78.72
  % Memory for SQL w/exec>1:   74.15   73.33
```

This little snippet gives us some insight into our shared pool utilization. The details shown above are:

❑ Memory Usage – The percentage of the shared pool in use. This number should stabilize in mid-70 percent to less than 90 percent range over time. If the percentage is too low, you are wasting memory. If the percentage is too high, you are aging components out of the shared pool, this will cause SQL to be hard parsed if it is executed again. In a right-sized system, your shared pool usage will stay in the 75 percent to less than 90 percent range.

❑ SQL with executions>1 – This is a measure of how many SQL statements were found in the shared pool that have been executed more than once. This number must be considered carefully in a system that tends to run in cycles, where a different set of SQL is executed during one part of the day versus another (for example, OLTP during the day, DSS at night). You'll have a bunch of SQL statements in your shared pool during the observed time that were not executed, only because the processes that would execute them did not run during the period of observation. Only if your system runs the same working set of SQL continuously will this number be near 100 percent. Here I show that almost 80 percent of the SQL in my shared pool was used more than once in the 13 minute observation window. The remaining 20 percent was there already probably – my system just had no cause to execute it.

❑ Memory for SQL w/exec>1 – This is a measure of how much of the memory the SQL you used frequently consumes, compared to the SQL you did not use frequently. This number will in general be very close to the percentage of SQL with executions greater than one, unless you have some queries that take an inordinate amount of memory. The usefulness of this particular value is questionable.

So, in general you would like to see about 75 to 85 percent of the shared pool being utilized over time in a steady state. The percentage of SQL with executions greater than one should be near 100 percent if the time window for the StatsPack report is big enough to cover all of your cycles. This is one statistic that is affected by the duration of time between the observations. You would expect it to increase as the amount of time between observations increases.

Now, onto the next section:

```
Top 5 Wait Events
~~~~~~~~~~~~~~~~~
                                                      Wait      % Total
Event                                       Waits   Time (cs)   Wt Time
------------------------------------------  ------  ---------   -------
SQL*Net more data from dblink                1,861        836     35.86
control file parallel write                    245        644     27.63
log file sync                                  150        280     12.01
db file scattered read                       1,020        275     11.80
db file sequential read                        483        165      7.08
                                            ------- ----------  -------
Wait Events for DB: ORA8I   Instance: ora8i   Snaps: 1 -3
  -> cs - centisecond -  100th of a second
  -> ms - millisecond - 1000th of a second
  -> ordered by wait time desc, waits desc (idle events last)
```

Here is your 'low hanging fruit', the events that are slowing you down more than anything else. The first step is to look at the Wait Time and see if it is even worth your time to bother tuning anything based on them. For example, I spent 8.36 seconds in a 13 minute time period waiting on data from a dblink. Is that worth my time to investigate and 'fix'? In this case, I would say no, the average wait was 0.004 seconds. Further, I know I have a background process running that is doing a large operation over a database link, the wait time is actually pretty small, all things considered.

So, suppose I did have something that needed attention. Here, what you need to do is first find out what the events mean. For example, if you look up 'log file sync' in the Oracle Reference Manual, you'll discover that it is:

> When a user session COMMITs, the session's redo information needs to be flushed to the redo logfile. The user session will post the LGWR to write the log buffer to the redo log file. When the LGWR has finished writing, it will post the user session.
>
> **Wait Time**: The wait time includes the writing of the log buffer and the post.

Now that I understand what the wait is, I would try to come up with a way to make it 'go away'. In the case of a log file sync, this means tuning LGWR. Basically, to make that wait go away you need to make the disks go faster, generate less redo, reduce contention for the log disks, and so on. Discovering the wait event is one thing, making it go away is another. There are some 200+ events that are timed in Oracle – none of them really have a cut and dry 'do this and they go away' solution.

One thing to keep in mind is that you will *always* be waiting on something. If you remove one roadblock, another will pop up. You will never get this list of large wait events to go away – you'll always have some. If you find that you are always 'tuning to go as fast as possible', you'll never be done. You can always make the system go one percent faster, but the amount of work and time you have to spend to get that one percent will increase exponentially over time. Tuning is something that must be done with a goal in mind, an end point. If you cannot say 'I am done when X is true', and X is something measurable, you are just wasting time.

The next section in the report:

```
Wait Events for DB: ORA8I  Instance: ora8i  Snaps: 1 -3
-> cs - centisecond -  100th of a second
-> ms - millisecond - 1000th of a second
-> ordered by wait time desc, waits desc (idle events last)
```

Event	Waits	Timeouts	Total Wait Time (cs)	Avg wait (ms)	Waits /txn
SQL*Net more data from dblin	1,861	0	836	4	5.5
control file parallel write	245	0	644	26	0.7
log file sync	150	0	280	19	0.4
db file scattered read	1,020	0	275	3	3.0
db file sequential read	483	0	165	3	1.4
control file sequential read	206	0	44	2	0.6
SQL*Net message from dblink	51	0	35	7	0.2
refresh controlfile command	21	0	28	13	0.1
log file parallel write	374	0	14	0	1.1
latch free	13	10	3	2	0.0
SQL*Net more data to client	586	0	2	0	1.7
single-task message	1	0	2	20	0.0
direct path read	716	0	1	0	2.1
direct path write	28	0	1	0	0.1
file open	28	0	1	0	0.1
SQL*Net message to dblink	51	0	0	0	0.2
db file parallel write	24	0	0	0	0.1
LGWR wait for redo copy	3	0	0	0	0.0
file identify	1	0	0	0	0.0

```
SQL*Net message from client          2,470          0    1,021,740    4137     7.3
virtual circuit status                  25         25       76,825   30730     0.1
pipe get                               739        739       76,106    1030     2.2
SQL*Net more data from clien           259          0            3       0     0.8
SQL*Net message to client            2,473          0            0       0     7.3
                              ----------------------------------------------------------
```

shows all of the wait events that occurred for clients of the database in the window of measurement. In addition to what was available in the Top 5 report, it shows the average wait time in thousands of seconds, and the number of times a transaction waited on it. You can use this to identify wait events that are relevant. I should point out in this listing, there are lots of events you should just ignore. For example, SQL*Net message from client – ignore it in systems where the client has think time. It represents the time the client sat there and didn't ask the database to do anything (on the other hand, if you see this during a data load – then the client is not feeding the database fast enough and it does indicate a problem). In this case, however, this just means the client was connected and didn't make any requests. The report heading notes that idle events last. Everything from SQL*Net message from client on down is an 'idle' event, some process was waiting to be told to do something. Ignore them for the most part.

```
Background Wait Events for DB: ORA8I  Instance: ora8i  Snaps: 1  -3
-> ordered by wait time desc, waits desc (idle events last)
                                                            Avg
                                                Total Wait    wait   Waits
Event                         Waits   Timeouts  Time (cs)    (ms)    /txn
---------------------------  ------  ---------  ----------  ------  ------
control file parallel write     245          0         644      26     0.7
control file sequential read     42          0          25       6     0.1
log file parallel write         374          0          14       0     1.1
db file parallel write           24          0           0       0     0.1
LGWR wait for redo copy           3          0           0       0     0.0
rdbms ipc message             1,379        741     564,886    4096     4.1
smon timer                        3          3      92,163  ######     0.0
pmon timer                      248        248      76,076    3068     0.7
                             ----------------------------------------------------------
```

The above section of the StatsPack report shows the wait events that occurred for the database 'background' processes (DBWR, LGRWR, and so on). Once again, idle waits are listed at the bottom of the report and generally should be ignored. These are useful for instance-wide tuning, to find out what the background processes are waiting on. It is easy for you to determine what is holding your session up, we've done that many times in the examples on bind variables and in other places by querying V$SESSION_EVENT. This report snippet shows the wait events for the background processes in much the same way that we showed them for our individual session.

```
SQL ordered by Gets for DB: ORA8I  Instance: ora8i  Snaps: 1 -3
-> End Buffer Gets Threshold:    10000
-> Note that resources reported for PL/SQL includes the resources used by
   all SQL statements called within the PL/SQL code.  As individual SQL
   statements are also reported, it is possible and valid for the summed
   total % to exceed 100

 Buffer Gets    Executions  Gets per Exec  % Total  Hash Value
--------------  ----------  -------------  -------  ------------
     713,388             1    713,388.0      56.2   1907729738
```

```
BEGIN sys.sync_users.do_it; END;

      485,161              1       485,161.0    38.3   1989876028
SELECT DECODE(SA.GRANTEE#,1,'PUBLIC',U1.NAME) "GRANTEE",U2.NAME
"GRANTED_ROLE",DECODE(OPTION$,1,'YES','NO') "ADMIN_OPTION"    FRO
M SYSAUTH$@ORACLE8.WORLD SA,DEFROLE$@ORACLE8.WORLD UD,USER$@ORAC
LE8.WORLD U1,USER$@ORACLE8.WORLD U2   WHERE SA.GRANTEE# = UD.USER
# (+)     AND SA.PRIVILEGE# = UD.ROLE# (+)    AND U1.USER# = SA.G

      239,778              2       119,889.0    18.9    617705294
BEGIN statspack.snap(10); END;
    ...
```

This section of the report shows us our 'TOP' SQL. In this section of the report, the SQL is ordered by `Buffer Gets`, in other words, how many logical I/Os it performed. As noted in the comment at the top, the buffer gets for a PL/SQL unit includes the buffer gets for *all* SQL executed by the block of code. Therefore, you will frequently see PL/SQL procedures at the top of this list, since the sum of the individual statements executed by the stored procedure are summed up.

In this particular example, I can see that there was a PL/SQL routine `sync_users.do_it`. It hit almost three quarters of a million block buffers in its single execution. Whether that is bad or not isn't clear from this report. The only thing this report can do is report on the facts – it makes no judgements based on those facts. In this case, I know that `sync_users` is a large batch job that is synchronizing the data dictionaries on two databases, making sure that a user created on one database, is created on the other and the all of the roles are the same and passwords in sync. I expect it to be large – as it turns out, this is the job that is waiting on the `dblink` wait event noticed above as well.

```
SQL ordered by Reads for DB: ORA8I  Instance: ora8i  Snaps: 1 -3
-> End Disk Reads Threshold:     1000

 Physical Reads  Executions  Reads per Exec % Total  Hash Value
 --------------- ----------- -------------- ------- ------------
        8,484              1        8,484.0    73.0   1907729738
BEGIN sys.sync_users.do_it; END;

        2,810              2        1,405.0    24.2    617705294
BEGIN statspack.snap(10); END;
...
```

This next section is very similar to the one above, but instead of reporting on logical I/O, it is reporting on physical I/O. This is showing me the SQL that incurs the most *read* activity on the system, the physical I/O. These are the queries and processes you might want to look at if you are finding yourself to be I/O bound. The `sync_users` routine might be in need of a little tuning – it is by far the largest consumer of disk resources on this particular system.

```
SQL ordered by Executions for DB: ORA8I  Instance: ora8i  Snaps: 1 -3
-> End Executions Threshold:     100

 Executions  Rows Processed    Rows per Exec   Hash Value
 ----------- ---------------- ---------------- ------------
      2,583              0             0.0   4044433098
SELECT TRANSLATE_TO_TEXT  FROM WWV_FLOW_DYNAMIC_TRANSLATIONS$
WHERE TRANSLATE_FROM_TEXT = :b1  AND TRANSLATE_TO_LANG_CODE = :b
```

```
  2

        2,065            2,065           1.0   2573952486
  SELECT DISPLAY_NAME   FROM WWC_PEOPLE_LABEL_NAMES  WHERE LABEL_N
  AME = :b1
```

This portion of the 'TOP' SQL report shows us the SQL that was executed the most during this period of time. This might be useful in order to isolate some very frequently executed queries to see if there is some way to change the logic, to avoid having to execute them so frequently. Perhaps a query is being executed inside a loop and it could be executed once outside the loop instead – simple algorithm changes might be made to reduce the number of times you have to execute that query. Even if they run blindingly fast, anything that is executed millions of times will start to eat up a large chunk of time.

```
  SQL ordered by Version Count for DB: ORA8I   Instance: ora8i   Snaps: 1 -3
  -> End Version Count Threshold:         20

  Version
     Count   Executions    Hash Value
  --------  ------------  ------------
        21         415     451919557
  SELECT SHORTCUT_NAME, ID    FROM WWV_FLOW_SHORTCUTS   WHERE FLOW_ID
   = :b1  AND (:b2 IS NULL   OR SHORTCUT_NAME = :b2 ) AND NOT EXIST
  S  (SELECT 1   FROM WWV_FLOW_PATCHES  WHERE FLOW_ID = :b1   AND I
  D = BUILD_OPTION  AND PATCH_STATUS = 'EXCLUDE' )   ORDER BY SHORT
  CUT_NAME, SHORTCUT_CONSIDERATION_SEQ

        21         110    1510890808
  SELECT DECODE(:b1,1,ICON_IMAGE,2,ICON_IMAGE2,3,ICON_IMAGE3) ICON
  _IMAGE,DECODE(:b1,1,ICON_SUBTEXT,2,ICON_SUBTEXT2,3,ICON_SUBTEXT3
  ) ICON_SUBTEXT,ICON_TARGET,ICON_IMAGE_ALT,DECODE(:b1,1,ICON_HEIG
  HT,2,NVL(ICON_HEIGHT2,ICON_HEIGHT),3,NVL(ICON_HEIGHT3,ICON_HEIGH
  T)) ICON_HEIGHT,DECODE(:b1,1,ICON_WIDTH,2,NVL(ICON_WIDTH2,ICON_H
```

This report shows the SQL ordered by how many versions of the SQL appear in the shared pool. There can be many reasons why there is more than one version of the same exact SQL statement in the shared pool. Some of the major causes for this are:

❑ Different users submit the same SQL, but different tables will actually be accessed.

❑ The same query is executed with a radically different environment, for example the optimizer goal is different.

❑ Fine Grained Access Control is being used to rewrite the query. Each version in the shared pool is really a very different query.

❑ The client uses different data types/lengths on the bind variables – one program binds a character string of length 10 and another binds a character string of length 20 – this will result in a new version of the SQL statement as well.

The following example shows you how you can get many versions of the same SQL query in the shared pool. We start by flushing the shared pool to remove all statements, and then we'll get three versions of the same query loaded in there:

```
tkyte@TKYTE816> connect tkyte/tkyte

tkyte@TKYTE816> alter system flush shared_pool;

System altered.

tkyte@TKYTE816> select * from t where x = 5;

no rows selected

tkyte@TKYTE816> alter session set optimizer_goal=first_rows;

Session altered.

tkyte@TKYTE816> select * from t where x = 5;

no rows selected


tkyte@TKYTE816> connect scott/tiger

scott@TKYTE816> select * from t where x = 5;

no rows selected

scott@TKYTE816> connect tkyte/tkyte

tkyte@TKYTE816> select sql_text, version_count
  2    from v$sqlarea
  3   where sql_text like 'select * from t where x = 5%'
  4  /

SQL_TEXT                VERSION_COUNT
------------------- -------------
select * from t wher           3
e x = 5


tkyte@TKYTE816> select loaded_versions, optimizer_mode,
  2          parsing_user_id, parsing_schema_id
  3    from v$sql
  4   where sql_text like 'select * from t where x = 5%'
  5  /

LOADED_VERSIONS OPTIMIZER_ PARSING_USER_ID PARSING_SCHEMA_ID
--------------- ---------- --------------- -----------------
              1 CHOOSE                  69                69
              1 FIRST_ROWS              69                69
              1 CHOOSE                  54                54
```

This shows why we have multiple versions in the shared pool. The first two are in there because even though the same user ID parsed them, they were parsed in different environments. The first time the optimizer goal was CHOOSE, the next time it was FIRST ROWS. Since a different optimizer mode can result in a different plan, we need two versions of that query. The last row is in there because it is a totally different query; the text is the same however. This query selects from SCOTT.T, not TKYTE.T – it is a totally separate query all together.

A high version count should be avoided for the same reason that you should use bind variables and avoid soft parsing queries whenever possible; you are doing more work then you need to. Sometimes multiple versions of a query must be kept, especially when it is caused by different accounts executing the same SQL against different tables, as was the case above with TKYTE.T and SCOTT.T. The other case, where you have different environments causing multiple versions, should typically be avoided whenever possible.

In my case above, the 21 versions were caused by 21 different user accounts parsing the same query against different tables.

```
Instance Activity Stats for DB: ORA8I  Instance: ora8i  Snaps: 1 -3

Statistic                                Total     per Second      per Trans
------------------------------      --------------    ------------    ------------
CPU used by this session            14,196,226       18,630.2        41,876.8
...
parse count (hard)                         127            0.2             0.4
parse count (total)                     12,530           16.4            37.0
parse time cpu                             203            0.3             0.6
parse time elapsed                         231            0.3             0.7
...
sorts (disk)                                 9            0.0             0.0
sorts (memory)                           2,242            2.9             6.6
sorts (rows)                           340,568          446.9         1,004.6
...
                                    --------------------------------------------
```

This part of the report, Instance Activity Stats, contains lots of very detailed numbers. We've already seen many of these numbers – they were used to compute the ratios and statistics at the beginning of the report. For example, looking at parse count (hard), and (total) we find:

```
tkyte@TKYTE816> select round( 100 *(1-127/12530),2 ) from dual;

ROUND(100*(1-127/12530),2)
--------------------------
                     98.99
```

which is exactly our Soft Parse % from the beginning of the report. This detailed data was used to compute many of the ratios and summaries above.

```
Tablespace IO Stats for DB: ORA8I  Instance: ora8i  Snaps: 1 -3
->ordered by IOs (Reads + Writes) desc
Tablespace
------------------------------
                 Av       Av      Av                       Av      Buffer  Av Buf
      Reads  Reads/s  Rd(ms)  Blks/Rd      Writes  Writes/s   Waits  Wt(ms)
-------------- ------- ------ ------- ------------ -------- ---------- ------
TEMP
      1,221        2     0.0      2.3         628         1         0     0.0
...
File IO Stats for DB: ORA8I  Instance: ora8i  Snaps: 1 -3
->ordered by Tablespace, File
```

Tablespace				Filename				
	Av	Av	Av			Av	Buffer	Av Buf
Reads	Reads/s	Rd(ms)	Blks/Rd	Writes	Writes/s		Waits	Wt(ms)
DRSYS				/d02/oradata/ora8i/drsys01.dbf				
14	0	7.9	2.4	0	0		0	
...								

The above two reports are I/O-oriented. In general, you are looking for an even distribution of reads and writes across devices here. You want to find out what files might be 'hot'. Once your DBA understands how the data is read and written, they may be able to get some performance gain by distributing I/O across disks more evenly.

```
Buffer Pool Statistics for DB: ORA8I  Instance: ora8i  Snaps: 1 -3
-> Pools  D: default pool,  K: keep pool,  R: recycle pool
```

			Free	Write	Buffer			
	Buffer	Consistent	Physical	Physical	Buffer	Buffer Complete		Busy
P	Gets	Gets	Reads	Writes	Waits	Waits		Waits
D	9,183	721,865	7,586	118	0	0		0

If we were using the multiple buffer pool feature, the above would show us the breakdown of usage by buffer pool. As it is, this is just reiterating information we saw at the beginning of the report.

```
Rollback Segment Stats for DB: ORA8I  Instance: ora8i  Snaps: 1 -3
->A high value for "Pct Waits" suggests more rollback segments may be required
```

	Trans Table	Pct	Undo Bytes			
RBS No	Gets	Waits	Written	Wraps	Shrinks	Extends
0	5.0	0.00	0	0	0	0
1	866.0	0.00	447,312	1	0	0

```
...
Rollback Segment Storage for DB: ORA8I  Instance: ora8i  Snaps: 1 -3
->Optimal Size should be larger than Avg Active
```

RBS No	Segment Size	Avg Active	Optimal Size	Maximum Size
0	663,552	7,372		663,552
1	26,206,208	526,774		26,206,208
2	26,206,208	649,805		26,206,208
...				

The above shows rollback segment activity. Again, you are looking for an even distribution across rollback segments (with the exception of the SYSTEM rollback segment of course). Also, the report headings have the most useful information to keep in mind while inspecting this section of the report – especially the advice about Optimal being larger then Avg Active if you use an optimal setting at all (the report above shows this database does not use optimal on the rollback segment size). As this is mostly DBA-related activity (the I/O and rollback segment information) we'll continue onto the next section:

```
Latch Activity for DB: ORA8I  Instance: ora8i Snaps: 1 -3
->"Get Requests", "Pct Get Miss" and "Avg Slps/Miss" are statistics for
  willing-to-wait latch get requests
->"NoWait Requests", "Pct NoWait Miss" are for no-wait latch get requests
->"Pct Misses" for both should be very close to 0.0
```

Latch Name	Get Requests	Pct Get Miss	Avg Slps /Miss	NoWait Requests	Pct NoWait Miss
Active checkpoint queue latch	271	0.0		0	
...					
virtual circuit queues	37	0.0		0	

```
Latch Sleep breakdown for DB: ORA8I  Instance: ora8i Snaps: 1 -3
-> ordered by misses desc
```

Latch Name	Get Requests	Misses	Sleeps	Spin & Sleeps 1->4
library cache	202,907	82	12	72/8/2/0/0
cache buffers chains	2,082,767	26	1	25/1/0/0/0

```
Latch Miss Sources for DB: ORA8I  Instance: ora8i Snaps: 1 -3
-> only latches with sleeps are shown
-> ordered by name, sleeps desc
```

Latch Name	Where	NoWait Misses	Sleeps	Waiter Sleeps
cache buffers chains	kcbgtcr: kslbegin	0	1	1
library cache	kglic	0	7	0
library cache	kglhdgn: child:	0	3	1
library cache	kglget: child: KGLDSBYD	0	2	0

```
Child Latch Statistics DB: ORA8I  Instance: ora8i Snaps: 1 -3
-> only latches with sleeps are shown
-> ordered by name, gets desc
```

Latch Name	Child Num	Get Requests	Misses	Sleeps	Spin & Sleeps 1->4
cache buffers chains	930	93,800	21	1	20/1/0/0/0
library cache	2	48,412	34	6	29/4/1/0/0
library cache	1	42,069	10	3	8/1/1/0/0
library cache	5	37,334	10	2	8/2/0/0/0
library cache	4	36,007	13	1	12/1/0/0/0

If you recall from Chapter 3 on *Locking and Concurrency*, latches are lightweight serialization devices used by Oracle. They are always either 'gotten' or not; they are not like enqueues where a session requests a lock and is put to sleep until it is available. With a latch, the requestor is told immediately 'you got it' or 'you didn't get it'. The requestor then 'spins' (consuming CPU) for a bit and tries again. If that doesn't work, it goes to 'sleep' for a bit, and tries again. The reports above show you this activity. For example, I can see that the library cache latch was missed 82 times out of 202,907 attempts. Further, 72 of the 82 attempts were successful the next time they tried, 8 on the second and 2 on the third. The ratio of Gets to Misses is very near 100 percent in this system (almost 100 percent of the gets were immediately successful) so there is nothing to do. On a system that does not use bind variables, or parses queries too frequently, you'll see lots of contention for the library cache latch. One other piece of information I can derive from this latch report above is that about 4.5 percent (93800/2082767) of my cache buffers chains latch requests were for one child latch out of (at least) 930. This probably indicates that I have a hot block – one that many processes are trying to access simultaneously. They all need a latch in order to access this block and this in resulting in some contention. That would be something to look into. The latch report is useful to identify what latch contention you are experiencing. We will need to go back to the *application*-level tuning to fix it. Latch contention is a symptom, not a cause of problems. In order to get rid of the symptom we must determine the cause. Unfortunately, you cannot generate a list of recommendations in the form of 'if you have contention for this latch, you need to do this' (if only it was so easy!). Rather, once you have identified that you in fact do have latch contention, you must go back to the application design and determine why you are contending for that resource.

```
Dictionary Cache Stats for DB: ORA8I  Instance: ora8i  Snaps: 1 -3
->"Pct Misses"  should be very low (< 2% in most cases)
->"Cache Usage" is the number of cache entries being used
->"Pct SGA"     is the ratio of usage to allocated size for that cache
```

Cache	Get Requests	Pct Miss	Scan Requests	Pct Miss	Mod Req	Final Usage	Pct SGA
dc_constraints	0		0		0	227	99
dc_database_links	9	0.0	0		0	7	88
dc_files	0		0		0	69	88
dc_free_extents	747	55.0	336	0.0	672	90	98
dc_global_oids	14	0.0	0		0	95	86
dc_histogram_data	0		0		0	0	0
dc_histogram_data_valu	0		0		0	0	0
dc_histogram_defs	94	21.3	0		0	1,902	100
dc_object_ids	190	0.0	0		0	2,392	100
dc_objects	345	2.9	0		0	6,092	100
dc_outlines	0		0		0	0	0
dc_profiles	132	0.0	0		0	2	33
dc_rollback_segments	192	0.0	0		0	33	77
dc_segments	637	0.6	0		340	3,028	100
dc_sequence_grants	6	0.0	0		0	6	6
dc_sequences	8	0.0	0		5	23	82
dc_synonyms	28	10.7	0		0	96	96
dc_tablespace_quotas	0		0		0	14	12
dc_tablespaces	1,033	0.0	0		0	100	94
dc_used_extents	672	50.0	0		672	5	6
dc_user_grants	1,296	0.2	0		0	756	82
dc_usernames	337	0.9	0		0	1,318	99
dc_users	9,892	0.0	0		1	865	100

This is a report on the dictionary cache. I don't like this report too much, since there is not very much I can do about the numbers reported back by it. The dictionary cache is totally controlled by Oracle, we cannot size the components of it. We can only size the shared pool size, as long as our shared pool is sized correctly – the above is supposed to take care of itself. As my shared pool is at 75 percent utilized, it is large enough. If my shared pool was 'full' and the hit ratios here were bad, increasing the shared pool would improve the hit ratios.

```
Library Cache Activity for DB: ORA8I  Instance: ora8i  Snaps: 1 -3
->"Pct Misses"  should be very low

                     Get       Pct        Pin       Pct                 Invali-
Namespace        Requests     Miss    Requests      Miss    Reloads     dations
---------------  ---------   ------  -----------   ------  ----------   --------
BODY                5,018      0.0        5,018      0.0          0          0
CLUSTER                 0                     0                   0          0
INDEX                   1      0.0            1      0.0          0          0
OBJECT                  0                     0                   0          0
PIPE                  765      0.0          765      0.0          0          0
SQL AREA            1,283      6.9       38,321      0.6         39          0
TABLE/PROCEDURE     3,005      0.3       11,488      0.6          1          0
TRIGGER                21      0.0           21      0.0          0          0
```

Here we are seeing the breakdown of the library cache hit ratio. On a finely tuned system the Pct Misses will be very near zero. On a development system, or a system where objects are frequently dropped and recreated, some of these ratios will be high, as will the Invalidations column. Sizing the shared pool and ensuring that you minimize hard parses by using bind variables, is the way to ensure good ratios in the above.

```
SGA Memory Summary for DB: ORA8I  Instance: ora8i  Snaps: 1 -3

SGA regions                     Size in Bytes
------------------------------  -----------------
Database Buffers                  134,217,728
Fixed Size                             69,616
Redo Buffers                          532,480
Variable Size                     130,187,264
                                -----------------
sum                               265,007,088

SGA breakdown difference for DB: ORA8I  Instance: ora8i  Snaps: 1 -3

Pool         Name                    Begin value      End value   Difference
-----------  ---------------------   -------------   -------------  -----------
java pool    free memory               17,838,080      17,838,080           0
java pool    memory in use              3,133,440       3,133,440           0
shared pool  KGFF heap                     54,128          54,128           0
shared pool  KGK heap                       5,840           5,840           0
shared pool  KQLS heap                  3,253,784       3,231,844     -21,940
shared pool  PL/SQL DIANA               4,436,044       4,413,960     -22,084
shared pool  PL/SQL MPCODE             15,378,764      15,546,652     167,888
shared pool  PLS non-lib hp                 2,096           2,096           0
shared pool  State objects                291,304         291,304           0
shared pool  VIRTUAL CIRCUITS             484,632         484,632           0
shared pool  db_block_buffers           2,228,224       2,228,224           0
```

shared pool db_block_hash_buckets	393,240	393,240	0
shared pool dictionary cache	6,547,348	6,586,032	38,684
shared pool event statistics per ses	1,017,600	1,017,600	0
shared pool fixed allocation callbac	960	960	0
shared pool free memory	27,266,500	27,013,928	-252,572
shared pool joxlod: in ehe	71,344	71,344	0
shared pool joxs heap init	244	244	0
shared pool library cache	28,105,460	28,168,952	63,492
shared pool message pool freequeue	231,152	231,152	0
shared pool miscellaneous	1,788,284	1,800,404	12,120
shared pool pl/sql source	42,536	42,536	0
shared pool processes	153,600	153,600	0
shared pool sessions	633,600	633,600	0
shared pool sql area	16,377,404	16,390,124	12,720
shared pool table columns	45,264	45,936	672
shared pool table definiti	11,984	12,944	960
shared pool transactions	294,360	294,360	0
shared pool trigger defini	8,216	8,216	0
shared pool trigger inform	5,004	5,064	60
shared pool type object de	48,040	48,040	0
shared pool view columns d	1,072	1,072	0
db_block_buffers	134,217,728	134,217,728	0
fixed_sga	69,616	69,616	0
log_buffer	512,000	512,000	0

This part of the report shows the utilization of the shared pool in some detail. You can see how over time, memory usage shifts from component to component, some sections giving up memory and others allocating more memory. I've found this section of the report most useful as a way to explain why something was reported in another section. For example, I received a series of StatsPack reports for analysis. They showed fairly constant hard and soft parse counts and then all of a sudden, the hard parses went through the roof for about an hour, then everything went back to normal. Using the reports, I was able to determine this at the same time the hard parse count shot up, the shared pool sql area memory usage decreased by a large amount, many tens of MB. Curious about this, I asked 'did someone flush the shared pool?' and the answer was 'of course, yes'. It was part of their standard operating procedure; every six hours they flushed the shared pool. Why? No one really knew, they just always did. In fact, a job was set up to do it. Disabling this job fixed the periodic performance issues, which were totally self-induced by flushing the shared pool (and hence flushing all of the plans that they spent the last six hours accumulating).

```
init.ora Parameters for DB: ORA8I   Instance: ora8i   Snaps: 1 -3

                                                        End value
Parameter Name                  Begin value             (if different)
-----------------------------   ---------------------   --------------
background_dump_dest            /export/home/ora816/admin/ora8i/b
compatible                      8.1.0, 8.1.6.0.0
control_files                   /d01/oradata/ora8i/control01.ctl,
core_dump_dest                  /export/home/ora816/admin/ora8i/c
db_block_buffers                16384

...
End of Report
```

The last part of the report is a listing of the `init.ora` parameters that differ from the default. These are useful in determining why something is occurring, similar to the shared pool memory report above. You can see quickly which parameters have been explicitly set and determine their effects on the system.

StatsPack Wrap-Up

StatsPack is a great tool to use on both production, and development systems. It will help you to determine the overall health of your database, as well as pinpoint potential bottlenecks. I strongly encourage people to use it continuously, as part of the day-to-day running of the system. There are plans to add additional analysis tools around the information collected by StatsPack, in particular some trend analysis, so you can not only see the delta between two points but you can see the trend over some arbitrary period of time.

Understanding the contents of the report is the first step. Understanding what to do about it is the next. You cannot look at any one number or statistic in isolation, as it takes some understanding of the system and its goals. In the above report we reviewed, unless I knew of the batch job `sync_users` and the fact that it used a database link heavily and that it was a background process – I might think I had a problem in the system. I don't however; `sync_users` is run in the background. The fact that it waits a little on a `dblink` is perfectly acceptable and within the constraints for my system. The report did point out that there is an application out there that is not making optimal use of bind variables in the system – we are hard parsing too frequently. I'll use the other tools presented in the earlier sections to troubleshoot that particular issue.

V$ Tables

In this section, I would like to review the primary V$ tables you will use in your application tuning efforts. There are over 180 of these tables and even though they are call 'dynamic performance tables', not all of them are performance-related. This section will show you the ones I use on a recurring basis. There are others, such as the V$ views used to monitor and tune multi-threaded server; this I won't be covering. All of these tables are documented in the *Oracle8i Reference* manual as well. I'm not going to repeat the material here but would rather like to draw you attention to the ones I think you should know about.

I am simply going to introduce these views to make you aware of them. Many of them we have used in various examples already. Some are new. When appropriate, a small example of using these views is included.

V$EVENT_NAME

We've seen the names of many 'events' in this section. We have seen how the event has a name and then up to three parameters p1, p2, and p3. We can either flip to the manuals every time we want to look up the meanings of p1, p2, and p3 for a given event, or we can simply query V$EVENT_NAME. For example, two of the events we've encountered in this chapter are `latch free` and `enqueue`. Using this view:

```
tkyte@TKYTE816>  select * from v$event_name where name = 'latch free'
  2  /

      EVENT# NAME                     PARAMETER1 PARAMETER2 PARAMETER3
  ---------- --------------------     ---------- ---------- ----------
```

```
            2 latch free              address    number     tries

tkyte@TKYTE816>  select * from v$event_name where name = 'enqueue'
  2  /

    EVENT# NAME                       PARAMETER1 PARAMETER2 PARAMETER3
---------- --------------------       ---------- ---------- ----------
        11 enqueue                    name|mode  id1        id2
```

we can quickly get a handle on the meaning of these parameters, especially if we've already read about them once or twice, and just need a quick reminder as to what is available.

V$FILESTAT and V$TEMPSTAT

V$FILESTAT and V$TEMPSTAT can give you a quick glimpse at the I/O done on your system, and how long Oracle has spent reading and writing any given file. You can either use StatsPack to get snapshots of this usage, or you can take a quick snapshot of this table yourself, wait a while, and then compare the differences.

V$LOCK

This is a view we've used a couple of times already in Chapter 3 on *Locking and Concurrency*. This view is used to tell you who has what locked. Remember, Oracle does not store row level locks externally from the data itself, so don't go looking for them in here. In this view, you'll be able to see who has TM (DML Enqueue) locks on tables, so you'll be able to tell that session 'x,y' has some rows locked in a given table but you cannot determine *which* rows they have locked.

V$MYSTAT

This view contains statistics for your session only. This is very useful to diagnose how *your* session is doing. The schema that creates this view must have direct access to the V$STATNAME and V$MYSTAT objects, for example:

```
sys@TKYTE816> grant select on v_$statname to tkyte;
    Grant succeeded.

sys@TKYTE816> grant select on v_$mystat to tkyte;
    Grant succeeded.
```

Notice that we used V_$STATNAME and not V$STATNAME. This is because V$STATNAME is really just a synonym for the view V_$STATNAME.

This view contains the statistic number, an internal code, not the name of the event that is being tracked. I typically install a view like this:

```
ops$tkyte@ORA8I.WORLD> create view my_stats
  2  as
  3  select a.name, b.value
  4    from v$statname a, v$mystat b
  5   where a.statistic# = b.statistic#
```

```
    6  /

View created.

ops$tkyte@ORA8I.WORLD> SELECT * FROM MY_STATS WHERE VALUE > 0;

NAME                                VALUE
------------------------------   ----------
logons cumulative                       1
logons current                          1
opened cursors cumulative             160
opened cursors current                  1
...
```

in my systems to make it easier to query. Once we have that set up, you can create queries that give you StatsPack-like information for your session. For example, we can compute the all-important `Soft Parse Ratio` like this:

```
ops$tkyte@ORA8I.WORLD> select round(100 *
  2             (1-max(decode(name,'parse count (hard)',value,null))/
  3                 max(decode(name,'parse count (total)',value,null))), 2
  4                      ) "Soft Parse Ratio"
  5      from my_stats
  6  /

Soft Parse Ratio
----------------
           84.03
```

If you create a set of queries like this, and put them in a 'logoff' trigger or embed them directly in your application, you can monitor the performance of your individual applications to see how many commits they perform, how many rollbacks, and so on by session and application.

V$OPEN_CURSOR

This view contains a list of every open cursor for all sessions. This is very useful for tracking down 'cursor leaks' and to see what SQL your session has been executing. Oracle will cache cursors even after you explicitly close them so don't be surprised to see cursors in there that you thought you closed (you might have). For example, in the same SQL*PLUS session I was using to compute the `Soft Parse Ratio` above I found:

```
ops$tkyte@ORA8I.WORLD> select * from v$open_cursor
  2  where sid = ( select sid from v$mystat where rownum = 1 );

SADDR      SID USER_NAME ADDRESS   HASH_VALUE SQL_TEXT
--------   --- --------- --------  ---------- ------------------------------
8C1706A0    92 OPS$TKYTE 8AD80D18   607327990 BEGIN DBMS_OUTPUT.DISABLE;
                                              END;

8C1706A0    92 OPS$TKYTE 8AD6BB54   130268528 select lower(user) || '@' ||
                                              decode(global_name,
                                              'ORACLE8.WO
```

```
8C1706A0  92 OPS$TKYTE 8AD8EDB4  230633120 select round(100 *
                                            (1-max(decode(name,'parse
                                            count (hard

8C1706A0  92 OPS$TKYTE 8AD7DEC0 1592329314 SELECT
                                            ATTRIBUTE,SCOPE,NUMERIC_VALUE,
                                            CHAR_VALUE,DATE_VALUE F

8C1706A0  92 OPS$TKYTE 8E16AC30 3347301380 select round( 100 *
                                            (1-max(decode(name,'parse
                                            count (hard)',

8C1706A0  92 OPS$TKYTE 8AD7AD70 1280991272 SELECT CHAR_VALUE FROM
                                            SYSTEM.PRODUCT_PRIVS WHERE
                                            (UPPER('

8C1706A0  92 OPS$TKYTE 8AD62080 1585371720 BEGIN
                                            DBMS_OUTPUT.ENABLE(1000000);
                                            END;

8C1706A0  92 OPS$TKYTE 8AD816B8 3441224864 SELECT USER FROM DUAL
8C1706A0  92 OPS$TKYTE 8ADF4D3C 1948987396 SELECT DECODE('A','A','1','2')
                                            FROM DUAL

8C1706A0  92 OPS$TKYTE 89D30A18 2728523820 select round(100 *
                                            (1-max(decode(name,'parse
                                            count (hard

8C1706A0  92 OPS$TKYTE 8865AB90 3507933882 select * from v$open_cursor
                                            where sid = ( select sid from
                                            v$

8C1706A0  92 OPS$TKYTE 8AD637B0  242587281 commit
8C1706A0  92 OPS$TKYTE 8AD70660 3759542639 BEGIN
                                            DBMS_APPLICATION_INFO.SET_MODU
                                            LE(:1,NULL); END;

13 rows selected.
```

As you can see, there are a number of cursors apparently open. However:

```
ops$tkyte@ORA8I.WORLD> select * from my_stats where name = 'opened cursors
current';


NAME                                VALUE
------------------------------- ----------
opened cursors current                   1
```

I really only have one cursor truly opened (and that is actually the cursor used to query how many open cursors I have). Oracle is caching the other cursors in the hope that I will execute them again.

V$PARAMETER

V$PARAMETER is useful to find various settings relevant to tuning, such as the block size, the sort area size, and so on. Its relevance to tuning is that it contains all of the init.ora parameter values, and many of these will have a bearing on our performance.

V$SESSION

V$SESSION contains a row for every session in the database. As with V$STATNAME shown earlier, you will need to be granted permissions by your DBA to use this view:

```
sys@TKYTE816> grant select on v_$session to tkyte;
  Grant succeeded.
```

To find your session's specific row, you can simply query:

```
ops$tkyte@ORA8I.WORLD> select * from v$session
  2  where sid = ( select sid from v$mystat where rownum = 1 )
  3  /
```

I usually use this view to see what else is going on in the database. For example, I frequently use a script called showsql that shows me a listing of every session, its status (active or not), the module, action, and client_info settings, and finally for active sessions, what SQL they happen to be running.

The MODULE, ACTION, and CLIENT_INFO fields are settable by you in your applications via a call to the procedures in the DBMS_APPLICATION_INFO package (see the Appendix A on *Necessary Supplied Packages* for details on this package). I would encourage you to instrument every application you build with calls to this package to set this field. It can really save time trying to figure out what session is running which application – if you put that information into the V$ view, it'll be obvious.

My showsql script is simply:

```
column username format a15 word_wrapped
column module format a15 word_wrapped
column action format a15 word_wrapped
column client_info format a15 word_wrapped
column status format a10
column sid_serial format a15
set feedback off
set serveroutput on

select username, ''''||sid||','||serial#||'''' sid_serial, status , module,
action, client_info
from v$session
where username is not null
/

column username format a20
column sql_text format a55 word_wrapped

set serveroutput on size 1000000
```

```
declare
    x number;
procedure p ( p_str in varchar2 )
is
   l_str    long := p_str;
begin
   loop
      exit when l_str is null;
      dbms_output.put_line( substr( l_str, 1, 250 ) );
      l_str := substr( l_str, 251 );
   end loop;
end;
begin
    for x in
    ( select username||'('||sid||','||serial#||
               ') ospid = ' ||   process ||
               ' program = ' || program username,
            to_char(LOGON_TIME,' Day HH24:MI') logon_time,
            to_char(sysdate,' Day HH24:MI') current_time,
            sql_address, LAST_CALL_ET
        from v$session
       where status = 'ACTIVE'
         and rawtohex(sql_address) <> '00'
         and username is not null order by last_call_et )
    loop
        dbms_output.put_line( '--------------------' );
        dbms_output.put_line( x.username );
        dbms_output.put_line( x.logon_time || ' ' ||
                         x.current_time||
                         ' last et = ' ||
                         x.LAST_CALL_ET);
        for y in ( select sql_text
                     from v$sqltext_with_newlines
                    where address = x.sql_address
                    order by piece )
        loop
            p( y.sql_text );
        end loop;
    end loop;
end;
/
```

and it produces output like this:

```
ops$tkyte@ORA8I.WORLD> @showsql

USERNAME         SID_SERIAL     STATUS     MODULE            ACTION CLIENT_INFO
---------------- -------------- ---------- ---------------- ------ -----------
OPS$TKYTE        '30,23483'     ACTIVE     01@ showsql.sql
CTXSYS           '56,32'        ACTIVE
--------------------
OPS$TKYTE(30,23483) ospid = 29832 program = sqlplus@aria (TNS V1-V3)
Sunday    20:34  Sunday     20:40 last et = 0
SELECT USERNAME || '(' || SID || ',' || SERIAL# || ') ospid
= ' || PROCESS || ' program = ' || PROGRAM  USERNAME,TO_CHAR(
```

```
LOGON_TIME,' Day HH24:MI') LOGON_TIME,TO_CHAR(SYSDATE,' Day HH24
:MI') CURRENT_TIME,SQL_ADDRESS,LAST_CALL_ET   FROM V$SESSION WH
ERE STATUS = 'ACTIVE'  AND RAWTOHEX(SQL_ADDRESS) != '00'  AND US
ERNAME IS NOT NULL  ORDER BY LAST_CALL_ET
--------------------
CTXSYS(56,32) ospid = 15610 program = ctxsrv@aria (TNS V1-V3)
Monday    11:52 Sunday     20:40 last et = 20
BEGIN      drilist.get_cmd( :sid, :mbox, :pmask, :cmd_type,:disp_
id, :disp_return_address, :disp_user, :disp_command, :disp_arg1,
:disp_arg2, :disp_arg3, :disp_arg4, :disp_arg5, :disp_arg6, :di
sp_arg7, :disp_arg8, :disp_arg9, :disp_arg10 ); :error_stack :=
drue.get_stack; exception when dr_def.textile_error then :error_
stack := drue.get_stack; when others then drue.text_on_stack(sql
errm); :error_stack := drue.get_stack; END;
ops$tkyte@ORA8I.WORLD>
```

As you can see, SQL*PLUS has filled in the MODULE column in V$SESSION with the name of the script that is being executed currently. This can be very useful, especially when your applications take advantage of it to show their progress.

V$SESSION_EVENT

We have used this view a number of times already. I use it frequently to see what is causing a procedure or query to 'wait' for a resource. You can get similar information from a trace file with the appropriate event set, but this makes it so easy to capture the current state of your session's events, run a process, and then display the differences. This is much easier then reviewing a trace file for similar information.

This view contains the wait events for all sessions in the system, so it is useful for seeing the major wait events for sessions, other than your own as well. Similar to the way we can turn SQL_TRACE on in another session using DBMS_SYSTEM, we can use V$SESSION_EVENT to see what wait events other sessions are experiencing.

V$SESSION_LONGOPS

We will look at this view in some detail in Appendix A on *Necessary Supplied Packages*. This view is used by long running processes such as index creates, backups, restores, and anything the cost based optimizer thinks will take more than six seconds of execution time, to report their progress. Your applications can use this view as well, via the DBMS_APPLICATION_INFO package. If you have a long running process or job, it should be instrumented with calls to DBMS_APPLICATION_INFO to report on its current progress. In this fashion, you can monitor your job easily and see if it is really 'stuck' or just taking its time to complete its task.

V$SESSION_WAIT

This view shows all sessions currently waiting for something and how long they have been waiting. This is typically used to monitor systems that appear to have 'hung' or are running very slowly.

V$SESSTAT

V$SESSTAT is similar to V$MYSTAT but it shows statistics for all sessions, not just yours. This is useful for monitoring another session that you have identified to see how it is doing.

For example, you can use this to monitor the soft parse ratio for a third party application you have installed on your machine. You might do this after observing the hard parse count increasing on your finely tuned system. By monitoring the soft parse ratio of just the third party application, you could quickly determine if they are the culprits of introducing lots of unique, non-bind variable SQL into your system or not.

V$SESS_IO

This is useful to see how much I/O your (or any other) session has done. I use this view in a fashion similar to V$MYSTAT and V$SESSION_EVENT. I take a snapshot, run some processes, and then review the 'difference' between the two points. This shows how much I/O the process performs. I could get this information from a TKPROF report as well, but this lets me aggregate the counts up easily. TKPROF will show the I/O performed by statement. This allows me to run an arbitrary set of statements and collect the I/O statistics for them.

VSQL, VSQLAREA

These views show us all of the SQL that is parsed and stored in the shared pool. We have already used both of these in various places in this section.

V$SQLAREA is an aggregate view. There will be one row per SQL query in this view. The VERSION_COUNT column tells us how many rows we could expect to find in the V$SQL table for that query. Try to avoid querying this view and use V$SQL instead. V$SQLAREA can be quite expensive, especially on an already busy system.

We can use the V$SQLAREA and V$SQL views to see what SQL our system executes, how many times this SQL is executed, parsed, how many logical and physical I/Os it does, and so on. We can use these views to find the SQL that is missing bind variables as well.

V$STATNAME

V$STATNAME contains the mapping from the statistic number to the statistic name. It is useful when joined with V$MYSTAT and V$SESSTAT to turn the statistic number into the readable name.

V$SYSSTAT

Whereas V$SESSTAT keeps statistics by session, V$SYSSTAT keeps them for the instance. As sessions come and go, their entries are added and removed in the V$SESSTAT view. The data in V$SYSSTAT persists until the database is shutdown. This is the information StatsPack uses to derive many of its ratios and such.

V$SYSTEM_EVENT

This is to events what the V$SYSSTAT view is to statistics. It contains instance-level wait event information. It is what StatsPack uses to derive many of its reports as well.

Summary

Tuning, when done 'after the fact', is a bit of luck and a lot of sleuthing. When done as part of the development process, it is straightforward and easy to do. I prefer straightforward and easy any day, especially when the other alternative involves 'luck'. Tuning after the fact is one of the hardest things to do. You have to figure out why the system is slow, where the system is slow, and how to make it go faster without ripping everything apart and doing it the way it should have been done in the first place. That last bit is what makes after-the-fact tuning so hard.

If you make performance part of the application from day one you will find tuning to be a science, not an art. Anyone can do it if it is part of the process. In order to achieve this goal, you will need to do things like set metrics by which applications can be tested against. You will need to have instrumented code, so you can diagnose where slowdowns are occurring. The instrumentation part is very important; the database is very much instrumented as shown in the above chapter. I can use this instrumentation to prove that the database is not the slow part. At that point, we still have a 'slow' system – the only thing we now know is that the database is not the slow part. At this point, if the code outside the database is not instrumented, we'll have to guess where the problem might be. Even for code running inside the database, application-level instrumentation is extremely useful for tracking down where things are running slow.

And just in case you missed it above, *bind variables are important*. I cannot tell you how many times I have seen systems just grind to a halt because the developers found it easier to use string concatenation for all of their queries instead of bind variables. These systems just do not work. It is just too easy to do it the right way in this case; don't make the mistake of not using them. Don't rely on crutches like CURSOR_SHARING as they introduce their own issues.

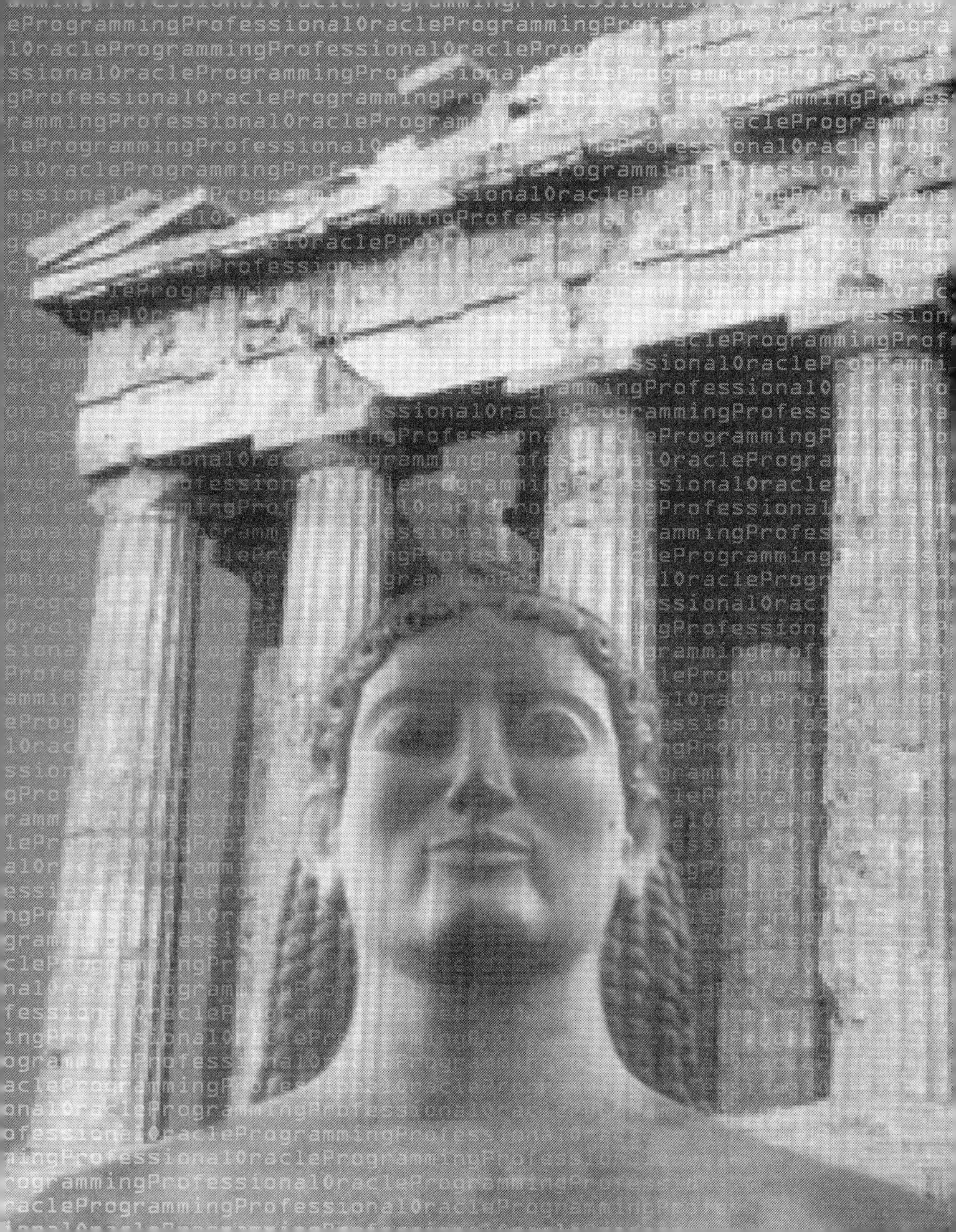

11

Optimizer Plan Stability

Oracle8i allows a developer to save a set of 'hints to the server' describing how to execute a specific SQL statement in the database. This feature is referred to as **Optimizer Plan Stability** and is implemented via a stored query plan outline, similar to an outline for a book. This chapter takes a detailed look at this feature, covering:

❑   Why you may want to use Optimizer Plan Stability in your applications, and the typical scenarios where it may be useful.

❑   Some interesting alternative uses of this feature as well – uses not necessarily intended by the developers of this feature.

❑   How to implement the feature and how to manage the stored plans in the database, via both DDL and the OUTLN_PKG package.

❑   Important caveats, including the importance of case sensitivity, issues with ALTER SESSION, OR-Expansion, and performance.

❑   Errors you may encounter, and what to do about them, including cases where no options are specified for ALTER OUTLINE, or if an outline already exists.

In order to execute the examples in this chapter you will need to have Oracle8i release 1 (version 8.1.5) or higher. Additionally, this must be an Enterprise or Personal version of Oracle8i as the Optimizer Plan Stability feature is not included in the Standard Edition.

An Overview of the Feature

For a given query or set of SQL statements, Optimizer Plan Stability allows us to save the optimal set of hints for their run-time execution, without having to 'hint' the query ourselves in the application. This allows us to:

1. Develop an application.

2. Test and tune the queries within it.

3. Have those finely tuned plans saved into the database for later use by the optimizer.

This feature helps to protect us from many changes to the underlying database. Typical changes in the underlying database that could cause query plans to change dramatically, include:

❑ Re-analyzing a table after changing the amount of data in it.

❑ Re-analyzing a table after changing the distribution of data in it.

❑ Re-analyzing the table using different parameters or methods.

❑ Changing various init.ora parameters that affect the optimizer's behavior such as db_block_buffers.

❑ Adding indexes.

❑ Upgrading the Oracle software to a new release.

Using Optimizer Plan Stability, however, we can preserve our existing execution plans, and isolate our application from these changes.

It should be noted that, in most cases, it is desirable that the query plans change over time in reaction to the events in the above list. If the distribution of data changes radically in a column, the optimizer is designed to change its query plan to accommodate this. If an index is added, the optimizer is designed to recognize that, and take advantage of it. Optimizer Plan Stability can be used to help prevent these changes from happening, which might be useful in an environment where changes must be made gradually, after testing. For example, before permitting the general use of a new index, you might want to test queries that may be affected one-by-one to ensure that the addition of that index does not adversely affect some other system component. The same would be true of a change to an initialization parameter or of a database upgrade.

A key point to remember about Optimizer Plan Stability is that it is implemented via **hints**. Hints are not mandates; hints are not rules. While the hinting mechanism used by Optimizer Plan Stability is a stronger one than is exposed to us via the documented hinting mechanism, the optimizer is still, as always, free to follow them or not at run-time. This is a double-edged sword – it sounds like a defect but in reality it is a feature. If changes are made to the database that render a set of hints obsolete (as will happen if you, say, drop an index) then Oracle will ignore the hints and generate the best plan it can.

A quick example will demonstrate what Optimizer Plan Stability offers. Below, we will see one method we can use to save a stored outline for a query. After storing the outline, we will make certain changes to the database (we will analyze the table) that causes the plan to change. Lastly, we'll see how, by enabling optimizer plan stability, we can have Oracle use the plan we stored in the first place – even in light of the changes we made. First, we create a copy of the SCOTT.EMP table and set up a primary key on it:

```
tkyte@TKYTE816> create table emp
  2  as
  3  select ename, empno from scott.emp group by ename, empno
  4  /

Table created.

tkyte@TKYTE816> alter table emp
  2  add constraint emp_pk
  3  primary key(empno)
  4  /

Table altered.
```

If you do not have access to the EMP table, you will need to have SELECT privileges granted to you. The primary key we created is used in the example; we generate a query that will use it. Next, we set the optimizer goal to CHOOSE:

```
tkyte@TKYTE816> alter session set optimizer_goal=choose
  2  /

Session altered.
```

This is done purely for the sake of consistency in running this example. Of course, in the absence of any statistics, the rule-based optimizer (RBO) is invoked. However, if your optimizer goal is set to some other value, FIRST_ROWS for example, the Cost Based Optimizer will be invoked and the change we make to the database later might not have any effect on the query plan. Finally, here is the execution plan for our query:

```
tkyte@TKYTE816> set autotrace traceonly explain
tkyte@TKYTE816> select empno, ename from emp where empno > 0

Execution Plan
----------------------------------------------------------
   0      SELECT STATEMENT Optimizer=CHOOSE
   1    0   TABLE ACCESS (BY INDEX ROWID) OF 'EMP'
   2    1     INDEX (RANGE SCAN) OF 'EMP_PK' (UNIQUE)
```

Let's assume this query comes from an interactive application where the end user would like to get some data very quickly, and the index access does this for us nicely. We are happy with this plan, and would like it to always be used, so the next thing to do is to create an outline for it. We create the outline explicitly (we can also create them implicitly, as is demonstrated in the *A Method to Implement Tuning* section):

```
tkyte@TKYTE816> create or replace outline MyOutline
  2  for category mycategory
  3  ON
  4  select empno, ename from emp where empno > 0
  5  /

Outline created.
```

The CREATE OR REPLACE OUTLINE command created our query outline, and stored it in the database (*where* it is stored and *how*, will be explained later in this chapter). Since we explicitly created the outline, we had the ability to name it (MYOUTLINE). Additionally, we placed this query outline into a specific **category** (MYCATEGORY).

Before moving on, it's worth pointing out that if you are working along with this example you may receive the following error from the above CREATE OUTLINE command:

```
select empno, ename from emp where empno > 0
                                  *

ERROR at line 4:
ORA-18005: create any outline privilege is required for this operation
```

If so, you need to have the DBA grant you the CREATE ANY OUTLINE privilege. All of the necessary privileges you may need for creating and manipulating outlines are covered in the *How Optimizer Plan Stability Works* section below.

OK, we have our outline that defines our required execution plan (it uses our index). Let's now make a change to the database – we will simply analyze our table:

```
tkyte@TKYTE816> analyze table emp compute statistics
  2  /

Table analyzed.
```

Now, let's take another look at the execution plan for our query:

```
tkyte@TKYTE816> set autotrace traceonly explain
tkyte@TKYTE816> select empno, ename from emp where empno > 0
  2  /

Execution Plan
----------------------------------------------------------
   0      SELECT STATEMENT Optimizer=CHOOSE (Cost=1 Card=14 Bytes=112)
   1    0   TABLE ACCESS (FULL) OF 'EMP' (Cost=1 Card=14 Bytes=112)
```

Instead of using our index, as we were with the RBO, we now have the statistics to allow the CBO to be invoked, and it is choosing a full table scan. The CBO has in fact chosen the correct plan. There are only 14 rows and it understands that *all of them* satisfy the predicate in this case. However, for our particular application, we still wish to use the index. In order to get back to our preferred plan, we need to use the Optimizer Plan Stability feature. To do that, we simply issue the following command:

```
tkyte@TKYTE816> alter session set use_stored_outlines = mycategory
  2  /

Session altered.
```

This enforces use of our MYCATEGORY stored outline. If we take a look at our execution plan:

```
tkyte@TKYTE816> set autotrace traceonly explain
tkyte@TKYTE816> select empno, ename from emp where empno > 0
  2  /

Execution Plan
----------------------------------------------------------
   0      SELECT STATEMENT Optimizer=CHOOSE (Cost=2 Card=14 Bytes=112)
   1    0   TABLE ACCESS (BY INDEX ROWID) OF 'EMP' (Cost=2 Card=14
   2    1     INDEX (RANGE SCAN) OF 'EMP_PK' (UNIQUE) (Cost=1 Card=14)
```

We find that we are back to using the original plan with the index again. This is the goal of optimizer plan stability – to allow you to 'freeze' the query plans for your finely tuned application as much as possible. It insulates you from changes to optimizer plans that take place at the database level (such as a DBA analyzing your tables, or changing some init.ora parameters, or upgrading the software). Like most features, it's a double-edged sword. The fact that it insulates you from external changes may be both good and bad. It can be good in that you will get performance results that are consistent over time (since your plan never changes). However, it could be bad in that you may miss out on a newer plan that could cause the query to run even faster.

Uses of Optimizer Plan Stability

In this section, we will explore various scenarios where you might choose to use this feature. We will use many of the features of outline generation in this section with minimal explanation, the details of how to use the commands, create outlines, manage them, and so on are in the later sections that follow.

A Method to Implement Tuning

Many times, people ask 'How can I hint a query in an existing application without actually hinting it?' Generally, they have access only to the binary code for the application and cannot make modifications to it, but need to be able to change the plan without modifying the application itself.

These people know the problem query, and have found that, through various session environment settings, the query can perform well. If they could inject a simple ALTER SESSION into the application (to enable or disable a hash join for example) or place a simple hint into the query (for example, /*+ RULE */ or /*+ ALL_ROWS */) it would run much better. Optimizer Plan Stability will give you this capability. You can independently create and store optimal query outlines **outside** of the existing application. You might utilize an ON LOGON database trigger (a method to run a snippet of code upon a user login to the database) or similar mechanism, causing the existing application to pick up your stored outline transparently.

For example, let's say you used SQL_TRACE to capture the SQL being performed by an application or report. You've used the TKPROF tool to analyze the resulting trace file and have found a query that runs very poorly. You've read through the Oracle-supplied *Designing and Tuning for Performance* guide, and tried out the hints that are documented. You find that if you execute the query with FIRST_ROWS optimization enabled, it runs very well, but if you enable FIRST_ROWS for the entire application, it affects overall performance in a very bad way. So, we'd like to have FIRST_ROWS optimization for this one query, and the default CHOOSE optimization for the remainder. Normally, we would just add a /*+ FIRST_ROWS */ hint to the query and be done with it. We cannot do this though, since we cannot modify the query. What we can do now is use the CREATE OUTLINE command, exactly as we did above, to create a named outline and then place it into the DEFAULT set of outlines, or some named category. We will set our environment such that the plan we want gets generated. For example, in this case we would have issued ALTER SESSION set optimizer_goal = first_rows, and then created the query outline. Then, we could utilize an ON LOGON trigger to enable this stored outline whenever the users of this application logged in.

This can be a little tricky to do since the query text for which we must generate the stored outline, must be exactly the same query text, byte-for-byte, as is embedded in the application itself. What we'll do here is demonstrate, in a step-by-step fashion, how we might perform this operation in the easiest way possible. We'll continue to use the EMP table query from the previous example – this is the query that we want to execute with FIRST_ROWS. The rest of the application should execute under CHOOSE. We have an 'application' that contains the following code:

```
tkyte@TKYTE816> create or replace procedure show_emps
  2  as
  3  begin
  4      for x in ( select ename, empno
  5                   from emp
  6                  where empno > 0 )
  7      loop
  8          dbms_output.put_line( x.empno || ',' || x.ename );
  9      end loop;
 10  end;
 11  /

Procedure created.
```

Now, we've executed this procedure using SQL_TRACE and determined from the TKPROF report that it is using an undesirable plan (See Chapter 10 on *Tuning Strategies and Tools* for more information on SQL_TRACE and TKPROF, and how you might enable them in various environments). Here, we will just use a simple ALTER SESSION command since it is a PL/SQL routine that we can run in SQL*PLUS:

```
tkyte@TKYTE816> alter session set sql_trace=true;

Session altered.

tkyte@TKYTE816> exec show_emps
7876,ADAMS
...
7521,WARD

PL/SQL procedure successfully completed.
```

Next, we run TKPROF on the resulting trace:

```
SELECT ENAME,EMPNO
FROM
 EMP  WHERE EMPNO > 0

call     count       cpu    elapsed disk      query    current       rows
-------  ------  -------- ---------- ----- ---------- ----------  ----------
```

```
Parse       2      0.01      0.01      0         0         0         0

Execute     2      0.00      0.00      0         0         0         0
Fetch      30      0.00      0.00      0        36        24        28
-------  ------  --------  --------  -----  ---------  --------  ----------
total      34      0.01      0.01      0        36        24        28

Misses in library cache during parse: 1
Optimizer goal: CHOOSE
Parsing user id: 224      (recursive depth: 1)


Rows     Row Source Operation
-------  -----------------------------------------------------
     14  TABLE ACCESS FULL EMP
```

The first thing to notice here is that the query in the TKPROF looks very different (in format) from the query in the application. This is a side effect of how PL/SQL processes SQL: it rewrites all static SQL, and the resulting query may look very different from the actual query in the original source code. When we create the stored outline, we must make sure we use the query that the database actually uses because Optimizer Plan Stability does exact string matching only – we must use the *exact* query the database sees, down to spaces, tabs and newlines. However, neither the text of the query in the PL/SQL routine nor the text in the TKPROF report is what we want! Fortunately, we can use the stored outline mechanisms themselves to capture the query we really need to work with. We will enable implicit stored outline generation, and this will capture the actual SQL text into a database table for us:

```
tkyte@TKYTE816> alter session set create_stored_outlines = hr_application;

Session altered.

tkyte@TKYTE816> exec show_emps
7876,ADAMS
...
7521,WARD

PL/SQL procedure successfully completed.

tkyte@TKYTE816> alter session set create_stored_outlines = FALSE;

Session altered.

tkyte@TKYTE816> set long 50000
tkyte@TKYTE816> select name, sql_text
  2    from user_outlines
  3    where category = 'HR_APPLICATION'
  4  /

NAME                             SQL_TEXT
-------------------------------  ---------------------------------------------------
SYS_OUTLINE_0104120951400008     SELECT ENAME,EMPNO   FROM EMP   WHERE EMPNO > 0
```

We used the ALTER SESSION command to enable automatic stored outline generation for a category named HR_APPLICATION, and ran our application.

The SET LONG command was used to ensure that SQL*PLUS would show us the entire SQL query; by default it would only show us the first 80 bytes.

We could have used an ON LOGON database trigger, such as the following, to achieve the same result:

```
tkyte@TKYTE816> create or replace trigger tkyte_logon
  2  after logon on database
  3  begin
  4      if ( user = 'TKYTE' ) then
  5          execute immediate
  6                  'alter session set use_stored_outlines = hr_application';
  7      end if;
  8  end;
  9  /

Trigger created.
```

> *You need the privileges* CREATE TRIGGER *and* ADMINISTER DATABASE TRIGGER *in order to create a* LOGON *trigger. Additionally, the owner of this trigger needs the* ALTER SESSION *privilege granted directly to them, rather than via a role.*

You would adopt this approach for an application where you cannot issue the ALTER SESSION command in any other fashion.

So, now that we have our query we are ready to generate the stored outline with the plan we would like to have the query use. It is interesting to notice that it is different from the query in the PL/SQL code – it is all in uppercase. It is also different from the query in the TKPROF report – that one had newlines in it. Since stored outline usage is *very* picky about using the *exact* same query, I'm going to show how to change the set of hints associated with outline we've captured in the easiest way possible. Notice how, in the above output from the query on the USER_OUTLINES view, we selected the NAME and the SQL_TEXT so we can easily identify the query we want to fix and now we know the stored outline name, SYS_OUTLINE_0104120951400008.

So, we can change our environment to FIRST_ROWS, rebuild our named outline, and we are done:

```
tkyte@TKYTE816> alter session set optimizer_goal=first_rows
  2  /

Session altered.

tkyte@TKYTE816> alter outline SYS_OUTLINE_0104120951400008 rebuild
  2  /

Outline altered.

tkyte@TKYTE816> alter session set optimizer_goal=CHOOSE;

Session altered.
```

We started by setting the optimizer goal to FIRST_ROWS instead of CHOOSE. We know that if we execute our query under FIRST_ROWS optimization, it gets the plan we want (we know this because that is the scenario we set up in this case – we would have discovered it through tuning and testing). Instead of executing the query now, we simply REBUILD the outline – the REBUILD will use our current environment to generate the plan for us.

Now to see that this actually works, we need to enable this category of outlines. For demonstration purposes, we will use a simple ALTER SESSION command interactively, but to make this transparent you might use the ON LOGON trigger to set this immediately upon logging onto the database. To verify this fix is in place, we will re-run the application:

```
tkyte@TKYTE816> alter session set optimizer_goal=CHOOSE;

Session altered.

tkyte@TKYTE816> alter session set USE_STORED_OUTLINES = hr_application;

Session altered.

tkyte@TKYTE816> alter session set sql_trace=true;

Session altered.

tkyte@TKYTE816> exec show_emps
7369,SMITH
...
7934,MILLER

PL/SQL procedure successfully completed.
```

We set the optimizer goal back to the default value, directed Oracle to use the stored outlines in the category HR_APPLICATION, and ran the application. Now the TKPROF report will show us:

```
SELECT ENAME, EMPNO
FROM
 EMP  WHERE EMPNO > 0


call     count       cpu    elapsed  disk      query    current       rows
-------  ------  --------  ---------- -----  ---------- ----------  ----------
Parse        1      0.01      0.01      0          0          1           0
Execute      1      0.00      0.00      0          0          0           0
Fetch       15      0.00      0.00      0         28          0          14
-------  ------  --------  ---------- -----  ---------- ----------  ----------
total       17      0.01      0.01      0         28          1          14

Misses in library cache during parse: 1
Optimizer goal: CHOOSE
Parsing user id: 224     (recursive depth: 1)

Rows     Row Source Operation
-------  ---------------------------------------------------
     14    TABLE ACCESS BY INDEX ROWID EMP
     15     INDEX RANGE SCAN (object id 28094)
```

This proves that our plan is now in effect. When we execute our application, this ALTER SESSION SET USE_STORED_OUTLINE has enabled the outlines we've stored. The one exact query we targeted will be optimized using the hints we stored – the hints generated with the FIRST_ROWS optimizer mode. The remaining queries in the application will be optimized exactly as they were before.

A Development Tool

Let's say you are building a new application that is to be delivered to lots of people. You are building the next 'killer app'. You will have little or no control over the target database environment – you might be installed into an instance that is 'all your own,' or you may be installed into an instance that has many other applications already running in it. These databases will have various init.ora settings that affect the optimizer such as DB_BLOCK_BUFFERS, DB_FILE_MULTIBLOCK_READ_COUNT, HASH_MULTIBLOCK_IO_COUNT, OPTIMIZER_GOAL, HASH_JOIN_ENABLED, and so on. They may or may not have parallel query enabled. They may or may not have a large SGA on a big machine. They might have version 8.1.6.1, 8.1.7, or 8.1.6.2. And so on. There are many factors that may influence the plan generated by the optimizer.

You will go to great lengths while developing your applications to get them to access the data in 'just the right way'. In your development tests and scaling tests, against real live large data sets on your machines, the application runs extremely well. Everything runs as expected. So why do people call your help desk with performance-related issues? It is because on their own machines, with their own configurations, the query plans are coming out slightly differently.

You can use Optimizer Plan Stability to level the playing field here. Once you have tuned your application in-house, tested it thoroughly against real data (appropriate number and mix of rows), the last step to undertake before shipping the application is to generate query outlines for all of your queries. This can be done very easily using the ON LOGON trigger, once again, but this time coding something like this:

```
sys@TKYTE816> create or replace trigger tkyte_logon
  2  after logon on database
  3  begin
  4     if ( user = 'TKYTE' ) then
  5        execute immediate
  6              'alter session set create_stored_outlines = KillerApp';
  7     end if;
  8  end;
  9  /

Trigger created.
```

> *This was executed as the user SYS who, by default, has all of the necessary privileges to do this trigger.*

Now, when I log in, every single query I execute will create an outline for me, name it and store it in the category KillerApp. I will run the full battery of tests against the application, exercising *all* of the SQL and, as I do that, I'm collecting the outlines for every query in the application.Once this is done, I can use the Oracle utility, EXP, to export my outlines, and install them as part of my import, using the utility IMP (this is discussed later in the chapter, in the section *Moving Outlines from Database to Database*). The applications we wrote will always issue the following command, right after they connect:

```
alter session set use_stored_outlines = KillerApp;
```

In this way, I know for sure that the query plan I worked so hard to achieve is being used, regardless of the settings on my customers' machines. This makes sense not just for 'external' customers, but also when moving an application from the test database instance, to the production instance. This will cut way down the number of times you hear 'Well it runs great in the test instance, but when we move it to the production instance it goes really slow'. This statement is usually followed by 'Both instances are exactly the same'. Then you discover they have different amounts of RAM, CPUs and their `init.ora` files are different to reflect the different hardware configuration. Any one of these factors can, and will, influence the optimizer, leading to different plans. Optimizer Plan Stability will avoid this issue altogether.

It should be noted however, that you might be missing out on the benefits of the latest and greatest optimizer enhancements. If you have installed new software, new features, it would be a good idea to disable this feature every now and again during the development and testing phase of your application, so that you can identify queries that would execute quicker with some new plan that the optimizer can come up with.

To See the Indexes Used

This is not actually one of the intended uses of stored outlines, more of a side effect – but, hey, it works! A frequently asked question is 'I have lots and lots of indexes in my database and I'm sure some of them are not being used, but I'm not sure which ones. How can I tell?' Well, one way is via the stored outlines – they'll list the name of every index they use in a query access plan. If you use an ON LOGON trigger to enable automatic outline generation, run your system for a while, and then disable it – you'll have a fairly inclusive list of what indexes are used in the system (and by which queries). As we see below, all of the 'hints' that stored outlines use are stored in a data dictionary table. It becomes very easy to see what indexes are used (and by what queries) and which are not. For example, using the output of our two examples above, we can see which queries use the index EMP_PK we have created in our database via:

```
tkyte@TKYTE816> select name, hint
  2  from user_outline_hints
  3  where hint like 'INDEX%EMP_PK%'
  4  /

NAME              HINT
----------------  --------------------
MYOUTLINE         INDEX(EMP EMP_PK)
FIRST_ROWS_EMP    INDEX(EMP EMP_PK)
```

We can use the NAME column from this query to go back to the actual SQL query stored in USER_OUTLINES, to see the original query text that is making use of this index.

To See what SQL is Executed by an Application

Again, this is a side effect rather than one of the actual intended uses of stored outlines, but it works. Frequently, people want to know what SQL their application actually executes. They cannot modify the application and setting SQL_TRACE ON is far too costly. Using an ON LOGON trigger for some users of the application, we can automatically capture, into the OUTLINE tables, all of the SQL the application executes at run-time. We can use this for tuning or analysis later.

You should be aware that this would only capture SQL as it is executed. In order to see an exhaustive list of the SQL an application might issue, you must cause that application to execute all of its SQL and this will entail using every feature and function in every combination.

How Optimizer Plan Stability Works

Optimizer Plan Stability works via the Oracle 'hinting' mechanism. Using our previous EMP example, we will be able to look at the hints that were stored for our query, and how they would be applied at run-time. We'll also look at the OUTLN schema, which holds all stored query outlines and their hints.

The first step in getting Optimizer Plan Stability working is to collect a query outline. Since we have already done that in the previous example, via the CREATE OUTLINE command, we'll use it here to look at how the database processes these outlines.

OUTLINES and OUTLINE_HINTS

There are only two views to consider with query outlines and they exhibit a master-detail relationship. The master table is the OUTLINES table (of which there are the three usual version: DBA_, ALL_, and USER_). The detail table is OUTLINE_HINTS (with, again, the three normal variants). The following sections explain what each of these are and how they are used:

The _OUTLINES Views

These views show the number of stored outlines in the database. DBA_OUTLINES has an entry for each and every stored outline by user, whereas ALL_ and USER_OUTLINES will only expose the rows relevant to the current user (the outlines *they* have created). Since DBA_OUTLINES and USER_OUTLINES only differ by one column (the DBA table has an OWNER column representing the schema that created the outline), we'll look at DBA_OUTLINES:

- ❏ NAME – The name of the outline you gave it using the CREATE OUTLINE command (in our example above, our names were MYOUTLINE or FIRST_ROWS_EMP). If you use the ALTER SESSION method to create a stored outline – we'll explore this method in full detail later in this chapter – and do not name it, then the system will generate an outline name for you. It should be noted that the name of an outline is unique by itself (the outline name is a primary key). I cannot have the same name in two different categories, nor can I have the same name with two different owners. This is discussed in more detail in the *Caveats* section.

- ❏ OWNER – The schema that created the outline. Outlines are not really 'owned' by anyone, so this name is somewhat of a misnomer. It should be 'creator'.

- ❏ CATEGORY – The category to which you assigned the schema (MYCATEGORY in our example). Query outlines may either belong to a specific named category, or to the generic DEFAULT category, which is used if no category name is specified. At run-time, a user or application will issue an ALTER SESSION SET USE_STORED_OUTLINES = <TRUE | category name> to specify which set of stored outlines should be used. Setting to TRUE will enable the use of outlines stored in the DEFAULT category. You may only have one category of stored outlines in use at any particular time.

- ❏ USED – This attribute tells us if the named outline has ever been used. It will have the value unused until the first time it is used to modify the query plan of a running query, at which point it will assume the value used.

- ❏ TIMESTAMP – The date and time the outline was originally created.

- ❏ VERSION – The database version that originally created the query outline.

- ❏ SQL_TEXT – The actual (verbatim) SQL query that was used to generate the outline. Only queries that match this text exactly, as noted above, will be candidates for using this stored outline.

So, for example, after executing our example queries from above, we have in USER_OUTLINES, the following information:

```
tkyte@TKYTE816> select * from user_outlines;

NAME            CATEGORY        USED TIMESTAMP VERSION    SQL_TEXT
--------------- --------------- ---- --------- ---------- --------------------
MYOUTLINE       MYCATEGORY      USED 11-APR-01 8.1.6.0.0  select empno, ename
                                                          from emp where empno
                                                          > 0

FIRST_ROWS_EMP  HR_APPLICATION  USED 12-APR-01 8.1.6.0.0  SELECT ENAME,EMPNO
                                                          FROM EMP  WHERE EMPNO
                                                          > 0
```

This shows all of the described information, as expected.

The _OUTLINE_HINTS Views

These views show the actual hints that must be applied to various internal phases of the developed query plan. The server internally rewrites our submitted query with these hints embedded in it in the appropriate locations, giving us the query plan we desire. We'll never see these hints in the query text itself – this is all done against internal query plan structures. Again, the only difference between the DBA_OUTLINE_HINTS view, and the USER_OUTLINE_HINTS and ALL_OUTLINE_HINTS views is the inclusion of an OWNER column identifying the schema that created the outline:

- ❏ NAME – The name of the stored outline. If generated with a CREATE OUTLINE statement, this will be some name you assigned. If generated via the ALTER SESSION method, this will be a system-assigned identifier like the SYS_OUTLINE_0104120957410010 name assigned to our stored outline in the example.

- ❏ OWNER – The name of the schema that created the query outline.

- ❏ NODE – The query or subquery to which this hint will apply. The outermost query will be assigned a node of 1 and subsequent subqueries embedded within the parent query will be assigned incremental ID numbers.

- ❏ STAGE – There are various stages at which these hints will be applied, during the compilation of a query. This number represents the stage that this particular hint will be 'written' into the query. These stages are internal compilation stages; part of the Oracle optimizer, something you normally do not have access to.

- ❏ JOIN_POS – Identifies the table to which this hint will be applied. For all hints that are not access method hints, this will be ZERO. For access method hints (for example, access this table by an INDEX), JOIN_POS will identify the table.

- ❏ HINT – The actual hint to be embedded in the query.

Looking at the results from out initial example, we have:

```
tkyte@TKYTE816> break on stage skip 1

tkyte@TKYTE816> select stage, name, node, join_pos, hint
  2    from user_outline_hints
  3    where name = 'MYOUTLINE'
  4    order by stage
  5  /

STAGE NAME        NODE   JOIN_POS HINT
----- ---------   ----   -------- --------------------
    1 MYOUTLINE   1             0 NOREWRITE
      MYOUTLINE   1             0 RULE

    2 MYOUTLINE   1             0 NOREWRITE

    3 MYOUTLINE   1             0 NO_EXPAND
      MYOUTLINE   1             0 ORDERED
      MYOUTLINE   1             0 NO_FACT(EMP)
      MYOUTLINE   1             1 INDEX(EMP EMP_PK)

7 rows selected.
```

This shows that at stage 1, the server will apply the NOREWRITE and RULE hints. The NOREWRITE hint will prevent query rewrite from taking place at run-time (if someone later adds a feature or enables a system/session parameter that could invoke QUERY_REWRITE). The RULE hint will use the rule-based optimizer at run-time, regardless of the current setting of the OPTIMIZER_GOAL or the presence (or lack thereof) of statistics on the table.

At stage 2, it will again prevent query rewrite from taking place. In stage 3, we are injecting the hints that will really make the query do what we want. It applies an ORDERED hint which makes use of the order of the tables in the FROM clause to join tables (since we accessed a single table in our example, this is somewhat superfluous). It applies a NO_EXPAND hint (this applies to object related conditions and since there are no object relations in our example, it is not really necessary). It then applies an internal, undocumented hint NO_FACT. Lastly, the access method hint INDEX() is to be used against table 1 (the JOIN_POS column), which is the EMP table using the index EMP_PK, our primary key.

So, those are the mechanics of Optimizer Plan Stability. You store a plan in a named or default category. At run-time your application chooses to 'use' a certain category of plans, and the database optimizer will merge the requisite hints into your query text to have the result plan come out the same way every time.

Creating Stored Outlines

There are two ways to generate plans. We've already loosely introduced them in the previous examples. One method is via SQL DDL, and the other is by setting a session state variable. We'll look at both and consider when each one might be used. In either case, however, you'll want to make sure the schema generating the outlines has the appropriate privileges needed to create and manage outlines.

Privileges Needed for Stored Outlines

When using stored outlines, there are four relevant privileges:

❑ CREATE ANY OUTLINE – Allows you to create outlines in the database. Without this privilege you will receive the error ORA-18005: create any outline privilege is required for this operation.

❑ ALTER ANY OUTLINE – Allows you to alter (rename, change the category of, or recompute the plan for) a query.

❑ DROP ANY OUTLINE – Allows you to drop any existing outline by name.

❑ EXECUTE ON OUTLN_PKG – Allows you to execute the OUTLINE package (see a little later for functionality).

It should be noted that these are ANY privileges. This means that if you have the ability to CREATE OR REPLACE ANY outline, you have the ability to overwrite someone else's outline, without their permission. Outlines, unlike most other database objects, are not really owned by anyone. They have a creator, but not an owner in the normal sense. If you can drop your own outlines, then you can also (inadvertently) drop anyone else's outline, so care must be exercised with these privileges. See *The Namespace of Outlines is Global* in the *Caveats* section for more information on this.

Using DDL

In order to create stored outlines using DDL, we use a SQL command of the following structure:

```
CREATE <OR REPLACE> OUTLINE OUTLINE_NAME
<FOR CATEGORY CATEGORY_NAME>
ON STATEMENT_TO_STORE_OUTLINE_FOR
```

Where:

❑ OUTLINE_NAME is the name that you have assigned to this particular outline. It should be something relevant to you, and your application. It follows the same naming constraints as any database object (30 characters, must start with a letter, and so on). Additionally, the OUTLINE_NAME must be unique in a database, not unique only for a particular user or category, as one might expect, so be very careful when using the OR REPLACE, as it will overwrite any existing outline of that name.

❑ CATEGORY_NAME is the name that you are using to group outlines together. This part of the CREATE statement is optional and if you do not specify a category, then the outline will be placed into the DEFAULT category. It is recommended that you explicitly name a category in all cases and do not rely on DEFAULT. Since only one category at a time may be used by a session, it will be important to generate a plan for every relevant query into this category.

❑ STATEMENT_TO_STORE_OUTLINE_FOR is any valid SQL DML statement.

Generating outlines via DDL is most useful if you have an application that stores all of its SQL statements externally. That is, you have a resource file of some sort that has all of the SQL you ever execute in it. In this case, it is a simple matter to generate a CREATE OUTLINE script from this resource file, and run it through the database. This ensures that you generate outlines for 100 percent of your queries (given that 100 percent of your queries exist in these resource files). It also safeguards against accidentally generating stored outlines for queries that are not relevant. For example, if you use the ON LOGON trigger and log into SQL*PLUS afterwards, you'll find that the queries SQL*PLUS runs on your behalf, have outlines generated for them.

Additionally, the DDL approach is useful when you have a small handful of individual queries for which you wish to generate outlines. For example, you might use this approach when using query outlines as a tuning tool. So, when you want to generate stored outlines for a small percentage of an application, you would use DDL to generate the outlines for just the queries you wanted, instead of every query you execute.

Using ALTER SESSION

This is a more general-purpose method for generating query outlines. It works in a similar manner to SQL_TRACE when tracing a program. From the time you issue an ALTER SESSION statement until you turn off the creation of stored outlines, every query you issue will have its outline saved (well, almost every query, see the *Caveats* section below for cases where your outline will not be saved).

You might use this method on any application where you want all of the plans to be stabilized. That is, when you want to know what the query plans for your SQL will be, regardless of the database version your application is installed in, regardless of the settings in the init.ora on that database, and so on. In order to do this for your application, you might utilize the ON LOGON trigger as demonstrated previously, and then fully exercise your entire application, executing every possible query. You would do this in your test database instance as part of your final testing before delivery. After you collect all of the plans, you would use the EXP tool to extract them, and utilize the IMP tool as part of your delivery mechanism. See *Moving Outlines From Database to Database* later for the exact details of that process.

You will also use this method when utilizing the database feature of **auto binding**. The *Caveats* section will go into more details on this feature, and its interaction with Optimizer Plan Stability.

The syntax of the ALTER SESSION method is very straightforward:

```
ALTER SESSION SET CREATE_STORED_OUTLINES = TRUE;
ALTER SESSION SET CREATE_STORED_OUTLINES = FALSE;
ALTER SESSION SET CREATE_STORED_OUTLINES = some_category_you_choose;
```

If you set CREATE_STORED_OUTLINES to TRUE, then Oracle will generate stored outlines into the DEFAULT category. The DEFAULT category is simply a category named DEFAULT – it must be enabled, as any other category would be. Once you set CREATE_STORED_OUTLINES to FALSE, Oracle will cease generating stored outlines in your session.

By setting CREATE_STORED_OUTLINES to some_category_you_choose, Oracle will generate query outlines for all queries issued, and store them into that named category. This is the preferred way of using this method. It is recommended, for clarity, that your application use a category of its own, especially if you are going to install your application into a shared database that might have lots of other applications utilizing this feature. It will prevent conflicts between these applications, and make it clear to whom a given outline belongs.

The OUTLN User

The schema OUTLN is now created in all Oracle8i databases, with a default password of OUTLN. The DBA *can* and *should* change the password of this account immediately after an install, just as they do for other accounts such as SYS and SYSTEM.

This schema holds two tables and some indexes that, by default, are in the SYSTEM tablespace. If you plan on using Optimizer Plan Stability heavily (especially with regards to using the ALTER SESSION method of capturing query plans), you might consider moving the objects out of the SYSTEM tablespace and into a tablespace you have set up just for them. One of the two tables contains a LONG column so cannot easily be moved, using the usual ALTER TABLE tablename MOVE syntax. Rather, we must use export and import to move these objects. The following steps describe how to move the entire OUTLN schema from the SYSTEM tablespace to the TOOLS tablespace:

1. Export the OUTLN user:

```
exp userid=outln/outln owner=outln
```

2. Alter the OUTLN user to change their default tablespace from SYSTEM to TOOLS, give them an unlimited quota on TOOLS and a 0k quota on SYSTEM:

```
alter user outln default tablespace tools;
revoke unlimited tablespace from outln;
alter user outln quota 0k on system;
alter user outln quota unlimited on tools;
```

3. Drop the OL$ and OL$HINTS table from the OUTLN schema:

```
drop table ol$;
drop table ol$hints;
```

4. Import the OUTLN user:

```
imp userid=outln/outln full=yes
```

Note that if a system is using outlines already, the above operation should be done in single user mode if at all possible, and in a database with no active end users.

You might consider monitoring the space utilization of the OL$ and OL$HINTS table and the corresponding indexes over time.

Moving Outlines from Database to Database

Having reviewed how to move the entire OUTLN schema from tablespace to tablespace within a database, let's look at how to export query outlines from your database, and import them into a totally different instance. This would be in support of using outlines to ensure Optimizer Plan Stability of an application you are going to install at various customer sites, or are moving from your test instance into your production instance.

The easiest way to do this is via a parameter file (to avoid any issues with sh escaping issues and NT command line nuances). I set up an exp.par file for export that looks like this:

```
query="where category='HR_APPLICATION'"
tables=(ol$,ol$hints)
```

This is set up to export all of the stored outlines for the HR_APPLICATION category. The only thing you'll change in the exp.par file from run to run would be the name of the category you are moving. We would then execute:

```
exp userid=outln/<password> parfile=exp.par
```

replacing <password> with the correct password for OUTLN of course. This will export only the rows in which we are interested. We would move the resulting expdat.dmp file to the target server, or run IMP over the network, to do a full import of it. This command would be:

```
imp userid=outln/outln full=y ignore=yes
```

We must use the IGNORE=YES clause this time since we are adding rows to an existing table, not trying to move it as we were in the last section. Optimizer Plan Stability fully supports export and import – you are allowed to do this. You should never directly modify the OL$ or OL$HINT tables, but you can use EXP/IMP to move them around from database to database. In fact, EXP/IMP is the only tool that will perform this task safely. Consider what would happen if you had a database with a stored outline called MYOUTLINE, you exported this outline, and took it to another database, but that other database *already* had an outline called MYOUTLINE. If you were to use any tool other than EXP/IMP, you would corrupt the outline in the other database. Suppose you just tried to copy the data over using SQL. Some of the rows might copy, but others would not, due to key conflicts. You would end up with bits and pieces of two stored outlines mixed together. Only import and export know the proper way to accomplish this task, and have special hooks to utilize to make sure an outline from one database does not overwrite the outlines in another database (discussed in more detail in *The OUTLN_PKG Package* section a little later).

Getting Just the Right Outline

The question 'How can we get just the right optimizer plan going?' might arise, if we are using this for a tuning tool. Earlier, I demonstrated how altering the session and running a specific query could generate a 'good' plan. This is by far the easiest method. If it were at all possible, you would simply issue the requisite ALTER SESSION directives to set up your session's environment appropriately, and then issue the CREATE OUTLINE for this query. Alternatively, if the query is already in the outline tables, rebuild it with the new environment as we did above. This second case is desirable as it guarantees the query text will match. This is possible in many cases, such as when:

❑ You want a specific query to use a certain optimization mode regardless of the OPTIMIZER_GOAL setting in the application at run-time. You can issue the ALTER SESSION to the appropriate mode, run the CREATE OUTLINE for that query, and that's it.

❑ You want to avoid the use of a specific feature such as QUERY_REWRITE_ENABLED, HASH_JOIN_ENABLED, or downgrade to a different OPTIMIZER_FEATURES_ENABLED. You would create a session, issue the ALTER SESSION to enable/disable various features, and then issue the CREATE OUTLINE command for the various queries.

Well, what happens when simply setting a session level attribute such as HASH_JOIN_ENABLED doesn't change the query plan in the manner you desire – when the only thing that has the desired effect is physically hinting the query itself? Well, you can certainly use hints with Optimizer Plan Stability, in that you can create a stored outline on a query containing hints, but that is probably not what you want. You want a query that is executed without the hints, to use this plan. However, in order to use this stored plan you must *execute* queries that *exactly* match the SQL used to generate the outline. You want to be able to store an outline for an un-hinted query, and have that query pick up that plan. Due to the implementation of Optimizer Plan Stability, we can, in fact, do that – just in a circuitous fashion. Here is how it would work.

Let's suppose we started with the query:

```
scott@TKYTE816> set autotrace traceonly explain
scott@TKYTE816> select * from emp, dept where emp.deptno = dept.deptno;


Execution Plan
----------------------------------------------------------
   0      SELECT STATEMENT Optimizer=CHOOSE
   1    0   NESTED LOOPS
   2    1     TABLE ACCESS (FULL) OF 'EMP'
   3    1     TABLE ACCESS (BY INDEX ROWID) OF 'DEPT'
   4    3       INDEX (UNIQUE SCAN) OF 'DEPT_PK' (UNIQUE)
```

We discovered through testing and tuning that the following query works much better for us:

```
scott@TKYTE816> select *
   2    from ( select /*+ use_hash(emp) */ * from emp ) emp,
   3         ( select /*+ use_hash(dept) */ * from dept ) dept
   4   where emp.deptno = dept.deptno
   5  /


Execution Plan
----------------------------------------------------------
   0      SELECT STATEMENT Optimizer=CHOOSE (Cost=3 Card=67 Bytes=7839)
   1    0   HASH JOIN (Cost=3 Card=67 Bytes=7839)
   2    1     TABLE ACCESS (FULL) OF 'EMP' (Cost=1 Card=82 Bytes=7134)
   3    1     TABLE ACCESS (FULL) OF 'DEPT' (Cost=1 Card=82 Bytes=2460)
```

The performance is incredible when compared to the nested loops query. *We would like the applications that issue the first query, to get the hash join plan rather than the nested loop plan, but we need this to happen without changing the application code* (for whatever reason, we cannot add hints to the code).

Well, since query plan outlines are based on character string comparisons, we can accomplish this using a different schema and some hinted views. Since the above objects are in the SCOTT schema, we are going to use the TKYTE schema to set up some views:

```
scott@TKYTE816> grant select on emp to tkyte;

Grant succeeded.

scott@TKYTE816> grant select on dept to tkyte;

Grant succeeded.

scott@TKYTE816> connect tkyte/tkyte
Connected.
tkyte@TKYTE816> drop table emp;

Table dropped.

tkyte@TKYTE816> drop table dept;

Table dropped.

tkyte@TKYTE816> create or replace view emp as
  2   select /*+ use_hash(emp) */ * from scott.emp emp
  3   /

View created.

tkyte@TKYTE816> create or replace view dept as
  2   select /*+ use_hash(dept) */  * from scott.dept dept
  3   /

View created.
```

Now we generate a stored outline for our application query:

```
tkyte@TKYTE816> create or replace outline my_outline
  2   for category my_category
  3   on select * from emp, dept where emp.deptno = dept.deptno;

Outline created.
```

So, in the TKYTE schema, we have our **hinted views** of the base objects and we've created a stored outline of the query we wanted in that schema. We could drop the views at this point if we wanted to – we have what we want, the stored outline using *hash* joins. Now, when we log in as SCOTT again, we see the following:

```
scott@TKYTE816> connect scott/tiger
scott@TKYTE816> alter session set use_stored_outlines=my_category;

Session altered.

scott@TKYTE816> set autotrace traceonly explain
scott@TKYTE816> select * from emp, dept where emp.deptno = dept.deptno;

Execution Plan
-----------------------------------------------------------
```

```
0          SELECT STATEMENT Optimizer=CHOOSE (Cost=3 Card=67 Bytes=7839)
1      0     HASH JOIN (Cost=3 Card=67 Bytes=7839)
2      1       TABLE ACCESS (FULL) OF 'EMP' (Cost=1 Card=82 Bytes=7134)
3      1       TABLE ACCESS (FULL) OF 'DEPT' (Cost=1 Card=82 Bytes=2460)
```

Simply by using the appropriate outline category, we are now picking up the desired plan. That is because the Optimizer Plan Stability does not, by design, resolve object references in the SQL text. It just stores a string, and when it gets another string that matches in the category you have enabled, it will utilize the stored hints. This is intended by design.

Utilizing this string-matching feature, we can use views and/or synonyms to create query outlines that utilize our hints in the generation of the final query plan. Combine this with the ALTER SESSION method above and it is safe to say you could generate most plans you need.

Managing Outlines

We will now take an in-depth look at the facilities used to manage outlines: using either DDL (ALTER and DROP), or the supplied OUTLN_PKG package.

Via DDL

In addition to the CREATE command, we also use the ALTER and DROP commands to manage query outlines. The ALTER command allows us to:

❑   RENAME a stored outline.

❑   REBUILD the plan for a stored outline.

❑   CHANGE the category a stored plan is in to another category

The DROP command simply drops a stored outline by name.

ALTER OUTLINE

The ALTER command has three variants and we will take a look at each one. To review how this command works, we will first create a stored outline and then alter it in various ways:

```
tkyte@TKYTE816> create or replace outline my_outline
  2  for category my_category
  3  on select * from all_objects
  4  /

Outline created.

tkyte@TKYTE816> select name, category, sql_text from user_outlines;

NAME                            CATEGORY        SQL_TEXT
------------------------------  --------------  --------------------
MY_OUTLINE                      MY_CATEGORY     select * from
                                                all_objects

tkyte@TKYTE816> select count(*) from user_outline_hints
```

```
                                                    where name = 'MY_OUTLINE';

  COUNT(*)
----------
       138
```

So, the outline we are working with is named MY_OUTLINE, in category MY_CATEGORY, and currently has 138 hints associated with it (your mileage may vary depending on your optimizer setting!).

The first use of the ALTER OUTLINE command simply allows us to rename a stored outline. The syntax for this command is:

```
alter outline outline_name rename to new_name
```

So, we will use this command to rename our outline from MY_OUTLINE to PLAN_FOR_ALL_OBJECTS as follows:

```
tkyte@TKYTE816> alter outline my_outline rename to plan_for_all_objects
  2  /

Outline altered.
```

A simple query verifies that it worked as planned:

```
tkyte@TKYTE816> select name, category, sql_text from user_outlines
  2  /

NAME                              CATEGORY         SQL_TEXT
-------------------------------   --------------   ---------------------
PLAN_FOR_ALL_OBJECTS              MY_CATEGORY      select * from
                                                   all_objects
```

The next step is to use the ALTER OUTLINE command to change the category in which this outline is currently stored. The syntax for this command is:

```
alter outline outline_name change category to new_category_name;
```

So, let's change the category of our stored outline from MY_CATEGORY to a category named DICTIONARY_PLANS:

```
tkyte@TKYTE816> alter outline plan_for_all_objects change category to
  2             dictionary_plans
  3  /

Outline altered.

tkyte@TKYTE816> select name, category, sql_text from user_outlines
  2  /
```

NAME	CATEGORY	SQL_TEXT
PLAN_FOR_ALL_OBJECTS	DICTIONARY_PLANS	select * from all_objects

Again, this is very straightforward. The ALTER command simply updated the category name for us in the OUTLN schema. To demonstrate the last usage of the ALTER command, we'll rebuild the query plan using the current environment. The basic syntax is as follows:

```
alter outline outline_name rebuild;
```

As it currently stands, we are logged into SQL*PLUS with the OPTIMIZER_GOAL set to CHOOSE. Since data dictionary objects are not analyzed, the optimizer being used by the above query is the rule-based optimizer (when the optimizer goal is CHOOSE, and no referenced objects are analyzed, we use the rule-based optimizer). We will set the optimizer goal to ALL_ROWS, forcing use of the cost-based optimizer, and rebuild the plan.

```
tkyte@TKYTE816> alter session set optimizer_goal = all_rows
  2  /

Session altered.

tkyte@TKYTE816> alter outline plan_for_all_objects rebuild
  2  /
Outline altered.
```

Looking at the number of resulting hints, we can confirm that the generated plan was in fact rebuilt and is different from the original plan:

```
tkyte@TKYTE816> SELECT COUNT (*)
  2    FROM USER_OUTLINE_HINTS
  3    WHERE NAME = 'PLAN_FOR_ALL_OBJECTS'
  4  /

  COUNT(*)
----------
       139
```

The plan is definitely different – we now have 139 hints – and it is now optimized using ALL_ROWS instead of CHOOSE.

DROP OUTLINE

The command to drop the outline is very simple. The syntax is:

```
drop outline outline_name;
```

Continuing our example, we will use this DDL command to drop our existing stored outline:

```
tkyte@TKYTE816> drop outline plan_for_all_objects
  2  /

Outline dropped.

tkyte@TKYTE816> select * from user_outlines;

no rows selected
```

That's about as simple as it gets. The following section details some more robust procedures to manipulate groups of outlines.

The OUTLN_PKG Package

We will now look at the OUTLN_PKG. This package is provided for two reasons:

❑ To allow you to perform bulk operations on outlines such as dropping all unused stored outlines, dropping all outlines in a category, and so on. The equivalent functionality is available via the ALTER and DROP commands, but only on a single outline at a time. The OUTLN_PKG offers an API to work on many outlines with one command.

❑ To provide the API for the Export and Import utilities to be able to export and import stored outlines.

We will describe and demonstrate the usage of the OUTLN_PKG functions for bulk operations. We will not look at the API calls in the package that are for the use of export and import. Those functions are undocumented and not intended to be invoked by any tool other than IMP and EXP.

The OUTLN_PKG is created by the dbmsol.sql and prvtol.plb scripts found in [ORACLE_HOME]/rdbms/admin. This script is executed by catproc.sql (found in the same place) and will be installed by default in your database. In addition to creating the OUTLN_PKG, this script inserts the necessary rows into the EXP dictionary tables to register its functions with the EXP/IMP tools. It should be installed by the user SYS or INTERNAL using SVRMGRL. As it is installed on an upgrade or an install of the database, it should never be necessary for you to run this script yourself.

The OUTLN_PKG has three entry points of interest to us:

❑ DROP_UNUSED – Drop any outline whose 'used' column is UNUSED. These are stored outlines that have been generated but never used to rewrite a query.

❑ DROP_BY_CAT – Drop all outlines in the same named category. If you determine that an entire category of stored outlines is no longer relevant, you may use this to drop all of them in one command, instead of calling DROP OUTLINE for each stored outline in turn.

❑ UPDATE_BY_CAT – Change the name of the category globally, for all stored outlines in the same category.

OUTLN_PKG.DROP_UNUSED

This procedure, which takes no inputs, drops every unused outline from *every* category. It simply finds every outline whose USED field is set to UNUSED, and does the equivalent of DROP OUTLINE outline_name against it. An example usage is:

```
tkyte@TKYTE816> exec outln_pkg.drop_unused;

PL/SQL procedure successfully completed.
```

Since this procedure works against all categories, care should be exercised in its use. You may inadvertently drop a stored outline in a category you should not have. This could interfere with someone else who had generated the outlines but had not yet used them.

OUTLN_PKG.DROP_BY_CAT

The DROP_BY_CAT procedure will remove all stored outlines in a given category. You might use this when testing, for example, to remove categories of stored outlines that did not meet your needs. Alternatively, you may use it to remove the outlines from a category. This will allow an application to start generating plans using the optimizer directly, where before it was using the outlines. Here is a brief example using this routine:

```
tkyte@TKYTE816> select category from user_outlines;

CATEGORY
--------------
DICTIONARY_PLANS

tkyte@TKYTE816> exec outln_pkg.drop_by_cat( 'DICTIONARY_PLANS' );

PL/SQL procedure successfully completed.

tkyte@TKYTE816> select category from user_outlines;

no rows selected
```

OUTLN_PKG.UPDATE_BY_CAT

This procedure allows you to rename an existing category, or to merge one category into another. The syntax of this procedure is simply:

```
outln_pkg.update_by_cat(old_category_name, new_category_name);
```

It works as follows:

- ❏ If the name new_category_name does not exist in the database yet, all existing outlines in old_category_name will now have the category new_category_name.

- ❏ If the category new_category_name does exist, all stored outlines from old_category_name that do not already have an entry in new_category_name will be moved into new_category_name.

- ❏ If the SQL_TEXT column of the stored outline in old_category_name has an exact match in the new_category_name category then *it will not be moved.*

Let's look at an example that demonstrates this feature:

```
tkyte@TKYTE816> create outline outline_1
  2  for category CAT_1
  3  on select * from dual
  4  /

Outline created.

tkyte@TKYTE816> create outline outline_2
  2  for category CAT_2
  3  on select * from dual
  4  /
Outline created.

tkyte@TKYTE816> create outline outline_3
  2  for category CAT_2
  3  on select * from dual A
  4  /
Outline created.
```

So, we have three stored outlines in two categories. The query SELECT * FROM DUAL has two stored outlines while the query SELECT * FROM DUAL A has one. Looking at what we have so far:

```
tkyte@TKYTE816> select category, name, sql_text
  2    from user_outlines
  3   order by category, name
  4  /

CATEGORY        NAME                                 SQL_TEXT
-------------   --------------------------------    --------------------
CAT_1           OUTLINE_1                            select * from dual
CAT_2           OUTLINE_2                            select * from dual
CAT_2           OUTLINE_3                            select * from dual A
```

we can see CAT_1 with 1 outline and CAT_2 with 2 outlines. Further, we clearly see that CAT_2 has a SQL_TEXT entry that already exists in CAT_1. Then we perform the merge:

```
tkyte@TKYTE816> exec outln_pkg.update_by_cat( 'CAT_2', 'CAT_1' );

PL/SQL procedure successfully completed.

tkyte@TKYTE816> select category, name, sql_text
  2    from user_outlines
  3   order by category, name
  4  /

CATEGORY        NAME                                 SQL_TEXT
-------------   --------------------------------    --------------------
CAT_1           OUTLINE_1                            select * from dual
CAT_1           OUTLINE_3                            select * from dual A
CAT_2           OUTLINE_2                            select * from dual
```

We can see the outlines from CAT_2 that did not already exist in CAT_1 were moved over. The stored outline for the duplicate query however, was not moved over. This is because there is uniqueness enforced on the columns (NAME) and (CATEGORY, SIGNATURE). Within a category, the SQL_TEXT must be unique. This is enforced by the generation of a unique signature for the SQL_TEXT. If you want to move OUTLINE_2 from CAT_2 into CAT_1, you will have to drop OUTLINE_1 from CAT_1 before you run UPDATE_BY_CAT.

```
tkyte@TKYTE816> drop outline outline_1;

Outline dropped.

tkyte@TKYTE816> exec outln_pkg.update_by_cat( 'CAT_2', 'CAT_1' );

PL/SQL procedure successfully completed.

tkyte@TKYTE816> select category, name, sql_text
  2    from user_outlines
  3    order by category, name
  4  /


CATEGORY          NAME                              SQL_TEXT
--------------    ----------------------------      --------------------
CAT_1             OUTLINE_2                         select * from dual
CAT_1             OUTLINE_3                         select * from dual A
```

Caveats

As with any feature, some nuances need to be noted in the way query outlines function. This section attempts to address some of them in turn.

Outline Names and Case

The OUTLN_PKG has two entry points that take in the name of an outline category, or an outline itself. Since it accepts a *string* as input, care must be taken with regards to the *case* used. Oracle will store object names by default in UPPERCASE but object names may be in mixed case if you used quoted identifiers. You must make certain that the case of the category name you pass into DROP_BY_CAT for example, matches the case of the category, as it is stored in the data dictionary. The following example will demonstrate this caveat for us:

```
tkyte@TKYTE816> create or replace outline my_outline
  2    for category my_category
  3    on select * from dual
  4  /

Outline created.

tkyte@TKYTE816> create or replace outline my_other_outline
  2    for category "My_Category"
  3    on select * from dual
  4  /
```

```
Outline created.

tkyte@TKYTE816> select name, category, sql_text from user_outlines;

NAME                             CATEGORY        SQL_TEXT
------------------------------   --------------  ---------------------
MY_OUTLINE                       MY_CATEGORY     select * from dual
MY_OTHER_OUTLINE                 My_Category     select * from dual
```

So we have our two outlines. Note that the category names are the same, but are in a different case. These are two distinctly different categories. We achieved this via the 'quoted' identifier in the second CREATE OUTLINE command. Now, it would seem natural enough to use lower case when dropping the category, but as we see below, this does not work:

```
tkyte@TKYTE816> exec outln_pkg.drop_by_cat( 'my_category' );

PL/SQL procedure successfully completed.

tkyte@TKYTE816> select name, category, sql_text from user_outlines;

NAME                             CATEGORY        SQL_TEXT
------------------------------   --------------  ---------------------
MY_OUTLINE                       MY_CATEGORY     select * from dual
MY_OTHER_OUTLINE                 My_Category     select * from dual
```

Both categories remain. This is because there is no category stored in all lower case characters. Now we will drop the upper case category:

```
tkyte@TKYTE816> exec outln_pkg.drop_by_cat( 'MY_CATEGORY' );

PL/SQL procedure successfully completed.

tkyte@TKYTE816> select name, category, sql_text from user_outlines

NAME                             CATEGORY        SQL_TEXT
------------------------------   --------------  ---------------------
MY_OTHER_OUTLINE                 My_Category     select * from dual
```

And now the lower case category:

```
tkyte@TKYTE816> exec outln_pkg.drop_by_cat( 'My_Category' );

PL/SQL procedure successfully completed.

tkyte@TKYTE816> select name, category, sql_text from user_outlines;

no rows selected
```

This side effect, of passing the name of an object instead of the 'object' itself, has been known to cause some confusion. Similar issues exist elsewhere with BFILES and DIRECTORY objects since they pass object names as strings as well.

I would strongly discourage you from using quoted identifiers. They will only lead to confusion in the long run and unless you always quote them, you cannot access them. I've seen more than one database tool go awry trying to work with mixed case identifiers.

ALTER SESSION Issue

It should be noted that if you do not have the CREATE ANY OUTLINE system privilege, either via a role or directly, the ALTER SESSION will silently succeed, but no outlines will be generated. Therefore, if you alter your session and notice no outlines being generated, this is the cause. You need to have CREATE ANY OUTLINE granted to you, or a role you have. This is true even if an ALTER SYSTEM command was used to generate query plans for every session. Only sessions that are authenticated using an account with the CREATE ANY OUTLINE privilege will actually create outlines.

DROP USER does not Drop Outlines

Normally, if you drop a user with the CASCADE option, all objects owned by that user are dropped from the database. Stored outlines are an exception to that rule. For example:

```
sys@TKYTE816> select owner, name from dba_outlines where owner = 'TKYTE';

OWNER                            NAME
-------------------------------- --------------------------------
TKYTE                            OUTLINE_1
TKYTE                            OUTLINE_2
TKYTE                            OUTLINE_3

sys@TKYTE816> drop user tkyte cascade;

User dropped.

sys@TKYTE816> select owner, name from dba_outlines where owner = 'TKYTE';

OWNER                            NAME
-------------------------------- --------------------------------
TKYTE                            OUTLINE_1
TKYTE                            OUTLINE_2
TKYTE                            OUTLINE_3
```

shows that even after dropping my account, the outlines from the previous example exists and would continue to be used.

'CURSOR_SHARING = FORCE' and Outlines

Oracle release 8.1.6 introduced a feature I refer to as 'auto binding'. In Chapter 10 in *Tuning Strategies and Tools*, I stressed the importance of using bind variables, and demonstrated a new feature in the database whereby the database kernel itself will rewrite queries that use constants to use bind variables instead. This feature, cursor sharing, has an anomaly with regards to stored outlines. Depending on *how* the outline was generated, we will either store the plan for a query with a bind variable, or not. An example will help to clarify. We will run the same exact query in a session where CURSOR_SHARING is enabled. In one case, we will generate the outline using DDL via the CREATE OUTLINE command and in the other case, we will use the ALTER SESSION command to have outlines generated for us. We can then compare the SQL_TEXT stored for each:

```
tkyte@TKYTE816> alter session set cursor_sharing = force;

Session altered.

tkyte@TKYTE816> create or replace outline my_outline
  2  for category my_category
  3  on select * from dual where dummy = 'X';

Outline created.

tkyte@TKYTE816> alter session set create_stored_outlines = true;

Session altered.

tkyte@TKYTE816> select * from dual where dummy = 'X';

D
-
X

tkyte@TKYTE816> alter session set create_stored_outlines = false;

Session altered.

tkyte@TKYTE816> select name, category, sql_text from user_outlines;
```

NAME	CATEGORY	SQL_TEXT
SYS_OUTLINE_0104122003150057	DEFAULT	select * from dual where dummy = :SYS_B_0
MY_OUTLINE	MY_CATEGORY	select * from dual where dummy = 'X'

As you can see, the stored queries are very different from each other. The one we generated via the CREATE OUTLINE command is exactly as we had entered it. The CURSOR_SHARING code was not executed in this case, since we did not actually run the query. The query text was stored verbatim. On the other hand, the query text for the implicitly generated outline shows the effect of the query rewrite for us. We can plainly see that our constant X was turned into a bind variable for us. This SQL was stored for us.

Depending on your needs, both methods may be applicable. It is just important to understand that there is a subtle different between the explicitly generated plan, and the implicitly generated one with CURSOR_SHARING enabled.

Outlines Use Simple Text Matching

The outline mechanism, the mechanism for finding and using a stored outline, is a very simple one. It does it purely by text matching. It is not like the matching that takes place in the shared pool with parsed query plans; it is much more straightforward.

With query outlines, Oracle stops at the matching of SQL text. No attempt is made to verify or ascertain that the underlying objects are in fact the same objects. We used this to our advantage in a previous section *Getting Just the Right Outline*. We created a schema in which we created hinted views named after 'real' base tables in another schema. We then generated outlines against queries on these views. These outlines were very much influenced by our hints. We then saw that when we ran the same exact query in the original schema with the 'real' tables (not the views), Oracle picked up the stored outline, even though the underlying tables were totally different. This is the expected designed behavior of this feature. It was intended that exact matches based on SQL text alone would get the same set of hints associated with them.

It should be noted that this string matching is *exact* string matching. Spaces, tabs, newlines, case – everything counts. These two queries:

```
select * from dual;
SELECT * FROM DUAL;
```

are different as far as stored outlines are concerned.

Outlines by Default are in the SYSTEM Tablespace

By default, outlines are stored in the SYSTEM tablespace. If you plan on making heavy use of stored outlines, you should consider moving them to another tablespace. The method for achieving that was given in the section on *The OUTLN User* earlier. The outline hints table can get very large very quickly (our one example shows a simple select * from all_objects generated over 100 rows in this hint table). Unless you want your system tablespace to grow extremely large, moving the OUTLN users objects to another tablespace is recommended.

OR-Expansion

Given that the query outline mechanism is done via hints, and is limited to what hinting can achieve, there is one case that bears pointing out as not being a suitable candidate for stored outlines. This is the class of queries that use **OR-Expansion**. OR-Expansion would take a query like:

```
select * from T where x = 5 or x = 6;
```

and rewrite it as:

```
select * from T where x = 5
Union All
select * from T where x = 6;
```

The outline mechanism does not have the ability to redistribute the hints to this internally rewritten plan. All of the stored hints would be applied to the first part of the UNION ALL query and not the subsequent queries. Oracle, in the readme supplied with the database ([ORACLE_HOME]/rdbms/doc/README.txt), states:

```
7.4.2 OR-Expansion
------------------
For execution plans that involve OR-expansion, you should avoid using stored
outlines if possible. This recommendation is due both to the nature of stored outlines, which
use hints to influence the execution plan, and to the nature of OR-expansion, which is
represented internally through a set of OR chains, each of which represents a distinct join
```

order. Hints are only useful for influencing a single join order, as there is no way to target a specific OR chain. Therefore an outline's hints are applied to the first OR chain represented internally. The net effect is that these hints simply get propagated across the remaining OR chains by the optimizer, often leading to suboptimal execution plans that differ from the originally saved plans.

Workaround:
Stored outlines that involve OR-expansion can be identified by querying the USER_OUTLINE_HINTS view for hint text containing USE_CONCAT. Issue the following query:

SELECT NAME, HINT FROM USER_OUTLINE_HINTS WHERE HINT LIKE 'USE_CONCAT%';

Any outline containing this hint should either be dropped using the DROP OUTLINE command or moved to an unused category with the following command:

ALTER OUTLINE <outline-name> CHANGE CATEGORY TO <unused-category-name>;

Performance

An obvious question is 'How does this facility affect my run-time performance?' The answer is, marginally. This feature adds marginal overhead during the parse phase of a query, with the most overhead occurring the first time the query plan is generated and saved (as might be expected).

What I did to test this was to set up a small PL/SQL block that would cause x number of 'simple' queries to be parsed, executed and fetched from (select * from T1, where T1 was a one row, one column table). In this fashion, I was measuring mostly the parse time. In order to set this up, I ran the following block to create 100 tables:

```
tkyte@TKYTE816> begin
  2      for i in 1 .. 100 loop
  3          begin
  4              execute immediate 'drop table t'||i;
  5          exception
  6              when others then null;
  7          end;
  8          execute immediate 'create table t'||i||' ( dummy char(1) )';
  9          execute immediate 'insert into t'||i||' values ( ''x'' )';
 10      end loop;
 11  end;
 12  /

PL/SQL procedure successfully completed.
```

So after creating 100 tables named T1 to T100 I ran a block of code just to get the shared SQL parsed and ready to go. We want to see the impact of creating outlines, not parsing the query:

```
tkyte@TKYTE816> declare l_tmp char(1); l_start number :=
                                       dbms_utility.get_time; begin
  2  select * into l_tmp from t1;
  3  select * into l_tmp from t2;
```

```
     4   select * into l_tmp from t3;
...  ...
...  ...
...  ...
    99   select * into l_tmp from t98;
   100   select * into l_tmp from t99;
   101   select * into l_tmp from t100;
   102   dbms_output.put_line( round( (dbms_utility.get_time-l_start)/100,
                                               2 )||' seconds' );
   103   end;
   104   /
.89 seconds
```

Once the cache was warmed up, I ran the block a couple of more times to see how long it would take:

```
tkyte@TKYTE816> declare l_tmp char(1); l_start number :=
                                       dbms_utility.get_time; begin
     2   select * into l_tmp from t1;
     3   select * into l_tmp from t2;
     4   select * into l_tmp from t3;
...  ...
...  ...
...  ...
    99   select * into l_tmp from t98;
   100   select * into l_tmp from t99;
   101   select * into l_tmp from t100;
   102   dbms_output.put_line( round( (dbms_utility.get_time-l_start)/100,
                                               2 )||' seconds' );
   103   end;
   104   /
.02 seconds
```

It was consistently taking about .02 seconds. Then I turned on outline creation:

```
tkyte@TKYTE816> alter session set create_stored_outlines = testing;

Session altered.

tkyte@TKYTE816> declare l_tmp char(1); l_start number :=
                                       dbms_utility.get_time; begin
     2   select * into l_tmp from t1;
     3   select * into l_tmp from t2;
     4   select * into l_tmp from t3;
...  ...
...  ...
...  ...
    99   select * into l_tmp from t98;
   100   select * into l_tmp from t99;
   101   select * into l_tmp from t100;
   102   dbms_output.put_line( round( (dbms_utility.get_time-l_start)/100,
                                               2 )||' seconds' );
   103   end;
   104   /
.82 seconds
```

The first time round, when it really did store the outlines for the first time, it took about .82 seconds. This is just about the same amount of time it took to parse the queries in the first place. What I discovered after this was that subsequent runs took .02 seconds. After the initial hit of storing the outlines, the run-time went back down to what it was before outline creation was enabled. Now, in a heavy, multi-user situation, your mileage may vary, you may have to perform some amount of tuning on the OUTLN tables (freelist adjustment for example) to handle a high level of concurrent insertions.

There is one thing to consider here. The standard mode is not to run with CREATE_STORED_OUTLINES = TRUE. Rather, this is done once for some period of time to capture the queries and their associated plans. It will be more typical to run with USE_STORED_OUTLINES = TRUE in production, not CREATE. The point being that, even if the overhead of generating the plans was excessive, you do not intend to run in this mode in production, in any event. Only in the test and development instances will the overhead would be acceptable.

Now, lets look at the overhead associated with actually *using* these stored plans on this simple query:

```
tkyte@TKYTE816> alter session set use_stored_outlines=testing;

Session altered.

tkyte@TKYTE816> select used, count(*) from user_outlines group by used;

USED        COUNT(*)
---------   ----------
UNUSED           100

tkyte@TKYTE816> declare l_tmp char(1); l_start number :=
                                      dbms_utility.get_time; begin
  2   select * into l_tmp from t1;
  3   select * into l_tmp from t2;
  4   select * into l_tmp from t3;
...   ...
...   ...
...   ...
 99   select * into l_tmp from t98;
100   select * into l_tmp from t99;
101   select * into l_tmp from t100;
102   dbms_output.put_line( round( (dbms_utility.get_time-l_start)/100,
                                      2 )||' seconds' );
103   end;
104   /
.32 seconds

PL/SQL procedure successfully completed.

tkyte@TKYTE816> select used, count(*) from user_outlines group by used;

USED        COUNT(*)
---------   ----------
USED             100

tkyte@TKYTE816> declare l_tmp char(1); l_start number :=
                                      dbms_utility.get_time; begin
  2   select * into l_tmp from t1;
```

```
   3  select * into l_tmp from t2;
   4  select * into l_tmp from t3;
 ...  ...
 ...  ...
 ...  ...
  99  select * into l_tmp from t98;
 100  select * into l_tmp from t99;
 101  select * into l_tmp from t100;
 102  dbms_output.put_line( round( (dbms_utility.get_time-l_start)/100,
                                          2 )||' seconds' );

 103  end;
 104  /
.03 seconds

PL/SQL procedure successfully completed.

tkyte@TKYTE816> declare l_tmp char(1); l_start number :=
                                      dbms_utility.get_time; begin

   2  select * into l_tmp from t1;
   3  select * into l_tmp from t2;
   4  select * into l_tmp from t3;
 ...  ...
 ...  ...
 ...  ...
  99  select * into l_tmp from t98;
 100  select * into l_tmp from t99;
 101  select * into l_tmp from t100;
 102  dbms_output.put_line( round( (dbms_utility.get_time-l_start)/100,
                                          2 )||' seconds' );

 103  end;
 104  /
.03 seconds

PL/SQL procedure successfully completed.
```

The first time we re-parse these queries after enabling stored outlines, it took 0.32 seconds to execute. When we compare this to the initial parse without stored outlines (without saving them or using them), we find the parse time to be not materially affected. We have verified as well, that we are using the stored outlines as the USED column went from UNUSED to USED in all cases after executing our block. We know based on this, that the hints were actually used in our queries. The subsequent re-execution of that block shows that once the hints have been merged and shared SQL kicks in, the effect of stored outlines on performance is totally gone.

In short, the utilization of stored outlines in your application will not materially affect the run-time performance after the parse of the query for the first time into the shared pool. The effect of using stored outlines, in as much as it influences the query plan, might affect your run-time, but the fact that stored outlines are being merged with your query will not.

The Namespace of Outlines is Global

At first glance, it would appear that outlines are much like any other database object, tables for example, and that their names must be unique within an OWNER. This is not the case however. The name of an outline must be unique database-wide, much like a tablespace or directory entry. The existence of an OWNER column and the USER_OUTLINES view is misleading, as no one truly owns an outline. The OWNER column is really the name of the user that created the outline.

We can see this easily with a small test:

```
tkyte@TKYTE816> create outline the_outline
  2  on select * from dual;

Outline created.

tkyte@TKYTE816> connect system

system@TKYTE816> select owner, name from dba_outlines;

OWNER                          NAME
------------------------------ ------------------------------
TKYTE                          THE_OUTLINE

system@TKYTE816> create outline the_outline
  2  on select * from dual;
on select * from dual
                    *
ERROR at line 2:
ORA-18004: outline already exists

system@TKYTE816> drop outline the_outline;

Outline dropped.

system@TKYTE816> select owner, name from dba_outlines;

no rows selected
```

So, as you can see, SYSTEM cannot create another outline called THE_OUTLINE, unless it used the CREATE OR REPLACE statement (which would overwrite my outline), or it drops the outline. (Note, there is no need for an OWNER.OUTLINE_NAME as for other objects).

This is something you will have to consider in order to avoid accidentally overwriting someone else's outline inadvertently. If you use implicit outline creation via the ALTER SESSION SET CREATE_STORED_OUTLINES, this issue is not relevant, as a unique name will always be generated. This only really affects outlines you yourself create, and name.

Errors you Might Encounter

This section will list the errors you may see when using outlines.

ORA-18001 "no options specified for ALTER OUTLINE"

```
// *Cause:  The parser detected that no clause was specified on the command
// *Action: Re-issue the command, specifying a valid ALTER OUTLINE clause.
```

You will receive this only when you use the ALTER outline command improperly. For example:

```
ops$tkyte@DEV816> alter outline xxxx
  2  /
```

```
alter outline xxxx
                 *
ERROR at line 1:
ORA-18001: no options specified for ALTER OUTLINE
```

The solution is clear; supply one of the three valid options (RENAME, REBUILD, CHANGE) to the command, and rerun it. See the *Managing Outlines* section for more information on this subject.

ORA-18002 *"the specified outline does not exist"*

```
// *Cause:  Either the outline did not exist to begin with, or a timing
//          window allowed for another thread to drop or alter the outline
//          midstream.
// *Action:
```

This error is pretty straightforward as well. The outline you referred to no longer exists – either it never did or someone else has dropped it.

ORA-18003 *"an outline already exists with this signature"*

```
// *Cause:  The signature generation algorithm generates signatures that are
//          are 16 bytes in length so it is highly unlikely that any 2
//          signatures will be identical. This message is raised in such a
//          rare case.
// *Action: Either re-issue the statement that led to the outline being
//          created with some whitespace added or force the outline to be
//          created in a different category.
```

I was unable to come up with a test case for this – you would have to be extremely unlucky to hit this particular error. The signatures of queries are computed to allow us to perform a fast lookup on them. Since the query text can be very long, the numeric signature is used instead for fast lookups.

ORA-18004 *"outline already exists"*

```
// *Cause:  An outline already exists, either with the specified name, or
//          for the specified SQL text.
// *Action:
```

This error is self-explanatory. You have attempted to CREATE a named outline but an outline with that name already exists. Your options are:

❏ Pick a new name.

❏ Use CREATE OR REPLACE and overwrite the existing outline.

❏ DROP the existing outline and then CREATE it.

ORA-18005-18007

These three errors are very inter-related, hence I will discuss all three at the same time:

❏ ORA-18005 "create any outline privilege is required for this operation".

❏ ORA-18006 "drop any outline privilege is required for this operation".

❏ ORA-18007 "alter any outline privilege is required for this operation".

These errors will occur when you attempt to perform an operation on an outline, but you do not have the requisite privilege. It can be somewhat confusing, especially when working with your own outlines. As indicated in the *Caveats* section however, outlines are not truly owned by anyone; their namespace is global (like a tablespace). Therefore, you may be able to CREATE an outline, but not subsequently DROP or ALTER it. You might be able to ALTER outlines but not CREATE or DROP them, and so on.

See the section on *Privileges Needed for Stored Outlines* for details on the privileges you need.

Summary

In this chapter, we thoroughly explored the Optimizer Plan Stability feature of Oracle8i. This feature was designed to allow a set of SQL statements performance to remain stable, regardless of changes in the database itself (for example, version upgrades, init.ora parameter changes, and so on). We have found some other useful functions of this feature, such as tuning applications that we cannot modify for whatever reason, finding out what indexes we really use, what SQL we really execute, and so on. Given that stored outlines are so transparent to an application, and add little or no overhead at run-time, their usefulness is increased. There are some crucial caveats to be aware of with regards to this feature, but once educated about them, stored outlines can be very powerful.

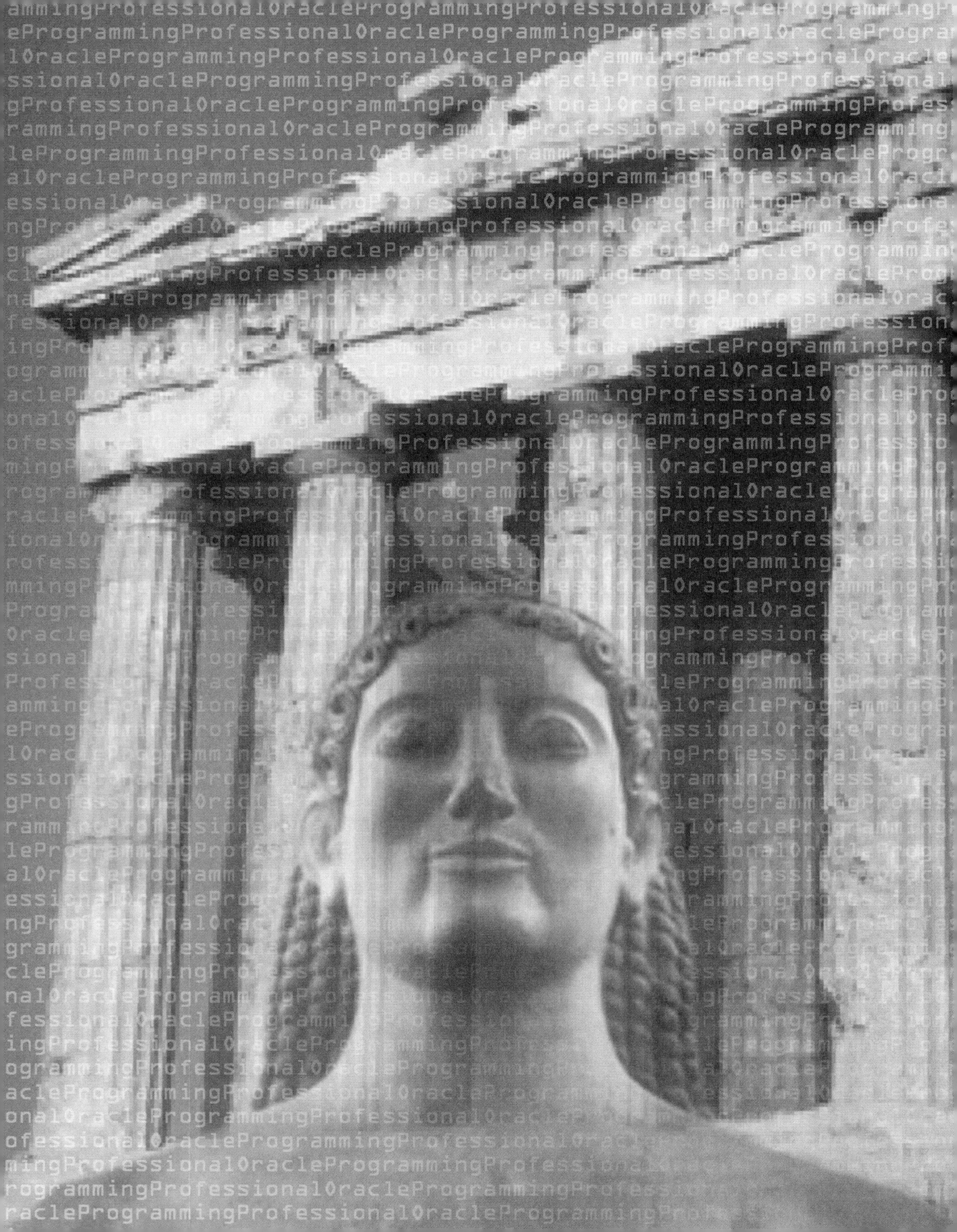

12

Analytic Functions

SQL is a very capable language and there are very few questions that it cannot answer. I find that I can come up with some convoluted SQL query to answer virtually any question you could ask from the data. However, the performance of some of these queries is not what it should be – nor is the query itself easy to write in the first place. Some of the things that are hard to do in straight SQL are actually very commonly requested operations, including:

- ❑ **Calculate a running total** – Show the cumulative salary within a department row by row, with each row including a summation of the prior rows' salary.

- ❑ **Find percentages within a group** – Show the percentage of the total salary paid to an individual in a certain department. Take their salary and divide it by the sum of the salary in the department.

- ❑ **Top-N queries** – Find the top N highest-paid people or the top N sales by region.

- ❑ **Compute a moving average** – Average the current row's value and the previous N rows values together.

- ❑ **Perform ranking queries** – Show the relative rank of an individual's salary within their department.

Analytic functions, which have been available since Oracle 8.1.6, are designed to address these issues. They add extensions to the SQL language that not only make these operations easier to code; they make them faster than could be achieved with the pure SQL approach. These extensions are currently under review by the ANSI SQL committee for inclusion in the SQL specification.

We'll start this chapter with an example that will give you a good idea of what analytic functions are about. From there we'll address the full syntax, describe the available functions and then run through some worked examples that tackle some of the above operations. As usual, we will finish by signposting some of the potential pitfalls of using these functions.

An Example

A quick example, which calculates a running total of salaries by department, and an explanation of what exactly is happening, will give you a good initial understanding of analytic functions:

```
tkyte@TKYTE816> break on deptno skip 1

tkyte@TKYTE816> select ename, deptno, sal,
  2      sum(sal) over
  3        (order by deptno, ename) running_total,
  4      sum(sal) over
  5        (partition by deptno
  6         order by ename) department_total,
  7      row_number() over
  8        (partition by deptno
  9         order by ename) seq
 10  from emp
 11  order by deptno, ename
 12  /
```

ENAME	DEPTNO	SAL	RUNNING_TOTAL	DEPARTMENT_TOTAL	SEQ
CLARK	10	2450	2450	2450	1
KING		5000	7450	7450	2
MILLER		1300	8750	8750	3
ADAMS	20	1100	9850	1100	1
FORD		3000	12850	4100	2
JONES		2975	15825	7075	3
SCOTT		3000	18825	10075	4
SMITH		800	19625	10875	5
ALLEN	30	1600	21225	1600	1
BLAKE		2850	24075	4450	2
JAMES		950	25025	5400	3
MARTIN		1250	26275	6650	4
TURNER		1500	27775	8150	5
WARD		1250	29025	9400	6

```
14 rows selected.
```

In the above code, we were able to compute a RUNNING_TOTAL for the entire query. This was done using the entire ordered resultset, via SUM(SAL) OVER (ORDER BY DEPTNO, ENAME). We were also able to compute a running total within each department, a total that would be reset at the beginning of the next department. The PARTITION BY DEPTNO in that SUM(SAL) caused this to happen – a partitioning clause was specified in the query in order to break the data up into groups. The ROW_NUMBER() function is used to sequentially number the rows returned in each group, according to our ordering criteria (a SEQ column was added to in order to display this position). So, we see that SCOTT is the fourth row in department 20, when ordered by ENAME. This ROW_NUMBER() feature has many uses elsewhere, for example to transpose or pivot resultsets (as we will discuss later).

This new set of functionality holds some exciting possibilities. It opens up a whole new way of looking at the data. It will remove a lot of procedural code and complex (or inefficient) queries that would have taken a long time to develop, to achieve the same result. Just to give you a flavor of how efficient these analytic functions can be, over the old 'pure relational ways', let's compare the performance of the above query with 1000 rows instead of just 14 rows. Both the new analytical functions and the 'old' relational methods are used here to test the performance of the query. The following two statements will set up a copy of the SCOOTT.EMP table with just the ENAME, DEPTNO, and SAL columns along with an index (the only one needed for this example). I am doing everything using DEPTNO and ENAME:

```
tkyte@TKYTE816> create table t
  2  as
  3  select object_name ename,
  4         mod(object_id,50) deptno,
  5         object_id sal
  6  from all_objects
  7  where rownum <= 1000
  8  /

Table created.

tkyte@TKYTE816> create index t_idx on t(deptno,ename);
Index created.
```

We execute our query on the new table, using AUTOTRACE in trace only mode to see how much work is done (you will need to have the PLUSTRACE role enabled):

```
tkyte@TKYTE816> set autotrace traceonly

tkyte@TKYTE816> select ename, deptno, sal,
  2    sum(sal) over
  3      (order by deptno, ename) running_total,
  4    sum(sal) over
  5      (partition by deptno
  6       order by ename) department_total,
  7    row_number() over
  8      (partition by deptno
  9       order by ename) seq
 10  from t emp
 11  order by deptno, ename
 12  /

1000 rows selected.

Elapsed: 00:00:00.61

Execution Plan
----------------------------------------------------------
   0      SELECT STATEMENT Optimizer=CHOOSE
   1    0   WINDOW (BUFFER)
   2    1     TABLE ACCESS (BY INDEX ROWID) OF 'T'
   3    2       INDEX (FULL SCAN) OF 'T_IDX' (NON-UNIQUE)

Statistics
----------------------------------------------------------
        0  recursive calls
        2  db block gets
      292  consistent gets
       66  physical reads
```

```
     0   redo size
106978   bytes sent via SQL*Net to client
  7750   bytes received via SQL*Net from client
    68   SQL*Net roundtrips to/from client
     0   sorts (memory)
     1   sorts (disk)
  1000   rows processed
```

This took 0.61 seconds and 294 logical I/Os. Now, repeat the same exact query using only 'standard' SQL functionality:

```
tkyte@TKYTE816> select ename, deptno, sal,
  2    (select sum(sal)
  3      from t e2
  4      where e2.deptno < emp.deptno
  5      or (e2.deptno = emp.deptno and e2.ename <= emp.ename ))
  6  running_total,
  7    (select sum(sal)
  8      from t e3
  9      where e3.deptno = emp.deptno
 10      and e3.ename <= emp.ename)
 11  department_total,
 12    (select count(ename)
 13      from t e3
 14      where e3.deptno = emp.deptno
 15      and e3.ename <= emp.ename)
 16  seq
 17  from t emp
 18  order by deptno, ename
 19  /

1000 rows selected.

Elapsed: 00:00:06.89

Execution Plan
----------------------------------------------------------
   0      SELECT STATEMENT Optimizer=CHOOSE
   1    0   TABLE ACCESS (BY INDEX ROWID) OF 'T'
   2    1     INDEX (FULL SCAN) OF 'T_IDX' (NON-UNIQUE)

Statistics
----------------------------------------------------------
      0   recursive calls
      0   db block gets
 665490   consistent gets
      0   physical reads
      0   redo size
 106978   bytes sent via SQL*Net to client
   7750   bytes received via SQL*Net from client
     68   SQL*Net roundtrips to/from client
      0   sorts (memory)
      0   sorts (disk)
   1000   rows processed

tkyte@TKYTE816> set autotrace off
```

You get the same exact answer from both queries, but what a difference these functions can make. The run time is many times longer and the number of logical I/Os is increased by many orders of magnitude. The analytical functions processed the resultset using significantly fewer resources and an astoundingly reduced amount of time. Not only that, but once you understand the syntax of the analytic functions, you will find them easier to code with then the equivalent standard SQL – just compare the syntax of the above two queries to see what a difference they can make.

How Analytic Functions Work

The first part of this section will contain the dry details of the syntax and definitions of terms. After that, we'll dive right into examples. I'll demonstrate many of the 26 new functions (not all of them, as many of the examples would be repetitive). The analytic functions utilize the same general syntax and many provide specialized functionality designed for certain technical disciplines not used by the everyday developer. Once you get familiar with the syntax – how to partition, how to define windows of data, and so on – using these functions will become very natural.

The Syntax

The syntax of the analytic function is rather straightforward in appearance, but looks can be deceiving. It starts with:

```
FUNCTION_NAME(<argument>,<argument>,...)
OVER
(<Partition-Clause> <Order-by-Clause> <Windowing Clause>)
```

There are up to four parts to an analytic function; it can be invoked with arguments, a partition clause, an order by clause, and a windowing clause. In the example shown in the above introduction:

```
4        sum(sal) over
5          (partition by deptno
6            order by ename) department_total,
```

In this case:

❏   **SUM** is our FUNCTION_NAME.

❏   **(SAL)** is the argument to our analytic function. Each function takes between zero and three arguments. The arguments are expressions – that could have been the SUM(SAL+COMM) just as well.

❏   OVER is a keyword that identifies this as an analytic function. Otherwise, the query parser would not be able to tell the difference between SUM() the aggregate function and SUM() the analytic function. The clause that follows the OVER keyword describes the slice of data that this analytic function will be performed 'over'.

❏   **PARTITION BY DEPTNO** is the optional partitioning clause. If no partitioning clause exists, the entire resultset is treated as a single large partition. You will use that to break a result set into **groups** and the analytic function will be applied to the group, not to the entire result set. In the introductory example when the partitioning clause was left out, the SUM of SAL was generated for the entire resultset. By partitioning by DEPTNO, the SUM of SAL by DEPTNO was computed– resetting the running total for each group.

❑ **ORDER BY ENAME** is the optional ORDER BY clause; some functions demand it, and some do not. Functions that depend on ordered data, such as LAG and LEAD that are used to access the 'previous' and 'next' rows in a result set, necessitate the use of an ORDER BY clause. Other functions, such as AVG do not. This clause is mandatory when using a windowing function of any sort (see below in the section on *The Windowing Clause* for more details). This specifies how the data is ordered within a group when computing the analytic function. You did not have to order by both DEPTNO and ENAME in this case since it is partitioned by DEPTNO – it is implied that the partitioning columns are part of the sort key by definition (the ORDER BY is applied to each partition in turn).

❑ **WINDOWING CLAUSE** was left out in this example. This is where the syntax gets a little confusing looking in some cases. We will delve into all of the permutations for the windowing clause in detail below.

Now we will look at each of the four parts of the analytic function in more detail to understand what is valid for each.

The Function Clause

Oracle provides 26 analytic functions for us to use. They fall into five major classes of functionality.

There are various **ranking** functions that are useful for finding the answers to TOP-N type queries. We have already used one such function, ROW_NUMBER, when generating the SEQ column in the previous example. This ranked people in their department based on their ENAME. We could have easily ranked them by SALARY or any other attribute.

There are **windowing** functions, which are useful for computing various aggregates. We saw two examples of this in the introductory example where we computed the SUM(SAL) over different groups. We could use many other functions in place of SUM, such as COUNT, AVG, MIN, MAX, and so on.

There are various **reporting** functions. These are very similar to the windowing functions above. In fact their names are the same: SUM, MIN, MAX, and so on. Whereas a windowing function is used to work on a window of data, as the running total in the earlier example did, a report function works on all of the rows in a partition or group. For example, if, in our initial query, we had simply asked for:

```
sum(sal) over () total_salary,
sum(sal) over (partition by deptno) total_salary_for_department
```

then, we would have received total sums for the group, not running totals as before. The key differentiator between a windowing function and a reporting function is the absence of an ORDER BY clause in the OVER statement. In the absence of the ORDER BY, the function is applied to every row in the group. With an ORDER BY clause, it is applied to a window (more on this in the section describing this clause).

There are also **LAG** and **LEAD** functions available. These functions allow you to look backwards or forwards in a result set to retrieve values. These are useful in order to avoid a self-join of data. For example, if you had a table that recorded patient visits by date and you wanted to compute the time between visits for each patient, the LAG function would come in handy. You could simply partition the data by patient and sort it by date. The LAG function would easily be able to return the data from the previous record for that patient. You could then just subtract the two dates. Prior to the introduction of analytic functions, this would have required a complex self-join of the patient data with itself in order to retrieve the data.

Lastly, there is a large set of **statistical** functions such as VAR_POP, VAR_SAMP, STDEV_POP, a set of linear regression functions, and so on. These functions compute the statistical values for any unordered partition.

At the close of this section on syntax, there is a table with each of the analytic functions listed and a brief explanation of the operation that they perform.

The Partition Clause

The PARTITION BY clause logically breaks a single result set into N groups, according to the criteria set by the partition expressions. The words 'partition' and 'group' are used synonymously here, and in the Oracle documentation. The analytic functions are applied to each group independently – they are 'reset' for each group. For example, above when we demonstrated a cumulative SAL function, we partitioned by DEPTNO. When the DEPTNO changed in the result set, we reset the cumulative SAL to ZERO and summation started anew.

If you omit a partitioning clause, then the entire result set is considered a single group. In the introductory example we used SUM(SAL) without a partitioning clause in order to obtain a running total for the entire result set.

It is interesting to note that each instance of an analytic function in a query may have an entirely different partitioning clause; the simple example we started this chapter with does this in fact. The column RUNNING_TOTAL did not supply a partitioning clause; hence, the entire result set was its target group. The column DEPARTMENTAL_TOTAL on the other hand, partitioned the result set by departments, allowing us to compute a running total within a department.

The partition clause has a simple syntax and is very similar in syntax to the GROUP BY clause you normally see with SQL queries:

```
PARTITION BY expression <, expression> <, expression>
```

The Order By Clause

The ORDER BY clause specifies how the data is sorted within each group (partition). This will definitely affect the outcome of any analytic function. The analytic functions are computed differently in the presence of an ORDER BY clause (or lack thereof). As a very simple example, consider what happens when we use AVG() with and without an ORDER BY clause:

```
scott@TKYTE816> select ename, sal, avg(sal) over ()
  2  from emp;
  3  /

ENAME            SAL AVG(SAL)OVER()
---------- --------- --------------
SMITH         800.00        2073.21
ALLEN        1600.00        2073.21
WARD         1250.00        2073.21
JONES        2975.00        2073.21
MARTIN       1250.00        2073.21
BLAKE        2850.00        2073.21
CLARK        2450.00        2073.21
SCOTT        3000.00        2073.21
KING         5000.00        2073.21
TURNER       1500.00        2073.21
```

```
   ADAMS          1100.00        2073.21
   JAMES           950.00        2073.21
   FORD           3000.00        2073.21
   MILLER         1300.00        2073.21

14 rows selected.

scott@TKYTE816> select ename, sal, avg(sal) over (ORDER BY ENAME)
  2    from emp
  3    order by ename
  4    /

ENAME             SAL AVG(SAL)OVER(ORDERBYENAME)
---------- ---------- ---------------------------
ADAMS         1100.00                     1100.00
ALLEN         1600.00                     1350.00
BLAKE         2850.00                     1850.00
CLARK         2450.00                     2000.00
FORD          3000.00                     2200.00
JAMES          950.00                     1991.67
JONES         2975.00                     2132.14
KING          5000.00                     2490.63
MARTIN        1250.00                     2352.78
MILLER        1300.00                     2247.50
SCOTT         3000.00                     2315.91
SMITH          800.00                     2189.58
TURNER        1500.00                     2136.54
WARD          1250.00                     2073.21

14 rows selected.
```

Without the ORDER BY clause, the average is computed over the entire group and the same value is given to every row (it is being used as a reporting function). When AVG() is used with the ORDER BY, the average for each row is the average of that row and all preceding rows (here it is used as a window function). For example, the average salary for ALLEN in the query with the ORDER BY clause is 1350 (the average of 1100 and 1600).

> *Jumping ahead, just a little, to the very next section on* The Windowing Clause – *it can be said that the existence of an ORDER BY in an analytic function will add a default window clause of RANGE UNBOUNDED PRECEDING. What this means is that the set of rows to be used in the computation is the current and all preceding rows in the current partition. Without the ORDER BY the default window is the entire partition.*

To get a real feel for how this works, it is instructive to use the same analytic function two times with a different ORDER BY each time. In the first example, a running total was computed for the entire EMP table using ORDER BY DEPTNO, ENAME. This caused the running total to be computed starting with the first row through the last row where the row order was specified by the ORDER BY function. If the order of the columns was reversed or the columns that were sorted changed all together, the results of our running total would be very different; the last row would have the same grand total but all of the intermediate values would be different. For example:

```
ops$tkyte@DEV816> select ename, deptno,
  2    sum(sal) over (order by ename, deptno) sum_ename_deptno,
  3    sum(sal) over (order by deptno, ename) sum_deptno_ename
  4  from emp
  5  order by ename, deptno
  6  /

ENAME         DEPTNO SUM_ENAME_DEPTNO SUM_DEPTNO_ENAME
---------- ---------- ---------------- ----------------
ADAMS          20             1100             9850
ALLEN          30             2700            21225
BLAKE          30             5550            24075
CLARK          10             8000             2450
FORD           20            11000            12850
JAMES          30            11950            25025
JONES          20            14925            15825
KING           10            19925             7450
MARTIN         30            21175            26275
MILLER         10            22475             8750
SCOTT          20            25475            18825
SMITH          20            26275            19625
TURNER         30            27775            27775
WARD           30            29025            29025

14 rows selected.
```

Both of the SUM(SAL) columns are equally correct; one of them is computing the SUM(SAL) by DEPTNO and then ENAME whereas the other does it by ENAME and then DEPTNO. Since the result set is order by (ENAME, DEPTNO) the SUM(SAL) that is computed in that order looks more correct but they both come to the same result, the grand total is 29025.

The syntax of an ORDER BY clause with analytic functions is as follows:

```
ORDER BY expression <ASC|DESC> <NULLS FIRST|NULLS LAST>,
```

It is exactly the same as an ORDER BY clause for a query but it will only order the rows within partitions and does not have to be the same as the ORDER BY for the query (or another partition for that matter). The NULLS FIRST and NULLS LAST clauses are new syntax with Oracle 8.1.6. They allow us to specify whether NULLS should come first or last in a sort. When using DESC sorts, especially with analytic functions, this new functionality is crucial. We will see why in the *Caveats* section towards the end.

The Windowing Clause

This is where the syntax gets a little complicated in appearance. Although it's not that hard in reality, the terms are a little confusing at first. Terms such as RANGE BETWEEN UNBOUNDED PRECEDING AND CURRENT ROW, which is the default window with an ORDER BY clause, are not terms that you use everyday. The syntax for a window clause is fairly complex to list out. Rather than trying to redraw the 'wire diagram' that you can review in the *Oracle8i SQL Reference Manual* yourself, I will list all of the variants of the windowing clause and explain the set of data that each would use, within a group. First, though, let's look at what the windowing clause does for you.

The windowing clause gives us a way to define a sliding or anchored window of data, on which the analytic function will operate, within a group. This clause can be used to have the analytic function compute its value based on any arbitrary sliding or anchored window within a group. For example, the range clause RANGE UNBOUNDED PRECEDING means 'apply the analytic function to every row in the current group from the first row in the group to the current row'. The default window is an anchored window that simply starts at the first row of a group and continues to the current row. If a window is used such as:

```
SUM(sal) OVER
   (PARTITION BY deptno
    ORDER BY ename
    ROWS 2 PRECEDING) department_total2,
```

This would create a sliding window within a group and compute the sum of the current row's SAL column plus the previous 2 rows in that group. If we need a report that shows the sum of the current employee's salary with the preceding two salaries within a department, it would look like this:

```
scott@TKYTE816> break on deptno

scott@TKYTE816> select deptno, ename, sal,
  2     sum(sal) over
  3        (partition by deptno
  4         order by ename
  5         rows 2 preceding) sliding_total
  6  from emp
  7  order by deptno, ename
  8  /

    DEPTNO ENAME           SAL SLIDING_TOTAL
---------- ---------- ---------- -------------
        10 CLARK          2450          2450
           KING           5000          7450
           MILLER         1300          8750

        20 ADAMS          1100          1100
           FORD           3000          4100
           JONES          2975          7075
           SCOTT          3000          8975
           SMITH           800          6775

        30 ALLEN          1600          1600
           BLAKE          2850          4450
           JAMES           950          5400
           MARTIN         1250          5050
           TURNER         1500          3700
           WARD           1250          4000

14 rows selected.
```

The relevant portion of the query here was:

```
  2     sum(sal) over
  3        (partition by deptno
  4         order by ename
  5         rows 2 preceding) sliding_total
```

The partition clause makes the SUM(SAL) be computed within each department, independent of the other groups (the SUM(SAL) is 'reset' as the department changes). The ORDER BY ENAME clause sorts the data within each department by ENAME; this allows the window clause, rows 2 preceding, to access the 2 rows prior to the current row in a group in order to sum the salaries. For example, if you note the SLIDING_TOTAL value for SMITH is 6775, which is the sum of 800, 3000, and 2975. That was simply SMITH's row plus the salary from the preceding two rows in the window.

We can set up windows based on two criteria: RANGES of data values or ROWS offset from the current row. We've seen the RANGE clause a couple of times, with a RANGE UNBOUNDED PRECEDING, for example. That says to get all rows in our partition that came before us as specified by the ORDER BY clause. It should be noted that in order to use a window, you must use an ORDER BY clause. We will now look at the ROW and RANGE windows and then finish up by describing the various ways in which the windows may be specified.

Range Windows

Range windows collect rows together based on a WHERE clause. If I say 'range 5 preceding' for example, this will generate a sliding window that has the set of all preceding rows in the group such that they are within 5 units of the current row. These units may either be numeric comparisons or date comparisons and it is not valid to use RANGE with datatypes other than numbers and dates.

If I have the EMP table with the date column HIREDATE and I specify:

```
count(*) over  (order by hiredate asc range 100 preceding)
```

then this will find all of the preceding rows in the partition such that the HIREDATE is within 100 days of the current row's HIREDATE. In this case, since the data is sorted by ASC (ascending, small to big), the values in the window would consist of all of the rows in the current group such that the HIREDATE was less then the current row's HIREDATE and within 100 days of it. If we used:

```
count(*) over  (order by hiredate desc range 100 preceding)
```

instead and sorted the partition DESC (descending, big to small) this would perform the same basic logic but since the data in the group is sorted differently, it will find a different set of rows for the window. In this case, it will find all of the rows preceding the current row, such that the HIREDATE was greater than the current rows HIREDATE and within 100 days of it. An example will help make this clearer. I will use a query that utilizes the FIRST_VALUE analytic function. This function returns the value of the expression using the FIRST row in a window. We can see where the window begins easily:

```
scott@TKYTE816> select ename, sal, hiredate, hiredate-100 windowtop,
  2     first_value(ename)
  3     over (order by hiredate asc
  4          range 100 preceding) ename_prec,
  5     first_value(hiredate)
  6     over (order by hiredate asc
  7          range 100 preceding) hiredate_prec
  8  from emp
  9  order by hiredate asc
 10  /
```

```
ENAME              SAL HIREDATE  WINDOW_TOP ENAME_PREC HIREDATE_
---------- ---------- --------- ---------- ---------- ---------
SMITH              800 17-DEC-80 08-SEP-80  SMITH      17-DEC-80
ALLEN             1600 20-FEB-81 12-NOV-80  SMITH      17-DEC-80
WARD              1250 22-FEB-81 14-NOV-80  SMITH      17-DEC-80

JONES             2975 02-APR-81 23-DEC-80  ALLEN      20-FEB-81
BLAKE             2850 01-MAY-81 21-JAN-81  ALLEN      20-FEB-81
CLARK             2450 09-JUN-81 01-MAR-81  JONES      02-APR-81

TURNER            1500 08-SEP-81 31-MAY-81  CLARK      09-JUN-81
MARTIN            1250 28-SEP-81 20-JUN-81  TURNER     08-SEP-81
KING              5000 17-NOV-81 09-AUG-81  TURNER     08-SEP-81
FORD              3000 03-DEC-81 25-AUG-81  TURNER     08-SEP-81
JAMES              950 03-DEC-81 25-AUG-81  TURNER     08-SEP-81
MILLER            1300 23-JAN-82 15-OCT-81  KING       17-NOV-81
SCOTT             3000 09-DEC-82 31-AUG-82  SCOTT      09-DEC-82
ADAMS             1100 12-JAN-83 04-OCT-82  SCOTT      09-DEC-82

14 rows selected.
```

We ordered the single partition by HIREDATE ASC. We used the analytic function FIRST_VALUE to find the value of the first ENAME in our window and the first HIREDATE in our window. If we look at the row for CLARK we can see that his HIREDATE was 09-JUN-81, and 100 days prior to that is the date 01-MAR-81. For convenience, this date is put into the column WINDOWTOP. The analytic function then defined as the window every row in the sorted partition that preceded the CLARK record and where the HIREDATE was between 09-JUN-81 and 01-MAR-81. The first value of ENAME for that window is JONES and this is the name that the analytic function returns in the column ENAME_PREC.

Looking at this from the HIREDATE DESC (descending) perspective, we see instead:

```
scott@TKYTE816> select ename, sal, hiredate, hiredate+100 windowtop,
  2     first_value(ename)
  3     over (order by hiredate desc
  4          range 100 preceding) ename_prec,
  5     first_value(hiredate)
  6     over (order by hiredate desc
  7          range 100 preceding) hiredate_prec
  8    from emp
  9    order by hiredate desc
 10   /

ENAME              SAL HIREDATE  WINDOWTOP  ENAME_PREC HIREDATE_
---------- ---------- --------- --------- ---------- ---------
ADAMS             1100 12-JAN-83 22-APR-83  ADAMS      12-JAN-83
SCOTT             3000 09-DEC-82 19-MAR-83  ADAMS      12-JAN-83
MILLER            1300 23-JAN-82 03-MAY-82  MILLER     23-JAN-82
FORD              3000 03-DEC-81 13-MAR-82  MILLER     23-JAN-82
JAMES              950 03-DEC-81 13-MAR-82  MILLER     23-JAN-82
KING              5000 17-NOV-81 25-FEB-82  MILLER     23-JAN-82
MARTIN            1250 28-SEP-81 06-JAN-82  FORD       03-DEC-81

TURNER            1500 08-SEP-81 17-DEC-81  FORD       03-DEC-81
CLARK             2450 09-JUN-81 17-SEP-81  TURNER     08-SEP-81

BLAKE             2850 01-MAY-81 09-AUG-81  CLARK      09-JUN-81
```

```
JONES            2975 02-APR-81 11-JUL-81  CLARK      09-JUN-81
WARD             1250 22-FEB-81 02-JUN-81  BLAKE      01-MAY-81
ALLEN            1600 20-FEB-81 31-MAY-81  BLAKE      01-MAY-81
SMITH             800 17-DEC-80 27-MAR-81  WARD       22-FEB-81
14 rows selected.
```

If we look at CLARK again – the window selected is different since the data in the partition is sorted differently. CLARK's window for RANGE 100 PRECEDING now goes back to TURNER since the HIREDATE for TURNER is the last HIREDATE **preceding** CLARK's record which is within 100 days of it.

At times it is a little confusing trying to figure out what the range will actually include. I find using FIRST_VALUE a handy method to help visualize the window and to verify that I have set up the parameters correctly. Now that we can clearly 'see' the windows for this example, we'll use them to compute something meaningful. We need to report each employee's salary *and* the average salary of everyone hired within the 100 preceding days *and* the average salary of everyone hired within 100 days subsequently. The query would look like this:

```
scott@TKYTE816> select ename, hiredate, sal,
  2      avg(sal)
  3      over (order by hiredate asc  range 100 preceding)
  4        avg_sal_100_days_before,
  5      avg(sal)
  6      over (order by hiredate desc  range 100 preceding)
  7        avg_sal_100_days_after
  8  from emp
  9  order by
  8  /

ENAME       HIREDATE      SAL AVG_SAL_100_DAYS_BEFORE AVG_SAL_100_DAYS_AFTER
----------  ---------  -------- ----------------------- ----------------------
SMITH       17-DEC-80   800.00                  800.00                1216.67
ALLEN       20-FEB-81  1600.00                 1200.00                2168.75
WARD        22-FEB-81  1250.00                 1216.67                2358.33
JONES       02-APR-81  2975.00                 1941.67                2758.33
BLAKE       01-MAY-81  2850.00                 2168.75                2650.00
CLARK       09-JUN-81  2450.00                 2758.33                1975.00
TURNER      08-SEP-81  1500.00                 1975.00                2340.00
MARTIN      28-SEP-81  1250.00                 1375.00                2550.00
KING        17-NOV-81  5000.00                 2583.33                2562.50
JAMES       03-DEC-81   950.00                 2340.00                1750.00
FORD        03-DEC-81  3000.00                 2340.00                1750.00
MILLER      23-JAN-82  1300.00                 2562.50                1300.00
SCOTT       09-DEC-82  3000.00                 3000.00                2050.00
ADAMS       12-JAN-83  1100.00                 2050.00                1100.00

14 rows selected.
```

Here, if we look at CLARK again, since we understand his window within the group, we can see that the average salary of 2758.33 is equal to (2450+2850+2975)/3. This is the average of the salaries for CLARK and the rows preceding CLARK (these are JONES and BLAKE) when the data is sorted in an ascending order. On the other hand, the average salary of 1975.00 is equal to (2450+1500)/2. These are the values of CLARK's salary and the rows preceding CLARK when the data is sorted in a descending order. Using this query we are able to compute the average salary of people hired within 100 days *before* and 100 day *after* CLARK simultaneously.

RANGE windows only work on NUMBERS and DATES since we cannot add or subtract N units from a VARCHAR2 in general. The other limitation they have is that there can only be one column in the ORDER BY – ranges are single dimensional in nature. We cannot do a range in N dimensional space.

Row Windows

Row windows are physical units; physical numbers of rows, to include in the window. Using the preceding example as a ROW partition:

```
count (*) over  ( order by x ROWS 5 preceding )
```

That window will consist of up to 6 rows; the current row and the five rows 'in front of' this row (where 'in front of' is defined by the ORDER BY clause). With ROW partitions, we do not have the limitations of the RANGE partition – the data may be of any type and the order by may include many columns. Here is an example similar to the one we just did above:

```
scott@TKYTE816> select ename, sal, hiredate,
  2     first_value(ename)
  3     over (order by hiredate asc
  4          rows 5 preceding) ename_prec,
  5     first_value(hiredate)
  6     over (order by hiredate asc
  7          rows 5 preceding) hiredate_prec
  8   from emp
  9   order by hiredate asc
 10   /

ENAME          SAL HIREDATE  ENAME_PREC HIREDATE_
---------- -------- --------- ---------- ---------
SMITH        800.00 17-DEC-80 SMITH      17-DEC-80
ALLEN       1600.00 20-FEB-81 SMITH      17-DEC-80
WARD        1250.00 22-FEB-81 SMITH      17-DEC-80
JONES       2975.00 02-APR-81 SMITH      17-DEC-80
BLAKE       2850.00 01-MAY-81 SMITH      17-DEC-80
CLARK       2450.00 09-JUN-81 SMITH      17-DEC-80
TURNER      1500.00 08-SEP-81 ALLEN      20-FEB-81
MARTIN      1250.00 28-SEP-81 WARD       22-FEB-81
KING        5000.00 17-NOV-81 JONES      02-APR-81
JAMES        950.00 03-DEC-81 BLAKE      01-MAY-81
FORD        3000.00 03-DEC-81 CLARK      09-JUN-81
MILLER      1300.00 23-JAN-82 TURNER     08-SEP-81
SCOTT       3000.00 09-DEC-82 MARTIN     28-SEP-81
ADAMS       1100.00 12-JAN-83 KING       17-NOV-81
14 rows selected.
```

Looking at CLARK again, we see that the first value in the window ROWS 5 PRECEDING is SMITH; the first row in the window preceding CLARK going back 5 rows. In fact, SMITH is the first value in all of the preceding rows, for BLAKE, JONES, and so on. This is because SMITH is the first record in this group (SMITH is the first value for SMITH even). Sorting the group in a descending fashion reverses the windows:

```
scott@TKYTE816> select ename, sal, hiredate,
  2     first_value(ename)
  3     over (order by hiredate desc
  4           rows 5 preceding) ename_prec,
  5     first_value(hiredate)
  6     over (order by hiredate desc
  7           rows 5 preceding) hiredate_prec
  8   from emp
  9   order by hiredate desc
 10   /

ENAME           SAL HIREDATE  ENAME_PREC HIREDATE_
---------- -------- --------- ---------- ---------
ADAMS       1100.00 12-JAN-83 ADAMS      12-JAN-83
SCOTT       3000.00 09-DEC-82 ADAMS      12-JAN-83
MILLER      1300.00 23-JAN-82 ADAMS      12-JAN-83
JAMES        950.00 03-DEC-81 ADAMS      12-JAN-83
FORD        3000.00 03-DEC-81 ADAMS      12-JAN-83
KING        5000.00 17-NOV-81 ADAMS      12-JAN-83
MARTIN      1250.00 28-SEP-81 SCOTT      09-DEC-82
TURNER      1500.00 08-SEP-81 MILLER     23-JAN-82
CLARK       2450.00 09-JUN-81 JAMES      03-DEC-81
BLAKE       2850.00 01-MAY-81 FORD       03-DEC-81
JONES       2975.00 02-APR-81 KING       17-NOV-81
WARD        1250.00 22-FEB-81 MARTIN     28-SEP-81
ALLEN       1600.00 20-FEB-81 TURNER     08-SEP-81
SMITH        800.00 17-DEC-80 CLARK      09-JUN-81

14 rows selected.
```

So now JAMES is the first value in the set of 5 rows preceding CLARK in the group. Now, we can compute the average salary of a given record with the (up to) 5 employees hired *before* them or *after* them as follows:

```
scott@TKYTE816> select ename, hiredate, sal,
  2     avg(sal)
  3     over (order by hiredate asc rows 5 preceding) avg_5_before,
  4       count(*)
  5     over (order by hiredate asc rows 5 preceding) obs_before,
  6       avg(sal)
  7     over (order by hiredate desc rows 5 preceding) avg_5_after,
  8       count(*)
  9     over (order by hiredate desc rows 5 preceding) obs_after
 10   from emp
 11   order by hiredate
 12   /

ENAME      HIREDATE      SAL AVG_5_BEFORE OBS_BEFORE AVG_5_AFTER OBS_AFTER
---------- --------- -------- ------------ ---------- ----------- ---------
SMITH      17-DEC-80   800.00       800.00       1.00     1987.50      6.00
ALLEN      20-FEB-81  1600.00      1200.00       2.00     2104.17      6.00
WARD       22-FEB-81  1250.00      1216.67       3.00     2045.83      6.00
JONES      02-APR-81  2975.00      1656.25       4.00     2670.83      6.00
BLAKE      01-MAY-81  2850.00      1895.00       5.00     2675.00      6.00
```

```
CLARK       09-JUN-81  2450.00     1987.50       6.00     2358.33     6.00
TURNER      08-SEP-81  1500.00     2104.17       6.00     2166.67     6.00
MARTIN      28-SEP-81  1250.00     2045.83       6.00     2416.67     6.00
KING        17-NOV-81  5000.00     2670.83       6.00     2391.67     6.00
JAMES       03-DEC-81   950.00     2333.33       6.00     1587.50     4.00
FORD        03-DEC-81  3000.00     2358.33       6.00     1870.00     5.00
MILLER      23-JAN-82  1300.00     2166.67       6.00     1800.00     3.00
SCOTT       09-DEC-82  3000.00     2416.67       6.00     2050.00     2.00
ADAMS       12-JAN-83  1100.00     2391.67       6.00     1100.00     1.00

14 rows selected.
```

Notice here I selected out a COUNT(*) as well. This is useful just to demonstrate how many rows went into making up a given average. We can see clearly that for ALLEN's record, the average salary computation for people hired *before* him used only 2 records whereas the computation for salaries of people hired *after* him used 6. At the point in the group where ALLEN's record is located there was only 1 preceding record so the analytic function just used as many as there were in the computation.

Specifying Windows

Now that we understand the differences between a RANGE and a ROWS window, we can investigate the ways in which we can specify these ranges.

In its simplest form, the window is specified with one of three mutually exclusive statements:

❑ **UNBOUNDED PRECEDING** – the window starts with the first row of the current partition and ends with the current row being processed.

❑ **CURRENT ROW** – the window starts (and ends) with the current row

❑ **Numeric Expression PRECEDING** – the window starts from the row that is Numeric Expression rows 'in front' of the current row for ROWS and starts from the row who's order by value is less then the current row by 'Numeric Expression' for RANGE

The CURRENT ROW range would probably never be used in the simple form as it would restrict the analytic function to the single row only, something for which an analytic function is not needed. In a more complex form, the window is specified with a BETWEEN clause. There, we might use the CURRENT ROW as either a starting point or ending point of the window. The start points and end points of the BETWEEN clause may be specified using all of the items in the list above plus one additional one:

Numeric Expression FOLLOWING – the window ends (or starts) from the row that is 'Numeric Expression' rows 'after' the current row for ROWS and starts (or ends) from the row who's order by value is more then the current row by 'Numeric Expression' for RANGE

Some examples of these windows would be:

```
scott@TKYTE816> select deptno, ename, hiredate,
  2         count(*) over (partition by deptno
  3                        order by hiredate nulls first
  4                        range 100 preceding) cnt_range,
  5         count(*) over (partition by deptno
  6                        order by hiredate nulls first
  7                        rows 2 preceding) cnt_rows
```

```
  8   from emp
  9   where deptno in (10, 20)
 10   order by deptno, hiredate
 11   /

     DEPTNO ENAME        HIREDATE    CNT_RANGE    CNT_ROWS
 ---------- ----------   ---------   ----------   ----------
         10 CLARK        09-JUN-81           1           1
            KING         17-NOV-81           1           2
            MILLER       23-JAN-82           2           3

         20 SMITH        17-DEC-80           1           1
            JONES        02-APR-81           1           2
            FORD         03-DEC-81           1           3
            SCOTT        09-DEC-82           1           3
            ADAMS        12-JAN-83           2           3

8 rows selected.
```

As you can see, the RANGE 100 PRECEDING counts only the rows in the current partition such that the HIREDATE is between HIREDATE-100 and HIREDATE+100 and that row preceded the current row in the window. In this case the count is always 1 or 2 indicating that in these departments, it was rare to have an employee hired within 100 days of another employee; it only happened twice. The ROWS 2 PRECEDING window however, varies from 1 to 3 rows depending on how far into the group we are. For the first row in the group, the count is one (there are no preceding rows). For the next row in the group there are 2. Finally for rows 3 and higher the COUNT(*) remains constant as we are counting only the current row and the preceding 2 rows.

Now we will take a look at using BETWEEN. All of the windows we have defined so far have ended at the current row and have looked 'backwards' in the resultset for more information. We can define a window such that the current row being processed is not the last row in the window, but is somewhere in the middle of the window. For example:

```
scott@TKYTE816> select ename, hiredate,
  2      first_value(ename) over
  3        (order by hiredate asc
  4         range between 100 preceding and 100 following),
  5      last_value(ename) over
  6        (order by hiredate asc
  7         range between 100 preceding and 100 following)
  8   from emp
  9   order by hiredate asc
 10   /

ENAME        HIREDATE  FIRST_VALU LAST_VALUE
----------   --------- ---------- ----------
SMITH        17-DEC-80 SMITH      WARD
ALLEN        20-FEB-81 SMITH      BLAKE
WARD         22-FEB-81 SMITH      BLAKE
JONES        02-APR-81 ALLEN      CLARK
BLAKE        01-MAY-81 ALLEN      CLARK
CLARK        09-JUN-81 JONES      TURNER
TURNER       08-SEP-81 CLARK      JAMES
MARTIN       28-SEP-81 TURNER     JAMES
```

```
KING        17-NOV-81  TURNER     MILLER
FORD        03-DEC-81  TURNER     MILLER
JAMES       03-DEC-81  TURNER     MILLER
MILLER      23-JAN-82  KING       MILLER
SCOTT       09-DEC-82  SCOTT      ADAMS
ADAMS       12-JAN-83  SCOTT      ADAMS

14 rows selected.
```

Using CLARK again, we can see this window extends back to JONES and down to TURNER. Instead of having a window consisting of the people hired 100 days before *or* after, the window now consists of people hired 100 days before *and* after the current record.

OK, now we have a good understanding of the syntax of the four components of the analytic function clause:

❑   The **function** itself

❑   The **partitioning clause** used to break the larger resultset into independent groups

❑   The **order by clause** used to sort data for the windowing functions within a group

❑   The **windowing clause** used to define the set of rows the analytic function will operate on

```
FUNCTION_NAME( <argument>,<argument>,... )
OVER
(<Partition-Clause> <Order-by-Clause> <Windowing Clause>)
```

We'll now take a brief look at all of the functions available.

The Functions

There are over 26 analytic functions available to use with this feature. Some of them have the same name as existing aggregate functions such as AVG and SUM. Others have new names and provide new functionality. What we will do in this section is simply list the available functions and give a short description of what their purpose is.

Analytic Function	Purpose
AVG (<distinct|all> expression)	Used to compute an average of an expression within a group and window. Distinct may be used to find the average of the values in a group after duplicates have been removed.

Analytic Function	Purpose
CORR (expression, expression)	Returns the coefficient of correlation of a pair of expressions that return numbers. It is shorthand for: COVAR_POP(expr1, expr2) / STDDEV_POP(expr1) * STDDEV_POP(expr2)). Statistically speaking, a correlation is the strength of an association between variables. An association between variables means that the value of one variable can be predicted, to some extent, by the value of the other. The correlation coefficient gives the strength of the association by returning a number between -1 (strong inverse correlation) and 1 (strong correlation). A value of 0 would indicate no correlation.
COUNT (<distinct> <*> <expression>)	This will count occurrences within a group. If you specify * or some non-null constant, count will count all rows. If you specify an expression, count returns the count of *non-null* evaluations of expression. You may use the DISTINCT modifier to count occurrences of rows in a group *after* duplicates have been removed.
COVAR_POP (expression, expression)	This returns the population covariance of a pair of expressions that return numbers.
COVAR_SAMP (expression, expression)	This returns the sample covariance of a pair of expressions that return numbers.
CUME_DIST	This computes the relative position of a row in a group. CUME_DIST will always return a number greater then 0 and less then or equal to 1. This number represents the 'position' of the row in the group of N rows. In a group of three rows, the cumulate distribution values returned would be 1/3, 2/3, and 3/3 for example.
DENSE_RANK	This function computes the relative rank of each row returned from a query with respect to the other rows, based on the values of the expressions in the ORDER BY clause. The data within a group is sorted by the ORDER BY clause and then a numeric ranking is assigned to each row in turn starting with 1 and continuing on up. The rank is incremented every time the values of the ORDER BY expressions change. Rows with equal values receive the same rank (nulls are considered equal in this comparison). A dense rank returns a ranking number without any gaps. This is in comparison to RANK below.
FIRST_VALUE	This simply returns the first value from a group.

Table continued on following page

Analytic Function	Purpose
LAG (expression, <offset>, <default>)	LAG gives you access to *other* rows in a resultset without doing a self-join. It allows you to treat the cursor as if it were an array in effect. You can reference rows that come before the current row in a given group. This would allow you to select 'the previous rows' from a group along with the current row. See LEAD for how to get 'the next rows'.
	Offset is a positive integer that defaults to 1 (the previous row). Default is the value to be returned if the index is out of range of the window (for the first row in a group, the default will be returned)
LAST_VALUE	This simply returns the last value from a group.
LEAD (expression, <offset>, <default>)	LEAD is the opposite of LAG. Whereas LAG gives you access to the a row preceding yours in a group – LEAD gives you access to the a row that comes after your row.
	Offset is a positive integer that defaults to 1 (the next row). Default is the value to be returned if the index is out of range of the window (for the last row in a group, the default will be returned).
MAX(expression)	Finds the maximum value of expression within a window of a group.
MIN(expression)	Finds the minimum value of expression within a window of a group.
NTILE (expression)	Divides a group into 'value of expression' buckets.
	For example; if expression = 4, then each row in the group would be assigned a number from 1 to 4 putting it into a percentile. If the group had 20 rows in it, the first 5 would be assigned 1, the next 5 would be assigned 2 and so on. In the event the cardinality of the group is not evenly divisible by the expression, the rows are distributed such that no percentile has more than 1 row more then any other percentile in that group and the lowest percentiles are the ones that will have 'extra' rows. For example, using expression = 4 again and the number of rows = 21, percentile = 1 will have 6 rows, percentile = 2 will have 5, and so on.
PERCENT_RANK	This is similar to the CUME_DIST (cumulative distribution) function. For a given row in a group, it calculates the rank of that row minus 1, divided by 1 less than the number of rows being evaluated in the group. This function will always return values from 0 to 1 inclusive.
RANK	This function computes the relative rank of each row returned from a query with respect to the other rows, based on the values of the expressions in the ORDER BY clause. The data within a group is sorted by the ORDER BY clause and then a numeric ranking is assigned to each row in turn starting with 1 and continuing on up. Rows with the same values of the ORDER BY expressions receive the same rank; however, if two rows do receive the same rank the rank numbers will subsequently 'skip'. If two rows are number 1, there will be no number 2 – rank will assign the value of 3 to the next row in the group. This is in contrast to DENSE_RANK, which does not skip values.

Analytic Function	Purpose
RATIO_TO_REPORT (expression)	This function computes the value of expression / (sum(expression)) over the group.
	This gives you the percentage of the total the current row contributes to the sum(expression).
REGR_ xxxxxxx (expression, expression)	These linear regression functions fit an ordinary-least-squares regression line to a pair of expressions. There are 9 different regression functions available for use.
ROW_NUMBER	Returns the offset of a row in an ordered group. Can be used to sequentially number rows, ordered by certain criteria.
STDDEV (expression)	Computes the standard deviation of the current row with respect to the group.
STDDEV_POP (expression)	This function computes the population standard deviation and returns the square root of the population variance. Its return value is same as the square root of the VAR_POP function.
STDDEV_SAMP (expression)	This function computes the cumulative sample standard deviation and returns the square root of the sample variance. This function returns the same value as the square root of the VAR_SAMP function would.
SUM(expression)	This function computes the cumulative sum of expression in a group.
VAR_POP (expression)	This function returns the population variance of a non-null set of numbers (nulls are ignored). VAR_POP function makes the following calculation for us:
	(SUM(expr*expr) – SUM(expr)*SUM(expr) / COUNT(expr)) / COUNT(expr)
VAR_SAMP (expression)	This function returns the sample variance of a non-null set of numbers (nulls in the set are ignored). This function makes the following calculation for us:
	(SUM(expr*expr) – SUM(expr)*SUM(expr) / COUNT(expr)) / (COUNT(expr) – 1)
VARIANCE (expression)	This function returns the variance of expression. Oracle will calculate the variance as follows:
	0 if the number of rows in expression = 1
	VAR_SAMP if the number of rows in expression > 1

Examples

Now we are ready for the fun part; what we can do with this functionality. I am going to demonstrate with a couple of examples that by no means exhaust what you can do with these new functions but will give you a good working set of examples to get going with.

The TOP-N Query

A question I hear frequently is, "How can I get the TOP-N records by some set of fields?" Prior to having access to these analytic functions, questions of this nature were extremely difficult to answer. Now, they are very easy.

There are some problems with TOP-N queries however; mostly in the way people phrase them. It is something to be careful about when designing your reports. Consider this seemingly sensible request:

I would like the top three paid sales reps by department

The problem with this question is that it is ambiguous. It is ambiguous because of repeated values, there might be four people who all make the same astronomical salary, what should we do then?

I can come up with at least three equally reasonable interpretations of that request – none of which might return three records! I could interpret the request as:

❑ Give me the set of sales people who make the top 3 salaries – that is, find the set of distinct salary amounts, sort them, take the largest three, and give me everyone who makes one of those values.

❑ Give me up to three people who make the top salary. If four people happen to make the largest salary, the answer would be no rows. If two people make the highest salary and two people make the same second highest; the answer will be only two rows (the two highest).

❑ Sort the sales people by salary from greatest to least. Give me the first three rows. If there are less then three people in a department, this will return less then three records.

After further questioning and clarification, most people want the first case; the rest will want the second or third case. Let's see how we can use this analytic functionality to answer any of the three and compare it to how we might do it without analytic functions.

We will use the SCOTT.EMP table for these examples. The first question we will answer is 'Give me the set of sales people making the top 3 salaries in each department':

```
scott@TKYTE816> select *
  2    from (select deptno, ename, sal,
  3            dense_rank()
  4              over (partition by deptno
  5                order by sal desc)
  6            dr from emp)
  7    where dr <= 3
  8  order by deptno, sal desc
  9  /
```

```
    DEPTNO ENAME              SAL          DR
---------- ----------  ----------  ----------
        10 KING              5000           1
           CLARK             2450           2
           MILLER            1300           3

        20 SCOTT             3000           1
           FORD              3000           1
           JONES             2975           2
           ADAMS             1100           3

        30 BLAKE             2850           1
           ALLEN             1600           2
           TURNER            1500           3

10 rows selected.
```

Here the DENSE_RANK() function was used to get the top three salaries. We assigned the dense rank to the salary column and sorted it in a descending order. If you recall from above, a dense rank does not skip numbers and will assign the same number to those rows with the same value. Hence, after the resultset is built in the inline view, we can simply select all of the rows with a dense rank of three or less, this gives us everyone who makes the top three salaries by department number. Just to show what would happen if we tried to use RANK and encountered these duplicate values:

```
scott@TKYTE816> select deptno, ename, sal,
  2          dense_rank()
  3          over (partition by deptno
  4                   order by sal desc) dr,
  5          rank()
  6          over (partition by deptno
  7                   order by sal desc) r
  8    from emp
  9   order by deptno, sal desc
 10   /

    DEPTNO ENAME              SAL          DR           R
---------- ----------  ----------  ----------  ----------
        10 KING              5000           1           1
           CLARK             2450           2           2
           MILLER            1300           3           3

        20 SCOTT             3000           1           1
           FORD              3000           1           1
           JONES             2975           2           3

           ADAMS             1100           3           4
           SMITH              800           4           5

        30 BLAKE             2850           1           1
           ALLEN             1600           2           2
           TURNER            1500           3           3
           WARD              1250           4           4
           MARTIN            1250           4           4
           JAMES              950           5           6

14 rows selected.
```

If we had used RANK, it would have left ADAMS (because he is ranked at 4) out of the resultset but ADAMS is one of the people in department 20 making the top 3 salaries so he belongs in the result. In this case, using RANK over DENSE_RANK would not have answered our specific query.

Lastly, we had to use an inline view and alias the dense rank column to DR. This is because we cannot use analytic functions in a WHERE or HAVING clause directly so we had to compute the view and then filter just the rows we wanted to keep. The use of an inline view with a predicate will be a common operation in many of our examples.

Now on to the question 'Give me up to three people who make the top salaries by department':

```
scott@TKYTE816> select *
  2  from (select deptno, ename, sal,
  3            count(*) over (partition by deptno
  4                           order by sal desc
  5                           range unbounded preceding)
  6            cnt from emp)
  7  where cnt <= 3
  8  order by deptno, sal desc
  9  /

    DEPTNO ENAME             SAL        CNT
---------- ---------- ---------- ----------
        10 KING             5000          1
           CLARK            2450          2
           MILLER           1300          3

        20 SCOTT            3000          2
           FORD             3000          2
           JONES            2975          3

        30 BLAKE            2850          1
           ALLEN            1600          2
           TURNER           1500          3

9 rows selected.
```

This one was a little tricky. What we are doing is counting all of the records that precede the current record in the window and sorting them by salary. The RANGE UNBOUNDED PRECEDING, which would be the default range here, makes a window that includes all of the records whose salary is larger than or equal to ours since we sorted by descending (DESC) order. By counting everyone who makes what we make or more, we can retrieve only rows such that the count (CNT) of people making the same or more is less then or equal to 3. Notice how for department 20, SCOTT and FORD both have a count of 2; they are the top two salary earners in that department hence they are both in the same window with regards to each other. It is interesting to note the subtle difference in this query:

```
scott@TKYTE816> select *
  2  from (select deptno, ename, sal,
  3            count(*) over (partition by deptno
  4                           order by sal desc, ename
  5                           range unbounded preceding)
  6            cnt from emp)
  7  where cnt <= 3
  8  order by deptno, sal desc
```

```
  9  /

    DEPTNO ENAME              SAL        CNT
---------- ----------  ----------  ----------
        10 KING              5000           1
           CLARK             2450           2
           MILLER            1300           3

        20 FORD              3000           1
           SCOTT             3000           2

           JONES             2975           3

        30 BLAKE             2850           1
           ALLEN             1600           2
           TURNER            1500           3

  9 rows selected.
```

Notice how adding the ORDER BY function affected the window. Previously both FORD and SCOTT had a count of two. That is because the window was built using only the salary column. A more specific window here changes the outcome of the COUNT. This just points out that the window function is computed based on the ORDER BY and the RANGE. When we sorted the partition just by salary, FORD preceded SCOTT when SCOTT was the current row and SCOTT preceded FORD when FORD was the current row. Only when we sort by both SAL and ENAME columns, did the SCOTT and FORD records have any sort of order with respect to each other.

To see that this approach, using the count, allows us to return three or less records, we can update the data to make it so that more than three people make the top salaries:

```
scott@TKYTE816> update emp set sal = 99 where deptno = 30;

6 rows updated.

scott@TKYTE816> select *
  2  from (select deptno, ename, sal,
  3        count(*) over (partition by deptno
  4                       order by sal desc
  5                       range unbounded preceding)
  6        cnt from emp)
  7  where cnt <= 3
  8  order by deptno, sal desc
  9  /

    DEPTNO ENAME              SAL        CNT
---------- ----------  ----------  ----------
        10 KING              5000           1
           CLARK             2450           2
           MILLER            1300           3

        20 SCOTT             3000           2
           FORD              3000           2
           JONES             2975           3

6 rows selected.
```

Now, department 30 no longer appears in the report, because all 6 people in that department make the same amount. The CNT field for all of them is 6, which is a number that is not less than or equal to 3.

Now for the last question of 'Sort the sales people by salary from greatest to least; give me the first three rows'. Using ROW_NUMBER() this is easy to accomplish:

```
scott@TKYTE816> select *
  2  from (select deptno, ename, sal,
  3               row_number() over (partition by deptno
  4                                  order by sal desc)
  5         rn from emp)
  6  where rn <= 3
  7  /

    DEPTNO ENAME             SAL         RN
---------- ---------- ---------- ----------
        10 KING             5000          1
           CLARK            2450          2
           MILLER           1300          3

        20 SCOTT            3000          1
           FORD             3000          2
           JONES            2975          3

        30 ALLEN              99          1
           BLAKE              99          2
           MARTIN             99          3

9 rows selected.
```

This query works by sorting each partition, in a descending order, based on the salary column and then assigning a sequential row number to each row in the partition as it is processed. We use a WHERE clause after doing this to get just the first three rows in each partition. Below, in the pivot example, we will use this same concept to turn rows into columns. It should be noted here however that the rows we got back for DEPTNO=30 are somewhat random. If you recall, department 30 was updated such that all 6 employees had the value of 99. You could control which of the three records came back via the ORDER BY to some degree. For instance, you could use ORDER SAL DESC, ENAME, to get the three highest paid in order of employee name when all three earn the same amount.

It is interesting to note that using the above method with ROW_NUMBER, you have the ability to get an arbitrary 'slice' of data from a group of rows. This may be useful in a stateless environment where you need to paginate through a set of data. For example, if you decide to display the EMP table sorted by ENAME five rows at a time, you could use a query similar to this:

```
scott@TKYTE816> select ename, hiredate, sal
  2  from (select ename, hiredate, sal,
  3               row_number() over (order by ename)
  4         rn from emp)
  5  where rn between 5 and 10
  6  order by rn
  7  /
```

```
ENAME        HIREDATE        SAL
----------   ----------   ----------
FORD         03-DEC-81        3000
JAMES        03-DEC-81         950
JONES        02-APR-81        2975
KING         17-NOV-81        5000
MARTIN       28-SEP-81        1250
MILLER       23-JAN-82        1300

6 rows selected.
```

One last thing, to demonstrate how truly powerful this functionality is, would be to see a comparison between queries that use the analytic function approach and queries that do not. What I did to test this was to create a table T, which is just a 'bigger' EMP table for all intents and purposes:

```
scott@TKYTE816> create table t
  2  as
  3  select object_name ename,
  4         mod(object_id,50) deptno,
  5         object_id sal
  6  from all_objects
  7  where rownum <= 1000
  8  /

Table created.

scott@TKYTE816> create index t_idx on t(deptno,sal desc);

Index created.

scott@TKYTE816> analyze table t
  2  compute statistics
  3  for table
  4  for all indexed columns
  5  for all indexes
  6  /

Table analyzed.
```

We've placed an index on this table that will be useful in answering the types of questions we have been asking of it. We would now like to compare the syntax and performance of the queries with and without analytic functions. For this, I used SQL_TRACE, TIMED_STATISTICS and TKPROF to compare the performance of the queries. See the chapter on *Tuning Strategies and Tools* for more details on using those tools and fully interpreting the following results:

```
scott@TKYTE816> select *
  2  from (select deptno, ename, sal,
  3        dense_rank() over (partition by deptno
  4                               order by sal desc)
  5        dr from t)
  6  where dr <= 3
  7  order by deptno, sal desc
  8  /
```

```
call       count       cpu    elapsed     disk      query    current        rows
------    ------  --------  ---------   ------  ---------  ---------   ----------
Parse          1      0.00       0.00        0          0          0            0
Execute        2      0.00       0.00        0          0          0            0
Fetch         11      0.01       0.07        7         10         17          150
------    ------  --------  ---------   ------  ---------  ---------   ----------
total         14      0.01       0.07        7         10         17          150
```

Misses in library cache during parse: 0
Optimizer goal: CHOOSE
Parsing user id: 54

```
Rows       Row Source Operation
-------    -------------------------------------------------------
    150    VIEW
    364      WINDOW SORT PUSHED RANK
   1000        TABLE ACCESS FULL T
```

****

```
scott@TKYTE816> select deptno, ename, sal
  2    from t e1
  3    where sal in (select sal
  4                     from (select distinct sal , deptno
  5                             from t e3
  6                             order by deptno, sal desc) e2
  7                     where e2.deptno = e1.deptno
  8                     and rownum <= 3)
  9    order by deptno, sal desc
 10    /
```

```
call       count       cpu    elapsed     disk      query    current        rows
------    ------  --------  ---------   ------  ---------  ---------   ----------
Parse          1      0.00       0.00        0          0          0            0
Execute        1      0.00       0.00        0          0          0            0
Fetch         11      0.80       0.80        0      10010      12012          150
------    ------  --------  ---------   ------  ---------  ---------   ----------
total         13      0.80       0.80        0      10010      12012          150
```

Misses in library cache during parse: 0
Optimizer goal: CHOOSE
Parsing user id: 54

```
Rows       Row Source Operation
-------    -------------------------------------------------------
    150    SORT ORDER BY
    150      FILTER
   1001        TABLE ACCESS FULL T
   1000        FILTER
   3700          COUNT STOPKEY
   2850            VIEW
   2850              SORT ORDER BY STOPKEY
  20654                SORT UNIQUE
  20654                  TABLE ACCESS FULL T
```

The queries opposite both answer the question of 'who make the top three salaries'. The analytic query can answer this question with almost no work at all – 0.01 CPU seconds and 27 logical I/Os. The relational query on the other hand, must do a lot more work – 0.80 CPU seconds and over 22,000 logical I/Os. For the non-analytical function query, we need to execute a subquery for each row in T to find the three biggest salaries for a given department. Not only does this query perform slower, but also it was hard to write. There are some tricks I could use in order to attempt to improve performance, some hints I might use but the query will only get less understandable and more 'fragile'. Fragile in the sense that any query that relies on hints is fragile. A hint is just a suggestion, the optimizer is free to ignore it at any time in the future. The analytic query clearly wins here for both performance and readability.

Now for the second question – 'give me up to the three people who make the top salary'.

```
scott@TKYTE816> select *
  2  from (select deptno, ename, sal,
  3         count(*) over (partition by deptno
  4                        order by sal desc
  5                        range unbounded preceding)
  6         cnt from t)
  7  where cnt <= 3
  8  order by deptno, sal desc
  9  /
```

call	count	cpu	elapsed	disk	query	current	rows
Parse	1	0.01	0.01	0	0	0	0
Execute	2	0.00	0.00	0	0	0	0
Fetch	11	0.02	0.12	15	10	17	150
total	14	0.03	0.13	15	10	17	150

```
Misses in library cache during parse: 0
Optimizer goal: CHOOSE
Parsing user id: 54

Rows     Row Source Operation
-------  -------------------------------------------------------
    150  VIEW
   1000  WINDOW SORT
   1000   TABLE ACCESS FULL T


*************************************

scott@TKYTE816> select deptno, ename, sal
  2  from t e1
  3  where (select count(*)
  4            from t e2
  5            where e2.deptno = e1.deptno
  6            and e2.sal >= e1.sal) <= 3
  7  order by deptno, sal desc
  8  /
```

call	count	cpu	elapsed	disk	query	current	rows
Parse	1	0.01	0.01	0	0	0	0
Execute	1	0.00	0.00	0	0	0	0
Fetch	11	0.60	0.66	0	4010	4012	150
total	13	0.61	0.67	0	4010	4012	150

```
Misses in library cache during parse: 0
Optimizer goal: CHOOSE
Parsing user id: 54
```

Rows	Row Source Operation
150	SORT ORDER BY
150	FILTER
1001	TABLE ACCESS FULL T
2000	SORT AGGREGATE
10827	INDEX FAST FULL SCAN (object id 27867)

Once again, the results are clear. 0.03 CPU seconds and 27 logical I/Os versus 0.61 CPU seconds and over 8000 logical I/Os. The clear winner here is the analytical function again. The reason, once again, is the fact that we need to execute a correlated subquery for each and every row in base table without the analytic functions. This query counts the number of records in the same department that make the same or greater salary. We only keep the records such that the count is less then or equal to 3. The results from the queries are the same; the run-time resources needed by both are radically different. In this particular case, I would say the query was no harder to code using either method, but performance-wise, there is no comparison.

Lastly, we need to get the first three highest paid employees we happen to see in a department. The results are:

```
scott@TKYTE816> select deptno, ename, sal
  2         from t e1
  3         where (select count(*)
  4                from t e2
  5                where e2.deptno = e1.deptno
  6                and e2.sal >= e1.sal ) <=3
  7         order by deptno, sal desc
  8  /
```

call	count	cpu	elapsed	disk	query	current	rows
Parse	1	0.00	0.00	0	0	0	0
Execute	2	0.00	0.00	0	0	0	0
Fetch	11	0.00	0.12	14	10	17	150
total	14	0.00	0.12	14	10	17	150

```
Misses in library cache during parse: 0
Optimizer goal: CHOOSE
Parsing user id: 54
```

```
Rows      Row Source Operation
-------   --------------------------------------------
   150    VIEW
  1000    WINDOW SORT
  1000     TABLE ACCESS FULL T


**************************************

scott@TKYTE816> select deptno, ename, sal
  2   from t e1
  3   where (select count(*)
  4          from t e2
  5          where e2.deptno = e1.deptno
  6          and e2.sal >= e1.sal
  7          and (e2.sal > e1.sal OR e2.rowid > e1.rowid)) < 3
  8   order by deptno, sal desc
  9   /
```

call	count	cpu	elapsed	disk	query	current	rows
Parse	1	0.00	0.00	0	0	0	0
Execute	1	0.00	0.00	0	0	0	0
Fetch	11	0.88	0.88	0	4010	4012	150
total	13	0.88	0.88	0	4010	4012	150

```
Misses in library cache during parse: 0
Optimizer goal: CHOOSE
Parsing user id: 54

Rows      Row Source Operation
-------   --------------------------------------------
   150    SORT ORDER BY
   150     FILTER
  1001      TABLE ACCESS FULL T
  2000      SORT AGGREGATE
  9827       INDEX FAST FULL SCAN (object id 27867)
```

Once again, performance-wise there is no comparison. The analytic function version simply outperforms the query that does not use analytic functions many times over. In this particular case, the analytic query is many orders of magnitude easier to code and understand as well. The correlated subquery we had to code is very complex. We need to count the number of records in a department such that salary is greater than or equal to the current row. Additionally, if the salary is not greater than ours (it is equal), we can only count this if the ROWID (any unique column would do) is greater than that record. That ensures we do not double count rows and just retrieve an arbitrary set of rows.

In each case, it is clear that the analytic functions not only ease the job of writing complex queries but that they can add substantial performance increases in the run-time performance of your queries. They allow you to do things you would not have considered doing in SQL otherwise due to the associated cost.

Pivot Query

A pivot query is when you want to take some data such as:

```
C1          C2          C3
-----       -----       ------
a1          b1          x1
a1          b1          x2
a1          b1          x3
...
```

and you would like to display in the following format:

```
C1          C2          C3(1)    C3(2)    C3(3)
-----       -----       ------   -----    ----
a1          b1          x1       x2       x3
...
```

This turns rows into columns. For example taking the distinct jobs within a department and making them be columns so the output would look like:

```
DEPTNO      JOB_1       JOB_2        JOB_3
----------  ----------  ----------   ----------
        10  CLERK       MANAGER      PRESIDENT
        20  ANALYST     ANALYST      CLERK
        30  CLERK       MANAGER      SALESMAN
```

instead of this:

```
DEPTNO      JOB
----------  ----------
        10  CLERK
        10  MANAGER
        10  PRESIDENT
        20  ANALYST
        20  CLERK
        20  MANAGER
        30  CLERK
        30  MANAGER
        30  SALESMAN
```

I'm going to show two examples for pivots. The first will be another implementation of the preceding question. The second shows how to pivot any resultset in a generic fashion and gives you a template for doing so.

In the first case, let's say you wanted to show the top 3 salary earners in each department as *columns*. The query needs to return exactly 1 row per department and the row would have 4 columns; the DEPTNO, the name of the highest paid employee in the department, the name of the next highest paid, and so on. Using this new functionality – this is almost easy (before these functions – this was virtually impossible):

```
ops$tkyte@DEV816> select deptno,
  2             max(decode(seq,1,ename,null)) highest_paid,
  3             max(decode(seq,2,ename,null)) second_highest,
  4             max(decode(seq,3,ename,null)) third_highest
  5    from (SELECT deptno, ename,
  6                 row_number() OVER
  7                    (PARTITION BY deptno
  8                     ORDER BY sal desc NULLS LAST) seq
  9          FROM emp)
 10    where seq <= 3
 11  /

    DEPTNO HIGHEST_PA SECOND_HIG THIRD_HIGH
---------- ---------- ---------- ----------
        10 KING       CLARK      MILLER
        20 SCOTT      FORD       JONES
        30 BLAKE      ALLEN      TURNER
```

This simply created an inner resultset that had a sequence assigned to employees by department number in order of salary. The decode in the outer query keeps only rows with sequences 1, 2, or 3 and assigns them to the correct 'column'. The GROUP BY gets rid of the redundant rows and we are left with our collapsed result. It may be easier to understand what I mean by that if you see the resultset without the GROUP BY and MAX:

```
scott@TKYTE816> select deptno,
  2         (decode(seq,1,ename,null)) highest_paid,
  3         (decode(seq,2,ename,null)) second_highest,
  4         (decode(seq,3,ename,null)) third_highest
  5    from (select deptno, ename,
  6          row_number() over
  7             (partition by deptno
  8              order by sal desc nulls last)
  9          seq from emp)
 10    where seq <= 3
 11  /

    DEPTNO HIGHEST_PA SECOND_HIG THIRD_HIGH
---------- ---------- ---------- ----------
        10 KING
        10            CLARK
        10                       MILLER

        20 SCOTT
        20            FORD
        20                       JONES

        30 ALLEN
        30            BLAKE
        30                       MARTIN

9 rows selected.
```

The MAX aggregate function will be applied by the GROUP BY column DEPTNO. In any given DEPTNO above only one row will have a non-null value for HIGHTEST_PAID, the remaining rows in that group will always be NULL. The MAX function will pick out the non-null row and keep that for us. Hence, the group by and MAX will 'collapse' our resultset, removing the NULL values from it and giving us what we want.

If you have a table T with columns C1, C2 and you would like to get a result like:

```
C1      C2(1)   C2(2)   ….   C2(N)
```

where column C1 is to stay *cross record* (going down the page) and column C2 will be pivoted to be *in record* (going across the page), the values of C2 are to become columns instead of rows – you will generate a query of the form:

```
Select c1,
   max(decode(rn,1,c2,null)) c2_1,
   max(decode(rn,2,c2,null)) c2_2,
   …
   max(decode(rn,N,c2,null)) c2_N
from (select c1, c2,
         row_number() over (partition by C1
                            order by <something>)
         rn from T
      <some predicate>)
group by C1
```

In the above example, C1 was simply DEPTNO and C2 was ENAME. Since we ordered by SAL DESC, the first three columns we retrieved were the top three paid employees in that department (bearing in mind that if four people made the top three, we would of course lose one).

The second example is a more generic 'I want to pivot my resultset'. Here, instead of having a single column C1 to anchor on and a single column C2 to pivot – we'll look at the more general case where C1 is a set of columns as is C2. As it turns out, this is very similar to the above. Suppose you want to report by JOB and DEPTNO the employees in that job and their salary. The report needs to have the employees going *across* the page as columns, however, not down the page, and the same with their salaries. Additionally, the employees need to appear from left to right in order of their salary. The steps would be:

```
scott@TKYTE816> select max(count(*)) from emp group by deptno, job;

MAX(COUNT(*))
-------------
            4
```

This tells us the number of columns; now we can generate the query:

```
scott@TKYTE816> select deptno, job,
  2     max(decode(rn, 1, ename, null)) ename_1,
  3     max(decode(rn, 1, sal, null)) sal_1,
  4     max(decode(rn, 2, ename, null)) ename_2,
  5     max(decode(rn, 2, sal, null)) sal_2,
  6     max(decode(rn, 3, ename, null)) ename_3,
  7     max(decode(rn, 3, sal, null)) sal_3,
  8     max(decode(rn, 4, ename, null)) ename_4,
```

```
  9    max(decode(rn, 4, sal, null)) sal_4
 10  from (select deptno, job, ename, sal,
 11        row_number() over (partition by deptno, job
 12                           order by sal, ename)
 13         rn from emp)
 14  group by deptno, job
 15  /
```

DEPTNO	JOB	ENAME_1	SAL_1	ENAME_2	SAL_2	ENAME_3	SAL_3	ENAME_	SAL_4
10	CLERK	MILLER	1300						
10	MANAGER	CLARK	2450						
10	PRESIDENT	KING	5000						
20	ANALYST	FORD	3000	SCOTT	3000				
20	CLERK	SMITH	800	ADAMS	1100				
20	MANAGER	JONES	2975						
30	CLERK	JAMES	99						
30	MANAGER	BLAKE	99						
30	SALESMAN	ALLEN	99	MARTIN	99	TURNER	99	WARD	99

```
9 rows selected.
```

We inserted values of 99 into the salary column of all the employees in department 30, earlier in the chapter. To pivot a resultset, we can generalize further. If you have a set of columns C1, C2, C3, ... CN and you want to keep columns C1 ... Cx *cross record* and Cx+1 ... CN *in record*, the syntax of the query would be:

```
Select C1, C2, ... CX,
   max(decode(rn,1,C{X+1},null)) cx+1_1,...max(decode(rn,1,CN,null)) CN_1
   max(decode(rn,2,C{X+1},null)) cx+1_2,...max(decode(rn,1,CN,null)) CN_2
   ...
   max(decode(rn,N,c{X+1},null)) cx+1_N,...max(decode(rn,1,CN,null)) CN_N
from (select C1, C2, ... CN
      row_number() over (partition by C1, C2, ... CX
                         order by <something>)
      rn from T
      <some predicate>)
group by C1, C2, ... CX
```

In the example above, we used C1 as DEPTNO, C2 as JOB, C3 as ENAME, and C4 as SAL.

One other thing that we must know is the *maximum* number of rows per partition that we anticipate. This will dictate the number of columns we will be generating. SQL needs to know the number of columns, there is no way around that fact, and without this knowledge we will not be able to pivot. This leads us into the next, more generic, example of pivoting. If we do not know the number of total columns until runtime, we'll have to use dynamic SQL to deal with the fact that the SELECT list is variable. We can use PL/SQL to demonstrate how to do this; this will result in a generic routine that can be reused whenever you need a pivot. This routine will have the following specification:

```
scott@TKYTE816> create or replace package my_pkg
  2  as
  3     type refcursor is ref cursor;
```

```
4    type array is table of varchar2(30);
5      procedure pivot(p_max_cols        in number   default NULL,
6                     p_max_cols_query in varchar2 default NULL,
7                     p_query          in varchar2,
8                     p_anchor         in array,
9                     p_pivot          in array,
10                    p_cursor in out refcursor);
12   end;

Package created.
```

Here, you must input values for either P_MAX_COLS or P_MAX_COLS_QUERY. SQL needs to know the number of columns in a query and this parameter will allow us to build a query with the proper number of columns. The value you should send in here will be the output of a query similar to:

```
scott@TKYTE816> select max(count(*)) from emp group by deptno, job;
```

This is the count of the discrete values that are currently in *rows,* which we will put into *columns.* You can either use a query to obtain this number, or insert the number yourself if you already know it.

The P_QUERY parameter is simply the query that gathers your data together. Using the example shown earlier the query would be:

```
10   from (select deptno, job, ename, sal,
11          row_number() over (partition by deptno, job
12                             order by sal, ename)
13        rn from emp)
```

The next two inputs are arrays of column names. The P_ANCHOR tells us what columns will stay *cross record* (down the page) and P_PIVOT states the columns that will go *in record* (across the page). In our example from above, P_ANCHOR = ('DEPTNO', 'JOB') and P_PIVOT = ('ENAME', 'SAL'). Skipping over the implementation for a moment, the entire call put together might look like this:

```
scott@TKYTE816> variable x refcursor

scott@TKYTE816> set autoprint on

scott@TKYTE816> begin
  2    my_pkg.pivot
  3    (p_max_cols_query => 'select max(count(*)) from emp
  4                          group by deptno,job',
  5    p_query => 'select deptno, job, ename, sal,
  6    row_number() over (partition by deptno, job
  7                       order by sal, ename)
  8    rn from emp a',
  9
 10      p_anchor => my_pkg.array('DEPTNO','JOB'),
 11      p_pivot  => my_pkg.array('ENAME', 'SAL'),
 12      p_cursor => :x);
 13   end;

PL/SQL procedure successfully completed.
```

```
   DEPTNO JOB         ENAME_ SAL_1 ENAME_2    SAL_2 ENAME_3    SAL_3 ENAME_ SAL_4
   ------ --------- ------ ----- ---------- ----- ---------- ----- ------ -----
       10 CLERK       MILLER 1300
       10 MANAGER     CLARK  2450
       10 PRESIDENT   KING   5000
       20 ANALYST     FORD   3000 SCOTT       3000
       20 CLERK       SMITH   800 ADAMS       1100
       20 MANAGER     JONES  2975
       30 CLERK       JAMES    99
       30 MANAGER     BLAKE    99
       30 SALESMAN    ALLEN    99 MARTIN        99 TURNER        99 WARD     99

   9 rows selected.
```

As you can see, that dynamically rewrote our query using the generalized template we developed. The implementation of the package body is straightforward:

```
scott@TKYTE816> create or replace package body my_pkg
  2  as
  3
  4  procedure pivot(p_max_cols       in number   default null,
  5                  p_max_cols_query in varchar2 default null,
  6                  p_query          in varchar2,
  7                  p_anchor         in array,
  8                  p_pivot          in array,
  9                  p_cursor in out refcursor)
 10  as
 11      l_max_cols number;
 12      l_query    long;
 13      l_cnames   array;
 14  begin
 15      -- figure out the number of columns we must support
 16      -- we either KNOW this or we have a query that can tell us
 17      if (p_max_cols is not null)
 18      then
 19          l_max_cols := p_max_cols;
 20      elsif (p_max_cols_query is not null)
 21      then
 22          execute immediate p_max_cols_query into l_max_cols;
 23      else
 24          raise_application_error(-20001, 'Cannot figure out max cols');
 25      end if;
 26
 27
 28      -- Now, construct the query that can answer the question for us...
 29      -- start with the C1, C2, ... CX columns:
 30
 31      l_query := 'select ';
 32      for i in 1 .. p_anchor.count
 33
 34      loop
 35          l_query := l_query || p_anchor(i) || ',';
 36      end loop;
 37
 38      -- Now add in the C{x+1}... CN columns to be pivoted:
```

```
39      -- the format is "max(decode(rn,1,C{X+1},null)) cx+1_1"
40
41      for i in 1 .. l_max_cols
42      loop
43        for j in 1 .. p_pivot.count
44          loop
45            l_query := l_query ||
46                      'max(decode(rn,'||i||',''||
47                      p_pivot(j)||',null)) ' ||
48                      p_pivot(j) || '_' || i || ',';
49          end loop;
50      end loop;
51
52      -- Now just add in the original query
53
54      l_query := rtrim(l_query,',') || ' from (' || p_query || ') group by ';
55
56      -- and then the group by columns...
57
58      for i in 1 .. p_anchor.count
59      loop
60          l_query := l_query || p_anchor(i) || ',';
61      end loop;
62      l_query := rtrim(l_query,',');
63
64      -- and return it
65
66      execute immediate 'alter session set cursor_sharing=force';
67      open p_cursor for l_query;
68      execute immediate 'alter session set cursor_sharing=exact';
69      end;
70
71   end;
72   /

Package body created.
```

It only does a little string manipulation to rewrite the query and open a REF CURSOR dynamically. In the likely event the query had a predicate with constants and such in it, we set cursor sharing on and then back off for the parse of this query to facilitate bind variables (see the section on tuning for more information on that). Now we have a fully parsed query that is ready to be fetched from.

Accessing Rows Around Your Current Row

Frequently people want to access data not only from the current row but the current row and the rows 'in front of' or 'behind' them. For example, let's say you needed a report that shows, by department all of the employees; their hire date; how many days before was the last hire; how many days after was the next hire. Using straight SQL this query would be nightmarish to write. It could be done but it would be quite difficult. Not only that but its performance would once again definitely be questionable. The approach I typically took in the past was either to 'select a select' or write a PL/SQL function that would take some data from the current row and 'find' the previous and next rows data. This worked, but introduce large overhead into both the development of the query (I had to write more code) and the run-time execution of the query.

Using analytic functions, this is easy and efficient to do. It would look like this:

```
scott@TKYTE816> select deptno, ename, hiredate,
  2          lag( hiredate, 1, null ) over ( partition by deptno
  3                                    order by hiredate, ename ) last_hire,
  4          hiredate - lag( hiredate, 1, null )
  5                       over ( partition by deptno
  6                              order by hiredate, ename ) days_last,
  7          lead( hiredate, 1, null )
  8           over ( partition by deptno
  9                    order by hiredate, ename ) next_hire,
 10          lead( hiredate, 1, null )
 11           over ( partition by deptno
 12                    order by hiredate, ename ) - hiredate days_next
 13  from emp
 14  order by deptno, hiredate
 15  /
```

DEPTNO	ENAME	HIREDATE	LAST_HIRE	DAYS_LAST	NEXT_HIRE	DAYS_NEXT
10	CLARK	**09-JUN-81**			17-NOV-81	161
	KING	17-NOV-81	**09-JUN-81**	161	**23-JAN-82**	67
	MILLER	**23-JAN-82**	17-NOV-81	67		
20	SMITH	17-DEC-80			02-APR-81	106
	JONES	02-APR-81	17-DEC-80	106	03-DEC-81	245
	FORD	03-DEC-81	02-APR-81	245	09-DEC-82	371
	SCOTT	09-DEC-82	03-DEC-81	371	12-JAN-83	34
	ADAMS	12-JAN-83	09-DEC-82	34		
30	ALLEN	20-FEB-81			22-FEB-81	2
	WARD	22-FEB-81	20-FEB-81	2	01-MAY-81	68
	BLAKE	01-MAY-81	22-FEB-81	68	08-SEP-81	130
	TURNER	08-SEP-81	01-MAY-81	130	28-SEP-81	20
	MARTIN	28-SEP-81	08-SEP-81	20	03-DEC-81	66
	JAMES	03-DEC-81	28-SEP-81	66		

```
14 rows selected.
```

The LEAD and LAG routines could be considered a way to 'index into your partitioned group'. Using these functions, you can access any individual row. Notice for example in the above printout, it shows that the record for KING includes the data (in bold font) from the prior row (LAST_HIRE) and the next row (NEXT_HIRE). We can access the fields in records preceding or following the current record in an ordered partition easily.

Before we look in more detail at LAG and LEAD, I would like to compare this to the way you would do this without analytic functions. Once again, I'll create an appropriately indexed table in an attempt to answer the question as quickly as possible:

```
scott@TKYTE816> create table t
  2  as
  3  select object_name ename,
  4         created hiredate,
  5             mod(object_id,50) deptno
  6  from all_objects
  7  /
```

```
Table created.

scott@TKYTE816> alter table t modify deptno not null;

Table altered.

scott@TKYTE816> create index t_idx on t(deptno,hiredate,ename)
  2  /

Index created.

scott@TKYTE816> analyze table t
  2  compute statistics
  3  for table
  4  for all indexes
  5  for all indexed columns
  6  /

Table analyzed.
```

I even added ENAME to the index in order to permit accessing *only* the index to answer the question and avoid the table access by ROWID. The query with the analytic function performed as follows:

```
scott@TKYTE816> select deptno, ename, hiredate,
  2  lag(hiredate, 1, null) over (partition by deptno
  3                                  order by hiredate, ename) last_hire,
  4      hiredate - lag(hiredate, 1, null)
  5      over (partition by deptno
  6            order by hiredate, ename) days_last,
  7      lead(hiredate, 1, null)
  8      over (partition by deptno
  9            order by hiredate, ename) next_hire,
 10      lead(hiredate, 1, null)
 11      over (partition by deptno
 12            order by hiredate, ename) - hiredate days_next
 13  from emp
 14  order by deptno, hiredate
 15  /
```

call	count	cpu	elapsed	disk	query	current	rows
Parse	1	0.01	0.01	0	0	0	0
Execute	2	0.00	0.00	0	0	0	0
Fetch	1313	0.72	1.57	142	133	2	19675
total	1316	0.73	1.58	142	133	2	19675

```
Misses in library cache during parse: 0
Optimizer goal: FIRST_ROWS
Parsing user id: 54

Rows     Row Source Operation
-------  ---------------------------------------------------
  19675  WINDOW BUFFER
  19675   INDEX FULL SCAN (object id 27899)
```

As compared to the equivalent query without the analytic functions:

```
scott@TKYTE816> select deptno, ename, hiredate,
  2  hiredate-(select max(hiredate)
  3          from t e2
  4          where e2.deptno = e1.deptno
  5          and e2.hiredate < e1.hiredate ) last_hire,
  6  hiredate-(select max(hiredate)
  7          from t e2
  8          where e2.deptno = e1.deptno
  9          and e2.hiredate < e1.hiredate ) days_last,
 10          (select min(hiredate)
 11          from t e3
 12          where e3.deptno = e1.deptno
 13          and e3.hiredate > e1.hiredate) next_hire,
 14          (select min(hiredate)
 15          from t e3
 16          where e3.deptno = e1.deptno
 17          and e3.hiredate > e1.hiredate) - hiredate days_next
 18      from t e1
 19      order by deptno, hiredate
 20  /
```

call	count	cpu	elapsed	disk	query	current	rows
Parse	1	0.01	0.01	0	0	0	0
Execute	1	0.00	0.00	0	0	0	0
Fetch	1313	2.48	2.69	0	141851	0	19675
total	1315	2.49	2.70	0	141851	0	19675

```
Misses in library cache during parse: 0
Optimizer goal: FIRST_ROWS
Parsing user id: 54
```

Rows	Row Source Operation
19675	INDEX FULL SCAN (object id 27899)

There is a significant difference between the performance of both queries; 135 Logical I/Os versus over 141000, 0.73 CPU seconds versus 2.49. The analytical function is once again the clear winner in this case. You should also consider the complexity of the queries as well. In my opinion, when we used LAG and LEAD it was not only easier to code, but it was also obvious what the query was retrieving. The 'select of a select' is a nice trick, but it is harder to write the code in the first place and with a quick read of the query, it is not at all obvious what you are retrieving. It takes more 'thought' to reverse engineer the second query.

Now for some details on the LAG and LEAD functions. These functions take three arguments:

```
lag( Arg1, Arg2, Arg3)
```

❑ **Arg1** is the expression to be returned from the other row

❑ **Arg2** is the offset into the partition from the current row you wish to retrieve. This is a positive integer offset from the current row. In the case of LAG, it is an index back into preceding rows. In the case of LEAD, it is an index forward into the rows to come. The default value for this argument is 1.

❑ **Arg3** is what to return by default when the index supplied by Arg2 goes out of the window. For example, the first row in every partition does not have a preceding row so LAG(..., 1) for that row will not be defined. You can allow it to return NULL by default or supply a value. It should be noted that windows are not used with LAG and LEAD – you may only use the PARTITION BY and ORDER BY, but not ROWS or RANGE.

So, in our example:

```
4              hiredate - lag( hiredate, 1, null )
5                     over ( partition by deptno
6                          order by hiredate, ename ) days_last,
```

We used LAG to find the record 'in front' of the current record by passing 1 as the second parameter (if there was no preceding record NULL would be returned by default). We partitioned the data by DEPTNO so each department was done independent of the others. We ordered the group by HIREDATE so that LAG(HIREDATE, 1, NULL) would return the largest HIREDATE that was less then the current record.

Caveats

With analytic functions, I have found very few caveats. They answer a whole new range of questions in a much more efficient way than was possible before their introduction. Once you master their syntax, the possibilities are limitless. It is very rarely that I will say you can get something for nothing but with analytic functions this seems to be the case. However, here are four things to be aware of.

PL/SQL and Analytic functions

In the areas of errors you might encounter, PL/SQL and analytic functions will be one. If I take a simple query and put it into a PL/SQL block such as:

```
scott@TKYTE816> variable x refcursor

scott@TKYTE816> set autoprint on

scott@TKYTE816> begin
  2   open :x for
  3   select mgr, ename,
  4          row_number() over (partition by mgr
  5                                  order by ename)
  6          rn from emp;
  7   end;
  8   /
          row_number() over (partition by mgr
                             *
ERROR at line 5:
ORA-06550: line 5, column 31:
PLS-00103: Encountered the symbol "(" when expecting one of the following:
, from into bulk
```

PL/SQL will reject it. The SQL parser used by PL/SQL does not understand this syntax as yet. Anytime I have that happen however (there are other constructs that will confuse PL/SQL as well) I use a dynamically opened ref cursor. An implementation of the above would look like this:

```
scott@TKYTE816> variable x refcursor

scott@TKYTE816> set autoprint on

scott@TKYTE816> begin
  2    open :x for
  3    'select mgr, ename,
  4           row_number() over (partition by mgr
  5                                  order by ename)
  6      rn from emp';
  7    end;
  8    /

PL/SQL procedure successfully completed.

       MGR ENAME           RN
---------- ---------- ----------
      7566 FORD               1
      7566 SCOTT              2
      7698 ALLEN              1
      7698 JAMES              2
      7698 MARTIN             3
      7698 TURNER             4
      7698 WARD               5
      7782 MILLER             1
      7788 ADAMS              1
      7839 BLAKE              1
      7839 CLARK              2
      7839 JONES              3
      7902 SMITH              1
           KING               1

14 rows selected.
```

What we have to do here is 'trick' the PL/SQL parser by not letting it see the constructs that it does not understand – the ROW_NUMBER() function in this case. Dynamically opened ref cursors are the way to accomplish this. They behave just like a *normal* cursor once we have them open, we fetch from them, close them and so on but the PL/SQL engine doesn't attempt to parse the statements at either compile time or run-time – so the syntax succeeds.

Another solution is to create a permanent VIEW using the query with the analytic functions and accessing the view in the PL/SQL block. For example:

```
scott@TKYTE816> create or replace view
  2    emp_view
  3    as
  4    select mgr, ename,
  5           row_number() over (partition by mgr
  6                                  order by ename) rn
  7      from emp
  8    /
```

```
View created.

scott@TKYTE816> begin
  2    open :x for
  3    'select mgr, ename,
  4              row_number() over (partition by mgr
  5                                 order by ename)
  6  rn from emp';
  7  end;
  8  /

PL/SQL procedure successfully completed.

     MGR ENAME                  RN
---------- ---------- ----------
    7566 FORD                   1
    7566 SCOTT                  2
```

Analytic Functions in the Where Clause

It should be noted that analytic functions are the last set of operations performed in a query except for the final ORDER BY clause. What this means is that we cannot use an analytic function directly in a predicate – you cannot use where or having clause on them. Rather we will have to use an inline view if we need to select from a resultset based on the outcome of an analytic function. Analytic functions can appear only in the select list or ORDER BY clause of a query.

We have seen many cases in this chapter we we've used the inline view capability – the *TOP-N Query* section had quite a few. For example to find the group of employees, by department, that made the top three salaries we coded:

```
scott@TKYTE816> select *
  2  from (select deptno, ename, sal,
  3          dense_rank() over (partition by deptno
  4                             order by sal desc) dr
  5           from emp)
  6  where dr <= 3
  7  order by deptno, sal desc
  8  /
```

Since the DENSE_RANK cannot be used in the where clause directly, we must push it into an inline view and alias it (DR in the above) so that we can later use DR in a predicate to get just the rows we want. We'll find this to be a common operation with analytic functions.

NULLS and Sorting

NULLS can affect the outcome of the analytic functions – especially when you use a descending sort. By default, NULLS are greater than any other value. Consider this for example:

```
scott@TKYTE816> select ename, comm from emp order by comm desc;

ENAME           COMM
---------- ----------
SMITH
JONES
CLARK
BLAKE
SCOTT
KING
JAMES
MILLER
FORD
ADAMS
MARTIN          1400
WARD             500
ALLEN            300
TURNER             0

14 rows selected.
```

If we applied our TOP-N logic to this, we may get:

```
scott@TKYTE816> select ename, comm, dr
  2  from (select ename, comm,
  3         dense_rank() over (order by comm desc)
  4        dr from emp)
  5  where dr <= 3
  6  order by comm
  8  /

ENAME           COMM          DR
---------- ---------- ----------
SMITH                          1
JONES                          1
CLARK                          1
BLAKE                          1
SCOTT                          1
KING                           1
JAMES                          1
MILLER                         1
FORD                           1
ADAMS                          1
MARTIN          1400           2
WARD             500           3

12 rows selected.
```

While this may technically be 'correct' it probably is not what you really wanted. You would either not want NULLS to be considered at all or to have NULLS be interpreted as 'small' in this case. So, we can either remove NULLS from consideration, using where comm is not null:

```
scott@TKYTE816> select ename, comm, dr
  2  from (select ename, comm,
  3          dense_rank() over (order by comm desc)
  4          dr from emp
  5          where comm is not null)
  6  where dr <= 3
  7  order by comm desc
  8  /

ENAME           COMM         DR
---------- ---------- ----------
MARTIN          1400          1
WARD             500          2
ALLEN            300          3
```

or we can use the NULLS LAST extension to the ORDER BY clause:

```
scott@TKYTE816> select ename, comm, dr
  2  from (select ename, comm,
  3          dense_rank() over (order by comm desc nulls last)
  4          dr from emp
  5          where comm is not null)
  6  where dr <= 3
  7  order by comm desc
  8  /

ENAME           COMM         DR
---------- ---------- ----------
MARTIN          1400          1
WARD             500          2
ALLEN            300          3
```

It should be noted that the NULLS LAST works on a normal ORDER BY as well; its use is not limited to the analytic functions.

Performance

So far, everything we've seen about analytic functions makes it look as if they are the silver bullet for performance tuning – if you use them everything will go fast. That's not an accurate representation of any technology or feature that I have ever come across anywhere. Anything can be abused and negatively impact on performance. Analytic functions are no different in this regard.

The one thing to be wary of with these functions is the extreme ease with which they allow you to sort and sift a set of data in ways that SQL never could. Each analytic function call in a select list may have different partitions, different windows and different sort orders. If they are not compatible with each other (not subsets of each other) you could be doing a massive amount of sorting and sifting. For example, early on we ran this query:

```
ops$tkyte@DEV816> select ename, deptno,
  2          sum(sal) over ( order by ename, deptno) sum_ename_deptno,
  3          sum(sal) over ( order by deptno, ename ) sum_deptno_ename
  4      from emp
  5    order by ename, deptno
  6  /
```

There are three ORDER BY clauses in this query, and as such, potentially three sorts involved. Two of the sorts might be done together since they sort on the same columns but the other sort will have to be done independently. This is not a *bad* thing, this is not cause for alarm, this should not cause you to outlaw the use of this feature. It is simply something to take into consideration. You can just as easily write the query that will consume all available machine resources using this feature as you can write queries that elegantly and efficiently answer your questions.

Summary

In this chapter, we thoroughly explored the syntax and implementation of analytic functions. We have seen how many common operations such as running totals, pivoting resultsets, accessing 'nearby' rows in the current row and so on are now easily achieved. Analytic functions open up a whole new potential for queries.

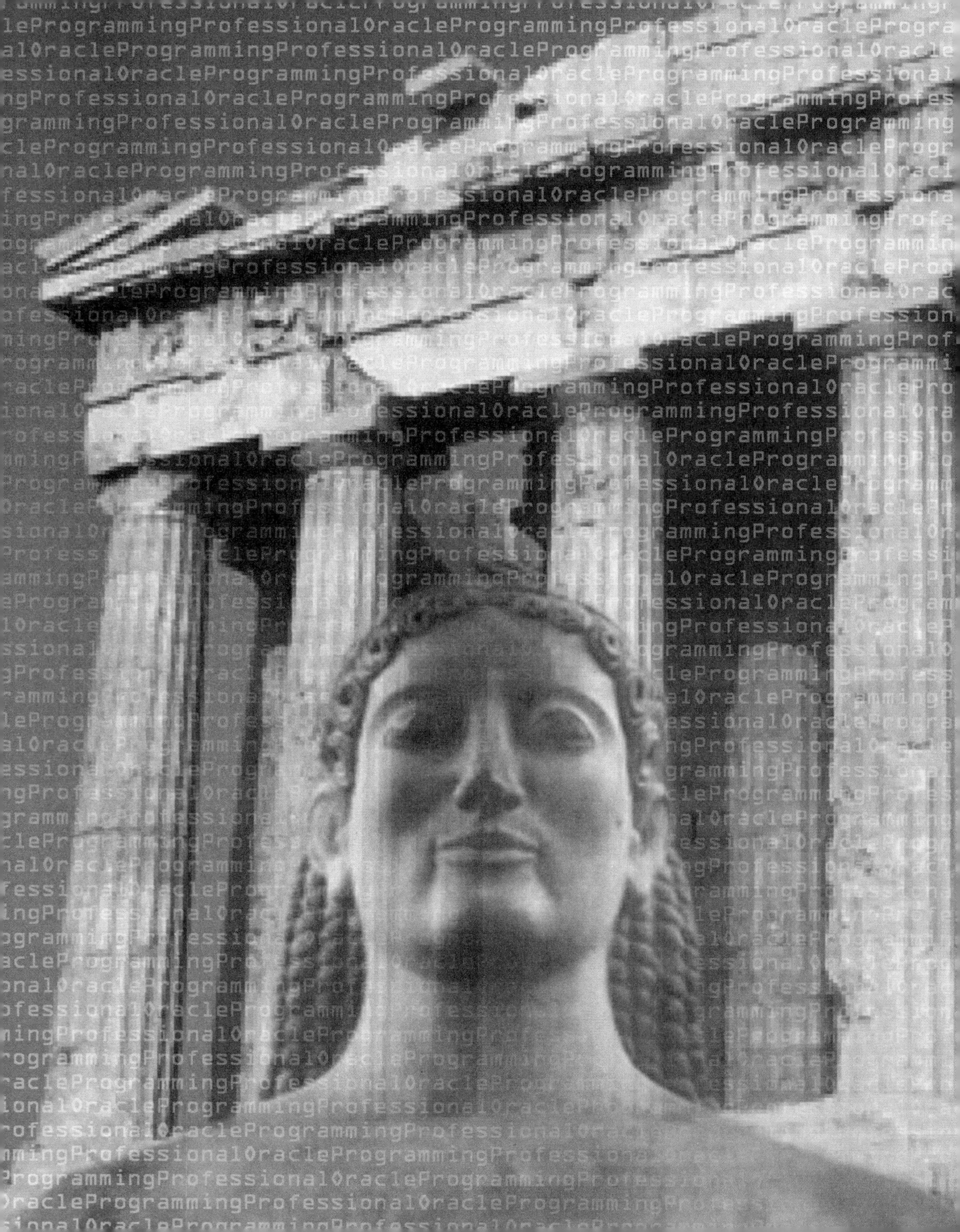
ProfessionalOracleProgramming

13

Materialized Views

Materialized views are a data warehousing/decision support system tool that can increase by many orders of magnitude the speed of queries that access a large number (maybe many hundreds of thousands or millions) of records. In basic terms, they allow a user to query potentially terabytes of detail data in seconds (or less). They accomplish this by transparently using pre-computed summarizations and joins of data. These pre-computed summaries would typically be very small compared to the original source data.

Say, for example, your company has a sales database loaded with the details of a million orders, and you want to get a breakdown of sales by region (a common enough query). Each and every record would be scanned, the data aggregated to the region level, and the calculation performed. Using a materialized view, we can store a summary of the sales data by region, and have the system maintain these summaries for us. If you have ten sales regions, this summary will have ten records, so instead of sifting through a million detail records, we'll query only ten. Furthermore, if someone asks a slightly different question, say for the sales in a specific region, then that query can also obtain the answer from the materialized view.

In this chapter you'll find out what materialized views are, what they can do and, most importantly, how they work – a lot of the 'magic' goes on behind the scenes. Having gone to the trouble of creating it, you'll find out how to make sure that your materialized view is used by *all* queries to which the view is capable of providing the answer (sometimes, *you* know Oracle could use the materialized view, but it is not able to do so simply because it lacks important information). Specifically, we will:

- ❑ Run through an example that will demonstrate the essential power of materialized views, and help you decide quickly whether it is a feature you might want to use.

- ❑ Discuss the various parameters and privileges that must be set in order to use this feature.

- ❑ Investigate, with examples, the use of constraints and dimensions to let the database know when to use a materialized view to answer a query in the most effective manner.

❑ Look at how to use the DBMS_OLAP package to analyze your views.

❑ Round off the chapter with two caveats you should be aware of when using materialized views.

A Brief History

Summary table management, another term for the materialized view, has actually been around for some time in tools such as **Oracle Discoverer** (an ad-hoc query and reporting tool). Using Discoverer, an administrator would set up various summary tables in the database. The tool would then parse queries before sending them to Oracle. If it determined that some summary table existed, which could answer the question more readily, it would rewrite the query to access the summary tables, rather than the underlying table that was originally specified in the query, and submit it to Oracle for processing. This was great, as long you used that tool to process your queries. If you ran a query in SQL*PLUS, or from your Java JDBC client, then the query rewrite would not (could not) take place. Furthermore, the synchronization between the details (original source data) and the summaries could not be performed or validated for you automatically, since the tool ran outside the database.

Furthermore, since version 7.0, the Oracle database itself has actually implemented a feature with many of the characteristics of summary tables – the **Snapshot**. This feature was initially designed to support replication, but I would use it myself to 'pre-answer' large queries. So, I would have snapshots that did not use a database link to replicate data from database to database, but rather just summarized or pre-joined frequently accessed data. This was good, but without any query rewrite capability, it was still problematic. The application had to know to use the summary tables in the first place, and this made the application more complex to code and maintain. If I added a new summary then I would have to find the code that could make use of it, and rewrite that code.

In Oracle 8.1.5 (Enterprise and Personal Editions) Oracle took the query rewriting capabilities from tools like Discoverer, the automated refresh and scheduling mechanisms from snapshots (that makes the summary tables 'self maintaining'), and combined these with the optimizer's ability to find the best plan out of many alternatives. This produced the materialized view.

With all of this functionality centralized in the database, now *every* application can take advantage of the **automated query rewrite facility**, regardless of whether access to the database is via SQL*PLUS, Oracle Forms, JDBC, ODBC, Pro*C, OCI, or some third party tool. Every Oracle 8i enterprise database can have summary table management. Also, since everything takes place inside the database, the details can be easily synchronized with the summaries, or at least the database knows when they *aren't* synchronized, and might bypass 'stale' summaries (you control its behavior in this case). By putting the functionality right in front of the data, anything that can access Oracle can take advantage of this functionality.

> *The same philosophy underpins features such as Fine Grained Access Control (see the section on Openness in Chapter 1 and also Chapter 21, which is dedicated to FGAC). The closer to the data these functions are, the broader the audience that can appreciate them. If you put security outside the database, in an application perhaps, only people who use the application can make use of it (hence the only access to the data is via the application).*

What you'll need to run the Examples

In order to run the examples in this chapter you'll need access to a Personal or Enterprise Edition of Oracle 8.1.5, or higher. This functionality is not provided in the Standard release. You will need a user account with the following privileges (at least):

❑   GRANT CREATE SESSION

❑   GRANT CREATE TABLE

❑   GRANT CREATE MATERIALIZED VIEW

❑   GRANT QUERY REWRITE

The first three privileges above may be granted to a role that you have been granted. The QUERY REWRITE privilege must be granted directly to you.

Additionally, you'll need access to a tablespace with about 30 – 50MB of free space.

Finally, you must be using the **C**ost-**B**ased **O**ptimizer (**CBO**) in order to make use of query rewrite. If you do not use the CBO, query rewrite will not take place. In these examples, our optimizer goal will be left at the default of CHOOSE; simply analyzing the tables will ensure we can take advantage of query rewrite.

An Example

A quick example will demonstrate what a materialized view entails. The concept demonstrated below is that of reducing the execution time of a long running query transparently, by summarizing data in the database. A query against a large table will be transparently rewritten into a query against a very small table, without any loss of accuracy in the answer. We'll start with a large table that contains a list of owners of objects, and the objects they own. This table is based on the ALL_OBJECTS data dictionary view:

```
tkyte@TKYTE816> create table my_all_objects
  2  nologging
  3  as
  4  select * from all_objects
  5  union all
  6  select * from all_objects
  7  union all
  8  select * from all_objects
  9  /

Table created.

tkyte@TKYTE816> insert /*+ APPEND */ into my_all_objects
  2  select * from my_all_objects;

65742 rows created.

tkyte@TKYTE816> commit;

Commit complete.
```

595

```
tkyte@TKYTE816> insert /*+ APPEND */ into my_all_objects
  2  select * from my_all_objects;

131484 rows created.

tkyte@TKYTE816> commit;

Commit complete.

tkyte@TKYTE816> analyze table my_all_objects compute statistics;

Table analyzed.
```

On my system, I have the Java option installed so the MY_ALL_OBJECTS table has about 250000 rows in it after the above. You may have to adjust the number of times you UNION ALL and INSERT, in order to achieve the same effect. Now, we'll execute a query against this table that shows the number of objects owned by each user. Initially, this will require a full scan of the large table we have above:

```
tkyte@TKYTE816> set autotrace on
tkyte@TKYTE816> set timing on
tkyte@TKYTE816> select owner, count(*) from my_all_objects group by owner;

OWNER                            COUNT(*)
------------------------------ ----------
A                                      36
B                                      24
CTXSYS                               2220
DBSNMP                                 48
DEMO                                   60
DEMO11                                 36
DEMO_DDL                              108
MDSYS                                2112
MV_USER                                60
ORDPLUGINS                            312
ORDSYS                               2472
OUR_TYPES                              12
OUTLN                                  60
PERFSTAT                              636
PUBLIC                             117972
SCHEDULER                              36
SCOTT                                  84
SEAPARK                                36
SYS                                135648
SYSTEM                                624
TESTING                               276
TKYTE                                  12
TTS_USER                               48
TYPES                                  36

24 rows selected.

Elapsed: 00:00:03.35

tkyte@TKYTE816> set timing off
tkyte@TKYTE816> set autotrace traceonly
tkyte@TKYTE816> select owner, count(*) from my_all_objects group by owner;
```

```
24 rows selected.

Execution Plan
----------------------------------------------------------
   0      SELECT STATEMENT Optimizer=CHOOSE (Cost=2525 Card=24 Bytes=120)
   1   0    SORT (GROUP BY) (Cost=2525 Card=24 Bytes=120)
   2   1      TABLE ACCESS (FULL) OF 'MY_ALL_OBJECTS' (Cost=547 Card=262968

Statistics
----------------------------------------------------------
      0   recursive calls
     27   db block gets
   3608   consistent gets
   3516   physical reads
      0   redo size
   1483   bytes sent via SQL*Net to client
    535   bytes received via SQL*Net from client
      3   SQL*Net roundtrips to/from client
      1   sorts (memory)
      0   sorts (disk)
     24   rows processed
```

In order to get the aggregate count, we must count 250000+ records on over 3600 blocks. Unfortunately, in our system we ask this question frequently, dozens of times every day. We are scanning almost 30MB of data. We could avoid counting the details each and every time by creating a materialized view of the data. The following demonstrates the basic steps needed to perform this operation. We'll discuss the GRANT and ALTER statements in more detail in the *How Materialized Views Work* section. In addition to the grants below, you might need the CREATE MATERIALIZED VIEW privilege as well, depending on what roles you have been granted and have enabled:

```
tkyte@TKYTE816> grant query rewrite to tkyte;

Grant succeeded.

tkyte@TKYTE816> alter session set query_rewrite_enabled=true;

Session altered.

tkyte@TKYTE816> alter session set query_rewrite_integrity=enforced;

Session altered.

tkyte@TKYTE816> create materialized view my_all_objects_aggs
  2  build immediate
  3  refresh on commit
  4  enable query rewrite
  5  as
  6  select owner, count(*)
  7    from my_all_objects
  8   group by owner
  9  /

Materialized view created.

tkyte@TKYTE816> analyze table my_all_objects_aggs compute statistics;
Table analyzed.
```

Basically, what we've done is pre-calculate the object count, and define this summary information as a materialized view. We have asked that the view be immediately built and populated with data. You'll notice that we have also specified REFRESH ON COMMIT and ENABLE QUERY REWRITE, but more on these in a moment. Also notice that we may have created a materialized view, but when we ANALYZE, we are analyzing a table. A materialized view creates a real table, and this table may be indexed, analyzed, and so on.

First, let's see the view in action by issuing the same query again (the query that we used to define the view itself):

```
tkyte@TKYTE816> set timing on
tkyte@TKYTE816> select owner, count(*)
  2    from my_all_objects
  3    group by owner;

OWNER                           COUNT(*)
------------------------------ ----------
A                                     36
B                                     24
...
TYPES                                 36

24 rows selected.

Elapsed: 00:00:00.10

tkyte@TKYTE816> set timing off

tkyte@TKYTE816> set autotrace traceonly
tkyte@TKYTE816> select owner, count(*)
  2    from my_all_objects
  3    group by owner;

24 rows selected.


Execution Plan
----------------------------------------------------------
   0      SELECT STATEMENT Optimizer=CHOOSE (Cost=1 Card=24 Bytes=216)
   1    0   TABLE ACCESS (FULL) OF 'MY_ALL_OBJECTS_AGGS' (Cost=1 Card=Valve)

Statistics
----------------------------------------------------------
          0  recursive calls
         12  db block gets
          7  consistent gets
          0  physical reads
          0  redo size
       1483  bytes sent via SQL*Net to client
        535  bytes received via SQL*Net from client
          3  SQL*Net roundtrips to/from client
          0  sorts (memory)
          0  sorts (disk)
         24  rows processed

tkyte@TKYTE816> set autotrace off
```

From over 3,600 consistent gets (logical I/Os), to just 12. No physical I/O this time around as the data was found in the cache. Our buffer cache will be much more efficient now as it has less to cache. I could not even begin to cache the previous query's working set, but now I can. Notice how our query plan shows we are now doing a full scan of the MY_ALL_OBJECTS_AGGS table, even though we queried the detail table MY_ALL_OBJECTS. When the SELECT OWNER, COUNT(*)... query is issued, the database automatically directs it to our materialized view.

Let's take this a step further by adding a new row to the MY_ALL_OBJECTS table, and committing the change:

```
tkyte@TKYTE816> insert into my_all_objects
  2  ( owner, object_name, object_type, object_id )
  3  values
  4  ( 'New Owner', 'New Name', 'New Type', 1111111 );

1 row created.

tkyte@TKYTE816> commit;

Commit complete.
```

Now, we issue effectively the same query again, but this time we're just looking at our newly inserted row:

```
tkyte@TKYTE816> set timing on
tkyte@TKYTE816> select owner, count(*)
  2     from my_all_objects
  3     where owner = 'New Owner'
  4     group by owner;

OWNER                          COUNT(*)
------------------------------ ----------
New Owner                             1

Elapsed: 00:00:00.01
tkyte@TKYTE816> set timing off

tkyte@TKYTE816> set autotrace traceonly
tkyte@TKYTE816> select owner, count(*)
  2     from my_all_objects
  3     where owner = 'New Owner'
  4     group by owner;


Execution Plan
----------------------------------------------------------
   0      SELECT STATEMENT Optimizer=CHOOSE (Cost=1 Card=1 Bytes=9)
   1    0    TABLE ACCESS (FULL) OF 'MY_ALL_OBJECTS_AGGS' (Cost=1 Card=Valve)

Statistics
----------------------------------------------------------
          0  recursive calls
         12  db block gets
          6  consistent gets
          0  physical reads
          0  redo size
        430  bytes sent via SQL*Net to client
        424  bytes received via SQL*Net from client
```

```
        2   SQL*Net roundtrips to/from client
        0   sorts (memory)
        0   sorts (disk)
        1   rows processed

tkyte@TKYTE816> set autotrace off
```

The analysis shows that we scanned the materialized view and found the new row. By specifying REFRESH ON COMMIT in our original definition of the view, we requested that Oracle maintain synchronization between the view and the details – when we update the details, the summary will be maintained as well. It cannot maintain synchronization in every case of an arbitrary materialized view, but in the case of a single table summary (as we have) or joins with no aggregation, it can.

Now, one last query:

```
tkyte@TKYTE816> set timing on
tkyte@TKYTE816> select count(*)
  2    from my_all_objects
  3    where owner = 'New Owner';

   COUNT(*)
----------
          1

Elapsed: 00:00:00.00

tkyte@TKYTE816> set timing off

tkyte@TKYTE816> set autotrace traceonly
tkyte@TKYTE816> select count(*)
  2    from my_all_objects
  3    where owner = 'New Owner';


Execution Plan
----------------------------------------------------------
   0       SELECT STATEMENT Optimizer=CHOOSE (Cost=1 Card=1 Bytes=9)
   1    0    SORT (AGGREGATE)
   2    1      TABLE ACCESS (FULL) OF 'MY_ALL_OBJECTS_AGGS' (Cost=1 Card=Valve)

Statistics
----------------------------------------------------------
        0   recursive calls
       12   db block gets
        5   consistent gets
        0   physical reads
        0   redo size
      367   bytes sent via SQL*Net to client
      424   bytes received via SQL*Net from client
        2   SQL*Net roundtrips to/from client
        0   sorts (memory)
        0   sorts (disk)
        1   rows processed
tkyte@TKYTE816> set autotrace off
```

We can see that Oracle is smart enough to use the view even when the query appears to be slightly different. There was no GROUP BY clause here, yet the database recognized that the materialized view could still be used. This is what makes materialized views 'magical'. The end users do not have to be aware of these summary tables. The database will realize for us that the answer already exists and, as long as we enable query rewrite (which we did), will automatically rewrite the query to use them. This feature allows you to immediately impact existing applications, without changing a single query.

Uses of Materialized Views

This is relatively straightforward and is answered in a single word – *performance*. By calculating the answers to the really hard questions up front (and once only), we will greatly reduce the load on our machine. We will experience:

- ❏ **Less physical reads** – There is less data to scan through.

- ❏ **Less writes** – We will not be sorting/aggregating as frequently.

- ❏ **Decreased CPU consumption** — We will not be calculating aggregates and functions on the data, as we will have already done that.

- ❏ **Markedly faster response times** – Our queries will return incredibly quickly when a summary is used, as opposed to the details. This will be a function of the amount of work we can avoid by using the materialized view, but many orders of magnitude is not out of the question.

Materialized views will increase your need for one resource – more permanently allocated disk. We need extra storage space to accommodate the materialized views, of course, but for the price of a little extra disk space, we can reap a lot of benefit.

Materialized views work best in a read-only, or read-intensive environment. They are *not* designed for use in a high-end OLTP environment. They will add overhead to modifications performed on the base tables in order to capture the changes. There are concurrency issues with regards to using the REFRESH ON COMMIT option. Consider our summary example from before. Any rows that are inserted or deleted from this table will have to update one of 24 rows in the summary table in order to maintain the count in real time. What this means is that, at most, you can have 24 people committing at the same time (assuming they all affect a different owner that is). This does not preclude the use of materialized views in an OLTP environment. For example if you use full refreshes on a recurring basis (during off-peak time) there will be no overhead added to the modifications, and there would be no concurrency issues. This would allow you to report on yesterday's activities, for example, and not query the live OLTP data for reports.

How Materialized Views Work

Materialized views may appear to be hard to work with at first. There will be cases where you create a materialized view, and *you know* that the view holds the answer to a certain question but, for some reason, Oracle does not. If you dig deep enough, you'll discover why, and it always comes back to the fact that Oracle is just a piece of software, and can only work with the information disk provided with it. The more meta data provided, the more pieces of information about the underlying data you can give to Oracle, the better. These pieces of information are mundane things that you might not even think about in a data warehouse environment, such as NOT NULL constraints, primary keys, foreign keys and so on. The meta data provided by these keys and constraints gives the optimizer more information, and hence, more of a chance.

*Not only do keys and constraints, such as those listed above preserve data integrity, they also add information **about** the data, into the data dictionary, which can be used in query rewrites – hence the term **met adata**. See the 'Constraints' section for further information.*

In the following sections we will look at what you have to do to set up materialized views, some examples of using them, and how adding more information, more meta data, to the database will make materialized views work more often.

Setting Up

There is one mandatory INIT.ORA parameter necessary for materialized views to function, and this is the COMPATIBLE parameter. The value of COMPATIBLE should be set to 8.1.0, or above, in order for query rewrites to be functional. If this value is not set appropriately, query rewrite will not be invoked.

There are two other relevant parameters that may be set at either the system-level (via the INIT.ORA file), or the session-level (via the ALTER SESSION command). They are:

❑ QUERY_REWRITE_ENABLED – Unless the value of this parameter is set to TRUE, query rewrites will not take place. The default value is FALSE.

❑ QUERY_REWRITE_INTEGRITY – This parameter controls *how* Oracle rewrites queries and may be set to one of three values:

ENFORCED – Queries will be rewritten using only constraints and rules that are enforced and guaranteed by Oracle. There are mechanisms by which we can tell Oracle about other inferred relationships, and this would allow for more queries to be rewritten, but since Oracle does not enforce those relationships, it would not make use of these facts at this level.

TRUSTED – Queries will be rewritten using the constraints that are enforced by Oracle, as well as any relationships existing in the data that we have told Oracle about, but are not enforced by the database. For example, in our initial example we could have created the physical table MY_ALL_OBJECTS_AGGS manually using a parallel, no-logging CREATE TABLE AS SELECT (to speed up the building of the summary table). We could have then created the materialized view, instructing it to use this pre-built table instead of creating the summary table itself. If we wish Oracle to use this pre-built table during a subsequent query rewrite, we must specify a value of TRUSTED. This is because we want Oracle to 'trust' that we have supplied the correct data in the pre-built table – Oracle does not enforce that the data in this table is correct.

STALE_TOLERATED – Queries will be rewritten to use materialized views even if Oracle knows the data contained in the materialized view is 'stale' (out-of-sync with the details). This might be useful in an environment where the summary tables are refreshed on a recurring basis, not on commit, and a slightly out-of-sync answer is acceptable.

In the example above, you saw the ALTER SESSION statements that enable this query rewrite magic. Since the example used only relationships and objects enforced by Oracle, the query rewrite integrity could be set to the highest level – ENFORCED.

I also needed to grant QUERY REWRITE privileges to myself. Now, the account I used happened to be a DBA account, which has QUERY REWRITE, so why did I need to grant the privilege directly to myself? The reason is that you cannot create compiled stored objects such as materialized views, stored procedures, and triggers that rely on privileges from a role (the DBA role in this case). See Chapter 23, *Invoker and Definers Rights*, for a full explanation of the use of roles and compiled stored objects. If you create a materialized view with QUERY REWRITE enabled, but do not have QUERY REWRITE system privilege yourself, you will receive the following error:

```
create materialized view my_all_objects_aggs
*
ERROR at line 1:
ORA-01031: insufficient privileges
```

Internal Mechanics

So, now that we can create a materialized view and show that it works, what are the steps Oracle will undertake to rewrite our queries? Normally, when QUERY_REWRITE_ENABLED is set to FALSE, Oracle will take your SQL as is, parse it, and optimize it. With query rewrites enabled, Oracle will insert an extra step into this process. After parsing, Oracle will attempt to rewrite the query to access some materialized view, instead of the actual table that it references. If it can perform a query rewrite, the rewritten query (or queries) is parsed and then optimized along with the original query. The query plan with the lowest cost from this set is chosen for execution. If it cannot rewrite the query, the original parsed query is optimized and executed as normal.

Query Rewrite

When query rewrite is enabled, Oracle will use the following steps to try and rewrite a query with a materialized view.

Full Exact Text Match

In this method, Oracle considers possible exact string matches in the set of available materialized views found in the data dictionary. In the example above, this is the method Oracle would have used for the very first query that used the materialized view. The algorithm used is 'friendlier' (more flexible) than a shared pool comparison (which demands an exact byte-for-byte match) as it ignores whitespace, case of characters, and other formatting.

Partial Text Match

Starting with the FROM clause, the optimizer compares the remaining text of the materialized view's defining query. This allows for mismatches between items in the SELECT list. If the data you need can be generated from the materialized view (if your SELECT list can be satisfied) Oracle will rewrite the query using the materialized view. The query SELECT LOWER(OWNER) FROM MY_ALL_OBJECTS GROUP BY OWNER; would be an example of a partial text match.

General Query Rewrite Methods

These enable the use of a materialized view even if it contains only part of the data, more data than requested, or data that can be converted. The optimizer tests the materialized view's definition against the individual components of the query (SELECT, FROM, WHERE, GROUP BY) to find a match. The checks that Oracle performs against these components are:

❑ **Data sufficiency** – Can the required data be obtained from a given materialized view? If you ask for column X, and column X is not in the materialized view and, furthermore, it is not retrievable via some join with the materialized view, then Oracle will not rewrite the query to use that view. For example, the query SELECT DISTINCT OWNER FROM MY_ALL_OBJECTS, using our previous example, can be rewritten using our materialized view – the OWNER column is available. The query SELECT DISTINCT OBJECT_TYPE FROM MY_ALL_OBJECTS cannot be satisfied using the materialized view, as the view does not have sufficient data.

❑ **Join compatibility** – Ensures that any JOIN required by the submitted query can be satisfied by the materialized view.

We can look at an example of join compatibility using MY_ALL_OBJECTS and the following tables:

```
tkyte@TKYTE816> create table t1 ( owner varchar2(30), flag char(1) );

Table created.

tkyte@TKYTE816> create table t2 ( object_type varchar2(30), flag char(1) );

Table created.
```

The following query is join-compatible with the materialized view – the query can and will be rewritten using the materialized view:

```
tkyte@TKYTE816> select a.owner, count(*), b.owner
  2      from my_all_objects a, t1 b
  3    where a.owner = b.owner
  4      and b.flag is not null
  5    group by a.owner, b.owner
  6  /
```

The database can see that using our materialized view, or the actual base table would result in the same answer. However, the following query, while similar, is not join-compatible:

```
tkyte@TKYTE816> select a.owner, count(*), b.object_type
  2      from my_all_objects a, t2 b
  3    where a.object_type = b.object_type
  4      and b.flag is not null
  5    group by a.owner, b.object_type
  6  /
```

The OBJECT_TYPE column is not in our materialized view, so Oracle cannot rewrite this query using the materialized view.

Grouping Compatibility

This is required if both the materialized view and the query contain a GROUP BY clause. If the materialized view is grouped at the same level, or is grouped at a higher level of detail than is needed, the query will be rewritten to use the materialized view. The query SELECT COUNT(*) FROM MY_ALL_OBJECTS GROUP BY 1; applied against our first example would be a case where the materialized view is grouped at a higher level of detail than is needed. The database can rewrite this query to use our materialized view even though the grouping for the query is not the same as the grouping for the materialized view.

Aggregate Compatibility

This is required if both query and materialized view contain aggregates. It will ensure that the materialized view can satisfy the required aggregates. It can perform some interesting rewrites in some cases. For example, it will recognize that AVG(X) is the same as SUM(X)/COUNT(X), so a query that requires AVG(X) can be satisfied by a materialized view with the SUM and COUNT.

In many cases, simple application of the above rules will allow Oracle to rewrite a query to use a materialized view. In other cases (as we will see in an example below), the database will need a little more help from you. You will need to give it additional information in order for it to recognize that it can use a materialized view to answer a question.

Making sure your View gets used

In this section, we'll look at ways to do this, first by using **constraints** to help us make use of a query rewrite, and then by using **dimensions**, which are a means of describing complex relationships – hierarchies of data.

Constraints

I've been asked in the past, 'Why should I use a primary key? Why not just use a unique index?' Well, the answer is that you could, but doesn't the fact you used a primary key say something over and above just using a unique index? In fact it does – it can say a lot. The same goes for the use of foreign keys, NOT NULL constraints and others. Not only do they protect the data, but they also add information *about* the data into the data dictionary. Using this additional information, Oracle is able to perform a query rewrite more often, in many complex cases.

Consider the following small example. We will copy the EMP and DEPT tables from the SCOTT schema, and create a materialized view that pre-joins the tables together. This materialized view differs from our first example in that it is a REFRESH ON DEMAND materialized view. This means that in order for changes to be applied to it, we will have to refresh it manually:

```
tkyte@TKYTE816> create table emp as select * from scott.emp;

Table created.

tkyte@TKYTE816> create table dept as select * from scott.dept;

Table created.

tkyte@TKYTE816> alter session set query_rewrite_enabled=true;

Session altered.

tkyte@TKYTE816> alter session set query_rewrite_integrity=enforced;

Session altered.

tkyte@TKYTE816> create materialized view emp_dept
  2  build immediate
  3  refresh on demand
  4  enable query rewrite
  5  as
  6  select dept.deptno, dept.dname, count (*)
  7    from emp, dept
  8   where emp.deptno = dept.deptno
  9   group by dept.deptno, dept.dname
 10  /

Materialized view created.

tkyte@TKYTE816> alter session set optimizer_goal=all_rows;

Session altered.
```

Since the underlying tables and the resulting materialized view are very small, we force the use of the cost-based optimizer using the ALTER SESSION command, instead of analyzing tables as we would normally. If Oracle knew how small these tables were, it would not do some of the optimizations we would like. Using the 'default' statistics, it will behave as if the tables were fairly large.

Now, we have withheld a lot of information from Oracle here. It does not understand the relationship between EMP and DEPT, does not know which columns are primary keys, and so on. Now, let's run a query, and see what happens:

```
tkyte@TKYTE816> set autotrace on
tkyte@TKYTE816> select count(*) from emp;

  COUNT(*)
----------
        14


Execution Plan
----------------------------------------------------------
   0      SELECT STATEMENT Optimizer=ALL_ROWS (Cost=1 Card=1)
   1    0   SORT (AGGREGATE)
   2    1     TABLE ACCESS (FULL) OF 'EMP' (Cost=1 Card=82)
```

The query has been directed at the underlying EMP table. Now, you and I know that the COUNT(*) query could easily, and more efficiently (especially if the number of employees in each department was large, and there were lots of departments), have been answered from the materialized view. There, we have all of the information we need to get the count of employees. We know this because we are aware of things about the data that we kept from Oracle:

❑   DEPTNO is the primary key of DEPT – This means that each EMP record will join to, at most, one DEPT record.

❑   DEPTNO in EMP is a foreign key to DEPTNO in DEPT – If the DEPTNO in EMP is not a Null value, then it will be joined to a row in DEPT (we won't lose any non-Null EMP records during a join).

❑   DEPTNO in EMP is NOT NULL – This coupled with the foreign key constraint tells us we won't lose *any* EMP records.

These three facts imply that if we join EMP to DEPT, each EMP row will be observed in the resultset *at least* once and *at most* once. Since we never told Oracle these facts, it was not able to make use of the materialized view. So, let's make Oracle aware of them:

```
tkyte@TKYTE816> alter table dept
  2  add constraint dept_pk primary key(deptno);

Table altered.

tkyte@TKYTE816> alter table emp
  2  add constraint emp_fk_dept
  3  foreign key(deptno) references dept(deptno);

Table altered.

tkyte@TKYTE816> alter table emp modify deptno not null;
```

```
                       Table altered.

tkyte@TKYTE816> set autotrace on
tkyte@TKYTE816> select count(*) from emp;

  COUNT(*)
----------
        14

Execution Plan
----------------------------------------------------------
   0      SELECT STATEMENT Optimizer=ALL_ROWS (Cost=1 Card=1 Bytes=13)
   1    0   SORT (AGGREGATE)
   2    1     TABLE ACCESS (FULL) OF 'EMP_DEPT' (Cost=1 Card=82 Bytes=1066)
```

Now Oracle is able to rewrite the query using the EMP_DEPT materialized view. Any time that you know Oracle *could* use a materialized view, but it is *not* doing so (and you have verified you can use materialized views in general), take a closer look at the data and ask yourself 'What piece of information have I withheld from Oracle?' Nine times out of ten, you'll find a missing piece of meta data that, when included, allows Oracle to rewrite the query.

So, what happens if this is a true data warehouse, and there are tens of millions of records in the above tables? You don't really want the additional effort of verifying a foreign key relationship – you already did that in your data scrubbing routine, didn't you? In this case, you can create a non-validated constraint, one that is used to inform the database about a relationship, but it has not been validated by the database itself. Let's look at the above example again, but this time we'll simulate the loading of data into an existing data warehouse (our example above is our data warehouse). We'll drop our constraints, load the data, refresh the materialized views, and add our constraints back. We'll start with dropping the constraints:

```
tkyte@TKYTE816> alter table emp drop constraint emp_fk_dept;

Table altered.

tkyte@TKYTE816> alter table dept drop constraint dept_pk;

Table altered.

tkyte@TKYTE816> alter table emp modify deptno null;

Table altered.
```

Now, in order to simulate our load, I will insert a single new row into EMP (not much of a load, I know, but enough for demonstration purposes). Then, we will refresh our materialized view and tell Oracle to consider it as FRESH:

```
tkyte@TKYTE816> insert into emp (empno,deptno) values ( 1, 1 );

1 row created.

tkyte@TKYTE816> exec dbms_mview.refresh( 'EMP_DEPT' );

PL/SQL procedure successfully completed.
```

```
tkyte@TKYTE816> alter materialized view emp_dept consider fresh;

Materialized view altered.
```

Now we tell Oracle about the relationships between EMP and DEPT:

```
tkyte@TKYTE816> alter table dept
  2    add constraint dept_pk primary key(deptno)
  3    rely enable NOVALIDATE
  4  /

Table altered.

tkyte@TKYTE816> alter table emp
  2    add constraint emp_fk_dept
  3    foreign key(deptno) references dept(deptno)
  4    rely enable NOVALIDATE
  5  /

Table altered.

tkyte@TKYTE816> alter table emp modify deptno not null NOVALIDATE;

Table altered.
```

So here we have told Oracle that there is a foreign key from EMP to DEPT as before. However this time, because we will have scrubbed our data prior to loading it into the warehouse, we tell Oracle not to perform any validating checks. The NOVALIDATE option bypasses the checking of existing data we loaded, and RELY tells Oracle to trust the integrity of the data. Basically, we have told Oracle to trust that if it joins EMP to DEPT by DEPTNO, every row in EMP will be retrieved at least once, and at most once.

In fact, in this case, we have 'lied' to the database. We have inserted a row into EMP that has no corresponding row in DEPT. We are now ready to query:

```
tkyte@TKYTE816> alter session set query_rewrite_integrity=enforced;

Session altered.

tkyte@TKYTE816> select count(*) from emp;

  COUNT(*)
----------
        15

Execution Plan
----------------------------------------------------------
   0      SELECT STATEMENT Optimizer=ALL_ROWS (Cost=1 Card=1)
   1    0   SORT (AGGREGATE)
   2    1     TABLE ACCESS (FULL) OF 'EMP' (Cost=1 Card=164)
```

Since we set QUERY_REWRITE_INTEGRITY=ENFORCED Oracle did not rewrite the query to use the materialized view. We must go down a level in query integrity. We need Oracle to 'trust' us:

```
tkyte@TKYTE816> alter session set query_rewrite_integrity=trusted;

Session altered.

tkyte@TKYTE816> select count(*) from emp;

  COUNT(*)
----------
        14


Execution Plan
----------------------------------------------------------
   0      SELECT STATEMENT Optimizer=ALL_ROWS (Cost=1 Card=1 Bytes=13)
   1    0   SORT (AGGREGATE)
   2    1     TABLE ACCESS (FULL) OF 'EMP_DEPT' (Cost=1 Card=82 Bytes=1066)
```

In this case, Oracle did in fact rewrite the query, but the side effect is that our newly inserted row has not been counted. The 'wrong' answer is returned because the 'fact' that each row in EMP should be preserved in a join to DEPT is not a fact, given the data we loaded. When the materialized view refreshed, it did not get the newly added EMP row. The data we told Oracle to rely on was not reliable. This demonstration highlights two important points:

❑   You can use materialized views in a large data warehouse very efficiently without having to perform lots of extra, typically redundant, verifications of the data.

❑   **BUT**, you had better be 100 percent sure that your data is scrubbed if you ask Oracle to rely on it.

Dimensions

Use of dimensions is another method by which we can give even more information to Oracle. Suppose we have a table of details giving a transaction date and a customer ID. The transaction date points to another table that gives full details of what month the transaction date was in, what quarter of your fiscal year it represents, what fiscal year it was in, and so on. Now, suppose you created a materialized view that stored aggregated sales information at the monthly level. Can Oracle use that view to answer a query for sales data for a particular quarter or year? Well, *we* know that transaction date implies month, month implies quarter, and quarter implies year, so the answer is that it *can*, but Oracle doesn't know this (yet), so although it can, it won't.

Using a database object called a DIMENSION, we can alert Oracle to these facts so that it will use them to rewrite queries in more cases. A dimension declares a parent/child relationship between pairs of columns. We can use it to describe to Oracle that, within a row of a table, the MONTH column implies the value you'll find in the QTR column, the QTR column implies the value you'll find in the YEAR column, and so on. Using a dimension, we can have a materialized view that has fewer details than the detailed records (summarized to the monthly level perhaps). This may still be at a higher level of aggregation than the query requests (the query wants data by quarter, say), but Oracle will recognize that it can use the materialized view to get the answer.

Here is a simple example. We will set up a SALES table to store the transaction date, a customer ID, and the total number of sales. This table will have about 350000 rows in it. Another table, TIME_HIERARCHY, will store the mapping of transaction date to month, to quarter, to year. If we join the two together, we can obtain aggregate sales by month, quarter, year, and so on. Likewise, if we had a table that mapped a customer ID to a zip code, and the zip code to a region, we could easily join this table to SALES, and aggregate by zip code or region.

In a conventional database schema (one without materialized views and other structures) these operations would succeed, but they would be very slow. For every row in the sales data, we would have to perform an indexed read into the lookup table to convert either the transaction date or customer ID into some other value (a NESTED LOOP JOIN) in order to group by this other value. Enter the materialized view. We can store a summarized rollup of the details, perhaps at the monthly level for the transaction date, and at the zip code level for the customer information. Now, rolling up to quarters or by region becomes a very fast operation.

We'll start by creating the SALES table, and load it with some random test data, generated using the ALL_OBJECTS view.

```
tkyte@TKYTE816> create table sales
  2  (trans_date date, cust_id int, sales_amount number );

Table created.

tkyte@TKYTE816> insert /*+ APPEND */ into sales
  2  select trunc(sysdate,'year')+mod(rownum,366) TRANS_DATE,
  3         mod(rownum,100) CUST_ID,
  4         abs(dbms_random.random)/100 SALES_AMOUNT
  5    from all_objects
  6  /

21921 rows created.

tkyte@TKYTE816> commit;

Commit complete.
```

These details will represent one year's worth of data. I set up the TRANS_DATE to simply be the first day of this year plus a number between 1 and 365. The CUST_ID is a number between 0 and 99. The total number of sales is some typically 'large' number (it was a really good year).

My ALL_OBJECTS view contains about 22000 rows, so after four inserts that consecutively double the size of the table, we'll have about 350000 records. I am using the /*+ APPEND */ hint simply to avoid the redo log that would otherwise be generated by these large inserts:

```
tkyte@TKYTE816> begin
  2      for i in 1 .. 4
  3      loop
  4          insert /*+ APPEND */ into sales
  5          select trans_date, cust_id, abs(dbms_random.random)/100
  6            from sales;
  7          commit;
  8      end loop;
  9  end;
 10  /

PL/SQL procedure successfully completed.

tkyte@TKYTE816> select count(*) from sales;

  COUNT(*)
----------
    350736
```

Now we need to set up our TIME_HIERARCHY table, to roll up the date field by month, year, quarter, and so on:

```
tkyte@TKYTE816> create table time_hierarchy
  2   (day primary key, mmyyyy, mon_yyyy, qtr_yyyy, yyyy)
  3   organization index
  4   as
  5   select distinct
  6       trans_date    DAY,
  7       cast (to_char(trans_date,'mmyyyy') as number) MMYYYY,
  8       to_char(trans_date,'mon-yyyy') MON_YYYY,
  9       'Q' || ceil( to_char(trans_date,'mm')/3) || ' FY'
 10           || to_char(trans_date,'yyyy') QTR_YYYY,
 11       cast( to_char( trans_date, 'yyyy' ) as number ) YYYY
 12     from sales
 13   /

Table created.
```

In this case, it was simple enough. We generated:

❑   MMYYYY – The month, including the year

❑   MON_YYYY – Same as above but we 'spelled' out the month

❑   QTR_YYYY – The quarter of the year, including the year

❑   YYYY – The year itself

In general, the computations required to create this table could be much more complex. For example, fiscal year quarters, typically, are not so easily computed, and neither are fiscal years. They do not generally follow the calendar year.

We'll now create the materialized view, SALES_MV. The summary we are creating rolls the data up from individual days to months. We would expect our materialized view to have about 1/30 the number of rows of our SALES table, if the data was evenly distributed:

```
tkyte@TKYTE816> analyze table sales compute statistics;

Table analyzed.

tkyte@TKYTE816> analyze table time_hierarchy compute statistics;

Table analyzed.

tkyte@TKYTE816> create materialized view sales_mv
  2   build immediate
  3   refresh on demand
  4   enable query rewrite
  5   as
  6   select sales.cust_id, sum(sales.sales_amount) sales_amount,
  7          time_hierarchy.mmyyyy
  8     from sales, time_hierarchy
  9    where sales.trans_date = time_hierarchy.day
 10    group by sales.cust_id, time_hierarchy.mmyyyy
 11   /
```

```
Materialized view created.

tkyte@TKYTE816> set autotrace on
tkyte@TKYTE816> select time_hierarchy.mmyyyy, sum(sales_amount)
  2    from sales, time_hierarchy
  3    where sales.trans_date = time_hierarchy.day
  4    group by time_hierarchy.mmyyyy
  5  /

    MMYYYY SUM(SALES_AMOUNT)
---------- -----------------
     12001        3.2177E+11
     12002        1.0200E+10
     22001        2.8848E+11
     32001        3.1944E+11
     42001        3.1012E+11
     52001        3.2066E+11
     62001        3.0794E+11
     72001        3.1796E+11
     82001        3.2176E+11
     92001        3.0859E+11
    102001        3.1868E+11
    112001        3.0763E+11
    122001        3.1305E+11

13 rows selected.

Execution Plan
----------------------------------------------------------
   0      SELECT STATEMENT Optimizer=CHOOSE (Cost=4 Card=327 Bytes=850VALVE)
   1    0   SORT (GROUP BY) (Cost=4 Card=327 Bytes=8502)
   2    1     TABLE ACCESS (FULL) OF 'SALES_MV' (Cost=1 Card=327 Bytes
```

So far, so good – Oracle rewrote the query to use the view, SALES_MV. However, let's see what happens if we issue a query that calls for a higher level of aggregation:

```
tkyte@TKYTE816> set timing on
tkyte@TKYTE816> set autotrace on
tkyte@TKYTE816> select time_hierarchy.qtr_yyyy, sum(sales_amount)
  2    from sales, time_hierarchy
  3    where sales.trans_date = time_hierarchy.day
  4    group by time_hierarchy.qtr_yyyy
  5  /

QTR_YYYY                                            SUM(SALES_AMOUNT)
-------------------------------------------------- -----------------
Q1 FY2001                                                 9.2969E+11
Q1 FY2002                                                 1.0200E+10
Q2 FY2001                                                 9.3872E+11
Q3 FY2001                                                 9.4832E+11
Q4 FY2001                                                 9.3936E+11

Elapsed: 00:00:05.58
```

```
Execution Plan
------------------------------------------------------------
   0        SELECT STATEMENT Optimizer=CHOOSE (Cost=8289 Card=5 Bytes=14)
   1     0   SORT (GROUP BY) (Cost=8289 Card=5 Bytes=145)
   2     1    NESTED LOOPS (Cost=169 Card=350736 Bytes=10171344)
   3     2     TABLE ACCESS (FULL) OF 'SALES' (Cost=169 Card=350736 B
   4     2     INDEX (UNIQUE SCAN) OF 'SYS_IOT_TOP_30180' (UNIQUE)

Statistics
------------------------------------------------------------
        0  recursive calls
       15  db block gets
   351853  consistent gets
...
```

We see that Oracle doesn't have the knowledge we have. It does not yet know that it could have used the materialized view to answer this particular query, so it used the original SALES table instead, and had to do a lot of work to get the answer. The same thing would happen if we requested data aggregated by fiscal year.

So, let's use a DIMENSION to alert Oracle to the fact that the materialized view would be useful in answering this question. First, we'll create the DIMENSION:

```
tkyte@TKYTE816> create dimension time_hierarchy_dim
  2          level day      is time_hierarchy.day
  3          level mmyyyy   is time_hierarchy.mmyyyy
  4          level qtr_yyyy is time_hierarchy.qtr_yyyy
  5          level yyyy     is time_hierarchy.yyyy
  6  hierarchy time_rollup
  7  (
  8   day child of
  9   mmyyyy child of
 10   qtr_yyyy child of
 11   yyyy
 12  )
 13  attribute mmyyyy
 14  determines mon_yyyy;

Dimension created.
```

This tells Oracle that the DAY column of the TIME_HIERARCHY table implies MMYYYY, which in turn implies QTR_YYYY. Finally, QTR_YYYY implies YYYY. Also stated is the fact that MMYYYY and MON_YYYY are synonymous – there is a one-to-one mapping between the two. So, any time Oracle sees MON_YYYY used, it understands it as if MMYYYY was used. Now that Oracle has a greater understanding of the relationships between the data we can see a marked improvement in our query response times:

```
tkyte@TKYTE816> set autotrace on
tkyte@TKYTE816> select time_hierarchy.qtr_yyyy, sum(sales_amount)
  2    from sales, time_hierarchy
  3  where sales.trans_date = time_hierarchy.day
  4  group by time_hierarchy.qtr_yyyy
  5  /
```

```
QTR_YYYY                                              SUM(SALES_AMOUNT)
------------------------------------------------- -----------------
Q1 FY2001                                                 9.2969E+11
Q1 FY2002                                                 1.0200E+10
Q2 FY2001                                                 9.3872E+11
Q3 FY2001                                                 9.4832E+11
Q4 FY2001                                                 9.3936E+11

Elapsed: 00:00:00.20

Execution Plan
----------------------------------------------------------
   0      SELECT STATEMENT Optimizer=CHOOSE (Cost=7 Card=5 Bytes=195)
   1    0   SORT (GROUP BY) (Cost=7 Card=5 Bytes=195)
   2    1     HASH JOIN (Cost=6 Card=150 Bytes=5850)
   3    2       VIEW (Cost=4 Card=46 Bytes=598)
   4    3         SORT (UNIQUE) (Cost=4 Card=46 Bytes=598)
   5    4           INDEX (FAST FULL SCAN) OF 'SYS_IOT_TOP_30180' (UNI
   6    2       TABLE ACCESS (FULL) OF 'SALES_MV' (Cost=1 Card=327 Byt

Statistics
----------------------------------------------------------
          0  recursive calls
         16  db block gets
         12  consistent gets
...
```

Well, we went from more than 350000 logical reads to 12 – not too bad at all. If you run this example, you'll be able to see the difference. The first query took a while (about six seconds), the answer to the second query was on the screen before our hands left the *Enter* key (about a fifth of a second).

We can use this DIMENSION feature many times on the same base fact table. Consider if we assign a ZIP_CODE and REGION attribute to every customer in our database:

```
tkyte@TKYTE816> create table customer_hierarchy
  2  ( cust_id primary key, zip_code, region )
  3  organization index
  4  as
  5  select cust_id,
  6    mod( rownum, 6 ) || to_char(mod( rownum, 1000 ), 'fm0000') zip_code,
  7    mod( rownum, 6 ) region
  8    from ( select distinct cust_id from sales)
  9  /

Table created.

tkyte@TKYTE816> analyze table customer_hierarchy compute statistics;

Table analyzed.
```

Next, we recreate our materialized view to be a summary that shows us SALES_AMOUNT by ZIP_CODE and MMYYYY:

```
tkyte@TKYTE816> drop materialized view sales_mv;

Materialized view dropped.

tkyte@TKYTE816> create materialized view sales_mv
  2  build immediate
  3  refresh on demand
  4  enable query rewrite
  5  as
  6  select customer_hierarchy.zip_code,
  7         time_hierarchy.mmyyyy,
  8         sum(sales.sales_amount) sales_amount
  9    from sales, time_hierarchy, customer_hierarchy
 10   where sales.trans_date = time_hierarchy.day
 11     and sales.cust_id = customer_hierarchy.cust_id
 12   group by customer_hierarchy.zip_code, time_hierarchy.mmyyyy
 13  /

Materialized view created.
```

We'll try to execute a query now, which will show us sales by ZIP_CODE and MMYYYY, and demonstrate that I used the materialized view as expected:

```
tkyte@TKYTE816> set autotrace
tkyte@TKYTE816> select customer_hierarchy.zip_code,
  2         time_hierarchy.mmyyyy,
  3         sum(sales.sales_amount) sales_amount
  4    from sales, time_hierarchy, customer_hierarchy
  5   where sales.trans_date = time_hierarchy.day
  6     and sales.cust_id = customer_hierarchy.cust_id
  7   group by customer_hierarchy.zip_code, time_hierarchy.mmyyyy
  8  /

1250 rows selected.

Execution Plan
----------------------------------------------------------
   0      SELECT STATEMENT Optimizer=CHOOSE (Cost=1 Card=409 Bytes=204
   1    0   TABLE ACCESS (FULL) OF 'SALES_MV' (Cost=1 Card=409 Bytes=2

Statistics
----------------------------------------------------------
         28  recursive calls
         12  db block gets
        120  consistent gets
...
```

However, when we ask for information at a different level of aggregation (rolling MMYYYY up to YYYY and ZIP_CODE up to REGION), we see that Oracle does not recognize that it can use the materialized view:

```
tkyte@TKYTE816> select customer_hierarchy.region,
  2         time_hierarchy.yyyy,
  3         sum(sales.sales_amount) sales_amount
  4    from sales, time_hierarchy, customer_hierarchy
  5   where sales.trans_date = time_hierarchy.day
```

```
    6        and sales.cust_id = customer_hierarchy.cust_id
    7     group by customer_hierarchy.region, time_hierarchy.yyyy
    8  /
9 rows selected.

Execution Plan
----------------------------------------------------------
    0       SELECT STATEMENT Optimizer=CHOOSE (Cost=8289 Card=9 Bytes=26
    1    0    SORT (GROUP BY) (Cost=8289 Card=9 Bytes=261)
    2    1     NESTED LOOPS (Cost=169 Card=350736 Bytes=10171344)
    3    2      NESTED LOOPS (Cost=169 Card=350736 Bytes=6663984)
    4    3       TABLE ACCESS (FULL) OF 'SALES' (Cost=169 Card=350736
    5    3        INDEX (UNIQUE SCAN) OF 'SYS_IOT_TOP_30185' (UNIQUE)
    6    2       INDEX (UNIQUE SCAN) OF 'SYS_IOT_TOP_30180' (UNIQUE)

Statistics
----------------------------------------------------------
          0  recursive calls
         15  db block gets
     702589  consistent gets
...
```

Oracle understands the time dimension we set up, but it does not yet have any information about how CUST_ID, ZIP_CODE, and REGION relate to each other in our CUSTOMER_HIERARCHY table. What we do to correct this is to rebuild our dimension with two hierarchies in it – one describing the TIME_HIERARCHY and the other describing the CUSTOMER_HIERARCHY table:

```
tkyte@TKYTE816> drop dimension time_hierarchy_dim
  2  /

Dimension dropped.

tkyte@TKYTE816> create dimension sales_dimension
  2      level cust_id    is customer_hierarchy.cust_id
  3      level zip_code   is customer_hierarchy.zip_code
  4      level region     is customer_hierarchy.region
  5      level day        is time_hierarchy.day
  6      level mmyyyy     is time_hierarchy.mmyyyy
  7      level qtr_yyyy   is time_hierarchy.qtr_yyyy
  8      level yyyy       is time_hierarchy.yyyy
  9  hierarchy cust_rollup
 10  (
 11      cust_id child of
 12      zip_code child of
 13      region
 14  )
 15  hierarchy time_rollup
 16  (
 17      day child of
 18      mmyyyy child of
 19      qtr_yyyy child of
 20      yyyy
 21  )
 22  attribute mmyyyy
```

```
  23  determines mon_yyyy;

Dimension created.
```

We dropped the original time hierarchy and created a new, more descriptive one explaining all of the relevant relationships. Now Oracle will understand that the SALES_MV we created is able to answer many more questions. For example, if we ask our 'REGION by YYYY' question again:

```
tkyte@TKYTE816> select customer_hierarchy.region,
  2             time_hierarchy.yyyy,
  3             sum(sales.sales_amount) sales_amount
  4    from sales, time_hierarchy, customer_hierarchy
  5   where sales.trans_date = time_hierarchy.day
  6     and sales.cust_id = customer_hierarchy.cust_id
  7   group by customer_hierarchy.region, time_hierarchy.yyyy
  8  /

    REGION     YYYY SALES_AMOUNT
---------- ---------- ------------
         0     2001   5.9598E+11
         0     2002   3123737106
         1     2001   6.3789E+11
         2     2001   6.3903E+11
         2     2002   3538489159
         3     2001   6.4069E+11
         4     2001   6.3885E+11
         4     2002   3537548948
         5     2001   6.0365E+11

9 rows selected.

Execution Plan
----------------------------------------------------------
   0      SELECT STATEMENT Optimizer=CHOOSE (Cost=11 Card=9 Bytes=576)
   1    0   SORT (GROUP BY) (Cost=11 Card=9 Bytes=576)
   2    1     HASH JOIN (Cost=9 Card=78 Bytes=4992)
   3    2       HASH JOIN (Cost=6 Card=78 Bytes=4446)
   4    3         VIEW (Cost=3 Card=19 Bytes=133)
   5    4           SORT (UNIQUE) (Cost=3 Card=19 Bytes=133)
   6    5             INDEX (FAST FULL SCAN) OF 'SYS_IOT_TOP_30180' (U
   7    3         TABLE ACCESS (FULL) OF 'SALES_MV' (Cost=1 Card=409 B
   8    2       VIEW (Cost=3 Card=100 Bytes=700)
   9    8         SORT (UNIQUE) (Cost=3 Card=100 Bytes=700)
  10    9           INDEX (FULL SCAN) OF 'SYS_IOT_TOP_30185' (UNIQUE)

Statistics
----------------------------------------------------------
          0   recursive calls
         16   db block gets
         14   consistent gets
...
```

Oracle was able to make use of *both* hierarchies in the dimension here, and can now make use of the materialized view. Due to the dimensions we created, it performed simple lookups to convert the CUST_ID column into REGION (since CUST_ID implies ZIP_CODE implies REGION), the MMYYYY column into QTR_YYYY, and answered our question almost instantly. Here, we reduced the number of logical I/Os from more than 700,000 to 16. When you consider that the size of the SALES table will only grow over time, and the size of the SALES_MV will grow much more slowly (180 records or so per month), we can see that this query will scale very well.

DBMS_OLAP

The last piece to the materialized view puzzle is the DBMS_OLAP package. This package is used for the following purposes:

❑ **To estimate the size of a materialized view,** in terms of the number of rows and bytes of storage.

❑ **To validate that your dimension objects are correct,** given the primary/foreign key relationships you have set up.

❑ **To recommend additional materialized views, and to name views that should be dropped,** based on either actual utilization and structure, or just structure alone.

❑ **To evaluate the utilization of a materialized view,** using procedures that are provided, which will report on the actual usefulness of your materialized views whether they are actually being used or not.

Unfortunately, the utilization routines are beyond the scope of what I can cover in one chapter. It involves the setting up of Oracle Trace and the Enterprise Manager Performance Pack, but we shall take a look at the other three.

In order to use the DBMS_OLAP package, you must have external procedures set up, as most of the DBMS_OLAP code is actually stored in a C library. See Chapter 18, *C-Based External Procedures*, for set-up instructions if you receive an error such as the following:

```
ERROR at line 1:
ORA-28575: unable to open RPC connection to external procedure agent
ORA-06512: at "SYS.DBMS_SUMADV", line 6
ORA-06512: at "SYS.DBMS_SUMMARY", line 559
ORA-06512: at line 1
```

Estimating Size

The ESTIMATE_SUMMARY_SIZE routine will report the estimated number of rows and bytes of storage that the materialized view will consume. Since hindsight is 20/20, we can ask DBMS_OLAP to estimate a figure and then compare that figure to what we get in reality.

In order to run this procedure, you will need to ensure that you have a PLAN_TABLE installed in your schema. You will find the CREATE TABLE statement in the [ORACLE_HOME]/rdbms/admin directory on your database server, in a file named utlxplan.sql. If you execute this script, it will create the PLAN_TABLE for you. This table is used by the EXPLAIN PLAN facility that in turn is used by DBMS_OLAP to estimate the size of the materialized view. With this table in place, we can use the built-in ESTIMATE_SUMMARY_SIZE routine to get an estimate of the number of rows/bytes a materialized view would need if we were to build it. I start with a DELETE STATISTICS on our SALES_MV materialized view. DBMS_OLAP would not normally have access to a materialized view to actually see what the sizes are, so we have to hide it (otherwise DBMS_OLAP will get the exact answer from the data dictionary):

```
tkyte@TKYTE816> analyze table sales_mv DELETE statistics;
Table analyzed.

tkyte@TKYTE816> declare
  2      num_rows number;
  3      num_bytes number;
  4  begin
  5      dbms_olap.estimate_summary_size
  6      ( 'SALES_MV_ESTIMATE',
  7        'select customer_hierarchy.zip_code,
  8                time_hierarchy.mmyyyy,
  9                sum(sales.sales_amount) sales_amount
 10          from sales, time_hierarchy, customer_hierarchy
 11         where sales.trans_date = time_hierarchy.day
 12           and sales.cust_id = customer_hierarchy.cust_id
 13         group by customer_hierarchy.zip_code, time_hierarchy.mmyyyy',
 14      num_rows,
 15      num_bytes );
 16
 17      dbms_output.put_line( num_rows || ' rows' );
 18      dbms_output.put_line( num_bytes || ' bytes' );
 19  end;
 20  /
409 rows
36401 bytes

PL/SQL procedure successfully completed.
```

The first parameter to this routine is the name of the plan to be stored in the plan table. This name is not excessively relevant, except that you will want to DELETE FROM PLAN_TABLE WHERE STATEMENT_ID = 'SALES_MV_ESTIMATE' after you are done. The second parameter is the query that will be used to instantiate the materialized view. DBMS_OLAP will analyze this query using the statistics on all of the underlying tables to guess the size of this object. The remaining two parameters are the outputs from DBMS_OLAP – the rows and byte count estimates, with values of 409 and 36401, respectively. Now let's calculate the true valves:

```
tkyte@TKYTE816> analyze table sales_mv COMPUTE statistics;
Table analyzed.

tkyte@TKYTE816> select count(*) from sales_mv;

  COUNT(*)
----------
      1250

tkyte@TKYTE816> select blocks * 8 * 1024
  2    from user_tables
  3   where table_name = 'SALES_MV'
  4  /

BLOCKS*8*1024
-------------
        40960
```

So, the ESTIMATE_SUMMARY_SIZE routine did very well on the size of the table, but underestimated the number of rows. This is typical of anything that 'estimates' – it will get some things right, and miss on others. I would use this routine for a rough 'best guess' as to the size of an object.

Dimension Validation

This routine takes any given dimension, and checks that the hierarchies you have defined are valid. For example, in our example earlier, it would ensure that a CUST_ID implied a ZIP_CODE implied a REGION. To see this routine at work, we'll create a 'bad' example to work from. We'll start by creating a table that has a row for every day of this year with the day, month and year as attributes:

```
tkyte@TKYTE816> create table time_rollup
  2  ( day      date,
  3    mon      number,
  4    year     number
  5  )
  6  /

Table created.

tkyte@TKYTE816> insert into time_rollup
  2  select dt, to_char(dt,'mm'), to_char(dt,'yyyy')
  3    from ( select trunc(sysdate,'year')+rownum-1 dt
  4             from all_objects where rownum < 366 )
  5  /

365 rows created.
```

So, here we have set up a time roll-up similar to our previous example. This time however, I did not preserve the year in the month attribute, just the two digits that represent the month. If we add one more row to this table:

```
tkyte@TKYTE816> insert into time_rollup values
  2  ( add_months(sysdate,12),
  3    to_char(add_months(sysdate,12),'mm'),
  4    to_char(add_months(sysdate,12),'yyyy') );

1 row created.
```

We can see the problem. We will be saying that DAY implies MONTH, and MONTH implies YEAR, but it is not true in this case. We'll have one month that implies one of *two* different years. DBMS_OLAP will do a sanity check for us to show us our error. First we'll set up the dimension:

```
tkyte@TKYTE816> create dimension time_rollup_dim
  2      level day is time_rollup.day
  3      level mon is time_rollup.mon
  4      level year is time_rollup.year
  5  hierarchy time_rollup
  6  (
  7          day child of mon child of year
  8  )
  9  /

Dimension created.
```

And then validate it:

```
tkyte@TKYTE816> exec dbms_olap.validate_dimension( 'time_rollup_dim', user, false,
false );

PL/SQL procedure successfully completed.
```

It looks like it succeeded, but we really have to check the table it *creates* and populates for us:

```
tkyte@TKYTE816> select * from mview$_exceptions;

OWNER TABLE_NAME    DIMENSION_NAME    RELATIONSHI BAD_ROWID
----- -----------   ---------------   ----------- ------------------
TKYTE TIME_ROLLUP   TIME_ROLLUP_DIM   CHILD OF    AAAGkxAAGAAAAcKAA7
TKYTE TIME_ROLLUP   TIME_ROLLUP_DIM   CHILD OF    AAAGkxAAGAAAAcKAA8
TKYTE TIME_ROLLUP   TIME_ROLLUP_DIM   CHILD OF    AAAGkxAAGAAAAcKAA9
...


32 rows selected.
```

If we look at the rows the MVIEW$_EXCEPTIONS point us to, we'll find that they are the rows for the month of MARCH (I ran this in March). Specifically:

```
tkyte@TKYTE816> select * from time_rollup
  2  where rowid in ( select bad_rowid from mview$_exceptions );

DAY          MON         YEAR
---------    ----------  ----------
01-MAR-01    3           2001
02-MAR-01    3           2001
03-MAR-01    3           2001
04-MAR-01    3           2001
...
30-MAR-01    3           2001
31-MAR-01    3           2001
26-MAR-02    3           2002

32 rows selected.
```

The problem is evident at this point, MON does not imply YEAR – the dimension is invalid. It would be unsafe to use this dimension, as the wrong answer would result.

It is recommended that your dimensions be validated after they are modified to ensure the integrity of the results you receive from the materialized views that make use of them.

Recommending Materialized Views

One of the more interesting uses of the DBMS_OLAP package is to have it tell you what materialized views you should consider creating. The RECOMMEND routines do just that.

There are two versions of this routine:

❑ RECOMMEND_MV looks at the structure of the table, the foreign keys that are in place, existing materialized views, statistics on everything, and then develops a list of prioritized recommendations.

❑ RECOMMEND_MV_W goes one step further. If you are using Oracle Trace and the Enterprise Manager Performance Packs, it will look at the queries the system processes, and recommend materialized views based on that real-life information.

As a simple example, we'll ask DBMS_OLAP to take a look at our existing 'fact' table, SALES.

> *A fact table is a table in a star schema that, quite simply, contains facts. The SALES table we used above is a fact table. A fact table typically has two types of columns. There are columns that contain facts (values like the SALES_AMOUNT in our sales table), and there are columns that are foreign keys to dimension tables (list TRANS_DATE in our sales table).*

Let's see what DBMS_OLAP has to say. Before we can do that, we'll need to add the foreign keys. The RECOMMEND routine won't look at the DIMENSION to see what can be done – it needs to see the foreign keys to determine the relationships between tables:

```
tkyte@TKYTE816> alter table sales add constraint t_fk_time
  2  foreign key( trans_date) references time_hierarchy
  3  /

Table altered.

tkyte@TKYTE816> alter table sales add constraint t_fk_cust
  2  foreign key( cust_id) references customer_hierarchy
  3  /

Table altered.
```

Once we've done that, we are ready to look at our fact table, SALES:

```
tkyte@TKYTE816> exec dbms_olap.recommend_mv( 'SALES', 10000000000, '' );

PL/SQL procedure successfully completed.
```

Here we asked RECOMMEND_MV to:

1. Look at the table SALES.

2. Consider a large amount of space to be used for the materialized views (we just passed a really big number).

3. Not feel that it needs to keep any particular materialized view (we passed ` ` as the list of views to KEEP).

Next, we can either query the tables it populates directly or, more conveniently, use a sample routine to print the contents. To install the sample routine and run the report you will:

```
tkyte@TKYTE816> @C:\oracle\RDBMS\demo\sadvdemo

Package created.

Package body created.

Package created.

Package body created.

tkyte@TKYTE816> exec demo_sumadv.prettyprint_recommendations
Recommendation Number = 1
Recommended Action is CREATE new summary:
SELECT CUSTOMER_HIERARCHY.CUST_ID, CUSTOMER_HIERARCHY.ZIP_CODE,
CUSTOMER_HIERARCHY.REGION , COUNT(*), SUM(SALES.SALES_AMOUNT),
COUNT(SALES.SALES_AMOUNT)
FROM TKYTE.SALES, TKYTE.CUSTOMER_HIERARCHY
WHERE SALES.CUST_ID = CUSTOMER_HIERARCHY.CUST_ID
GROUP BY CUSTOMER_HIERARCHY.CUST_ID, CUSTOMER_HIERARCHY.ZIP_CODE,
CUSTOMER_HIERARCHY.REGION
Storage in bytes is 2100
Percent performance gain is 43.2371266138567
Benefit-to-cost ratio is .0205891079113603
Recommendation Number = 2
...

PL/SQL procedure successfully completed.
```

DBMS_OLAP looked at the dimensions and existing materialized views, and is now making suggestions for additional materialized views that may usefully be created, given the meta data (primary keys, foreign keys, and dimensions) we have entered into the database.

If we used Oracle Trace we could go a step further with this recommendation process. Oracle Trace is capable of capturing the *actual* queries asked of the system, and recording details about them. These will be used by DBMS_OLAP to perform even more focused recommendations, recommendations based not only on what is possible, but based on the reality of the types of questions you actually ask of the data. Materialized views that are possible but would not be used by you based on your workload are not recommended. Other materialized views that are possible, and would be used by you, would be recommended, since they would be used by queries that your system actually executes.

Caveats

There are a few considerations to be aware of with regards to using materialized views. We will briefly cover some of them here.

Materialized Views are Not Designed for OLTP Systems

As mentioned above, materialized views typically add overhead to individual transactions and, if created with REFRESH ON COMMIT, will introduce contention. The overhead arises from the need to track the changes made by a transaction – these changes will either be maintained in the session state or in log tables. In a high-end OLTP system, this overhead is not desirable. The concurrency issue comes into play with a REFRESH ON COMMIT materialized view, due to the fact that many rows in the detail fact table point to a single row in a summary table. An update to any one of perhaps thousands of records, will need to modify a single row in the summary. This will naturally inhibit concurrency in a high update situation.

This does not preclude the use of materialized views with OLTP, in particular materialized views that are REFRESHed ON DEMAND, with a *full* refresh. A full refresh does not add the overhead of tracking transaction-level changes. Rather, at some point in time, the defining query for the materialized view is executed, and the results simply replace the existing materialized view. Since this is done on demand (or on a timed basis), the refresh may be scheduled for a time when the load is light. The resulting materialized view is especially relevant for reporting purposes – your OLTP data can be transformed using SQL into something that is easy and fast to query, every night. The next day, your online reports of yesterday's activities run as fast as possible, and easily co-exist with your OLTP system.

Query Rewrite Integrity

As we discussed above – this has three modes:

- ❑ ENFORCED – Will only use a materialized view if there is no chance of getting incorrect or stale data.

- ❑ TRUSTED – Oracle will use a materialized view even if some of the constraints it is relying on are something Oracle did not validate or enforce. This is typical in a data warehouse environment, where many constraints may be present but have not been enforced by Oracle.

- ❑ STALE_TOLERATED – Oracle will use a materialized view even if it knows the data it is derived from has changed. This is typical in a reporting environment such as described in the preceding caveat.

You must understand the ramifications of using each of these modes. ENFORCED will give you the right answer every time, at the expense of not using some materialized views that would speed up the query response time. TRUSTED, if what Oracle has been asked to 'trust' turns out to be false, may give a result that would not be achieved if the original source data had been queried instead. We saw an example of this early on with the EMP_DEPT materialized view. STALE_TOLERATED should be used in reporting systems where getting a value that existed a while ago is acceptable. If up-to-the-minute information is mandatory, STALE_TOLERATED should not be used.

Summary

Materialized views are a powerful data warehouse/decision support system feature. A single materialized view may be used by many different, but related, queries. Best of all, it is 100 percent transparent to the application, and the end user. You do not have to teach people what summaries are available – you inform Oracle what is possible via constraints, referential integrity, and dimensions. It does the rest for you.

Materialized views are the natural evolution, and merging, of features found in the database and decision support tools. No more are the summary table management features of Oracle's Discoverer (and other like tools) limited to these environments. Now every client, from the lowly SQL*PLUS to your custom developed applications, to off-the-shelf reporting tools can take advantage of the fact that the answer has already been stored for them.

Add to all this the DBMS_OLAP tool. It will not only estimate how much additional storage you need to support a materialized view, but it can watch how your existing views are used. Based on this, it will recommend dropping some and creating others – to the point of even supplying you with the query it feels you should use in the materialized view.

All in all, materialized views in a read-only/read-intensive environment will definitely pay you back for the additional storage through reduced query response time and reduced resources needed to actually process the queries.

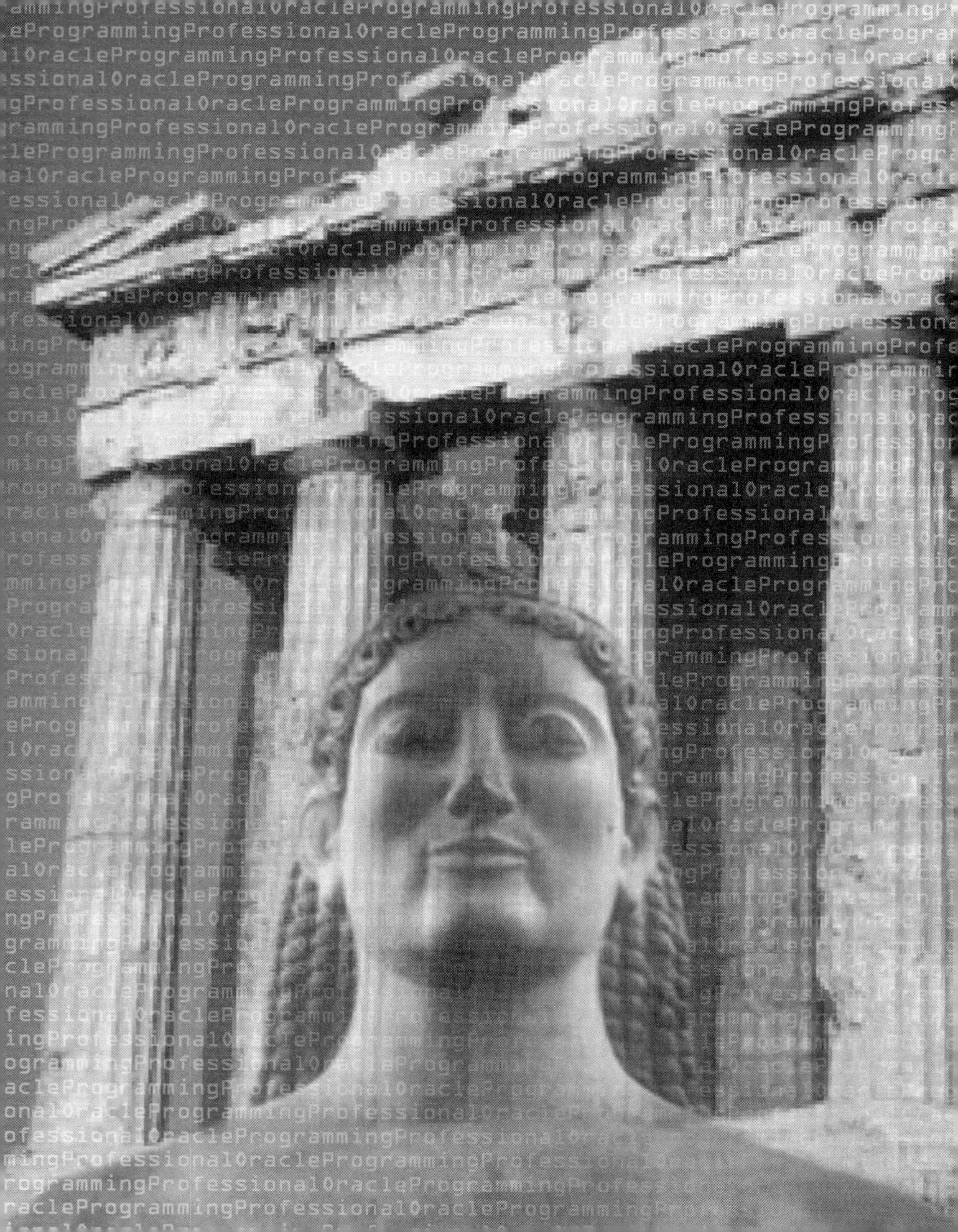

14

Partitioning

Partitioning in Oracle was first introduced in Oracle 8.0. It is the ability to physically break a table or index into many smaller more manageable pieces. As far as the application accessing the database is concerned, there is logically only one table or one index. Physically, there may be many dozens of physical partitions that comprise the table or index. Each partition is an independent object that may be manipulated either by itself or as part of the larger object.

Partitioning is designed to facilitate the management of very large tables and indexes, by implementing the divide and conquer logic. For example, say you have a 10GB index in your database. If for some reason, you need to rebuild this index and it is not partitioned, you will have to rebuild the entire 10 GB index as a single unit of work. While it is true we could rebuild the index online, the amount of resources necessary to completely rebuild the entire 10 GB index is huge. We'll need at least 10 GB of free storage elsewhere to hold a copy of both indexes, we'll need a temporary transaction log table to record the changes made against the base table during the long time we spend rebuilding the index, and so on. On the other hand, if the index itself had been partitioned into ten, 1 GB partitions, we could rebuild each index partition individually, one by one. Now we need 10 percent of the free space we needed previously. Likewise, the index rebuild goes much faster (say ten times faster perhaps) and so the amount of transactional changes that need to be merged into the new index is much less, and so on.

In short, partitioning can make what would be otherwise daunting, or in some cases unfeasible, operations as easy as they are in a small database.

The Uses of Partitioning

There are three main reasons for using partitioning:

❏   To increase availability

❑ To ease administration burdens

❑ To enhance DML and query performance

Increased Availability

Increased availability is derived from the fact that partitions are independent entities. The availability (or lack thereof) of a single partition in an object does not mean the object itself is unavailable. The optimizer is aware of the partitioning scheme you have implemented and will remove un-referenced partitions from the query plan accordingly. If a single partition is unavailable in a large object and your query can eliminate this partition from consideration, Oracle will successfully process the query for you. For example, we'll set up a hash-partitioned table with two partitions, each in a separate tablespace, and insert some data into it. For each row inserted into this table, the value of the EMPNO column is hashed to determine which partition (and hence tablespace in this case) the data will be placed into. Then, using the partition-extended tablename, we'll inspect the contents of each partition:

```
tkyte@TKYTE816> CREATE TABLE emp
  2  ( empno    int,
  3    ename    varchar2(20)
  4  )
  5  PARTITION BY HASH (empno)
  6  ( partition part_1 tablespace p1,
  7    partition part_2 tablespace p2
  8  )
  9  /

Table created.

tkyte@TKYTE816> insert into emp select empno, ename from scott.emp
  2  /

14 rows created.

tkyte@TKYTE816> select * from emp partition(part_1);

     EMPNO ENAME
---------- --------------------
      7369 SMITH
      7499 ALLEN
      7654 MARTIN
      7698 BLAKE
      7782 CLARK
      7839 KING
      7876 ADAMS
      7934 MILLER
8 rows selected.

tkyte@TKYTE816> select * from emp partition(part_2);

     EMPNO ENAME
---------- --------------------
      7521 WARD
      7566 JONES
      7788 SCOTT
      7844 TURNER
      7900 JAMES
      7902 FORD
6 rows selected.
```

Now, we'll make some of the data unavailable by taking one of the tablespaces offline. We will run a query that hits every partition to show that the query will fail. We will then show that a query that does not access the offline tablespace will function as normal – Oracle will eliminate the offline partition from consideration. I use a bind variable in this particular example just to demonstrate that even though Oracle does not know at query optimization time which partition will be accessed, it is able to perform this elimination nonetheless:

```
tkyte@TKYTE816> alter tablespace p1 offline;

Tablespace altered.

tkyte@TKYTE816> select * from emp
  2  /
select * from emp
              *
ERROR at line 1:
ORA-00376: file 4 cannot be read at this time
ORA-01110: data file 4: 'C:\ORACLE\ORADATA\TKYTE816\P1.DBF'

tkyte@TKYTE816> variable n number
tkyte@TKYTE816> exec :n := 7844

PL/SQL procedure successfully completed.

tkyte@TKYTE816> select * from emp where empno = :n
  2  /

     EMPNO ENAME
---------- --------------------
      7844 TURNER
```

As you can see, we put one of the tablespaces offline, simulating a disk failure. The effect of this is that if we try to access the entire table, we of course cannot. However, if we attempt to access data that resides in the online partition, it is successful. When the optimizer can eliminate partitions from the plan, it will. This fact increases availability for those applications that use the partition key in their queries.

Partitions also increase availability due to the fact that downtime is reduced. If you have a 100 GB table for example, and it is partitioned into fifty 2 GB partitions, you can recover from errors that much faster. If one of the 2 GB partitions is damaged, the time to recover is now the time it takes to restore and recover a 2 GB partition, not a 100 GB table. So availability is increased in two ways; one is that many users may never even notice the data was unavailable due to partition elimination and the other is reduced downtime in the event of an error because of the significantly reduced amount of work that is performed.

Reduced Administrative Burden

The administrative burden relief is derived from the fact that performing operations on small objects is inherently easier, faster, and less resource intensive than performing the same operation on a large object. For example, if you discover that 50 percent of the rows in your table are 'chained' rows (see Chapter 6 on *Tables* for details on chained/migrated rows), and you would like to fix this, having a partitioned table will facilitate the operation. In order to 'fix' chained rows, you must typically rebuild the object – in this case a table. If you have one 100 GB table, you will need to perform this operation in one very large 'chunk' serially using ALTER TABLE MOVE. On the other hand, if you have 25 4GB partitions, you can rebuild each partition one by one. Alternatively, if you are doing this off-hours, you can even do the ALTER TABLE MOVE statements in parallel, in separate sessions, potentially reducing the amount of time it takes. If you are using locally partitioned indexes on this partitioned table then the index rebuilds will take significantly less time as well. Virtually everything you can do to a non-partitioned object, you can do to an individual partition of a partitioned object.

Another factor to consider, with regard to partitions and administration, is the use of 'sliding windows' of data in data warehousing and archiving. In many cases, you need to keep the last N units of time data online. For example, you need to keep the last twelve months online or the last five years. Without partitions, this was generally a massive INSERT followed by a massive DELETE. Lots of DML, lots of redo and rollback generated. Now with partitions we can simply:

❑ Load a separate table with the new months (or years, or whatever) data.

❑ Index the table fully. (These steps could even be done in another instance and transported to this database.)

❑ Slide it onto the *end* of the partitioned table.

❑ Slide the oldest partition off the other end of the partitioned table.

So, we can now very easily support extremely large objects containing time-sensitive information. The old data can easily be removed from the partitioned table and simply *dropped* if you do not need it, or it can be archived off elsewhere. New data can be loaded into a separate table, so as to not affect the partitioned table until the loading, indexing, and so on, is complete. We will take a look at a complete example of a sliding window later.

Enhanced DML and Query Performance

The last general benefit of partitioning is in the area of enhanced query and DML performance. We'll take a look at each individually to see what benefits we might expect.

Enhanced DML performance refers to the potential to perform parallel DML (or PDML). During PDML Oracle uses many threads or processes to perform your INSERT, UPDATE, or DELETE instead of a single serial process. On a multi-CPU machine with plenty of I/O bandwidth, the potential speed-up may be large for mass DML operations. Unlike parallel query (the processing of a SELECT statement by many processes/threads), PDML requires partitioning (there is a special case of a parallel, direct path insert via the /*+ APPEND */ hint that does not require partitioning). If your tables are not partitioned, you cannot perform these operations in parallel. Oracle will assign a maximum degree of parallelism to the object, based on the number of physical partitions it has.

You should not look to PDML as a feature to speed up your OLTP based applications. There is often confusion with regards to this. Many times, I hear 'Parallel operations must be faster than serial operations – they just have to be'. This is not always the case. Some operations performed in parallel may be many times slower than the same thing done serially. There is a certain overhead associated with setting up parallel operations; more co-ordination that must take place. Additionally, parallel operations are not things you should consider doing in a mainly online, OLTP system – it just would not make sense. Parallel operations are designed to fully, and totally, maximize the utilization of a machine. They are designed so that a single user can completely use all of the disks, CPU, and memory on the machine. In a data warehouse – lots of data, few users – this is something you want to achieve. In an OLTP system (tons of users all doing short, fast transactions) giving a user the ability to fully take over the machine resources is not a very scalable solution.

This sounds contradictory – we use parallel query to scale up, how could it not be scalable? When applied to an OLTP system, the statement is quite accurate however. Parallel query is not something that scales up as the number of concurrent users scale up. Parallel query was designed to allow a single session to generate as much work as a hundred concurrent sessions would. In our OLTP system, we really do not want a single user to generate the work of a hundred users.

PDML is useful in a large data warehousing environment to facilitate bulk updates to massive amounts of data. The PDML operation is executed much in the way a distributed query would be executed by Oracle, with each partition acting like a separate database instance. Each partition is updated by a separate thread with its own transaction (and hence its own rollback segment hopefully) and after they are all done, the equivalent of a fast two phase commit is performed to commit the separate, independent transactions. Due to this architecture, there are certain limitations associated with PDML. For example, triggers are not supported during a PDML operation. This is a reasonable limitation in my opinion since triggers would tend to add a large amount of overhead to the update and you are using PDML in order to go fast – the two features don't go together. Also, there are certain declarative RI constraints that are not supported during the PDML, since each partition is done as a separate transaction in the equivalent of a separate session. Self-referential integrity is not supported for example. Consider the deadlocks and other locking issues that would occur if it were supported.

In the area of query performance, partitioning comes into play with two types of specialized operations:

❑ **Partition Elimination** – Some partitions of data are not considered in the processing of the query. We saw an example of partition elimination in the example where we took one of two tablespaces offline, and the query still functioned. The offline tablespace (partition in this case) was eliminated from consideration.

❑ **Parallel Operations** – Such as partition-wise joins for objects partitioned on the join keys, or parallel index scans, whereby index partitions may be scanned in parallel.

Again, much like PDML, you should not look toward partitions as a way to massively improve performance in an OLTP system. Partition elimination is useful where you have full scans of large objects. Utilizing partition elimination, you can avoid full scanning large pieces of an object. That is where the increase in performance would be derived from this feature. However, in an OLTP environment *you are not full scanning* large objects (if you are, you have a serious design flaw). Even if you partition your indexes, the speed up you achieve by scanning a smaller index is miniscule – if you actually achieve a speed up at all. If some of your queries use an index *and* they cannot be used to eliminate all but one partition, you may find your queries actually run slower after partitioning since you now have 5, 10, or 20 small indexes to scan, instead of one larger index. We will investigate this in much more detail later when we look at the types of partitioned indexes available to us. There are opportunities to gain efficiency in an OLTP system with partitions – they may be used to increase concurrency by decreasing contention for example. They can be used to spread the modifications of a single table out over many physical partitions. Instead of having a single table segment with a single index segment – you might have 20 table partitions and 20 index partitions. It could be like having 20 tables instead of one – hence decreasing contention for this shared resource during modifications.

As for parallel operations, as stated previously, you do not want to be doing a parallel query in an OLTP system. You would reserve your use of parallel operations for the DBA to perform rebuilds, creating indexes, analyzing tables, and so on. The fact is that in an OLTP system your queries should already be characterized by very fast index accesses– partitioning will not speed that up very much, if at all. This does not mean 'avoid partitioning for OLTP', it means do not expect massive improvements in performance by simply adding partitioning. Your applications are not able to take advantage of the times where partitioning is able to enhance query performance in this case.

Now, in a data warehouse/decision support system, partitioning is not only a great administrative tool, but it is something to speed up processing. For example, you may have a large table, on which you need to perform an ad-hoc query. You always do the ad-hoc query by sales quarter – each sales quarter contains hundreds of thousands of records and you have millions of online records. So, you want to query a relatively small slice of the entire data set but it is not really feasible to index it based on the sales quarter. This index would point to hundreds of thousands of records and doing the index range scan in this way would be terrible (refer to Chapter 7 on *Indexes* for more details on this). A full table scan is called for to process many of your queries, but we end up having to scan millions of records, most of which won't apply to our query. Using an intelligent partitioning scheme, we can segregate the data by quarter so that when we go to query the data for any given quarter, we will end up full scanning just that quarter's data. This is the best of all possible solutions.

In addition, in a warehousing/decision support system environment, parallel query is used frequently. Here, operations such as parallel index range scans, or parallel fast full index scans are not only meaningful, but also beneficial to us. We want to maximize our use of all available resources, and parallel query is the way to do it. So, in this environment, partitioning stands a very good chance of speeding up processing.

If I were to put the benefits of partitioning in some sort of order, it would be:

1. Increases availability of data – good for all system types

2. Eases administration of large objects by removing large objects from the database – good for all system types

3. Improves the performance of certain DML and queries – beneficial mainly in a large warehouse environment

4. Reduces contention on high insert OLTP systems (such as an audit trail table) by spreading the inserts out across many separate partitions (spreads the hot spots around)

How Partitioning Works

In this section, we'll look at the partitioning schemes offered by Oracle 8i. There are three partitioning schemes for tables and two for indexes. Within the two schemes for index partitioning, there are various classes of partitioned indexes. We'll look at the benefits of each and at the differences between them. We'll also look at when to apply which schemes to different application types.

Table Partitioning Schemes

There are currently three methods by which you can partition tables in Oracle:

❑ **Range Partitioning** – You may specify ranges of data that should be stored together. For example, everything that has a timestamp in the month of Jan-2001 will be stored in partition 1, everything with a timestamp of Feb-2001 in partition 2, and so on. This is probably the most commonly used partitioning mechanism in Oracle 8i.

❑ **Hash Partitioning** – We saw this in the first example in this chapter. A column, or columns, has a hash function applied to it and the row will be placed into a partition according to the value of this hash.

❑ **Composite Partitioning** – This is a combination of range and hash. It allows you to first apply range partitioning to some data, and then within that range, have the ultimate partition be chosen by hash.

The following code and diagrams provide a visual demonstration of these different methods. Additionally, the CREATE TABLE statements are set up in such a way as to give an overview of the syntax of a partitioned table. The first type we will look at is a range partitioned table:

```
tkyte@TKYTE816> CREATE TABLE range_example
  2  ( range_key_column date,
  3    data              varchar2(20)
  4  )
  5  PARTITION BY RANGE (range_key_column)
  6  ( PARTITION part_1 VALUES LESS THAN
  7        (to_date('01-jan-1995','dd-mon-yyyy')),
  8    PARTITION part_2 VALUES LESS THAN
  9        (to_date('01-jan-1996','dd-mon-yyyy'))
 10  )
 11  /

Table created.
```

The following diagram shows that Oracle will inspect the value of the RANGE_KEY_COLUMN and based on its value, insert it into one of the two partitions:

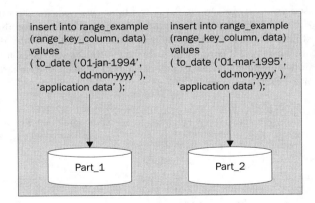

You might wonder what would happen if the column used to determine the partition is modified. There are two cases to consider:

❑ The modification would not cause a different partition to be used; the row would still belong in this partition. This is supported in all cases.

❑ The modification would cause the row to move across partitions. This is supported *if* row movement is enabled for the table, otherwise an error will be raised.

633

We can observe these behaviors easily. Below we'll insert a row into PART_1 of the above table. We will then update it to a value that allows it to remain in PART_1 – and that'll succeed. Next, we'll update the RANGE_KEY_COLUMN to a value that would cause it to belong in PART_2 – that will raise an error since we did not explicitly enable row movement. Lastly, we'll alter the table to support row movement and see the side effect of doing so:

```
tkyte@TKYTE816> insert into range_example
  2  values ( to_date( '01-jan-1994', 'dd-mon-yyyy' ), 'application data' );

1 row created.

tkyte@TKYTE816> update range_example
  2  set range_key_column = range_key_column+1
  3  /

1 row updated.
```

As expected, this succeeds, the row remains in partition PART_1. Next, we'll observe the behavior when the update would cause the row to move:

```
tkyte@TKYTE816> update range_example
  2  set range_key_column = range_key_column+366
  3  /
update range_example
       *
ERROR at line 1:
ORA-14402: updating partition key column would cause a partition change
```

That immediately raised an error. In Oracle 8.1.5 and later releases, we can enable row movement on this table to allow the row to move from partition to partition. This functionality is not available on Oracle 8.0 – you must delete the row and re-insert it in that release. You should be aware of a subtle side effect of doing this, however. It is one of two cases where the ROWID of a row will change due to an update (the other is an update to the primary key of an IOT – index organized table. The universal ROWID will change for that row too):

```
tkyte@TKYTE816> select rowid from range_example
  2  /

ROWID
------------------
AAAHeRAAGAAAAAKAAA

tkyte@TKYTE816> alter table range_example enable row movement
  2  /

Table altered.

tkyte@TKYTE816> update range_example
  2  set range_key_column = range_key_column+366
  3  /

1 row updated.
```

```
tkyte@TKYTE816> select rowid from range_example
  2  /

ROWID
------------------
AAAHeSAAGAAAABKAAA
```

So, as long as you understand that the ROWID of the row will change on this update, enabling row movement will allow you to update partition keys.

The next example is that of a *hash*-partitioned table. Here Oracle will apply a hash function to the partition key to determine in which of the N partitions the data should be placed. Oracle recommends that N be a number that is a power of 2 (2, 4, 8, 16, and so on) to achieve the best overall distribution. Hash partitioning is designed to achieve a good spread of data across many different devices (disks). The hash key chosen for a table should be a column or set of columns that are as unique as possible in order to provide for a good spread of values. If you chose a column that has only four values and you use two partitions then they may very well all end up hashing to the same partition quite easily, bypassing the value of partitioning in the first place!

We will create a hash table with two partitions in this case:

```
tkyte@TKYTE816> CREATE TABLE hash_example
  2  ( hash_key_column    date,
  3    data               varchar2(20)
  4  )
  5  PARTITION BY HASH (hash_key_column)
  6  ( partition part_1 tablespace p1,
  7    partition part_2 tablespace p2
  8  )
  9  /

Table created.
```

The diagram shows that Oracle will inspect the value in the hash_key_column, hash it, and determine which of the two partitions a given row will appear in:

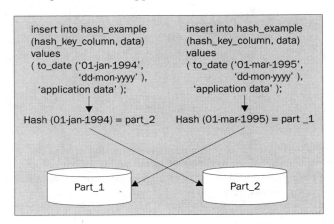

Lastly, we'll look at an example of composite partitioning, which is a mixture of range and hash. Here we are using a different set of columns to range partition by from the set of columns used to hash on. This is not mandatory – we could use the same set of columns for both:

```
tkyte@TKYTE816> CREATE TABLE composite_example
  2  ( range_key_column   date,
  3    hash_key_column    int,
  4    data               varchar2(20)
  5  )
  6  PARTITION BY RANGE (range_key_column)
  7  subpartition by hash(hash_key_column) subpartitions 2
  8  (
  9  PARTITION part_1
 10      VALUES LESS THAN(to_date('01-jan-1995','dd-mon-yyyy'))
 11      (subpartition part_1_sub_1,
 12       subpartition part_1_sub_2
 13      ),
 14  PARTITION part_2
 15      VALUES LESS THAN(to_date('01-jan-1996','dd-mon-yyyy'))
 16      (subpartition part_2_sub_1,
 17       subpartition part_2_sub_2
 18      )
 19  )
 20  /

Table created.
```

In composite partitioning, Oracle will first apply the range partitioning rules to figure out which range the data falls into. Then, it will apply the hash function to decide which physical partition the data should finally be placed into:

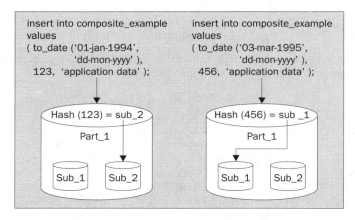

In general, range partitioning is useful when you have data that is logically segregated by some value(s). Time-based data immediately comes to the forefront as a classic example. Partition by 'Sales Quarter'. Partition by 'Fiscal Year'. Partition by 'Month'. Range partitioning is able to take advantage of partition elimination in many cases, including use of exact equality and ranges – less than, greater than, between, and so on.

Hash partitioning is suitable for data that has no natural ranges by which you can partition. For example, if you had to load a table full of census-related data, there might not be an attribute by which it would make sense to range partition by. However, you would still like to take advantage of the administrative, performance, and availability enhancements offered by partitioning. Here, you would simply pick a unique or almost unique set of columns to hash on. This would achieve an even distributionof data across as many partitions as you like. Hash partitioned objects can take advantage of partition elimination when exact equality or IN (value, value, ...) is used but not when ranges of data are used.

Composite partitioning is useful when you have something logical by which you can range partition, but the resulting range partitions are still too large to manage effectively. You can apply the range partitioning and then further divide each range by a hash function. This will allow you to spread I/O requests out across many disks in any given large partition. Additionally, you may achieve partition elimination at three levels now. If you query on the range partition key, Oracle is able to eliminate any range partitions that do not meet your criteria. If you add the hash key to your query, Oracle can eliminate the other hash partitions within that range. If you just query on the hash key (not using the range partition key), Oracle will query only those hash sub-partitions that apply from each range partition.

It is recommended that if there is something by which it makes sense to range partition your data, you should use that over hash partitioning. Hash partitioning adds many of the salient benefits of partitioning, but is not as useful as range partitioning when it comes to partition elimination. Using hash partitions within range partitions is advisable when the resulting range partitions are too large to manage or when you want to utilize PDML or parallel index scanning against a single range partition.

Partitioning Indexes

Indexes, like tables, may be partitioned. There are two possible methods to partition indexes. You may either:

❑ **Equi-partition the index with the table** – also known as a **local index**. For every table partition, there will be an index partition that indexes just that table partition. All of the entries in a given index partition point to a single table partition and all of the rows in a single table partition are represented in a single index partition.

❑ **Partition the index by range** – also known as a **global index**. Here the index is partitioned by range, and a single index partition may point to *any* (and all) table partitions.

The following diagrams display the difference between a local and a global index:

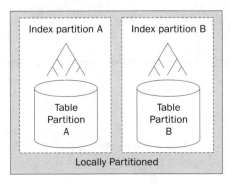
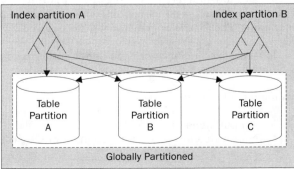

In the case of a globally partitioned index, note that the number of index partitions may in fact be different than the number of table partitions.

Since global indexes may be partitioned by range only, you must use local indexes if you wish to have a hash or composite partitioned index. The local index will be partitioned using the same scheme as the underlying table.

Local Indexes

Local indexes are what most partition implementations have used in my experience. This is because most of the partitioning implementations I've seen have been data warehouses. In an OLTP system, global indexes would be more common. Local indexes have certain properties that make them the best choice for most data warehouse implementations. They support a more available environment (less down time) since problems will be isolated to one range or hash of data. A global index on the other hand, since it can point to many table partitions, may become a point of failure, rendering all partitions inaccessible to certain queries. Local indexes are more flexible when it comes to partition maintenance operations. If the DBA decides to move a table partition, only the associated local index partition needs to be rebuilt. With a global index all index partitions must be rebuilt. The same is true with 'sliding window' implementations where old data is aged out of the partition and new data is aged in. No local indexes will be in need of a rebuild but all global indexes will be. In some cases, Oracle can take advantage of the fact that the index is locally partitioned with the table, and will develop optimized query plans based on that. With global indexes, there is no such relationship between the index and table partitions. Local indexes also facilitate a partition point-in-time recovery operation. If a single partition needs to be recovered to an earlier point in time than the rest of the table for some reason, all locally partitioned indexes can be recovered to that same point in time. All global indexes would need to be rebuilt on this object.

Oracle makes a distinction between these two types of local indexes:

❏ **Local prefixed indexes** – These are indexes such that the partition keys are on the leading edge of the index definition. For example, if a table is range partitioned on the TIMESTAMP column, a local prefixed index on that table would have TIMESTAMP as the first column in its column list.

❏ **Local non-prefixed indexes** – These indexes do *not* have the partition key on the leading edge of their column list. The index may or may not contain the partition key columns.

Both types of indexes are able take advantage of partition elimination, both can support uniqueness (as long as the non-prefixed index includes the partition key), and so on. The fact is that a query that uses a local prefixed index will always *allow* for index partition elimination, whereas a query that uses a local non-prefixed index might not. This is why local non-prefixed indexes are said to be 'slower'; they do not *enforce* partition elimination (but they do support it). Additionally, as we'll see below, the optimizer will treat local non-prefixed indexes differently from local prefixed indexes when performing certain operations. The Oracle documentation stresses that:

local prefixed indexes provide better performance than local non-prefixed indexes because they minimize the number of indexes probed

It should really read more like:

locally partitioned indexes that are used in QUERIES that reference the entire partition key in them provide better performance than for QUERIES that do not reference the partition key

There is nothing inherently better about a local prefixed index, as opposed to a local non-prefixed index, when that index is used as the initial path to the table in a query. What I mean by that is that if the query can start with SCAN AN INDEX as the first step, there isn't much difference between a prefixed and non-prefixed index. Below, when we are looking at using partitioned indexes in joins, we'll see the difference between a prefixed and non-prefixed index.

For the query that starts with an index access, it all really depends on the predicate in your query. A small example will help demonstrate this. We'll set up a table, PARTITIONED_TABLE, and create a local prefixed index LOCAL_PREFIXED on it. Additionally, we'll add a local non-prefixed index LOCAL_NONPREFIXED:

```
tkyte@TKYTE816> CREATE TABLE partitioned_table
  2  ( a int,
  3    b int
  4  )
  5  PARTITION BY RANGE (a)
  6  (
  7  PARTITION part_1 VALUES LESS THAN(2) ,
  8  PARTITION part_2 VALUES LESS THAN(3)
  9  )
 10  /

Table created.

tkyte@TKYTE816> create index local_prefixed on partitioned_table (a,b) local;

Index created.

tkyte@TKYTE816> create index local_nonprefixed on partitioned_table (b) local;

Index created.
```

Now, we'll insert some data into one partition and mark the indexes UNUSABLE:

```
tkyte@TKYTE816> insert into partitioned_table values ( 1, 1 );

1 row created.

tkyte@TKYTE816> alter index local_prefixed modify partition part_2 unusable;

Index altered.

tkyte@TKYTE816> alter index local_nonprefixed modify partition part_2 unusable;

Index altered.
```

Setting these index partitions to UNUSABLE will prevent Oracle from accessing these specific index partitions. It will be as is they suffered 'media failure' – they are unavailable. So, now we'll query the table to see what index partitions are needed by different queries:

```
tkyte@TKYTE816> set autotrace on explain
tkyte@TKYTE816> select * from partitioned_table where a = 1 and b = 1;

         A         B
```

```
       ---------- ----------
                1          1


Execution Plan
-------------------------------------------------------------
    0          SELECT STATEMENT Optimizer=CHOOSE (Cost=1 Card=1 Bytes=26)
    1     0      INDEX (RANGE SCAN) OF 'LOCAL_PREFIXED' (NON-UNIQUE) (Cost=1
```

So, the query that uses LOCAL_PREFIX succeeds. The optimizer was able to exclude PART_2 of LOCAL_PREFIX from consideration because we specified A=1 in the query. Partition elimination kicked in for us. For the second query:

```
tkyte@TKYTE816> select * from partitioned_table where b = 1;
ERROR:
ORA-01502: index 'TKYTE.LOCAL_NONPREFIXED' or partition of such index is in
unusable state


no rows selected

Execution Plan
-------------------------------------------------------------
    0          SELECT STATEMENT Optimizer=CHOOSE (Cost=1 Card=2 Bytes=52)
    1     0      PARTITION RANGE (ALL)
    2     1        TABLE ACCESS (BY LOCAL INDEX ROWID) OF 'PARTITIONED_TABLE'
    3     2          INDEX (RANGE SCAN) OF 'LOCAL_NONPREFIXED' (NON-UNIQUE)
```

Here the optimizer was *not* able to remove PART_2 of LOCAL_NONPREFIXED from consideration. Herein lies a performance issue with local non-prefixed indexes. They do not *make* you use the partition key in the predicate as a prefixed index does. It is not that prefixed indexes are better, it is that in order to use them, you must use a query that allows for partition elimination.

If we drop LOCAL_PREFIXED index, and rerun the original successful query:

```
tkyte@TKYTE816> select * from partitioned_table where a = 1 and b = 1;


            A          B
       ---------- ----------
                1          1

Execution Plan
-------------------------------------------------------------
    0          SELECT STATEMENT Optimizer=CHOOSE (Cost=1 Card=1 Bytes=26)
    1     0      TABLE ACCESS (BY LOCAL INDEX ROWID) OF 'PARTITIONED_TABLE'
    2     1        INDEX (RANGE SCAN) OF 'LOCAL_NONPREFIXED' (NON-UNIQUE) (Cost=1
```

Well, this might be a surprising result. This is almost the same exact plan for the query that just failed, but this time it works. That is because the optimizer is able to perform partition elimination even for non-prefixed local indexes (there is no PARTITION RANGE (ALL) step in this plan).

If you frequently query the above table with the queries:

```
select ... from partitioned_table where a = :a and b = :b;
select ... from partitioned_table where b = :b;
```

then, you might consider using a local non-prefixed index on (b,a) – that index would be useful for both of the above queries. The local prefixed index on (a,b) would only be useful for the first query.

However, when it comes to using the partitioned indexes in joins, the results may be different. In the above examples, Oracle was able to look at the predicate and at optimization time determine that it would be able to eliminate partitions (or not). This was clear from the predicate (even if the predicate used bind variables this would be true). When the index is used as the initial, primary access method, there are no real differences between prefixed and non-prefixed indexes. When we join to a local prefixed index, however, this changes. Consider a simple range partitioned table such as:

```
tkyte@TKYTE816> CREATE TABLE range_example
  2  ( range_key_column date,
  3    x               int,
  4    data            varchar2(20)
  5  )
  6  PARTITION BY RANGE (range_key_column)
  7  ( PARTITION part_1 VALUES LESS THAN
  8         (to_date('01-jan-1995','dd-mon-yyyy')),
  9    PARTITION part_2 VALUES LESS THAN
 10         (to_date('01-jan-1996','dd-mon-yyyy'))
 11  )
 12  /

Table created.

tkyte@TKYTE816> alter table range_example
  2  add constraint range_example_pk
  3  primary key (range_key_column,x)
  4  using index local
  5  /

Table altered.

tkyte@TKYTE816> insert into range_example values ( to_date( '01-jan-1994' ), 1,
'xxx' );

1 row created.

tkyte@TKYTE816> insert into range_example values ( to_date( '01-jan-1995' ), 2,
'xxx' );

1 row created.
```

This table will start out with a local prefixed primary key index. In order to see the difference between the prefixed and non-prefixed indexes, we'll need to create another table. We will use this table to drive a query against our RANGE_EXAMPLE table above. The TEST table will simply be used as the driving table in a query that will do a 'nested loops' type of join to the RANGE_EXAMPLE table:

```
tkyte@TKYTE816> create table test ( pk , range_key_column , x,
  2                              constraint test_pk primary key(pk) )
  3  as
  4  select rownum, range_key_column, x from range_example
  5  /
```

```
Table created.

tkyte@TKYTE816> set autotrace on explain

tkyte@TKYTE816> select * from test, range_example
  2    where test.pk = 1
  3    and test.range_key_column = range_example.range_key_column
  4    and test.x = range_example.x
  5  /

        PK RANGE_KEY          X RANGE_KEY          X DATA
---------- --------- ---------- --------- ---------- --------------------
         1 01-JAN-94          1 01-JAN-94          1 xxx


Execution Plan
----------------------------------------------------------
   0      SELECT STATEMENT Optimizer=CHOOSE (Cost=2 Card=1 Bytes=69)
   1    0   NESTED LOOPS (Cost=2 Card=1 Bytes=69)
   2    1     TABLE ACCESS (BY INDEX ROWID) OF 'TEST' (Cost=1 Card=1
   3    2       INDEX (RANGE SCAN) OF 'TEST_PK' (UNIQUE) (Cost=1 Card=1)
   4    1     PARTITION RANGE (ITERATOR)
   5    4       TABLE ACCESS (BY LOCAL INDEX ROWID) OF 'RANGE_EXAMPLE'
   6    5         INDEX (UNIQUE SCAN) OF 'RANGE_EXAMPLE_PK' (UNIQUE)
```

The query plan of the above would be processed in the following manner:

1. Use the index TEST_PK to find the rows in the table TEST that match the predicate test.pk = 1.

2. Access the table TEST to pick up the remaining columns in TEST – the range_key_column and x specifically.

3. Using these values we picked up in (2), use the RANGE_EXAMPLE_PK to find the rows in a single partition of RANGE_EXAMPLE.

4. Access the single RANGE_EXAMPLE partition to pick up the data column.

That seems straightforward enough – but look what happens when we turn the index into a non-prefixed index by reversing range_key_column and x:

```
tkyte@TKYTE816> alter table range_example
  2    drop constraint range_example_pk
  3  /

Table altered.

tkyte@TKYTE816> alter table range_example
  2    add constraint range_example_pk
  3    primary key (x,range_key_column)
  4    using index local
  5  /

Table altered.
```

```
tkyte@TKYTE816> select * from test, range_example
  2    where test.pk = 1
  3    and test.range_key_column = range_example.range_key_column
  4    and test.x = range_example.x
  5  /

        PK RANGE_KEY          X RANGE_KEY          X DATA
---------- --------- ---------- --------- ---------- --------------------
         1 01-JAN-94          1 01-JAN-94          1 xxx


Execution Plan
----------------------------------------------------------
   0      SELECT STATEMENT Optimizer=CHOOSE (Cost=2 Card=1 Bytes=69)
   1    0   NESTED LOOPS (Cost=2 Card=1 Bytes=69)
   2    1     TABLE ACCESS (BY INDEX ROWID) OF 'TEST' (Cost=1 Card=1
   3    2       INDEX (RANGE SCAN) OF 'TEST_PK' (UNIQUE) (Cost=1 Card=1)
   4    1     PARTITION RANGE (ITERATOR)
   5    4       TABLE ACCESS (FULL) OF 'RANGE_EXAMPLE' (Cost=1 Card=164
```

All of a sudden, Oracle finds this new index to be too expensive to use. This is one case where the use of a prefixed index would provide a measurable benefit.

The bottom line here is that you should not be afraid of non-prefixed indexes or consider them as major performance inhibitors. If you have many queries that could benefit from a non-prefixed index as outlined above, then you should consider using it. The main concern is to ensure that your queries contain predicates that allow for index partition elimination whenever possible. The use of prefixed local indexes enforces that consideration. The use of non-prefixed indexes does not. Consider also, how the index will be used – if it will be used as the first step in a query plan, there are not many differences between the two types of indexes. If, on the other hand, the index is intended to be used primarily as an access method in a join, as above, consider prefixed indexes over non-prefixed indexes. If you can use the local prefixed index, try to use it.

Local Indexes and Uniqueness

In order to enforce uniqueness, and that includes a UNIQUE constraint or PRIMARY KEY constraints, your partitioning key must be included in the constraint itself. This is the largest impact of a local index, in my opinion. Oracle only enforces uniqueness within an index partition, never across partitions. What this implies, for example, is that you cannot range partition on a TIMESTAMP field, and have a primary key on the ID which is enforced using a locally partitioned index. Oracle will utilize a single *global* index to enforce uniqueness.

For example, if you execute the following CREATE TABLE statement in a schema that owns no other objects (so we can see exactly what objects are created by looking at every segment this user owns) we'll find:

```
tkyte@TKYTE816> CREATE TABLE partitioned
  2  ( timestamp date,
  3    id          int primary key
  4  )
  5  PARTITION BY RANGE (timestamp)
  6  (
  7  PARTITION part_1 VALUES LESS THAN
  8  ( to_date('01-jan-2000','dd-mon-yyyy') ) ,
  9  PARTITION part_2 VALUES LESS THAN
```

```
 10  ( to_date('01-jan-2001','dd-mon-yyyy') )
 11  )
 12  /

Table created.

tkyte@TKYTE816> select segment_name, partition_name, segment_type
  2     from user_segments;

SEGMENT_NAME      PARTITION_NAME    SEGMENT_TYPE
----------------  ----------------  ------------------
PARTITIONED       PART_2            TABLE PARTITION
PARTITIONED       PART_1            TABLE PARTITION
SYS_C003582                         INDEX
```

The SYS_C003582 index is not partitioned – it cannot be. This means you lose many of the availability features of partitions in a data warehouse. If you perform partition operations, as you would in a data warehouse, you lose the ability to do them independently. That is, if you add a new partition of data, your single global index must be rebuilt – virtually every partition operation will require a rebuild. Contrast that with a local index only implementation whereby the local indexes never need to be rebuilt unless it is their partition that was operated on.

If you try to trick Oracle by realizing that a primary key can be enforced by a non-unique index as well as a unique index, you'll find that it will not work either:

```
tkyte@TKYTE816> CREATE TABLE partitioned
  2  ( timestamp date,
  3    id         int
  4  )
  5  PARTITION BY RANGE (timestamp)
  6  (
  7  PARTITION part_1 VALUES LESS THAN
  8  ( to_date('01-jan-2000','dd-mon-yyyy') ) ,
  9  PARTITION part_2 VALUES LESS THAN
 10  ( to_date('01-jan-2001','dd-mon-yyyy') )
 11  )
 12  /

Table created.

tkyte@TKYTE816> create index partitioned_index
  2  on partitioned(id)
  3  LOCAL
  4  /

Index created.

tkyte@TKYTE816> select segment_name, partition_name, segment_type
  2     from user_segments;

SEGMENT_NAME      PARTITION_NAME    SEGMENT_TYPE
----------------  ----------------  ------------------
PARTITIONED       PART_2            TABLE PARTITION
PARTITIONED       PART_1            TABLE PARTITION
```

```
PARTITIONED_INDEX PART_2            INDEX PARTITION
PARTITIONED_INDEX PART_1            INDEX PARTITION

tkyte@TKYTE816> alter table partitioned
  2   add constraint partitioned_pk
  3   primary key(id)
  4   /
alter table partitioned
*
ERROR at line 1:
ORA-01408: such column list already indexed
```

Here, Oracle attempts to create a global index on ID but finds that it cannot since an index already exists. The above statements would work if the index we created was not partitioned – Oracle would have used that index to enforce the constraint.

The reason that uniqueness cannot be enforced, unless the partition key is part of the constraint, is twofold. Firstly, if Oracle allowed this it would void most all of the advantages of partitions. Availability and scalability would be lost, as each, and every, partition would always have to be *available* and *scanned* to do any inserts and updates. The more partitions you have, the less available the data is. The more partitions you have, the more index partitions you must scan, the less scalable partitions become. Instead of providing availability and scalability, this would actually decrease both.

Additionally, Oracle would have to effectively **serialize** inserts and updates to this table at the transaction level. This is because of the fact that if we add ID=1 to PART_1, Oracle would have to somehow *prevent* anyone else from adding ID=1 to PART_2. The only way to do this would be to prevent them from modifying index partition PART_2 since there isn't anything to really 'lock' in that partition.

In an OLTP system, unique constraints must be system enforced (enforced by Oracle) to ensure the integrity of data. This implies that the logical model of your system will have an impact on the physical design. Uniqueness constraints will either drive the underlying table partitioning scheme, driving the choice of the partition keys, or alternatively, these constraints will point you towards the use of *global* indexes instead. We'll take a look at global indexes in more depth now.

Global Indexes

Global indexes are partitioned using a scheme different from their underlying table. The table might be partitioned by the TIMESTAMP column into ten partitions, and a global index on that table could be partitioned into five partitions by the REGION column. Unlike local indexes, there is only one class of global index, and that is a **prefixed global index**. There is no support for a global index whose index key does not begin with the partition key.

Following on from our previous example, here is a quick example of the use of a global index. It shows that a global partitioned index can be used to enforce uniqueness for a primary key, so you can have partitioned indexes that enforce uniqueness, but do not include the partition key of TABLE. The following example creates a table partitioned by TIMESTAMP that has an index that is partitioned by ID:

```
tkyte@TKYTE816> CREATE TABLE partitioned
  2  ( timestamp date,
  3    id        int
  4  )
```

```
    5   PARTITION BY RANGE (timestamp)
    6   (
    7   PARTITION part_1 VALUES LESS THAN
    8   ( to_date('01-jan-2000','dd-mon-yyyy') ) ,
    9   PARTITION part_2 VALUES LESS THAN
   10   ( to_date('01-jan-2001','dd-mon-yyyy') )
   11   )
   12   /

Table created.

tkyte@TKYTE816> create index partitioned_index
    2   on partitioned(id)
    3   GLOBAL
    4   partition  by range(id)
    5   (
    6   partition part_1 values less than(1000),
    7   partition part_2 values less than (MAXVALUE)
    8   )
    9   /

Index created.
```

Note the use of MAXVALUE in this index. MAXVALUE can be used in any range-partitioned table as well as in the index. It represents an 'infinite upper bound' on the range. In our examples so far, we've used hard upper bounds on the ranges (values less than <some value>). However, a global index has a requirement that the highest partition (the last partition) must have a partition bound whose value is MAXVALUE. This ensures that all rows in the underlying table can be placed in the index.

Now, completing this example, we'll add our primary key to the table:

```
tkyte@TKYTE816> alter table partitioned add constraint
    2   partitioned_pk
    3   primary key(id)
    4   /

Table altered.
```

It is not evident from the above that Oracle is using the index we created to enforce the primary key (it is to me because I know that Oracle is using it) so we can prove it by a magic query against the 'real' data dictionary. You'll need an account that has SELECT granted on the base tables, or the SELECT ANY TABLE privilege, in order to execute this query:

```
tkyte@TKYTE816> select  t.name    table_name
    2        , u.name    owner
    3        , c.name    constraint_name
    4        , i.name    index_name
    5        , decode(bitand(i.flags, 4), 4, 'Yes',
    6               decode( i.name, c.name, 'Possibly', 'No') ) generated
    7   from sys.cdef$ cd
    8        , sys.con$  c
    9        , sys.obj$  t
   10        , sys.obj$  i
```

```
11        , sys.user$ u
12   where cd.type#        between 2 and 3
13     and     cd.con#    = c.con#
14     and     cd.obj#    = t.obj#
15     and     cd.enabled = i.obj#
16     and      c.owner#      = u.user#
17     and      c.owner# = uid
18   /


TABLE_NAME    OWNER CONSTRAINT_NAME  INDEX_NAME        GENERATE
------------- ----- --------------- ----------------- --------
PARTITIONED   TKYTE PARTITIONED_PK   PARTITIONED_INDEX No
```

This query shows us the index used to enforce a given constraint, and tries to 'guess' as to whether the index name is a system generated one or not. In this case, it shows us that the index being used for our primary key is in fact the PARTITIONED_INDEX we just created (and the name was definitely not system generated).

To show that Oracle will not allow us to create a *non*-prefixed global index, we only need try:

```
tkyte@TKYTE816> create index partitioned_index2
  2  on partitioned(timestamp,id)
  3  GLOBAL
  4  partition  by range(id)
  5  (
  6  partition part_1 values less than(1000),
  7  partition part_2 values less than (MAXVALUE)
  8  )
  9  /
partition  by range(id)
                    *
ERROR at line 4:
ORA-14038: GLOBAL partitioned index must be prefixed
```

The error message is pretty clear. The global index *must* be prefixed.

So, when would you use a global index? We'll take a look at two system types, data warehouse and OLTP, and see when they might apply.

Data Warehousing and Global Indexes

It is my opinion that these two things are mutually exclusive. A data warehouse implies certain things; large amounts of data coming in and going out, high probability of a failure of a disk somewhere, and so on. Any data warehouse that uses a 'sliding window' would want to avoid the use of global indexes. Here is an example of what I mean by a sliding window of data and the impact of a global index on it:

```
tkyte@TKYTE816> CREATE TABLE partitioned
  2  ( timestamp date,
  3    id        int
  4  )
  5  PARTITION BY RANGE (timestamp)
```

```
  6  (
  7  PARTITION fy_1999 VALUES LESS THAN
  8  ( to_date('01-jan-2000','dd-mon-yyyy') ) ,
  9  PARTITION fy_2000 VALUES LESS THAN
 10  ( to_date('01-jan-2001','dd-mon-yyyy') ) ,
 11  PARTITION the_rest VALUES LESS THAN
 12  ( maxvalue )
 13  )
 14  /

Table created.

tkyte@TKYTE816> insert into partitioned partition(fy_1999)
  2  select to_date('31-dec-1999')-mod(rownum,360), object_id
  3  from all_objects
  4  /

21914 rows created.

tkyte@TKYTE816> insert into partitioned partition(fy_2000)
  2  select to_date('31-dec-2000')-mod(rownum,360), object_id
  3  from all_objects
  4  /

21914 rows created.

tkyte@TKYTE816> create index partitioned_idx_local
  2  on partitioned(id)
  3  LOCAL
  4  /

Index created.

tkyte@TKYTE816> create index partitioned_idx_global
  2  on partitioned(timestamp)
  3  GLOBAL
  4  /

Index created.
```

So, this sets up our 'warehouse' table. The data is partitioned by fiscal year and we have the last two years worth of data online. This table has two indexes; one is LOCAL and the other GLOBAL. Notice that I left an empty partition THE_REST at the end of the table. This will facilitate sliding new data in quickly. Now, it is the end of the year and we would like to:

1. Remove the oldest fiscal year data. We do not want to lose this data forever, we just want to age it out and archive it.

2. Add the newest fiscal year data. It will take a while to load it, transform it, index it, and so on. We would like to do this work without impacting the availability of the current data, if at all possible.

The steps I might take would be:

```
tkyte@TKYTE816> create table fy_1999 ( timestamp date, id int );

Table created.

tkyte@TKYTE816> create index fy_1999_idx on fy_1999(id)
  2  /

Index created.

tkyte@TKYTE816> create table fy_2001 ( timestamp date, id int );

Table created.

tkyte@TKYTE816> insert into fy_2001
  2  select to_date('31-dec-2001')-mod(rownum,360), object_id
  3  from all_objects
  4  /

21922 rows created.

tkyte@TKYTE816> create index fy_2001_idx on fy_2001(id) nologging
  2  /

Index created.
```

What I've done here is to set up an empty 'shell' table and index for the oldest data. What we will do is turn the current full partition into an empty partition and create a 'full' table, with the FY_1999 data in it. Also, I've completed all of the work necessary to have the FY_2001 data ready to go. This would have involved verifying the data, transforming it – whatever complex tasks you need to undertake to get it ready.

Now we are ready to update the 'live' data:

```
tkyte@TKYTE816> alter table partitioned
  2  exchange partition fy_1999
  3  with table fy_1999
  4  including indexes
  5  without validation
  6  /

Table altered.

tkyte@TKYTE816> alter table partitioned
  2  drop partition fy_1999
  3  /

Table altered.
```

This is all you need to do to 'age' the old data out. We turned the partition into a full table and the empty table into a partition. This was a simple data dictionary update – no large amount of I/O took place, it just happened. We can now export that table (perhaps using a transportable tablespace) out of our database for archival purposes. We could re-attach it quickly if we ever need to.

Next, we want to slide in the new data:

```
tkyte@TKYTE816> alter table partitioned
  2  split partition the_rest
  3  at ( to_date('01-jan-2002','dd-mon-yyyy') )
  4  into ( partition fy_2001, partition the_rest )
  5  /

Table altered.

tkyte@TKYTE816> alter table partitioned
  2  exchange partition fy_2001
  3  with table fy_2001
  4  including indexes
  5  without validation
  6  /

Table altered.
```

Again, this was instantaneous – a simple data dictionary update. Splitting the empty partition takes very little real-time since there never was, and never will be data in it. That is why I placed an extra empty partition at the end of the table, to facilitate the split. Then, we exchange the newly created empty partition with the full table and the full table with an empty partition. The new data is online.

Looking at our indexes however, we'll find:

```
tkyte@TKYTE816> select index_name, status from user_indexes;

INDEX_NAME             STATUS
---------------------- ----------
FY_1999_IDX            VALID
FY_2001_IDX            VALID
PARTITIONED_IDX_GLOBAL UNUSABLE
PARTITIONED_IDX_LOCAL  N/A
```

The global index is of course unusable after this operation. Since each index partition can point to any table partition *and* we just took away a partition and added a partition, that index is invalid. It has entries that point into the partition we dropped. It has *no* entries that point into the partition we just added. Any query that would make use of this index will fail:

```
tkyte@TKYTE816> select count(*)
  2  from partitioned
  3  where timestamp between sysdate-50 and sysdate;
select count(*)
*
ERROR at line 1:
ORA-01502: index 'TKYTE.PARTITIONED_IDX_GLOBAL' or partition of such index is in
unusable state
```

We could set `SKIP_UNUSABLE_INDEXES=TRUE`, but then we lose the performance the index was giving us (this works in Oracle 8.1.5 and later versions; prior to that, `SELECT` statement would still try to use the `UNUSABLE` index). We need to rebuild this index in order to make the data truly usable again. The sliding window process, which so far has resulted in virtually no downtime, will now take a very long time to complete while we rebuild the global index. All of the data must be scanned and the entire index reconstructed from the table data. If the table is many hundreds of gigabytes in size, this will take considerable resources.

Any partition operation will cause this global index invalidation to occur. If you need to move a partition to another disk, your global indexes must be rebuilt (only the local index partitions on *that* partition would have to be rebuilt). If you find that you need to split a partition into two smaller partitions at some point in time, all global indexes must be rebuilt (only the pairs of individual local index partitions on those two new partitions would have to be rebuilt). And so on. For this reason, global indexes in a data warehousing environment should be avoided. Their use may dramatically affect many operations.

OLTP and Global Indexes

An OLTP system is characterized by the frequent occurence of many small, to very small, read and write transactions. In general, sliding windows of data are not something with which you are concerned. Fast access to the row, or rows, you need is paramount. Data integrity is vital. Availability is also very important.

Global indexes make sense in OLTP systems. Table data can only be partitioned by one key – one set of columns. However, you may need to access the data in many different ways. You might partition `EMPLOYEE` data by location. You still need fast access to `EMPLOYEE` data however by:

❑ `DEPARTMENT` – departments are geographically dispersed, there is no relationship between a department and a location.

❑ `EMPLOYEE_ID` – while an employee ID will determine a location, you don't want to have to search by `EMPLOYEE_ID` and `LOCATION`, hence partition elimination cannot take place on the index partitions. Also, `EMPLOYEE_ID` by itself must be *unique*.

❑ `JOB_TITLE`

There is a need to access the `EMPLOYEE` data by many different keys in different places in your application, and speed is paramount. In a data warehouse, we would just use locally partitioned indexes on the above key values, and use parallel index range scans to collect the data fast. In these cases we don't necessarily need to utilize index partition elimination, but in an OLTP system, however, we do need to utilize it. Parallel query is not appropriate for these systems; we need to provide the indexes appropriately. Therefore, we will need to make use of global indexes on certain fields.

Therefore the goals we need to meet are:

❑ Fast Access

❑ Data Integrity

❑ Availability

Global indexes can do this for us in an OLTP system, since the characteristics of this system are very different from a data warehouse. We will probably not be doing sliding windows, we will not be splitting partitions (unless we have a scheduled downtime), we will not be moving data and so on. The operations we perform in a data warehouse are not done on a live OLTP system in general.

Here is a small example that shows how we can achieve the above three goals with global indexes. I am going to use simple, single partition global indexes, but the results would not be different with partitioned global indexes (except for the fact that availability and manageability would *increase* as we add index partitions):

```
tkyte@TKYTE816> create table emp
  2  (EMPNO              NUMBER(4) NOT NULL,
  3   ENAME              VARCHAR2(10),
  4   JOB                VARCHAR2(9),
  5   MGR                NUMBER(4),
  6   HIREDATE           DATE,
  7   SAL                NUMBER(7,2),
  8   COMM               NUMBER(7,2),
  9   DEPTNO             NUMBER(2) NOT NULL,
 10   LOC                VARCHAR2(13) NOT NULL
 11  )
 12  partition by range(loc)
 13  (
 14  partition p1 values less than('C') tablespace p1,
 15  partition p2 values less than('D') tablespace p2,
 16  partition p3 values less than('N') tablespace p3,
 17  partition p4 values less than('Z') tablespace p4
 18  )
 19  /

Table created.

tkyte@TKYTE816> alter table emp add constraint emp_pk
  2  primary key(empno)
  3  /

Table altered.

tkyte@TKYTE816> create index emp_job_idx on emp(job)
  2  GLOBAL
  3  /

Index created.

tkyte@TKYTE816> create index emp_dept_idx on emp(deptno)
  2  GLOBAL
  3  /

Index created.

tkyte@TKYTE816> insert into emp
  2  select e.*, d.loc
  3    from scott.emp e, scott.dept d
  4   where e.deptno = d.deptno
  5  /

14 rows created.
```

So, we start with a table that is partitioned by location, LOC, according to our rules. There exists a global unique index on the EMPNO column as a side effect of the ALTER TABLE ADD CONSTRAINT. This shows we can support data integrity. Additionally, we've added two more global indexes on DEPTNO and JOB, to facilitate accessing records quickly by those attributes. Now we'll put some data in there and see what is in each partition:

```
tkyte@TKYTE816> select empno,job,loc from emp partition(p1);

no rows selected

tkyte@TKYTE816> select empno,job,loc from emp partition(p2);

     EMPNO JOB       LOC
---------- --------- -------------
      7900 CLERK     CHICAGO
      7844 SALESMAN  CHICAGO
      7698 MANAGER   CHICAGO
      7654 SALESMAN  CHICAGO
      7521 SALESMAN  CHICAGO
      7499 SALESMAN  CHICAGO
6 rows selected.

tkyte@TKYTE816> select empno,job,loc from emp partition(p3);

     EMPNO JOB       LOC
---------- --------- -------------
      7902 ANALYST   DALLAS
      7876 CLERK     DALLAS
      7788 ANALYST   DALLAS
      7566 MANAGER   DALLAS
      7369 CLERK     DALLAS

tkyte@TKYTE816> select empno,job,loc from emp partition(p4);

     EMPNO JOB       LOC
---------- --------- -------------
      7934 CLERK     NEW YORK
      7839 PRESIDENT NEW YORK
      7782 MANAGER   NEW YORK
```

This shows the distribution of data, by location, into the individual partitions. We can now run some queries to check out performance:

```
tkyte@TKYTE816> select empno,job,loc from emp where empno = 7782;

     EMPNO JOB       LOC
---------- --------- -------------
      7782 MANAGER   NEW YORK

Execution Plan
----------------------------------------------------------
   0      SELECT STATEMENT Optimizer=CHOOSE (Cost=1 Card=4 Bytes=108)
   1    0   TABLE ACCESS (BY GLOBAL INDEX ROWID) OF 'EMP' (Cost=1 Card
   2    1     INDEX (RANGE SCAN) OF 'EMP_PK' (UNIQUE) (Cost=1 Card=4)


tkyte@TKYTE816> select empno,job,loc from emp where job = 'CLERK';

     EMPNO JOB       LOC
---------- --------- -------------
      7900 CLERK     CHICAGO
      7876 CLERK     DALLAS
```

```
         7369 CLERK      DALLAS
         7934 CLERK      NEW YORK


Execution Plan
-----------------------------------------------------------
    0      SELECT STATEMENT Optimizer=CHOOSE (Cost=1 Card=4 Bytes=108)
    1    0    TABLE ACCESS (BY GLOBAL INDEX ROWID) OF 'EMP' (Cost=1 Card
    2    1      INDEX (RANGE SCAN) OF 'EMP_JOB_IDX' (NON-UNIQUE) (Cost=1
```

And sure enough, our indexes are used and provide high speed OLTP access to the underlying data. If they were partitioned, they would have to be prefixed and would enforce index partition elimination; hence, they are scalable as well. Lastly, let's look at the area of availability. The Oracle documentation claims that globally partitioned indexes make for 'less available' data than locally partitioned indexes. I don't fully agree with this blanket characterization, I believe that in an OLTP system they are as highly available as a locally partitioned index. Consider:

```
tkyte@TKYTE816> alter tablespace p1 offline;

Tablespace altered.

tkyte@TKYTE816> alter tablespace p2 offline;

Tablespace altered.

tkyte@TKYTE816> alter tablespace p3 offline;

Tablespace altered.

tkyte@TKYTE816> select empno,job,loc from emp where empno = 7782;

    EMPNO JOB        LOC
---------- ---------- -------------
     7782 MANAGER    NEW YORK


Execution Plan
-----------------------------------------------------------
    0      SELECT STATEMENT Optimizer=CHOOSE (Cost=1 Card=4 Bytes=108)
    1    0    TABLE ACCESS (BY GLOBAL INDEX ROWID) OF 'EMP' (Cost=1 Card
    2    1      INDEX (RANGE SCAN) OF 'EMP_PK' (UNIQUE) (Cost=1 Card=4)
```

Here, even though most of the underlying data is unavailable in the table, we can still gain access to any bit of data available via that index. As long as the EMPNO we want is in a tablespace that is available, our GLOBAL index works for us. On the other hand, if we *had* been using the 'highly available' local index in the above case, we might have been prevented from accessing the data! This is a side effect of the fact that we partitioned on LOC but needed to query by EMPNO; we would have had to probe each local index partition and would have failed on the index partitions that were not available.

Other types of queries however will not (and cannot) function at this point in time:

```
tkyte@TKYTE816> select empno,job,loc from emp where job = 'CLERK';
select empno,job,loc from emp where job = 'CLERK'
```

```
                                  *
    ERROR at line 1:
    ORA-00376: file 13 cannot be read at this time
    ORA-01110: data file 13: 'C:\ORACLE\ORADATA\TKYTE816\P2.DBF'
```

The CLERK data is in all of the partitions – the fact that three of the tablespaces are offline does affect us. This is unavoidable unless we had partitioned on JOB, but then we would have had the same issues with queries that needed data by LOC. Any time you need to access the data from many different 'keys', you will have this issue. Oracle will give you the data whenever it can.

Note, however, that if the query can be answered from the index, avoiding the TABLE ACCESS BY ROWID, the fact that the data is unavailable is not as meaningful:

```
    tkyte@TKYTE816> select count(*) from emp where job = 'CLERK';

      COUNT(*)
    ----------
             4


    Execution Plan
    ----------------------------------------------------------
       0      SELECT STATEMENT Optimizer=CHOOSE (Cost=1 Card=1 Bytes=6)
       1    0   SORT (AGGREGATE)
       2    1     INDEX (RANGE SCAN) OF 'EMP_JOB_IDX' (NON-UNIQUE) (Cost=1
```

Since Oracle didn't need the table in this case, the fact that most of the partitions were offline doesn't affect this query. As this type of optimization (answer the query using just the index) is common in an OLTP system, there will be many applications that are not affected by the data that is offline. All we need to do now is make the offline data available as fast as possible (restore it, recover it).

Summary

Partitioning is extremely useful in scaling up large database objects in the database. This scaling is visible from the perspective of performance scaling, availability scaling, as well as administrative scaling. All three are extremely important to different people. The DBA is concerned with administrative scaling. The owners of the system are concerned with availability. Downtime is lost money and anything that reduces downtime, or reduces the impact of downtime, boosts the payback for a system. The end users of the system are concerned with performance scaling – no one likes to use a slow system after all.

We also looked at the fact that in an OLTP system, partitions may not increase performance, especially if applied improperly. Partitions can increase performance of certain classes of queries but those queries are generally not applied in an OLTP system. This point is important to understand as many people associate partitioning with 'free performance increase'. This does not mean that partitions should *not* be used in OLTP systems, as they do provide many other salient benefits in this environment – just don't expect a massive increase in throughput. Expect reduced downtime. Expect the same good performance (it will not slow you down when applied appropriately). Expect easier manageability, which may lead to increased performance due to the fact that some maintenance operations are performed by the DBAs more frequently because they can be.

We investigated the various table-partitioning schemes offered by Oracle – range, hash, and composite – and talked about when they are most appropriately used. We spent the bulk of our time looking at partitioned indexes, examining the difference between prefixed and non-prefixed, and local and global indexes. We found that global indexes are perhaps not appropriate in most data warehouses whereas an OLTP system would most likely make use of them frequently.

Partitioning is an ever-growing feature within Oracle with many enhancements planned for the next release. Over time, I see this feature becoming more relevant to a broader audience as the size and scale of database applications grow. The Internet and its database hungry nature are leading to more and more extremely large collections of data and partitioning is a natural tool to help manage that problem.

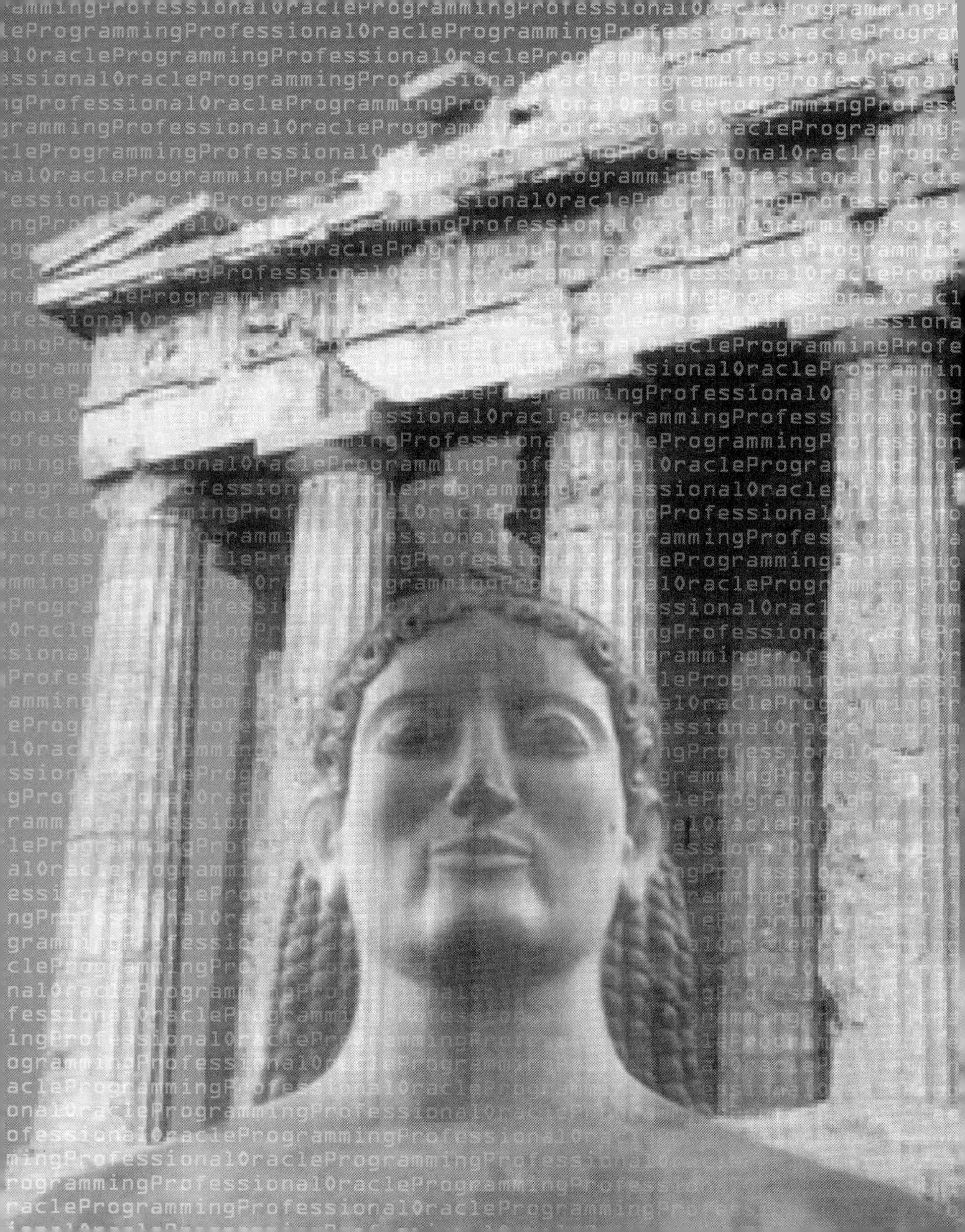

15

Autonomous Transactions

Autonomous transactions allow you to create a new **transaction within a transaction** that may commit or roll back changes, independently of its parent transaction. They allow you to suspend the currently executing transaction, start a new one, do some work and commit or roll back, all without affecting the currently executing transaction state. Autonomous transactions provide a new method of controlling transactions in PL/SQL, and may be used in:

- ❑ Top-level anonymous blocks
- ❑ Local, standalone, or packaged functions and procedures
- ❑ Methods or object types
- ❑ Database triggers

In order to execute the examples in this chapter, you will need Oracle 8.1.5 or higher. Any edition, Standard, Enterprise, or Personal may be used, as this feature is available with all of them.

After looking at a first example of a simple autonomous transaction, we will:

- ❑ Look at how to use them, including how to implement auditing that cannot be rolled back, prevent mutating tables, write to the database from a SELECT statement, and as a means to develop more modular code.
- ❑ See how they work. We'll investigate transactional control and scope, how to end an autonomous transaction and how to issue savepoints.
- ❑ Round off the chapter with caveats and errors that you should look out for when using this feature in your applications.

An Example

In order to show what this feature can do, we'll start with a quick example that demonstrates the effects of autonomous transactions. What we'll do is create a simple table to hold a message, along with two procedures: one 'regular' procedure, and the other coded as an autonomous transaction. The procedures will modify the table we created. We'll use these objects to show what work persists (is committed) in the database under various circumstances:

```
tkyte@TKYTE816> create table t ( msg varchar2(25) );

Table created.

tkyte@TKYTE816> create or replace procedure Autonomous_Insert
  2    as
  3            pragma autonomous_transaction;
  4    begin
  5            insert into t values ( 'Autonomous Insert' );
  6            commit;
  7    end;
  8    /

Procedure created.

tkyte@TKYTE816> create or replace procedure NonAutonomous_Insert
  2    as
  3    begin
  4            insert into t values ( 'NonAutonomous Insert' );
  5            commit;
  6    end;
  7    /

Procedure created.
```

The procedures simply insert their name into the message table and commit – very simple. Note the use of the PRAGMA AUTONOMOUS_TRANSACTION. This directive tells the database that this procedure, when executed, is to be executed as a new autonomous transaction, independently of its parent transaction. Now, let's observe the behavior of the non-autonomous transaction in an anonymous block of PL/SQL code:

```
tkyte@TKYTE816> begin
  2            insert into t values ( 'Anonymous Block' );
  3            NonAutonomous_Insert;
  4            rollback;
  5    end;
  6    /

PL/SQL procedure successfully completed.

tkyte@TKYTE816> select * from t;

MSG
-------------------------
Anonymous Block
NonAutonomous Insert
```

As you can see, the work performed by the anonymous block, its insert, was committed by the procedure NonAutonomous_Insert. Both rows of data were committed, and the rollback had nothing to roll back. Compare this to the behavior of the autonomous transaction procedure:

```
tkyte@TKYTE816> delete from t;

2 rows deleted.

tkyte@TKYTE816> commit;

Commit complete.

tkyte@TKYTE816> begin
  2          insert into t values ( 'Anonymous Block' );
  3          Autonomous_Insert;
  4          rollback;
  5  end;
  6  /

PL/SQL procedure successfully completed.

tkyte@TKYTE816> select * from t;

MSG
------------------------------
Autonomous Insert
```

Here, only the work done by, and committed, in the autonomous transaction persists. The INSERT done in the anonymous block is rolled back by the ROLLBACK statement on line 4. The autonomous transaction procedure's COMMIT has no effect on the parent transaction started in the anonymous block. This simple example captures the essence of autonomous transactions and what they do.

In the absence of autonomous transactions, the COMMIT in the procedure NonAutonomous_Insert committed not only the work it performed (the INSERT of NonAutonomous Insert), but also any outstanding work the session had performed and not yet committed (such as the insert of Anonymous Block in the anonymous block). The rollback rolled back no work, since the procedure call already committed both INSERTs. We see that this is not the case with autonomous transactions. The work performed in the procedure marked with AUTONOMOUS_TRANSACTION was committed; however, the work performed outside the autonomous transaction was rolled back.

Oracle has supported autonomous transactions internally for quite a while. We see them all of the time in the form of recursive SQL. For example, when selecting from a non-cached sequence, a recursive transaction is performed for you to increment the sequence immediately in the SYS.SEQ$ table. The update of the sequence was immediately committed and visible to other transactions, but your transaction was not committed yet. Additionally, if you roll back your transaction, the increment to the sequence remained in place – it was not rolled back with your transaction, as it had already been committed. Space management, auditing, and other internal operations are performed in a similar, recursive fashion. This feature has now been exposed for all to use.

Now that we have seen what an autonomous transaction is, we'll take a look at reasons for using them.

Why Use Autonomous Transactions?

In this section we will explore various scenarios where you might choose to use this feature.

Auditing that Can Not be Rolled Back

A question that, in the past, was frequently posed by application developers was, 'How can I audit an *attempt* to modify secure information?' What they want to do is not only *prevent* the attempted modification from taking place, but also create a permanent record of the attempt. The approach in the past that many have tried to use (and failed) was triggers. The trigger would detect the update and, upon discovering a user modifying data they should not, the trigger would create an audit record and fail the update. Unfortunately, when you failed the update, you also rolled back the audit record – it was an all or nothing failure. Now, with autonomous transactions we can securely capture the audit of an attempted operation, as well as roll back that operation, giving us the ability to tell the end user, 'You cannot modify that data, and we have a record of you attempting to modify it'. It is interesting to note that the native Oracle AUDIT capability gave us the ability to capture unsuccessful attempts to modify information using autonomous transactions for many years. The exposure of this feature to the Oracle developer, allows us to create our own, more customized auditing.

Here is a small example. What we will do is copy the EMP table from the SCOTT schema. We will also create an audit trail table that will be used to capture *who* tried to update this EMP table and *when* they tried to do it, along with a descriptive message of what they tried to modify. A trigger, coded as an autonomous transaction, will be placed in the EMP table to capture this information for us:

```
tkyte@TKYTE816> create table emp
  2  as
  3  select * from scott.emp;

Table created.

tkyte@TKYTE816> grant all on emp to scott;

Grant succeeded.

tkyte@TKYTE816> create table audit_tab
  2  ( username   varchar2(30) default user,
  3    timestamp  date default sysdate,
  4    msg        varchar2(4000)
  5  )
  6  /

Table created.
```

The next thing is to create a trigger to audit update activity on the EMP table. Note the use of the autonomous transaction. The logic employed by this trigger is to prevent anyone from updating the record of an employee that does not work for him or her. The CONNECT BY query is adept at resolving the entire hierarchy for us, given the current user. It will verify that the record you are attempting to update is of someone that reports to you at some level:

```
tkyte@TKYTE816> create or replace trigger EMP_AUDIT
  2  before update on emp
  3  for each row
  4  declare
  5      pragma autonomous_transaction;
  6      l_cnt   number;
  7  begin
  8
  9      select count(*) into l_cnt
 10        from dual
 11       where EXISTS ( select null
 12                        from emp
 13                       where empno = :new.empno
 14                       start with mgr = ( select empno
 15                                            from emp
 16                                           where ename = USER )
 17                     connect by prior  empno = mgr );
 18
 19      if ( l_cnt = 0 )
 20      then
 21          insert into audit_tab ( msg )
 22          values ( 'Attempt to update ' || :new.empno );
 23          commit;
 24
 25          raise_application_error( -20001, 'Access Denied' );
 26      end if;
 27  end;
 28  /

Trigger created.
```

So, we have set up the EMP table that has a nice hierarchical structure (EMPNO/MGR recursive relationship). We have an AUDIT_TAB into which we want to record failed attempts to modify information. We have a trigger to enforce our rule that only your manager, or your manager's manager (and so on) may modify your record.

The things to notice in the above trigger are:

❑   PRAGMA AUTONOMOUS_TRANSACTION is applied to the trigger definition. This entire trigger is an autonomous transaction of the parent transaction. A quick word on the term 'pragma'. A pragma is simply a compiler directive, a method to instruct the compiler to perform some compilation option. There are other pragmas available, see the *PL/SQL User's Guide and Reference* in Oracle's documentation and look in the index for a list of them under pragma.

❑   This trigger on EMP reads *from* EMP in the query. More on why this is 'earth shattering' in a moment.

❑   This trigger commits. This has never been possible before – triggers could never commit work. This trigger is not committing the work that actually fired the trigger. Rather, it is only committing the work that the trigger has performed (the audit record).

So, let's see how this works then:

```
tkyte@TKYTE816> update emp set sal = sal*10;
update emp set sal = sal*10
       *
ERROR at line 1:
ORA-20001: Access Denied
ORA-06512: at "TKYTE.EMP_AUDIT", line 22
ORA-04088: error during execution of trigger 'TKYTE.EMP_AUDIT'


tkyte@TKYTE816> column msg format a30 word_wrapped
tkyte@TKYTE816> select * from audit_tab;

USERNAME                         TIMESTAMP MSG
------------------------------   --------- ------------------------------
TKYTE                            15-APR-01 Attempt to update 7369
```

So, the trigger caught me and was able to prevent the update from occurring while at the same time creating a permanent record of the attempt (notice how it used the DEFAULT keyword on the CREATE TABLE above to automatically have the USER and SYSDATE values inserted for us). Now, let's log in as a user who can actually do an update and try some things out:

```
tkyte@TKYTE816> connect scott/tiger

scott@TKYTE816> update tkyte.emp set sal = sal*1.05 where ename = 'ADAMS';

1 row updated.

scott@TKYTE816> update tkyte.emp set sal = sal*1.05 where ename = 'SCOTT';
update tkyte.emp set sal = sal*1.05 where ename = 'SCOTT'
                *
ERROR at line 1:
ORA-20001: Access Denied
ORA-06512: at "TKYTE.EMP_AUDIT", line 22
ORA-04088: error during execution of trigger 'TKYTE.EMP_AUDIT'
```

In the default EMP table, the employee ADAMS works for SCOTT so the first update succeeds. The second update, where SCOTT tries to give himself a raise, fails since SCOTT does not report to SCOTT. Logging back into the schema where the AUDIT_TAB is located, we see:

```
scott@TKYTE816> connect tkyte/tkyte
tkyte@TKYTE816> select * from audit_tab;

USERNAME                         TIMESTAMP MSG
------------------------------   --------- ------------------------
TKYTE                            15-APR-01 Attempt to update 7369
SCOTT                            15-APR-01 Attempt to update 7788
```

The attempt by SCOTT to perform this update is there. The last thing we want to look at is why it is relevant that we read *from* EMP in the trigger on EMP – 'why is this earth shattering?' This leads us directly into the next section.

A Method to Avoid a Mutating Table

A mutating table error can happen for a number of reasons. The most predominant cause is trying to read the table upon which a trigger is firing. In the example above, we clearly read from the table that fired the trigger. If we comment out two lines of this trigger, and we could attempt to use it as follows:

```
tkyte@TKYTE816> create or replace trigger EMP_AUDIT
  2  before update on emp
  3  for each row
  4  declare
  5      -- pragma autonomous_transaction;
  6      l_cnt   number;
  7  begin
  8
  9      select count(*) into l_cnt
 10        from dual
 11       where EXISTS ( select null
 12                        from emp
 13                       where empno = :new.empno
 14                       start with mgr = ( select empno
 15                                            from emp
 16                                           where ename = USER )
 17                     connect by prior  empno = mgr );
 18
 19      if ( l_cnt = 0 )
 20      then
 21          insert into audit_tab ( msg )
 22          values ( 'Attempt to update ' || :new.empno );
 23          -- commit;
 24
 25          raise_application_error( -20001, 'Access Denied' );
 26      end if;
 27  end;
 28  /

tkyte@TKYTE816> update emp set sal = sal*10;
update emp set sal = sal*10
       *
ERROR at line 1:
ORA-04091: table TKYTE.EMP is mutating, trigger/function may not see it
ORA-06512: at "TKYTE.EMP_AUDIT", line 6
ORA-04088: error during execution of trigger 'TKYTE.EMP_AUDIT'
```

The fact is that without autonomous transactions, the above trigger would be difficult to write, even if all it wanted to do was to verify that you were updating a row you should be allowed to (and not even auditing). Typically, it would actually take a package and three triggers to code without the AUTONOMOUS_TRANSACTION. This does not mean that we will use autonomous transactions to 'fix' mutating table errors any time we hit them – they must be used cautiously and with knowledge of how the transaction is really progressing. In the *Caveats* section later, we will explore the reasons for this. The mutating table error is actually for your protection; an understanding of why it happens is important. Do not fall into the trap of believing that autonomous transactions have removed mutating triggers as an issue!

Performing DDL in Triggers

This is a frequently asked question, 'How can I create a database object whenever I insert a row into such and such a table?' The database object varies from question to question. Sometimes people want to create a database USER when they insert into some table, sometimes they want to create a table or sequence. Since DDL always issues a commit right before and right after it executes (or a commit and a rollback depending on the success or failure of the DDL), doing DDL in a trigger was not possible. Now, autonomous transactions make this possible.

In the past, one might have used DBMS_JOB to schedule the DDL to execute after the transaction commits. This is still a viable option and *in almost all cases is still the correct, optimal option*. The nice thing about using DBMS_JOB to schedule the DDL is that it offers a way of making the DDL transactional. If the trigger queues a job to be executed, and that job creates a user account, upon rollback of the parent transaction, the job we queued to create the user will be rolled back as well. The row representing the job will be 'un-inserted'. No record in your PEOPLE table and no database account. Using autonomous transactions in the same scenario, you will have created the database account, but have no record in the PEOPLE table. The drawback to the DBMS_JOB approach is that there will necessarily be a small lag between the time you commit, and the time at which the job actually runs. The user would be created after you commit, soon after, but not immediately. Which method you use will be based upon your requirements. Again, in almost every case, the argument should be made for DBMS_JOB.

The example we will use to demonstrate doing DDL in triggers is the case where you want to CREATE a user in the database upon INSERT into a table and DROP that user upon DELETE. In this example below, I am going out of my way to avoid the condition where you could end up with a user created, but no row in the table or, upon a delete, be left with a record in the table, but no user account. My method is to use an INSTEAD OF TRIGGER on a view of the APPLICATION_USERS_TBL table. INSTEAD OF triggers are handy devices that allow us to provide the logic to be performed during the modification of rows in a view *instead* of the default processing Oracle would do. In Chapter 20 on *Using Object Relational Features*, we demonstrate how we can use INSTEAD OF triggers to allow for updates to complex views, which Oracle would not permit updates to otherwise. Here, we will use them to perform the act of creating a USER, and inserting the row into a real table (or dropping the user and deleting the row). This will ensure that either both the USER gets created and the row inserted, or neither take place. If the trigger was just on the table itself, we would not be able to ensure that either both, or neither took place – the *view* will allow us to link the two events together. Instead of inserting or deleting the real physical table, all applications will insert and delete from the view. The view will have an INSTEAD OF trigger on it, so it can procedurally process the changes row by row. In this fashion, I will be able to guarantee that if a row exists in the real table, the user account is created. If a row is removed from the real table, the user account is dropped. The example will show best how I accomplished this. I will point out the relevant parts as we get to them.

We will start by creating the schema that will hold this application:

```
tkyte@TKYTE816> create user demo_ddl identified by demo_ddl;

User created.

tkyte@TKYTE816> grant connect, resource to demo_ddl with admin option;

Grant succeeded.

tkyte@TKYTE816> grant create user to demo_ddl;
Grant succeeded.
```

```
tkyte@TKYTE816> grant drop user to demo_ddl;
Grant succeeded.

tkyte@TKYTE816> connect demo_ddl/demo_ddl
demo_ddl@TKYTE816>
```

So, we have just created a user, and we want that user to grant CONNECT and RESOURCE to other users. (Note that CONNECT and RESOURCE are used for convenience here. You would use your own set of privileges as dictated by your needs.) Hence, we need to grant CONNECT and RESOURCE to this schema using the WITH ADMIN OPTION so the user can grant them to others. Additionally, since we want to create and drop users in the trigger, we must be granted the CREATE and DROP user privileges directly, as above. We need these grants to be directly to this schema, not via a role, since triggers always execute with definers rights and in that mode, roles are not enabled (see Chapter 23 on *Invoker and Definer Rights* for more information on this topic).

Next, we create the application table to hold our users. We will place a trigger on this table for the BEFORE INSERT or DELETE event. This trigger will be used to make sure no one ever inserts or deletes this table directly (including the owner). The reason is that we need all inserts/deletes to take place against the view so the DDL gets done as well.

In the code below, MY_CALLER is a small routine that I frequently use (along with the WHO_CALLED_ME routine). You can find the code for those routines in the *Necessary Supplied Packages* guide at the back of this book, in the section on DBMS_UTILITY. This function simply returns the name of the procedure/function/trigger that caused the code to execute. If MY_CALLER is *not* the trigger on the views (yet to be created), it will not allow you to perform this operation.

```
demo_ddl@TKYTE816> create table application_users_tbl
  2  ( uname          varchar2(30) primary key,
  3    pw             varchar2(30),
  4    role_to_grant  varchar2(4000)
  5  );

Table created.

demo_ddl@TKYTE816> create or replace trigger application_users_tbl_bid
  2  before insert or delete on application_users_tbl
  3  begin
  4      if ( my_caller not in ( 'DEMO_DDL.APPLICATION_USERS_IOI',
  5                              'DEMO_DDL.APPLICATION_USERS_IOD' ) )
  6      then
  7          raise_application_error(-20001, 'Cannot insert/delete directly');
  8      end if;
  9  end;
 10  /

Trigger created.
```

Now we will create the view and INSTEAD OF trigger that does the actual work. We will place an INSTEAD OF INSERT trigger on this view to create the accounts. We will put an INSTEAD OF DELETE trigger on this view as well. The DELETE will cause a DROP USER statement to be executed. You could extend this to add support for INSTEAD OF UPDATE triggers to enable the addition of roles and changing of passwords via an UPDATE as well.

When the `INSTEAD OF INSERT` trigger fires, it will execute two statements:

❑ A single statement similar to `GRANT CONNECT, RESOURCE TO SOME_USERNAME IDENTIFIED BY SOME_PASSWORD`.

❑ An `INSERT` into the `APPLICATION_USERS_TBL` defined above.

The reason I used a `GRANT`, instead of `CREATE USER` and then `GRANT`, is that this statement performs a `COMMIT`, `CREATE USER`, `GRANT`, and `COMMIT` in one step. The advantage to this is that if the single statement above fails, we don't have to manually drop a user as we would if we used two statements to create and grant to the user. The `CREATE USER` statement might succeed and the `GRANT` could fail. We still need to catch errors, however, from the `GRANT` in order to delete the row we just inserted.

Since we do this `INSERT` and `GRANT` for each row inserted into the view, we can safely say that if a row exists in the real table, the account was successfully created, else it was not. There is still a very small window for potential failure, which we can never fully get rid of. If after we insert the row into the `APPLICATION_USERS_TBL`, the `GRANT` fails for some reason, and we are prevented from deleting the row we just inserted (due to the system crashing, or the tablespace with the `APPLICATION_USERS_TBL` going offline, and so on), we will have this inconsistency. Don't forget a `GRANT` is really a `COMMIT/GRANT/COMMIT` as all DDL is, so before the `GRANT` fails, it already committed the `INSERT`. The window is, however, sufficiently small to feel secure in this technique.

Now, let's implement the view, and the triggers on the view as described:

```
demo_ddl@TKYTE816> create or replace view
  2  application_users
  3  as
  4  select * from application_users_tbl
  5  /

View created.

demo_ddl@TKYTE816> create or replace trigger application_users_IOI
  2  instead of insert on application_users
  3  declare
  4    pragma    autonomous_transaction;
  5  begin
  6    insert into application_users_tbl
  7    ( uname, pw, role_to_grant )
  8    values
  9    ( upper(:new.uname), :new.pw, :new.role_to_grant );
 10
 11    begin
 12      execute immediate
 13        'grant ' || :new.role_to_grant ||
 14        ' to ' || :new.uname ||
 15        ' identified by ' || :new.pw;
 16    exception
 17      when others then
 18          delete from application_users_tbl
 19            where uname = upper(:new.uname);
 20          commit;
 21          raise;
 22    end;
 23  end;
 24  /

Trigger created.
```

So, the INSTEAD OF INSERT trigger on this table first inserts a row into the APPLICATION_USERS_TBL. It then executes the GRANT to create the user. The GRANT is really COMMIT/GRANT/COMMIT so as soon as we execute it, the row in APPLICATION_USER_TBL is committed for us. If the GRANT succeeds, it has already committed the autonomous transaction, and the trigger exits. If on the other hand, the GRANT fails (the user already exists, invalid username, whatever), we catch the error, explicitly UNDO the insert, and commit that delete. We then re-raise the error.

We do the INSERT and then the DDL in this instance, because undoing the INSERT is much easier than undoing the user creation – I'd rather DELETE than DROP in order to undo work. In the end, this trigger ensures either we have a row in the APPLICATION_USERS_TBL and a user is created, or neither action takes place.

Now for the delete trigger to remove the row and drop the user:

```
demo_ddl@TKYTE816> create or replace trigger application_users_IOD
  2  instead of delete on application_users
  3  declare
  4    pragma   autonomous_transaction;
  5  begin
  6      execute immediate 'drop user ' || :old.uname;
  7      delete from application_users_tbl
  8       where uname = :old.uname;
  9      commit;
 10  end;
 11  /

Trigger created.
```

In this case, I've purposely reversed the order of operation. Here, we do DDL and then DML, whereas before we did DML then DDL. The reason is once again ease of error recovery. If the DROP USER fails, we have nothing to 'undo'. The probability of the DELETE failing is (hopefully) zero. We have no constraints that would make it so the row cannot be deleted. If there was a high probability that the DELETE could fail due to some integrity constraints, we might reverse the order of these operations, and make it look more like the INSTEAD OF INSERT trigger.

Now we can test it by inserting a user to create, checking that they are there, and then finally by 'deleting' the user.

```
demo_ddl@TKYTE816> select * from all_users where username = 'NEW_USER';

no rows selected

demo_ddl@TKYTE816> insert into application_users values
  2  ( 'new_user', 'pw', 'connect, resource' );

1 row created.

demo_ddl@TKYTE816> select * from all_users where username = 'NEW_USER';

USERNAME                          USER_ID CREATED
------------------------------ ---------- ---------
NEW_USER                              235 15-APR-01

demo_ddl@TKYTE816> delete from application_users where uname = 'NEW_USER';
```

```
1 row deleted.

demo_ddl@TKYTE816> select * from all_users where username = 'NEW_USER';

no rows selected
```

(Note the USER_ID you might see if you do this example on your own database will most likely be different to 235 as above. This is to be expected.) Lastly, we'll verify we cannot insert or delete from the 'real' table as well.

```
demo_ddl@TKYTE816> insert into application_users_tbl values
  2  ( 'new_user', 'pw', 'connect, resource' );
insert into application_users_tbl values
             *

ERROR at line 1:
ORA-20001: Cannot insert/delete directly
ORA-06512: at "DEMO_DDL.APPLICATION_USERS_TBL_BID", line 5
ORA-04088: error during execution of trigger 'DEMO_DDL.APPLICATION_USERS_TBL_BID'

demo_ddl@TKYTE816> delete from application_users_tbl;
delete from application_users_tbl
            *
ERROR at line 1:
ORA-20001: Cannot insert/delete directly
ORA-06512: at "DEMO_DDL.APPLICATION_USERS_TBL_BID", line 5
ORA-04088: error during execution of trigger 'DEMO_DDL.APPLICATION_USERS_TBL_BID'
```

So there it is. The triggers are capable of adding and dropping users upon inserts and deletes from a database table. Using the INSTEAD OF triggers, we can make this 'safe' by providing compensating transactions when needed, to ensure our application database tables stay in sync with our DDL commands. You might even take this one step further and utilize database EVENT triggers that fire during the DROP of a user account, just to ensure that you do not have accounts being dropped without going through your view.

Writing to the Database

Oracle 7.1 introduced the ability to extend the SQL set of functions with any new function you could think of writing in PL/SQL. This is an extremely powerful feature, especially today, when these functions may be written in Java and C, in addition to PL/SQL. In the past, the one thing that all functions called from SQL must promise, is to **W**rite **N**o **D**atabase **S**tate (**WNDS**). If your function did an INSERT, UPDATE, DELETE, CREATE, ALTER, COMMIT, and so on, or called any function or procedure that performed on of these operations, it simply could not be called from SQL.

Using autonomous transactions, we can now write to the database state in functions called from SQL. There are few reasons for doing this, but two that I've seen in the past more than once are:

❑ **Really strict auditing.** I want to know what data each person saw. I need to record the ID of each record they queried from the system.

❑ **My report generator only lets me run SQL SELECT statements.** I really need to call a stored procedure that does some inserts from this report (to populate a parameter table for the report, perhaps).

Let's look at how each one might be implemented.

Really Strict Auditing

I have seen certain government settings where, for privacy reasons, they need to track who has seen various elements of any given record. For example, the tax office keeps very detailed records as to how much you make, what you own, and so on. This is extremely sensitive information. Whenever someone queries up someone's record and sees this sensitive information, they need to audit that. This is so they can audit over time to see if people are getting into records they should not be, or to retroactively find out who had access to certain information after a leak to the press, or some other exposure.

With autonomous transactions and views, we can do this in a way that is very non-intrusive and, to the casual end user using whatever tools, is totally transparent. They will not be able to get around it, and it will not get in their way. It will, of course, add additional overhead to the query, but this is really suited to those occasions where you pull up one record at a time, not hundreds or thousands of records. Given this constraint, the implementation is quite simple. Using the EMP table as a template, we can implement an audit on the HIREDATE, SALARY, and COMMISSION columns, so whenever someone views a SALARY for example, we know *who* looked at it, and even what record that they saw. We'll start by creating an audit trail table for our EMP table, which we copied from SCOTT previously in this chapter:

```
tkyte@TKYTE816> create table audit_trail
  2  ( username  varchar2(30),
  3    pk        number,
  4    attribute varchar2(30),
  5    dataum    varchar2(255),
  6    timestamp date
  7  )
  8  /

Table created.
```

Next, we'll create a series of overloaded functions in an audit trail package. These functions will each be passed the primary key value of the row being selected, as well as the column value and name of the column. We use overloaded functions so that dates would be preserved as dates, and numbers as numbers, allowing us to convert them into a standard format for storing in the character string DATAUM above:

```
tkyte@TKYTE816> create or replace package audit_trail_pkg
  2  as
  3      function record( p_pk in number,
  4                       p_attr in varchar2,
  5                       p_dataum in number ) return number;
  6      function record( p_pk in number,
  7                       p_attr in varchar2,
  8                       p_dataum in varchar2 ) return varchar2;
  9      function record( p_pk in number,
 10                       p_attr in varchar2,
 11                       p_dataum in date ) return date;
 12  end;
 13  /

Package created.
```

So, now we are ready to implement the package body itself. Here each RECORD function above, calls the same internal procedure LOG. LOG is the autonomous transaction that inserts into the audit trail table, and commits. Notice in particular, how the date RECORD function below formats the date column into a string that preserves the time component for us:

```
tkyte@TKYTE816> create or replace package body audit_trail_pkg
  2  as
  3
  4  procedure log( p_pk in number,
  5                 p_attr in varchar2,
  6                 p_datum in varchar2 )
  7  as
  8      pragma autonomous_transaction;
  9  begin
 10      insert into audit_trail values
 11      ( user, p_pk, p_attr, p_datum, sysdate );
 12      commit;
 13  end;
 14
 15  function record( p_pk in number,
 16                   p_attr in varchar2,
 17                   p_datum in number ) return number
 18  is
 19  begin
 20      log( p_pk, p_attr, p_datum );
 21      return p_datum;
 22  end;
 23
 24  function record( p_pk in number,
 25                   p_attr in varchar2,
 26                   p_datum in varchar2 ) return varchar2
 27  is
 28  begin
 29      log( p_pk, p_attr, p_datum );
 30      return p_datum;
 31  end;
 32
 33  function record( p_pk in number,
 34                   p_attr in varchar2,
 35                   p_datum in date ) return date
 36  is
 37  begin
 38      log( p_pk, p_attr,
 39          to_char(p_datum,'dd-mon-yyyy hh24:mi:ss') );
 40      return p_datum;
 41  end;
 42
 43  end;
 44  /

Package body created.

tkyte@TKYTE816> create or replace view emp_v
  2  as
  3  select empno , ename, job,mgr,
  4         audit_trail_pkg.record( empno, 'sal', sal ) sal,
```

```
      5          audit_trail_pkg.record( empno, 'comm', comm ) comm,
      6          audit_trail_pkg.record( empno, 'hiredate', hiredate ) hiredate,
      7       deptno
      8    from emp
      9  /

View created.
```

So, what we have created is a view that exposes the three columns HIREDATE, SAL, and COMM via a PL/SQL function. The PL/SQL function is our audit function that will silently record who looked at what, and when. This view is suitable for direct 'lookup'-type queries such as the following:

```
tkyte@TKYTE816> select empno, ename, hiredate, sal, comm, job
  2      from emp_v where ename = 'KING';

    EMPNO ENAME       HIREDATE          SAL       COMM JOB
--------- ---------- ---------- ---------- ---------- ---------
     7839 KING        17-NOV-81        5000            PRESIDENT

tkyte@TKYTE816> column username format a8
tkyte@TKYTE816> column pk format 9999
tkyte@TKYTE816> column attribute format a8
tkyte@TKYTE816> column dataum format a20

tkyte@TKYTE816> select * from audit_trail;

USERNAME    PK ATTRIBUT DATAUM               TIMESTAMP
-------- ----- -------- -------------------- ---------
TKYTE     7839 hiredate 17-nov-1981 00:00:00 15-APR-01
TKYTE     7839 sal      5000                 15-APR-01
TKYTE     7839 comm                          15-APR-01

tkyte@TKYTE816> select empno, ename from emp_v where ename = 'BLAKE';

    EMPNO ENAME
--------- ----------
     7698 BLAKE

tkyte@TKYTE816> select * from audit_trail;

USERNAME    PK ATTRIBUT DATAUM               TIMESTAMP
-------- ----- -------- -------------------- ---------
TKYTE     7839 hiredate 17-nov-1981 00:00:00 15-APR-01
TKYTE     7839 sal      5000                 15-APR-01
TKYTE     7839 comm                          15-APR-01
```

As you can see from the above, I can tell that TKYTE viewed the HIREDATE, SAL, and COMM columns on the listed date. The second query did not retrieve information on these columns and therefore, no additional audit records were produced.

The reason I said the above view is appropriate for 'lookup'-type queries is because it will tend to 'over-audit' in some cases. There may be cases where it reports that someone looked at some piece of information, when in fact they did not actually see it. It was filtered later in a complex query, or it was aggregated up to some value not associated with a single individual. For example, the following shows that using an aggregate, or using a column in the WHERE clause, will cause this to be audited 'as seen'.

We start by clearing out the audit trail table; just to make it obvious what is going in:

```
tkyte@TKYTE816> delete from audit_trail;

3 rows deleted.

tkyte@TKYTE816> commit;

Commit complete.

tkyte@TKYTE816> select avg(sal) from emp_v;

  AVG(SAL)
----------
2077.14286

tkyte@TKYTE816> select * from audit_trail;

USERNAME    PK ATTRIBUT DATAUM               TIMESTAMP
--------- ----- -------- -------------------- ---------
TKYTE      7499 sal      1600                 15-APR-01
...
TKYTE      7934 sal      1300                 15-APR-01

14 rows selected.

tkyte@TKYTE816> select ename from emp_v where sal >= 5000;

ENAME
----------
KING

tkyte@TKYTE816> select * from audit_trail;

USERNAME    PK ATTRIBUT DATAUM               TIMESTAMP
--------- ----- -------- -------------------- ---------
TKYTE      7499 sal      1600                 15-APR-01
...
TKYTE      7934 sal      1300                 15-APR-01

28 rows selected.
```

The aggregate query recorded each salary we 'looked' at in order to get the AVG(SAL). The WHERE SAL >= 5000 query similarly recorded each salary we looked at, in order to get the answer. There is no good solution for these cases, other than not to use this view to answer these types of questions. In the case of the AVG(SAL), you would want to expose only the SAL column, maybe other information, and use this view in your application when you needed the average salary, for example. That is, query a view that does not associate the SAL column with an individual, you can see the salaries, but *not* who the salaries belong to. The other question, SAL >= 5000, is hard to answer without recording each salary. For this I might use a stored procedure that returned a REF CURSOR. The stored procedure can safely query the EMP table using a predicate on SAL, but only select out other information, minus the SAL column. The user would not know how much the person made, only that it was above some value. You would restrict your usage of the EMP_V to the times when you wanted to show both the person-related information (EMPNO and ENAME) and SAL.

So in this context, running DML from SQL is of a very specialized use, and must be used cautiously.

When the Environment Only Allows SELECTs

This is a truly handy use of autonomous transactions in SQL statements. In many cases, people are using tools that only allow them to process SQL SELECT statements, or perhaps they can do INSERTs and such, but really need to call a stored procedure but they are unable to. Autonomous transactions make it so we can ultimately call any stored procedure or function using a SQL SELECT statement.

Let's say you've set up a stored procedure that puts some values into a table. It puts these values into this table so that a query run later in that session can restrict its values, based on the contents of that table. If this table is not populated, your report does not run. You are in an environment that does not permit you to run stored procedures, only 'regular' SQL. However, you *really* need to run this procedure. How can we do this? The following demonstrates how this would work:

```
tkyte@TKYTE816> create table report_parm_table
  2  ( session_id   number,
  3    arg1         number,
  4    arg2         date
  5  )
  6  /

Table created.

tkyte@TKYTE816> create or replace
  2  procedure set_up_report( p_arg1 in number, p_arg2 in date )
  3  as
  4  begin
  5      delete from report_parm_table
  6      where session_id = sys_context('userenv','sessionid');
  7
  8      insert into report_parm_table
  9      ( session_id, arg1, arg2 )
 10      values
 11      ( sys_context('userenv','sessionid'), p_arg1, p_arg2 );
 12  end;
 13  /

Procedure created.
```

So what we have here is an existing stored procedure that writes to the database state – it is part of an already instituted system. We would like to call it from a SQL SELECT statement, since this is the only method available to us. We will need to wrap this SET_UP_REPORT procedure in a small PL/SQL function, because the only thing SQL can call are functions. Additionally, we need the wrapper to supply the AUTONOMOUS_TRANSACTION pragma for us:

```
tkyte@TKYTE816> create or replace
  2  function set_up_report_F( p_arg1 in number, p_arg2 in date )
  3  return number
  4  as
  5      pragma autonomous_transaction;
  6  begin
  7      set_up_report( p_arg1, p_arg2 );
  8      commit;
  9      return 1;
 10  exception
```

```
 11        when others then
 12            rollback;
 13            return 0;
 14   end;
 15   /

Function created.

tkyte@TKYTE816> select set_up_report_F( 1, sysdate ) from dual
  2  /

SET_UP_REPORT_F(1,SYSDATE)
-------------------------
                        1

tkyte@TKYTE816> select * from report_parm_table
  2
```

It might be interesting to see what would happen if we tried to call this function from SQL, without the autonomous transaction. If you recompile the above function with the pragma you would receive:

```
tkyte@TKYTE816> select set_up_report_F( 1, sysdate ) from dual
  2  /
select set_up_report_F( 1, sysdate ) from dual
       *
ERROR at line 1:
ORA-14552: cannot perform a DDL, commit or rollback inside a query or DML
ORA-06512: at "TKYTE.SET_UP_REPORT_F", line 10
ORA-14551: cannot perform a DML operation inside a query
ORA-06512: at line 1
```

This is exactly what the autonomous transaction is avoiding. So, we now have a function that can be called from SQL, and does an actual insert into a database table. It is important to note that the wrapper function must commit (or rollback), before returning to avoid the ORA-06519 error (see the *Errors You Might Encounter* section for more information) that would happen otherwise. Additionally, the function needs to return something – anything, but it *has* to return something; I am returning 1 for success, 0 for failure. Lastly, the important thing to note is that the function can only accept IN parameters – not IN/OUT or OUT. This is because the SQL layer will not permit parameters of this mode.

I would like to caveat this approach. Normally, I would do this at the end, but this directly applies to calling functions that modify the database from SQL. It can have dangerous side effects due to the way the database optimizes and executes queries. The above example was relatively 'safe'. DUAL is a single row table, we selected our function, and it should be called only once. There were no joins, no predicates, no sorts, and no side effects. This should be reliable. There are other cases where our function may be called less than we thought it should, more than we thought, or luckily, exactly as many times as we thought. In order to demonstrate this, I will use a somewhat contrived example. We will have a simple COUNTER table that an autonomous transaction will update with every call made to it. In this fashion, we can run queries, and see how many times our function is actually called:

```
tkyte@TKYTE816> create table counter ( x int );

Table created.
```

```
tkyte@TKYTE816> insert into counter values (0);

1 row created.

tkyte@TKYTE816> create or replace function f return number
  2  as
  3          pragma autonomous_transaction;
  4  begin
  5          update counter set x = x+1;
  6          commit;
  7          return 1;
  8  end;
  9  /

Function created.
```

So, this is the function and COUNTER table. Every time F is called, X will be incremented by 1. Let's try it out:

```
tkyte@TKYTE816> select count(*)
  2     from ( select f from emp )
  3  /

  COUNT(*)
----------
        14

tkyte@TKYTE816> select * from counter;

         X
----------
         0
```

Apparently, our function never got called. It looks like it should have been called 14 times but it was not. Just to show that F works we use the following:

```
tkyte@TKYTE816> select count(*)
  2  from ( select f from emp union select f from emp )
  3  /

  COUNT(*)
----------
         1

tkyte@TKYTE816> select * from counter;

         X
----------
        28
```

This is what we expected. The function F was called 28 times – 14 times for each query in the UNION statement. Since a UNION does a SORT DISTINCT as a side effect of processing, the COUNT(*) from the union is 1 (this is correct) and the number of calls was 28, which is what we expected. What if we modify the query just a little, though:

```
tkyte@TKYTE816> update counter set x = 0;

1 row updated.

tkyte@TKYTE816> commit;

Commit complete.

tkyte@TKYTE816> select f from emp union ALL select f from emp
  2  /

         F
----------
         1
...
         1

28 rows selected.

tkyte@TKYTE816> select * from counter;

         X
----------
        32
```

28 rows came back *but* our function was apparently called 32 times! Beware of side effects. Oracle never promised to either call your function (first example above) or call it a deterministic number of times (last example). Be extremely wary of using this functionality (writing to the database in a function called in SQL) when any table other than DUAL is involved, and you have joins, sorts, and so on. The results may be surprising.

To Develop More Modular Code

Autonomous transactions also allow for the development of more modular code. Traditionally, one would write a series of packages that performed some operations. These operations would do some modifications in the database and then, depending on the outcome, either commit or roll them back. This is all well and good if your procedures are the only thing to be concerned with. In a large-scale application, however, it is rare that your simple package would be the only thing going on. It is most likely a small piece of a much larger pie.

In a typical procedure, if you commit, you commit not only your work, but also all of the outstanding work performed in your session *before* the procedure was called. By committing you are making permanent your work, and that other work. The problem is, that other work might not be 100 percent complete as yet. Therefore, your commit introduces the potential for an error in the invoking routine. It has lost the ability to roll back its changes in the event of a failure, and it might not even be aware of that.

Using autonomous transactions, you may now create self-contained transactions that take place without affecting the invoking transactions state. This could be extremely useful for many types of routines such as auditing, logging, and other services. It allows you to develop code that may be safely called from a variety of environments, all without effecting these environments in an adverse way. These are valid uses for autonomous transactions – auditing, logging, and other service-oriented routines. I, in general, do not believe in committing in a stored procedure except in cases such as those. I believe transaction control should be only in the hands of the client application. Care must be taken to ensure that you do not abuse autonomous transactions. If your code should be invoked as a logical part of a much larger transaction (for example, you are supplying the ADDRESS_UPDATE package in an HR system), then coding it as an autonomous transaction would not be appropriate. The invoker would like to be able to call your functionality, and other related packages, committing all of the work (or not) as a whole. So, if you had utilized an autonomous transaction, the invoker would lose this control, and building larger transactions from these smaller transactions would not be possible. Additionally, one of the attributes of an autonomous transaction is that it cannot see any of the uncommitted work performed by its caller. We'll hear more on that in the *How They Work* section. This would mean that your autonomous transaction would not be able to see the uncommitted updates to the rest of the HR information. You need to understand how your code will ultimately be used in order to utilize this functionality correctly.

How They Work

This section will describe how autonomous transactions work, and what you can expect from them. We will investigate transactional control flow with regards to autonomous transactions. We will also see how autonomous transactions affect the scope of various elements such as packaged variables, session settings, database changes, and locks. We will explore the correct way to end an autonomous transaction, and finally wrap up with a section on savepoints.

Transactional Control

The transaction control flow of an autonomous transaction begins with a BEGIN, and ends at the END. What I mean by this is that given the following block of code:

```
declare
    pragma autonomous_transaction;
    X number default func;          (1)
begin                               (2)
    ...
end;                                (3)
```

the autonomous transaction begins at (2), not at (1). It begins with the first executable section. If FUNC is in fact a function that performs operations in the database, it is not part of the autonomous transaction! It will be part of the parent transaction. Additionally, the order of items in the DECLARE block is not relevant – the PRAGMA can come first or last. The entire DECLARE block is part of the parent transaction, not the autonomous transaction. An example will make this clear:

```
tkyte@TKYTE816> create table t ( msg varchar2(50) );

Table created.

tkyte@TKYTE816> create or replace function func return number
  2  as
  3  begin
  4          insert into t values
  5          ( 'I was inserted by FUNC' );
  6          return 0;
  7  end;
  8  /

Function created.
```

So, we have a function that does some work in the database. Let's call this function in the DECLARE block of an autonomous transaction now:

```
tkyte@TKYTE816> declare
  2          x  number default func;
  3          pragma autonomous_transaction;
  4  begin
  5          insert into t values
  6          ( 'I was inserted by anon block' );
  7          commit;
  8  end;
  9  /

PL/SQL procedure successfully completed.

tkyte@TKYTE816> select * from t;

MSG
--------------------------------------------------
I was inserted by FUNC
I was inserted by anon block
```

Right now, both rows are there. However, one of the rows has yet to be committed. We can observe this by rolling back:

```
tkyte@TKYTE816> rollback;

Rollback complete.

tkyte@TKYTE816> select * from t;

MSG
--------------------------------------------------
I was inserted by anon block
```

As you can see, after executing the anonymous block, it appears that both rows are in table T, and committed. This is misleading however. The row inserted by the function is in fact, still outstanding. It is part of the parent transaction, and is still uncommitted. By rolling back, we can see that it goes away, but the row inserted in the autonomous transaction remains as expected.

So, an autonomous transaction begins at the *very next* BEGIN *after* the PRAGMA, and is in effect for the entire time that BEGIN block is still in scope. Any functions or procedures that the autonomous transaction calls, any triggers that it causes to fire, and so on are part of its autonomous transaction, and will commit or be rolled back along with it.

Autonomous transactions can be nested, so that one can cause another to occur. These new autonomous transactions behave in exactly the same fashion as the parent autonomous transaction – they begin with the first BEGIN, they have transactional control until the end statement is reached, and they are totally independent of their parent transaction. The only limit to the depth of nesting of autonomous transactions is the init.ora parameter TRANSACTIONS, which governs the total number of concurrent transactions possible in the server at the same time. Normally, this defaults to 1.1 times the number of SESSIONS, and if you plan on using lots of autonomous transactions, you may have to increase this parameter.

Scope

By **scope**, I mean the ability to see values of various things within the database. We are concerned with four different elements here. We will look at the scope of:

- ❏ Packaged variables.
- ❏ Session settings/parameters.
- ❏ Database changes.
- ❏ Locks.

and consider each in turn.

Packaged Variables

An autonomous transaction creates a new transaction state but not a new 'session'. Therefore, any variables that are in the scope (are visible) of both the parent and the autonomous transaction, will be identical in nature to both, since variable assignment is not covered by transactional boundaries (you cannot rollback a PL/SQL assignment to a variable). So, not only can an autonomous transaction see the parent transaction's variable state, but it can also modify it, and the parent will see these changes.

What this means is that changes to variables, since they are explicitly not affected by commits and rollbacks, fall outside of the domain of the autonomous transaction, and will behave exactly as they would in the absence of autonomous transactions. In way of a simple example to demonstrate this, I'll create a package that has a global variable. The 'parent transaction' (our session) will set this value to some known state, and an autonomous transaction will then modify it. The parent transaction will see the effects of that modification:

```
tkyte@TKYTE816> create or replace package global_variables
  2  as
  3          x number;
  4  end;
  5  /

Package created.

tkyte@TKYTE816> begin
  2          global_variables.x := 5;
  3  end;
  4  /

PL/SQL procedure successfully completed.

tkyte@TKYTE816> declare
  2          pragma autonomous_transaction;
  3  begin
  4          global_variables.x := 10;
  5          commit;
  6  end;
  7  /

PL/SQL procedure successfully completed.
```

```
tkyte@TKYTE816> set serveroutput on
tkyte@TKYTE816> exec dbms_output.put_line( global_variables.x );
10

PL/SQL procedure successfully completed.
```

This change to the global variable by the autonomous transaction will be in place regardless of the ultimate outcome of the autonomous transaction.

Session Settings/Parameters

Again, since autonomous transactions create a new transaction but not a new session, the session state of the parent transaction is the same as the session state of the child. They both share the same exact session, but they just are running in separate transactions. The session is established when the application connected to the database. An autonomous transaction does not 'reconnect' to the database again, it just shares the same connection or session. Therefore, any session-level changes made in the parent will be visible to the child and furthermore, if the child makes any session-level changes via the ALTER SESSION command, these changes will be in effect for the parent transaction as well. It should be noted that the SET TRANSACTION command, which by definition works at the transaction-level, affects only the transaction in which it was issued. So for example, an autonomous transaction that issues a SET TRANSACTION USE ROLLBACK SEGMENT command will set the rollback segment only for *its* transaction, not for the parent. An autonomous transaction that issues SET TRANSACTION ISOLATION LEVEL SERIALIZABLE affects only its transaction, but an autonomous transaction that issues an ALTER SESSION SET ISOLATION_LEVEL=SERIALIZABLE will change the parent's isolation level, for their *next* transaction. Additionally, a parent READ ONLY transaction can invoke an autonomous transaction that modifies the database. The autonomous transaction is not forced to be read-only as well.

Database Changes

Now, this is where things start to get interesting – database changes. Here, things can get a little murky. Database changes made, but not yet committed by a parent transaction, are *not* visible to the autonomous transactions. Changes made, and already committed by the parent transaction, are always visible to the child transaction. Changes made by the autonomous transaction *may or may not* be visible to the parent transaction depending on its isolation level.

I said before though, that this is where things get murky. I was pretty clear above in saying that changes made by the parent transaction are not visible to the child but that's not 100 percent of the story. A cursor opened by the child autonomous transaction will not see these uncommitted changes, but a cursor opened by the parent and fetched from by the child, will. The following case shows how this works. We will recreate our EMP table (it has all kinds of auditing routines on it), and then code a package that modifies it, and prints it out. In this package, we'll have a global cursor that selects from EMP. There will be a single autonomous transaction. It simply fetches from a cursor and prints the results. It'll check first to see if the cursor is opened, and if not, it will open it. This will show us the difference in results we get, depending on who opened a given cursor. The cursor's resultset is always consistent with respect to the point in time it was opened, and the transaction it was opened in:

```
tkyte@TKYTE816> drop table emp;

Table dropped.

tkyte@TKYTE816> create table emp as select * from scott.emp;
```

```
Table created.

tkyte@TKYTE816> create or replace package my_pkg
  2  as
  3
  4          procedure run;
  5
  6  end;
  7  /

Package created.

tkyte@TKYTE816> create or replace package body my_pkg
  2  as
  3
  4
  5  cursor global_cursor is select ename from emp;
  6
  7
  8  procedure show_results
  9  is
 10          pragma autonomous_transaction;
 11          l_ename emp.ename%type;
 12  begin
 13          if ( global_cursor%isopen )
 14          then
 15                  dbms_output.put_line( 'NOT already opened cursor' );
 16          else
 17                  dbms_output.put_line( 'Already opened' );
 18                  open global_cursor;
 19          end if;
 20
 21          loop
 22                  fetch global_cursor into l_ename;
 23                  exit when global_cursor%notfound;
 24                  dbms_output.put_line( l_ename );
 25          end loop;
 26          close global_cursor;
 27  end;
 28
 29
 30  procedure run
 31  is
 32  begin
 33          update emp set ename = 'x';
 34
 35          open global_cursor;
 36          show_results;
 37
 38          show_results;
 39
 40          rollback;
 41  end;
 42
 43  end;
 44  /
```

```
Package body created.

tkyte@TKYTE816> exec my_pkg.run
NOT already opened cursor
x
...
x
Already opened
SMITH
...
MILLER

PL/SQL procedure successfully completed.
```

When the cursor is opened in the parent's transaction state, the autonomous transaction can see these uncommitted rows – they were all x. The cursor opened in the autonomous transaction might as well have been opened in another session all together when it comes to this uncommitted data. It will never be able to see these uncommitted rows. We see the images of the data as they existed *before* the update took place.

So, this shows how a child autonomous transaction will react to uncommitted changes made by the parent as far as SELECTs go. What about the parent with regards to seeing data changes, made by the child? Well, this will depend on the parent's isolation level. If you use the default isolation level of READ COMMITTED, the parent will be able to see the changes. If you are using SERIALIZABLE transactions however, you will not be able to see the changes made, even though you made them. For example:

```
tkyte@TKYTE816> create table t ( msg varchar2(4000) );

Table created.

tkyte@TKYTE816> create or replace procedure auto_proc
  2   as
  3           pragma autonomous_transaction;
  4   begin
  5           insert into t values ( 'A row for you' );
  6           commit;
  7   end;
  8   /

Procedure created.

tkyte@TKYTE816> create or replace
  2   procedure proc( read_committed in boolean )
  3   as
  4   begin
  5           if ( read_committed ) then
  6                   set transaction isolation level read committed;
  7           else
  8                   set transaction isolation level serializable;
  9           end if;
 10
 11           auto_proc;
 12
 13           dbms_output.put_line( '---------' );
```

```
 .14              for x in ( select * from t ) loop
  15                  dbms_output.put_line( x.msg );
  16              end loop;
  17              dbms_output.put_line( '--------' );
  18              commit;
  19   end;
  20   /

Procedure created.

tkyte@TKYTE816> exec proc( TRUE )
--------
A row for you
--------

PL/SQL procedure successfully completed.

tkyte@TKYTE816> delete from t;

1 row deleted.

tkyte@TKYTE816> commit;

Commit complete.

tkyte@TKYTE816> exec proc( FALSE )
--------
--------

PL/SQL procedure successfully completed.
```

As you can see, when the procedure is run in READ COMMITTED mode, we see the committed changes.
When run in SERIALIZABLE mode, we cannot see the changes. This is because the changes in the
autonomous transaction happened in another transaction all together, and the isolation mode of
SERIALIZABLE dictates that we could only see our transactions changes (it is as if our transaction was
the only transaction in the database in this mode, we are not permitted to see others' changes).

Locks

In the previous section, we explored what happens with regards to a child autonomous transaction
reading a parent's committed and uncommitted changes, as well as a parent reading a child autonomous
transaction's changes. Now we will look at what happens with regards to locks.

Since the parent and child have two totally different transactions, they will not be able to share locks in
any way shape or form. If the parent transaction has a resource locked that the child autonomous
transaction also needs to lock, you will deadlock yourself. The following demonstrates this issue:

```
tkyte@TKYTE816> create or replace procedure child
  2   as
  3           pragma autonomous_transaction;
  4           l_ename emp.ename%type;
  5   begin
  6           select ename into l_ename
  7                   from emp
```

```
     8                      where ename = 'KING'
     9                         FOR UPDATE;
    10            commit;
    11  end;
    12  /

Procedure created.

tkyte@TKYTE816> create or replace procedure parent
     2  as
     3            l_ename emp.ename%type;
     4  begin
     5            select ename into l_ename
     6                    from emp
     7                   where ename = 'KING'
     8                      FOR UPDATE;
     9            child;
    10            commit;
    11  end;
    12  /

Procedure created.

tkyte@TKYTE816> exec parent
BEGIN parent; END;

*
ERROR at line 1:
ORA-00060: deadlock detected while waiting for resource
ORA-06512: at "TKYTE.CHILD", line 6
ORA-06512: at "TKYTE.PARENT", line 9
ORA-06512: at line 1
```

Care must be taken to avoid a child deadlocking with its parent. The child will always 'lose' in this case, and the offending statement will be rolled back.

Ending an Autonomous Transaction

To end the autonomous transaction, we must always issue a full-blown COMMIT or ROLLBACK, or execute DDL, which does a COMMIT for us. The autonomous transaction itself will start automatically when the autonomous transaction makes any database changes, locks resources, or issues transaction control statements such as SET TRANSACTION or SAVEPOINT. The autonomous transaction must be explicitly terminated before control returns to the parent transaction (else an error will occur). A ROLLBACK to SAVEPOINT is not sufficient, even if this leaves no outstanding work, as it does not terminate the transaction state.

If an autonomous transaction exits 'normally' (not via a propagated exception), and neglects to COMMIT or ROLLBACK, it will receive the following error:

```
tkyte@TKYTE816> create or replace procedure child
     2  as
     3            pragma autonomous_transaction;
     4            l_ename emp.ename%type;
```

```
  5  begin
  6          select ename into l_ename
  7                   from emp
  8                  where ename = 'KING'
  9                    FOR UPDATE;
 10  end;
 11  /

Procedure created.

tkyte@TKYTE816> exec child
BEGIN child; END;

*
ERROR at line 1:
ORA-06519: active autonomous transaction detected and rolled back
ORA-06512: at "TKYTE.CHILD", line 6
ORA-06512: at line 1
```

So, just as an autonomous transaction must take care to avoid deadlocks with the parent transaction, it must also take care to cleanly terminate any transaction it begins (to avoid having it rolled back).

Savepoints

In Chapter 4 on *Transactions*, we described savepoints, and how they affect transactions in your application. Savepoints are scoped to the current transaction only. That is, an autonomous transaction cannot rollback to a savepoint issued in the calling routine's transaction. This savepoint just does not exist in the autonomous transaction's environment. Consider what happens if we try:

```
tkyte@TKYTE816> create or replace procedure child
  2  as
  3          pragma autonomous_transaction;
  4          l_ename emp.ename%type;
  5  begin
  6
  7          update emp set ename = 'y' where ename = 'BLAKE';
  8          rollback to Parent_Savepoint;
  9          commit;
 10  end;
 11  /

Procedure created.

tkyte@TKYTE816> create or replace procedure parent
  2  as
  3          l_ename emp.ename%type;
  4  begin
  5          savepoint Parent_Savepoint;
  6          update emp set ename = 'x' where ename = 'KING';
  7
  8          child;
  9          rollback;
 10  end;
```

```
 11  /

Procedure created.

tkyte@TKYTE816> exec parent
BEGIN parent; END;

*
ERROR at line 1:
ORA-01086: savepoint 'PARENT_SAVEPOINT' never established
ORA-06512: at "TKYTE.CHILD", line 8
ORA-06512: at "TKYTE.PARENT", line 8
ORA-06512: at line 1
```

As far as the autonomous transaction was concerned, this savepoint never had been issued. If we remove the autonomous transaction from child above and re-execute, it works just fine. The autonomous transaction cannot affect the calling transaction's 'state'.

This does not mean that autonomous transactions cannot use savepoints – they can. They have to just use their *own* savepoints. For example, the following code demonstrates that a savepoint issued in the child transaction works. The one update inside the savepoint was rolled back as expected and the other persisted:

```
tkyte@TKYTE816> create or replace procedure child
  2  as
  3          pragma autonomous_transaction;
  4          l_ename emp.ename%type;
  5  begin
  6
  7      update emp set ename = 'y' where ename = 'BLAKE';
  8      savepoint child_savepoint;
  9      update emp set ename = 'z' where ename = 'SMITH';
 10      rollback to child_savepoint;
 11      commit;
 12  end;
 13  /

Procedure created.

tkyte@TKYTE816> create or replace procedure parent
  2  as
  3          l_ename emp.ename%type;
  4  begin
  5          savepoint Parent_Savepoint;
  6          update emp set ename = 'x' where ename = 'KING';
  7
  8          child;
  9          commit;
 10  end;
 11  /

Procedure created.
```

```
tkyte@TKYTE816> select ename
  2    from emp
  3    where ename in ( 'x', 'y', 'z', 'BLAKE', 'SMITH', 'KING' );

ENAME
----------
SMITH
BLAKE
KING

tkyte@TKYTE816> exec parent

PL/SQL procedure successfully completed.

tkyte@TKYTE816> select ename
  2    from emp
  3    where ename in ( 'x', 'y', 'z', 'BLAKE', 'SMITH', 'KING' );

ENAME
----------
SMITH
y
x
```

Caveats

As with any feature, there are some nuances that need to be noted in the way this feature functions. This section attempts to address them each in turn. We will look at features that are mutually exclusive with autonomous transactions, the environments that may use them, differences in behavior you will notice using them, and other such issues.

No Distributed Transactions

Currently (at least up to Oracle 8.1.7), it is not feasible to use autonomous transactions in a distributed transaction. You will not receive a clear error message with regards to this. Rather, an internal error will be raised in various (but not all) cases. It is planned that autonomous transactions can be used in distributed transactions safely in the future. For now, if you are using a Database Link, do not use an autonomous transaction.

PL/SQL Only

Autonomous transactions are available with PL/SQL only. They can be extended to Java, and other languages, by invoking the Java, or other language routine, from a PL/SQL block that is an autonomous transaction. So, if you need a Java stored procedure to be invoked as an autonomous transaction, you must create a stored procedure in PL/SQL that is an autonomous transaction and call the Java from that.

The Entire Transaction Rolls Back

If an autonomous transaction exits in error, due to an exception that was not caught and handled, it's entire transaction, not just the offending statement, is rolled back. What this means is that a call to an

689

autonomous transaction is an 'all-or-nothing' event. It either exits successfully having saved all of its work, *or* it exits with an exception and all of its *uncommitted* work is undone. Note that I stressed uncommitted in that sentence. An autonomous transaction can in fact commit many times during its execution, only its uncommitted work is rolled back. Normally, if a procedure exits with an exception, and you catch and handle that exception, it's uncommitted work is preserved – not so with an autonomous transaction. For example:

```
tkyte@TKYTE816> create table t ( msg varchar2(25) );

Table created.

tkyte@TKYTE816> create or replace procedure auto_proc
  2  as
  3      pragma AUTONOMOUS_TRANSACTION;
  4      x number;
  5  begin
  6      insert into t values ('AutoProc');
  7      x := 'a'; -- This will fail
  8      commit;
  9  end;
 10  /

Procedure created.

tkyte@TKYTE816> create or replace procedure Regular_Proc
  2  as
  3      x number;
  4  begin
  5      insert into t values ('RegularProc');
  6      x := 'a'; -- This will fail
  7      commit;
  8  end;
  9  /

Procedure created.

tkyte@TKYTE816> set serveroutput on

tkyte@TKYTE816> begin
  2      insert into t values ('Anonymous');
  3      auto_proc;
  4  exception
  5      when others then
  6              dbms_output.put_line( 'Caught Error:' );
  7              dbms_output.put_line( sqlerrm );
  8          commit;
  9  end;
 10  /
Caught Error:
ORA-06502: PL/SQL: numeric or value error: character to number conversion error

PL/SQL procedure successfully completed.

tkyte@TKYTE816> select * from t;
```

```
MSG
------------------------
Anonymous
```

Only the anonymous block's data is preserved. Contrast this to a 'regular' block's behavior:

```
tkyte@TKYTE816> delete from t;

1 row deleted.

tkyte@TKYTE816> commit;

Commit complete.

tkyte@TKYTE816> begin
  2         insert into t values ('Anonymous');
  3         regular_proc;
  4   exception
  5       when others then
  6                   dbms_output.put_line( 'Caught Error:' );
  7                   dbms_output.put_line( sqlerrm );
  8           commit;
  9   end;
 10   /
Caught Error:
ORA-06502: PL/SQL: numeric or value error: character to number conversion error

PL/SQL procedure successfully completed.

tkyte@TKYTE816> select * from t;

MSG
------------------------
Anonymous
RegularProc
```

Here, since we caught and handled the error, the rows from both the failed procedure and the anonymous block survived.

What this means in the end is that you cannot just slap PRAGMA AUTONOMOUS_TRANSACTION onto existing stored procedures, and expect the same behavior from them. There will be subtle differences.

Transaction-Level Temporary Tables

If you are using GLOBAL TEMPORARY tables, one thing you must be aware of is the fact that a transaction-level temporary table cannot be used by more than one transaction, in a single session, at the same time. Temporary tables are managed at the session-level, and when they are created in the mode that makes them 'transactional' (on commit, delete rows), they can only be used by either the parent, or the child transaction, but not both. For example, the following shows that an autonomous transaction, which attempts to read or write a *transaction*-level temporary table that is already in use in the session, will fail:

```
tkyte@TKYTE816> create global temporary table temp
  2  (  x int )
  3  on commit delete rows
  4  /

Table created.

tkyte@TKYTE816> create or replace procedure auto_proc1
  2  as
  3          pragma autonomous_transaction;
  4  begin
  5     insert into temp values ( 1 );
  6     commit;
  7  end;
  8  /

Procedure created.

tkyte@TKYTE816> create or replace procedure auto_proc2
  2  as
  3          pragma autonomous_transaction;
  4  begin
  5          for x in ( select * from temp )
  6          loop
  7                  null;
  8          end loop;
  9     commit;
 10  end;
 11  /

Procedure created.

tkyte@TKYTE816> insert into temp values ( 2 );

1 row created.

tkyte@TKYTE816> exec auto_proc1;
BEGIN auto_proc1; END;

*
ERROR at line 1:
ORA-14450: attempt to access a transactional temp table already in use
ORA-06512: at "TKYTE.AUTO_PROC1", line 5
ORA-06512: at line 1


tkyte@TKYTE816> exec auto_proc2;
BEGIN auto_proc2; END;

*
ERROR at line 1:
ORA-14450: attempt to access a transactional temp table already in use
ORA-06512: at "TKYTE.AUTO_PROC2", line 5
ORA-06512: at line 1
```

This is the error you will get if you attempt to use the same temporary table by both transactions. It should be noted that this only happens with simultaneous transactions in the *same session*. Many concurrent transactions can, and do, use transaction-level temporary tables simultaneously when each transaction is owned by a separate session.

Mutating Tables

At first glance, autonomous transactions look like the answer to all of your mutating table problems. They might only be the beginning of a *new* set of logic problems however.

Let's say you wanted to enforce a rule that the average salary of all employees cannot be less than half of the maximum salary for anyone in their department. You might start with a procedure and trigger that looks like:

```
tkyte@TKYTE816> create or replace
  2  procedure sal_check( p_deptno in number )
  3  is
  4          avg_sal number;
  5          max_sal number;
  6  begin
  7          select avg(sal), max(sal)
  8            into avg_sal, max_sal
  9            from emp
 10        where deptno = p_deptno;
 11
 12          if ( max_sal/2 > avg_sal )
 13          then
 14                  raise_application_error(-20001,'Rule violated');
 15          end if;
 16  end;
 17  /

Procedure created.

tkyte@TKYTE816> create or replace trigger sal_trigger
  2  after insert or update or delete on emp
  3  for each row
  4  begin
  5          if (inserting or updating) then
  6                  sal_check(:new.deptno);
  7          end if;
  8
  9          if (updating or deleting) then
 10                  sal_check(:old.deptno);
 11          end if;
 12  end;
 13  /

Trigger created.

tkyte@TKYTE816>
tkyte@TKYTE816> update emp set sal = sal*1.1;
update emp set sal = sal*1.1
      *
```

```
ERROR at line 1:
ORA-04091: table TKYTE.EMP is mutating, trigger/function may not see it
ORA-06512: at "TKYTE.SAL_CHECK", line 6
ORA-06512: at "TKYTE.SAL_TRIGGER", line 3
ORA-04088: error during execution of trigger 'TKYTE.SAL_TRIGGER'
```

This didn't work too well. We hit the mutating table error right away because we quite simply cannot read the table that we are in the process of modifying. So, we immediately think 'mutating tables equals autonomous transactions', and apply an autonomous transaction to our procedure:

```
tkyte@TKYTE816> create or replace
  2  procedure sal_check( p_deptno in number )
  3  is
  4          pragma autonomous_transaction;
  5          avg_sal number;
  6          max_sal number;
  7  begin
...

Procedure created.
```

and sure enough, it appears to have fixed the issue:

```
tkyte@TKYTE816> update emp set sal = sal*1.1;

14 rows updated.

tkyte@TKYTE816> commit;

Commit complete.
```

Upon closer inspection though, we find that we have a fatal flaw in our design. During testing we found that could easily happen:

```
tkyte@TKYTE816> update emp set sal = 99999.99 where ename = 'WARD';

1 row updated.

tkyte@TKYTE816> commit;

Commit complete.

tkyte@TKYTE816> exec sal_check(30);
BEGIN sal_check(30); END;

*
ERROR at line 1:
ORA-20001: Rule violated
ORA-06512: at "TKYTE.SAL_CHECK", line 14
ORA-06512: at line 1
```

I updated WARD with a very high salary; WARD works in department 30, and his salary is now very much higher than half of the average salary in that department. The trigger did not detect this, but after the fact, running the same code, the trigger does let us see that the rule was violated. Why? Because our autonomous transaction cannot see any of the changes we are making. Hence, the update of the salary to a large amount appears OK, because the procedure is validating the table, as it existed *before* our update began! It would be the next unlucky end user who would trigger this violation (as we artificially forced by running the SAL_CHECK procedure).

Any time you use an autonomous transaction to avoid a mutating table, you must make sure you are doing the right thing. In the *Auditing that Can Not be Rolled Back* example, I used an autonomous transaction in a 'safe' way. The logic of my trigger is not affected by the fact that I am seeing the table as it existed *before* the transaction took place. In this example above, my trigger is affected greatly by this fact. Special care must be taken, and every trigger that uses an autonomous transaction should be verified for correctness.

Errors You Might Encounter

There are a few errors you might expect to encounter with autonomous transactions. They are listed here for completeness, but we have already seen each of them in the above examples.

ORA-06519 "active autonomous transaction detected and rolled back"

```
// *Cause:  Before returning from an autonomous PL/SQL block, all autonomous
//          transactions started within the block must be completed (either
//          committed or rolled back). If not, the active autonomous
//          transaction is implicitly rolled back and this error is raised.
// *Action: Ensure that before returning from an autonomous PL/SQL block,
//          any active autonomous transactions are explicitly committed
//          or rolled back.
```

You will receive this error any time you exit an autonomous transaction, and neglect to either commit or roll it back yourself. The action taken will be to roll back your autonomous transaction and propagate this error to the invoker. You should always ensure that all exit paths from your autonomous procedures either commit or rollback, to avoid this issue altogether. This error is always the result of an error in the logic of your code.

ORA-14450 "attempt to access a transactional temp table already in use"

```
// *Cause:  An attempt was made to access a transactional temporary table
//          that has been already populated by a concurrent transaction of
//          the same session.
// *Action: do not attempt to access the temporary table until the
//          concurrent transaction has committed or aborted.
```

As demonstrated above, a global temporary table created with ON COMMIT DELETE ROWS may be utilized by exactly one transaction in any given session. Care must be taken to not have both a parent and child transaction attempt to utilize the same temporary table.

ORA-00060 "deadlock detected while waiting for resource"

```
// *Cause:  Transactions deadlocked one another while waiting for resources.
// *Action: Look at the trace file to see the transactions and resources
//          involved. Retry if necessary.
```

This is not really an autonomous transaction error, but I've included it here due to the increased probability of hitting this particular error when using them. Since the parent transaction is suspended during the execution of the child transaction, and will not be able to resume processing until the child transaction completes, a deadlock that would not occur if two concurrently executing sessions were used may very well occur when using autonomous transactions. It will occur when we attempt to update the same data from two separate transactions in a single session. Care must be taken to ensure that the child does not attempt to lock the same resources the parent might have locked already.

Summary

In this chapter we thoroughly explored the feature of autonomous transactions. We have seen how they can be used to generate more modular, safe code. We have seen how they can be used to do things that have previously not been possible, such as performing DDL in a trigger or running any stored function via a SELECT statement, regardless of whether that function wrote to the database or not. We also saw that it is not wise to think you know exactly how many times a function called from SQL will actually be called, so be careful when writing to the database state in that fashion. We have seen how this feature can be used to avoid a mutating table error, as well as how this feature might lead to the 'wrong' result when used incorrectly to solve this problem.

Autonomous transactions are a powerful feature that Oracle itself has been using for years in the guise of recursive SQL. It is now available for you to use in your applications as well. A thorough understanding of transactions, how they work, where they start, and when they end, is mandatory before utilizing this feature, as various side effects can occur. For example, a session can deadlock itself, a parent transaction may or may not see the results of the child autonomous transaction, a child autonomous transaction cannot see outstanding work of the parent, and so on.

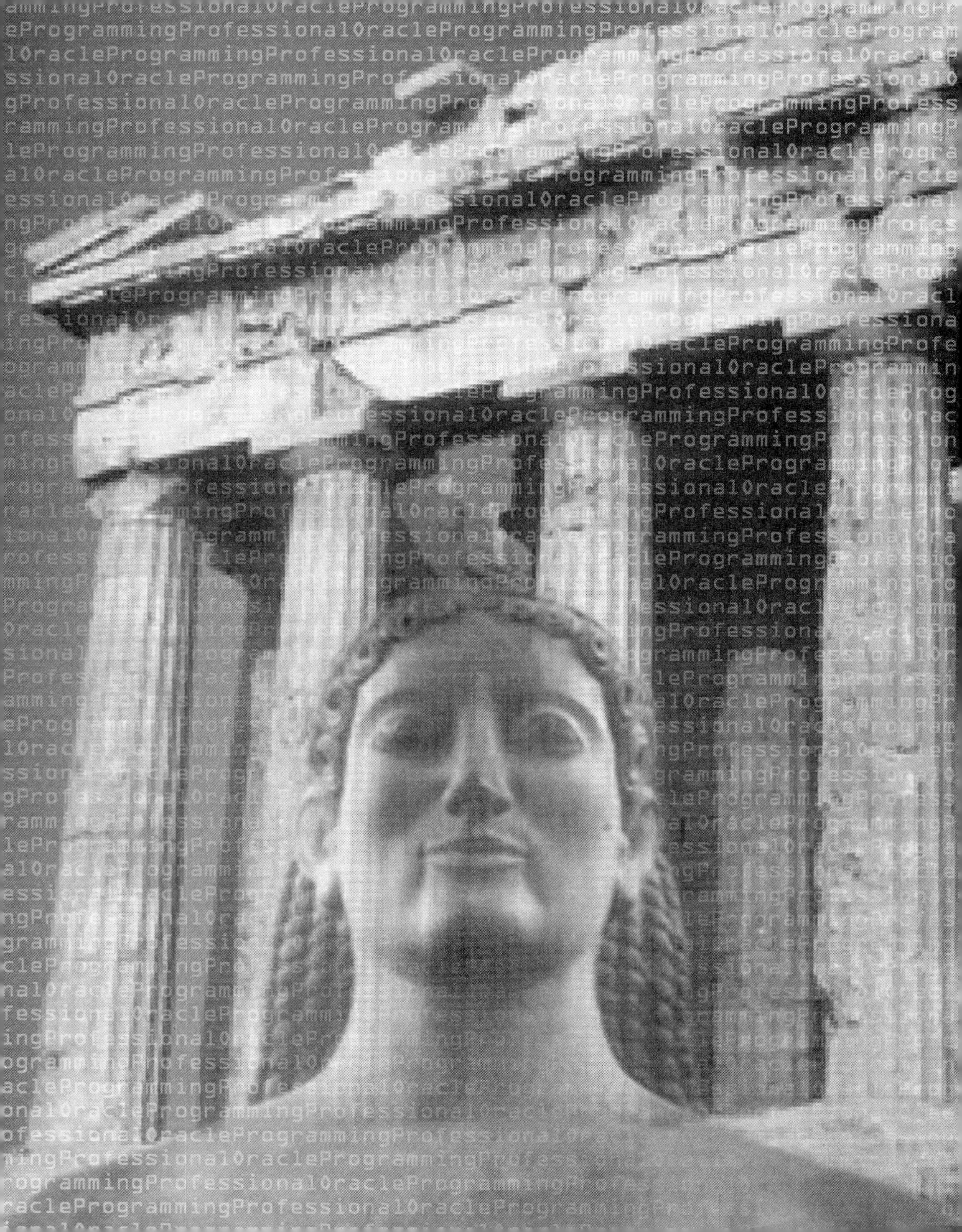

16

Dynamic SQL

Normally, a program is developed with all of the SQL it uses hard coded into it. This is typically referred to as **static SQL**. Many useful programs however, do not know what SQL they will be executing until run-time. This is where **dynamic SQL** comes in – it is SQL your program executes at run-time, which was not known at compile-time. Maybe your program generates queries on the fly based on user input; maybe it is a data load program you have developed. SQL*PLUS is a great example of this sort of program, as is any ad-hoc query or reporting tool. SQL*PLUS can execute and display the results of any SQL statement, and it definitely was not compiled knowing all of the SQL you would want to execute.

In this chapter, we will discuss how and why you may want to use dynamic SQL in your programs and the kinds of scenarios where this would be of benefit to your application. We will concentrate on dynamic SQL in PL/SQL, as this is the environment in which most people will be using dynamic SQL in a pre-compiler format. Since dynamic SQL is the norm in Java via JDBC (and in order to perform dynamic SQL in SQLJ you must use JDBC) and in C via OCI, it would not be relevant to discuss them in that context – there is only dynamic SQL and no such thing as static SQL, so discussion of this as a special topic would be pointless. Specifically, we will:

- ❑ Demonstrate the different implications of the use of dynamic or static SQL.

- ❑ Look in detail at how you can use dynamic SQL in your programs through the DBMS_SQL supplied package.

- ❑ Examine the **native dynamic SQL** feature.

- ❑ Deal with some of the problems that you may face when using dynamic SQL in your applications. These include the fact that it breaks the dependency chain and it also makes the code more fragile and difficult to tune.

In order to perform all of the dynamic SQL examples in this section, you will need to have Oracle 8.1.5 or higher. Native dynamic SQL was introduced in that release and is a core feature of all subsequent Oracle editions. The majority of the DBMS_SQL examples require only Oracle 7.1 and up, with the exception of functions that employ array processing – a feature that was added to DBMS_SQL in version 8.0.

Dynamic SQL versus Static SQL

Dynamic SQL is a natural choice in API approaches to database programming, such as ODBC, JDBC, and OCI. Static SQL on the other hand is more natural in pre-compiler environments such as Pro*C, SQLJ, and PL/SQL (yes, it is fair to think of the PL/SQL compiler as a pre-compiler). In API-based approaches, *only* dynamic SQL is supported. In order to execute a query you, the programmer, build the query in a string, parse the string, bind inputs into it, execute it, fetch rows if need be, and then finally close the statement. In a static SQL environment almost all of that work will be performed for you. By way of comparison, let's create two PL/SQL programs that do the same thing, but where one uses dynamic SQL and the other static SQL. Here's the dynamic SQL version:

```
scott@TKYTE816> create or replace procedure DynEmpProc( p_job in varchar2 )
  2  as
  3      type refcursor is ref cursor;
  4
  5      -- We must allocate our own host
  6      -- variables and resources using dynamic sql.
  7      l_cursor    refcursor;
  8      l_ename     emp.ename%type;
  9  begin
 10
 11      -- We start by parsing the query
 12      open l_cursor for
 13      'select ename
 14         from emp
 15       where job = :x' USING in p_job;
 16
 17      loop
 18          -- and explicitly FETCHING from the cursor.
 19          fetch l_cursor into l_ename;
 20
 21          -- We have to do all error handling
 22          -- and processing logic ourselves.
 23          exit when l_cursor%notfound;
 24
 25          dbms_output.put_line( l_ename );
 26      end loop;
 27
 28      -- Make sure to free up resources
 29      close l_cursor;
 30  exception
 31      when others then
 32          -- and catch and handle any errors so
 33          -- as to not 'leak' resources over time
 34          -- when errors occur.
 if ( l_cursor%isopen )
```

```
36          then
37              close l_cursor;
38          end if;
39          RAISE;
40  end;
41  /

Procedure created.
```

and here is the static SQL counterpart:

```
scott@TKYTE816> create or replace procedure StaticEmpProc(p_job in varchar2)
  2  as
  3  begin
  4      for x in ( select ename from emp where job = p_job )
  5      loop
  6          dbms_output.put_line( x.ename );
  7      end loop;
  8  end;
  9  /

Procedure created.
```

The two procedures do exactly the same thing:

```
scott@TKYTE816> set serveroutput on size 1000000
scott@TKYTE816> exec DynEmpProc( 'CLERK' )
SMITH
ADAMS
JAMES
MILLER

PL/SQL procedure successfully completed.

scott@TKYTE816> exec StaticEmpProc( 'CLERK' )
SMITH
ADAMS
JAMES
MILLER

PL/SQL procedure successfully completed.
```

However, it is clear that dynamic SQL will require significantly more coding on your part. I find that, from a programming standpoint, static SQL is more efficient while coding (I can develop an application faster using static SQL) but dynamic SQL is more flexible at run-time (my program can do things I did not explicitly code into it at run-time). Also, static SQL, especially static SQL in PL/SQL, will execute much more efficiently than dynamic SQL. Using static SQL, the PL/SQL engine can do in a single interpreted line of code what might take five or six lines of interpreted code with dynamic SQL. For this reason, I use static SQL whenever possible and drop down to dynamic SQL only when I have to. Both methods are useful; one is not inherently better than the other and there are efficiencies and features to be gained from both.

Why Use Dynamic SQL?

There are many reasons for using dynamic SQL in PL/SQL. Some of the more common ones are:

- ❑ To develop generic routines to perform common operations such as unloading data to flat files. In Chapter 9 on *Data Loading*, we demonstrate such a routine.

- ❑ To develop generic routines to load data into as yet unknown tables. We will explore the use of dynamic SQL to load any table.

- ❑ To dynamically invoke other PL/SQL routines at run-time. We discuss this topic in Chapter 23 on *Invoker and Definer Rights* procedures. We'll investigate this further in this chapter.

- ❑ To generate predicates (for example the where clause) on the fly at run-time based on inputs. This is perhaps the number one reason people use dynamic SQL. We will explore how to do this (and how not to do this!) in this chapter.

- ❑ To execute DDL. Since PL/SQL does not permit you to code static DDL statements in your application, dynamic SQL is the only way to achieve this. This will permit us to issue statements that begin with CREATE, ALTER, GRANT, DROP, and so on.

We will explore the above using two main PL/SQL constructs. Firstly, the DBMS_SQL supplied package. This package has been around for a while – since version 7.1 of Oracle. It supplies a procedural method for executing dynamic SQL that is similar to an API-based approach (such as JDBC or ODBC). Secondly, **native dynamic SQL** (this is the EXECUTE IMMEDIATE verb in PL/SQL). This is a declarative method of performing dynamic SQL in PL/SQL and in most cases, is syntactically easier than DBMS_SQL as well as being faster.

Note that *most*, but not *all*, of the procedural DBMS_SQL package still represents a vital and important approach in PL/SQL. We will compare and contrast the two methods and try to spell out when you might want to use one over the other. Once you determine that you need dynamic SQL (static SQL would be best in most cases), you will choose DBMS_SQL or native dynamic SQL after determining the following.

DBMS_SQL will be used when:

- ❑ You do not know the number or types of columns with which you will be working. DBMS_SQL includes procedures to 'describe' a resultset. Native dynamic SQL does not. With native dynamic SQL, you need to know what the resultset will look like at compile-time if PL/SQL is to process the results.

- ❑ You do not know the number or types of possible bind variables with which you will be working. DBMS_SQL allows us to procedurally bind inputs into our statements. Native dynamic SQL requires us to be aware of the number and types of bind variables at compile-time (but we will investigate an interesting workaround to this issue).

- ❑ You will be fetching or inserting thousands of rows and can employ array processing. DBMS_SQL permits array processing, the ability to fetch N rows in a single call instead of a row at a time. Native dynamic SQL in general does not, but there is a workaround demonstrated below.

- ❑ You will be executing the same statement many times in the same session. DBMS_SQL will allow us to parse the statement once and execute it many times over. Native dynamic SQL will cause a soft parse with each and every execution. See Chapter 10 on *Tuning Strategies and Tools* for why this extra parsing is not desirable.

Native dynamic SQL should be used when:

- ❑ You know the number and types of columns with which you will be working.

- ❑ You know the number and types of bind variables (we can also use application contexts to use the easier native dynamic SQL to get around the fact we don't know the number and types).

- ❑ You will be doing DDL.

- ❑ You will be executing the statement very few (one optimally) times.

How to Use Dynamic SQL

We will look at the basics involved in using both the supplied DBMS_SQL database package as well as the native dynamic SQL feature.

DBMS_SQL

The DBMS_SQL package is a supplied built-in package with the database. It is installed by default into the SYS schema and the privilege to execute this package is granted to PUBLIC. That means you should have no trouble accessing it or building compiled stored objects that reference it – no additional or special grants need to be made. One of the nice things about this package is that the documentation is always just a couple of keystrokes away. If you are using DBMS_SQL and need a quick refresher, you can simply execute the following script:

```
scott@TKYTE816> set pagesize 30
scott@TKYTE816> set pause on
scott@TKYTE816> prompt remember to hit ENTER to start reading
remember to hit ENTER to start reading

scott@TKYTE816> select text
  2      from all_source
  3    where name = 'DBMS_SQL'
  4      and type = 'PACKAGE'
  5    order by line
  6  /


TEXT
--------------------------------------------------------------------------
package dbms_sql is


------------
--   OVERVIEW
--
--   This package provides a means to use dynamic SQL to access the database.
--


------------------------
--   RULES AND LIMITATIONS
...
```

In fact, if you need an overview and examples, the above trick works nicely for any of the supplied DBMS_ *or* UTL_ *packages.*

DBMS_SQL is a procedural approach to dynamic SQL. It represents a very similar approach to that used in any other language, such as Java using JDBC or C using OCI. In general, a process using DBMS_SQL will have the following structure:

❏ Call OPEN_CURSOR to obtain a cursor handle.

❏ Call PARSE to parse a statement. A single cursor handle may be used with many different parsed statements. Only one statement at a time will be in effect however.

❏ Call BIND_VARIABLE or BIND_ARRAY to supply any input to the statement.

❏ If it is a query (SELECT statement) you will call DEFINE_COLUMN or DEFINE_ARRAY to tell Oracle how you want the output (as arrays or scalars and of what types).

❏ Call EXECUTE to have the statement run and do its work.

❏ If it was a query, you will call FETCH_ROWS to have Oracle fetch data. You will use COLUMN_VALUE to retrieve these values by position in the select list.

❏ Otherwise, if it was a PL/SQL block of code or a DML statement with a RETURN clause, you can call VARIABLE_VALUE to retrieve OUT values from the block by name.

❏ Call CLOSE_CURSOR.

The pseudo-code steps for dynamically processing a query are:

```
1) Open a cursor
2) Parse a statement
3) Optionally describe the statement to discover the outputs
4) For I in number of bind variables (inputs)
     Bind the I'th input to the statement
5) For I in number of output columns
     Define the I'th column, tell Oracle what type of variable you will be
     fetching into
6) Execute the statement
7) While Fetch Rows succeeds
     Loop
8)   For I in number of output columns
     Call column value to retrieve the value of the I'th column
   End while loop
9) Close cursor
```

And the pseudo-code steps for a PL/SQL block or DML statement are:

```
1) Open a cursor
2) Parse a statement
3) For I in number of bind variables (inputs and outputs)
     Bind the I'th input to the statement
4) Execute the statement
5) For I in number of output bind variables
     Call variable value to retrieve the value of the I'th output
6) Close cursor
```

Lastly, when simply executing DDL (which can have no bind variables) or PL/SQL or DML statements that need no bind variables, the above set of steps is simplified to (although, for this type of statement, I would prefer not to use DBMS_SQL but rather to use native dynamic SQL in all such cases):

```
1) Open a cursor
2) Parse a statement
3) Execute the statement
4) Close cursor
```

Consider the following example of using DBMS_SQL with a query, which can count the number of rows in any database table to which you have access:

```
scott@TKYTE816> create or replace
  2  function get_row_cnts( p_tname in varchar2 ) return number
  3  as
  4          l_theCursor       integer;
  5          l_columnValue     number  default NULL;
  6          l_status          integer;
  7  begin
  8
  9          -- Step 1, open the cursor.
 10          l_theCursor := dbms_sql.open_cursor;
```

We begin a block with an exception handler. If we get an error in this next block of code, we need to have the exception handler close our cursor that we just opened, in order to avoid a 'cursor leak' whereby an opened cursor handle is lost when an error throws us out of this routine.

```
 11          begin
 12
 13          -- Step 2, parse the query.
 14          dbms_sql.parse(  c               => l_theCursor,
 15                           statement       => 'select count(*) from ' || p_tname,
 16                           language_flag   => dbms_sql.native );
 17
```

Notice the language flag is set to the constant supplied in the DBMS_SQL package named NATIVE. This causes the query to be parsed using the rules of the database that the code is executing in. It could be set to DBMS_SQL.V6 or DBMS_SQL.V7 as well. I use NATIVE in all cases.

We did not need step 3 or 4 from the pseudo-code above, as we *know* the outputs and there are no bind variables in this simple example.

```
 18          -- Step 5, define the output of this query as a NUMBER.
 19          dbms_sql.define_column ( c       => l_theCursor,
 20                                   position => 1,
 21                                   column   => l_columnValue );
 22
```

DEFINE does this by being an overloaded procedure so it can tell when you defined a number, DATE, or VARCHAR.

```
 23          -- Step 6, execute the statement.
 24          l_status := dbms_sql.execute(l_theCursor);
 25
```

If this were a DML statement, L_STATUS would be the number of rows returned. For a SELECT, the return value is not meaningful.

```
26              -- Step 7, fetch the rows.
27              if ( dbms_sql.fetch_rows( c => l_theCursor) > 0 )
28              then
29                  -- Step 8, retrieve the outputs.
30                  dbms_sql.column_value( c        => l_theCursor,
31                                         position => 1,
32                                         value    => l_columnValue );
33              end if;
34
35              -- Step 9, close the cursor.
36              dbms_sql.close_cursor( c => l_theCursor );
37              return l_columnValue;
38          exception
39              when others then
40                  dbms_output.put_line( '===> ' || sqlerrm );
41                  dbms_sql.close_cursor( c => l_theCursor );
42                  RAISE;
43          end;
44  end;
45  /

Function created.

scott@TKYTE816> set serveroutput on
scott@TKYTE816> begin
  2      dbms_output.put_line('Emp has this many rows ' ||
  3                          get_row_cnts('emp'));
  4  end;
  5  /
Emp has this many rows 14

PL/SQL procedure successfully completed.

scott@TKYTE816> begin
  2      dbms_output.put_line('Not a table has this many rows ' ||
  3                          get_row_cnts('NOT_A_TABLE'));
  4  end;
  5  /
===> ORA-00942: table or view does not exist
begin
*
ERROR at line 1:
ORA-00942: table or view does not exist
ORA-06512: at "SCOTT.GET_ROW_CNTS", line 60
ORA-06512: at line 2
```

In the above example, we started by allocating a cursor via the call to DBMS_SQL.OPEN_CURSOR. It should be noted that this cursor is specific to DBMS_SQL – it cannot be returned to a VB application to be fetched from and it cannot be used as a PL/SQL cursor. In order to retrieve data from this cursor we must use DBMS_SQL. We then parsed a query SELECT COUNT(*) FROM TABLE, where the value of TABLE is supplied by the caller at run-time – it is concatenated into the query. We must 'glue' the name of the table into the query and not use a bind variable, since bind variables can *never* be used where an identifier (table name or column name for example) is needed. After parsing the query, we used DBMS_SQL.DEFINE_COLUMN to specify that we would like the first (and in this case only) output column in the SELECT list to be retrieved as a NUMBER. The fact we want it retrieved as a number is implicit here – DBMS_SQL.DEFINE_COLUMN is an overloaded procedure with entry points for VARCHARs, NUMBERs, DATEs, BLOB, CLOB, and so on. The output data type we want is implied by the entry point we use, since L_COLUMNVALUE above is a number, the number version of DEFINE_COLUMN is invoked. Next, we call DBMS_SQL.EXECUTE. If we were performing an INSERT, UPDATE, or DELETE type of statement, EXECUTE would return the number of rows affected. In the case of a query, the return value is not defined and may just be ignored. After executing the statement, we call DBMS_SQL.FETCH_ROWS. FETCH_ROWS returns the number of rows actually fetched. In our case above, since we bound to scalar types (not arrays) FETCH_ROWS will return 1 until no more data exists at which point it will return 0. After each row we fetch, we call DBMS_SQL.COLUMN_VALUE for each column in the select list to retrieve its value. Lastly, we finish the routine by closing the cursor via DBMS_SQL.CLOSE_CURSOR.

Next, we will demonstrate how to use DBMS_SQL to process parameterized PL/SQL blocks or DML statements dynamically. I find this functionality very useful when loading an arbitrary file from the operating system using UTL_FILE (an API to allow PL/SQL to read text files) for example. We provide such a utility as an example in Chapter 9 on *Data Loading*. There we use DBMS_SQL to dynamically build an INSERT statement with some number of columns, the number of which is only known at run-time and varies from call to call. It would not be possible to use native dynamic SQL to load an arbitrary table with an arbitrary number of columns, since it needs to know the number of bind variables at compile-time. This particular example is designed to show the mechanics of DBMS_SQL with regards to PL/SQL blocks and DML (it would actually be easier to code the following example using native dynamic SQL because we obviously know the number of bind variables at compile-time in this case):

```
scott@TKYTE816> create or replace
  2  function update_row( p_owner     in varchar2,
  3                       p_newDname  in varchar2,
  4                       p_newLoc    in varchar2,
  5                       p_deptno    in varchar2,
  6                       p_rowid     out varchar2 )
  7  return number
  8  is
  9      l_theCursor     integer;
 10      l_columnValue   number  default NULL;
 11      l_status        integer;
 12      l_update        long;
 13  begin
 14      l_update := 'update ' || p_owner || '.dept
 15                   set dname = :bv1, loc = :bv2
 16                 where deptno = to_number(:pk)
 17             returning rowid into :out';
 18
 19      -- Step 1, open the cursor.
 20      l_theCursor := dbms_sql.open_cursor;
 21
```

We begin a subblock with an exception handler. If we get an error in this block of code, we need to have the exception handler close our cursor we just opened in order to avoid a 'cursor leak' whereby an opened cursor handle is lost when an error throws us out of this routine.

```
22     begin
23         -- Step 2, parse the query.
24         dbms_sql.parse( c               => l_theCursor,
25                         statement       => l_update,
26                         language_flag => dbms_sql.native );
27
28         -- Step 3, bind all of the INPUTS and OUTPUTS.
29         dbms_sql.bind_variable( c       => l_theCursor,
30                                 name    => ':bv1',
31                                 value   => p_newDname );
32         dbms_sql.bind_variable( c       => l_theCursor,
33                                 name    => ':bv2',
34                                 value   => p_newLoc );
35         dbms_sql.bind_variable( c       => l_theCursor,
36                                 name    => ':pk',
37                                 value   => p_deptno );
38         dbms_sql.bind_variable( c       => l_theCursor,
39                                 name    => ':out',
40                                 value   => p_rowid,
41                                 out_value_size => 4000 );
42
```

Note that even though the *returning* variables are all OUT only parameters, we must 'bind' them on input. We also must send the maximum size that we expect them to be on the way out as well (OUT_VALUE_SIZE) so that Oracle will set aside the space for them.

```
43             -- Step 4, execute the statement. Since this is a DML
44             -- statement, L_STATUS is be the number of rows updated.
45             -- This is what we'll return.
46
47             l_status := dbms_sql.execute(l_theCursor);
48
49             -- Step 5, retrieve the OUT variables from the statement.
50             dbms_sql.variable_value( c       => l_theCursor,
51                                      name    => ':out',
52                                      value   => p_rowid );
53
54             -- Step 6, close the cursor.
55             dbms_sql.close_cursor( c => l_theCursor );
56             return l_columnValue;
57     exception
58         when dup_val_on_index then
59             dbms_output.put_line( '===> ' || sqlerrm );
60             dbms_sql.close_cursor( c => l_theCursor );
61             RAISE;
62     end;
63 end;
64 /

Function created.

scott@TKYTE816> set serveroutput on
scott@TKYTE816> declare
  2     l_rowid    varchar(50);
  3     l_rows     number;
```

```
   4  begin
   5      l_rows := update_row('SCOTT','CONSULTING','WASHINGTON',
                                '10',l_rowid );
   6
   7      dbms_output.put_line( 'Updated ' || l_rows || ' rows' );
   8      dbms_output.put_line( 'its rowid was ' || l_rowid );
   9  end;
  10  /
Updated 1 rows
its rowid was AAAGnuAAFAAAAESAAA


PL/SQL procedure successfully completed.
```

So, this shows the mechanics of using DBMS_SQL to execute a block of code providing inputs and retrieving outputs. Let me reiterate – the above block of code would typically be implemented using native dynamic SQL (we'll implement the above routine in native dynamic SQL in a moment). We used DBMS_SQL merely to show how the API worked. In other sections of the book, specifically Chapter 9 on *Data Loading*, we show why DBMS_SQL is still extremely useful. In that chapter we examine the code for a PL/SQL 'data loader' and 'data unloader'. There, DBMS_SQL shows its true power – the ability to process an unknown number of columns of different types, either on input (INSERTs) or output (SELECTs).

We have now covered perhaps 75 percent of the functionality of the DBMS_SQL package. A little later, when we take a look at executing the same statement, dynamically, many times, we'll take a look at the array interface and compare the use of DBMS_SQL to native dynamic SQL in this scenario. However, for the time being, this concludes our overview of DBMS_SQL. For a complete list of the subroutines available and their inputs/outputs, I would refer you to the *Oracle8i Supplied PL/SQL Packages Reference*, where each routine is enumerated.

Native Dynamic SQL

Native dynamic SQL was introduced in Oracle 8i. It introduces to PL/SQL a declarative method for executing dynamic SQL. Most of the work is done with one clause, EXECUTE IMMEDIATE, but with a little help from OPEN FOR. The syntax for EXECUTE IMMEDIATE is as follows:

```
EXECUTE IMMEDIATE 'some statement'
[INTO {variable1, variable2, ... variableN | record}]
[USING [IN | OUT | IN OUT] bindvar1, ... bindvarN]
[{RETURNING | RETURN} INTO output1 [, ..., outputN]...];
```

where:

❑   some statement is any SQL or PL/SQL statement.

❑   variable1, variable2, ... variableN or record is a PL/SQL variable to be fetched into (as the result of single row SELECT).

❑   bindvar1, ... bindvarN is a set of PL/SQL variables to be used for input and/or output.

❑   output1, ... outputN is a set of PL/SQL variables to be used for output from a RETURN clause in DML.

By way of an example, I will implement the code for the GET_ROW_CNTS and UPDATE_ROW functions, that we previously implemented using DBMS_SQL, using EXECUTE IMMEDIATE. First, the GET_ROW_CNTS function:

```
scott@TKYTE816> create or replace
  2    function get_row_cnts( p_tname in varchar2 ) return number
  3    as
  4        l_cnt number;
  5    begin
  6            execute immediate
  7               'select count(*) from ' || p_tname
  8                into l_cnt;
  9
 10            return l_cnt;
 11    end;
 12    /

Function created.

scott@TKYTE816> set serveroutput on
scott@TKYTE816> exec dbms_output.put_line( get_row_cnts('emp') );
 14

PL/SQL procedure successfully completed.
```

Using a simple SELECT...INTO...with EXECUTE IMMEDIATE, you can see that we have drastically cut down the amount of code we needed to write. The nine procedural steps needed by DBMS_SQL are rolled into one step using native dynamic SQL. It is not always just one step – sometimes it is three, as we'll see below – but you get the point. Native dynamic SQL is much more efficient from a coding perspective in this scenario (we'll investigate it from a performance perspective in a moment). You may also have noticed the removal of the EXCEPTION block here – it is not necessary, since everything is *implicit*. There is no cursor for me to close, no cleanup necessary. Oracle does all of the work.

Now, we will implement UPDATE_ROW using native dynamic SQL:

```
scott@TKYTE816> create or replace
  2    function update_row( p_owner      in varchar2,
  3                         p_newDname in varchar2,
  4                         p_newLoc   in varchar2,
  5                         p_deptno   in varchar2,
  6                         p_rowid      out varchar2 )
  7    return number
  8    is
  9    begin
 10        execute immediate
 11                  'update ' || p_owner || '.dept
 12                     set dname = :bv1, loc = :bv2
 13                   where deptno = to_number(:pk)
 14              returning rowid into :out'
 15        using p_newDname, p_newLoc, p_deptno
 16        returning into p_rowid;
 17
 18        return sql%rowcount;
 19    end;
 20    /

Function created.
```

```
scott@TKYTE816> set serveroutput on
scott@TKYTE816> declare
   2        l_rowid    varchar(50);
   3        l_rows     number;
   4  begin
   5        l_rows := update_row( 'SCOTT', 'CONSULTING',
   6                              'WASHINGTON', '10', l_rowid );
   7
   8        dbms_output.put_line( 'Updated ' || l_rows || ' rows' );
   9        dbms_output.put_line( 'its rowid was ' || l_rowid );
  10  end;
  11  /
Updated 1 rows
its rowid was AAAGnuAAFAAAAESAAA

PL/SQL procedure successfully completed.
```

Once again, the reduction in code is tremendous – one step instead of six; easier to read, easier to maintain. In these two cases, native dynamic SQL is clearly superior to DBMS_SQL.

In addition to the EXECUTE IMMEDIATE, native dynamic SQL supports the dynamic processing of a REF CURSOR, also known as a cursor variable. Cursor variables have been around for a while in Oracle (since version 7.2, in fact). Initially, they allowed a stored procedure to OPEN a query (resultset) and return it to a client. They are the methods by which a stored procedure returns a resultset to a client when using a VB, JDBC, ODBC, or OCI program. Later, in version 7.3, they were generalized so that PL/SQL could use a cursor variable not only in the OPEN statement, but in a FETCH statement as well (the client could be another PL/SQL routine). This allowed a PL/SQL routine to accept a resultset as input and process it. This gave us a way to centralize certain processing of different queries – a single routine could FETCH from many different queries (resultsets) for the first time. Until Oracle 8i, however, REF CURSORS were purely static in nature. You had to know at compile-time (stored procedure creation time) exactly what the SQL query was going to be. This was very limiting, as you could not dynamically change the predicate, change the table(s) being queried, and so on. Starting with Oracle 8i, native dynamic SQL allows us to dynamically open a REF CURSOR using any arbitrary query. The syntax for this is simply:

```
OPEN ref_cursor_variable FOR 'select ...'
USING bind_variable1, bind_variabl2, ...;
```

So, using a ref cursor with dynamic SQL, we can implement a generic procedure that queries a table differently given different inputs, and returns the resultset to the client for further processing:

```
scott@TKYTE816> create or replace package my_pkg
   2  as
   3        type refcursor_Type is ref cursor;
   4
   5        procedure get_emps( p_ename  in varchar2 default NULL,
   6                            p_deptno in varchar2 default NULL,
   7                            p_cursor in out refcursor_type );
   8  end;
   9  /

Package created.
```

```
scott@TKYTE816> create or replace package body my_pkg
  2   as
  3       procedure get_emps( p_ename  in varchar2 default NULL,
  4                           p_deptno in varchar2 default NULL,
  5                           p_cursor in out refcursor_type )
  6       is
  7           l_query long;
  8           l_bind  varchar2(30);
  9       begin
 10           l_query := 'select deptno, ename, job from emp';
 11
 12           if ( p_ename is not NULL )
 13           then
 14               l_query := l_query || ' where ename like :x';
 15               l_bind := '%' || upper(p_ename) || '%';
 16           elsif ( p_deptno is not NULL )
 17           then
 18               l_query := l_query || ' where deptno = to_number(:x)';
 19               l_bind := p_deptno;
 20           else
 21               raise_application_error(-20001,'Missing search criteria');
 22           end if;
 23
 24           open p_cursor for l_query using l_bind;
 25       end;
 26   end;
 27   /

Package body created.

scott@TKYTE816> variable C refcursor
scott@TKYTE816> set autoprint on
scott@TKYTE816> exec my_pkg.get_emps( p_ename =>  'a', p_cursor => :C )

PL/SQL procedure successfully completed.


    DEPTNO ENAME      JOB
---------- ---------- ---------
        20 ADAMS      CLERK
        30 ALLEN      SALESMAN
        30 BLAKE      MANAGER
        10 CLARK      MANAGER
        30 JAMES      CLERK
        30 MARTIN     SALESMAN
        30 WARD       SALESMAN

7 rows selected.

scott@TKYTE816> exec my_pkg.get_emps( p_deptno=> '10', p_cursor => :C )

PL/SQL procedure successfully completed.
```

```
       DEPTNO ENAME      JOB
------------- ---------- ----------
           10 CLARK      MANAGER
           10 KING       PRESIDENT
           10 MILLER     CLERK
```

Any time you have more than one row returned from a dynamic query, you must use the above method instead of EXECUTE IMMEDIATE.

So, compared to the DBMS_SQL routines above, this EXECUTE IMMEDIATE and OPEN method is trivial to code and to implement. Does that mean we should never use DBMS_SQL again? The answer to that is definitely *no*. The above examples show how easy dynamic SQL can be when we know the number of bind variables at compile-time. If we did not know this, we could not use EXECUTE IMMEDIATE as easily as we did above. It needs to know the number of bind variables beforehand. DBMS_SQL is more flexible in that respect. In addition to the bind variables, there is the issue of defined columns – columns that are output from a SQL SELECT statement. If you do not know the number and types of these columns, you again cannot use EXECUTE IMMEDIATE. You may be able to use OPEN FOR if the client that will receive the REF CURSOR is not another PL/SQL routine.

In terms of performance, EXECUTE IMMEDIATE will outperform DBMS_SQL for all statements that are parsed and executed only once (all of our examples so far have been of the 'execute once' type). DBMS_SQL has more overhead in this regard, simply because we must make five or six procedure calls to accomplish what is done in one EXECUTE IMMEDIATE.

However, DBMS_SQL makes a comeback in the performance arena when you use it to execute a parsed statement over and over again. EXECUTE IMMEDIATE has no mechanism to 'reuse' parsed statements. It must always parse them, and the overhead of doing that over and over again soon outweighs the benefits of making fewer procedure calls. This is especially relevant in a multi-user environment. Lastly, EXECUTE IMMEDIATE and OPEN cannot utilize array processing as easily as DBMS_SQL and, as we shall see, this alone can have a huge impact on performance.

DBMS_SQL versus Native Dynamic SQL

Now that we've discussed how to implement various routines using either DBMS_SQL or native dynamic SQL, we'll investigate when you should use one over the other. It boils down to some very clear cases. The things that will impact your choice are:

❑ Whether you know the bind variables at compile-time or not. If you do not, DBMS_SQL will most likely be the correct choice.

❑ Whether you know all of the outputs at compile-time or not. If you do not, DBMS_SQL most likely will be the correct choice.

❑ Whether you need to use a REF CURSOR to return a resultset from a stored procedure. If you do, you will have to use OPEN FOR.

❑ Whether you will be executing a given statement once, or many times in a session. If you find you will dynamically execute the same statement many times, DBMS_SQL will give better performance.

❑ Whether you need to employ array processing dynamically.

We'll investigate three of these cases below (in fact, four really – because we will look at examples that execute a statement many times, both with and without array processing.

Bind Variables

Bind variables have a great impact on the performance of your system. Without them, performance will be terrible. With them, performance will be enhanced. It is as simple as that. We have looked at methods to perform **auto binding** in Chapter 10 on *Tuning Strategies and Tools* (via the CURSOR_SHARING parameter). This helps immensely but still adds overhead as the database must rewrite your query and remove information that could be vital to the optimizer, instead of you doing it right in your code yourself.

So, let's say you wanted to create a procedure that creates a query dynamically, based on user inputs. The query will always have the same outputs – the same SELECT list – but the WHERE clause will vary depending on user input. We need to use bind variables for performance reasons. How can we do this using native dynamic SQL and DBMS_SQL? To see the methods, we'll start with a sample routine specification. The procedure we will develop will look like this:

```
scott@TKYTE816> create or replace package dyn_demo
  2  as
  3      type array is table of varchar2(2000);
  4
  5
  6      /*
  7       * DO_QUERY will dynamically query the emp
  8       * table and process the results. You might
  9       * call it like this:
 10       *
 11       * dyn_demo.do_query( array( 'ename', 'job' ),
 12       *                    array( 'like',  '=' ),
 13       *                    array( '%A%',   'CLERK' ) );
 14       *
 15       * to have it query up:
 16       *
 17       * select * from emp where ename like '%A%' and job = 'CLERK'
 18       *
 19       * for example.
 20       */
 21      procedure do_query( p_cnames    in array,
 22                          p_operators in array,
 23                          p_values    in array );
 24
 25  end;
 26  /

Package created.
```

It is natural to do this with DBMS_SQL – the package was built for this type of situation. We can procedurally loop through our arrays of columns and values, and build the WHERE clause. We can parse that query and then loop through the arrays again to bind the values to the placeholders. Then we can execute the statement, fetch the rows and process them. It could be coded as follows:

```
scott@TKYTE816> create or replace package body dyn_demo
  2  as
  3
  4  /*
  5   * DBMS_SQL-based implementation of dynamic
  6   * query with unknown bind variables
```

```
 7   */
 8   g_cursor int default dbms_sql.open_cursor;
 9
10
11   procedure do_query( p_cnames        in array,
12                       p_operators in array,
13                       p_values      in array )
14   is
15       l_query       long;
16       l_sep         varchar2(20) default ' where ';
17       l_comma       varchar2(1) default '';
18       l_status      int;
19       l_colValue    varchar2(4000);
20   begin
21       /*
22        * This is our constant SELECT list - we'll always
23        * get these three columns. The predicate is what
24        * changes.
25        */
26       l_query := 'select ename, empno, job from emp';
27
28       /*
29        * We build the predicate by putting:
30        *
31        * cname operator :bvX
32        *
33        * into the query first.
34        */
35       for i in 1 .. p_cnames.count loop
36           l_query := l_query || l_sep || p_cnames(i) || ' ' ||
37                                           p_operators(i) || ' ' ||
38                                           ':bv' || i;
39           l_sep := ' and ';
40       end loop;
41
42       /*
43        * Now we can parse the query
44        */
45       dbms_sql.parse(g_cursor, l_query, dbms_sql.native);
46
47       /*
48        * and then define the outputs. We fetch all three
49        * columns into a VARCHAR2 type.
50        */
51       for i in 1 .. 3 loop
52           dbms_sql.define_column( g_cursor, i, l_colValue, 4000 );
53       end loop;
54
55       /*
56        * Now, we can bind the inputs to the query
57        */
58       for i in 1 .. p_cnames.count loop
59           dbms_sql.bind_variable( g_cursor, ':bv'||i, p_values(i), 4000);
60       end loop;
61
62       /*
```

```
63         * and then execute it. This defines the resultset
64         */
65         l_status := dbms_sql.execute(g_cursor);
66
67         /*
68         * and now we loop over the rows and print out the results.
69         */
70         while( dbms_sql.fetch_rows( g_cursor ) > 0 )
71         loop
72             l_comma := '';
73             for i in 1 .. 3 loop
74                 dbms_sql.column_value( g_cursor, i, l_colValue );
75                 dbms_output.put( l_comma || l_colValue  );
76                 l_comma := ',';
77             end loop;
78             dbms_output.new_line;
79         end loop;
80     end;
81
82     end dyn_demo;
83     /

Package body created.

scott@TKYTE816> set serveroutput on
scott@TKYTE816> begin
  2         dyn_demo.do_query( dyn_demo.array( 'ename', 'job' ),
  3                            dyn_demo.array( 'like',  '=' ),
  4                            dyn_demo.array( '%A%',   'CLERK' ) );
  5     end;
  6     /
ADAMS,7876,CLERK
JAMES,7900,CLERK

PL/SQL procedure successfully completed.
```

As you can see, it is very straightforward and it follows the steps for DBMS_SQL outlined in the beginning. Now, we would like to implement the same thing using native dynamic SQL. Here we run into a snag however. The syntax for opening a query dynamically with bind variables using native dynamic SQL is:

```
OPEN ref_cursor_variable FOR 'select ...'
USING variable1, variable2, variable3, ...;
```

The problem here is that we do not know at compile-time how large our USING list is – will there be one variable, two variables, no variables? The answer is: we do not know. So, we need to parameterize our query but cannot use bind variables in the traditional sense. We can however, borrow a feature intended for use elsewhere. When we investigate *Fine Grained Access Control* in Chapter 21, we review what an **application context** is and how to use it. An application context is basically a method to place a variable/value pair into a namespace. This variable/value pair may be referenced in SQL using the built-in SYS_CONTEXT function. We can use this application context to parameterize a query by placing our bind values into a namespace and referencing them via the built-in SYS_CONTEXT routine in the query.

So, instead of building a query like:

```
select ename, empno, job
  from emp
 where ename like :bv1
   and job = :bv2;
```

as we did above, we will build a query that looks like:

```
select ename, empno, job
  from emp
 where ename like SYS_CONTEXT('namespace','ename')
   and job = SYS_CONTEXT('namespace','job');
```

The code to implement this could look like this:

```
scott@TKYTE816> REM SCOTT must have GRANT CREATE ANY CONTEXT TO SCOTT;
scott@TKYTE816> REM or a role with that for this to work
scott@TKYTE816> create or replace context bv_context using dyn_demo
  2  /

Context created.

scott@TKYTE816> create or replace package body dyn_demo
  2  as
  3
  4  procedure do_query( p_cnames    in array,
  5                      p_operators in array,
  6                      p_values    in array )
  7  is
  8      type rc is ref cursor;
  9
 10      l_query      long;
 11      l_sep        varchar2(20) default ' where ';
 12      l_cursor     rc;
 13      l_ename      emp.ename%type;
 14      l_empno      emp.empno%type;
 15      l_job        emp.job%type;
 16  begin
 17      /*
 18       * This is our constant SELECT list - we'll always
 19       * get these three columns. The predicate is what
 20       * changes.
 21       */
 22      l_query := 'select ename, empno, job from emp';
 23
 24      for i in 1 .. p_cnames.count loop
 25          l_query := l_query || l_sep ||
 26                      p_cnames(i) || ' ' ||
 27                      p_operators(i) || ' ' ||
 28                      'sys_context( ''BV_CONTEXT'', ''' ||
 29                                  p_cnames(i) || ''' )';
 30          l_sep := ' and ';
 31          dbms_session.set_context( 'bv_context',
 32                                  p_cnames(i),
```

```
33                                        p_values(i) );
34        end loop;
35
36        open l_cursor for l_query;
37        loop
38            fetch l_cursor into l_ename, l_empno, l_job;
39            exit when l_cursor%notfound;
40            dbms_output.put_line( l_ename ||','|| l_empno ||','|| l_job );
41        end loop;
42        close l_cursor;
43    end;
44
45    end dyn_demo;
46    /

Package body created.

scott@TKYTE816> set serveroutput on
scott@TKYTE816> begin
  2          dyn_demo.do_query( dyn_demo.array( 'ename', 'job' ),
  3                             dyn_demo.array( 'like',  '=' ),
  4                             dyn_demo.array( '%A%',   'CLERK' ) );
  5    end;
  6    /
ADAMS,7876,CLERK
JAMES,7900,CLERK

PL/SQL procedure successfully completed.
```

So, it is not as straightforward as using DBMS_SQL with regards to bind variables – it requires a *trick*. Once you understand how to do this, you should opt for using native dynamic SQL over DBMS_SQL *as long as the query has a fixed number of outputs and you use an application context*. You must create and use an application context to support bind variables in order to do the above type of work efficiently. In the end, you will find the above example, using REF CURSORS with native dynamic SQL, to be faster. On simple queries, where the processing of the query itself could be ignored, native dynamic SQL is almost twice as fast at fetching the data as DBMS_SQL.

Number of Outputs Unknown at Compile-Time

Here the answer is cut and dry – if the client that will fetch and process the data is PL/SQL, you must use DBMS_SQL. If the client that will fetch and process the data is a 3GL application using ODBC, JDBC, OCI, and so on, you will use native dynamic SQL.

The situation we will look at is that you are given a query at run-time and you have no idea how many columns are in the select list. You need to process this in PL/SQL. We will find we cannot use native dynamic SQL since we would need to code the following:

```
FETCH cursor INTO variable1, variable2, variable3, ...;
```

at some point in our code, but we cannot do this since we do not know how many variables to place there until run-time. This is one case where DBMS_SQL's use will be mandatory, since it gives us the ability to use constructs such as:

```
41          while ( dbms_sql.fetch_rows(l_theCursor) > 0 )
42          loop
43              /* Build up a big output line, this is more efficient than calling
44               * DBMS_OUTPUT.PUT_LINE inside the loop.
45               */
46              l_cnt := l_cnt+1;
47              l_line := l_cnt;
48              /* Step 8 - get and process the column data. */
49              for i in 1 .. l_colCnt loop
50                  dbms_sql.column_value( l_theCursor, i, l_columnValue );
51                  l_line := l_line || ',' || l_columnValue;
52              end loop;
53
54              /* Now print out this line. */
55              dbms_output.put_line( l_line );
56          end loop;
```

We can procedurally iterate over the columns, indexing each one as if it were an array. The above construct comes from the following piece of code:

```
scott@TKYTE816> create or replace
  2  procedure  dump_query( p_query in varchar2 )
  3  is
  4      l_columnValue    varchar2(4000);
  5      l_status         integer;
  6      l_colCnt         number default 0;
  7      l_cnt            number default 0;
  8      l_line           long;
  9
 10      /* We'll be using this to see how many columns
 11       * we have to fetch so we can define them and
 12       * then retrieve their values.
 13       */
 14      l_descTbl        dbms_sql.desc_tab;
 15
 16
 17      /* Step 1 - open cursor. */
 18      l_theCursor      integer default dbms_sql.open_cursor;
 19  begin
 20
 21      /* Step 2 - parse the input query so we can describe it. */
 22      dbms_sql.parse( l_theCursor,  p_query, dbms_sql.native );
 23
 24      /* Step 3 - now, describe the outputs of the query. */
 25      dbms_sql.describe_columns( l_theCursor, l_colCnt, l_descTbl );
 26
 27      /* Step 4 - we do not use in this example, no BINDING needed.
 28       * Step 5 - for each column, we need to define it, tell the database
 29       * what we will fetch into. In this case, all data is going
 30       * to be fetched into a single varchar2(4000) variable.
 31       */
 32      for i in 1 .. l_colCnt
 33      loop
```

```
34              dbms_sql.define_column( l_theCursor, i, l_columnValue, 4000 );
35          end loop;
36
37          /* Step 6 - execute the statement. */
38          l_status := dbms_sql.execute(l_theCursor);
39
40          /* Step 7 - fetch all rows. */
41          while ( dbms_sql.fetch_rows(l_theCursor) > 0 )
42          loop
43              /* Build up a big output line, this is more efficient than calling
44               * DBMS_OUTPUT.PUT_LINE inside the loop.
45               */
46              l_cnt := l_cnt+1;
47              l_line := l_cnt;
48              /* Step 8 - get and process the column data. */
49              for i in 1 .. l_colCnt loop
50                  dbms_sql.column_value( l_theCursor, i, l_columnValue );
51                  l_line := l_line || ',' || l_columnValue;
52              end loop;
53
54              /* Now print out this line. */
55              dbms_output.put_line( l_line );
56          end loop;
57
58          /* Step 9 - close cursor to free up resources.. */
59          dbms_sql.close_cursor(l_theCursor);
60      exception
61          when others then
62              dbms_sql.close_cursor( l_theCursor );
63              raise;
64      end dump_query;
65      /

Procedure created.
```

Additionally, DBMS_SQL gives us an API called DBMS_SQL.DESCRIBE_COLUMNS, which will tell us the number of columns in a query, their data types, and their names among other pieces of information. As an example of this, we'll look at a generic routine to dump the results of an arbitrary query to a flat file. It differs from the other example we have of this in Chapter 9 on *Data Loading*, where we look at a SQL-Unloader tool. This example dumps data to a fixed width file, where each column always appears in the same position in the output file. It does this by inspecting the output of DBMS_SQL.DESCRIBE_COLUMNS, which tells us the maximum width of a column, in addition to the number of columns we have selected. Before we look at the full example, we'll take a look at the DESCRIBE_COLUMNS routine first. After we parse a SELECT query, we can use this routine to interrogate the database as to what we can expect when we fetch from the query. This routine will populate an array of records with information regarding the column name, data type, max length, and so on.

Here is an example that shows how to use DESCRIBE_COLUMNS and dumps out the data it returns for an arbitrary query so we can see what sort of information is available:

```
scott@TKYTE816> create or replace
  2  procedure  desc_query( p_query in varchar2 )
  3  is
  4      l_columnValue    varchar2(4000);
  5      l_status         integer;
```

```
 6      l_colCnt         number default 0;
 7      l_cnt            number default 0;
 8      l_line           long;
 9
10      /* We'll be using this to see what our query SELECTs
11       */
12      l_descTbl        dbms_sql.desc_tab;
13
14
15      /* Step 1 - open cursor. */
16      l_theCursor      integer default dbms_sql.open_cursor;
17   begin
18
19      /* Step 2 - parse the input query so we can describe it. */
20      dbms_sql.parse( l_theCursor, p_query, dbms_sql.native );
21
22      /* Step 3 - now, describe the outputs of the query.
23       * L_COLCNT will contain the number of columns selected
24       * in the query. It will be equal to L_DESCTBL.COUNT
25       * actually and so it is redundant really. L_DESCTBL
26       * contains the useful data about our SELECTed columns.
27       */
28
29      dbms_sql.describe_columns( c       => l_theCursor,
30                                 col_cnt => l_colCnt,
31                                 desc_t  => l_descTbl );
32
33      for i in 1 .. l_colCnt
34      loop
35          dbms_output.put_line
36          ( 'Column Type..........' || l_descTbl(i).col_type );
37          dbms_output.put_line
38          ( 'Max Length...........' || l_descTbl(i).col_max_len );
39          dbms_output.put_line
40          ( 'Name.................' || l_descTbl(i).col_name );
41          dbms_output.put_line
42          ( 'Name Length..........' || l_descTbl(i).col_name_len );
43          dbms_output.put_line
44          ( 'ObjColumn Schema Name.' || l_descTbl(i).col_schema_name );
45          dbms_output.put_line
46          ( 'Schema Name Length....' || l_descTbl(i).col_schema_name_len );
47          dbms_output.put_line
48          ( 'Precision.............' || l_descTbl(i).col_precision );
49          dbms_output.put_line
50          ( 'Scale.................' || l_descTbl(i).col_scale );
51          dbms_output.put_line
52          ( 'Charsetid.............' || l_descTbl(i).col_Charsetid );
53          dbms_output.put_line
54          ( 'Charset Form..........' || l_descTbl(i).col_charsetform );
55          if ( l_desctbl(i).col_null_ok ) then
56              dbms_output.put_line( 'Nullable..............Y' );
57          else
58              dbms_output.put_line( 'Nullable..............N' );
59          end if;
60          dbms_output.put_line( '------------------------' );
```

```
61        end loop;
62
63        /* Step 9 - close cursor to free up resources. */
64        dbms_sql.close_cursor(l_theCursor);
65   exception
66       when others then
67           dbms_sql.close_cursor( l_theCursor );
68           raise;
69   end desc_query;
70   /

Procedure created.

scott@TKYTE816> set serveroutput on
scott@TKYTE816> exec desc_query( 'select rowid, ename from emp' );
Column Type..........11
Max Length...........16
Name.................ROWID
Name Length..........5
ObjColumn Schema Name.
Schema Name Length....0
Precision............0
Scale................0
Charsetid............0
Charset Form.........0
Nullable.............Y
-----------------------
Column Type..........1
Max Length...........10
Name.................ENAME
Name Length..........5
ObjColumn Schema Name.
Schema Name Length....0
Precision............0
Scale................0
Charsetid............31
Charset Form.........1
Nullable.............Y
-----------------------

PL/SQL procedure successfully completed.
```

Unfortunately, the COLUMN TYPE is simply a number, not the name of the data type itself, so unless you know that Column Type 11 is a ROWID and 1 is a VARCHAR2, you won't be able to decode these. The *Oracle Call Interface Programmer's Guide* has a complete list of all internal data type codes and their corresponding data type names. This is a copy of that list:

Data type Name	Code
VARCHAR2, NVARCHAR2	1
NUMBER	2
LONG	8
ROWID	11
DATE	12
RAW	23

Data type Name	Code
LONG RAW	24
CHAR, NCHAR	96
User-defined type (object type, VARRAY, nested table)	108
REF	111
CLOB, NCLOB	112
BLOB	113
BFILE	114
UROWID	208

Now we are ready for the full routine that can take almost any query and dump the results to a flat file (assuming you have setup UTL_FILE, see the Appendix A on *Necessary Supplied Packages* for more details on this):

```
scott@TKYTE816> create or replace
  2  function  dump_fixed_width( p_query      in varchar2,
  3                              p_dir        in varchar2 ,
  4                              p_filename   in varchar2 )
  5  return number
  6  is
  7      l_output        utl_file.file_type;
  8      l_theCursor     integer default dbms_sql.open_cursor;
  9      l_columnValue   varchar2(4000);
 10      l_status        integer;
 11      l_colCnt        number default 0;
 12      l_cnt           number default 0;
 13       l_line          long;
 14      l_descTbl       dbms_sql.desc_tab;
 15      l_dateformat    nls_session_parameters.value%type;
 16  begin
 17      select value into l_dateformat
 18        from nls_session_parameters
 19       where parameter = 'NLS_DATE_FORMAT';
 20
 21      /* Use a date format that includes the time. */
 22      execute immediate
 23      'alter session set nls_date_format=''dd-mon-yyyy hh24:mi:ss'' ';
 24      l_output := utl_file.fopen( p_dir, p_filename, 'w', 32000 );
 25
 26      /* Parse the input query so we can describe it. */
 27      dbms_sql.parse( l_theCursor,  p_query, dbms_sql.native );
 28
 29      /* Now, describe the outputs of the query. */
 30      dbms_sql.describe_columns( l_theCursor, l_colCnt, l_descTbl );
 31
 32      /* For each column, we need to define it, to tell the database
 33       * what we will fetch into. In this case, all data is going
 34       * to be fetched into a single varchar2(4000) variable.
 35       *
```

```
36          * We will also adjust the max width of each column. We do
37          * this so when we OUTPUT the data. Each field starts and
38          * stops in the same position for each record.
39          */
40        for i in 1 .. l_colCnt loop
41            dbms_sql.define_column( l_theCursor, i, l_columnValue, 4000 );
42
43            if ( l_descTbl(i).col_type = 2 )  /* number type */
44            then
45                L_descTbl(i).col_max_len := l_descTbl(i).col_precision+2;
46            elsif ( l_descTbl(i).col_type = 12 ) /* date type */
47            then
48                    /* length of my format above */
49                    l_descTbl(i).col_max_len := 20;
50            end if;
51          end loop;
52
53        l_status := dbms_sql.execute(l_theCursor);
54
55        while ( dbms_sql.fetch_rows(l_theCursor) > 0 )
56        loop
57            /* Build up a big output line. This is more efficient than
58             * calling UTL_FILE.PUT inside the loop.
59             */
60            l_line := null;
61            for i in 1 .. l_colCnt loop
62                dbms_sql.column_value( l_theCursor, i, l_columnValue );
63                l_line := l_line ||
64                        rpad( nvl(l_columnValue,' '),
65                        l_descTbl(i).col_max_len );
66            end loop;
67
68            /* Now print out that line and increment a counter. */
69            utl_file.put_line( l_output, l_line );
70            l_cnt := l_cnt+1;
71        end loop;
72
73        /* Free up resources. */
74        dbms_sql.close_cursor(l_theCursor);
75        utl_file.fclose( l_output );
76
77        /* Reset the date format ... and return. */
78        execute immediate
79        'alter session set nls_date_format=''' || l_dateformat || ''' ';
80        return l_cnt;
81    exception
82        when others then
83            dbms_sql.close_cursor( l_theCursor );
84            execute immediate
85            'alter session set nls_date_format=''' || l_dateformat || ''' ';
86
87    end dump_fixed_width;
88    /

Function created.
```

So, this function uses the DBMS_SQL.DESCRIBE_COLUMNS routine to find the number of columns based on their data type. I have modified some of the maximum length settings to adjust for the size of the date format I am using and decimals/signs in numbers. As currently coded, the above routine would not unload LONGs, LONG RAW, CLOBs, and BLOBs. It could be modified easily to handle CLOBs and even LONGs. You would need to bind specifically for those types and use DBMS_CLOB to retrieve the CLOB data and DBMS_SQL.COLUMN_VALUE_LONG for the LONG data. It should be noted that you quite simply *would not* be able to achieve the above using native dynamic SQL – it just is not possible when the SELECT list is not known in PL/SQL.

Executing the Same Statement Dynamically Many Times

This will be a trade-off between DBMS_SQL and native dynamic SQL. The trade-off is one of code and complexity versus performance. To demonstrate this, I will develop a routine that inserts many rows into a table dynamically. We are using dynamic SQL since we don't know the name of the table in to which we are inserting until run-time. We'll set up four routines to compare and contrast:

Routine	Meaning
DBMSSQL_ARRAY	Uses array processing in PL/SQL to bulk insert rows
NATIVE_DYNAMIC_ARRAY	Uses simulated array processing with object type tables
DBMSSQL_NOARRAY	Uses row at a time processing to insert records
NATIVE_DYNAMIC_NOARRAY	Uses row at a time processing to insert records

The first method will be the most scalable and best performing. In my tests on various platforms, methods one and two were basically *tied* in a single user test – given a machine with no other users, they were more or less equivalent. On some platforms, native dynamic SQL was marginally faster – on others DBMS_SQL was the quicker of the two. In a multi-user environment, however, due to the fact that native dynamic SQL is parsed every time it is executed, the DBMS_SQL array approach will be more scalable. It removes the need to soft parse the query for each and every execution. Another thing to consider is that in order to simulate array processing in native dynamic SQL, we had to resort to a trick. The code is no easier to write in either case. Normally, native dynamic SQL is much easier to code than DBMS_SQL but not in this case.

The only clear conclusion we will come to from this is that methods three and four are much slower than one and two – many times slower in fact. The following results were obtained on a single user Solaris platform although the results on Windows were similar. You should test on your platform to see which makes the most sense for you.

```
scott@TKYTE816> create or replace type vcArray as table of varchar2(400)
  2  /

Type created.

scott@TKYTE816> create or replace type dtArray as table of date
  2  /

Type created.

scott@TKYTE816> create or replace type nmArray as table of number
  2  /

Type created.
```

These types are needed in order to simulate array processing with native dynamic SQL. They will be our array types – native dynamic SQL cannot be used with PL/SQL table types at all. Now, here is the specification of the package we'll use to test with:

```
scott@TKYTE816> create or replace package load_data
  2  as
  3
  4  procedure dbmssql_array( p_tname      in varchar2,
  5                           p_arraysize in number default 100,
  6                           p_rows      in number default 500 );
  7
  8  procedure dbmssql_noarray( p_tname in varchar2,
  9                             p_rows  in number default 500 );
 10
 11
 12  procedure native_dynamic_noarray( p_tname  in varchar2,
 13                                    p_rows   in number default 500 );
 14
 15  procedure native_dynamic_array( p_tname      in varchar2,
 16                                  p_arraysize in number default 100,
 17                                  p_rows      in number default 500 );
 18  end load_data;
 19  /

Package created.
```

Each of the above procedures will dynamically insert into some table specified by P_TNAME. The number of rows inserted is controlled by P_ROWS and, when using array processing, the array size used is dictated by the P_ARRAYSIZE parameter. Now for the implementation:

```
scott@TKYTE816> create or replace package body load_data
  2  as
  3
  4  procedure dbmssql_array( p_tname      in varchar2,
  5                           p_arraysize in number default 100,
  6                           p_rows      in number default 500 )
  7  is
  8      l_stmt      long;
  9      l_theCursor integer;
 10      l_status    number;
 11      l_col1      dbms_sql.number_table;
 12      l_col2      dbms_sql.date_table;
 13      l_col3      dbms_sql.varchar2_table;
 14      l_cnt       number default 0;
 15  begin
 16      l_stmt := 'insert into ' || p_tname ||
 17              ' q1 ( a, b, c ) values ( :a, :b, :c )';
 18
 19      l_theCursor := dbms_sql.open_cursor;
 20      dbms_sql.parse(l_theCursor, l_stmt, dbms_sql.native);
 21          /*
 22           * We will make up data here. When we've made up ARRAYSIZE
 23           * rows, we'll bulk insert them. At the end of the loop,
 24           * if any rows remain, we'll insert them as well.
 25           */
```

```
26        for i in 1 .. p_rows
27        loop
28              l_cnt := l_cnt+1;
29          l_col1( l_cnt ) := i;
30          l_col2( l_cnt ) := sysdate+i;
31          l_col3( l_cnt ) := to_char(i);
32
33          if (l_cnt = p_arraysize)
34          then
35             dbms_sql.bind_array( l_theCursor, ':a', l_col1, 1, l_cnt );
36             dbms_sql.bind_array( l_theCursor, ':b', l_col2, 1, l_cnt );
37             dbms_sql.bind_array( l_theCursor, ':c', l_col3, 1, l_cnt );
38             l_status := dbms_sql.execute( l_theCursor );
39                  l_cnt := 0;
40          end if;
41        end loop;
42        if (l_cnt > 0 )
43        then
44             dbms_sql.bind_array( l_theCursor, ':a', l_col1, 1, l_cnt );
45             dbms_sql.bind_array( l_theCursor, ':b', l_col2, 1, l_cnt );
46             dbms_sql.bind_array( l_theCursor, ':c', l_col3, 1, l_cnt );
47             l_status := dbms_sql.execute( l_theCursor );
48        end if;
49        dbms_sql.close_cursor( l_theCursor );
50   end;
51
```

So, this is the routine that uses DBMS_SQL to array-insert N rows at a time. We use the overloaded BIND_VARIABLE routine that allows us to send in a PL/SQL table type with the data to be loaded. We send in the array bounds telling Oracle where to start and stop in our PL/SQL table – in this case, we always start at index 1 and end at index L_CNT. Notice that the table name in the INSERT statement has a correlation name Q1 associated with it. I did this so that when we go to analyze the performance using TKPROF, we'll be able to identify which INSERT statements were used by particular routines. Overall the code is fairly straightforward. Next, we implement the DBMS_SQL that does not use array processing:

```
52   procedure dbmssql_noarray( p_tname      in varchar2,
53                              p_rows       in number default 500 )
54   is
55       l_stmt       long;
56       l_theCursor  integer;
57       l_status     number;
58   begin
59       l_stmt := 'insert into ' || p_tname ||
60                 ' q2 ( a, b, c ) values ( :a, :b, :c )';
61
62       l_theCursor := dbms_sql.open_cursor;
63       dbms_sql.parse(l_theCursor, l_stmt, dbms_sql.native);
64           /*
65            * We will make up data here. When we've made up ARRAYSIZE
66            * rows, we'll bulk insert them. At the end of the loop,
67            * if any rows remain, we'll insert them as well.
68            */
69       for i in 1 .. p_rows
70       loop
71          dbms_sql.bind_variable( l_theCursor, ':a', i );
```

```
72              dbms_sql.bind_variable( l_theCursor, ':b', sysdate+i );
73              dbms_sql.bind_variable( l_theCursor, ':c', to_char(i) );
74              l_status := dbms_sql.execute( l_theCursor );
75          end loop;
76          dbms_sql.close_cursor( l_theCursor );
77      end;
78
```

This is very similar in appearance to the previous routine, with just the arrays missing. If you find yourself coding a routine that looks like the above logic, you should give serious consideration to using array processing. As we'll see in a moment, it can make a big difference in the performance of your application. Now for the native dynamic SQL routine:

```
79      procedure native_dynamic_noarray( p_tname   in varchar2,
80                                        p_rows    in number default 500 )
81      is
82      begin
83          /*
84           * Here, we simply make up a row and insert it.
85           * A trivial amount of code to write and execute.
86           */
87          for i in 1 .. p_rows
88          loop
89              execute immediate
90                  'insert into ' || p_tname ||
91                  ' q3 ( a, b, c ) values ( :a, :b, :c )'
92              using i, sysdate+i, to_char(i);
93          end loop;
94      end;
95
```

This is without array processing. Very simple, very small – easy to code but among the worst performing due to the excessive amount of parsing that must take place. Lastly, an example of simulating array inserts using native dynamic SQL:

```
96      procedure native_dynamic_array( p_tname     in varchar2,
97                                      p_arraysize in number default 100,
98                                      p_rows      in number default 500 )
99      is
100         l_stmt      long;
101         l_theCursor integer;
102         l_status    number;
103         l_col1      nmArray := nmArray();
104         l_col2      dtArray := dtArray();
105         l_col3      vcArray := vcArray();
106         l_cnt       number  := 0;
107     begin
108         /*
109          * We will make up data here. When we've made up ARRAYSIZE
110          * rows, we'll bulk insert them. At the end of the loop,
111          * if any rows remain, we'll insert them as well.
112          */
113         l_col1.extend( p_arraysize );
114         l_col2.extend( p_arraysize );
```

```
115        l_col3.extend( p_arraysize );
116        for i in 1 .. p_rows
117        loop
118             l_cnt := l_cnt+1;
119          l_col1( l_cnt ) := i;
120          l_col2( l_cnt ) := sysdate+i;
121          l_col3( l_cnt ) := to_char(i);
122
123          if (l_cnt = p_arraysize)
124          then
125                  execute immediate
126                  'begin
127                  forall i in 1 .. :n
128                       insert into ' || p_tname || '
129                  q4 ( a, b, c ) values ( :a(i), :b(i), :c(i) );
130                  end;'
131                  USING l_cnt, l_col1, l_col2, l_col3;
132                  l_cnt := 0;
133          end if;
134        end loop;
135        if (l_cnt > 0 )
136        then
137              execute immediate
138              'begin
139              forall i in 1 .. :n
140                   insert into ' || p_tname || '
141              q4 ( a, b, c ) values ( :a(i), :b(i), :c(i) );
142              end;'
143              USING l_cnt, l_col1, l_col2, l_col3;
144        end if;
145  end;
146
147  end load_data;
148  /

Package body created.
```

As you can see, this is a little obscure. Our code is writing code that will be dynamically executed. This dynamic code uses the FORALL syntax to bulk insert arrays. Since the EXECUTE IMMEDIATE statement can only use SQL types, we had to define types for it to use. Then we had to dynamically execute a statement:

```
begin
    forall i in 1 .. :n
        insert into t (a,b,c) values (:a(I), :b(I), :c(I));
end;
```

binding in the number of rows to insert and the three arrays. As we will see below, the use of array processing speeds up the inserts many times. You have to trade this off with the ease of coding the native dynamic SQL routine without arrays, however – it is hard to beat one line of code! If this was a one-time program where performance was not crucial, I might go down that path. If this was a reusable routine, one that would be around for a while, I would choose DBMS_SQL when the need for speed was present and the number of bind variables unknown and native dynamic SQL when the performance was acceptable and the number of bind variables was well known.

Lastly, we cannot forget about the discussion from Chapter 10, *Tuning Strategies and Tools*, where we saw that avoiding soft parses is desirable – DBMS_SQL can do this, native dynamic SQL cannot. You need to look at what you are doing and chose the appropriate approach. If you are writing a data loader that will be run once a day and parse the queries a couple of hundred times, native dynamic SQL would work great. On the other hand, if you are writing a routine that uses the same dynamic SQL statement dozens of times by many dozens of users concurrently, you'll want to use DBMS_SQL so you can parse once and run many times.

I ran the above routines using this test block of code (a single user system remember!):

```
create table t (a int, b date, c varchar2(15));

alter session set sql_trace=true;
truncate table t;
exec load_data.dbmssql_array('t', 50, 10000);

truncate table t;
exec load_data.native_dynamic_array('t', 50, 10000);

truncate table t;
exec load_data.dbmssql_noarray('t', 10000)

truncate table t;
exec load_data.native_dynamic_noarray('t', 10000)
```

What we find from the TKPROF report is this:

```
BEGIN load_data.dbmssql_array( 't', 50, 10000 ); END;
```

call	count	cpu	elapsed	disk	query	current	rows
Parse	1	0.01	0.00	0	0	0	0
Execute	1	2.58	2.83	0	0	0	1
Fetch	0	0.00	0.00	0	0	0	0
total	2	2.59	2.83	0	0	0	1

```
BEGIN load_data.native_dynamic_array( 't', 50, 10000 ); END;
```

call	count	cpu	elapsed	disk	query	current	rows
Parse	1	0.00	0.00	0	0	0	0
Execute	1	2.39	2.63	0	0	0	1
Fetch	0	0.00	0.00	0	0	0	0
total	2	2.39	2.63	0	0	0	1

So overall, the execution profiles were very similar, 2.59 CPU seconds and 2.30 CPU seconds. The devil is in the details here, however. If you look at the code above, I make sure each and every insert was a little different from the other inserts by sticking a Q1, Q2, Q3, and Q4 correlation name in them. In this fashion, we can see how many parses took place. The DBMS_SQL array routine used Q1 and the native dynamic SQL routine used Q4. The results are:

```
insert into t q1 ( a, b, c ) values ( :a, :b, :c )

call     count        cpu    elapsed disk      query    current        rows
-------  ------   --------  ---------- -----  ----------  ----------  ----------
Parse        1      0.00        0.01      0           0           0           0
```

and:

```
begin
     forall i in 1 .. :n
         insert into t q4 ( a, b, c ) values ( :a(i), :b(i), :c(i) );
end;

call     count        cpu    elapsed disk      query    current        rows
-------  ------   --------  ---------- -----  ----------  ----------  ----------
Parse      200      0.10        0.07      0           0           0           0

INSERT INTO T Q4 ( A,B,C ) VALUES ( :b1,:b2,:b3 )

call     count        cpu    elapsed disk      query    current        rows
-------  ------   --------  ---------- -----  ----------  ----------  ----------
Parse      200      0.07        0.04      0           0           0           0
```

As you can see, the DBMS_SQL routine was able to get away with a single parse, but the native dynamic SQL had to parse 400 times. On a heavily loaded system, with lots of concurrent users, this may really affect performance and is something to consider. Since it can be avoided and the DBMS_SQL code is not significantly harder to code in this particular case, I would give the nod to DBMS_SQL as the correct implementation for this type of work. It is a close call but for scalability reasons, I would go with it.

The results of the non-array processing routines were terrible, relatively speaking:

```
BEGIN load_data.dbmssql_noarray( 't', 10000 ); END;

call     count        cpu    elapsed disk      query    current        rows
-------  ------   --------  ---------- -----  ----------  ----------  ----------
Parse        1      0.00        0.00      0           0           0           0
Execute      1      7.66        7.68      0           0           0           1
Fetch        0      0.00        0.00      0           0           0           0
-------  ------   --------  ---------- -----  ----------  ----------  ----------
total        2      7.66        7.68      0           0           0           1

BEGIN load_data.native_dynamic_noarray( 't', 10000 ); END;

call     count        cpu    elapsed disk      query    current        rows
-------  ------   --------  ---------- -----  ----------  ----------  ----------
Parse        1      0.00        0.00      0           0           0           0
Execute      1      6.15        6.25      0           0           0           1
Fetch        0      0.00        0.00      0           0           0           0
-------  ------   --------  ---------- -----  ----------  ----------  ----------
total        2      6.15        6.25      0           0           0           1
```

Here, it looks like the native dynamic SQL would be the way to go. However, I would still probably go with `DBMS_SQL` if I were not to implement array processing. It is purely because of this:

```
insert into t q2 ( a, b, c ) values ( :a, :b, :c )

call     count       cpu    elapsed  disk       query      current       rows
-------  ------   -------- ---------- -----  ---------- ----------  ----------
Parse        1      0.00       0.00     0           0          0           0

insert into t q3 ( a, b, c ) values ( :a, :b, :c )

call     count       cpu    elapsed  disk       query      current       rows
-------  ------   -------- ---------- -----  ---------- ----------  ----------
Parse    10000      1.87       1.84     0           0          0           0
```

This shows 10,000 soft parses using native dynamic SQL and one soft parse using `DBMS_SQL`. In a multi-user environment, the `DBMS_SQL` implementation will scale better.

We see similar results when processing lots of rows from a dynamically executed query. Normally, you can array-fetch from a `REF CURSOR`, but only a strongly typed `REF CURSOR`. That is, a `REF CURSOR` whose structure is known by the compiler at compile-time. Native dynamic SQL only supports weakly typed `REF CURSORS` and hence, does not support the `BULK COLLECT`. If you attempt to `BULK COLLECT` a dynamically opened `REF CURSOR` you'll receive a:

```
ORA-01001: Invalid Cursor
```

Here is a comparison of two routines, both of which fetch all of the rows from `ALL_OBJECTS` and count them. The routine that utilizes `DBMS_SQL` with array processing is almost twice as fast:

```
scott@TKYTE816> create or replace procedure native_dynamic_select
  2  as
  3      type rc is ref cursor;
  4      l_cursor rc;
  5      l_oname  varchar2(255);
  6      l_cnt           number := 0;
  7      l_start  number default dbms_utility.get_time;
  8  begin
  9      open l_cursor for 'select object_name from all_objects';
 10
 11      loop
 12          fetch l_cursor into l_oname;
 13          exit when l_cursor%notfound;
 14          l_cnt := l_cnt+1;
 15      end loop;
 16
 17      close l_cursor;
 18      dbms_output.put_line( L_cnt || ' rows processed' );
 19      dbms_output.put_line
 20      ( round( (dbms_utility.get_time-l_start)/100, 2 ) || ' seconds' );
 21  exception
 22      when others then
 23          if ( l_cursor%isopen )
 24          then
```

```
 25                 close l_cursor;
 26          end if;
 27          raise;
 28   end;
 29   /

Procedure created.

scott@TKYTE816> create or replace procedure dbms_sql_select
  2    as
  3        l_theCursor      integer default dbms_sql.open_cursor;
  4        l_columnValue    dbms_sql.varchar2_table;
  5        l_status         integer;
  6        l_cnt            number := 0;
  7        l_start  number default dbms_utility.get_time;
  8    begin
  9
 10        dbms_sql.parse( l_theCursor,
 11                        'select object_name from all_objects',
 12                        dbms_sql.native );
 13
 14        dbms_sql.define_array( l_theCursor, 1, l_columnValue, 100, 1 );
 15        l_status := dbms_sql.execute( l_theCursor );
 16        loop
 17            l_status := dbms_sql.fetch_rows(l_theCursor);
 18            dbms_sql.column_value(l_theCursor,1,l_columnValue);
 19
 20            l_cnt := l_status+l_cnt;
 21            exit when l_status <> 100;
 22        end loop;
 23        dbms_sql.close_cursor( l_theCursor );
 24        dbms_output.put_line( L_cnt || ' rows processed' );
 25        dbms_output.put_line
 26        ( round( (dbms_utility.get_time-l_start)/100, 2 ) || ' seconds' );
 27    exception
 28        when others then
 29            dbms_sql.close_cursor( l_theCursor );
 30            raise;
 31    end;
 32    /

Procedure created.

scott@TKYTE816> set serveroutput on

scott@TKYTE816> exec native_dynamic_select
19695 rows processed
1.85 seconds

PL/SQL procedure successfully completed.

scott@TKYTE816> exec native_dynamic_select
19695 rows processed
1.86 seconds

PL/SQL procedure successfully completed.
```

```
scott@TKYTE816> exec dbms_sql_select
19695 rows processed
1.03 seconds

PL/SQL procedure successfully completed.

scott@TKYTE816> exec dbms_sql_select
19695 rows processed
1.07 seconds

PL/SQL procedure successfully completed.
```

Again, it is a trade-off of performance versus coding effort. Utilizing array processing in DBMS_SQL takes a considerable amount more coding then native dynamic SQL but the pay off is greatly increased performance.

Caveats

As with any feature, there are some nuances that need to be noted in the way this feature functions. This section attempts to address them each in turn. There are three major caveats that come to mind with dynamic SQL in stored procedures. They are:

- ❑ It breaks the dependency chain.
- ❑ It makes the code more 'fragile'.
- ❑ It is much harder to tune to have predictable response times.

It Breaks the Dependency Chain

Normally, when you compile a procedure into the database, everything it references and everything that references it is recorded in the data dictionary. For example, I create a procedure:

```
ops$tkyte@DEV816> create or replace function count_emp return number
  2   as
  3           l_cnt number;
  4   begin
  5           select count(*) into l_cnt from emp;
  6           return l_cnt;
  7   end;
  8   /

Function created.

ops$tkyte@DEV816> select referenced_name, referenced_type
  2     from user_dependencies
  3    where name = 'COUNT_EMP'
  4      and type = 'FUNCTION'
  5   /

REFERENCED_NAME                                                REFERENCED_T
-------------------------------------------------------------- ------------
STANDARD                                                       PACKAGE
SYS_STUB_FOR_PURITY_ANALYSIS                                   PACKAGE
EMP                                                            TABLE
3 rows selected.
```

Now, let's compare the last iteration of our native dynamic SQL function GET_ROW_CNTS from above to the COUNT_EMP procedure:

```
ops$tkyte@DEV816> select referenced_name, referenced_type
  2     from user_dependencies
  3     where name = 'GET_ROW_CNTS'
  4       and type = 'FUNCTION'
  5   /

REFERENCED_NAME                                                 REFERENCED_T
--------------------------------------------------------------- ------------
STANDARD                                                        PACKAGE
SYS_STUB_FOR_PURITY_ANALYSIS                                    PACKAGE
2 rows selected.
```

The function with a static reference to EMP shows this reference in the dependency table. The other function does not, because it is not dependent on the EMP table. In this case, it is perfectly OK because we derive much added value from the use of dynamic SQL – the ability to generically get the row count of any table. In the above, we were using dynamic SQL just for the sake of it, however – this broken dependency would be a bad thing. It is extremely useful to find out what your procedures reference and what references them. Dynamic SQL will obscure that relationship.

The Code is More Fragile

When using static SQL only, I can be assured that when I compile the program, the SQL I have embedded in there will in fact be syntactically correct – it has to be, we verified that completely at compile-time. When using dynamic SQL, I'll only be able to tell at run-time if the SQL is OK. Further, since we build the SQL on the fly, we need to test every possible code path to check that all of the SQL we generate is OK. This means that a given set of inputs, which cause the procedure to generate SQL in one way, might not work while a different set of inputs will. This is true of *all* code but the use of dynamic SQL introduces another way for your code to 'break'.

Dynamic SQL makes it possible to do many things that you could not do otherwise, but static SQL should be used whenever possible. Static SQL will be faster, cleaner, and less fragile.

It is Harder to Tune

This is not as obvious, but an application that dynamically builds queries is hard to tune. Normally, we can look at the exhaustive set of queries an application will use, identify the ones that will be potential performance issues and tune them to death. If the set of queries the application will use isn't known until *after* the application actually executes, we have no way of knowing how it will perform. Suppose you create a stored procedure that dynamically builds a query based on user inputs on a web screen. Unless you test each and every query that may be generated by your routine you'll never know if you have all of the correct indexes in place and so on to have a well tuned system. With just a low number of columns (say five) there are already dozens of combinations of predicates that you could come up with. This does not mean 'never use dynamic SQL', it means be prepared to be on the lookout for these types of issues – queries you never anticipated being generated by the system.

Summary

In this chapter we thoroughly explored dynamic SQL in stored procedures. We have seen the differences between native dynamic SQL and DBMS_SQL, showing when to use one over the other. Both implementations have their time and place.

Dynamic SQL allows you to write procedures that are otherwise impossible – generic utilities to dump data, to load data, and so on. Further examples of dynamic SQL-based routines can be found on the Apress web site, such as a utility to load dBASE III files into Oracle via PL/SQL, printing the results of a query down the page in SQL*PLUS (see *Invoker and Definer Rights*, Chapter 23), pivoting resultsets (see *Analytic Functions*, Chapter 12 for details on this), and much more.

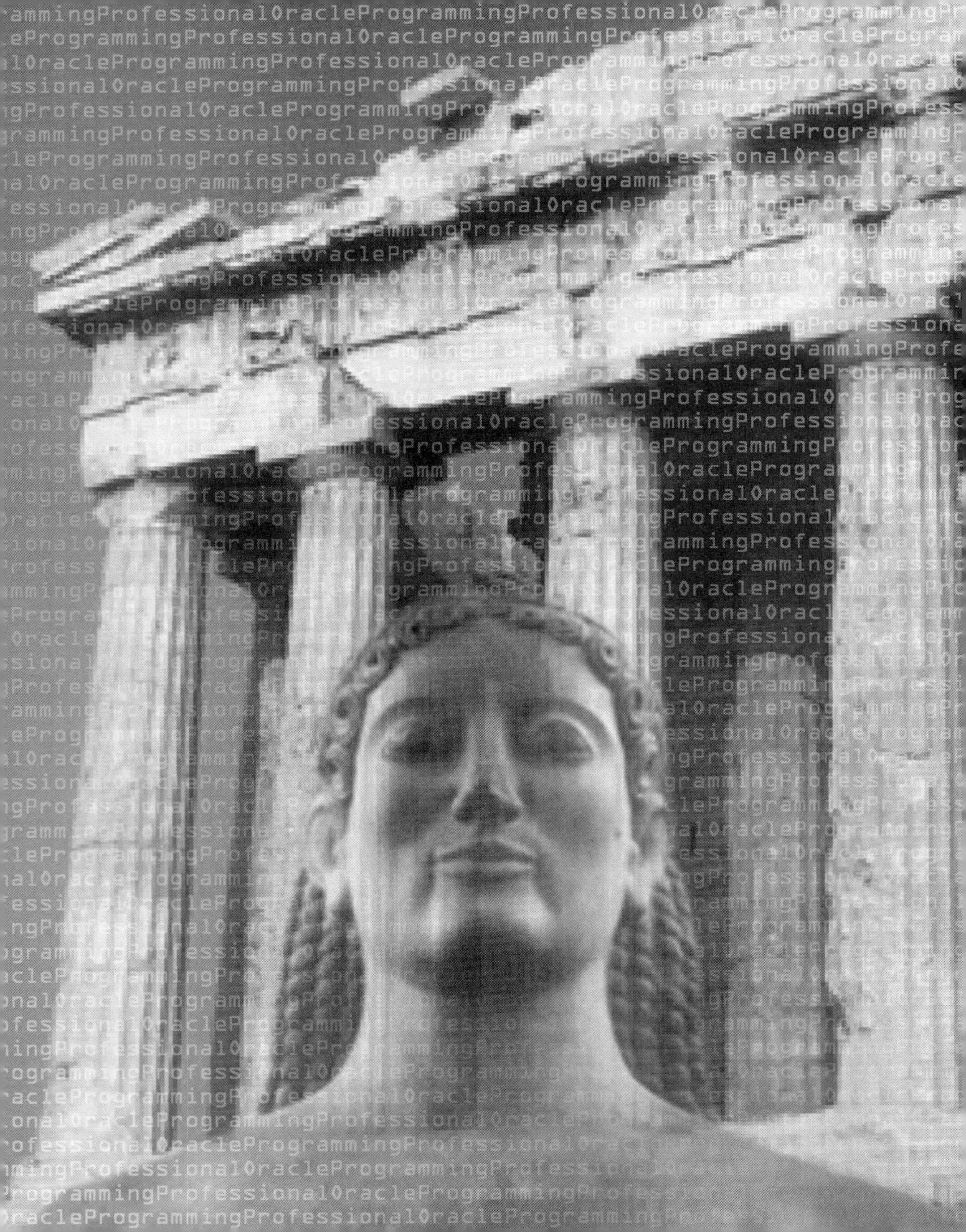

17

interMedia

interMedia is a collection of features, tightly integrated into the Oracle database, that enable you to load rich content into the database, securely manage it, and ultimately, deliver it for use in an application. Rich content is widely used in most web applications today, and includes text, data, images, audio files, and video.

This chapter focuses on one of my favorite components of interMedia: **interMedia Text**. I find that interMedia Text is typically an under-utilized technology. This stems from a lack of understanding of what it is, and what it does. Most people understand what interMedia Text can do from a high level, and how to 'text-enable' a table. Once you delve beneath the surface though, you'll discover that interMedia Text is a brilliantly crafted feature of the Oracle database.

After a quick overview of interMedia's history we will:

- ❑ Discuss the potential uses of interMedia Text such as searching for text, indexing data from many different sources of data and searching XML applications, amongst others.
- ❑ Take a look at how the database actually implements this feature.
- ❑ Cover some of the mechanisms of interMedia Text such as indexing, the ABOUT operator, and section searching.

A Brief History

During my work on a large development project in 1992, I had my first introduction to interMedia Text or, as it was called then, **SQL*TextRetrieval**. At that time, one of my tasks was to integrate a variety of different database systems in a larger, distributed network of databases. One of these database products was proprietary in every way possible. It lacked a SQL interface for database definition and amounts of textual data. Our job was to write a SQL interface to it.

Sometime in the middle of this development project, our Oracle sales consultant delivered information about the next generation of Oracle's SQL*TextRetrieval product, to be called **TextServer3**. One of the advantages of TextServer3 was that it was highly optimized for the client-server environment. Along with TextServer3 came a somewhat obtuse C-based interface, but at least now I had the ability to store all of my textual data within an Oracle database, and also to access other data within the same database via SQL. I was hooked.

In 1996, Oracle released the next generation of TextServer, called **ConText Option**, which was dramatically different from previous versions. No longer did I have to store and manage my textual content via a C or Forms-based API. I could do everything from SQL. ConText Option provided many PL/SQL procedures and packages that enabled me to store text, create indexes, perform queries, perform index maintenance, and so on, and I never had to write a single line of C. Of the many advances ConText Option delivered, two in my opinion are most noteworthy. First and foremost, ConText Option was no longer on the periphery of database integration. It shipped with Oracle7, and was a separately licensed, installable option to the database, and for all practical purposes, was tightly integrated with the Oracle7 database. Secondly, ConText Option went beyond standard text-retrieval, and offered linguistic analysis of text and documents, enabling an application developer to build a system that could 'see' beyond just the words and actually exploit the overall meaning of textual data. And don't forget that all of this was accessible via SQL, which made use of these advanced features dramatically easier.

One of the advanced features of the Oracle8i database is the extensibility framework. Using the services provided, developers were now given the tools to create custom, complex data types, and also craft their own core database services in support of these data types. With the extensibility framework, new index types could be defined, custom statistics collection methods could be employed, and custom cost and selectivity functions could be integrated into an Oracle database. Using this information, the query optimizer could now intelligently and efficiently access these new data types. The ConText Option team recognized the value of these services, and went about creating the current product, interMedia Text, which was first released with Oracle8i in 1999.

Uses of interMedia Text

There are countless ways in which interMedia Text can be exploited in applications, including:

- ❑ **Searching for text** – You need to quickly build an application that can efficiently search textual data.

- ❑ **Managing a variety of documents** – You have to build an application that permits searching across a mix of document formats, including text, Microsoft Word, Lotus 1-2-3, and Microsoft Excel.

- ❑ **Indexing text from many data sources** – You need to build an application that manages textual data not only from an Oracle database, but also from a file system as well as the Internet.

- ❑ **Building applications beyond just text** – Beyond searching for words and phrases, you are tasked to build a knowledge base with brief snapshots or 'gists' about each document, or you need to classify documents based upon the concepts they discuss, rather than just the words they contain.

- ❑ **Searching XML applications** – interMedia Text gives the application developer all the tools needed to build systems which can query not only the content of XML documents, but also perform these queries confined to a specific structure of the XML document.

And, of course, the fact that this functionality is in an Oracle database means that you can exploit the inherent scalability and security of Oracle, and apply this to your textual data.

Searching for Text

There are, of course, a number of ways that you can use to search for text within the Oracle database, without using the interMedia functionality. In the following example, we create a simple table, insert a couple of rows then use the standard INSTR function and LIKE operator to search the text column in the table:

```
SQL> create table mytext
  2  ( id        number primary key,
  3    thetext varchar2(4000)
  4  )
  5  /

Table created.

SQL> insert into mytext
  2  values( 1, 'The headquarters of Oracle Corporation is ' ||
  3              'in Redwood Shores, California.');

1 row created.

SQL> insert into mytext
  2  values( 2, 'Oracle has many training centers around the world.');

1 row created.

SQL> commit;

Commit complete.

SQL> select id
  2      from mytext
  3    where instr( thetext, 'Oracle') > 0;

        ID
----------
         1
         2

SQL> select id
  2      from mytext
  3    where thetext like '%Oracle%';

        ID
----------
         1
         2
```

Using the SQL INSTR function, we can search for the occurrence of a substring within another string. Using the LIKE operator we can also search for patterns within a string. There are many times when the use of the INSTR function or LIKE operator is ideal, and anything more would be overkill, especially when searching across fairly small tables.

However, these methods of locating text will typically result in a full tablescan, and they tend to be very expensive in terms of resources. Furthermore, they are actually fairly limited in functionality. They would not, for example, be of use if you needed to build an application that answered questions such as:

❑ Find all rows that contain 'Oracle' near the word 'Corporation', and no more than 10 words apart.

❑ Find all rows that contain 'Oracle' or 'California', and rank in relevance order.

❑ Find all rows that have the same linguistic root as 'train' (for example, trained, training, trains).

❑ Perform a case-insensitive search across a document library.

Such queries just scratch the surface of what cannot be done via traditional means, but which can easily be accomplished through the use of interMedia Text. In order to demonstrate how easily interMedia can answer questions such as those posed above, we first need to create a simple interMedia Text index on our text column:

In order to use the interMedia Text PL/SQL packages, the user must be granted the role CTXAPP.

```
SQL> create index mytext_idx
  2  on mytext( thetext )
  3  indextype is CTXSYS.CONTEXT
  4  /

Index created.
```

With the creation of the new index type, CTXSYS.CONTEXT, we have 'Text-enabled' our existing table. We can now make use of the variety of operators that interMedia Text supports, for sophisticated handling of textual content. The following examples demonstrate the use of the CONTAINS query operator to answer three of the above four questions (don't worry about the intricacies of the SQL syntax for now, as this will be explained a little later):

```
SQL> select id
  2      from mytext
  3      where contains( thetext, 'near((Oracle,Corporation),10)') > 0;

        ID
----------
         1

SQL> select score(1), id
  2      from mytext
  3      where contains( thetext, 'oracle or california', 1 ) > 0
  4      order by score(1) desc
  5  /

  SCORE(1)        ID
---------- ----------
         4         1
         3         2
```

```
SQL> select id
  2    from mytext
  3    where contains( thetext, '$train') > 0;

       ID
----------
        2
```

Every bit as important as functionality, is the performance aspects of an interMedia Text index, which surpasses traditional relational methods of locating text within a column. Being truly a new index type within the Oracle database, information that is maintained about the data being indexed can be exploited during query plan creation. Thus, the Oracle kernel is given the optimal path to locating textual data within a column indexed by interMedia Text.

Managing a Variety of Documents

Beyond the ability to index plain text columns in a database, interMedia Text is also bundled with document filters for a huge variety of document formats. interMedia Text will automatically filter Microsoft Word 2000 for Windows, Microsoft Word 98 for the Macintosh, Lotus 1-2-3 spreadsheets, Adobe Acrobat PDF, and even Microsoft PowerPoint presentation files. In total, over 150 document and file filters are bundled with interMedia Text.

> *The availability of filters is dependent upon the specific release of Oracle 8i. For example, Oracle 8.1.5 and Oracle 8.1.6 were released before the introduction of Microsoft Word 2000 for Windows. Hence, there is no filter for this document format in interMedia Text 8.1.5 or 8.1.6, but it is present in interMedia Text with Oracle 8.1.7.*

The filtering technology that is bundled with interMedia Text is licensed from Inso Corporation and, as far as accuracy and efficiency of filters go, I feel that these are the best on the market. The list of current file formats supported is documented in an appendix of the *Oracle8i interMedia Text Reference*.

> *At the time of writing, the Inso filters were not available on the Linux platform, and there were no plans to eventually make them available, which is unfortunate. This doesn't mean that interMedia Text cannot be exploited on a Linux platform, but it does mean that if you are deploying Oracle 8i on a Linux system, you'll either need to restrict your document types to plain text or HTML, or you'll have to create what is called a USER_FILTER object.*

Indexing Text from Many Data Sources

interMedia Text is not just about storing files inside a database. An interMedia Text **datastore object** allows you to specify exactly where your text/data is stored. A datastore object basically supplies information to the interMedia Text index, letting it 'know' where your data is located. This information can only be specified at index creation time.

As we saw in an earlier example, the data for an interMedia Text index can come directly from the database, being stored internally in a column. This is the DIRECT_DATASTORE datastore object, and is the default datastore if none is specified. The database column type can be CHAR, VARCHAR, VARCHAR2, BLOB, CLOB, or BFILE. Also, please note that you can create an interMedia Text index on a column of type LONG or LONG RAW, but these are deprecated datatypes since the release of Oracle 8 and you absolutely should *not* use them for any new applications.

Another interesting datastore type that is based upon text stored internally in a column is the DETAIL_DATASTORE. The master/detail relationship is very common in any database application. Stated in simple terms, it describes a relationship from a single row in a master or parent table, to zero or more rows in a detail table, with typically a foreign-key constraint from the detail table to the master table. A purchase order is a good example of a master/detail relationship, with typically one row for a purchase order itself, and zero or more rows in the detail table making up the line items of the purchase order. A DETAIL_DATASTORE lets the application developer maintain this logical relationship.

Let's look at an example. Basically, we need to create a masterdetail structure that permits us to perform an interMedia Text query on a master table, but with the actual source of the data for the interMedia Text being derived from a detail table. To demonstrate, we first need to create our masterdetail tables and load them with data:

```
SQL> create table purchase_order
  2  ( id                    number primary key,
  3    description           varchar2(100),
  4    line_item_body        char(1)
  5  )
  6  /

Table created.

SQL> create table line_item
  2  ( po_id           number,
  3    po_sequence     number,
  4    line_item_detail varchar2(1000)
  5  )
  6  /

Table created.

SQL> insert into purchase_order ( id, description )
  2  values( 1, 'Many Office Items' )
  3  /

1 row created.

SQL> insert into line_item( po_id, po_sequence, line_item_detail )
  2  values( 1, 1, 'Paperclips to be used for many reports')
  3  /

1 row created.

SQL> insert into line_item( po_id, po_sequence, line_item_detail )
  2  values( 1, 2, 'Some more Oracle letterhead')
  3  /

1 row created.

SQL> insert into line_item( po_id, po_sequence, line_item_detail )
  2  values( 1, 3, 'Optical mouse')
  3  /

1 row created.

SQL> commit;

Commit complete.
```

Note that the column LINE_ITEM_BODY is essentially a 'dummy' column, as it simply exists so that we can create the interMedia Text index on a column in the master table. I never inserted any data into it. Now, prior to index creation, we need to set the interMedia Text preferences so that the index can locate the data to be indexed:

```
SQL> begin
  2    ctx_ddl.create_preference( 'po_pref', 'DETAIL_DATASTORE' );
  3    ctx_ddl.set_attribute( 'po_pref', 'detail_table', 'line_item' );
  4    ctx_ddl.set_attribute( 'po_pref', 'detail_key', 'po_id' );
  5    ctx_ddl.set_attribute( 'po_pref', 'detail_lineno', 'po_sequence' );
  6    ctx_ddl.set_attribute( 'po_pref', 'detail_text', 'line_item_detail' );
  7  end;
  8  /

PL/SQL procedure successfully completed.
```

First we create a user-defined preference PO_PREF. It is a DETAIL_DATASTORE that will store all the information necessary to locate the data from the detail table. In subsequent lines, we define the name of the detail table, the key that joins to the master table, how the rows are ordered, and finally, the column that is actually getting indexed.

Now, we just create our index and see it in action:

```
SQL> create index po_index on purchase_order( line_item_body )
  2    indextype is ctxsys.context
  3    parameters( 'datastore po_pref' )
  4  /

Index created.

SQL> select id
  2      from purchase_order
  3    where contains( line_item_body, 'Oracle' ) > 0
  4  /

        ID
----------
         1
```

Although we created the index on LINE_ITEM_BODY, we could have specified the master table column DESCRIPTION when creating the index. However, bear in mind that any changes to *this* column (this is *not* a dummy column) will initiate a re-index operation on the master row and all associated detail rows.

interMedia Text also supports data sources external to the database – specifically, files external to the database as well as Uniform Resource Locators (URLs). In many work environments, files are commonly stored on a network-accessible shared file system. Rather than imposing the requirement to build an application that stores all text and document data within the Oracle database, the FILE_DATASTORE datastore object allows Oracle to manage the text index itself, and not the storage and security of the files. Using a FILE_DATASTORE, you would not store the text of the document in a column. Rather, you store a file system reference to the file, which must be accessible from the database *server* file system. So, even though you might be using a Windows client, for example, if the Oracle database was running on your favorite flavor of UNIX, your reference to the file would follow UNIX file system syntax, as in /export/home/tkyte/MyWordDoc.doc. Note that this type of external file access is unrelated to an alternative form of external file access from an Oracle database using BFILEs.

Another type of datastore external to the database is a URL_DATASTORE. This is very much like a FILE_DATASTORE datastore object, but instead of storing a file system reference in a column in the Oracle database, you can store a URL. At the time of indexing a row, interMedia Text will actually fetch the data over HTTP from the database server itself. Again, Oracle is not storing or managing the data itself. The index is constructed from the filtered contents from the HTTP stream, and the actual data fetched from the URL is discarded. FTP (file transfer protocol) is also a valid protocol when using a URL_DATASTORE, so interMedia Text can also index files accessible via FTP from the database server. With Oracle 8.1.7 and later, you can also embed the username and password directly in an FTP URL (for example, ftp://uid:pwd@ftp.bogus.com/tmp/test.doc).

Some people actually think that the URL_DATASTORE is good for building your own Web-crawling robot, but not much else (by the way, it does not have this Web-crawling capability out-of-the-box). This is not true. Colleagues of mine have architected a very large, distributed, Internet-accessible system with many different database nodes. A requirement of this system was to provide a single, unified search interface to all of the textual data across the nodes. They could have constructed a system with interMedia Text indexes on the database tables on each node, and then the query could be composed of many smaller, distributed queries against each node. However, rather than follow a route that may have led to non-optimal performance, they architected a solution that dedicated a single server to interMedia Text, and the indexes were created exclusively using the URL_DATASTORE datastore object. In this system, the distributed nodes were responsible for inserting URLs of new or modified content into the search data node. In this fashion, every time a new document was created or an existing one was modified, the machine responsible for indexing the content was given the URL to retrieve that content. So, instead of the indexing machine crawling all of the possible documents looking for new/modified content, the content providers notified the indexing machine of new content.. Not only did the distributed query go away, but also there was now a single point of truth, which resulted in less administration.

It's an Oracle Database, After All

One of the most compelling reasons to use interMedia Text rather than a file system-based solution is the fact that it's an Oracle database. Firstly, an Oracle database is transactional in nature, whereas a file system is not. The integrity of your data will not be compromised, and the ACID properties of a relational database are also observed by interMedia Text.

> *For a definition of the ACID properties of a relational database, please reference Chapter 4 on Transactions.*

Secondly, in Oracle, the database manipulation language is SQL, and interMedia Text is wholly accessible from SQL. This enables an application developer to choose from a huge variety of tools that can 'talk' SQL. Then, if you were so inclined (not my recommendation), you could build an interMedia Text application that was accessible from Microsoft Excel, communicating over an ODBC driver to the Oracle database.

Having fulfilled many DBA roles in my career, I appreciate the fact that once all of my data is contained inside the Oracle database, when I backup my database I am backing up my application and all of its data. In the event of a recovery situation, I can restore the application and its data to any point in time. In a file system-based approach, I would always need to ensure that my database *and* file system were backed up, and hopefully, they were relatively consistent when the backup was performed.

One important caveat to this point, though, is that if you are using interMedia Text to index information contained outside of an Oracle database, your backup strategy is slightly altered. If you are using the URL_DATASTORE or FILE_DATASTORE datastores for your content, interMedia Text is only maintaining references to the content, and not managing the content as well. Thus, content can typically become stale, be deleted, or become unavailable as time passes and this can have an impact on your application. Additionally, no longer do you have a complete backup of your entire application when you backup the Oracle database. You will also need to develop a separate backup strategy for any content managed externally from the Oracle database.

Generating Themes

Go to your favorite web search engine, type in a frequently occurring word on the Internet like 'database', and wait for the plethora of search results to return. Text indexing is very powerful and can be used in many applications. This is particularly true when the domain of information is very large, since it becomes difficult for an end user to sift through all of the data. interMedia Text has integrated features that let you transform all of this data into useful information.

Integrated into interMedia Text is an extensible knowledge base, used during indexing and analysis of the text, which confers considerable linguistic capabilities on this feature. Not only can we search the text, we can *analyze the meaning* of text. So, at index creation time, we can optionally generate themes for the interMedia Text index itself. This allows us to create applications that can, for example, analyze documents and classify them by theme, rather than by specific words or phrases.

When theme generation was first available in an Oracle database, I ran a quick test to see what it could do. I fed into a table in an Oracle database over one thousand news-clippings from various computer journals. I created an interMedia Text index on the column that was used to store the actual text of the articles, and then generated the themes for each article. I searched for all documents that had a theme of 'database', and the results included a news article that did not contain a single occurrence of the actual word 'database' and yet interMedia Text generated database as a theme. At first I thought that this was an error with interMedia Text itself but after a little careful thought, I realized that this was actually a very powerful feature – the ability to locate text in a database, based upon the *meaning* of the text. It is not statistical analysis, or some form of word-counting, it truly is linguistic analysis of the text.

A small example illustrates these capabilities:

```
SQL> create table mydocs
  2  ( id       number primary key,
  3    thetext varchar2(4000)
  4  )
  5  /

Table created.

SQL> create table mythemes
  2  ( query_id number,
  3    theme    varchar2(2000),
  4    weight   number
  5  )
  6  /

Table created.

SQL> insert into mydocs( id, thetext )
```

```
  2  values( 1,
  3  'Go to your favorite Web search engine, type in a frequently
  4  occurring word on the Internet like ''database'', and wait
  5  for the plethora of search results to return.'
  6  )
  7  /

1 row created.

SQL> commit;

Commit complete.

SQL> create index my_idx on mydocs(thetext) indextype is ctxsys.context;

Index created.

SQL> begin
  2      ctx_doc.themes( index_name => 'my_idx',
  3                      textkey    => '1',
  4                      restab     => 'mythemes'
  5      );
  6  end;
  7  /

PL/SQL procedure successfully completed.

SQL> select theme, weight from mythemes order by weight desc;

THEME                                      WEIGHT
------------------------------------------ ----------
occurrences                                    12
search engines                                 12
Internet                                       11
result                                         11
returns                                        11
databases                                      11
searches                                       10
favoritism                                      6
type                                            5
plethora                                        4
frequency                                       3
words                                           3

12 rows selected.
```

Our PL/SQL procedure takes the table pointed to by the index MY_IDX, finds the row with key = 1 and retrieves the data that is indexed. It then runs that data through a thematic analyzer. This analyzer generates, and assigns a weight to, all of the 'themes' of the document (for example, a paper on banking might extract themes like 'money', 'credit', and so on). It puts these themes into the results table MYTHEMES.

Now if I did this for all of the data within my application, my end users would now have the ability to search, not only for those rows which contained a certain word, but also be able to search for those rows which were most similar in meaning to the text in a particular row.

Note that with more information for interMedia Text to analyze, the themes can be calculated with much greater accuracy than the simple sentence shown in the example above.

Also note that I created an `ID` column with a primary key constraint. In interMedia Text in Oracle 8i 8.1.6 and earlier, the existence of a primary key was required before you could create an interMedia Text index on the same table. In Oracle 8i 8.1.7 and later, interMedia Text no longer requires the existence of a primary key.

Searching XML Applications

People frequently ask me how they can efficiently search within a document that has embedded markup, like HTML or XML. Fortunately, interMedia Text makes this trivial through the use of an object called **sections**.

This solution really comes together when you combine the features of XML parsing and section definition with a `URL_DATASTORE`. If XML lives up to its billing as *the* communication medium through which heterogeneous systems communicate, then an application developer armed with interMedia Text can quickly create a searchable, online knowledgebase of data from a variety of systems. A full example of indexing XML is presented later in this chapter.

How interMedia Text Works

This section will describe how interMedia Text is implemented and what you can expect from your use of it.

As mentioned earlier, interMedia Text was built using the Oracle-provided extensibility framework. Using this facility, the interMedia Text team was able to introduce into Oracle the equivalent of a text-specific type of index. If we take a look at some of the underlying database objects, we can pull back the covers, and begin to learn how this is truly implemented. The database objects that make up interMedia Text are always owned by user `CTXSYS`:

```
SQL> connect ctxsys/ctxsys
Connected.

SQL> select indextype_name, implementation_name
  2    from user_indextypes;

INDEXTYPE_NAME                  IMPLEMENTATION_NAME
------------------------------  ------------------------------
CONTEXT                         TEXTINDEXMETHODS
CTXCAT                          CATINDEXMETHODS
```

Here, we see that there are actually two index types owned within the interMedia Text schema. The first index type is `CONTEXT`, one which most interMedia Text users are familiar with. The second index type, `CTXCAT`, is a catalog index type, and provides a subset of the functionality available with a `CONTEXT` index type. The catalog index type, which was introduced with Oracle 8.1.7, is ideal for textual data that can be classified as short text fragments.

```
SQL> select library_name, file_spec, dynamic from user_libraries;

LIBRARY_NAME                     FILE_SPEC                                D
-------------------------------- ---------------------------------------- -
DR$LIB                                                                    N
DR$LIBX                          O:\Oracle\Ora81\Bin\oractxx8.dll         Y
```

Here, we can see that there are two libraries associated with interMedia Text. The library DR$LIB is not dynamic, and hence, is a library of trusted code within the Oracle database itself. The other library, DR$LIBX, is a shared library, and is on the dependant operating system. As the above query was performed against a database running in a Windows environment, the file specification to this shared library is Windows-specific. If you perform the same query in a UNIX environment, you will see something different. These libraries are specific to interMedia Text. They contain a collection of methods, so that the Oracle kernel can handle these interMedia Text index types.

```
SQL> select operator_name, number_of_binds from user_operators;

OPERATOR_NAME                    NUMBER_OF_BINDS
-------------------------------- ---------------
CATSEARCH                                      2
CONTAINS                                       8
SCORE                                          5
```

Within the extensibility framework, you can also define a rather unique database object called an **operator**. An operator is referenced by an index type, and has a number of bindings associated with each operator. Very much like in PL/SQL, where you can define a function with the same name but different parameter types, the extensibility framework lets you define an operator that maps to different user-defined methods, based upon the signature of its use.

```
SQL> select distinct method_name, type_name from user_method_params order by
  2   type_name;

METHOD_NAME                      TYPE_NAME
-------------------------------- ------------------------------
ODCIGETINTERFACES                CATINDEXMETHODS
ODCIINDEXALTER                   CATINDEXMETHODS
ODCIINDEXCREATE                  CATINDEXMETHODS
ODCIINDEXDELETE                  CATINDEXMETHODS
ODCIINDEXDROP                    CATINDEXMETHODS
ODCIINDEXGETMETADATA             CATINDEXMETHODS
ODCIINDEXINSERT                  CATINDEXMETHODS
ODCIINDEXTRUNCATE                CATINDEXMETHODS
ODCIINDEXUPDATE                  CATINDEXMETHODS
ODCIINDEXUTILCLEANUP             CATINDEXMETHODS
ODCIINDEXUTILGETTABLENAMES       CATINDEXMETHODS
RANK                             CTX_FEEDBACK_ITEM_TYPE
ODCIGETINTERFACES                TEXTINDEXMETHODS
ODCIINDEXALTER                   TEXTINDEXMETHODS
ODCIINDEXCREATE                  TEXTINDEXMETHODS
ODCIINDEXDROP                    TEXTINDEXMETHODS
ODCIINDEXGETMETADATA             TEXTINDEXMETHODS
ODCIINDEXTRUNCATE                TEXTINDEXMETHODS
ODCIINDEXUTILCLEANUP             TEXTINDEXMETHODS
ODCIINDEXUTILGETTABLENAMES       TEXTINDEXMETHODS
ODCIGETINTERFACES                TEXTOPTSTATS

21 rows selected.
```

After viewing these results, it should start to become clear how a developer could exploit the extensibility framework within the Oracle database. Associated with each type are sets of named methods, which the Oracle extensibility framework defines by a unique name. For example, the methods associated with the maintenance of an index, `ODCIIndexInsert`, `ODCIIndexUpdate`, and `ODCIIndexDelete` are invoked by Oracle when data that is associated with an index is created, modified, or deleted. Thus, when maintenance needs to be performed on an interMedia Text index for a new row, the Oracle engine invokes the method associated with `ODCIIndexInsert`. This custom routine then performs whatever operations are necessary against the interMedia Text index, and then signals to the Oracle database that it is complete.

Now that we've seen the underlying architecture of the implementation of interMedia Text, let's take a look at some of the database objects associated with this custom index type when you actually create an interMedia Text index.

```
SQL> select table_name
  2    from user_tables
  3    where table_name like '%MYTEXT%';

TABLE_NAME
------------------------------
MYTEXT

SQL> create index mytext_idx
  2  on mytext( thetext )
  3  indextype is ctxsys.context
  4  /

Index created.

SQL> select table_name
  2    from user_tables
  3    where table_name like '%MYTEXT%';

TABLE_NAME
------------------------------
DR$MYTEXT_IDX$I
DR$MYTEXT_IDX$K
DR$MYTEXT_IDX$N
DR$MYTEXT_IDX$R
MYTEXT
```

We started in our SQL*PLUS session, by querying from the USER_TABLES views for all tables that contained the name MYTEXT. After creating our table MYTEXT, and an interMedia Text index on this same table, we see that we now have a total of five tables that contain this name, including our original table.

There are a total of four tables that are automatically created whenever you create an interMedia Text index. These table names will always have a prefix of DR$, then the index name, and then a suffix of either $I, $K, $N, or $R. These tables will always be created in the same Oracle schema that owns the interMedia Text index. Let's examine them in greater detail.

```
SQL> desc dr$mytext_idx$i;
 Name                                    Null?    Type
 -------------------------------------   -------- --------------------
 TOKEN_TEXT                              NOT NULL VARCHAR2(64)
 TOKEN_TYPE                              NOT NULL NUMBER(3)
 TOKEN_FIRST                             NOT NULL NUMBER(10)
 TOKEN_LAST                              NOT NULL NUMBER(10)
 TOKEN_COUNT                             NOT NULL NUMBER(10)
 TOKEN_INFO                                       BLOB

SQL> desc dr$mytext_idx$k;
 Name                                    Null?    Type
 -------------------------------------   -------- --------------------
  DOCID                                           NUMBER(38)
  TEXTKEY                                NOT NULL ROWID

SQL> desc dr$mytext_idx$n;
 Name                                    Null?    Type
 -------------------------------------   -------- --------------------
 NLT_DOCID                              NOT NULL NUMBER(38)
 NLT_MARK                               NOT NULL CHAR(1)

SQL> desc dr$mytext_idx$r;
 Name                                    Null?    Type
 -------------------------------------   -------- --------------------
 ROW_NO                                          NUMBER(3)
 DATA                                            BLOB
```

Every interMedia Text index will have a set of tables created with a similar structure as the ones above. The token table DR$MYTEXT_IDX$I is the primary table of any interMedia Text index. This table is used to maintain an entry for every token indexed, as well as a bitmap of all documents that contain this token. Other binary information is stored in this table to maintain the proximity information of the tokens within the columns themselves. Note that I'm careful to use the word 'token' in this context, as interMedia Text has the ability to index several multi-byte languages, including Chinese, Japanese, and Korean. It would be inaccurate to say the DR$I table is used to index 'words'.

The DR$K and DR$R tables are merely mapping tables between a ROWID and a document identifier.

The last table, the DR$N table, or 'negative row table', is used to maintain a list of documents/rows which have been deleted. In effect, when you delete a row from a table that has an interMedia Text index defined on it, the physical removal of this row's information from the interMedia Text index is deferred. Using this internal table, the row is referenced by a document identifier, and marked for cleanup during the next rebuild or optimization.

Also, note that the DR$K and DR$N tables are created as index-organized tables. If at any time either of these tables is referenced from interMedia Text code, it will typically reference both columns contained in the table. For efficiency, and to avoid any extra I/O, these were implemented as index-organized tables.

Let me summarize this section by saying that although it's interesting to look at how interMedia Text is implemented within the Oracle extensibility framework, it is by no means essential information to effectively using interMedia Text. On the contrary, many developers have built quite sophisticated applications using interMedia Text, but were not completely aware of the purpose of these underlying tables.

interMedia Text Indexing

Using the sample table we created in the previous section, let's step through the actual process of inserting text, and controlling when interMedia Text actually processes our changes:

```
SQL> delete from mytext;

2 rows deleted.

SQL> insert into mytext( id, thetext )
  2  values( 1, 'interMedia Text is quite simple to use');

1 row created.

SQL> insert into mytext( id, thetext )
  2  values( 2, 'interMedia Text is powerful, yet easy to learn');

1 row created.

SQL> commit;

Commit complete.
```

So at this point, do you think we should be able to query for the token text, which would return both rows from our table? The answer is really, 'maybe'. If the index is not synchronized, then the underlying interMedia Text index will not have been updated with our changes yet. To synchronize an index means to bring it up to date with the pending changes. So, how do we tell if there are pending updates to the interMedia Text index?

```
SQL> select pnd_index_name, pnd_rowid from ctx_user_pending;

PND_INDEX_NAME                   PND_ROWID
------------------------------   ------------------
MYTEXT_IDX                       AAAGF1AABAAAIV0AAA
MYTEXT_IDX                       AAAGF1AABAAAIV0AAB
```

By querying the CTX_USER_PENDING view, we're able to determine that there are two rows associated with the MYTEXT_IDX interMedia Text index that are pending update. This view, CTX_USER_PENDING, is a view on the CTXSYS-owned table DR$PENDING. Any time a new row is inserted into our table MYTEXT, a row will also be inserted into the table DR$PENDING for the MYTEXT_IDX interMedia Text index. Both of these inserts occur within the same physical transaction, so that if the transaction, which inserted into the MYTEXT table was rolled back, the insert into DR$PENDING would also be rolled back.

There are three different ways in which an interMedia Text index can be synchronized. These can be performed in a number of different scenarios, and for a number of different reasons. Later, I will talk about why you would choose one method over the other.

The simplest method to synchronize an index is to run the program ctxsrv. This program runs in a fashion similar to a UNIX daemon. You start this program, let it run in the background, and it will automatically take care of periodically synchronizing the index. This method is advisable when you are dealing with a small set (under 10,000 rows), and each row does not comprise a great deal of text.

Another method to synchronize the index is to issue the ALTER INDEX statement. It is usually not an issue to allow the queue of pending requests to build up and process the synchronization actions to the index in batch. In many cases, this is the preferred method of synchronizing an index, as it will minimize overall index fragmentation. The syntax used to 'sync' an index is:

```
alter index [schema.]index rebuild [online]
            parameters( 'sync [memory memsize]' )
```

You would want to rebuild an index online to make it available during the 'sync' process. Additionally, you can specify the amount of memory to be used during the synchronization process. The more memory specified for the 'sync' process, then the larger the indexing batch size can be, which will ultimately result in a more compact interMedia Text index.

Although some may argue that this truly isn't a repeatable way to synchronize an index, I assert that a third way to synchronize an index is to simply create the index itself. When you issue the CREATE INDEX statement for an index of type CONTEXT, it will result in the creation of the index, as well as the indexing of any column data upon which the index was created. This usually throws people for a loop when they have existing data in their table. They create their index, and then they add subsequent rows to the table. As the changes incurred by the new rows aren't realized until the index is synchronized, many people have come to me complaining that the only way to bring their index up to date is to drop and then recreate! It truly is a way to keep your index in synchronization, albeit a wholly inefficient one which I would strongly discourage.

The semantics of SQL inherently prevent two distinct users from issuing an ALTER INDEX REBUILD on the same index concurrently, but there are no restrictions from rebuilding or synchronizing multiple interMedia Text indexes at the same time.

Continuing with our example, we will synchronize our index:

```
SQL> alter index mytext_idx rebuild online parameters('sync memory 20M');

Index altered.

SQL> select pnd_index_name, pnd_rowid from ctx_user_pending;

no rows selected
```

At this point, our index is synchronized, and we should be ready to perform a query using it:

```
SQL> select id
  2    from mytext
  3   where contains( thetext, 'easy') > 0
  4  /

        ID
----------
         2
```

Let's explore a little further, and look at the data in one of the internal tables that was created when we created the interMedia Text index:

```
SQL> select token_text, token_type from dr$mytext_idx$i;

TOKEN_TEXT                                                      TOKEN_TYPE
-------------------------------------------------------------- ----------
EASY                                                                    0
INTERMEDIA                                                              0
LEARN                                                                   0
POWERFUL                                                                0
QUITE                                                                   0
SIMPLE                                                                  0
TEXT                                                                    0
USE                                                                     0
YET                                                                     0
interMedia Text                                                        1
learning                                                               1

TOKEN_TEXT                                                      TOKEN_TYPE
-------------------------------------------------------------- ----------
powerfulness                                                           1
simplicity                                                            1
```

By querying the DR$I table associated with the index MYTEXT_IDX, we are able to examine some of the information that interMedia Text processed during index synchronization.

Firstly, notice that many of the values for TOKEN_TEXT are in all uppercase. These are the actual words from our text itself, and are stored in a case-normalized fashion. If we so desired, we could have directed interMedia Text to create an index in mixed case when we issued the CREATE INDEX statement.

The next thing you should notice is that there are a number of tokens where TOKEN_TYPE=1, which are stored in mixed case. More importantly though, you should note that the data 'simplicity' and 'learning' are not contained in either of the rows in the MYTEXT table. So where did this data come from? The default setting for the **lexer** (a lexer is used to determine how to break apart a block of text into individual tokens) in the English language is to generate theme index information as well. Thus, every row where TOKEN_TEXT=1, is a generated theme from interMedia Text's linguistic analysis.

Lastly, something you may not notice right away is the *absence* of certain words in this table. The words is and to are not part of the table of tokens, although they were part of the data in our table. These are considered **stopwords**, and are considered poor information to index, as they are frequently occurring in much English text, and can be classified essentially as noise. The words is, to, and about 120 others are part of the default **stoplist** for the English language, which was used, by default, when we created the index. Oracle delivers interMedia Text with default stoplists for over 40 different languages. Keep in mind that there is no requirement for you to use a stoplist, and you can also create your own customized stoplist.

To conclude this section, I want to issue a word of caution. While it is quite interesting to look at how interMedia Text is implemented, especially by looking at the tokens generated when we create an index, you should *never* create other database objects on these internally implemented structures. As an example, you should not create a view on top of the DR$MYTEXT_IDX$I table. Nor should you create a trigger on the DR$MYTEXT_IDX$K table. The structure of this implementation is subject to change and most likely will change in subsequent releases of the product.

About ABOUT

With the introduction of the ABOUT operator, Oracle has greatly simplified the use of themes in queries, and has also dramatically improved the precision of queries overall. In the English language implementation, the ABOUT operator will search for all the rows that match the normalized representation of the concept provided. I mentioned earlier that the default setting was True for generation of theme index information in the English language. This theme index information will be used to locate other rows that match in concept. If for some reason you decided not to generate theme index information, the ABOUT operator would revert to a simple token-based search.

```
SQL> select id from mytext where contains(thetext,'about(databases)') > 0;

no rows selected
```

As expected, there are no rows in our example table that are about the concept 'databases'.

```
SQL> select id from mytext where contains(thetext,'about(simply)') > 0;

        ID
----------
         1
```

There is one row that is about the concept simply. To be accurate, there is one row that is similar in concept to the normalized version of the word simply. To prove this:

```
SQL> select id from mytext where contains(thetext,'simply') > 0;

no rows selected
```

When we remove the ABOUT operator from our query, no rows are returned, our thetext column has no occurrences of the word simply. There is one row that matches in concept to the normalized root of simply though.

The concept associated with a word is not the same as the linguistic root of a word. Use of the stem operator ($) in interMedia Text, enables the user to search for inflectional or derivational stems of a word. Thus, a stem search on the word 'health' may include in the result, documents that contain the word 'healthy'. An ABOUT search of health may also return documents that contain the word wellness though.

The ABOUT operator is very easy to include in your applications, and permits application developers to exploit the power of theme generation, and linguistic analysis with little effort. The ABOUT operator moves an application from enabling the end user to search using words, to now searching across concepts. Quite powerful, indeed.

Section Searching

The last topic I'll cover in-depth is **section searching**. Sections enable granular query access to a document, and can greatly improve the precision of these queries. A section can really be nothing more than an application developer-defined sequence of characters to delimit the start and end of a logical unit of a document. The popularity of several standard markup languages, such as HTML and XML, will show the power of section searching within interMedia Text.

A typical document has commonly occurring logical elements that comprise its structure. Most documents have some form of name, may have a heading, may have boilerplate information, most likely have a body, and can contain a table of contents, glossary, appendix, and so on. All of these things are logical units that make up the structure of a document.

As an example of where this could be useful, consider a fictitious Department of Defense. It may be adequate just to find all documents in our library that contains the phrase 'Hellfire missile'. It may be even more meaningful to find all documents in our library that contain the phrase 'Hellfire missile' in the title of the document, or perhaps in the glossary of the document. interMedia Text provides a way to let an application developer define the sequence of characters that portray these logical sections of the structure of a document. Additionally, interMedia Text supports searching *within* these same logical sections.

interMedia Text uses the term '**sections**' to specify these logical units, or grouping of text within a document. A collection of section identifiers is aggregated into a **section group**, and it is this section group that can be referenced when creating an interMedia Text index.

Hypertext Markup Language, or HTML, originally started as a way to denote structure within a document, but it quickly transformed into a language that was part structural representation, and part visual rendering. Regardless, interMedia Text ships with the default components to let an application developer create a section of logical structural unit out of every markup tag contained within a document.

In the same fashion, XML support is native in interMedia Text starting with Oracle 8.1.6. Given an arbitrary XML document, you can easily (and automatically, if you wish) define sections for every XML element within that document.

Let's first take a look at the following HTML example:

```
SQL> create table my_html_docs
  2  ( id number primary key,
  3    html_text varchar2(4000))
  4  /

Table created.

SQL> insert into my_html_docs( id, html_text )
  2  values( 1,
  3  '<html>
  4  <title>Oracle Technology</title>
  5  <body>This is about the wonderful marvels of 8i and 9i</body>
  6  </html>' )
  7  /

1 row created.

SQL> commit;

Commit complete.

SQL> create index my_html_idx on my_html_docs( html_text )
  2  indextype is ctxsys.context
  3  /

Index created.
```

At this point, we should be able to locate a row, based upon any indexed word in the HTML document.

```
SQL> select id from my_html_docs
  2    where contains( html_text, 'Oracle' ) > 0
  3  /

        ID
----------
         1

SQL> select id from my_html_docs
  2    where contains( html_text, 'html' ) > 0
  3  /

        ID
----------
         1
```

We can easily construct a query to locate all rows that contain the word Oracle, but we immediately have a couple of things we'd like to change about our current solution. Firstly, the actual markup elements themselves should not be indexed, as these will be commonly occurring, and are not part of the actual content of the document. Secondly, we're able to search for words within our HTML document, but not with respect to the structural element that contains them. We know that we have a row that contains Oracle somewhere in the content, but it could be in the heading, the body, the footer, the title, and so on.

Let's assume that our application requirement is to be able to search within the titles of our HTML documents. To easily accomplish this, we will create a section group containing a field section for TITLE, and then drop and recreate the index:

```
SQL> begin
  2    ctx_ddl.create_section_group('my_section_group','BASIC_SECTION_GROUP');
  3    ctx_ddl.add_field_section(
  4       group_name   => 'my_section_group',
  5       section_name => 'Title',
  6       tag          => 'title',
  7       visible      => FALSE );
  8  end;
  9  /

PL/SQL procedure successfully completed.

SQL> drop index my_html_idx;

Index dropped.

SQL> create index my_html_idx on my_html_docs( html_text )
  2    indextype is ctxsys.context
  3    parameters( 'section group my_section_group' )
  4  /

Index created.
```

We have created a new section group called MY_SECTION_GROUP, and added a field section with a name of Title. Note that our section name maps to the tag title, and that this section will not be visible. If a field section is marked as visible, the text contained within the tags will be treated as part of the containing document. If a field section is marked as not visible, then the contents between the field section start and end tags are treated as separate from the containing document, and will only be searchable when querying within the field section.

Like most modern markup languages (for example, XML, HTML, WML), in interMedia Text a start tag begins with <, and ends with >. Additionally, an end tag begins with the sequence </, and ends with >.

```
SQL> select id
  2    from my_html_docs
  3    where contains( html_text, 'Oracle' ) > 0
  4  /

no rows selected
```

A query that previously returned our single row now returns zero rows, and all we have done is define a section group for the interMedia Text index. Remember that I defined the field section as not visible, so the text contained within the title tags is treated as a sub-document.

```
SQL> select id
  2    from my_html_docs
  3    where contains( html_text, 'Oracle within title' ) > 0
  4  /

        ID
----------
         1
```

We are now able to execute a query that restricts our text search to only the title field sections across all of our documents. And if we try and search for the text of the tag itself we see that interMedia Text does not index the text of the tags themselves:

```
SQL> select id
  2    from my_html_docs
  3    where contains( html_text, 'title' ) > 0
  4  /

no rows selected
```

Although earlier I defined my own section group type based upon the section group BASIC_SECTION_GROUP, interMedia ships with pre-defined section group system preferences for HTML and XML, called HTML_SECTION_GROUP and XML_SECTION_GROUP respectively. The use of this section group does not automatically define sections for every possible HTML and XML element. You would still need to define these yourself, but by the use of these section groups, interMedia Text will now know how to correctly transform your marked up document to text. If we now apply this to our example:

```
SQL> drop index my_html_idx;

Index dropped.

SQL> create index my_html_idx on my_html_docs( html_text )
  2   indextype is ctxsys.context
  3   parameters( 'section group ctxsys.html_section_group' )
  4  /

Index created.

SQL> select id
  2     from my_html_docs
  3    where contains( html_text, 'html') > 0
  4  /

no rows selected
```

By simply specifying the preference of the HTML_SECTION_GROUP section group, we now avoid indexing all of the elements that are HTML markup tags within our document. This will not only improve the accuracy of all queries against our documents, but will also reduce the overall size of the interMedia Text index. For example, lets say for whatever reason, I wanted to search for the word title across all of my HTML documents. If I did not use the HTML_SECTION_GROUP for my interMedia Text index, I might end up with every HTML document that had a title section (that is, a section in the HTML document delimited by the <title> and </title> tags) in my result. By ignoring the tags and focusing solely on the content of my HTML documents, my search accuracy is greatly improved.

Now, switching our focus to processing of XML documents, let's say you had a requirement to manage a collection of XML documents, and also provide an interface with which to query within the structural elements of an XML document. To further compound the issue, your collection of XML documents may not all conform to the same structural definition contained in a DTD (Document Type Definition).

Following the previous examples, you may think that your only option is to determine all the searchable elements over all of your XML documents, and then go about defining interMedia Text sections for every one of these elements. Fortunately, interMedia Text includes a facility to automatically create and index sections out of every tag contained within a document.

Introduced with interMedia Text in Oracle 8.1.6, the AUTO_SECTION_GROUP operates just like the XML_SECTION_GROUP section group, but removes the burden from the application developer to define, in advance, all of the sections. The AUTO_SECTION_GROUP section group will instruct interMedia Text to automatically create sections for any non-empty tags within a document. Whereas, an application developer can map an arbitrary section name to a tag, these generated sections will be defined with the same name as the tag itself.

```
SQL> create table my_xml_docs
  2   ( id       number primary key,
  3     xmldoc varchar2(4000)
  4   )
  5  /

Table created.

SQL> insert into my_xml_docs( id, xmldoc )
```

```
  2  values( 1,
  3  '<appointment type="personal">
  4      <title>Team Meeting</title>
  5      <start_date>31-MAR-2001</start_date>
  6      <start_time>1100</start_time>
  7      <notes>Review projects for Q1</notes>
  8      <attendees>
  9          <attendee>Joel</attendee>
 10          <attendee>Tom</attendee>
 11      </attendees>
 12  </appointment>' )
 13  /

1 row created.

SQL> commit;

Commit complete.

SQL> create index my_xml_idx on my_xml_docs( xmldoc )
  2  indextype is ctxsys.context
  3  parameters('section group ctxsys.auto_section_group')
  4  /

Index created.
```

At this point, without any further intervention, interMedia Text has automatically created sections for every tag contained within our XML documents. So if we wanted to locate all documents that contained the word projects in a note element, we would issue:

```
SQL> select id
  2     from my_xml_docs
  3   where contains( xmldoc, 'projects within notes' ) > 0
  4  /

         ID
----------
          1
```

The auto-sectioning process creates a special kind of section called a **zone section**. Whereas our previous examples showing section definition demonstrated the use of field sections, zone sections are a different type of section. Unlike field sections, zone sections can overlap one another, and can also be nested. As the AUTO_SECTION_GROUP section group instructs interMedia Text to create zone sections out of all non-empty tags, we can now issue queries like:

```
SQL> select id
  2     from my_xml_docs
  3   where contains( xmldoc, 'projects within appointment' ) > 0
  4  /

         ID
----------
          1
```

```
SQL> select id
  2    from my_xml_docs
  3    where contains( xmldoc, 'Joel within attendees' ) > 0
  4  /

        ID
----------
         1
```

The section specified in these two previous queries do not directly contain the search terms, but the search terms are nested within the structure of these sections. Zone sections, and the use of auto-sectioning, enable users to control the scope of a search across an XML document. It can be as broad or narrow as you see fit.

With the use of section groups, you can instruct interMedia Text to index attributes of tags themselves. Again with the AUTO_SECTION_GROUP section group, attribute values of sections are also automatically created and indexed.

So, if we wished to locate all appointments that are personal, that is, all XML documents that contain the string personal as an attribute called type within the tag appointment, we would issue:

```
SQL> select id
  2      from my_xml_docs
  3    where contains( xmldoc, 'personal within appointment@type' ) > 0
  4  /

        ID
----------
         1
```

As you can see, the definition and indexing of sections is a very powerful feature of interMedia Text. One point you want to remember, though, is that you do *not* always want to use the AUTO_SECTION_GROUP. Although there is a facility to instruct interMedia Text and the auto-sectioner not to index certain tags, you may end up indexing and creating sections for many document elements, which may pollute the index itself. This will increase the overall size of the index and possibly degrade performance. It is a powerful feature, but it should be used with prudence.

Caveats

There are a number of issues you should be aware of when using interMedia Text. Not all of these are readily apparent, but I will address the most common ones that I have come across in my experience.

It is NOT Document Management

Rather than a caveat, this is more of a common 'mischaracterization' of interMedia Text. Upon the mention of interMedia Text, I have heard customers, and Oracle employees alike, refer to this as Oracle's document management solution. Without question, interMedia Text is *not* document management.

Document management is a science in its own right. A document management solution is a system with a feature set that assists in the life cycle of documents. This can include basic check-in and check-out functionality, multiple versions and subversions of documents, access control lists, a logical collection structure, text query interface, and also a mechanism to publish documents.

interMedia Text itself is not document management. interMedia Text can be exploited in a document management system, and provides many of the building blocks that you would find in complete systems. As a matter of fact, Oracle has tightly integrated the features of interMedia Text with the Oracle Internet File System, which can be used for content management, and provides much of the basic document management functionality.

Index Synchronization

There are many times when you would want to build a system and run the process `ctxsrv` in the background to periodically synchronize your interMedia Text index, and keep it in synchronization in almost real-time. One of the issues that can arise from performing many frequent index synchronizations for a large document set, is that the interMedia Text index can end up in a non-compact, fragmented state.

There is no hard and fast rule that states that you should periodically synchronize your indexes in batches, versus synchronizing them with `ctxsrv` as soon as they are committed. Much of this is dependent upon the nature of your application, how frequently text is updated, if at all, how many documents are in the total set, and how large your documents are.

A good example is my **AskTom** web site. This is a site used by Oracle customers to ask technical questions about Oracle products. The questions are reviewed, followed up with a (hopefully) descriptive response and, optionally, published. Once these questions and answers are published, they are inserted into a table that is indexed with an interMedia Text index. This table of published questions and answers is searchable via a page on the **AskTom** web site.

This system has a relatively small number of total rows (less than 10,000 at the time of this writing). There are hardly ever any updates to the system; once the questions and answers are published, they are almost never updated, or deleted. The number of total rows inserted on any given day is usually 25 or less, and these occur throughout the day. We perform index synchronization via the `ctxsrv` process running in the background, which is ideal for this system as it is primarily search-only, with very few inserts and updates.

On the other hand, if you were preparing to periodically load one million documents into a table over the next week, it would be ill-advised to index these using `ctxsrv`. You typically want the batch size to be as large as possible without causing memory paging when interMedia Text synchronizes an index. Letting these requests build up in the queue, and then processing in a large batch will result in a more compact index.

Regardless of whichever method is chosen, you should periodically optimize your interMedia Text indexes using the `ALTER INDEX REBUILD` syntax. The optimization process will not only result in a more compact state of your index, but the information maintained from previous logical deletions will be cleaned up as well.

Indexing Information Outside the Database

interMedia Text does not constrain the location of your textual data to the database. You could choose to store your textual data directly in a database, but you can also use interMedia Text to index information contained in documents on the server file system, or even documents accessible via a URL.

When your data is maintained in an Oracle database, any updates to this data are automatically processed by interMedia Text. When the source of your data is outside of the database though, the onus is now on the application developer to ensure that data updated outside of the database is synchronized with the index.

The easiest way to trigger an update on an individual row is to update one of the columns indexed by an interMedia Text index. As an example, if I used the following table and index to maintain my list of indexed URLs:

```
SQL> create table my_urls
  2  ( id number primary key,
  3    theurl varchar2(4000)
  4  )
/

Table created.

SQL> create index my_url_idx on my_urls( theurl )
  2  indextype is ctxsys.context
  3  parameters( 'datastore ctxsys.url_datastore' )
  4  /

Index created.
```

I could easily trigger a 'refresh' of a particular row by issuing:

```
SQL> update my_urls
  2     set theurl = theurl
  3   where id = 1
  4  /

0 rows updated.
```

Document Services

By **document services**, I mean the set of services provided by interMedia Text to filter 'on-demand' a document into text or HTML, and also, optionally, to highlight the hits in a document as the result of a search.

Another common misconception that some people have is that interMedia Text maintains all information needed to reconstruct an entire document. This misconception leads people to believe that once a document is indexed, the actual source of the document can be discarded. This is true if all you will ever do are queries against the indexed information, but it is not true if you want to employ some of these document services.

For example, if you create an interMedia Text index using a URL_DATASTORE, and you wish to generate an HTML rendition of a row via the CTX_DOC.FILTER procedure; if the URL is not accessible, the call to CTX_DOC.FILTER will fail. interMedia Text needs to access the original document to perform this operation. This also applies to files that reside outside of the database on the file system, indexed using the FILE_DATASTORE preference.

The Catalog Index

There are many situations where an interMedia Text index provides much more functionality than is required by the application. The use of an interMedia Text index also entails certain maintenance functions to keep the index synchronized, optimized, and so on. In order to support applications where the full functionality of an interMedia Text index is not required, a new index type called the **catalog** index, or ctxcat for short was introduced with the release of interMedia Text in Oracle 8.1.7.

Typically, the majority of textual data is *not* stored in a database system as a large collection of documents. In many database applications, text is typically not formatted, occurs in small fragments, is not broken up into logical sections, and the sections are so small as to inhibit high quality linguistic analysis. Also, these types of database-centric applications often perform queries against the textual data combined with other relational constraints. For example, consider a database used to log reported problems, along with a description of how to resolve them. It may have, say, an 80 character free-form subject field (what the problem is about) and a large text field with the problem resolution and description. It might also store other pieces of structured information, such as the date the problem was reported, the analyst working on it, the product on which the problem occurred, and so on. Here we have a combination of text (not a document persay) and structured data. It will be frequently queried to find the answers to questions such as, 'find all problems regarding the database (a product) version 8.1.6 (another attribute) that contains a reference to "ORA-01555" in the subject (a text search)'. It is for these types of applications that the catalog index was created.

As you might expect from a 'cut-down' version of the full index, there are a number of limitations to ctxcat. The types of query operators supported by a catalog index are a subset of the operators supported in a 'full' interMedia Text index. The text that you wish to index with ctxcat must be contained in the Oracle database and must be plain text. Furthermore, ctxcat does not support multiple languages within the same index. However, given these limitations, the catalog index performs exceedingly well in many applications.

One nice feature of the catalog index is the lack of index maintenance. DML performed against a catalog index is entirely transactional. Hence, there is no requirement to periodically synchronize a catalog index, or run the ctxsrv process for periodic synchronization.

Another compelling reason to use a catalog index is its inherent support for structured queries. The application developer can define index sets, which are used by the catalog index to process efficiently both text search, and a query across other structural data. An index set allows interMedia to store some of the structured relational information in its index, along with the text it is indexing. This will allow interMedia using both a text search and structured search at the same time, in order to find documents that meet very specific criteria Let's take a look at a short example:

```
SQL> create table mynews
  2  ( id number primary key,
  3    date_created date,
  4    news_text varchar2(4000) )
  5  /
```

```
Table created.

SQL> insert into mynews
  2  values( 1, '01-JAN-1990', 'Oracle is doing well' )
  3  /

1 row created.

SQL> insert into mynews
  2  values( 2, '01-JAN-2001', 'I am looking forward to 9i' )
  3  /

1 row created.

SQL> commit;

Commit complete.

SQL> begin
  2      ctx_ddl.create_index_set( 'news_index_set' );
  3      ctx_ddl.add_index( 'news_index_set', 'date_created' );
  4  end;
  5  /

SQL> create index news_idx on mynews( news_text )
  2  indextype is ctxsys.ctxcat
  3  parameters( 'index set news_index_set' )
  4  /

Index created.
```

Note that the index type I specified to create a catalog index is CTXSYS.CTXCAT. Additionally, I created an index set NEWS_INDEX_SET, and added the column DATE_CREATED to this index set. This will enable interMedia Text to efficiently process any queries that include constraints on both the columns NEWS_TEXT and DATE_CREATED.

```
SQL> select id
  2    from mynews
  3   where catsearch( news_text, 'Oracle', null ) > 0
  4     and date_created < sysdate
  5  /

        ID
----------
         1

SQL> select id
  2    from mynews
  3   where catsearch( news_text, 'Oracle', 'date_created < sysdate' ) > 0
  4  /

        ID
----------
         1
```

Here, we can see both methods of locating all rows that contain Oracle in the text of the news, and where the DATE_CREATED is earlier than today. The first query would first use interMedia to find all of the rows that might satisfy our query and would then access those rows to see if the DATE_CREATED was less than SYSDATE. The second, more efficient query, would use the interMedia index, which has incorporated the DATE_CREATED column, to find only those rows that satisfy the text query *and* the DATE_CREATED < SYSDATE constraint simultaneously. Rather than using the CONTAINS operator, a search using the catalog index uses the CATSEARCH operator. As we had previously defined an index set which contains the DATE_CREATED column, I was also able to specify the structured condition of our query directly in the CATSEARCH operator. Using this information, Oracle can very efficiently process both constraints in the query.

There are a number of restrictions on the type of conditions that can be specified in the structure constraints of the CATSEARCH operator, specifically that it only supports AND, OR, and NOT logical operators, but for a large number of applications, the catalog index is suitable, and often preferred.

Errors You May Encounter

In my dealings with application developers and customers who use interMedia Text, I tend to see the same few issues cropping up time and again. They are the ones I cover in this section.

Index Out of Date

A number of people have come to me inquiring why some of their information is indexed, but not any new rows they recently added. The most common cause of this is that the interMedia Text index is simply out of sync. If you query the view CTX_USER_PENDING, you can quickly assess if there are pending indexing requests. If so, simply synchronize the index using one of the methods described earlier.

Another common cause for this apparent lack of indexed information is errors, especially during the filtering process. If you are attempting to index documents with the Inso filters, and the document format is not supported, this will result in errors, and the specific document will not be indexed. If you query the view CTX_USER_INDEX_ERRORS, this should provide suitable information in tracking down the indexing issue.

External Procedure Errors

In the version of interMedia Text supplied with Oracle 8.1.5 and 8.1.6, all filtering of text was handled via the Inso filters through external procedures. External procedures are functions that are typically written in C, stored in a shared library on the database server, and invoked from PL/SQL. These external procedures run in an address space that is separate from the Oracle server itself.

If you have documents to be filtered by interMedia Text, but external procedures are not properly configured on the database server, this will typically result in one or more of the following errors:

```
ORA-29855: error occurred in the execution of ODCIINDEXCREATE routine

ORA-20000: interMedia text error:
DRG-50704: Net8 listener is not running or cannot start external procedures

ORA-28575: unable to open RPC connection to external procedure agent
```

You should refer to the *Net8 Administrator's Guide* for complete configuration information about external procedures, but here is a very quick and dirty check to see if external procedures are working. From the database server (not on your local client), you want to execute from a telnet session (or command window if your database server is installed on Microsoft Windows) the command `tnsping extproc_connection_data`. If you don't see a result of OK, as in:

```
oracle8i@cmh:/> tnsping extproc_connection_data

TNS Ping Utility for Solaris: Version 8.1.7.0.0 - Production on 30-MAR-2001
13:46:59

(c) Copyright 1997 Oracle Corporation.  All rights reserved.

Attempting to contact (ADDRESS=(PROTOCOL=IPC)(KEY=EXTPROC))
OK (100 msec)
```

then your configuration of external procedures is incorrect.

External procedures are not required for interMedia Text filtering as of Oracle 8.1.7. The filtering process has been folded into the database server itself.

The Road Ahead

With the Oracle 9i release, interMedia Text is undergoing another name change, and will be referred to as Oracle Text. All of the functionality that is present in the Oracle 8i release of interMedia Text will also be present in Oracle Text, but the Oracle 9i release also introduces many powerful new features.

One of the most desired features in interMedia Text was automatic classification of documents, based upon their content. interMedia Text gave the application developer all of the tools necessary to construct a system to generate the themes and summaries of documents, which could then be used to develop a pseudo-document classification system. With Oracle Text, document classification is now a native feature. This feature facilitates the construction of a system that permits the end user to ask, 'which queries match this document?'

Oracle Text also improves upon the native support of XML documents. An XML document is composed of content, as well as structural metadata. The elements of an XML document have implicit relationships, and the structural metadata can be used to convey these relationships. XPath, a W3C recommendation (http://www.w3.org/TR/xpath) provides a way to obtain certain elements of an XML document, based upon the content and relative structure of the document elements. Oracle Text introduces a new XPATH operator, which enables SQL queries based upon the structural elements of a document.

These are just a few of the new features coming to interMedia Text/Oracle Text with the Oracle 9i release.

Summary

In this chapter, we examined the rich feature set of interMedia Text, and how it can be easily exploited in a variety of applications. Although this chapter covered many facets of interMedia Text, there are still many more things I haven't covered. You can use a thesaurus, define a custom lexer, generate HTML renditions of all of your documents regardless of format, store your query expressions for later use, and even define your own custom stopword lists.

interMedia Text itself is a very broad topic, and one which can't be covered in a single chapter. Besides being very feature-rich, interMedia Text is quite easy to use and understand. After reading this chapter, you should now have a clear understanding of how interMedia Text is implemented, and also how you can exploit the power of interMedia Text in many of your applications.

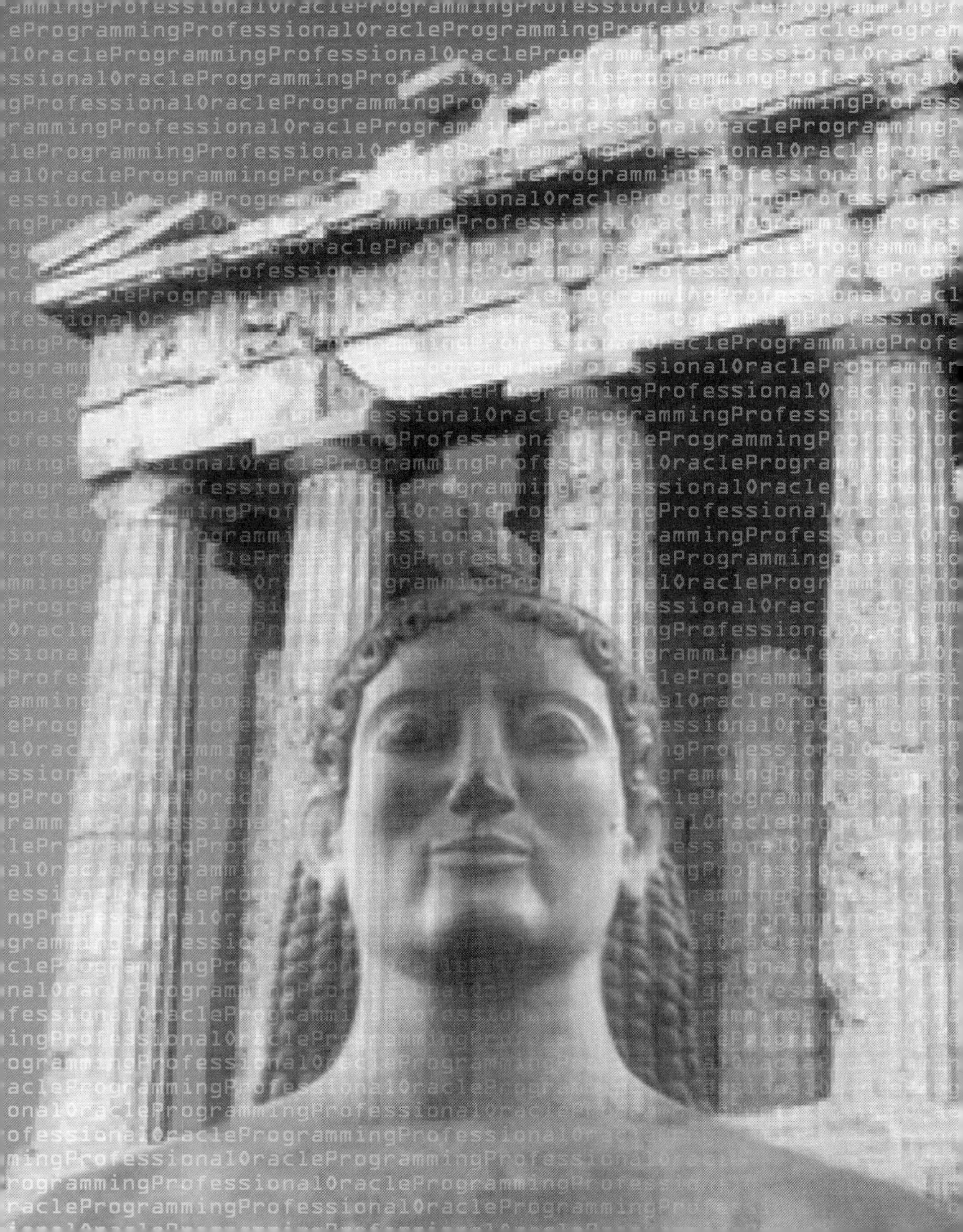
ProfessionalOracleProgramming

18

C-Based External Procedures

In the beginning, PL/SQL, and only PL/SQL, was used as a language with which to program the Oracle server, and Oracle client applications, *within the server itself.* Starting with version 8.0 of Oracle, the ability to implement stored procedures in other languages was introduced. This feature is called **external procedures** and covers both C (or anything that is C callable) and Java-based stored procedures. In this chapter, we will focus exclusively on C; the next chapter covers Java.

This chapter will cover external procedures from an architectural perspective, showing you how they have been implemented by the Oracle kernel developers. Additionally, we will see how you must configure your server to support them, and how you *should* configure your server for safety reasons. We will demonstrate how to write an external procedure using Oracle's Pro*C. This external procedure will be used to write the contents of any LOB to the server's file system. Before we get to that example though, we will work through a 'primer' example that demonstrates how to send and receive all interesting datatypes to and from PL/SQL and C. This primer will also develop a generic template useful for developing all subsequent C based external procedures quickly. We will cover how the C code should be implemented, with a mind towards being able to support this server-side code. We will also look at the implementation of the SQL binding we create for this external procedure. We will learn how we make it callable from SQL and PL/SQL, and how we should code the binding layer for ease of use on part of the people who will actually use our developed code. Lastly, we will cover the pros and cons of external procedures, and cover any miscellaneous server errors (ORA-XXXX errors) you might encounter.

The Pro*C example that will be developed in this chapter supplies a missing piece of server functionality. Oracle supplies the package DBMS_LOB to manipulate large objects (LOB). Within this package is a procedure, loadfromfile, which reads an arbitrary file from the OS file system, into the database and stores it there. However, they do not supply a function, writetofile, to take the contents of a LOB and write it to the OS – a common requirement. We will rectify this issue, and create for ourselves a LOB_IO package. This package allows us to write any BLOB, CLOB, or BFILE object to a separate file outside of the database (so for BFILEs we have effectively given ourselves a copy command since the source BFILE is already located outside of the database).

When Are They Used?

A single language or environment is not capable of providing every single feature and function you could ever want. Every language has shortcomings, things it cannot do, which you really want to do – there are features missing, things overlooked. When I'm writing in C, sometimes Assembler comes in handy. When I'm writing in Java, sometimes PL/SQL comes in handy. The point being that you don't always drop down to a 'lower level' language – sometimes you take a step up to a higher level. External procedures would be considered a 'step down' to a lower level language. You will typically use them to integrate existing C callable code you already have (a DLL – Dynamic Link Library on Windows; supplied by some third party you would like to call from the database), or to extend the functionality of some existing packages, as we are. This is the same technology Oracle itself uses to extend the server's capabilities – for example we saw how interMedia makes use of this feature in the previous chapter, and in Chapter 13 on *Materialized Views* we saw how DBMS_OLAP makes use of this capability.

The first external procedure I wrote was a 'simple TCP/IP' client. With it, in version 8.0.3 of the database, I gave PL/SQL the ability to open a TCP/IP socket to an existing server and send and receive messages. The server I could connect to could have been a Net News Transport Protocol (NNTP) server, an Internet Message Access Protocol (IMAP) server, a Simple Mail Transfer Protocol (SMTP) server, a Post Office Protocol (POP) server, a web server, or so on. By 'teaching' PL/SQL how to use a socket, I opened a whole new spectrum of opportunities. I could now:

❑ Send e-mail from a trigger using SMTP

❑ Incorporate e-mail into the database using POP

❑ Index a newsgroup through interMedia text using NNTP

❑ Access virtually *any* network based service available to me

Instead of thinking of the server as a *server*, I started thinking of it as a client – a client of all of these other servers. Once I got their data into my database, I could do a lot of things with it (index it, search it, serve it up in a different way, and so on).

Over time, this became such a frequently used tool that it is now an integrated feature of the database. Starting with release 8.1.6 of the Oracle server, all of the services that had been provided in the simple TCP/IP client are now implemented in the UTL_TCP package.

Since that time, I have written a couple of other external procedures. Some to get the system clock down to a finer resolution than the built-in SYSDATE function would return, others to execute operating system commands, or get the system's timezone, or to list the contents of a directory. The most recent one that I have developed, and the one that we will explore here, is a function to take the contents of any LOB, be it a Character LOB (CLOB), Binary LOB (BLOB), or BFILE, and write it to a named file. Another nice side effect of this package will be functionality similar to UTL_FILE, but for binary files (which UTL_FILE cannot generate). Since the server supports the concept of a Temporary LOB, and has functions to WRITE to a Temporary LOB, this new package we are going to implement will give us the ability to write an arbitrary binary file from PL/SQL. So in short, what we will get from this package is:

❑ The capability to export any LOB to an external file on the server.

❑ The capability to write any binary file of up to virtually any size with any data (this is similar to UTL_FILE which works with text data, but fails with arbitrary binary data).

As you can see by some of the examples above, the reasons for using an external procedure can be many and varied. Typically, you are using it to:

❑ Supply missing functionality.

❑ Integrate existing code, perhaps from a legacy system that performs data validation.

❑ Speed up your processing. Compiled C will be able to perform some computationally expensive operation faster than interpreted PL/SQL or Java.

As always, the choice to use something like external procedures comes with certain cost. There is the cost of developing the code in C, which is more complex , in my opinion, than developing in PL/SQL. There is the cost of portability – or the potential inability to be portable. If you develop a DLL on Windows, there is no guarantee that source code you wrote would function on a UNIX machine, or vice versa. I'm of the opinion that you should only use an external procedure when the language (PL/SQL) gives you no other opportunity.

How Are They Implemented?

External procedures run in a process physically separate from the database. This is for reasons of safety. While it would be technically possible for the existing database server processes to dynamically load your DLL (on Windows) or .so (Shared Object code on Solaris) at run-time, it would expose the server to unnecessary risk. Your code would have access to the same memory space as the server processes do, and this might include areas of memory such as the Oracle SGA. This could allow developed code to accidentally corrupt, or otherwise damage, kernel data structures, possibly leading to loss of data, or a crashed database instance. In order to avoid this, external processes are executed as a separate process that does not share those memory areas with the server.

In most cases, the separate process would be configured to execute as a user *other than the Oracle software account.* The reason for this is much the same as why they are run in a separate process – safety. For example, we are going to create an external procedure that is capable of writing files to disk (as the example we will develop below does). Let's say you are on UNIX, and the external procedure is executing as the Oracle software owner. Someone calls your new function and asks to write a BLOB to /d01/oracle/data/system.dbf. Since the Oracle software owner is the user ID executing this code, we will be able to do this, thus inadvertently overwriting our system tablespace with the contents of some BLOB. We might not even notice that this happened until we shutdown and restarted our database (many days later). If we had run the external procedure as some less privileged user, this could not happen (that user would not have WRITE on the system.dbf file). So, for this reason, when we get to the section on configuring the server for external procedures, we'll find out how to set up a 'safe' EXTPROC (EXTernal PROCedure) listener that runs under a different OS account. This is very similar to why web servers typically execute as the user nobody on UNIX, or in some low-privileged account in Windows.

So, when you invoke an external procedure, Oracle will create an OS process called EXTPROC for you. It does this by contacting the Net8 listener. The Net8 listener will create the EXTPROC process for us in much the same way as it spawns dedicated servers or shared servers. This can be seen in Windows NT by using the NT Resource Toolkit utility tlist to print a tree of processes and subprocesses. For example, I started a session that accessed an external procedure, and then issued tlist –t, and I see the following:

```
C:\bin>tlist -t
System Process (0)
System (8)
  smss.exe (140)
    csrss.exe (164)
    winlogon.exe (160)
      services.exe (212)
        svchost.exe (384)
        SPOOLSV.EXE (412)
        svchost.exe (444)
        regsvc.exe (512)
        stisvc.exe (600)
        ORACLE.EXE (1024)
          ORADIM.EXE (1264)
        TNSLSNR.EXE (1188)
          EXTPROC.EXE (972)
      lsass.exe (224)
  ...
```

This shows that the TNSLSNR.EXE process is the parent process of the EXTPROC.EXE. The EXTPROC process and your server process can now communicate. More importantly, the EXTPROC process is able to dynamically load your developed DLL (or .so/.sl/.a file on UNIX).

So, architecturally it looks like this:

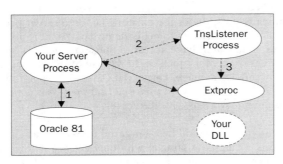

Where:

1. You have your initial connection to the database. You are running in either your dedicated server, or some shared server process.

2. You make a call to an external procedure. Since this is your first call, your process will get in touch with the TNSLISTENER (Net8 listener) process.

3. The Net8 listener will start (or find in a pool of already started) an external procedure process for you. This external procedure will load the requisite DLL (or .so/.sl/.a file on UNIX).

4. You can now 'talk' to the external procedure process, which will marshal your data between SQL and C.

Configuring Your Server

We will now cover the requisite setup we must do to enable an external procedure to execute. This will involve setting up the LISTENER.ORA and TNSNAMES.ORA files on the server, not on the client machine. Upon install, these files should have automatically been configured for you with the external procedure (EXTPROC) services. If so, your LISTENER.ORA configuration file will resemble:

```
# LISTENER.ORA Network Configuration File: C:\oracle\network\admin\LISTENER.ORA
# Generated by Oracle configuration tools.

LISTENER =
  (DESCRIPTION_LIST =
    (DESCRIPTION =
      (ADDRESS_LIST =
        (ADDRESS = (PROTOCOL = TCP)(HOST = tkyte-del)(PORT = 1521))
      )
      (ADDRESS_LIST =
        (ADDRESS = (PROTOCOL = IPC)(KEY = EXTPROC1))
      )
    )
  )

SID_LIST_LISTENER =
  (SID_LIST =
    (SID_DESC =
      (SID_NAME = PLSExtProc)
      (ORACLE_HOME = C:\oracle)
      (PROGRAM = extproc)
    )
    (SID_DESC =
      (GLOBAL_DBNAME = tkyte816)
      (ORACLE_HOME = C:\oracle)
      (SID_NAME = tkyte816)
    )
  )
```

These are the important things in the listener file for external procedures:

❑ (ADDRESS = (PROTOCOL = IPC)(KEY = EXTPROC1)) – Set up an IPC-based address. Remember the value of the KEY. You can make it whatever you want; just remember what it is. On various operating systems, the KEY is case sensitive as well keep that in mind.

❑ (SID_DESC = (SID_NAME = PLSExtProc,) – Remember the SID_NAME, call it PLSExtProc or something similar. By default, this SID will be configured to be PLSExtProc.

You may configure your LISTENER.ORA file manually using a plain text editor, or using the Net8 Assistant. It is strongly recommended that you use the Net8 assistant as the slightest configuration file error – such as a mis-matched parenthesis – will render these configuration files useless. If using the Net8 Assistant, follow the steps outlined in the online help under NetAssistantHelp, Local, Listeners, How To.., and finally Configure External Procedures for the Listener.

After modifying the LISTENER.ORA file remember to stop and start your listener using the commands Lsnrctl stop and Lsnrctl start on the command line.

The next file is the TNSNAMES.ORA file. This file needs to be in the directory that the server will use to resolve names. Typically, a TNSNAMES.ORA file is found on a client as it is used to find the server. This is one case where the server needs it to find a service itself. The TNSNAMES.ORA file will have an entry similar to:

```
# TNSNAMES.ORA Network Configuration File:C:\oracle\network\admin\TNSNAMES.ORA
# Generated by Oracle configuration tools.

EXTPROC_CONNECTION_DATA =
  (DESCRIPTION =
    (ADDRESS_LIST =
      (ADDRESS = (PROTOCOL = IPC)(KEY = EXTPROC1))
    )
    (CONNECT_DATA =
      (SID = PLSExtProc)
      (PRESENTATION = RO)
    )
  )
```

These are the important things in this configuration:

❑ EXTPROC_CONNECTION_DATA – This is the service name the database will be looking for. You must use this name. See the caveat below with regards to the names.default_domain setting in your SQLNET.ORA configuration file.

❑ (ADDRESS = (PROTOCOL = IPC)(KEY = EXTPROC1)) – This should be the same as in the LISTENER.ORA file. In particular, the KEY = component must match.

❑ (CONNECT_DATA =(SID = PLSExtProc), – The SID = must match the SID in the (SID_DESC = (SID_NAME = PLSExtProc) from the LISTENER.ORA.

The following is a caveat on the EXTPROC_CONNECTION_DATA name. If your SQLNET.ORA specifies some default domain, it needs to be on the TNSNAMES entry. So if you have a SQLNET.ORA with a setting such as:

```
names.default_domain = world
```

you would need to specify EXTPROC_CONNECTION_DATA.world, not just EXTPROC_CONNECTION_DATA in the TNSNAMES.ORA file.

Any errors in the above configuration files will almost certainly lead to the error ORA-28575 shown below:

```
declare
*
ERROR at line 1:
ORA-28575: unable to open RPC connection to external procedure agent
ORA-06512: at "USERNAME.PROCEDURE_NAME", line 0
ORA-06512: at line 5
```

Upon receiving this error, the steps that might be useful to resolve this error are as follows:

- ❏ Verify the extproc program is available and executable.
- ❏ Verify the database environment is properly set up for extprocs.
- ❏ Verify the listener is correctly configured.

We'll take an in depth look at each of these steps now. They assume you have actually hit this error for some reason.

Verify the extproc Program

The first sanity check after you've configured extprocs and received the ORA-28575 is to verify the existence and execution of the extproc program itself. This is easily done from the command line in either Windows or UNIX. You should do this when logged in with the credentials of the user that will be *starting the listener* (since that is the process that will execute the extproc), to verify that execute permissions for this user are in place. You will simply do the following:

```
C:\oracle\BIN>.\extproc.exe


Oracle Corporation --- SATURDAY  AUG 05 2000 14:57:19.851

Heterogeneous Agent based on the following module(s):
   - External Procedure Module


C:\oracle\BIN>
```

You are looking for output similar to the above. Note that I have run this from the [ORACLE_HOME]\bin directory as this is where we would find the extproc.exe program. If you cannot run this program, that would be an indication of a corrupted installation or some operating system configuration that must be corrected.

Verify the Database Environment

There are a couple of things to check in the database environment. First and foremost is to verify that the *correct* TNSNAMES.ORA is being used, and that it is configured correctly. For example, on my UNIX machine, using truss I can see that:

```
$ setenv TNS_ADMIN /tmp

$ truss sqlplus /@ora8i.us.oracle.com |& grep TNSNAMES

access("/export/home/tkyte/.TNSNAMES.ORA", 0)      Err#2 ENOENT
access("/tmp/TNSNAMES.ORA", 0)                     Err#2 ENOENT
access("/var/opt/oracle/TNSNAMES.ORA", 0)          Err#2 ENOENT
access("/export/home/oracle8i/network/admin/TNSNAMES.ORA", 0) = 0
...
```

So, Oracle looked in:

- ❏ My home directory for a TNSNAMES.ORA file.
- ❏ The directory specified by the environment variable TNS_ADMIN.
- ❏ The /var/opt/oracle directory.
- ❏ And lastly $ORACLE_HOME/network/admin/.

for a TNSNAMES.ORA file. A common mistake is to configure the TNSNAMES.ORA file in the [ORACLE_HOME]/network/admin directory, but have a TNS_ADMIN environment variable that causes Oracle to find a different TNSNAMES.ORA elsewhere. So, make sure you have configured the correct TNSNAMES.ORA (if there is any confusion, you can simply set the TNS_ADMIN environment variable *before starting* the server; this will ensure the copy *you* want Oracle to use is in fact being used).

Once you have verified that the correct TNSNAMES.ORA is being used, we can look for configuration errors in that file. You would follow the steps outlined above to make sure the (ADDRESS = (PROTOCOL = IPC)(KEY = EXTPROC1)) and (CONNECT_DATA =(SID = PLSExtProc)) components are correctly set up. You do this by comparing them to the LISTENER.ORA configuration. If you use the Net8 Assistant to set this up, you will not have to concern yourself with matching parentheses. If you do it manually, be very careful. One mismatched, or out of place, parenthesis will make it impossible to use an entry.

Once you have verified these settings appear correct, we will look at the TNSNAMES.ORA entry name used. It must be EXTPROC_CONNECTION_DATA. It cannot be anything else, although it may have a domain appended to it. Verify the spelling of this entry. Check your SQLNET.ORA configuration file at this time. Oracle looks for the SQLNET.ORA file in the same way it looks for the TNSNAMES.ORA file. Beware that it does not have to be in the same directory as the TNSNAMES.ORA file – it may be in one of the other locations. If it either of:

- ❏ names.directory_path
- ❏ names.default_domain

are set, we must verify that we are in compliance with them.

If we have the names.default_domain set for example to (WORLD), we must ensure this domain appears in the TNSNAMES.ORA entry. Instead of EXTPROC_CONNECTION_DATA, it must be EXTPROC_CONNECTION_DATA.WORLD.

If we have the names.directory_path set we must verify that it contains TNSNAMES in it. If the names.directory_path is set to (HOSTNAME,ONAMES) for example, then Net8 will use the Host Naming Method to resolve the EXTPROC_CONNECTION_DATA connect string, and then the Oracle Names Server after that fails. Since neither of these methods will find EXTPROC_CONNECTION_DATA, our connection will fail, and the extproc call will fail. Simply add TNSNAMES to this list to allow Oracle to see the EXTPROC_CONNECTION_DATA entry in the local TNSNAMES.ORA file.

Verify the Listener

The issues for the listener are similar to the issues for the database environment. There are two things to consider when verifying the listener configuration:

❑ Are you using the correct LISTENER.ORA configuration file?

❑ Is this file set up correctly?

Again, just as we did with the database server environment, we must ensure we are using the correct environment for the listener, allowing it to discover the LISTENER.ORA we want it to. We have the same considerations, in that the listener will look in various places for the configuration files. If there is any doubt as to which set of configuration files is being used, the TNS_ADMIN environment variable should be set *prior* to starting the listener. This will ensure that the configuration files we want it to use are in fact being used. Once you have verified that the correct configuration files are being used, you would use the information above with regards to the LISTENER.ORA file to ensure it is properly configured.

Once this is done, we should be able to, from the database server environment, use tnsping to tnsping extproc_connection_data (with any default domain appended). For example, my default domain is us.oracle.com and I am able to:

```
C:\oracle\network\ADMIN>tnsping extproc_connection_data.us.oracle.com

TNS Ping Utility for 32-bit Windows: Version 8.1.6.0.0 - Production on 06-AUG-2000
09:34:32

(c) Copyright 1997 Oracle Corporation.  All rights reserved.

Attempting to contact (ADDRESS=(PROTOCOL=IPC)(KEY=EXTPROC1))
OK (40 msec)
```

This indicates and verifies that the database server and listener environment is correctly configured. We should have no problems with the ORA-28575: unable to open RPC connection to external procedure agent at this point.

The First Test

It is recommended to test the installation of external procedures with the demonstration programs. The reason for this is two-fold:

❑ Oracle support is aware of, and can help set up/configure the demonstration program. If we work with an example they know about, we'll be able to resolve any issues much faster.

❑ The supplied demonstration program will illustrate the correct approach for compiling and linking on your platform.

The demonstration program is found in your [ORACLE_HOME]/plsql/demo directory on all releases of Oracle 8i. The steps we should follow to make the demonstration are exposed in the following sections.

Compile extproc.c Code

First, we compile the extproc.c code into a DLL or .so/.sl/.a file. The process for doing this on Windows is to simply cd to the ORACLE_HOME\plsql\demo directory and type make (Oracle has supplied a make.bat file in that directory):

```
C:\oracle\plsql\demo>make
Microsoft (R) 32-bit C/C++ Optimizing Compiler Version 10.00.5270 for 80x86
Copyright (C) Microsoft Corp 1984-1995. All rights reserved.

extproc.c
Microsoft (R) 32-Bit Incremental Linker Version 3.00.5270
Copyright (C) Microsoft Corp 1992-1995. All rights reserved.

/out:extproc.dll
/dll
/implib:extproc.lib
/debug
..\..\oci\lib\msvc\oci.lib
msvcrt.lib
/nod:libcmt
/DLL
/EXPORT:UpdateSalary
/EXPORT:PercentComm
/EXPORT:PercentComm_ByRef
/EXPORT:EmpExp
/EXPORT:CheckEmpName
/EXPORT:LobDemo
extproc.obj
C:\oracle\plsql\demo>
```

In UNIX, you will do much the same thing, but the command to compile is different. There, it will look like:

```
$ make -f demo_plsql.mk extproc.so
/usr/ccs/bin/make -f /export/home/ora816/rdbms/demo/demo_rdbms.mk extproc_callback
SHARED_LIBNAME=extproc.so OBJS="extproc.o"
...
```

After the command completes, you will have a .dll file on Windows or a .so/.sl/.a file on UNIX; the extension depends on platform. For example, Solaris is .so, HP/UX will be .sl.

Set Up the SCOTT/TIGER Account

For this demonstration program to work correct, we will need a SCOTT/TIGER demo account. If your database does not have a SCOTT/TIGER account, you can set one up by issuing:

```
SQL> grant connect, resource to scott identified by tiger;
```

This will create the SCOTT user, and give it the ability to connect to the database and create objects like tables and packages. You will most like want to assign this to use a default tablespace other than SYSTEM, and a temporary tablespace as well.

```
SQL> alter user scott default tablespace tools temporary tablespace temp;
```

Given that we have the SCOTT/TIGER account, we must provide it with one additional grant before proceeding. The SCOTT user will need the CREATE LIBRARY privilege. This privilege will allow SCOTT to issue the create library statement needed for external procedures. We will discuss this later. As this is a fairly powerful privilege, you will want to consider revoking it from SCOTT after running the example. To accomplish this you will need the following line:

```
SQL> grant create library to SCOTT;
```

when connected as someone who has the CREATE LIBRARY privilege with the ADMIN option themselves (for example, SYSTEM or some other DBA account).

Lastly, you will want to ensure the EMP/DEPT demo tables are in the SCOTT schema and populated with data. You can verify this via:

```
SQL> select count(*) from emp;

  COUNT(*)
----------
        14

SQL> select count(*) from dept;

  COUNT(*)
----------
         4
```

If these tables do not exist or do not have any data, you can rebuild them by executing demodrop.sql (to remove them) and demobld.sql (to create and populate them). These scripts are found in [ORACLE_HOME]\sqlplus\demo, and are meant to be executed via SQL*PLUS when logged in as SCOTT.

Create the demolib Library

The next step in the demonstration is to create the library object in Oracle. This object is simply a mapping of a library name (some 30 character name you choose) to a physical operating system file. This OS file is your compiled binary we made in the first step. The user who issues the CREATE LIBRARY statement must have the CREATE LIBRARY privilege granted to them, either via a ROLE or directly. This privilege is considered a fairly powerful one and should be given out only to those accounts you trust with the privilege. It will allow them to execute any arbitrary C code they wish on your server machine using the account the extproc service executes with. This is one of the reasons you would want to configure the extproc service to execute under some account other than the Oracle software owner (to avoid the inadvertent or malicious overwriting of your SYSTEM tablespace for example).

In order to accomplish this step, you use SQL*PLUS and execute:

```
SQL> connect scott/tiger
Connected.
SQL> create or replace library demolib as
```

```
     2  'c:\oracle\plsql\demo\extproc.dll';
     3  /

Library created.
```

The name DEMOLIB is what the developers of the demo chose as the name of their library; you must use DEMOLIB. The file name c:\oracle\plsql\demo\extproc.dll may be different for you – I built the example directly in the demo directory of my ORACLE_HOME. You may have a different ORACLE_HOME than I do, or you might have built the demo in some other directory entirely. You should use the actual path name of the extproc.dll you built in the first step.

Installing and Running

The last step in the demo is to install the PL/SQL code that maps to routines in the demolib library. We are not interested at this point in what they look like as much as we are in what they output. We are using this demo to test external procedures. We'll look at how we code them soon.

Now we will simply execute:

```
SQL> connect scott/tiger
Connected.
SQL> @extproc
```

when in the [ORACLE_HOME]\plsql\demo directory. What we expect to see is:

```
SQL> @extproc

Package created.

No errors.

Package body created.

No errors.
ENAME       : ALLEN
JOB         : SALESMAN
SALARY      : 1600
COMMISSION  : 300
Percent Commission : 18.75
ENAME       : MARTIN
JOB         : SALESMAN
SALARY      : 1250
COMMISSION  : 1400
Percent Commission : 112
Return value from CheckEmpName : 0
old_ename value on return      : ANIL
ENAME       : 7369
HIREDATE    : 17-DEC-80
Employee Experience Test Passed.
*****************************************

PL/SQL procedure successfully completed.
… (other feedback would be here as well)…
```

This shows that external procedures are correctly configured, and ready to be used on the system. The first procedure executes many of the routines in the `extproc.dll` we created. This shows conclusively that all is configured correctly.

In the event of an incorrectly configured system, you would expect to see:

```
SQL> @extproc

Package created.

No errors.

Package body created.

No errors.
BEGIN demopack.demo_procedure; END;

*
ERROR at line 1:
ORA-28575: unable to open RPC connection to external procedure agent
ORA-06512: at "SCOTT.DEMOPACK", line 61
ORA-06512: at "SCOTT.DEMOPACK", line 103
ORA-06512: at line 1
```

This implies that it is time to revisit the section earlier on *Configuring Your Server*, and run through the verification steps.

Our First External Procedure

Given that our development environment is set up as above and ready to go for external procedures, we will now develop our first. This external procedure example will simply pass many different types of variables (strings, numbers, dates, arrays, and so on) and show how the corresponding C code would look to receive them. Our external procedure will manipulate some of these variables, changing the values of OUT or IN/OUT parameters, based on the values of some of the IN or IN/OUT parameters.

I will demonstrate how I prefer to map these variables, as there are many possible mappings and shortcuts. I am showing the method I myself prefer to use which, while more verbose than absolutely necessary, provides me with the maximum information at run-time. Additionally, I will introduce a template upon which I built all of my external procedures. This template implements many of the constructs you need to use in any real application such as:

❑ **State management** – External procedures can and will 'lose' their state (current values of 'static' or 'global' variables). This is due to the EXTPROC caching that is implemented. Therefore, we need a mechanism for establishing and persisting a state in our C programs.

❑ **Tracing mechanisms** – External procedures run on the server behind other processes. While it is possible on various platforms to debug these routines using a conventional debugger, it is quite difficult and, when the bugs only arise when many people use the external procedure concurrently, can be impossible. We need a facility to generate copious trace files on demand to 'debug from afar'. These are similar in nature to the trace files Oracle generates in response to an `alter session set sql_trace = true` – the only goal is to provide runtime information in a readable file for debugging/tuning purposes.

❑ **Parameter setting** – We need a facility to parameterize our external procedures so we can easily change their behavior externally, using a parameter file, much like we do with the init.ora file and the database.

❑ **Generic Error Handling** – We need a facility to easily report meaningful errors to the end user.

The Wrapper

The way I like to start is with the PL/SQL prototype – I come up with the specification of the PL/SQL routines I would like to implement. The routines I would like to implement in this example will be a series of procedures that accept an IN parameter and an OUT (or IN/OUT) parameter. We will write one for each type of interesting data type (the ones we will use frequently). They will demonstrate how to pass as inputs and receive as outputs each of these types correctly. Additionally, I would like to have some functions that show how to return some of these interesting types as well. To me, the interesting types are:

❑ STRINGs (up to the 32KB PL/SQL limit)

❑ NUMBERs (of any scale/precision)

❑ DATEs

❑ INTEGERs (binary_integers)

❑ BOOLEANs

❑ RAWs (upto 32KB)

❑ LOBs (for all data >32KB)

❑ Arrays of STRINGs

❑ Arrays of NUMBERs

❑ Arrays of DATEs

In order to do this, we'll need to set up some collection types first. These represent our arrays of STRINGs, NUMBERs and DATEs:

```
tkyte@TKYTE816> create or replace type numArray as table of number
  2  /
Type created.

tkyte@TKYTE816> create or replace type dateArray as table of date
  2  /
Type created.

tkyte@TKYTE816> create or replace type strArray as table of varchar2(255)
  2  /
Type created.
```

Now we are ready for the package specification. This is a series of overloaded procedures to test passing parameters with. Each routine has an IN and an OUT parameter with the exception of the CLOB version which has an IN/OUT parameter. The client must initialize the LOB IN OUT implementation and the external procedure will fill it in:

```
tkyte@TKYTE816> create or replace package demo_passing_pkg
  2  as
  3      procedure pass( p_in in number, p_out out number );
  4
  5      procedure pass( p_in in date, p_out out date );
  6
  7      procedure pass( p_in in varchar2, p_out out varchar2 );
  8
  9      procedure pass( p_in in boolean, p_out  out boolean );
 10
 11      procedure pass( p_in in CLOB, p_out in out CLOB );
 12
 13      procedure pass( p_in in numArray, p_out out numArray );
 14
 15      procedure pass( p_in in dateArray, p_out out dateArray );
 16
 17      procedure pass( p_in in strArray, p_out out strArray );
```

We cannot use overloading on the RAW and INT procedures below as we did above since PASS(RAW, RAW) would be confused with PASS(VARCHAR2,VARCHAR2) and PASS(INT,INT) gets confused with PASS(NUMBER,NUMBER) by Oracle. Therefore, we make an exception for these two and create named routines for them:

```
 19      procedure pass_raw( p_in in RAW, p_out out RAW );
 20
 21      procedure pass_int( p_in   in binary_integer,
 22                          p_out  out binary_integer );
```

And lastly, we'll implement some functions to return values in order to demonstrate how that works. We'll implement one to return each type of interesting SCALAR type:

```
 25      function return_number return number;
 26
 27      function return_date return date;
 28
 29      function return_string return varchar2;
 30
 31  end demo_passing_pkg;
 32  /

Package created.
```

The CREATE TYPES represent our array types. We have defined new SQL types; numArray to be a nested table type of numbers, dateArray as a nested table of dates, and strArray as a nested table of VARCHAR2(255)s. We have now created the spec of the package we want to implement so we're ready for the rest of it. I'll introduce this piece-by-piece now. We'll start with the library definition:

```
tkyte@TKYTE816> create or replace library demoPassing
  2  as
  3  'C:\demo_passing\extproc.dll'
  4  /
Library created.
```

That, as you might recall from testing the SCOTT/TIGER example above, simply defines to Oracle where the library named demoPassing physically is stored – in this case, the file C:\demo_passing\extproc.dll. The fact that we have not yet built this DLL is not relevant yet. We need the library object in order to compile the PL/SQL body that we are going to create. The extproc.dll will come later. We can execute the create library successfully without actually having the library yet.

Now, onto the package body:

```
tkyte@TKYTE816> create or replace package body demo_passing_pkg
  2  as
  3
  4       procedure pass(  p_in    in  number,
  5                        p_out   out number )
  6       as
  7       language C
  8       name "pass_number"
  9       library demoPassing
 10       with context
 11       parameters (
 12                    CONTEXT,
 13                    p_in    OCINumber,
 14                    p_in    INDICATOR short,
 15                    p_out   OCINumber,
 16                    p_out   INDICATOR short );
```

So, in looking at that, it starts off normal enough with CREATE OR REPLACE PACKAGE and PROCEDURE Pass (...) as ..., but then it diverges from a normal stored procedure. We are creating a call specification now, not embedding PL/SQL code. A call specification is the method by which Oracle maps the PL/SQL types to the external routine's native data types. For example, the above is mapping the p_in number parameter to the C data type OCINumber. A line-by-line explanation of what we are doing in this case is:

❑   Line 7: language C – We identify the language. We are doing C, though it could have been language Java as well (but that's in the next chapter).

❑   Line 8: name "pass_number" – We identify the name of the subroutine in C we will be calling in our demoPassing library. We have to use a quoted identifier in order to preserve case (since C preserves case). Normally, all identifiers in Oracle are folded to uppercase, quoting them preserves their case. This name must match exactly the name of the C routine in text and case.

❑   Line 9: library demoPassing – We identify the name of the library that will contain our code. This name matches the name we used in the CREATE LIBRARY statement above.

❑   Line 10: with context – This is optional but I always pass it. This context is needed in order to return meaningful error messages, and to use the OCI or Pro*C routines.

❑   Line 11: parameters – This is the beginning of our parameter list. Here, we will explicitly specify the order and types of parameters being passed. This, like the with context, is optional but I always use it to be explicit. Rather than accept the defaults and sometimes 'guess' what is going to be passed, I explicitly tell Oracle what I'm expecting, and what order I'm expecting them in.

❏ Line 12: CONTEXT – This keyword, since it is first, tells Oracle to pass the OCIExtProcContext * parameter as the first parameter. I could place it anywhere in the parameter list but typically it is first. The OCIExtProcContext is a datatype defined by OCI and represents our session in the database.

❏ Line 13: p_in OCINumber – Here, I am telling Oracle that the next parameter I expect in my C routine is an OCINumber. In this case an OCINumber * a pointer to an OCINumber. See below for a table of data type mappings.

❏ Line 14: p_in INDICATOR short – Here, I am telling Oracle that the next parameter I expect in my C routine is an indicator variable of type short that will tell me if p_in was passed with a NULL value or not. This is not mandatory; however I always pass a NULL INDICATOR variable with each and every variable. If you do not, you have no way to detect Nulls in your external procedures, or return a Null value yourself.

❏ Line 15: p_out OCINumber – Here, I am telling Oracle that the next parameter I expect after that indicator variable is another OCINumber. In this case, it will be an OCINumber *. See below for a table of data type mappings.

❏ Line 16: p_out INDICATOR short – Here, I am telling Oracle the next parameter I expect is an indicator variable for the p_out parameter, and that it should be a C short. Since p_out is an OUT parameter, this indicator variable is for me to set to tell the caller if the OUT parameter is NULL or not NULL. Hence, this parameter will be passed as a short * (a pointer), so that I can set the value, not just read it.

Given that, we will skip ahead for a moment and look at the C prototype that will go with this SQL call specification we've just created. Given the above input, our C prototype will be:

```
18      --void pass_number
19      -- (
20      -- OCIExtProcContext  * ,   /*  1 : With-Context  */
21      --         OCINumber  * ,   /*  2 : P_IN  */
22      --             short     ,   /*  3 : P_IN (Indicator) */
23      --         OCINumber  * ,   /*  4 : P_OUT  */
24      --             short  *    /*  5 : P_OUT (Indicator) */
25      -- );
```

Now, we will finish looking at the annotated PL/SQL package body that maps the rest of the procedures/functions. Here is the routine that passes Oracle dates back and forth; they will be mapped to the C datatype OCIDate supplied by OCI:

```
27      procedure pass( p_in in date, p_out out date )
28      as
29      language C name "pass_date" library demoPassing
30      with context parameters
31      ( CONTEXT,
32        p_in   OCIDate, p_in   INDICATOR short,
33        p_out  OCIDate, p_out  INDICATOR short );
34
35      -- void pass_date
36      -- (
37      -- OCIExtProcContext  * ,   /*  1 : With-Context  */
38      --             OCIDate  * ,   /*  2 : P_IN  */
```

```
39      --                short    ,   /*   3 : P_IN (Indicator) */
40      --              OCIDate   *,   /*   4 : P_OUT  */
41      --                short   *    /*   5 : P_OUT (Indicator) */
42      --    );
```

Next, we see how to pass the varchar2 type back and forth – in this case Oracle will map the STRING type of a C char * – a character string pointer.

```
45      procedure pass(  p_in in varchar2, p_out  out  varchar2 )
46      as
47      language C name "pass_str" library demoPassing
48      with context parameters
49      ( CONTEXT,
50        p_in   STRING, p_in  INDICATOR short,
51        p_out  STRING, p_out INDICATOR short, p_out  MAXLEN int );
52
53      -- void pass_str
54      --   (
55      --   OCIExtProcContext  *,   /*   1 : With-Context  */
56      --              char   *,   /*   2 : P_IN */
57      --              short   ,   /*   3 : P_IN (Indicator) */
58      --              char   *,   /*   4 : P_OUT  */
59      --              short  *,   /*   5 : P_OUT (Indicator) */
60      --              int    *    /*   6 : P_OUT (Maxlen) */
61      --    );
```

In the above, we see the first use of MAXLEN. This instructs Oracle to pass to our external procedure the maximum width of the OUT parameter p_out. Since we are returning a string, it is very useful to know what the maximum length of that string may be, to avoid a buffer overwrite. For all string types that are mapped as an OUT parameter the use of the MAXLEN parameter is strongly encouraged.

Next, we see how to pass the PL/SQL BOOLEAN type; this will be mapped to a C int type:

```
64      procedure pass( p_in in boolean, p_out out boolean )
65      as
66      language C name "pass_bool" library demoPassing
67      with context parameters
68      ( CONTEXT,
69        p_in  int, p_in  INDICATOR short,
70        p_out int, p_out INDICATOR short );
71
72      -- void pass_bool
73      --   (
74      --   OCIExtProcContext  *,   /*   1 : With-Context  */
75      --              int    ,   /*   2 : P_IN  */
76      --              short   ,   /*   3 : P_IN (Indicator) */
77      --              int   *,   /*   4 : P_OUT  */
78      --              short  *    /*   5 : P_OUT (Indicator) */
79      --    );
```

Next, we see the CLOB example. Here we pass the PL/SQL CLOB type to a C OCILobLocator type. Notice in this case, we must be ready to receive a pointer to a pointer for the OUT parameter. This allows the C code to change not only the contents of what the LOB locator points to, but also change the LOB locator itself – allowing us to point it to a totally different LOB if we wanted to:

```
83        procedure pass( p_in in clob, p_out in out clob )
84        as
85        language C name "pass_clob" library demoPassing
86        with context parameters
87        ( CONTEXT,
88          p_in   OCILobLocator, p_in   INDICATOR short,
89          p_out  OCILobLocator, p_out  INDICATOR short );
90
91        -- void pass_clob
92        --   (
93        --   OCIExtProcContext   *,   /*   1 : With-Context   */
94        --       OCILobLocator   *,   /*   2 : P_IN   */
95        --           short    ,   /*   3 : P_IN (Indicator) */
96        --       OCILobLocator  **,   /*   4 : P_OUT   */
97        --           short    *   /*   5 : P_OUT (Indicator) */
98        --   );
```

Next are the three routines that pass arrays, Oracle collection types, back and forth. Since the mappings for each are so similar – we'll present all three at once. The C routines for each have the same exact prototypes – the `OCIColl` type is passed to each, regardless of the collection type being passed:

```
100       procedure pass( p_in in numArray, p_out out numArray )
101       as
102       language C name "pass_numArray" library demoPassing
103       with context parameters
104       ( CONTEXT,
105         p_in  OCIColl, p_in  INDICATOR short,
106         p_out OCIColl, p_out INDICATOR short );
107
108       -- void pass_numArray
109       --   (
110       --   OCIExtProcContext   *,   /*   1 : With-Context   */
111       --           OCIColl   *,   /*   2 : P_IN   */
112       --           short    ,   /*   3 : P_IN (Indicator) */
113       --           OCIColl  **,   /*   4 : P_OUT   */
114       --           short    *   /*   5 : P_OUT (Indicator) */
115       --   );
116
117       procedure pass( p_in in dateArray, p_out out dateArray )
118       as
119       language C name "pass_dateArray" library demoPassing
120       with context parameters
121       ( CONTEXT,
122         p_in  OCIColl, p_in  INDICATOR short,
123         p_out OCIColl, p_out INDICATOR short );
124
125       procedure pass( p_in in strArray, p_out out strArray )
126       as
127       language C name "pass_strArray" library demoPassing
128       with context parameters
129       ( CONTEXT,
130         p_in  OCIColl, p_in  INDICATOR short,
131         p_out OCIColl, p_out INDICATOR short );
```

Next we have the routine that passes raw data back and forth. Here, we use both the MAXLEN (which we observed with the VARCHAR2s above) and the LENGTH attribute. We must pass a length with a RAW type as RAWs contain binary information, including binary zeroes, which means our C program would not be able to determine the actual string length, and Oracle would not be able to figure out how big the raw data we were returning is. For RAW types both LENGTH and MAXLEN are crucial. LENGTH must be passed and MAXLEN should be passed.

```
134    procedure pass_raw( p_in in raw, p_out out raw )
135    as
136    language C name "pass_raw " library demoPassing
137    with context parameters
138    ( CONTEXT,
139      p_in  RAW, p_in  INDICATOR short, p_in  LENGTH int,
140      p_out RAW, p_out INDICATOR short, p_out MAXLEN int,
141      p_out LENGTH int );
142    -- void pass_long_raw
143    --  (
144    --   OCIExtProcContext *,  /*  1 : With-Context  */
145    --       unsigned char *,  /*  2 : P_IN  */
146    --             short   ,  /*  3 : P_IN (Indicator) */
147    --             int    ,  /*  4 : P_IN (Length) */
148    --       unsigned char *,  /*  5 : P_OUT  */
149    --             short *,  /*  6 : P_OUT (Indicator) */
150    --             int  *,  /*  7 : P_OUT (Maxlen) */
151    --             int  *  /*  8 : P_OUT (Length) */
152    --  );
```

Next we have the routine to pass a PL/SQL BINARY_INTEGER back and forth to C. In this case, the BINARY_INTEGER type is mapped to the native int type in C:

```
154    procedure pass_int(p_in in binary_integer, p_out out binary_integer )
155    as
156    language C name "pass_int" library demoPassing
157    with context parameters
158    ( CONTEXT,
159      p_in  int, p_in  INDICATOR short,
160      p_out int, p_out INDICATOR short );
161
162      -- void pass_int
163      --  (
164      --   OCIExtProcContext *,  /*  1 : With-Context  */
165      --             int   ,  /*  2 : P_IN  */
166      --             short   ,  /*  3 : P_IN (Indicator) */
167      --             int  *,  /*  4 : P_OUT  */
168      --             short *  /*  5 : P_OUT (Indicator) */
169      --  );
```

Here are the wrappers for our three functions to return NUMBERs, DATEs, and STRINGs. We encounter a new keyword here; RETURN. When we map to a function, we must use the RETURN keyword as the last parameter in the parameter list. It is actually the return type of the function and not a formal parameter to/from the function itself. In the above, I have three parameters in the SQL wrapper, but only two parameters in the C prototype I will be using. The RETURN OCINumber parameter really defines the type I will be *returning* from the function, as denoted by OCINumber *return_number. I do include an indicator even for my return value, since I want to be able to return Null at some time. If I did not include this indicator, I would have no mechanism to be able to return a Null value. As we will see with the string example, I can return the LENGTH attribute as well, but not MAXLEN, as this is only available with OUT parameters where the Oracle sets up storage. With return values, since we are responsible for allocating memory, the MAXLEN attribute would not make sense.

```
173      function return_number return number
174      as
175      language C name "return_number" library demoPassing
176      with context parameters
177      ( CONTEXT, RETURN INDICATOR short, RETURN OCINumber );
178
179        -- OCINumber *return_number
180        --   (
181        --   OCIExtProcContext   *,   /*   1 : With-Context   */
182        --                short   *   /*   2 : RETURN (Indicator) */
183        --   );
184
185      function return_date return date
186      as
187      language C name "return_date" library demoPassing
188      with context parameters
189      ( CONTEXT, RETURN INDICATOR short, RETURN OCIDate );
190
191        -- OCIDate *return_date
192        --   (
193        --   OCIExtProcContext   *,   /*   1 : With-Context   */
194        --                short   *   /*   2 : RETURN (Indicator) */
195        --   );
196
197      function return_string return varchar2
198      as
199      language C name "return_string" library demoPassing
200      with context parameters
201      (CONTEXT, RETURN INDICATOR short, RETURN LENGTH int, RETURN STRING );
202
203        -- char *return_string
204        --   (
205        --   OCIExtProcContext   *,   /*   1 : With-Context   */
206        --                short   *,  /*   2 : RETURN (Indicator) */
207        --                  int   *   /*   3 : RETURN (Length)   */
208        --   );
209
210   end demo_passing_pkg;
211   /
```

```
Package body created.
```

There you can see in last function, that I am using the LENGTH attribute as well as the INDICATOR. This is so I can let Oracle know how long the string I'm returning is.

So, to recap, what we have now is:

❑   A package specification outlining the package we wish to implement.

❑   A series of new SQL array types that we can use.

❑ A library object in the database mapping to our yet to be created `extproc.dll`.

❑ A package body that is really just a SQL call specification around our C functions. It instructs Oracle what data (indicators, parameters, contexts and so on) to send to our external procedure and how (data type-wise) to send it.

At this point after seeing the example, it might be a good time to take a look at a data type mapping table. That is, when given a SQL type X, what external types are available? Then, given the external type we choose, what is the C type that will actually be used? These data type mapping tables are available in the *Oracle Application Developers Guide – Fundamentals* and are included here for your reference. Note that an external data type is not a C type (nor is it a SQL or PL/SQL type). You will need to refer to the second table to get the real C type you should use.

SQL or PL/SQL Data Type	External Data Type	Default Type
BINARY_INTEGER, BOOLEAN, PLS_INTEGER	[unsigned]char, [unsigned]short, [unsigned]int, [unsigned]long, sb1, sb2, sb4, ub1, ub2, ub4, size_t	int
NATURAL, NATURALN, POSITIVE, POSITIVEN, SIGNTYPE	[unsigned]char, [unsigned]short, [unsigned]int, [unsigned]long, sb1, sb2, sb4, ub1, ub2, ub4, size_t	unsigned int
FLOAT, REAL	Float	float
DOUBLE PRECISION	Double	double
CHAR, CHARACTER, LONG, NCHAR, NVARCHAR2, ROWID, VARCHAR2, VARCHAR	string, ocistring	string
LONG RAW, RAW	raw, ociraw	raw
BFILE, BLOB, CLOB, NCLOB	ociloblocator	ociloblocator
NUMBER, DEC, DECIMAL, INT, INTEGER, NUMERIC, SMALLINT	[unsigned]char, [unsigned]short, [unsigned]int, [unsigned]long, sb1, sb2, sb4, ub1, ub2, ub4, size_t, ocinumber	ocinumber
DATE	Ocidate	ocidate
Abstract Data Types (ADTs)	Dvoid	dvoid
Collections (nested tables, VARRAYS)	Ocicoll	ocicoll

So, the above table maps the SQL or PL/SQL types to an external data type. I recommend always using the default type as listed above as they are the easiest to handle in your C code. An external data type looks a lot like a C type but we need to go one step further. Since each SQL or PL/SQL type may be in, in out, out, or a return value from a function, we must go one step further in determining the actual C Type. In general, variables that are 'returned' or are in are passed by value, whereas variables that are in out, out or passed explicitly by reference are passed via pointers, by reference. The following table shows us what C type we would use given an external data type and a parameter mode:

External Data Type	C Type for IN Parameters and RETURN values	C Type for IN OUT, OUT and by REFERENCE Variables
[unsigned] char	[unsigned] char	[unsigned] char *
[unsigned] short	[unsigned] short	[unsigned] short *
[unsigned] int	[unsigned] int	[unsigned] int *
[unsigned] long	[unsigned] long	[unsigned] long *
size_t	size_t	size_t *
sb1	sb1	sb1 *
sb2	sb2	sb2 *
sb4	sb4	sb4 *
ub1	ub1	ub1 *
ub2	ub2	ub2 *
ub4	ub4	ub4 *
float	float	float *
double	double	double *
string	char *	char *
raw	unsigned char *	unsigned char *
Ociloblocator	OCILobLocator *	OCILobLocator * *
Ocinumber	OCINumber *	OCINumber *
Ocistring	OCIString *	OCIString *
Ociraw	OCIRaw *	OCIRaw *
Ocidate	OCIDate *	OCIDate *
Ocicoll	OCIColl *	OCIColl **
Adt	dvoid *	dvoid *

The C Code

Now we are ready for the C code to implement our library. We will start with the common template I use for all external procedures. This template includes standard header files I frequently use, the Oracle OCI header file we need, and three functions debugf, oci_error, and raise_application_error. These functions will help us in meeting our goals of having a tracing mechanism (debugf) and generic error handling (oci_error and raise_application_error). I simply copy this file any time I'm starting a new extproc project, and use it to start.

```c
#include <stdio.h>
#include <stdlib.h>
#include <stdarg.h>
#include <time.h>
#include <string.h>
#include <errno.h>
#include <ctype.h>

#include <oci.h>

#ifdef WIN_NT
#define INI_FILE_NAME "c:\\temp\\extproc.ini"
#else
#define INI_FILE_NAME "/tmp/extproc.ini"
#endif

#define strupr(a) {char * cp; for(cp=a;*cp;*cp=toupper(*cp), cp++);}
```

The above is the very beginning of my C template. I include 'popular' header files, ones that I use frequently, as well as define where my parameter file will be. There are many ways we could set this at run-time. For example, if I was building an external procedure for execution on Windows, I might use the Windows functions RegOpenKeyEx, RegQueryInfoKey, and RegEnumValue to retrieve the location of the parameter file from the registry. On UNIX, I might use an environment variable. In this example, I simply 'hard code' the location into the external procedure. This is a valid approach as you could simply demand that your initialization parameter file be placed in some known location (for example, /etc/your_extproc.ora on UNIX, and c:\your_extproc\your_extproc.ora on Windows).

Now onto the code itself. The next part defines our context. It holds what normally might be global variables in a typical program. We cannot (should not – it is wholly unreliable) use global variables in an external procedure. Also, since static data will be reinitialized between calls globals would not work correctly anyway. We will use the OCI context management API calls to get and set a global context for our extproc. You would add any state variables you needed to preserve from call to call in this structure below yourself.

The global variables I have defined are:

❑ OCIExtProcContext * ctx – The context that is passed to each of our external procedures. We'll need this in various calls, such as error handling.

❑ OCIEnv * envhp – The OCI environment pointer. We'll need this in almost every OCI function call we make.

❑ `OCISvcCtx * svchp` – The OCI service handle. We'll need this in some, but not all, OCI function calls.

❑ `OCIError * errhp` – The OCI error handle. This will be used in almost all OCI function calls to handle errors with.

❑ `int curr_lineno` and `char * curr_filename` – These will be used by our tracing routine. We will remember the source code file and line number that is making a trace call so when we print out the message, we'll know exactly what source code file, and line in that file, caused the message to be printed – very handy for 'debugging from afar'. In Chapter 10, *Tuning Strategies and Tools*, I spoke of heavily instrumenting code – this is a good example of where this is really crucial.

❑ `ub1 debugf_flag` – A flag that will tell us if we are printing trace messages or not. If this flag is not set, we will 'short circuit' the `debugf` calls (`debugf` is defined below). This will allow us to retain the tracing calls in our code even during production, so we can easily turn it on if we ever need it.

❑ `char debugf_path[255]` – This controls the directory to which we will write our debugging messages.

❑ `char debugf_filename[50]` – This controls the name of the file in the directory we will write our debugging messages to.

```
typedef struct myCtx
{
  OCIExtProcContext * ctx;          /* Context passed to all external procs */
  OCIEnv *            envhp;        /* OCI environment handle */
  OCISvcCtx *         svchp;        /* OCI Service handle */
  OCIError *          errhp;        /* OCI Error handle */

  int                 curr_lineno;
  char *              curr_filename;

  ub1                 debugf_flag;
  char                debugf_path[255];
  char                debugf_filename[50];

  /* add your own state variables here... */
}
  myCtxStruct;
```

Next in the source code template, we have `debugf`, our tracing routine. It is a C function that works very much like the standard C `fprintf` does and even accepts a varying number of input arguments (the ... in the argument list). The first argument to it is the 'context'; our state described above. I always assume this state pointer is named `myCtx` (my macro for `debugf` makes that assumption). This `debugf` routine shows a couple of things. It introduces much of the OCI file-handling API, which is modeled loosely after the C `fopen/fread/fwrite/fclose` API family. The `debugf` routine, which is only called if the flag `myCtx->debugf_flag` is actually set, simply opens a file, builds a message, writes it, and closes the file.

This shows how our context is used as well. It contains our 'session' state and holds important variables such as the `OCIEnv` and `OCIError` structures we need for all OCI API calls. It shows how we can set the state simply by manipulating variables in the structure (as the `debugf` macro does). The `debugf` macro will 'short circuit' calls to the actual `_debugf()` subroutine. By this, I mean that if either `myCtx` or `myCtx->debugf_flag` is not set, the context state is never changed, and the `_debugf()` routine is never called. This means that you can safely leave all of your debugging statements in your production code, as its existence does not materially affect run-time performance in the long run (when `debugf_flag` is set to false).

```
void _debugf( myCtxStruct * myCtx, char * fmt, ... )
{
va_list            ap;
OCIFileObject * fp;
time_t             theTime = time(NULL);
char               msg[8192];
ub4                bytes;

    if ( OCIFileOpen( myCtx->envhp, myCtx->errhp, &fp,
                      myCtx->debugf_filename,
                      myCtx->debugf_path,
                      OCI_FILE_WRITE_ONLY, OCI_FILE_APPEND|OCI_FILE_CREATE,
                      OCI_FILE_TEXT ) != OCI_SUCCESS ) return;

    strftime( msg, sizeof(msg),
              "%y%m%d %H%M%S GMT ", gmtime(&theTime) );
    OCIFileWrite( myCtx->envhp, myCtx->errhp, fp, msg, strlen(msg), &bytes );

    va_start(ap,fmt);
    vsprintf( msg, fmt, ap );
    va_end(ap);
    strcat( msg,"\n");

    OCIFileWrite( myCtx->envhp, myCtx->errhp, fp, msg, strlen(msg), &bytes );
    OCIFileClose( myCtx->envhp, myCtx->errhp, fp );
}
```

This next bit of code introduces a macro interface to `debugf`. This macro is a more convenient way to use `debugf`. Instead of having to pass the `_LINE_`, `_FILE_` each time we call; we just code:

```
debugf( myCtx, "This is some format %s", some_string );
```

and this macro will set them in our context and then call `_debugf` for us.

```
void _debugf( myCtxStruct * myCtx, char * fmt, ... );
#define debugf \
if ((myCtx!=NULL) && (myCtx->debugf_flag)) \
    myCtx->curr_lineno = __LINE__, \
    myCtx->curr_filename = __FILE__, \
    _debugf
```

Next in the template is an error handling utility, raise_application_error. This should be a familiar name to a PL/SQL developer. raise_application_error is a PL/SQL built-in function to raise errors as exceptions. This function has the same exact purpose. If your external procedure calls this function prior to returning, the return values from your external procedure are ignored, and an exception will be raised to the caller instead. This makes handling errors from an external procedure no different than any other PL/SQL routine as far as the caller is concerned.

```c
static int raise_application_error( myCtxStruct * myCtx,
                                    int           errCode,
                                    char *        errMsg, ...)
{
char    msg[8192];
va_list ap;

    va_start(ap,errMsg);
    vsprintf( msg, errMsg, ap );
    va_end(ap);

    debugf( myCtx,  "raise application error( %d, %s )", errCode, msg );
    if ( OCIExtProcRaiseExcpWithMsg(myCtx->ctx,errCode,msg,0) ==
                                    OCIEXTPROC_ERROR )
    {
      debugf( myCtx,   "Unable to raise exception" );
    }
    return -1;
}
```

Next is another error handling routine, lastOciError. This function takes the current session context and, using the OCIError structure in it, retrieves the last OCI error text that occurred. It retrieves this text into some memory that has been allocated using OCIExtProcAllocCallMemory(). Any memory allocated by this function will be automatically freed for us upon returning from the external procedure. This function is most frequently used in a call to raise_application_error after a failed OCI call. It simply lets the caller know the cause of the OCI error we encountered.

```c
static char * lastOciError( myCtxStruct * myCtx )
{
sb4       errcode;
char      * errbuf = (char*)OCIExtProcAllocCallMemory( myCtx->ctx, 256 );

    strcpy( errbuf, "unable to retrieve message\n" );
    OCIErrorGet( myCtx->errhp, 1, NULL, &errcode, errbuf,
                 255, OCI_HTYPE_ERROR );
    errbuf[strlen(errbuf)-1] = 0;
    return errbuf;
}
```

Now for the 'workhorse' routine of the external procedure template; init. It is responsible for establishing and retrieving our state, and processing any parameters we have set up in our initialization file. It is a lot to digest in one fell swoop, but it is actually quite straightforward once we introduce the OCI API calls we are utilizing.

The goal of the `init` routine is to set up our `myCtxStruct`, and to call any OCI initialization functions we need. This function starts by getting the OCI environment handles. It does this in one of two ways. If we are using just OCI (no Pro*C) we simply call `OCIExtProcGetEnv` with the context that was sent to our external procedure. This OCI API retrieves these handles for us. If we are using both OCI and Pro*C, we must instead use `EXEC SQL REGISTER CONNECT :ctx`. This sets up the Pro*C layer. We still have to retrieve the OCI environment handles, but this time, we must use the Pro*C-supplied API calls to do that – `SQLEnvGet`, `SQLSvcCtxGet`. You would comment or uncomment the appropriate method depending on your needs.

```
/*------------- include this for Pro*C external procedures only!! --------
#define SQLCA_INIT
EXEC SQL INCLUDE sqlca;
  -----------------------------------------------------------------------*/

static myCtxStruct * init( OCIExtProcContext * ctx )
{
ub1          false = 0;
myCtxStruct *myCtx = NULL;
OCIEnv      *envhp;
OCISvcCtx   *svchp;
OCIError    *errhp;
ub4          key = 1;


    if ( OCIExtProcGetEnv( ctx, &envhp, &svchp, &errhp ) != OCI_SUCCESS )
    {
        OCIExtProcRaiseExcpWithMsg(ctx,20000,
                                "failed to get OCI Connection",0);
        return NULL;
    }

/*----- replace the above OCIExtProcGetEnv() call with the following -----
----- when using Pro*C -------------------------------------------------

    EXEC SQL REGISTER CONNECT USING :ctx;
    if ( sqlca.sqlcode < 0 )
    {
        OCIExtProcRaiseExcpWithMsg(ctx,20000,sqlca.sqlerrm.sqlerrmc,70);
        return NULL;
    }
    if ( ( SQLEnvGet(0, &envhp ) != OCI_SUCCESS )  ||
         ( OCIHandleAlloc(envhp, (dvoid**)&errhp,
                    OCI_HTYPE_ERROR,0,0) != OCI_SUCCESS )  ||
         ( SQLSvcCtxGet(0, NULL, 0, &svchp ) != OCI_SUCCESS ) )
    {
        OCIExtProcRaiseExcpWithMsg(ctx,20000,"failed to get OCI ENV",0);
        return NULL;
    }
    ----------------------------------------------------------------*/
```

Once we have the OCI environment, the first thing we do is call `OCIContextGetValue()` to retrieve our context. This API call takes the OCI environment and a 'key', and attempts to retrieve a pointer. The 'key' in this case is some 64-bit number. You may store as many contexts as you like, but we'll just be using one at this time.

```
        if ( OCIContextGetValue( envhp, errhp, (ub1*)&key, sizeof(key),
                                 (dvoid**)&myCtx ) != OCI_SUCCESS )
        {
            OCIExtProcRaiseExcpWithMsg(ctx,20000,"failed to get OCI Context",0);
            return NULL;
        }
```

If we retrieve a Null pointer at this time, which simply indicates we have not set a context as yet, we will allocate sufficient memory for one and set it. The call to `OCIMemoryAllocate` is used to allocate a block of memory that will stay valid for the life of the process. Once we've allocated this memory, we save it in our context using `OCIContextSetValue`. This function will associate our pointer (which will never change) with the key we choose for the duration of our session. The very next call to `OCIContextGetValue` with the same key in the same session will retrieve this pointer for us.

```
        if ( myCtx == NULL )
        {
            if ( OCIMemoryAlloc( envhp, errhp, (dvoid**)&myCtx,
                                 OCI_DURATION_PROCESS,
                                 sizeof(myCtxStruct),
                                 OCI_MEMORY_CLEARED ) != OCI_SUCCESS )
            {
                OCIExtProcRaiseExcpWithMsg(ctx,20000,
                                         "failed to get OCI Memory",0);
                return NULL;
            }
            myCtx->ctx   = ctx;
            myCtx->envhp = envhp;
            myCtx->svchp = svchp;
            myCtx->errhp = errhp;
            if ( OCIContextSetValue( envhp, errhp,
                                     OCI_DURATION_SESSION, (ub1*)&key,
                                     sizeof(key), myCtx ) != OCI_SUCCESS )
            {
                raise_application_error(myCtx, 20000, "%s",
                                        lastOciError(myCtx));
                return NULL;
            }
```

Continuing onwards, since we retrieved a Null pointer that indicates we had never processed our parameters. We do so in the next block of code. We use the supplied parameter management API calls to process files that follow the same rules as the Oracle `init.ora` parameter file. See Chapter 2, *Architecture* for a description of those files. I typically use this file to control debug tracing, and any other state variable defaults I would like in my program. The initialization file we are using for example, might look like this:

```
debugf = true
debugf_filename = extproc2.log
debugf_path = /tmp/
```

This enables tracing (`debugf = true`) to a file `/tmp/extproc2.log`. You could add additional parameters to this file and modify the `init` code appropriate to read and set them in your session's context. The process for reading and processing a parameter file takes the following steps:

1. *Call* `OCIExtractInit` *to initialize the parameter processing library.*

2. Call `OCIExtractSetNumKeys` to let the OCI API know the number of key names you are going to ask for. This must match the number of parameters entered into the parameter file.

3. Call `OCIExtractSetKey` the number of times you told `OCIExtractSetNumKeys()`.

4. Call `OCIExtractFromFile` to process the parameter file.

5. Call `OCIExtractTo<some datatype>` to retrieve each of the parameter values in turn.

6. Call `OCIExtractTerm` to terminate the parameter processing library and allow it to return any resources it might have allocated to the system.

```
if (( OCIExtractInit( envhp, errhp ) != OCI_SUCCESS )  ||
    ( OCIExtractSetNumKeys( envhp, errhp, 3 ) != OCI_SUCCESS ) ||
    ( OCIExtractSetKey( envhp, errhp, "debugf",
                        OCI_EXTRACT_TYPE_BOOLEAN,
                        0, &false, NULL, NULL ) != OCI_SUCCESS ) ||
    ( OCIExtractSetKey( envhp, errhp, "debugf_filename",
                        OCI_EXTRACT_TYPE_STRING,
                        0, "extproc.log",
                        NULL, NULL ) != OCI_SUCCESS )  ||
    ( OCIExtractSetKey( envhp, errhp, "debugf_path",
                        OCI_EXTRACT_TYPE_STRING,
                        0, "", NULL, NULL ) != OCI_SUCCESS )  ||
    ( OCIExtractFromFile( envhp, errhp, 0,
                          INI_FILE_NAME ) != OCI_SUCCESS ) ||
    ( OCIExtractToBool( envhp, errhp, "debugf", 0,
                        &myCtx->debugf_flag ) != OCI_SUCCESS ) ||
    ( OCIExtractToStr( envhp, errhp, "debugf_filename", 0,
                       myCtx->debugf_filename,
                       sizeof(myCtx->debugf_filename ) )
                                        != OCI_SUCCESS ) ||
    ( OCIExtractToStr( envhp, errhp, "debugf_path",
                       0, myCtx->debugf_path,
                       sizeof(myCtx->debugf_path ) )
                                        != OCI_SUCCESS ) ||
    ( OCIExtractTerm( envhp, errhp ) != OCI_SUCCESS ))
{
    raise_application_error(myCtx, 20000, "%s",
                            lastOciError(myCtx));
    return NULL;
}
}
```

The following is the block of code that will be executed on the second and subsequent calls to `init` by our session. Since `OCIContextGetValue` returns our context for the second and subsequent calls, we simply set up our data structure to point to it:

```
        else
        {
            myCtx->ctx   = ctx;
            myCtx->envhp = envhp;
            myCtx->svchp = svchp;
            myCtx->errhp = errhp;
        }
```

The last thing we do in `init` before returning, is to call the `OCIFileInit` routine. This initializes the OCI file-handling API for us, and makes it so we can open and read/write OS files. We could use the standard C `fopen`, `fclose`, `fread`, `fwrite` routines. This just makes it a little more portable and makes handling errors very consistent from platform-to-platform. You may add additional `init` calls here yourself as well. For example, if you choose to use the `OCIFormat*` (similar to `vsprintf` in C) routines, you could add a call to `OCIFormatInit` here. Don't forget to add a corresponding `OCIFormatTerm` call to your `term` routine below as well.

```
        if ( OCIFileInit( myCtx->envhp, myCtx->errhp ) != OCI_SUCCESS )
        {
            raise_application_error(myCtx, 20000, "%s", lastOciError(myCtx));
            return NULL;
        }
        return myCtx;
    }
```

Now for the `term` referred to above. This is my termination routine, a cleanup routine, and it must be called after any successful call to `init` above. It should be the last thing you call in your routine before returning from C to SQL:

```
    static void term( myCtxStruct * myCtx )
    {
        OCIFileTerm( myCtx->envhp, myCtx->errhp );
    }
```

That's the end of my template. I use the same source code template for every external procedure project I do (minor modifications for pure OCI versus Pro*C plus OCI). This saves a lot of time and provides a lot of functionality.

Now we start adding our code. The first part I start with, right after the generic component, is a listing of all error codes we will return, beginning with 20001. It is convenient to list them all here, as it will allow us to easily set up a `pragma exception_init` mapping in PL/SQL for each error code in our PL/SQL. This will let PL/SQL programs catch named exceptions instead of having to inspect error codes. We will not demonstrate this with this particular example; however, when we get to the Pro*C example below we will. Error numbers must be in the range of 20,000 to 20,999 as these are the ones supported by Oracle; the remaining error codes are reserved for its use.

```
    #define ERROR_OCI_ERROR      20001
    #define ERROR_STR_TOO_SMALL  20002
    #define ERROR_RAW_TOO_SMALL  20003
    #define ERROR_CLOB_NULL      20004
    #define ERROR_ARRAY_NULL     20005
```

Next comes our first real routine. This procedure is the implementation of the pass_number routine we specced out in PL/SQL above. It takes a PL/SQL Number IN and sets an OUT PL/SQL NUMBER. Our sample routine below will:

❑ Access the OCI Number type, which is an internal Oracle data type using supplied OCI functions. In this example we will convert the Oracle NUMBER into a C double using the built-in OCINumberToReal. We could convert the NUMBER into a string using OCINumberToText or to a C int type using OCINumberToInt. There are almost 50 OCI number functions you can use to perform various operations on this internal type. All of the available functions are found in the Oracle Call Interface Programmer's Guide.

❑ We will perform an operation on the C DOUBLE. In this case, we will simply negate it; if it was positive we'll make it negative and vice versa.

❑ We will set the OUT NUMBER parameter to this negated value and return.

We will also see a portability macro we place in front of each routine that is callable from PL/SQL. This macro will 'export' a function. This is needed only on the Windows platform, and is technically not necessary on UNIX. I typically put it in regardless of the platform I am building on, as the need to move the extproc library from Windows to UNIX, and vice versa arises frequently for me. Doing this all of the time just makes it easier. The embedded comments explain the code in detail as we go along:

```
#ifdef WIN_NT
_declspec (dllexport)
#endif
void pass_number
  ( OCIExtProcContext * ctx        /* CONTEXT */,

    OCINumber *        p_inum      /* OCINumber */,
    short              p_inum_i    /* INDICATOR short */,

    OCINumber *        p_onum      /* OCINumber */,
    short *            p_onum_i    /* INDICATOR short */ )
{
double      l_inum;
myCtxStruct*myCtx;
```

Before we can do *anything*, we must retrieve our session context. This gets the OCI environment, our parameters, and so on. It will be the first call we make in all of our extproc routines:

```
    if ( (myCtx = init( ctx )) == NULL ) return;
    debugf( myCtx,  "Enter Pass Number" );
```

Now, we'll access the first parameter. We passed it as an OCINumber type. We now can use the many OCINumber* functions on it. In this case, we'll get the Oracle Number converted into a C DOUBLE using OCINumberToReal. We could convert into an Int, Long, Float, or formatted string just as easily.

First, we must check to see if the passed Number is *Not Null*, if so process, else in this case; do nothing except call term() and return. If we successfully access the first parameter, we negate it and then construct an OCINumber from it using OCINumberFromReal. If that is successful, we set the null indicator p_onum_I to not Null – to let the caller know there is a value stored in there. Then we are done, we call term to clean up and return:

```
        if ( p_inum_i == OCI_IND_NOTNULL )
        {
            if ( OCINumberToReal( myCtx->errhp, p_inum, sizeof(l_inum), &l_inum )
                    != OCI_SUCCESS )
            {
                raise_application_error(myCtx,ERROR_OCI_ERROR,
                                    "%s",lastOciError(myCtx));
            }
            else
            {
                debugf( myCtx,  "The first parameter is %g", l_inum );
                l_inum = -l_inum;
                if ( OCINumberFromReal( myCtx->errhp, &l_inum,
                                    sizeof(l_inum), p_onum) != OCI_SUCCESS )
                {
                    raise_application_error(myCtx,ERROR_OCI_ERROR,
                                        "%s",lastOciError(myCtx));
                }
                else
                {
                    *p_onum_i = OCI_IND_NOTNULL;
                    debugf( myCtx,
                        "Set OUT parameter to %g and set indicator to NOTNULL",
                            l_inum );
                }
            }
        }
    term(myCtx);
}
```

and that's it. Our first routine makes use of all of our helper routines; raise_application_error, lastOciError, init, term, and debugf. Later, when we test this routine, we will inspect the results of our debugf calls. They will confirm that routine does what it is supposed to (and provide a handy tool for debugging later on).

Note how I am careful to return from only one location in this routine. If you return from more than one place, make sure to call term(myCtx) at each location.

Now, we move onto the remaining routines. The next routine deals with dates as IN and OUT parameters. We will:

❑ Retrieve the IN DATE parameter.

❑ Format it as a string using the OCI API calls for tracing purposes (there are about 16 OCI API calls you can use to manipulate a DATE data type).

❑ Add one month to it using the supplied OCI API.

❑ Assign the new date to the OUT parameter.

❑ Convert the newly assigned date into string, and print it.

❑ And finally call term and return it.

```
#ifdef WIN_NT
_declspec (dllexport)
#endif
void pass_date
 ( OCIExtProcContext * ctx          /* CONTEXT */,

   OCIDate *            p_idate    /* OCIDATE */,
   short                p_idate_i  /* INDICATOR short */,

   OCIDate *            p_odate    /* OCIDATE */,
   short *              p_odate_i  /* INDICATOR short */
 )
{
char      buffer[255];
ub4       buff_len;
char      * fmt = "dd-mon-yyyy hh24:mi:ss";
myCtxStruct*myCtx;

    if ( (myCtx = init( ctx )) == NULL ) return;
    debugf( myCtx,  "Enter Pass Date" );

    if ( p_idate_i == OCI_IND_NOTNULL )
    {
        buff_len = sizeof(buffer);
        if ( OCIDateToText( myCtx->errhp, p_idate, fmt, strlen(fmt),
                         NULL, -1, &buff_len, buffer ) != OCI_SUCCESS )
        {
            raise_application_error(myCtx,ERROR_OCI_ERROR,
                                "%s",lastOciError(myCtx));
        }
        else
        {
            debugf( myCtx,  "The date input parameter was set to '%.*s'",
                    buff_len, buffer );

            if ( OCIDateAddMonths( myCtx->errhp, p_idate, 1, p_odate )
                    != OCI_SUCCESS )
            {
                raise_application_error(myCtx,ERROR_OCI_ERROR,
                                    "%s",lastOciError(myCtx));
            }
            else
            {
                *p_odate_i = OCI_IND_NOTNULL;

                buff_len = sizeof(buffer);
                if ( OCIDateToText( myCtx->errhp, p_odate, fmt,
                                strlen(fmt), NULL, -1,
                                &buff_len, buffer ) != OCI_SUCCESS )
                {
                    raise_application_error(myCtx,ERROR_OCI_ERROR,
                                        "%s",lastOciError(myCtx));
                }
                else
                {
                    debugf( myCtx,
```

```
                                    "The date output parameter was set to '%.*s'",
                                    buff_len, buffer );
                    }
                }
            }
        }
        term(myCtx);}
```

Now we will see what is involved in passing a string back and forth. STRINGs are somewhat easier then NUMBERs and DATEs as they are passed simply as ASCII Null Terminated Strings. We will make use of the MAXLEN parameter with all OUT strings. The MAXLEN parameter tells us the maximum size of the output string buffer, which may change from call to call. This is because the caller supplies the buffer, and every time they call us, it may be with a different OUT parameter of a different length. This allows our external procedure to detect a buffer overwrite before it happens, and avoid it. We can then report back to the caller that the buffer they provided was too small (and what size it should have been).

```c
#ifdef WIN_NT
_declspec (dllexport)
#endif
void pass_str
  ( OCIExtProcContext * ctx          /* CONTEXT */,

    char *              p_istr       /* STRING */,
    short               p_istr_i     /* INDICATOR short */,

    char *              p_ostr       /* STRING */,
    short *             p_ostr_i     /* INDICATOR short */,
    int *               p_ostr_ml    /* MAXLEN int */
  )
{
myCtxStruct*myCtx;

    if ( (myCtx = init( ctx )) == NULL ) return;
    debugf( myCtx,  "Enter Pass Str" );

    if ( p_istr_i == OCI_IND_NOTNULL )
    {
    int     l_istr_l = strlen(p_istr);

        if ( *p_ostr_ml > l_istr_l )
        {

            strcpy( p_ostr, p_istr );
            strupr( p_ostr );
            *p_ostr_i = OCI_IND_NOTNULL;
        }
        else
        {
            raise_application_error( myCtx, ERROR_STR_TOO_SMALL,
                "output buffer of %d bytes needs to be at least %d bytes",
                *p_ostr_ml, l_istr_l+1 );
        }
    }
    term(myCtx);
}
```

The next routine demonstrates a `binary_integer` type. A `binary_integer` in PL/SQL is a 32-bit signed integer. It is the simplest type to send and receive by far. It is passed in a fashion that is very intuitive to a C programmer. This routine will simply inspect the input value and assign it (times 10) to the output variable:

```
#ifdef WIN_NT
_declspec (dllexport)
#endif
void pass_int
  ( OCIExtProcContext * ctx          /* CONTEXT */,

    int                 p_iINT       /* int */,
    short               p_iINT_i     /* INDICATOR short */,

    int *               p_oINT       /* int */,
    short *             p_oINT_i     /* INDICATOR short */
  )
{
myCtxStruct*myCtx;

    if ( (myCtx = init( ctx )) == NULL ) return;
    debugf( myCtx,  "Enter Pass Int" );

    if ( p_iINT_i == OCI_IND_NOTNULL )
    {
        debugf( myCtx,  "This first INT parameter is %d", p_iINT );

        *p_oINT = p_iINT*10;
        *p_oINT_i = OCI_IND_NOTNULL;

        debugf( myCtx,  "Set the INT out parameter to %d", *p_oINT );
    }
    term(myCtx);
}
```

Now for a PL/SQL BOOLEAN. The PL/SQL BOOLEAN type will be mapped to a C int in this case. A value of 1 indicates true and 0 indicates false as you would expect. This routine will simply inspect the INPUT (if not Null) and set the output to the negative of the input. Again, since this maps nicely to native C types, this is very easy to code. No special environment handles or API calls to massage the data. This routine simply sets the output equal to the negation of the input:

```
#ifdef WIN_NT
_declspec (dllexport)
#endif
void pass_bool
  ( OCIExtProcContext * ctx          /* CONTEXT */,

    int                 p_ibool      /* int */,
    short               p_ibool_i    /* INDICATOR short */,

    int *               p_obool      /* int */,
    short *             p_obool_i    /* INDICATOR short */ )
```

```
   {
myCtxStruct*myCtx;

    if ( (myCtx = init( ctx )) == NULL ) return;
    debugf( myCtx,  "Enter Pass Boolean" );

    if ( p_ibool_i == OCI_IND_NOTNULL )
    {
        *p_obool = !p_ibool;
        *p_obool_i = OCI_IND_NOTNULL;
    }
    term(myCtx);
}
```

We will now pass and return a RAW parameter. Since PL/SQL VARCHAR2 type variables are limited to 32 KB in length, we will always utilize the easier-to-interface-with RAW external type. This maps to a C unsigned char * which is just a pointer to byte data. With RAWs we will *always* receive the LENGTH attribute. This is mandatory; else we have no way to determine the number of bytes we should access. We will also *always* receive the MAXLEN attribute for all OUT parameters that have a varying length to avoid the potential of buffer overwrites. This attribute, while technically not mandatory, is just far too important to leave out. This routine simply copies the input buffer into the output buffer:

```
#ifdef WIN_NT
_declspec (dllexport)
#endif
void pass_raw
  ( OCIExtProcContext * ctx      /* CONTEXT */,

    unsigned char *  p_iraw      /* RAW */,
    short            p_iraw_i    /* INDICATOR short */,
    int              p_iraw_l    /* LENGHT INT */,

    unsigned char *  p_oraw      /* RAW */,
    short *          p_oraw_i    /* INDICATOR short */,
    int *            p_oraw_ml   /* MAXLEN int */,
    int *            p_oraw_l    /* LENGTH int */
  )
{
myCtxStruct*myCtx;

    if ( (myCtx = init( ctx )) == NULL ) return;
    debugf( myCtx, "Enter Pass long raw" );

    if ( p_iraw_i == OCI_IND_NOTNULL )
    {
        if ( p_iraw_l <= *p_oraw_ml )
        {
            memcpy( p_oraw, p_iraw, p_iraw_l );

            *p_oraw_l = p_iraw_l;
            *p_oraw_i = OCI_IND_NOTNULL;
        }
        else
        {
```

```
            raise_application_error( myCtx, ERROR_RAW_TOO_SMALL,
                    "Buffer of %d bytes needs to be %d",
                    *p_oraw_ml, p_iraw_l );
        }
    }
    else
    {
        *p_oraw_i = OCI_IND_NULL;
        *p_oraw_l =  0;
    }
    term(myCtx);
}
```

For our last `scalar` subroutine, we'll tackle LOBs. LOBs are not any harder or more complex then DATEs or NUMBERs. There are various OCI API calls that allow us to read and write them, copy them, compare them, and so on. In this example, we'll use API calls to determine the length, and then copy the input LOB to the OUTPUT LOB. This procedure requires the caller to initialize the LOB (either by selecting a LOB locator from an existing row in a table, or by utilizing `dbms_lob.createtemporary`). It should be noted that while we are demonstrating with a CLOB here, that the BLOB and BFILE implementations would be very similar – an OCILobLocator is used for all three types. More information on the functions you may use with the OCILobLocator type may be found in the *Oracle Call Interface Programmer's Guide*. This demonstration routine will simply copy the input CLOB to the output CLOB.

```c
#ifdef WIN_NT
_declspec (dllexport)
#endif
void pass_clob
  ( OCIExtProcContext * ctx          /* CONTEXT */,

    OCILobLocator *      p_iCLOB     /* OCILOBLOCATOR */,
    short                p_iCLOB_i   /* INDICATOR short */,

    OCILobLocator * *  p_oCLOB       /* OCILOBLOCATOR */,
    short *            p_oCLOB_i     /* INDICATOR short */
  )
{
ub4          lob_length;
myCtxStruct* myCtx;

    if ( (myCtx = init( ctx )) == NULL ) return;
    debugf( myCtx,  "Enter Pass Clob" );
    if ( p_iCLOB_i == OCI_IND_NOTNULL && *p_oCLOB_i == OCI_IND_NOTNULL )
    {
        debugf( myCtx,  "both lobs are NOT NULL" );

        if ( OCILobGetLength( myCtx->svchp, myCtx->errhp,
                        p_iCLOB, &lob_length ) != OCI_SUCCESS )
        {
            raise_application_error(myCtx,ERROR_OCI_ERROR,
                                "%s",lastOciError(myCtx));
        }
        else
        {
```

```
                  debugf( myCtx,   "Length of input lob was %d", lob_length );
                  if ( OCILobCopy(myCtx->svchp, myCtx->errhp, *p_oCLOB, p_iCLOB,
                              lob_length, 1, 1) != OCI_SUCCESS )
                  {
                      raise_application_error(myCtx,ERROR_OCI_ERROR,
                                          "%s",lastOciError(myCtx));
                  }
                  else
                  {

                      debugf( myCtx,   "We copied the lob!");
                  }
              }
          }
          else
          {
              raise_application_error( myCtx, ERROR_CLOB_NULL,
                              "%s %s clob was NULL",
                              (p_iCLOB_i == OCI_IND_NULL)?"input":"",
                              (*p_oCLOB_i== OCI_IND_NULL)?"output":"" );
          }
          term(myCtx);
      }
```

The following three routines demonstrate how to pass arrays of data back and forth between a stored procedure, and an external procedure. If you recall above, we created some SQL nested table types – a numArray, dateArray, and strArray. We will demonstrate with these types. In general, our routines will show how many array elements there are, dump their contents and populate the OUT array with those elements.

In these array routines, we will utilize the OCIColl* set of API calls. There are about 15 API calls we can use on collection (array) types to iterate over them, get or set their values, and so on. The ones we use below (the most common) are:

❑ OCICollSize to retrieve the number of elements in a collection.

❑ OCICollGetElem to retrieve the i'th element of an array.

❑ OCICollAppend to add an element to the end of an array.

Refer to the *Oracle Call Interface Programmer's Guide* for an exhaustive list of available functions.

We'll start with the array of numbers. This routine will simply iterate over all of the values in the IN collection, print them out, and assign them to the OUT collection:

```
#ifdef WIN_NT
_declspec (dllexport)
#endif
void pass_numArray
  ( OCIExtProcContext * ctx          /* CONTEXT */,
    OCIColl *           p_in         /* OCICOL  */,
    short               p_in_i       /* INDICATOR short */,
    OCIColl **          p_out        /* OCICOL  */,
    short *             p_out_i      /* INDICATOR short */
  )
  {
```

```
ub4         arraySize;
double      tmp_dbl;
boolean     exists;
OCINumber *ocinum;
int         i;
myCtxStruct*myCtx;

    if ( (myCtx = init( ctx )) == NULL ) return;
    debugf( myCtx,  "Enter Pass numArray" );

    if ( p_in_i == OCI_IND_NULL )
    {
        raise_application_error( myCtx, ERROR_ARRAY_NULL,
                                    "Input array was NULL" );
    }
    else

    if ( OCICollSize( myCtx->envhp, myCtx->errhp,
                    p_in, &arraySize ) != OCI_SUCCESS )
    {
        raise_application_error(myCtx,ERROR_OCI_ERROR,
                                "%s",lastOciError(myCtx));
    }
    else
    {
        debugf( myCtx,  "IN Array is %d elements long", arraySize );

        for( i = 0; i < arraySize; i++ )
        {
            if (OCICollGetElem( myCtx->envhp, myCtx->errhp, p_in, i,
                            &exists, (dvoid*)&ocinum, 0 ) != OCI_SUCCESS )
            {
                raise_application_error(myCtx,ERROR_OCI_ERROR,
                                        "%s",lastOciError(myCtx));
                break;
            }
            if (OCINumberToReal( myCtx->errhp, ocinum,
                            sizeof(tmp_dbl), &tmp_dbl ) != OCI_SUCCESS )
            {
                raise_application_error(myCtx,ERROR_OCI_ERROR,"%s",
                                        lastOciError(myCtx));
                break;
            }
            debugf( myCtx,  "p_in[%d] = %g", i, tmp_dbl );
            if ( OCICollAppend( myCtx->envhp, myCtx->errhp, ocinum, 0,
                            *p_out ) != OCI_SUCCESS )
            {
                raise_application_error(myCtx,ERROR_OCI_ERROR,
                                        "%s",lastOciError(myCtx));
                break;
            }
            debugf( myCtx,  "Appended to end of other array" );
        }
        *p_out_i = OCI_IND_NOTNULL;
    }
    term(myCtx);
}
```

Now, the next two routines do STRINGs and DATEs. They are very much similar to the number example above since they all work on OCIColl *. The strArray example is interesting in that it introduces a new OCI type – an OCIString (which is *not* a simple char *). We must do some double indirection with OCIString types. We'll do for strings and dates exactly what we did for numbers above:

```c
#ifdef WIN_NT
_declspec (dllexport)
#endif
void pass_strArray
  ( OCIExtProcContext * ctx          /* CONTEXT */,
    OCIColl *           p_in         /* OCICOL  */,
    short               p_in_i       /* INDICATOR short */,
    OCIColl **          p_out        /* OCICOL  */,
    short *             p_out_i       /* INDICATOR short */
  )
{
ub4        arraySize;
boolean    exists;
OCIString * * ocistring;
int        i;
text       *txt;
myCtxStruct*myCtx;

    if ( (myCtx = init( ctx )) == NULL ) return;
    debugf( myCtx,  "Enter Pass strArray" );

    if ( p_in_i == OCI_IND_NULL )
    {
        raise_application_error( myCtx, ERROR_ARRAY_NULL,
                                 "Input array was NULL" );
    }
    else if ( OCICollSize( myCtx->envhp, myCtx->errhp,
                    p_in, &arraySize ) != OCI_SUCCESS )
    {
        raise_application_error(myCtx,ERROR_OCI_ERROR,
                        "%s",lastOciError(myCtx));
    }
    else
    {
        debugf( myCtx,  "IN Array is %d elements long", arraySize );
        for( i = 0; i < arraySize; i++ )
        {
            if (OCICollGetElem( myCtx->envhp, myCtx->errhp, p_in, i, &exists,
                          (dvoid*)&ocistring, 0) != OCI_SUCCESS )
            {
                raise_application_error(myCtx,ERROR_OCI_ERROR,
                                "%s",lastOciError(myCtx));
                break;
            }
            txt = OCIStringPtr( myCtx->envhp, *ocistring );

            debugf( myCtx,  "p_in[%d] = '%s', size = %d, exists = %d",
                    i, txt, OCIStringSize(myCtx->envhp,*ocistring), exists );

            if ( OCICollAppend( myCtx->envhp,myCtx->errhp, *ocistring,
```

```
                                          0, *p_out ) != OCI_SUCCESS )
                {
                        raise_application_error(myCtx,ERROR_OCI_ERROR,
                                                "%s",lastOciError(myCtx));
                        break;
                }
                debugf( myCtx,  "Appended to end of other array" );
            }
            *p_out_i = OCI_IND_NOTNULL;
        }
        term(myCtx);
}


#ifdef WIN_NT
_declspec (dllexport)
#endif
void pass_dateArray
  ( OCIExtProcContext * ctx          /* CONTEXT */,

    OCIColl *           p_in         /* OCICOL  */,
    short               p_in_i       /* INDICATOR short */,

    OCIColl **          p_out        /* OCICOL  */,
    short *             p_out_i      /* INDICATOR short */
  )
{
ub4         arraySize;
boolean     exists;
OCIDate *   ocidate;
int         i;
char      * fmt = "Day, Month YYYY hh24:mi:ss";
ub4         buff_len;
char        buffer[255];
myCtxStruct*myCtx;

    if ( (myCtx = init( ctx )) == NULL ) return;
    debugf( myCtx,  "Enter Pass dateArray" );

    if ( p_in_i == OCI_IND_NULL )
    {
        raise_application_error( myCtx, ERROR_ARRAY_NULL,
                                        "Input array was NULL" );
    }
    else if ( OCICollSize( myCtx->envhp, myCtx->errhp,
                        p_in, &arraySize ) != OCI_SUCCESS )
    {
        raise_application_error(myCtx,ERROR_OCI_ERROR,
                                "%s",lastOciError(myCtx));
    }
    else
    {
        debugf( myCtx,  "IN Array is %d elements long", arraySize );

        for( i = 0; i < arraySize; i++ )
        {
            if (OCICollGetElem( myCtx->envhp, myCtx->errhp, p_in, i,
```

```
                                &exists, (dvoid*)&ocidate, 0 ) != OCI_SUCCESS )
            {
                raise_application_error(myCtx,ERROR_OCI_ERROR,
                                        "%s",lastOciError(myCtx));
                break;
            }

            buff_len = sizeof(buffer);
            if ( OCIDateToText( myCtx->errhp, ocidate, fmt, strlen(fmt),
                        NULL, -1, &buff_len, buffer ) != OCI_SUCCESS )
            {
                raise_application_error(myCtx,ERROR_OCI_ERROR,
                                        "%s",lastOciError(myCtx));
                break;
            }

            debugf( myCtx,   "p_in[%d] = %.*s", i, buff_len, buffer );

            if ( OCICollAppend( myCtx->envhp,myCtx->errhp, ocidate,
                            0, *p_out ) != OCI_SUCCESS )
            {
                raise_application_error(myCtx,ERROR_OCI_ERROR,
                                        "%s",lastOciError(myCtx));
                break;
            }
            debugf( myCtx,   "Appended to end of other array" );
        }
        *p_out_i = OCI_IND_NOTNULL;
    }
    term(myCtx);
}
```

Lastly, we'll look at functions that return values. This looks a little unusual because in PL/SQL we simply have functions that return a value and take no inputs but the C routines we should map to *must* have some inputs. That is, the simplest function in PL/SQL that takes no inputs, will map to a C routine that does have formal parameters. These formal parameters will be used by the external routine to tell Oracle things such as:

❑ Whether the function returned a Null or not Null value via an indicator.

❑ The current length of a STRING or RAW type.

So, we have seen these parameters before but they are just unexpected in a function.

```
#ifdef WIN_NT
_declspec (dllexport)
#endif
OCINumber * return_number
  ( OCIExtProcContext * ctx,
    short *             return_i )
{
double      our_number = 123.456;
OCINumber * return_value;
myCtxStruct*myCtx;
```

```
      *return_i = OCI_IND_NULL;
      if ( (myCtx = init( ctx )) == NULL ) return NULL;
      debugf( myCtx,  "Enter return Number" );
```

Here we must allocate storage for the number we are returning. We cannot just use a stack variable as it will go out of scope when we return. Using `malloc` would be a cause for a memory leak. Using a static variable would not work either as due to `extproc` caching, someone else can come along and alter the values we are pointing to after we return (but before Oracle has copied the value). Allocating storage is the only correct way to do this:

```
      return_value =
            (OCINumber *)OCIExtProcAllocCallMemory(ctx, sizeof(OCINumber) );

      if( return_value == NULL )
      {
          raise_application_error( myCtx, ERROR_OCI_ERROR,"%s","no memory" );
      }
      else
      {
          if ( OCINumberFromReal( myCtx->errhp, &our_number,
                      sizeof(our_number), return_value ) != OCI_SUCCESS )
          {
              raise_application_error(myCtx,ERROR_OCI_ERROR,
                                      "%s",lastOciError(myCtx));
          }
          *return_i = OCI_IND_NOTNULL;
      }
      term(myCtx);
      return return_value;
}
```

Returning a `date` is very similar to returning a `number`. The same memory issues apply. We'll allocate storage for our `date`, fill it in, set the indicator, and return:

```
#ifdef WIN_NT
_declspec (dllexport)
#endif
OCIDate * return_date
 ( OCIExtProcContext * ctx,
   short *             return_i )
{
OCIDate * return_value;
myCtxStruct*myCtx;

      if ( (myCtx = init( ctx )) == NULL ) return NULL;
      debugf( myCtx,  "Enter return Date" );

      return_value =
            (OCIDate *)OCIExtProcAllocCallMemory(ctx, sizeof(OCIDate) );

      if( return_value == NULL )
      {
          raise_application_error( myCtx, ERROR_OCI_ERROR, "%s","no memory" );
```

```
    }
    else
    {
        *return_i = OCI_IND_NULL;
        if ( OCIDateSysDate( myCtx->errhp, return_value ) != OCI_SUCCESS )
        {
            raise_application_error(myCtx,ERROR_OCI_ERROR,
                                    "%s",lastOciError(myCtx));
        }
        *return_i = OCI_IND_NOTNULL;
    }
    term(myCtx);
    return return_value;
}
```

With the string (the VARCHAR) return type we'll use two parameters – the indicator variable and the LENGTH field. This time, much like an OUT parameter, we set the LENGTH field to let the caller know how long the returned string is.

Many of the same considerations apply for returning strings as above; we'll allocate storage, set the indicator, supply the value, and return it:

```
#ifdef WIN_NT
_declspec (dllexport)
#endif
char * return_string
  ( OCIExtProcContext * ctx,
    short *             return_i,
    int    *            return_l )
{
char * data_we_want_to_return = "Hello World!";

char * return_value;
myCtxStruct*myCtx;

    if ( (myCtx = init( ctx )) == NULL ) return NULL;
    debugf( myCtx,  "Enter return String" );

    return_value = (char *)OCIExtProcAllocCallMemory(ctx,
                                    strlen(data_we_want_to_return)+1 );

    if( return_value == NULL )
    {
        raise_application_error( myCtx, ERROR_OCI_ERROR, "%s","no memory" );
    }
    else
    {
        *return_i = OCI_IND_NULL;
        strcpy( return_value, data_we_want_to_return );
        *return_l = strlen(return_value);
        *return_i = OCI_IND_NOTNULL;

    }
    term(myCtx);
    return return_value;
}
```

This concludes the C code necessary to demonstrate the passing of all 'interesting' types as IN and IN/OUT parameters or return via functions. We were also introduced to a great number of the OCI external procedure functions such as those for storing and retrieving a context to maintain state, process parameter files, and create/write OS files. What it explicitly did not show is:

❑ Sending and receiving *complex* object types to external procedures. They are similar to the array examples (as they send and receive simple object types). They would utilize the OCI object navigation features to manipulate the object type inputs and outputs.

❑ Returning every single type. We only covered strings, dates, and numbers. The remaining types are very similar (easier in fact since for ints and such, you do not even have to allocate storage).

Next, we will look at makefiles that we can use to build this external procedure on either UNIX or Windows.

Building the extproc

First we will look at a general purpose makefile for Windows:

```
CPU=i386

MSDEV       = c:\msdev                                          (1)
ORACLE_HOME = c:\oracle                                         (2)

!include <$(MSDEV)\include\win32.mak>                           (3)

TGTDLL  = extproc.dll                                           (4)
OBJS    = extproc.obj                                           (5)

NTUSER32LIBS    = $(MSDEV)\lib\user32.lib    \                  (6)
                  $(MSDEV)\lib\msvcrt.lib    \
                  $(MSDEV)\lib\oldnames.lib  \
                  $(MSDEV)\lib\kernel32.lib  \
                  $(MSDEV)\lib\advapi32.lib

SQLLIB = $(ORACLE_HOME)\precomp\lib\msvc\orasql8.lib  \         (7)
             $(ORACLE_HOME)\oci\lib\msvc\oci.lib

INCLS  = -I$(MSDEV)\include \                                   (8)
           -I$(ORACLE_HOME)\oci\include \
           -I.

CFLAGS = $(INCLS) -DWIN32 -DWIN_NT -D_DLL                       (9)

all: $(TGTDLL)                                                  (10)

clean:                                                          (11)
        erase *.obj *.lib *.exp

$(TGTDLL): $(OBJS)                                              (12)
        $(link) -DLL $(dllflags) \
          /NODEFAULTLIB:LIBC.LIB -out:$(TGTDLL) \
          $(OBJS) \
          $(NTUSER32LIBS) \
          $(SQLLIB)
```

*The **bold numbers** in parentheses are not part of the* makefile *but are there simply for reference below.*

1. *This is the path to where my C compiler is installed. I am using Microsoft Visual C/C++, which is the supported compiler on Windows. I will use this symbolic later in the makefile when I need to refer to this path.*

2. My ORACLE_HOME. This is used to find include files for OCI/Pro*C, and the Oracle supplied libraries.

3. I include the standard Microsoft makefile template. This gives symbolics for things like $(link) and $(dllflags), which may change from release to release of the compiler.

4. TGTDLL is the name of the DLL I am creating.

5. OBJS is a list of the object files I am using for this build. If I separated the code into many files, there would be more than one obj file listed here. In this simple, small example, we have only one obj file.

6. NTUSER32LIBS is a list of standard system libraries I am linking in.

7. SQLLIB is a list of Oracle supplied libraries we need. In this example, I am linking in *both* the Pro*C and OCI libraries, although we only make use of the OCI libraries at this time. It does not hurt to include Pro*C.

8. INCLS are the list of directories in which I have files I need to include. In here, I have the system header files, as well as the Oracle header files and the current working directory.

9. CFLAGS is the standard C macro used by the compiler. I define –DWIN_NT to allow the conditional code we have for NT, to compile on NT (the _declspec(dllexport) for example).

10. The all: target by default will build the DLL.

11. The clean: target removes temporary files created during a compile.

12. TGTDLL is the command that really creates the DLL for us. It will compile and link all of the code.

As a developer, I use and reuse this makefile constantly. Typically, I change only line (4), the output name), and line (5), the list of object code files. Other than that, the remaining components of the makefile, once configured to your system, is ready to go.

All we need do now is issue the nmake command and we should see something like:

```
C:\Documents and Settings\Thomas Kyte\Desktop\extproc\demo_passing>nmake

Microsoft (R) Program Maintenance Utility   Version 1.60.5270
Copyright (c) Microsoft Corp 1988-1995. All rights reserved.
```

```
        cl -Ic:\msdev\include  -Ic:\oracle\oci\include  -I. -DWIN32 -DWIN_NT -
D_DLL /c extproc.c
Microsoft (R) 32-bit C/C++ Optimizing Compiler Version 10.00.5270 for 80x86
Copyright (C) Microsoft Corp 1984-1995. All rights reserved.

extproc.c
        link -DLL   /NODEFAULTLIB:LIBC.LIB -out:extproc.dll  extproc.obj
c:\msdev\lib\user32.lib
  c:\msdev\lib\msvcrt.lib   c:\msdev\lib\oldnames.lib   c:\msdev\lib\kernel32.lib
c:\msdev\lib\adv
api32.lib  c:\oracle\precomp\lib\msvc\orasql8.lib   c:\oracle\oci\lib\msvc\oci.lib
Microsoft (R) 32-Bit Incremental Linker Version 3.00.5270
Copyright (C) Microsoft Corp 1992-1995. All rights reserved.

   Creating library extproc.lib and object extproc.exp
```

and that's it; our `extproc.dll` is built and ready to go. Now, let's port this to UNIX, using this `makefile` here:

```
MAKEFILE= $(ORACLE_HOME)/rdbms/demo/demo_rdbms.mk          (1)

INCLUDE= -I$(ORACLE_HOME)/rdbms/demo \                     (2)
        -I$(ORACLE_HOME)/rdbms/public \
        -I$(ORACLE_HOME)/plsql/public \
        -I$(ORACLE_HOME)/network/public

TGTDLL= extproc.so                                        (3)
OBJS  = extproc.o                                         (4)

all: $(TGTDLL)                                            (5)

clean:
    rm *.o                                                (6)

$(TGTDLL): $(OBJS)
    $(MAKE) -f $(MAKEFILE) extproc_callback \             (7)
      SHARED_LIBNAME=$(TGTDLL) OBJS=$(OBJS)

CC=cc                                                     (8)
CFLAGS= -g -I. $(INCLUDE) -Wall                           (9)
```

1. *Again, the **bold numbers** in parentheses are not part of the* `makefile` *but are there simply for reference below.*

2. The name/location of the standard Oracle `makefile`. I will use this `makefile` to cleanly compile and link with the required Oracle libraries on each platform/release. As these vary widely from release-to-release, version-to-version, and platform-to-platform, using this `makefile` is *highly* recommended.

3. A list of directories to search for includes. I have listed the Oracle directories here.

4. The name of the output library.

5. All of the files that make up this library.

6. The default target to make.

7. A target to remove temporary files created during the make.

8. The actual target itself. This uses the standard `makefile` supplied by Oracle, to build the extproc. This removes all issues with regards to library names/locations.

9. The name of the C compiler we want to use.

10. The standard set of options you want to pass to the C compiler.

Given the way we wrote the code, we are done with porting. All we need do is issue `make` and see something like the following:

```
$ make
cc -g -I. -I/export/home/ora816/rdbms/demo -I/export/home/ora816/rdbms/public -
I/export/home/ora816/plsql/public -I/export/home/ora816/network/public -Wall    -c
extproc.c -o extproc.o
make  -f /export/home/ora816/rdbms/demo/demo_rdbms.mk extproc_callback \
  SHARED_LIBNAME=extproc.so OBJS=extproc.o
make[1]: Entering directory `/aria-export/home/tkyte/src/demo_passing'
ld -G -L/export/home/ora816/lib -R/export/home/ora816/lib -o extproc.so extproc.o
-lclntsh `sed -e 's/-ljava//g' /export/home/ora816/lib/ldflags`        -lnsgr8 -
lnzjs8 -ln8 -lnl8 -lnro8 `sed -e 's/-ljava//g' /export/home/ora816/lib/ldflags`
-lnsgr8 -lnzjs8 -ln8 -lnl8 -lclient8  -lvsn8 -lwtc8 -lcommon8 -lgeneric8 -lwtc8 -
lmm -lnls8  -lcore8 -lnls8 -lcore8 -lnls8 `sed -e 's/-ljava//g'
/export/home/ora816/lib/ldflags`        -lnsgr8 -lnzjs8 -ln8 -lnl8 -lnro8 `sed -e
's/-ljava//g' /export/home/ora816/lib/ldflags`        -lnsgr8 -lnzjs8 -ln8 -lnl8 -
lclient8 -lvsn8 -lwtc8 -lcommon8 -lgeneric8 -ltrace8 -lnls8  -lcore8 -lnls8 -
lcore8 -lnls8 -lclient8 -lvsn8 -lwtc8 -lcommon8 -lgeneric8 -lnls8  -lcore8 -
lnls8 -lcore8 -lnls8    `cat /export/home/ora816/lib/sysliblist` `if [ -f
/usr/lib/libsched.so ] ; then echo -lsched ; else true; fi`   -
R/export/home/ora816/lib -laio  -lposix4 -lkstat -lm  -lthread \
/export/home/ora816/lib/libpls8.a
make[1]: Leaving directory `/aria-export/home/tkyte/src/demo_passing'
```

then we have our `extproc.so` file for Solaris.

Installing and Running

Now that we have our call specification, the create library, create types, and `demo_passing` package spec and body in `extproc.sql`, and `extproc.dll` (or `extproc.so`), we are ready to install the example into the database. To do so, we will simply execute `@extproc.sql` and then run a series of anonymous blocks to exercise our external procedure. You will need to customize the CREATE LIBRARY statement to point to your `.dll` or `.so`:

```
create or replace library demoPassing as
'C:\<LOCATION OF YOUR DLL>\extproc.dll';
```

but the rest should compile 'as is'.

So, after we run `extproc.sql`, we will test our external procedures as such:

```
SQL> declare
  2        l_input    number;
  3        l_output number;
  4  begin
  5      dbms_output.put_line( 'Pass Number' );
  6
  7      dbms_output.put_line('first test passing nulls to see that works');
  8      demo_passing_pkg.pass( l_input, l_output );
  9      dbms_output.put_line( 'l_input = '||l_input||
                                       ' l_output = '||l_output );
 10
 11      l_input := 123;
 12      dbms_output.put_line
              ( 'Now test passing non-nulls to see that works' );
 13      dbms_output.put_line( 'We expect the output to be -123' );
 14      demo_passing_pkg.pass( l_input, l_output );
 15      dbms_output.put_line
              ( 'l_input = '||l_input||' l_output = '||l_output );
 16  end;
 17  /
Pass Number
first test passing nulls to see that works
l_input =  l_output =
Now test passing non-nulls to see that works
We expect the output to be -123
l_input = 123 l_output = -123

PL/SQL procedure successfully completed.
```

I have a simple anonymous block to test each procedure/function in turn. We won't embed the output from each one from here on. Rather, there is a `test_all.sql` script included in the example code that exercises each procedure/function, and produces output similar to the above. You may execute this after installing the demo to see each one working.

Now, if you remember in the C code, we had a series of `debugf` statements. If, before executing the above block of PL/SQL, I simply make sure an `ext_proc.log` file exists in my temporary directory, we can see the output of `debugf`. It will look like this:

```
000809 185056 GMT (      extproc.c,176) Enter Pass Number
000809 185056 GMT (      extproc.c,183) Oci Environment Retrieved
000809 185056 GMT (      extproc.c,176) Enter Pass Number
000809 185056 GMT (      extproc.c,183) Oci Environment Retrieved
000809 185056 GMT (      extproc.c,209) The first parameter is 123
000809 185056 GMT (      extproc.c,230) Set OUT parameter to -123 and set indicator
to NOTNULL
```

This shows that on August 9, 2000 (`000809`) at 6:50:56PM (`185056`) GMT, the source code file `extproc.c` executed on line 176, the `debugf` statement that said `Enter Pass Number`. It goes on to record the rest of the `debugf` statements we executed. As you can see, having a trace file that we can turn on and off at will could be very handy in a debugging situation. Since external procedures run *on the server*, they can be notoriously hard to debug. While the opportunity to use a conventional debugger does exist, the practicality of that option is very limited.

LOB to File External Procedure (LOB_IO)

Oracle 8.0 introduced a set of new data types:

❑ CLOB – **C**haracter **L**arge **OB**ject.

❑ BLOB – **B**inary **L**arge **OB**ject.

❑ BFILE – **B**inary **FILE.**

Using a CLOB or BLOB, I can store upto 4 GBs of unstructured data in the database. Using a BFILE I can access OS files residing on the database server's filesystem in a read-only fashion. Oracle supplies a DBMS_LOB package with many utility routines to manipulate a LOB. It even provides a function to loadfromfile for loading a LOB from an existing OS file. What Oracle does not provide however, is a function to write a LOB to an OS file. UTL_FILE could be used for the CLOB type in many cases, but it could never be used for the BLOB type. We will implement a routine now using an external procedure written in C with Pro*C that permits us to write all CLOBs and BLOBs to a file.

The LOB_IO Call Specification

Again, we will start with a CREATE LIBRARY statement, then define our package specification, then a package body to map to the C routines, and finally, we'll implement our C routine using Pro*C. Starting with the library specification we have:

```
tkyte@TKYTE816> create or replace library lobToFile_lib
  2  as 'C:\extproc\lobtofile\extproc.dll'
  3  /
Library created.
```

And then the specificiation of the package we are creating. It starts with three overloaded functions to write a LOB to a file on our server. They are called in identical fashion and all return the number of bytes written to disk. The exceptions they might throw are listed below them.

```
tkyte@TKYTE816> create or replace package lob_io
  2  as
  3
  4      function write( p_path in varchar2,
  5                      p_filename in varchar2, p_lob in blob )
  6      return binary_integer;
  7
  8      function write( p_path in varchar2,
  9                      p_filename in varchar2, p_lob in clob )
 10      return binary_integer;
 11
 12      function write( p_path in varchar2,
 13                      p_filename in varchar2, p_lob in bfile )
 14      return binary_integer;
 15
 16      IO_ERROR exception;
 17      pragma exception_init( IO_ERROR, -20001 );
 18
 19      CONNECT_ERROR exception;
```

```
20        pragma exception_init( CONNECT_ERROR, -20002 );
21
22        INVALID_LOB exception;
23        pragma exception_init( INVALID_LOB, -20003 );
24
25        INVALID_FILENAME exception;
26        pragma exception_init( INVALID_FILENAME, -20004 );
27
28        OPEN_FILE_ERROR exception;
29        pragma exception_init( OPEN_FILE_ERROR, -20005 );
30
31        LOB_READ_ERROR exception;
32        pragma exception_init( LOB_READ_ERROR, -20006 );
33
34  end;
35  /
Package created.
```

Here we have taken every error code we might raise (the #define ERROR_ codes we define at the top of our extproc below) and have mapped them to named exceptions in PL/SQL. This is a nice touch that allows the user of our package to either catch a *named* exception like this:

```
exception
    when lob_io.IO_ERROR then
        ...
    when lob_io.CONNECT_ERROR then
        ...
```

or if they prefer, error codes and error messages instead of named exceptions like this:

```
exception
   when others then
        if (sqlcode = -20001 ) then -- (it was an IO error)
        ...
      elsif( sqlcode = -20002 )  then -- (it was a connect error)
            … and so on
```

It is also a nice way to determine exactly what errors might possible by raised by the external procedure without having to inspect the C code directly.

Now for the package body – this simply maps the PL/SQL specification from above to the C routine in our lobToFile library:

```
tkyte@TKYTE816> create or replace package body lob_io
  2  as
  3
  4  function write(p_path in varchar2,p_filename in varchar2,p_lob in blob)
  5  return binary_integer
  6  as
  7  language C name "lobToFile" library lobtofile_lib
  8  with context parameters ( CONTEXT,
  9    p_path       STRING,        p_path       INDICATOR short,
 10    p_filename STRING,          p_filename INDICATOR short,
```

```
11      p_lob       OCILOBLOCATOR, p_lob        INDICATOR short,
12      RETURN INDICATOR short );
13
14
15   function write(p_path in varchar2,p_filename in varchar2,p_lob in clob)
16   return binary_integer
17   as
18   language C name "lobToFile" library lobtofile_lib
19   with context parameters ( CONTEXT,
20      p_path      STRING,          p_path      INDICATOR short,
21      p_filename STRING,          p_filename INDICATOR short,
22      p_lob       OCILOBLOCATOR, p_lob        INDICATOR short,
23      RETURN INDICATOR short );
24
25
26   function write(p_path in varchar2,p_filename in varchar2,
                                                p_lob in bfile)
27   return binary_integer
28   as
29   language C name "lobToFile" library lobtofile_lib
30   with context parameters ( CONTEXT,
31      p_path      STRING,          p_path      INDICATOR short,
32      p_filename STRING,          p_filename INDICATOR short,
33      p_lob       OCILOBLOCATOR, p_lob        INDICATOR short,
34      RETURN INDICATOR short );
35
36   end lob_io;
37   /

Package body created.
```

It is somewhat interesting to note that all three functions map to the *same exact external C function*. I did not write a separate routine for CLOBs, BLOBs, and BFILEs. Since the LOB is passed as an OCILOBLOCATOR, they can all use the same routine. As usual, I am passing an indicator variable for each formal parameter, and one for the return value. While not mandatory, they are strongly encouraged.

The LOB_IO Pro*C Code

Now we'll inspect the Pro*C code we will generate to implement the lobtofile_lib library. I'm leaving the generic code we discussed in the first example out for brevity (the implementation of debugf, raise_application_error, ociLastError, term, and init are the same, with the exception that we use EXEC SQL REGISTER CONNECT in Pro*C applications in the init function) and will jump right into the code itself. It should be noted that the following code goes at the end of our 'template' code from above and that the relevant sections regarding connections with Pro*C would be uncommented in the template. We start with all of the errors we will possibly return. This set of error codes should match exactly with the named exceptions and their SQLCodes in our PL/SQL package specification. There is nothing to ensure that this is the case as this is purely a convention I use, but it is a good practice.

```
#define ERROR_FWRITE               20001
#define ERROR_REGISTER_CONNECT     20002
#define ERROR_BLOB_IS_NULL         20003
#define ERROR_FILENAME_IS_NULL     20004
```

```
#define ERROR_OPEN_FILE          20005
#define ERROR_LOB_READ           20006
```

Next comes an internal routine, not available to PL/SQL directly, which will be used by the main lobToFile routine to write bytes to a file. It also keeps a running total of the number of bytes written to the file:

```
static int writeToFile( myCtxStruct *        myCtx,
                        OCIFileObject *      output,
                        char *               buff,
                        int                  bytes,
                        int *                totalWritten )
{
ub4    bytesWritten;

    debugf( myCtx, "Writing %d bytes to output", bytes );
    if ( OCIFileWrite( myCtx->envhp, myCtx->errhp, output,
                    buff, bytes, &bytesWritten ) != OCI_SUCCESS )
    {
        return raise_application_error
                ( myCtx,
                  ERROR_FWRITE,
                  "Error writing to file '%s'",
                  lastOciError(myCtx) );
    }

    if ( bytesWritten != bytes )
    {
        return raise_application_error
                ( myCtx,
                  ERROR_FWRITE,
                  "Error writing %d bytes to file, only %d written",
                  bytes, bytesWritten );
    }
    *totalWritten += bytesWritten;
    return 0;
}
```

The first parameter to this routine is our session context. This context must be passed down to any routine so that we can call utilities such as raise_application_error. The next parameter is the output file we will be writing to. We are using the portable OCIFile functions to perform our I/O. It is expected that this file be already opened prior to calling writeToFile. Following that are the pointers to the buffer to write to, along with the number of bytes it currently is pointing to. Lastly is a counter variable we are using to keep a running total with.

Now for the main, (and the last) routine. This routine does all of the real work; it takes a LOB locator as an input (any of BLOB, CLOB, or BFILE) and writes the contents to the named file:

```
#ifdef WIN_NT
_declspec (dllexport)
#endif
int lobToFile( OCIExtProcContext * ctx,
            char *              path,
short                 path_i,
            char *              filename,
```

```
            short                    filename_i,
            OCIBlobLocator    *      blob,
            short                    blob_i,
            short *                  return_indicator )
{
```

This next part of the code defines the structure we will fetch into. It contains a leading byte count and then 64 KB of data space. We'll fetch 64 KB at a time from the LOB and write it to disk. It then goes onto define some other local variables we need:

```
typedef struct long_varraw
{
  ub4   len;
  text buf[65536];
} long_varraw;

EXEC SQL TYPE long_varraw IS LONG VARRAW(65536);

long_varraw     data;      /* we'll fetch into this */
ub4             amt;       /* this will be how much was fetched */
ub4             buffsize = sizeof(data.buf);  /* this is the amt we ask for*/
int             offset = 1; /* where in the lob we are currently reading */
OCIFileObject*  output = NULL; /* file we write to */
int             bytesWritten = 0; /* how many bytes we WROTE in total */
myCtxStruct *   myCtx;

    *return_indicator = OCI_IND_NULL;
    if ( (myCtx=init(ctx)) == NULL )  return 0;
```

We begin by inspecting the Null indicators. If either is set, we must fail the request. This points out the importance of *always* passing an indicator to an external procedure in C. You never know when the end user of your code will slip you a Null by accident. If we attempt to access filename or BLOB without checking first *and* they are Null – we may very well 'crash' (our extproc will crash) as they are not initialized.

```
    if ( blob_i == OCI_IND_NULL )
    {
        raise_application_error
               ( myCtx,
                 ERROR_BLOB_IS_NULL,
                 "Null lob passed to lobToFile, invalid argument" );
    }
    else if ( filename_i == OCI_IND_NULL || path_i == OCI_IND_NULL )
    {
        raise_application_error
               ( myCtx,
                 ERROR_FILENAME_IS_NULL,
                 "Null Filename/path passed to lobToFile, invalid argument");
    }
```

Now, open the output file. We open with the intent to 'write' in 'binary' mode We just want to dump bytes from the database to a file.

```
        else if ( OCIFileOpen( myCtx->envhp, myCtx->errhp, &output,
                        filename, path,
                        OCI_FILE_WRITE_ONLY, OCI_FILE_CREATE,
                        OCI_FILE_BIN ) != OCI_SUCCESS )
        {
            raise_application_error( myCtx,
                            ERROR_OPEN_FILE,
                            "Error opening file '%s'",
                            lastOciError(myCtx) );
        }
        else
        {
            debugf( myCtx, "lobToFile( filename => '%s%s', lob => %X )",
                    path, filename, blob );
```

We will now read the LOB using Pro*C in a *non-polling* method. This is important, as you cannot 'poll' for a LOB in an external procedure. Hence, we will never ask for more than we can receive in one call (non-polling). We start at offset 1 (the first byte) and will read BUFSIZE (64 KB in this case) bytes at a time. Every time through, we'll increment our offset by the amount we just read and we'll exit the loop when the amount read is less then the amount requested – indicating we have read the entire BLOB;

```
        for( offset = 1, amt = buffsize;
             amt == buffsize;
             offset += amt )
        {
            debugf( myCtx, "Attempt to read %d bytes from LOB", amt );
            EXEC SQL LOB
                    READ :amt
                    FROM :blob
                    AT   :offset
                    INTO :data
                    WITH LENGTH :buffsize;
```

Check for any *and* all errors, we'll convert that into *our* error message and add the real error message onto the PL/SQL error stack.

Note how we are careful to clean up any and all resources (the open file) before we return. This is important. You do not want to 'leak' resources if possible. We do this by returning from only one location (below) and calling term before we do so:

```
            if ( sqlca.sqlcode < 0 )
                break;

            if ( writeToFile(myCtx, output, data.buf, amt, &bytesWritten) )
                break;
        }
    }
```

All we need do now is close the file and return:

```
        if ( output != NULL )
        {
            debugf( myCtx, "Done and closing file" );
            OCIFileClose( myCtx->envhp, myCtx->errhp, output );
        }

        *return_indicator = OCI_IND_NOTNULL;
        debugf( myCtx, "Returning a value of %d for total bytes written",
                bytesWritten );

        term( myCtx );
        return bytesWritten;
}
```

Building the extproc

The process for building `lobtofile` is virtually identical as it was for the `demo_passing` library above. The generic `makefile` was utilized on both Windows and UNIX with minimal modification. On Windows we use:

```
CPU=i386

MSDEV       = c:\msdev
ORACLE_HOME = c:\oracle

!include <$(MSDEV)\include\win32.mak>

TGTDLL = extproc.dll
OBJS   = lobtofile.obj

NTUSER32LIBS   = $(MSDEV)\lib\user32.lib   \
                 $(MSDEV)\lib\msvcrt.lib   \
                 $(MSDEV)\lib\oldnames.lib   \
                 $(MSDEV)\lib\kernel32.lib   \
                 $(MSDEV)\lib\advapi32.lib

SQLLIB = $(ORACLE_HOME)\precomp\lib\msvc\orasql8.lib   \
         $(ORACLE_HOME)\oci\lib\msvc\oci.lib

INCLS  = -I$(MSDEV)\include   \
         -I$(ORACLE_HOME)\oci\include   \
         -I.

CFLAGS = $(INCLS) -DWIN32 -DWIN_NT -D_DLL

all: $(TGTDLL)

clean:
    erase *.obj *.lib *.exp lobtofile.c

$(TGTDLL): $(OBJS)
    $(link) -DLL $(dllflags)   \
        /NODEFAULTLIB:LIBC.LIB -out:$(TGTDLL)   \
        $(OBJS)   \
```

```
               $(NTUSER32LIBS) \
               $(SQLLIB) \

lobtofile.c: lobtofile.pc
        proc \
          include=$(ORACLE_HOME)\network\public \
          include=$(ORACLE_HOME)\proc\lib \
          include=$(ORACLE_HOME)\rdbms\demo \
          include=$(ORACLE_HOME)\oci\include \
          include=$(MSDEV) \include \
          lines=yes \
          parse=full \
          iname=lobtofile.pc
```

The only alterations are in **bold** font. We changed the name of the OBJ files we are linking in and we added the rule to convert lobtofile.pc into lobtofile.c for us. We simply invoke the command line Pro*C precompiler and tell it where our include files are (INCLUDE=), that we would like line numbers preserved in our .c file (lines=yes), that we would like to take full advantage of its ability to understand C (parse=full), and that the input filename to convert is lobtofile.pc (iname=). Now all we need do is issue nmake and our DLL will be built.

On UNIX, the makefile is:

```
MAKEFILE= $(ORACLE_HOME)/rdbms/demo/demo_rdbms.mk

INCLUDE= -I$(ORACLE_HOME)/rdbms/demo \
         -I$(ORACLE_HOME)/rdbms/public \
         -I$(ORACLE_HOME)/plsql/public \
         -I$(ORACLE_HOME)/network/public

TGTDLL= extproc.so
OBJS  = lobtofile.o


all: $(TGTDLL)

clean:
    rm *.o


lobtofile.c: lobtofile.pc
    proc \
        include=$(ORACLE_HOME)/network/public \
        include=$(ORACLE_HOME)/proc/lib \
        include=$(ORACLE_HOME)/rdbms/demo \
        include=$(ORACLE_HOME)/rdbms/public \
        lines=yes \
        iname=lobtofile.pc

extproc.so: lobtofile.c lobtofile.o
    $(MAKE) -f $(MAKEFILE) extproc_callback \
      SHARED_LIBNAME=extproc.so OBJS="lobtofile.o"

CC=cc
CFLAGS= -g -I. $(INCLUDE)
```

Again, the same exact alterations we made on Windows, we make on UNIX. We simply add the Pro*C precompile command and change the name of the object code we are linking. Type make and we have our .so file.

Now we are ready to test and use it.

Installing and Using LOB_IO

All we need to do now is run our CREATE LIBRARY, CREATE PACKAGE, and CREATE PACKAGE BODY. This installs the LOB_IO package into our database. To test it, we will use a couple of anonymous PL/SQL blocks. The first block we will execute exercises our error detection and handling. We will call our external procedure and deliberately pass it bad inputs, bad directory names, and the like. Here it is with comments explaining what we are expecting to see at each step:

```
SQL> REM for NT
SQL> REM define PATH=c:\temp\
SQL> REM define CMD=fc /b

SQL> REM for UNIX
SQL> define PATH=/tmp/
SQL> define CMD="diff -s"

SQL> drop table demo;
Table dropped.

SQL> create table demo( theBlob blob, theClob clob );
Table created.

SQL> /*
DOC> * the following block tests all of the error conditions we
DOC> * can test for. It does not test for IO_ERROR (we'd need a full
DOC> * disk or something for that) or CONNECT_ERROR (that should *never*
DOC> * happen)
DOC> */
SQL>
SQL> declare
  2      l_blob    blob;
  3      l_bytes number;
  4  begin
  5
  6      /*
  7       * Try a NULL blob
  8       */
  9      begin
 10          l_bytes := lob_io.write( '&PATH', 'test.dat', l_blob );
 11      exception
 12          when lob_io.INVALID_LOB then
 13              dbms_output.put_line( 'invalid arg caught as expected' );
 14              dbms_output.put_line( rpad('-',70,'-') );
 15      end;
```

```
16
17      /*
18       * Now, we'll try with a real blob and a NULL filename
19       */
20      begin
21          insert into demo (theBlob) values( empty_blob() )
22          returning theBlob into l_blob;
23
24          l_bytes := lob_io.write( NULL, NULL, l_blob );
25      exception
26          when lob_io.INVALID_FILENAME then
27              dbms_output.put_line( 'invalid arg caught as expected again' );
28              dbms_output.put_line( rpad('-',70,'-') );
29      end;
30
31      /*
32       * Now, try with an OK blob but a directory that does not exist
33       */
34      begin
35          l_bytes := lob_io.write( '/nonexistent/directory', 'x.dat', l_blob );
36      exception
37          when lob_io.OPEN_FILE_ERROR then
38              dbms_output.put_line( 'caught open file error expected' );
39              dbms_output.put_line( sqlerrm );
40              dbms_output.put_line( rpad('-',70,'-') );
41      end;
42
43      /*
44       * Lets just try writing it out to see that work
45       */
46      l_bytes := lob_io.write( '&PATH', '1.dat', l_blob );
47      dbms_output.put_line( 'Writing successful ' || l_bytes || ' bytes' );
48      dbms_output.put_line( rpad('-',70,'-') );
49
50      rollback;
51
52      /*
53       * Now we have a non-null blob BUT we rolled back so its an
54       * invalid lob locator.  Lets see what our extproc returns
55       * now...
56       */
57      begin
58          l_bytes := lob_io.write( '&PATH', '1.dat', l_blob );
59      exception
60          when lob_io.LOB_READ_ERROR then
61              dbms_output.put_line( 'caught lob read error expected' );
62              dbms_output.put_line( sqlerrm );
63              dbms_output.put_line( rpad('-',70,'-') );
64      end;
65  end;
66  /
old  10:            l_bytes := lob_io.write( '&PATH', 'test.dat', l_blob );
new  10:            l_bytes := lob_io.write( '/tmp/', 'test.dat', l_blob );
old  46:        l_bytes := lob_io.write( '&PATH', '1.dat', l_blob );
new  46:        l_bytes := lob_io.write( '/tmp/', '1.dat', l_blob );
old  58:            l_bytes := lob_io.write( '&PATH', '1.dat', l_blob );
```

```
new  58:           l_bytes := lob_io.write( '/tmp/', '1.dat', l_blob );

invalid arg caught as expected
-------------------------------------------------------------------
invalid arg caught as expected again
-------------------------------------------------------------------
caught open file error expected
ORA-20005: Error opening file 'ORA-30152: File does not exist'
-------------------------------------------------------------------
Writing successful 0 bytes
-------------------------------------------------------------------

PL/SQL procedure successfully completed.
```

As you can see, everything happened as expected. We forced many errors to happen and they happened exactly as planned. Now, let's use our package as it was intended. In order to test this, I'll create a *directory* object mapped to my temporary directory (/tmp on UNIX, C:\temp\ on Windows). A directory object is used by BFILEs to permit reading of files in a given directory. In the OS filesystem (/tmp or C:\temp\) I'll place a file to test with called something.big. This is just a fairly large file to test with. Its contents are not relevant. We will load this file into a CLOB, then a BLOB, and finally a temporary BLOB. We'll use our routine to write each of these to a separate file. We'll finish up by using OS utilities (diff on UNIX, FC on Windows) to compare the generated files with the original input file:

```
SQL> create or replace directory my_files as '&PATH.';
old  1: create or replace directory my_files as '&PATH.'
new  1: create or replace directory my_files as '/tmp/'

Directory created.

SQL>
SQL> declare
  2      l_blob    blob;
  3      l_clob    clob;
  4      l_bfile    bfile;
  5  begin
  6      insert into demo
  7      values ( empty_blob(), empty_clob() )
  8      returning theBlob, theClob into l_blob, l_clob;
  9
 10      l_bfile := bfilename ( 'MY_FILES', 'something.big' );
 11
 12      dbms_lob.fileopen( l_bfile );
 13
 14      dbms_lob.loadfromfile( l_blob, l_bfile,
 15                         dbms_lob.getlength( l_bfile ) );
 16
 17      dbms_lob.loadfromfile( l_clob, l_bfile,
 18                         dbms_lob.getlength( l_bfile ) );
 19
 20      dbms_lob.fileclose( l_bfile );
 21      commit;
 22  end;
 23  /

PL/SQL procedure successfully completed.
```

So, this has now loaded the file `something.big` into our database, once into a BLOB and then into a CLOB data element. Now, we'll write them back out:

```
SQL> declare
  2      l_bytes number;
  3      l_bfile    bfile;
  4  begin
  5      for x in ( select theBlob from demo )
  6      loop
  7          l_bytes := lob_io.write( '&PATH','blob.dat', x.theBlob );
  8          dbms_output.put_line( 'Wrote ' || l_bytes ||' bytes of blob' );
  9      end loop;
 10
 11      for x in ( select theClob from demo )
 12      loop
 13          l_bytes := lob_io.write( '&PATH','clob.dat', x.theclob );
 14          dbms_output.put_line( 'Wrote ' || l_bytes ||' bytes of clob' );
 15      end loop;
 16
 17      l_bfile := bfilename ( 'MY_FILES', 'something.big' );
 18      dbms_lob.fileopen( l_bfile );
 19      l_bytes := lob_io.write( '&PATH','bfile.dat', l_bfile );
 20      dbms_output.put_line( 'Wrote ' || l_bytes || ' bytes of bfile' );
 21      dbms_lob.fileclose( l_bfile );
 22  end;
 23  /
old   7:            l_bytes := lob_io.write( '&PATH','blob.dat', x.theBlob );
new   7:            l_bytes := lob_io.write( '/tmp/','blob.dat', x.theBlob );
old  13:            l_bytes := lob_io.write( '&PATH','clob.dat', x.theclob );
new  13:            l_bytes := lob_io.write( '/tmp/','clob.dat', x.theclob );
old  19:        l_bytes := lob_io.write( '&PATH','bfile.dat', l_bfile );
new  19:        l_bytes := lob_io.write( '/tmp/','bfile.dat', l_bfile );
Wrote 1107317 bytes of blob
Wrote 1107317 bytes of clob
Wrote 1107317 bytes of bfile

PL/SQL procedure successfully completed.
```

This shows that we successfully called our external procedure, and wrote the file out three times. Each time it was the same exact size (as expected). Now, we'll create a temporary LOB, copy the file into it, and write that out, just to make sure we can work with temporary LOBs as well:

```
SQL> declare
  2      l_tmpblob blob;
  3      l_blob    blob;
  4      l_bytes       number;
  5  begin
  6    select theBlob into l_blob from demo;
  7
  8    dbms_lob.createtemporary(l_tmpblob,TRUE);
  9
 10    dbms_lob.copy(l_tmpblob,l_blob,dbms_lob.getlength(l_blob),1,1);
 11
 12    l_bytes := lob_io.write( '&PATH','tempblob.dat', l_tmpblob );
 13    dbms_output.put_line( 'Wrote ' || l_bytes ||' bytes of temp_blob' );
 14
 15        DBMS_LOB.FREETEMPORARY(l_tmpblob);
```

```
   16  END;
   17  /
old 12:        l_bytes := lob_io.write( '&PATH','tempblob.dat', l_tmpblob );
new 12:        l_bytes := lob_io.write( '/tmp/','tempblob.dat', l_tmpblob );
Wrote 1107317 bytes of temp_blob

PL/SQL procedure successfully completed.
```

So, that was successful and, fortunately, it wrote the same number of bytes out for us. The last step is to use the OS utilities to verify the files we just wrote out are the same as what we loaded:

```
SQL> host &CMD &PATH.something.big &PATH.blob.dat
Files /tmp/something.big and /tmp/blob.dat are identical

SQL> host &CMD &PATH.something.big &PATH.clob.dat
Files /tmp/something.big and /tmp/clob.dat are identical

SQL> host &CMD &PATH.something.big &PATH.bfile.dat
Files /tmp/something.big and /tmp/bfile.dat are identical

SQL> host &CMD &PATH.something.big &PATH.tempblob.dat
Files /tmp/something.big and /tmp/tempblob.dat are identical
```

and that concludes this new feature; LOB_IO.

Errors You May Encounter

The following is a list of common errors you may encounter when using external procedures. Some of them we have talked about already, for example, the error you'll get if your listener or TNSNAMES.ORA file is not configured correctly, but many we have not. We'll look at them now, explaining when they would happen, and what you can do to correct them.

All of these errors are documented in the *Oracle 8i Error Messages Manual* as well.

ORA-28575 "unable to open RPC connection to external procedure agent"

```
28575, 00000, "unable to open RPC connection to external procedure agent"
// *Cause:  Initialization of a network connection to the extproc agent did
//          not succeed. This problem can be caused by network problems,
//          incorrect listener configuration, or incorrect transfer code.
// *Action: Check listener configuration in LISTENER.ORA and TNSNAMES.ORA, or
//          check Oracle Names Server.
```

This error almost always indicates an incorrectly configured TNSNAMES.ORA or LISTENER.ORA. We covered the possible causes and solutions for this error earlier in the *Configuring Your Server* section.

ORA-28576 "lost RPC connection to external procedure agent"

```
28576, 00000, "lost RPC connection to external procedure agent"
// *Cause:  A fatal error occurred in either an RPC network connection,
//          the extproc agent, or the invoked 3GL after communication had
//          been established successfully.
// *Action: First check the 3GL code you are invoking; the most likely
//          cause of this error is abnormal termination of the
//          invoked "C" routine. If this is not the case, check for
//          network problems. Correct the problem if you find it. If all
//          components appear to be normal but the problem persists, the
//          problem could be an internal logic error in the RPC transfer
//          code.  Contact your customer support representative.
//
```

This error, when reported against an external procedure you have written, almost certainly implies a bug in your developed code. This error occurs when the external process 'disappears'. This will happen if your program 'crashes'. For example, I added:

```
char * return_string
  ( OCIExtProcContext * ctx,
    short *             return_i,
    int    *            return_l )
{
  ...
    *return_i = OCI_IND_NOTNULL;
    *(char*)NULL = 1;
    return return_value;
}
```

to the bottom of my return_string example. After a recompile, I find the following:

```
ops$tkyte@ORA816.US.ORACLE.COM> exec dbms_output.put_line(
demo_passing_pkg.return_string )
BEGIN dbms_output.put_line( demo_passing_pkg.return_string ); END;

*
ERROR at line 1:
ORA-28576: lost RPC connection to external procedure agent
```

will always happen (until I debug and fix the code, of course).

ORA-28577 "argument %s of external procedure %s has unsupported datatype %s"

```
28577, 00000, "argument %s of external procedure %s has unsupported datatype %s"
// *Cause:  While transferring external procedure arguments to the agent,
//          an unsupported datatype was detected.
// *Action: Check your documentation for the supported datatypes of external
//          procedure arguments.
```

This error will occur if you try to pass a data type from PL/SQL to an external procedure that is not supported by this interface. In particular, an example of this would be a PL/SQL table type. If, in the demo_passing example, we had declared the numArray type in the package spec as:

```
       ...
       type numArray is table of number index by binary_integer;

       procedure pass( p_in in numArray, p_out out numArray );
       ...
```

instead of as a SQL nested table type as we did, we would find at run-time that:

```
  1  declare
  2       l_input    demo_passing_pkg.numArray;
  3       l_output   demo_passing_pkg.numArray;
  4  begin
  5       demo_passing_pkg.pass( l_input, l_output );
  6* end;
SQL> /
declare
*
ERROR at line 1:
ORA-28577: argument 2 of external procedure pass_numArray has unsupported datatype
ORA-06512: at "OPS$TKYTE.DEMO_PASSING_PKG", line 0
ORA-06512: at line 5
```

This is because the passing of PL/SQL table types is not supported (we can pass collections, but not PL/SQL table types).

ORA-28578 "protocol error during callback from an external procedure"

```
    28578, 00000, "protocol error during callback from an external procedure"
    // *Cause:  An internal protocol error occurred while trying to execute a
    //          callback to the Oracle server from the user's 3GL routine.
    // *Action: Contact Oracle customer support.
```

Hopefully, we never see this error and the one shown below. It would indicate an internal error within Oracle. The only thing to do upon receiving this error is to attempt to reproduce it with a very small testcase and report it to Oracle support.

ORA-28579 "network error during callback from external procedure agent"

```
    ORA-28579 "network error during callback from external procedure agent"
    // *Cause:  An internal network error occurred while trying to execute a
    //          callback to the Oracle server from the user's 3GL routine.
    // *Action: Contact Oracle customer support.
```

ORA-28580 "recursive external procedures are not supported"

```
    // *Cause:  A callback from within a user's 3GL routine resulted in the
    //          invocation of another external procedure.
    // *Action: Make sure that the SQL code executed in a callback does not directly
    //          call another external procedure, or indirectly results in another
    //          external procedure, such as triggers calling external
    //          procedures, PL/SQL procedures calling external procedures, etc.
```

This error will occur when you do a callback *from* an external procedure into the database, and the procedure you call performs another callout to another external procedure. In short, an external procedure cannot directly, or indirectly, call another external procedure. We can demonstrate this by modifying our LOB_IO .pc file. In this file, I added:

```
{ int x;

exec sql execute begin
    :x := demo_passing_pkg.return_number;
end; end-exec;

if ( sqlca.sqlcode < 0 )
{
    return raise_application_error
            ( ctx,
              20000,
              "Error:\n%.70s",
              sqlca.sqlerrm.sqlerrmc );
}
}
```

right after the REGISTER CONNECT call. Now, whenever I execute lob_io, we will receive:

```
ops$tkyte@DEV8I.WORLD> declare x clob; y number; begin y := lob_io.write( 'x', x
); end;
  2  /
declare x clob; y number; begin y := lob_io.write( 'x', x ); end;
*
ERROR at line 1:
ORA-20000: Error:
ORA-28580: recursive external procedures are not supported
ORA-06512:
ORA-06512: at "OPS$TKYTE.LOB_IO", line 0
ORA-06512: at line 1
```

The only solution is never to call another external procedure from an external procedure.

ORA-28582 "a direct connection to this agent is not allowed"

```
$ oerr ora 28582
28582, 00000, "a direct connection to this agent is not allowed"
// *Cause:  A user or a tool tried to establish a direct connection to either
//        an external procedure agent or a Heterogeneous Services agent,
//        for example: "SVRMGR> CONNECT SCOTT/TIGER@NETWORK_ALIAS".This type
//        of connection is not allowed.
//*Action: When executing the CONNECT statement, make sure your database
link
//        or network alias is not pointing to a Heterogeneous Option agent or
//        an external procedure agent.
```

We should never see this error. It will only happen when you attempt to connect to a database, and accidently use a service name that is configured to connect to an extproc service.

ORA-06520 "PL/SQL: Error loading external library"

```
$ oerr ora 6520
06520, 00000, "PL/SQL: Error loading external library"
// *Cause:  An error was detected by PL/SQL trying to load the external
//          library dynamically.
// *Action: Check the stacked error (if any) for more details.
```

This error should be followed up immediately by an OS-specific error. For example, to see this error I simply do the following:

```
$ cp lobtofile.pc extproc.so
```

I copied my source code over my .so file and that is defintely going to cause problems! Now when I run the external procedure, I receive:

```
declare x clob; y number; begin y := lob_io.write( 'x', x ); end;
*
ERROR at line 1:
ORA-06520: PL/SQL: Error loading external library
ORA-06522: ld.so.1: extprocPLSExtProc: fatal:
/export/home/tkyte/src/lobtofile/extproc.so: unknown file type
ORA-06512: at "OPS$TKYTE.LOB_IO", line 0
ORA-06512: at line 1
```

So, as you can see, the error stack contains the OS error which tells us this is an unknown type of file, and this will help you diagnose this error (in this case, it is easy to diagnose – extproc.so is actually some C code).

ORA-06521 "PL/SQL: Error mapping function"

```
$ oerr ora 6521
06521, 00000, "PL/SQL: Error mapping function"
// *Cause:  An error was detected by PL/SQL trying to map the mentioned
//          function dynamically.
// *Action: Check the stacked error (if any) for more details.
```

This error is typically the result of one of these two things:

❑   A typo in the name of the procedure either in the wrapper or in the C source code.

❑   Forgetting to export the function on Windows (_declspec(dllexport)).

To see this error, I modified the lobtofile.pc source code to have:

```
#ifdef WIN_NT
_declspec (dllexport)
#endif
int xlobToFile( OCIExtProcContext * ctx,
               char *              filename,
```

I added an x to the filename. Now when we run this, we receive:

```
declare x clob; y number; begin y := lob_io.write( 'x', x ); end;
*
ERROR at line 1:
ORA-06521: PL/SQL: Error mapping function
ORA-06522: ld.so.1: extprocPLSExtProc: fatal: lobToFile: can't find symbol
ORA-06512: at "OPS$TKYTE.LOB_IO", line 0
ORA-06512: at line 1
```

This shows that the error is can't find symbol, meaning we have a mismatch between the name name in the PL/SQL wrapper, and the name of the function in the external library. Either we have a typo, or we've forgotten to export the name (on Windows).

ORA-06523 "Maximum number of arguments exceeded"

```
$ oerr ora 6523
06523, 00000, "Maximum number of arguments exceeded"
// *Cause:  There is an upper limit on the number of arguments that one
//          can pass to the external function.
// *Action: Check the port specific documentation on how to calculate the
//          upper limit.
```

You will get this error if you have an unusually large parameter list. The number of elements that may be passed to an external procedure is about 128 (less if you pass doubles as they take 8 bytes, not 4). If you get this error, and you really need to send that many inputs, the easiest work-around is to use a collection type. For example:

```
 1  declare
 2      l_input    strArray := strArray();
 3      l_output   strArray := strArray();
 4  begin
 5      dbms_output.put_line( 'Pass strArray' );
 6      for i in 1 .. 1000 loop
 7          l_input.extend;
 8          l_input(i) := 'Element ' || i;
 9      end loop;
10      demo_passing_pkg.pass( l_input, l_output );
11      dbms_output.put_line( 'l_input.count = ' || l_input.count ||
12                           ' l_output.count = ' || l_output.count );
13      for i in 1 .. l_input.count loop
14          if ( l_input(i) != l_output(i) ) then
15              raise program_error;
16          end if;
17      end loop;
18* end;
SQL> /
Pass strArray
l_input.count = 1000 l_output.count = 1000

PL/SQL procedure successfully completed.
```

shows that I can send 1,000 strings, many times the limit on the number of scalars, to an external procedure via a collection.

ORA-06525 "Length Mismatch for CHAR or RAW data"

```
06525, 00000, "Length Mismatch for CHAR or RAW data"
// *Cause:  The length specified in the length variable has an illegal
//          value. This can happen if you have requested requested a PL/SQL
//          INOUT, OUT or RETURN raw variable to be passed as a RAW with
//          no corresponding length variable. This error can also happen
//          if there is a mismatch in the length value set in the length
//          variable and the length in the orlvstr or orlraw.
//
// *Action: Correct the external procedure code and set the length variable
//          correctly.
```

This error, if you follow my usage for sending and returning parameters, will only occur on the RAW type and a string that is returned from a function. The solution is very straightforward – you must set the length correctly. For a Null RAW OUT parameter, the length must be set to 0, as I did in the examples above. For a non Null RAW OUT parameter, the length must be set to some value less than or equal to MAXLEN. Likewise, for a string that we will return, the length must be set correctly (to less than MAXLEN but since you are responsible for setting the storage for the string, there is no MAXLEN so LENGTH must be less than or equal to 32760, which is the largest PL/SQL can handle).

ORA-06526 "Unable to load PL/SQL library"

```
$ oerr ora 6526
06526, 00000, "Unable to load PL/SQL library"
// *Cause:  PL/SQL was unable to instantiate the library referenced by this
//          referenced in the EXTERNAL syntax. This is a serious error and
//          should normally not happen.
//
// *Action: Report this problem to customer support.
```

This is an internal error. We should not see this, but if it appears, there are two things that can happen:

Firstly, this error can be accompanied by some other error with some more details. It might look like this:

```
ERROR at line 1: ORA-6526: Unable to load PL/SQL library
ORA-4030: out of process memory when trying to allocate 65036 bytes (callheap,KQL
tmpbuf)
```

This one is self-explanatory – we've run out of memory. We need to reduce the amount of memory we are using elsewhere.

Alternatively, the error message that accompanies the ORA-6526 doesn't lead us to any positive conclusions. In this case, we must contact support.

ORA-06527 "External procedure SQLLIB error: %s"

```
$ oerr ora 6527
06527, 00000, "External procedure SQLLIB error: %s"
// *Cause:  An error occurred in sqllib during execution of a Pro* external
```

```
//          procedure.
//
// *Action: The message text indicates the actual SQLLIB error that
//          occurred.  Consult the Oracle Error Messages and Codes manual
//          for a complete description of the error message and follow
//          the appropriate action.
```

This one is self-explanatory. The error message will contain more information.

Summary

In this chapter, we have covered the main issues surrounding external procedures such as:

❑   Maintaining a state using contexts.

❑   Using the OS-independent file APIs.

❑   Making our external procedure code parameterized using external parameter files.

❑   How to instrument our code (using debugf) to allow for 'debugging from afar'.

❑   How to code defensively (*always* pass the context, *always* pass the Null indicators, and so on).

❑   How to use a generic template to get your external procedures 'jump started' quickly, with lots of functionality.

❑   The differences between a pure OCI external procedure and one that uses Pro*C.

❑   How to map and pass the relevant PL/SQL data types to and from C.

❑   How to pass collections of data back and forth as well.

Given the generic template and makefiles above, you have all you need to write an external procedure from start to finish in a couple of minutes now. The tricky part is mapping the datatypes and the tables above, but that is easily accomplished by following the two tables in *The Wrapper* section – they tell you 'given this type, you will use that type'. Then, just follow the guidelines I have for passing the parameters in the example above (always send the context, always send the MAXLEN attribute for strings and raws, always send the Null indicator, and so on). If you do that, you'll be writing external procedures in no time.

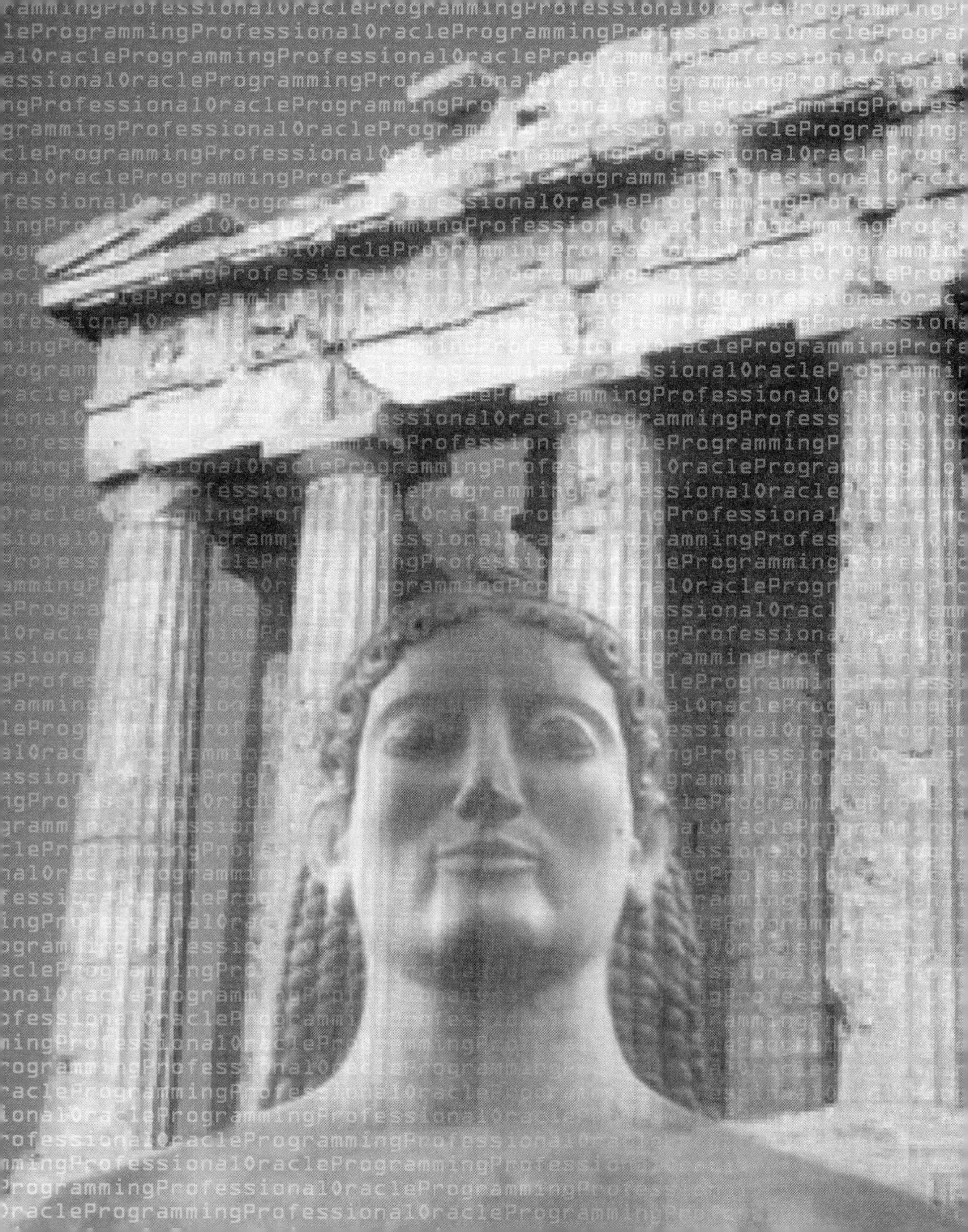

Java Stored Procedures

Oracle 8.1.5 introduced the ability to choose Java as a language to implement a stored procedure. PL/SQL has always been the natural choice and for 99 percent of what you need to do, it is still the right choice. Oracle 8.0 previously gave us the ability to implement a stored procedure in C, a feature we covered in Chapter 18, *C-Based External Routines.* Java-based stored procedures (another form of an external routine) are a natural extension of this capability, providing us with the ability to use Java where before, we might have used C or C++.

In short, this is just another choice. When you set about to develop a stored procedure, you now have at least three choices – PL/SQL, Java and C. I've listed them in my order of preference here. PL/SQL does most of the real database work, Java comes into play for things PL/SQL cannot do (mostly OS interfaces), and C comes into play when I have existing C code, or because there is some reason I cannot do it in Java.

This chapter is not an introduction to Java, JDBC, or SQLJ programming. It assumes you have at least a cursory knowledge of Java and would be able to read through small bits of Java code. It also assumes at least a cursory knowledge of JDBC and SQLJ – although if you have a little Java experience, you should be able to read through the JDBC and SQLJ parts without issue.

Why Use Java Stored Procedures?

Java external routines differ from C-based routines in that, much like PL/SQL, the Java runs natively in Oracle's JVM, right in the address space of the database. With C-based external procedures, we had to configure a listener, set up the TNSNAMES.ORA file, and have a separate process running. None of this is necessary with Java because, as an interpreted language, it is deemed as being 'safe' in much the same way as PL/SQL. It is not possible to develop a Java routine that overwrites some part of the SGA. This has its pros and cons, as we will discuss. The fact that it is running in the same address space allows the interaction between Java and the database to be a little smoother – there is less context switching between processes at the OS level, for example. On the downside, however, the Java code is always running as the 'Oracle software owner', meaning a Java stored procedure could overwrite the database's INIT.ORA parameter file (or some other, even more important set of files, such as the data files) if it has been given the appropriate privileges.

I find myself using a little Java every now and then to do things I cannot do in PL/SQL. For example, in Appendix A, *Necessary Supplied Packages*, I show how I implemented a TCP/IP socket package using Java. I did this in Oracle 8.1.5 before UTL_TCP was available (which is really written in Java as well), and still find it preferable. I also use Java to send e-mail from the database. Again, a package already exists, UTL_SMTP (built on Java as well), that can send simple e-mails, but Java makes many other options available, including the ability to send (and receive) e-mails with attachments.

I use UTL_FILE a lot, to read and write files in PL/SQL. One of the things missing in UTL_FILE is the ability to get a directory listing. PL/SQL cannot do this – Java can quite easily.

Occasionally, it would be convenient to run an operating system command or program from within the database. Again, PL/SQL won't facilitate this, but Java easily does. On a few occasions, I need to know the time zone on the server – PL/SQL cannot find this out but Java can (we explore that functionality in Appendix A, *Necessary Supplied Packages*, on UTL_TCP). Need the time down to milliseconds? In Oracle 8i, Java can do it.

If we need to connect to a DB2 database to run a query every now and then, we could do this with the Transparent Gateway to DB2. This would give us full heterogeneous database joins, distributed transactions, transparent two-phase commits, and many other options. But, if we only need to run a simple query or update on DB2, without any of the other fancy features, then we could simply load the DB2 Java JDBC drivers into the database, and do it that way (this doesn't only apply to DB2, of course).

Basically, any of the millions of non-interactive (no user interface) pieces of Java code that are out there, can be loaded into Oracle and used. That is why you will use snippets of Java here and there in your applications.

In short, my philosophy is to use Java only when it is sensible and useful to do so. I still find PL/SQL to be the right choice for the vast majority of my stored procedures. I can write one or two lines of PL/SQL code to achieve the same thing that would need many lines of Java/JDBC code. SQLJ cuts down on the code I might have to write, but it will not perform as well as PL/SQL and SQL together. The run-time performance of PL/SQL interacting with SQL is simply better than that for Java/JDBC, as you might expect. PL/SQL is designed around SQL, the integration between the two is very tight. PL/SQL data types are in general SQL data types and all SQL data types are PL/SQL data types – there is no impedance mismatch between the two. SQL access in Java, on the other hand, is by the means of an API added to the language. Every SQL type must be converted to some Java type and back again, all SQL access is procedural – there is no tight coupling between the two. In short, if you are manipulating data in the database, PL/SQL is the way to go. If you need to jump out of the database for a moment (to send an e-mail perhaps), Java is the most appropriate tool. If you need to search through stored e-mails in your database, use PL/SQL. If you need to get the e-mails into your database in the first place, then use Java.

How They Work

You will find Java external routines ('external routine' being synonymous with 'stored procedure') to be much easier to implement than C-based external routines. For example, in the previous chapter on *C-Based External Routines*, we had to be concerned with the following issues:

- ❑ **State management** – External procedures can, and will, 'lose' their state (current values of 'static' or 'global' variables). This is due to the DLL caching that is implemented. Therefore, we need a mechanism for establishing and persisting a state in our C programs.

- ❑ **Tracing mechanisms** – External procedures run on the server in their *own* process, outside of the server processes. While it is possible, on various platforms, to debug these routines using a conventional debugger, it is quite difficult and can be impossible if the bugs only arise when many people use the external procedure concurrently. We need a facility to generate copious trace files on demand to 'debug from afar'.

- ❑ **Parameter setting** – We need a facility that allows us to parameterize our external procedures so that we can easily change their behavior externally, using a parameter file, much like we do with the `init.ora` file and the database.

- ❑ **Generic Error Handling** – We need a facility to easily report meaningful errors to the end user.

With Java you'll find that state management, tracing, and generic error handling, are not a problem. For state management, we just declare variables in our Java classes. For simple tracing requirements we can use `System.out.println`. Generic error handling is taken care of with a call to the `RAISE_APPLICATION_ERROR` PL/SQL function. All of this is demonstrated in the following code:

```
tkyte@TKYTE816> create or replace and compile
  2  java source named "demo"
  3  as
  4  import java.sql.SQLException;
  5
  6  public class demo extends Object
  7  {
  8
  9  static int counter = 0;
 10
 11  public static int IncrementCounter() throws SQLException
 12  {
 13      System.out.println( "Enter IncrementCounter, counter = "+counter);
 14      if ( ++counter >= 3 )
 15      {
 16          System.out.println( "Error! counter="+counter);
 17          #sql {
 18          begin raise_application_error( -20001, 'Too many calls' ); end;
 19          };
 20      }
 21      System.out.println( "Exit IncrementCounter, counter = "+counter);
 22      return counter;
 23  }
 24  }
 25  /

Java created.
```

We maintain a state through a static `counter` variable. Our simple `demo` routine will increment the counter each time it is called and on the third, and any subsequent, call it will raise an error for us.

Notice how for small snippets of code such as this, we can just use SQL*PLUS to load our Java code straight into the database, have it compiled into byte code and stored for us. There is no need for an external compiler, no JDK installs – just a SQL CREATE OR REPLACE statement. I prefer to do most of my Java stored procedures this way. It makes it very easy to install on any platform. I don't have to prompt for a username/password as I would with the LOADJAVA command (a command line tool to load Java source, classes, or jar files into the database). I don't have to worry about classpaths, and so on. In the Appendix A on *Necessary Supplied Packages*, we will take a look at LOADJAVA, in particular the DBMS_JAVA package interface to LOADJAVA.

This method (using CREATE OR REPLACE) of loading small Java routines into the database is particularly appropriate for people wanting to get their feet wet using this technology. Rather then installing the JDBC drivers, a JDK, an environment to compile in, setting up classpaths – you just compile straight into the database, in exactly the same way you would with PL/SQL. You would find compile time errors in the same way you do with PL/SQL as well, for example:

```
tkyte@TKYTE816> create or replace and compile
  2  java source named "demo2"
  3  as
  4
  5  public class demo2 extends Object
  6  {
  7
  8  public static int my_routine()
  9  {
 10      System.out.println( "Enter my_routine" );
 11
 12      return counter;
 13  }
 14  }
 15  /

Warning: Java created with compilation errors.

tkyte@TKYTE816> show errors java source "demo2"
Errors for JAVA SOURCE demo2:

LINE/COL ERROR
-------- -------------------------------------------------------
0/0      demo2:8: Undefined variable: counter
0/0      Info: 1 errors
```

That shows me that `my_routine` defined on line 8 is accessing a variable I did not declare – I don't have to guess at the error in the code it is shown to me. I've found many times that the frustrations of trying to get the JDBC/JDK/CLASSPATH setup correctly can be overcome in seconds using this easy approach.

Now, back to the working example. There is another important detail to note in the demo class above. The entry point method that is called from SQL, `IncrementCounter`, is static. It must be static (not everything must be static. You can use 'regular' methods from then on out). The SQL layer needs at least one method it can call, without having to pass the implicit instance data as a hidden parameter, hence the need for a static method.

Now that I have a small Java routine loaded up, I need to create a call specification for it in PL/SQL. This step is very similar to that seen in Chapter18, *C-Based External Procedures*, where we mapped the C data types to the SQL data types. We are doing the same exact thing here; only this time we are mapping Java data types to SQL data types:

```
tkyte@TKYTE816> create or replace
  2  function java_counter return number
  3  as
  4  language java
  5  name 'demo.IncrementCounter() return integer';
  6  /

Function created.
```

Now we are ready to call it:

```
tkyte@TKYTE816> set serveroutput on

tkyte@TKYTE816> exec dbms_output.put_line( java_counter );
1
PL/SQL procedure successfully completed.

tkyte@TKYTE816> exec dbms_output.put_line( java_counter );
2
PL/SQL procedure successfully completed.

tkyte@TKYTE816> exec dbms_output.put_line( java_counter );
BEGIN dbms_output.put_line( java_counter ); END;

*
ERROR at line 1:
ORA-29532: Java call terminated by uncaught Java exception:
oracle.jdbc.driver.OracleSQLException:
ORA-20001: Too many calls
ORA-06512: at line 1
ORA-06512: at "TKYTE.JAVA_COUNTER", line 0
ORA-06512: at line 1
```

We can see the state management is done for us as evidenced by the counter being incremented from 1 to 2 to 3. We can see that we can communicate errors easily enough, but where did our System.out.println calls go? By default, they will go into a trace file. If you have access to V$PROCESS, V$SESSION, and V$PARAMETER, we can determine the name of the trace file in a dedicated server configuration this way (this example is setup for Windows – it would be similar on UNIX but the filename you select would be slightly different):

```
tkyte@TKYTE816>select c.value||'\ORA'||to_char(a.spid,'fm00000')||'.trc'
  2         from v$process a, v$session b, v$parameter c
  3        where a.addr = b.paddr
  4          and b.audsid = userenv('sessionid')
  5          and c.name = 'user_dump_dest'
  6  /

C.VALUE||'\ORA'||TO_CHAR(A.SPID,'FM00000')||'.TRC'
------------------------------------------------------------
```

```
C:\oracle\admin\tkyte816\udump\ORA01236.trc

tkyte@TKYTE816> edit C:\oracle\admin\tkyte816\udump\ORA01236.trc
```

When I looked at that file, I found:

```
Dump file C:\oracle\admin\tkyte816\udump\ORA01236.TRC
Tue Mar 27 11:15:48 2001
ORACLE V8.1.6.0.0 - Production vsnsta=0
vsnsql=e vsnxtr=3
Windows 2000 Version 5.0 , CPU type 586
Oracle8i Enterprise Edition Release 8.1.6.0.0 - Production
With the Partitioning option
JServer Release 8.1.6.0.0 - Production
Windows 2000 Version 5.0 , CPU type 586
Instance name: tkyte816
Redo thread mounted by this instance: 1
Oracle process number: 12
Windows thread id: 1236, image: ORACLE.EXE

*** 2001-03-27 11:15:48.820
*** SESSION ID:(8.11) 2001-03-27 11:15:48.810
Enter IncrementCounter, counter = 0
Exit IncrementCounter, counter = 1
Enter IncrementCounter, counter = 1
Exit IncrementCounter, counter = 2
Enter IncrementCounter, counter = 2
Error! counter=3
oracle.jdbc.driver.OracleSQLException: ORA-20001: Too many calls
ORA-06512: at line 1
...
```

I could use the DBMS_JAVA package to redirect this output to the SQL*PLUS screen as well, to avoid having to use the trace files while debugging the routine. We'll come back to the DBMS_JAVA package in this section from time to time, but for a complete overview see the section on it in Appendix A, *Necessary Supplied Packages*.

One thing that is clear from this small example, is that when compared to a C-based external procedure, this is easy. I need no special setup on the server (other than having Java itself installed in the database). I need no external compiler. Many of the facilities we had to code in C are provided out of the box for us. This is easy.

The one thing that I skipped over, are the parameters to configure your Java routines. The reason for doing this is because Java supplies built-in functionality for this, in the form of the java.util.Properties class. You would simply use the load method of this class to load a previously saved set of properties either from a LOB in a database table, or from an OS file – whichever is more flexible for you.

In the remainder of this section, I will give a couple of useful examples of Java stored procedures, such as the ones listed in the *Why Use Java Stored Procedures* section of this chapter. Before we do that, I would like to implement the same DEMO_PASSING_PKG for Java that we did for C, just to get a grasp on how to pass the common data types back and forth between SQL and Java external routines.

Passing Data

The routines I would like to implement in this example will be a series of procedures that accept an `IN` parameter, and an `OUT` (or `IN OUT`) parameter. We will write one for each type of interesting data type (the ones we will use frequently). They will demonstrate the correct way to pass as inputs, and receive as outputs, each of these types. Additionally, I would like to have some functions that show how to return some of these interesting types as well. To me the interesting types with Java are:

- ❑ `Strings` (up to 32k)
- ❑ `Numbers` (of any scale/precision)
- ❑ `Dates`
- ❑ `Integers` (`binary_integers`)
- ❑ `RAWs` (up to 32k)
- ❑ `LOBS` (for all data > 32k)
- ❑ Arrays of `Strings`
- ❑ Arrays of `Numbers`
- ❑ Arrays of `Dates`

This list is a little different from that for C-based external routines. Specifically, `BOOLEAN` is not represented. This is because there currently exists no mapping between the PL/SQL `BOOLEAN` type, and the Java types. We cannot use `BOOLEAN`s as parameters in our Java external procedures.

There are also the arbitrarily complex data types you can create with the object relational extensions. For those, I would recommend you consider using the Oracle-supplied Java tool **JPublisher**. This tool will create Java classes that wrap the object types for you automatically. For more information on JPublisher please refer to the 'Oracle8i JPublisher User's Guide', part of the Oracle supplied documentation set. As with C-based external routines, we will not be going into object types in Java external routines, beyond the simple collections of scalar types.

Our Java class will be a re-implementation of the C-based external routine we coded earlier, only this time it is, of course, written in Java. We'll begin with the SQL definition of our three collection types – these are the same definitions we used in the C External Procedures example as well:

```
tkyte@TKYTE816> create or replace type numArray as table of number;
Type created.

tkyte@TKYTE816> create or replace type dateArray as table of date;
Type created.

tkyte@TKYTE816> create or replace type strArray as table of varchar2 (255);
Type created.
```

Now, the PL/SQL call specification for our example will be as follows. It will be a series of overloaded procedures and functions to test passing parameters to and from Java stored procedures. Each routine has an `IN` and an `OUT` parameter to show data being sent to and returned from the Java code.

The first routine passes the number type. Oracle Numbers will be passed to Java `BigDecimal` types. They could be passed to `int`, `string`, and other types but could suffer from the loss of precision. `BigDecimal` can hold an Oracle number safely.

Notice how the OUT parameter is passed as an array of BigDecimal types to the Java layer. This will be true of all OUT parameters passed to Java. In order to modify a parameter passed to Java, we must pass an 'array' of parameters (there will only be a single element in this array) and modify that array element. Below, in the implementation of the Java code, we'll see what that means in our source code.

```
tkyte@TKYTE816> create or replace package demo_passing_pkg
  2  as
  3      procedure pass( p_in in number, p_out out number )
  4      as
  5      language java
  6      name 'demo_passing_pkg.pass( java.math.BigDecimal,
  7                                   java.math.BigDecimal[] )'
```

Next, Oracle Dates are mapped to the Timestamp type. Again, they could have been mapped to a variety of different types – such as a String but in order to avoid any loss of information during the implicit conversions, I chose the Timestamp type, which can accurately reflect the data contained in the Oracle Date type.

```
  8
  9      procedure pass( p_in in date, p_out out date )
 10      as
 11      language java
 12      name 'demo_passing_pkg.pass( java.sql.Timestamp,
 13                                   java.sql.Timestamp[] )';
```

VARCHAR2s are very straightforward – they are passed to the java.lang.String type as you might expect.

```
 14
 15      procedure pass( p_in in varchar2, p_out out varchar2 )
 16      as
 17      language java
 18      name 'demo_passing_pkg.pass( java.lang.String,
 19                                   java.lang.String[] )';
```

For the CLOB type, we use the Oracle supplied Java type oracle.sql.CLOB. Using this type, we'll easily be able to get the input and output streams used to read and write CLOB types.

```
 20
 21      procedure pass( p_in in CLOB, p_out in out CLOB )
 22      as
 23      language java
 24      name 'demo_passing_pkg.pass( oracle.sql.CLOB,
 25                                   oracle.sql.CLOB[] )';
```

Now for the collection types: we see that we will use the same Oracle supplied type regardless of the type of collection we are actually passing. That is why in this case, the Java routines are not overloaded routines as they have all been so far (all of the Java routines have been named demo_passing_pkg.pass so far). Since each of the collection types are passed as the exact same Java type – we cannot use overloading in this case – rather we have a routine named after the type we are actually passing:

```
26
27        procedure pass( p_in in numArray, p_out out numArray )
28        as
29        language java
30        name 'demo_passing_pkg.pass_num_array( oracle.sql.ARRAY,
31                                               oracle.sql.ARRAY[] )';
32
33        procedure pass( p_in in dateArray, p_out out dateArray )
34        as
35        language java
36        name 'demo_passing_pkg.pass_date_array( oracle.sql.ARRAY,
37                                                oracle.sql.ARRAY[] )';
38
39        procedure pass( p_in in strArray, p_out out strArray )
40        as
41        language java
42        name 'demo_passing_pkg.pass_str_array( oracle.sql.ARRAY,
43                                               oracle.sql.ARRAY[] )';
```

The next two routines demonstrate the mapping we will use for the RAW and INT types. The SQL RAW type will be mapped to the native Java byte type. Likewise, we will use the native Java type int for simple integers:

```
44
45        procedure pass_raw( p_in in RAW, p_out out RAW )
46        as
47        language java
48        name 'demo_passing_pkg.pass( byte[], byte[][] )';
49
50        procedure pass_int( p_in    in number,
51                            p_out   out number )
52        as
53        language java
54        name 'demo_passing_pkg.pass_int( int, int[] )';
```

Lastly, for completeness, we will demonstrate using functions to return the basic scalar types as well:

```
55
56        function return_number return number
57        as
58        language java
59        name 'demo_passing_pkg.return_num() return java.math.BigDecimal';
60
61        function return_date return date
62        as
63        language java
64        name 'demo_passing_pkg.return_date() return java.sql.Timestamp';
65
66        function return_string return varchar2
67        as
68        language java
69        name 'demo_passing_pkg.return_string() return java.lang.String';
70
71  end demo_passing_pkg;
72  /

Package created.
```

This is basically the same package specification (minus the BOOLEAN) interface that we used for the C-based external routines. In this example, I have put the binding layer right into the specification itself, to avoid having to code an entirely redundant package body (every function is implemented in Java).

Now for the Java code that implements the above. We'll start with the definition of the demo_passing_pkg Java class:

```
tkyte@TKYTE816> set define off

tkyte@TKYTE816> create or replace and compile
  2    java source named "demo_passing_pkg"
  3    as
  4    import java.io.*;
  5    import java.sql.*;
  6    import java.math.*;
  7    import oracle.sql.*;
  8    import oracle.jdbc.driver.*;
  9
 10    public class demo_passing_pkg extends Object
 11    {
```

This first routine, shown below, demonstrates the only way to pass an OUT parameter to Java; we actually pass an 'array' and the first element in the array is the only element in the array. When we modify the value in the array, we will have modified the OUT parameter. That is why all of these methods have their second parameter as an array. p_out[0] is something we can set and it will be sent 'out' of the method. Any changes we make to p_in on the other hand will not be returned.

The other interesting thing to note in this routine is the lack of need for an indicator variable! Java supports the concept of null in its object types as does SQL and PL/SQL. It is not tri-valued logic like SQL is, however – there is no X IS NOT NULL operation, we can just compare an object to null directly. Don't get confused and try to code something like p_in <> NULL in PL/SQL, it'll never work correctly!

```
 12    public static void pass( java.math.BigDecimal p_in,
 13                             java.math.BigDecimal[] p_out )
 14    {
 15        if ( p_in != null )
 16        {
 17            System.out.println
 18            ( "The first parameter is " + p_in.toString() );
 19
 20            p_out[0] = p_in.negate();
 21
 22            System.out.println
 23            ( "Set out parameter to " + p_out[0].toString() );
 24        }
 25    }
```

The next routine operates on Oracle Date types. This is virtually identical to the above routine but we use the methods of the Timestamp class to manipulate the date. Our goal in this routine is to add one month to the date:

```
26
27   public static void pass( java.sql.Timestamp p_in,
28                            java.sql.Timestamp[] p_out )
29   {
30       if ( p_in != null )
31       {
32           System.out.println
33           ( "The first parameter is " + p_in.toString() );
34
35           p_out[0] = p_in;
36
37           if ( p_out[0].getMonth() < 11 )
38               p_out[0].setMonth( p_out[0].getMonth()+1 );
39           else
40           {
41               p_out[0].setMonth( 0 );
42               p_out[0].setYear( p_out[0].getYear()+1 );
43           }
44           System.out.println
45           ( "Set out parameter to " + p_out[0].toString() );
46       }
47   }
```

Now for the simplest of data types; the `String` type. If you remember the C version with six formal parameters, null indicators, `strlens`, `strcpys`, and so on – this is trivial in comparison:

```
48
49   public static void pass( java.lang.String p_in,
50                            java.lang.String[] p_out )
51   {
52       if ( p_in != null )
53       {
54           System.out.println
55           ( "The first parameter is " + p_in.toString() );
56
57           p_out[0] = p_in.toUpperCase();
58
59           System.out.println
60           ( "Set out parameter to " + p_out[0].toString() );
61       }
62   }
```

In the CLOB routine, we have a little bit of work to do. This routine implements a 'copy' routine to show how to pass LOBs back and forth. It shows that in order to modify/read the contents of the LOB, we just use standard Java input/output stream types. In this example `is` is my input stream and `os` is the output stream. The logic in this routine does this copy 8K at a time. It just loops, reads, writes, and then exits when there is no more to read:

```
63
64   public static void pass( oracle.sql.CLOB p_in,
65                            oracle.sql.CLOB[] p_out )
66   throws SQLException, IOException
67   {
68       if ( p_in != null && p_out[0] != null )
```

```
69       {
70           System.out.println
71           ( "The first parameter is " + p_in.length() );
72           System.out.println
73           ( "The first parameter is '" +
74               p_in.getSubString(1,80) + "'" );
75
76           Reader is = p_in.getCharacterStream();
77           Writer os = p_out[0].getCharacterOutputStream();
78
79           char buffer[] = new char[8192];
80           int length;
81
82           while( (length=is.read(buffer,0,8192)) != -1 )
83               os.write(buffer,0,length);
84
85           is.close();
86           os.close();
87
88           System.out.println
89           ( "Set out parameter to " +
90               p_out[0].getSubString(1,80) );
91       }
92   }
```

This next routine is a private (internal) routine. It simply prints out meta-data about the
`oracle.sql.ARRAY` that is passed to it. Each of the three array types we send down to Java will make
use of this routine just to report what size/type that they are:

```
93
94   private static void show_array_info( oracle.sql.ARRAY p_in )
95   throws SQLException
96   {
97       System.out.println( "Array is of type      " +
98                           p_in.getSQLTypeName() );
99       System.out.println( "Array is of type code " +
100                          p_in.getBaseType() );
101      System.out.println( "Array is of length    " +
102                          p_in.length() );
103  }
```

Now, we will look at the routines that manipulate the arrays. Arrays are easy to use once you figure out
how to get the data out of them and then back in. Getting the data out is very easy; the `getArray()`
method will return the base data array for us. We simply need to cast the return value from
`getArray()` to the appropriate type and we then have a Java array of that type. Putting the data back
into an array is a little more complex. We must first create a descriptor (metadata) about the array and
then create a new array object with that descriptor and the associated values. The following set of
routines will demonstrate this for each of the array types in turn. Note that the code is virtually identical
– with the exception of the times, we actually access the Java array of data. All these routines do is show
us the meta-data of the `oracle.sql.ARRAY` type, print out the contents of the array, and finally copy
the input array to the output array:

```
104
105   public static void pass_num_array( oracle.sql.ARRAY p_in,
106                                     oracle.sql.ARRAY[] p_out )
107   throws SQLException
108   {
109       show_array_info( p_in );
110       java.math.BigDecimal[] values = (BigDecimal[])p_in.getArray();
111
112       for( int i = 0; i < p_in.length(); i++ )
113           System.out.println( "p_in["+i+"] = " + values[i].toString() );
114
115       Connection conn = new OracleDriver().defaultConnection();
116       ArrayDescriptor descriptor =
117           ArrayDescriptor.createDescriptor( p_in.getSQLTypeName(), conn );
118
119       p_out[0] = new ARRAY( descriptor, conn, values );
120
121   }
122
123   public static void
124   pass_date_array( oracle.sql.ARRAY p_in, oracle.sql.ARRAY[] p_out )
125   throws SQLException
126   {
127       show_array_info( p_in );
128       java.sql.Timestamp[] values = (Timestamp[])p_in.getArray();
129
130       for( int i = 0; i < p_in.length(); i++ )
131           System.out.println( "p_in["+i+"] = " + values[i].toString() );
132
133       Connection conn = new OracleDriver().defaultConnection();
134       ArrayDescriptor descriptor =
135           ArrayDescriptor.createDescriptor( p_in.getSQLTypeName(), conn );
136
137       p_out[0] = new ARRAY( descriptor, conn, values );
138
139   }
140
141   public static void
142   pass_str_array( oracle.sql.ARRAY p_in, oracle.sql.ARRAY[] p_out )
143   throws java.sql.SQLException,IOException
144   {
145       show_array_info( p_in );
146       String[] values = (String[])p_in.getArray();
147
148       for( int i = 0; i < p_in.length(); i++ )
149           System.out.println( "p_in["+i+"] = " + values[i] );
150
151       Connection conn = new OracleDriver().defaultConnection();
152       ArrayDescriptor descriptor =
153           ArrayDescriptor.createDescriptor( p_in.getSQLTypeName(), conn );
154
155       p_out[0] = new ARRAY( descriptor, conn, values );
156
157   }
```

Passing RAW data is much like the String type in other words it is trivial. It is a very easy type to work with:

```
158
159   public static void pass( byte[] p_in, byte[][] p_out )
160   {
161       if ( p_in != null )
162           p_out[0] = p_in;
163   }
```

To pass an int is *problematic* and I do not recommend it. There is no way to pass Null – an int is a 'base data type' in Java they are not objects – hence they cannot be Null. Since there is no concept of a Null indicator here, we would have to actually pass our own if we wanted to support nulls and the PL/SQL layer would have to check a flag to see if the variable was Null or not. This is here for completeness but is not a good idea, especially for in parameters – the Java routine cannot tell that it should not be reading the value since there is no concept of Nulls!

```
164
165   public static void pass_int( int p_in, int[] p_out )
166   {
167       System.out.println
168       ( "The in parameter was " + p_in );
169
170       p_out[0] = p_in;
171
172       System.out.println
173       ( "The out parameter is " + p_out[0] );
174   }
```

Finally, we come to the function. If you recall from the C based external procedures – this was hard to implement in C. We had memory allocations, nulls to deal with, manual conversions from C types to Oracle types and so on. Each C routine was ten or more lines of code. Here, it is as simple as a return statement:

```
175
176   public static String return_string()
177   {
178       return "Hello World";
179   }
180
181   public static java.sql.Timestamp return_date()
182   {
183       return new java.sql.Timestamp(0);
184   }
185
186   public static java.math.BigDecimal return_num()
187   {
188       return new java.math.BigDecimal( "44.3543" );
189   }
190
191   }
192   /

Java created

tkyte@TKYTE816> set define on
```

In general, it is easier to code than in C due to the fact that Java does a lot of work under the covers for us. In the C example, there were about 1000 lines to provide similar functionality. The memory allocation that we had to be so careful with in C is not a factor in Java it'll throw an exception for us if we do something wrong. The Null indicators that were prevalent in C are non-existent in Java. This does raise a problem if you bind to a non-object Java type, but as noted above in the PASS_INT routine, I would recommend against that if Nulls are part of your environment.

Now we are ready to call the routines, since everything is in place. For example I can:

```
tkyte@TKYTE816> set serveroutput on size 1000000
tkyte@TKYTE816> exec dbms_java.set_output( 1000000 )

tkyte@TKYTE816> declare
  2          l_in strArray := strArray();
  3          l_out strArray := strArray();
  4   begin
  5          for i in 1 .. 5 loop
  6              l_in.extend;
  7              l_in(i) := 'Element ' || i;
  8          end loop;
  9
 10          demo_passing_pkg.pass( l_in, l_out );
 11          for i in 1 .. l_out.count loop
 12              dbms_output.put_line( 'l_out(' || i || ') = ' || l_out(i) );
 13          end loop;
 14   end;
 15   /
Array is of type        SECOND.STRARRAY
Array is of type code 12
Array is of length      5
p_in[0] = Element 1
p_in[1] = Element 2
p_in[2] = Element 3
p_in[3] = Element 4
p_in[4] = Element 5
l_out(1) = Element 1
l_out(2) = Element 2
l_out(3) = Element 3
l_out(4) = Element 4
l_out(5) = Element 5

PL/SQL procedure successfully completed.
```

The first eight lines of output were generated by the Java routine, the last five by PL/SQL. This shows that we were able to pass the array from PL/SQL to Java, and receive an array back just as easily. The Java routine simply copied the input array to the output array after printing out the array metadata and values.

Useful Examples

I firmly believe that if you can do something in a single SQL statement you should. Never use a CURSOR FOR loop, for example, when a simple update will do. I also believe that when you cannot do it in SQL, you should attempt to do it in PL/SQL. Never write a Java or C external routine unless it is impossible to accomplish your task in PL/SQL, or if the speedup you get with C is overwhelming. If you cannot do it for technical reasons in PL/SQL, Java should be the next choice. However, there is overhead associated with Java, in terms of memory required, CPU used, and the JVM startup time. PL/SQL has some of this as well, but it is already running – it is not yet another thing to run.

That aside, there are certain things that you quite simply cannot do in PL/SQL, but at which Java excels. The following are some of the truly useful snippets of Java I rely on every day. You should not look at this as an exhaustive list of what can be done, rather just as the tip of the iceberg. Later, in Appendix A on *Necessary Supplied Packages*, we'll see some larger examples of Java usage in Oracle.

Getting a Directory Listing

UTL_FILE, a utility we use in a couple of places in this book, is great for reading and writing text files. A very common requirement, however, is to process all of the files in a given directory. For that task, it falls short. There are no built-in methods anywhere in SQL or PL/SQL to read a directory listing. Well, Java can do that for us easily. Here is how:

```
tkyte@TKYTE816> create global temporary table DIR_LIST
  2  ( filename varchar2(255) )
  3  on commit delete rows
  4  /
Table created.
```

In this implementation, I have chosen to use a temporary table as the way for the Java stored procedure to return its results. I found this most convenient as it allows me to sort and select the returned filenames easily.

The snippet of Java code we need is:

```
tkyte@TKYTE816> create or replace
  2      and compile java source named "DirList"
  3  as
  4  import java.io.*;
  5  import java.sql.*;
  6
  7  public class DirList
  8  {
  9  public static void getList(String directory)
 10                     throws SQLException
 11  {
 12      File path = new File( directory );
 13      String[] list = path.list();
 14      String element;
 15
 16      for(int i = 0; i < list.length; i++)
 17      {
 18          element = list[i];
 19          #sql { INSERT INTO DIR_LIST (FILENAME)
 20                 VALUES (:element) };
 21      }
 22  }
 23
 24  }
 25  /

Java created.
```

I chose to use SQLJ here for programming efficiency. I'm already connected to the database, and doing this through JDBC would have taken quite a few lines of code. SQLJ makes doing SQL in Java almost as easy as in PL/SQL. Now, of course, we need to create our call specification:

```
tkyte@TKYTE816> create or replace
  2   procedure get_dir_list( p_directory in varchar2 )
  3   as language java
  4   name 'DirList.getList( java.lang.String )';
  5   /

Procedure created.
```

One last detail here before we run this procedure. We need to give it permissions to do what it wants to do; read a directory. Now, in this example I am the DBA so I can grant this to myself but normally, you will have to request this ability from the DBA. If you recall in the introduction to this section I said:

> "... the Java code is always running as the 'Oracle software owner', meaning a Java stored procedure could overwrite the database's INIT.ORA parameter file (or some other, even more important set of files, such as the data files) if it has been given the appropriate privileges."

This is how Oracle protects itself from this, you must explicitly be given a privilege in order to do many things that would be damaging. If we had attempted to use this procedure before getting the privileges, we would have received the following error:

```
tkyte@TKYTE816>  exec get_dir_list( 'c:\temp' );
BEGIN get_dir_list( 'c:\temp' ); END;

*
ERROR at line 1:
ORA-29532: Java call terminated by uncaught Java exception:
java.security.AccessControlException:
the Permission (java.io.FilePermission c:\temp read) has not been granted by
dbms_java.grant_permission to
SchemaProtectionDomain(TKYTE|PolicyTableProxy(TKYTE))
ORA-06512: at "TKYTE.GET_DIR_LIST", line 0
ORA-06512: at line 1
```

So, we'll authorize ourselves to do this:

```
tkyte@TKYTE816> begin
  2           dbms_java.grant_permission
  3           ( USER,
  4           'java.io.FilePermission',
  5           'c:\temp',
  6       'read');
  7   end;
  8   /

PL/SQL procedure successfully completed.
```

and we are ready to go:

```
tkyte@TKYTE816> exec get_dir_list( 'c:\temp' );

PL/SQL procedure successfully completed.

tkyte@TKYTE816> select * from dir_list where rownum < 5;

FILENAME
---------------------------------
a.sql
abc.dat
activation
activation8i.zip
```

The permissions are part of the Java2 Standard Edition (J2SE) and you can read more about them at http://java.sun.com/j2se/1.3/docs/api/java/security/Permission.html. In Appendix A, *Necessary Supplied Packages*, we'll explore DBMS_JAVA and its uses in more detail as well.

There is one other thing of which you should be aware. Oracle 8.1.6 was the first version of Oracle to support the J2SE permissions. In Oracle 8.1.5 this would have been accomplished via a role. Unfortunately when I say 'a role' I mean basically a single role; JAVASYSPRIV. It would be similar to granting DBA to every user just because they needed to create a view – it is far too powerful. Once I have JAVASYSPRIV, I can do anything I want. Use caution with this role if you have 8.1.5 and consider using a later release with the infinitely more granular privilege model.

Running an OS Command

If I had a nickel for every time I was asked how to run an OS command, I would not be writing this book – I'd be on vacation! Before Java, this was really hard. Now it is almost trivial. There are probably a hundred ways to implement the following snippet of code but this works well:

```
tkyte@TKYTE816> create or replace and compile
  2  java source named "Util"
  3  as
  4  import java.io.*;
  5  import java.lang.*;
  6
  7  public class Util extends Object
  8  {
  9
 10    public static int RunThis(String[] args)
 11    {
 12    Runtime rt = Runtime.getRuntime();
 13    int        rc = -1;
 14
 15    try
 16    {
 17        Process p = rt.exec(args[0]);
 18
 19        int bufSize = 4096;
 20        BufferedInputStream bis =
 21         new BufferedInputStream(p.getInputStream(), bufSize);
 22        int len;
 23        byte buffer[] = new byte[bufSize];
 24
```

```
25          // Echo back what the program spit out
26          while ((len = bis.read(buffer, 0, bufSize)) != -1)
27              System.out.write(buffer, 0, len);
28
29          rc = p.waitFor();
30      }
31      catch (Exception e)
32      {
33          e.printStackTrace();
34          rc = -1;
35      }
36      finally
37      {
38          return rc;
39      }
40      }
41  }
42  /

Java created.
```

It is setup to run any program and capture the output to either a TRACE file on the server or, if you use DBMS_JAVA, to the DBMS_OUTPUT buffer. Now, this is a pretty powerful feature – we could run any command as the Oracle software account using this – were it not for the privileges we need. In this case, I want to be able to get a process listing - using /usr/bin/ps on UNIX and \bin\tlist.exe on Windows. In order to do that I need two privileges:

```
tkyte@TKYTE816> BEGIN
  2         dbms_java.grant_permission
  3         ( USER,
  4          'java.io.FilePermission',
  5          -- '/usr/bin/ps',  -- for UNIX
  6          c:\bin\tlist.exe',  -- for WINDOWS
  7          'execute');
  8
  9         dbms_java.grant_permission
 10         ( USER,
 11          'java.lang.RuntimePermission',
 12          '*',
 13          'writeFileDescriptor' );
 14  end;
 15  /

PL/SQL procedure successfully completed.
```

You may not have the tlist.exe *on your system. It is part of the Windows Resource Toolkit and not available on all Windows systems. This is purely illustrative of what you can do – not having access to* tlist.exe *is not a 'show stopper' for us here. You can use this technique to run any program. Beware however, you should consider carefully what programs you grant execute on using* DBMS_JAVA. *For example, if you granted execute on* c:\winnt\system32\cmd.exe, *you would be in effect granting execute on ALL programs – a very dangerous idea indeed.*

The first allows me to run a very specific program. If I was daring, I could put * in place of the program name. This would let me run anything. I do not think that it would be wise, however; you should explicitly list only the fully qualified paths to programs you are sure of. The second privilege allows my run-time to produce output. Here I must use a *, as I do not know what output might be created (stdout for example).

Now we need our binding layer:

```
tkyte@TKYTE816> create or replace
  2  function RUN_CMD( p_cmd  in varchar2) return number
  3  as
  4  language java
  5  name 'Util.RunThis(java.lang.String[]) return integer';
  6  /

Function created.

tkyte@TKYTE816> create or replace procedure rc( p_cmd in varchar2 )
  2  as
  3    x number;
  4  begin
  5    x := run_cmd(p_cmd);
  6    if ( x <> 0 )
  7    then
  8         raise program_error;
  9    end if;
 10  end;
 11  /

Procedure created.
```

Here, I created a small layer on top of the binding layer to let me run this easily as a procedure. Now we will see how this works:

```
tkyte@TKYTE816> set serveroutput on size 1000000
tkyte@TKYTE816> exec dbms_java.set_output(1000000)

PL/SQL procedure successfully completed.

tkyte@TKYTE816> exec rc('C:\WINNT\system32\cmd.exe /c dir')
Volume in drive C has no label.
Volume Serial Number is F455-B3C3
Directory of C:\oracle\DATABASE
05/07/2001  10:13a       <DIR>          .
05/07/2001  10:13a       <DIR>          ..
11/04/2000  06:28p       <DIR>          ARCHIVE
11/04/2000  06:37p                  47  inittkyte816.ora
11/04/2000  06:28p              31,744  ORADBA.EXE
05/07/2001  09:07p               1,581  oradim.log
05/10/2001  07:47p               2,560  pwdtkyte816.ora
05/06/2001  08:43p               3,584  pwdtkyte816.ora.hold
01/26/2001  11:31a               3,584  pwdtkyte816.xxx
04/19/2001  09:34a              21,309  sqlnet.log
05/07/2001  10:13a               2,424  test.sql
01/30/2001  02:10p             348,444  xml.tar
               9 File(s)        415,277 bytes
               3 Dir(s)  13,600,501,760 bytes free

PL/SQL procedure successfully completed.
```

And that's it, we have just got a directory listing from the OS.

Getting Time Down to the Milliseconds

The examples are getting smaller, shorter, and faster. That's the point actually. With a tiny bit of Java functionality dropped in here and there at the right points, you can achieve a great deal of functionality.

In Oracle 9i, this function will be rendered moot; support for timestamps more granular than one second is provided. Until then, if you need it, we can get it:

```
tkyte@TKYTE816> create or replace java source
  2  named "MyTimestamp"
  3  as
  4  import java.lang.String;
  5  import java.sql.Timestamp;
  6
  7  public class MyTimestamp
  8  {
  9      public static String getTimestamp()
 10      {
 11        return (new
 12           Timestamp(System.currentTimeMillis())).toString();
 13      }
 14  };
 15  /

Java created.

tkyte@TKYTE816>  create or replace function my_timestamp return varchar2
  2  as language java
  3  name 'MyTimestamp.getTimestamp() return java.lang.String';
  4  /

Function created.

tkyte@TKYTE816>  select my_timestamp,
  2  to_char(sysdate,'yyyy-mm-dd hh24:mi:ss') from dual
  3  /

MY_TIMESTAMP                    TO_CHAR(SYSDATE,'YY
------------------------        -------------------
2001-03-27 19:15:59.688    2001-03-27 19:15:59
```

Possible Errors

Most of the errors you will encounter using this feature are related to compiling code, and parameter mismatches. Some of the more frequent ones are listed here.

ORA-29549 Java Session State Cleared

You will hit errors like this:

```
select my_timestamp, to_char(sysdate,'yyyy-mm-dd hh24:mi:ss') from dual
                                                                   *
ERROR at line 1:
ORA-29549: class TKYTE.MyTimestamp has changed, Java session state cleared
```

continuously when developing. All it means is that the class you had used earlier in the session was recompiled, typically by you. Any state associated with that class is wiped out. You may simply re-run the statement that failed again, and a new state will be instantiated.

You should avoid reloading Java classes on an active production system for this reason. Any session that used the Java class will receive this error the next time they use the Java class again.

Permissions Errors

Just as we received previously:

```
ERROR at line 1:
ORA-29532: Java call terminated by uncaught Java exception:
java.security.AccessControlException:
the Permission (java.io.FilePermission c:\temp read) has not been granted by
dbms_java.grant_permission to
SchemaProtectionDomain(TKYTE|PolicyTableProxy(TKYTE))
ORA-06512: at "TKYTE.GET_DIR_LIST", line 0
ORA-06512: at line 1
```

Fortunately, the error message has the explicit privileges you must obtain in order to be successful listed right there. You must have an appropriately privileged user use the DBMS_JAVA GRANT_PERMISSION routine for you.

ORA-29531 no method X in class Y

Taking the RunThis example from above and changing the call specification to:

```
tkyte@TKYTE816> create or replace
  2    function RUN_CMD( p_cmd  in varchar2) return number
  3    as
  4    language java
  5    name 'Util.RunThis(String[]) return integer';
  7  /

Function created.
```

will raise this error for me. Note that in the parameter list to Util.RunThis, I specified STRING, not java.lang.String.

```
tkyte@TKYTE816> exec rc('c:\winnt\system32\cmd.exe /c dir')
java.lang.NullPointerException
at oracle.aurora.util.JRIExtensions.getMaximallySpecificMethod(JRIExtensions.java)
at oracle.aurora.util.JRIExtensions.getMaximallySpecificMethod(JRIExtensions.java)
BEGIN RC('c:\winnt\system32\cmd.exe /c dir'); END;

*
ERROR at line 1:
ORA-29531: no method RunThis in class Util
ORA-06512: at "TKYTE.RUN_CMD", line 0
ORA-06512: at "TKYTE.RC", line 5
ORA-06512: at line 1
```

The solution here is that you must use *fully* qualified type names in the mapping. Even though java.lang is implicitly imported into a Java program, it is not imported into the SQL layer. When you get this error, you need to look at your data type mapping and ensure that you are using *fully* qualified data types, and that they match the actual types exactly. The Java method to be used is found by its signature, and its signature is built from the data types used. The smallest difference in the inputs, the outputs, or the case of the name will cause the signatures to be different and Oracle will not find your code.

Summary

In this chapter, we explored how to implement stored procedures in Java. This does not mean that you should run out and re-code all of your PL/SQL in Java stored procedures. It does mean that when you hit the wall with what PL/SQL can do, typically when you attempt to reach out of the database and do operating system interactions, Java should be the first thing you think of.

Using the material presented in this chapter you should be able to pass all of the mainstream SQL datatypes from a PL/SQL layer down to Java, and send them back, including arrays of information. You have a handful of useful snippets of Java that can be of immediate use and as you peruse the Java documentation, you'll find dozens more that apply in your installation.

Used judiciously, a little Java can go a long way in your implementation.

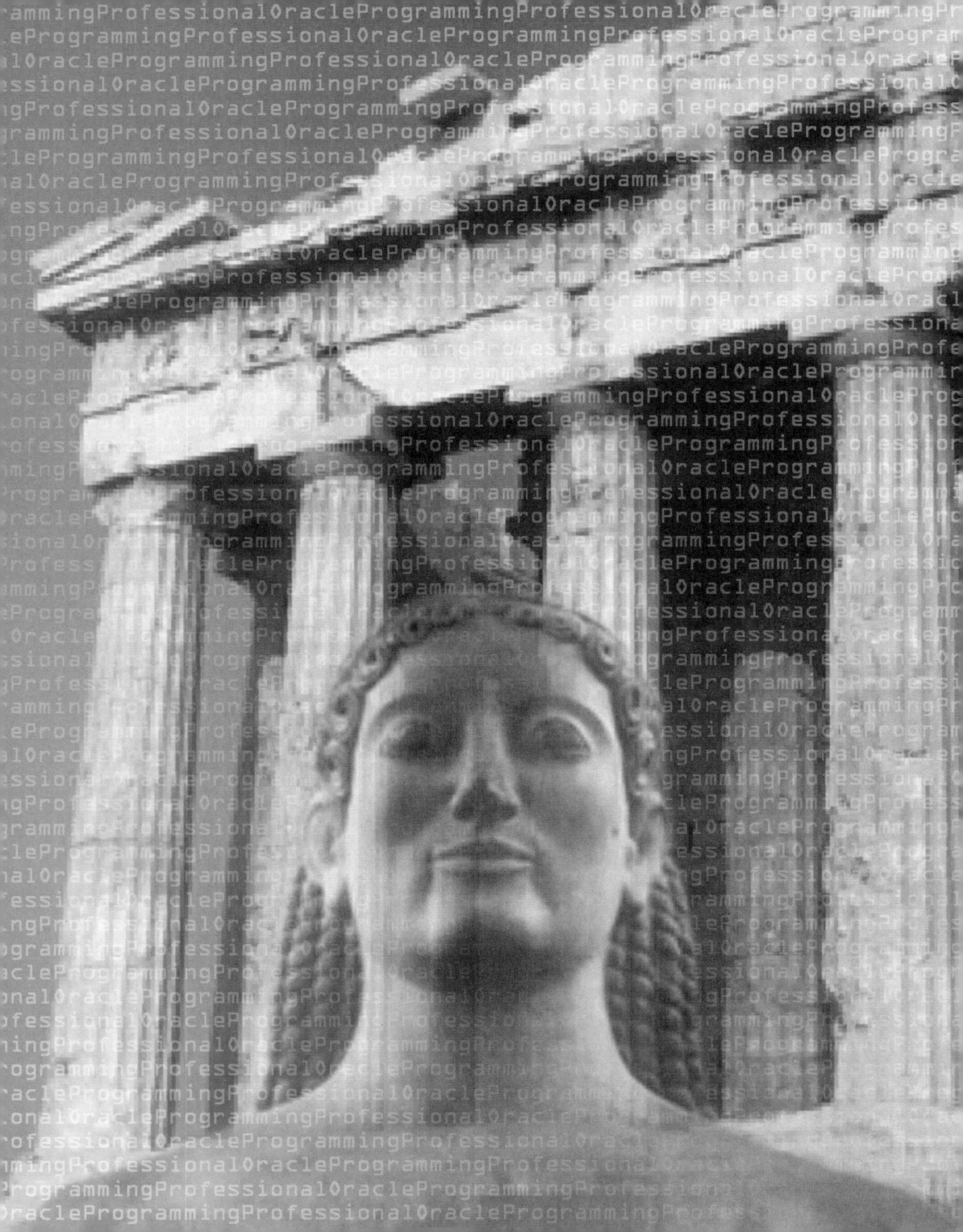
ProfessionalOracleProgramming

20

Using Object Relational Features

Starting with Oracle 8, Oracle has given us the ability to use **object relational features** in the database. In short, the object relational features in Oracle allow you to extend the set of data types available in the database to go beyond simple NUMBERs, DATEs, and STRINGs. You can set up your own types that include:

❑ One or more attributes, where each attribute may be a scalar type, or a set (array) of other object/data types.

❑ One or more methods that operate on this type.

❑ One or more static methods.

❑ An optional comparison method used for sorting and equality/inequality comparisons.

You can then use this new type you have created in order to create database tables, specify columns of a table, create views, or as an excellent way to extend the SQL and PL/SQL languages. Once created, your data type is available to be used in the same manner as the basic data type DATE.

What I would like to do in this chapter is cover how I use the object relational features in Oracle. Just as important, will be how I do *not* use the feature. I will explain the components of this technology as I introduce them. However this should not be considered a complete overview of everything that you can possibly do with the object relational features in Oracle. This is covered in a 200 page manual from Oracle titled *Application Developer's Guide – Object-Relational Features*. The goal of this chapter is to expose why and how you would want to use these capabilities.

Oracle's object relational features are accessible using many languages. Languages such as Java via JDBC, Visual Basic with **OO4O** (**O**racle **O**bjects for **O**le), **OCI** (**O**racle **C**all **I**nterface), PL/SQL, and Pro*C can all easily make use of this functionality. Oracle provides various tools to make using object relational features in these languages easy. For example, when using Java/JDBC, one might take advantage of Oracle's JPublisher, a utility that generates Java classes that represent database object types, collection types, and PL/SQL packages for you (it is a code generator that removes any complexity associated with mapping complex SQL types to Java types). OCI has a built-in client side object cache used to efficiently manipulate and work with objects. Pro*C has the **OTT** (**O**bject **T**ype **T**ranslator) tool to generate C/C++ structs for use in that language. In this book, we will not be investigating using these languages or tools specifically; each is documented in depth with the Oracle Server documentation. Rather we will focus on the implementation and creation of objects types in the database itself.

Reasons for Using These Features

The reason I use the object relational features in Oracle is predominantly as a means to extend the PL/SQL language in a natural fashion. The object type is an excellent way to extend PL/SQL with new functionality in the same way a class structure does this in C++ or Java. We will take a look at an example of doing this in the following section.

Object types can be used to enforce standardization as well. I can create a new type, say ADDRESS_TYPE, which encapsulates the definition of an address – the discrete components that make it up. I can even add convenience functions (methods) around this type, perhaps to return the address in a format suitable for printing on labels for example. Now, whenever I create a table needing a column that is an address, I can simply declare it is as ADDRESS_TYPE. The attributes that constitute an address will be added to my table for me automatically. We will walk through an example of this as well.

Object types can be used to present an object relational view of strictly relational data. That is, I could take the simple EMP/DEPT example, and build an object relational view of it to expose each row of the DEPT table as if it contained a collection of EMP objects. Instead of joining EMP to DEPT, I can simply query the DEPT object view to see the DEPT and EMP information in a single row. In the next section, we'll take a look at this example as well.

Object types may also be used to create object tables. We covered the pros and cons of object tables in Chapter 6 on *Tables*. Object tables have many hidden columns, side effects, and 'magic' happening behind them. Additionally, you usually need a strictly relational view of data for a variety of purposes (in particular, for the large number of existing utilities and report generators that do not 'understand' these new object types). I tend to not use them myself for this reason. I do use object views of relational data, which gives me the same effect in the end as an object table. However, I control the physical storage of everything. For this reason, we will not go into depth on object tables in this chapter.

How Object Relational Features Work

In this section we will look at using the object relational features in Oracle to perform the following goals:

- ❏ Impose standard data types on a system.
- ❏ Naturally extend the PL/SQL language.
- ❏ Present object relational views of inherently relational data.

Adding Data Types to your System

We will start with the basics here, the simple ADDRESS_TYPE. We will look at the syntax involved, what is possible, what side effects we might observe, and so on. In order to begin, we'll need a simple type to start with:

```
tkyte@TKYTE816> create or replace type Address_Type
  2  as object
  3  ( street_addr1    varchar2(25),
  4    street_addr2    varchar2(25),
  5    city            varchar2(30),
  6    state           varchar2(2),
  7    zip_code        number
  8  )
  9  /

Type created.
```

This is the most basic sort of CREATE TYPE statement we can use. We'll add more features to it as we progress in this example. It is the most basic because it is a type composed only of other pre-existing scalar types; it has no methods, no comparison functions, nothing 'fancy'. We can immediately begin to use this type in our tables and PL/SQL code however:

```
tkyte@TKYTE816> create table people
  2  ( name            varchar2(10),
  3    home_address    address_type,
  4    work_address    address_type
  5  )
  6  /

Table created.

tkyte@TKYTE816> declare
  2      l_home_address address_type;
  3      l_work_address address_type;
  4  begin
  5      l_home_address := Address_Type( '123 Main Street', null,
  6                                      'Reston', 'VA', 45678 );
  7      l_work_address := Address_Type( '1 Oracle Way', null,
  8                                      'Redwood', 'CA', 23456 );
  9
 10      insert into people
 11      ( name, home_address, work_address )
 12      values
 13      ( 'Tom Kyte', l_home_address, l_work_address );
 14  end;
 15  /

PL/SQL procedure successfully completed.

tkyte@TKYTE816> select * from people;
```

```
NAME        HOME_ADDRESS(STREET_  WORK_ADDRESS(STREET_
----------  --------------------  --------------------
Tom Kyte    ADDRESS_TYPE('123 Ma  ADDRESS_TYPE('1 Orac
            in Street', NULL, 'R  le Way', NULL, 'Redw
            eston', 'VA', 45678)  ood', 'CA', 23456)
```

So, as you can see, using the new type in a CREATE TABLE is as easy as using the NUMBER type. Additionally, declaring variables of type ADDRESS_TYPE in PL/SQL is straightforward as well – PL/SQL is immediately aware of the new types. The new bit of functionality we see in the PL/SQL code is on lines 5 through 8. Here we are invoking the object constructor for the new type. The default object constructor in the type allows us to set all of the attributes of the object type to some value. There is, by default, only one default constructor and it must be invoked with a value for every attribute in the type. In the section on *Using Types to Extend PL/SQL*, we'll see how to write our own custom constructors using static member functions.

Once we create and set variables of the type ADDRESS_TYPE, we can use them as bind variables in SQL very easily, as demonstrated above. We just insert the NAME, HOME_ADDRESS, and WORK_ADDRESS, and we are done. A simple SQL query retrieves the data. We can use SQL to not only gain access to the column HOME_ADDRESS, but to each of the components of HOME_ADDRESS as well. For example:

```
tkyte@TKYTE816> select name, home_address.state, work_address.state
  2    from people
  3  /
select name, home_address.state, work_address.state
                                      *
ERROR at line 1:
ORA-00904: invalid column name


tkyte@TKYTE816> select name, P.home_address.state, P.work_address.state
  2    from people P
  3  /

NAME        HOME_ADDRESS.STATE    WORK_ADDRESS.STATE
----------  --------------------  --------------------
Tom Kyte    VA                    CA
```

I've shown both the incorrect and correct method to do this. The first example is probably what most people would naturally try. It obviously does not work. To access the components of an object type, we must use a correlation name, as I did in the second query. Here I alias the table PEOPLE with P (any valid identifier could have been used, including the word PEOPLE itself). Then, when I want to reference the individual components of the addresses, I use the alias.

So, what does the physical table PEOPLE actually look like? What Oracle shows us, and what is *really* there, are quite different, as you might expect if you read Chapter 6 on *Tables*, and saw the nested table or object table example:

```
tkyte@TKYTE816> desc people
 Name                                    Null?    Type
 --------------------------------------- -------- ---------------
 NAME                                             VARCHAR2(10)
 HOME_ADDRESS                                     ADDRESS_TYPE
 WORK_ADDRESS                                     ADDRESS_TYPE
```

```
tkyte@TKYTE816> select name, length
  2     from sys.col$
  3    where obj# = ( select object_id
  4                     from user_objects
  5                    where object_name = 'PEOPLE' )
  6  /

NAME                     LENGTH
-------------------- ----------
NAME                         10
HOME_ADDRESS                  1
SYS_NC00003$                 25
SYS_NC00004$                 25
SYS_NC00005$                 30
SYS_NC00006$                  2
SYS_NC00007$                 22
WORK_ADDRESS                  1
SYS_NC00009$                 25
SYS_NC00010$                 25
SYS_NC00011$                 30
SYS_NC00012$                  2
SYS_NC00013$                 22

13 rows selected.
```

Oracle tells us we have three columns, the real data dictionary, however says thirteen. We can see our scalar columns hidden in there. Even though there is a little bit of magic and some hidden columns here, using scalar object types (no nested tables) in this fashion is very straightforward. This is the sort of magic we can live with. If we use the SET DESCRIBE option in SQL*PLUS, we can get SQL*PLUS to show us the entire hierarchy of our type:

```
tkyte@TKYTE816> set describe depth all
tkyte@TKYTE816> desc people
 Name                                    Null?    Type
 --------------------------------------- -------- ---------------------------
 NAME                                             VARCHAR2(10)
 HOME_ADDRESS                                     ADDRESS_TYPE
   STREET_ADDR1                                   VARCHAR2(25)
   STREET_ADDR2                                   VARCHAR2(25)
   CITY                                           VARCHAR2(30)
   STATE                                          VARCHAR2(2)
   ZIP_CODE                                       NUMBER
 WORK_ADDRESS                                     ADDRESS_TYPE
   STREET_ADDR1                                   VARCHAR2(25)
   STREET_ADDR2                                   VARCHAR2(25)
   CITY                                           VARCHAR2(30)
   STATE                                          VARCHAR2(2)
   ZIP_CODE                                       NUMBER
```

This is very handy for determining what attributes are available to us.

871

Now, lets take our ADDRESS_TYPE one step further. We would like to have a convenient routine that returns a nicely formatted address for us in one field. We can do this by adding a `member function` to the type body:

```
tkyte@TKYTE816> alter type Address_Type
  2  REPLACE
  3  as object
  4  (  street_addr1    varchar2(25),
  5     street_addr2    varchar2(25),
  6     city            varchar2(30),
  7     state           varchar2(2),
  8     zip_code        number,
  9     member function toString return varchar2
 10  )
 11  /

Type altered.

tkyte@TKYTE816> create or replace type body Address_Type
  2  as
  3      member function toString return varchar2
  4      is
  5      begin
  6          if ( street_addr2 is not NULL )
  7          then
  8              return street_addr1 || chr(10) ||
  9                     street_addr2 || chr(10) ||
 10                     city || ', ' || state || ' ' || zip_code;
 11          else
 12              return street_addr1 || chr(10) ||
 13                     city || ', ' || state || ' ' || zip_code;
 14          end if;
 15      end;
 16  end;
 17  /

Type body created.

tkyte@TKYTE816> select name, p.home_address.toString()
  2      from people P
  3  /

NAME
--------------------
P.HOME_ADDRESS.TOSTRING()
---------------------------
Tom Kyte
123 Main Street
Reston, VA 45678
```

Here, we are looking at our first example of an **object method**. Each method is invoked with an implicit SELF parameter. We could have prefixed STREET_ADDR1, STREET_ADDR2, and so on with:

```
SELF.street_addr1 || chr(10) || SELF.street_addr2 ...
```

but it is implied for us. You might be looking at this and saying, 'well, that's nice but it is nothing we couldn't do with a relational table and a PL/SQL package.' You would be correct. However, there are advantages to using the object type with methods, as I have done above.

❑ **It serves as a better encapsulation mechanism** – The ADDRESS_TYPE encapsulates and enforces our concept of what an address is, what attributes it has, and what functionality is available.

❑ **It tightly binds methods to specific data** – This is a more subtle point but extremely important. If we implemented the above using scalar columns and a PL/SQL function to format them into a nice printable address, we could call this function with any data we wanted. I could pass in an EMPLOYEE_NUMBER as the zip code, a FIRST_NAME as the street address, and so on. By coupling the method with the attribute data, the TOSTRING method can *only* work on address data. The people who call this method do not have to be aware of the proper data to be passed – the proper data is 'just there already'.

However, there is a disadvantage to the object type that you must be aware of. In Oracle 8i, the object type is not very 'alterable'. You can add methods to the type via the ALTER statement, but you can neither *remove* nor *add* additional attributes once you have a table created using that type, nor can you remove methods once you've added them. The only thing you can do, pretty much, is add methods, or change their implementation (type body). In other words, schema evolution is not well supported using the type. If you discovered over time that you needed another attribute in the ADDRESS_TYPE object, you would have to rebuild objects that have that type embedded in them. This does not affect object types that are not used as columns in database tables, or as the type in a CREATE TABLE OF TYPE statement. That is, if you use object types solely in object views and as a method to extend PL/SQL (the following two sections) you can ignore this caveat.

One special set of methods associated with object types are the MAP and ORDER methods. These are used when sorting, comparing, or grouping instances of object types. If an object type does not have a MAP or ORDER function, you will find the following to be true:

```
tkyte@TKYTE816> select * from people order by home_address;
select * from people order by home_address
                     *
ERROR at line 1:
ORA-22950: cannot ORDER objects without MAP or ORDER method


tkyte@TKYTE816> select * from people where home_address > work_address;
select * from people where home_address > work_address
                                        *
ERROR at line 1:
ORA-22950: cannot ORDER objects without MAP or ORDER method


tkyte@TKYTE816> select * from people where home_address = work_address;

no rows selected
```

You cannot order by the object type and you cannot use them in 'greater than' or 'less than' searches. The only thing you can do with them is to use them in direct equality comparisons. Then Oracle does an attribute-by-attribute compare for us to see if they are equal. The solution to the above is to add a MAP or an ORDER method – one or the other (an object type may only have a MAP or an ORDER method, but not both).

A MAP method is simply a function that works on a single instance of an object, and returns some scalar type that Oracle will use to compare to other object types. For example, if the object type in question represented a point with an X and Y co-ordinate, the MAP function might return the square root of (X*X+Y*Y) – the distance from the origin. An ORDER method on the other hand receives two object instances; SELF and something to compare to SELF. The ORDER method returns 1 if SELF is greater than the other object, –1 if SELF is less than the other object, or 0 if they are equal. A MAP method is the preferred mechanism as it can be much faster and can even be invoked in a parallel query (whereas the ORDER method cannot). A MAP method has to be invoked once on an object instance and then Oracle can sort it – an ORDER function might be called hundreds or thousands of times with the same inputs to sort a large set. I'll demonstrate both examples using the ADDRESS_TYPE from above. First the ORDER method:

```
tkyte@TKYTE816> alter type Address_Type
  2    REPLACE
  3    as object
  4    (  street_addr1    varchar2(25),
  5       street_addr2    varchar2(25),
  6       city            varchar2(30),
  7       state           varchar2(2),
  8       zip_code        number,
  9       member function toString return varchar2,
 10       order member function order_function( compare2 in Address_type )
 11       return number
 12    )
 13    /

Type altered.

tkyte@TKYTE816> create or replace type body Address_Type
  2    as
  3        member function toString return varchar2
  4        is
  5        begin
  6            if ( street_addr2 is not NULL )
  7            then
  8                return street_addr1 || chr(10) ||
  9                        street_addr2 || chr(10) ||
 10                        city || ', ' || state || ' ' || zip_code;
 11            else
 12                return street_addr1 || chr(10) ||
 13                        city || ', ' || state || ' ' || zip_code;
 14            end if;
 15        end;
 16
 17        order member function order_function(compare2 in Address_type)
 18        return number
 19        is
 20        begin
 21            if (nvl(self.zip_code,-99999) <> nvl(compare2.zip_code,-99999))
 22            then
 23                return sign(nvl(self.zip_code,-99999)
 24                            - nvl(compare2.zip_code,-99999));
 25            end if;
 26            if (nvl(self.city,chr(0)) > nvl(compare2.city,chr(0)))
 27            then
```

```
28                    return 1;
29            elsif (nvl(self.city,chr(0)) < nvl(compare2.city,chr(0)))
30            then
31                    return -1;
32            end if;
33            if ( nvl(self.street_addr1,chr(0)) >
34                          nvl(compare2.street_addr1,chr(0))   )
35            then
36                    return 1;
37            elsif ( nvl(self.street_addr1,chr(0)) <
38                          nvl(compare2.street_addr1,chr(0))   )
39            then
40                    return -1;
41            end if;
42            if ( nvl(self.street_addr2,chr(0)) >
43                          nvl(compare2.street_addr2,chr(0))   )
44            then
45                    return 1;
46            elsif ( nvl(self.street_addr2,chr(0)) <
47                          nvl(compare2.street_addr2,chr(0))   )
48            then
49                    return -1;
50            end if;
51            return 0;
52        end;
53    end;
54    /
```

Type body created.

This would compare two addresses using the following algorithm:

1. If the ZIP_CODES differ, return −1 if SELF is less than COMPARE2, else return 1.

2. If the CITY differ, return −1 if SELF is less than COMPARE2, else return 1.

3. If the STREET_ADDR1 differ, return −1 if SELF is less than COMPARE2, else return 1.

4. If the STREET_ADDR2 differ, return −1 if SELF is less than COMPARE2, else return 1.

5. Else return 0 (they are the same).

As you can see, we have to worry about Nulls in the comparison and such. The logic is long and complex. It is definitely not efficient. Any time you are thinking of coding an ORDER member function, you should try to find a way to make it into a MAP member function instead. The above logic, I realize a better way would be to code it as a MAP member function. Note that if you have already altered the type to have the ORDER member function from above, you will have to drop the table that depends on this type, drop the type itself, and start over. Member functions cannot be removed, only added via the ALTER TYPE command and we need to get rid of the existing ORDER member function. The full example of the following would have a DROP TABLE PEOPLE, DROP TYPE ADDRESS_TYPE, and a CREATE TYPE command preceding the ALTER TYPE:

```
tkyte@TKYTE816> alter type Address_Type
  2   REPLACE
  3   as object
  4   ( street_addr1    varchar2(25),
  5     street_addr2    varchar2(25),
  6     city            varchar2(30),
  7     state           varchar2(2),
  8     zip_code        number,
  9     member function toString return varchar2,
 10     map member function mapping_function return varchar2
 11   )
 12   /

Type altered.

tkyte@TKYTE816> create or replace type body Address_Type
  2   as
  3       member function toString return varchar2
  4       is
  5       begin
  6           if ( street_addr2 is not NULL )
  7           then
  8               return street_addr1 || chr(10) ||
  9                      street_addr2 || chr(10) ||
 10                      city || ', ' || state || ' ' || zip_code;
 11           else
 12               return street_addr1 || chr(10) ||
 13                      city || ', ' || state || ' ' || zip_code;
 14           end if;
 15       end;
 16
 17       map member function mapping_function return varchar2
 18       is
 19       begin
 20           return to_char( nvl(zip_code,0), 'fm00000' ) ||
 21                  lpad( nvl(city,' '), 30 ) ||
 22                  lpad( nvl(street_addr1,' '), 25 ) ||
 23                  lpad( nvl(street_addr2,' '), 25 );
 24       end;
 25   end;
 26   /

Type body created.
```

By returning a fixed length string with the ZIP_CODE, then CITY, then STREET_ADDR fields, Oracle will do the sorting and comparisons for us.

Before we continue onto the next use of object types (my favorite use – as a means to extend PL/SQL), I would like to introduce the other collection type, VARRAYS. In Chapter 6 on *Tables*, we investigated nested tables and their implementation. We saw that they are nothing more than a parent/child table pair, implemented with a hidden surrogate key in the parent table and a NESTED_TABLE_ID in the child table. A VARRAY is, in many ways, similar to a nested table but is implemented very differently.

A VARRAY (or nested table) would be used to store an array of data associated with a single row. For example, if you had the need to store additional addresses with the PEOPLE table (perhaps an array of previous home addresses from oldest to newest), we could do the following:

```
tkyte@TKYTE816> create or replace type Address_Array_Type
  2  as varray(25) of Address_Type
  3  /

Type created.

tkyte@TKYTE816> alter table people add previous_addresses Address_Array_Type
  2  /

Table altered.

tkyte@TKYTE816> set describe depth all
tkyte@TKYTE816> desc people
 Name                                   Null?    Type
 -------------------------------------- -------- --------------------
 NAME                                            VARCHAR2(10)
 HOME_ADDRESS                                    ADDRESS_TYPE
    STREET_ADDR1                                 VARCHAR2(25)
    STREET_ADDR2                                 VARCHAR2(25)
    CITY                                         VARCHAR2(30)
    STATE                                        VARCHAR2(2)
    ZIP_CODE                                     NUMBER

METHOD
------
 MEMBER FUNCTION TOSTRING RETURNS VARCHAR2

METHOD
------
 MAP MEMBER FUNCTION MAPPING_FUNCTION RETURNS VARCHAR2
 WORK_ADDRESS                                   ADDRESS_TYPE
    STREET_ADDR1                                 VARCHAR2(25)
    STREET_ADDR2                                 VARCHAR2(25)
    CITY                                         VARCHAR2(30)
    STATE                                        VARCHAR2(2)
    ZIP_CODE                                     NUMBER

METHOD
------
 MEMBER FUNCTION TOSTRING RETURNS VARCHAR2

METHOD
------
 MAP MEMBER FUNCTION MAPPING_FUNCTION RETURNS VARCHAR2
 PREVIOUS_ADDRESSES                             ADDRESS_ARRAY_TYPE
    STREET_ADDR1                                 VARCHAR2(25)
    STREET_ADDR2                                 VARCHAR2(25)
    CITY                                         VARCHAR2(30)
    STATE                                        VARCHAR2(2)
    ZIP_CODE                                     NUMBER
```

```
METHOD
------
 MEMBER FUNCTION TOSTRING RETURNS VARCHAR2

METHOD
------
 MAP MEMBER FUNCTION MAPPING_FUNCTION RETURNS VARCHAR2
```

So, now our table has the ability to optionally store up to 25 previous addresses. The question is; what went on behind the covers in order to facilitate this? If we query the 'real' data dictionary, we'll see:

```
tkyte@TKYTE816> select name, length
  2    from sys.col$
  3    where obj# = ( select object_id
  4                     from user_objects
  5                     where object_name = 'PEOPLE' )
  6  /

NAME                      LENGTH
-------------------- ----------
NAME                          10
HOME_ADDRESS                   1
SYS_NC00003$                  25
SYS_NC00004$                  25
SYS_NC00005$                  30
SYS_NC00006$                   2
SYS_NC00007$                  22
WORK_ADDRESS                   1
SYS_NC00009$                  25
SYS_NC00010$                  25
SYS_NC00011$                  30
SYS_NC00012$                   2
SYS_NC00013$                  22
PREVIOUS_ADDRESSES          2940

14 rows selected.
```

Oracle has added a 2,940 byte column to support our VARRAY implementation. The data for our VARRAY will be stored inline (in the row itself). This raises an interesting question; what will happen if our array could exceed 4,000 bytes (the largest structured column that Oracle supports)? If we drop the column and recreate it as a VARRAY(50), we can see what happens:

```
tkyte@TKYTE816> alter table people drop column previous_addresses
  2  /

Table altered.

tkyte@TKYTE816> create or replace type Address_Array_Type
  2  as varray(50) of Address_Type
  3  /

Type created.
```

```
tkyte@TKYTE816> alter table people add previous_addresses Address_Array_Type
  2  /

Table altered.

tkyte@TKYTE816> select object_type, object_name,
  2              decode(status,'INVALID','*','') status,
  3              tablespace_name
  4  from user_objects a, user_segments b
  5  where a.object_name = b.segment_name (+)
  6  order by object_type, object_name
  7  /

OBJECT_TYPE   OBJECT_NAME                         S TABLESPACE_NAME
-----------   --------------------------------    - -------------------------------
LOB           SYS_LOB0000026301C00014$$             DATA

TABLE         PEOPLE                                DATA

TYPE          ADDRESS_ARRAY_TYPE
              ADDRESS_TYPE

TYPE BODY     ADDRESS_TYPE


tkyte@TKYTE816> select name, length
  2      from sys.col$
  3      where obj# = ( select object_id
  4                     from user_objects
  5                     where object_name = 'PEOPLE' )
  6  /

NAME                  LENGTH
--------------------  ----------
NAME                      10
HOME_ADDRESS               1
SYS_NC00003$              25
SYS_NC00004$              25
SYS_NC00005$              30
SYS_NC00006$               2
SYS_NC00007$              22
WORK_ADDRESS               1
SYS_NC00009$              25
SYS_NC00010$              25
SYS_NC00011$              30
SYS_NC00012$               2
SYS_NC00013$              22
PREVIOUS_ADDRESSES      3852

14 rows selected.
```

What we see here now is that Oracle created a LOB for us. If the data in the VARRAY is under about 4,000 bytes, the data will be stored inline. If the data exceeds this, the VARRAY will be moved out-of-line into the LOB segment (just as any LOB would be).

VARRAYs are either stored as a RAW column inline, or as a LOB when they get too large. The overhead of a VARRAY (as compared to a nested table) is very small, making them a good choice as a method to store repeating data. VARRAYs can be searched on by un-nesting them, making them as flexible as nested tables in this respect:

```
tkyte@TKYTE816> update people
    2      set previous_addresses = Address_Array_Type(
    3                      Address_Type( '312 Johnston Dr', null,
    4                                    'Bethlehem', 'PA', 18017 ),
    5                      Address_Type( '513 Zulema St', 'Apartment #3',
    6                                    'Pittsburg', 'PA', 18123 ),
    7                      Address_Type( '840 South Frederick St', null,
    8                                    'Alexandria', 'VA', 20654 ) );

1 row updated.

tkyte@TKYTE816> select name, prev.city, prev.state, prev.zip_code
    2      from people p, table( p.previous_addresses ) prev
    3    where prev.state = 'PA';

NAME                    CITY                            ST   ZIP_CODE
--------------------    ----------------------------    --   ----------
Tom Kyte                Bethlehem                       PA      18017
Tom Kyte                Pittsburg                       PA      18123
```

One big difference here is that in the nested table implementation, we could have created an index on the nested table's STATE column, and the optimizer would have been able to use that. Here, the STATE column cannot be indexed.

The main differences between nested tables and VARRAYs can be summarized as follows:

Nested Table	VARRAY
'Array' elements have no specific order. The data in the collection may be returned in a very different order than it was in when you inserted it.	VARRAYs are true arrays. The data will remain inherently ordered as you left it. In our example above, the addresses are appended to the array. This implies that the oldest address is the first address, and the last previous address is the last address found in the array. A nested table implementation would need another attribute in order to identify the relative age of an address.
Nested tables are physically stored as a parent child table with surrogate keys.	VARRAYs are stored as a RAW column or as a LOB. There is minimal overhead introduced for the functionality.
Nested tables have no upper bound as to the number of elements that can be stored.	VARRAYs have an upper bound on the number of elements that can be stored. This maximum upper bound is defined at the time the type itself is created.

Nested Table	VARRAY

Nested tables may be modified (inserted/updated/deleted) from, using SQL.	VARRAYs must be procedurally modified. You cannot:
	
	`INSERT INTO`
	
	`TABLE ( SELECT P.PREVIOUS_ADDRESSES FROM PEOPLE P )`
	
	`VALUES ...`
	
	as you could with a nested table. To add an address, you would have to use procedural code (see example below).

Nested tables will perform a relational JOIN to bring the collect back with the row. For small collections, this may be expensive	VARRAYs do not join. The data is accessed inline for small collections, and as a LOB segment for large collections. In general, there will be less overhead associated with accessing a VARRAY compared to a nested table. There is potentially more overhead associated with updating a VARRAY as compared to a nested table however, since the entire VARRAY must be replaced – not just an element of it.

In the table above, I mentioned that VARRAYs cannot be modified using SQL and the TABLE clause, we must procedurally process them. You will most likely write a stored procedure to facilitate the modification of VARRAY columns. The code would look something like this:

```
tkyte@TKYTE816> declare
  2      l_prev_addresses    address_Array_Type;
  3  begin
  4          select p.previous_addresses into l_prev_addresses
  5            from people p
  6           where p.name = 'Tom Kyte';
  7
  8          l_prev_addresses.extend;
  9          l_prev_addresses(l_prev_addresses.count) :=
 10           Address_Type( '123 Main Street', null,
 11                         'Reston', 'VA', 45678 );
 12
 13          update people
 14             set previous_addresses = l_prev_addresses
 15           where name = 'Tom Kyte';
 16  end;
 17  /

PL/SQL procedure successfully completed.

tkyte@TKYTE816> select name, prev.city, prev.state, prev.zip_code
  2      from people p, table( p.previous_addresses ) prev
  3  /
```

NAME	CITY	ST	ZIP_CODE
Tom Kyte	Bethlehem	PA	18017
Tom Kyte	Pittsburg	PA	18123
Tom Kyte	Alexandria	VA	20654
Tom Kyte	Reston	VA	45678

Adding Data Types Wrap-Up

In this section, we reviewed the advantages and disadvantages of using the Oracle type extensions in your database tables. You must decide if the ability to create new data types, with standard column definitions and methods that may operate one those types unambiguously, is overshadowed by the inability to evolve these types over time (add/remove attributes).

> *I would like to point out that in Oracle 9i, this changes radically as the ability to evolve the type schema over time is added.*

We also reviewed the use of VARRAYs versus nested tables as a physical storage mechanism. We have seen how VARRAYs are excellent for storing a bounded set of ordered items compared to a nested table. You will find VARRAYs useful in many cases where you need to store a list of items, such as previous addresses, phone numbers, names of pets, and so on. Any time you have a list of items that do not necessitate an entire table all to themselves, VARRAYs will be useful.

Judicious use of types can add much to your system and its design. Using Oracle object types as columns in a table (as opposed to a table created as a TYPE, seen in Chapter 6 on *Tables*) is useful to enforce standardization, and ensure that the procedures (methods) are invoked with the correct inputs. The downside is the current lack of true schema evolution for the types, once you have created a table, which uses that type.

Using Types to Extend PL/SQL

This is where the object relational features of Oracle excel. PL/SQL is a very flexible, and capable, language as evidenced by the fact that Advanced Replication was written entirely in PL/SQL way back in Oracle 7.1.6. Oracle Applications (Human Resources, Financial Applications, CRM applications, and so on) are developed using PL/SQL as one of the predominant languages. In spite of its agility as a programming language, there will be times when you want to extend its capabilities – just as you would in Java C, C++ or any language. Object types are the way to do this. They add functionality to PL/SQL similar to what the **class** adds to Java or C++.

In this section, I would like to create an example that demonstrates how I use object types to make PL/SQL programming easier. Here I would like to create a File Type built on top of UTL_FILE. UTL_FILE is a supplied Oracle package that allows PL/SQL to perform text I/O operations (reading and writing) on the server's file system. It is a procedural API similar to the C language's F family of functions (fopen, fclose, fread, fwrite, and so on). We would like to encapsulate the functionality of UTL_FILE in an easier-to- use object type.

Creating a New PL/SQL Data Type

UTL_FILE works by returning a PL/SQL RECORD type. This will complicate our implementation slightly but can be worked around. The reason it complicates things is because a SQL object type can only contain SQL types, not PL/SQL types. Hence, we cannot create an object type that contains a PL/SQL RECORD in it, but we must if we want to encapsulate the functionality. In order to solve this, we'll use a small PL/SQL package in conjunction with our type.

I'll start with the type specification – our prototype for what we will build:

```
tkyte@TKYTE816> create or replace type FileType
  2  as object
  3  ( g_file_name    varchar2(255),
  4    g_path         varchar2(255),
  5    g_file_hdl     number,
  6
  7    static function open( p_path        in varchar2,
  8                          p_file_name   in varchar2,
  9                          p_mode        in varchar2 default 'r',
 10                          p_maxlinesize in number default 32765 )
 11    return FileType,
 12
 13    member function isOpen return boolean,
 14    member procedure close,
 15    member function get_line return varchar2,
 16    member procedure put( p_text in varchar2 ),
 17    member procedure new_line( p_lines in number default 1 ),
 18    member procedure put_line( p_text in varchar2 ),
 19    member procedure putf( p_fmt   in varchar2,
 20                           p_arg1 in varchar2 default null,
 21                           p_arg2 in varchar2 default null,
 22                           p_arg3 in varchar2 default null,
 23                           p_arg4 in varchar2 default null,
 24                           p_arg5 in varchar2 default null ),
 25    member procedure flush,
 26
 27    static procedure write_io( p_file      in  number,
 28                               p_operation in  varchar2,
 29                               p_parm1     in  varchar2 default null,
 30                               p_parm2     in  varchar2 default null,
 31                               p_parm3     in  varchar2 default null,
 32                               p_parm4     in  varchar2 default null,
 33                               p_parm5     in  varchar2 default null,
 34                               p_parm6     in  varchar2 default null )
 35  )
 36  /

Type created.
```

It looks a lot like the UTL_FILE package itself (if you are not familiar with UTL_FILE, you might want to read up on it in Appendix A on *Necessary Supplied Packages*). It provides almost the same functionality as the package, just more intuitively as you'll see (in my opinion). Now, if you remember from the ADDRESS_TYPE example above I said each object type has one default constructor, and that you must set each of the attributes of the object type to some value in that constructor. No user-defined code may execute as a side effect of this default constructor. In other words, this default constructor can be used only to set *every* attribute of the object type. This is not very useful. The static function OPEN in the above type will be used to demonstrate how we can create our own, infinitely more useful (and complex), constructors for our types. Notice how OPEN, part of the FILETYPE object type, returns a FILETYPE itself. It will do the necessary setup work, and then return a fully instantiated object type for us. This is the main use of static member functions in object types – they provide the ability to create your own complex object constructors. Static functions and procedures in an object type differ from member procedures and functions in that they do not get an implicit SELF parameter. These functions are very similar in nature to a packaged procedure or function. They are useful for coding common utility routines that many of the other member functions would invoke, but do not themselves need access to the instance data (the object attributes). WRITE_IO in the above object type will be an example of just such a routine. I use this one routine to do all of the UTL_FILE calls that write to a file so as to not have to repeat the same 14-line exception block every time.

Now, you will notice that the UTL_FILE.FILE_TYPE data type is not referenced in this object type, and in fact, it cannot be. The object type attributes can only be SQL types). We must save this record elsewhere. In order to do this, I am going to use a PL/SQL package as follows:

```
tkyte@TKYTE816> create or replace package FileType_pkg
  2  as
  3      type utl_fileArrayType is table of utl_file.file_type
  4          index by binary_integer;
  5
  6      g_files utl_fileArrayType;
  7
  8      g_invalid_path_msg constant varchar2(131) default
  9      'INVALID_PATH: File location or filename was invalid.';
 10
 11      g_invalid_mode_msg constant varchar2(131) default
 12      'INVALID_MODE: The open_mode parameter %s in FOPEN was invalid.';
 13
 14      g_invalid_filehandle_msg constant varchar2(131) default
 15      'INVALID_FILEHANDLE: The file handle was invalid.';
 16
 17      g_invalid_operation_msg constant varchar2(131) default
 18      'INVALID_OPERATION: The file could not be opened or operated '||
 19      'on as requested.';
 20
 21      g_read_error_msg constant varchar2(131) default
 22      'READ_ERROR: An operating system error occurred during '||
 23      'the read operation.';
 24
 25      g_write_error_msg constant varchar2(131) default
 26      'WRITE_ERROR: An operating system error occurred during '||
 27      'the write operation.';
 28
 29      g_internal_error_msg constant varchar2(131) default
 30      'INTERNAL_ERROR: An unspecified error in PL/SQL.';
 31
 32      g_invalid_maxlinesize_msg constant varchar2(131) default
 33      'INVALID_MAXLINESIZE: Specified max linesize %d is too '||
 34      'large or too small';
 35  end;
 36  /
Package created.
```

This package will be used at run-time to hold any, and all, `UTL_FILE.FILE_TYPE` records for us. Each object type instance (variable) we declare of `FILE_TYPE` will allocate themselves an empty 'slot' in the `G_FILES` array above. This shows a method to implement 'private' data in Oracle object types. We will store the real runtime data in this packaged array variable `G_FILES` and storing only the handle (the index into the array) in the object type. In Oracle's current object implementation, all data in an object type is `PUBLIC` data. There is no way to hide an attribute in the type, to make it inaccessible to the users of that type. For example, given the `FILE_TYPE` above, it will be legitimate for us to access the `G_FILE_NAME` instance variable directly. If that were not desirable, we would 'hide' this variable in a PL/SQL package in the same fashion that we are going to 'hide' the PL/SQL record type there. No one can access the data in the PL/SQL package unless we grant `EXECUTE` on that package to them, therefore it is protected data.

This package is also used to hold some constants for us. Object types do not support constant data, hence the package becomes a nice holding place for that as well.

I tend to name a package that supports a type like this, after the type itself. So, since we created the type `FILETYPE`, I have a `FILETYPE_PKG` to go along with it. Now we are ready for the `FILETYPE` type body. This will contain the implementation of all of our member and static functions and procedures from above. I'll present the code with comments about what it is doing interspersed throughout:

```
tkyte@TKYTE816> create or replace type body FileType
  2  as
  3
  4  static function open( p_path       in varchar2,
  5                        p_file_name  in varchar2,
  6                        p_mode       in varchar2 default 'r',
  7                        p_maxlinesize in number default 32765 )
  8  return FileType
  9  is
 10      l_file_hdl number;
 11      l_utl_file_dir varchar2(1024);
 12  begin
 13      l_file_hdl := nvl( fileType_pkg.g_files.last, 0 )+1;
 14
 15      filetype_pkg.g_files(l_file_hdl) :=
 16          utl_file.fopen( p_path, p_file_name, p_mode, p_maxlinesize );
 17
 18      return fileType( p_file_name, p_path, l_file_hdl );
```

The above portion of the static member function OPEN is responsible for finding an empty slot in our private data (hidden in the `filetype_pkg` package). It does this by adding one to the LAST attribute of the table. If the table is empty, LAST returns NULL so we NVL this value – the first entry we will allocate will be the array index 1. The next one will be 2 and so on. Our CLOSE function *deletes* the entries as we close the file so we will reuse space in this array over time as we open and close files. The remainder of the function is very straightforward; it opens the requested file and returns a fully instantiated instance of a `FILETYPE` object for us to use. The rest of the `FILETYPE.OPEN` method is an exception block to catch and handle all of the errors that `UTL_FILE.FOPEN` might raise:

```
 19  exception
 20      when utl_file.invalid_path then
 21          begin
 22              execute immediate 'select value
 23                                  from v$parameter
```

```
24                            where name = ``utl_file_dir'''
25            into l_utl_file_dir;
26         exception
27            when others then
28                 l_utl_file_dir := p_path;
29         end;
30         if ( instr( l_utl_file_dir||',', p_path ||',' ) = 0 )
31         then
32            raise_application_error
33            ( -20001,'The path ` || p_path ||
34              ` is not in the utl_file_dir path "` ||
35                 l_utl_file_dir || '"' );
36         else
37            raise_application_error
38            (-20001,fileType_pkg.g_invalid_path_msg);
39         end if;
40      when utl_file.invalid_mode then
41         raise_application_error
42         (-20002,replace(fileType_pkg.g_invalid_mode_msg,'%s',p_mode) );
43      when utl_file.invalid_operation then
44         raise_application_error
45         (-20003,fileType_pkg.g_invalid_operation_msg);
46      when utl_file.internal_error then
47         raise_application_error
48         (-20006,fileType_pkg.g_internal_error_msg);
49      when utl_file.invalid_maxlinesize then
50         raise_application_error
51         (-20007, replace(fileType_pkg.g_invalid_maxlinesize_msg,
52                     '%d',p_maxlinesize));
53  end;
```

This exception block is designed to catch and re-raise all UTL_FILE exceptions in a better way than UTL_FILE does natively. Instead of receiving the SQLERRMR of USER DEFINED EXCEPTION in the invoking routine as you would normally, we'll receive something meaningful like THE OPEN MODE PARAMETER WAS INVALID. Additionally, for the INVALID_PATH exception, which is raised if the file could not be opened due to an invalid path or filename, we go out of our way to provide a meaningful error message. If the OWNER of this type has been granted SELECT on SYS.V_$PARAMETER, we will retrieve the entire UTL_FILE_DIR INIT.ORA parameter and verify the path we are attempting to use is in fact set up to be used. If it is not we return an error message stating that this is the case. Of all of the errors raised by UTL_FILE, this one exception is by far the most 'popular'. Having an error message this meaningful will save many hours of 'debugging' for the novice UTL_FILE user.

Continuing on, we have the is Open method:

```
55  member function isOpen return boolean
56  is
57  begin
58      return utl_file.is_open( .filetype_pkg.g_files(g_file_hdl) );
59  end;
```

It is simply a layer on top of the existing UTL_FILE.IS_OPEN. Since this UTL_FILE function never raises any errors, it is a very easy routine to implement. The next method is GET_LINE, its logic is a little more involved:

```
61   member function get_line return varchar2
62   is
63       l_buffer varchar2(32765);
64   begin
65       utl_file.get_line( filetype_pkg.g_files(g_file_hdl), l_buffer );
66       return l_buffer;
67   exception
68       when utl_file.invalid_filehandle then
69           raise_application_error
70           (-20002,fileType_pkg.g_invalid_filehandle_msg);
71       when utl_file.invalid_operation then
72           raise_application_error
73           (-20003,fileType_pkg.g_invalid_operation_msg);
74       when utl_file.read_error then
75           raise_application_error
76           (-20004,fileType_pkg.g_read_error_msg);
77       when utl_file.internal_error then
78           raise_application_error
79           (-20006,fileType_pkg.g_internal_error_msg);
80   end;
```

Here we use a local variable of type VARCHAR2(32765),which is the largest PL/SQL variable you can have and is the largest line UTL_FILE can actually read. Again, much like the OPEN method above, we catch and handle each and every error that UTL_FILE.GET_LINE can raise and convert it into a RAISE_APPLICATION_ERROR call. This allows us to get meaningful error messages from the GET_LINE function now (and makes GET_LINE a function, not a procedure, which is done for convenience).

Now for another static procedure; WRITE_IO. The sole purpose of WRITE_IO is to avoid having to code the same exception handler in six times for each of the WRITE oriented routines, because they all throw the same exceptions. This function is here purely for convenience and simply calls one of six UTL_FILE functions and handles the errors generically:

```
82   static procedure write_io( p_file      in number,
83                              p_operation in varchar2,
84                              p_parm1     in varchar2 default null,
85                              p_parm2     in varchar2 default null,
86                              p_parm3     in varchar2 default null,
87                              p_parm4     in varchar2 default null,
88                              p_parm5     in varchar2 default null,
89                              p_parm6     in varchar2 default null )
90   is
91       l_file utl_file.file_type default  filetype_pkg.g_files(p_file);
92   begin
93       if    (p_operation='close')    then
94           utl_file.fclose(l_file);
95       elsif (p_operation='put')      then
96           utl_file.put(l_file,p_parm1);
97       elsif (p_operation='new_line') then
98           utl_file.new_line( l_file,p_parm1 );
99       elsif (p_operation='put_line') then
100          utl_file.put_line( l_file, p_parm1 );
101      elsif (p_operation='flush')    then
102          utl_file.fflush( l_file );
103      elsif (p_operation='putf' )    then
104          utl_file.putf(l_file,p_parm1,p_parm2,
```

```
105                      p_parm3,p_parm4,p_parm5,
106                      p_parm6);
107        else raise program_error;
108        end if;
109   exception
110        when utl_file.invalid_filehandle then
111            raise_application_error
112            (-20002,fileType_pkg.g_invalid_filehandle_msg);
113        when utl_file.invalid_operation then
114            raise_application_error
115            (-20003,fileType_pkg.g_invalid_operation_msg);
116        when utl_file.write_error then
117            raise_application_error
118            (-20005,fileType_pkg.g_write_error_msg);
119        when utl_file.internal_error then
120            raise_application_error
121            (-20006,fileType_pkg.g_internal_error_msg);
122   end;
```

The six remaining methods simply call the WRITE_IO method to do their work:

```
124   member procedure close
125   is
126   begin
127        fileType.write_io(g_file_hdl, 'close' );
128        filetype_pkg.g_files.delete(g_file_hdl);
129   end;
130
131   member procedure put( p_text in varchar2 )
132   is
133   begin
134        fileType.write_io(g_file_hdl, 'put',p_text );
135   end;
136
137   member procedure new_line( p_lines in number default 1 )
138   is
139   begin
140        fileType.write_io(g_file_hdl, 'new_line',p_lines );
141   end;
142
143   member procedure put_line( p_text in varchar2 )
144   is
145   begin
146        fileType.write_io(g_file_hdl, 'put_line',p_text );
147   end;
148
149   member procedure putf
150   ( p_fmt  in varchar2, p_arg1 in varchar2 default null,
151     p_arg2 in varchar2 default null, p_arg3 in varchar2 default null,
152     p_arg4 in varchar2 default null, p_arg5 in varchar2 default null )
153   is
154   begin
155        fileType.write_io
156        (g_file_hdl, 'putf', p_fmt, p_arg1,
157          p_arg2, p_arg3, p_arg4, p_arg5);
```

```
158   end;
159
160   member procedure flush
161   is
162   begin
163       fileType.write_io(g_file_hdl, 'flush' );
164   end;
165
166   end;
167   /

Type body created.
```

Now, you'll notice in the above that I catch each, and every UTL_FILE exception, and raise another error using RAISE_APPLICATION_ERROR. This is the main reason I decided to encapsulate UTL_FILE in the first place. UTL_FILE uses 'USER-DEFINED EXCEPTIONS' to raise errors. These exceptions are defined by the developers of UTL_FILE and when they raise these exceptions, the error message Oracle associates with that is simply 'USER-DEFINED EXCEPTION'. This is not very meaningful and doesn't help us figure out what went wrong. I prefer to use RAISE_APPLICATION_ERROR, which allows me to set the SQLCODE and SQLERRM returned to the client. To see the effect this can have on us, we just need to look at the following small example which demonstrates the types of error messages we will receive from UTL_FILE and FILETYPE:

```
tkyte@TKYTE816> declare
  2       f utl_file.file_type := utl_file.fopen( 'c:\temp\bogus',
  3                                               'foo.txt', 'w' );
  4   begin
  5       utl_file.fclose( f );
  6   end;
  7   /
declare
*
ERROR at line 1:
ORA-06510: PL/SQL: unhandled user-defined exception
ORA-06512: at "SYS.UTL_FILE", line 98
ORA-06512: at "SYS.UTL_FILE", line 157
ORA-06512: at line 2


tkyte@TKYTE816> declare
  2       f fileType := fileType.open( 'c:\temp\bogus', '
  3                                    foo.txt', 'w' );
  4   begin
  5       f.close;
  6   end;
  7   /
declare
*
ERROR at line 1:
ORA-20001: The path c:\temp\bogus is not in the utl_file_dir path "c:\temp,
c:\oracle"
ORA-06512: at "TKYTE.FILETYPE", line 54
ORA-06512: at line 2
```

It is not hard to tell which one is easier to figure out what exactly the error is. The second error message, since the owner of the type had access to V$PARAMETER, is *very* precise as to the exact cause of the error; the directory I used was invalid, it was not in the UTL_FILE_DIR init.ora parameter. Even if the owner didn't have access to V$PARAMETER, the error would have been:

```
*
ERROR at line 1:
ORA-20001: INVALID_PATH: File location or filename was invalid.
ORA-06512: at "TKYTE.FILETYPE", line 59
ORA-06512: at line 2
```

which is still much more useful than user-defined exception.

Another thing to notice in this type is that I am able to set up my preferred defaults for routines. For example, prior to Oracle 8.0.5, UTL_FILE was limited to a maximum line size of 1,023 bytes per line. If you tried to print out a line of text that exceeded this, UTL_FILE would raise an exception. By default, this behavior persists in Oracle 8i. Unless you call UTL_FILE.FOPEN and tell it to use a particular line size, it will still default to 1,023. I myself would rather have this default to the maximum size of 32 KB by default. I also implemented a default open mode at the start of the code of 'R' for read. Since 90 percent of the time I use UTL_FILE I'm using it to read a file, this made the most sense for me.

Now to exercise the package and show how each function/procedure works. The first example will create a file (assumes that we are running on Windows NT, that the c:\temp directory exists, and that the UTL_FILE_DIR init.ora parameter contains c:\temp) and write some known data to it. It will then close that file, saving the data. This demonstrates the WRITE functionality of the FILETYPE type:

```
tkyte@TKYTE816> declare
  2      f fileType := fileType.open( 'c:\temp', 'foo.txt', 'w' );
  3  begin
  4      if ( f.isOpen )
  5      then
  6          dbms_output.put_line( 'File is OPEN' );
  7      end if;
  8
  9      for i in 1 .. 10 loop
 10          f.put( i || ',' );
 11      end loop;
 12      f.put_line( 11 );
 13
 14      f.new_line( 5 );
 15      for i in 1 .. 5
 16      loop
 17          f.put_line( 'line ' || i );
 18      end loop;
 19
 20      f.putf( '%s %s', 'Hello', 'World' );
 21
 22      f.flush;
 23
 24      f.close;
 25  end;
 26  /
File is OPEN

PL/SQL procedure successfully completed.
```

The second half of the example demonstrates reading a file using `FILETYPE`. It will open the file we just wrote and verify the data we read in is exactly the data we expect:

```
tkyte@TKYTE816> declare
  2      f fileType := fileType.open( 'c:\temp', 'foo.txt' );
  3  begin
  4      if ( f.isOpen )
  5      then
  6          dbms_output.put_line( 'File is OPEN' );
  7      end if;
  8
  9      dbms_output.put_line
 10      ( 'line 1: (should be 1,2,...,11)' || f.get_line );
 11
 12      for i in 2 .. 6
 13      loop
 14          dbms_output.put_line
 15          ( 'line ' || i || ': (should be blank)' || f.get_line);
 16      end loop;
 17
 18      for i in 7 .. 11
 19      loop
 20          dbms_output.put_line
 21          ( 'line ' || to_char(i+1) ||
 22            ': (should be line N)' || f.get_line);
 23      end loop;
 24
 25      dbms_output.put_line
 26      ( 'line 12: (should be Hello World)' || f.get_line);
 27
 28      begin
 29          dbms_output.put_line( f.get_line );
 30          dbms_output.put_line( 'the above is an error' );
 31      exception
 32          when NO_DATA_FOUND then
 33              dbms_output.put_line( 'got a no data found as expected' );
 34      end;
 35      f.close;
 36  end;
 37  /
File is OPEN
line 1: (should be 1,2,...,11)1,2,3,4,5,6,7,8,9,10,11
line 2: (should be blank)
line 3: (should be blank)
line 4: (should be blank)
line 5: (should be blank)
line 6: (should be blank)
line 8: (should be line N)line 1
line 9: (should be line N)line 2
line 10: (should be line N)line 3
line 11: (should be line N)line 4
line 12: (should be line N)line 5
line 12: (should be Hello World)Hello World
got a no data found as expected

PL/SQL procedure successfully completed.
```

We have encapsulated the UTL_FILE type using an Oracle object type. We have a nice layer on top of the supplied package that works the way we want it to exactly. In 'object programming' terms we have just extended the UTL_FILE class – implementing it with methods that work as we prefer, instead of exactly the way the Oracle developers set it up. We haven't reinvented UTL_FILE, simply repackaged it. This is a good overall programming technique; if the implementation of UTL_FILE changes, or a bug is introduced during an upgrade, the odds are you can work around it in your type body, avoiding having to change hundreds or thousands of dependent routines. For example, in one release of UTL_FILE, opening a non-existent file in A mode didn't work; it would not create the file as it should have. The work around was to code:

```
begin
    file_stat := utl_file.fopen(file_dir,file_name,'a');
exception
    -- if file does not exist, fopen will fail with
    -- mode 'a' - bug:371510
    when utl_file.invalid_operation then
        -- let any other exception propagate
        -- to the outer block as normal
        file_stat := utl_file.fopen(file_dir,file_name,'w');
end;
```

Now, if you opened a file in APPEND mode in 100 routines, you would have a lot of fixing to do. If on the other hand, you had this nice layer, you would be able to fix it in one location and be done with it.

Unique Uses for Collections

Another use of object types in PL/SQL is the use of collection types, and their potential to interact with SQL and PL/SQL easily. There are three things collection types can do in SQL and PL/SQL that people frequently ask how to do. These are:

❑   The ability to SELECT * from PLSQL_FUNCTION – You can write a PL/SQL routine and query from it, instead of querying from a database table.

❑   The ability to array fetch into a table of records – PL/SQL gives us the ability to BULK COLLECT (fetch more than one row at a time) into PL/SQL tables natively. Unfortunately, this works only with PL/SQL tables of SCALARs. I cannot do the following:

```
select c1, c2 BULK COLLECT INTO record_type from T
```

so I must code:

```
select c1, c2 BULK COLLECT INTO table1, table2 from T
```

Using collection types, I can array fetch into a 'record type'.

❑   The ability to insert a record – Instead of inserting column by column, I can insert a single record.

SELECT * from PLSQL_FUNCTION

In order to demonstrate this ability, we will revisit a bind variable issue (I cannot leave this topic alone). A common requirement I see frequently is the stated need to issue a query such as:

```
select * from t where c in ( :bind_variable )
```

where the BIND_VARIABLE is a list of values. That is, the value of BIND_VARIABLE is '1, 2, 3' perhaps, and you want the above query to be executed as if it were:

```
select * from t where c in ( 1, 2, 3 )
```

This would return rows where c = 1 or 2 or 3, but it will really be executed as:

```
select * from t where c in ( '1,2,3' )
```

This will return rows where c = '1,2,3' – a single string. This usually arises from a user interface where the end user is supplied with a list box of values, and may select one or more (any number) items from the list. In order to avoid having to create unique queries for each request (we know how bad that would be) we need a method of binding a varying number of elements in an in list. Well, since we can SELECT * FROM PLSQL_FUNCTION, we are in business. This demonstrates how:

```
tkyte@TKYTE816> create or replace type myTableType
  2  as table of number;
  3  /

Type created.
```

The type we created is the one our PL/SQL function will return. This type *must* be defined at the SQL level via the CREATE TYPE statement. It cannot be a type inside of a PL/SQL package, the goal is to retrieve this data via SQL, hence we need a SQL type. This also proves that I am not totally biased against nested tables. In fact, they are the collection of choice when it comes to programming in PL/SQL, in this fashion. A VARRAY would limit us to some artificial upper bound in the array – the nested table implementation is limited only by the available memory on your system.

```
tkyte@TKYTE816> create or replace
  2  function str2tbl( p_str in varchar2 ) return myTableType
  3  as
  4      l_str    long default p_str || ',';
  5      l_n         number;
  6      l_data      myTableType := myTabletype();
  7  begin
  8      loop
  9          l_n := instr( l_str, ',' );
 10          exit when (nvl(l_n,0) = 0);
 11          l_data.extend;
 12          l_data( l_data.count ) :=
 13              ltrim(rtrim(substr(l_str,1,l_n-1)));
 14          l_str := substr( l_str, l_n+1 );
 15      end loop;
 16      return l_data;
 17  end;
 18  /

Function created.
```

So, we have a PL/SQL function that will take a comma-delimited string of values, and parse it out into a SQL Type MYTABLETYPE. All we need to do now is find a way to retrieve this, using SQL. Using the TABLE operator and a CAST, we can do this easily:

```
tkyte@TKYTE816> variable bind_variable varchar2(30)
tkyte@TKYTE816> exec :bind_variable := '1,3,5,7,99'

PL/SQL procedure successfully completed.


BIND_VARIABLE
-------------------------------
1,3,5,7,99

tkyte@TKYTE816> select *
  2    from TABLE ( cast ( str2tbl(:bind_variable) as myTableType ) )
  3  /

COLUMN_VALUE
------------
           1
           3
           5
           7
          99
```

Now, using this as an IN subquery becomes trivial:

```
tkyte@TKYTE816> select *
  2    from all_users
  3  where user_id in
  4      ( select *
  5          from TABLE ( cast ( str2tbl(:bind_variable) as myTableType ) )
  6      )
  7  /

USERNAME                         USER_ID CREATED
------------------------------ --------- ---------
SYSTEM                                 5 04-NOV-00
```

You can use this functionality in many places now. You can now take a PL/SQL variable and apply an ORDER BY to it, you can return sets of data that was generated by the PL/SQL routine back to the client easily, you can apply WHERE clauses to PL/SQL variables, and so on.

Going one step further here, we can return full multi-column result-sets this way as well. For example:

```
tkyte@TKYTE816> create type myRecordType as object
  2  ( seq int,
  3    a int,
  4    b varchar2(10),
  5    c date
  6  )
  7  /

Type created.

tkyte@TKYTE816> create table t ( x int, y varchar2(10), z date );
Table created.
```

```
tkyte@TKYTE816> create or replace type myTableType
  2  as table of myRecordType
  3  /

Type created.

tkyte@TKYTE816> create or replace function my_function return myTableType
  2  is
  3      l_data myTableType;
  4  begin
  5      l_data := myTableType();
  6
  7      for i in 1..5
  8      loop
  9          l_data.extend;
 10          l_data(i) := myRecordType( i, i, 'row ' || i, sysdate+i );
 11      end loop;
 12      return l_data;
 13  end;
 14  /

Function created.

tkyte@TKYTE816> select *
  2      from TABLE ( cast( my_function() as mytableType ) )
  3     where c > sysdate+1
  4     order by seq desc
  5  /

       SEQ          A B          C
---------- ---------- ---------- ---------
         5          5 row 5      29-MAR-01
         4          4 row 4      28-MAR-01
         3          3 row 3      27-MAR-01
         2          2 row 2      26-MAR-01
```

Bulk Fetching into RECORD Types

So, we've seen how we can use the collection type to SELECT * FROM PLSQL_FUNCTION, now we'll see that we can use it to do a bulk fetch into the equivalent of a PL/SQL record type. We cannot actually do a bulk fetch into a true PL/SQL record type, but we can fetch into a SQL nested table type easily. For this, we will need two object types, a scalar type that represents our record, and a table of that type. For example:

```
tkyte@TKYTE816> create type myScalarType
  2  as object
  3  ( username varchar2(30),
  4    user_id  number,
  5    created  date
  6  )
  7  /

Type created.
```

```
tkyte@TKYTE816> create type myTableType as table of myScalarType
  2  /

Type created.
```

Now we are ready to select into a variable of MYTABLETYPE as follows:

```
tkyte@TKYTE816> declare
  2      l_users    myTableType;
  3  begin
  4      select cast( multiset(select username, user_id, created
  5                              from all_users
  6                             order by username )
  7                  as myTableType )
  8        into l_users
  9        from dual;
 10
 11      dbms_output.put_line( 'Retrieved '|| l_users.count || ' rows');
 12  end;
 13  /
Retrieved 25 rows

PL/SQL procedure successfully completed.
```

We can substitute the query against ALL_USERS with any query that fetches a VARCHAR2(30), number and a date. The query can be arbitrarily complex, involve joins, and so on. The trick is to cast the results of that subquery as being of our object type. We can then fetch that entire result set into our local variable using the standard SELECT . . . INTO syntax.

Inserting Using a RECORD Type

Given that we can SELECT * FROM COLLECTION_VARIABLE, where the collection variable is either a local variable or a PL/SQL function that returns a nested table type, it is not too hard to figure out how to INSERT using this method. We simply define a variable of our nested table type, and fill it up with as many records as we would like to insert. The following example demonstrates what a single row insert would look like:

```
tkyte@TKYTE816> create table t as select * from all_users where 1=0;

Table created.

tkyte@TKYTE816> declare
  2      l_users    myTableType :=
  3                      myTableType( myScalarType( 'tom', 1, sysdate ) );
  4  begin
  5          insert into t
  6          select * from TABLE ( cast( l_users as myTableType ) );
  7  end;
  8  /
tkyte@TKYTE816> select * from t;

USERNAME            USER_ID CREATED
--------------- ---------- ---------
tom                       1 24-MAR-01
```

When dealing with a table that has many columns, this little trick can come in handy.

Using Types to Extend PL/SQL Wrap-Up

In this section, we have seen how we can effectively use Oracle object types, not as a storage mechanism, but rather as a way to extend PL/SQL in the same way classes are used in Java or C++ to provide generic functionality.

We have also seen some interesting uses for the nested table type. The ability to SELECT * from a PLSQL_FUNCTION raises some interesting opportunities. Varying sized IN lists is just the beginning. The opportunities are limitless here. You could write a small routine that uses UTL_FILE to read an OS file, parse each line around commas, and return a result set that is the contents of the flat file to be inserted into some other table, or joined to a table for example.

Using object types in this fashion breathes new life into an established language. Once you've created a type or two for yourself, you'll begin to find applications for this technique in much of your code. It is a logical way to tightly couple data and functionality together – one of the primary goals of object-oriented programming. To not offend the purists, I won't call this *pure* object-oriented programming in PL/SQL, but it certainly is something very close to that.

Object Relational Views

This is a fairly powerful feature for those of you who want to work with the object relational features, but still must present a relational view of the data to many applications. This allows you to use the standard VIEW mechanism to synthesize objects from relational tables. You don't have to create tables of a TYPE, with all of the mysterious columns and such – you can create a view of standard tables you have created (and probably already have). These views will behave just like an object table of that type would – without much of the overhead of hidden keys, surrogate keys, and other nuances.

In this section, we will use the EMP and DEPT tables to present a department-oriented view of the data. This is similar to the example of the nested table we used in Chapter 6 on *Tables*, where by we had the EMP_TAB_TYPE as a nested table of EMP_TYPE, and the DEPT table had a column of this nested table type. Here, we will model the EMP_TYPE and the EMP_TAB_TYPE once again, but we will also create a DEPT_TYPE object type as well and a view of that type.

It is interesting to note that this approach of using object views allows us to have the best of both worlds (relational and object relational). For example, we might have an application that needs a department-oriented view of the data. Their view starts at the department and the employees in the department are naturally modeled as a collection inside the department. Another application however needs a different perspective. For example, when you walk up to a security guard and identify yourself as an employee, they will need to have an employee-oriented view of the data. Department in this case is inferred by the employee, not the other way around where the view was that department infers employees. This is the power of the relational model – many different views can efficiently be supported simultaneously. The object model does not support many different views of the same data as easily (if at all) or efficiently. By using many different object views of the relational data, we can satisfy everyone.

The Types

The types used in this example are borrowed from Chapter 6 on *Tables*, with the addition of the DEPT_TYPE. They are:

```
scott@TKYTE816> create or replace type emp_type
  2   as object
  3   (empno        number(4),
  4    ename        varchar2(10),
  5    job          varchar2(9),
  6    mgr          number(4),
  7    hiredate     date,
  8    sal          number(7, 2),
  9    comm         number(7, 2)
 10   );
 11   /

Type created.

scott@TKYTE816> create or replace type emp_tab_type
  2   as table of emp_type
  3   /

Type created.

scott@TKYTE816> create or replace type dept_type
  2   as object
  3   ( deptno number(2),
  4     dname   varchar2(14),
  5     loc     varchar2(13),
  6     emps    emp_tab_type
  7   )
  8   /

Type created.
```

Once again, a department is modeled as being an object with a department number, a name, a location, and employees.

The O-R View

It is easy from the above type definitions, to synthesize our data for this view from the existing relational data. It would look like:

```
scott@TKYTE816> create or replace view dept_or
  2   of dept_type
  3   with object identifier(deptno)
  4   as
  5   select deptno, dname, loc,
  6          cast ( multiset (
  7                  select empno, ename, job, mgr, hiredate, sal, comm
  8                    from emp
  9                   where emp.deptno = dept.deptno )
```

```
 10                    as emp_tab_type )
 11      from dept
 12   /

View created.
```

We are already familiar with the role of the CAST and the MULTISET – we are just turning a correlated subquery into a nested table collection here. For each row in DEPT, we will query out all of the employees. We've told Oracle which column(s) identify a row uniquely in the view using the WITH OBJECT IDENTIFIER clause. This allows Oracle to synthesize an object reference for us, giving us the ability to treat this view as if it were an object table.

As soon as we have the view, we can start using it:

```
scott@TKYTE816> select dname, d.emps
  2      from dept_or d
  3   /

DNAME             EMPS(EMPNO, ENAME, JOB, MGR, HIREDATE, S
--------------    ----------------------------------------
ACCOUNTING        EMP_TAB_TYPE(EMP_TYPE(7782, 'CLARK',
                  'MANAGER', 7839, '09-JUN-81', 2450,
                  NULL), EMP_TYPE(7839, 'KING',
                  'PRESIDENT', NULL, '17-NOV-81', 5000,
                  NULL), EMP_TYPE(7934, 'MILLER', 'CLERK',
                  7782, '23-JAN-82', 1300, NULL))

RESEARCH          EMP_TAB_TYPE(EMP_TYPE(7369, 'SMITH',
                  'CLERK', 7902, '17-DEC-80', 800, NULL),
                  EMP_TYPE(7566, 'JONES', 'MANAGER', 7839,
                  '02-APR-81', 2975, NULL), EMP_TYPE(7788,
                  'SCOTT', 'ANALYST', 7566, '09-DEC-82',
                  3000, NULL), EMP_TYPE(7876, 'ADAMS',
                  'CLERK', 7788, '12-JAN-83', 1100, NULL),
                  EMP_TYPE(7902, 'FORD', 'ANALYST', 7566,
                  '03-DEC-81', 3000, NULL))

SALES             EMP_TAB_TYPE(EMP_TYPE(7499, 'ALLEN',
                  'SALESMAN', 7698, '20-FEB-81', 1600,
                  300), EMP_TYPE(7521, 'WARD', 'SALESMAN',
                  7698, '22-FEB-81', 1250, 500),
                  EMP_TYPE(7654, 'MARTIN', 'SALESMAN',
                  7698, '28-SEP-81', 1250, 1400),
                  EMP_TYPE(7698, 'BLAKE', 'MANAGER', 7839,
                  '01-MAY-81', 2850, NULL), EMP_TYPE(7844,
                  'TURNER', 'SALESMAN', 7698, '08-SEP-81',
                  1500, 0), EMP_TYPE(7900, 'JAMES',
                  'CLERK', 7698, '03-DEC-81', 950, NULL))

OPERATIONS        EMP_TAB_TYPE()

4 rows selected.
```

```
scott@TKYTE816> select deptno, dname, loc, count(*)
  2      from dept_or d, table ( d.emps )
  3    group by deptno, dname, loc
  4  /

    DEPTNO DNAME            LOC             COUNT(*)
---------- --------------- -------------- ----------
        10 ACCOUNTING       NEW YORK               3
        20 RESEARCH         DALLAS                 5
        30 SALES            CHICAGO                6

3 rows selected.
```

So, we are on our way. We have the relational tables and the object-relational view. Externally, it is difficult to tell which is the view, and which are the tables. The functionality of an object table is available to us – we have object references on this table, the nested table is set up, and so on. The advantage here is that we specify how to join EMP to DEPT using the existing natural parent/child relationship.

So, we have created an object-relational view that exposes the data for querying. It does not however work when it comes to modifications yet:

```
scott@TKYTE816> update TABLE ( select p.emps
  2                        from dept_or p
  3                       where deptno = 20 )
  4      set ename = lower(ename)
  5  /
   set ename = lower(ename)
       *
ERROR at line 4:
ORA-25015: cannot perform DML on this nested table view column


scott@TKYTE816> declare
  2      l_emps   emp_tab_type;
  3  begin
  4      select p.emps into l_emps
  5        from dept_or  p
  6       where deptno = 10;
  7
  8      for i in 1 .. l_emps.count
  9      loop
 10          l_emps(i).ename := lower(l_emps(i).ename);
 11      end loop;
 12
 13      update dept_or
 14         set emps = l_emps
 15       where deptno = 10;
 16  end;
 17  /
declare
*
ERROR at line 1:
ORA-01733: virtual column not allowed here
ORA-06512: at line 13
```

We need to 'train' our view how to update itself. We have a somewhat, complex mapping of relational data to object-relational – it can be arbitrarily complex in fact. So, how can we 'train' our view to update itself? Oracle provides a mechanism called an INSTEAD OF trigger for this purpose. We can code the logic that should execute INSTEAD OF Oracle's logic when we modify the contents of the view. For illustrative purposes, we will train the above view to allow it to update itself.

Oracle allows us to place INSTEAD OF triggers on the view DEPT_OR as well as any nested table type included in the view. If we place a trigger on the nested table columns, it will allow us to process the first update from above – the UPDATE of the nested table column as if it where a table. The trigger for this would look like:

```
scott@TKYTE816> create or replace trigger EMPS_IO_UPDATE
  2  instead of UPDATE on nested table emps of dept_or
  3  begin
  4      if ( :new.empno = :old.empno )
  5      then
  6          update emp
  7              set ename = :new.ename, job = :new.job, mgr = :new.mgr,
  8                  hiredate = :new.hiredate, sal = :new.sal, comm = :new.comm
  9              where empno = :old.empno;
 10      else
 11          raise_application_error(-20001,'Empno cannot be updated' );
 12      end if;
 13  end;
 14  /

Trigger created.
```

As you can see, this trigger will fire INSTEAD OF UPDATE on the nested table column EMPS of the DEPT_OR view. It will be called for each and every row modified in the nested table and has access to the :OLD and :NEW values – just like a 'normal' trigger would. In this case, it is clear what we need to do. We need to update the existing EMP row by EMPNO, setting the columns to their new values. One thing I enforce in this trigger is that an UPDATE to the primary key is not allowed (hey, we might be using object-relational features, but that doesn't mean we should violate the basic tenets of relational database design!).

Now if we execute:

```
scott@TKYTE816> update TABLE ( select p.emps
  2                      from dept_or p
  3                      where deptno = 20 )
  4      set ename = lower(ename)
  5  /

5 rows updated.

scott@TKYTE816> select ename from emp where deptno = 20;

ENAME
----------
smith
jones
scott
```

```
    adams
    ford

scott@TKYTE816> select ename
  2      from TABLE( select p.emps
  3                    from dept_or p
  4                   where deptno = 20 );

ENAME
----------
smith
jones
scott
adams
ford
```

We see that the update of the nested table successfully translates into the relational table updates as expected. Coding the relevant INSERT and DELETE triggers are equally as easy, the UPDATE is the most complex case, and so we'll stop there.

At this point, it we execute:

```
scott@TKYTE816> declare
  2      l_emps    emp_tab_type;
  3  begin
  4      select p.emps into l_emps
  5        from dept_or  p
  6       where deptno = 10;
  7
  8      for i in 1 .. l_emps.count
  9      loop
 10          l_emps(i).ename := lower(l_emps(i).ename);
 11      end loop;
 12
 13      update dept_or
 14         set emps = l_emps
 15       where deptno = 10;
 16  end;
 17  /
declare
*
ERROR at line 1:
ORA-01732: data manipulation operation not legal on this view
ORA-06512: at line 13
```

We find that it still does not work. This might seem surprising. Should it not fire our trigger from above? In fact, no it will not. Only updates to the nested table that use the collection un-nesting will fire this trigger – only when we treat the nested table as a table will that fire the trigger. Here, we are simply updating a column in the DEPT_OR table – we are not doing a set operation on the nested table itself. In order to support this style of code (and to support updates to the other scalar attributes of the DEPT_OR view itself), we need an INSTEAD OF trigger on the DEPT_OR view. The logic of this trigger will be to process the :OLD.EMPS and :NEW.EMPS as sets and:

1. Remove *all* records from EMP such that their EMPNO was in the :OLD set but is not seen in the :NEW set. The SQL operator MINUS is excellent for this.

2. Update every EMP record such that their EMPNO is in the set of EMPNOs such that their :NEW record differs from their :OLD record. Again MINUS is excellent for finding that set easily.

3. INSERT into EMP all :NEW records where the EMPNO of the :NEW record was not in the :OLD set of values.

This implementation is:

```
scott@TKYTE816> create or replace trigger DEPT_OR_IO_UPDATE
  2  instead of update on dept_or
  3  begin
  4      if ( :new.deptno = :old.deptno )
  5      then
  6          if updating('DNAME') or updating('LOC')
  7          then
  8              update dept
  9                 set dname = :new.dname, loc = :new.loc
 10               where deptno = :new.deptno;
 11          end if;
 12
 13          if ( updating('EMPS') )
 14          then
 15              delete from emp
 16               where empno in
 17               ( select empno
 18                    from TABLE(cast(:old.emps as emp_tab_type))
 19                  MINUS
 20                  select empno
 21                     from TABLE(cast(:new.emps as emp_tab_type))
 22               );
 23              dbms_output.put_line( 'deleted ' || sql%rowcount );
```

This first MINUS gives us the set of EMPNOs that were in the :OLD but are not seen in the :NEW set, we need to remove those records from the EMP table as they no longer exist in the collection. Next, we'll modify the changed collection records:

```
 24
 25              update emp E
 26                 set ( deptno, ename, job, mgr,
 27                       hiredate, sal, comm ) =
 28                     ( select :new.deptno, ename, job, mgr,
 29                              hiredate, sal, comm
 30                         from TABLE(cast(:new.emps as emp_tab_type)) T
 31                        where T.empno = E.empno
 32                     )
 33               where empno in
 34               ( select empno
 35                    from (select *
 36                            from TABLE(cast(:new.emps as emp_tab_type))
```

```
37                           MINUS
38                         select *
39                           from TABLE(cast(:old.emps as emp_tab_type))
40                         )
41                     );
42             dbms_output.put_line( 'updated ' || sql%rowcount );
```

That MINUS returned everything in :NEW minus anything in :OLD; which is the set of modified records. We used this in a subquery to get the set of EMPNOs we need to update in the EMP table and then used a correlated subquery to actually set those values. Lastly, we will add all new records:

```
43
44           insert into emp
45           ( deptno, empno, ename, job, mgr, hiredate, sal, comm )
46           select :new.deptno,empno,ename,job,mgr,hiredate,sal,comm
47             from ( select *
48                      from TABLE(cast(:new.emps as emp_tab_type))
49                     where empno in
50                        ( select empno
51                            from TABLE(cast(:new.emps as emp_tab_type))
52                          MINUS
53                         select empno
54                            from TABLE(cast(:old.emps as emp_tab_type))
55                        )
56                  );
57          dbms_output.put_line( 'inserted ' || sql%rowcount );
58       else
59          dbms_output.put_line( 'Skipped processing nested table' );
60       end if;
61    else
62       raise_application_error(-20001,'deptno cannot be udpated' );
63    end if;
64 end;
65 /

Trigger created.
```

That MINUS generated the set of EMPNOs in the :NEW collection that were not present in the :OLD collection; this presents a list of rows to add to EMP.

This looks like a monster trigger, but is actually straightforward. To recap, it begins by seeing if the scalar columns of DEPT_OR were modified. If so, it applies the changes to the DEPT table. Next, if the nested table column was updated (all of its values replaced), it reflects those changes to the EMP table. What we need to do to reflect those changes is:

1. DELETE any records in EMP that were removed from the EMPS nested table column.

2. UPDATE any records in EMP that had their values modified in the EMPS nested table column.

3. INSERT any records into EMP that were added to EMP's nested table column.

Fortunately, the SQL MINUS operator and the ability to TABLE the nested column variable make this easy for us. Now we can process:

```
scott@TKYTE816> declare
  2      l_emps   emp_tab_type;
  3  begin
  4      select p.emps into l_emps
  5        from dept_or  p
  6       where deptno = 10;
  7
  8      for i in 1 .. l_emps.count
  9      loop
 10          l_emps(i).ename := lower(l_emps(i).ename);
 11      end loop;
 12
 13      update dept_or
 14         set emps = l_emps
 15       where deptno = 10;
 16  end;
 17  /
deleted 0
updated 3
inserted 0

PL/SQL procedure successfully completed.

scott@TKYTE816> declare
  2      l_emps   emp_tab_type;
  3  begin
  4      select p.emps into l_emps
  5        from dept_or  p
  6       where deptno = 10;
  7
  8
  9      for i in 1 .. l_emps.count
 10      loop
 11          if ( l_emps(i).ename = 'miller' )
 12          then
 13              l_emps.delete(i);
 14          else
 15              l_emps(i).ename := initcap( l_emps(i).ename );
 16          end if;
 17      end loop;
 18
 19      l_emps.extend;
 20      l_emps(l_emps.count) :=
 21          emp_type(1234, 'Tom', 'Boss',
 22                   null, sysdate, 1000, 500 );
 23
 24      update dept_or
 25         set emps = l_emps
 26       where deptno = 10;
 27  end;
 28  /
deleted 1
updated 2
inserted 1

PL/SQL procedure successfully completed.
```

```
scott@TKYTE816> update dept_or set dname = initcap(dname);
Skipped processing nested table
Skipped processing nested table
Skipped processing nested table
Skipped processing nested table

4 rows updated.

scott@TKYTE816> commit;

Commit complete.
```

The trigger translates our operations on the object instance into the equivalent modifications against the base relational tables.

This capability, to expose our relational data as object-relational views, allows us to maximize the benefits of both the relational model and the object relational model.

The relational model shows its strength in its ability to answer almost any question you might have of the underlying data, easily and efficiently. Whether your view of the data is a departmental view (query a department and related employees) or employee-oriented (you specify an employee number and need to see departmental information), we can support you. You can use the relational tables directly or we can generate an object type model that exposes your view of the data, pulls all of the requisite data together, and gives it to you easily. Consider the results of these two queries:

```
scott@TKYTE816> select * from dept_or where deptno = 10;

    DEPTNO DNAME        LOC            EMPS(EMPNO, ENAME, JOB, MGR, HIREDATE, S
--------- ----------- -------------  ----------------------------------------
        10 Accounting  NEW YORK       EMP_TAB_TYPE(EMP_TYPE(7782, 'Clark',
                                      'MANAGER', 7839, '09-JUN-81', 2450,
                                      NULL), EMP_TYPE(7839, 'King',
                                      'PRESIDENT', NULL, '17-NOV-81', 5000,
                                      NULL), EMP_TYPE(1234, 'Tom', 'Boss',
                                      NULL, '25-MAR-01', 1000, 500))
scott@TKYTE816> select dept.*, empno, ename, job, mgr, hiredate, sal, comm
  2  from emp, dept
  3  where emp.deptno = dept.deptno
  4  and dept.deptno = 10
  5  /

DEPTNO DNAME        LOC        EMPNO ENAME JOB         MGR  HIREDATE    SAL  COMM
------ ----------- --------- ----- ----- --------- ---- --------- ----- ----
    10 Accounting  NEW YORK   7782 Clark MANAGER   7839 09-JUN-81  2450
    10 Accounting  NEW YORK   7839 King  PRESIDENT      17-NOV-81  5000
    10 Accounting  NEW YORK   1234 Tom   Boss           25-MAR-01  1000  500
```

They return similar data. The first one concisely gives you all of the information about a department in a single row. It could come back with many nested table types, which in SQL would take many queries.

It can do a lot of work in the server assembling the answer for you, and shipping it back in a single row. If you are in an environment where network round trips are to be avoided when possible (long latency times) this could be extremely beneficial. Not to mention that a single SELECT * FROM T can do the work of many SQL statements. Also, notice that repeating columns of data don't occur with the object view. The DEPTNO, DNAME, and LOC columns are not repeated for each employee; they are returned only once, which may be more intuitive for many applications.

The second query requires the developer to have more knowledge of the data (that's not a bad thing mind you, just something to consider). They must know how to join the data together and, if there were many other tables to join to, they might very well need many separate queries they would have to assemble back together themselves to get the same answer. As a matter of example by what I mean by that, suppose in your model that a department has a fiscal year budget. It is stored relationally as:

```
scott@TKYTE816> create table dept_fy_budget
  2  ( deptno    number(2) references dept,
  3    fy        date,
  4    amount    number,
  5    constraint dept_fy_budget_pk primary key(deptno,fy)
  6  )
  7  /

Table created.
```

You have some data in there representing this year and the last couple of year's FY budgets by department. Your application needs the department view that has all of the scalar data surrounding the department (name, location). It also needs the employee related information (the EMP_TAB_TYPE). It also however, needs the FY budget information as well. In order to get that relationally, the application programmer will have to code:

```
scott@TKYTE816> select dept.*, empno, ename, job, mgr, hiredate, sal, comm
  2  from emp, dept
  3  where emp.deptno = dept.deptno
  4  and dept.deptno = 10
  5  /

DEPTNO DNAME      LOC      EMPNO ENAME JOB        MGR  HIREDATE   SAL  COMM
------ ---------- -------- ----- ----- ---------- ---- --------- ----- ----
    10 Accounting NEW YORK  7782 Clark MANAGER    7839 09-JUN-81 2450
    10 Accounting NEW YORK  7839 King  PRESIDENT       17-NOV-81 5000
    10 Accounting NEW YORK  1234 Tom   Boss            25-MAR-01 1000  500

3 rows selected.

scott@TKYTE816> select fy, amount
  2  from dept_fy_budget
  3  where deptno = 10
  4  /

FY        AMOUNT
--------- ----------
01-JAN-99        500
01-JAN-00        750
01-JAN-01       1000

3 rows selected.
```

It is not possible to write a *single* relational query that retrieves this data in one call. We can use some Oracle extensions (the CURSOR function in SQL) to return rows that return result sets themselves:

```
scott@TKYTE816> select
  2  dept.deptno, dept.dname,
  3  cursor(select empno from emp where deptno = dept.deptno),
  4  cursor(select fy, amount from dept_fy_budget where deptno = dept.deptno)
  5    from dept
  6  where deptno = 10
  7  /

DEPTNO DNAME             CURSOR(SELECTEMPNOFR CURSOR(SELECTFY,AMOU
------ --------------    -------------------- --------------------
    10 ACCOUNTING        CURSOR STATEMENT : 3 CURSOR STATEMENT : 4

CURSOR STATEMENT : 3

     EMPNO
----------
      7782
      7839
      7934

3 rows selected.

CURSOR STATEMENT : 4

FY            AMOUNT
--------- ----------
01-JAN-99        500
01-JAN-00        750
01-JAN-01       1000

3 rows selected.

1 row selected.
```

In this case, 1 row was selected and this row returned two more cursors to the client. The client fetched data from each cursor and displayed the results. This works nicely, but requires a knowledge of the underlying data and how to put it together (how to write the correlated subqueries to generate the cursors). We can instead model this data using the object-relational extensions and recreate our view as follows:

```
scott@TKYTE816> create or replace type dept_budget_type
  2  as object
  3  ( fy        date,
  4    amount number
  5  )
  6  /

Type created.

scott@TKYTE816> create or replace type dept_budget_tab_type
  2  as table of dept_budget_type
  3  /
Type created.
```

```
scott@TKYTE816> create or replace type dept_type
  2  as object
  3  ( deptno number(2),
  4    dname  varchar2(14),
  5    loc        varchar2(13),
  6    emps       emp_tab_type,
  7    budget dept_budget_tab_type
  8  )
  9  /

Type created.

scott@TKYTE816> create or replace view dept_or
  2  of dept_type
  3  with object identifier(deptno)
  4  as
  5  select deptno, dname, loc,
  6         cast ( multiset (
  7              select empno, ename, job, mgr, hiredate, sal, comm
  8                from emp
  9               where emp.deptno = dept.deptno )
 10            as emp_tab_type ) emps,
 11         cast ( multiset (
 12              select fy, amount
 13                from dept_fy_budget
 14               where dept_fy_budget.deptno = dept.deptno )
 15            as dept_budget_tab_type ) budget
 16      from dept
 17  /

View created.
```

Now remember, the above is work we do once, the complexity is hidden from the application. The application will simply code:

```
scott@TKYTE816> select * from dept_or where deptno = 10
  2  /

    DEPTNO DNAME        LOC      EMPS(EMPNO, ENAME, J BUDGET(FY, AMOUNT)
---------- -----------  -------  -------------------- --------------------
        10 Accounting   NEW YORK EMP_TAB_TYPE(EMP_TYP DEPT_BUDGET_TAB_TYPE
                                 E(7782, 'Clark',      (DEPT_BUDGET_TYPE('0
                                 'MANAGER', 7839,      1-JAN-99', 500),
                                 '09-JUN-81', 2450,    DEPT_BUDGET_TYPE('01
                                 NULL),                -JAN-00', 750),
                                 EMP_TYPE(7839,        DEPT_BUDGET_TYPE('01
                                 'King', 'PRESIDENT',  -JAN-01', 1000))
                                 NULL, '17-NOV-81',
                                 5000, NULL),
                                 EMP_TYPE(1234,
                                 'Tom', 'Boss', NULL,
                                 '25-MAR-01', 1000,
                                 500))

1 row selected.
```

Again, they get back one row, one object instance, which represents their view of the data. This can be quite handy indeed. The complexity of the underlying physical model is removed and it is easy to see how you might populate a GUI screen with this data. Languages such as Java JDBC, Visual Basic with OO4O (Oracle Objects for Ole), OCI (Oracle Call Interface), PL/SQL, and Pro*C can all make use of this functionality easily. Using the relational model, it is a little more cumbersome as you get more and more complex one to many relationships. With the object-relational model, it is a little more natural. Of course, we would have to modify our INSTEAD OF triggers to support modifications to the underlying relational data as well, so it is not totally completed but the gist is there.

Summary

In this chapter, we reviewed the major uses of Oracle object types and extensibility. There are four ways to use them, three of which we looked at in depth.

We covered its use as a method to impose standard data types on a system. Using the ADDRESS_TYPE we were able to not only enforce a common naming convention and data type usage, but to provide for data specific methods and functionality.

We covered its use as a method to naturally extend the PL/SQL language. Here, we took a supplied package and wrapped it in an object type layer. This protects us from future changes in the implementation of the supplied package, as well as giving us a more 'object' way to programming in PL/SQL, similar to the class structure in C++ or Java. Additionally, we saw how using collection types gives us the extremely interesting ability to SELECT * FROM PLSQL_FUNCTION. This ability in itself is worth looking into the object features for.

Finally, we investigated how to use this feature as a method to present object relational views of inherently relational data. As we saw, this allows us to easily present an application-specific object view of the relational data to as many different applications as we like. The main benefit of this approach is that the SQL required in the client becomes almost 'trivial' to code. There are no joins, no multiple queries to assemble the answer together. A simple single row FETCH should return everything we need in one call.

The fourth option, to create tables of a type, was covered in the Chapter 6 on *Tables*. As they behave just like object views (or is that the other way around?) their use has been covered as well. I tend to not use object tables. I lean towards object views of relation tables for many of the reasons of the covered above. The most prevalent reason being that you almost *always* need the relational view at the end of the day in order to provide the many specific application views of the data. Object-relational views are excellent for modeling application specific views of the data.

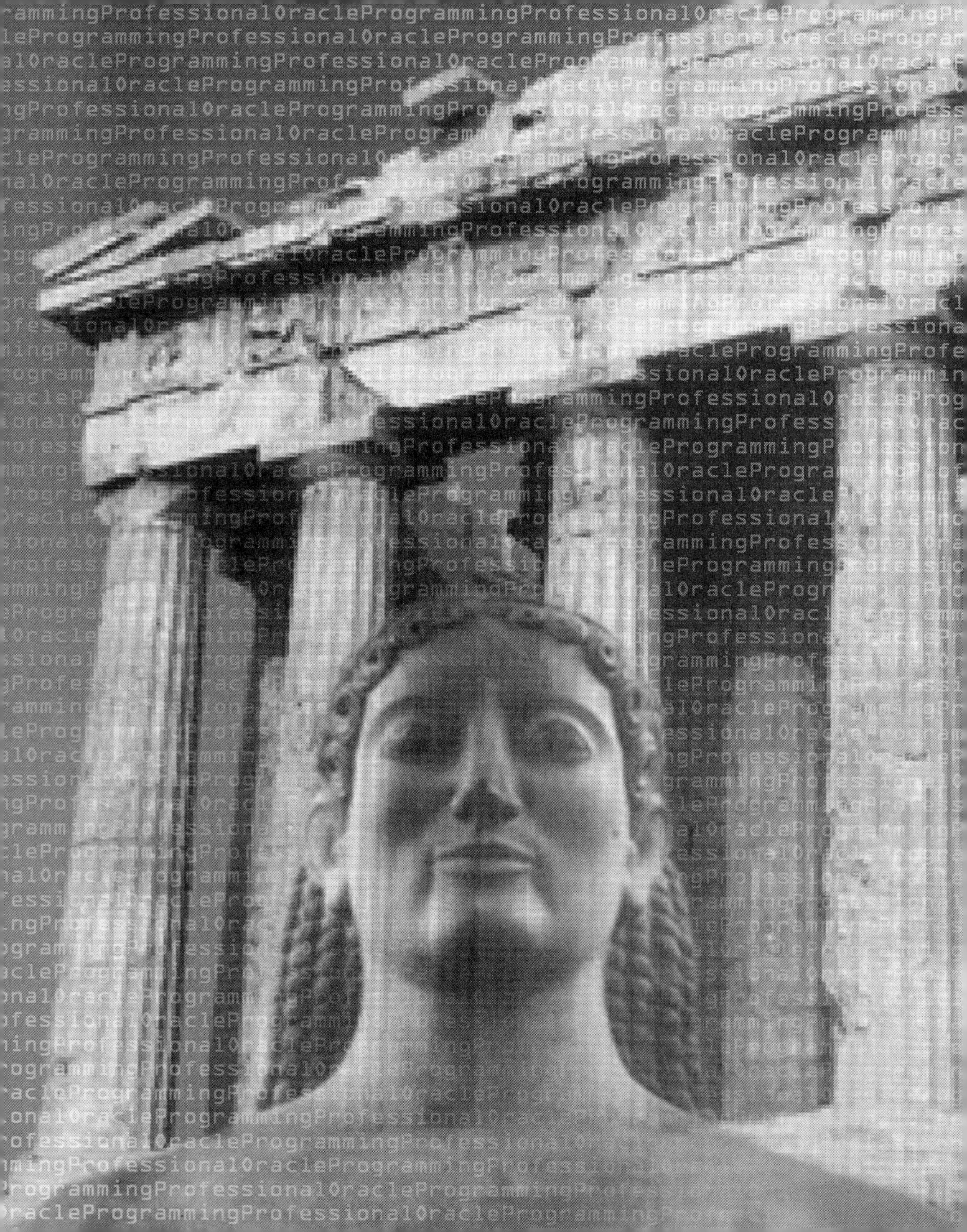

21

Fine Grained Access Control

Fine Grained Access Control (**FGAC**) in Oracle 8i gives you the ability to dynamically attach, at runtime, a predicate (the WHERE clause) to all queries issued against a database table or view. You now have the ability to procedurally modify the query at run-time – a dynamic view capability. You may evaluate who is running the query, which terminal they are running the query from, when they are running it (as in time of day), and then build the predicate based on those specific set of circumstances. With the use of **application contexts**, you may securely add additional information to the environment (such as an application role the user may have), and access this in your procedure or predicate as well.

You will see FGAC referred to with various names in different publications. The following are synonymous terms for this feature:

❏ Fine Grained Access Control

❏ **V**irtual **P**rivate **D**atabase (**VPD**)

❏ **R**ow **L**evel **S**ecurity or DBMS_RLS (based on the PL/SQL package DBMS_RLS that implements this feature)

In order to execute the examples found in this chapter, you will need Oracleion 8.1.5), or higher. In addition, this feature is available only in the Enterprise and Personal Editions of Oracle; these examples will not work in the Standard Edition.

In this chapter, we will cover:

❏ The reasons why it would be advantageous to use this feature, such as it's ease of maintenance, the fact that it is performed in the server itself, takes into account the evolution of application and also allows for easier development, and so on.

❏ Two examples in the *How it Works* section, demonstrating both security policies and application contexts.

❑ An extensive list of issues you should be aware of such as, FGAC's behavior with respect to referential integrity, cursor caching, import and export matters, and debugging nuances.

❑ Some of the errors you may come across when attempting to implementing FGAC in your applications.

An Example

Say you have a security policy that determines what rows different groups of people may see. Your security policy will develop and return a predicate based on who is logged in, and what role they have. FGAC will allow you to rewrite the basic query SELECT * FROM EMP as follows:

Logged in user	Query rewritten to	Comments
| Employee | ```
select *
    from ( select * from emp
  where ename = USER )
``` | Employees may only see their own records. |
| Manager | ```
select *
    from ( select *
        from emp
      where mgr =
        ( select empno
            from emp
          where ename = USER )
        or ename = USER
    )
``` | Managers may see their record, and the records of people that work for them. |
| HR rep. | ```
select *
    from (select *
        from emp
      where deptno =
SYS_CONTEXT( 'OurApp', ptno' )
        )
``` | HR representatives may see anyone in a given department. This introduces the syntax for retrieving variables from an application context, the SYS_CONTEXT() built-in function. |

Why Use this Feature?

In this section we will explore the various reasons and cases where you might choose to use this feature.
```

Ease of Maintenance

FGAC allows you to have one table and one stored procedure, to manage what used to take many views, or database triggers, or lots of application logic.

The multiple-view approach was common. The application developers would create many different database accounts, such as EMPLOYEE, MANAGER, HR_REP, and install into each of these accounts, a complete set of views that selected exactly the right data. Using the above introductory example, each database account would have a separate EMP view, with a customized predicate specifically for that group of users. In order to control what the end users could see, create, modify, and remove they would also need up to four different views for the EMP table, one each for SELECT, INSERT, UPDATE, and DELETE. This quickly leads to a proliferation of database objects – every time you need to add another group of users, it means another set of views to manage and maintain.

If you change the security policy (for example, if you want managers to see not only their direct reports, but also the ones that are two levels down), you would have to recreate the view in the database, invalidating all objects that refer to it. Not only did this approach lead to a proliferation of views in the database, it also forced users to log in using various common accounts, which compromised accountability. A further side effect of this approach is that a lot of code must be duplicated in the database. If I have a stored procedure that operates on the EMP table, I would have to install the stored procedure into each individual account. The same would hold true for many other objects (triggers, functions, packages, and so on). Now I must update N accounts every time I roll out a patch to my software, to ensure everyone is executing the same code base.

Another approach uses database triggers along with views. Here, instead of creating a database view for each of SELECT, INSERT, UPDATE, and DELETE, we would use a database trigger to review, row-by-row, the changes an individual was making and either accept or reject them. This implementation would not only cause the same proliferation of views as outlined above, but it would also add the overhead of a trigger (sometimes complex trigger) firing for each, and every, row modified.

A final option is to put all of the security in the application, be it a client application in a client-server environment, or a middle-tier server application. The application would look at who is logged on, and use the right query for that user. The application in effect, implements its own FGAC. The serious drawback to this approach (and any approach that uses an application to enforce access to data) is that the data in the database is useful *only* to the application. It precludes the use of any ad-hoc query tools, report generation tools, and the like because the data is not secured unless accessed via the application. When the security is tied up in the application, it is not easy to extend the application to new interfaces – the usability of the data is reduced.

FGAC allows you to manage this complexity and avoid any sort of loss of functionality using just two objects – the original table or view, and a database package or function. You can update the database package at any point in time to immediately put in place a new set of security polices. Rather than having to look at dozens of views to see all of the security policies in place on an object, you can get all of this information in one place.

Performed in the Server

Many times, given the complexity of managing and maintaining so many views, developers will encode the application logic into the application itself, as discussed above. The application will look at who is logged on and what they are requesting, and then submit the appropriate query. This protects the data only when the data is accessed via the application thus the probability that the data will be compromised at some point is increased, since all one needs to do is log into the database with some tool, other than your application, and query the data.

Using FGAC we place the security logic, which determines what data the user should see, in the database. In this way we are ensuring that the data is protected, regardless of the tool used to access it.

The need for this is clearly visible today. In the early to mid-1990s, the client-server model ruled (and before that, host-based programming was the norm). Most client-server applications (and pretty much all host-based ones) have embedded within them, the logic that is used to access the application. Today, it is very much 'en vogue' to use an application server and host the application logic there. As these client-server applications are migrated to the new architecture, people are extracting the security logic from the client-server applications, and embedding it in the application server. This has lead to a double implementation of the security logic (the client-server applications don't totally go away), so there are two places to maintain and debug the logic. Even worse, it doesn't solve the problem when the next programming paradigm comes along. What happens after application servers go out of fashion? What happens when your users want to use a third-party tool that can access the data directly? If the security is all locked up in the middle-tier logic, they won't be able to. If the security is right there with the data, then not only are you ready for any yet to be invented technology, but you are also ready right now for free, secure access to the data.

Easier Application Development

FGAC takes the security logic out of the application logic. The application developer can concentrate on the application itself, not the logic of accessing the underlying data to keep it secure. Since FGAC is done entirely in the database server, the applications immediately inherit this logic. In the past, the application developers had to encode the security logic into the application, making the applications harder to develop initially, and also making them especially hard to maintain. If the application is responsible for mediating access to the data, and you access the same data from many locations in the application, a simple change to your security policy may affect dozens of application modules. Using FGAC, all relevant application modules automatically inherit your new security policies without having to be modified.

Evolutionary Application Development

In many environments, security policies are not well defined initially, and can change over time. As companies merge, or as health care providers tighten the access to patient databases, or as privacy laws are introduced, these security policies will need to change. Placing the access control as close to the data as possible, allows for this evolution with minimal impact on applications and tools. There is one place where the new security logic is implemented, and all applications and tools that access the database automatically inherit the new logic.

Avoids Shared User Accounts

Using FGAC, each user can and should, log in with unique credentials. This supplies complete accountability, and you can audit actions at the user level. In the past, many applications, when faced with having different views of the data for different users, make the choice to set up shared accounts. For example, every employee would use the EMPLOYEE account to access the employee views; every manager would use the MANAGER account, and so on. This removes the ability to audit actions at the user level. You can no longer see that TKYTE is logged in (as an employee), but only that EMPLOYEE (whoever that may be) is logged in.

You can use still use FGAC with shared accounts if desired. However, this feature removes the *necessity* for shared accounts.

Supports Shared User Accounts

This is a corollary to the preceding section. FGAC does not mandate the use of a logon per user; it simply facilitates it. Using a feature called an **application context,** as we will see below, we'll be able to use FGAC in a 'single account' environment, as may arise in a connection pool with an application server. Some connection pools mandate that you use a single database account to log in with. FGAC works well with those environments as well.

Hosting an Application as an ASP

FGAC allows you to take an existing application and host it for many different customers in an **A**pplication **S**ervice **P**rovider (**ASP**) environment, without having to change the application. Lets say you had an HR application, which you wanted to put on the Internet, and charge access fees. Since you have many different customers, and each wants to ensure their data cannot be seen by anyone else, you have to come up with a plan for protecting this information. Your choices are:

- ❑ Install, configure, and maintain a separate database instance per customer base.

- ❑ Recode any stored procedure the application uses to be an **invoker rights routine,** as described in Chapter 23 on *Invoker and Definers Rights*, and implement a schema per customer base.

- ❑ Use a single install of the database instance, and a single schema with FGAC.

The first option is less than desirable. The overhead of having a database instance per customer base, where a customer might only have a handful of users, prevents this option from being viable. For very large customers, with hundreds or thousands of users, this makes sense. For the plethora of small customers, each of which contribute five or six end users, a database per customer is not workable. You probably couldn't afford to do it.

The second option potentially involves recoding the application. The goal here would be to for each customer schema to have its own set of database tables. Any stored procedures would have to be coded in such a fashion that they would operate on the tables visible to the currently logged in user account (the customer). Normally, stored procedures see the same objects that the *definer* of the procedure would see – we would have to go out of our way to ensure we used invokers rights routines, and never use any hard-coded schema names in the application. For example, we could never SELECT * FROM SCOTT.EMP, only SELECT * FROM EMP. This would apply not only to PL/SQL routines, but any external code in languages such as Java or Visual Basic would have to follow these rules as well (since they have no schema names). It is not desirable for this reason, as well as the fact that you now have many hundreds of schemas to manage.

The third option, using FGAC, is the least intrusive of the three and also the easiest to implement. Here, for example, we could add a column to each table that must be protected, and this column would contain the company identifier. We would utilize a trigger to maintain this column (so the application does not have to do so). The trigger would utilize an application context, set by an ON LOGON trigger, to supply this value. The security policy would return a predicate that selected only the rows for the company you are allowed to see. The security policy would not only limit the data by company, but would also add any other predicates necessary to limit access to data. Returning to our HR application – not only would we add WHERE COMPANY = VALUE, but also the predicates defined according to whether you were an employee, manager or HR representative. Going a step further, you could implement partitioning to physically segregate the data of larger customers for recoverability and availability options.

How it Works

FGAC is implemented in Oracle 8i with two primary constructs:

- ❏ **An application context** – This is a namespace with a corresponding set of attribute/value pairs. For example, in the context named OurApp, we could access variables DeptNo, Mgr, and so on. An application context is always bound to some PL/SQL package. This package is the only method for setting values in the context. To get the DeptNo attribute set to a value in the OurApp context, you must call a specific package – the one bound to the OurApp context. This package is trusted to set values correctly in the OurApp context (you wrote it, that's why it is trusted to set the context correctly). This prevents users with malicious intent, from setting values in an application context that would give them access to information they should not have access to. Anyone can read the values of an application context, but only one package may set these values.

- ❏ **A security policy** – A security policy is simply a function you develop that will return a predicate used to filter data dynamically when a query is executed. This function will be bound to a database table or view, and may be invoked for some or all of the statements that access the table. What this means is you can have one policy that is used for SELECT, another for INSERT, and a third for UPDATE and DELETE. Typically this function will make use of values in an application context to determine the correct predicate to return (for example, it will look at 'who' is logged in, 'what' they are trying to do, and restrict the rows they can operate on to some set). It should be noted that the user SYS (or INTERNAL) never have security policies applied to them (the policy functions are quite simply never invoked), and they will be able to see/modify all of the data.

Also worth mentioning are other Oracle 8i features that enhance the implementation of FGAC, such as:

- ❏ SYS_CONTEXT **function** – this function is used in SQL or PL/SQL to access the application context values. See the *Oracle SQL Reference* manual for all of the details on this function, and a list of default values you'll find in the USERENV context that Oracle automatically sets up. You'll find things like the session username, the IP address of the client, and other goodies hidden in there.

- ❏ **Database logon triggers** – This function allows you to run some code upon a user logging into the database. This is extremely useful for setting up the initial, default application context.

- ❏ DBMS_RLS **package** – This package provides the API for us to add, remove, refresh, enable, and disable security policies. It is callable from any language/environment that can connect to Oracle.

In order to use this feature, the developer will need the following privileges in addition to the standard CONNECT and RESOURCE (or equivalent) roles:

- ❏ EXECUTE_CATALOG_ROLE – This allows the developer to execute the DBMS_RLS package. Alternatively, you may just grant execute on DBMS_RLS to the account when connected as SYS.

- ❏ CREATE ANY CONTEXT – This allows the developer to create application contexts.

An application context is created using a simple SQL command:

```
SQL> create or replace context OurApp using Our_Context_Pkg;
```

Here `OurApp` is the name of the context and `Our_Context_Pkg` is the PL/SQL package that is allowed to set values in the context. Application contexts are an important feature for the FGAC implementation for two reasons:

❑ **It supplies you with a trusted way to set variables in a namespace** – Only the PL/SQL package associated with a context may set values in that context. This ensures the integrity of the values in this context. Since you will use this context to restrict or permit access to data, the integrity of the values in the context must be assured.

❑ **References to the application context values in a SQL query are treated as bind variables** – For example, if you set value of a `DeptNo` attribute in the context `OurApp`, and implemented a policy to return a `WHERE` clause `deptno = SYS_CONTEXT('OurApp', 'DeptNo')`, it will be subject to shared SQL usage since the `SYS_CONTEXT` reference is similar to `deptno = :b1`. Everyone might use different values for `Deptno`, but they will all reuse the same parsed and optimized query plans.

Example 1: Implementing a Security Policy

We will implement a very simple security policy as a quick demonstration of this feature. The policy we will implement is:

❑ If the current user is the `OWNER` of the table, you can see all rows in the table, else,

❑ You can only see rows 'you own', rows where the name in the `OWNER` column is your username.

❑ Additionally, you can only add rows such that you are the `OWNER` of that row. If you attempt to add a row for someone else, it will be rejected.

The PL/SQL function we would need to create for this would look like this:

```
tkyte@TKYTE816> create or replace
  2  function security_policy_function( p_schema in varchar2,
  3                  p_object in varchar2 )
  4  return varchar2
  5  as
  6  begin
  7      if ( user = p_schema ) then
  8          return '';
  9      else
 10          return 'owner = USER';
 11      end if;
 12  end;
 13  /

Function created.
```

The above shows the general structure of a security policy function. This will always be a function that returns a `VARCHAR2`. The return value will be a predicate that will be added to the query against the table. It will in effect, be added as a predicate against the table or view you applied this security policy to using an inline view as follows:

```
The query:              SELECT * FROM T

Will be rewritten as: SELECT * FROM ( SELECT * FROM T WHERE owner = USER)
or:                     SELECT * FROM ( SELECT * FROM T )
```

Additionally, all security policy functions must accept two IN parameters – the name of the schema that *owns* the object and the name of the object, to which function is being applied. These may be used in any way you see fit in the security policy function.

So in this example, the predicate owner = USER will be dynamically appended to all queries against the table to which this function is bound, effectively restricting the number of rows that would be available to the user. Only if the currently logged in user is owner of the table will an empty predicate be returned. Returning an empty predicate is like returning 1=1 or True. Returning Null is the same as returning an empty predicate as well. The above could have returned Null instead of an empty string to achieve the same effect.

To tie this function to a table, we use the PL/SQL procedure DBMS_RLS.ADD_POLICY, which will be shown later. In the example we have the following table set up, and the user is logged in as TKYTE:

```
tkyte@TKYTE816> create table data_table
  2  (   some_data    varchar2(30),
  3      OWNER        varchar2(30) default USER
  4  )
  5  /

Table created.

tkyte@TKYTE816> grant all on data_table to public;

Grant succeeded.

tkyte@TKYTE816> create public synonym data_table for data_table;

Synonym created.

tkyte@TKYTE816> insert into data_table ( some_data ) values ( 'Some Data' );

1 row created.

tkyte@TKYTE816> insert into data_table ( some_data, owner )
  2  values ( 'Some Data Owned by SCOTT', 'SCOTT' );

1 row created.

tkyte@TKYTE816> commit;

Commit complete.

tkyte@TKYTE816> select * from data_table;

SOME_DATA                        OWNER
------------------------------   ------------------------------
Some Data                        TKYTE
Some Data Owned by SCOTT          SCOTT
```

Now we would attach the security function that we wrote to this table with the following call to the package DBMS_RLS:

```
tkyte@TKYTE816> begin
    2      dbms_rls.add_policy
    3      ( object_schema    => 'TKYTE',
    4        object_name      => 'data_table',
    5        policy_name      => 'MY_POLICY',
    6        function_schema  => 'TKYTE',
    7        policy_function  => 'security_policy_function',
    8        statement_types  => 'select, insert, update, delete' ,
    9        update_check     => TRUE,
   10        enable           => TRUE
   11      );
   12  end;
   13  /

PL/SQL procedure successfully completed.
```

The ADD_POLICY routine is one of the key routines in the DBMS_RLS package we'll be using. It is what allows you to add your security policy to the table in question. The parameters we passed in detail are:

❑ OBJECT_SCHEMA – The name of the owner of the table or view. If left as Null (this is the default), it will be interpreted as the currently logged in user. I passed in my username for completeness in the above example.

❑ OBJECT_NAME – The name of the table or view the policy will be placed on.

❑ POLICY_NAME – Any unique name you would like to assign to this policy. You will use this name later if you wish to enable/disable, refresh, or drop this policy.

❑ FUNCTION_SCHEMA – The name of the owner of the function that returns the predicate. It works in the same way as the OBJECT_SCHEMA. If left to its default of Null, the currently logged in username will be used.

❑ POLICY_FUNCTION – The name of the function that returns the predicate.

❑ STATEMENT_TYPES – Lists the types of statements this policy will be applied to. Can be any combination of INSERT, UPDATE, SELECT, and DELETE. The default is all four – I've listed them here for completeness.

❑ UPDATE_CHECK – This applies to the processing of INSERTs and UPDATEs only. If set to True (the default is False), this will verify that the data you just INSERTed or UPDATEd is visible by you, using that predicate. That is, when set to True, you cannot INSERT any data that would not be SELECTed from that table using the returned predicate.

❑ ENABLE – Specifies whether the policy is enabled or not. This defaults to True.

Now after executing the ADD_POLICY call, all DML against the DATA_TABLE table will have the predicate which is returned by SECURITY_POLICY_FUNCTION applied to it, regardless of the environment submitting the DML operation. In other words, regardless of the application accessing the data. To see this in action:

```
tkyte@TKYTE816> connect system/manager
system@TKYTE816> select * from data_table;
```

```
no rows selected

system@TKYTE816> connect scott/tiger
scott@TKYTE816> select * from data_table;

SOME_DATA                        OWNER
------------------------------   --------------------
Some Data Owned by SCOTT         SCOTT
```

So, this shows that we have effectively filtered the rows – the user SYSTEM sees no data in this table. This is because the predicate WHERE OWNER = USER is satisfied by none of the existing rows of data. When we log in as SCOTT however, the single row owned by SCOTT becomes visible. Going further with some DML against the table:

```
sys@TKYTE816> connect scott/tiger

scott@TKYTE816> insert into data_table ( some_data )
  2  values ( 'Some New Data' );

1 row created.

scott@TKYTE816> insert into data_table ( some_data, owner )
  2  values ( 'Some New Data Owned by SYS', 'SYS' )
  3  /
insert into data_table ( some_data, owner )
            *
ERROR at line 1:
ORA-28115: policy with check option violation


scott@TKYTE816> select * from data_table;

SOME_DATA                        OWNER
------------------------------   ------------------------------
Some Data Owned by SCOTT         SCOTT
Some New Data                    SCOTT
```

We are allowed to create data we can see, but the error ORA-28115 is raised because when we added the policy we specified, we made the call to dbms_rls.add_policy

```
...
9       update_check    => TRUE );
...
```

This is analogous to creating a view with the CHECK OPTION enabled. This will enable us to only create data that we can also select. The default is to allow you to create data you cannot select.

Now, due to the way in which we coded our security policy, we know the OWNER of the table can see all rows, and can create any row. To see this in action, we'll just log in as TKYTE and attempt these operations:

```
scott@TKYTE816> connect tkyte/tkyte
```

```
tkyte@TKYTE816> insert into data_table ( some_data, owner )
  2  values ( 'Some New Data Owned by SYS', 'SYS' )
  3  /

1 row created.

tkyte@TKYTE816> select * from data_table
  2  /

SOME_DATA                            OWNER
----------------------------         ----------------------------
Some Data                            TKYTE
Some Data Owned by SCOTT             SCOTT
Some New Data                        SCOTT
Some New Data Owned by SYS           SYS
```

So, this shows that TKYTE is not affected by this policy. One interesting thing to note is that if we log in as SYS, the following behavior is noted:

```
tkyte@TKYTE816> connect sys/change_on_install
Connected.

sys@TKYTE816> select * from data_table;

SOME_DATA                            OWNER
----------------------------         ----------------------------
Some Data                            TKYTE
Some Data Owned by SCOTT             SCOTT
Some New Data                        SCOTT
Some New Data Owned by SYS           SYS
```

The security policy is not used when logged in as the special user SYS (or INTERNAL, or as SYSDBA). This is the expected, desired behavior. The SYSDBA accounts are powerful administrative accounts, and are allowed to see all data. This is particularly important to note when exporting information. Unless you do the export as a SYSDBA, you must be aware that the security policy will be applied when you export. You will *not* get all of the data if you use a non-SYSDBA account and a conventional path export!

Example 2: Using Application Contexts

In this example, we would like to implement a Human Resources Security Policy. We will use the sample EMP and DEPT tables, which are owned by SCOTT and add one additional table that allows us to designate people to be HR representatives for various departments. Our requirements for this are:

❑   A manager of a department can:

Read their own record, the records of all the employees that report directly to them, the records of all the people that report to these employees, and so on (hierarchy).

Update records of the employees that report directly to them.

❑   An employee can:

Read their own record.

❏   An HR representative can:

Read all the records for the department they are working in (HR reps only work on one
department at a time in our application).

Update all records for the given department.

Insert into the given department.

Delete from the given department.

As stated, our application will use copies of the existing EMP and DEPT tables from the SCOTT schema,
with the addition of a HR_REPS table to allow us to assign an HR representative to a department. When
you log in, we would like your role to be automatically assigned and set up for you. That is, upon login,
if you are an HR representative, the HR representative role will be in place, and so on

To begin, we will need some accounts in our database. These accounts will represent the application
owner and the application end users. In this example, TKYTE is the owner of the application, and will
have a copy of the EMP and DEPT tables from the SCOTT demo account. The end users are named after
people in the EMP table (in other words, KING, BLAKE, and so on). We used the following script to set
this up. First we drop and recreate the user TKYTE and grant CONNECT and RESOURCE to him:

```
sys@TKYTE816> drop user tkyte cascade;

User dropped.

sys@TKYTE816> create user tkyte identified by tkyte
  2   default tablespace data
  3   temporary tablespace temp;

User created.

sys@TKYTE816> grant connect, resource to tkyte;

Grant succeeded.
```

Next are the minimum privileges required to set up FGAC. The role EXECUTE_CATALOG may be used
in place of EXECUTE ON DBMS_RLS:

```
sys@TKYTE816> grant execute on dbms_rls to tkyte;

Grant succeeded.

sys@TKYTE816> grant create any context to tkyte;

Grant succeeded.
```

The next privilege is needed to create the database trigger on logon, which we will need to create later:

```
sys@TKYTE816> grant administer database trigger to tkyte;
Grant succeeded.
```

Now we create the employee and manager accounts to represent the application users. Every user in the EMP table will have an account named after them with the exception of SCOTT. In some databases the user SCOTT already exist:

```
sys@TKYTE816> begin
  2      for x in (select ename
  3              from scott.emp  where ename <> 'SCOTT')
  4      loop
  5         execute immediate 'grant connect to ' || x.ename  ||
  6                 ' identified by ' || x.ename;
  7      end loop;
  8  end;
  9  /

PL/SQL procedure successfully completed.

sys@TKYTE816> connect scott/tiger

scott@TKYTE816> grant select on emp to tkyte;

Grant succeeded.

scott@TKYTE816> grant select on dept to tkyte;

Grant succeeded.
```

The simple application schema we will use is as follows. It starts with the EMP and DEPT tables copied from the SCOTT schema. We've added declarative referential integrity to these tables as well:

```
scott@TKYTE816> connect tkyte/tkyte

tkyte@TKYTE816> create table dept as select * from scott.dept;

Table created.

tkyte@TKYTE816> alter table dept add constraint dept_pk primary key(deptno);

Table altered.

tkyte@TKYTE816> create table emp_base_table as select * from scott.emp;

Table created.

tkyte@TKYTE816> alter table emp_base_table add constraint
  2 emp_pk primary key(empno);

Table altered.

tkyte@TKYTE816> alter table emp_base_table add constraint emp_fk_to_dept
  2  foreign key (deptno) references dept(deptno);

Table altered.
```

Now we'll add some indexes and additional constraints. We create indexes that will be used our application context functions for performance. We need to find out quickly if a specific user is a manager of a department:

```
tkyte@TKYTE816> create index emp_mgr_deptno_idx on emp_base_table(mgr);

Index created.
```

Also, we need to convert a username into an EMPNO quickly, and enforce uniqueness of the usernames in this application:

```
tkyte@TKYTE816> alter table emp_base_table
  2  add constraint
  3  emp_ename_unique unique(ename);

Table altered.
```

Next, we create a view EMP from the EMP_BASE_TABLE. We will place our security policy on this view, and our applications will use it to query, insert, update, and delete. Why we are using a view will be explained later:

```
tkyte@TKYTE816> create view emp as select * from emp_base_table;

View created.
```

Now we will create the table that manages our assigned HR representatives. We are using an indexed organized table (IOT) for this, since we only the query, SELECT * FROM HR_REPS WHERE USERNAME = :X AND DEPTNO = :Y, we have no need for a traditional table structure:

```
tkyte@TKYTE816> create table hr_reps
  2  ( username     varchar2(30),
  3        deptno       number,
  4        primary key(username,deptno)
  5  )
  6  organization index;

Table created.
```

We now make the assignments of HR representatives:

```
tkyte@TKYTE816> insert into hr_reps values ( 'KING', 10 );

1 row created.

tkyte@TKYTE816> insert into hr_reps values ( 'KING', 20 );

1 row created.

tkyte@TKYTE816> insert into hr_reps values ( 'KING', 30 );

1 row created.

tkyte@TKYTE816> insert into hr_reps values ( 'BLAKE', 10 );

1 row created.
```

```
tkyte@TKYTE816> insert into hr_reps values ( 'BLAKE', 20 );

1 row created.

tkyte@TKYTE816> commit;

Commit complete.
```

Now that we have the application tables EMP, DEPT, and HR_REPS created, let's create a procedure that will let us set an application context. This application context will contain three pieces of information; the currently logged in users EMPNO, USERNAME, and the role they are using (one of EMP, MGR, or HR_REP). Our dynamic predicate routine will use the role stored in application context to decide what the WHERE clause should look like for the given user.

We use the EMP_BASE_TABLE and HR_REPS tables to make this determination. This answers the question you were thinking about, 'why do we have a table EMP_BASE_TABLE and a view EMP that is simply SELECT * FROM EMP_BASE_TABLE?' There are two reasons for this:

❑   We use the data in the employee table to enforce our security policy.

❑   We read this table while attempting to set an application context.

In order to read the employee data, we need the application context to be set, but in order to set the application context we need to read the employee data. It's a 'chicken and egg' problem, which comes first? Our solution is to create a view that all applications will use (the EMP view) and enforce our security on this view. The original EMP_BASE_TABLE will be used by our security policy to enforce the rules. From the EMP_BASE_TABLE we can discover who is a manager of a given department, and who works for a given manager. The application and the end users will never use the EMP_BASE_TABLE, only our security policy will. This last point is achieved by not granting any privileges on the base table – the database will enforce that for us.

In this example, we have chosen to have the context set automatically upon logon. This is a standard procedure, when possible, to have the application context set up automatically. There may be times when you need to override this behavior. If upon logon, you do not have sufficient information to determine what the context should be, you may need to manually set the context via a procedure call. This would frequently occur when using a middle tier that logs all users in via the same common user. This middle tier would have to call a database procedure passing in the name of the 'real' user to get the application context set correctly.

The following is our 'trusted' procedure to set the context. It is trusted in that *we* have confidence in its functionality since *we* wrote it. It helps to enforce our policies by only setting the appropriate username, role name, and employee number in our context. Later, when we access these values, we can trust that it was set accurately and safely. This procedure will be executed automatically by an ON LOGON trigger. As it is coded, it is ready to support a 3-tier application that uses a connection pool, with a single database account as well. We would grant execute on this procedure to the user account used by the connection pool, and it would execute this procedure, sending the username as a parameter, instead of letting the procedure use the currently logged in username.

```
tkyte@TKYTE816> create or replace
  2    procedure set_app_role( p_username in varchar2
  3                            default sys_context('userenv','session_user') )
  4    as
```

```
5        l_empno      number;
6        l_cnt        number;
7        l_ctx        varchar2(255) default 'Hr_App_Ctx';
8    begin
9         dbms_session.set_context( l_ctx, 'UserName', p_username );
10        begin
11          select empno into l_empno
12            from emp_base_table
13           where ename = p_username; ;
14          dbms_session.set_context( l_ctx, 'Empno', l_empno );
15        exception
16          when NO_DATA_FOUND then
17              -- Person not in emp table - might be an HR rep.
18              NULL;
19        end;
20
21
22        -- First, let's see if this person is a HR_REP, if not, then
23        -- try MGR, if not, then set the EMP role on.
24
25        select count(*) into l_cnt
26          from dual
27         where exists
28          ( select NULL
29              from hr_reps
30             where username = p_username
31          );
32
33        if ( l_cnt <> 0 )
34        then
35            dbms_session.set_context( l_ctx, 'RoleName', 'HR_REP' );
36          else
37          -- Lets see if this person is a MGR, if not, give them
38          -- the EMP role.
39
40          select count(*) into l_cnt
41            from dual
42           where exists
43            ( select NULL
44                from emp_base_table
45               where mgr = to_number(sys_context(l_ctx,'Empno'))
46            );
47          if ( l_cnt <> 0 )
48          then
49             dbms_session.set_context(l_ctx, 'RoleName', 'MGR');
50          else
51          -- Everyone may use the EMP role.
52             dbms_session.set_context( l_ctx, 'RoleName', 'EMP' );
53          end if;
54      end if;
55   end;
56   /

Procedure created.
```

Next, we create our application context. The name of the context is HR_APP_CTX (the same as we used in the preceding procedure). When we create the context, notice how we bind it to the procedure we just created – only that procedure can set attribute values in that context now:

```
tkyte@TKYTE816> create or replace context Hr_App_Ctx using SET_APP_ROLE
  2  /

Context created.
```

Lastly, to make everything automatic, we'll use an on logon database event trigger to automatically call our procedure to set the context values:

```
tkyte@TKYTE816> create or replace trigger APP_LOGON_TRIGGER
  2  after logon on database
  3  begin
  4          set_app_role;
  5  end;
  6  /

Trigger created.
```

What we've done so far is to create a procedure that finds the correct role for the currently logged in user. As designed, this procedure will be called at most once per session, ensuring the RoleName attribute is set once upon logon to a static value. Since we will return different predicates based on the value of RoleName in our security policy, we cannot permit a user to change their role after it has been set, in Oracle 8.1.5 and 8.1.6. If we did, we would have a potential problem with cached cursors and 'old' predicates (see the *Caveats* section for a description of the problem we would encounter – it is mostly solved in 8.1.7). Additionally, we look up the current user's EMPNO. This does two things for us:

❑   It verifies the end user is an employee – If we get an error NO_DATA_FOUND, we know the person is not an employee. Since their EMPNO attribute never gets set, this person will see no data unless they are an HR representative.

❑   It puts frequently used values into the application context. – We can now quickly access the EMP table by the current users EMPNO, which we will do in the predicate function below.

Next, we create the database application context object, and bind it to the SET_APP_ROLE procedure we just created. This makes it so *only* that procedure can set values in this context. This is what makes an application context secure and trustworthy. We know exactly what piece of code can set values in it, and we trust it to do this correctly (we wrote it after all). The following demonstrates what happens when any other procedure attempts to set our context:

```
tkyte@TKYTE816> begin
  2      dbms_session.set_context( 'Hr_App_Ctx',
  3                                'RoleName', 'MGR' );
  4  end;
  5  /
begin
*
ERROR at line 1:
ORA-01031: insufficient privileges
ORA-06512: at "SYS.DBMS_SESSION", line 58
ORA-06512: at line 2
```

Now, to test the logic of our procedure, we will attempt to use the stored procedure as various users, and see what roles we can set and what values are placed into the context. We'll begin with SMITH. This person is just an EMP. They manage no one and are not an HR representative. We'll use the SESSION_CONTEXT view that is publicly available, to see what values get set in our context:

```
tkyte@TKYTE816> connect smith/smith

smith@TKYTE816> column namespace format a10
smith@TKYTE816> column attribute format a10
smith@TKYTE816> column value      format a10
smith@TKYTE816> select * from session_context;

NAMESPACE  ATTRIBUTE  VALUE
---------- ---------- ----------
HR_APP_CTX ROLENAME   EMP
HR_APP_CTX USERNAME   SMITH
HR_APP_CTX EMPNO      7369
```

We can see that this works as expected. SMITH gets his username, employee number, and RoleName attribute set in the HR_APP_CTX context successfully.

Next, connecting as a different user, we see how the procedure works, and can look at a different way to inspect a session's context values:

```
smith@TKYTE816> connect blake/blake

blake@TKYTE816> declare
  2      l_AppCtx      dbms_session.AppCtxTabTyp;
  3      l_size        number;
  4  begin
  5      dbms_session.list_context( l_AppCtx, l_size );
  6      for i in 1 .. l_size loop
  7          dbms_output.put( l_AppCtx(i).namespace || '.' );
  8          dbms_output.put( l_AppCtx(i).attribute || ' = ' );
  9          dbms_output.put_line( l_AppCtx(i).value );
 10      end loop;
 11  end;
 12  /
HR_APP_CTX.ROLENAME = HR_REP
HR_APP_CTX.USERNAME = BLAKE
HR_APP_CTX.EMPNO = 7698

PL/SQL procedure successfully completed.
```

This time, we logged in as BLAKE who is the manager for department 30, and HR representative for departments 10 and 30. When BLAKE logs in, we see the context is set appropriately – he is an HR_REP, and his employee number and username are set. This also demonstrates how to list the attribute/value pairs in a session's context using the DMBS_SESSION.LIST_CONTEXT package. This package is executable by the general public, hence all users will be able to use this method to inspect their session's context values, in addition to the SESSION_CONTEXT view above.

Now that we have our session context being populated the way we want, we can set about to write our security policy function. These are the functions that will be called by the database engine at run-time to provide a dynamic predicate. The dynamic predicate will restrict what the user can read or write. We have a separate function for SELECTs versus UPDATEs versus INSERT/DELETE. This is because each of these statements allows access to different sets of rows. We are allowed to SELECT more data than we can UPDATE (we can see our employee record but not modify it, for example). Only special users can INSERT or DELETE, hence those predicates are different from the other two:

```
blake@TKYTE816> connect tkyte/tkyte

tkyte@TKYTE816> create or replace package hr_predicate_pkg
  2  as
  3      function select_function( p_schema in varchar2,
  4                      p_object in varchar2 ) return varchar2;
  5
  6      function update_function( p_schema in varchar2,
  7                      p_object in varchar2 ) return varchar2;
  8
  9      function insert_delete_function( p_schema in varchar2,
 10                      p_object in varchar2 ) return varchar2;
 11  end;
 12  /

Package created.
```

The implementation of the HR_PREDICATE_PKG is as follows. We begin with some global variables:

```
tkyte@TKYTE816> create or replace package body hr_predicate_pkg
  2  as
  3
  4  g_app_ctx constant varchar2(30) default 'Hr_App_Ctx';
  5
  6  g_sel_pred      varchar2(1024) default NULL;
  7  g_upd_pred      varchar2(1024) default NULL;
  8  g_ins_del_pred varchar2(1024) default NULL;
  9
```

The G_APP_CTX is the name of our application context. In the event that we might want to rename this at some point in time, we used a constant global variable to hold this name and use the variable in the subsequent code. This will let us simply change the constant, and recompile the package to use a different context name if we ever want to. The other three global variables will hold our predicates. This particular example was coded in Oracle 8.1.6. In this release, there is an issue with regards to cursor caching and FGAC (see the *Caveats* section for all of the details). In Oracle 8.1.7 and up, this programming technique does not need to be employed. In this case, what it means to us is that you cannot change your role *after* logging in. We generate the predicates once per session, and return the same ones for every query. We do not generate them once per query, so any changes to the role will not take effect until you log off and log back in (or reset your session state via a call to DBMS_SESSION.RESET_PACKAGE).

Now, for the first of our predicate functions. This one generates the predicate for a SELECT on our EMP view. Notice that all it does is set the global variable G_SEL_PRED (**G**lobal **SEL**ect **PRED**icate) depending on the value of the RoleName attribute in our context. If the context attribute is not set, this routine raises an error, which will subsequently fail the query:

```
10
11   function select_function( p_schema in varchar2,
12                             p_object in varchar2) return varchar2
13   is
14   begin
15
16       if ( g_sel_pred is NULL )
17       then
18           if ( sys_context( g_app_ctx, 'RoleName' ) = 'EMP' )
19           then
20             g_sel_pred:=
21                   'empno=sys_context('''||g_app_ctx||''',''EmpNo'')';
22           elsif ( sys_context( g_app_ctx, 'RoleName' ) = 'MGR' )
23           then
24               g_sel_pred :=
25                 'empno in ( select empno
26                       from emp_base_table
27                   start with empno =
28                           sys_context('''||g_app_ctx||''',''EmpNo'')
29               connect by prior empno = mgr)';
30
31           elsif ( sys_context( g_app_ctx, 'RoleName' ) = 'HR_REP' )
32           then
33               g_sel_pred := 'deptno in
34                       ( select deptno
35                           from hr_reps
36                         where username =
37                       sys_context('''||g_app_ctx||''',''UserName'') )';
38
39           else
40               raise_application_error( -20005, 'No Role Set' );
41           end if;
42       end if;
43
44       return g_sel_pred;
45   end;
46
```

And now for the routine that provides the predicate for updates. The logic is much the same as the previous routine, however the predicates returned are different. Notice the use of 1=0 for example, when the RoleName is set to EMP. An employee cannot update any information. MGRs can update the records of those that work for them (but not their own record). The HR_REPs can update anyone in the departments they manage:

```
47   function update_function( p_schema in varchar2,
48                             p_object in varchar2 ) return varchar2
49   is
50   begin
51       if ( g_upd_pred is NULL )
52       then
53           if ( sys_context( g_app_ctx, 'RoleName' ) = 'EMP' )
54           then
55               g_upd_pred := '1=0';
56
57           elsif ( sys_context( g_app_ctx, 'RoleName' ) = 'MGR' )
58           then
```

```
59                      g_upd_pred :=
60                          ' empno in ( select empno
61                                       from emp_base_table
62                                       where mgr =
63                                       sys_context('''||g_app_ctx||
64                                             ''','''EmpNo''') )';
65
66              elsif ( sys_context( g_app_ctx, 'RoleName' ) = 'HR_REP' )
67              then
68                  g_upd_pred := 'deptno in
69                          ( select deptno
70                              from hr_reps
71                              where username =
72                          sys_context('''||g_app_ctx||''','''UserName''') )';
73
74              else
75                  raise_application_error( -20005, 'No Role Set' );
76              end if;
77          end if;
78
79          return g_upd_pred;
80      end;
```

Lastly, is the predicate function for INSERTs and DELETEs. In this case, 1=0 is returned for both EMPs and MGRs alike – neither are allowed to CREATE or DELETE records, only HR_REPS may do so:

```
81
82      function insert_delete_function( p_schema in varchar2,
83                          p_object in varchar2) return varchar2
84      is
85      begin
86          if ( g_ins_del_pred is NULL )
87          then
88              if ( sys_context(g_app_ctx, 'RoleName' ) in ( 'EMP', 'MGR' ) )
89              then
90                  g_ins_del_pred := '1=0';
91              elsif ( sys_context( g_app_ctx, 'RoleName' ) = 'HR_REP' )
92              then
93                  g_ins_del_pred := 'deptno in
94                          ( select deptno
95                              from hr_reps
96                              where username =
97                          sys_context('''||g_app_ctx||''','''UserName''') )';
98              else
99                  raise_application_error( -20005, 'No Role Set' );
100             end if;
101         end if;
102         return g_ins_del_pred;
103     end;
104
105     end;
106 /
```

Package body created.

In the past, before we had FGAC, having one table with the above three predicates could only have been achieved with the use of many views, one each to SELECT, UPDATE, and INSERT/DELETE from for each role. FGAC simplifies this to just one view with a dynamic predicate.

The last step in the process is to associate our predicates with each of the DML operations, and the EMP table itself. This is accomplished as follows:

```
tkyte@TKYTE816> begin
  2      dbms_rls.add_policy
  3      ( object_name      => 'EMP',
  4        policy_name      => 'HR_APP_SELECT_POLICY',
  5        policy_function  => 'HR_PREDICATE_PKG.SELECT_FUNCTION',
  6        statement_types  => 'select' );
  7   end;
  8   /

PL/SQL procedure successfully completed.

tkyte@TKYTE816> begin
  2      dbms_rls.add_policy
  3      ( object_name      => 'EMP',
  4        policy_name      => 'HR_APP_UPDATE_POLICY',
  5        policy_function  => 'HR_PREDICATE_PKG.UPDATE_FUNCTION',
  6        statement_types  => 'update' ,
  7        update_check     => TRUE );
  8   end;
  9   /

PL/SQL procedure successfully completed.

tkyte@TKYTE816> begin
  2      dbms_rls.add_policy
  3      ( object_name      => 'EMP',
  4        policy_name      => 'HR_APP_INSERT_DELETE_POLICY',
  5        policy_function  => 'HR_PREDICATE_PKG.INSERT_DELETE_FUNCTION',
  6        statement_types  => 'insert, delete' ,
  7        update_check     => TRUE );
  8   end;
  9   /

PL/SQL procedure successfully completed.
```

So, for each of the DML operations, we have associated a different predicate function. When the user queries the EMP table, the predicate generated by the HR_PREDICATE_PKG.SELECT_FUNCTION will be invoked. When the user updates the table, the update function in that package will be used, and so on.

Now, to test the application. We will create a package HR_APP. This package represents our application. It has entry points to:

❑   Retrieve data (procedure listEmps)

❑   Update data (procedure updateSal)

❑   Delete data (procedure deleteAll)

❑   Insert new data (procedure insertNew)

We will log in as various users, with different roles, and monitor the behavior of our application. This will show us FGAC at work.

The following is our specification for our application:

```
tkyte@TKYTE816> create or replace package hr_app
  2  as
  3      procedure listEmps;
  4
  5      procedure updateSal;
  6
  7      procedure deleteAll;
  8
  9      procedure insertNew( p_deptno in number );
 10  end;
 11  /

Package created.
```

And now the package body. It is a somewhat contrived example as the UPDATE routine attempts to update as many rows as possible with a constant value. This is so that we can see exactly how many, and also which, rows are affected. The other routines are similar in nature – reporting back what they are able to do, and how many rows they are able to do it to:

```
tkyte@TKYTE816> create or replace package body hr_app
  2  as
  3
  4  procedure listEmps
  5  as
  6      l_cnt number default 0;
  7  begin
  8      dbms_output.put_line
  9      ( rpad('ename',10) || rpad('sal', 6 )  || ' ' ||
 10        rpad('dname',10) || rpad('mgr',5) || ' ' ||
 11        rpad('dno',3) );
 12      for x in ( select ename, sal, dname, mgr, emp.deptno
 13                   from emp, dept
 14                  where emp.deptno = dept.deptno )
 15      loop
 16          dbms_output.put_line(rpad(nvl(x.ename,'(null)'),10) ||
 17                                  to_char(x.sal,'9,999') || ' ' ||
 18                                  rpad(x.dname,10) ||
 19                                  to_char(x.mgr,'9999') || ' ' ||
 20                                  to_char(x.deptno,'99') );
 21          l_cnt := l_cnt + 1;
 22      end loop;
 23      dbms_output.put_line( l_cnt || ' rows selected' );
 24  end;
 25
 26
 27  procedure updateSal
 28  is
 29  begin
 30      update emp set sal = 9999;
 31      dbms_output.put_line( sql%rowcount || ' rows updated' );
```

```
32   end;
33
34   procedure deleteAll
35   is
36   begin
37       delete from emp where empno <> sys_context('Hr_app_Ctx','EMPNO' );
38       dbms_output.put_line( sql%rowcount || ' rows deleted' );
39   end;
40
41   procedure insertNew( p_deptno in number )
42   as
43   begin
44       insert into emp (empno, deptno, sal) values (123, p_deptno, 1111);
45   end;
46
47   end hr_app;
48   /
Package body created.

tkyte@TKYTE816> grant execute on hr_app to public
  2  /

Grant succeeded.
```

So, this is our 'application'. The listEmps routine shows every record we can see in the EMP view. The updateSal routine updates every record we are allowed to. The deleteAll routine deletes every record we are allowed to, with the exception of our own record. The insertNew routine tries to create a new employee in the department we request. This application simply tests all of the DML operations we might attempt on the EMP view (it is a rather contrived application to say the least).

Now, as different users, we will log in, and test the functionality of our application. First, we will log in and review our application context values:

```
tkyte@TKYTE816> connect adams/adams

adams@TKYTE816> column namespace format a10
adams@TKYTE816> column attribute format a10
adams@TKYTE816> column value     format a10
adams@TKYTE816> select * from session_context;

NAMESPACE  ATTRIBUTE   VALUE
---------- ----------- ----------
HR_APP_CTX ROLENAME    EMP
HR_APP_CTX USERNAME    ADAMS
HR_APP_CTX EMPNO       7876

adams@TKYTE816> set serveroutput on
```

Now, since we are just an EMP we expect that listEmps will show our record, and nothing else:

```
adams@TKYTE816> exec tkyte.hr_app.listEmps
ename    sal    dname     mgr   dno
ADAMS    1,100  RESEARCH  7788  20
```

```
1 rows selected

PL/SQL procedure successfully completed.
```

Again, since we are a just an EMP, we do not expect to be able to UPDATE and DELETE. The following tests that:

```
adams@TKYTE816> exec tkyte.hr_app.updateSal

0 rows updated

PL/SQL procedure successfully completed.

adams@TKYTE816> exec tkyte.hr_app.deleteAll

0 rows deleted

PL/SQL procedure successfully completed.
```

Lastly, we'll test the INSERT. Here, we will get an error back from the database. This differs from the UPDATE and DELETE cases above, in this particular example. The attempts to UPDATE or DELETE did not fail, since we precluded the user from seeing any data to UPDATE or DELETE in the first place. When we go to INSERT however, the row is created, found to be in violation of the policy, and then removed. The database raises an error in this case:

```
adams@TKYTE816> exec tkyte.hr_app.insertNew(20);
BEGIN tkyte.hr_app.insertNew(20); END;

*
ERROR at line 1:
ORA-28115: policy with check option violation
ORA-06512: at "TKYTE.HR_APP", line 36
ORA-06512: at line 1
```

So, the above shows we can see only our record. We cannot UPDATE any data whatsoever, we cannot DELETE any records, and INSERTing a new employee fails as well. This is exactly what we intended and it happens transparently. The application, HR_APP, does nothing special to enforce these rules. The database is doing it for us now, from logon to logoff, no matter what tool or environment we use to connect.

Next, we log in as a MGR and see what happens. First, we will once again print out our context to see what is in there, and then list out the employees we can 'see':

```
adams@TKYTE816> @connect jones/jones

jones@TKYTE816> set serveroutput on

jones@TKYTE816> select * from session_context;

NAMESPACE    ATTRIBUTE    VALUE
----------   ----------   ----------
HR_APP_CTX   ROLENAME     MGR
HR_APP_CTX   USERNAME     JONES
```

```
HR_APP_CTX EMPNO        7566

jones@TKYTE816> exec tkyte.hr_app.listEmps
ename      sal    dname        mgr    dno
SMITH          800 RESEARCH    7902   20
JONES        2,975 RESEARCH    7839   20
SCOTT        9,999 RESEARCH    7566   20
ADAMS        1,100 RESEARCH    7788   20
FORD         3,000 RESEARCH    7566   20
5 rows selected


PL/SQL procedure successfully completed.
```

This shows that this time, we can see many more than one record in the EMP table. In fact, we 'see' all of department 20 – JONES is the MGR of department 20 in the EMP table. Next, we'll run the UPDATE routine and review the changes made:

```
jones@TKYTE816> exec tkyte.hr_app.updateSal
2 rows updated

PL/SQL procedure successfully completed.

jones@TKYTE816> exec tkyte.hr_app.listEmps
ename      sal    dname        mgr    dno
SMITH          800 RESEARCH    7902   20
JONES        2,975 RESEARCH    7839   20
SCOTT        9,999 RESEARCH    7566   20
ADAMS        1,100 RESEARCH    7788   20
FORD         9,999 RESEARCH    7566   20
5 rows selected
```

As per our logic, we can UPDATE only the records of our direct reports. The UPDATE affected only the two records that represent the employees reporting directly to JONES. Next we try to DELETE and INSERT. Since we are a MGR and not an HR_REP, we will not be able to DELETE any records and the INSERT will fail:

```
jones@TKYTE816> exec tkyte.hr_app.deleteAll
0 rows deleted

PL/SQL procedure successfully completed.

jones@TKYTE816> exec tkyte.hr_app.insertNew(20)
BEGIN tkyte.hr_app.insertNew(20); END;

*
ERROR at line 1:
ORA-28115: policy with check option violation
ORA-06512: at "TKYTE.HR_APP", line 44
ORA-06512: at line 1
```

So, this time as a MGR we can:

❑ See more than just our data. We see everyone who reports to us, and their reports, and so on (a hierarchy).

❑ UPDATE some of the data. Specifically, we can UPDATE only those records belonging to people who report directly to us, as required.

❑ Still not DELETE or INSERT any data, as required.

Lastly, we'll log in as an HR_REP and review the behavior of our application in this role. We'll start again by showing the application context state and print out the rows we can see. This time, we'll see the entire EMP table – KING has access to all three departments:

```
jones@TKYTE816> connect king/king

king@TKYTE816> select * from session_context;

NAMESPACE    ATTRIBUTE   VALUE
----------   ----------  ----------
HR_APP_CTX   ROLENAME    HR_REP
HR_APP_CTX   USERNAME    KING
HR_APP_CTX   EMPNO       7839

king@TKYTE816> exec tkyte.hr_app.listEmps
ename      sal     dname       mgr   dno
CLARK      2,450   ACCOUNTING  7839  10
KING       5,000   ACCOUNTING  10
MILLER     1,300   ACCOUNTING  7782  10
SMITH        800   RESEARCH    7902  20
JONES      2,975   RESEARCH    7839  20
SCOTT      9,999   RESEARCH    7566  20
ADAMS      1,100   RESEARCH    7788  20
FORD       9,999   RESEARCH    7566  20
ALLEN      1,600   SALES       7698  30
WARD       1,250   SALES       7698  30
MARTIN     1,250   SALES       7698  30
BLAKE      2,850   SALES       7839  30
TURNER     1,500   SALES       7698  30
JAMES        950   SALES       7698  30
14 rows selected

PL/SQL procedure successfully completed.
```

Now, we'll execute an UPDATE to see what data we can modify. In this case, every row will be updated:

```
king@TKYTE816> exec tkyte.hr_app.updateSal
14 rows updated

PL/SQL procedure successfully completed.

king@TKYTE816> exec tkyte.hr_app.listEmps
ename      sal     dname       mgr   dno
CLARK      9,999   ACCOUNTING  7839  10
KING       9,999   ACCOUNTING  10
```

```
MILLER      9,999 ACCOUNTING 7782  10
SMITH       9,999 RESEARCH   7902  20
JONES       9,999 RESEARCH   7839  20
SCOTT       9,999 RESEARCH   7566  20
ADAMS       9,999 RESEARCH   7788  20
FORD        9,999 RESEARCH   7566  20
ALLEN       9,999 SALES      7698  30
WARD        9,999 SALES      7698  30
MARTIN      9,999 SALES      7698  30
BLAKE       9,999 SALES      7839  30
TURNER      9,999 SALES      7698  30
JAMES       9,999 SALES      7698  30
14 rows selected

PL/SQL procedure successfully completed.
```

The value of 9,999 in the SAL column verifies that we modified every row in the table. Next, we'll try out the DELETE. Remember, the DeleteAll API call we developed earlier will not DELETE the currently logged in users record by design:

```
king@TKYTE816> exec tkyte.hr_app.deleteAll
13 rows deleted

PL/SQL procedure successfully completed.
```

This shows we can DELETE records for the first time. Let's try creating one:

```
king@TKYTE816> exec tkyte.hr_app.insertNew(20)

PL/SQL procedure successfully completed.

king@TKYTE816> exec tkyte.hr_app.listEmps
ename      sal    dname     mgr    dno
KING       9,999 ACCOUNTING  10
(null)     1,111 RESEARCH    20
2 rows selected

PL/SQL procedure successfully completed.
```

Sure enough, it worked this time, as the rules for an HR_Rep were implemented. This completes the testing of our three roles. Our requirements have been met, we secured the data, and did it transparently to the application.

Caveats

As with any feature, there are some nuances that need to be noted in the way this feature functions. This section attempts to address them, each in turn.

Referential Integrity

FGAC may or may not work the way you expect it to with regards to referential integrity. It depends on what you think should happen I suppose. I myself wasn't really sure *what* would happen right away.

As it turns out, referential integrity will bypass FGAC. With it, I can read a table, delete from it, and update it, even if I cannot issue the SELECT, DELETE, or INSERT against that table. This is the way it is supposed to work, so it is something you must consider in your design when using FGAC.

We will look at the cases of:

❑ Discovering data values I should not be able to see. This is what is known as a **covert channel**. I cannot directly query the data. However, I can prove the existence (or lack thereof) of some data values in a table using a foreign key.

❑ Being able to delete from a table via an ON DELETE CASCADE integrity constraint.

❑ Being able to update a table via an ON UPDATE SET NULL integrity constraint.

We will look at these three cases using a somewhat contrived example with two tables P (parent), and C (child):

```
tkyte@TKYTE816> create table p ( x int primary key );

Table created.

tkyte@TKYTE816> create table c ( x int references p on delete cascade );

Table created.
```

The Covert Channel

The covert channel here is that we can discover primary key values of rows in P by inserting into C, and watching what happens. I'll be able to determine if a row exists in P or not, via this method. We'll start by implementing a predicate function that always returns a WHERE clause that evaluates to False:

```
tkyte@TKYTE816> create or replace function pred_function
  2  ( p_schema in varchar2, p_object in varchar2 )
  3  return varchar2
  4  as
  5  begin
  6          return '1=0';
  7  end;
  8  /

Function created.
```

and using this predicate function to restrict SELECT access on P:

```
tkyte@TKYTE816> begin
  2          dbms_rls.add_policy
  3          ( object_name => 'P',
  4            policy_name => 'P_POLICY',
```

```
    5          policy_function => 'pred_function',
    6          statement_types => 'select' );
    7  end;
    8  /

PL/SQL procedure successfully completed.
```

Now, we can still INSERT into P (and UPDATE/DELETE from P), we just cannot SELECT anything from it. We'll start by putting a value into P:

```
tkyte@TKYTE816> insert into p values ( 1 );

1 row created.

tkyte@TKYTE816> select * from p;
no rows selected
```

Our predicate prevents us from seeing this row, but we can tell it is there simply by inserting into C:

```
tkyte@TKYTE816> insert into c values ( 1 );
1 row created.

tkyte@TKYTE816> insert into c values ( 2 );
insert into c values ( 2 )
*
ERROR at line 1:
ORA-02291: integrity constraint (TKYTE.SYS_C003873) violated - parent key not
found
```

So, we can now see that the value 1 must be in P, and the value 2 is not, by the fact that C can have a row with 1 but not 2. Referential integrity is able to read through FGAC. This may be confusing to an application such as an ad-hoc query tool that generates queries based on relationships in the data dictionary. If it queries C, all rows come back. If it joins P and C, no data will be found.

It should also be noted that a similar covert channel exists from the parent to the child. If the policy above were placed on C instead of P, and C did not have the ON DELETE CASCADE clause (in other words, just a references), we would be able to determine what values of X were in C by deleting from P. DELETEs on P would raise an error if there were child rows in C and succeed otherwise, even though we cannot SELECT any rows from C normally.

Deleting Rows

This is exposed via the ON DELETE CASCADE referential integrity clause. If we drop the policy on P and instead, use the same function as a DELETE policy on C as follows:

```
tkyte@TKYTE816> begin
    2      dbms_rls.drop_policy
    3      ( 'TKYTE', 'P', 'P_POLICY' );
    4  end;
    5  /

PL/SQL procedure successfully completed.
```

```
tkyte@TKYTE816> begin
  2      dbms_rls.add_policy
  3      ( object_name => 'C',
  4        policy_name => 'C_POLICY',
  5        policy_function => 'pred_function',
  6        statement_types => 'DELETE' );
  7  end;
  8  /

PL/SQL procedure successfully completed.
```

we'll find we can delete *no* rows in C using SQL:

```
tkyte@TKYTE816> delete from C;

0 rows deleted.
```

The policy we put in place prevents this. We can see that there is a row in C (from the prior INSERT above):

```
tkyte@TKYTE816> select * from C;

         X
----------
         1
```

The simple act of deleting the parent row:

```
tkyte@TKYTE816> delete from P;

1 row deleted.
```

will in fact read through the FGAC policy once again, and DELETE that row in C for us:

```
tkyte@TKYTE816> select * from C;

no rows selected
```

Updating Rows

A very similar condition to the DELETE example exists with regards to ON DELETE SET NULL. Here, we will change the example so that we can use referential integrity to update rows in C we cannot update via SQL. We'll start by rebuilding C with an ON DELETE SET NULL constraint:

```
tkyte@TKYTE816> drop table c;

Table dropped.

tkyte@TKYTE816> create table c ( x int references p on delete set null );

Table created.
```

```
tkyte@TKYTE816> insert into p values ( 1 );

1 row created.

tkyte@TKYTE816> insert into c values ( 1 );

1 row created.
```

Next, we'll associate that same predicate function from above with the table C on UPDATE, and set the UPDATE_CHECK flag to TRUE. This will prevent us from updating any rows:

```
tkyte@TKYTE816> begin
  2      dbms_rls.add_policy
  3      ( object_name => 'C',
  4        policy_name => 'C_POLICY',
  5        policy_function => 'pred_function',
  6        statement_types => 'UPDATE',
  7            update_check => TRUE );
  8  end;
  9  /

PL/SQL procedure successfully completed.

tkyte@TKYTE816> update c set x = NULL;

0 rows updated.

tkyte@TKYTE816> select * from c;

         X
----------
         1
```

So, we are not able to update any rows in C using SQL. However, a simple DELETE on the parent table P shows us:

```
tkyte@TKYTE816> delete from p;
1 row deleted.

tkyte@TKYTE816> select * from c;

         X
----------
```

In this fashion, we can update C in a roundabout way. There is another way to demonstrate this, so we'll start by resetting the example:

```
tkyte@TKYTE816> delete from c;

1 row deleted.

tkyte@TKYTE816> insert into p values ( 1 );
```

```
   1 row created.

   tkyte@TKYTE816> insert into c values ( 1 );

   1 row created.
```

and then rewriting the function so we can update rows in C to any value *except Null*:

```
   tkyte@TKYTE816> create or replace function pred_function
     2  ( p_schema in varchar2, p_object in varchar2 )
     3  return varchar2
     4  as
     5  begin
     6          return 'x is not null';
     7  end;
     8  /

   Function created.

   tkyte@TKYTE816> update c set x = NULL;
   update c set x = NULL
                 *
   ERROR at line 1:
   ORA-28115: policy with check option violation
```

This update failed because the predicate X IS NOT NULL was not satisfied after the update. Now when we DELETE from P again:

```
   tkyte@TKYTE816> delete from p;

   1 row deleted.

   tkyte@TKYTE816> select * from c;

           X
   ----------
```

the row in C is set to the value we could not set using SQL.

Cursor Caching

One important implementation feature of our security predicate function shown earlier, in section *Example 1: Implementing a Security Policy*, is the fact that during a given session, this function returns a constant predicate – this is critical. If we look at the function we used above once more, we see the logic is:

```
   ...
     5  as
     6  begin
     7      if ( user = p_schema ) then
     8          return '';
     9      else
    10          return 'owner = USER';
```

```
 11        end if;
 12   end;
...
```

This predicate function returns either no predicate or owner = USER. During a given session it will consistently return the same predicate. There is no chance that we would retrieve the predicate owner = USER and, later in that same session, retrieve the empty predicate. To understand why this is absolutely critical to a correctly designed FGAC application, we must understand when the predicate is associated with a query, and how different environments such as PL/SQL, Pro*C, OCI, JDBC, ODBC, and so on, handle this.

Let's say we wrote a predicate function that looked something like this:

```
SQL> create or replace function rls_examp
  2  ( p_schema in varchar2, p_object in varchar2 )
  3  return varchar2
  4  as
  5  begin
  6          if ( sys_context( 'myctx', 'x' ) is not null )
  7          then
  8                  return 'x > 0';
  9          else
 10                  return '1=0';
 11          end if;
 12  end;
 13  /

Function created.
```

This says that if the attribute x is set in the context, the predicate should be x > 0. If the context attribute x is not set, the predicate is 1=0. If we create a table T, put data into it, and add the policy and context as follows:

```
SQL> create table t ( x int );

Table created.

SQL> insert into t values ( 1234 );

1 row created.

SQL> begin
  2      dbms_rls.add_policy
  3      ( object_schema    => user,
  4        object_name => 'T',
  5      policy_name => 'T_POLICY',
  6        function_schema => user,
  7        policy_function => 'rls_examp',
  8        statement_types => 'select' );
  9  end;
 10  /

PL/SQL procedure successfully completed.
```

```
SQL> create or replace procedure set_ctx( p_val in varchar2 )
  2  as
  3  begin
  4          dbms_session.set_context( 'myctx', 'x', p_val );
  5  end;
  6  /

Procedure created.

SQL> create or replace context myctx using set_ctx;

Context created.
```

it would appear that if the context is set, we would see one row. If the context is not set, we would see zero rows. In fact, if we test in SQL*PLUS using just SQL, the following would be the case:

```
SQL> exec set_ctx( null );

PL/SQL procedure successfully completed.

SQL> select * from t;

no rows selected

SQL> exec set_ctx( 1 );

PL/SQL procedure successfully completed.

SQL> select * from t;

         X
----------
      1234
```

So, it would appear that we are set to go. The dynamic predicate is working as we expected. In fact, if we use PL/SQL (or Pro*C, or well-coded OCI/JDBC/ODBC applications, as well as many other execution environments) we find that the above does not hold true. For example, lets code a small PL/SQL routine:

```
SQL> create or replace procedure dump_t
  2  ( some_input in number default NULL )
  3  as
  4  begin
  5          dbms_output.put_line
  6          ( '*** Output from SELECT * FROM T' );
  7
  8          for x in (select * from t ) loop
  9                  dbms_output.put_line( x.x );
 10          end loop;
 11
 12          if ( some_input is not null )
 13          then
 14                  dbms_output.put_line
 15                  ( '*** Output from another SELECT * FROM T' );
```

```
16
17                          for x in (select * from t ) loop
18                              dbms_output.put_line( x.x );
19                          end loop;
20            end if;
21  end;
22  /

Procedure created.
```

This routine simply issues a SELECT * FROM T once in the procedure if no inputs are passed, and twice in the procedure if some input is passed. Let's execute this procedure and observe the outcome. We'll start by running the procedure with the context value set to Null (hence the predicate would be 1=0, in other words, no rows):

```
SQL> set serveroutput on

SQL> exec set_ctx( NULL )

PL/SQL procedure successfully completed.


SQL> exec dump_t
*** Output from SELECT * FROM T

PL/SQL procedure successfully completed.
```

As expected, no data was returned. Now, let's set the context value so the predicate will be x > 0. We will call DUMP_T in a manner so has it execute *both* queries this time. What will happen in Oracle 8.1.5 and 8.1.6 is the following:

```
SQL> exec set_ctx( 1 )

PL/SQL procedure successfully completed.

SQL> exec dump_t( 0 )
*** Output from SELECT * FROM T
*** Output from another SELECT * FROM T
1234

PL/SQL procedure successfully completed.
```

The first query, the one that was executed with the Null context initially, *still returns no data.* Its cursor was cached; it was not re-parsed.

When we run the procedure with the context attribute 'x' set to Null, we get the expected results (because it's the first time in this session we are running this procedure). We set the context attribute 'x' to a non-Null value, and find we get 'ambiguous' results. The first SELECT * FROM T in the procedure still returns no rows – it is apparently still using the predicate 1=0. The second query (which we did not execute the first time) returns, what appears to be, the correct results. It is apparently using the predicate x > 0 as we expect.

Why did the first SELECT in this procedure not use the predicate we anticipated? It is because of an optimization called **cursor caching**. PL/SQL, and many other execution environments, do not really 'close' a cursor when you close a cursor. The above example may be easily reproduced in Pro*C for example if, the pre-compile option release_cursor is left to default to NO. If you take the same code and pre-compile with release_cursor=YES, the Pro*C program would behave more like queries in SQL*PLUS. The predicate used by DBMS_RLS is assigned to a query during the PARSE phase. The first query SELECT * FROM T is getting parsed during the first execution of the stored procedure, when the predicate was in fact 1=0. The PL/SQL engine is caching this parsed cursor for you. The second time we execute the stored procedure, PL/SQL simply reused the parsed cursor from the first SELECT * FROM T. This parsed query has the predicate 1=0. The predicate function was not invoked at all this time around. Since we also passed some inputs to the procedure, PL/SQL executed the second query. This query however, did not already have an opened, parsed cursor for it, so it parsed during this execution, when the context attribute was not Null. The second SELECT * FROM T has the predicate x>0 associated with it. This is the cause of the ambiguity. Since we have no control over the caching of these cursors in general, a security predicate function that may return more then one predicate per session should be avoided at all cost. Subtle, hard to detect bugs in your application will be the result otherwise. Earlier, in the HR example, we demonstrated how to implement a security predicate function that cannot return more than one predicate per session. This ensured that:

❏   Your results are consistent from query to query with respect to FGAC.

❏   You are never tempted to change the predicate in the middle of a session. Strange, and unpredictable results will be the outcome if you do.

❏   You are made to enforce your security policy in this single predicate for a user, rather than attempting to return a predicate customized for the current environment in which the user is running.

In Oracle 8.1.7 and up, you should expect the following outcome:

```
tkyte@dev817> exec dump_t( 0 )
*** Output from SELECT * FROM T
1234
*** Output from another SELECT * FROM T
1234

PL/SQL procedure successfully completed.
```

In 8.1.7 and up, the database will now re-parse this query if the session context has changed, and it has a security policy associated with it to avoid issues as described above. We need to stress the *session context changing* bit of the previous statement. If we do not use a session context to determine our predicate, this cursor caching issue comes back into play. Consider a system where the predicates are stored as data in a database table, a sort of a table driven policy function. Here, if the contents of the data table changes, causing the predicate that is returned to change, we get into the same issues with 8.1.7 as we did in 8.1.6 and before. If we change the above example to include a database table:

```
tkyte@TKYTE816> create table policy_rules_table
  2  ( predicate_piece varchar2(255)
  3  );

Table created.

tkyte@TKYTE816> insert into policy_rules_table values ( 'x > 0' );

1 row created.
```

and change the policy function to be table driven:

```
tkyte@TKYTE816> create or replace function rls_examp
  2  ( p_schema in varchar2, p_object in varchar2 )
  3  return varchar2
  4  as
  5      l_predicate_piece varchar2(255);
  6  begin
  7      select predicate_piece into l_predicate_piece
  8        from policy_rules_table;
  9
 10      return l_predicate_piece;
 11  end;
 12  /

Function created.
```

we will now expect the following output from DUMP_T if we change the predicate *after* executing DUMP_T with no inputs, but *before* executing it with inputs:

```
tkyte@DEV817> exec dump_t
*** Output from SELECT * FROM T
1234

PL/SQL procedure successfully completed.

tkyte@DEV817> update policy_rules_table set predicate_piece = '1=0';

1 row updated.

tkyte@DEV817> exec dump_t(0)
*** Output from SELECT * FROM T
1234
*** Output from another SELECT * FROM T

PL/SQL procedure successfully completed.
```

Notice how during the first execution, the predicate was x>0; this returned the row from table T. After we executed this procedure, we modified the predicate (this update could be done from another session, by an administrator for example). When we executed DUMP_T for the second time, passing it an input so as to have it execute the second query in addition to the first, we see that the first query is still using the old predicate x>0, whereas the second query is obviously using the second predicate 1=0 we just put into the POLICY_RULES table. You must use caution with regards to this cursor caching, even in 8.1.7 and up unless you use an application context as well as the table.

I would like to point out that it is *very safe to change the value of* SYS_CONTEXT in the middle of an application. Their changes will take effect and be used on the next execution of the query. Since they are bind variables, they are evaluated during the 'execute' phase of the query, and not during the parse, so their values do not remain fixed at parse-time. It is only the text of the predicate itself that should not change during the execution of an application. Here is a small example demonstrating this. We will log out, and log back in (to clear out our previous session from above with the cached cursors), and re-implement our RLS_EXAMP function. Then, we'll do the same sort of logic we did above, and see what happens:

```
tkyte@TKYTE816> connect tkyte/tkyte

tkyte@TKYTE816> create or replace function rls_examp
  2  ( p_schema in varchar2, p_object in varchar2 )
  3  return varchar2
  4  as
  5  begin
  6          return 'x > sys_context(''myctx'',''x'')';
  7  end;
  8  /

Function created.

tkyte@TKYTE816> set serveroutput on

tkyte@TKYTE816> exec set_ctx( NULL )

PL/SQL procedure successfully completed.

tkyte@TKYTE816> exec dump_t
*** Output from SELECT * FROM T

PL/SQL procedure successfully completed.

tkyte@TKYTE816> exec set_ctx( 1 )

PL/SQL procedure successfully completed.

tkyte@TKYTE816> exec dump_t( 0 )
*** Output from SELECT * FROM T
1234
*** Output from another SELECT * FROM T
1234

PL/SQL procedure successfully completed.
```

This time, both queries return the same result. This simply because they both use the same WHERE clause, and dynamically access the value of the application context in the query itself.

I should mention that there are cases where changing the predicate in the middle of a session may be desirable. The client applications that access objects, which employ policies that can change predicates in the middle of a session must be coded in a specific fashion to take advantage of this. For example, in PL/SQL, we would have to code the application using dynamic SQL entirely, to avoid the cursor caching. If you are employing this dynamic predicate method, then you should bear in mind that the results will depend on how the client application is coded, therefore you should not be enforcing a security policy with this use of the feature. We will not be discussing this possible use of the DBMS_RLS feature, but rather will concentrate on its intended use, which is to secure data.

Export/Import

We mentioned this issue previously. Care must be taken when using the EXP tool to export data, and IMP to import it. Since the two issues are different, we'll look at each in turn. For this caveat, we'll extend the prior example by changing the policy T_POLICY. We'll have it so that it will be in effect for INSERTs, as well as SELECTs this time:

```
tkyte@TKYTE816> begin
  2      dbms_rls.drop_policy( 'TKYTE', 'T', 'T_POLICY' );
  3  end;
  4  /
PL/SQL procedure successfully completed.

tkyte@TKYTE816> begin
  2      dbms_rls.add_policy
  3      ( object_name => 'T',
  4        policy_name => 'T_POLICY',
  5        policy_function => 'rls_examp',
  6        statement_types => 'select, insert',
  7        update_check    => TRUE );
  8  end;
  9  /
PL/SQL procedure successfully completed.
```

Once we do this, the following behavior will be observed:

```
tkyte@TKYTE816> delete from t;

1 row deleted.

tkyte@TKYTE816> commit;

Commit complete.

tkyte@TKYTE816> exec set_ctx( null );

PL/SQL procedure successfully completed.

tkyte@TKYTE816> insert into t values ( 1 );
insert into t values ( 1 )
                  *
ERROR at line 1:
ORA-28115: policy with check option violation

tkyte@TKYTE816> exec set_ctx( 0 ) ;

PL/SQL procedure successfully completed.

tkyte@TKYTE816> insert into t values ( 1 );

1 row created.
```

So now the context must be set to SELECT and INSERT data.

Export Issues

By default EXP will execute in a 'conventional' path mode. It will use SQL to read all of the data. If we use EXP to extract the table T from the database, the following will be observed (note that T has 1 row in it right now due to our INSERT above):

```
C:\fgac>exp userid=tkyte/tkyte tables=t

Export: Release 8.1.6.0.0 - Production on Mon Apr 16 16:29:25 2001
(c) Copyright 1999 Oracle Corporation.  All rights reserved.


Connected to: Oracle8i Enterprise Edition Release 8.1.6.0.0 - Production
With the Partitioning option
JServer Release 8.1.6.0.0 - Production
Export done in WE8ISO8859P1 character set and WE8ISO8859P1 NCHAR character set

About to export specified tables via Conventional Path ...
EXP-00079: Data in table "T" is protected. Conventional path may only be exporting
partial table.
. . exporting table                             T              0 rows exported
Export terminated successfully with warnings.
```

Notice that EXP was kind enough to notify us that the table we exported *may* be only partially exported, since the conventional path was used. The solution to this is to use the SYS (or any account connected as SYSDBA) account to export. FGAC is not in effect for the SYS user:

```
C:\fgac>exp userid=sys/manager tables=tkyte.t

Export: Release 8.1.6.0.0 - Production on Mon Apr 16 16:35:21 2001
(c) Copyright 1999 Oracle Corporation.  All rights reserved.


Connected to: Oracle8i Enterprise Edition Release 8.1.6.0.0 - Production
With the Partitioning option
JServer Release 8.1.6.0.0 - Production
Export done in WE8ISO8859P1 character set and WE8ISO8859P1 NCHAR character set

About to export specified tables via Conventional Path ...
Current user changed to TKYTE
. . exporting table                             T              1 rows exported
Export terminated successfully without warnings.
```

Another valid option would be to use DBMS_RLS.ENABLE_POLICY to disable the policy temporarily, and re-enable it after the export. This is not entirely desirable as the table is left unprotected during this period of time.

> *In some versions of Oracle 8.1.5, a direct path export bypassed FGAC erroneously. That is, by adding* direct=true, *all of the data would be exported. You should not rely on this, as it has since been corrected in all later releases. In these releases you will get:*

```
About to export specified tables via Direct Path ...
EXP-00080: Data in table "T" is protected. Using conventional mode.
EXP-00079: Data in table "T" is protected. Conventional path may only...
```

EXP will automatically drop into a conventional path export for protected tables.

Import Issues

This is only an issue if you have a FGAC policy on a table that is in effect for INSERTs with the UPDATE_CHECK set to True. In this case, IMP may reject some rows if your predicate function returns a predicate they cannot satisfy. In the above example, this is the case. Unless we set the context, no rows can be inserted (the context value is Null). Hence, if we take the above EXP we created, and try to import the data back in:

```
C:\fgac>imp userid=tkyte/tkyte full=y ignore=y

Import: Release 8.1.6.0.0 - Production on Mon Apr 16 16:37:33 2001

(c) Copyright 1999 Oracle Corporation.  All rights reserved.


Connected to: Oracle8i Enterprise Edition Release 8.1.6.0.0 - Production
With the Partitioning option
JServer Release 8.1.6.0.0 - Production

Export file created by EXPORT:V08.01.06 via conventional path

Warning: the objects were exported by SYS, not by you

import done in WE8ISO8859P1 character set and WE8ISO8859P1 NCHAR character set
. importing SYS's objects into TKYTE
. . importing table                             "T"
IMP-00058: ORACLE error 28115 encountered
ORA-28115: policy with check option violation
IMP-00017: following statement failed with ORACLE error 28101:
 "BEGIN  DBMS_RLS.ADD_POLICY('TKYTE', 'T','T_POLICY','TKYTE','RLS_EXAMP','SE"
 "LECT,INSERT',TRUE,TRUE); END;"
IMP-00003: ORACLE error 28101 encountered
ORA-28101: policy already exists
ORA-06512: at "SYS.DBMS_RLS", line 0
ORA-06512: at line 1
Import terminated successfully with warnings.
```

and our rows are not inserted. Once again, the work around is to import as SYS or SYSDBA:

```
C:\fgac>imp userid=sys/manager full=y ignore=y

Import: Release 8.1.6.0.0 - Production on Mon Apr 16 16:40:56 2001

(c) Copyright 1999 Oracle Corporation.  All rights reserved.


Connected to: Oracle8i Enterprise Edition Release 8.1.6.0.0 - Production
With the Partitioning option
JServer Release 8.1.6.0.0 - Production

Export file created by EXPORT:V08.01.06 via conventional path
import done in WE8ISO8859P1 character set and WE8ISO8859P1 NCHAR character set
. importing SYS's objects into SYS
. importing TKYTE's objects into TKYTE
. . importing table                             "T"           1 rows imported
```

Another valid option would be to use `DBMS_RLS.ENABLE_POLICY` to disable the policy temporarily, and re-enable it after the import. As with `EXP`, this is not entirely desirable as the table is left unprotected during that period of time.

Debugging

One utility I use frequently when writing predicate functions is a simple 'debug' package. This package, authored by Christopher Beck, also of Oracle, allows us to instrument our code with 'print' statements. This package also allows us to liberally put in our code, statements like:

```
create function foo ...
as
    ...
begin
    debug.f( 'Enter procedure foo' );
    if ( some_condition ) then
        l_predicate := 'x=1';
    end if;

    debug.f( 'Going to return the predicate ''%s''', l_predicate );
    return l_predicate;
end;
```

So, `debug.f` works similarly to the C `printf` function, and is implemented using `UTL_FILE`. It creates programmer-managed trace files on the database server. These trace files contain your debug statements, things you can use to see what is happening in your code. Since the database kernel is invoking your code in the background, debugging it can be hard. Traditional tools like `DBMS_OUTPUT` and the PL/SQL debugger are not very useful here. Having these trace files can save lots of time. The scripts you can download (see the Apress web site) contain this debug package, and comments on setting it up and using it.

This package is extremely invaluable is diagnosing exactly what is going on in your security policy functions, and I strongly urge you to use it, or something like it. Without a tracing facility like this, figuring out exactly what is going wrong is nearly impossible.

Errors You Might Encounter

During the implementation of the above application, I ran into many errors, and had to debug my application. Since FGAC happens totally in the server, it can be a little obtuse to diagnose errors, and debug your application. The following sections will help you successfully debug and diagnose errors.

ORA-28110: policy function or package <function name> has error.

This indicates that the package or function the policy is bound to has an error, and cannot be recompiled. If you issue the SQL*PLUS command, SHOW ERRORS FUNCTION <FUNCTION NAME> or SHOW ERRORS PACKAGE BODY <PACKAGE NAME>, you will discover what the errors are.

This invalidation may happen because:

❑　Some object your function references was dropped, or is itself invalid.

❑　The code you compiled into the database has a syntactical error, or cannot be compiled for some reason.

The most common cause of this error is that the predicate function associated with a table has an error. For example, consider the function from the previous examples:

```
tkyte@TKYTE816> create or replace function rls_examp
  2  ( p_schema in varchar2, p_object in varchar2 )
  3  return varchar2
  4  as
  5  begin
  6          this is an error
  7          return 'x > sys_context(''myctx'',''x'')';
  8  end;
  9  /

Warning: Function created with compilation errors.
```

Let's say we didn't notice at compile-time that the function did not compile cleanly. We assume the function compiled, and we could execute it as normal. Now, whenever we execute any queries on T we receive:

```
tkyte@TKYTE816> exec set_ctx( 0 ) ;

PL/SQL procedure successfully completed.

tkyte@TKYTE816> select * from t;
select * from t
              *
ERROR at line 1:
ORA-28110: policy function or package TKYTE.RLS_EXAMP has error
```

So, this is telling us that we have an error, specifically that the function TKYTE.RLS_EXAMP is in error (it cannot be successfully compiled). A query you might find useful in discovering these issues before they happen is:

```
tkyte@TKYTE816> column pf_owner format a10
tkyte@TKYTE816> column package format a10
tkyte@TKYTE816> column function format a10
tkyte@TKYTE816> select pf_owner, package, function
  2    from user_policies a
  3   where exists ( select null
  4                    from all_objects
  5                   where owner = pf_owner
  6                     and object_type in ( 'FUNCTION', 'PACKAGE',
  7                                          'PACKAGE BODY' )
  8                     and status = 'INVALID'
  9                     and object_name in ( a.package, a.function )
 10                 )
 11  /

PF_OWNER   PACKAGE    FUNCTION
---------- ---------- ----------
TKYTE                 RLS_EXAMP
```

This query lists all *invalid* security policy functions for you. So, currently it confirms what we already know – that TKYTE.RLS_EXAMP is invalid. The solution now is pretty straightforward. We issue:

```
tkyte@TKYTE816> show errors function rls_examp
Errors for FUNCTION RLS_EXAMP:

LINE/COL ERROR
-------- ----------------------------------------------------------------
6/10     PLS-00103: Encountered the symbol "AN" when expecting one of the
         following:
         := . ( @ % ;
```

Looking at line 6, it is the line that reads `this is an error`. Correct this and the ORA-28110 will go away.

ORA-28112: failed to execute policy function.

An `ORA-28112: failed to execute policy function` results if SELECT or DML is performed on a table with an associated policy function, and the policy function has policy-related (not predicate) errors. This means the function is valid (it can be executed), but it raised some exception and did not it, allowing the database kernel to receive the exception.

An `ORA-28112` will generate a trace file in the directory specified by the USER_DUMP_DEST init.ora parameter. This file will *not* have the ORA-28112, but it will have the phrase `Policy function execution error`.

For example, let's say we had coded the following logic (continuing the example from earlier):

```
tkyte@TKYTE816> create or replace function rls_examp
  2  ( p_schema in varchar2, p_object in varchar2 )
  3  return varchar2
  4  as
  5          l_uid number;
  6  begin
  7          select user_id
  8            into l_uid
  9            from all_users
 10           where username = 'SOME_USER_WHO_DOESNT_EXIST';
 11
 12      return 'x > sys_context(''myctx'',''x'')';
 13  end;
 14  /

Function created.
```

The intention of the above routine is to raise the exception NO_DATA_FOUND, and not to handle it. This is to see what happens when an exception is allowed to propagate back to the database kernel. Now let's cause this routine to be invoked:

```
tkyte@TKYTE816> exec set_ctx( 0 ) ;

PL/SQL procedure successfully completed.

tkyte@TKYTE816> select * from t;
select * from t
              *
ERROR at line 1:
ORA-28112: failed to execute policy function
```

This indicates that the policy function exists, and is valid, but raised an error during execution. A trace file accompanies this error. If we look in the directory specified by the `init.ora` parameter, `USER_DUMP_DEST` and find our trace file, we'll find at the bottom of this file:

```
...
*** SESSION ID:(8.405) 2001-04-16 17:03:00.193
*** 2001-04-16 17:03:00.193
---------------------------------------------------------
Policy function execution error:
Logon user     : TKYTE
Table or View  : TKYTE.T
Policy name    : T_POLICY
Policy function: TKYTE.RLS_EXAMP
ORA-01403: no data found
ORA-06512: at "TKYTE.RLS_EXAMP", line 7
ORA-06512: at line 1
```

This information is critical in determining the error in our procedure. It points us right to line 7, the `SELECT ... INTO` statement, and tells us that it returned NO DATA FOUND.

ORA-28113: policy predicate has error.

An `ORA-28113: policy predicate has error` results if `SELECT` or DML is performed on a table with an associated policy function, and the policy function returns a predicate that is syntactically incorrect. This predicate, when merged with the original query, is not valid SQL.

An `ORA-28113` will generate a trace file in the directory specified by the `USER_DUMP_DEST` `init.ora` parameter. This file will have the `ORA-28113` error message, as well as information about the current session and the predicate that failed.

For example, let's say we had coded the following logic. It returns a predicate that compares X to a non-existent column in the table (at least it will try to):

```
tkyte@TKYTE816> create or replace function rls_examp
  2  ( p_schema in varchar2, p_object in varchar2 )
  3  return varchar2
  4  as
  5  begin
  6      return 'x = nonexistent_column';
  7  end;
  8  /

Function created.
```

so a query such as:

```
select * from t
```

will be rewritten as:

```
select * from ( select * from t where x = nonexistent_column )
```

Obviously, since our table T does not have this column, it will fail. The query cannot execute.

```
tkyte@TKYTE816> select * from t;
select * from t
               *
ERROR at line 1:
ORA-28113: policy predicate has error
```

This indicates that the predicate was successfully retrieved from the function, but when used in the query, it raised some other error. In reviewing the trace file retrieved from the database server machine, we find at the bottom:

```
...
*** SESSION ID:(8.409) 2001-04-16 17:08:10.669
*** 2001-04-16 17:08:10.669
...
--------------------------------------------------------------
Error information for ORA-28113:
Logon user      : TKYTE
Table or View   : TKYTE.T
Policy name     : T_POLICY
Policy function: TKYTE.RLS_EXAMP
RLS predicate   :
x = nonexistent_column
ORA-00904: invalid column name
```

This shows us the information we need, at a minimum, to fix the problem – the predicate that caused the error, as well as the SQL error message that accompanies the incorrect predicate.

ORA-28106: input value for argument #2 is not valid.

You will receive this error from a call to DBMS_SESSION.SET_CONTEXT if the attribute name is not a valid Oracle identifier. An application context's attribute names must be valid Oracle identifiers (in other words, you could use them for names of columns in tables, or as PL/SQL variable names). The only solution is to change the name of your attribute. For example, you cannot have a context attribute named SELECT, so you would have to pick an alternate name instead.

Summary

In this chapter we thoroughly explored FGAC. There are many pros to this feature, and very few cons. In fact, it is hard to think of any cons to this feature at all. We have seen how this feature:

❑ **Simplifies application development.** It separates access control from the application, and puts it with the data.

❑ **Ensures data in the database is always protected.** No matter what tool accesses the data, we are ensured our security policy is invoked and cannot be bypassed.

❑ **Allows for evolutionary changes** to security policies with no impact on client applications.

❑ **Simplifies the management of database objects**. It reduces the total number of database objects needed to support an application.

❑ **It performs well.** Actually, it performs as well as the SQL you add will allow it to. If the predicate you return makes it very hard for the optimizer to develop a fast plan, it is not the fault of FGAC – this is a SQL query tuning issue. The use of the application contexts allow us to reap the benefits of shared SQL, and reduce the number of database objects we must have. FGAC will not impact performance any more than performing this operation in any other fashion.

We have also seen that it may be difficult to debug, as FGAC happens in the background and the conventional tools such as a debugger or DBMS_OUTPUT will not work. Packages such as debug.f, referred to in the *Errors You Might Encounter* section, make debugging and tracing this feature much easier.

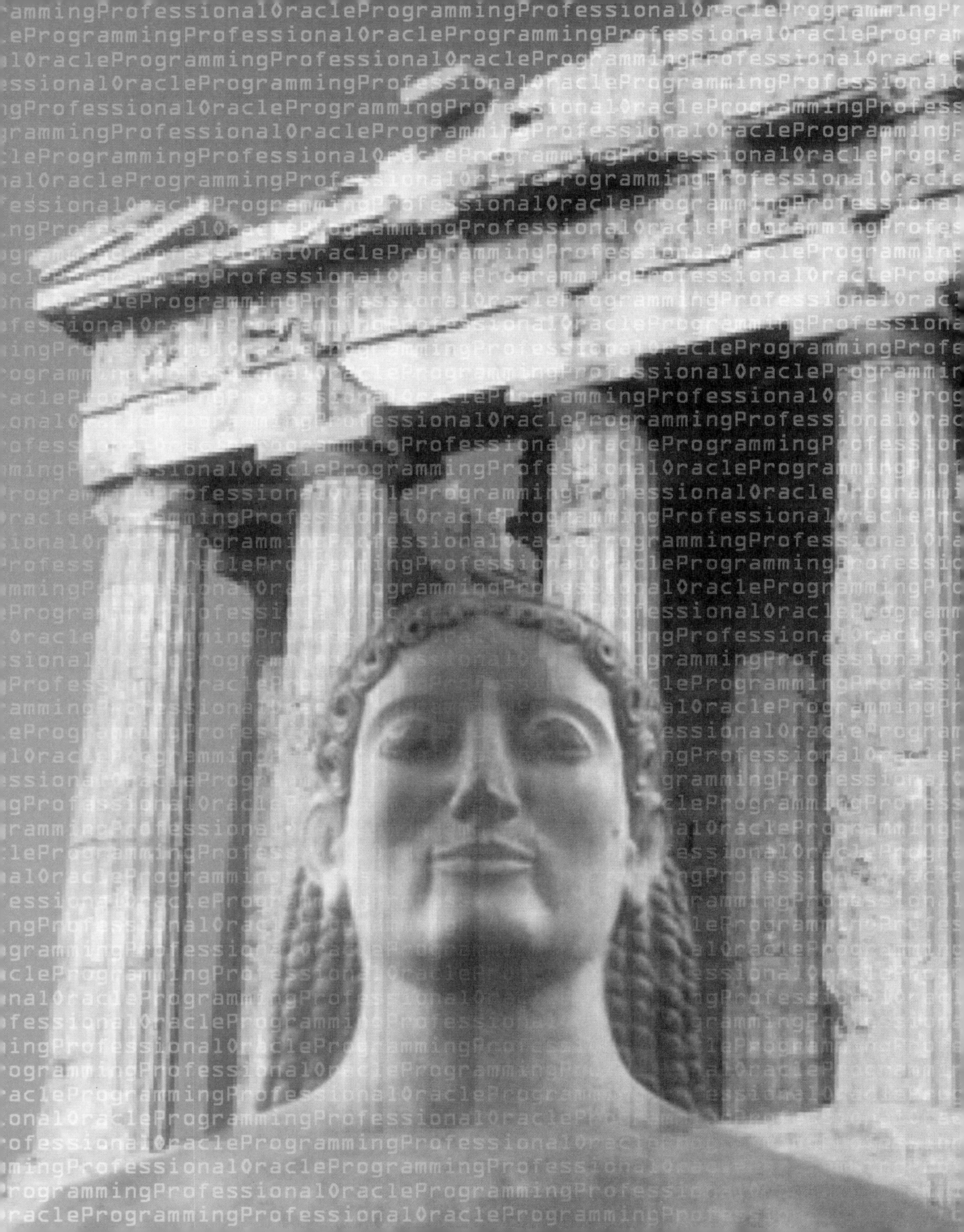

22

n-Tier Authentication

n-Tier, or proxy, authentication is the ability for middle tier software to log onto the database using its 'own' credentials on another user's behalf, in order to perform some operation in the database. This allows us to build middle tier applications that use their own authentication scheme, perhaps via X509 certificates, or by some other single sign-on process, to securely log into a database on your behalf without having to know your database password. As far as the database is concerned, you are logged in. However, the credentials that are used to log in are not yours; they are those of the middle tier.

In this chapter, we'll take a look at the features of n-Tier authentication and at how to implement this new Oracle 8i functionality in your applications. Specifically, we will:

- ❏ Introduce the feature and look at why you might want to use it in your applications.

- ❏ Develop an OCI program that will allow you to use this proxy authentication scheme to log in to the database.

- ❏ Investigate the ALTER USER command that enables this feature in the database.

- ❏ Discuss the auditing options that allow you to track the operations of the proxy account.

Currently, in Oracle 8i, n-tier authentication is limited to Oracle Call Interface (OCI) programs written in C or C++. Looking ahead to Oracle 9i, this feature will be available in JDBC as well, thus greatly expanding the audience that can make use of this feature.

Why Use n-Tier Authentication?

In the days of client-server and host-based systems, authentication was easy. The client (your application) prompted the end user for their credentials (username and password) and presented these credentials to the database server. The database verified those credentials, and you were connected:

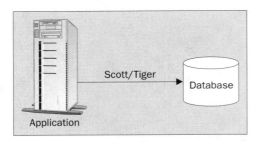

Now we have the Web and with it an n-Tier architecture where, for example, a client (your browser) presents credentials to a middle tier application server running a JavaServer Page (JSP), which in turn makes a callout to a CORBA object that finally accesses the database. The credentials presented to the middle tier may or may not be the same as the database username and password from the client server days – it might be credentials that permit access to a directory service, so the middle tier can discover who you are and what access privileges you have. It may be credentials presented in the form of an X.509 certificate that carries your identity and privileges. In any case, they are not necessarily credentials that the middle tier can use to log you into the database.

The fact is that the client is no longer talking to the database directly; there are one, two, or more layers in between. You could of course, make the end user pass their database username and password to the JSP, which would pass it to the CORBA object, which would pass it to the database but that thwarts the use of other technologies and authentication mechanisms, especially single sign-on mechanisms.

Consider the following example – a fairly typical web-based application today:

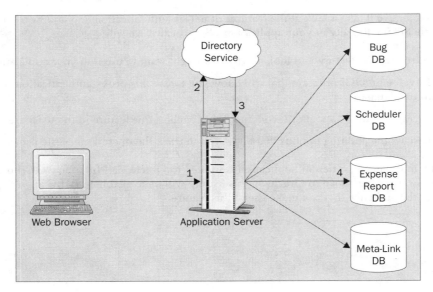

The client is really just a web browser, displaying HTML, which submits requests to a web/application server over HTTP (1). The application itself resides in the web/application server, perhaps as a Java servlet, Apache module, and so on. In the above diagram, the middle tier application server uses a directory service, perhaps running LDAP, to which it transmits the credentials you supplied (2). The directory service is used as a means to authenticate the browser session. If authentication is successful, the application server is notified (3) and, finally, the application server logs in to one of many existing databases (4) to retrieve data and process transactions.

The 'credentials' passed from browser to application server in (1) can take many forms – a username/password, a cookie from a single sign-on server, a digital certificate of some sorts – anything. The only thing that is generally true is that we did not pass our database username and password.

The problem is, of course, that the application server needs a database login and password to authenticate the user to a back end database. Furthermore the username/password combination will be different in each case. In the above example, we have four databases:

- ❑ A `Bug` database, which might recognize me as, say, `TKYTE`.
- ❑ An `Expense Report` database which might recognize me as `TKYTE_US`.
- ❑ A `Scheduler` database which might recognize me as `WEB$TKYTE`.
- ❑ ...And so on...

Stop and think for a moment – how many usernames and passwords do you have? I have at least 15 that I can remember off of the top of my head. Furthermore, although my identity in the database is never changing, my password changes frequently. Now, wouldn't it be nice if we could authenticate ourselves once – to the application server – and then the App server itself could access each of the backend databases on our behalf (in other words, by proxy), without needing to be given the specific password for each of these databases? This is what n-Tier authentication is all about.

The feature that enables this in the database is a simple connection option. In Oracle 8i the `ALTER USER` command has been modified to support the `GRANT CONNECT THROUGH` clause (this is discussed in full detail later, in the *Granting the Privilege* section). Consider access to the `Expense Report` database in the above application:

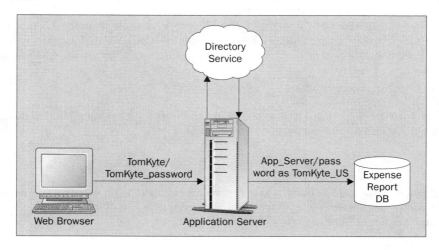

The directory service stores the mapping information that associates TomKyte with the database client TKYTE_US. Once that information has been successfully retrieved, the application server account (the proxy) can then log into the database, **using its own credentials**, on behalf of the client in the database, TKYTE_US. The application server does not need to know TKYTE_US's password.

To allow this to happen, the administrator of the Expense Report database would need to grant the schema APP_SERVER permission to connect as the client:

```
alter user tykte_us grant connect through app_server
```

The application server will execute in the database with the identity and privileges of TKYTE_US, and it will be as if TKYTE_US logged directly into the database.

In this manner, Oracle 8i extends the security model so that the application server can securely act on behalf of the client, without requiring the database password of the client, or requiring many privileges that allow it to access objects or procedures that it has no need to access. In addition, auditing has been extended to include operations performed by the application server on behalf of a client. That is, we can see that the application server, on behalf of a client, performed some operation (see the *Auditing Proxy Accounts* section for full details).

We'll now move on to discuss how to implement this feature. As indicated in the introduction, this feature is currently only accessible via the Oracle Call Interface (OCI) programs written in C or C++.

The Mechanics of n-Tier Authentication

In this section, we'll take one of the supplied OCI demonstration programs that implements a mini-SQL*PLUS, and modify it to use the proxy authentication scheme to log in to the database. This will give us a small, interactive SQL tool that will let us explore how this works, and what side effects we can expect to see. As a bonus, you'll have a tool that, provided you have been granted the appropriate privileges, will allow you to log in as another user and perform ad-hoc operations on their behalf, all the while being audited as yourself. You could use this, for example, to GRANT SELECT on another user's table without having to know their password.

The necessary C code that we will graft into the cdemo2.c example (found in [ORACLE_HOME]\rdbms\demo) will just be a login routine. Once we've done that, we'll be able to login using OS Authentication to the SCOTT account and enable the CONNECT role, as follows:

```
C:\> cdemo2 / scott CONNECT
```

Alternatively, we can login using a username and password to a database remote to the SCOTT account and enable the roles RESOURCE and PLUSTRACE:

```
C:\> cdemo2 user/pass@database scott RESOURCE,PLUSTRACE
```

The C routine that we need to build n-Tier demonstrates how to login using this n-Tier authentication – we'll take a look at it piecebypiece. Once we are logged in, the rest of the application is just standard OCI code, no different from any other OCI program.

The beginning of the C code includes the standard `oci.h` header file found in `ORACLE_HOME]\rdbms\demo`. This `include` file holds the necessary function prototypes and defines all OCI programs. Next, we declare a couple of variables local to our login routine. Specifically, we have the normal OCI handles for a connection – but notice that we have two `OCISession` handles. One is for the account we will present the credentials for (login with) and the other will be for the account we want to 'become'. The remaining local variables are pretty self-explanatory – they hold the username, password, database, and all of the roles we want enabled for us:

```c
#include <oci.h>

void checkerr( OCIError * errhp, sword status);


Lda_Def connect8i( int argc, char * argv[] )
{
OCIEnv      *environment_handle;
OCIServer   *data_server_handle;
OCIError    *error_handle;
OCISvcCtx   *application_server_service_handle;
OCISession  *first_client_session_handle;
OCISession  *application_server_session_handle;

char        *username;
char        *password;
char        *database;
char         temp[255];
char         role_buffer[1024];
char        *roles[255];
int          nroles;
```

Next, we validate the command line arguments passed to this routine. If the number of arguments is not equal to four, we have not been passed enough information and we'll just print out a usage and exit. Otherwise, we'll parse (using the standard C function `strtok`) the inputs. Since `strtok` is destructive (it changes the string it is parsing), we copy the arguments into local variables before breaking them up:

```c
if ( argc != 4 )
{
  printf( "usage: %s proxy_user/proxy_pass real_account_name role1,...\n",
          argv[0] );
  printf( "           proxy_user/proxy_pass can just be /\n" );
  printf( "           real_account_name is what you want to connect to\n" );
  exit(1);
}
strcpy( temp, argv[1] );
username = strtok( temp, "/" );
password = strtok( NULL, "@" );
database = strtok( NULL, "" );

strcpy( role_buffer, argv[3] );
for( nroles = 0, roles[nroles] = strtok(role_buffer,",");
     roles[nroles] != NULL;
     nroles++, roles[nroles] = strtok(NULL,",") );
```

Now we do some general initialization and allocation of contexts. This is standard for all OCI routines:

```
OCIInitialize( OCI_DEFAULT, NULL, NULL, NULL, NULL );

OCIEnvInit( &environment_handle, OCI_DEFAULT, 0, NULL );

OCIHandleAlloc( (dvoid *) environment_handle,
                (dvoid **) &error_handle,
                OCI_HTYPE_ERROR, 0, NULL );
```

Next, we allocate and initialize the server and service contexts used by the 'application server'. In this case, the application server is going to be our mini-SQL*PLUS tool cdemo2. This code attaches us to the server but does not yet begin a session:

```
checkerr(error_handle,
    OCIHandleAlloc(environment_handle,
                   (dvoid **)&data_server_handle,
                   OCI_HTYPE_SERVER,
                   0, NULL)
        );

checkerr(error_handle,
    OCIHandleAlloc((dvoid *) environment_handle,
                   (dvoid **) &application_server_service_handle,
                   OCI_HTYPE_SVCCTX, 0, NULL)
        );

checkerr(error_handle,
    OCIServerAttach(data_server_handle,
                    error_handle,
                    (text *)database?database:"",
                    strlen(database?database:""), 0)
        );

checkerr(error_handle,
    OCIAttrSet((dvoid *) application_server_service_handle,
               OCI_HTYPE_SVCCTX,
               (dvoid *) data_server_handle,
               (ub4) 0,
               OCI_ATTR_SERVER,
               error_handle)
        );
```

Now we are ready to initialize and then authenticate the application server session handle. In this case, either external authentication or username/password is being used:

```
checkerr(error_handle,
    OCIHandleAlloc((dvoid *) environment_handle,
                   (dvoid **)&application_server_session_handle,
                   (ub4) OCI_HTYPE_SESSION,
                   (size_t) 0,
                   (dvoid **) 0)
        );
```

Having initialized our session handle, we now need to add the authentication information. We permit either OS-based authentication (which would not require our application server to pass any username and password at all to the server) or standard username/password authentication. We'll put the code for username/password-based authentication first:

```
if (username != NULL && password != NULL && *username && *password)
    {
        checkerr(error_handle,
            OCIAttrSet((dvoid *) application_server_session_handle,
                    (ub4) OCI_HTYPE_SESSION,
                    (dvoid *) username, (ub4) strlen((char *)username),
                    (ub4) OCI_ATTR_USERNAME, error_handle)
            );

        checkerr( error_handle,
            OCIAttrSet((dvoid *) application_server_session_handle,
                    (ub4) OCI_HTYPE_SESSION,
                    (dvoid *) password,
                    (ub4) strlen((char *)password),
                    (ub4) OCI_ATTR_PASSWORD,
                    error_handle)
            );

        checkerr(error_handle,
            OCISessionBegin (application_server_service_handle,
                        error_handle,
                        application_server_session_handle,
                        OCI_CRED_RDBMS,
                        (ub4) OCI_DEFAULT)
            );
    }
```

Now, the code to handle OS authentication:

```
else
    {
        checkerr(error_handle,
            OCISessionBegin(application_server_service_handle,
                        error_handle,
                        application_server_session_handle,
                        OCI_CRED_EXT,
                        OCI_DEFAULT)
            );
    }
```

We are now ready to initialize the session for our client (the user who is logging in, and on whose behalf we have been trusted to execute processes). First we initialize the session:

```
checkerr(error_handle,
        OCIHandleAlloc((dvoid *) environment_handle,
                    (dvoid **)&first_client_session_handle,
                    (ub4) OCI_HTYPE_SESSION,
                    (size_t) 0,
                    (dvoid **) 0)
        );
```

Then we set the username to be associated with this session:

```
checkerr( error_handle,
    OCIAttrSet((dvoid *) first_client_session_handle,
            (ub4) OCI_HTYPE_SESSION,
            (dvoid *) argv[2],
            (ub4) strlen(argv[2]),
            OCI_ATTR_USERNAME,
            error_handle)
        );
```

Next, we add the list of roles we want enabled for this session – if we skip this call, all default roles for that user would be enabled:

```
checkerr( error_handle,
    OCIAttrSet((dvoid *) first_client_session_handle,
            (ub4) OCI_HTYPE_SESSION,
            (dvoid *) roles,
            (ub4) nroles,
            OCI_ATTR_INITIAL_CLIENT_ROLES,
            error_handle)
        );
```

Now we are ready to begin our actual session. First, we associate our client session (who we want to be seen as in the database) with our application server session (our proxy account):

```
checkerr(error_handle,
    OCIAttrSet((dvoid *) first_client_session_handle,
            (ub4) OCI_HTYPE_SESSION,
            (dvoid *) application_server_session_handle,
            (ub4) 0,
            OCI_ATTR_PROXY_CREDENTIALS,
            error_handle)
        );

checkerr(error_handle,
    OCIAttrSet((dvoid *)application_server_service_handle,
            (ub4) OCI_HTYPE_SVCCTX,
            (dvoid *)first_client_session_handle,
            (ub4)0,
            (ub4)OCI_ATTR_SESSION,
            error_handle)
        );
```

And then we begin the session:

```
checkerr(error_handle,
    OCISessionBegin(application_server_service_handle,
                error_handle,
                first_client_session_handle,
                OCI_CRED_PROXY,
                OCI_DEFAULT)
        );
```

Now, since this is a version 7 OCI program (cdemo2.c is a v.7 program), we need to convert our Oracle 8i login data into something usable. Here we convert a version 8 connection into a version 7 OCI LDA (Login Data Area) and return it:

```
checkerr(error_handle,
         OCISvcCtxToLda( application_server_service_handle,
                         error_handle,
                         &lda )
         );

    return lda;
}
```

The last bit of code is the checkerr routine that we referenced many times above. It is used to verify that the return codes from the OCI functions above indicate success, otherwise it prints out the error message and exits:

```
void checkerr(OCIError * errhp, sword status)
{
text          errbuf[512];
sb4           errcode = 0;

  switch (status)
  {
  case OCI_SUCCESS:
    break;
  case OCI_SUCCESS_WITH_INFO:
    (void) printf("Error - OCI_SUCCESS_WITH_INFO\n");
    break;
  case OCI_NEED_DATA:
    (void) printf("Error - OCI_NEED_DATA\n");
    break;
  case OCI_NO_DATA:
    (void) printf("Error - OCI_NODATA\n");
    break;
  case OCI_ERROR:
    (void) OCIErrorGet((dvoid *)errhp, (ub4) 1, (text *) NULL, &errcode,
                        errbuf, (ub4) sizeof(errbuf), OCI_HTYPE_ERROR);
    (void) printf("Error - %.*s\n", 512, errbuf);
    exit(1);
    break;
  case OCI_INVALID_HANDLE:
    (void) printf("Error - OCI_INVALID_HANDLE\n");
    break;
  case OCI_STILL_EXECUTING:
    (void) printf("Error - OCI_STILL_EXECUTE\n");
    break;
  case OCI_CONTINUE:
    (void) printf("Error - OCI_CONTINUE\n");
    break;
  default:
    break;
  }
}
```

Now, we need to modify `cdemo2.c` and inject our new code. The existing code in that sample program looks like this:

```
...
static sword numwidth = 8;

main()
{
    sword col, errno, n, ncols;
    text *cp;

    /* Connect to ORACLE. */
    if (connect_user())
        exit(-1);
...
```

The modification is very straightforward, we simply need to add the code in bold:

```
...
static sword numwidth = 8;

Lda_Def connect8i( int argc, char * argv[] );

main( int argc, char * argv[] )
{
    sword col, errno, n, ncols;
    text *cp;

    /* Connect to ORACLE. */
    /*
    if (connect_user())
        exit(-1);
    */
    lda = connect8i( argc, argv );
...
```

Next, add the entire contents of the code from above (the `connect8i` and `checkerr` subroutines) to the bottom of the source code file. Save that file and compile.

On UNIX, the command to compile this will be:

```
$ make -f $ORACLE_HOME/rdbms/demo/demo_rdbms.mk cdemo2
```

On Windows NT, I used this `makefile`:

```
CPU=i386

WORK_DIR        = .\

!include <\msdev\include\win32.mak>

OBJDIR    = $(WORK_DIR)\    #
EXEDIR    =   $(WORK_DIR)\    #  dir where all the .exe will be put
```

```
ORACLE_HOME = \oracle

TARGET    = $(EXEDIR)cdemo2.exe


SAMPLEOBJS   = cdemo2.obj

LOCAL_DEFINE = -DWIN_NT

SYSLIBS = \msdev\lib\msvcrt.lib \
          \msdev\lib\oldnames.lib \
          \msdev\lib\kernel32.lib  \
          \msdev\lib\advapi32.lib  \
          \msdev\lib\wsock32.lib

NTUSER32LIBS  = \msdev\lib\user32.lib \
                \msdev\lib\advapi32.lib \
                \msdev\lib\libc.lib

SQLLIB  = $(ORACLE_HOME)\oci\lib\msvc\oci.lib

INCLS   = -I\msdev\include \
          -I$(ORACLE_HOME)\oci\include
CFLAGS  = $(cdebug) $(cflags) $(INCLS) $(LOCAL_DEFINE)
LINKOPT = /nologo /subsystem:console /machine:I386 /nodefaultlib

$(TARGET): $(SAMPLEOBJS) $(SQLLIB)
    $(link) $(LINKOPT) \
    -out:$(TARGET) $(SAMPLEOBJS) \
        $(NTUSER32LIBS) \
        $(SYSLIBS) \
        $(SQLLIB)
```

And then just used nmake to compile it:

```
c:\oracle\rdbms\demo>nmake
```

Now we are ready to try it:

```
c:\oracle\rdbms\demo>cdemo2 tkyte/tkyte scott connect,resource
Error - ORA-28150: proxy not authorized to connect as client
```

So, we do not have success yet but we are very close. We need to give our proxy (TKYTE) the authority to connect as the database client (SCOTT). Log into SQL*PLUS and issue:

```
sys@TKYTE816> alter user scott grant connect through tkyte;
User altered.
```

We'll explain more about that new command in a moment, along with all of its options. Now we just want to see this work. Notice the **bolded** prompt – I am not in SQL*PLUS here, I am in the cdemo2 application, it just looks a lot like SQL*PLUS:

```
c:\oracle\rdbms\demo>cdemo2 tkyte/tkyte scott connect,resource

OCISQL> SELECT user, substr(sys_context('userenv','proxy_user'),1,30)
   2      FROM dual;

USER                            SUBSTR(SYS_CONTEXT('USERENV','PRO
------------------------------  ------------------------------
SCOTT                           TKYTE

1 row processed.

OCISQL> select * from session_roles;

ROLE
------------------------------
CONNECT
RESOURCE

2 rows processed.

OCISQL> select distinct authentication_type from v$session_connect_info
   2      where sid = ( select sid from v$mystat where rownum =1 );

AUTHENTICATION_TYPE
--------
PROXY

1 row processed.

OCISQL> exit

C:\oracle\RDBMS\demo>
```

That's it. We've successfully logged in as SCOTT without knowing SCOTT's password. Additionally, we've seen how we can verify that we are proxied in, by comparing USER to SYS_CONTEXT's PROXY_USER, or by looking in the V$SESSION_CONNECT_INFO view. Also, we can clearly see that the roles CONNECT and RESOURCE are enabled. If we connected like this:

```
c:\oracle\rdbms\demo>cdemo2 tkyte/tkyte scott connect

OCISQL> select * from session_roles;

ROLE
------------------------------
CONNECT

1 row processed.
```

We can see that only CONNECT is enabled – we control what roles the 'application server' enables.

Granting the Privilege

The basic syntax of the ALTER USER command is as follows:

```
Alter user <username> grant connect through <proxy user><,proxy user>...
```

This gives the usernames listed in the proxy user list the ability to connect as username. By default, these listed users will have all of that user's roles available to them. There is a variation of this command:

```
Alter user <username> grant connect through <proxy> WITH NONE;
```

This allows the proxy account to connect as username but only with their base privileges – no roles will be enabled. Additionally, we can use:

```
Alter user <username> grant connect through <proxy> ROLE rolename,rolename,...
```

or:

```
Alter user <username> grant connect through <proxy> ROLE ALL EXCEPT
rolename,rolename,...
```

The purpose of the above two statements would be to give a proxy account the ability to connect as a given user, but only with certain application roles enabled. You do not have to give the application server proxy account all of the privileges, just the necessary roles to accomplish the job. By default, Oracle tries to enable all default roles for the user and the PUBLIC role. This would be appropriate if the application server was only allowed to assume the HR role for a given user, and none of the other application roles that user was able to use.

There is, of course, also a method to revoke:

```
Alter user <username> REVOKE connect through <proxy user><,proxy user>...
```

There is an administrative view, PROXY_USERS, which you may use to review all granted proxy accounts. Right now, given that we issued the ALTER user SCOTT GRANT CONNECT through tkyte; command – our PROXY_USERS view has:

```
TKYTE@TKYTE816> select * from proxy_users;

PROXY     CLIENT   ROLE        FLAGS
--------  -------- ----------  -----------------------------------
TKYTE     SCOTT                PROXY MAY ACTIVATE ALL CLIENT ROLES
```

Auditing Proxy Accounts

The new syntax of the audit command with regards to proxy accounts is:

```
AUDIT <operation> BY <proxy>, <proxy> ... ON BEHALF OF <client>, <client>..;
```

or:

```
AUDIT <operation> BY <proxy>, <proxy> ON BEHALF OF ANY;
```

The new part is the BY <proxy> and ON BEHALF OF. It allows us to specifically audit operations performed by specific proxy users on behalf of any specific or all accounts.

For example, suppose you enabled auditing by setting AUDIT_TRAIL=TRUE in your init.ora and restarting the instance. We could then use:

```
sys@TKYTE816> audit connect by tkyte on behalf of scott;
Audit succeeded.
```

Now, if I use our modified cdemo2.c to connect:

```
C:\oracle\RDBMS\demo>cdemo2 tkyte/tkyte scott connect

OCISQL> exit
```

I'll find this record in DBA_AUDIT_TRAIL:

```
OS_USERNAME          : Thomas?Kyte
USERNAME             : SCOTT
USERHOST             :
TERMINAL             : TKYTE-DELL
TIMESTAMP            : 08-may-2001 19:19:29
OWNER                :
OBJ_NAME             :
ACTION               : 101
ACTION_NAME          : LOGOFF
NEW_OWNER            :
NEW_NAME             :
OBJ_PRIVILEGE        :
SYS_PRIVILEGE        :
ADMIN_OPTION         :
GRANTEE              :
AUDIT_OPTION         :
SES_ACTIONS          :
LOGOFF_TIME          : 08-may-2001 19:19:30
LOGOFF_LREAD         : 23
LOGOFF_PREAD         : 0
LOGOFF_LWRITE        : 6
LOGOFF_DLOCK         : 0
COMMENT_TEXT         : Authenticated by: PROXY: TKYTE
SESSIONID            : 8234
ENTRYID              : 1
STATEMENTID          : 1
RETURNCODE           : 0
PRIV_USED            : CREATE SESSION
```

It is interesting to note that if either SCOTT or TKYTE connects via SQL*PLUS, no audit trail record is created. Auditing is strictly limited to:

```
connect by tkyte on behalf of scott;
```

I can still audit connects by TKYTE or SCOTT if I want, I just chose not to in this case. This just shows that we can still have accountability in the database (we can tell it was SCOTT that performed some action), but we can also tell when it was an application server executing on behalf of SCOTT.

Caveats

In general, n-Tier authentication works exactly like you might expect it to. If you connect:

```
C:\oracle\RDBMS\demo>cdemo2 tkyte/tkyte scott connect
```

It will be as if SCOTT logged in directly. Features like *Invoker and Definer Rights* (Chapter 23) work as if SCOTT logged in. *Fine Grained Access Control* (Chapter 21) work as if SCOTT logged in. Login triggers for SCOTT will fire as expected. And so on. I have not found any feature to be negatively affected by the use of n-Tier authentication.

There is one implementation detail that might be an issue, however. When using n-Tier authentication, the server will enable a set of roles for you. If you use the OCI_ATTR_INITIAL_CLIENT_ROLES attribute that we used above, you might expect this set of roles to be limited only to those you specify. However, the roles that have been granted to PUBLIC are always enabled as well. For example, if we grant the PLUSTRACE role to PUBLIC (PLUSTRACE is the AUTOTRACE role we've been making use of throughout this book to do performance tracing in SQL*PLUS):

```
sys@TKYTE816> grant plustrace to public;
Grant succeeded.
```

Now, when we connect with our mini-SQL*PLUS:

```
c:\oracle\rdbms\demo>cdemo2 tkyte/tkyte scott connect

OCISQL> select * from session_roles;

ROLE
------------------------------
CONNECT
PLUSTRACE

2 rows processed.
```

You'll notice that in addition to the CONNECT role being enabled, the PLUSTRACE role is also enabled. This might not seem like a bad thing at first. However, if you've used the ALTER USER command to pass on only a few roles to some user:

```
sys@TKYTE816> alter user scott grant connect through tkyte with role CONNECT;
User altered.
```

You'll now discover that:

```
c:\oracle\rdbms\demo>cdemo2 tkyte/tkyte scott connect
Error - ORA-28156: Proxy user 'TKYTE' not authorized to set role 'PLUSTRACE' for
client 'SCOTT'
```

The user, TKYTE, is not allowed to enable this role when connecting on SCOTT's behalf. The only solutions to this issue are:

1. Do not grant roles to PUBLIC

2. Or, always add that role to the list of roles in the ALTER USER command.

For example, if we issue:

```
sys@TKYTE816> alter user scott grant connect through tkyte with role
  2  connect, plustrace;

User altered.
```

Then the following works as expected:

```
c:\oracle\rdbms\demo>cdemo2 tkyte/tkyte scott connect

OCISQL> select * from session_roles;

ROLE
-------------------------------
CONNECT
PLUSTRACE
```

Summary

In this chapter, we learned about the proxy authentication or n-Tier authentication capabilities available to us when programming in OCI. This feature allows a middle tier application server to act as a trusted agent into the database, on behalf of a client known to the application. We have seen how Oracle allows us to restrict the set of roles available to the application server proxy account, so that the proxy account can only perform application specific operations. Further, we have seen how auditing has been enhanced to support this new feature. We can audit actions specifically performed by proxy accounts on behalf of any given user or all users. We can clearly see when a given user, via the application proxy account, performed an action, and when it was done by the user directly.

We modified one of Oracle's simple demonstration programs to provide us with a simple SQL*PLUS-like environment to test this feature. The environment it provides is optimal for testing out various pieces of this functionality, and will help you see how it works interactively.

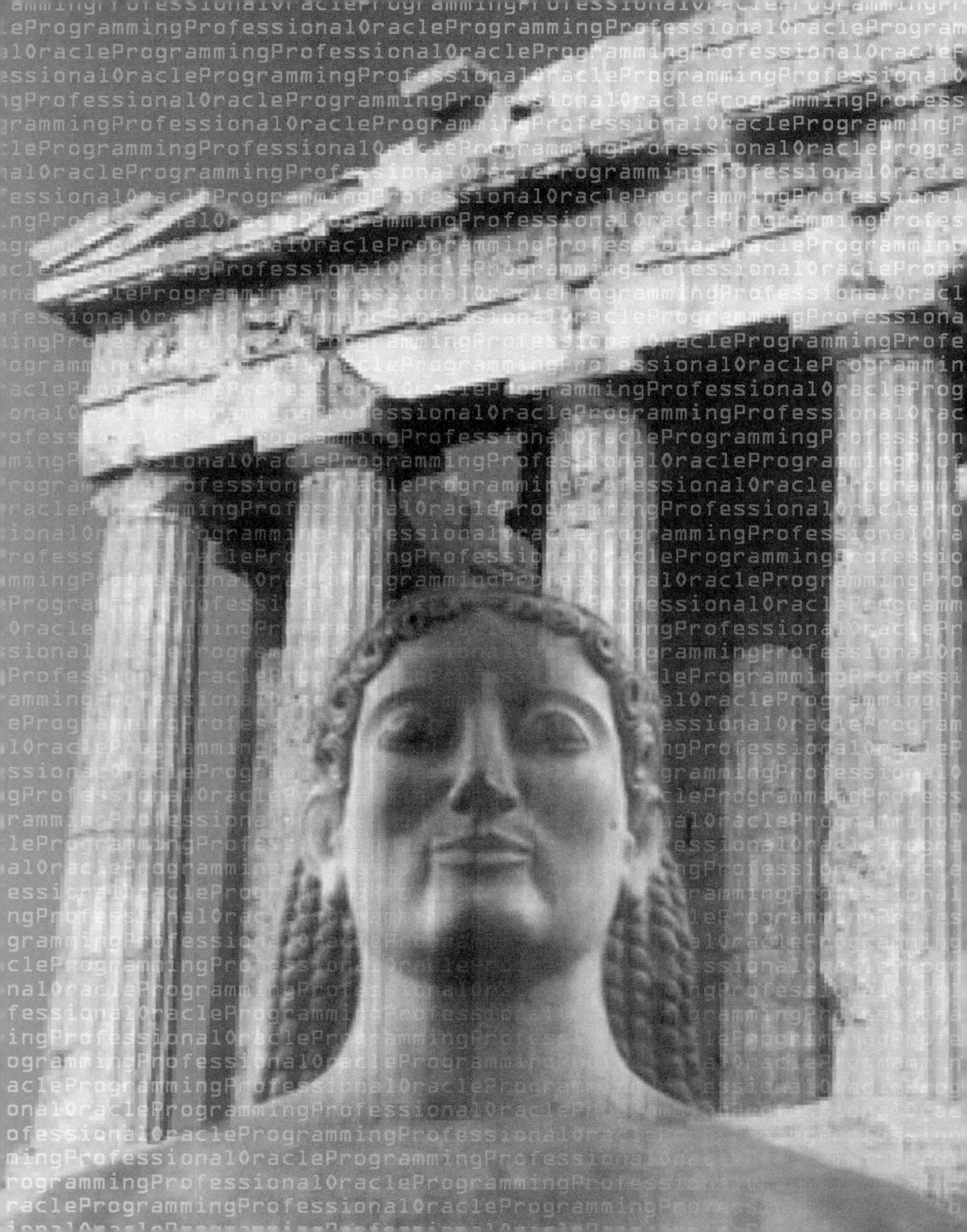

23

Invoker and Definer Rights

To begin with, some definitions are called for to ensure that we all understand exactly the same thing by the terms **invoker** and **definer**:

❑ **Definer** – The schema (username) of the owner of the compiled stored object. Compiled stored objects include packages, procedures, functions, triggers, and views.

❑ **Invoker** – The schema whose privileges are currently in effect in the session. This may or may not be the same as the currently logged in user.

Prior to Oracle 8i, all compiled stored objects were executed with the privileges and name resolution of the definer of the object. That is, the set of privileges granted directly to the owner (definer) of the stored object were used at compile-time to figure out:

❑ What objects (tables, and so on) to actually access.

❑ Whether the definer had the necessary privileges to access them.

This static, compile-time binding went as far as to limit the set of privileges to only those granted to the definer directly (in other words, no roles were ever enabled during the compilation or execution of a stored procedure). Additionally, when anyone executes a routine with definer's rights, this routine will execute with the base set of privileges of the definer of the routine, not the invoker that executes the procedure.

Beginning in Oracle 8i, we have a feature called **invoker rights**, which allow us to create procedures, packages, and functions that execute with the privilege set of the invoker at run-time, rather than the definer. In this chapter we will look at:

❑ When you should use invoker rights routines, covering uses such as data dictionary applications, generic object types, and implementing your own 'access control'.

❑ When to use definer rights procedures, covering their scalability compared to invoker rights, and also ways in which they can implement security on the database.

❑ How each of these features works.

❑ Issues which need to be considered when implementing the feature, such as considering the shared pool utilization, performance of procedures, the need for greater error handling abilities in the code, and also using Java to implement invoker rights.

An Example

With the introduction of invoker rights, we can now, for example, develop a stored procedure that executes with the privilege set of the invoker at run-time. This allows us to create a stored procedure that might execute properly and correctly for one user (one who had access to all of the relevant objects), but not for another (who didn't). The reason we can do this is that access to the underlying objects is not defined at compile-time, (although the definer must have access to these objects, or at least objects with these names, in order to compile the PL/SQL code), but rather at run-time. This run-time access is based on the privileges *and roles* of the current schema/user in effect. It should be noted that invoker rights are not available in the creation of views or triggers. Views and triggers are created with definer rights only.

This invoker rights feature is very easy to implement and test, as it only demands you add one line to a procedure or package to use it. For example, consider the following routine, which prints out:

❑ CURRENT_USER – The name of the user under whose privileges the session is currently executing.

❑ SESSION_USER – The name of the user who originally created this session, who is logged in. This is constant for a session.

❑ CURRENT_SCHEMA – The name of the default schema that will be used to resolve references to unqualified objects.

To create the procedure with definer rights, we would code:

```
tkyte@TKYTE816> create or replace procedure definer_proc
  2  as
  3  begin
  4      for x in
  5      ( select sys_context( 'userenv', 'current_user' ) current_user,
  6               sys_context( 'userenv', 'session_user' ) session_user,
  7               sys_context( 'userenv', 'current_schema' ) current_schema
  8          from dual )
  9      loop
 10          dbms_output.put_line( 'Current User:   ' || x.current_user );
 11          dbms_output.put_line( 'Session User:   ' || x.session_user );
 12          dbms_output.put_line( 'Current Schema: ' || x.current_schema );
 13      end loop;
 14  end;
 15  /

Procedure created.
tkyte@TKYTE816> grant execute on definer_proc to scott;

Grant succeeded.
```

To create the same procedure with invoker rights, you would code:

```
tkyte@TKYTE816> create or replace procedure invoker_proc
  2  AUTHID CURRENT_USER
  3  as
  4  begin
  5     for x in
  6     ( select sys_context( 'userenv', 'current_user' ) current_user,
  7              sys_context( 'userenv', 'session_user' ) session_user,
  8              sys_context( 'userenv', 'current_schema' ) current_schema
  9         from dual )
 10     loop
 11         dbms_output.put_line( 'Current User:   ' || x.current_user );
 12         dbms_output.put_line( 'Session User:   ' || x.session_user );
 13         dbms_output.put_line( 'Current Schema: ' || x.current_schema );
 14     end loop;
 15  end;
 16  /

Procedure created.

tkyte@TKYTE816> grant execute on invoker_proc to scott;

Grant succeeded.
```

That's it; one line and the procedure will now execute with the privileges and name resolution of the invoker, not the definer. To see exactly what this means, we'll run the above routines and examine the two outputs. First the definer rights routine:

```
tkyte@TKYTE816> connect scott/tiger

scott@TKYTE816> exec tkyte.definer_proc
Current User:   TKYTE
Session User:   SCOTT
Current Schema: TKYTE

PL/SQL procedure successfully completed.
```

For the definer rights procedure, the current user, and the schema whose privileges the session is currently executing under, is TKYTE inside of the procedure. The session user is the logged on user, SCOTT, which will be constant for this session. In this scenario, all unqualified schema references will be resolved using TKYTE as the schema (for example, the query SELECT * FROM T will be resolved as SELECT * FROM TKYTE.T).

The invoker rights routine behaves very differently:

```
scott@TKYTE816> exec tkyte.invoker_proc
Current User:   SCOTT
Session User:   SCOTT
Current Schema: SCOTT

PL/SQL procedure successfully completed.
```

The current user is SCOTT, not TKYTE. The current user in the invoker rights routine will be different for every user that directly runs this procedure. The session user is SCOTT, as expected. The current schema however, is also SCOTT, meaning that if this procedure executed the SELECT * FROM T, it would execute as SELECT * FROM SCOTT.T. This shows the fundamental differences between a definer and an invoker rights routine – the schema whose privileges the procedure executes under is the invoker of the routine. Also, the current schema is dependent on the invoker of the routine. Different objects may be accessed via this routine when executed by different users.

Additionally, it is interesting to see the effect that changing our current schema has on these routines:

```
scott@TKYTE816> alter session set current_schema = system;

Session altered.

scott@TKYTE816> exec tkyte.definer_proc
Current User:    TKYTE
Session User:    SCOTT
Current Schema:  TKYTE

PL/SQL procedure successfully completed.

scott@TKYTE816> exec tkyte.invoker_proc
Current User:    SCOTT
Session User:    SCOTT
Current Schema:  SYSTEM

PL/SQL procedure successfully completed.
```

As you can see, the definer rights routine does not change its behavior at all. Definer rights procedures are 'static' with regards to the current user, and the current schema. These are fixed at compile-time and are not affected by subsequent changes in the current environment. The invoker rights routine, on the other hand, is much more dynamic. The current user is set according to the invoker at run-time, and the current schema may change from execution to execution, even within the same session.

This is an extremely powerful construct when used correctly, and in the correct places. It allows PL/SQL stored procedures and packages to behave more like a compiled Pro*C application might. A Pro*C application (or ODBC, JDBC, or any 3GL) executes with the privilege set and name resolution of the currently logged in user (invoker). We can now write code in PL/SQL which, in the past, we had to write using a 3GL outside of the database.

When to Use Invoker Rights

In this section we will explore the various reasons and cases where you might choose to use this feature. We will concentrate on invoker rights since it is new and is still the exception. Stored procedures have previously always been executed in Oracle using definer rights.

The need for invoker rights arises most often when some generic piece of code is to be developed by one person but reused by many others. The developer will not have access to the objects that the end users will have. Rather, the end users' privileges will determine which objects this code may access. Another potential use of this feature is to produce a single set of routines that will centralize data retrieval from many different schemas. With definer rights procedures, we have seen how the current user (the privilege user) and the current schema (the schema used to resolve unqualified references) are static, fixed at the time of compilation. A definer rights procedure would access the same set of objects each time it was executed (unless you wrote dynamic SQL of course). An invoker rights routine allows you to write one routine that can access similar structures in different schemas, based on who executes the procedure.

So, lets take a look at some typical cases where you will use invoker rights routines.

Developing Generic Utilities

In this case, you might develop a stored procedure that uses dynamic SQL to take any query, execute it, and produce a comma-separated file. Without invoker rights, one of the following would have to be true in order to allow this procedure to be generally useful to everyone:

❏ **The definer of the procedure would have to have read access to virtually every object in the database** – For example, via the SELECT ANY TABLE privilege. Otherwise, when we run this procedure to produce a flat file from some table, the procedure would fail because the definer lacked the necessary SELECT privileges on this particular table. Here, we would like the procedure to execute with our privileges, not the definer's privileges.

❏ **Everyone would have the source code and be able to install their own copy of the code** – This is undesirable for obvious reasons – it produces a maintenance nightmare. If a bug is found in the original code, or an upgrade changes the way in which the code must be written, we now have many dozens of copies to go out and 'upgrade'. Additionally, objects we could access via a role will still not be available to us in this copied procedure.

In general, the second option above was the most frequently applied method of developing generic code. This is not a very satisfying approach, but is the 'safest' from a security perspective. Using invoker rights procedures however, I now can write that routine *once*, grant execute on it to many people, and they can use it with their own privileges and name resolution. We'll look at a small example here. I frequently need to view tables in SQL*PLUS that are very 'wide', in other words, they have many columns. If I just do a SELECT * FROM T on that table, SQL*PLUS will wrap all of the data on my terminal. For example:

```
tkyte@DEV816> select * from dba_tablespaces where rownum = 1;

TABLESPACE_NAME                     INITIAL_EXTENT NEXT_EXTENT MIN_EXTENTS
--------------------------------- --------------- ----------- -----------
MAX_EXTENTS PCT_INCREASE MIN_EXTLEN STATUS    CONTENTS  LOGGING
----------- ------------ ---------- --------- --------- ---------
EXTENT_MAN ALLOCATIO PLU
---------- --------- ---
SYSTEM                                      16384       16384           1
        505           50        0 ONLINE    PERMANENT LOGGING
DICTIONARY USER      NO
```

All of the data is there, but it is extremely hard to read. What if I could get the output like this instead:

```
tkyte@DEV816> exec print_table('select * from dba_tablespaces where rownum = 1');

TABLESPACE_NAME                : SYSTEM
```

```
INITIAL_EXTENT            : 16384
NEXT_EXTENT               : 16384
MIN_EXTENTS               : 1
MAX_EXTENTS               : 505
PCT_INCREASE              : 50
MIN_EXTLEN                : 0
STATUS                    : ONLINE
CONTENTS                  : PERMANENT
LOGGING                   : LOGGING
EXTENT_MANAGEMENT         : DICTIONARY
ALLOCATION_TYPE           : USER
PLUGGED_IN                : NO
-------------------

PL/SQL procedure successfully completed.
```

Now, that's more like it! I can actually see what column is what. Every time someone sees me using my
PRINT_TABLE procedure, they want a copy. Rather then give them the code, I tell them to just use mine
since it was created using AUTHID CURRENT_USER. I do not need access to their tables. This procedure
will be able to access them (not only that but it can access tables via a role, something a definer rights
procedure cannot do). Let us look at the code, and see how it behaves. We'll start by creating a utility
account to hold this generic code as well as an account that can be used to test the security features:

```
tkyte@TKYTE816> grant connect to another_user identified by another_user;

Grant succeeded.

tkyte@TKYTE816> create user utils_acct identified by utils_acct;

User created.

tkyte@TKYTE816> grant create session, create procedure to utils_acct;

Grant succeeded.
```

What I have done here is to create a user with very few privileges. Just enough to log on and create a
procedure. I will now install the utility code into this schema:

```
tkyte@TKYTE816> utils_acct/utils_acct

utils_acct@TKYTE816> create or replace
  2  procedure print_table( p_query in varchar2 )
  3  AUTHID CURRENT_USER
  4  is
  5      l_theCursor      integer default dbms_sql.open_cursor;
  6      l_columnValue    varchar2(4000);
  7      l_status         integer;
  8      l_descTbl        dbms_sql.desc_tab;
  9      l_colCnt         number;
 10  begin
 11      dbms_sql.parse( l_theCursor, p_query, dbms_sql.native );
 12      dbms_sql.describe_columns( l_theCursor, l_colCnt, l_descTbl);
 13
 14      for i in 1 .. l_colCnt loop
```

```
15              dbms_sql.define_column(l_theCursor, i, l_columnValue, 4000);
16          end loop;
17
18          l_status := dbms_sql.execute(l_theCursor);
19
20          while ( dbms_sql.fetch_rows(l_theCursor) > 0 ) loop
21              for i in 1 .. l_colCnt loop
22                  dbms_sql.column_value( l_theCursor, i, l_columnValue );
23                  dbms_output.put_line( rpad( l_descTbl(i).col_name, 30 )
24                                        || ': ' ||
25                                        l_columnValue );
26              end loop;
27              dbms_output.put_line( '-----------------' );
28          end loop;
29      exception
30          when others then
31              dbms_sql.close_cursor( l_theCursor );
32              RAISE;
33      end;
34  /

Procedure created.

utils_acct@TKYTE816> grant execute on print_table to public;

Grant succeeded.
```

I'll now go one step further. I'll actually make it so that we cannot log in to the UTILS_ACCT account at all. This will prevent a normal user from guessing the UTILS_ACCT password, and placing a Trojan horse in place of the PRINT_TABLE procedure. Of course, a DBA with the appropriate privileges will be able to reactivate this account and log in as this user anyway – there is no way to prevent this:

```
utils_acct@TKYTE816> connect tkyte/tkyte

tkyte@TKYTE816> revoke create session, create procedure
  2   from utils_acct;

Revoke succeeded.
```

So, what we have is an account with some code in it but that is effectively locked, since it no longer has CREATE SESSION privileges. When we log in as SCOTT, we'll find that not only can we still use this procedure (even though UTILS_ACCT is a non-functional account with no privileges), but also that it can access our tables. We will then verify that other users cannot use it to access our tables as well (unless they could do so with a straight query), thus showing the procedure executes with the privileges of the invoker:

```
scott@TKYTE816> exec utils_acct.print_table('select * from scott.dept')
DEPTNO                        : 10
DNAME                         : ACCOUNTING
LOC                           : NEW YORK
-----------------
...

PL/SQL procedure successfully completed.
```

This shows that SCOTT can use the procedure, and it can access SCOTT's objects. However, ANOTHER_USER might discover the following:

```
scott@TKYTE816> connect another_user/another_user

another_user@TKYTE816> desc scott.dept
ERROR:
ORA-04043: object scott.dept does not exist

another_user@TKYTE816> set serverout on
another_user@TKYTE816> exec utils_acct.print_table('select * from scott.dept' );
BEGIN utils_acct.print_table('select * from scott.dept' ); END;

*
ERROR at line 1:
ORA-00942: table or view does not exist
ORA-06512: at "UTILS_ACCT.PRINT_TABLE", line 31
ORA-06512: at line 1
```

Any user in the database who does not have access to SCOTT's tables cannot use this routine to get access to it. For completeness, we'll log back in as SCOTT, and grant ANOTHER_USER the appropriate privilege to complete the example:

```
another_user@TKYTE816> connect scott/tiger

scott@TKYTE816> grant select on dept to another_user;

Grant succeeded.

scott@TKYTE816> connect another_user/another_user

another_user@TKYTE816> exec utils_acct.print_table('select * from scott.dept' );
DEPTNO                   : 10
DNAME                    : ACCOUNTING
LOC                      : NEW YORK
-----------------
...

PL/SQL procedure successfully completed.
```

This effectively shows the use of invoker rights with regards to generic applications.

Data Dictionary Applications

People have always wanted to create procedures that would display the information in the data dictionary in a nicer format than a simple SELECT can achieve, or to create a DDL extraction tool perhaps. With definer rights procedures, this was very difficult. If you used the USER_* views (for example, USER_TABLES), the tables would be the set that the definer of the procedure owned, and never the invoker's tables. This is because the USER_* and ALL_* views all include in their predicate:

```
where o.owner# = userenv('SCHEMAID')
```

The USERENV('SCHEMAID') function returns the user ID of the schema under which the procedure executes. In a stored procedure that is defined with definer rights (the default), and this was, in effect, a constant value – it would always be the user ID of the person who owned the procedure. This means any procedure they write, which accesses the data dictionary would see *their* objects, never the objects of the person executing the query. Furthermore, *roles were never active* (we will revisit this fact below) inside of a stored procedure, so if you had access to a table in someone else's schema via a role, your stored procedure could not see that object. In the past, the only solution to this conundrum, was to create the stored procedure on the DBA_* views (after getting *direct* grants on all of them), and implementing your own security, to ensure people could only see what they would have seen via the ALL_* or USER_* views. This is less than desirable, as it leads to writing lots of code, getting a grant on each of the DBA_* tables, and, unless you are careful, you will risk exposing objects that should not be visible.

Invoker rights to the rescue here. Now, not only can we create a stored procedure that accesses the ALL_* and USER_* views, we can do it as the currently logged in user, using their privileges, and even their roles. We will demonstrate this with the implementation of a 'better' DESCRIBE command. This is will be the minimal implementation – once you see what it can do, you can make it do anything you want:

```
tkyte@TKYTE816> create or replace
  2  procedure desc_table( p_tname in varchar2 )
  3  AUTHID CURRENT_USER
  4  as
  5  begin
  6      dbms_output.put_line('Datatypes for Table ' || p_tname );
  7      dbms_output.new_line;
  8
  9      dbms_output.put_line( rpad('Column Name',31) ||
 10                            rpad('Datatype',20)    ||
 11                            rpad('Length',11) ||
 12                            'Nullable' );
 13      dbms_output.put_line( rpad('-',30,'-') || ' ' ||
 14                            rpad('-',19,'-') || ' ' ||
 15                            rpad('-',10,'-') || ' ' ||
 16                            '--------' );
 17      for x in
 18      ( select column_name,
 19               data_type,
 20               substr(
 21               decode( data_type,
 22                       'NUMBER', decode( data_precision, NULL, NULL,
 23                           '('||data_precision||','||data_scale||')' ),
 24                       data_length),1,11) data_length,
 25               decode( nullable,'Y','null','not null') nullable
 26          from user_tab_columns
 27         where table_name = upper(p_tname)
 28         order by column_id )
 29      loop
 30          dbms_output.put_line( rpad(x.column_name,31) ||
 31                                rpad(x.data_type,20)    ||
 32                                rpad(x.data_length,11) ||
 33                                x.nullable );
 34      end loop;
```

```
35
36        dbms_output.put_line( chr(10) || chr(10) ||
37                          'Indexes on ' || p_tname );
38
39      for z in
40      ( select a.index_name, a.uniqueness
41          from user_indexes a
42        where a.table_name = upper(p_tname)
43          and index_type = 'NORMAL' )
44      loop
45          dbms_output.put( rpad(z.index_name,31) ||
46                              z.uniqueness );
47          for y in
48          ( select decode(column_position,1,'(',', ')||
49                                  column_name column_name
50              from user_ind_columns b
51            where b.index_name = z.index_name
52            order by column_position )
53          loop
54              dbms_output.put( y.column_name );
55          end loop;
56          dbms_output.put_line( ')' || chr(10) );
57      end loop;
58
59  end;
60  /

Procedure created.

tkyte@TKYTE816> grant execute on desc_table to public
  2  /

Grant succeeded.
```

This procedure queries the USER_INDEXES and USER_IND_COLUMNS views heavily. Under definer rights (without the AUTHID CURRENT_USER) this procedure would be able to show the information for only *one* user (and always the same user). In the invoker rights model, however, this procedure will execute with the identity and privileges of the user who is logged in at run-time. So, even though TKYTE owns this procedure, we can execute it as the user SCOTT, and receive output similar to the following:

```
tkyte@TKYTE816> connect scott/tiger

scott@TKYTE816> set serveroutput on format wrapped
scott@TKYTE816> exec tkyte.desc_table( 'emp' )
Datatypes for Table emp

Column Name                     Datatype            Length     Nullable
------------------------------- ------------------- ---------- --------
EMPNO                           NUMBER              (4,0)      not null
ENAME                           VARCHAR2            10         null
JOB                             VARCHAR2            9          null
MGR                             NUMBER              (4,0)      null
HIREDATE                        DATE                7          null
SAL                             NUMBER              (7,2)      null
COMM                            NUMBER              (7,2)      null
```

```
DEPTNO                     NUMBER              (2,0)      null


Indexes on emp
EMP_PK                     UNIQUE(EMPNO)


PL/SQL procedure successfully completed.
```

Generic Object Types

The reasoning here is similar to above, but is more powerful in nature. Using the Oracle 8 feature that allows you to create your own object types with their own methods for manipulating data, you can now create member functions and procedures that act under the privilege domain of the currently logged in user. This allows you to create generic types, install them once in the database, and let everyone use them. If we did not have invoker rights, the owner of the object type would need to have very powerful privileges (as described above), or we would have to install the object type into each schema that wanted it.

Invoker rights is the mode in which the Oracle supplied types (for interMedia support, these are the ORDSYS.* types) have always operated, making it so that you can install them once per database, and everyone can use them with their privilege set intact. The relevance of this is that the ORDSYS object types read and write database tables. The set of database tables that they read and write are totally dependent on who is running them at the time. This is what allows them to be very generic and general purpose. The object types are installed in the ORDSYS schema, but ORDSYS does not have access to the tables on which it actually operates. Now, in Oracle 8i, you can do the same.

Implementing your own Access Control

Oracle 8i introduced a feature called **F**ine **G**rained **A**ccess **C**ontrol (FGAC) that allows you to implement a security policy to prevent unauthorized access to data. Typically, this might be accomplished by adding a column to every table, say a column named COMPANY. This column would be populated automatically by a trigger, and every query would be modified to include WHERE COMPANY = SYS_CONTEXT (...) to restrict access to just the rows the particular user was authorized to access (see Chapter 21, *Fine Grained Access Control*, for full details).

Another approach would be to create a schema (set of tables) per company. That is, each company would get its own copy of the database tables installed, and populated. There would be no chance of anyone accessing someone else's data, since this data is physically stored in a totally different table. This approach is very viable and has many advantages (as well as disadvantages) over FGAC. The problem is, however, that you would like to maintain one set of code for all users. You do not want to have ten copies of the same large PL/SQL package cached in the shared pool. You do not want to have to remember to update ten copies of the same code when a bug is found and fixed. You do not want people to be running potentially different versions of the code at any time. Invoker rights supports this model (many sets of tables, one copy of code).

With invoker rights, I can write one stored procedure that accesses tables based on the currently logged in users access privileges *and* name resolution. As demonstrated in the PRINT_TABLE example, we can do this in dynamic SQL, but it works with static SQL as well. Consider this example. We will install the EMP/DEPT tables into both the SCOTT schema as well as my TKYTE schema. A third party will write the application that uses the EMP and DEPT tables to print a report. This third party will not have access to either SCOTT or TKYTE's EMP or DEPT table, (they will have their own copy for testing). We will see that when SCOTT executes the procedure, it will display data from SCOTT's schema and when TKYTE executes the procedure, it utilizes his own tables:

```
tkyte@TKYTE816> connect scott/tiger

scott@TKYTE816> grant select on emp to public;

Grant succeeded.

scott@TKYTE816> grant select on dept to public;

Grant succeeded.

scott@TKYTE816> connect tkyte/tkyte

tkyte@TKYTE816> create table dept as select * from scott.dept;

Table created.

tkyte@TKYTE816> create table emp as select * from scott.emp;

Table created.

tkyte@TKYTE816> insert into emp select * from emp;

14 rows created.

tkyte@TKYTE816> create user application identified by pw
  2              default tablespace users quota unlimited on users;

User created.

tkyte@TKYTE816> grant create session, create table,
  2                  create procedure to application;

Grant succeeded.

tkyte@TKYTE816> connect application/pw

application@TKYTE816> create table emp as select * from scott.emp where 1=0;

Table created.

application@TKYTE816> create table dept as
  2                  select * from scott.dept where 1=0;

Table created.
```

So, at this point we have three users, each with their own EMP/DEPT tables in place. The data in all three tables is distinctly different. SCOTT has the 'normal' set of EMP data, TKYTE has two times the normal amount, and APPLICATION has just empty tables. Now, we will create the application:

```
application@TKYTE816> create or replace procedure emp_dept_rpt
  2    AUTHID CURRENT_USER
  3    as
  4    begin
  5      dbms_output.put_line( 'Salaries and Employee Count by Deptno' );
  6      dbms_output.put_line( chr(9)||'Deptno   Salary   Count' );
  7      dbms_output.put_line( chr(9)||'------   ------   ------' );
  8      for x in ( select dept.deptno, sum(sal) sal, count(*) cnt
  9               from emp, dept
 10               where dept.deptno = emp.deptno
 11               group by dept.deptno )
 12      loop
 13          dbms_output.put_line( chr(9) ||
 14                  to_char(x.deptno,'99999') || ' ' ||
 15                  to_char(x.sal,'99,999') || ' ' ||
 16                  to_char(x.cnt,'99,999') );
 17      end loop;
 18      dbms_output.put_line( '=====================================' );
 19    end;
 20    /

Procedure created.

application@TKYTE816> grant execute on emp_dept_rpt to public
  2    /

Grant succeeded.

application@TKYTE816> set serveroutput on format wrapped
application@TKYTE816> exec emp_dept_rpt;
Salaries and Employee Count by Deptno
      Deptno   Salary   Count
      ------   ------   ------
=====================================

PL/SQL procedure successfully completed.
```

This shows that when APPLICATION executes the procedure it shows the empty tables, as expected. Now, when SCOTT, and then TKYTE run the same exact application:

```
tkyte@TKYTE816> connect scott/tiger

scott@TKYTE816> set serveroutput on format wrapped
scott@TKYTE816> exec application.emp_dept_rpt
Salaries and Employee Count by Deptno
      Deptno   Salary   Count
      ------   ------   ------
          10    8,750       3
          20   10,875       5
          30    9,400       6
=====================================

PL/SQL procedure successfully completed.

scott@TKYTE816> connect tkyte/tkyte
```

```
tkyte@TKYTE816> set serveroutput on format wrapped
tkyte@TKYTE816> exec application.emp_dept_rpt
Salaries and Employee Count by Deptno
        Deptno   Salary   Count
        ------   ------   ------
            10   17,500        6
            20   21,750       10
            30   18,800       12
========================================

PL/SQL procedure successfully completed.
```

we see that it actually accesses different tables in different schemas. As we will see in the *Caveats* section, however, care must be taken to ensure that the schemas are synchronized. Not only must the same table names exist, but also the data type, order, and number of columns should be the same when using static SQL.

When to Use Definer Rights

Definer rights routines will continue to be the predominant method used with compiled stored objects. There are two major reasons for this, both of which address critical issues:

❑ **Performance** – A database using definer rights routines when possible, will be inherently more scalable and better performing than a database using invoker rights routines.

❑ **Security** – Definer rights routines have some very interesting and useful security aspects that make them the correct choice almost all of the time.

Performance and Scalability

A definer rights procedure is really a great thing in terms of security and performance. In the *How they Work* section, we will see that, due to the static binding at compile-time, much in the way of efficiency can be gained at run-time. All of the security validations, dependency mechanisms, and so on are done once at compile-time. With an invoker rights routine, much of this work must be done at run-time. Not only that, but it may have to be performed many times in a single session, after an ALTER SESSION or SET ROLE command. Anything that can change the run-time execution environment will cause an invoker rights routine to change its behavior as well. A definer rights routine is static with regards to this, invoker rights routines are not.

Additionally, as we'll see in the *Caveats* section later in this chapter, an invoker rights routine will incur higher shared pool utilization than will a definer rights routine. Since the execution environment of the definer rights routine is static, *all* static SQL executed by them is guaranteed to be sharable in the shared pool. As we have seen in other sections of this book, the shared pool is a data structure we must take care to not abuse (via the use of bind variables, avoiding excessive parsing, and so on). Using definer rights routines ensure maximum usage of the shared pool. An invoker rights routine on the other hand defeats the shared pool in some respects. Instead of the single query SELECT * FROM T meaning the same thing to all people when it is in a procedure, it may very well mean different things to different people. We'll have more SQL in our shared pool. Using definer rights procedures ensures the best overall shared pool utilization.

Security

In a nutshell, definer rights allow us to create a procedure that operates safely and correctly on some set of database objects. We can then allow other people to execute this procedure via the GRANT EXECUTE ON <procedure> TO <user>/public/<role> command. These people can run this procedure to access our tables in a read/write fashion (via the code in the procedure only), without being able to actually read or write our tables in any other way. In other words, we have just made a trusted process that can modify or read our objects in a safe way, and can give other people the permission to execute this trusted process without having to give them the ability to read or write our objects via any other method. They will not be using SQL*PLUS to insert into your Human Resources table. The ability to do this is provided *only* via your stored procedure, with all of your checks and audits in place. This has huge implications in the design of your application, and how you allow people to use your data. No longer would you GRANT INSERT on a table as you do with a client-server application that does straight SQL inserts. Instead, you would GRANT EXECUTE on a procedure that can validate and verify the data, implement other auditing and security checks, and not worry about the integrity of your data (your procedure knows what to do and it's the only game in town).

Compare this to how typical client-server applications, or even many 3-tier applications work. In a client-sever application, the INSERT, UPDATE and DELETE statements, and so on, are coded directly into the client application. The end user must have been granted INSERT, UPDATE and DELETE directly on the base tables in order to run this application. Now the whole world has access to your base tables via any interface that can log into Oracle. If you use a definer rights procedure, you have no such issue. Your trusted procedure is the *only* mechanism for modifying the tables. This is very powerful.

Frequently people ask, 'How can I make it so that only my application myapp.exe is able to perform operation X in the database?' That is, they want their .exe to be able to INSERT into some table, but they do not want any other application to be able to do the same thing. The *only secure way* to do this is to put the database logic of myapp.exe into the database – do not ever put an INSERT, UPDATE, DELETE, or SELECT into the client application. Only if you put the application directly in the database, removing the need for the client application to directly INSERT, or whatever into your table, can you make it so that *only* your application can access the data. By placing your application's database logic in the database, your application now becomes nothing more then a presentation layer. It does not matter if your application (the database component of it) is invoked via SQL*PLUS, by your GUI application, or by some yet to be implemented interface, it is your application that is running in the database.

How they Work

This is where things can get confusing; exactly what privileges are active and when. Before we get into how the invoker rights procedures work, we will take a look at definer rights procedures and how *they* work (and have always worked). After we understand definer rights, and why they work the way they do, we'll look at the different ways invoker rights procedures will behave under various calling circumstances.

Definer Rights

In the definer rights model, a stored procedure is compiled using the privileges granted directly to the person who 'owns' the procedure. By 'granted directly', I mean all object and system privileges granted to that account, or granted to PUBLIC, not inclusive of any roles the user or PUBLIC may have. In short, in a definer rights procedure, roles have no meaning or presence either at compile-time or during run-time execution. The procedures are compiled using only directly granted privileges. This fact is documented in *Oracle Application Developer's Guide* as follows:

Privileges Required to Create Procedures and Functions

To create a stand-alone procedure or function, or package specification or body, you must meet the following prerequisites:

You must have the CREATE PROCEDURE system privilege to create a procedure or package in your schema, or the CREATE ANY PROCEDURE system privilege to create a procedure or package in another user's schema.

Attention: To create without errors (to compile the procedure or package successfully) requires the following additional privileges:

❑ The owner of the procedure or package must have been explicitly granted the necessary object privileges for all objects referenced within the body of the code.

❑ The owner cannot have obtained required privileges through roles.

If the privileges of a procedure's or package's owner change, the procedure must be reauthenticated before it is executed. If a necessary privilege to a referenced object is revoked from the owner of the procedure (or package), the procedure cannot be executed.

Although it doesn't explicitly state this, a grant to PUBLIC is as good as a grant to the owner of the procedure as well. This requirement, the need for a direct grant in definer rights procedure, leads to the sometimes confusing situation demonstrated below. Here, we will see that we can query the object in SQL*PLUS, and we can use an anonymous block to access the object, but we cannot create a stored procedure on this object. We'll start by setting up the appropriate grants for this scenario:

```
scott@TKYTE816> revoke select on emp from public;

Revoke succeeded.

scott@TKYTE816> grant select on emp to connect;

Grant succeeded.

scott@TKYTE816> connect tkyte/tkyte

tkyte@TKYTE816> grant create procedure to another_user;

Grant succeeded.
```

and now we'll see that ANOTHER_USER can query the SCOTT.EMP table:

```
tkyte@TKYTE816> connect another_user/another_user

another_user@TKYTE816> select count(*) from scott.emp;

  COUNT(*)
----------
        14
```

Likewise, ANOTHER_USER can also execute an anonymous PL/SQL block:

```
another_user@TKYTE816> begin
  2    for x in ( select count(*) cnt from scott.emp )
  3    loop
  4          dbms_output.put_line( x.cnt );
  5    end loop;
  6  end;
  7  /
14

PL/SQL procedure successfully completed.
```

However, when we try to create a procedure identical to the PL/SQL above, we find this:

```
another_user@TKYTE816> create or replace procedure P
  2  as
  3  begin
  4    for x in ( select count(*) cnt from scott.emp )
  5    loop
  6          dbms_output.put_line( x.cnt );
  7    end loop;
  8  end;
  9  /

Warning: Procedure created with compilation errors.

another_user@TKYTE816> show err
Errors for PROCEDURE P:

LINE/COL ERROR
-------- -------------------------------------------------------
4/14     PL/SQL: SQL Statement ignored
4/39     PLS-00201: identifier 'SCOTT.EMP' must be declared
6/9      PL/SQL: Statement ignored
6/31     PLS-00364: loop index variable 'X' use is invalid
```

I cannot create a procedure (or in fact any compiled stored object, such as a view or trigger) that accesses SCOTT.EMP. This is expected, and documented behavior. In the above example, ANOTHER_USER is a user with the CONNECT role. The CONNECT role was granted SELECT on SCOTT.EMP. This privilege from the role CONNECT, is not available in the definer rights stored procedure however, hence the error message. What I tell people to do to avoid this confusion, is to SET ROLE NONE in SQL*PLUS, and try out the statement they want to encapsulate in a stored procedure. For example:

```
another_user@TKYTE816> set role none;

Role set.

another_user@TKYTE816> select count(*) from scott.emp;
select count(*) from scott.emp
                      *
ERROR at line 1:
ORA-00942: table or view does not exist
```

If it won't work in SQL*PLUS without roles, it will definitely not work in a definer rights stored procedure either.

Compiling a Definer Rights Procedure

When we compile the procedure into the database, a couple of things happen with regards to privileges. We will list them here briefly, and then go into more detail:

❑ All of the objects, which the procedure statically accesses (anything not accessed via dynamic SQL), are verified for existence. Names are resolved via the standard scoping rules as they apply to the definer of the procedure.

❑ All of the objects it accesses are verified to ensure that the required access mode will be available. That is, if an attempt to UPDATE T is made, Oracle will verify that the definer, or PUBLIC, has the ability to UPDATE T without use of any roles.

❑ A dependency between this procedure and the referenced objects is set up and maintained. If this procedure issues SELECT FROM T, then a dependency between T and this procedure is recorded

If, for example, I have a procedure P that attempted to SELECT * FROM T, the compiler will first resolve T into a fully qualified reference. T is an ambiguous name in the database – there may be to choose from. Oracle will follow its scoping rules to figure out what T really is. Any synonyms will be resolved to their base objects, and the schema name will be associated with the object. It does this name resolution using the rules for the currently logged in user (the definer). That is, it will look for an object called T that is owned by this user, and use that first (this includes private synonyms), then it will look at public synonyms, and try to find T, and so on.

Once it determines exactly what T refers to, Oracle will determine if the mode in which we are attempting to access T is permitted. In this case, if the definer owns the object T, or has been granted SELECT on T directly (or if PUBLIC was granted SELECT privileges), then the procedure will compile. If the definer does not have access to an object called T by a direct grant, then the procedure P will not compile. So, when the object (the stored procedure that references T) is compiled into the database, Oracle will do these checks. If they 'pass', Oracle will compile the procedure, store the binary code for the procedure, and set up a dependency between this procedure, and this object T. This dependency is used to invalidate the procedure later, in the event something happens to T that necessitates the stored procedure's recompilation. For example if at a later date, we REVOKE SELECT ON T from the owner of this stored procedure, Oracle will mark all stored procedures this user has, which are dependent on T, and that refer to T, as INVALID. If we ALTER T ADD . . . some column, Oracle can invalidate all of the dependent procedures. This will cause them to be recompiled automatically upon their next execution.

What is interesting to note is not only what is stored, but what is *not* stored when we compile the object. Oracle does not store the exact privilege used to get access to T. We only know that the procedure P is dependent on T. We do not know if the reason we were allowed to see T was due to:

❑ A grant given to the definer of the procedure (GRANT SELECT ON T TO USER)

❑ A grant to PUBLIC on T (GRANT SELECT ON T TO PUBLIC)

❑ The user having the SELECT ANY TABLE privilege

The reason it is interesting to note what is not stored, is that a REVOKE of any of the above will cause the procedure P to become invalid. If all three privileges were in place when the procedure was compiled, a REVOKE of *any* of them will invalidate the procedure, forcing it to be recompiled before it is executed again.

Now that the procedure is compiled into the database, and the dependencies are all set up, we can execute the procedure, and be assured that it knows what T is, and that T is accessible. If something happens to either the table T, or to the set of base privileges available to the definer of this procedure that might affect our ability to access T, our procedure will become invalid, and will need to be recompiled.

Definer Rights and Roles

This leads us on to why roles are not enabled during the compilation and execution of a stored procedure in definer rights mode. Oracle is not storing exactly *why* you are allowed to access T, *only that you are*. Any change to your privileges that might cause access to T to be removed, will cause the procedure to become invalid, and necessitate its recompilation. Without roles, this means only REVOKE SELECT ANY TABLE or REVOKE SELECT ON T from the definer account or from PUBLIC.

With roles enabled, it greatly expands the number of occasions where we could invalidate this procedure. To illustrate what I mean by this, let's imagine for a moment that roles did give us privileges on stored objects. Now, almost every time *any role* we had was modified, any time a privilege was revoked from a role, or from a role that had been assigned to a role (and so on, roles can and are granted to roles), we run the risk of invalidating many procedures (even procedures where we were not relying on a privilege from the modified role).

Consider the impact of revoking a system privilege from a role. It would be comparable to revoking a powerful system privilege from PUBLIC (don't do it, just think about it – or do it on a test database first). If PUBLIC had been granted SELECT ANY TABLE, revoking that privilege would cause virtually every procedure in the database to be made invalid. If procedures relied on roles, virtually every procedure in the database would constantly become invalid due to small changes in permissions. Since one of the major benefits of procedures is the 'compile once, run many' model, this would be disastrous for performance.

Also consider that roles may be:

❑ **Non-default** – If I have a non-default role, enable it, and compile a procedure that relies on those privileges, when I log out I no longer have that role. Should my procedure become *invalid*? Why? Why not? I could easily argue both sides.

❑ **Password protected** – If someone changes the password on a ROLE, should everything that might need this role need to be recompiled? I might be granted this role but, not knowing the new password, I can no longer enable it. Should the privileges still be available? Why, or why not? Again, there are cases for and against.

The bottom line with regard to roles in procedures with definer rights is:

❑ You have thousands, or tens of thousands of end users. They don't create stored objects (they should not). We need roles to manage these people. Roles are designed for these people (end users).

❑ You have far fewer application schemas (things that hold stored objects). For these we want to be explicit as to exactly what privileges we need, and why. In security terms, this is called the concept of 'least privileges'. You want to specifically say what privilege you need, and why you need it. If you inherit lots of privileges from roles, you cannot do this effectively. You can manage to be explicit, since the number of development schemas is *small* (but the number of end users is *large*).

❑ Having the direct relationship between the definer and the procedure makes for a much more efficient database. We recompile objects *only when we need to*, not when *we might need to*. It is a large enhancement in efficiency.

Invoker Rights

There is a big difference between invoker rights procedures and definer rights procedures (and anonymous blocks of PL/SQL) with regard to how they use privileges, and resolve references to objects. In terms of executing SQL statements, invoker rights procedures are similar to an anonymous block of PL/SQL, but they execute very much like a definer rights procedure with respect to other PL/SQL statements. Additionally, roles *may* be enabled in an invoker rights procedure, depending on how it was accessed – unlike definer rights, which disallows the use of roles to provide access to objects in stored procedures.

We will explore two pieces of these invoker rights procedures:

❑   'SQL' pieces – anything we SELECT, INSERT, UPDATE, DELETE, *and* anything we dynamically execute using DBMS_SQL or EXECUTE IMMEDIATE (including PL/SQL code dynamically executed).

❑   'PL/SQL' pieces – static references to object types in variable declarations, calls to other stored procedures, packages, functions, and so on.

These two 'pieces' are treated very differently in invoker rights procedures. The 'SQL pieces' are in fact resolved at compile-time (to determine their structure and such), but are resolved once again at run-time. This is what allows a stored procedure with a SELECT * FROM EMP access to totally different EMP tables at run-time, when executed by different users. The 'PL/SQL' pieces however, are statically bound at compile-time, much as they are in a definer rights procedure. So, if your invoker rights procedure has code such as:

```
...
AUTHID CURRENT_USER
as
begin
   for x in ( select * from T ) loop
          proc( x.c1 );
   end loop;
...
```

then the reference to T will be resolved at run-time (as well as compile-time, to understand what SELECT * means) dynamically, allowing for a different T to be used by each person. The reference to PROC however, will be resolved only at compile-time, and our procedure will be statically bound to a single PROC. The invoker of this routine does not need EXECUTE ON PROC, but they do need SELECT on an object called T. Not to confuse the issue, but if we desire the call to PROC to be resolved at run-time, we have the mechanism for doing so. We can code:

```
...
AUTHID CURRENT_USER
as
begin
   for x in ( select * from T ) loop
          execute immediate 'begin proc( :x ); end;' USING x.c1;
   end loop;
...
```

In the above case, the reference to PROC will be resolved using the invoker set of privileges, and they must have EXECUTE granted to them (or to some role, if roles are active).

Resolving References and Conveying Privileges

Let's look at how privileges are conveyed within an invoker rights procedure. When we do this, we'll have to consider the various environments, or call stacks, that might invoke our procedure:

❏   A direct invocation by an end user.

❏   An invocation by a definer rights procedure.

❏   An invocation by another invoker rights procedure.

❏   An invocation by a SQL statement.

❏   An invocation by a view that references an invoker rights procedure.

❏   An invocation by a trigger.

With the exact same procedure, the result in each of the above environments could, potentially, be different. In each case, an invoker rights procedure may very well access totally different database tables and objects at run-time.

So, we'll begin by looking at how objects are bound, and what privileges are available in an invoker rights procedure at run-time when executing in each of the above environments. The case of the view and trigger will be considered the same, since both execute with definer rights only. Also, since PL/SQL static objects *are always resolved at compile-time in all environments*, we will not consider them. They are always resolved with respect to the definer's schema and access rights. The currently logged in user does not need access to referenced PL/SQL object. The following table describes the behavior you should expect for each environment:

Environment	SQL objects and dynamically invoked PL/SQL	Are roles enabled?
A direct invocation by an end user. For example: SQL> exec p;	References to these objects are resolved using the current user's default schema and privileges. Unqualified references to objects will be resolved in their schema. All objects must be accessible to the currently logged in user. If the procedure SELECTs from T, the currently logged in user must have SELECT on T as well (either directly or via some role).	Yes. All of the roles enabled prior to the execution of the procedure are available inside of the procedure. They will be used to allow or deny access to all SQL objects and dynamically invoked PL/SQL.

Environment	SQL objects and dynamically invoked PL/SQL	Are roles enabled?

An invocation by a definer rights procedure (P1), where P2 is an invoker rights procedure. For example:
 	
`procedure p1`
 	
`is`
 	
`begin`
 	
`  p2;`
 	
`end;`
	These are resolved using the definer schema, the schema of the calling procedure. Unqualified objects will be resolved in this other schema, not the schema of the currently logged in user, and not the schema that created the invoker rights procedure, but the schema of the calling procedure. In our example, the owner of P1 would always be the 'invoker' inside of P2.	No. There are no roles enabled since the definer rights procedure was invoked. At the point of entry into the definer rights procedure, all roles were disabled and will remain so until the definer rights procedure returns.

An invocation by another invoker rights procedure.	Same as direct invocation by an end user.	Yes. Same as direct invocation by an end user.
An invocation by a SQL statement.	Same as direct invocation by an end user.	Yes. Same as direct invocation by an end user.
An invocation by a VIEW or TRIGGER that references an invoker rights procedure.	Same as an invocation by definer rights procedure.	No. Same as an invocation by definer rights procedure.

So, as you can see, the execution environment can have a dramatic effect on the run-time behavior of an invoker rights routine. The exact same PL/SQL stored procedure, when run directly, may access a wholly different set of objects than it will when executed by another stored procedure, even when logged in as the same exact user.

To demonstrate this, we will create a procedure that shows what roles are active at run-time and access a table that has data in it, which tells us who 'owns' that table. We will do this for each of the above cases, except for the invoker rights routine called from an invoker rights routine, since this is exactly the same as just calling the invoker rights routine directly. We'll start by setting up the two accounts we'll use for this demonstration:

```
tkyte@TKYTE816> drop user a cascade;

User dropped.

tkyte@TKYTE816> drop user b cascade;

User dropped.

tkyte@TKYTE816> create user a identified by a default tablespace data temporary
```

```
tablespace temp;

User created.

tkyte@TKYTE816> grant connect, resource to a;

Grant succeeded.

tkyte@TKYTE816> create user b identified by b default tablespace data temporary
tablespace temp;

User created.

tkyte@TKYTE816> grant connect, resource to b;

Grant succeeded.
```

This sets up are two users, A and B, each with two roles, CONNECT and RESOURCE. Next, we will have the user A create an invoker rights routine, and then a definer rights routine and a view, each of which calls the invoker rights routine. Each execution of the procedure will tell us how many roles are in place, who the current user is (the schema whose privilege set we are executing under), what the current schema is, and finally what table is being used by the query. We start by creating a table identifiable to user A:

```
tkyte@TKYTE816> connect a/a

a@TKYTE816> create table t ( x varchar2(255) );

Table created.

a@TKYTE816> insert into t values ( 'A's table' );

1 row created.
```

Next, user A creates the invoker rights function, definer rights procedure, and the view:

```
a@TKYTE816> create function Invoker_rights_function return varchar2
  2   AUTHID CURRENT_USER
  3   as
  4          l_data varchar2(4000);
  5   begin
  6      dbms_output.put_line( 'I am an IR PROC owned by A' );
  7      select 'current_user=' ||
  8              sys_context( 'userenv', 'current_user' ) ||
  9              ' current_schema=' ||
 10              sys_context( 'userenv', 'current_schema' ) ||
 11              ' active roles=' || cnt ||
 12              ' data from T=' || t.x
 13          into l_data
 14            from (select count(*) cnt from session_roles), t;
 15
 16      return l_data;
 17   end;
```

```
 18  /

Function created.

a@TKYTE816> grant execute on Invoker_rights_function to public;

Grant succeeded.

a@TKYTE816> create procedure Definer_rights_procedure
  2  as
  3          l_data varchar2(4000);
  4  begin
  5     dbms_output.put_line( 'I am a DR PROC owned by A' );
  6     select 'current_user=' ||
  7            sys_context( 'userenv', 'current_user' ) ||
  8           ' current_schema=' ||
  9            sys_context( 'userenv', 'current_schema' ) ||
 10           ' active roles=' || cnt ||
 11           ' data from T=' || t.x
 12         into l_data
 13         from (select count(*) cnt from session_roles), t;
 14
 15     dbms_output.put_line( l_data );
 16     dbms_output.put_line
 17             ( 'Going to call the INVOKER rights procedure now...' );
 17     dbms_output.put_line( Invoker_rights_function );
 18  end;
 19  /

Procedure created.

a@TKYTE816> grant execute on Definer_rights_procedure to public;

Grant succeeded.

a@TKYTE816> create view V
  2  as
  3  select invoker_rights_function from dual
  4  /

View created.

a@TKYTE816> grant select on v to public
  2  /

Grant succeeded.
```

Now we will log in as user B, create a table T with an identifying row, and execute the above procedures:

```
a@TKYTE816> connect b/b

b@TKYTE816> create table t ( x varchar2(255) );

Table created.
```

```
b@TKYTE816> insert into t values ( 'B''s table' );

1 row created.

b@TKYTE816> exec dbms_output.put_line( a.Invoker_rights_function )
I am an IR PROC owned by A
current_user=B current_schema=B active roles=3 data from T=B's table

PL/SQL procedure successfully completed.
```

This shows that when user B directly invokes the invoker rights routine owned by A, the privileges are taken from user B at run-time (current_user=B). Further, since the current_schema is user B, the query selected from B.T, not A.T. This is evidenced by the data from T=B's table in the above output. Lastly, we see that there are three roles active in the session at the point in time we executed the query (I have PLUSTRACE, used by AUTOTRACE, granted to PUBLIC in my database – this is the third role). Now, let's compare that to what happens when we invoke through the definer rights procedure:

```
b@TKYTE816> exec a.Definer_rights_procedure
I am a DR PROC owned by A
current_user=A current_schema=A active roles=0 data from T=A's table
Going to call the INVOKER rights procedure now...
I am an IR PROC owned by A
current_user=A current_schema=A active roles=0 data from T=A's table

PL/SQL procedure successfully completed.
```

This shows that the definer rights routine executed with user A's privileges, minus roles (active roles=0). Further, the definer rights routine is statically bound to the table A.T, and will not see the table B.T.

The most important thing to note is the effect seen when we call the invoker rights routine from the definer rights routine. Notice that the *invoker* this time is A, not B. The invoker is the schema that is currently in place at the time of the call to the invoker rights routine. It will *not* execute as user B as it did before, but this time it will execute as user A. Thus, the current_user and current_schema are set to user A and so the table the invoker rights routine accesses will be A's table. Another important fact is that the roles are not active in the invoker rights routine this time around. When we entered the definer rights routine, the roles were disabled, and they remain disabled until we exit the definer rights routine again.

Now, let's see what the effects of calling the invoker rights function from SQL:

```
b@TKYTE816> select a.invoker_rights_function from dual;

INVOKER_RIGHTS_FUNCTION
-----------------------------------------------------------------
current_user=B current_schema=B active roles=3 data from T=B's table

b@TKYTE816> select * from a.v;

INVOKER_RIGHTS_FUNCTION
-----------------------------------------------------------------
current_user=A current_schema=A active roles=0 data from T=B's table
```

We can see that calling the invoker rights routine from SQL directly, as we did by selecting it from DUAL, is the same as calling the routine directly. Further, calling the routine from a view, as we did with the second query, shows that it will behave as if it were called from a definer rights routine, since views are always stored using definer rights.

Compiling an Invoker Rights Procedure

We will now explore what happens when we compile an invoker rights procedure into the database. This might be surprising, but the answer to this is the *same exact thing as what happens when we compile a Definer rights procedure.* The steps are:

❑ All of the objects it statically accesses (anything not accessed via dynamic SQL) are verified for existence. Names are resolved via the standard scoping rules as they apply to the definer of the procedure. Roles are *not* enabled.

❑ All of the objects it accesses are verified to ensure that the required access mode will be available. That is, if an attempt to UPDATE T is made, Oracle will verify the definer, or PUBLIC has the ability to UPDATE T without use of any roles.

❑ A dependency between this procedure and the referenced objects is set up and maintained. If this procedure SELECTS FROM T, then a dependency between T and this procedure is recorded

What this means is that an invoker rights routine, at *compile-time*, is treated exactly the same as a definer rights routine. This is an area of confusion for many. They have heard that roles are enabled in invoker rights routines, and this is, in fact, accurate. *However* (and this is a big however), they are not in effect during the compilation process. This means that the person who compiles the stored procedure, the owner of the stored procedure, still needs to have direct access to all statically referenced tables. Recall the example we used in the *Definer Rights* section, where we showed that SELECT COUNT (*) FROM EMP succeeded in SQL and in PL/SQL with an anonymous block, but failed in the stored procedure compilation. The exact same thing would still happen with an invoker rights routine. The rules spelled out in the *Oracle 8i Application Developer's Guide* on *Privileges Required to Create Procedures and Functions* remain in place. You still need direct access to the underlying objects.

The reason for this is due to the dependency mechanism employed by Oracle. If an operation performed in the database would cause a definer rights procedure to become invalid (for example, the REVOKE statement), the corresponding invoker rights procedure would also become invalid. The only true difference between invoker rights procedures and definer rights is their run-time execution behavior. In terms of dependencies, invalidation, and the privileges required by the owner of the procedure, they are exactly the same.

There are ways to work around this issue, and for many uses of invoker rights procedures it won't be an issue at all. However, it does indicate the need for **template objects**, in some cases. In the next section we'll see what template objects are, and how we can use them to get around the need for a direct grant.

Using Template Objects

Now that we know that at compile-time, an invoker rights procedure is really no different to a definer rights procedure we can understand the need to have access to all of the objects directly. If we are designing invoker rights procedures in which we intend to make use of roles, we, as the definer, will need direct grants, not the role. This may not be possible for whatever reason (it just takes someone saying 'no, I won't grant you select on that table') and we need to work around that.

Enter template objects. A template object is basically an object to which the defining schema has direct access, and which looks just like the object you actually want to access at run-time. Think of it like a C struct, a Java Class, a PL/SQL record, or a data structure. It is there to let PL/SQL know the number of columns, the types of columns, and so on. An example will help here. Let's say you wanted to create a procedure that queries the DBA_USERS table, and displays, in a nice format, a CREATE USER statement for any existing user. You might attempt to write a procedure as a DBA, such as:

```
tkyte@TKYTE816> create or replace
  2  procedure show_user_info( p_username in varchar2 )
  3  AUTHID CURRENT_USER
  4  as
  5      l_rec    dba_users%rowtype;
  6  begin
  7      select *
  8        into l_rec
  9        from dba_users
 10       where username = upper(p_username);
 11
 12      dbms_output.put_line( 'create user ' || p_username  );
 13      if ( l_rec.password = 'EXTERNAL' ) then
 14          dbms_output.put_line( ' identified externally' );
 15      else
 16          dbms_output.put_line
 17          ( ' identified by values ''' || l_rec.password || '''' );
 18      end if;
 19      dbms_output.put_line
 20      ( ' temporary tablespace ' || l_rec.temporary_tablespace ||
 21        ' default tablespace ' || l_rec.default_tablespace ||
 22        ' profile ' || l_rec.profile );
 23  exception
 24      when no_data_found then
 25          dbms_output.put_line( '*** No such user ' || p_username );
 26  end;
 27  /

Warning: Procedure created with compilation errors.

tkyte@TKYTE816> show err
Errors for PROCEDURE SHOW_USER_INFO:

LINE/COL ERROR
-------- -----------------------------------------------------------------
4/13     PLS-00201: identifier 'SYS.DBA_USERS' must be declared
4/13     PL/SQL: Item ignored
6/5      PL/SQL: SQL Statement ignored
8/12     PLS-00201: identifier 'SYS.DBA_USERS' must be declared
12/5     PL/SQL: Statement ignored
12/10    PLS-00320: the declaration of the type of this expression is
         incomplete or malformed

18/5     PL/SQL: Statement ignored
19/35    PLS-00320: the declaration of the type of this expression is
         incomplete or malformed
```

This procedure fails to compile, not because SYS.DBA_USERS does not really exist, but rather because we have the ability to access DBA_USERS via a role, and roles are not enabled during the *compilation* of stored procedures, ever. So, what can we do to get this procedure to compile? For one, we could create our own DBA_USERS table. This will allow our procedure to successfully compile. However, since this table will not be the 'real' DBA_USERS table, it will not give us the result we desire *unless* we execute it as another user who can access the real DBA_USERS view:

```
tkyte@TKYTE816> create table dba_users
  2  as
  3  select * from SYS.dba_users where 1=0;

Table created.

tkyte@TKYTE816> alter procedure show_user_info compile;

Procedure altered.

tkyte@TKYTE816> exec show_user_info( USER );
*** No such user TKYTE

PL/SQL procedure successfully completed.

tkyte@TKYTE816> connect system/manager

system@TKYTE816> exec tkyte.show_user_info( 'TKYTE' )
create user TKYTE
identified by values '698F1E51F530CA57'
temporary tablespace TEMP default tablespace DATA profile DEFAULT

PL/SQL procedure successfully completed.
```

We now have a procedure that, when executed by someone other than the *definer*, sees the correct DBA_USERS (if the invoker is not allowed to see DBA_USERS, they will receive table or view does not exist). When the definer runs the procedure, they get no such user ... since their template object DBA_USERS is empty. Everyone else though, gets the expected results. In many cases this is perfectly acceptable. An example of this is when you expect to run the same set of code against many different tables. In this case however, we wish for this procedure to execute against exactly one table, DBA_USERS. So, back to the drawing board, how can we get this procedure to work for all users, including the definer? The answer is to use a template object of a different kind. We will create a table that is structurally the same as DBA_USERS, but give it a different name, say DBA_USERS_TEMPLATE. We'll use this table simply to define a record to fetch into. We will then dynamically access DBA_USERS in all cases:

```
system@TKYTE816> connect tkyte/tkyte

tkyte@TKYTE816> drop table dba_users;

Table dropped.

tkyte@TKYTE816> create table dba_users_TEMPLATE
  2  as
  3  select * from SYS.dba_users where 1=0;

Table created.
```

```
tkyte@TKYTE816> create or replace
  2  procedure show_user_info( p_username in varchar2 )
  3  AUTHID CURRENT_USER
  4  as
  5      type rc is ref cursor;
  6
  7      l_rec    dba_users_TEMPLATE%rowtype;
  8      l_cursor rc;
  9  begin
 10      open l_cursor for
 11       'select *
 12          from dba_users
 13         where username = :x'
 14      USING upper(p_username);
 15
 16      fetch l_cursor into l_rec;
 17      if ( l_cursor%found ) then
 18
 19          dbms_output.put_line( 'create user ' || p_username  );
 20          if ( l_rec.password = 'EXTERNAL' ) then
 21              dbms_output.put_line( ' identified externally' );
 22          else
 23              dbms_output.put_line
 24              ( ' identified by values ''' || l_rec.password || '''' );
 25          end if;
 26          dbms_output.put_line
 27          ( ' temporary tablespace ' || l_rec.temporary_tablespace ||
 28            ' default tablespace ' || l_rec.default_tablespace ||
 29            ' profile ' || l_rec.profile );
 30      else
 31          dbms_output.put_line( '*** No such user ' || p_username );
 32      end if;
 33      close l_cursor;
 34  end;
 35  /

Procedure created.

tkyte@TKYTE816> exec show_user_info( USER );
create user TKYTE
identified by values '698F1E51F530CA57'
temporary tablespace TEMP default tablespace DATA profile DEFAULT

PL/SQL procedure successfully completed.
```

So, in this case, we used the table DBA_USERS_TEMPLATE as a simple way to create a record type to fetch into. We could have described DBA_USERS and set up our own record type and all the rest of it, but I just find it easier to let the database do the work for me. In the event we upgrade to the next release of Oracle, we can simply recreate the template table, our procedure will recompile itself, and any new/additional columns or data type changes will be accounted for automatically.

Caveats

As with any feature, there are some nuances that need to be noted in the way this feature functions. This section attempts to address some of them.

Invoker Rights and Shared Pool Utilization

When using invoker rights to have a single procedure access data in different schemas, depending on who is running the query at run-time, you must be aware of the penalty you will pay in the shared pool. When using definer rights procedures, there is at most one copy of a SQL statement in the shared pool for each query in the procedure. Definer rights stored procedures make excellent use of the shared SQL facility (see Chapter 10 on *Tuning Strategies and Tools* for why this is an extremely important consideration). Invoker rights procedures, by design, on the other hand might not.

This is neither a terrible nor a good thing. Rather, it is something you must be aware of and size your shared pool accordingly. When using invoker rights procedures, we will use the shared pool in much the same way as you would if you wrote a client-server application using ODBC or JDBC that directly invoked DML. Each user may be executing the same exact query, but each query may actually be different. So, while we might all be issuing SELECT * FROM T, since we all may have different T tables, we will each get our own copy of the query plan and related information in the shared pool. This is necessary, since we each have a different T with different access rights and totally different access plans.

We can see the effect on the shared pool easily via an example. I have created the following objects in one schema:

```
tkyte@TKYTE816> create table t ( x int );

Table created.

tkyte@TKYTE816> create table t2 ( x int );

Table created.

tkyte@TKYTE816> create public synonym T for T;

Synonym created.

tkyte@TKYTE816> create or replace procedure dr_proc
  2  as
  3      l_cnt number;
  4  begin
  5      select count(*) into l_cnt from t DEMO_DR;
  6  end;
  7  /

Procedure created.

tkyte@TKYTE816> create or replace procedure ir_proc1
  2  authid current_user
  3  as
  4      l_cnt number;
  5  begin
```

```
  6        select count(*) into l_cnt from t DEMO_IR_1;
  7   end;
  8   /

Procedure created.

tkyte@TKYTE816> create or replace procedure ir_proc2
  2   authid current_user
  3   as
  4        l_cnt number;
  5   begin
  6        select count(*) into l_cnt from tkyte.t DEMO_IR_2;
  7   end;
  8   /

Procedure created.

tkyte@TKYTE816> create or replace procedure ir_proc3
  2   authid current_user
  3   as
  4        l_cnt number;
  5   begin
  6        select count(*) into l_cnt from t2 DEMO_IR_3;
  7   end;
  8   /

Procedure created.

tkyte@TKYTE816> grant select on t to public;

Grant succeeded.

tkyte@TKYTE816> grant execute on dr_proc to public;

Grant succeeded.

tkyte@TKYTE816> grant execute on ir_proc1 to public;

Grant succeeded.

tkyte@TKYTE816> grant execute on ir_proc2 to public;

Grant succeeded.

tkyte@TKYTE816> grant execute on ir_proc3 to public;

Grant succeeded.
```

We have created two tables T and T2. A public synonym T for TKYTE.T exists. Our four procedures all access either T or T2. The definer rights procedure, being statically bound at compile-time, does not need a schema qualifier. The invoker rights procedure, IR_PROC1 will access T via the public synonym. The second procedure IR_PROC2 will use a fully qualified reference, and the third procedure IR_PROC3 will access T2 in an unqualified way. Note that there is no public synonym for T2 – it is my intention to have IR_PROC3 access many different T2s at run-time.

Next, I created ten users via this script:

```
tkyte@TKYTE816> begin
  2          for i in 1 .. 10 loop
  3              begin
  4                  execute immediate 'drop user u' || i || ' cascade';
  5              exception
  6                  when others then null;
  7              end;
  8              execute immediate 'create user u'||i || ' identified by pw';
  9              execute immediate 'grant create session, create table to u'||i;
 10              execute immediate 'alter user u' || i || ' default tablespace
 11                                 data quota unlimited on data';
 12          end loop;
 13  end;
 14  /

PL/SQL procedure successfully completed.
```

and for each user, we executed:

```
create table t2 ( x int );
exec tkyte.dr_proc
exec tkyte.ir_proc1
exec tkyte.ir_proc2
exec tkyte.ir_proc3
```

This would log in as that user, create T2, and then run the four procedures in question. Now, after doing this for each of the ten users, we can inspect our shared pool, specifically the V$SQLAREA view, to see what happened, using the PRINT_TABLE procedure shown earlier in the chapter:

```
tkyte@TKYTE816> set serveroutput on size 1000000
tkyte@TKYTE816> begin
  2     print_table ('select sql_text, sharable_mem, version_count,
  3                          loaded_versions, parse_calls, optimizer_mode
  4                     from v$sqlarea
  5                    where sql_text like ''% DEMO\__R%'' escape ''\''
  6                      and lower(sql_text) not like ''%v$sqlarea%'' ');
  7  end;
  8  /

SQL_TEXT                       : SELECT COUNT(*)   FROM OPS$TKYTE.T DEMO_IR_2
SHARABLE_MEM                   : 4450
VERSION_COUNT                  : 1
LOADED_VERSIONS                : 1
PARSE_CALLS                    : 10
OPTIMIZER_MODE                 : CHOOSE
-----------------
SQL_TEXT                       : SELECT COUNT(*)   FROM T DEMO_DR
SHARABLE_MEM                   : 4246
VERSION_COUNT                  : 1
LOADED_VERSIONS                : 1
PARSE_CALLS                    : 10
OPTIMIZER_MODE                 : CHOOSE
```

```
-----------------
SQL_TEXT              : SELECT COUNT(*)    FROM T DEMO_IR_1
SHARABLE_MEM          : 4212
VERSION_COUNT         : 1
LOADED_VERSIONS       : 1
PARSE_CALLS           : 10
OPTIMIZER_MODE        : CHOOSE
-----------------
SQL_TEXT              : SELECT COUNT(*)    FROM T2 DEMO_IR_3
SHARABLE_MEM          : 31941
VERSION_COUNT         : 10
LOADED_VERSIONS       : 10
PARSE_CALLS           : 10
OPTIMIZER_MODE        : MULTIPLE CHILDREN PRESENT
-----------------

PL/SQL procedure successfully completed.
```

Even though the SQL text is exactly the same for SELECT COUNT(*) FROM T2 DEMO_IR_3, we can clearly see that there are ten different copies of this code in the shared pool. Each user in fact, needs their own optimized plan, as the objects referenced by this same query are totally different. In the cases where the underlying objects were identical, and the privileges were in place, we shared the SQL plans as expected.

So, the bottom line is that if you are using invoker rights to host one copy of code to access many different schemas, you must be prepared to have a larger shared pool to cache these query plans and such. This leads us into the next caveat.

Performance

When using invoker rights procedures, as you are now aware, each user might need to have their own special query plan generated for them. The cost of this additional parsing can be huge. Parsing a query is one of the most CPU-intensive things we do. We can see the 'cost' of parsing unique queries, as an invoker rights routine might do, by using TKPROF to time the parse of statements. In order to execute the following example, you will need the ALTER SYSTEM privilege:

```
tkyte@TKYTE816> alter system flush shared_pool;

System altered.

tkyte@TKYTE816> alter system set timed_statistics=true;

System altered.

tkyte@TKYTE816> alter session set sql_trace=true;

Session altered.

tkyte@TKYTE816> declare
  2      type rc is ref cursor;
  3      l_cursor rc;
  4  begin
  5      for i in 1 .. 500 loop
```

```
    6              open l_cursor for 'select * from all_objects t' || i;
    7              close l_cursor;
    8          end loop;
    9      end;
   10  /


PL/SQL procedure successfully completed.
```

This will cause 500 unique statements (each has a different table alias) to be parsed (similar to an invoker rights routine run by 500 different users with 500 different schemas). Looking at the TKPROF report summary for this session we see:

```
...

OVERALL TOTALS FOR ALL RECURSIVE STATEMENTS

call      count    cpu   elapsed   disk  query   current    rows
-------  ------  -----  --------  -----  -----  ---------  ------
Parse     1148  17.95     18.03      0     55         15       0
Execute   1229   0.29      0.25      0      0          0       0
Fetch     1013   0.14      0.17      0   2176          0     888
-------  ------  -----  --------  -----  -----  ---------  ------
total     3390  18.38     18.45      0   2231         15     888

Misses in library cache during parse: 536

   504  user  SQL statements in session.
   648  internal SQL statements in session.
  1152  SQL statements in session.
     0  statements EXPLAINed in this session.
```

Now we run a block that does not parse a unique statement 500 times, such as:

```
tkyte@TKYTE816> alter system flush shared_pool;

System altered.

tkyte@TKYTE816> alter system set timed_statistics=true;

System altered.

tkyte@TKYTE816> alter session set sql_trace=true;

Session altered.

tkyte@TKYTE816> declare
    2      type rc is ref cursor;
    3      l_cursor rc;
    4  begin
    5      for i in 1 .. 500 loop
    6              open l_cursor for 'select * from all_objects t';
    7              close l_cursor;
    8          end loop;
    9      end;
```

```
   10  /

PL/SQL procedure successfully completed.
```

we find from the TKPROF report that:

```
...

OVERALL TOTALS FOR ALL RECURSIVE STATEMENTS

call      count     cpu    elapsed    disk  query current      rows
-------   ------   -----  ----------  ----- ------ -------   ------
Parse      614     0.74     0.53        1     55     9           0
Execute    671     0.09     0.31        0      0     0           0
Fetch      358     0.08     0.04        8    830     0         272
-------   ------   -----  ----------  ----- ------ -------   ------
total     1643     0.91     0.88        9    885     9         272

Misses in library cache during parse: 22

 504   user  SQL statements in session.
 114   internal SQL statements in session.
 618   SQL statements in session.
   0   statements EXPLAINed in this session.
```

This is, quite simply, a *huge* difference. 500 unique statements (emulating the behavior of an invoker rights routine that accesses different tables each time), 17.95 CPU seconds of parse time. 500 of the same statement (emulating a standard definer rights routine), 0.74 CPU seconds of parse time. That is 24 times the effort!

This is definitely something to watch out for. In many cases, where SQL is not reused, the system will spend more time parsing queries than actually executing them! To find out why this is so, see the Chapter 10 on *Tuning Strategies and Tools*, where I talk of the vital importance of bind variables to make queries reusable.

This is not a reason to avoid using invoker rights routines. By all means use them, but be aware of the implications of doing so.

Code must be more Robust in Handling Errors

Normally, if I were to code a stored procedure such as:

```
...
begin
   for x in ( select pk from t ) loop
       update y set c = c+0.5 where d = x.pk;
   end loop;
end;
...
```

I could feel very confident that if that procedure were *valid*, it would run. In the definer rights model, this is the case. I know for a fact that T and Y exist. I know for a fact that T is readable and that Y is updateable.

Under invoker rights, I lose all of these facts. I no longer know if T exists and if it does, does it have a column called PK? If it does exist, do I have SELECT on it? If I have SELECT on it, is the SELECT via a role, meaning if I invoke this procedure from a definer rights routine, it won't work, but a direct invocation would? Does Y exist? And so on. In short, all of the facts we have ever taken for granted, are removed from us in invoker rights routines. So, while invoker rights routines open up a new way for us to program, in some ways they make it harder.

In the above, our code should be prepared to handle many of the possible (and probable) cases such as:

❑   T does not exist.

❑   T exists, but we do not have the required privileges on it.

❑   T exists, but it does not have a PK column.

❑   T exists, and has a column called PK, but the column's data type is different from the type at compilation.

❑   All of the above with regards to Y.

Since the update on Y only happens when there is some data in T, we may be able to run this procedure successfully many times, but one day when data is put into T the procedure fails. In fact, we never were able to see Y, but because this is the first time we had ever 'tried' to see Y, the procedure had failed. Only when a code path is executed will it fail!

To have a 'bullet-proof' routine that catches the possible errors, we would need to code:

```
create or replace procedure P
authid current_user
as
    no_such_table exception;
    pragma exception_init(no_such_table,-942);

    insufficient_privs exception;
    pragma exception_init(insufficient_privs,-1031);

    invalid_column_name exception;
    pragma exception_init(invalid_column_name,-904);

    inconsistent_datatypes exception;
    pragma exception_init(inconsistent_datatypes,-932);
begin
    for x in ( select pk from t ) loop
            update y set c = c+0.5 where d = x.pk;
    end loop;
exception
    when NO_SUCH_TABLE then
        dbms_output.put_line( 'Error Caught: ' || sqlerrm );
    when INSUFFICIENT_PRIVS then
        dbms_output.put_line( 'Error Caught: ' || sqlerrm );
    when INVALID_COLUMN_NAME then
        dbms_output.put_line( 'Error Caught: ' || sqlerrm );
    when INCONSISTENT_DATATYPES then
        dbms_output.put_line( 'Error Caught: ' || sqlerrm );
... (a variety of other errors go here)...
end;
/
```

Side Effects of Using SELECT *

Using a SELECT * can be very dangerous in a PL/SQL routine that accesses different tables, when run by different users such as in invoker rights code. The data may appear to come out 'scrambled', or in a different order. This is because the record that is set up, and fetched into, is defined at compile-time, not at run-time. Hence, the * is expanded at *compile-time* for the PL/SQL objects (the record types) but expanded at *run-time* for the query. If you have an object with the same name, but a different column ordering, in different schemas and access this via an invoker rights routine with a SELECT *, be prepared for this side effect:

```
tkyte@TKYTE816> create table t ( msg varchar2(25), c1 int, c2 int );

Table created.

tkyte@TKYTE816> insert into t values ( 'c1=1, c2=2', 1, 2 );

1 row created.

tkyte@TKYTE816> create or replace procedure P
  2  authid current_user
  3  as
  4  begin
  5      for x in ( select * from t ) loop
  6              dbms_output.put_line( 'msg= ' || x.msg );
  7              dbms_output.put_line( 'C1 = ' || x.c1 );
  8              dbms_output.put_line( 'C2 = ' || x.c2 );
  9      end loop;
 10  end;
 11  /

Procedure created.

tkyte@TKYTE816> exec p
msg= c1=1, c2=2
C1 = 1
C2 = 2

PL/SQL procedure successfully completed.

tkyte@TKYTE816> grant execute on P to u1;

Grant succeeded.
```

So what we have above is a procedure that simply shows us what is in the table T. It prints out a MSG column, which I am using in this example to show what I expect the answer to be. It prints out C1 and C2's values. Very simple, very straightforward. Now, let's see what happens when I execute it as another user with their own T table:

```
tkyte@TKYTE816> @connect u1/pw

u1@TKYTE816> drop table t;

Table dropped.
```

```
u1@TKYTE816> create table t ( msg varchar2(25), c2 int, c1 int );

Table created.

u1@TKYTE816> insert into t values ( 'c1=2, c2=1', 1, 2 );

1 row created.
```

Notice here that I created the table with C1 and C2 reversed! Here, I am expecting that C1 = 2 and C2 = 1. When we run the procedure however, we get this:

```
u1@TKYTE816> exec tkyte.p
msg= c1=2, c2=1
C1 = 1
C2 = 2

PL/SQL procedure successfully completed.
```

It is not exactly what we expected – until we think about it. PL/SQL, at compile-time, set up the implicit record X for us. The record X is simply a data structure with three elements, MSG VARCHAR2, C1 NUMBER, and C2 NUMBER. When the SELECT * columns were expanded during the parse phase of the query as user TKYTE, they got expanded to be MSG, C1, and C2 in that order. As U1 however, they got expanded to MSG, C2, and C1. Since the data types all matched up with the implicit record X, we did not receive an INCONSISTENT DATATYPE error (this could also happen if the data types were not compatible). The fetch succeeded, but put column C2 into record attribute C1. This is the expected behavior, and yet another good reason to not use SELECT * in production code.

Beware of the 'Hidden' Columns

This is very similar to the SELECT * caveat above. Again this ties into how the PL/SQL routine with invoker rights is compiled, and how names and references to objects are resolved. In this case, we will consider an UPDATE statement that, if executed directly in SQL*PLUS would give a totally different answer than when executed in an invoker rights routine. It does the 'correct' thing in both environments – it just does them very differently.

When PL/SQL code is compiled into the database, each and every static SQL query is parsed, and all identifiers are discovered in them. These identifiers might be database column names or they might reference PL/SQL variables (bind variables). If they are database column names, they are left in the query 'as is'. If they are PL/SQL variable names, they are replaced in the query with a :BIND_VARIABLE reference. This replacement is done at compile-time, never at run-time. So, if we take an example:

```
tkyte@TKYTE816> create table t ( c1 int );

Table created.

tkyte@TKYTE816> insert into t values ( 1 );

1 row created.

tkyte@TKYTE816> create or replace procedure P
  2    authid current_user
```

```
  3  as
  4          c2  number default 5;
  5  begin
  6          update t set c1 = c2;
  7  end;
  8  /

Procedure created.

tkyte@TKYTE816> exec p

PL/SQL procedure successfully completed.

tkyte@TKYTE816> select * from t;

        C1
----------
         5

tkyte@TKYTE816> grant execute on P to u1;

Grant succeeded.
```

All looks normal so far. C1 is a database column in the table T, and C2 is a PL/SQL variable name. The statement UPDATE T SET C1 = C2 is processed by PL/SQL at compile-time to be UPDATE T SET C1 = :BIND_VARIABLE, and the value of :BIND_VARIABLE is passed in at run-time. Now, if we log in as U1, and create our own T table:

```
tkyte@TKYTE816> connect u1/pw

u1@TKYTE816> drop table t;

Table dropped.

u1@TKYTE816> create table t ( c1 int, c2 int );

Table created.

u1@TKYTE816> insert into t values ( 1, 2 );

1 row created.

u1@TKYTE816> exec tkyte.p

PL/SQL procedure successfully completed.

u1@TKYTE816> select * from t;

        C1         C2
---------- ----------
         5          2
```

This might seem right or wrong, depending on how you look at it. We just executed UPDATE T SET C1 = C2, which if we were to execute at the SQL*PLUS prompt, would result in C1 being set to 2, not 5. However, since PL/SQL rewrote this query at compile-time to not have any references to C2, it does the same exact thing to our copy of T, as it did to the other copy of T – it set the column C1 to 5. This PL/SQL routine cannot 'see' the column C2, since C2 does not exist in the object it was compiled against.

At first, this seems confusing, since we do not get to see the rewritten update normally, but once you are aware of it, it makes perfect sense.

Java and Invoker Rights

PL/SQL, by default, compiles with definer rights. You must go out of your way to make it run as the invoker. Java on the other hand, goes the other way. *Java by default, uses invoker rights.* If you want definer rights you must specify this when you load it.

As an example, I've created a table T such as:

```
ops$tkyte@DEV816> create table t ( msg varchar2(50) );

Table created.

ops$tkyte@DEV816> insert into t values ( 'This is T owned by ' || user  );

1 row created.
```

I have also created, and loaded two Java stored procedures (you will need the CREATE PUBLIC SYNONYM privilege to complete this example). These Java stored procedures are very much like the PL/SQL examples above. They will access a table T that contains a row describing who 'owns' this table, and they will print out the session user, current user (privilege schema), and current schema:

```
tkyte@TKYTE816> host type ir_java.java
import java.sql.*;
import oracle.jdbc.driver.*;

public class ir_java
{
public static void test() throws SQLException
  {
  Connection cnx = new OracleDriver().defaultConnection();

  String sql =
      "SELECT MSG, sys_context('userenv','session_user'), "+
              "sys_context('userenv','current_user'), "+
              "sys_context('userenv','current_schema') "+
        "FROM T";

    Statement stmt = cnx.createStatement();
    ResultSet rset = stmt.executeQuery(sql);

    if (rset.next())
       System.out.println( rset.getString(1) +
                      " session_user=" + rset.getString(2)+
                      " current_user=" + rset.getString(3)+
                      " current_schema=" + rset.getString(4) );
    rset.close();
```

```
        stmt.close();
    }
}

tkyte@TKYTE816> host dropjava -user tkyte/tkyte ir_java.java

tkyte@TKYTE816> host loadjava -user tkyte/tkyte -synonym -grant u1 -verbose -
resolve ir_java.java
initialization complete
loading   : ir_java
creating  : ir_java
resolver  :
resolving : ir_java
synonym   : ir_java
```

By default, the above routine is loaded with invoker rights. Now we'll load the same routine but with a different name. When we `loadjava` this routine, we'll specify it as a definer rights routine:

```
tkyte@TKYTE816> host type dr_java.java
import java.sql.*;
import oracle.jdbc.driver.*;

public class dr_java
{
... same code as above ...
}

tkyte@TKYTE816> host dropjava -user tkyte/tkyte dr_java.java

tkyte@TKYTE816> host loadjava -user tkyte/tkyte -synonym -definer -grant u1 -
verbose -resolve dr_jav
initialization complete
loading   : dr_java
creating  : dr_java
resolver  :
resolving : dr_java
synonym   : dr_java
```

Now, the only difference between IR_JAVA and DR_JAVA is their class name, and the fact that DR_JAVA was loaded with -definer.

Next, I created the PL/SQL call specs so we can run these procedures from SQL*PLUS. Notice that there are four versions here. All calls to Java stored procedures are ultimately via the SQL layer. Since this SQL layer is really just a PL/SQL binding, we can specify the AUTHID clause here as well. We need to see what happens when an invoker/definer rights PL/SQL layer calls the invoker/definer rights Java procedure:

```
tkyte@TKYTE816> create OR replace procedure ir_ir_java
  2   authid current_user
  3   as language java name 'ir_java.test()';
  4   /

Procedure created.

tkyte@TKYTE816> grant execute on ir_ir_java to u1;
```

```
Grant succeeded.

tkyte@TKYTE816> create OR replace procedure dr_ir_java
  2   as language java name 'ir_java.test()';
  3   /

Procedure created.

tkyte@TKYTE816> grant execute on dr_ir_java to u1;

Grant succeeded.

tkyte@TKYTE816> create OR replace procedure ir_dr_java
  2   authid current_user
  3   as language java name 'dr_java.test()';
  4   /

Procedure created.

tkyte@TKYTE816> grant execute on ir_dr_java to u1;

Grant succeeded.

tkyte@TKYTE816> create OR replace procedure dr_dr_java
  2   authid current_user
  3   as language java name 'dr_java.test()';
  4   /

Procedure created.

tkyte@TKYTE816> grant execute on dr_dr_java to u1;

Grant succeeded.
```

Now we need to create and populate the table T in the TKYTE schema:

```
tkyte@TKYTE816> drop table t;

Table dropped.

tkyte@TKYTE816> create table t ( msg varchar2(50) );

Table created.

tkyte@TKYTE816> insert into t values ( 'This is T owned by ' || user  );

1 row created.
```

So now we are ready to test this using U1, who will just happen to have a table T with a row identifying the owner as well:

```
tkyte@TKYTE816> @connect u1/pw

u1@TKYTE816> drop table t;
```

```
    Table dropped.

    u1@TKYTE816> create table t ( msg varchar2(50) );

    Table created.

    u1@TKYTE816> insert into t values ( 'This is T owned by ' || user  );

    1 row created.

    u1@TKYTE816> set serveroutput on size 1000000
    u1@TKYTE816> exec dbms_java.set_output(1000000);

    PL/SQL procedure successfully completed.

    u1@TKYTE816> exec tkyte.ir_ir_java
    This is T owned by U1 session_user=U1 current_user=U1 current_schema=U1

    PL/SQL procedure successfully completed.
```

This shows that when the invoker rights Java stored procedure is called via an invoker rights PL/SQL layer, it behaves as an invoker rights routine. U1 is the current user and current schema, the SQL in the Java stored procedure accessed U1.T, not TKYTE.T. Now, let's call that same bit of Java via a definer rights layer:

```
    u1@TKYTE816> exec tkyte.dr_ir_java
    This is T owned by TKYTE session_user=U1 current_user=TKYTE current_schema=TKYTE

    PL/SQL procedure successfully completed.
```

Now, even though the Java stored procedure is an invoker rights routine, it is behaving as if it were a definer rights routine. This is expected, as we saw above. When an invoker rights routine is called by a definer rights routine, it will behave much like the definer rights routine. There are no roles; the current schema is statically fixed, as is the current user. This routine queries TKYTE.T not U1.T as before, and the current user/schema is fixed at TKYTE.

Continuing on, we'll see what happens when an invoker rights PL/SQL layer calls the definer rights loaded Java stored procedure:

```
    u1@TKYTE816> exec tkyte.ir_dr_java
    This is T owned by TKYTE session_user=U1 current_user=TKYTE current_schema =TKYTE

    PL/SQL procedure successfully completed.
```

This shows that by loading the Java with -definer, it runs using definer rights, even when called by an invoker rights layer. The last example should be obvious by now. We have a definer rights PL/SQL layer invoking a Java definer rights routine:

```
    u1@TKYTE816> exec tkyte.dr_dr_java
    This is T owned by TKYTE session_user=U1 current_user=TKYTE current_schema =TKYTE

    PL/SQL procedure successfully completed.
```

And of course, it executes as a definers rights routine, as expected.

1023

Given the above, you might not even notice the Java stored procedure is loaded with invoker rights by default, since the PL/SQL call spec is typically the invoker of the Java stored procedure, and this by default compiles with definer rights. Typically, the schema that loads the Java is the schema that creates the call spec, and if they create it with definer rights, the Java appears to have definer rights as well (and for all intents and purposes it does in that case). I would hazard a guess that most people are not aware of the fact that Java is loaded this way, as it almost never appears to be an invoker rights routine. Only if the call spec is created in the schema with AUTHID CURRENT_USER does it make itself apparent.

The other case where it 'matters' that Java is loaded with invoker rights by default, is when the call spec is defined in a wholly different schema from that of the Java bytecode. Using the same loaded Java code above, I had U1 create some call specs to invoke the Java in TKYTE's schema. In order to do this, U1 was granted CREATE PROCEDURE. Also, this relies on the fact that when the Java code was loaded, we used -synonym, which created a public synonym for the loaded Java and -grant U1, which gave U1 direct access to this Java code. This is the result:

```
u1@TKYTE816> create OR replace procedure ir_java
  2   authid current_user
  3   as language java name 'ir_java.test()';
  4   /

Procedure created.

u1@TKYTE816> exec ir_java
This is T owned by U1 session_user=U1 current_user=U1 current_schema=U1

PL/SQL procedure successfully completed.
```

So this shows that this invoker rights procedure (in fact a definer rights procedure would have the same effect) owned by U1 runs the SQL in the Java code as if U1 had loaded it. It shows that the Java code is loaded with invoker rights. If it were not, the SQL in the Java code would execute with the name resolution and privileges of TKYTE, not U1. This next example shows the definer rights loaded by the U1 schema. Java does execute in the domain of TKYTE:

```
u1@TKYTE816> create OR replace procedure dr_java
  2   as language java name 'dr_java.test()';
  3   /

Procedure created.

u1@TKYTE816> exec dr_java
This is T owned by TKYTE session_user=U1 current_user=TKYTE current_schema =TKYTE

PL/SQL procedure successfully completed.
```

This shows that the Java code loaded with definer rights runs as TKYTE, not as U1. We had to force this Java code to load with definer rights using -definer, showing the Java stored procedure is 'backwards' with regards to this when compared to PL/SQL.

Errors You Might Encounter

Beyond what we just discussed in the *Caveats* section, there are no special errors you can expect when using definer or invoker rights. When using invoker rights, it is important to understand more fully how PL/SQL processes embedded SQL so as to avoid issues with SELECT * changing the order of columns, 'hidden' columns at run-time, and so on. Additionally, with invoker rights, your PL/SQL code that would normally run without any issues whatsoever may fail to run at various places for different users. The reason being that objects are being resolved differently. In different schemas, the required privileges may not be in place, data types might be different, and so on.

In general, with invoker rights procedures, your code must be a little more robust, and you must expect errors where errors would not normally occur. Static references no longer guarantee clean running code. It will be more like maintaining an ODBC or JDBC program with straight SQL calls. You control the 'linkage' of your program (*you* know what subroutines in your client application will be called), but you have no control over when the SQL will execute until you actually execute it. The SQL invoked in an invoker rights PL/SQL routine will behave just like it would in a JDBC client application. Until you test every execution path with every user, you will never be 100 percent sure that it will execute flawlessly in production. Hence, you must code much more error handling than otherwise necessary in a traditional stored procedure.

Summary

In this chapter we thoroughly explored the concepts of definer rights and invoker rights procedures. We learned how easy it is to enable invoker rights, but we also learned of the price that is to be paid with regards to:

❑ Error detection and handling.

❑ Subtle errors that could be introduced by different table structures at run-time.

❑ Additional shared SQL area overhead potential.

❑ Additional parse times incurred.

At first glance, these seem too high a price to pay – and in many cases it is. In other cases, such as the generic routine to print out comma-separated data from any query, or to print out the results of a query down the screen instead of across the screen, it is an invaluable feature. Without it, we just could not accomplish what we set out to do.

Invoker rights routines make the most sense in the following cases:

❑ When the SQL to be processed is dynamic in nature (as these examples are).

❑ When the SQL to be processed is set up to enforce security by the SCHEMAID, as in the case of the data dictionary (or your own application).

❑ When you need roles to be in place, invoker rights routines are the only way to do it.

Invoker rights *can* be used to provide access to different schemas based on the current schema (as returned by SYS_CONTEXT('USERENV', 'CURRENT_SCHEMA')), but care must be taken here to ensure the schemas are consistent with each other, and that the necessary privileges are in place (or that your code is set up to handle the lack of access gracefully). You must also be prepared to pay the price in shared pool utilization, and additional overhead with regards to parsing.

Definer rights procedures are still the correct implementation for almost all stored procedures. Invoker rights routines is a powerful tool, but should only be used where appropriate.

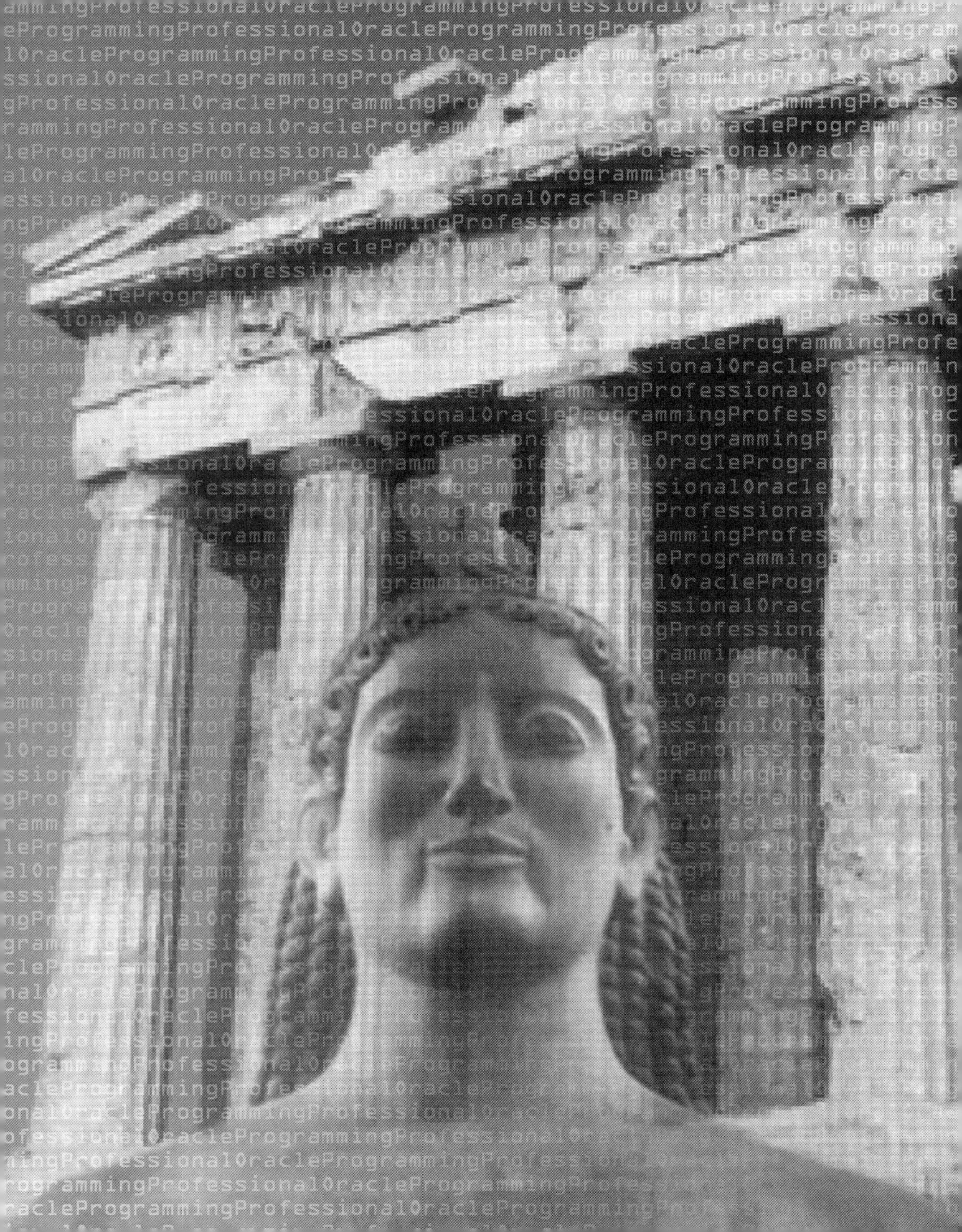

Necessary Supplied Packages

In this section of the book, we will cover the supplied database packages that, in my opinion, everyone needs to be aware of. Each of these packages is documented in the Oracle document entitled *Oracle8i Supplied PL/SQL Packages Reference.* The supplied documentation typically shows the entry points (externalized procedures and functions) of the supplied package, and gives you an overview of each function/procedure's usage. In this section we will describe in more detail when you might (or might not) choose to use such a package. We will not go into depth on each and every procedure in every package. Rather, we will discuss the most commonly used package entry points, and show how they are used. For a comprehensive list of all procedures available in a given package, along with all possible parameters, I will refer you to the aforementioned document.

This appendix will serve as a 'jumping off' point for using these supplied packages. After you are done with it, you will have a good feel for the intended use of many of them. We do not cover every supplied package in this section. This does not imply that they are not useful, just that their use falls outside the scope of typical development. We will explore the packages that applications will employ in most cases.

The packages we will cover are:

- ❑ DBMS_ALERT and DBMS_PIPE – Inter-process communication facilities in the database. DBMS_ALERT can be used to signal all interested sessions that some event has taken place. DBMS_PIPE allows two sessions to 'talk' to each other, much like a TCP/IP socket.

- ❑ DBMS_APPLICATION_INFO – Allows an application to register useful information in the V$ tables. Extremely useful to monitor what your stored procedure is doing, and register other information.

- ❑ DBMS_JAVA – A PL/SQL package useful for working with Java stored procedures.

- ❑ DBMS_JOB – A database job scheduler. Used when you have that stored procedure you want to execute every night at 2am, or when you just want to run something in the background.

- ❑ DBMS_LOB – For working with **Large OB**jects (**LOB**s) in the database.

- ❑ DBMS_LOCK – To create your own user-defined locks, separate and distinct from Oracle's row row or table level locks.

- ❑ DBMS_LOGMNR – To review and analyze the contents of your online redo log files

- ❑ DBMS_OBFUSCATION_TOOLKIT – Provides data encryption in the database.

- ❑ DBMS_OUTPUT – Provides simple screen I/O capabilities for PL/SQL in SQL*PLUS and SVRMGRL.

- ❑ DBMS_PROFILER – A PL/SQL source code profiler built into the database.

- ❑ DBMS_UTILITY – A 'hodge-podge' collection of useful procedures.

- ❑ UTL_FILE – Provides text file I/O for PL/SQL. Allows PL/SQL to read and write text files on the server.

- ❑ UTL_HTTP – Provides access to the **HTTP** (**H**yper **T**ext **T**ransfer **P**rotocol) protocol from within PL/SQL. Allows PL/SQL to 'grab' web pages.

- ❑ UTL_RAW – Provides conversion between the RAW and VARCHAR2 types. Extremely useful when working with TCP/IP, BLOBs and BFILEs, and encryption.

- ❑ UTL_SMTP – Provides access to the **SMTP** (**S**imple **M**ail **T**ransfer **P**rotocol) from within PL/SQL. Specifically, it allows you to send an e-mail from PL/SQL.

- ❑ UTL_TCP –Provide TCP/IP socket abilities for PL/SQL. Allows PL/SQL to open a connection to any TCP/IP service.

Why Use the Supplied Packages?

The reasoning behind using the supplied packages is simple, it is much easier and more maintainable to develop using supplied functionality then it is to build your own. If Oracle supplies a package for doing something (for example, data encryption) it would not be productive to write your own. Often, I find people implementing functionality that they did not know already existed in the database, purely out of ignorance. Knowing what tools you have available to you will make your life much easier.

About The Supplied Packages

The supplied packages from Oracle all begin with either DBMS_ or UTL_. Historically, packages that were created by Server Technologies (the guys who write the database) begin with DBMS_. The UTL_ packages were derived from other sources. The UTL_HTTP package, for performing HTTP calls from PL/SQL (to retrieve web pages and such), is an example of such an external package. The Application Server Division at Oracle developed this package in order to support the concept of **ICX** (**I**nter-**C**artridge e**X**change) with **OAS** (the **O**racle **A**pplication **S**erver), which has now been replaced with **iAS**, (the **i**nternet **A**pplication **S**erver). This naming difference does not mean anything to us, the developers, really – it is just interesting to note.

Most of these packages are stored in a compiled, wrapped format in the database. This wrapped format protects the code from snooping eyes. We can see the specification of the code but we cannot see the code itself. If you were to select the code of DBMS_OUTPUT PACKAGE BODY from the database itself, it might look like something like this:

```
tkyte@TKYTE816> select text
  2   from all_source
  3   where name = 'DBMS_OUTPUT'
  4   and type = 'PACKAGE BODY'
  5   and line < 10
  6   order by line
  7   /

TEXT
-------------------------------------------------

package body dbms_output wrapped
0
abcd
abcd
abcd
abcd
abcd
abcd
abcd

9 rows selected.
```

Not very useful. What is very useful however, is if we select out the *specification* of the PACKAGE:

```
tkyte@TKYTE816> select text
  2     from all_source
  3    where name = 'DBMS_OUTPUT'
  4      and type = 'PACKAGE'
  5      and line < 26
  6    order by line
  7   /

TEXT
-------------------------------------------------------------------------

package dbms_output as

     ------------
     --  OVERVIEW
     --
     --   These procedures accumulate information in a buffer (via "put" and
     --   "put_line") so that it can be retrieved out later (via "get_line" or
     --   "get_lines").  If this package is disabled then all
     --   calls to this package are simply ignored.  This way, these routines
     --   are only active when the client is one that is able to deal with the
     --   information.  This is good for debugging, or SP's that want to want
     --   to display messages or reports to sql*dba or plus (like 'describing
     --   procedures', etc.).  The default buffer size is 20000 bytes.  The
     --   minimum is 2000 and the maximum is 1,000,000.
```

```
    -----------
    --   EXAMPLE
    --
    --   A trigger might want to print out some debugging information.  To do
    --   do this the trigger would do
    --      dbms_output.put_line('I got here:'||:new.col||' is the new value');
    --   If the client had enabled the dbms_output package then this put_line
    --   would be buffered and the client could, after executing the statement
    --   (presumably some insert, delete or update that caused the trigger to
    --   fire) execute

  25 rows selected.
```

Hidden in the database is an online source of documentation. Each of these packages has a specification that has a nice overview of what the package is, what each function or procedure does, and how to use it. This is obviously very handy when you don't have the documentation, but is also useful even when you do, since the specification sometimes contains data that the documentation doesn't mention, or has further examples that are useful.

We will now look at the various packages I find useful in day-to-day work with Oracle. These are the packages, which not only *I* use frequently, but find *others* using as well. Additionally, we'll introduce some new packages, or ways to do things to work around some of the limitations of these built-in packages – limits people frequently hit, in my experience.

DBMS_ALERT and DBMS_PIPE

The two packages, DBMS_ALERT and DBMS_PIPE, are very powerful inter-process communication packages. Both allow for one session to talk to another session in the database. DBMS_ALERT is very much like a UNIX operating system 'signal', and DBMS_PIPE is very much like a UNIX 'named pipe'. Since a lot of confusion exists over which package to use and when, I've decided to handle them together.

The package DBMS_ALERT is designed to allow a session to signal the occurrence of some event in the database. Other sessions that are interested in this event would be notified of its occurrence. Alerts are designed to be transactional in nature, meaning that you might signal an alert in a trigger, or some stored procedure, but until your transaction actually commits, the alert will not be sent out to the waiting sessions. If you rollback, your alert is never sent. It is important to understand that the session wishing to be notified of the alert in the database must either occasionally 'poll' for the event (ask the database if it has been signaled), or block (wait) in the database, waiting for the event to occur.

The package DBMS_PIPE on the other hand, is a more generic inter-process communication package. It allows one or more sessions to 'read' on one end of a named pipe, and one or more sessions to 'write' messages onto this pipe. Only one of the 'read' sessions will ever get the message (and at least one session will), and it is not possible to direct a given message on a single named pipe to a specific session. It will be somewhat arbitrary as to which session will read a given message written to a pipe when there is more then one 'reader' available. Pipes are, by design, not transactional in nature – as soon as you send a message, the message will become available to other sessions. You do not need to commit, and committing or rolling back will not affect the outcome of sending the pipe.

Why You Might Use Them

The major difference between alerts and pipes is the transactional (or not) nature of the two. Alerts are useful when you desire to transmit a message to one or more sessions *after* it has been successfully committed to the database. Pipes are useful when you desire to transmit a message to a single session *immediately*. Examples of when you might use alerts are:

❑   You have a GUI chart to display stock data on a screen. When the stock information is modified in the database, the application should be notified so that it knows to update the screen

❑   You wish to put a notification dialogue up in an application when a new record is placed into a table so the end user can be notified of 'new work'

Examples of when you might choose to use a database pipe would be:

❑   You have a process running on some other machine in the network that can perform an operation for you. You would like to send a message to this process to ask it to do something for you. In this way, a database pipe is much like a TCP/IP socket.

❑   You would like to queue some data up in the SGA so that another process will ultimately come along, read out and process. In this fashion, you are using a database pipe like a non-persistent FIFO queue that can be read by many different sessions.

There are other examples of both, but these cover the main uses of alerts and pipes, and give a good characterization of when you might use one over the other. You use alerts when you want to notify a community of users of an event that has definitely taken place (after the commit). You use pipes when you want to immediately send a message to some other session out there (and typically wait for a reply).

Now that we understand the basic intention of alerts and pipes, we'll take a look at some of the implementation details of each.

Set Up

DBMS_ALERT and DBMS_PIPE are both installed by default in the database. Unlike many of the supplied packages, EXECUTE on these packages is not granted to PUBLIC. In Oracle 8.0 and up, EXECUTE on these packages is granted to the EXECUTE_CATALOG_ROLE. In prior releases, these packages had no default grants whatsoever.

Since EXECUTE is granted to a role, and not to PUBLIC, you will find that you cannot create a stored procedure that is dependent on these packages, since roles are never enabled during the compilation of a procedure/package. You must have EXECUTE granted directly to your account.

DBMS_ALERT

The DBMS_ALERT package is very small, consisting of only seven entry points. I shall discuss the six of most interest here. The application that wishes to receive an alert will be primarily interested in:

❑   REGISTER – To register interest in a named alert. You may call REGISTER many times in a session with different names, in order to be notified when any one of a number of events occurs.

- ❏ REMOVE – To remove your interest in an event, in order to prevent the server from attempting to notify of you an event.

- ❏ REMOVEALL – To remove your interest in all named alerts you registered for.

- ❏ WAITANY – To wait for any of the named alerts, in which you have registered your interest, to be fired. This routine will tell you the name of the event that was fired, and provide access to the brief message that might accompany it. You may either wait for a specific duration of time, or not wait at all (to allow for an occasional 'poll' from the application to see if any event has taken place, but not block waiting for an event to occur).

- ❏ WAITONE – To wait for a specific named alert to be fired. Like WAITANY, you may wait for a specified duration of time, or not wait at all.

And the application that wishes to signal, or fire an alert, is interested only in the routine:

- ❏ SIGNAL – To signal an alert upon the commit of the current transaction. A rollback will 'unsignal'.

So, DBMS_ALERT is very easy to use. A client application interested in being notified of an event might contain code such as:

```
tkyte@TKYTE816> begin
  2      dbms_alert.register( 'MyAlert' );
  3  end;
  4  /

PL/SQL procedure successfully completed.

tkyte@TKYTE816> set serveroutput on
tkyte@TKYTE816> declare
  2      l_status    number;
  3      l_msg       varchar2(1800);
  4  begin
  5      dbms_alert.waitone( name    => 'MyAlert',
  6                          message => l_msg,
  7                          status  => l_status,
  8                          timeout => dbms_alert.maxwait );
  9
 10      if ( l_status = 0 )
 11      then
 12          dbms_output.put_line( 'Msg from event is ' || l_msg );
 13      end if;
 14  end;
 15  /
```

They simply register their interest in the named alert, MyAlert, and then call DBMS_ALERT.WAITONE to wait for this alert to be fired. Notice that since DBMS_ALERT.MAXWAIT is used, a constant from the DBMS_ALERT package, this code will just 'sit there'. It is blocked in the database waiting for this event to occur. The interested client application might use a much smaller timeout period specified in seconds (perhaps 0, meaning no waiting should occur) so it could poll for an event. For example, an Oracle Forms application might have a timer that goes off every minute and calls DBMS_ALERT.WAITONE to see if some event has occurred. If so, the screen will be updated. A Java thread might become active every so often to check for an event, and update some shared data structure, and so on.

Now, in order to signal this alert, all we need to do is:

```
tkyte@TKYTE816> exec dbms_alert.signal( 'MyAlert', 'Hello World' );

PL/SQL procedure successfully completed.

tkyte@TKYTE816> commit;

Commit complete.
```

in another session. You should immediately see:

```
...
 15  /
Msg from event is Hello World

PL/SQL procedure successfully completed.
```

in the session that was blocked waiting for the alert, so this session will no longer be blocked. This simple example shows the most commonly used format of DBMS_ALERT. Some sessions wait on a named alert, and another session signals it. Until the signaling session commits, the alert does not go through. You'll see this yourself easily using two SQL*PLUS sessions.

It gets more interesting with alerts when we ask ourselves:

❑   What happens when many messages get 'signaled' at more or less the same time by different sessions?

❑   What happens if I call signal repeatedly – how many alerts will be generated in the end?

❑   What happens if more than one session signals an alert after I registered interest in it, but before I've called one of the wait routines? Same question, only what happens when more than one session signals an alert between my calls to wait?

The answers to these questions will point out some of the side effects of alerts; some of the things you need to be aware of when using them. I'll also suggest ways to avoid some of the issues these questions raise.

Concurrent Signals by More than One Session

If we re-execute our small test from above, have the one session register its interest in MyAlert, wait on it, and then start up two additional sessions, we can easily see what happens when more than one session signals an alert simultaneously. In this test, both of the other two sessions will execute:

```
tkyte@TKYTE816> exec dbms_alert.signal( 'MyAlert', 'Hello World' );
```

and nothing else (no commit). What you will observe in this case is that the session, which issued the second signal, is blocked. This shows that if N sessions attempt to signal the same named event concurrently, N-1 of them will block on the DBMS_ALERT.SIGNAL call. Only one of the sessions will continue forward. Alerts are serial in nature, and care must be taken to avoid issues with this.

The database is designed to provide highly concurrent access to data. DBMS_ALERT is one of those tools that can definitely limit scalability in this area. If you place an INSERT trigger on a table and this trigger places a DBMS_ALERT.SIGNAL call when fired then, if the table is subject to frequent INSERT statements, you will serialize all INSERTs on that particular table whenever someone is registered for that alert. For this reason, you may want to consider limiting the number of overall sessions that might signal an alert. For example, if you have a live data feed coming into your database so that there is only one session inserting data into this table, DBMS_ALERT would be appropriate. On the other hand, if this is an audit trail table that everyone must INSERT into frequently, DBMS_ALERT would not be an appropriate technology.

One method to avoid this serialization by many sessions could be to use DBMS_JOB (detailed in its own section in this appendix). You might write a procedure in which the only thing you do is signal the alert and commit:

```
tkyte@TKYTE816> create table alert_messages
  2  ( job_id      int primary key,
  3    alert_name varchar2(30),
  4    message     varchar2(2000)
  5  )
  6  /

Table created.

tkyte@TKYTE816> create or replace procedure background_alert( p_job in int )
  2  as
  3      l_rec alert_messages%rowtype;
  4  begin
  5      select * into l_rec from alert_messages where job_id = p_job;
  6
  7      dbms_alert.signal( l_rec.alert_name, l_rec.message );
  8      delete from alert_messages where job_id = p_job;
  9      commit;
 10  end;
 11  /

Procedure created.
```

Then, your database trigger would look like this:

```
tkyte@TKYTE816> create table t ( x int );
Table created.

tkyte@TKYTE816> create or replace trigger t_trigger
  2  after insert or update of x on t for each row
  3  declare
  4          l_job number;
  5  begin
  6          dbms_job.submit( l_job, 'background_alert(JOB);' );
  7          insert into alert_messages
  8          ( job_id, alert_name, message )
  9          values
 10          ( l_job, 'MyAlert', 'X in T has value ' || :new.x );
 11  end;
 12  /

Trigger created.
```

to have the alert signaled by a background process *after* you commit. In this fashion:

❑ Alerts are still transactional

❑ They will not serialize your foreground processes (interactive applications)

The drawback is that jobs are not necessarily run *right* away; it might be a little while before the alert gets out. In many cases, I have found this to be acceptable (it is important to notify the waiting process that something has occurred, but a short lag time is generally OK). Advanced queues (AQ) also supply a highly scalable method of signaling events in the database. They are more complex to use than DBMS_ALERT, but offer more flexibility in this area.

Repeated Calls to Signal by a Session

Now the question is, what if I signal the same named alert many times in my application, and then commit? How many alerts actually get signaled? Here, the answer is simple: *one*. DBMS_ALERT works very much like a UNIX signal would. The UNIX OS uses signals to notify processes of events that have occurred in the operating system. One such event for example is 'I/O is ready', meaning that one of the files (or sockets or such) you have open is ready for more I/O. You might use this signal when building a TCP/IP-based server for example. The OS will notify you when a socket you have opened, has data that is waiting to be read on it, rather than you going to each socket, and peeking into it to see if it has more data ready. If the OS determines five times that the socket has data to be read, and it did not get a chance to notify you yet, it will not tell you five times, it will only tell you once. You get the event, 'socket X is ready to be read'. You do not get all of the prior events about that socket. DBMS_ALERT works in the same exact fashion.

Returning to our simple example from above, we would run the snippet of code that registers its interest in an event, and calls the WAITONE routine to wait for this event. In another session, we will execute:

```
tkyte@TKYTE816> begin
  2   for i in 1 .. 10 loop
  3      dbms_alert.signal( 'MyAlert', 'Message ' || i );
  4   end loop;
  5   end;
  6   /

PL/SQL procedure successfully completed.

tkyte@TKYTE816> commit;

Commit complete.
```

In the other window, we will see the feedback:

```
Msg from event is Message 10

PL/SQL procedure successfully completed.
```

Only the very last message we signaled will get out – the intervening messages will never be seen. You must be aware the DBMS_ALERT will, by design, drop messages by a session. It is not a method to deliver a sequence of messages, it is purely a signaling mechanism. It gives you the ability to tell a client application 'something has happened'. If you rely on each and every event you ever signal to be received by all sessions, you will be disappointed (and most likely have a bug in your code on your hands).

Again, DBMS_JOB can be used to some extent to resolve this issue if it is paramount for each event to be signaled. However, at this point, an alternate technology comes to mind. Advanced queues, (a topic outside the scope of this book), can be used to satisfy that requirement in a much better fashion.

Many Calls to Signal by Many Sessions before a Wait Routine is Called

This is the last question; what happens if more than one session signals an alert after I registered interest in it, but before I've called one of the wait routines? Same question, only what happens when more than one session signals an alert between my calls to wait? The answer is the same as when a single session makes many calls to DBMS_ALERT.SIGNAL. Only the *last* event is remembered, and signaled out. You can see this by placing a PAUSE in the simple SQL*PLUS script we have been using so that it reads like this:

```
begin
    dbms_alert.register( 'MyAlert' );
end;
/
pause
```

Now, in some other sessions, call the DBMS_ALERT.SIGNAL with unique messages (so you can distinguish them) and commit each message. For example, modify our simple loop from above as follows:

```
tkyte@TKYTE816> begin
  2    for i in 1 .. 10 loop
  3        dbms_alert.signal( 'MyAlert', 'Message ' || i );
  4        commit;
  5    end loop;
  6  end;
  7  /
PL/SQL procedure successfully completed.
```

After you do that and return to this original session, simply hit the *Enter* key, and the block of code that calls WAITONE will execute. Since the alert we are waiting on has been signaled already, this block of code will return immediately, and will show us we received the *last* message that was signaled by this alert. All of the other intervening messages from the other sessions are lost, by design.

Summary

The DBMS_ALERT package is suitable for those cases where you wish to notify a large audience of interested clients about events in the database. These named events should be signaled by as few sessions as possible, due to inherent serialization issues with DBMS_ALERT. Since messages will by design be 'lost', DBMS_ALERT is suitable as an *event* notification process. You can use it to notify an interested client that data in a table T has changed for example, but to try and use it to notify these clients of the changes of individual rows in T would not work (due to the fact that only the 'last' message is saved). DBMS_ALERT is a very simple package to use and requires little to no set up.

DBMS_PIPE

DBMS_PIPE is a package supplied to allow two sessions to communicate with each other. It is an inter-process communication device. One session can write a 'message' on a pipe, and another session can 'read' this message. In UNIX, the same concept exists in the form of a named pipe in the operating system. With named pipes, we can allow one process to write data to another process.

The DBMS_PIPE package, unlike DBMS_ALERT, is a 'real time' package. As soon as you call the SEND_MESSAGE function, the message is sent. It does not wait for a COMMIT; it is not transactional. This makes DBMS_PIPE suitable for cases where DBMS_ALERT is not (and vice-versa). We can use DBMS_PIPE to allow two sessions to have a conversation (not something we can do with DBMS_ALERT). Session one could ask session two to perform some operation. Session two could do it, and return the results to session one. For example, assume session two is a C program that can read a thermometer attached to the serial port of the computer it is running on, and return the temperature to session one. Session one needs to record in a database table the current temperature. It can send a 'give me the temperature' message to session two, which would find out what this is, and write the answer back to session one. Session one and session two may or may not be on the same computer – all we know is that they are both connected to the database. I am using the database much like I might use a TCP/IP network to perform communication between two processes. In the case of DBMS_PIPE however, I do not need to know a hostname and a port number to connect to, like you would with TCP/IP – just the name of the database pipe upon which to write my request.

There are two types of pipes available in the database – **public** and **private**. A public pipe can either be created explicitly via a call to CREATE_PIPE, or you may just implicitly create one upon sending a message on it. The major difference between an explicit and implicit pipe is that the pipe created via the CREATE_PIPE call should be removed by your application when it is done using it, whereas the implicit pipe will age out of the SGA after it hasn't been accessed for a while. A public pipe is set up such that *any* session, which has access to the DBMS_PIPE package can read and write messages on the pipe. Therefore, public pipes are not suitable for sensitive or even just 'important' data. Since pipes are typically used to perform a conversation of sorts, and a public pipe allows anyone to read or write this conversation, a malicious user could either remove messages from your pipe, or add additional 'garbage' messages onto your pipe. Either action would have the effect of breaking the conversation or protocol between the sessions. For this reason, most applications will use a private pipe.

Private pipes may be read or written, only by sessions that operate under the effective user ID of the *owner* of the pipe and the special users SYS and INTERNAL. This means *only* definer rights (see the Chapter 23, *Invoker and Definer Rights*) stored procedures owned by the owner of the pipe or sessions logged in as the owner of the pipe, SYS, or INTERNAL can read or write on this pipe. This significantly enhances the reliability of pipes as no other session or piece of code can corrupt or intercept your protocol.

A pipe is an object that will live in the SGA of your Oracle instance. It is not a disk-based mechanism at all. Data in a pipe will not survive a shutdown and startup – any information in this pipe at shutdown will be flushed, and will not be in the pipe again upon startup.

The most common usage of pipes is to build your own customized services or servers. Prior to the introduction of external procedures in Oracle 8.0, this was the only way to implement a stored procedure in a language other than PL/SQL. You would create a 'pipe' server. In fact, ConText (the precursor to interMedia text) was implemented using database pipes in Oracle 7.3, onwards. Over time, some of its functionality was implemented via external procedures, but much of the indexing logic is still implemented via database pipes.

Due to the fact that any number of sessions can attempt to read off of a pipe, and any number may attempt to write on a given pipe, we must implement some logic to ensure that we can deliver messages to the correct session. If we are going to create our own customized service (for example the thermometer demonstration from earlier) and add it to the database, we must make sure that the answer for session A's question gets to session A, and not session B. In order to satisfy that very typical requirement, we generally write our requests in one message onto a pipe with a well-known name, and include in this message, a unique name of a pipe we expect to read our response on. We can show this in the following figure:

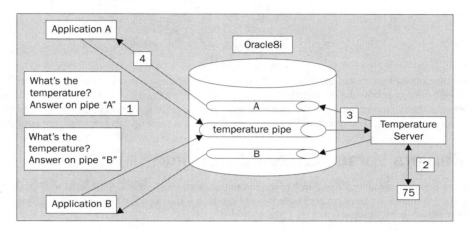

- ❑ **Step 1** – Session A will write it's request, 'What is the temperature? Answer on pipe A ' onto the well-known pipe named 'temperature pipe'. At the same time, other sessions may be doing the same thing. Each message will be queued into the pipe in a 'first in, first out' fashion.

- ❑ **Step 2** – The temperature server will read a single message out of the pipe, and query whatever service it is providing access to.

- ❑ **Step 3** – The temperature server will use the unique pipe name, which the session requesting the information wrote onto the pipe, to write a response (pipe A in this example). We use an implicit queue for this response (so the response pipe disappears right after we are done). If we planned on making many such calls, we would want to use an explicitly created pipe to keep it in the SGA during our session (but we would have to remember to clean it out upon logout!).

- ❑ **Step 4** – Session A reads the response back from the pipe it told the temperature server to write the answer on.

The same sequence of events would take place for Session B. The temperature server would read its request, query the temperature, look at the message to find the name of the pipe to answer on, and write the response back.

One of the interesting aspects of database pipes is that many sessions can *read* from the pipe. Any given message placed onto the pipe will be read by exactly one session, but many sessions can be reading at the same time. This allows us to 'scale' up the above picture. In the above, it is obvious we could have many sessions requesting data from the 'temperature server', and it would serially process them one after the other. There is nothing stopping us from starting more than one temperature server as thus:

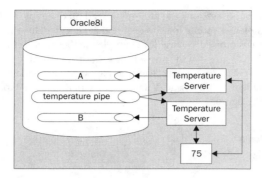

We can now service two concurrent requests. If we started five of them, we could do five at a time. This is similar to connection pooling, or how the multi-threaded server in Oracle itself works. We have a pool of processes ready to do work, and the maximum amount of concurrent work we can do at any point in time is dictated by the number of processes we start up. This aspect of database pipes allows us to scale up this particular implementation easily.

Pipe Servers versus External Routines

Oracle8 release 8.0 introduced the ability to implement a stored procedure in C directly, and Oracle8i gave us the ability to implement the stored procedure in Java. Given this, is the need for DBMS_PIPE and 'pipe servers' gone? The short answer is *no*, absolutely not.

When we covered external routines, we described their architecture. C-based external routines for example, execute in an address space separate from the PL/SQL stored procedure. There exists a one-to-one mapping between the number of sessions concurrently using an external procedure, and the number of separate address spaces created. That is, if 50 sessions concurrently call the external routine, there will be 50 EXTPROC processes or threads at least. C-based external routines are architected in a manner similar to the dedicated server mode of Oracle. Just as Oracle will create a dedicated server for each concurrent session, it will also create an EXTPROC instance for every concurrent external routine call. Java external routines are executed in much the same fashion – one-to-one. For every session using a Java external routine, there will be a separate JVM instance running in the server with its own state and resources.

A pipe server on the other hand works like the MTS architecture does in Oracle. You create a pool of shared resources (start up N pipe servers), and they will service the requests. If more requests come in concurrently than can be handled, the requests will be queued. This is very analogous to the MTS mode of Oracle, whereby requests will be queued in the SGA, and dequeued by a shared server as soon as they completed processing the prior request they were working on. The temperature example we walked through earlier is a good example of this. The first diagram depicts a single pipe server running; one temperature at a time will be retrieved and returned to a client. The second diagram depicts two pipe servers running to service all of the requests. Never more than two concurrent requests will be processed. The thermometer will never have more than two clients hitting it.

The reason this is important is that it gives us a great capability to limit concurrent accesses to this shared resource. If we used external routines, and 50 sessions simultaneously requested the temperature, they may very well 'crash' the thermometer if it was not designed to scale up to so many requests. Replace the thermometer with many other shared resources, and you may find the same problem arises. It can handle a couple of concurrent requests, but if you tried to hit it with many simultaneous requests, either it would fail, or performance would suffer to the point of making it non-functional.

Another reason why a pipe server might make sense is in accessing some shared resource that takes a long time to 'connect to'. For example, I worked on a project a couple of years ago at a large university. They needed access to some mainframe transactions (then needed to call up to a mainframe to get some student information). The initial connection to the mainframe might take 30 to 60 seconds to complete but after that, it was very fast (as long as we didn't overload the mainframe with tons of concurrent requests). Using a pipe server, we were able to initiate the connection to the server *once*, when the pipe server started up. This single pipe server would run for days using that initial connection. Using an external routine we would have to initiate the connect once per database session. An implementation that used external routines would quite simply not work in this environment due to the high startup costs associated with the mainframe connection. The pipe server not only gave them the ability to limit the number of concurrent mainframe requests, but it also provided the ability to do the expensive mainframe connection *once*, and then reuse this connection many hundreds of thousands of times.

If you are familiar with the reasoning behind using connection pooling software in a 3-tier environment, you are already familiar with why you would want to use pipes in certain circumstances. They provide the ability to reuse the outcome of a long running operation (the connection to the database in the case of the connection pooling software) over an over, and they give you the ability to limit the amount of resources you consume concurrently (the size of your connection pool).

One last difference between a pipe server and external routines is where the pipe server can run. Suppose in the temperature server example, the database server was executing on Windows. The temperature probe is located on a UNIX machine. The only object libraries available to access it are on UNIX. Since a pipe server is just a client of the database like any other client, we can code it, compile it, and run it on UNIX. The pipe server need not be on the same machine, or even platform, as the database itself. An external routine on the other hand, must execute on the same machine with the database server itself – they cannot execute on remote machines. Therefore, a pipe server can be used in circumstances where an external routine cannot.

Online Example

On the Apress web site (http://www.apress.com), you'll find an example of a small pipe server. It answers the frequently asked question, 'How can I run a host command from PL/SQL?' With the addition of Java to the database and C external procedures, we could easily implement a host command function with either technology. However, what if I do not have access to a C compiler, or I don't have the Java component of the database available – what then? The example shows how we could very simply setup a small 'pipe server' that can do host commands using nothing more than SQL*PLUS and the csh scripting language. It is fairly simple, consisting of only a few lines of csh, and even fewer of PL/SQL. It shows much of the power of database pipes though, and should give you some ideas for other interesting implementations.

Summary

Database pipes are a powerful feature of the Oracle database that allow for any two sessions to have a 'conversation' with each other. Modeled after pipes in UNIX, they allow you to develop your own protocol for sending and receiving messages. The small example available on the Apress web site demonstrates how easy it can be to create a 'pipe server', an external process that receives requests from database sessions and does something 'special' on their behalf. Database pipes are not transactional, differentiating them from database alerts, but it is this non-transactional feature that makes them so useful in many cases. Amongst many others, I have used database pipes to add features to the database such as:

❑ Sending e-mail.

❑ Printing files.

❑ Integrating non-Oracle, non-SQL data sources.

❑ Implementing the equivalent of DBMS_LOB.LOADFROMFILE for LONGs and LONG RAWs.

DBMS_APPLICATION_INFO

This is one of the most under-utilized features in the set of supplied packages, yet I cannot think of a single application that would not benefit from its use. Have you ever asked yourself:

❑   I wonder what that session is doing, what form is it running, what code module is executing?

❑   I wonder how far along that stored procedure is?

❑   I wonder how far along that batch job is?

❑   I wonder what bind variable values were being used on that query?

DBMS_APPLICATION_INFO is the package that can be used to answer all of these questions, and more. It allows us to set up to three columns in our row of the V$SESSION table – the CLIENT_INFO, ACTION, and MODULE columns. It provides functions not only to set these values, but also to return them. Further, there is a parameter to the built-in USERENV or SYS_CONTEXT function that will allow us to access the CLIENT_INFO column easily in any query. I can SELECT USERENV('CLIENT_INFO') FROM DUAL for example, or use WHERE SOME_COLUMN = SYS_CONTEXT('USERENV', 'CLIENT_INFO') in my queries. The values we set in the V$ tables are immediately visible. We do not need to commit them to 'see' them, making them very useful for communicating with the 'outside'. Lastly, it allows us to set values in the dynamic performance view V$SESSION_LONGOPS (**LONG OP**eration**S**) as well – useful for recording the progress of long running jobs.

Many Oracle tools, such as SQL*PLUS, already make use of this facility. For example, I have a script, SHOWSQL.SQL, which I use to see what SQL people are currently running in the database (this is available on the Apress web site at http://www.apress.com). Part of this script dumps out the V$SESSION table for all entries where CLIENT_INFO, MODULE, or ACTION is NOT NULL. Whenever I run it, I see, for example:

```
USERNAME              MODULE           ACTION           CLIENT_INFO
--------------------  ---------------  ---------------  ----------------------
OPS$TKYTE(107,19225)  01@ showsql.sql
OPS$TKYTE(22,50901)   SQL*Plus
```

The first line shows my current session running the script SHOWSQL.SQL with a level of 01. This means that this script has not called another script yet. If I were to create a script TEST.SQL with just @SHOWSQL in it, then SQL*PLUS would set 02 in front of SHOWSQL to show that it is nested. The second line shows another SQL*PLUS session. It is not running any scripts right now (it may have been executing a command entered on the command line directly). If you add the appropriate calls to DBMS_APPLICATION_INFO to your application, you can do the same thing, enhancing the abilities of you and your DBA to monitor your application.

The calls to set these values in the V$SESSION table are simply:

❑   SET_MODULE – This API call allows you to set both the MODULE, and ACTION columns in V$SESSION. The name of the module is limited to 48 bytes and the value of the action is limited to 32 bytes. The name of the module would typically be your application name. The initial action might be something like STARTUP or INITIALIZING to indicate the program is just starting.

❑   SET_ACTION – This API calls allows you to set the ACTION column in V$SESSION. ACTION should be a descriptive term to let you know where in your program you are. You might set action to be the name of the currently active form in a forms application for example, or the name of a subroutine in a Pro*C or PL/SQL routine.

❑   SET_CLIENT_INFO – This API call allows you to store up to 64 bytes of any sort of application specification information you might wish to keep. A common use of this is to parameterize views (see below) and queries.

There are corresponding API calls to read this information back out as well. In addition to setting values in the V$SESSION table, this package allows you to set information in the V$SESSION_LONGOPS dynamic performance view. This view allows you to store more than one row of information in various columns. We will take an in depth look at this functionality in a moment.

Using the Client Info

The SET_CLIENT_INFO call gives us the ability to not only set a value in a column of the V$SESSION table, but also gives us access to that variable via the built-in function userenv (Oracle 7.3 and up) or sys_context (preferred function in Oracle 8i and up). For example, with this we can create a **parameterized view**, a view whose results depend on the value in the CLIENT_INFO field. The following example demonstrates this concept:

```
scott@TKYTE816> exec dbms_application_info.set_client_info('KING');

PL/SQL procedure successfully completed.

scott@TKYTE816> select userenv('CLIENT_INFO') from dual;

USERENV('CLIENT_INFO')
------------------------------------
KING
```

```
scott@TKYTE816> select sys_context('userenv','client_info')from dual;

SYS_CONTEXT('USERENV','CLIENT_INFO')
------------------------------------
KING

scott@TKYTE816> create or replace view
  2   emp_view
  3   as
  4   select ename, empno
  5     from emp
  6    where ename = sys_context( 'userenv', 'client_info');

View created.

scott@TKYTE816> select * from emp_view;

ENAME           EMPNO
---------- ----------
KING             7839

scott@TKYTE816> exec dbms_application_info.set_client_info('BLAKE');

PL/SQL procedure successfully completed.

scott@TKYTE816> select * from emp_view;

ENAME           EMPNO
---------- ----------
BLAKE            7698
```

As you can see, we can set this value and we can also easily use it in queries where we could use a constant. This allows us to create complex views with predicates that get their values at run-time. One of the issues with views can be in the area of predicate merging. If the optimizer were able to 'merge' the predicate into the view definition, it would run really fast. If not, it runs really slow. This feature, using the client info, allows us to 'merge' the predicate ahead of time when the optimizer cannot. The application developer must set the value and just SELECT * from the view. Then, the 'right' data will come out.

Another place where I make use of this functionality is to store the bind variables I am using in my query (and other pieces of information), so I can see what my procedures are doing very quickly. For example, if you have a long running process you might instrument it like this:

```
tkyte@TKYTE816> declare
  2       l_owner varchar2(30) default 'SYS';
  3       l_cnt   number default 0;
  4   begin
  5       dbms_application_info.set_client_info( 'owner='||l_owner );
  6
  7       for x in ( select * from all_objects where owner = l_owner )
  8       loop
  9           l_cnt := l_cnt+1;
 10           dbms_application_info.set_action( 'processing row ' || l_cnt );
 11       end loop;
 12   end;
 13   /
```

Now, using that `SHOWSQL.SQL` script once again, I can see:

```
tkyte@TKYTE816> @showsql

USERNAME                              SID   SERIAL# PROCESS   STATUS
------------------------------ ---------- ---------- --------- ----------
TKYTE                                   8       206 780:716   ACTIVE
TKYTE                                  11       635 1004:1144 ACTIVE
--------------------
TKYTE(11,635) ospid = 1004:1144 program = SQLPLUS.EXE
Saturday  15:59  Saturday  16:15
SELECT *   FROM ALL_OBJECTS  WHERE OWNER = :b1

USERNAME         MODULE           ACTION           CLIENT_INFO
---------------- ---------------- ---------------- ---------------------------
TKYTE(8,206)     01@ showsql.sql
TKYTE(11,635)    SQL*Plus         processing row   owner=SYS
                                  5393
```

Session `(11,635)` is running the query `SELECT * FROM ALL_OBJECTS WHERE OWNER = :B1`. The report also shows me that `owner=SYS` in this case, and at the point in time we were looking at it, it had already processed `5,393` rows. In the next section, we'll see how using `SESSION LONGOPS` can take this a step further, if you know how many operations or steps your procedure will be performing.

Using V$SESSION_LONGOPS

Many operations in the database may take a considerable amount of time. Parallel execution, Recovery Manager, large sorts, loads, and so on fall into this category. These long running operations take advantage of their ability to set values in the dynamic performance view, `V$SESSION_LONGOPS` to let us know how far along in their work they are, and so can your applications. This view displays the status of various database operations that run for longer than six seconds. That is, functions the database performs that the Oracle developers felt would normally take longer than six seconds have been instrumented to populate the `V$SESSION_LONGOPS` view. This does not mean anything that takes longer than six seconds will automatically appear in this view. These operations currently include many backup and recovery functions, statistics gathering, and query execution. More operations are added for every Oracle release.

Changes made to this view are immediately visible to other sessions, without the need to commit your transaction. For any process that updates this view, you will be able to monitor their progress from another session by querying the `V$SESSION_LONGOPS` view. You too have the ability to populate rows in this view, typically one row, but you may use others if you like.

The API to set the values in this view is defined as:

```
PROCEDURE SET_SESSION_LONGOPS
 Argument Name                  Type                    In/Out Default?
 ------------------------------ ----------------------- ------ --------
 RINDEX                         BINARY_INTEGER          IN/OUT
 SLNO                           BINARY_INTEGER          IN/OUT
 OP_NAME                        VARCHAR2                IN     DEFAULT
 TARGET                         BINARY_INTEGER          IN     DEFAULT
 CONTEXT                        BINARY_INTEGER          IN     DEFAULT
 SOFAR                          NUMBER                  IN     DEFAULT
 TOTALWORK                      NUMBER                  IN     DEFAULT
 TARGET_DESC                    VARCHAR2                IN     DEFAULT
 UNITS                          VARCHAR2                IN     DEFAULT
```

with the following meanings:

- ❏ RINDEX – Tells the server which row to modify in the V$SESSION_LONGOPS view. If you set this value to DBMS_APPLICATION_INFO.SET_SESSION_LONGOPS_NOHINT, a new row will be allocated in this view for you, and the index of this row will be returned in RINDEX. Subsequent calls to SET_SESSION_LONGOPS with the same value for RINDEX will update this already existing row.

- ❏ SLNO – An internal value. You should initially pass a Null number in, and ignore its value otherwise. You should pass the same value in with each call.

- ❏ OP_NAME – The name of the long running process. It is limited to 64 bytes in size, and should be set to some string that will be easily identified and provides some meaning to you.

- ❏ TARGET – Typically used to hold the object ID that is the target of the long running operation (for example, the object ID of the table being loaded). You may supply any number you wish here, or leave it Null.

- ❏ CONTEXT – A user-defined number. This number would have meaning only to you. It is simply any number you wish to store.

- ❏ SOFAR – This is defined as any number you want to store, but if you make this number be some percentage or indicator of the amount of work done, the database will attempt to estimate your time to completion for you. For example, if you have 25 things to do, and they all take more or less the same amount of time, you could set SOFAR to the number of things done so far, and then set the next parameter TOTALWORK. The server will figure out how long it took you to get to where you are, and estimate how long it will take you to complete.

- ❏ TOTALWORK – This is defined as any number you want to store, but the same caveat for SOFAR applies here. If SOFAR is a percentage of TOTALWORK, representing your progress, the server will compute the time remaining to complete your task.

- ❏ TARGET_DESC – This is used to describe the contents of the TARGET input from above. If the TARGET actually contained an object ID, this might contain the object name for that object ID.

- ❏ UNITS – A descriptive term that categorizes what SOFAR and TOTALWORK are measured in. Units might be 'files', 'iterations', or 'calls' for example.

These are the values you can set. When you look at the V$SESSION_LONGOPS view, you'll see it has many more columns than these however:

```
ops$tkyte@ORA8I.WORLD> desc v$session_longops
 Name                                      Null?    Type
 ----------------------------------------- -------- ----------------------
 SID                                                NUMBER
 SERIAL#                                            NUMBER
 OPNAME                                             VARCHAR2(64) **
 TARGET                                             VARCHAR2(64) **
 TARGET_DESC                                        VARCHAR2(32) **
 SOFAR                                              NUMBER **
 TOTALWORK                                          NUMBER **
 UNITS                                              VARCHAR2(32) **
 START_TIME                                         DATE
 LAST_UPDATE_TIME                                   DATE
 TIME_REMAINING                                     NUMBER
```

ELAPSED_SECONDS	NUMBER
CONTEXT	NUMBER **
MESSAGE	VARCHAR2(512)
USERNAME	VARCHAR2(30)
SQL_ADDRESS	RAW(4)
SQL_HASH_VALUE	NUMBER
QCSID	NUMBER

*The columns marked with * * are the ones you have control over, and can set.*

The meanings are as follows:

❑   The SID and SERIAL# columns are used to join back to V$SESSION, to pick up the session information.

❑   The START_TIME column marks the time this record was created (typically your first call to DBMS_APPLICATION_INFO.SET_SESSION_LONGOPS).

❑   The LAST_UPDATE_TIME column represents the time of your last call to SET_SESSION_LONGOPS.

❑   The TIME_REMAINING is an estimate in seconds of the time to completion. It is equal to ROUND(ELAPSED_SECONDS*((TOTALWORK/SOFAR)-1)).

❑   The ELAPSED_SECONDS column is the time in seconds since the start of the long running operation, and the last update time.

❑   The MESSAGE column is a derived column. It concatenates together pieces of the OPNAME, TARGET_DESC, TARGET, SOFAR, TOTALWORK, and UNITS column to make a readable description of the work in process.

❑   The USERNAME is the name of the user this process is executing under.

❑   The SQL_ADDRESS and SQL_HASH_VALUE may be used to look into V$SQLAREA to see what SQL statement this process was last executing.

❑   The QCSID is used with parallel query. It would be the session of the parallel coordinator.

So, what can you expect from this particular view? A small example will clearly show what it can provide for you. In one session, if you run a block of code such as:

```
tkyte@TKYTE816> declare
  2      l_nohint number default
            dbms_application_info.set_session_longops_nohint;
  3      l_rindex number default l_nohint;
  4      l_slno   number;
  5  begin
  6      for i in 1 .. 25
  7      loop
  8          dbms_lock.sleep(2);
  9          dbms_application_info.set_session_longops
 10          ( rindex => l_rindex,
 11            slno   => l_slno,
 12  op_name => 'my long running operation',
```

```
 13              target      =>  1234,
 14              target_desc =>  '1234 is my target',
 15              context     =>  0,
 16              sofar       =>  i,
 17              totalwork   =>  25,
 18              units       =>  'loops'
 19          );
 20      end loop;
 21  end;
 22  /
```

This is a long running operation that will take 50 seconds to complete (the DBMS_LOCK.SLEEP just sleeps for two seconds). In another session, we can monitor this session via the query below (see the Chapter 23 on *Invoker and Definer Rights* for the definition of the PRINT_TABLE utility used in this code):

```
tkyte@TKYTE816> begin
  2      print_table( 'select b.*
  3                     from v$session a, v$session_longops b
  4                    where a.sid = b.sid
  5                      and a.serial# = b.serial#' );
  6  end;
  7  /
SID                             : 11
SERIAL#                         : 635
OPNAME                          : my long running operation
TARGET                          : 1234
TARGET_DESC                     : 1234 is my target
SOFAR                           : 2
TOTALWORK                       : 25
UNITS                           : loops
START_TIME                      : 28-apr-2001 16:02:46
LAST_UPDATE_TIME                : 28-apr-2001 16:02:46
TIME_REMAINING                  : 0
ELAPSED_SECONDS                 : 0
CONTEXT                         : 0
MESSAGE                         : my long running operation: 1234 is my target
                                  1234: 2 out of 25 loops done
USERNAME                        : TKYTE
SQL_ADDRESS                     : 036C3758
SQL_HASH_VALUE                  : 1723303299
QCSID                           : 0
-----------------

PL/SQL procedure successfully completed.

ops$tkyte@ORA8I.WORLD> /
SID                             : 11
SERIAL#                         : 635
OPNAME                          : my long running operation
TARGET                          : 1234
TARGET_DESC                     : 1234 is my target
SOFAR                           : 6
TOTALWORK                       : 25
UNITS                           : loops
START_TIME                      : 28-apr-2001 16:02:46
LAST_UPDATE_TIME                : 28-apr-2001 16:02:55
TIME_REMAINING                  : 29
ELAPSED_SECONDS                 : 9
```

```
        CONTEXT                 : 0
        MESSAGE                 : my long running operation: 1234 is my target
                                  1234: 6 out of 25 loops done
        USERNAME                : TKYTE
        SQL_ADDRESS             : 036C3758
        SQL_HASH_VALUE          : 1723303299
        QCSID                   : 0
        -----------------

PL/SQL procedure successfully completed.

ops$tkyte@ORA8I.WORLD> /
        SID                     : 11
        SERIAL#                 : 635
        OPNAME                  : my long running operation
        TARGET                  : 1234
        TARGET_DESC             : 1234 is my target
        SOFAR                   : 10
        TOTALWORK               : 25
        UNITS                   : loops
        START_TIME              : 28-apr-2001 16:02:46
        LAST_UPDATE_TIME        : 28-apr-2001 16:03:04
        TIME_REMAINING          : 27
        ELAPSED_SECONDS         : 18
        CONTEXT                 : 0
        MESSAGE                 : my long running operation: 1234 is my target
                                  1234: 10 out of 25 loops done
        USERNAME                : TKYTE
        SQL_ADDRESS             : 036C3758
        SQL_HASH_VALUE          : 1723303299
        QCSID                   : 0
        -----------------

PL/SQL procedure successfully completed.
```

The first question you might ask is, 'why did I join V$SESSION_LONGOPS to V$SESSION if I did not actually select any information from V$SESSION?' This is because the view V$SESSION_LONGOPS will contain values from rows of current, as well as legacy sessions. This view is not 'emptied out' when you log out. The data you left there remains until some other session comes along, and reuses your slot. Therefore, to see long operations information for current sessions only, you want to join or use a sub-query to get current sessions only.

As you can see from the rather simple example, this information could be quite invaluable to you and your DBA, as far as monitoring long running stored procedures, batch jobs, reports, and so on, goes. A little bit of instrumentation can save a lot of guesswork in production. Rather than trying to 'guess' where a job might be and how long it might take to complete, you can get an accurate view of where it is, and an educated guess as to the length of time it will take to complete.

Summary

Here, we have looked at the DBMS_APPLICATION_INFO package, an often overlooked and under-utilized package. Every application can, and should, make use of this particular package, just to register itself in the database so the DBA, or anyone monitoring the system, can tell what applications are using it. For any process that takes more than a few seconds, the use of V$SESSION_LONGOPS is critical. To show that a process is not 'hanging' but is moving along at a steady pace, this feature is the only way to go. Oracle Enterprise Manager (OEM), and many third party tools, are aware of these views and will automatically integrate your information into their display.

DBMS_JAVA

The DBMS_JAVA package is somewhat of an enigma. It is a PL/SQL package but it is not documented in the *Supplied PL/SQL Packages Reference* guide. It is designed to support Java in the database, so you might expect to find it in the *Supplied Java Packages Reference* guide (but you won't). It is actually documented in the *Oracle8i Java Developer's Guide.* We've used it many times in this book already without really going through it, so here we will cover the procedures I use within this package, how to use them, and what they do.

The DBMS_JAVA package has almost 60 procedures and functions, only a very small handful of which are useful to us as developers. The bulk of this package is in support of debuggers (not for us to debug with, but for others to write debuggers for us), various internal convenience routines, and the export/import utilities. We will skip these functions and procedures altogether.

LONGNAME and SHORTNAME

These are utility routines to convert between a 'short' 30-character identifier (all Oracle identifiers are 30 characters or less), and the 'long' Java name. If you look in the data dictionary, you will typically find a 'hashed' name for the Java classes that are loaded into the database. This is because they come with really long names, which the server cannot deal with. These two routines allow you to see what the 'real' name is, given a short name (OBJECT_NAME column in USER_OBJECTS), and what the short name would be given a long name. Here is an example of the usage of each when logged in as the user SYS (who happens to own lots of Java code, if you have Java installed in the database):

```
sys@TKYTE816> column long_nm format a30 word_wrapped
sys@TKYTE816> column short_nm format a30

sys@TKYTE816> select dbms_java.longname(object_name) long_nm,
  2           dbms_java.shortname(dbms_java.longname(object_name)) short_nm
  3    from user_objects where object_type = 'JAVA CLASS'
  4      and rownum < 11
  5  /

LONG_NM                          SHORT_NM
------------------------------   ------------------------------
com/visigenic/vbroker/ir/Const   /1001a851_ConstantDefImpl
antDefImpl

oracle/sqlj/runtime/OraCustomD   /10076b23_OraCustomDatumClosur
atumClosure

com/visigenic/vbroker/intercep   /10322588_HandlerRegistryHelpe
tor/HandlerRegistryHelper
...

10 rows selected.
```

As you can see, using LONGNAME on the OBJECT NAME turns it into the original class name for the Java class. If we take this long name and pass it through SHORTNAME, we get back the hashed-shortened name Oracle uses internally.

Setting Compiler Options

You may specify most compiler options for the Java compiler in the database, in one of two places; the command line when using loadjava, or in the JAVA$OPTIONS database table. A setting on the command line will always override the JAVA$OPTIONS table. This only applies if you use the Oracle Java compiler in the database, of course. If you use a standalone Java compiler outside of the database (JDeveloper perhaps), you will set compiler options in that environment.

There are three compiler options we may set, and they all relate to the SQLJ compiler (a pre-compiler for Java, converts embedded SQL statements into JDBC calls) built-in to the database. They are:

Option	Meaning	Values
ONLINE	Whether type checking is done at compile-time (online), or run-time.	**True**/False
DEBUG	Whether the Java code is compiled with debugging enabled. Equivalent to javac -g in a command line environment.	**True**e/False
ENCODING	Identifies the source file encoding for the compiler.	**Latin1** is the default

*The values in **bold** are the default settings.*

We'll demonstrate the use of DBMS_JAVA to set compiler options using the online SQLJ pre-compiler option. Normally, this option defaults to True, and will cause the SQLJ pre-compiler to attempt to perform semantic checking on our SQLJ code. What this means is that the SQLJ pre-compiler would normally verify each and every referenced database object exists, that the host variable bind types match, and so on. If you would like this checking to be performed at run-time (perhaps the tables your SQLJ code will access are not yet created, but you would like to install your code cleanly), we can use the DBMS_JAVA.SET_COMPILER_OPTIONS routine to disable this type checking.

As an example, we'll use this snippet of code. It attempts to INSERT into a table that does not exist in the database:

```
tkyte@TKYTE816> create or replace and compile
  2  java source named "bad_code"
  3  as
  4  import java.sql.SQLException;
  5
  6  public class bad_code extends Object
  7  {
  8  public static void wont_work() throws SQLException
  9  {
 10      #sql {
 11          insert into non_existent_table values ( 1 )
 12      };
 13  }
 14  }
 15  /

Java created.

tkyte@TKYTE816> show errors java source "bad_code"
Errors for JAVA SOURCE bad_code:

LINE/COL ERROR
-------- -----------------------------------------------------------------
0/0      bad_code:7: Warning: Database issued an error: PLS-00201:
         identifier 'NON_EXISTENT_TABLE' must be declared

0/0      insert into non_existent_table values ( 1 )
0/0      ^^^^^^^^^^^^^^^^^^^^^^
0/0      ;
0/0      #sql {
0/0      ^
0/0      Info: 1 warnings
```

Now, we'll set the compiler option ONLINE to FALSE. In order to do this, we have to disconnect and connect again. There is an issue whereby the Java run-time will look for the existence of the JAVA$OPTIONS table once it starts up. If this table does not exist, it never attempts to read it again in that session. The DBMS_JAVA.SET_COMPILER_OPTION routine will create this table for us, but only if it is invoked prior to the Java run-time being started. So, we need a 'clean' session for this to work.

In the following example, we establish a new session, and then see that the JAVA$OPTIONS table does not exist. We'll set the compiler option, and see that the table has been created for us. Lastly, we'll create the same Java routine as above, and see that it compiles without warnings this time, due to the compiler option setting:

```
tkyte@TKYTE816> disconnect
Disconnected from Oracle8i Enterprise Edition Release 8.1.6.0.0 - Production
With the Partitioning option
JServer Release 8.1.6.0.0 - Production

tkyte@TKYTE816> connect tkyte/tkyte
Connected.
tkyte@TKYTE816> column value format a10
tkyte@TKYTE816> column what format a10

tkyte@TKYTE816> select * from java$options;
select * from java$options
              *
ERROR at line 1:
ORA-00942: table or view does not exist

tkyte@TKYTE816> begin
  2            dbms_java.set_compiler_option
  3            ( what       => 'bad_code',
  4              optionName => 'online',
  5              value      => 'false' );
  6  end;
  7  /

PL/SQL procedure successfully completed.

tkyte@TKYTE816> select * from java$options;

WHAT        OPT                  VALUE
---------- -------------------- ----------
bad_code   online               false

tkyte@TKYTE816> create or replace and compile
  2  java source named "bad_code"
  3  as
  4  import java.sql.SQLException;
  5
  6  public class bad_code extends Object
  7  {
  8  public static void wont_work() throws SQLException
  9  {
 10     #sql {
 11            insert into non_existent_table values ( 1 )
 12     };
 13  }
 14  }
 15  /

Java created.

tkyte@TKYTE816> show errors java source "bad_code"
No errors.
```

The SET_COMPILER_OPTION takes three inputs in this case:

- ❑ WHAT – A pattern to be matched against. Normally, Java programs would use packages and hence, the above name would be a.b.c.bad_code, not just bad_code. If you want to set an option for a package a.b.c, you may. Then, anything that matched a.b.c would use this option, unless there was a more specific pattern, which matches this package. Given a WHAT of a.b.c, and a.b.c.bad_code, then a.b.c.bad_code would be used, since it matches more of the name.

- ❑ OPTIONNAME – One of the three values ONLINE, DEBUG, or ENCODING.

- ❑ VALUE – The value for that option.

There are two routines related to SET_COMPILER_OPTION. They are:

- ❑ GET_COMPILER_OPTION – This returns the value of a given compiler option, even if the value is defaulted.

- ❑ RESET_COMPILER_OPTION – This removes any row from the JAVA$OPTIONS table that matches the WHAT pattern, and the OPTIONNAME.

Here are examples of both in action. We'll begin by using GET_COMPILER_OPTION to see the value of the online option:

```
tkyte@TKYTE816> set serveroutput on
tkyte@TKYTE816> begin
  2          dbms_output.put_line
  3          ( dbms_java.get_compiler_option( what       => 'bad_code',
  4                                            optionName => 'online' ) );
  5   end;
  6   /
false

PL/SQL procedure successfully completed.
```

and now we'll reset it using RESET_COMPILER_OPTION:

```
tkyte@TKYTE816> begin
  2          dbms_java.reset_compiler_option( what       =>  'bad_code',
  3                                           optionName => 'online' );
  4   end;
  5   /

PL/SQL procedure successfully completed.
```

Now we'll see that GET_COMPILER_OPTION will always return us a value for the compiler option, even though the JAVA$OPTIONS table is now empty (the RESET deleted the row):

```
tkyte@TKYTE816> begin
  2          dbms_output.put_line
  3          ( dbms_java.get_compiler_option( what       => 'bad_code',
  4                                           optionName => 'online' ) );
  5   end;
  6   /
```

```
true

PL/SQL procedure successfully completed.

tkyte@TKYTE816> select * from java$options;

no rows selected
```

SET_OUTPUT

This procedure is a lot like the SQL*PLUS command SET SERVEROUTPUT ON. Just as you need to use it to enable DBMS_OUTPUT, we need to use DBMS_JAVA.SET_OUTPUT to enable the results of System.out.println and System.err.print calls to come to the screen in SQL*PLUS. If you fail to call:

```
SQL> set serveroutput on size 1000000
SQL> exec dbms_java.set_output( 1000000 )
```

before running a Java stored procedure in SQL*PLUS, you must be aware that any of its System.out.println messages will be written to a trace file in the directory specified by the USER_DUMP_DEST init.ora parameter on the server. This procedure is truly useful when debugging Java stored procedures, as you can put calls to System.out.println in the code, much as you would put DBMS_OUTPUT.PUT_LINE calls in your PL/SQL. Later, you can disable this in your Java code by redirecting System.out to the 'bit bucket'.

So, if you ever wondered where your System.out calls where going in a Java stored procedure, now you know. They were going to a trace file. Now you can cause that output to come to your screen in SQL*PLUS.

loadjava and dropjava

These functions provide PL/SQL APIs to perform the job of the command line utilities loadjava and dropjava. As you might expect with these internal routines, you do not need to specify a -u username/password, or specify the type of JDBC driver to use – you are already connected! These routines will load the Java objects into the currently logged in schema. The supplied routines are:

```
PROCEDURE loadjava(options varchar2)
PROCEDURE loadjava(options varchar2, resolver varchar2)
PROCEDURE dropjava(options varchar2)
```

We could use this to load the activation8i.zip file, which we also use in the UTL_SMTP section, and more information on JavaMail API can be found at http://java.sun.com/products/javamail/index.html. For example:

```
sys@TKYTE816> exec dbms_java.loadjava( '-r -v -f -noverify -synonym -g p
ublic c:\temp\activation8i.zip' )
initialization complete
loading  : com/sun/activation/registries/LineTokenizer
creating : com/sun/activation/registries/LineTokenizer
```

```
loading  : com/sun/activation/registries/MailcapEntry
creating : com/sun/activation/registries/MailcapEntry
loading  : com/sun/activation/registries/MailcapFile
creating : com/sun/activation/registries/MailcapFile
loading  : com/sun/activation/registries/MailcapParseException
creating : com/sun/activation/registries/MailcapParseException
...
```

Permission Procedures

These are strange ones indeed. Do a DESCRIBE on DBMS_JAVA in the database, and tell me if you see GRANT_PERMISSION in that package. You won't, although you know it must exist since you've seen me use it quite a few times. It does exist, as do a couple of other permission-related functions. We'll describe the GRANT_PERMISSION/REVOKE_PERMISSION here, and its usage. For complete details on using the permissions routines, and all of the options, refer to the *Oracle Java Developers Guide*. Chapter 5 in this manual, *Security for Oracle 8i Java Applications*, covers these functions.

In Oracle 8.1.5, the granularity of privileges in Java was very coarse. You either had JAVAUSERPRIV or JAVASYSPRIV, pretty much. This would be like having just RESOURCE and DBA roles in the database – in both cases these roles may offer too much functionality to the end users. With Oracle 8.1.6, the Java in the database supports the Java 2 security classes. Now we have very granular privileges we can grant and revoke, just like the database has for its privilege set. For a general discussion and overview of these permission classes, I'll refer you to this web page http://java.sun.com/j2se/1.3/docs/api/java/security/Permission.html.

So, the two main APIs we'll use here are GRANT_PERMISSION and REVOKE_PERMISSION. The question is, how do I find out what permissions I need? The easiest way is to install the Java, run it, and see what it tells you it needs. For example, I will refer you to the UTL_SMTP section. In there, I create the stored procedure SEND to send mail. I also show you the two grants we need to perform with GRANT_PERMISSION in order to get that to work. The way in which I discover exactly what those grants was to run SEND and see how it fails. For example:

```
tkyte@TKYTE816> set serveroutput on size 1000000
tkyte@TKYTE816> exec dbms_java.set_output( 1000000 )

PL/SQL procedure successfully completed.

tkyte@TKYTE816> declare
  2      ret_code number;
  3  begin
  4      ret_code := send(
  5                      p_from => 'me@here.com',
  6                      p_to => 'me@here.com',
  7                      p_cc => NULL,
  8                      p_bcc => NULL,
  9                      p_subject => 'Use the attached Zip file',
 10                      p_body => 'to send email with attachments....',
 11                      p_smtp_host => 'aria.us.oracle.com',
 12                      p_attachment_data => null,
 13                      p_attachment_type => null,
 14                      p_attachment_file_name => null );
 15      if ret_code = 1 then
```

```
16          dbms_output.put_line ('Successful sent message...');
17      else
18          dbms_output.put_line ('Failed to send message...');
19      end if;
20  end;
21  /
java.security.AccessControlException: the Permission (java.util.Property
Permission * read,write) has
not been granted by dbms_java.grant_permission to
SchemaProtectionDomain(TKYTE|PolicyTableProxy(TKYTE))
```

Now, that is about as clear as you can get. It is telling me that TKYTE needs the permission type java.util.PropertyPermission with * and read and write. This is how I knew I needed to execute:

```
sys@TKYTE816> begin
  2      dbms_java.grant_permission(
  3          grantee => 'TKYTE',
  4          permission_type => 'java.util.PropertyPermission',
  5          permission_name => '*',
  6          permission_action => 'read,write'
  7      );
```

After I did this, I discovered the error:

```
java.security.AccessControlException: the Permission (java.net.SocketPer
mission aria.us.oracle.com resolve) has not been granted by
dbms_java.grant_permission to
SchemaProtectionDomain(TKYTE|PolicyTableProxy(TKYTE))
```

and after granting that, it told me I needed CONNECT in addition to RESOLVE. This is how I knew to add:

```
  8      dbms_java.grant_permission(
  9          grantee => 'TKYTE',
 10          permission_type => 'java.net.SocketPermission',
 11          permission_name => '*',
 12          permission_action => 'connect,resolve'
 13      );
 14  end;
 15  /
```

to the privileges that this schema had. Note that I used * in the permission_name so I could actually resolve and connect to any host, not just my SMTP server.

Now, the opposite of GRANT_PERMISSION is REVOKE_PERMISSION. It operates exactly as you might think. If you pass it the same exact parameters you pass to GRANT_PERMISSION, it will revoke that privilege from the schema.

Summary

In this section, we covered using the DBMS_JAVA package to perform various operations for us. We started out by looking at how Oracle, which has a 30-character name limit, handles the very long names used in Java. It hashes a unique, 30-character name for each of the long Java names. The DBMS_JAVA package gives us a function to convert either a short name back into its corresponding long name, or to convert a long name into its short name representation.

Next we investigated using DBMS_JAVA to set, retrieve, and reset various Java compiler options. We saw how this feature uses the JAVA$OPTIONS table to permanently store default compiler options for us, and how we can use it to reset these values back to their defaults. Then we looked briefly at the SET_OUTPUT routine. This redirects the output generated by System.out.println Java calls to a SQL*PLUS or SVRMGRL session, much in the same way SET SERVEROUTPUT ON does for the PL/SQL routine DBMS_OUTPUT. We also saw how the DBMS_JAVA package provides an alternative method of loading Java source code, class files and jars into the database, via a stored procedure call in Oracle8i release 2 (version 8.1.6) and up. Lastly, we looked at the permission procedures provided by this package in Oracle8i release 2 and up. This interface allows us to grant very granular privileges to our Java routines, allowing us to strictly control what they can, and cannot do.

All in all, if you are using Java inside the Oracle database, you will find these routines invaluable in your day-to-day programming.

DBMS_JOB

The DBMS_JOB package allows you to schedule one-off or recurring jobs in your database. A job is a stored procedure, anonymous PL/SQL block, or external procedure written in C or Java. These jobs are run in the background by the server processes themselves. They can be run on a recurring basis (every night at 2am), or one time (run this job right after I commit, and then remove it from the job queue). If you are familiar with the cron or at utilities in UNIX or Windows, you already have a good understanding of the DBMS_JOB package. They are run in the same environment (user, characterset, and so on) they were submitted in (minus roles). Jobs are run in an environment much as a definer rights stored procedure is – without any roles being enabled. We can see this by the following example:

The routines used in this example are explained in detail further down in this section.

```
tkyte@TKYTE816> create table t ( msg varchar2(20), cnt int );

Table created.

tkyte@TKYTE816> insert into t select 'from SQL*PLUS', count(*) from
               session_roles;

1 row created.

tkyte@TKYTE816> variable n number
tkyte@TKYTE816> exec dbms_job.submit(:n,'insert into t select ''from job'',
               count(*) from session_roles;');

PL/SQL procedure successfully completed.

tkyte@TKYTE816> print n
```

```
         N
----------
        81

tkyte@TKYTE816> exec dbms_job.run(:n);

PL/SQL procedure successfully completed.

tkyte@TKYTE816> select * from t;

MSG                      CNT
-------------------- ----------
from SQL*PLUS                10
from job                      0
```

As you can see, in SQL*PLUS we had 10 roles active, in the job environment, we had none. Typically, since most people submit a stored procedure call as the job, this will not affect anything, since the stored procedure runs without roles in the first place. The only time you might notice this is if you try to schedule a stored procedure to which you have access via a *role*. This will not work – there are no roles enabled in jobs, ever.

Many times, people ask what the best method is for hiding a username/password associated with a batch job (for example, to analyze tables periodically) that is scheduled via cron, or some utility on Windows NT/2000. They are worried about the password being stored in file (as they should be), or being visible in the ps output on UNIX, and so on. My answer to this is to not use the OS to schedule operations against the database at all, but rather, write a stored procedure that performs your operation, and schedule it using DBMS_JOB. In this fashion, there is no stored username and password, and the job will only actually execute if the database is available. If the database is not available, the job will not run of course, as the database is responsible for running the job.

Another frequent question is, 'How can I speed this up?' You are faced with some long operation, and the end user does not want to wait. Sometimes the answer is that it cannot be sped up. For example, I've been sending e-mails from the database for many years. I've used different mechanisms over time; database pipes, UTL_HTTP, external procedures, and Java. They all worked at about the same speed, but they were slow. It takes a while for SMTP to finish its stuff sometimes. It definitely took too long in my application, where anything longer than quarter of a second *is* too long. The SMTP send might take 2 to 3 seconds at times. We cannot make it go faster, but we can give it the *perception* of being faster. Instead of sending the e-mail when the user hit the submit button on the application, we would submit a JOB that would send the e-mail as soon as we committed. This had two nice side effects. The first was that the operation appeared to be much faster, the second was that it made e-mail 'transactional'. One of the properties of DBMS_JOB is that the job will be visible in the queue, only after you commit. If you roll back, the job is dequeued, and will never be executed. By using DBMS_JOB, not only did we make the application appear faster, but we made it more robust as well. No longer did we send e-mail alerts out from a trigger on an update of a row that got rolled back. Both the row was updated and we sent the e-mail, or the row was not updated and we did not send the e-mail.

So, DBMS_JOB has many uses. It can make 'non transactional' things transactional (like sending an e-mail, or creating a table upon an insert into another table). It can appear to speed things up, especially when you do not need any output from the really slow operation. It can schedule and automate many of the tasks you normally write scripts for outside of the database. It is one of those truly useful packages.

In order for DBMS_JOB to function correctly, we need to do a little set up in the database. There are two init.ora parameters that must be set:

- ❑ job_queue_interval – Specifies the frequency in seconds by which the job queues will be inspected for jobs that are ready to run. If you schedule a job to run every 30 seconds, but set job_queue_interval to 60 (the default), your job will never run every 30 seconds – it'll run every 60 seconds at best.

- ❑ job_queue_processes – Specifies the number of background processes available to run jobs. This is an integer number between 0 (the default) and 36. This value may be changed without restarting the database via the ALTER SYSTEM SET JOB_QUEUE_PROCESSES=<nn> command. If this value is left at 0, jobs in the job queue will never run automatically. These job queue processes are visible in the UNIX environment, where they will have the name ora_snpN_$ORACLE_SID where the N will be a number (0, 1, 2, ..., job_queue_processes-1). On Windows, the job queues execute as threads and will not be externally visible.

Many systems run with a value of 60 for job_queue_interval (in other words, check the queues every minute), and 1 for the job_queue_processes (run at most one job at a time). If you use jobs heavily, or make use of features that use the job queues as well (replication, and materialized views are two features that make use of the job queues), you might consider adding an additional job_queue_processes.

Once the job queues are set up to run automatically, we are ready to start using them. The main routine you will use with DBMS_JOB is the SUBMIT routine. Its interface is as follows:

```
PROCEDURE SUBMIT
 Argument Name                  Type                    In/Out Default?
 ------------------------------ ----------------------- ------ --------
 JOB                            BINARY_INTEGER          OUT
 WHAT                           VARCHAR2                IN
 NEXT_DATE                      DATE                    IN     DEFAULT
 INTERVAL                       VARCHAR2                IN     DEFAULT
 NO_PARSE                       BOOLEAN                 IN     DEFAULT
 INSTANCE                       BINARY_INTEGER          IN     DEFAULT
 FORCE                          BOOLEAN                 IN     DEFAULT
```

where the arguments to the SUBMIT routine have the following meanings:

- ❑ JOB – A job identifier. It is *system*-assigned (it is an OUT only parameter). You can use this to query the USER_JOBS or DBA_JOBS views by job ID to see information about that job. Additionally, some routines such as RUN and REMOVE take the job ID as their only input, to uniquely identify the job to run or be removed.

- ❑ WHAT – The SQL text of what will be run. It must be a valid PL/SQL statement or block of code. For example, to run a stored procedure P, you might pass the string P; (with the semi-colon) to this routine. Whatever you submit in the WHAT parameter, will be wrapped in the following PL/SQL block:

```
DECLARE
    job BINARY_INTEGER := :job;
    next_date DATE := :mydate;
    broken BOOLEAN := FALSE;
BEGIN
```

```
        WHAT
    :mydate := next_date;
    IF broken THEN :b := 1; ELSE :b := 0; END IF;
END;
```

This is why you need to add the ; to any statement. In order to just replace the WHAT with your code, it will need a semi-colon.

❑   NEXT_DATE – The next (or since we are just submitting, the first) time to run the job. The default is SYSDATE – run as soon as possible (after committing).

❑   INTERVAL – A string containing a date function that calculates the next time to run the job. You can consider this function to be 'selected from dual'. If you pass in the string sysdate+1, the database will in effect execute SELECT sysdate+1 INTO :NEXT_DATE FROM DUAL. See below for some caveats on setting the interval of a job to prevent 'sliding'.

❑   NO_PARSE – Determines whether the WHAT parameter is parsed upon submission. By parsing the string, you can be reasonably sure the string is in fact, executable. In general, NO_PARSE should always be left with its default of False. When set to True, the WHAT parameter is accepted 'as is' with no validity checking.

❑   INSTANCE – Only meaningful in Parallel Server mode, a mode Oracle can run in, on a loosely coupled cluster of machines. This would specify the instance upon which this job should be executed. By default, this will have a value of ANY_INSTANCE.

❑   FORCE – Again, this is only meaningful in Parallel Server mode. If set to True (the default), you may submit the job with any instance number, even if that instance is not available at the time of job submission. If set to False, submit will fail the request if the associated instance is not available.

There are other entry points into the DBMS_JOB package as well. SUBMIT is the one you will use to schedule a job, and the others allow you to manipulate the scheduled jobs, and perform operations such as RUN it, REMOVE it, and CHANGE it. Below is a listing of the commonly used ones, what they expect as input, and what they do:

Entry Point	Inputs	Description
REMOVE	job number	Removes a job from the job queue. You should note that if the job is running, this cannot stop it. It will be removed from the queue so it will not execute again, but it will not stop an executing job. In order to stop a running job, you may use the ALTER SYSTEM command to kill the session.
CHANGE	job number WHAT, NEXT_DATE, INTERVAL, INSTANCE, FORCE	This acts like an UPDATE statement would on the JOBS view. It allows you to change any of the settings of the job.

Entry Point	Inputs	Description
BROKEN	job number BROKEN (Boolean) NEXT_DATE	Allows you to 'break' or 'unbreak' a job. A broken job will not execute. A job that has failed 16 times in a row will automatically be set to broken, and Oracle will stop trying to execute it.
RUN	job number	Runs a job right now in the foreground (in your session). Useful for trying to debug why a job is failing.

Now that we have a working knowledge of how DBMS_JOB works, and what functions are available to us, we'll look at how to run a job once, how to set up a recurring job correctly, and how to monitor our jobs and find out what errors they have encountered.

Running a Job Once

Many of the jobs I run are 'one-off' jobs. I use DBMS_JOB much as one would use the & in UNIX, or the start command in Windows, to run a process in the background. The example I gave above with regards to sending e-mail is a good example. I use DBMS_JOB to make the sending of e-mail not only transactional, but also appear to be fast. Here is one implementation of this to demonstrate how to run a job once. We'll start with a small stored procedure to send e-mail using the supplied UTL_SMTP package:

```
tkyte@TKYTE816> create or replace
  2  PROCEDURE send_mail (p_sender      IN VARCHAR2,
  3                       p_recipient IN VARCHAR2,
  4                       p_message   IN VARCHAR2)
  5  as
  6     -- Note that you have to use a host
  7     -- that supports SMTP and that you have access to.
  8     -- You do not have access to this host and must change it
  9     l_mailhost VARCHAR2(255) := 'aria.us.oracle.com';
 10     l_mail_conn utl_smtp.connection;
 11  BEGIN
 12     l_mail_conn := utl_smtp.open_connection(l_mailhost, 25);
 13     utl_smtp.helo(l_mail_conn, l_mailhost);
 14     utl_smtp.mail(l_mail_conn, p_sender);
 15     utl_smtp.rcpt(l_mail_conn, p_recipient);
 16     utl_smtp.open_data(l_mail_conn );
 17     utl_smtp.write_data(l_mail_conn, p_message);
 18     utl_smtp.close_data(l_mail_conn );
 19     utl_smtp.quit(l_mail_conn);
 20  end;
 21  /

Procedure created.
```

Now, to time how long this takes, I'll run it twice:

```
tkyte@TKYTE816> set serveroutput on
tkyte@TKYTE816> declare
  2          l_start number := dbms_utility.get_time;
  3  begin
  4          send_mail( 'anyone@outthere.com',
  5                     'anyone@outthere.com', 'hey there' );
  6          dbms_output.put_line
  7          ( round( (dbms_utility.get_time-l_start)/100, 2 ) ||
  8            ' seconds' );
  9  end;
 10  /
.81 seconds

PL/SQL procedure successfully completed.

tkyte@TKYTE816> /
.79 seconds

PL/SQL procedure successfully completed.
```

It looks like it will consistently take the order of 8 tenths of a second to send a mail during the best of times. As far as I am concerned, that is far too long. We can do much better – well, we can 'apparently' do much better. We'll use jobs to give this the appearance of being much faster, and gain the benefit of a 'transactional' e-mail as well.

We will start by creating a table to store the e-mail, and a procedure we could run against it to send e-mail. This procedure will ultimately become our background job. A question is, why am I using a table to store the emails? Why not just pass parameters to the job? The reason is bind variables, and the shared pool. Since all jobs are created using the WHAT parameter, and the database will simply 'execute' this string at run-time, we want to make sure that the WHAT parameter we submit is something that will be in the shared pool. We could easily just submit a job such as:

```
dbms_job.submit( x, 'send_mail(''someone@there.com'',
                     ''someone@there.com'', ''hello'' );' );
```

but that would have the effect of flooding our shared pool with hundreds or thousands of unique statements, killing our performance. Since we plan on sending lots of e-mails (anything more than one is lots, and would mandate the use of bind variables), we need to be able to submit something like:

```
dbms_job.submit( x, 'background_send_mail( constant );' );
```

Well, as it turns out, there is an easy way to do this. We simply need to create a table that contains a field for each parameter we really wanted to send to the routine (sender, recipient, and message in this case), plus an ID primary key field. For example:

```
tkyte@TKYTE816> create table send_mail_data( id        number primary key,
  2                           sender    varchar2(255),
  3                           recipient varchar2(255),
  4                           message   varchar2(4000),
  5                           senton    date default NULL );

Table created.
```

Here I added an `ID` column as a primary key, and in this case, a sent on senton column. We'll use this table not only as a place to queue up outgoing e-mails, but also to keep a persistent log of e-mails sent, and when they were sent (very handy, trust me, for when people say 'but I didn't get the notification'). Now all we need to do is figure out a way to generate a key for this table, and get it to our background process using a constant string. Fortunately `DBMS_JOB` already does that for us. When we schedule a job, it automatically creates a job ID for it, and returns this to us. Since the block of code it wraps around our `WHAT` parameter includes this job ID, we can simply pass it to ourselves! This means that our `FAST_SEND_MAIL` routine will look like this:

```
tkyte@TKYTE816> create or replace
  2  PROCEDURE fast_send_mail (p_sender      IN VARCHAR2,
  3                            p_recipient   IN VARCHAR2,
  4                            p_message     IN VARCHAR2)
  5  as
  6          l_job     number;
  7  begin
  8          dbms_job.submit( l_job, 'background_send_mail( JOB );' );
  9          insert into send_mail_data
 10          ( id, sender, recipient, message )
 11          values
 12          ( l_job, p_sender, p_recipient, p_message );
 13  end;
 14  /

Procedure created.
```

This routine will submit a job, `BACKGROUND_SEND_MAIL`, and pass it the `JOB` parameter. If you refer to the `WHAT` parameter description above, you'll see the block of code includes three local variables we have access to – we are simply passing ourselves one of them. The very next thing we do in this procedure is to insert the e-mail into our `QUEUE` table, for delivery later. So, `DBMS_JOB` creates the primary key, and then we insert the primary key with the associated data into this table. That's all we need to do. Now we need to create the `BACKGROUND_SEND_MAIL` routine and it is simply:

```
tkyte@TKYTE816> create or replace
  2  procedure background_send_mail( p_job in number )
  3  as
  4          l_rec     send_mail_data%rowtype;
  5  begin
  6          select * into l_rec
  7            from send_mail_data
  8           where id = p_job;
  9
 10          send_mail( l_rec.sender, l_rec.recipient, l_rec.message );
 11          update send_mail_data set senton = sysdate where id = p_job;
 12  end;
 13  /

Procedure created.
```

It reads out the data we saved, calls the slow `SEND_MAIL` routine, and then updates the record, to record the fact that we actually sent the mail. Now, we can run `FAST_SEND_MAIL`, and see how fast it really is:

```
tkyte@TKYTE816> declare
  2              l_start number := dbms_utility.get_time;
  3  begin
  4              fast_send_mail( 'panda@panda.com',
  5                              'snake@snake.com', 'hey there' );
  6              dbms_output.put_line
  7              ( round( (dbms_utility.get_time-l_start)/100, 2 ) ||
  8                ' seconds' );
  9  end;
 10  /
.03 seconds

PL/SQL procedure successfully completed.

tkyte@TKYTE816> /
.02 seconds

PL/SQL procedure successfully completed.
```

As far as our end users are concerned, this FAST_SEND_MAIL is 26 to 40 times *faster* than the original send mail. It is not really faster, but it just appears to be that much faster (and that is what really counts). The actual sending of the mail will happen in the background after they commit. This is an important note here. If you run this example, make sure you COMMIT when using the DBMS_JOB example, else the e-mail will never get sent. The job will not be visible to the job queue processes until you do (your session can see the job in the USER_JOBS view, but the job queue processes won't see it until you commit). Don't take this as a limitation, it is actually a feature – we've just made e-mail transactional. If you ROLLBACK, so does your send mail. When you COMMIT, it'll be delivered.

Ongoing Jobs

The other main use of DBMS_JOB is to schedule recurring jobs in the database. As mentioned previously, many people try to use OS utilities such as cron or at to run jobs in the database, but then encounter the issue of, 'How do I protect the password?' and such. My answer to this is always to use the job queues. In addition to removing the need to store credentials anywhere, this ensures the jobs are only run if in fact, the database is up and running. It will also retry the job time and time again in the event of a failure. For example, if the first time we attempted to run the job, the database link it uses was unavailable, it will put the job back onto the queue, and will retry it later. The database will do this 16 times, waiting a little longer each time, before ultimately marking the job 'broken'. See the next section, *Monitoring Jobs And Finding The Errors*, for more details on that. These are things cron and at won't do for you. Also, since the jobs are in the database, we can just run queries to find their status – when they last ran, if they ran, and so on. Everything is integrated.

Other Oracle features such as replication and materialized views implicitly use the job queues themselves as part of their day-to-day functioning. The way a snapshot pulls its changes, or a materialized view refreshes, is by the job queues running the stored procedures that perform these operations.

Let's say you wanted to schedule an analysis of all of the tables in a certain schema to take place every night at 3am. The stored procedure for doing such a thing could be:

```
scott@TKYTE816> create or replace procedure analyze_my_tables
  2  as
  3  begin
  4      for x in ( select table_name from user_tables )
  5      loop
  6          execute immediate
  7              'analyze table ' || x.table_name || ' compute statistics';
  8      end loop;
  9  end;
 10  /

Procedure created.
```

Now, in order to schedule this to run *tonight* at 3am (tomorrow morning really), and every day thereafter at 3am, we will use the following:

```
scott@TKYTE816> declare
  2      l_job number;
  3  begin
  4      dbms_job.submit( job       => l_job,
  5                       what      => 'analyze_my_tables;',
  6                       next_date => trunc(sysdate)+1+3/24,
  7                       interval  => 'trunc(sysdate)+1+3/24' );
  8  end;
  9  /

PL/SQL procedure successfully completed.

scott@TKYTE816> select job, to_char(sysdate,'dd-mon'),
  2                    to_char(next_date,'dd-mon-yyyy hh24:mi:ss'),
  3                    interval, what
  4  from user_jobs
  5  /

 JOB TO_CHA TO_CHAR(NEXT_DATE,'D INTERVAL              WHAT
---- ------ -------------------- -------------------- --------------------
  33 09-jan 10-jan-2001 03:00:00 trunc(sysdate)+1+3/24 analyze_my_tables;
```

So, the next date for this job to run will be 3am on the 10th of January. We used a 'real' date for that, not a string as we did for interval. We used a date function so that no matter when it is executed, no matter what time during the day, it will always return 3am *tomorrow* morning. This is an important fact. We use the same exact function for the INTERVAL parameter as a string. We are using a function that always returns 3am tomorrow, regardless of when it is executed. The reason this is important is to prevent jobs from **sliding**. It might seem that since the first time the job is run, it'll be run at 3am, we could use an interval simply of sysdate+1. If we ran this at 3am on Tuesday, it should give us 3am on Wednesday. It would – *if* the jobs were guaranteed to run precisely on time, but they are not. Jobs are processed in the queue sequentially based on their time to be run. If I have one job queue process, and two jobs to be run at 3am, obviously one of them will not run at 3am exactly. It will have to wait for the first to finish to completion, and then it will be executed. Even if I have no overlapping jobs, the job queues are inspected at discrete points in time, say every 60 seconds. I might pick up the job to be run at 3am at 3:00:45am. If it used a simple sysdate+1 function, it might compute its next time to run as '3:00:46am' tomorrow. Tomorrow at 3:00:45am, this job would not be ready to run yet, and would be picked up on the next inspection of the queue at 3:01:45am. This job would slowly slip over time. Even more dramatic, let's say the tables were being operated on at 3am one morning, so the analysis failed. The stored procedure would fail, and the job queues would retry the job later. Now the job will 'slip' by many minutes for the next day since it runs at a time much later than 3am. For this reason, to prevent the job from slipping, you must use a function that returns a *fixed* point in time if you want the job to always be scheduled at a *particular* point in time. If it is important that this job runs at 3am, you must use a function that *always* returns 3am, and is not dependent on the time of day it is executed.

Many of these 'non-sliding' functions are typically very easy to write – others not so. For example, I was once requested to implement a job that would collect STATSPACK statistics Monday through Friday at 7am, and 3pm only. Well, the INTERVAL for this was certainly non-intuitive, but let's have a look at the pseudo-code:

```
if it is before 15:00
then
    return TODAY at 15:00
  (eg: if we are running at 7am, we want to run at 3pm today)
else
    return today + either 3 (if it is Friday) or 1 (otherwise) at 7am
end if
```

So, what we needed to do then, was turn this logic into a nice DECODE statement – or if that is too complex, I could have used a PL/SQL function to perform the complex logic. I used the interval:

```
decode(sign(15-to_char(sysdate,'hh24')),
          1, trunc(sysdate)+15/24,
          trunc( sysdate + decode(to_char(sysdate,'d'), 6, 3, 1))+7/24)
```

The decode starts with the SIGN(15-TO_CHAR(SYSDATE,'HH24')). SIGN is a function that returns -1, 0, or 1 if the resulting number is negative, zero, or positive respectively. If this number was positive, it would imply that it was *before* 3pm in the afternoon (the hour was less than 15), and hence the next time we should run would be TRUNC(SYSDATE)+15/24 (15 hours after midnight today). On the other hand, if the sign came back 0 or -1, then we would use the TRUNC(SYSDATE + DECODE(TO_CHAR(SYSDATE,'D'), 6, 3, 1))+7/24. This would use the DECODE to look at the current day of the week to see if we should add three days (on Friday to get to Monday), or one day (every other day of the week). We would add that many days to SYSDATE, truncate this date back to midnight, and add 7 hours to it.

There are times when a 'sliding' date is OK, and even desired. For example, if you would like a job to collect some statistics from the V$ tables every 30 minutes while the database is up and running, it would be totally appropriate to use an interval of SYSDATE+1/24/2 which adds a half hour to a date.

Custom Scheduling

There are times, such as the above, where the NEXT_DATE is hard to compute in a simple SQL statement, or where the next time the job runs is dependent on some complex procedural set of rules. In this case, we can have the job itself set the next date to run.

If you recall from above, the PL/SQL block that runs a job is:

```
DECLARE
    job BINARY_INTEGER := :job;
    next_date DATE := :mydate;
    broken BOOLEAN := FALSE;
BEGIN
        WHAT
    :mydate := next_date;
    IF broken THEN :b := 1; ELSE :b := 0; END IF;
END;
```

We have already seen how we can make use of the fact that JOB is available there in the *Running a Job Once* section. We can use it as a primary key into a parameter table to make maximum use of shared SQL. Well, we can also make use of the NEXT_DATE variable as well. As you can see in the above block of code, Oracle uses the bind variable :mydate as an *input* into the routine, to set the NEXT_DATE variable, but it also retrieves this value after *what* (your procedure) executes. If your procedure happens to modify this value, the value of NEXT_DATE, Oracle will use this as the next date to run the job. As an example, we'll set up a small procedure P that will write some informative message to a table T, and set it's NEXT_DATE:

```
tkyte@TKYTE816> create table t ( msg varchar2(80) );
Table created.

tkyte@TKYTE816> create or replace
  2  procedure p( p_job in number, p_next_date in OUT date )
  3  as
  4      l_next_date date default p_next_date;
  5  begin
  6      p_next_date := trunc(sysdate)+1+3/24;
  7
  8      insert into t values
  9      ( 'Next date was "' ||
 10        to_char(l_next_date,'dd-mon-yyyy hh24:mi:ss') ||
 11        '" Next date IS ' ||
 12        to_char(p_next_date,'dd-mon-yyyy hh24:mi:ss') );
 13  end;
 14  /
Procedure created.
```

Now we will schedule this job using the method from the section, *Running a Job Once*. That is, without an INTERVAL:

```
tkyte@TKYTE816> variable n number

tkyte@TKYTE816> exec dbms_job.submit( :n, 'p(JOB,NEXT_DATE);' );
PL/SQL procedure successfully completed.

tkyte@TKYTE816> select what, interval,
  2         to_char(last_date,'dd-mon-yyyy hh24:mi:ss') last_date,
  3         to_char(next_date,'dd-mon-yyyy hh24:mi:ss') next_date
  4    from user_jobs
  5   where job = :n
  6  /

WHAT                       INTERVAL LAST_DATE            NEXT_DATE
-------------------------- -------- -------------------- --------------------
p(JOB,NEXT_DATE);          null                          28-apr-2001 18:23:01
```

In this case, we send the JOB and the NEXT_DATE as parameters to our procedure. These will be supplied by the job queue at run-time. As you can see, this job has not yet run (LAST_DATE is Null), the INTERVAL is set to null so that the NEXT_DATE will be computed as SELECT NULL FROM DUAL. Normally, this means the job would run once, and be removed from the job queue. However, when this job runs, we'll discover:

```
tkyte@TKYTE816> exec dbms_job.run( :n );

PL/SQL procedure successfully completed.

tkyte@TKYTE816> select * from t;

MSG
------------------------------------------------------------------
Next date was "" Next date IS 29-apr-2001 03:00:00

tkyte@TKYTE816> select what, interval,
  2         to_char(last_date,'dd-mon-yyyy hh24:mi:ss') last_date,
  3         to_char(next_date,'dd-mon-yyyy hh24:mi:ss') next_date
  4     from user_jobs
  5    where job = :n
  6  /

WHAT                       INTERVAL LAST_DATE            NEXT_DATE
-------------------------- -------- -------------------- --------------------
p(JOB,NEXT_DATE);          null     28-apr-2001 18:23:01 29-apr-2001 03:00:00
```

that the NEXT_DATE is filled in. It is the NEXT_DATE computed in the procedure itself, and the job is still in the queue. As long as this job continues to fill in the NEXT_DATE field, it will remain in the job queue. If it ever exits successfully without setting NEXT_DATE, it will be removed from the queue.

This is very useful for those jobs with hard to compute NEXT_DATE values, or NEXT_DATE values that depend on data found in other database tables.

Monitoring the Jobs and Finding the Errors

There are three main views used to monitor jobs in the database. They are simply:

- ❏ USER_JOBS – A list of all jobs submitted by the currently logged in user. There is also a public synonym, ALL_JOBS that references this view. ALL_JOBS is the same as USER_JOBS.

- ❏ DBA_JOBS – A comprehensive list of all jobs scheduled in the database.

- ❏ DBA_JOBS_RUNNING – A list of currently executing jobs.

Everyone has access to USER_JOBS as normal, and the DBA_* views are limited to people with the DBA privilege, or those who have been granted SELECT on these particular views directly. These views will give you information such as:

- ❏ LAST_DATE/LAST_SEC – Tells you when the job last ran. LAST_DATE is an Oracle date/time. LAST_SEC is a character string that has only the time component (hour:minute:second) formatted into it.

❑ THIS_DATE/THIS_SEC – If the job is currently running, this will be filled in with the time it started execution. Like LAST_DATE/LAST_SEC, THIS_DATE is a date/time, and THIS_SEC is a character string with only the time component.

❑ NEXT_DATE/NEXT_SEC – The time the job is schedule to be executed NEXT.

❑ TOTAL_TIME – The total time in seconds, which the job has spent executing. Includes times from other runs – this is a cumulative count.

❑ BROKEN – A Yes/No flag that shows if a job that is 'broken'. Broken jobs are not run by the job queue processes. A job will 'break' itself after 16 failures. You may use the DBMS_JOB.BROKEN API call to 'break' a job (temporarily prevent it from executing).

❑ INTERVAL – The date function to be evaluated at the beginning of the job's next execution, to determine when to run the job next.

❑ FAILURES – The number of times in a row the job has failed. A successful execution of the job will reset this count be to 0.

❑ WHAT – The body of the job, in other words, what to do.

❑ NLS_ENV – The **NLS** (National Language Support) environment that the job will be executed in. Includes things such as the language, the date format, the number format, and so on. The entire NLS environment is inherited from the environment that submits the job. If you change this environment and submit a job, the job will run with this modified environment.

❑ INSTANCE – Only valid in Parallel Server mode. This is the ID of the instance the job can execute on, or in DBA_JOBS_RUNNING, the instance it is running on.

Suppose you look into these views and see some jobs with a positive value in the FAILURES column – where would you go to see the error message for that job? It is not stored in the database, rather it can be found in the alert log for the database. For example, let's say you create a procedure such as:

```
tkyte@TKYTE816> create or replace procedure run_by_jobs
  2  as
  3          l_cnt    number;
  4  begin
  5          select user_id into l_cnt from all_users;
  6          -- other code here
  7  end;
  8  /

Procedure created.

tkyte@TKYTE816> variable n number
tkyte@TKYTE816> exec dbms_job.submit( :n, 'run_by_jobs;' );

PL/SQL procedure successfully completed.

tkyte@TKYTE816> commit;

Commit complete.

tkyte@TKYTE816> exec dbms_lock.sleep(60);

PL/SQL procedure successfully completed.
```

```
tkyte@TKYTE816> select job, what, failures
  2     from user_jobs
  3    where job = :n;

        JOB WHAT                                    FAILURES
---------- ------------------------------ ----------
         35 run_by_jobs;                                  1
```

If you have more than one user in your database (as all databases do) this procedure will most definitely *fail*. The SELECT ... INTO will always return too many rows; we have a programming error. Since this happens in the background however, it is hard for us to see what exactly might be wrong. Fortunately the error is recorded in the alert log for the database. If we were to edit that file and go to the bottom, we would find:

```
Tue Jan 09 13:07:51 2001
Errors in file C:\oracle\admin\tkyte816\bdump\tkyte816SNP0.TRC:
...
ORA-12012: error on auto execute of job 35
ORA-01422: exact fetch returns more than requested number of rows
ORA-06512: at "SCOTT.RUN_BY_JOBS", line 5
ORA-06512: at line 1
```

It tells us that job 35 (our job) failed to execute. More importantly, it tells us exactly *why* it failed; the same error stack you would get if you ran this in SQL*PLUS. This information is crucial to diagnosing why a job is failing. With this information we can fix it and get it to run correctly.

This is pretty much all there is to monitoring jobs. You need to either keep an eye on your alert.log (something your DBA should already be doing), or monitor the DBA_JOBS table from time to time to ensure things are running smoothly.

Summary

DBMS_JOB is an excellent facility inside the database for running procedures in the background. It has uses in the automated scheduling of routine tasks such as analyzing your tables, performing some archival operation, cleaning up scratch tables – whatever. It has application functionality in the area of making long running operations 'apparently fast' (and apparently fast is all that matters to the end user really). It removes the need to code OS-dependent scripts to perform database operations on a recurring basis. Even better, it removes the need to hard code usernames and passwords in a script to log into the database. The job always runs as the person who submitted it – no credentials are required. Lastly, unlike an OS scheduling facility, these *database* jobs run only when the database is actually available. If the system is down when a job is scheduled to run, it will not run (obviously, if the database isn't up, the job queues are not up). All in all, DBMS_JOB is a robust facility for which I've found many uses.

DBMS_LOB

DBMS_LOB is a package supplied to manipulate **Large OB**jects (**LOB**s) in the database. LOBs are new data types available with Oracle 8, and upwards. LOBs support the storage, and retrieval of up to 4 GB of arbitrary data in a single database column. They replace the, now deprecated, data types LONG and LONG RAW. LONG types in Oracle had many shorting comings, such as:

❑   You could only have one per table

❑   You could not manipulate them in a stored procedure once they grew beyond 32 KB

❑   You could not piece-wise modify them readily

❑   Many database operations, such as INSERT INTO T SELECT LONG_COL FROM T2, were not supported

❑   You could not reference them in a WHERE clause

❑   You could not replicate them

❑   And so on...

The LOB data type overcomes all of these limitations.

Rather than go over each and every function/procedure of the DBMS_LOB package (there are some 25 of them), I am going to answer the most common questions that come up regarding using the DBMS_LOB package and LOBs. Much of it is either self-explanatory, or is well covered in the standard Oracle documentation. For LOBs there are two main documents you are concerned with:

❑ *Oracle8i Supplied PL/SQL Packages Reference* – An overview of the DBMS_LOB package, and every procedure within, along with a definition of all of the inputs and outputs. Handy to have for reference purposes. You should give this a quick read through to get an understanding of the functions you can perform on LOBs.

❑ *Oracle8i Application Developer's Guide – Large Objects (LOBs)* – An entire document dedicated to explaining how to program using LOBs in various languages and environments. A must read for the developer who will be using LOBs.

Additionally, many of the nuances of working with LOBs is language-specific. How you do something in Java, will be different in C, will be different in PL/SQL, and so on. To this end, Oracle Corporation has actually developed an *Application Developer's Guide* by language, for languages such as PL/SQL, OCI, Pro*C, COBOL, VB, and Java detailing how LOBs interact with each language. There is also a comprehensive *Application Developer's Guide* on LOBs, as mentioned above, that is useful, regardless of the language used. I would urge anyone who is considering using LOBs in their applications to read this document, as well as the language-specific guide for their language of choice. These documents answer most of the questions you will ask.

What I will cover here are the answers to the frequently asked questions about LOBs, from, 'How can I show them on the web?', to, 'How can I convert between BLOBs and CLOBs?' – things that aren't covered so well in the standard documentation. LOBs are extremely easy to use once you familiarize yourself with the DBMS_LOB package (see the *Oracle 8i Supplied PL/SQL Packages Reference* for an overview of this package) and if you haven't done so already, you should do so now before reading this section as it assumes you are ready to go and do things with LOBs.

How do I Load LOBs?

There are quite a few methods available for loading LOBs. In Chapter 9 on *Data Loading* for example, I demonstrate how the SQLLDR tool may be used to load LOBs into the database. Additionally, the *Application Developer's Guide* for each language provided by Oracle demonstrate how to create and retrieve a LOB using a specific host language (it's a little different in each). In my opinion however, if I had a directory full of files to load, the use of a BFILE, a DIRECTORY object, and the LOADFROMFILE routine would by far be the way to go.

In Chapter 9 on *Data Loading*, we covered the topic of using DBMS_LOB.LOADFROMFILE in depth. I will refer you to that section for all of the details. Also, the section on *Conversions* here, contains a full example of loading a CLOB using LOADFROMFILE.

substr

This is just a quick note on the substr function provided by the DBMS_LOB package. Every other substr function I have ever seen (including the one provided with SQL and PL/SQL) has the following arguments in the following order:

```
substr( the-string, from-character, for-number-of-characters );
```

So, the substr('hello', 3, 2) would be ll – the third and fourth characters (from character 3, for 2 characters). DBMS_LOB.SUBSTR however, defines them as:

```
dbms_lob.substr( the-lob, for-number-of-characters, from-character )
```

So that same `substr` with DBMS_LOB would return `ell`. A very small simple test confirms this behavior:

```
tkyte@TKYTE816> create table t ( str varchar2(10), lob clob );

Table created.

tkyte@TKYTE816> insert into t values ( 'hello', 'hello' );

1 row created.

tkyte@TKYTE816> select substr( str, 3, 2 ),
  2         dbms_lob.substr( lob, 3, 2) lob
  3    from t
  4  /

SU LOB
-- --------------------
ll ell
```

I am constantly doing it backwards myself. It is just one of those things we have to remember to watch out for!

SELECT FOR UPDATE and Java

In order to modify a database-based LOB (not a temporary LOB), the row that contains the LOB in the database must be locked by our session. This is a common point of confusion to Java/JDBC programmers. Consider the small Java program below. It simply:

❑   Inserts a record (hence you would assume its locked)

❑   Reads out the LOB locator just created

❑   Attempts to use this LOB locator with DBMS_LOB.WRITEAPPEND

As it turns out – this Java program will always encounter the error:

```
java Test
java.sql.SQLException: ORA-22920: row containing the LOB value is not locked
ORA-06512: at "SYS.DBMS_LOB", line 715
ORA-06512: at line 1
```

Apparently, the LOB we inserted is not locked by our session any more. This is an unfortunate side effect of the default 'transactional' mode of JDBC – by default it does not support transactions! After every statement, it commits work immediately. In the following application, unless you add `conn.setAutoCommit (false);` immediately after the `getConnection` – it will fail. That one line of code should (in my opinion) be the first line of code after *every connect* in a JDBC program!

```
import java.sql.*;
import java.io.*;
import oracle.jdbc.driver.*;
import oracle.sql.*;

// You need a table:
// create table demo ( id int primary key, theBlob blob );
// in order for this application to execute.
```

```
class Test {

public static void main (String args [])
   throws SQLException , FileNotFoundException, IOException
{
    DriverManager.registerDriver
      (new oracle.jdbc.driver.OracleDriver());

    Connection conn = DriverManager.getConnection
        ("jdbc:oracle:thin:@aria:1521:ora8i",
         "scott", "tiger");

    // If this program is to work, uncomment this next line!
    // conn.setAutoCommit(false);

    Statement stmt = conn.createStatement();

    // Insert an empty BLOB into the table
    // create it new for the very first time.
    stmt.execute
    ( "insert into demo (id,theBlob) " +
      "values (1,empty_blob())" );

    // Now, we will read it back out so we can
    // load it.
    ResultSet rset = stmt.executeQuery
                    ("SELECT theBlob " +
                        "FROM demo "+
                      "where id = 1 ");

    if(rset.next())
    {
        // Get the BLOB to load into.
        BLOB l_mapBLOB = ((OracleResultSet)rset).getBLOB(1);

        // Here is the data we will load into it.
        File binaryFile = new File("/tmp/binary.dat");
        FileInputStream instream =
             new FileInputStream(binaryFile);

        // We will load about 32 KB at a time. That's
        // the most dbms_lob can handle (PL/SQL limit).
        int chunk = 32000;
        byte[] l_buffer = new byte[chunk];

        int l_nread = 0;

        // We'll use the easy writeappend routine to add
        // our chunk of file to the end of the BLOB.
        OracleCallableStatement cstmt =
            (OracleCallableStatement)conn.prepareCall
            ( "begin dbms_lob.writeappend( :1, :2, :3 ); end;" );

        // Read and write, read and write, until done.
        cstmt.registerOutParameter( 1, OracleTypes.BLOB );
        while ((l_nread= instream.read(l_buffer)) != -1)
        {
            cstmt.setBLOB(  1, l_mapBLOB );
            cstmt.setInt(   2, l_nread );
            cstmt.setBytes( 3, l_buffer );
```

```
                        cstmt.executeUpdate();

                        l_mapBLOB = cstmt.getBLOB(1);
                }
                // Close up the input file and callable statement.
                instream.close();
                cstmt.close();
        }
        // Close out the statements.
        rset.close();
        stmt.close();
        conn.close ();
    }

    }
```

This is a general shortcoming of JDBC, and it affects LOB operations in particular. I cannot tell you how many people are surprised to find that an API would presume to commit for them – something that must be done by the application itself. Only an ex-ODBC programmer might be expecting that! The same thing will happen in ODBC in its default mode of auto commit as well.

Conversions

Frequently, people have their data in a BLOB, and need it for some reason to appear as a CLOB. Typically, someone has loaded a mixture of text and binary data into a BLOB column, and this person would like to parse the text. Parsing the BLOB is difficult since the database will constantly try to convert the raw BLOB data into hexadecimal, which is not the desired effect. In other cases, people have data in a LONG or LONG RAW that they would like to process as if it were a CLOB or BLOB, given the APIs for these types are so superior to anything available for LONGs and LONG RAWs.

Fortunately, these conversions are easy to solve. We can convert:

❑   BLOB data into VARCHAR2

❑   VARCHAR2 into RAW

❑   LONGs into CLOBs

❑   LONG RAWs into BLOBs

We'll deal first with the BLOB to VARCHAR2, and vice versa, conversion and then look at the LONG to CLOB, or LONG RAW to BLOB conversion.

From BLOB to VARCHAR2 and Back Again

The UTL_RAW package has two very handy routines in it for us to use with BLOBs. We'll cover this package in more depth later on in thesection on UTL_RAW. These two routines are:

❑   CAST_TO_VARCHAR2 – Takes a RAW input and just changes the data type from RAW to VARCHAR2. No conversion of data actually happens, it is all really just a data type change.

❑   CAST_TO_RAW – Take a VARCHAR2 as input and makes it RAW. It doesn't change the data, just changes the data type again.

So, if you know the BLOB you have is actually text information, and in the right characterset, and everything, these functions are truly useful. Let's say someone used the LOADFROMFILE routine we briefly looked at earlier to load a series of files into a BLOB column. We would like to have the ability to view them in SQL*PLUS (masking out any 'bad' characters that would cause SQL*PLUS to behave improperly). We can use UTL_RAW to do this for us. First, we will load up some files into a DEMO table:

```
scott@DEV816> create table demo
  2  ( id              int primary key,
  3    theBlob         blob
  4  )
  5  /

Table created.

scott@DEV816> create or replace directory my_files as '/export/home/tkyte';

Directory created.

scott@DEV816> create sequence blob_seq;

Sequence created.

scott@DEV816> create or replace
  2  procedure load_a_file( p_dir_name in varchar2,
  3                         p_file_name in varchar2 )
  4  as
  5      l_blob      blob;
  6      l_bfile     bfile;
  7  begin
  8      -- First we must create a LOB in the database. We
  9      -- need an empty CLOB, BLOB, or a LOB created via the
 10      -- CREATE TEMPORARY API call to load into.
 11
 12      insert into demo values ( blob_seq.nextval, empty_blob() )
 13      returning theBlob into l_Blob;
 14
 15      -- Next, we open the BFILE we will load
 16      -- from.
 17
 18      l_bfile := bfilename( p_dir_name, p_file_name );
 19      dbms_lob.fileopen( l_bfile );
 20
 21
 22      -- Then, we call LOADFROMFILE, loading the CLOB we
 23      -- just created with the entire contents of the BFILE
 24      -- we just opened.
 25      dbms_lob.loadfromfile( l_blob, l_bfile,
 26                             dbms_lob.getlength( l_bfile ) );
 27
 28      -- Close out the BFILE we opened to avoid running
 29      -- out of file handles eventually.
 30
 31      dbms_lob.fileclose( l_bfile );
 32  end;
 33  /
```

```
Procedure created.

scott@DEV816> exec load_a_file( 'MY_FILES', 'clean.sql' );

PL/SQL procedure successfully completed.

scott@DEV816> exec load_a_file( 'MY_FILES', 'expdat.dmp' );

PL/SQL procedure successfully completed.
```

So, now I have two files loaded up. One is the script I am working on right here – clean.sql. The other is some expdat.dmp (export file) I have. Now I will write a routine that is callable from SQL to allow me to view any arbitrary 4000 byte slice of a BLOB in SQL*PLUS. We can only view 4,000 bytes, as this is a SQL limitation on the size of a VARCHAR2 data type. The CLEAN function below works much as SUBSTR would work on a regular string, but it takes a BLOB as input and optionally FROM_BYTE and FOR_BYTES arguments. These allow us to pick off an arbitrary substring of the BLOB to display. Note here how we use UTL_RAW.CAST_TO_VARCHAR2 to convert the RAW into a VARCHAR2. If we did not use this routine, the RAW bytes would be converted into hexadecimal before being placed into the VARCHAR2 field. By using this routine, we simply 'change the data type' from RAW to VARCHAR2, and no translation whatsoever takes place:

```
scott@DEV816> create or replace
  2  function clean( p_raw in blob,
  3                  p_from_byte in number default 1,
  4                  p_for_bytes in number default 4000 )
  5  return varchar2
  6  as
  7      l_tmp varchar2(8192) default
  8          utl_raw.cast_to_varchar2(
  9              dbms_lob.substr(p_raw,p_for_bytes,p_from_byte)
 10                          );
 11      l_char    char(1);
 12      l_return varchar2(16384);
 13      l_whitespace varchar2(25) default
 14                  chr(13) || chr(10) || chr(9);
 15      l_ws_char    varchar2(50) default
 16                  'rnt';
 17
 18  begin
 19      for i in 1 .. length(l_tmp)
 20      loop
 21          l_char := substr( l_tmp, i, 1 );
 22
 23          -- If the character is 'printable' (ASCII non-control)
 24          -- then just add it. If it happens to be a \, add another
 25          -- \ to it, since we will replace newlines and tabs with
 26          -- \n and \t and such, so need to be able to tell the
 27          -- difference between a file with \n in it, and a newline.
 28
 29          if ( ascii(l_char) between 32 and 127 )
 30          then
 31              l_return := l_return || l_char;
 32              if ( l_char = '\' ) then
 33                  l_return := l_return || '\';
```

```
34              end if;
35
36          -- If the character is a 'whitespace', replace it
37          -- with a special character like \r, \n, \t
38
39          elsif ( instr( l_whitespace, l_char ) > 0 )
40          then
41              l_return := l_return ||
42                      '\' ||
43                      substr( l_ws_char, instr(l_whitespace,l_char), 1 );
44
45          -- Else for all other non-printable characters
46          -- just put a '.'.
47
48          else
49              l_return := l_return || '.';
50          end if;
51      end loop;
52
53      -- Now, just return the first 4000 bytes as
54      -- this is all that the SQL will let us see. We
55      -- might have more than 4000 characters since CHR(10) will
56      -- become \n (double the bytes) and so, this is necessary.
57
58      return substr(l_return,1,4000);
59  end;
60  /

Function created.

scott@DEV816> select id,
  2         dbms_lob.getlength(theBlob) len,
  3         clean(theBlob,30,40) piece,
  4         dbms_lob.substr(theBlob,40,30) raw_data
  5    from demo;

        ID  LEN PIECE                  RAW_DATA
---------- ----- -------------------- ------------------------------
         1 3498 \ndrop sequence        0A64726F702073657175656E636520
                blob_seq;\n\ncreate    626C6F625F7365713B0A0A63726561
                table d                7465207461626C652064

         2 2048 TE\nRTABLES\n1024\n0   54450A525441424C45530A31303234
                \n28\n4000\n........    0A300A32380A343030300A0001001F
                ......                 00010001000000000000
```

As you can see, we can view the textual component of the BLOB in SQL*PLUS as clear text now using CLEAN. If we just use DBMS_LOB.SUBSTR, which returns a RAW, we get a hexadecimal dump. Looking at the hexadecimal dump, we can see the first byte of the first BLOB is 0A, which is a CHR(10), which is a newline. We can see in our text dump of the BLOB, that our CLEAN function converted the 0A into \n (newline). This just confirms our routine is working as expected. Further, in the second BLOB, we can see many binary zeroes (hexadecimal 00) in the raw dump of the expdat.dmp data. We can see that we turned them into . in our CLEAN function, as many of these special characters, if dumped to the terminal directly, would display in a non-sensical fashion.

In addition to the CAST_TO_VARCHAR2 function, UTL_RAW contains the CAST_TO_RAW function. As demonstrated above, you may have plain ASCII text stored in a BLOB. If you want to be able to use STRINGs to update this data, you would have to know how to encode the string in hexadecimal. For example:

```
scott@DEV816> update demo
   2      set theBlob = 'Hello World'
   3    where id = 1
   4   /
    set theBlob = 'Hello World'
                     *
ERROR at line 2:
ORA-01465: invalid hex number
```

does not work. The implicit conversion from VARCHAR2 to RAW assumes the string Hello World is a string of hexadecimal characters. Oracle would take the first two bytes, convert them from hexadecimal to decimal, and assign this number as byte 1 of the RAW data, and so on. We could either take the time to figure out what the hexadecimal representation of Hello World was, or we could simply cast our VARCHAR2 into a RAW type – just change the data type and don't change the bytes contained therein. For example:

```
scott@DEV816> update demo
   2      set theBlob = utl_raw.cast_to_raw('Hello World')
   3    where id = 1
   4   /

1 row updated.

scott@DEV816> commit;

Commit complete.

scott@DEV816> select id,
   2         dbms_lob.getlength(theBlob) len,
   3         clean(theBlob) piece,
   4         dbms_lob.substr(theBlob,40,1) raw_data
   5    from demo
   6   where id =1;

        ID   LEN PIECE                   RAW_DATA
---------- ----- -------------------- ------------------------------
         1    11 Hello World              48656C6C6F20576F726C64
```

Using UTL_RAW.CAST_TO_RAW('Hello World') is typically much easier than converting Hello World into 48656C6C6F20576F726C64.

Converting From LONG/LONG RAW to a LOB

Converting from a LONG or LONG RAW to a LOB is rather straightforward. The supplied SQL function TO_LOB does the job for us. TO_LOB is a rather restricted function however, in that:

❑   It can only be used in an INSERT or CREATE TABLE AS SELECT statement.

❑   It can only be used in SQL, not in PL/SQL.

The ramification of the first restriction is that you *cannot* perform a statement such as:

```
alter table t add column clob_column;
update t set clob_column = to_lob( long_column );
alter table t drop column long_column;
```

The above will fail with:

```
ORA-00932: inconsistent datatypes
```

during the UPDATE. In order to bulk convert existing tables with LONGs/LONG RAWs, you must create a new table. This is probably for the best in any case, since LONGs and LONG RAWs were stored 'inline', in other words, with the table data itself. If we simply converted them to LOBs and then removed the LONG column, we would leave the table in pretty bad shape. There would be lots of allocated, but not used, space in the table now. Rebuilding these objects is for the best.

The ramification of the second restriction is that you cannot use TO_LOB in a PL/SQL block. In order to use TO_LOB in PL/SQL we must use dynamic SQL. We'll demonstrate this in a moment.

We will take a look at two ways of using TO_LOB in the following examples. One is in the use of the TO_LOB function in a CREATE TABLE AS SELECT or INSERT INTO statement. The other is useful when the source data must remain in a LONG or LONG RAW column for the time being. For example, a legacy application needs it to be in a LONG. You would like other applications to be able to access it as a LOB, giving PL/SQL the opportunity to have full access to it via the piece-wise DBMS_LOB functions, such as READ and SUBSTR for example.

We'll start by synthesizing some LONG and LONG RAW data:

```
ops$tkyte@DEV816> create table long_table
  2  ( id        int primary key,
  3    data      long
  4  )
  5  /

Table created.

ops$tkyte@DEV816> create table long_raw_table
  2  ( id        int primary key,
  3    data      long raw
  4  )
  5  /

Table created.

ops$tkyte@DEV816> declare
  2      l_tmp    long := 'Hello World';
  3      l_raw    long raw;
  4  begin
  5      while( length(l_tmp) < 32000 )
  6      loop
  7          l_tmp := l_tmp || ' Hello World';
  8      end loop;
  9
 10      insert into long_table
 11      ( id, data ) values
```

```
12          ( 1, l_tmp );
13
14          l_raw := utl_raw.cast_to_raw( l_tmp );
15
16          insert into long_raw_table
17          ( id, data ) values
18          ( 1, l_raw );
19
20          dbms_output.put_line( 'created long with length = ' ||
21                                length(l_tmp) );
22  end;
23  /
created long with length = 32003

PL/SQL procedure successfully completed.
```

Performing a Mass One-Time Conversion Illustration

So, we have two tables, each with one row and either a LONG or a LONG RAW column. We can do a conversion from LONG to CLOB as easily as a CREATE TABLE AS SELECT statement now:

```
ops$tkyte@DEV816> create table clob_table
  2  as
  3  select id, to_lob(data) data
  4    from long_table;

Table created.
```

Additionally, we could have created the table at another point in time, and use the INSERT INTO variant to populate this table:

```
ops$tkyte@DEV816> insert into clob_table
  2  select id, to_lob(data)
  3    from long_table;

1 row created.
```

The following simply shows that the TO_LOB function does not operate in a PL/SQL block, and that this is to be expected:

```
ops$tkyte@DEV816> begin
  2      insert into clob_table
  3      select id, to_lob(data)
  4        from long_table;
  5  end;
  6  /
begin
*
ERROR at line 1:
ORA-06550: line 3, column 16:
PLS-00201: identifier 'TO_LOB' must be declared
ORA-06550: line 2, column 5:
PL/SQL: SQL Statement ignored
```

This is easy to work around using dynamic SQL (you will just have to dynamically execute the INSERT, not statically as above). Now that we've seen how to convert a LONG or LONG RAW into a CLOB or BLOB, we'll consider performance of the conversion. Typically, tables with LONGs and LONG RAWs are huge. By definition they are big tables – we are using them to store very large objects. They are in many cases, many gigabytes in size. The question is, how can we perform a bulk conversion in a timely fashion? I suggest using the following features:

❑ Unrecoverable operations such as a direct path INSERT and NOLOGGING LOBs

❑ Parallel DML (parallel INSERTs specifically)

❑ Parallel query

Here is an example using these features. I have a rather large IMAGE table, which contains many hundreds of uploaded files (uploaded from the Web). The fields in this table are the NAME of the document, the MIME_TYPE (for example, application/MS-Word), the IMG_SIZE of the document in bytes, and finally the document itself in a LONG RAW. I would like to convert this table into an equivalent table where the document is stored in a BLOB column. I might start by creating the new table:

```
scott@DEV816> CREATE TABLE "SCOTT"."T"
  2   ("NAME" VARCHAR2(255),
  3    "MIME_TYPE" VARCHAR2(255),
  4    "IMG_SIZE" NUMBER,
  5    "IMAGE" BLOB)
  6   PCTFREE 0 PCTUSED 40
  7   INITRANS 1
  8   MAXTRANS 255
  9   NOLOGGING
 10   TABLESPACE "USERS"
 11   LOB ("IMAGE") STORE AS
 12   (TABLESPACE "USERS"
 13    DISABLE STORAGE IN ROW CHUNK 32768
 14    PCTVERSION 10
 15    NOCACHE
 16    NOLOGGING
 17   ) ;

Table created.
```

Notice the TABLE and the LOB are NOLOGGING – this is important. You can alter them instead of creating them this way. Now, to convert the data from the existing IMAGE table, I would execute:

```
scott@DEV816> ALTER SESSION ENABLE PARALLEL DML;

Session altered.

scott@DEV816> INSERT /*+ APPEND PARALLEL(t,5) */ INTO t
  2   SELECT /*+ PARALLEL(long_raw,5) */
  3             name, mime_type, img_size, to_lob(image)
  4     FROM long_raw;
```

This performs a direct path, parallel insert into non-logged BLOBs. As a matter of comparison, I ran the INSERT INTO with and without logging enabled, and this was the result (using a subset of rows to be converted):

```
scott@DEV816> create table t
  2  as
  3  select name, mime_type, img_size, to_lob(image) image
  4  from image where 1=0;
Table created.

scott@DEV816> set autotrace on

scott@DEV816> insert into t
  2  select name, mime_type, img_size, to_lob(image) image
  3  from image;
99 rows created.

Execution Plan
----------------------------------------------------------
   0      INSERT STATEMENT Optimizer=CHOOSE
   1    0   TABLE ACCESS (FULL) OF 'IMAGE'

Statistics
----------------------------------------------------------
       1242  recursive calls
      36057  db block gets
      12843  consistent gets
       7870  physical reads
   34393500  redo size
       1006  bytes sent via SQL*Net to client
        861  bytes received via SQL*Net from client
          4  SQL*Net roundtrips to/from client
          2  sorts (memory)
          0  sorts (disk)
         99  rows processed
```

Note how that generated 34 MB of redo (if you add up the bytes of the 99 images, then I have 32 MB of data). Now, using the CREATE for T I have above with the NOLOGGING clauses and just using a direct path insert, I find:

```
scott@DEV816> INSERT /*+ APPEND */ INTO t
  2  SELECT name, mime_type, img_size, to_lob(image)
  3    FROM image;

99 rows created.

Execution Plan
----------------------------------------------------------
   0      INSERT STATEMENT Optimizer=CHOOSE
   1    0   TABLE ACCESS (FULL) OF 'IMAGE'

Statistics
----------------------------------------------------------
       1242  recursive calls
      36474  db block gets
      13079  consistent gets
       6487  physical reads
```

```
   1355104  redo size
      1013  bytes sent via SQL*Net to client
       871  bytes received via SQL*Net from client
         4  SQL*Net roundtrips to/from client
         2  sorts (memory)
         0  sorts (disk)
        99  rows processed
```

I generated about 1 MB of log. This conversion ran dramatically faster, and generated much less redo log. Of course, as is the case with all unrecoverable operations, you must ensure that a database backup takes place in the near future to ensure the recoverability of these new objects. Otherwise, you may find yourself reconverting the converted data in the event of a disk failure!

> *The above example is not actually executable by itself. I just happened to have an IMAGE table lying around, which had about 200 MB of data in it. This is used to demonstrate large, one-time conversions, and the differences that NOLOGGING clauses had on the size of the redo log generated.*

Performing an 'on the fly' Conversion

In many cases, you would like to be able to access (read) a LONG or LONG RAW from various environments, but find that you cannot. For example, when using PL/SQL, if the LONG RAW exceeds 32KB in size, you will find it to be quite impossible to access it. Other languages and interfaces have issues with LONGs and LONG RAWs as well. Well, using the TO_LOB function and a temporary table, we can easily convert a LONG or LONG RAW into a CLOB or BLOB on the fly. This is very handy for example when using OAS4.x or WebDB with its file upload functionality. These tools will upload documents over the Web into a database table, but unfortunately, the data type of the column they upload into is a LONG RAW. This makes accessing this column via PL/SQL virtually impossible. The functions below show how to provide access to this data via a BLOB, a snap.

We will start with a temporary table to hold the converted CLOB/BLOB, and a sequence to identify our row:

```
ops$tkyte@DEV816> create global temporary table lob_temp
  2  ( id     int primary key,
  3    c_lob clob,
  4    b_lob blob
  5  )
  6  /

Table created.

ops$tkyte@DEV816> create sequence lob_temp_seq;

Sequence created.
```

Now we'll create functions TO_BLOB and TO_CLOB. These functions use the following logic to convert a LONG or LONG RAW on the fly:

❑ The end user of this function will select the row ID from the table with the LONG or LONG RAW, instead of selecting the LONG or LONG RAW column. They will pass to us the column name of the LONG column, the table name and the row ID, identifying the row they want.

❑ We will get a sequence number to identify the row we will create in the temporary table.

- ❏ Using dynamic SQL, we will TO_LOB their LONG or LONG RAW column. The use of dynamic SQL not only makes this routine generic (works for any LONG column in any table), but it also solves the issue that TO_LOB cannot be invoked in PLSQL directly.

- ❏ We read the BLOB or CLOB we just created, back out, and return it to the caller.

Here is the code for TO_BLOB and TO_CLOB:

```
ops$tkyte@DEV816> create or replace
  2  function to_blob( p_cname in varchar2,
  3                     p_tname in varchar2,
  4                     p_rowid in rowid ) return blob
  5  as
  6      l_blob blob;
  7      l_id   int;
  8  begin
  9      select lob_temp_seq.nextval into l_id from dual;
 10
 11      execute immediate
 12         'insert into lob_temp (id,b_lob)
 13          select :id, to_lob( ' || p_cname || ' )
 14            from ' || p_tname ||
 15          ' where rowid = :rid '
 16       using IN l_id, IN p_rowid;
 17
 18      select b_lob into l_blob from lob_temp where id = l_id ;
 19
 20      return l_blob;
 21  end;
 22  /

Function created.

ops$tkyte@DEV816> create or replace
  2  function to_clob( p_cname in varchar2,
  3                     p_tname in varchar2,
  4                     p_rowid in rowid ) return clob
  5  as
  6      l_clob clob;
  7      l_id   int;
  8  begin
  9      select lob_temp_seq.nextval into l_id from dual;
 10
 11      execute immediate
 12         'insert into lob_temp (id,c_lob)
 13          select :id, to_lob( ' || p_cname || ' )
 14            from ' || p_tname ||
 15          ' where rowid = :rid '
 16       using IN l_id, IN p_rowid;
 17
 18      select c_lob into l_clob from lob_temp where id = l_id ;
 19
 20      return l_clob;
 21  end;
 22  /

Function created.
```

Now, to demonstrate their usage, we can use a simple PL/SQL block. We convert the LONG RAW into a BLOB, and show its length and a little of the data it holds:

```
ops$tkyte@DEV816> declare
  2      l_blob    blob;
  3      l_rowid rowid;
  4  begin
  5      select rowid into l_rowid from long_raw_table;
  6      l_blob := to_blob( 'data', 'long_raw_table', l_rowid );
  7      dbms_output.put_line( dbms_lob.getlength(l_blob) );
  8      dbms_output.put_line(
  9          utl_raw.cast_to_varchar2(
 10              dbms_lob.substr(l_blob,41,1)
 11                          )
 12                      );
 13  end;
 14  /
32003
Hello World Hello World Hello World Hello

PL/SQL procedure successfully completed.
```

The code to test TO_CLOB is virtually the same, with the exception that we do not need to utilize the UTL_RAW functionality:

```
ops$tkyte@DEV816> declare
  2      l_clob    clob;
  3      l_rowid rowid;
  4  begin
  5      select rowid into l_rowid from long_table;
  6      l_clob := to_clob( 'data', 'long_table', l_rowid );
  7      dbms_output.put_line( dbms_lob.getlength(l_clob) );
  8      dbms_output.put_line( dbms_lob.substr(l_clob,41,1) );
  9  end;
 10  /
32003
Hello World Hello World Hello World Hello

PL/SQL procedure successfully completed.
```

How to Write a BLOB/CLOB to Disk

This functionality is missing from the DBMS_LOB package. We have methods to load LOBs from files, but not create a file from a LOB. I mention it here, simply because we have a solution for it in this book. If you refer to Chapters 18 and 19 on *C-Based External Procedures* and *Java Stored Procedures*, I provide both the C and Java code for an external procedure that will write any BLOB, CLOB, or TEMPORARY LOB to a file on the server's file system. Both implementations perform the same function – just using different languages. Use whichever is appropriate with your server (for example, if you do not have the Java option, but you have Pro*C and a C compiler, then the C-based external procedure would be more appropriate for you).

Displaying a LOB on the Web Using PL/SQL

This is a frequently asked question. This example assumes you have one of the following installed and running on your system:

❑ WebDB's lightweight listener.

❑ OAS 2.x, 3.x or 4.x with the PL/SQL cartridge.

❑ iAS with the mod_plsql module.

Without one of the above three, this example will not work. It relies on the PL/SQL Web Toolkit (commonly referred to as the HTP functions), and the PL/SQL cartridge or module.

Another assumption we must make is that the character set of the web server (the client of the database) is the same as the database itself. This is due to the fact that the PL/SQL cartridge or module uses VARCHAR2s as the data type to return pages from the database. If the client's character set (the web server is the client in this case) is different from the database's character set, then character set conversion will take place. This conversion will typically corrupt a BLOB. For example, say you are running the web server on Windows NT. The typical character set for a client on Windows NT is WE8ISO8859P1 – Western European 8bit. Now, say the database is running on Solaris. The default and typical character set on that platform is US7ASCII – a 7bit character set. If you attempt to return a BLOB through a VARCHAR2 interface given these two character sets, you'll find that the 'high bit' is stripped off of the data as it comes out of the database. The data will be changed. Only if both the client (the web server) and the database server have the same character set will the data be passed 'as is', unchanged.

So, given that you have the above two assumptions satisfied, we can now see how to use the PL/SQL web toolkit to display a BLOB on the Web. We'll continue using the example from above (conversions) with the DEMO table. We'll load one more file:

```
ops$tkyte@DEV816> exec load_a_file( 'MY_FILES', 'demo.gif' );

PL/SQL procedure successfully completed.
```

a GIF file. Now, we need a package that can retrieve this GIF, and display it on the Web. It might look like this:

```
ops$tkyte@DEV816> create or replace package image_get
  2  as
  3        -- You might have a procedure named
  4        -- after each type of document you want
  5        -- to get, for example:
  6        -- procedure pdf
  7        -- procedure doc
  8        -- procedure txt
  9        -- and so on. Some browsers (MS IE for example)
 10        -- seem to prefer file extensions over
 11        -- mime types when deciding how to handle
 12        -- documents.
 13        procedure gif( p_id in demo.id%type );
 14  end;
 15  /

Package created.
```

```
ops$tkyte@DEV816> create or replace package body image_get
   2  as
   3
   4  procedure gif( p_id in demo.id%type )
   5  is
   6      l_lob   blob;
   7      l_amt   number default 32000;
   8      l_off   number default 1;
   9      l_raw   raw(32000);
  10  begin
  11
  12      -- Get the LOB locator for
  13      -- our document.
  14      select theBlob into l_lob
  15        from demo
  16       where id = p_id;
  17
  18      -- Print out the mime header for this
  19      -- type of document.
  20      owa_util.mime_header( 'image/gif' );
  21
  22      begin
  23          loop
  24              dbms_lob.read( l_lob, l_amt, l_off, l_raw );
  25
  26              -- It is vital to use htp.PRN to avoid
  27              -- spurious line feeds getting added to your
  28              -- document.
  29              htp.prn( utl_raw.cast_to_varchar2( l_raw ) );
  30              l_off := l_off+l_amt;
  31              l_amt := 32000;
  32          end loop;
  33      exception
  34          when no_data_found then
  35              NULL;
  36      end;
  37  end;
  38
  39  end;
  40  /

Package body created.
```

So, now if I had a **DAD** (Database Access Descriptor; part of the normal setup for the PL/SQL cartridge and module) set up called mydad I can use the URL:

```
http://myhost:myport/pls/mydata/image_get.gif?p_id=3
```

to retrieve my image. Here we are passing P_ID=3 argument into image_get.gif, asking it to find the LOB locator we stored in the row with id=3. We could embed this image in a page using the IMG tag as such:

```
<html>
<head><title>This is my page</title></head>
<body>
Here is my GIF file
<img src=http://myhost:myport/pls/mydata/image_get.gif?p_id=3>
</body>
</html>
```

Summary

LOBs provide much more functionality than the now deprecated LONG data type. This section answered some of the questions I receive frequently regarding LOB manipulations. We discussed how to load LOBs into the database. We saw how to convert from a BLOB to a CLOB, and back again. We investigated how you might efficiently convert all of your existing legacy LONG and LONG RAW data into CLOB and BLOB data using unrecoverable and parallel operations. Lastly, we discussed how you might use the PL/SQL Web Toolkit to retrieve the contents of a CLOB or BLOB, and display this on a web page.

DBMS_LOCK

The DBMS_LOCK package exposes, to the programmer, the locking mechanism used by Oracle itself. It allows them to create their own named locks. These locks can be monitored in the same way as any other Oracle lock. They will show up in the dynamic performance view V$LOCK with a type of UL (**user lock**). Also any standard tool such as Oracle Enterprise Manager, and the UTLOCKT.SQL script (found in [ORACLE_HOME]/rdbms/admin) will display them as well. In addition to exposing the locking mechanism for a programmer to use, DBMS_LOCK has one other utility function, a SLEEP function, which allows a PL/SQL program to pause for a given number of seconds.

The DBMS_LOCK package has many uses, for example:

❑ You have a routine that uses UTL_FILE to write audit messages to an operating system file. Only one process at a time should write to this file. On some operating systems, such as Solaris, many can write simultaneously (the OS does not prevent it). This results in inter-leaved audit messages that are hard or impossible to read. DBMS_LOCK can be used to serialize access to this file.

❑ To prevent mutually exclusive operations from occurring concurrently. For example, assume you have a data purge routine that can run only when other sessions that need the data are not running. These other sessions cannot begin while a purge is happening – they must wait. The purge session would attempt to get a named lock in X (exclusive) mode. The other sessions would attempt to get this same named lock in S (shared) mode. The X lock request will block while any S locks are present, and the S lock request will block while the X lock is held. You will have made it so the purge session will wait until there are no 'normal' sessions, and if the purge session is executing, all other sessions will be blocked until it is finished.

These are two common uses of this package. They work well as long as all sessions co-operate in the use of locks (there is nothing stopping a session from using UTL_FILE to open and write to that audit file without getting the appropriate lock). As an example, we will implement a solution to a mutual exclusion problem that many applications could benefit from. This problem arises from two sessions attempting to INSERT into the same table, and that table has a primary key or unique constraint on it. If both sessions attempt to use the same value for the constrained columns, the second (and third, and so on) sessions will block indefinitely, waiting for the first session to commit or rollback. If the first session commits, these blocked sessions will get an error. Only if the first session rolls back will one of the subsequent sessions have their INSERT succeed. The gist of this is that people will wait for a while to find out they cannot do what they wanted to.

This issue is avoidable when using UPDATE, because we can lock the row we want to update in a non-blocking fashion, prior to updating it. That is, instead of just executing:

```
update emp set ename = 'King' where empno = 1234;
```

you can code:

```
select ename from emp where empno = 1234 FOR UPDATE NOWAIT;
update emp set ename = 'King' where empno = 1234;
```

The use of the FOR UPDATE NOWAIT on the SELECT will have the effect of locking the row for your session (making it so the UPDATE will not block), or returning an ORA-54 'Resource Busy' error. If we do not get an error from the SELECT, the row is locked for us.

When it comes to INSERTs however, we have no such method. There is no existing row to SELECT and lock, and hence, no way to prevent others from inserting a row with the same value, thus blocking our session and causing us to wait indefinitely. Here is where DBMS_LOCK comes into play. To demonstrate this, we will create a table with a primary key and a trigger that will prevent two (or more) sessions from inserting the same values simultaneously. We will place a trigger on this table as well. This trigger will use DBMS_UTILITY.GET_HASH_VALUE (see the DBMS_UTILITY section later in this appendix for more information) to hash the primary key into some number between 0 and 1,073,741,823 (the range of lock ID numbers permitted for our use by Oracle). In this example, I've chosen a hash table of size 1,024, meaning we will hash our primary keys into one of 1,024 different lock IDs. Then, we will use DBMS_LOCK.REQUEST to allocate an exclusive lock based on that ID. Only one session at a time will be able to do this, so if someone else tries to insert a record into our table with the same primary key, their lock request will fail (and the error RESOURCE BUSY will be raised to them):

```
tkyte@TKYTE816> create table demo ( x int primary key );

Table created.

tkyte@TKYTE816> create or replace trigger demo_bifer
  2   before insert on demo
  3   for each row
  4   declare
  5       l_lock_id    number;
  6       resource_busy    exception;
  7       pragma exception_init( resource_busy, -54 );
  8   begin
  9       l_lock_id :=
 10           dbms_utility.get_hash_value( to_char( :new.x ), 0, 1024 );
 11
 12       if ( dbms_lock.request
```

```
13                    (   id                  => l_lock_id,
14                        lockmode            => dbms_lock.x_mode,
15                        timeout             => 0,
16                        release_on_commit   => TRUE ) = 1 )
17          then
18              raise resource_busy;
19          end if;
20  end;
21  /

Trigger created.
```

If, in two separate sessions you execute:

```
tkyte@TKYTE816> insert into demo values ( 1 );

1 row created.
```

it will succeed in the first one, but immediately issue:

```
tkyte@TKYTE816> insert into demo values ( 1 );
insert into demo values ( 1 )
            *
ERROR at line 1:
ORA-00054: resource busy and acquire with NOWAIT specified
ORA-06512: at "TKYTE.DEMO_BIFER", line 15
ORA-04088: error during execution of trigger 'TKYTE.DEMO_BIFER'
```

in the second session (unless the first session commits, and then a UNIQUE CONSTRAINT violation will be the error message).

The concept here is to take the *primary key* of the table in the trigger, and put it in a character string. We can then use DBMS_UTILITY.GET_HASH_VALUE to come up with a 'mostly unique' hash value for the string. As long as we use a hash table smaller than 1,073,741,823, we can 'lock' that value exclusively using DBMS_LOCK. We could use the DBMS_LOCK routine ALLOCATE_UNIQUE as well, but it comes with some amount of overhead. ALLOCATE_UNIQUE creates a unique lock identifier in the range of 1,073,741,824 to 1,999,999,999. It does this using another database table, and a recursive (autonomous) transaction. The hashing approach uses less resource, and avoids this recursive SQL call.

After hashing, we take this value, and use DBMS_LOCK to request that lock ID to be exclusively locked with a timeout of zero (it returns immediately if someone else has locked that value). If we timeout, we raise ORA-54 RESOURCE BUSY. Else, we do nothing – it is OK to INSERT, we won't block.

Of course, if the primary key of your table is an INTEGER, and you don't expect the key to go over 1 billion, you can skip the hash, and just use the number as the lock ID as well.

You'll need to play with the size of the hash table (1,024 in my example) to avoid artificial RESOURCE BUSY messages, due to different strings hashing to the same number. The size of the hash table will be application (data) specific and will be influenced by the number of concurrent insertions as well. Also, the owner of the trigger will need EXECUTE on DBMS_LOCK granted directly to them (not via a role). Lastly, you might find you run out of ENQUEUE_RESOURCES if you insert lots of rows this way without committing. If you do, you need to modify the init.ora parameter ENQUEUE_RESOURCES to be high enough (you'll get an error message about ENQUEUE_RESOURCES if you hit this). You might instead add a flag to the trigger to allow people to turn the check on and off. If I was going to insert hundreds/thousands of records, I might not want this check enabled for example.

We can 'see' our locks in the V$LOCK table, as well as the number of primary keys hashed to (the lock) it. For example, using our DEMO table from above with the trigger in place:

```
tkyte@TKYTE816> insert into demo values ( 1 );

1 row created.

tkyte@TKYTE816> select sid, type, id1
  2    from v$lock
  3    where sid = ( select sid from v$mystat where rownum = 1 )
  4  /

       SID TY          ID1
---------- -- ----------
         8 TX       589913
         8 TM        30536
         8 UL          827

tkyte@TKYTE816> begin
  2          dbms_output.put_line
  3          ( dbms_utility.get_hash_value( to_char(1), 0, 1024 ) );
  4  end;
  5  /
827

PL/SQL procedure successfully completed.
```

Notice the UL lock, our user lock, with an ID1 of 827. It just so happens that 827 is the hash value of TO_CHAR(1), our primary key.

To complete this example, we need to discuss what would happen if your application permits an UPDATE to the primary key. Ideally, you would not UPDATE a primary key, but some applications do. We would have to consider what would happen if one session updates the primary key:

```
tkyte@TKYTE816> update demo set x = 2 where x = 1;

1 row updated.
```

and another session attempts to INSERT a row with that newly updated primary key value:

```
tkyte@TKYTE816> INSERT INTO DEMO VALUES (2);
```

This second session will block once again. The issue here is that every process that can modify the primary key is not yet participating in our modified locking scheme. In order to solve this issue, the case whereby you UPDATE the primary key, we need to modify the times our trigger will fire to be:

```
before insert OR UPDATE OF X on demo
```

If the trigger we coded fires before any INSERT, or the UPDATE of the column X, our expected behavior will be observed (and the UPDATE will become non-blocking as well).

Summary

DBMS_LOCK exposes the internal Oracle locking mechanism for our applications to exploit. As demonstrated above, we can use this functionality to implement our own custom locking that goes above, and beyond the supplied functionality. We reviewed potential uses for this facility such as a serialization device for accessing a shared resource (an OS file for example), or as a method to coordinate various conflicting processes. We took an in-depth look at using DBMS_LOCK as a tool to prevent blocking INSERTs. This example demonstrated how to use DBMS_LOCK, and how to see your locks in the V$LOCK table itself. Lastly, we closed with the importance of ensuring all sessions coordinate their activities with regards to your custom locking, by discussing how an UPDATE of a primary key could subvert our non-blocking insert logic.

DBMS_LOGMNR

The LogMiner packages, DBMS_LOGMNR and DBMS_LOGMNR_D, allow for analysis of Oracle's redo log files. You would make use of this feature for some of the following reasons:

- ❑ You want to find out when a table was 'accidentally' dropped, and by whom.

- ❑ You want to perform some auditing on a given table, or set of tables, to see who has been modifying what pieces of it. You can do this auditing 'after the fact'. Normally, you might use the AUDIT command, but this must be enabled ahead of time, and it only tells you someone modified the table – not what they modified. LogMiner is good for post-facto 'who did that' discovery, and to see what data changed exactly.

- ❑ You would like to 'undo' a given transaction. In order to undo it, we'll need to see what it did, and get the PL/SQL for undoing it.

- ❑ You would like to get some empirical counts of rows modified in an average transaction.

- ❑ You would like to perform a historical analysis of how the database has been used over time.

- ❑ You would like to find out why your database is suddenly generating 10 MB of log every minute. It never used to do this, and now it is all of a sudden. Are there any obvious culprits to be found in a quick review of the logs?

- ❑ You would like to see what is really happening 'under the cover'. The contents of the redo logs show you what actually happened when you did that INSERT on a table with a trigger that does an UPDATE of another table. All of the effects of your transaction are recorded in the log. LogMiner is an excellent exploration tool.

LogMiner provides you the tools to do all this, and more. What I will provide here is a quick overview of how to use LogMiner, and then explain some of the caveats of its use that are not spelled out in the *Supplied PL/SQL Packages Reference* guide shipped with Oracle. As with all of the other packages, it is recommended that you read the section in the *Supplied PL/SQL Packages Reference* on DBMS_LOGMNR and DBMS_LOGMNR_D to get an overview of the functions and procedures they contain, and how they are used. Below in the *Options and Usage* section, we will give an overview of these procedures, and their inputs as well.

LogMiner works best on archived redo log files, although it can be used with online redo log files that are not active. Attempting to use an active online redo log file could lead to an error message or just confusion on your part, as the redo log file will contain a mixture of old and new transaction data. An interesting thing to note about LogMiner is that you do not need to analyze a log file in the database that originally created it. It doesn't even have to be the same exact database version (you can analyze version 8.0 archive files in an 8.1 database). You can move an archived redo log file to another system, and analyze it there instead. This can be quite convenient for auditing and looking at historical usage patterns, without impacting the existing system. In order to do this however, you must use a database that is on the same hardware platform (byte-ordering, word sizes, and so on will be affected by this). Also, you will want to make sure that the database block sizes are the same (or that the database doing the analysis has a block size *at least* as big as the database originating the redo log), and have the same character set.

Using LogMiner is a two-step process. Step one involves creating a data dictionary for LogMiner to operate with. This is what allows a redo log file from one database to be analyzed on another – LogMiner does not use the existing data dictionary, it uses the data dictionary that was exported to an external file by the DBMS_LOGMNR_D package. LogMiner can be used without this data dictionary, but you will find the resulting output virtually unreadable. We'll take a look at what this would look like later.

Step two involves importing the redo log files and starting LogMiner. Once LogMiner is started, you can review the contents of the redo log files using SQL. There are four V$ views associated with LogMiner. The main view is V$LOGMNR_CONTENTS. This is the view you will use to review the contents of the redo log files you have loaded. We will take a look at this view in more detail in the example and at the end of this section we have a table that defines each column. The other three views are:

❑ V$LOGMNR_DICTIONARY – This view contains information about the dictionary file that has been loaded. This is the dictionary you created in step one. In order to make sense of the contents of a redo log file, we need to have a dictionary file that tells us what object name goes with what object ID, what the columns and data types of each table are, and so on. This view contains at most, one row for the currently loaded dictionary only.

❑ V$LOGMNR_LOGS – This view contains information about the redo log files you have requested LogMiner to load into the system. The contents of these redo log files will be found in V$LOGMNR_CONTENTS. This view tells you about the redo log file itself. Attributes such as the name of the redo log file, the database name of the database it came from, the SCNs (system change numbers) contained in it and so on, are found here. This view will have an entry per log file you are analyzing.

❑ V$LOGMNR_PARAMETERS – This view shows the parameters that were passed to LogMiner during it's start up. This view will have one entry after you call the start up routine for log miner.

An important point to note here is that because LogMiner's memory allocation comes from the PGA, LogMiner cannot be used in an MTS environment. This is because with MTS, you will be assigned to a different shared server (process or thread) each time you make a request into the database. The data you loaded into Process One (Shared Server One) is simply not available to Process Two (Shared Server Two). You must be using a dedicated server configuration for LogMiner to function. Also, the output is only visible in a single session, and only for the life of that session. If further analysis is needed, you must either reload the information, or make it permanent, perhaps using a CREATE TABLE AS SELECT. If you are analyzing a large amount of data, making the data permanent via a CREATE TABLE AS SELECT or INSERT INTO makes even more sense. You would then be able to index this information whereas with the V$LOGMNR_CONTENTS table, you will always be performing a full scan of a V$ table, since it has no indexes. This full scanning of a V$ table can be quite resource-intensive.

Overview

What we'll do now is present an overview of how to use the LogMiner facility. After that, we'll look at all of the inputs to the two LogMiner supplied packages, and what they mean. Then, we will investigate using LogMiner to find out when some operation took place in the database. After that, we'll take a quick look at how LogMiner affects your session's memory usage, and how it caches the redo log files internally. Lastly, we'll look at some of the limitations of LogMiner that are not mentioned in the documentation.

Step 1: Creating the Data Dictionary

In order for LogMiner to map internal object IDs and columns to their appropriate tables, it needs a data dictionary. It will not use the data dictionary already present in the database. Rather, it relies on an external file to provide the data dictionary. LogMiner works this way in order to allow redo log files from *other* databases to be analyzed in different one. Additionally, the data dictionary that is current today in your database may not support all of the objects that were in the database when the redo log file was generated, hence the need to be able to import a data dictionary.

To see the purpose of this data dictionary file, we'll look at some output from LogMiner without having a data dictionary loaded. We'll do this by loading an archived redo log file and starting LogMiner. Then a quick query in V$LOGMNR_CONTENTS to see what is there:

```
tkyte@TKYTE816> begin
  2      sys.dbms_logmnr.add_logfile
  3      ( 'C:\oracle\oradata\tkyte816\archive\TKYTE816T001S01263.ARC',
  4        sys.dbms_logmnr.NEW );
  5  end;
  6  /

PL/SQL procedure successfully completed.

tkyte@TKYTE816> begin
  2      sys.dbms_logmnr.start_logmnr;
  3  end;
  4  /

PL/SQL procedure successfully completed.

tkyte@TKYTE816> column sql_redo format a30
tkyte@TKYTE816> column sql_undo format a30
tkyte@TKYTE816> select scn, sql_redo, sql_undo from v$logmnr_contents
  2  /

       SCN SQL_REDO                        SQL_UNDO
---------- ------------------------------  ------------------------------
6.4430E+12
6.4430E+12 set transaction read write;
6.4430E+12 update UNKNOWN.Objn:30551 set   update UNKNOWN.Objn:30551 set
           Col[2] = HEXTORAW('787878') wh  Col[2] = HEXTORAW('534d495448'
           ere ROWID = 'AAAHdXAAGAAAAJKAA ) where ROWID = 'AAAHdXAAGAAAA
           A';                             JKAAA';

6.4430E+12
6.4430E+12 commit;
```

```
tkyte@TKYTE816> select utl_raw.cast_to_varchar2(hextoraw('787878')) from dual;

UTL_RAW.CAST_TO_VARCHAR2(HEXTORAW('787878'))
-------------------------------------------------------------------
xxx

tkyte@TKYTE816> select utl_raw.cast_to_varchar2(hextoraw('534d495448')) from dual;

UTL_RAW.CAST_TO_VARCHAR2(HEXTORAW('534D495448'))
-------------------------------------------------------------------
SMITH
```

This output is fairly unreadable. We know that object number 30551 was updated and column 2 was modified. Further, we can turn the HEXTORAW('787878') into a character string. We could go to the data dictionary and find out that object 30551 is:

```
tkyte@TKYTE816> select object_name
  2   from all_objects
  3   where data_object_id = 30551;

OBJECT_NAME
-------------------------------
EMP
```

but only if we are in the same database in which the redo log file was originally generated, and only if that object still exists. Further we could DESCRIBE EMP and discover that column 2 is ENAME. Therefore, the SQL_REDO column from LogMiner is really UPDATE EMP SET ENAME = 'XXX' WHERE ROWID = ... Fortunately, we do not need to go through this laborious conversion each and every time we use log miner. We'll find that by building and then loading a dictionary, we'll get much better results. The following example shows what output we could expect if we build a dictionary file for LogMiner to work with, and then load it.

We start by creating the dictionary file. Creating this data dictionary file is rather straightforward. The prerequisites for doing this are:

❑ UTL_FILE has been configured in your init.ora file so that there is at least one directory that can be written to. See the section on UTL_FILE for information on setting this up. DBMS_LOGMNR_D, the package that builds the data dictionary file, relies on UTL_FILE to perform I/O.

❑ The schema that will execute the DBMS_LOGMNR_D package has been granted EXECUTE ON SYS.DBMS_LOGMNR_D, or has a role that is able to execute this package. By default, the EXECUTE_CATALOG_ROLE has the privilege to run this package.

Once you have UTL_FILE set up and EXECUTE ON DBMS_LOGMNR_D, creating the data dictionary file is trivial. There is only one call inside of DBMS_LOGMNR_D, and this is called BUILD. You would simply execute something along the lines of:

```
tkyte@TKYTE816> set serveroutput on

tkyte@TKYTE816> begin
  2       sys.dbms_logmnr_d.build( 'miner_dictionary.dat',
  3                                'c:\temp' );
```

```
   4  end;
   5  /
LogMnr Dictionary Procedure started
LogMnr Dictionary File Opened
TABLE: OBJ$ recorded in LogMnr Dictionary File
TABLE: TAB$ recorded in LogMnr Dictionary File
TABLE: COL$ recorded in LogMnr Dictionary File
TABLE: SEG$ recorded in LogMnr Dictionary File
TABLE: UNDO$ recorded in LogMnr Dictionary File
TABLE: UGROUP$ recorded in LogMnr Dictionary File
TABLE: TS$ recorded in LogMnr Dictionary File
TABLE: CLU$ recorded in LogMnr Dictionary File
TABLE: IND$ recorded in LogMnr Dictionary File
TABLE: ICOL$ recorded in LogMnr Dictionary File
TABLE: LOB$ recorded in LogMnr Dictionary File
TABLE: USER$ recorded in LogMnr Dictionary File
TABLE: FILE$ recorded in LogMnr Dictionary File
TABLE: PARTOBJ$ recorded in LogMnr Dictionary File
TABLE: PARTCOL$ recorded in LogMnr Dictionary File
TABLE: TABPART$ recorded in LogMnr Dictionary File
TABLE: INDPART$ recorded in LogMnr Dictionary File
TABLE: SUBPARTCOL$ recorded in LogMnr Dictionary File
TABLE: TABSUBPART$ recorded in LogMnr Dictionary File
TABLE: INDSUBPART$ recorded in LogMnr Dictionary File
TABLE: TABCOMPART$ recorded in LogMnr Dictionary File
TABLE: INDCOMPART$ recorded in LogMnr Dictionary File
Procedure executed successfully - LogMnr Dictionary Created

PL/SQL procedure successfully completed.
```

It is recommended that you issue a SET SERVEROUTPUT ON prior to executing DBMS_LOGMNR_D, as this will allow informational messages from DBMS_LOGMNR_D to be printed. This can be extremely useful when trying to diagnose an error from DBMS_LOGMNR_D. What the above command did was to create a file C:\TEMP\MINER_DICTIONARY.DAT. This is a plain text, ASCII file that you may edit to see what is in there. This file consists of a lot of SQL-like statements that are parsed and executed by the LogMiner start routine. Now that we have a dictionary file on hand, we are ready to see what the contents of V$LOGMNR_CONTENTS might look like now:

```
tkyte@TKYTE816> begin
   2      sys.dbms_logmnr.add_logfile
   3      ( 'C:\oracle\oradata\tkyte816\archive\TKYTE816T001S01263.ARC',
   4          sys.dbms_logmnr.NEW );
   5  end;
   6  /

PL/SQL procedure successfully completed.

tkyte@TKYTE816> begin
   2      sys.dbms_logmnr.start_logmnr
   3      ( dictFileName => 'c:\temp\miner_dictionary.dat' );
   4  end;
   5  /

PL/SQL procedure successfully completed.
```

```
tkyte@TKYTE816> column sql_redo format a30
tkyte@TKYTE816> column sql_undo format a30
tkyte@TKYTE816> select scn, sql_redo, sql_undo from v$logmnr_contents
  2 /

       SCN SQL_REDO                        SQL_UNDO
---------- ------------------------------ ------------------------------
6.4430E+12
6.4430E+12 set transaction read write;
6.4430E+12 update TKYTE.EMP set ENAME = ' update TKYTE.EMP set ENAME = '
           xxx' where ROWID = 'AAAHdXAAGA SMITH' where ROWID = 'AAAHdXAA
           AAAJKAAA';                      GAAAAJKAAA';

6.4430E+12
6.4430E+12 commit;
```

Now that's more like it – we can actually read the SQL that LogMiner generates for us, which would 'replay' (or undo) the transaction we are looking at. Now we are ready to go into Step 2 – Using LogMiner.

Step 2: Using Log Miner

Here, we will take the dictionary file we just generated, and use it to review the contents of some archived redo log files. Before we load a redo log file, we will generate one with some known transactions in it. For the first time around, this will make it easier to see what we have. We'll be able to correlate what we find in the V$LOGMNR_CONTENTS view with what we just did. For this to work, it is important to have a 'test' database, one where you can be ensured you are the only one logged in. This allows us to artificially constrain just exactly what gets put into the redo log. Also, it would be necessary to have the ALTER SYSTEM privilege in this database so we can force a log file archive. Lastly, this is easiest to do if the database is in archive log mode with automatic archiving. In this fashion, finding the redo log file is trivial (it will be the one just archived – we'll see below how to find this). If you are using a NOARCHIVELOGMODE database, you will need to find the active log, and determine which log file was active just prior to it. So, to generate our sample transaction we could:

```
tkyte@TKYTE816> alter system archive log current;

System altered.

tkyte@TKYTE816> update emp set ename = lower(ename);

14 rows updated.

tkyte@TKYTE816> update dept set dname = lower(dname);

4 rows updated.

tkyte@TKYTE816> commit;

Commit complete.

tkyte@TKYTE816> alter system archive log current;

System altered.
```

```
tkyte@TKYTE816> column name format a80
tkyte@TKYTE816> select name
  2    from v$archived_log
  3   where completion_time = ( select max(completion_time)
  4                               from v$archived_log )
  5  /

NAME
--------------------------------------------------------------------
C:\ORACLE\ORADATA\TKYTE816\ARCHIVE\TKYTE816T001S01267.ARC
```

Now, given that we were the only user logged in doing work, the archive redo log we just generated will have our two updates in it and nothing else. This last query against V$ARCHIVED_LOG shows us the name of the archive redo log file we actually want to analyze. We can load this into LogMiner and get started by using the following SQL. It will add the last archive redo log file to the LogMiner list, and then start LogMiner:

```
tkyte@TKYTE816> declare
  2        l_name v$archived_log.name%type;
  3  begin
  4
  5        select name into l_name
  6          from v$archived_log
  7         where completion_time = ( select max(completion_time)
  8                                     from v$archived_log );
  9
 10        sys.dbms_logmnr.add_logfile( l_name, sys.dbms_logmnr.NEW );
 11  end;
 12  /

PL/SQL procedure successfully completed.

tkyte@TKYTE816> begin
  2        sys.dbms_logmnr.start_logmnr
  3        ( dictFileName => 'c:\temp\miner_dictionary.dat' );
  4  end;
  5  /

PL/SQL procedure successfully completed.
```

The first call, to DBMS_LOGMNR.ADD_LOGFILE, loaded an archive redo log file into LogMiner. I passed in the name of the archived redo log file, as well as the option of DBMS_LOGMNR.NEW. Since this is the first log file I am adding in, I used DBMS_LOGMNR.NEW. The other options are ADDFILE to add another log file to an existing list of files and REMOVEFILE to remove a file from consideration. After we load the log files we are interested in, we can call DBMS_LOGMNR.START_LOGMNR and tell it the name of the dictionary file we created. We used a minimal call to START_LOGMNR here, passing just the name of the dictionary file. We will look at some of the other options to START_LOGMNR in the next section *Options and Usage*.

Now that we've loaded a log file and started LogMiner, we are ready to take our first look at the contents of V$LOGMNR_CONTENTS. V$LOGMNR_CONTENTS has lots of information in it and for now, we'll look at a very small slice of the data available. Specifically, we'll investigate the SCN, SQL_REDO, and SQL_UNDO columns. In case you are not familiar with it, the SCN is a simple timing mechanism that Oracle uses to guarantee ordering of transactions, and to enable recovery from failure. They are also used to guarantee read-consistency, and checkpointing in the database. Think of the SCN as a ticker – every time someone commits, the SCN is incremented by one. Here is a sample query from our example above where we lowercased the names in EMP and DEPT tables:

```
tkyte@TKYTE816> column sql_redo format a20 word_wrapped
tkyte@TKYTE816> column sql_undo format a20 word_wrapped

tkyte@TKYTE816> select scn, sql_redo, sql_undo from v$logmnr_contents
  2  /

        SCN SQL_REDO              SQL_UNDO
---------- -------------------- --------------------
6.4430E+12 set transaction read
           write;

6.4430E+12 update TKYTE.EMP set update TKYTE.EMP set
           ENAME = 'smith'      ENAME = 'SMITH'
           where ROWID =        where ROWID =
           'AAAHdYAAGAAAAJKAAA' 'AAAHdYAAGAAAAJKAAA'
           ;                    ;

6.4430E+12
6.4430E+12 update TKYTE.EMP set update TKYTE.EMP set
           ENAME = 'allen'      ENAME = 'ALLEN'
           where ROWID =        where ROWID =
           'AAAHdYAAGAAAAJKAAB' 'AAAHdYAAGAAAAJKAAB'
           ;                    ;

...(many similar rows snipped out)...

6.4430E+12 update TKYTE.DEPT    update TKYTE.DEPT
           set DNAME = 'sales'  set DNAME = 'SALES'
           where ROWID =        where ROWID =
           'AAAHdZAAGAAAAKKAAC' 'AAAHdZAAGAAAAKKAAC'
           ;                    ;

6.4430E+12 update TKYTE.DEPT    update TKYTE.DEPT
           set DNAME =          set DNAME =
           'operations' where   'OPERATIONS' where
           ROWID =              ROWID =
           'AAAHdZAAGAAAAKKAAD' 'AAAHdZAAGAAAAKKAAD'
           ;                    ;

6.4430E+12 commit;

22 rows selected.
```

As you can see, our two SQL statements generated many more than two SQL statements from the redo log. The redo log contains the bits and bytes that we changed – not SQL. Therefore our multi-row statement UPDATE EMP SET ENAME = LOWER(ENAME) is presented by LogMiner as a series of single row updates. LogMiner currently *cannot* be used to retrieve the actual SQL performed at run-time. It can only reproduce equivalent SQL, SQL that does the same thing but in many individual statements.

Now, we'll go one step further with this example. The V$LOGMNR_CONTENTS view has 'placeholder' columns. These placeholder columns are useful for finding particular updates for up to five columns in your table. The placeholder columns can tell us the name of the changed column, and show us the 'before' value of the column, and the 'after' column value. Since these columns are broken out from the SQL, it would be very easy to find the transaction such that the ENAME column was updated (the name placeholder column would have ENAME) from KING (the before image placeholder column would have KING in it) to king. We'll do another quick UPDATE example, and set up the necessary column mapping file to demonstrate this. The column mapping file (colmap for short) is used to tell LogMiner which columns are of interest to you by table. We can map up to five columns per table to be mapped, into these placeholder columns. The format of a colmap file is simply:

```
colmap = TKYTE DEPT (1, DEPTNO, 2, DNAME, 3, LOC);
colmap = TKYTE EMP (1, EMPNO, 2, ENAME, 3, JOB, 4, MGR, 5, HIREDATE);
```

This will map the DEPT DEPTNO column to the first placeholder column when we are looking at a row for the DEPT table. It will map the EMP EMPNO column to this placeholder column when we are looking at an EMP row.

The column mapping file in general has lines that consist of the following (items in **bold** are constants, <sp> represent a single, mandatory space)

colmap<sp>=<sp>OWNER**<sp>**TABLE_NAME**<sp>(**1,**<sp>**CNAME**[,<sp>**2,**<sp>**CNAME**]...);**

The case of everything is important – the OWNER must be uppercase, the table name must be the 'correct' case (uppercase is usually the correct case unless you've used quoted identifiers to create objects). The spaces are mandatory as well. In order to make using the column mapping file a little easier, I use a script such as:

```
set linesize 500
set trimspool on
set feedback off
set heading off
set embedded on
spool logmnr.opt
select
    'colmap = ' || user || ' ' || table_name || ' (' ||
  max( decode( column_id, 1,          column_id , null ) ) ||
  max( decode( column_id, 1, ', '||column_name, null ) ) ||
  max( decode( column_id, 2, ', '||column_id , null ) ) ||
  max( decode( column_id, 2, ', '||column_name, null ) ) ||
  max( decode( column_id, 3, ', '||column_id , null ) ) ||
  max( decode( column_id, 3, ', '||column_name, null ) ) ||
  max( decode( column_id, 4, ', '||column_id , null ) ) ||
  max( decode( column_id, 4, ', '||column_name, null ) ) ||
  max( decode( column_id, 5, ', '||column_id , null ) ) ||
  max( decode( column_id, 5, ', '||column_name, null ) ) || ');' colmap
 from user_tab_columns
group by user, table_name
/
spool off
```

in SQL*PLUS to generate the logmnr.opt file for me. For example, if I execute this script in a schema that contains only the EMP and DEPT tables from the SCOTT/TIGER account, I will see:

```
tkyte@TKYTE816> @colmap
colmap = TKYTE DEPT (1, DEPTNO, 2, DNAME, 3, LOC);
colmap = TKYTE EMP (1, EMPNO, 2, ENAME, 3, JOB, 4, MGR, 5, HIREDATE);
```

It always picks the first five columns of the table. If you desire a different set of five columns, just edit the resulting logmnr.opt file this creates, and change the column names. For example, the EMP table has three more columns that are not shown in the above colmap – SAL, COMM, and DEPTNO. If you wanted to see the SAL column instead of the JOB column, the colmap would simply be:

```
tkyte@TKYTE816> @colmap
colmap = TKYTE DEPT (1, DEPTNO, 2, DNAME, 3, LOC);
colmap = TKYTE EMP (1, EMPNO, 2, ENAME, 3, SAL, 4, MGR, 5, HIREDATE);
```

Important considerations for the colmap file, beyond its needs to have the correct case and whitespace, are

- *The file must be named* logmnr.opt. No other name may be used.
- This file must be *in the same directory* as your dictionary file.
- You *must be using a dictionary file* in order to use a colmap file.

So, we will now modify all of the columns in the DEPT table. I am using four different UPDATEs, each against a different row and set of columns. This is so we'll see better the effect of the placeholder columns:

```
tkyte@TKYTE816> alter system archive log current;

tkyte@TKYTE816> update dept set deptno = 11
  2    where deptno = 40
  3  /

tkyte@TKYTE816> update dept set dname = initcap(dname)
  2    where deptno = 10
  3  /

tkyte@TKYTE816> update dept set loc = initcap(loc)
  2    where deptno = 20
  3  /

tkyte@TKYTE816> update dept set dname = initcap(dname),
  2                        loc = initcap(loc)
  3    where deptno = 30
  4  /

tkyte@TKYTE816> commit;

tkyte@TKYTE816> alter system archive log current;
```

We can review the column-by-column changes now by loading the newly generated archived redo log file and starting Log Miner with the option USE_COLMAP. Note that I did generate the logmnr.opt file using the script above and I placed that file in the same directory with my dictionary file:

```
tkyte@TKYTE816> declare
  2          l_name v$archived_log.name%type;
  3  begin
  4
  5      select name into l_name
  6        from v$archived_log
  7       where completion_time = ( select max(completion_time)
  8                                   from v$archived_log );
  9
 10      sys.dbms_logmnr.add_logfile( l_name, sys.dbms_logmnr.NEW );
 11  end;
 12  /

PL/SQL procedure successfully completed.
```

```
tkyte@TKYTE816> begin
  2      sys.dbms_logmnr.start_logmnr
  3      ( dictFileName => 'c:\temp\miner_dictionary.dat',
  4        options => sys.dbms_logmnr.USE_COLMAP );
  5  end;
  6  /

PL/SQL procedure successfully completed.

tkyte@TKYTE816> select scn, ph1_name, ph1_undo, ph1_redo,
  2               ph2_name, ph2_undo, ph2_redo,
  3               ph3_name, ph3_undo, ph3_redo
  4    from v$logmnr_contents
  5   where seg_name = 'DEPT'
  6  /

       SCN PH1_NA PH1 PH1 PH2_N PH2_UNDO   PH2_REDO   PH3 PH3_UNDO PH3_REDO
---------- ------ --- --- ----- ---------- ---------- --- -------- --------
6.4430E+12 DEPTNO 40  11
6.4430E+12                  DNAME accounting Accounting
6.4430E+12                                             LOC DALLAS   Dallas
6.4430E+12                  DNAME sales      Sales     LOC CHICAGO  Chicago
```

So, this output clearly shows us (from line 1 for example) that DEPTNO had a before image value of 40 (PH1) and became 11. This makes sense, since we did SET DEPTNO = 11 WHERE DEPTNO = 40. Notice that the remaining columns in that first row of output are Null. This is because Oracle logs changed bytes only; there is no before/after image of the DNAME and LOC columns for that row. The second row shows the update of the DNAME column from accounting to Accounting, and no changes for DEPTNO or LOC, as these columns were not affected. The last row shows that when we modified two columns with our UPDATE statement, they both show up in the placeholder columns.

As you can see, using the placeholder columns can be very convenient if you are trying to locate a specific transaction in a large set of redo. If you know that the transaction updated the X table, and changed the Y column from a to b, finding this transaction will be a breeze.

Options and Usage

These are the two packages that implement the LogMiner functionality – DBMS_LOGMNR and DBMS_LOGMNR_D. The DBMS_LOGMNR_D (the _D stands for 'dictionary') package has exactly one procedure in it, which is BUILD. This is used the build the data dictionary used by the DBMS_LOGMNR package when loading a redo log file. It will map object IDs to table names, determine data types, map column positions to column name, and so on. Using the DBMS_LOGMNR_D.BUILD routine is very straightforward. It takes two parameters:

❑ DICTIONARY_FILENAME – The name of the dictionary file to be created. In our examples, we have been using the file name miner_dictionary.dat.

❑ DICTIONARY_LOCATION – The path to where this file will be created. This routine uses UTL_FILE to create the file, so this path must be a valid path as set in the utl_file_dir init.ora parameter See the UTL_FILE section later in this appendix for more details on configuring UTL_FILE.

That's it for BUILD. Neither parameter is optional, so both must be supplied. If you receive an error from this routine similar to the following:

```
tkyte@TKYTE816> exec sys.dbms_logmnr_d.build( 'x.dat', 'c:\not_valid\' );
BEGIN sys.dbms_logmnr_d.build( 'x.dat', 'c:\not_valid\' ); END;


*
ERROR at line 1:
ORA-01309: specified dictionary file cannot be opened
ORA-06510: PL/SQL: unhandled user-defined exception
ORA-06512: at "SYS.DBMS_LOGMNR_D", line 793
ORA-06512: at line 1
```

it will mean that the directory you are attempting to use is not set in the utl_file_dir init.ora parameter.

The DBMS_LOGMNR package itself has only three routines:

❑   ADD_LOGFILE – To register the set of log files to be analyzed.

❑   START_LOGMNR – To populate the V$LOGMNR_CONTENTS view

❑   END_LOGMNR – To release all resources allocated by the LogMiner processing. This should be called before exiting your session to release resources cleanly, or when you are done using LogMiner.

The ADD_LOGFILE routine, as we have seen above, is called before actually starting LogMiner. It simply builds a list of log files that START_LOGMNR will process, and populate into the V$LOGMNR_CONTENTS view for us. The inputs to ADD_LOGFILE are:

❑   LOGFILENAME – The fully qualified filename of the archived redo log file you want to analyze.

❑   OPTIONS – Specifies how to add (or remove) this file. We use the DBMS_LOGMNR constants:

DBMS_LOGMNR.NEW – Start a new list. If a list already exists, this will empty the list

DBMS_LOGMNR.ADD – Add to an already started list or empty list

DBMS_LOGMNR.REMOVEFILE – Remove a file from the list

If we wanted to analyze the last two archive redo log files, we would call ADD_LOGFILE twice. For example:

```
tkyte@TKYTE816> declare
  2      l_cnt   number default 0;
  3  begin
  4      for x in (select name
  5                  from v$archived_log
  6                  order by completion_time desc )
  7      loop
  8          l_cnt := l_cnt+1;
  9          exit when ( l_cnt > 2 );
 10
 11          sys.dbms_logmnr.add_logfile( x.name );
 12      end loop;
 13
```

```
14        sys.dbms_logmnr.start_logmnr
15        ( dictFileName => 'c:\temp\miner_dictionary.dat',
16          options => sys.dbms_logmnr.USE_COLMAP );
17  end;
18  /

PL/SQL procedure successfully completed.
```

Within that same session, after we've started LogMiner, we may call ADD_LOGFILE to add more log files, remove uninteresting ones, or if you use DBMS_LOGMNR.NEW, reset the list of log files to be just that one new file. Calling DBMS_LOGMNR.START_LOGMNR after making changes to the list will effectively flush the V$LOGMNR_CONTENTS view, and repopulate it with the contents of the log files that are on the list now.

Moving onto DBMS_LOGMNR.START_LOGMNR, we see that we have many inputs. In the above examples, we have only been using two out of the six available to us. We've used the dictionary file name and the options (to specify we wanted to use a colmap file). The available inputs in full are:

❑ STARTSCN and ENDSCN – If you know the system change number range you are interested in exactly, this will limit the rows in V$LOGMNR_CONTENTS to be between these values. This is useful after you've loaded a full log file, and determined the upper and lower SCNs you are interested in. You can restart LogMiner with this range to cut down on the size of V$LOGMNR_CONTENTS. These values default to 0, implying they are not used by default.

❑ STARTTIME and ENDTIME – Instead of using the SCN, you can supply a date/time range. Only log entries that fall between the start and end time will be visible in the V$LOGMNR_CONTENTS view. These values are ignored if STARTSCN and ENDSCN are used, and default to 01-Jan-1988 and 01-Jan-2988.

❑ DICTFILENAME – The fully qualified path to the dictionary file created by DBMS_LOGMNR_D.BUILD.

❑ OPTIONS – Currently there is only one option to DBMS_LOGMNR.START_LOGMNR and this is DBMS_LOGMNR.USE_COLMAP. This directs LogMiner to look for a logmnr.opt file in the same directory in which it finds the DICTFILENAME. It is important to note that the name of the colmap file must be logmnr.opt, and it must reside in the same directory as the dictionary file.

The last procedure in DBMS_LOGMNR is simply the DBMS_LOGMNR.END_LOGMNR routine. This terminates the LogMiner session, and empties out the V$LOGMNR_CONTENTS view. After you call DBMS_LOGMNR.END_LOGMNR, any attempt to query the view will result in:

```
tkyte@TKYTE816> exec dbms_logmnr.end_logmnr;

PL/SQL procedure successfully completed.

tkyte@TKYTE816> select count(*) from v$logmnr_contents;
select count(*) from v$logmnr_contents
                     *
ERROR at line 1:
ORA-01306: dbms_logmnr.start_logmnr() must be invoked before selecting from
v$logmnr_contents
```

Using Log Miner to Find Out When...

This is one of the more common uses of LogMiner I've seen. Someone 'accidentally' dropped a table. You would like to get it back, or just find out who did it. Or maybe someone updated an important table and you don't know whom, but no one will own up to it. In any case, something happened, you do not have auditing enabled, but you have been running in archive log mode, and have the backups. You would like to restore your backups and do a point-in-time recovery to the point in time *immediately* prior to the DROP TABLE. In this fashion, you can restore and recover that table, stop recovery (hence not dropping the table again), and then export this table from the restored database and import it into the correct database. This allows you to restore the table with all of the changes intact.

In order to do this, we'll need to know either the exact time or the SCN of the DROP TABLE. Since clocks are out of sync, and people are probably panicked, they may give bad information in this case. What we can do is load up the archived log files from around the time of the DROP TABLE, and find the exact SCN of the point we want to recover.

We'll do another quick example here to isolate the statements you might see in LogMiner when a table is dropped. I'm using locally managed tablespaces, so if you are using dictionary-managed tablespaces, you may see more SQL than I do below. This extra SQL you see with a dictionary-managed tablespace will be the SQL executed to return the extents back to the system, and free up the space allocated to the table. So, here we go to drop the table:

```
tkyte@TKYTE816> alter system archive log current;

System altered.

tkyte@TKYTE816> drop table dept;

Table dropped.

tkyte@TKYTE816> alter system archive log current;

System altered.
```

Now, we want to locate the SQL_REDO that represents the DROP TABLE. If you recall, the actual SQL executed at run-time is not reported by LogMiner. Rather, the equivalent SQL is reported. We will not see a DROP TABLE statement – we will see data dictionary modifications. The one we are looking for will be a DELETE against SYS.OBJ$, which is the base table for holding all objects. Part of dropping a table involves deleting a row from SYS.OBJ$. Fortunately, when LogMiner builds the SQL_REDO to process a DELETE, it includes the column values in the SQL along with the row ID. We can use this fact to search for the DELETE of DEPT from OBJ$. Here is how:

```
tkyte@TKYTE816> declare
  2      l_name v$archived_log.name%type;
  3  begin
  4      select name into l_name
  5        from v$archived_log
  6       where completion_time = ( select max(completion_time)
  7                                   from v$archived_log );
  8
  9      sys.dbms_logmnr.add_logfile( l_name, sys.dbms_logmnr.NEW );
 10  end;
 11  /
```

```
PL/SQL procedure successfully completed.

tkyte@TKYTE816> begin
  2      sys.dbms_logmnr.start_logmnr
  3      ( dictFileName => 'c:\temp\miner_dictionary.dat',
  4        options => sys.dbms_logmnr.USE_COLMAP );
  5  end;
  6  /

PL/SQL procedure successfully completed.

tkyte@TKYTE816> select scn, sql_redo
  2      from v$logmnr_contents
  3    where sql_redo like 'delete from SYS.OBJ$ %''DEPT''%'
  4  /

SCN SQL_REDO
---------------- --------------------------------------------
    6442991097246 delete from SYS.OBJ$ where OBJ# = 30553
                  and DATAOBJ# = 30553 and OWNER# = 337 an
                  d NAME = 'DEPT' and NAMESPACE = 1 and SU
                  BNAME IS NULL and TYPE# = 2 and CTIME =
                  TO_DATE('29-APR-2001 12:32:11', 'DD-MON-
                  YYYY HH24:MI:SS') and MTIME = TO_DATE('2
                  9-APR-2001 12:32:11', 'DD-MON-YYYY HH24:
                  MI:SS') and STIME = TO_DATE('29-APR-2001
                   12:32:11', 'DD-MON-YYYY HH24:MI:SS') an
                  d STATUS = 1 and REMOTEOWNER IS NULL and
                   LINKNAME IS NULL and FLAGS = 0 and OID$
                   IS NULL and SPARE1 = 6 and ROWID = 'AAA
                  AASAABAAAFz3AAZ';
```

That is all there is to it. Now that we have found that the SCN was 6442991097246, we can do a point in time recovery elsewhere to recover this table, and restore it to our system. We can recover it to the very point in time immediately prior to it being dropped.

PGA Usage

LogMiner uses PGA memory in order to perform its task. We have mentioned previously, that this implies you cannot use DBMS_LOGMNR with MTS. What we haven't looked at is how much PGA memory LogMiner might actually use.

The log files on my system are 100 MB each. I loaded up two of them for analysis, measuring the before and after PGA memory use:

```
tkyte@TKYTE816> select a.name, b.value
  2      from v$statname a, v$mystat b
  3    where a.statistic# = b.statistic#
  4      and lower(a.name) like '%pga%'
  5  /
```

```
NAME                             VALUE
------------------------------ ----------
session pga memory               454768
session pga memory max           454768

tkyte@TKYTE816> declare
  2          l_name varchar2(255) default
  3                  'C:\oracle\ORADATA\tkyte816\archive\TKYTE816T001S012';
  4  begin
  5          for i in 49 .. 50
  6      loop
  7          sys.dbms_logmnr.add_logfile( l_name || i || '.ARC' );
  8      end loop;
  9
 10      sys.dbms_logmnr.start_logmnr
 11      ( dictFileName => 'c:\temp\miner_dictionary.dat',
 12        options => sys.dbms_logmnr.USE_COLMAP );
 13  end;
 14  /

PL/SQL procedure successfully completed.

tkyte@TKYTE816> select a.name, b.value
  2      from v$statname a, v$mystat b
  3    where a.statistic# = b.statistic#
  4      and lower(a.name) like '%pga%'
  5  /

NAME                             VALUE
------------------------------ ----------
session pga memory             11748180
session pga memory max         11748180
```

So, 200 MB of archive redo log is currently taking about 11.5 MB of PGA memory. This means that either the archived redo was mostly 'fluff', or that Oracle doesn't actually cache the entire redo log file in RAM. The answer is that Oracle doesn't actually cache the entire redo log file in RAM. Rather, it reads it from disk as needed. Only some information in cached in RAM.

If we actually query the V$LOGMNR_CONTENTS view right now and measure the amount of PGA memory in use after this operation, we'll see that the memory requirements for this will go up as we access it:

```
tkyte@TKYTE816> create table tmp_logmnr_contents unrecoverable
  2  as
  3  select * from v$logmnr_contents
  4  /
Table created.

tkyte@TKYTE816> select a.name, b.value
  2      from v$statname a, v$mystat b
  3    where a.statistic# = b.statistic#
  4      and lower(a.name) like '%pga%'
  5  /
```

```
NAME                                    VALUE
-----------------------------   ----------
session pga memory                   19965696
session pga memory max               19965696
```

So, as you can see, our session now needs almost 20 MB of PGA memory.

Log Miner Limits

LogMiner has some serious limits that you need to be aware of. These limits are in regards to using Oracle object types and chained rows.

Oracle Object Types

Object types are somewhat supported by LogMiner. LogMiner is not able to rebuild the SQL you would typically use to access object types, and it is not able to support all object types. A quick example demonstrates best some of the limitations in this area. We'll start with a small schema with some common object types such as VARRAYs and nested tables in it:

```
tkyte@TKYTE816> create or replace type myScalarType
  2  as object
  3  ( x int, y date, z varchar2(25) );
  4  /

Type created.

tkyte@TKYTE816> create or replace type myArrayType
  2  as varray(25) of myScalarType
  3  /

Type created.

tkyte@TKYTE816> create or replace type myTableType
  2  as table of myScalarType
  3  /

Type created.

tkyte@TKYTE816> drop table t;

Table dropped.

tkyte@TKYTE816> create table t ( a int, b myArrayType, c myTableType )
  2  nested table c store as c_tbl
  3  /

Table created.

tkyte@TKYTE816> begin
  2      sys.dbms_logmnr_d.build( 'miner_dictionary.dat',
  3                              'c:\temp' );
  4  end;
  5  /
```

```
PL/SQL procedure successfully completed.

tkyte@TKYTE816> alter system switch logfile;

System altered.

tkyte@TKYTE816> insert into t values ( 1,
  2                   myArrayType( myScalarType( 2, sysdate, 'hello' ) ),
  3                   myTableType( myScalarType( 3, sysdate+1, 'GoodBye' ) )
  4                                    );

1 row created.

tkyte@TKYTE816> alter system switch logfile;

System altered.
```

So, in the above example, we created some object types, added a table that utilizes these types, re-exported our data dictionary, and then finally did some isolated DML on this object. Now we are ready to see what LogMiner is able to tell us about these operations:

```
tkyte@TKYTE816> begin
  2      sys.dbms_logmnr.add_logfile( 'C:\oracle\rdbms\ARC00028.001',
  3                                    dbms_logmnr.NEW );
  4  end;
  5  /

PL/SQL procedure successfully completed.

tkyte@TKYTE816> begin
  2      sys.dbms_logmnr.start_logmnr
  3        ( dictFileName => 'c:\temp\miner_dictionary.dat' );
  4  end;
  5  /

PL/SQL procedure successfully completed.

tkyte@TKYTE816> select scn, sql_redo, sql_undo
  2      from v$logmnr_contents
  3  /

       SCN SQL_REDO                   SQL_UNDO
---------- -------------------- --------------------
    824288
    824288
    824288
    824288 set transaction read
           write;

    824288 insert into          delete from
           TKYTE.C_TBL(NESTED_T TKYTE.C_TBL where
           ABLE_ID,X,Y,Z)       NESTED_TABLE_ID =
           values               HEXTORAW('252cb5fad8
           (HEXTORAW('252cb5fad 784e2ca93eb432c2d35b
```

```
               8784e2ca93eb432c2d35   7c') and X = 3 and Y
               b7c'),3,TO_DATE('23-    =
               JAN-2001 16:21:44',     TO_DATE('23-JAN-2001
               'DD-MON-YYYY            16:21:44',
               HH24:MI:SS'),'GoodBy    'DD-MON-YYYY
               e');                    HH24:MI:SS') and Z =
                                       'GoodBye' and ROWID
                                       =
                                       'AAAFaqAADAAAAGzAAA'
                                       ;

    824288
    824288
    824288
    824288    insert into            delete from TKYTE.T
               TKYTE.T(A,B,SYS_NC00   where A = 1 and B =
               00300004$) values      Unsupported Type and
               (1,Unsupported         SYS_NC0000300004$ =
               Type,HEXTORAW('252cb   HEXTORAW('252cb5fad8
               5fad8784e2ca93eb432c   784e2ca93eb432c2d35b
               2d35b7c'));            7c') and ROWID =
                                      'AAAFapAADAAAARjAAA'
                                      ;

    824288

10 rows selected.
```

As you can see, our original single `INSERT`:

```
tkyte@TKYTE816> insert into t values ( 1,
  2                     myArrayType( myScalarType( 2, sysdate, 'hello' ) ),
  3                     myTableType( myScalarType( 3, sysdate+1, 'GoodBye' ) )
  4                                   );
1 row created.
```

was turned into two `INSERT`s. One for the child table (the nested table), and one for the parent able `T`. LogMiner does not reproduce the single `INSERT` – equivalent SQL was produced. As we look closer however, we will notice that in the `INSERT INTO T`, we see `Unsupported Type` as one of the column values. Looking back at the original `INSERT`, we can see that the unsupported type is in fact our `VARRAY`. LogMiner is not capable of reproducing this particular construct.

This does not remove *all* of the usefulness of LogMiner with regards to objects. It does prevent us from using it to undo or redo transactions, since it cannot faithfully reproduce the necessary SQL. However, we can still use it to analyze historical trends, perform auditing, and the like. Perhaps of more interest is that it gives us the ability to see how Oracle physically implements object types under the covers. For example, look at the insert into `T`:

```
insert into tkyte.t ( a, b, SYS_NC0000300004$) values ...
```

It is pretty clear to us what `A` and `B` are. They are our `INT` and `MyArrayType` (`VARRAY`) columns. However, where is `C` and what is this `SYS_NC0000300004$` column? Well, `C` is our nested table, and nested tables are actually physically stored as a parent/child table. `C` is not stored *in* `T`; it is stored in a wholly separate table. The column `SYS_NC0000300004$` is actually a surrogate primary key on `T`, and is used as a foreign key in `C_TBL` – the nested table. If we look at the `INSERT` into the nested table:

```
insert into tkyte.c_tbl( nested_table_id, x, y, z ) values ...
```

we can see that the NESTED_TABLE_ID was added to our nested table, and this column is, in fact, used to join to the T.SYS_NC0000300004$ column. Further, looking at the value that is put into both of these columns:

```
HEXTORAW('252cb5fad8784e2ca93eb432c2d35b7c')
```

we can see that Oracle is, by default, using a system-generated 16 byte RAW value to join C_TBL with T. Therefore, through LogMiner analysis, we can gain a better understanding of how various features in Oracle are implemented. Here, we have seen how a nested table type is really nothing more than a parent/child table with a surrogate key in the parent table, and a foreign key in the child table.

Chained or Migrated Rows

LogMiner currently does not handle chained or migrated rows. A chained row is a row that spans more than one Oracle block. A migrated row is a row that started on one block when it was inserted, but due to an UPDATE, grew too large to fit on this block with the other rows that were there, and was therefore 'moved' to a new block. A migrated row retains its original row ID – the block it was originally on has a pointer to the new location for the row. A migrated row is a special type of chained row. It is a chained row where no data will be found on the first block, and all of the data will be found on the second block.

In order to see what LogMiner does with chained rows, we will artificially create one. We'll start with a table that has nine CHAR(2000) columns. I am using an 8 KB block size for my database so if all nine columns have values, they will be 18,000 bytes in size, which is too big to fit on a block. This row will have to be chained onto at least three blocks. The table we'll use to demonstrate this limitation is as follows:

```
tkyte@TKYTE816> create table t ( x int primary key,
  2                             a char(2000),
  3                             b char(2000),
  4                             c char(2000),
  5                             d char(2000),
  6                             e char(2000),
  7                             f char(2000),
  8                             g char(2000),
  9                             h char(2000),
 10                             i char(2000) );

Table created.
```

Now, to demonstrate the issue, we'll insert a row into T with a value for only column X and column A. The size of this row will be about 2,000 plus bytes. Since B, C, D, and so on are Null, they will consume no space whatsoever. This row will fit on a block. We will then update this row, and supply values for B, C, D, and E. Since CHARs are always blank padded, this will cause the size of the row to increase from 2,000 plus bytes to 10,000 plus bytes, forcing it to chain onto two blocks. We'll then update every column in the row, growing the row to 18 KB, forcing it to span three blocks. We can then dump the redo with LogMiner, and see what it does with it:

```
tkyte@TKYTE816> begin
  2      sys.dbms_logmnr_d.build( 'miner_dictionary.dat',
  3                               'c:\temp' );
  4  end;
  5  /

PL/SQL procedure successfully completed.
```

```
tkyte@TKYTE816> alter system archive log current;

System altered.

tkyte@TKYTE816> insert into t ( x, a ) values ( 1, 'non-chained' );

1 row created.

tkyte@TKYTE816> commit;

Commit complete.

tkyte@TKYTE816> update t set a = 'chained row',
  2                b = 'x', c = 'x',
  3                d = 'x', e = 'x'
  4    where x = 1;

1 row updated.

tkyte@TKYTE816> commit;

Commit complete.

tkyte@TKYTE816> update t set a = 'chained row',
  2                b = 'x', c = 'x',
  3                d = 'x', e = 'x',
  4                f = 'x', g = 'x',
  5                h = 'x', i = 'x'
  6    where x = 1;

1 row updated.

tkyte@TKYTE816> commit;

Commit complete.

tkyte@TKYTE816> alter system archive log current;

System altered.
```

Now that we've created the exact case we want to analyze, we can dump it via LogMiner. Don't forget, we need to *rebuild* your data dictionary file after we create table T, or the output will be unreadable!

```
tkyte@TKYTE816> declare
  2        l_name v$archived_log.name%type;
  3  begin
  4
  5      select name into l_name
  6        from v$archived_log
  7       where completion_time = ( select max(completion_time)
  8                                   from v$archived_log );
  9
 10      sys.dbms_logmnr.add_logfile( l_name, dbms_logmnr.NEW );
 11  end;
 12  /
```

```
PL/SQL procedure successfully completed.

tkyte@TKYTE816> begin
  2        sys.dbms_logmnr.start_logmnr
  3        ( dictFileName => 'c:\temp\miner_dictionary.dat' );
  4   end;
  5   /

PL/SQL procedure successfully completed.

tkyte@TKYTE816> select scn, sql_redo, sql_undo
  2      from v$logmnr_contents
  3    where sql_redo is not null or sql_undo is not null
  4   /

            SCN  SQL_REDO                          SQL_UNDO
---------------  --------------------------------  --------------------------
  6442991118354  set transaction read write;
  6442991118354  insert into TKYTE.T(X,A) va       delete from TKYTE.T where X
                 lues (1,'non-chained                  = 1 and A = 'non-chained
                               ');                       ' and ROWID
                                                     = 'AAAHdgAAGAAAACKAAA';

  6442991118355  commit;
  6442991118356  set transaction read write;
  6442991118356  Unsupported (Chained Row)         Unsupported (Chained Row)
  6442991118356  Unsupported (Chained Row)         Unsupported (Chained Row)
  6442991118357  commit;
  6442991118358  set transaction read write;
  6442991118358  Unsupported (Chained Row)         Unsupported (Chained Row)
  6442991118358  Unsupported (Chained Row)         Unsupported (Chained Row)
  6442991118358  Unsupported (Chained Row)         Unsupported (Chained Row)
  6442991118359  commit;

12 rows selected.
```

As you can see, the original INSERT we did was reported by Log Miner as you would expect. The UPDATE however, since it caused the row to be chained, is not reported by LogMiner. Instead it reports Unsupported (Chained Row). It is interesting to note that it reports this twice for our first UPDATE, and three times for the second. LogMiner is reporting changes by database block. If your row is on two blocks, there will be two change entries in V$LOGMNR_CONTENTS. If your database block is on three blocks, then there will be three entries. You just need to be aware of the fact that LogMiner cannot faithfully reproduce the SQL to redo or undo actions against chained and migrated rows.

Other limits

LogMiner has some other limitations similar to the above. In addition to the above it does not currently support:

❑   Analysis of IOTs.

❑   Analysis of clustered tables and indexes.

V$LOGMNR_CONTENTS

The V$LOGMNR_CONTENTS table contains a row for every logical change to the database retrieved from the processed redo log files. We have already used this view many times, but have utilized a small fraction of the columns within it. The following table describes all of the columns available in this view with a more detailed description of what is available in them, than is available in the Oracle documentation:

PRIVATE COLUMN	DESCRIPTION
SCN	**S**ystem **C**hange **N**umbers associated with the transaction that made this change.
TIMESTAMP	Date when redo record was generated. Timestamps cannot be used to infer ordering of redo records. Since the SCN is assigned upon COMMIT, only the SCN can be used to infer ordering of redo records. Ordering by timestamp in a multi-user system will result in the wrong order.
THREAD#	Identifies the thread that generated the redo record.
LOG_ID	Identifies the log file within the V$LOGMNR_FILES table that contains the redo record. This is a foreign key to the V$LOGMNR_FILES view.
XIDUSN	Transaction **ID** (**XID**) **U**ndo **S**egment **N**umber (**USN**). The transaction identifier is constructed from the XIDUSN, XIDSLOT, and XIDSQN, and is used to identify the transaction that generated the change. These three fields taken together uniquely identify the transaction.
XIDSLOT	Transaction ID slot number. Identifies the transaction table entry number.
XIDSQN	Transaction ID sequence number.
RBASQN	Uniquely identifies the log that contained this redo record, among a group of redo logs. A **RBA** (**R**edo **B**lock **A**ddress) is composed of the RBASQN, RBABLK, and RBABYTE fields.
RBABLK	The block number within the log file.
RBABYTE	The byte offset within the block.
UBAFIL	**UBA** (Undo Block Address) file number identifying the file containing the undo block. The UBA is constructed from the UBAFIL, UBABLK, UBASQN, and UBAREC, and is used to identify the undo generated for the change.
UBABLK	UBA block number.
UBAREC	UBA record index.
UBASQN	UBA undo block sequence number.
ABS_FILE#	Data block absolute file number. The ABS_FILE#, together with the REL_FILE#, DATA_BLOCK#, DATA_OBJ#, DATA_DOBJ, identify the block changed by the transaction.
REL_FILE#	Data block relative file number. The file number is relative to the tablespace of the object.

Table continued on following page

PRIVATE COLUMN	DESCRIPTION
DATA_BLOCK#	Data block number.
DATA_OBJ#	Data block object number.
DATA_DOBJ#	Data block data object number identifying the object within the tablespace.
SEG_OWNER	Name of the user owning the object.
SEG_NAME	Name of the structure the segment was allocated for (in other words, table name, cluster name, and so on). Partitioned tables will have a segment name constructed of two parts; the table name followed by a comma-separated partition name (for example, (TableName,PartitionName)).
SEG_TYPE	The type of the segment in numeric form.
SEG_TYPE_NAME	The type of segment in string form (in other words, TABLE, INDEX, and so on) Only the type, TABLE, will be supported in the initial release. Other segment types will be reported as UNSUPPORTED.
TABLE_SPACE_NAME	Name of the tablespace.
ROW_ID	Row ID.
SESSION#	Identifies session that generated the redo. A Null value will be reported if the session number is not available from the redo log.
SERIAL#	Serial number of the session, which generated the redo. The SESSION# and SERIAL# can be used to uniquely identify the Oracle session. A Null value will be reported if the session number is not available from the redo log.
USERNAME	Name of the user initiating the operation that generated the redo record. The user name will always be Null if the archive auditing option is not enabled. This auditing is enabled via the init.ora parameter TRANSACTION_AUDITING.
SESSION_INFO	String containing login username, client information, OS username, machine name, OS terminal, OS PID, OS program name.
ROLLBACK	A value of 1 (True) identifies operations and SQL statements that were generated as a result of a rollback request, 0 (False) otherwise.
OPERATION	Type of SQL operation. Only INSERT, DELETE, UPDATE, COMMIT, and BEGIN_TRANSACTION will be reported. All other operations will be reported as UNSUPPORTED or INTERNAL_OPERATION.
SQL_REDO, SQL_UNDO	The SQL_REDO and SQL_UNDO columns contain SQL-compliant statements that represent the logical redo and undo operations decoded from one or more archive log records. A Null value indicates that no valid SQL statement can be generated for this redo record. Some redo records may not be translatable. In this case, the SQL_REDO and SQL_UNDO will be Null, and the STATUS column will contain the string UNSUPPORTED.

PRIVATE COLUMN	DESCRIPTION
RS_ID	RS_ID (Record Set ID). uniquely identifies the set of records used to generate a SQL statement (a set may be a single record). It can be used to determine when multiple records generate a single SQL statement. The RS_ID will be identical for all records within the set. The SQL statement will appear only in the last row the record set. The SQL_REDO and SQL_UNDO columns for all other rows, within the set, will be Null. Note that the RS_ID/SSN pair together provide a unique SQL identifier for every SQL statement generated (see SSN).
SSN	The SSN (SQL Sequence Number) can be used to identify multiple rows, with valid SQL_REDO statements, that are generated from a single redo record (in other words, array inserts, direct loads). All such rows will have the same RS_ID, but a unique SSN. The SSN is an incrementing value starting at 1 for each new RS_ID.
CSF	CSF (Continuation SQL Flag) set to 1 (True) indicates that either a LogMiner-generated REDO_SQL or UNDO_SQL statement is larger than the maximum size of the VARCHAR2 (currently 4000 characters) data type. SQL statements exceeding this limit will span multiple rows.
	The next row entry will contain the remainder of the SQL statement. The RS_ID, SSN pair will be identical for all continued rows corresponding to the same SQL statement. The last of the continued rows will have CSF set to 0 (False) to indicate the end of the SQL continuation.
STATUS	Indicates the status of the translation. Null value indicates a successful translation, UNSUPPORTED will indicate that this version of LogMiner does not support the SQL translation, READ_FAILURE will indicate an internal operating system failure to read from the log file, TRANSLATION_ERROR will indicate that LogMiner was unable to complete the translation (this may be due to a corrupted log or an out of date dictionary file).
PH1_NAME	Placeholder column name. Placeholder columns are generic columns that can be assigned to specify database table columns, via an optional LogMiner mapping file.
PH1_REDO	Placeholder column redo value.
PH1_UNDO	Placeholder column undo value.
PH2_NAME	Placeholder column name.
PH2_REDO	Placeholder column redo value.
PH2_UNDO	Placeholder column undo value.
PH3_NAME	Placeholder column name.
PH3_REDO	Placeholder column redo value.
PH3_UNDO	Placeholder column undo value.
PH4_NAME	Placeholder column name.
PH4_REDO	Placeholder column redo value.
PH4_UNDO	Placeholder column undo value.
PH5_NAME	Placeholder column name.
PH5_REDO	Placeholder column redo value.
PH5_UNDO	Placeholder column undo value.

Summary

LogMiner is not a tool you will use every day – I cannot anticipate any application that would actually use it as part of its processing. It is an easy way to see what the database does however, and is an excellent exploration tool in this regard. We have seen how LogMiner can be useful in finding out 'who did what and when' after the fact – this is the use of LogMiner I've seen more often than others. You have the errant program that is doing something it wasn't supposed to, or you have a privileged person doing things they shouldn't be (and not owning up to it). If auditing wasn't turned on, you have no other way to go back in time, and see what happened. In a pinch, this tool can be used to undo an errant transaction as well, given that it supplies you the SQL UNDO and REDO statements. In general, you'll find that LogMiner is a good 'stealth' tool. It won't be on the top ten list of executed procedures, but when you need it, it's good to know it is there.

DBMS_OBFUSCATION_TOOLKIT

In this section, we'll take a look at encryption of data. We will discuss the supplied DBMS_OBFUSCATION_TOOLKIT package for Oracle 8.1.6 and 8.1.7. We will look at another implementation (a wrapper) that could be placed on top of this package, increasing its functionality. We will discuss some of the caveats with regards to using this package and perhaps most importantly, we'll touch on the subject of key management.

In Oracle 8.1.6, database packages for encryption were introduced. These packages have been enhanced for Oracle 8.1.7 to include support wider ranging encryption key sizes and MD5 hashing. In Oracle 8.1.6, support for single **DES** (Data Encryption Standard) encryption using a 56-bit key is provided. In Oracle 8.1.7, support for both single and triple DES encryption is provided, allowing for the use of 56, 112, or 168-bit keys. DES is implemented using a **symmetric key cipher**. What this means simply, is that the same key used to encrypt data, is used to decrypt data. DES encrypts data in 64-bit (8 byte) blocks using a 56-bit key. We'll see below how this 8-byte fact affects us when using the encryption routines. The DES algorithm ignores 8 bits of the 64-bit key that is supplied. However, developers must supply a 64-bit (8 byte) key to the algorithm. Triple DES (**3DES**) is a far stronger cipher than DES. The resulting encrypted data is much harder to break using an exhaustive search. It would take $2**112$ attempts using two-key (16 byte key) 3DES, or $2**168$ attempts using three-key (24 byte key) 3DES, as opposed to $2**56$ attempts with single-key DES.

To quote the executive summary of **rfc1321** (for a full description of rfc1321, the website is http://www.ietf.org/rfc.html), the new MD5:

> ... takes as input a message of arbitrary length and produces as output a 128-bit "fingerprint" or "message digest" of the input. It is conjectured that it is computationally infeasible to produce two messages having the same message digest, or to produce any message having a given prespecified target message digest. The MD5 algorithm is intended for digital signature applications, where a large file must be "compressed" in a secure manner before being encrypted with a private (secret) key under a public-key cryptosystem such as RSA.

In essence, MD5 is a way to verify data integrity, and is much more reliable than checksum and many other commonly used methods.

In order to run the DES3 and MD5 examples below, you will need access to an Oracle 8.1.7 database. The DES examples require the use of Oracle 8.1.6, or higher.

The encryption and MD5 routines have the following constraints that make them a bit unwieldy to use 'out of the box' in the DBMS_OBFUSCATION_TOOLKIT package. They are:

❑ The data being encrypted must have a length that is evenly divisible by 8. A 9-byte VARCHAR2 field for example, must be padded out to 16 bytes. Any attempt to encrypt or decrypt a piece of data that does not have a length evenly divisible by 8, will fail with an error.

❑ The key used to encrypt the data must be 8 bytes long for DESEncrypt, and either 16 or 24 bytes for DES3Decrypt.

❑ There are different routines to be called depending on whether you are using 56 bit encryption (DESENCRYPT and DESDECRYPT) versus 112/168bit encryption (DES3ENCRYPT and DES3DECRYPT). I personally find it nicer to have one set of routines for all three.

❑ The encryption routines in Oracle 8.1.6 are procedures and therefore, they are not callable from SQL (procedures cannot be called from SQL).

❑ The 'out of the box' encryption routines support encryption of up to 32 KB of data. They do not encrypt/decrypt LOBs.

❑ The encryption routines in Oracle 8.1.7 include functions. However, these functions are overloaded in such a way (see the example below) that also makes them not callable from SQL.

❑ The MD5 routines are likewise overloaded in such a way as to make them not callable from SQL.

I find the first constraint, that the data length must be a multiple of 8, to be the hardest to satisfy in an application. Typically, I just have some data, like a salary amount or some other sensitive data, and want to encrypt it. I do not really want to be bothered with ensuring it is a multiple of 8 bytes in length. Fortunately, we can easily implement our own encryption wrapper package to hide this, and most all of the other issues. The fact that the key must be 8, 16 or, 24 bytes in length is something that you must do yourself, however.

What I intend to do here is to create a wrapper package, that is installable in 8.1.6 and later versions, which provides support for all of the encryption functionality, and adds support for:

❑ Calling the functions from SQL

❑ Single function calls regardless of the key length

❑ Encryption/decryption of LOBs callable from both PL/SQL and SQL

❑ Installing successfully regardless of which version of the database (8.1.6 or 8.1.7) you are using. That is, it is not dependent on DES3Encrypt/Decrypt, and MD5 support.

The Wrapper

We'll start with the package specification. Here we will define an API that provides functions to encrypt and decrypt VARCHAR, RAW, BLOB, and CLOB data. The algorithm used (single key DES or 3DES with 16 or 24 byte keys) will be decided, based on the key length. In our API, the length of the key you send in implies the algorithm.

The API is set up so that the key may be passed in with each call, or it may optionally be set for the package by calling SETKEY. The advantage of using SETKEY is that a certain amount of work must be performed to look at the key length and figure out which algorithm to use. If you set the key once and call the routines many times, we can avoid performing this iterative work over and over. Another detail about the key we must use is that if you are working with RAW or BLOB data, you must use a RAW key. If you want to use a VARCHAR2 as the key for RAW/BLOB data, you must cast it to be a RAW using the UTL_RAW package discussed in a later section of this appendix. On the other hand, if you are working with VARCHAR2 and CLOB data, the key must be a VARCHAR2.

In addition to providing a layer on top of encryption, this package provides access to the MD5 CHECKSUM routines if installed (version 8.1.7 and up).

This wrapper package adds a couple of new possible errors to the documented set of DBMS_OBFUSCATION_TOOLKIT errors (which this package will simply propagate). The following 'new' errors will only occur when using version 8.1.6:

❑   PLS-00302: component 'MD5' must be declared

❑   PLS-00302: component 'DES3ENCRYPT' must be declared

❑   PLS-00302: component 'THREEKEYMODE' must be declared

You will get these errors if you attempt to use the 8.1.7 functionality of DES3 encryption or MD5 hashing, in the 8.1.6 database.

Here is our suggested wrapper package specification. Explanation of the procedures and functions listed below follow the code:

```
create or replace package crypt_pkg
as

function encryptString( p_data in varchar2,
                        p_key  in varchar2 default NULL ) return varchar2;
function decryptString( p_data in varchar2,
                        p_key  in varchar2 default NULL ) return varchar2;

function encryptRaw( p_data in raw, p_key in raw default NULL ) return raw;
function decryptRaw( p_data in raw, p_key in raw default NULL ) return raw;

function encryptLob( p_data in clob,
                     p_key  in varchar2 default NULL ) return clob;
function encryptLob( p_data in blob,
                     p_key  in raw default NULL ) return blob;
function decryptLob( p_data in clob,
                     p_key  in varchar2 default NULL ) return clob;
function decryptLob( p_data in blob,
```

```
                        p_key  in raw default NULL ) return blob;

   subtype checksum_str is varchar2(16);
   subtype checksum_raw is raw(16);

   function md5str( p_data in varchar2 ) return checksum_str;
   function md5raw( p_data in raw ) return checksum_raw;
   function md5lob( p_data in clob ) return checksum_str;
   function md5lob( p_data in blob ) return checksum_raw;

   procedure setKey( p_key in varchar2 );

end;
/
```

The functions ENCRYPTSTRING and DECRYPTSTRING are used to encrypt/decrypt any STRING, DATE, or NUMBER data up to 32 KB in size. 32 KB is the maximum size of a PL/SQL variable, and is considerably larger than the maximum size that can be stored in a database table, where the limit is 4,000 bytes. These functions are callable from SQL directly so you'll be able to encrypt data in the database using an INSERT or UPDATE statement, and retrieve decrypted data using a simple SELECT. The KEY parameter is optional. If you have set a key via the SETKEY procedure, we do not need to pass it with each and every call.

Next we have ENCRYPTRAW and DECRYPTRAW. These functions are to the RAW data type what the previous two functions are to VARCHAR2s. Note how we purposely avoided function overloading the encrypt/decrypt routines for RAW and VARCHAR2 data by naming them differently. We did this because of the following issue:

```
tkyte@TKYTE816> create or replace package overloaded
  2  as
  3          function foo( x in varchar2 ) return number;
  4          function foo( x in raw ) return number;
  5  end;
  6  /

Package created.

tkyte@TKYTE816> select overloaded.foo( 'hello' ) from dual;
select overloaded.foo( 'hello' ) from dual
       *
ERROR at line 1:
ORA-06553: PLS-307: too many declarations of 'FOO' match this call


tkyte@TKYTE816> select overloaded.foo( hextoraw( 'aa' ) ) from dual;
select overloaded.foo( hextoraw( 'aa' ) ) from dual
       *
ERROR at line 1:
ORA-06553: PLS-307: too many declarations of 'FOO' match this call
```

The database does not distinguish between RAW and VARCHAR2 in the signature of an overloaded function. We would have no way to call these functions from SQL. Even if we used different parameter names for the inputs to these routines (as DBMS_OBFUSCATION_TOOLKIT currently does), they cannot be *called* from SQL because named parameter notation cannot be *used* in SQL. The only viable solution to this conundrum is to use functions with unique names to identify the routine we really want.

Next we have the ENCRYPTLOB and DECRYPTLOB functions. These are overloaded functions designed to work with either CLOBs or BLOBs. Oracle is able to successfully overload, based on these types, so we'll take advantage of this fact. Since we are limited to encrypting at most 32 KB of data by the DBMS_OBFUSCATION_TOOLKIT routine, these wrapper APIs will implement an algorithm that encrypts 32 KB chunks of a LOB. The resulting LOB will be a series of encrypted 32 KB chunks of data. The decrypt wrapper we implement understands how the data was packed by the LOB encryption routines, and will decrypt the pieces for us and re-assemble them back into our original LOB.

Next, we have the routines for the MD5 CHECKSUMs. To better define what these routines return, we've set up the subtypes:

```
subtype checksum_str is varchar2(16);
subtype checksum_raw is raw(16);
```

and defined our routines to return these types. You can declare variables of this type yourself:

```
tkyte@TKYTE816> declare
  2      checksum_variable    crypt_pkg.checksum_str;
  3  begin
  4  null;
  5  end;
  6  /

PL/SQL procedure successfully completed.
```

This saves you from having to guess how big the checksum return types are. We've provided for four different CHECKSUM routines, one each for VARCHAR2 (includes the DATE and NUMBER types), RAW, CLOB, and BLOB data. It should be noted that the MD5 checksum will only be computed on the first 32 KB of the CLOB or BLOB data, as this is the largest variable PL/SQL can work with.

The implementation of the package below will not only give us an easier to use encryption package, but it also shows a couple of useful concepts. Firstly, it shows how you can easily create your own wrapper layer to provide for a more customized interface to the database packages. In this case, we are working around some perceived limitations of the DBMS_OBFUSCATION_TOOLKIT package. Secondly, it shows one method for developing a package that is protected from enhancements in the supplied database packages over time. We would like to provide a single wrapper package that works both in 8.1.6 and 8.1.7, but which provides total access to the 8.1.7 functionality. If we used static SQL to access the DESENCRYPT, DES3DECRYPT, and MD5 routines, we would need a different package for 8.1.6 because MD5 and the DES3 functions do not exist in 8.1.6. The dynamic invocation we'll utilize below allows us to develop a package that can be used by both versions of the database. It also reduces the amount of code has to be written.

Here is the implementation of the CRYPT_PKG with explanations of what is taking place intermixed with the code:

```
create or replace package body crypt_pkg
as
-- package globals
g_charkey           varchar2(48);
g_stringFunction    varchar2(1);
g_rawFunction       varchar2(1);
g_stringWhich       varchar2(75);
g_rawWhich          varchar2(75);
g_chunkSize         CONSTANT number default 32000;
```

The package begins with a few global variables. They are:

❑ G_CHARKEY – This stores the RAW or VARCHAR2 key for use by the encryption routines. It is 48 bytes long to support holding a 24 byte RAW key (which will be doubled in length due to the hexadecimal conversion caused by placing a RAW string in a VARCHAR2 variable).

❑ G_STRINGFUNCTION and G_RAWFUNCTION – Contains either Null or the string '3' after a call to SETKEY. We will dynamically add this string to the routine name at run-time so we either run DESENCRYPT or DES3ENCRYPT, depending on the key size. In short, this is used to construct the appropriate function name we need to call.

❑ G_STRINGWHICH and G_RAWWHICH – Used with DES3EN/DECRYPT only. Adds the fourth optional parameter to force 3 key mode, when doing 3DES in 3 key mode. Whereas the string function variables above tell us whether to call DESENCRYPT or DES3ENCRYPT, this tells us what value we need to pass in for the key mode (two key or three key).

❑ G_CHUNKSIZE – A constant that controls the size of the LOB chunk we'll encrypt/decrypt. It also controls the maximum amount of data sent to the MD5 checksum routines when working with LOBs. It is *crucial* that this number is a multiple of 8 – the implementation below counts on it!

Continuing on, we have six small 'private' routines to implement. These are helper functions used by the other routines in the package:

```
function padstr( p_str in varchar2 ) return varchar2
as
    l_len number default length(p_str);
begin
    return to_char(l_len,'fm00000009') ||
            rpad(p_str, ( trunc(l_len/8)+sign(mod(l_len,8)) )*8, chr(0));
end;


function padraw( p_raw in raw ) return raw
as
    l_len number default utl_raw.length(p_raw);
begin
    return utl_raw.concat( utl_raw.cast_to_raw(to_char(l_len,'fm00000009')),
                            p_raw,
                            utl_raw.cast_to_raw( rpad(chr(0),
                            (8-mod(l_len,8))*sign(mod(l_len,8)),
                            chr(0))));
end;
```

It you recall from the description of the DES encryption algorithm, it was stated that '*DES encrypts data in 64-bit (8 byte) blocks...*' A side effect of this is that the DBMS_OBFUSCATION_TOOLKIT package works *only* on data whose length is a multiple of 8. If you have a string that is 7 bytes long, it must be padded to 8 bytes. A 9 byte string must be padded out to 16 bytes. The above two routines encode and pad out strings and RAW data. They encode the string or RAW by placing the original length into the string/RAW itself. Then they pad out the string with binary zeros (CHR(0)) to make it a multiple of 8 bytes in length. For example, the string Hello World will be encoded as follows:

```
tkyte@TKYTE816> select length(padstr), padstr, dump(padstr) dump
  2    from
  3    ( select to_char(l_len,'fm00000009') ||
  4            rpad(p_str,
  5               (trunc(l_len/8)+sign(mod(l_len,8)) )*8,
  6            chr(0)) padstr
  7        from ( select length( 'Hello World' ) l_len,
  8                     'Hello World' p_str
  9               from dual
 10             )
 11    )
 12  /

LENGTH(PADSTR) PADSTR                        DUMP
-------------- ------------------------      ------------------------------
           24 00000011Hello World           Typ=1 Len=24: 48,48,48,48,48,4
                                             8,49,49,72,101,108,108,111,32,
                                             87,111,114,108,100,0,0,0,0,0
```

The final length of the encoded string is 24 bytes (LENGTH(PADSDTR)), and the original length was 11 (this is visible in the first 8 characters of the PADSTR column). Looking at the DUMP column, which shows the ASCII values of the bytes in the string, we can see it ends with 5 binary zeroes. We needed to pad out 5 bytes to make the 11 byte Hello World string a multiple of 8. Next, we have the routines that 'undo' the padding we did above:

```
function unpadstr( p_str in varchar2 ) return varchar2
is
begin
    return substr( p_str, 9, to_number(substr(p_str,1,8)) );
end;

function unpadraw( p_raw in raw ) return raw
is
begin
    return utl_raw.substr( p_raw, 9,
        to_number( utl_raw.cast_to_varchar2(utl_raw.substr(p_raw,1,8)) ) );
end;
```

They are straightforward enough. They assume the first 8 bytes of the string or RAW is the original length of the string, and return the SUBSTR of this encoded data appropriately.

Continuing on, we have the last of our internal helper routines:

```
procedure wa( p_clob in out clob, p_buffer in varchar2 )
is
begin
    dbms_lob.writeappend(p_clob,length(p_buffer),p_buffer);
end;

procedure wa( p_blob in out blob, p_buffer in raw )
is
begin
    dbms_lob.writeappend(p_blob,utl_raw.length(p_buffer),p_buffer);
end;
```

These simply make it easier to call DBMS_LOB.WRITEAPPEND, by shortening the name to WA, and by passing in the length of the buffer to write for us, which in our case is always the current length of the buffer.

Now we hit our first externally callable routine SETKEY:

```
procedure setKey( p_key in varchar2 )
as
begin
    if ( g_charkey = p_key OR p_key is NULL ) then
        return;
    end if;
    g_charkey := p_key;

    if ( length(g_charkey) not in ( 8, 16, 24, 16, 32, 48 ) )
    then
        raise_application_error( -20001,
                            'Key must be 8, 16, or 24 bytes' );
    end if;

    select decode(length(g_charkey),8,'','3'),
           decode(length(g_charkey),8,'',16,'',
               24,', which=>dbms_obfuscation_toolkit.ThreeKeyMode'),
           decode(length(g_charkey),16,'','3'),
           decode(length(g_charkey),16,'',32,'',
               48,', which=>dbms_obfuscation_toolkit.ThreeKeyMode')
       into g_stringFunction, g_stringWhich, g_rawFunction, g_rawWhich
       from dual;
end;
```

This routine is used whether you call it or not. The remaining externally callable routines below will call SETKEY regardless of whether you do or not. This routine will compare your key P_KEY to the one in the global variable G_CHARKEY. If they compare, or no key was provided, this routine simply returns. It has no work to perform. If the P_KEY is different from G_CHARKEY however, this routine will continue. The first thing it does is a sanity check to verify that the key is a valid multiple of 8. The key must be 8, 16 or 24 bytes in length. Since this routine may be passed RAW data, which causes each byte to be expanded into a 2 byte hexadecimal code, 16, 32, and 48 are valid lengths as well. This check does not fully guarantee the key will work however. For example, you could send a 4 byte RAW key that will appear as 8 bytes to us. You will get a run-time error from DBMS_OBFUSCATION_TOOLKIT later in that case.

The SELECT with a DECODE is a used to set up the remaining global variables. Since we cannot tell the difference between a RAW and VARCHAR2 string at this point, we set up all four possible variables. The key thing to note about this piece of code is that if the length of the key is 8 bytes (16 bytes when RAW), then the FUNCTION variable will be set to a Null string. If the key length is 16 or 24 bytes (32 or 48 bytes when RAW), the FUNCTION variable will be set to the string '3'. This is what will cause us to call DESENCRYPT or DES3Encrypt later. The other thing to notice here is the setting of the WHICH global variable. This is used to set the optional parameter to the DES3ENCRYPT routine. If the key length is 8 or 16 bytes (16 or 32 bytes RAW), we set this string to Null – we do not pass a parameter. If the key length is 24 bytes (48 bytes RAW), we set this string to pass THREEKEYMODE to the ENCRYPT/DECRYPT routines to instruct them to use this larger key.

Now we are ready to see the functions that do the actual work for us:

```
function encryptString( p_data in varchar2,
                        p_key  in varchar2 default NULL ) return varchar2
as
    l_encrypted long;
begin
    setkey(p_key);
    execute immediate
    'begin
        dbms_obfuscation_toolkit.des' || g_StringFunction || 'encrypt
        ( input_string => :1, key_string => :2, encrypted_string => :3' ||
        g_stringWhich || ' );
     end;'
     using IN padstr(p_data), IN g_charkey, IN OUT l_encrypted;

    return l_encrypted;
end;

function encryptRaw( p_data in raw,
                     p_key  in raw default NULL ) return raw
as
    l_encrypted long raw;
begin
    setkey(p_key);
    execute immediate
    'begin
        dbms_obfuscation_toolkit.des' || g_RawFunction || 'encrypt
        ( input => :1, key => :2, encrypted_data => :3' ||
        g_rawWhich || ' );
     end;'
     using IN padraw( p_data ), IN hextoraw(g_charkey), IN OUT l_encrypted;

    return l_encrypted;
end;
```

The ENCRYPTSTRING and ENCRYPTRAW functions work in a similar manner to each other. They both *dynamically* call either DESENCRYPT or DES3ENCRYPT. This dynamic call not only reduces the amount of code we have to write as it avoids the IF THEN ELSE we would have use to statically call either routine, but it also makes it so the package can be installed in 8.1.6 or 8.1.7, without change. Since we do not statically reference DBMS_OBFUSCATION_TOOLKIT, we can compile against either version. This dynamic invocation is a technique that is useful any time you are not certain what might or might not be installed in the database. I've used it in the past when writing utility routines that needed to be installed in 7.3, 8.0, and 8.1. Over time, additional functionality was added to the core packages, and when the code was running in 8.1, we wanted to take advantage of it. When we were running in 7.3, the code would still function; it just wouldn't be able to benefit from the newer functionality. The same concept applies here. When installed in an 8.1.7 database, the above code can, and will call DES3ENCRYPT. When installed in 8.1.6, any attempt to invoke the DES3ENCRYPT will result in a run-time error (instead of preventing you from installing this package). The calls to DESENCRYPT will function as expected in 8.1.6.

These functions work simply by creating a dynamic string using the FUNCTION and WHICH we set in the SETKEY routine. We will either add the number 3 to the procedure name, or not. We will add the optional fourth parameter to DES3ENCRYPT when we want three key mode. Then we execute the string, send the data and key to be encrypted, and receive the encrypted data as output. Notice how we bind the PADSTR or PADRAW of the original data. The data that is encrypted is the encoded string, which is padded out to the proper length.

Now for the inverse of the above two functions:

```
function decryptString( p_data in varchar2,
                        p_key  in varchar2 default NULL ) return varchar2
as
    l_string long;
begin
    setkey(p_key);
    execute immediate
    'begin
        dbms_obfuscation_toolkit.des' || g_StringFunction || 'decrypt
        ( input_string => :1, key_string => :2, decrypted_string => :3' ||
        g_stringWhich || ' );
     end;'
     using IN p_data, IN g_charkey, IN OUT l_string;

    return unpadstr( l_string );
end;

function decryptRaw( p_data in raw,
                     p_key  in raw default NULL ) return raw
as
    l_string long raw;
begin
    setkey(p_key);
    execute immediate
    'begin
        dbms_obfuscation_toolkit.des' || g_RawFunction || 'decrypt
        ( input => :1, key => :2, decrypted_data => :3 ' ||
        g_rawWhich || ' );
     end;'
     using IN p_data, IN hextoraw(g_charkey), IN OUT l_string;

    return unpadraw( l_string );
end;
```

DECRYPTSTRING and DECRYPTRAW work in a similar manner as the ENCRYPT routines above functionally. The only difference is they call DECRYPT instead of ENCRYPT in the DBMS_OBFUSCATION_TOOLKIT package, and call UNPAD to decode the string or RAW data.

Now onto the routines for encrypting LOBs:

```
function encryptLob( p_data in clob,
                     p_key  in varchar2 ) return clob
as
    l_clob      clob;
    l_offset    number default 1;
    l_len       number default dbms_lob.getlength(p_data);
begin
    setkey(p_key);
    dbms_lob.createtemporary( l_clob, TRUE );
    while ( l_offset <= l_len )
    loop
        wa( l_clob, encryptString(
            dbms_lob.substr( p_data, g_chunkSize, l_offset ) ) );
        l_offset := l_offset + g_chunksize;
    end loop;
    return l_clob;
end;


function encryptLob( p_data in blob,
                     p_key  in raw ) return blob
as
    l_blob      blob;
    l_offset    number default 1;
    l_len       number default dbms_lob.getlength(p_data);
begin
    setkey(p_key);
    dbms_lob.createtemporary( l_blob, TRUE );
    while ( l_offset <= l_len )
    loop
        wa( l_blob, encryptRaw(
            dbms_lob.substr( p_data, g_chunkSize, l_offset ) ) );
        l_offset := l_offset + g_chunksize;
    end loop;
    return l_blob;
end;
```

These are overloaded procedures for BLOBs and CLOBs. They work by creating a temporary LOB to write the encrypted data into. Since we change the length of a string/RAW data when encrypted to preserve its original length and pad it out, doing this 'in place' using the existing LOB would not be possible. For example, if you had a 64 KB LOB, we would take the first 32 KB, and make it 'larger' than 32 KB. Now we would need to slide over the last 32 KB of the existing LOB to make room for this larger chunk of data. Also, it would make it not possible to call these functions from SQL, since the LOB locator would have to be IN/OUT, and IN/OUT parameters would preclude this from being called from SQL. So, we simply copy the encrypted data into a new LOB which the caller can use anywhere, even in an INSERT or UPDATE statement.

The algorithm used to encrypt and encode the LOB data is as follows. We start at byte 1 (L_OFFSET) and encrypt G_CHUNKSIZE bytes of data. This is appended to the temporary LOB we created. We add G_CHUNKSIZE to the offset, and continue looping until we have processed the entire LOB. At the end, we return the temporary LOB to the caller.

Next for the decryption routines for LOB data:

```
function decryptLob( p_data in clob,
                     p_key  in varchar2 default NULL ) return clob
as
    l_clob      clob;
    l_offset    number default 1;
    l_len       number default dbms_lob.getlength(p_data);
begin
    setkey(p_key);
    dbms_lob.createtemporary( l_clob, TRUE );
    loop
        exit when l_offset > l_len;
        wa( l_clob, decryptString(
                dbms_lob.substr( p_data, g_chunksize+8, l_offset ) ) );
        l_offset := l_offset + 8 + g_chunksize;
    end loop;
    return l_clob;
end;

function decryptLob( p_data in blob,
                     p_key  in raw default NULL ) return blob
as
    l_blob      blob;
    l_offset    number default 1;
    l_len       number default dbms_lob.getlength(p_data);
begin
    setkey(p_key);
    dbms_lob.createtemporary( l_blob, TRUE );
    loop
        exit when l_offset > l_len;
        wa( l_blob, decryptRaw(
                dbms_lob.substr( p_data, g_chunksize+8, l_offset ) ) );
        l_offset := l_offset + 8 + g_chunksize;
    end loop;
    return l_blob;
end;
```

Once again, for the same reasons as before, we utilize a temporary LOB to perform the decryption. This time however, there is one additional reason for the temporary LOB. If we did not use a temporary LOB to decrypt the data into, we would actually be decrypting the data in the DATABASE. Subsequent SELECTs would see already decrypted data if we didn't copy it into a new LOB! Here, the temporary LOB usage is even more important than before.

The logic employed here is to loop over the chunks in the LOB as before. We start at offset 1 (the first byte) in the LOB and SUBSTR off G_CHUNKSIZE+8 bytes. The additional 8 bytes caters for the 8 bytes the PADSTR/PADRAW functions added to the data when we encoded it. So, all we do is walk through the LOB G_CHUNKSIZE+8 bytes at a time, decrypting the data, and appending it to the temporary LOB. This is what gets returned to the client.

And now for the last part of the CRYPT_PKG, the interface to the MD5 routines:

```
function md5str( p_data in varchar2 ) return checksum_str
is
    l_checksum_str  checksum_str;
begin
    execute immediate
    'begin :x := dbms_obfuscation_toolkit.md5( input_string => :y ); end;'
    using OUT l_checksum_str, IN p_data;

    return l_checksum_str;
end;

function md5raw( p_data in raw ) return checksum_raw
is
    l_checksum_raw    checksum_raw;
begin
    execute immediate
    'begin :x := dbms_obfuscation_toolkit.md5( input => :y ); end;'
    using OUT l_checksum_raw, IN p_data;

    return l_checksum_raw;
end;

function md5lob( p_data in clob ) return checksum_str
is
    l_checksum_str  checksum_str;
begin
    execute immediate
    'begin :x := dbms_obfuscation_toolkit.md5( input_string => :y ); end;'
    using OUT l_checksum_str, IN dbms_lob.substr(p_data,g_chunksize,1);

    return l_checksum_str;
end;

function md5lob( p_data in blob ) return checksum_raw
is
    l_checksum_raw  checksum_raw;
begin
    execute immediate
    'begin :x := dbms_obfuscation_toolkit.md5( input => :y ); end;'
    using OUT l_checksum_raw, IN dbms_lob.substr(p_data,g_chunksize,1);

    return l_checksum_raw;
end;

end;
/
```

The MD5 routines act as a passthrough to the native DBMS_OBFUSCATION_TOOLKIT routines. The one thing they do differently is that they are not overloaded, allowing them to be called directly from SQL. You should note that the MD5 LOB routines only compute the CHECKSUM based on the first G_CHUNKSIZE bytes of data. This is due to the limitation of PL/SQL in regards to variable sizes.

Now we will briefly test out and demonstrate the functionality of this package. The following examples were executed in an Oracle 8.1.7 database. If executed in 8.1.6, you should expect the DES3 and MD5 examples to fail at run-time:

```
tkyte@DEV817> declare
  2       l_str_data     varchar2(25) := 'hello world';
  3       l_str_enc      varchar2(50);
  4       l_str_decoded  varchar2(25);
  5
  6       l_raw_data     raw(25) := utl_raw.cast_to_raw('Goodbye');
  7       l_raw_enc      raw(50);
  8       l_raw_decoded  raw(25);
  9
 10  begin
 11       crypt_pkg.setkey( 'MagicKey' );
 12
 13       l_str_enc      := crypt_pkg.encryptString( l_str_data );
 14       l_str_decoded  := crypt_pkg.decryptString( l_str_enc );
 15
 16       dbms_output.put_line( 'Encoded In hex = ' ||
 17                             utl_raw.cast_to_raw(l_str_enc)  );
 18       dbms_output.put_line( 'Decoded = '  || l_str_decoded );
 19
 20       crypt_pkg.setkey( utl_raw.cast_to_raw('MagicKey') );
 21
 22       l_raw_enc      := crypt_pkg.encryptRaw( l_raw_data );
 23       l_raw_decoded  := crypt_pkg.decryptRaw( l_raw_enc );
 24
 25       dbms_output.put_line( 'Encoded = ' || l_raw_enc );
 26       dbms_output.put_line( 'Decoded = '  ||
 27                             utl_raw.cast_to_varchar2(l_raw_decoded) );
 28  end;
 29  /
Encoded In hex = 7004DB310AC6A8F210F8467278518CF988DF554B299B35EF
Decoded = hello world
Encoded = E3CC4E04EF3951178DEB9AFAE9C99096
Decoded = Goodbye

PL/SQL procedure successfully completed.
```

This shows the basic functionality of the ENCRYPT and DECRYPT routines. Here, I am calling them procedurally – below we will do it in SQL. I test against both string and RAW data in this example. On line 11 of the code, I call SETKEY to set the encryption key, to be used for encoding and decoding of the VARCHAR2 data elements, to the string MAGICKEY. This saves me from having to repeatedly pass this string into these routines. Then I encrypt the string into L_STR_ENC. I then decrypt this string just to make sure everything is working as expected. On lines 16-18 I print out the results. Since the encrypted data can contain various characters that drive terminal emulators crazy, I print out the encrypted string using UTL_RAW.CAST_TO_RAW on line 17. This has the effect of just changing the data type of the VARCHAR2 into a RAW, as mentioned previously. The underlying data is not changed at all. Since RAW data is implicitly converted to a string of hexadecimal digits, we can use this as a convenient way to dump data to the screen in hexadecimal.

On lines 20 through 27 I do the same thing to RAW data. I must call SETKEY once again, this time with 8 bytes of RAW data. For convenience sake, I use UTL_RAW.CAST_TO_RAW to change a VARCHAR2 key into a RAW key. I could have used HEXTORAW and passed a string of hexadecimal characters as well. I then encrypt the data, and decrypt the encrypted data. When I print it out, I just print the encrypted data (it'll display in hexadecimal), and I cast the data I decrypted back to VARCHAR2 so we can see that it worked. The output confirms the package functions.

Next, we'll look at how this might work in SQL. We'll test out the triple DES encryption in two key mode this time:

```
tkyte@DEV817> drop table t;

Table dropped.

tkyte@DEV817> create table t
  2  ( id int primary key, data varchar2(255) );

Table created.

tkyte@DEV817> insert into t values
  2  ( 1, crypt_pkg.encryptString( 'This is row 1', 'MagicKeyIsLonger' ) );

1 row created.

tkyte@DEV817> insert into t values
  2  ( 2, crypt_pkg.encryptString( 'This is row 2', 'MagicKeyIsLonger' ) );

1 row created.

tkyte@DEV817> select utl_raw.cast_to_raw(data) encrypted_in_hex,
  2         crypt_pkg.decryptString(data,'MagicKeyIsLonger') decrypted
  3    from t
  4  /

ENCRYPTED_IN_HEX                                         DECRYPTED
------------------------------------------------------- -------------
0B9A809515519FA6A34F150941B318DA441FBB0C790E9481 This is row 1
0B9A809515519FA6A34F150941B318DA20A936F9848ADC13 This is row 2
```

So, simply by using a 16 byte key as input to the CRYPT_PKG.ENCRYPTSTRING routine, we automatically switched over to the DES3ENCRYPT routine, within the DBMS_OBFUSCATION_TOOLKIT package. This example shows how easy it is to use the CRYPT_PKG in SQL. All of the functions are callable from SQL and can be used anywhere where SUBSTR, for example, could be used. The CRYPT_PKG could be used in the SET clause of an UPDATE, the VALUES clause of an INSERT, the SELECT clause of a SQL query, and even in the WHERE clause of any statement if you like.

Now we will look at how this package may be used on LOBs and demonstrate the MD5 routines as well. We'll use a 50 KB CLOB as our test case. First we must load the LOB into the database:

```
tkyte@DEV817> create table demo ( id int, theClob clob );

Table created.

tkyte@DEV817> create or replace directory my_files as
  2                          '/d01/home/tkyte';

Directory created.

tkyte@DEV817> declare
  2        l_clob    clob;
  3        l_bfile   bfile;
```

```
  4  begin
  5      insert into demo values ( 1, empty_clob() )
  6      returning theclob into l_clob;
  7
  8      l_bfile := bfilename( 'MY_FILES', 'htp.sql' );
  9      dbms_lob.fileopen( l_bfile );
 10
 11      dbms_lob.loadfromfile( l_clob, l_bfile,
 12                             dbms_lob.getlength( l_bfile ) );
 13
 14      dbms_lob.fileclose( l_bfile );
 15  end;
 16  /

PL/SQL procedure successfully completed.
```

The above procedure has loaded some data into the CLOB. Now we would like to perform some operations on it. Again, we will use SQL, as this is a fairly natural way to interact with the data. We'll start by computing a CHECKSUM based on the first 32 KB of the CLOB:

```
tkyte@DEV817> select dbms_lob.getlength(theclob) lob_len,
  2             utl_raw.cast_to_raw( crypt_pkg.md5lob(theclob) ) md5_checksum
  3    from demo;

   LOB_LEN MD5_CHECKSUM
---------- --------------------------------
     50601 307D19748889C2DEAD879F89AD45D1BA
```

Again, we use the UTL_RAW.CAST_TO_RAW to convert the VARCHAR2 returned from the MD5 routines into a hexadecimal string for display. The VARCHAR2 string will most likely contain data that is 'unprintable' on your terminal, or it may contain embedded newlines, tabs, and other control characters. The above code shows how easy it is to use the MD5 routines – just send it some data and it will compute the CHECKSUM.

Next, we want to see how one might encrypt and decrypt a LOB. We'll do it with a simple UPDATE. Notice that this time our encryption key is 24 bytes long. We will be using the DES3ENCRYPT routine with the optional which => ThreeKeyMode parameter set. This gives us 3 key, triple DES encryption:

```
tkyte@DEV817> update demo
  2             set theClob = crypt_pkg.encryptLob( theClob,
  3                               'MagicKeyIsLongerEvenMore' )
  4    where id = 1;

1 row updated.

tkyte@DEV817> select dbms_lob.getlength(theclob) lob_len,
  2             utl_raw.cast_to_raw( crypt_pkg.md5lob(theclob) ) md5_checksum
  3    from demo;

   LOB_LEN MD5_CHECKSUM
---------- --------------------------------
     50624 FCBD33DA2336C83685B1A62956CA2D16
```

Here we can see by the fact that the length has changed from 50,601 to 50,624 bytes, and that the MD5 CHECKSUM is different, that we have in fact modified the data. What we did, if you recall from the algorithm above, is to take the first 32,000 bytes of the CLOB, added 8 bytes onto the front of this 32,000 bytes as part of the string encryption, and encrypted it. Then, we retrieved the remaining 18,601 bytes. We padded this out to 18,608 bytes (divisible by 8 evenly), and added 8 bytes to remember the original length. This gives us our expanded length of 50,624 bytes.

Lastly, we will look at how to retrieve the CLOB decrypted from the database:

```
tkyte@DEV817> select dbms_lob.substr(
  2                          crypt_pkg.decryptLob(theClob), 100, 1 ) data
  3    from demo
  4   where id = 1;

DATA
----------------------------------------
set define off
create or replace package htp as
/* STRUCTURE tags */
procedure htmlOpen;
procedure
```

An interesting thing to note here is that I did not pass in the encryption key. Since we save this key in the package state, it is not necessary here. The package will remember it from call to call, but not session to session. I could send the key, but I do not need to. The key is stored in a package body global variable, so it is not visible to anything other than the functions in the package body, and cannot be seen by other sessions.

Caveats

Currently, there exists a situation with the DBMS_OBFUSCATION_TOOLKIT whereby data encrypted on a 'little endian' system cannot be decrypted using the same key on a 'big endian' system. 'Endian' has to do with he ordering of bytes in a multi-byte number. Intel platforms (NT, many Linuxes, and Solaris x86 run on Intel) have a little endian byte ordering. Sparc and Risc typically have a big endian. Data that is encrypted on Windows NT using a key of '12345678' cannot be decrypted on Sparc Solaris using the same key. The following example demonstrates the issue (and shows the workaround). On Windows NT:

```
tkyte@TKYTE816> create table anothert ( encrypted_data varchar2(25) );

Table created.

tkyte@TKYTE816> insert into anothert values
  2    ( crypt_pkg.encryptString( 'hello world', '12345678' ) );

1 row created.

tkyte@TKYTE816> select crypt_pkg.decryptstring( encrypted_data ) from anothert;

CRYPT_PKG.DECRYPTSTRING(ENCRYPTED_DATA)
-------------------------------------------------------------------
hello world

tkyte@TKYTE816> host exp userid=tom/kyte tables=anothert
```

I ftp this EXPDAT.DMP file to my Sparc Solaris machine, and load the data into it. Then, when I attempt to query it out I receive:

```
ops$tkyte@DEV816> select
  2   crypt_pkg.decryptstring( encrypted_data, '12345678' )
  3   from t;
crypt_pkg.decryptstring( encrypted_data, '12345678' )
      *
ERROR at line 2:
ORA-06502: PL/SQL: numeric or value error: character to number conversion
ORA-06512: at "OPS$TKYTE.CRYPT_PKG", line 84
ORA-06512: at "OPS$TKYTE.CRYPT_PKG", line 215
ORA-06512: at line 1

ops$tkyte@DEV816> select
  2   crypt_pkg.decryptstring( encrypted_data, '43218765' )
  3   from t;

CRYPT_PKG.DECRYPTSTRING(ENCRYPTED_DATA,'43218765')
--------------------------------------------------------------------hello
world
```

The error above is coming from my wrapper package. I am taking the first 8 bytes of data in the string, and assuming that it is a number. Since the key could not successfully decrypt the data, the first 8 bytes is in fact *not* my length field – it is some garbage set of characters.

Apparently, our 8 byte (or 16 or 24 byte) key is addressed internally as a series of 4 byte integers. We must reverse the bytes in every 4 byte group in our key, in order to decrypt data on one system that was encrypted on another with a different byte order. Therefore, if I use the key '12345678' on Windows NT (Intel), I must use the key '43218765' on Sparc Solaris. We take the first 4 bytes and reverse them, then take the next 4 bytes and reverse them (and so on for larger keys).

This is an important fact to keep in mind if you either move the data from NT to Sparc Solaris for example, or use database links to query the data out. You must be prepared to physically reorder the bytes to decrypt successfully. This particular issue is corrected in the patch release of Oracle 8.1.7.1 and up, and the need for the byte swapping is removed.

Key Management

I would like to briefly talk about key management here for a moment. Encryption is only part of the solution to making data 'secure'. The primary reason people quote for encrypting data in the database is to make it so the DBA, who can query any table, cannot make sense of the data in the table. For example, you are an online web site taking customer orders. People are giving you their credit card numbers. You are storing them in the database. You would like to assure that neither the DBA, who must be able to backup your database, nor the malicious hacker that breaks into your database, could read this highly sensitive information. If you stored it in clear text, it would be easy for someone to see it, if they gained DBA access to your database. If it is stored encrypted this would not be the case.

The encrypted data is only as secure as the key you use to encrypt the data. The key that is used is the magic component here. If the key is discovered, the data might as well not be encrypted (as evidenced by the fact that we can simply select to decrypt data if we were given the key).

Therefore key generation and key protection are two things you must give a lot of thought to. There are many paths you could follow. What follows are some ideas, and concepts that you can use, but each has its own specific issues.

The Client Application Manages and Stores Keys

One approach is to keep the keys out of the database, perhaps even on another machine (just don't lose them – it'll take you a couple hundred CPU years to guess what they might be!). In this scenario, the client application, be it software in a middle tier application server, or a client-server application, manages the keys on its system. The client software determines if the user accessing the data is permitted to decrypt it or not, and sends the key to the database.

If you choose to do this, to transmit the key over the network, we must add yet one more layer of encryption and this is data stream encryption for the Net8 traffic. Bind variables and string literals are transmitted unencrypted by default. In this situation, since the keys are so critical, you would need to make use of a technology such as the **ASO** (Advanced Security Option). This Net8 option provides full data stream encryption so that no one can 'sniff' your keys from the network.

As long as the key is securely maintained by the client application (this is up to you to ensure), and you use ASO, this would be a viable solution.

Store the Keys in the Same Database

Here, you would store the keys in the database itself with the data. This is not a perfect solution, as you now know that a DBA with enough time on their hands (or a hacker who has gotten into a DBA account) could possibly discover your keys and the data that was encrypted by them. What you need to do in a case like this, is to make it as hard as possible to put the keys together with the data. This is a hard thing to do because both are in the same database.

One approach is to never directly relate the key table to the data table. For example, you have a table with CUSTOMER_ID, CREDIT_CARD, and other data. The CUSTOMER_ID is immutable; it is the primary key (and we all know you never update a primary key). You might set up another table:

```
ID       number primary key,
DATA varchar2(255)
```

This is the table in which we will store our keys, one key per customer ID. We will provide a packaged function that will return the key if and only if the *appropriate* user in the *appropriate* environment is executing it (similar to the concept behind FGAC; you can only get to the data if you have set up the correct application context).

This package would provide two basic functions:

❑ **Function 1: The addition of a new customer** – In this case, the function would perform some operation on the customer ID to 'scramble' it (convert it into another string). This function would be deterministic so that given the same customer ID we would always get the same output. Some ideas for how to mangle this customer ID, or any string in fact, follow below. It would also generate a random key for this customer. Some ideas on how to generate that key follow. It would then use dynamic SQL to insert the row into the key table (which is not going to be named KEY_TABLE or anything obvious like that).

❑ **Function 2: The retrieval of a key for a customer** – This function would take a customer ID, run it through the same deterministic function as above, and then using dynamic SQL, it would look up the key for this customer, and return it. It will only perform these functions if the current user is executing in the appropriate environment.

The reason for the use of dynamic SQL is that it may become obvious to people that this package is the one performing the key management. A user may be able to query ALL_DEPENDENCIES to find all of the tables this package statically references. By using dynamic SQL, there will be no correlation between this package, and the key table. We are not preventing a really smart person from deducing the key table here, just making it as hard as we possibly can.

As for how to scramble the customer ID (or any set of immutable data related to this row, the primary key is a good candidate as long as you never update it), we can use many algorithms. If I was using Oracle 8.1.7, I may send this piece of information concatenated with some constant value (commonly referred to as a 'salt') to the MD5 routines, to generate a 16 byte CHECKSUM. I would use this as my key. Using Oracle 8.1.6, I might do the same sort of operation, but use DBMS_UTILITY.GET_HASH_VALUE with a very large hash table size. I could use an XOR algorithm after reversing the bytes in the CUSTOMER_ID. Any algorithm that would be hard to guess given the resulting output data would suffice.

By now, you should be saying, 'Ahh but the DBA can just read the code out, see the algorithm, and figure this all out.' Not if you *wrap* the code. Wrapping PL/SQL code is very straightforward (see the WRAP utility that is documented in the *PL/SQL User's Guide and Reference*). This will take your source code and 'obfuscate' it. You will load the wrapped version of the code into the database. Now no one can read your code. There are no 'reverse wrap' tools available. Just make sure to maintain a good copy of your algorithm somewhere safe. Since there are no reverse wrap, tools you will not be able to resurrect your code from the database if you need to.

Now, to generate a key for this customer, we need a randomizer of sorts. There are many ways we could do this. We could use the same basic routines we used to obfuscate the CUSTOMER_ID. We could use a random number generator (such as DBMS_RANDOM or one we develop ourselves). The goal is to generate something that cannot be 'guessed', based on anything else.

Personally speaking, this would be my preferred choice, storing the keys in the database. If I let the client application manage them, there is the risk of the client application 'losing' the keys due to a media failure, or some other system catastrophe. If I use the next method, storing them in the file system, I stand the same sort of risk. Only if I store the keys in the database can I be ensured that the encrypted data can in fact be decrypted – my database is always in 'sync', and backup and recovery is assured.

Store the Keys in the File System with the Database

You could also store the keys used to encrypt the data in files within the file system and, using a C external procedure, access them. I suggest using a C external procedure because the goal here is to prevent the DBA from 'seeing' them, and quite often the DBA has access to the Oracle software account. UTL_FILE, BFILES, and Java stored procedures doing I/O, run as the Oracle software account user. If the DBA can become the Oracle software owner, they can see the files. If they can see the files, they can see the keys. Using an external procedure written in C, the EXTPROC service can run under a wholly different account by running the listener for the EXTPROC service as another user. In this fashion, the Oracle account cannot 'see' the keys. Only via the EXTPROC listener can I gain access to them. This just adds a layer of assuredness to your solution. See Chapter 18 on *C-Based External Procedures* for more information regarding this approach.

Summary

We have spent quite a bit of time looking at the DBMS_OBFUSCATION_TOOLKIT package in this section. Here, we have seen how to effectively create a wrapper package that provides the functionality in the way we would like to (feel free to write your own wrappers if you don't like my implementation). We've learned also how to use dynamic SQL to create packages that can be installed into databases with different capabilities (8.1.6 versus 8.1.7 encryption capabilities in this case). We investigated a cross-platform issue that accompanies the DMBS_OBFUSCATION_TOOLKIT package, that of byte ordering in the keys. We learned how to solve this issue, if it occurs, by rearranging the bytes in the key itself. An interesting enhancement to the CRYPT_PKG above would be to have it automatically detect if you were on a little or big endian system, and swap the bytes in the key on one of them for you, so you would not even be aware of these differences. This would be an excellent idea given that in version 8.1.7.1, the need to reverse the bytes goes away and you could just remove the code that does this, and be fully functional again.

Lastly, we looked at the very important area of key management. I spent a lot of time working on a nice wrapper package to make encryption and decryption look easy. The hard part is still left up to you – how to secure the keys. You have to consider the fact that if you believe your keys have been compromised, you would have to come up with a new set of keys, and need to decrypt/encrypt all your existing data to protect it. Planning ahead will avoid you from having to do such things.

DBMS_OUTPUT

The DBMS_OUTPUT package is one that people frequently misunderstand. They misunderstand how it works, what it does, and it's limits. In this section I will address these misunderstandings. I will also address some alternative implementations that give you DBMS_OUTPUT-like functionality, but without some of the limits found in the native package.

DBMS_OUTPUT is a simple package designed to give the appearance that PL/SQL has the ability to perform simple screen I/O operations. It is designed so that it appears PL/SQL can print Hello World on your screen for example. You've seen me use it many hundreds of times in this book. An example is:

```
ops$tkyte@DEV816> exec dbms_output.put_line( 'Hello World' );
Hello World

PL/SQL procedure successfully completed.
```

What you didn't see is that I had to issue a SQL*PLUS (or SVRMGRL) command in order to make this work. We can turn this screen I/O on and off like this:

```
ops$tkyte@DEV816> set serveroutput off
ops$tkyte@DEV816> exec dbms_output.put_line( 'Hello World' );

PL/SQL procedure successfully completed.

ops$tkyte@DEV816> set serveroutput on
ops$tkyte@DEV816> exec dbms_output.put_line( 'Hello World' );
Hello World

PL/SQL procedure successfully completed.
```

In reality, PL/SQL has no capability to perform screen I/O (that's why I said it was designed to give PL/SQL the *appearance* of being able to do this). In fact, it is SQL*PLUS that is doing the screen I/O – it is impossible for PL/SQL to write to our terminal. PL/SQL is being executed in a totally separate process, typically running on a different machine elsewhere in the network. SQL*PLUS, SVRMGRL, and other tools however, can write to our screens quite easily. You will notice that if you use DBMS_OUTPUT in your Java or Pro*C programs (or any program) the DBMS_OUTPUT data goes into the 'bit bucket', and never gets displayed. This is because your application would be responsible for displaying the output.

How DBMS_OUTPUT Works

DBMS_OUTPUT is a package with a few entry points. The ones you will use the most are:

- ❑   PUT – Puts a string, NUMBER, or DATE into the output buffer, without adding a newline.

- ❑   PUT_LINE – Puts a STRING, NUMBER, or DATE into the output buffer and adds a newline.

- ❑   NEW_LINE – Puts a newline into the output stream.

- ❑   ENABLE/DISABLE – Enables or disables the buffering of data in the package. Effectively turns DBMS_OUTPUT on and off procedurally.

These procedures write to an internal buffer; a PL/SQL table stored in the package body of DBMS_OUTPUT. The limit the total length of a line (the sum of all bytes put into the buffer by you, without calling either PUT_LINE or NEW_LINE to terminate that line) is set to 255 bytes. All of the output your procedure generates is buffered in this table, and will not be visible to you in SQL*PLUS until *after* your procedure completes execution. PL/SQL is not writing to a terminal anywhere, it is simply stuffing data into a PL/SQL table.

As your procedure makes calls to DBMS_OUTPUT.PUT_LINE, the DBMS_OUTPUT package stores this data into an array (PL/SQL table), and returns control to your procedure. It is not until you are done that you will see any output. Even then, you will *only* see output if the client you are using is aware of DBMS_OUTPUT, and goes out of its way to print it out. SQL*PLUS for example, will issue calls to DBMS_OUTPUT.GET_LINES to get some of the DBMS_OUTPUT buffer, and print it on your screen. If you run a stored procedure from your Java/JDBC application, and expect to see the DBMS_OUTPUT output appear with the rest of your System.out.println data, you will be disappointed. Unless the client application makes a conscious effect to retrieve and print the data, it is just going into the bit bucket. We will demonstrate how to do this from Java/JDBC later in this chapter.

This fact that the output is buffered until the procedure completes, is the number one point of confusion with regards to DBMS_OUTPUT. People see DBMS_OUTPUT and read about it, and then they try to use it to monitor a long running process. That is, they'll stick DBMS_OUTPUT.PUT_LINE calls all over their code, and run the procedure in SQL*PLUS. They wait for the output to start coming to the screen, and are very disappointed when it does not (because it cannot). Without an understanding of how it is implemented, it is not clear why the data doesn't start appearing. Once you understand that PL/SQL (and Java and C external routines) running in the database cannot perform screen I/O, and that DBMS_OUTPUT is really just buffering the data in a big array, it becomes clear. This is when you should go back to the section on DBMS_APPLICATION_INFO, and read about the long operations interface! DBMS_APPLICATION_INFO is the tool you want to use to monitor long running processes, not DBMS_OUTPUT.

So, what is DBMS_OUTPUT useful for then? It is great for printing out simple reports and making utilities. See Chapter 23 on *Invoker and Definer Rights* for a PRINT_TABLE procedure that uses DBMS_OUTPUT to generate output like this:

```
SQL> exec print_table( 'select * from all_users where username = user' );
USERNAME                       : OPS$TKYTE       .
USER_ID                        : 334
CREATED                        : 02-oct-2000 10:02:12
-----------------

PL/SQL procedure successfully completed.
```

It prints the data *down* the screen instead of wrapping it across. Great for printing that really wide row, which would consume lots of horizontal space, and wrap on your screen, making it pretty unreadable.

Now that we know that DBMS_OUTPUT works by putting data into a PL/SQL table, we can look further at the implementation. When we enable DBMS_OUTPUT, either by calling DBMS_OUTPUT.ENABLE, or by using SET SERVEROUTPUT ON, we are not only enabling the capture of the data, but also we are setting a maximum limit on how much data we will capture. By default, if I issue:

```
SQL> set serveroutput on
```

I have enabled 20,000 bytes of DBMS_OUTPUT buffer. If I exceed this, I will receive:

```
begin
*
ERROR at line 1:
ORA-20000: ORU-10027: buffer overflow, limit of 20000 bytes
ORA-06512: at "SYS.DBMS_OUTPUT", line 106
ORA-06512: at "SYS.DBMS_OUTPUT", line 65
ORA-06512: at line 3
```

I can increase this limit via a call to SET SERVEROUTPUT (or DBMS_OUTPUT.ENABLE):

```
SQL> set serveroutput on size 1000000

SQL> set serveroutput on size 1000001
SP2-0547: size option 1000001 out of range (2000 through 1000000)
```

As you can see from the error message however, the limit is 20,000 bytes through 1,000,000 bytes. The limit of the number of bytes *you* can put into the buffer is somewhat less than the amount you set, perhaps *much* less. DBMS_OUTPUT has a simple packing algorithm it uses to place the data into the PL/SQL table. It does not put the i'th row of your output into the i'th array element, rather it densely packs the array. Array element #1 might have your first five lines of output encoded into it. In order to do this (to encode many lines into one line), they necessarily introduce some overhead. This overhead, the data they use to remember where your data is, and how big it is, is included in the byte count limit. So, even if you SET SERVEROUTPUT ON SIZE 1000000, you will get somewhat less than one million bytes of output.

Can you figure out how many bytes you will get? Sometimes yes and sometimes no. If you have a fixed size output line, every line is the same length, then the answer is yes. We can compute the number of bytes you will get exactly. If your data is of varying width, then no, we cannot calculate the number of bytes you will be able to output before you actually output it. Below, I explain the algorithm Oracle uses to pack this data.

We know that Oracle stores the data in an array. The maximum total number of lines in this array is set based upon your SET SERVEROUTPUT ON SIZE setting. The DBMS_OUTPUT array will never have more than IDXLIMIT lines where IDXLIMIT is computed as:

```
idxlimit := trunc((xxxxxx+499) / 500);
```

So, if you SET SERVEROUTPUT ON SIZE 1000000, DBMS_OUTPUT will use 2,000 array elements at most. DBMS_OUTPUT will store at most 504 bytes of data in each array element, and typically less. DBMS_OUTPUT packs the data into a row in the array, in the following format:

```
their_buffer(1) = '<sp>NNNyour data here<sp>NNNyour data here...';
their_buffer(2) = '<sp>NNNyour data here<sp>NNNyour data here...';
```

So, for each line of your output, there is a 4-byte overhead for a space, and a 3-digit number. Each line in the DBMS_OUTPUT buffer will not exceed 504 bytes, and DBMS_OUTPUT will not wrap your data from line to line. So, for example, if you use the maximum line length and always write 255 bytes per line, DBMS_OUTPUT will be able to pack one line per array element above. This is because $(255+4) * 2 = 518$, 518 is bigger than 504, and DBMS_OUTPUT will not split your line between two of its array elements. Two lines will simply not fit in one of DBMS_OUTPUT's lines. Therefore, even though you asked for a buffer of 1,000,000 bytes, you will only get 510,000 – a little more then *half* of what you asked for. The 510,000 comes from the fact you are printing lines of 255 bytes, and they will allow for a maximum of 2,000 lines (remember IDXLIMIT from above); $255*2000 = 510,000$. On the other hand, if you used a fixed line size of 248 bytes, they will get two lines for each of their lines, resulting in you being able to print out $248 * 2 * 2000 = 992,000$ – a little more than 99 percent of what you asked for. In fact, this is the best you can hope for with DBMS_OUTPUT – 992,000 bytes of your data. It is impossible to get more printed out.

As I said previously, with a fixed size line, it is very easy to determine the number of lines you will be able to print. If you give me a number, say 79, 80, or 81 bytes per line, I can simply determine:

```
ops$tkyte@ORA8I.WORLD> select trunc(504/(79+4)) * 79 * 2000 from dual;

TRUNC(504/(79+4))*79*2000
-------------------------
                   948000

ops$tkyte@ORA8I.WORLD> select trunc(504/(80+4)) * 80 * 2000 from dual;

TRUNC(504/(80+4))*80*2000
-------------------------
                   960000

ops$tkyte@ORA8I.WORLD> select trunc(504/(81+4)) * 81 * 2000 from dual;

TRUNC(504/(81+4))*81*2000
-------------------------
                   810000
```

As you can see, the amount of data we can output varies widely, depending on the size of our output line!

The trouble with varying length output is that the amount of output we can produce is unpredictable. It depends on how you do the output, and the mix of line sizes DBMS_OUTPUT receives. If you output the same lines, just in a different order, you may be able to print more or less lines. This is a direct result of the packing algorithm.

This is one of the most confusing aspects of DBMS_OUTPUT. You might run your procedure once and have it produce a report of 700,000 bytes successfully, and run it then tomorrow and have it fail with ORA-20000: ORU-10027: buffer overflow at 650,000 bytes of output. This is simply due to the way DBMS_OUTPUT packs the data in the buffer. Further on in this section, we will look at some alternatives to DBMS_OUTPUT that remove this ambiguity.

A reasonable question to ask is, 'Why do they do this packing?' The reason is that when DBMS_OUTPUT was introduced in version 7.0, PL/SQL table memory allocation was very different. If you allocated a slot in a PL/SQL table, enough storage for the maximum array element size was allocated immediately. This means that since DBMS_OUTPUT uses a VARCHAR2(500), 500 bytes would be allocated for a DBMS_OUTPUT.PUT_LINE('hello world') – the same as for the output of a really big string. 2,000 lines of output would take 1,000,000 bytes of data, even if you printed out hello world 2,000 times, something that should actually take about 22 KB. So, this packing was implemented in order to prevent this over-allocation of memory in the PGA for the buffering array. In the latest releases of Oracle (8.0 and up) this is no longer the case. Array elements are dynamically sized and this packing isn't technically necessary any longer. So, you might say this is a legacy side effect from code written in prior releases.

The last thing about how DBMS_OUTPUT works I would like to mention has to do with the trimming of leading blanks on output lines. It is a mistaken belief that this is a DBMS_OUTPUT 'feature'. It is actually a SQL*PLUS 'feature' (although I know of many who disagree with the 'feature' tag on this one). To see what I mean, we can run a small test:

```
ops$tkyte@ORA8I.WORLD> exec dbms_output.put_line( '      hello world' );
hello world

PL/SQL procedure successfully completed.
```

When I call DBMS_OUTPUT with '   hello world', the leading blanks are trimmed away. It is assumed that DBMS_OUTPUT is doing this but really it isn't. It is SQL*PLUS doing the trimming. The simple solution to this is to use the extended syntax on the SET SERVEROUTPUT command. The full syntax is of that command is:

```
set serveroutput {ON|OFF} [SIZE n]
        [FORMAT   {WRAPPED|WORD_WRAPPED|TRUNCATED}]
```

The formats have the following meanings:

❑ WRAPPED – SQL*PLUS wraps the server output within the line size specified by SET LINESIZE, beginning new lines when required.

❑ WORD_WRAPPED – Each line of server output is wrapped within the line size specified by SET LINESIZE. Lines are broken on word boundaries. SQL*PLUS left-justifies each line, *skipping all leading whitespace*. This is the default.

❑   TRUNCATED – When enabled, each line of server output is truncated to the line size specified by SET LINESIZE.

It is easiest just to see the effect of each format in action, to understand what each does:

```
SQL>set linesize 20
SQL>set serveroutput on format wrapped
SQL>exec dbms_output.put_line( '          Hello      World         !!!!!' );
    Hello      World
    !!!!!

PL/SQL procedure successfully completed.

SQL>set serveroutput on format word_wrapped
SQL>exec dbms_output.put_line( '          Hello      World         !!!!!' );
Hello      World
!!!!!

PL/SQL procedure successfully completed.

SQL>set serveroutput on format truncated
SQL>exec dbms_output.put_line( '          Hello      World         !!!!!' );
    Hello      World

PL/SQL procedure successfully completed.
```

DBMS_OUTPUT and Other Environments

By default, tools such as SQL*PLUS and SVRMGRL are DBMS_OUTPUT-aware. Most other environments are not. For example, your Java/JDBC program is definitely not DBMS_OUTPUT-aware. In this section, we'll see how to make Java/JDBC DBMS_OUTPUT-aware. The same principles used below apply equally to any programming environment. The methods I use with Java can be easily applied to Pro*C, OCI, VB, or any number of these environments.

We'll start with a small PL/SQL routine that generates some output data:

```
scott@TKYTE816> create or replace
  2   procedure emp_report
  3   as
  4   begin
  5       dbms_output.put_line
  6     ( rpad( 'Empno', 7 ) ||
  7       rpad('Ename',12) ||
  8       rpad('Job',11) );
  9
 10       dbms_output.put_line
 11     ( rpad( '-', 5, '-' ) ||
 12       rpad(' -',12,'-') ||
 13       rpad(' -',11,'-') );
 14
```

```
 15        for x in ( select * from emp )
 16        loop
 17            dbms_output.put_line
 18            ( to_char( x.empno, '9999' ) || ' ' ||
 19                rpad( x.ename, 12 ) ||
 20                rpad( x.job, 11 ) );
 21        end loop;
 22  end;
 23  /

Procedure created.

scott@TKYTE816> set serveroutput on format wrapped
scott@TKYTE816> exec emp_report
Empno   Ename        Job
-----   ----------   ---------
 7369   SMITH        CLERK
 7499   ALLEN        SALESMAN
 ...
 7934   MILLER       CLERK

PL/SQL procedure successfully completed.
```

Now, we'll set up a class to allow Java/JDBC to easily perform DBMS_OUTPUT for us:

```java
import java.sql.*;

class DbmsOutput
{
/*
 * Our instance variables. It is always best to
 * use callable or prepared statements, and prepare (parse)
 * them once per program execution, rather then once per
 * execution in the program. The cost of reparsing is
 * very high. Also, make sure to use BIND VARIABLES!
 *
 * We use three statements in this class. One to enable
 * DBMS_OUTPUT, equivalent to SET SERVEROUTPUT on in SQL*PLUS,
 * another to disable it, like SET SERVEROUTPUT OFF.
 * The last is to 'dump' or display the results from DBMS_OUTPUT
 * using system.out.
 *
 */
private CallableStatement enable_stmt;
private CallableStatement disable_stmt;
private CallableStatement show_stmt;


/*
 * Our constructor simply prepares the three
 * statements we plan on executing.
 *
 * The statement we prepare for SHOW is a block of
 * code to return a string of DBMS_OUTPUT output. Normally,
 * you might bind to a PL/SQL table type, but the JDBC drivers
```

```
 * don't support PL/SQL table types. Hence, we get the output
 * and concatenate it into a string. We will retrieve at least
 * one line of output, so we may exceed your MAXBYTES parameter
 * below. If you set MAXBYTES to 10, and the first line is 100
 * bytes long, you will get the 100 bytes. MAXBYTES will stop us
 * from getting yet another line, but it will not chunk up a line.
 *
 */
public DbmsOutput( Connection conn ) throws SQLException
{
    enable_stmt  = conn.prepareCall( "begin dbms_output.enable(:1); end;" );
    disable_stmt = conn.prepareCall( "begin dbms_output.disable; end;" );

    show_stmt = conn.prepareCall(
        "declare " +
        "    l_line varchar2(255); " +
        "    l_done number; " +
        "    l_buffer long; " +
        "begin " +
        "  loop " +
        "    exit when length(l_buffer)+255 > :maxbytes OR l_done = 1; " +
        "    dbms_output.get_line( l_line, l_done ); " +
        "    l_buffer := l_buffer || l_line || chr(10); " +
        "  end loop; " +
        " :done := l_done; " +
        " :buffer := l_buffer; " +
        "end;" );
}


/*
 * ENABLE simply sets your size and executes
 * the DBMS_OUTPUT.ENABLE call
 *
 */
public void enable( int size ) throws SQLException
{
    enable_stmt.setInt( 1, size );
    enable_stmt.executeUpdate();
}


/*
 * DISABLE only has to execute the DBMS_OUTPUT.DISABLE call
 */
public void disable() throws SQLException
{
    disable_stmt.executeUpdate();
}


/*
 * SHOW does most of the work. It loops over
 * all of the DBMS_OUTPUT data, fetching it, in this
 * case, 32,000 bytes at a time (give or take 255 bytes).
 * It will print this output on STDOUT by default (just
 * reset what System.out is to change or redirect this
 * output).
 */
```

```
public void show() throws SQLException
{
int                done = 0;

    show_stmt.registerOutParameter( 2, java.sql.Types.INTEGER );
    show_stmt.registerOutParameter( 3, java.sql.Types.VARCHAR );

    for(;;)
    {
        show_stmt.setInt( 1, 32000 );
        show_stmt.executeUpdate();
        System.out.print( show_stmt.getString(3) );
        if ( (done = show_stmt.getInt(2)) == 1 ) break;
    }
}


/*
 * CLOSE closes the callable statements associated with
 * the DbmsOutput class. Call this if you allocate a DbmsOutput
 * statement on the stack and it is going to go out of scope,
 * just as you would with any callable statement, resultset,
 * and so on.
 */
public void close() throws SQLException
{
    enable_stmt.close();
    disable_stmt.close();
    show_stmt.close();
}
}
```

In order to demonstrate its use, I've set up the following small Java/JDBC test program. Here dbserver is the name of the database server and ora8i is the service name of the instance:

```
import java.sql.*;

class test {

public static void main (String args [])
    throws SQLException
{
    DriverManager.registerDriver
       (new oracle.jdbc.driver.OracleDriver());

    Connection conn = DriverManager.getConnection
          ("jdbc:oracle:thin:@dbserver:1521:ora8i",
           "scott", "tiger");
    conn.setAutoCommit (false);

    Statement stmt = conn.createStatement();

    DbmsOutput dbmsOutput = new DbmsOutput( conn );

    dbmsOutput.enable( 1000000 );
```

```
        stmt.execute
        ( "begin emp_report; end;" );
        stmt.close();

        dbmsOutput.show();

        dbmsOutput.close();
        conn.close();
    }
    }
```

Now we will test it, by first compiling it, and then running it:

```
$ javac test.java

$ java test
Empno  Ename       Job
-----  ----------  ---------
 7369  SMITH       CLERK
 7499  ALLEN       SALESMAN
 7521  WARD        SALESMAN

 ...
```

So, this shows how to teach Java to do DBMS_OUTPUT for us. Just as SQL*PLUS does, you'll have to call DbmsOutput.show() after executing any statement that might cause some output to be displayed. After we execute an INSERT, UPDATE, DELETE, or stored procedure call, SQL*PLUS is calling DBMS_OUTPUT.GET_LINES to get the output. Your Java (or C, or VB) application would call SHOW to display the results.

Getting Around the Limits

DBMS_OUTPUT has two major limitations that I've found:

❑   The length of a 'line' is limited to 255 bytes. You must inject a new line at least every 255 bytes.

❑   The total output you can produce is limited to between 200,000 bytes (if you output 1 byte per line) and 992,000 bytes (if you output 248 bytes per line). This is sufficient for many operations, but a show stopper for others, especially since the amount of output you can generate is a function of the lengths of the strings, and the order in which you print them.

So, what can we do? I'll suggest three alternatives to get around these various limits. The next two sections demonstrate these alternatives.

Using A Small Wrapper Function or Another Package

Sometimes the 255 byte line limit is just a nuisance. You want to print some debug statements, and the thing you are printing is 500 characters long. You just want to print it, and the format of it is not as relevant as just being able to see it. In this case, we can write a small wrapper routine. I have one permanently installed in all of my database instances, in part to get around the 255 bytes per line, and in part because DBMS_OUTPUT.PUT_LINE is 20 characters long, which is a lot of typing. I use a procedure P frequently. P is simply:

```
procedure p( p_string in varchar2 )
is
    l_string long default p_string;
begin
    loop
      exit when l_string is null;
      dbms_output.put_line( substr( l_string, 1, 248) );
      l_string := substr( l_string, 251 );
    end loop;
end;
```

It does not word-wrap output, it does nothing fancy. It simply takes a string up to 32 KB in size, and prints it out. It will break my large strings into many strings of 248 bytes each (248 being the 'best' number we calculated above, giving us the maximum output), and output them. It will change the data (so it is not suitable for increasing the line width of a routine that is creating a flat file), and will cause my one line of data to be printed on perhaps many lines.

All it does is solve a simple problem. It removes the error message:

```
ops$tkyte@ORA8I.WORLD> exec dbms_output.put_line( rpad('*',256,'*') )
BEGIN dbms_output.put_line( rpad('*',256,'*') ); END;


*
ERROR at line 1:
ORA-20000: ORU-10028: line length overflow, limit of 255 bytes per line
ORA-06512: at "SYS.DBMS_OUTPUT", line 99
ORA-06512: at "SYS.DBMS_OUTPUT", line 65
ORA-06512: at line 1
```

from occurring when I am just printing some debug, or a report.

A more robust method of getting around this limit, especially useful if you are creating a flat file data dump, is to not use DBMS_OUTPUT at all, but rather to use UTL_FILE and write *directly* to a file. UTL_FILE has a 32 KB limit per line of output, and does not have a byte limit on the size of a file. Using UTL_FILE, you can only create a file on the server so it is not appropriate if you were using SQL*PLUS on a network-connected client, and spooling to a local file on the client. If your goal was to create a flat file for data loading, and creating the file on the server is OK, UTL_FILE would be the correct approach.

So, this covers two of the three alternatives, now for the last one.

Creating DBMS_OUTPUT Functionality

This is a general-purpose solution that works well in all environments. What we will do here is reinvent the wheel, only we'll invent a 'better' wheel. We will create a DBMS_OUTPUT-like package that:

❑ Has a 4,000 byte per line limit (this is a SQL limit unfortunately, not a PL/SQL limit).

❑ No limit on the number of output lines.

❑ Can be spooled on the client, like DBMS_OUTPUT.

❑ SQL*PLUS will not blank-trim the front of the string in any mode.

❑ Can be fetched into a resultset on a client using a cursor (the *output* will be available via a query).

We'll begin by creating a SQL type. This type will be our DBMS_OUTPUT buffer. Since it is a SQL type, we can SELECT * from it easily. Since virtually everything can do a SELECT *, any tool should be able to display our output easily.

```
ops$tkyte@ORA8I.WORLD> create or replace type my_dbms_output_type
  2  as table of varchar2(4000)
  3  /

Type created.
```

Now we move on to the specification for our DBMS_OUTPUT-like package. This package is set up much like the real DBMS_OUTPUT. It does not have the routines GET_LINE and GET_LINES. These will not be needed, given our implementation. The routines PUT, PUT_LINE, and NEW_LINE work just like their counterparts in DBMS_OUTPUT. The functions GET, FLUSH, and GET_AND_FLUSH are new – they have no counterpart in DBMS_OUTPUT. These routines will be used to retrieve the output once the stored procedure has executed. The function GET will simply return the buffered data, but it will not 'erase' it. You can call GET over and over to retrieve the same buffer (DBMS_OUTPUT always flushes the buffer). The function FLUSH allows you to reset the buffer, in other words empty it out. The function GET_AND_FLUSH, as you might guess, returns the buffer, and clears it out - the next calls to this package will function against an empty buffer:

```
tkyte@TKYTE816> create or replace package my_dbms_output
  2  as
  3      procedure enable;
  4      procedure disable;
  5
  6      procedure put( s in varchar2 );
  7      procedure put_line( s in varchar2 );
  8      procedure new_line;
  9
 10      function get return my_dbms_output_type;
 11      procedure flush;
 12      function get_and_flush return my_dbms_output_type;
 13  end;
 14  /

Package created.
```

We will be using some of the methods we discussed Chapter 20 on *Using Object Relational Features*, specifically the capability of being able to *SELECT * from PLSQL_FUNCTION*, which is how our DBMS_OUTPUT package will work. The functions you are most interested in are the ENABLE, DISABLE, PUT, PUT_LINE, and NEW_LINE routines. These work more or less like their DBMS_OUTPUT counterparts, the major difference being that ENABLE takes no parameters, and that MY_DBMS_OUTPUT is enabled by default (whereas DBMS_OUTPUT is disabled by default). You are limited by the amount of RAM you can allocate on your system (so beware!). Next, we implement the package body. The implementation of this package is very straightforward. We have a package global variable that is our output buffer. We add lines of text to it and extend this variable when necessary. To flush it, we assign an empty table to it. As it is so straightforward, it is presented here without further comment:

```
tkyte@TKYTE816> create or replace package body my_dbms_output
  2   as
  3
  4   g_data         my_dbms_output_type := my_dbms_output_type();
  5   g_enabled      boolean default TRUE;
  6
  7       procedure enable
  8       is
  9       begin
 10           g_enabled := TRUE;
 11       end;
 12
 13       procedure disable
 14       is
 15       begin
 16           g_enabled := FALSE;
 17       end;
 18
 19       procedure put( s in varchar2 )
 20       is
 21       begin
 22           if ( NOT g_enabled ) then return; end if;
 23           if ( g_data.count <> 0 ) then
 24               g_data(g_data.last) := g_data(g_data.last) || s;
 25           else
 26               g_data.extend;
 27               g_data(1) := s;
 28           end if;
 29       end;
 30
 31       procedure put_line( s in varchar2 )
 32       is
 33       begin
 34           if ( NOT g_enabled ) then return; end if;
 35           put( s );
 36           g_data.extend;
 37       end;
 38
 39       procedure new_line
 40       is
 41       begin
 42           if ( NOT g_enabled ) then return; end if;
 43           put( null );
 44           g_data.extend;
 45       end;
 46
 47
 48       procedure flush
 49       is
 50           l_empty        my_dbms_output_type := my_dbms_output_type();
 51       begin
 52           g_data := l_empty;
 53       end;
 54
 55       function get return my_dbms_output_type
 56       is
```

```
57        begin
58            return g_data;
59        end;
60
61        function get_and_flush return my_dbms_output_type
62        is
63            l_data        my_dbms_output_type := g_data;
64            l_empty       my_dbms_output_type := my_dbms_output_type();
65        begin
66            g_data := l_empty;
67            return l_data;
68        end;
69  end;
70  /

Package body created.
```

Now, in order to make this package useful, we need some method of getting at the buffer easily. You can call MY_DBMS_OUTPUT.GET or GET_AND_FLUSH, and retrieve the object type yourself, or you can use one of the two views below. The first view, MY_DBMS_OUTPUT_PEEK, provides a SQL interface to the GET routine. It allows you to query the output buffer over and over again, in effect, allowing you to 'peek' into the buffer without resetting it. The second view, MY_DBMS_OUTPUT_VIEW, allows you to query the buffer once – any subsequent calls to PUT, PUT_LINE, NEW_LINE, GET, or GET_AND_FLUSH will work on an empty output buffer. A SELECT * FROM MY_DBMS_OUTPUT_VIEW is similar to calling DBMS_OUTPUT.GET_LINES. It resets everything:

```
tkyte@TKYTE816> create or replace
  2  view my_dbms_output_peek ( text )
  3  as
  4  select *
  5    from TABLE ( cast( my_dbms_output.get()
  6                         as my_dbms_output_type ) )
  7  /

View created.

tkyte@TKYTE816> create or replace
  2  view my_dbms_output_view ( text )
  3  as
  4  select *
  5    from TABLE ( cast( my_dbms_output.get_and_flush()
  6                         as my_dbms_output_type ) )
  7  /

View created.
```

Now we are ready to demonstrate how this works. We will run a procedure to generate some data into the buffer, and then see how to display and interact with it:

```
tkyte@TKYTE816> begin
  2           my_dbms_output.put_line( 'hello' );
  3           my_dbms_output.put( 'Hey ' );
  4           my_dbms_output.put( 'there ' );
  5           my_dbms_output.new_line;
  6
  7      for i in 1 .. 20
  8      loop
  9           my_dbms_output.put_line( rpad( ' ', i, ' ' ) || i );
 10      end loop;
 11  end;
 12  /

PL/SQL procedure successfully completed.

tkyte@TKYTE816> select *
  2      from my_dbms_output_peek
  3  /

TEXT
-----------------------------------------------------------------------
hello
Hey there
 1
  2
...
                   19
                    20


23 rows selected.
```

The interesting thing to note here is that SQL*PLUS, not being aware of MY_DBMS_OUTPUT, will not display the results automatically. You need to help it along, and execute a query to dump the results.

Since we are just using SQL to access the output, it should be easy for you to rewrite your own DbmsOutput Java/JDBC class. It will be a simple ResultSet object, nothing more. As a last comment on this snippet of code, the output buffer is still there waiting for us:

```
tkyte@TKYTE816> select *
  2      from my_dbms_output_peek
  3  /

TEXT
-----------------------------------
hello
Hey there
 1
  2
...
                   19
                    20

23 rows selected.
```

and not only is it waiting for us, we also can WHERE on it, sort it, join it, and so on (like any table could be):

```
tkyte@TKYTE816> select *
  2      from my_dbms_output_peek
  3    where text like '%1%'
  4  /

TEXT
-------------------------------------
 1
          10
          11

...
                  18
                  19


11 rows selected.
```

Now, if this is not the desired behavior (to be able to query and re-query this data) we would SELECT from MY_DBMS_OUTPUT_VIEW instead:

```
tkyte@TKYTE816> select *
  2      from my_dbms_output_view
  3  /

TEXT
-------------------------------
hello
Hey there
 1
 ...
                  19
                  20


23 rows selected.

tkyte@TKYTE816> select *
  2      from my_dbms_output_view
  3  /

no rows selected
```

In this fashion, we get to see the data only once.

This new implementation of DBMS_OUTPUT raises the 255 bytes per line limit to 4,000 bytes per line, and effectively removes the size limitation on the number of total output bytes (you are still limited by available RAM on your server though). It introduces some new functionality (you can query your output, sort it, and so on) as well. It removes the SQL*PLUS default feature of blank-trimming. Lastly, unlike UTL_FILE, the results of MY_DBMS_OUTPUT can be spooled to a client file in the same way DBMS_OUTPUT output could, making it a viable replacement for client-side functions.

You might ask why I used an object type instead of a temporary table in this implementation. The answer is one of code, and overhead. The amount of code to manage the temporary table, to have at least an additional column to remember the proper order of the data, as compared to this simple implementation, is large. Also, a temporary table incurs some amount of I/O activities and overhead. Lastly, it would be hard to implement the 'flushing view' effect I have above, whereby we empty the output buffer automatically simply by selecting from it. In short, using the object type lead to a lighter weight implementation. If I planned on using this to generate tens of MB of output, I might very well reconsider my choice of buffering mechanisms, and use a temporary table. For moderate amounts of data, this implementation works well.

Summary

In this section, we have covered how the DBMS_OUTPUT package is actually implemented. Now that you know how it works, you will not become a victim of the side effects of this. You are now able to anticipate that you won't get the buffer size you asked for, and that the size of this output buffer will seem arbitrary at times. You'll be aware that it is not possible to produce an output line that exceeds 255 bytes without a newline. You know that you cannot see DBMS_OUTPUT output until *after* the procedure or statement completes execution, and even then, *only* if the environment you are using to query the database supports DBMS_OUTPUT.

In addition to gaining an understanding of how DBMS_OUTPUT works, we have also seen how to solve many of the major limitations, typically by using other features to accomplish our goals. Solutions such as UTL_FILE to produce flat files and simple functions like P to not only save on typing, but also to print larger lines. In the extreme case, we looked implementing your own equivalent functionality that does not suffer from some of the limits.

DBMS_OUTPUT is a good example of how something seemingly trivial can, in fact, be a very complex piece of software with unintended side effects. When you read through the DBMS_OUTPUT documentation in Oracle's *Supplied PL/SQL Packages Reference* guide, it sounds so simple and straightforward. Then issues like the total number of output bytes you can generate, and so on, crop up. Knowledge of how the package works helps us avoid these issues, either by just being aware that they are there, or by using alternative methods to implement our applications.

DBMS_PROFILER

The profiler is a long awaited (by me anyway) feature. It provides us with a source code profiler for our PL/SQL applications. In the past, you would tune your PL/SQL applications using SQL_TRACE and TKPROF. This would help you identify and tune your long running SQL, but trying to discover where the bottlenecks in 5,000 lines of PL/SQL code are (which you might not have even written yourself) was pretty near impossible. You typically ended up instrumenting the code with lots of calls to DBMS_UTILITY.GET_TIME to measure elapsed time, in an attempt to find out what was slow.

Well, you no longer have to do this – we have the DBMS_PROFILER package. I am going to demonstrate how I use it. I myself use little of its total functionality – I just use it to find the really bad areas, and go straight there. I use it in a very simplistic fashion. It is set up and designed to do much more than presented here, however.

The statistics gathering takes place in database tables. These tables are set up to hold the statistics for many different runs of the code. This is OK for some people, but I like to just keep the last run or two, in there only. Any more than that and it gets too confusing. Sometimes, too much information is just that – too much information.

Your DBA may have to install the profiler in your database. The procedure for installing this package is simple:

- ❏ cd [ORACLE_HOME]/rdbms/admin.
- ❏ using SVRMGRL you would connect as SYS or INTERNAL.
- ❏ Run profload.sql.

In order to actually use the profiler after that, you will need to have the profiling tables installed. You can install these once per database, but I recommend that developers have their own copy. Fortunately, the DBMS_PROFILER package is built with invoker rights and unqualified table names, so that we can install the tables in each schema, and the profiler package will use them correctly. The reason you each want your own tables, is so that you only see the results of your profiling runs, not those of your co-workers. In order to get a copy of the profiling tables in your schema, you would run [ORACLE_HOME]\rdbms\admin\proftab.sql in SQL*PLUS. After you run proftab.sql, you'll need to run profrep.sql as well. This script creates views and packages to operate on the profiler tables in order to generate reports. This script is found in [ORACLE_HOME]\plsql\demo\profrep.sql. You should run this in your schema as well, after creating the tables.

I like to keep a small script around to reset these tables, and clear them out every so often. After I've done a run or two and have analyzed the results, I run this script. I have the following in a script I call profreset.sql:

```
-- uses deletes because of foreign key constraints
delete from plsql_profiler_data;
delete from plsql_profiler_units;
delete from plsql_profiler_runs;
```

Now we are ready to start profiling. I'm going to demonstrate the use of this package by running two different implementations of a factorial algorithm. One is recursive, and the other is iterative. We'll use the profiler to see which one is faster, and what components of the code are 'slow' in each implementation. The test driver for this is simply:

```
tkyte@TKYTE816> @profreset
tkyte@TKYTE816> create or replace
  2  function fact_recursive( n int ) return number
  3  as
  4  begin
  5          if ( n = 1 )
  6          then
  7                  return 1;
  8          else
  9                  return n * fact_recursive(n-1);
 10          end if;
 11  end;
 12  /

Function created.

tkyte@TKYTE816> create or replace
  2  function fact_iterative( n int ) return number
  3  as
  4          l_result number default 1;
  5  begin
  6          for i in 2 .. n
  7          loop
  8                  l_result := l_result * i;
  9          end loop;
 10          return l_result;
 11  end;
 12  /
```

```
Function created.

tkyte@TKYTE816> set serveroutput on

tkyte@TKYTE816> exec dbms_profiler.start_profiler( 'factorial recursive' )

PL/SQL procedure successfully completed.

tkyte@TKYTE816> begin
  2          for i in 1 .. 50 loop
  3                  dbms_output.put_line( fact_recursive(50) );
  4          end loop;
  5  end;
  6  /
30414093201713378043612608166064768844300000000000000000000000000000
...
30414093201713378043612608166064768844300000000000000000000000000000

PL/SQL procedure successfully completed.

tkyte@TKYTE816> exec dbms_profiler.stop_profiler

PL/SQL procedure successfully completed.

tkyte@TKYTE816> exec dbms_profiler.start_profiler( 'factorial iterative' )

PL/SQL procedure successfully completed.

tkyte@TKYTE816> begin
  2          for i in 1 .. 50 loop
  3                  dbms_output.put_line( fact_iterative(50) );
  4          end loop;
  5  end;
  6  /
30414093201713378043612608166064768844300000000000000000000000000000
...
30414093201713378043612608166064768844300000000000000000000000000000

PL/SQL procedure successfully completed.

tkyte@TKYTE816> exec dbms_profiler.stop_profiler

PL/SQL procedure successfully completed.
```

In order to collect statistics for a profiler run, we must call START_PROFILER. We name each run with some meaningful name, and then start running the code. I ran the factorial routines 50 times each before ending the statistics collection for a given run. Now, we are ready to analyze the results.

In [ORACLE_HOME]/plsql/demo there is a script profsum.sql. Don't run it– some of the queries in that script can take a considerable amount of time to execute (could take hours), and the amount of data it produces is very large. Below is the modified profsum.sql I use myself. It provides much of the same information, but the queries execute quickly, and many of the really detailed reports are cut out. Also, some of the queries would include the timings for the STOP_PROFILER call in it, and others would not, skewing the observations from query to query. I've adjusted all of the queries to not include the timings of the profiler package itself.

My `profsum.sql` is the following, and this of course is available for download at
htpp://www.apress.com:

```
set echo off
set linesize 5000
set trimspool on
set serveroutput on
set termout off

column owner format a11
column unit_name format a14
column text format a21 word_wrapped
column runid format 9999
column secs  format 999.99
column hsecs format 999.99
column grand_total  format 9999.99
column run_comment format a11 word_wrapped
column line# format 99999
column pct format 999.9
column unit_owner format a11

spool profsum.out

/* Clean out rollup results, and recreate. */
update plsql_profiler_units set total_time = 0;

execute prof_report_utilities.rollup_all_runs;

prompt =
prompt =
prompt ====================
prompt Total time
select grand_total/1000000000 as grand_total
  from plsql_profiler_grand_total;

prompt =
prompt =
prompt ====================
prompt Total time spent on each run
select runid,
       substr(run_comment,1, 30) as run_comment,
       run_total_time/1000000000 as secs
  from (select a.runid, sum(a.total_time)  run_total_time, b.run_comment
          from plsql_profiler_units a, plsql_profiler_runs b
         where a.runid = b.runid group by a.runid, b.run_comment )
 where run_total_time > 0
 order by runid asc;

prompt =
prompt =
prompt ====================
prompt Percentage of time in each module, for each run separately
```

```
select p1.runid,
       substr(p2.run_comment, 1, 20) as run_comment,
       p1.unit_owner,
       decode(p1.unit_name, '', '<anonymous>',
                   substr(p1.unit_name,1, 20)) as unit_name,
       p1.total_time/1000000000 as secs,
       TO_CHAR(100*p1.total_time/p2.run_total_time, '999.9') as percentage
  from plsql_profiler_units p1,
       (select a.runid, sum(a.total_time)  run_total_time, b.run_comment
          from plsql_profiler_units a, plsql_profiler_runs b
         where a.runid = b.runid group by a.runid, b.run_comment ) p2
 where p1.runid=p2.runid
   and p1.total_time > 0
   and p2.run_total_time > 0
   and  (p1.total_time/p2.run_total_time)  >= .01
 order by p1.runid asc, p1.total_time desc;

column secs form 9.99
prompt =
prompt =
prompt ====================
prompt Percentage of time in each module, summarized across runs
select p1.unit_owner,
       decode(p1.unit_name, '', '<anonymous>', substr(p1.unit_name,1, 25)) as
unit_name,
       p1.total_time/1000000000 as secs,
       TO_CHAR(100*p1.total_time/p2.grand_total, '99999.99') as percentage
  from plsql_profiler_units_cross_run p1,
       plsql_profiler_grand_total p2
 order by p1.total_time DESC;

prompt =
prompt =
prompt ====================
prompt Lines taking more than 1% of the total time, each run separate
select p1.runid as runid,
       p1.total_time/10000000 as Hsecs,
        p1.total_time/p4.grand_total*100 as pct,
       substr(p2.unit_owner, 1, 20) as owner,
       decode(p2.unit_name, '', '<anonymous>', substr(p2.unit_name,1, 20)) as
unit_name,
       p1.line#,
       ( select p3.text
           from all_source p3
          where p3.owner = p2.unit_owner and
                p3.line = p1.line# and
                p3.name=p2.unit_name and
                p3.type not in ( 'PACKAGE', 'TYPE' )) text
  from plsql_profiler_data p1,
       plsql_profiler_units p2,
       plsql_profiler_grand_total p4
 where (p1.total_time >= p4.grand_total/100)
   AND p1.runID = p2.runid
   and p2.unit_number=p1.unit_number
 order by p1.total_time desc;
prompt =
prompt =
prompt ====================
prompt Most popular lines (more than 1%), summarize across all runs
```

```
select p1.total_time/10000000 as hsecs,
        p1.total_time/p4.grand_total*100 as pct,
       substr(p1.unit_owner, 1, 20) as unit_owner,
       decode(p1.unit_name, '', '<anonymous>',
                 substr(p1.unit_name,1, 20)) as unit_name,
       p1.line#,
       ( select p3.text from all_source p3
           where (p3.line = p1.line#) and
                 (p3.owner = p1.unit_owner) AND
                 (p3.name = p1.unit_name) and
                 (p3.type not in ( 'PACKAGE', 'TYPE' ) ) ) text
  from  plsql_profiler_lines_cross_run p1,
        plsql_profiler_grand_total p4
 where (p1.total_time >= p4.grand_total/100)
 order by p1.total_time desc;

execute prof_report_utilities.rollup_all_runs;

prompt =
prompt =
prompt ====================
prompt  Number of lines actually executed in different units (by unit_name)

select p1.unit_owner,
       p1.unit_name,
       count( decode( p1.total_occur, 0, null, 0))  as lines_executed ,
       count(p1.line#) as lines_present,
       count( decode( p1.total_occur, 0, null, 0))/count(p1.line#) *100
                                    as pct
  from plsql_profiler_lines_cross_run p1
 where (p1.unit_type in ( 'PACKAGE BODY', 'TYPE BODY',
                          'PROCEDURE', 'FUNCTION' )  )
 group by p1.unit_owner, p1.unit_name;


prompt =
prompt =
prompt ====================
prompt  Number of lines actually executed for all units
select count(p1.line#) as lines_executed
  from plsql_profiler_lines_cross_run p1
 where (p1.unit_type in ( 'PACKAGE BODY', 'TYPE BODY',
                          'PROCEDURE', 'FUNCTION' )  )
    AND p1.total_occur > 0;


prompt =
prompt =
prompt ====================
prompt  Total number of lines in all units
select count(p1.line#) as lines_present
  from plsql_profiler_lines_cross_run p1
 where (p1.unit_type in ( 'PACKAGE BODY', 'TYPE BODY',
                          'PROCEDURE', 'FUNCTION' )  );

spool off
set termout on
edit profsum.out
set linesize 131
```

I have gone out of my way to make that report fit into an 80-column screen, you could be more generous with some of the column formats if you don't use Telnet frequently.

Now, let's look at the output of our factorial run, the results of running the above `profsum.sql` script:

```
Total time

GRAND_TOTAL
-----------
       5.57
```

This tells us the grand total of our run times across both runs was 5.57 seconds. Next, we'll see a breakdown by run:

```
Total time spent on each run

RUNID RUN_COMMENT    SECS
----- -----------  -------
   17 factorial      3.26
      recursive

   18 factorial      2.31
      iterative
```

This shows us already that the recursive routine is not nearly as efficient as the iterative version, it took almost 50 percent longer to execute. Next, we will look at the amount of time spent in each module (package or procedure) in both runs, and the raw percentage of time by run:

```
Percentage of time in each module, for each run separately

RUNID RUN_COMMENT UNIT_OWNER  UNIT_NAME       SECS PERCEN
----- ----------- ----------- --------------- ------- ------
   17 factorial   TKYTE       FACT_RECURSIVE  1.87   57.5
      recursive

   17 factorial   SYS         DBMS_OUTPUT     1.20   36.9
      recursive

   17 factorial   <anonymous> <anonymous>      .08    2.5
      recursive

   17 factorial   <anonymous> <anonymous>      .06    1.9
      recursive

   18 factorial   SYS         DBMS_OUTPUT     1.24   53.6
      iterative

   18 factorial   TKYTE       FACT_ITERATIVE   .89   38.5
      iterative

   18 factorial   <anonymous> <anonymous>      .08    3.4
      iterative

   18 factorial   <anonymous> <anonymous>      .06    2.7
      iterative

8 rows selected.
```

In this example, we see that in the recursive implementation, 57 percent of our run-time is spent in our routine, 37 percent in DBMS_OUTPUT, and the rest in miscellaneous routines. In our second run, the percentages are quite different. Our code is only 38 percent of the total run-time, and that it 38 percent of a smaller number! This already shows that the second implementation is superior to the first. More telling is the SECS column. Here, we can see that the recursive routine took 1.87 seconds, whereas the iterative routine took only .89. If we ignore DBMS_OUTPUT for a moment, we see that the iterative routine is two times faster than the recursive implementation.

It should be noted that you might not get exactly the same percentages (or even close) on your system. If you do not have SERVEROUTPUT ON in SQL*PLUS for example, DBMS_OUTPUT might not even show up on your system. If you run on a slower or faster machine, the numbers will be very different. For example, when I ran this on my Sparc Solaris machine, the GRAND_TOTAL time was about 1.0 seconds, and the percentages spent in each section of code were slightly different. Overall, the end result was much the same, percentage-wise.

Now we can look at the time spent in each module summarized across the runs. This will tell us what piece of code we spend most of our time in:

```
Percentage of time in each module, summarized across runs

UNIT_OWNER    UNIT_NAME        SECS PERCENTAG
-----------   -------------   ----- ---------
SYS           DBMS_OUTPUT      2.44    43.82
TKYTE         FACT_RECURSIVE   1.87    33.61
TKYTE         FACT_ITERATIVE    .89    16.00
<anonymous>   <anonymous>       .33     5.88
SYS           DBMS_PROFILER     .04      .69
```

Here, is it obvious we could cut our run-time almost in half by removing the single call to DBMS_OUTPUT. In fact, if you simply SET SERVEROUTPUT OFF, effectively disabling DBMS_OUTPUT, and rerun the test, you should find that it drops down to 3 percent or less of the total run-time. Currently however, it is taking the largest amount of time. What is more interesting than this, is that 33 percent of the total time is in the recursive routine and only 16 percent in the iterative – the iterative routine is much faster.

Now, let's look at some more details:

```
Lines taking more than 1% of the total time, each run separate

RUNID   HSECS     PCT OWNER UNIT_NAME       LINE TEXT
-----  -------   ------ ----- -------------- ---- --------------------
   17  142.47    25.6 TKYTE FACT_RECURSIVE    8 return n*fact_recursive(n-1);
   18   68.00    12.2 TKYTE FACT_ITERATIVE    7 l_result := l_result * i;
   17   43.29     7.8 TKYTE FACT_RECURSIVE    4 if ( n = 1 )
   17   19.58     3.5 SYS   DBMS_OUTPUT     116 a3 a0 51 a5 1c 6e 81 b0
   18   19.29     3.5 TKYTE FACT_ITERATIVE    5 for i in 2 .. n
   18   17.66     3.2 SYS   DBMS_OUTPUT     116 a3 a0 51 a5 1c 6e 81 b0
   17   14.76     2.7 SYS   DBMS_OUTPUT     118 1c 51 81 b0 a3 a0 1c 51
   18   14.49     2.6 SYS   DBMS_OUTPUT     118 1c 51 81 b0 a3 a0 1c 51
   18   13.41     2.4 SYS   DBMS_OUTPUT     142 :2 a0 a5 b b4 2e d b7 19
   17   13.22     2.4 SYS   DBMS_OUTPUT     142 :2 a0 a5 b b4 2e d b7 19
   18   10.62     1.9 SYS   DBMS_OUTPUT     166 6e b4 2e d :2 a0 7e 51 b4
```

```
    17     10.46      1.9  SYS     DBMS_OUTPUT     166 6e b4 2e d :2 a0 7e 51 b4
    17      8.11      1.5  SYS     DBMS_OUTPUT      72 1TO_CHAR:
    18      8.09      1.5  SYS     DBMS_OUTPUT     144 8f a0 b0 3d b4 55 6a :3 a0
    18      8.02      1.4  SYS     DBMS_OUTPUT      72 1TO_CHAR:
    17      8.00      1.4  SYS     DBMS_OUTPUT     144 8f a0 b0 3d b4 55 6a :3 a0
    17      7.52      1.4  <ano>   <anonymous>       3
    18      7.22      1.3  <ano>   <anonymous>       3
    18      6.65      1.2  SYS     DBMS_OUTPUT     141 a0 b0 3d b4 55 6a :3 a0 7e
    18      6.21      1.1  <ano>   <anonymous>       1
    17      6.13      1.1  <ano>   <anonymous>       1
    18      5.77      1.0  SYS     DBMS_OUTPUT      81 1ORU-10028:: line length

22 rows selected.
```

Here, I am printing out the run-time in hundreds of seconds instead of seconds, and showing the percentages as well. No surprises here – we would expect that line 8 in the recursive routine and line 7 in the iterative routine would be the big ones. Here, we can see that they are. This part of the report gives you specific lines in the code to zero in on and fix. Notice the strange looking lines of code from DBMS_OUTPUT. This is what wrapped PL/SQL looks like in the database. It is just a bytecode representation of the actual source, designed to obscure it from prying eyes like yours and mine.

Now, the next report is similar to the one above, but it aggregates results across runs, whereas the numbers above show percentages within a run:

```
Most popular lines (more than 1%), summarize across all runs

   HSECS     PCT  OWNER  UNIT_NAME       LINE TEXT
  -------  ------ -----  --------------  ---- ---------------------
   142.47   25.6  TKYTE  FACT_RECURSIVE     8 return n * fact_recursive(n-1);
    68.00   12.2  TKYTE  FACT_ITERATIVE     7 l_result := l_result * i;
    43.29    7.8  TKYTE  FACT_RECURSIVE     4 if ( n = 1 )
    37.24    6.7  SYS    DBMS_OUTPUT      116 a3 a0 51 a5 1c 6e 81 b0
    29.26    5.3  SYS    DBMS_OUTPUT      118 1c 51 81 b0 a3 a0 1c 51
    26.63    4.8  SYS    DBMS_OUTPUT      142 :2 a0 a5 b b4 2e d b7 19
    21.08    3.8  SYS    DBMS_OUTPUT      166 6e b4 2e d :2 a0 7e 51 b4
    19.29    3.5  TKYTE  FACT_ITERATIVE     5 for i in 2 .. n
    16.88    3.0  <ano>  <anonymous>        1
    16.13    2.9  SYS    DBMS_OUTPUT       72 1TO_CHAR:
    16.09    2.9  SYS    DBMS_OUTPUT      144 8f a0 b0 3d b4 55 6a :3 a0
    14.74    2.6  <ano>  <anonymous>        3
    11.28    2.0  SYS    DBMS_OUTPUT       81 1ORU-10028:: line length overflow,
    10.17    1.8  SYS    DBMS_OUTPUT      147 4f 9a 8f a0 b0 3d b4 55
     9.52    1.7  SYS    DBMS_OUTPUT       73 1DATE:
     8.54    1.5  SYS    DBMS_OUTPUT      117 a3 a0 1c 51 81 b0 a3 a0
     7.36    1.3  SYS    DBMS_OUTPUT      141 a0 b0 3d b4 55 6a :3 a0 7e
     6.25    1.1  SYS    DBMS_OUTPUT       96 1WHILE:
     6.19    1.1  SYS    DBMS_OUTPUT       65 1499:
     5.77    1.0  SYS    DBMS_OUTPUT      145 7e a0 b4 2e d a0 57 b3

20 rows selected.
```

Lastly, we'll take a look at some of the code coverage statistics. This is useful not only for profiling and performance tuning, but testing as well. This tells you how many of the statements in the code we have executed, and shows the percentage of the code that has been 'covered':

```
Number of lines actually executed in different units (by unit_name)

UNIT_OWNER    UNIT_NAME        LINES_EXECUTED LINES_PRESENT    PCT
-----------   --------------   -------------- --------------  ------
SYS           DBMS_OUTPUT                  51             88    58.0
SYS           DBMS_PROFILER                 9             62    14.5
TKYTE         FACT_ITERATIVE                4              4   100.0
TKYTE         FACT_RECURSIVE                3              3   100.0


=
=
=====================
Number of lines actually executed for all units

LINES_EXECUTED
--------------
            67

=
=
====================
Total number of lines in all units

LINES_PRESENT
-------------
           157
```

This shows that of the 88 statements in the DBMS_OUTPUT package, we executed 51 of them. It is interesting to note how DBMS_PROFILER counts lines or statements here. It claims that FACT_ITERATIVE has 4 lines of code, but if we look at the source code:

```
function fact_iterative( n int ) return number
as
        l_result number default 1;
begin
        for i in 2 .. n
        loop
                l_result := l_result * i;
        end loop;
        return l_result;
end;
```

I don't see four of anything clearly. DBMS_PROFILER is counting statements, and not really lines of code. Here, the four statements are:

```
...
        l_result number default 1;
...
        for i in 2 .. n
...
            l_result := l_result * i;
...
        return l_result;
...
```

Everything else, while necessary to compile and execute the code, was not really executable code, and therefore, not statements. DBMS_PROFILER can be used to tell us how many executable statements we have in our code, and how many of them we actually executed.

Caveats

The only caveats I have with regards to DBMS_PROFILER, are the amount of data it generates, and the amount of your time it can consume.

The small test case we did above generated some 500-plus rows of observations in the PLSQL_PROFILER_DATA table. This table contains eleven number columns, and so it is not very 'wide', but it grows rapidly. Every statement executed will cause a row to be added to this table. You will need to monitor the space you need for this table, and make sure you clear it out every now and again. Typically, this is not a serious issue, but I have seen this table getting filled with thousands of rows for extremely complex PL/SQL routines (hundreds of thousands of rows).

The amount of your time it can consume, is a more insidious problem. No matter how much you tune, there will *always* be a line of code that consumes the most amount of time. If you remove this line of code from the top of the list, another one is just waiting to take its place. You will never get a report from DBMS_PROFILER that says, 'everything ran so fast, I won't even generate a report.' In order to use this tool effectively, you have to set some goals for yourself – give yourself a finish line. Either set a time boundary (I will tune this routine to the best of my ability for two hours), or a performance metric boundary (when the run-time is N units long, I will stop). Otherwise, you will find yourself (as I have from time to time) spending an inordinate amount of time fine-tuning a routine that just cannot get any faster.

DBMS_PROFILER is a nice tool with lots of detailed information. It is far too easy to get bogged down in the details.

Summary

In this section we have covered the uses of the DBMS_PROFILER package. One of its two main uses is source code profiling to detect where in the code time is being spent, or to compare two different algorithms. The other major use is as a code coverage tool, to report back the percentage of executable statements your test routines actually exercised in the application. While 100 percent code coverage does not assure you of bug free code – it certainly brings you a step closer though.

We also developed a report, based on the example profiler report provided by Oracle. This report extracts the basic information you need in order to use the DBMS_PROFILER tool successfully. It avoids the great detail you can go into, providing you with the aggregate view of what happened in your application, and more details on the most expensive parts. It may be the only report you really need to use with this tool in order to identify bottlenecks and tune your application.

DBMS_UTILITY

The DBMS_UTILITY package is a collection of miscellaneous procedures. It is where many, standalone procedures are placed. The DBMS_UTILITY package is installed in the database by default, and has EXECUTE granted to PUBLIC. The procedures in this package are not related to one another as they typically are in the other packages. For example, all of the entry points in the UTL_FILE package have a common goal and meaning – to perform I/O on a file. The entry points in DBMS_UTILITY are pretty much independent of one another.

In this section, we will look at many of these functions, and the important caveats and issues will be pointed out.

COMPILE_SCHEMA

The goal of the COMPILE_SCHEMA procedure is to attempt to make valid all *invalid* procedures, packages, triggers, views, types, and so on in a schema. This procedure works in Oracle 8.1.6 by using the SYS.ORDER_OBJECT_BY_DEPENDENCY view. This view returns objects in the order they depend on each other. In Oracle 8.1.7 and higher, this view is no longer used (why this is relevant will be shown below). If we compile the objects in the order that this view returns them, then at the end, all objects that *can* be valid, *should* be valid. This procedure runs the ALTER COMPILE command as the user who invoked the procedure (invoker rights).

It should be noted that COMPILE_SCHEMA demands you pass in a case-sensitive username. If you call:

```
scott@TKYTE816> exec DBMS_UTILITY.compile_schema( 'scott' );
```

It is probable that nothing will happen, unless you have a lowercase user named scott. You must pass in SCOTT.

There is however another issue with COMPILE_SCHEMA in 8.1 versions of the database prior to 8.1.6.2 (that is all 8.1.5, 8.1.6.0, and 8.1.6.1 versions). If you have a Java-enabled database, this will introduce some recursive dependencies into your system. This will cause COMPILE_SCHEMA to raise the error:

```
scott@TKYTE816> exec dbms_utility.compile_schema( user );
BEGIN dbms_utility.compile_schema( user ); END;

*
ERROR at line 1:
ORA-01436: CONNECT BY loop in user data
ORA-06512: at "SYS.DBMS_UTILITY", line 195
ORA-06512: at line 1
```

This is coming from the SYS.ORDER_OBJECT_BY_DEPENDENCY view, and is the reason why Oracle 8.1.7 and up do not use this view. If you encounter this error, we can create our own COMPILE_SCHEMA procedure that behaves exactly as the real COMPILE_SCHEMA. We can do this by compiling the objects in any order we feel like it. It is a common misconception that we must compile objects in some specific order – we can in fact do them in *any arbitrary order*, and still end up with the same outcome we would have, if we ordered by dependency. The logic is:

1. Pick any invalid object from a schema that we have not yet tried to compile.

2. Compile it.

3. Go back to step one until there are no more invalid objects that we have not yet tried to compile.

It is that simple – we need no special ordering. This is because a side effect of compiling an invalid object is that all invalid objects it depends on will be compiled in order to validate this one. We just have to keep compiling objects until we have no more invalid ones (well, we might have invalid ones, but that would be because they cannot be successfully compiled no matter what). What we might discover is that we need only to compile a *single* procedure to get 10 or 20 other objects compiled. As long as we don't attempt to manually recompile those 10 or 20 other objects (as this would invalidate the first object again) we are OK.

Since the implementation of this procedure is somewhat interesting, we'll demonstrate it here. We need to rely on an invoker rights routine to do the actual ALTER COMPILE command. However, we need access to the DBA_OBJECTS table to find the 'next' invalid object, and report on the status of the just-compiled object. We do not necessarily want the invoker of the routine to have to have access to DBA_OBJECTS. In order to achieve this, we will use a mixture of invoker rights routines and definer rights routines. We need to make sure that the top-level routine, the one called by the end user, is the invoker rights routine however, to ensure that roles are enabled.

Here is my implementation of a COMPILE_SCHEMA.

The user who runs this script must have had SELECT granted to them on the SYS.DBA_OBJECTS view directly (refer to Chapter 23, Invoker and Definer Rights for details on why this is).

Since this is a SQL*PLUS script, with some SQL*PLUS directives in it, I'll show the script here this time, not the results of actually running the script. I am using a SQL*PLUS substitution variable to fill in the schema name as we compile objects. I am doing this because of the invoker rights routine (the need to fully qualify objects if they should always access the *same* table, regardless of who is running it), and the fact that I personally do not like to rely on public synonyms. The script will be given to you in pieces below with commentary in between:

```
column u new_val uname
select user u from dual;

drop table compile_schema_tmp
/

create global temporary table compile_schema_tmp
( object_name varchar2(30),
  object_type varchar2(30),
  constraint compile_schema_tmp_pk
  primary key(object_name,object_type)
)
on commit preserve rows
/

grant all on compile_schema_tmp to public
/
```

We start the script by getting the currently logged in user's username into a SQL*PLUS substitution variable. We will use this later in our CREATE OR REPLACE procedures. We need to do this because our procedure is going to run as an invoker rights routine, and needs to access the table we just created above. If you recall in Chapter 23 on *Invoker and Definer Rights*, we discussed how references to tables in the procedure are be done using the default schema of the person running the procedure. Well, we only have one temporary table that all users will use, and it will be owned by whoever installs this package. Therefore, we need to hard code the username into the PL/SQL routine. The temporary table is used by our procedures to 'remember' what objects we have attempted to compile. We need to use ON COMMIT PRESERVE ROWS because of the fact that we are going to do DDL in our procedure (the ALTER COMPILE command is DDL), and DDL commits. Next, we can start in on the procedures we need:

```
create or replace
procedure get_next_object_to_compile( p_username in varchar2,
                                       p_cmd out varchar2,
                                       p_obj out varchar2,
                                       p_typ out varchar2 )
as
begin
    select 'alter ' || object_type || ' '
            || p_username || '.' || object_name ||
        decode( object_type, 'PACKAGE BODY', ' compile body',
                ' compile' ), object_name, object_type
      into p_cmd, p_obj, p_typ
      from dba_objects a
     where owner = upper(p_username)
       and status = 'INVALID'
       and object_type <> 'UNDEFINED'
```

```
                and not exists ( select null
                                   from compile_schema_tmp b
                                  where a.object_name = b.object_name
                                    and a.object_type = b.object_type
                               )
            and rownum = 1;

        insert into compile_schema_tmp
        ( object_name, object_type )
        values
        ( p_obj, p_typ );
    end;
    /
```

This is a definer rights procedure that accesses the DBA_OBJECTS view for us. This will return 'some' invalid object to be compiled, as long as we have not yet attempted to compile it. It just finds the first one. As we retrieve them, we 'remember' them in our temporary table. Note that this routine will throw the exception NO_DATA_FOUND when there are no objects left to be compiled in the requested schema – we'll use this fact in our next routine to stop processing. Next, we have our invoker rights routine that will actually do the compilation. This also shows why we needed the COLUMN U NEW_VAL UNAME directive above– we need to physically insert the *owner* of the temporary table in here to avoid having to use a synonym. Since we do this dynamically upon compiling the procedure, it makes it better than a synonym:

```
create or replace procedure compile_schema( p_username in varchar2 )
authid current_user
as
    l_cmd   varchar2(512);
    l_obj   dba_objects.object_name%type;
    l_typ   dba_objects.object_type%type;
begin
    delete from &uname..compile_schema_tmp;

    loop
        get_next_object_to_compile( p_username, l_cmd, l_obj, l_typ );

        dbms_output.put_line( l_cmd );
        begin
            execute immediate l_cmd;
            dbms_output.put_line( 'Successful' );
        exception
            when others then
                dbms_output.put_line( sqlerrm );
        end;
        dbms_output.put_line( chr(9) );
    end loop;

exception - get_next_object_to_compile raises this when done
    when no_data_found then NULL;
end;
/

grant execute on compile_schema to public
/
```

1175

And that's it. Now you can go into any schema that is able to compile some objects, and execute:

```
scott@TKYTE816> exec tkyte.compile_schema('scott')
alter PROCEDURE scott.ANALYZE_MY_TABLES compile
Successful

alter PROCEDURE scott.CUST_LIST compile
ORA-24344: success with compilation error

alter TYPE scott.EMP_MASTER compile
ORA-24344: success with compilation error

alter PROCEDURE scott.FOO compile
Successful

alter PACKAGE scott.LOADLOBS compile
Successful

alter PROCEDURE scott.P compile
Successful

alter PROCEDURE scott.RUN_BY_JOBS compile
Successful

PL/SQL procedure successfully completed.
```

So, this shows me the objects it attempted to compile, and the outcome. According to the above, we compile seven objects, two of which failed, and five of which succeeded. We compiled them in any order – the order was simply not relevant. This procedure should work in all situations.

ANALYZE_SCHEMA

The ANALYZE_SCHEMA routine does pretty much what it sounds like it would do – it performs an ANALYZE to collect statistics for the objects in a user's schema. It is recommended that you never do this on either SYS or SYSTEM. This is especially for SYS, as the recursive SQL generated by Oracle over the years was optimized for execution using the rule-based optimizer. Having statistics on SYS-owned tables will cause your database to operate slower than it should. You may use this procedure to analyze application schemas you have yourself developed.

The ANALYZE_SCHEMA procedure accepts five arguments:

❑ SCHEMA – The schema to be analyzed.

❑ METHOD – ESTIMATE, COMPUTE, or DELETE. If ESTIMATE, then either ESTIMATE_ROWS or ESTIMATE_PERCENT must be non-zero.

❑ ESTIMATE_ROWS – Number of rows to estimate.

❑ ESTIMATE_PERCENT – Percentage of rows to estimate. If ESTIMATE_ROWS is specified, then this parameter is ignored.

❑ METHOD_OPT [FOR TABLE] [FOR ALL [INDEXED] COLUMNS] [SIZE n] [FOR ALL INDEXES] – These options are the same options as you use with the ANALYZE command itself. You will find these options fully documented in the *Oracle8i SQL Reference* manual under the ANALYZE commands, *for clause*.

So, for example, to analyze all of the objects in SCOTT's schema, we can do the following. We start by first deleting and then collecting statistics:

```
scott@TKYTE816> exec dbms_utility.analyze_schema(user,'delete');

PL/SQL procedure successfully completed.

scott@TKYTE816> select table_name, num_rows, last_analyzed
  2  from user_tables;

TABLE_NAME                        NUM_ROWS LAST_ANAL
------------------------------- ---------- ---------
BONUS
CREATE$JAVA$LOB$TABLE
DEPT
...

12 rows selected.

scott@TKYTE816> exec dbms_utility.analyze_schema(user,'compute');

PL/SQL procedure successfully completed.

scott@TKYTE816> select table_name, num_rows, last_analyzed
  2  from user_tables;

TABLE_NAME                        NUM_ROWS LAST_ANAL
------------------------------- ---------- ---------
BONUS                                    0 03-FEB-01
CREATE$JAVA$LOB$TABLE                   58 03-FEB-01
DEPT                                     4 03-FEB-01
...

12 rows selected.
```

This simple shows that the ANALYZE COMPUTE actually did its job – the NUM_ROWS and LAST_ANALYZED columns got filled in.

In general, the ANALYZE_SCHEMA procedure is as straightforward as it sounds. If you have the need to specifically analyze certain objects in certain ways, it will not apply. This procedure does the same sort of analysis to each object type, and does not have exceptions. For example, if you are a large data warehouse, and you make use of histograms on specific columns, or sets of columns on certain tables only, ANALYZE_SCHEMA is not what you want. You can use ANALYZE_SCHEMA to get histograms either for every column or none of the columns – not just certain columns. Once you go beyond the 'simple' with regards to analyzing objects, ANALYZE_SCHEMA will not be useful any more. This routine works well for small to medium sized applications, where small to medium is a measure of the amount of data you have. If you have large volumes of data, you will want to analyze in parallel or use special options to analyze on various tables. This will exclude ANALYZE_SCHEMA from being of use to you.

If you do use ANALYZE_SCHEMA, you should be aware of the following two issues. The first has to do with ANALYZE_SCHEMA against a schema that is changing. The second is with respect to objects ANALYZE_SCHEMA does not analyze. We will look at both of these caveats in turn.

ANALYZE_SCHEMA with a Changing Schema

Suppose you start an ANALYZE_SCHEMA in the SCOTT schema. You've added some large tables so it will take a while. In another session, you drop or add some objects to SCOTT's schema. The object you drop hasn't been reached by ANALYZE_SCHEMA yet. When it does, you will receive the somewhat misleading message:

```
scott@TKYTE816> exec dbms_utility.analyze_schema(user,'compute');
BEGIN dbms_utility.analyze_schema(user,'compute'); END;

*
ERROR at line 1:
ORA-20000: You have insufficient privileges for an object in this schema.
ORA-06512: at "SYS.DBMS_UTILITY", line 258
ORA-06512: at line 1
```

Obviously, you have all of the privileges you need; you own the objects after all. The error here is that a table, which it is trying to analyze no longer exists, when it gets round to analyzing it. Instead of recognizing that the table does not exist anymore, it assumes it does, and the error must be that you do not have sufficient privileges to analyze it. Currently, there is nothing you can do about this other than:

❑ Restart the ANALYZE_SCHEMA.

❑ Do not drop objects while ANALYZE_SCHEMA is executing.

The other thing to be aware of is that objects added to the schema *after* the ANALYZE_SCHEMA begins will not be analyzed – it will not see them yet. This is fairly harmless, as the ANALYZE_SCHEMA will run to completion successfully.

ANALYZE_SCHEMA does not Analyze Everything

There is an open issue with respect to ANALYZE_SCHEMA. It will not analyze an index-organized table that has an overflow segment (see Chapter 7, *Indexes*, for more information regarding IOTs and overflows). For example if you run the following code:

```
scott@TKYTE816> drop table t;

Table dropped.

scott@TKYTE816> create table t ( x int primary key, y date )
  2   organization index
  3   OVERFLOW TABLESPACE  TOOLS
  4   /

Table created.

scott@TKYTE816> execute dbms_utility.analyze_schema('SCOTT','COMPUTE')

PL/SQL procedure successfully completed.

scott@TKYTE816> select table_name, num_rows, last_analyzed
  2      from user_tables
  3    where table_name = 'T';
TABLE_NAME                       NUM_ROWS LAST_ANAL
------------------------------ ---------- ---------
T
```

it did not get analyzed. However, if you leave off the OVERFLOW clause:

```
scott@TKYTE816> drop table t;

Table dropped.

scott@TKYTE816> create table t ( x int primary key, y date )
  2  organization index
  3  /

Table created.

scott@TKYTE816> execute dbms_utility.analyze_schema('SCOTT','COMPUTE')

PL/SQL procedure successfully completed.

scott@TKYTE816> select table_name, num_rows, last_analyzed
  2     from user_tables
  3     where table_name = 'T';

TABLE_NAME                      NUM_ROWS LAST_ANAL
------------------------------ ---------- ---------
T                                      0 03-FEB-01
```

it does. This does *not* mean you should leave the OVERFLOW off of your IOTs, but rather that you will have to manually analyze these objects.

ANALYZE_DATABASE

This will be an exceptionally short section. *Do not use this procedure.* It is not realistic on a database of any size, and has a nasty side effect of analyzing the data dictionary (these are SYS owned objects, and we should never analyze these). Do not use it. Simply ignore its existence.

FORMAT_ERROR_STACK

FORMAT_ERROR_STACK is a function that, at first glance, would appear to be very useful, but in retrospect, is not at all. In actuality, FORMAT_ERROR_STACK is simply a less functional implementation of SQLERRM (SQL ERRor Message). A simple demonstration will help you to understand what I mean:

```
scott@TKYTE816> create or replace procedure p1
  2  as
  3  begin
  4          raise program_error;
  5  end;
  6  /

Procedure created.
```

```
scott@TKYTE816> create or replace procedure p2
  2  as
  3  begin
  4          p1;
  5  end;
  6  /

Procedure created.

scott@TKYTE816> create or replace procedure p3
  2  as
  3  begin
  4          p2;
  5  end;
  6  /

Procedure created.

scott@TKYTE816> exec p3
BEGIN p3; END;

*
ERROR at line 1:
ORA-06501: PL/SQL: program error
ORA-06512: at "SCOTT.P1", line 4
ORA-06512: at "SCOTT.P2", line 4
ORA-06512: at "SCOTT.P3", line 4
ORA-06512: at line 1
```

If we have an error, and we do not catch it in an exception handle, the entire error stack is displayed for us, and would be available to use in a Pro*C, OCI, JDBC, and so on, program. You would expect that the DBMS_UTILITY.FORMAT_ERROR_STACK routine would return similar information. You will find however that it loses this important information:

```
scott@TKYTE816> create or replace procedure p3
  2  as
  3  begin
  4          p2;
  5  exception
  6          when others then
  7                  dbms_output.put_line( dbms_utility.format_error_stack );
  8  end;
  9  /
Procedure created.

scott@TKYTE816> exec p3
ORA-06501: PL/SQL: program error

PL/SQL procedure successfully completed.
```

As you can see, we actually lost the error stack by calling FORMAT_ERROR_STACK! This routine returns the same information SQLERRM would return:

```
scott@TKYTE816> create or replace procedure p3
  2   as
  3   begin
  4         p2;
  5   exception
  6         when others then
  7                 dbms_output.put_line( sqlerrm );
  8   end;
  9   /
Procedure created.

scott@TKYTE816> exec p3
ORA-06501: PL/SQL: program error

PL/SQL procedure successfully completed.
```

Before, I said FORMAT_ERROR_STACK was a less functional SQLERRM. This is because SQLERRM can, not only return the current error message, but it can also return any error message:

```
scott@TKYTE816> exec dbms_output.put_line( sqlerrm(-1) );
ORA-00001: unique constraint (.) violated

PL/SQL procedure successfully completed.
```

Unfortunately, there simply is no way currently to get the real error stack in PL/SQL. You must let fatal errors propagate up to the calling client routine, in order to get the actual line number of the code that raised the error in the first place.

FORMAT_CALL_STACK

Fortunately this function *is* truly useful compared to FORMAT_ERROR_STACK. This returns to us the current call stack. Using this, we can write some utility procedures such as MY_CALLER and WHO_AM_I. These routines call a procedure to determine what source code from which line number invoked it. This is very useful for debugging and logging purposes. Also, a procedure could modify its behavior based on who called it, or where it was called.

Before we introduce the code for MY_CALLER and WHO_AM_I, let us look at what the call stack provides for us, and what the output from these routines is destined to be. If we use the P1, P2, P3 example from above, and rewrite P1 to be:

```
scott@TKYTE816> create or replace procedure p1
  2   as
  3       l_owner      varchar2(30);
  4       l_name       varchar2(30);
  5       l_lineno     number;
  6       l_type       varchar2(30);
  7   begin
  8       dbms_output.put_line( '----------------------' );
  9       dbms_output.put_line( dbms_utility.format_call_stack );
 10       dbms_output.put_line( '----------------------' );
 11       who_called_me( l_owner, l_name, l_lineno, l_type );
```

```
12        dbms_output.put_line( l_type || ' ' ||
13                                l_owner || '.' || l_name ||
14                                '(' || l_lineno || ')' );
15        dbms_output.put_line( '----------------------' );
16        dbms_output.put_line( who_am_i );
17        dbms_output.put_line( '----------------------' );
18        raise program_error;
19   end;
20   /

Procedure created.
```

we will receive output such as:

```
scott@TKYTE816> exec p3
----------------------
----- PL/SQL Call Stack -----
   object      line   object
   handle      number name
  2f191e0          9   procedure SCOTT.P1
  39f0a9c          4   procedure SCOTT.P2
  3aae318          4   procedure SCOTT.P3
  3a3461c          1   anonymous block
----------------------
PROCEDURE SCOTT.P2(4)
----------------------
SCOTT.P1(16)
----------------------
BEGIN p3; END;

*
ERROR at line 1:
ORA-06501: PL/SQL: program error
ORA-06512: at "SCOTT.P2", line 8
ORA-06512: at "SCOTT.P3", line 4
ORA-06512: at line 1
```

So, we can see the entire call stack in P1. This shows that P1 was called by P2, P2 was called by P3, and P3 was called by an anonymous block. Additionally, we can procedurally retrieve the fact that our caller in P1 was the procedure SCOTT.P2, and that they called us from line 4. Lastly, we can see simply that we are the procedure SCOTT.P1.

So, now that we see what the call stack looks like, and what kind of output we would like to get, we can present the code to do it:

```
tkyte@TKYTE816> create or replace function my_caller return varchar2
  2
  3  as
  4      owner        varchar2(30);
  5      name         varchar2(30);
  6      lineno       number;
  7      caller_t     varchar2(30);
  8      call_stack   varchar2(4096) default dbms_utility.format_call_stack;
```

```
 9      n              number;
10      found_stack BOOLEAN default FALSE;
11      line           varchar2(255);
12      cnt            number := 0;
13   begin
14
15      loop
16          n := instr( call_stack, chr(10) );
17          exit when ( cnt = 3 or n is NULL or n = 0 );
18
19          line := substr( call_stack, 1, n-1 );
20          call_stack := substr( call_stack, n+1 );
21
22          if ( NOT found_stack ) then
23              if ( line like '%handle%number%name%' ) then
24                  found_stack := TRUE;
25              end if;
26          else
27              cnt := cnt + 1;
28              -- cnt = 1 is ME
29              -- cnt = 2 is MY Caller
30              -- cnt = 3 is Their Caller
31              if ( cnt = 3 ) then
32                  lineno := to_number(substr( line, 13, 6 ));
33                  line   := substr( line, 21 );
34                  if ( line like 'pr%' ) then
35                      n := length( 'procedure ' );
36                  elsif ( line like 'fun%' ) then
37                      n := length( 'function ' );
38                  elsif ( line like 'package body%' ) then
39                      n := length( 'package body ' );
40                  elsif ( line like 'pack%' ) then
41                      n := length( 'package ' );
42                  elsif ( line like 'anonymous block%' ) then
43                      n := length( 'anonymous block ' );
44                  else -- must be a trigger
45                      n := 0;
46                  end if;
47                  if ( n <> 0 ) then
48                      caller_t := ltrim(rtrim(upper(substr(line,1,n-1))));
49                      line := substr( line, n );
50                  else
51                      caller_t := 'TRIGGER';
52                      line := ltrim( line );
53                  end if;
54                  n := instr( line, '.' );
55                  owner := ltrim(rtrim(substr( line, 1, n-1 )));
56                  name  := ltrim(rtrim(substr( line, n+1 )));
57              end if;
58          end if;
59      end loop;
60      return owner || '.' || name;
61   end;
62   /
```

```
Function created.

tkyte@TKYTE816> create or replace function who_am_i return varchar2
  2  as
  3  begin
  4      return my_caller;
  5  end;
  6  /

Function created.
```

Now that you have these routines, you can do some interesting things. It has been used to

❑ **Perform auditing** – The audit routines log not only the *user* that performed some operation, but also the *code* that did it as well.

❑ **Perform debugging** – For example, if you litter your code with calls to DBMS_APPLICATION_INFO.SET_CLIENT_INFO(WHO_AM_I), you can query V$SESSION in another session to see where in your code you are currently. See the earlier section of this appendix on DBMS_APPLICATION_INFO for details on this package.

GET_TIME

This function returns a ticker that measures time in hundredths of a second. You cannot use GET_TIME to tell what time it is, a function it's name may imply, but rather you can use this to measure elapsed time. A common way to do this is:

```
scott@TKYTE816> declare
  2      l_start   number;
  3      n         number := 0;
  4  begin
  5
  6      l_start := dbms_utility.get_time;
  7
  8      for x in 1 .. 100000
  9      loop
 10          n := n+1;
 11      end loop;
 12
 13      dbms_output.put_line( ' it took ' ||
 14          round( (dbms_utility.get_time-l_start)/100, 2 ) ||
 15          ' seconds...' );
 16  end;
 17  /
it took .12 seconds...

PL/SQL procedure successfully completed.
```

so you can use GET_TIME to measure elapsed time in hundredths of a second. You should realize however, that GET_TIME will wrap around to *zero* and start counting again if your database is up long enough. Now, on most platforms this time to wrap is well over a year in length. The counter is a 32-bit integer, and this can hold hundredths of seconds for about 497 days. After that, the 32-bit integer will roll over to zero, and start over again. On some platforms, the operating system supplies this ticker in a smaller increment than hundredths of seconds. On these platforms the ticker may roll over sooner than 497 days. For example, on Sequent it is known that the timer will roll over every 71.58 minutes, since this operating system's ticker measures time in microseconds, leaving significantly less room in the 32-bit integer. On a 64-bit platform, the time may very well not roll over for many thousands of years.

A last note about GET_TIME. The same value that GET_TIME returns may be retrieved from a SELECT * FROM V$TIMER. The dynamic view and GET_TIME return the same values:

```
tkyte@TKYTE816> select hsecs, dbms_utility.get_time
  2  from v$timer;

    HSECS    GET_TIME
---------- ----------
   7944822    7944822
```

GET_PARAMETER_VALUE

This API allows anyone to get the value of a specific init.ora parameter. Even if you have no access to V$PARAMETER, and cannot run the SHOW PARAMETER command, you can use this to get the value of an init.ora parameter. It works like this:

```
scott@TKYTE816> show parameter utl_file_dir
ORA-00942: table or view does not exist

scott@TKYTE816> select * from v$parameter where name = 'utl_file_dir'
  2  /
select * from v$parameter where name = 'utl_file_dir'
                *
ERROR at line 1:
ORA-00942: table or view does not exist

scott@TKYTE816> declare
  2      intval number;
  3      strval varchar2(512);
  4  begin
  5      if ( dbms_utility.get_parameter_value( 'utl_file_dir',
  6                                             intval,
  7                                             strval ) = 0)
  8      then
  9          dbms_output.put_line( 'Value = ' || intval );
 10      else
 11          dbms_output.put_line( 'Value = ' || strval );
 12      end if;
 13  end;
 14  /
Value = c:\temp\

PL/SQL procedure successfully completed.
```

As you can see, even though SCOTT cannot query V$PARAMETER and the call to show parameter failed, he can still use this call to get the value. It should be noted that parameters set with True/False strings in the init.ora file will be reported back as returning a number type (this particular function will return 0), and a value of 1 indicates True while a value of 0 indicates False. Additionally, for multi-valued parameters, such as UTL_FILE_DIR, this routine only returns the first value. If I use an account that can do a SHOW PARAMETER in the same database:

```
tkyte@TKYTE816> show parameter utl_file_dir

NAME                                    TYPE    VALUE
------------------------------------    ------- -------------------------------
utl_file_dir                            string  c:\temp, c:\oracle
```

I can see more values.

NAME_RESOLVE

This routine will take the name of a:

❑   Top-level procedure

❑   Top-level function

❑   Database package name

❑   A synonym that points to a database package, or a top level procedure or function

and fully resolve the name for you. It can tell you if the object name you gave it is a procedure, function, or package, and what schema it belongs to. Here is a simple example:

```
scott@TKYTE816> declare
  2       type vcArray is table of varchar2(30);
  3       l_types vcArray := vcArray( null, null, null, null, 'synonym',
  4                                   null, 'procedure', 'function',
  5                                   'package' );
  6
  7       l_schema    varchar2(30);
  8       l_part1     varchar2(30);
  9       l_part2     varchar2(30);
 10       l_dblink    varchar2(30);
 11       l_type      number;
 12       l_obj#      number;
 13  begin
 14     dbms_utility.name_resolve( name => 'DBMS_UTILITY',
 15                                context       => 1,
 16                                schema        => l_schema,
 17                                part1         => l_part1,
 18                                part2         => l_part2,
 19                                dblink        => l_dblink,
 20                                part1_type    => l_type,
 21                                object_number => l_obj# );
 22     if l_obj# IS NULL
```

```
23    then
24      dbms_output.put_line('Object not found or not valid.');
25    else
26      dbms_output.put( l_schema || '.' || nvl(l_part1,l_part2) );
27      if l_part2 is not null and l_part1 is not null
28      then
29          dbms_output.put( '.' || l_part2 );
30      end if;
31
32      dbms_output.put_line( ' is a ' || l_types( l_type ) ||
33                              ' with object id ' || l_obj# ||
34                              ' and dblink "' || l_dblink || '"' );
35    end if;
36  end;
37  /
SYS.DBMS_UTILITY is a package with object id 2408 and dblink ""

PL/SQL procedure successfully completed.
```

In this case, NAME_RESOLVE took our synonym DBMS_UTILITY, and figured out for us that this was in fact a database package that is owned by SYS.

It should be noted that NAME_RESOLVE works only on procedures, functions, packages, and synonyms that point to one of these three object types. It explicitly will not work on a database table for example. You will receive the following error:

```
declare
*
ERROR at line 1:
ORA-06564: object emp does not exist
ORA-06512: at "SYS.DBMS_UTILITY", line 68
ORA-06512: at line 9
```

if you attempt to use it on the EMP table in the SCOTT schema for example.

In addition to not being able to do tables, indexes, and other objects, NAME_RESOLVE does not function as documented when it comes to resolving synonyms that point to remote objects over a database link. It is documented that if you pass NAME_RESOLVE a synonym to a remote package/procedure, then the TYPE will be set to synonym, and they will tell us the name of the database link. This is an issue with the NAME_RESOLVE code (the documentation is correct, the procedure does not function as it should). Currently, NAME_RESOLVE will never return SYNONYM as the type. Rather, it will resolve the remote object and return its name and an object ID of −1. For example, I have a database link set up, and I create a synonym X for DBMS_UTILITY@ora8i.world. When I NAME_RESOLVE this, I receive:

```
SYS.DBMS_UTILITY is a package with object id -1 and dblink ""

PL/SQL procedure successfully completed.
```

I should have been told that X was a synonym and the DBLINK OUT parameter would have been filled in. As you can see however, the DBLINK is Null, and the only indication we have that this is not a local package, is the fact that the object ID is set to −1. You should not rely on this behavior persisting in future releases of Oracle. It has been determined as an issue in the NAME_RESOLVE implementation, and is not a documentation issue. The documentation is correct, the observed behavior is wrong. When this gets corrected, NAME_RESOLVE will function differently on remote objects. For this reason, you will want to either avoid using NAME_RESOLVE on remote objects or make sure to 'wrap' the NAME_RESOLVE routine in some function of your own. This will make it so that when, and if, the behavior changes, you can easily modify your code to provide yourself with the old functionality, if that is what you depend on.

One last comment about NAME_RESOLVE. The parameters CONTEXT and OBJECT_NUMBER are under-documented and not documented, respectively. The CONTEXT parameter is documented briefly as:

.. . must be an integer between 0 and 8

In fact, it must be an integer between 1 and 7 or you'll receive:

```
declare
*
ERROR at line 1:
ORA-20005: ORU-10034: context argument must be 1 or 2 or 3 or 4 or 5 or
6 or 7
ORA-06512: at "SYS.DBMS_UTILITY", line 66
ORA-06512: at line 14
```

And if it is anything other than 1, you will receive one of the two following error messages:

```
ORA-04047: object specified is incompatible with the flag specified

ORA-06564: object OBJECT-NAME does not exist
```

So, the only valid value for context is 1. The OBJECT_NUMBER parameter is not documented at all. This is the OBJECT_ID value found in DBA_OBJECTS, ALL_OBJECTS and USER_OBJECTS. For example, given our first example where the OBJECT_ID was shown to be 2048 I can query:

```
scott@TKYTE816> select owner, object_name
  2  from all_objects
  3  where object_id = 2408;

OWNER                          OBJECT_NAME
------------------------------ ------------------------------
SYS                            DBMS_UTILITY
```

NAME_TOKENIZE

This utility routine simply takes a string that represents some object name, and breaks it into its component pieces for you. Objects are referenced via:

```
[schema].[object_name].[procedure|function]@[database link]
```

NAME_TOKENIZE simply takes a string in this form, and breaks it out into the three leading pieces and the last (database link) piece. Additionally, it tells us what byte it stopped parsing the object name at. Here is a small example showing what you might expect back from various object names you pass to it. Note that you do not have to use *real* object names (these tables and procedures do not have to exist), but you must use *valid* object identifiers. If you do not use a valid object identifier, NAME_TOKENIZE will raise an error. This makes NAME_TOKENIZE suitable as a method to discover whether a given string of characters will be a valid identifier or not:

```
scott@TKYTE816> declare
  2      l_a       varchar2(30);
  3      l_b       varchar2(30);
  4      l_c       varchar2(30);
  5      l_dblink varchar2(30);
```

```
 6          l_next    number;
 7
 8          type vcArray is table of varchar2(255);
 9          l_names vcArray :=
10              vcArray( 'owner.pkg.proc@database_link',
11                       'owner.tbl@database_link',
12                       'tbl',
13                       '"Owner".tbl',
14                       'pkg.proc',
15                       'owner.pkg.proc',
16                       'proc',
17                       'owner.pkg.proc@dblink with junk',
18                       '123' );
19  begin
20      for i in 1 .. l_names.count
21      loop
22      begin
23          dbms_utility.name_tokenize(name    => l_names(i),
24                                     a        => l_a,
25                                     b        => l_b,
26                                     c        => l_c,
27                                     dblink => l_dblink,
28                                     nextpos=> l_next );
29
30          dbms_output.put_line( 'name    ' || l_names(i) );
31          dbms_output.put_line( 'A       ' || l_a );
32          dbms_output.put_line( 'B       ' || l_b );
33          dbms_output.put_line( 'C       ' || l_c );
34          dbms_output.put_line( 'dblink  ' || l_dblink );
35          dbms_output.put_line( 'next    ' || l_next || ' ' ||
36                                     length(l_names(i)));
37          dbms_output.put_line( '-----------------------' );
38      exception
39          when others then
40              dbms_output.put_line( 'name    ' || l_names(i) );
41              dbms_output.put_line( sqlerrm );
42      end;
43      end loop;
44  end;
45  /
name    owner.pkg.proc@database_link
A       OWNER
B       PKG
C       PROC
dblink  DATABASE_LINK
next    28 28
```

As you can see, this breaks out the various bits and pieces of our object name for us. Here the NEXT is set to the length of the string – parsing ended when we hit the end of the string in this case. Since we used every possible piece of the object name, all four components are filled in. Now for the remaining examples:

```
name    owner.tbl@database_link
A       OWNER
B       TBL
C
dblink  DATABASE_LINK
next    23 23
```

```
------------------------
name    tbl
A       TBL
B
C
dblink
next    3 3
------------------------
```

Notice here how B and C are left Null. Even though an object identifier is
SCHEMA.OBJECT.PROCEDURE, NAME_TOKENIZE makes no attempt to put TBL into the B OUT
parameter. It simply takes the first part it finds, and puts it in A, the next into B, and so on. A, B, and C
do not represent specific pieces of the object name, just the first found, next found, and so on.

```
------------------------
name    "Owner".tbl
A       Owner
B       TBL
C
dblink
next    11 11
------------------------
```

Here is something interesting. In the previous examples, NAME_TOKENIZE uppercased everything. This
is because identifiers are in uppercase unless you use *quoted* identifiers. Here, we used a quoted
identifier. NAME_TOKENIZE will preserve this for us, and remove the quotes!

```
------------------------
name    pkg.proc
A       PKG
B       PROC
C
dblink
next    8 8
------------------------
name    owner.pkg.proc
A       OWNER
B       PKG
C       PROC
dblink
next    14 14
------------------------
name    proc
A       PROC
B
C
dblink
next    4 4
------------------------
name    owner.pkg.proc@dblink with junk
A       OWNER
B       PKG
C       PROC
dblink  DBLINK
next    22 31
------------------------
```

Here is an example where the parsing stopped *before* we ran out of string. NAME_TOKENIZE is telling us it stopped parsing at byte 22 out of 31. This is the space right before with junk. It simply ignores the remaining pieces of the string for us.

```
name    123
ORA-00931: missing identifier

PL/SQL procedure successfully completed.
```

And lastly, this shows if we use an invalid identifier, NAME_TOKENIZE will raise an exception. It checks all tokens for being valid identifiers before returning. This makes it useful as a tool to validate object names if you are building an application that will create objects in the Oracle database. For example, if you are building a data modeling tool, and would like to validate that the name the end user wants to use for a table or column name is valid, NAME_TOKENIZE will do the work for you.

COMMA_TO_TABLE, TABLE_TO_COMMA

These two utilities either take a comma-delimited string of *identifiers* and parse them into a PL/SQL table (COMMA_TO_TABLE), or take a PL/SQL table of any type of string, and make a comma-delimited string of them (TABLE_TO_COMMA). I stress the word identifiers above, because COMMA_TO_TABLE uses NAME_TOKENIZE to parse the strings, hence as we saw in that section, we need to use valid Oracle identifiers (or quoted identifiers). This still limits us to 30 characters per element in our comma-delimited string however.

This utility is most useful for applications that want to store a list of table names in a single string for example, and have them easily converted to an array in PL/SQL at run-time. Otherwise, it is of limited use. If you need a general purpose COMMA_TO_TABLE routine that works with comma-delimited strings of data, see Chapter 20, *Using Object Relational Features*. In the *SELECT * from PLSQL_FUNCTION* section, I demonstrate how to do this.

Here is an example using this routine, demonstrating how it deals with long identifiers and invalid identifiers:

```
scott@TKYTE816> declare
  2      type vcArray is table of varchar2(4000);
  3
  4      l_names   vcArray := vcArray( 'emp,dept,bonus',
  5                                    'a,  b  ,   c',
  6                                    '123, 456, 789',
  7                                    '"123", "456", "789"',
  8          '"This is a long string, longer then 32 characters","b",c');
  9      l_tablen number;
 10      l_tab     dbms_utility.uncl_array;
 11  begin
 12      for i in 1 .. l_names.count
 13      loop
 14          dbms_output.put_line( chr(10) ||
 15                              '[' || l_names(i) || ']' );
 16      begin
 17
 18          dbms_utility.comma_to_table( l_names(i),
 19                                       l_tablen, l_tab );
 20
```

```
21              for j in 1..l_tablen
22              loop
23                  dbms_output.put_line( '[' || l_tab(j) || ']' );
24              end loop;
25
26              l_names(i) := null;
27              dbms_utility.table_to_comma( l_tab,
28                                           l_tablen, l_names(i) );
29              dbms_output.put_line( l_names(i) );
30          exception
31              when others then
32                  dbms_output.put_line( sqlerrm );
33          end;
34      end loop;
35  end;
36  /
```

```
[emp,dept,bonus]
[emp]
[dept]
[bonus]
emp,dept,bonus
```

So, that shows that it can take the string emp,dept,bonus, break it into a table, and put it back together again.

```
[a,   b,      c]
[a]
[  b  ]
[    c]
a,   b,      c
```

This example shows that if you have whitespace in the list, it will be preserved. You would have to use the TRIM function to remove leading and trailing white space if you do not want any.

```
[123, 456, 789]
ORA-00931: missing identifier
```

This shows that to use this procedure on a comma-delimited string of numbers, we must go one step further as demonstrated below:

```
["123", "456", "789"]
["123"]
[ "456"]
[ "789"]
"123", "456", "789"
```

Here, it is able to extract the numbers from the string. Note however, how it not only retains the leading whitespace, but it also retains the quotes. It would be up to you to remove them if you so desire.

```
["This is a long string, longer than 32 characters","b",c]
ORA-00972: identifier is too long

PL/SQL procedure successfully completed.
```

And this last example shows that if the identifier is too long (longer than 30 characters), it will raise an error as well. These routines are only useful for strings of 30 characters or less. While it is true that TABLE_TO_COMMA will take larger strings than 30 characters, COMMA_TO_TABLE will not be able to undo this work.

DB_VERSION and PORT_STRING

The DB_VERSION routine was added in Oracle 8.0, in order to make it easier for applications to figure out what version of the database they were running in. We could have used this in our CRYPT_PKG (see the DBMS_OBFUSCATION_TOOLKIT section) for example, to tell users who attempted to use the DES3 routines in an Oracle 8.1.5 database that it would not work, instead of just trying to execute the DES3 routines and failing. It is a very simple interface as follows:

```
scott@TKYTE816> declare
  2      l_version          varchar2(255);
  3      l_compatibility varchar2(255);
  4  begin
  5      dbms_utility.db_version( l_version, l_compatibility );
  6      dbms_output.put_line( l_version );
  7      dbms_output.put_line( l_compatibility );
  8  end;
  9  /
8.1.6.0.0
8.1.6

PL/SQL procedure successfully completed.
```

And provides more version detail than the older function, PORT_STRING:

```
scott@TKYTE816> select dbms_utility.port_string from dual;

PORT_STRING
-----------------------------
IBMPC/WIN_NT-8.1.0
```

Using the PORT_STRING, not only would you have to parse the string, but you also cannot tell if you are in version 8.1.5 versus 8.1.6 versus 8.1.7. DB_VERSION will be more useful for this. On the other hand, the PORT_STRING does tell you what operating system you are on.

GET_HASH_VALUE

This function will take any string as input, and return a numeric HASH value for it. You could use this to build your own 'index by table' that was indexed by a string, or as we did in the DBMS_LOCK section, to facilitate the implementation of some other algorithm.

You should be aware that the algorithm used to implement GET_HASH_VALUE can, and has, changed from release to release, so you should not use this function to generate surrogate keys. If you find yourself storing the return value from this function in a table, you might be setting yourself up for a problem in a later release when the same inputs return a different hash value!

This function takes three inputs:

- ❏ The string to hash.
- ❏ The 'base' number to be returned. If you want the numbers to range from 0 to some number, use 0 for your base.
- ❏ The size of the hash table. Optimally this number would be a power of two.

As a demonstration of using the GET_HASH_VALUE, we will implement a new type, HASHTABLETYPE, to add to the PL/SQL language a hash type. This is very similar to a PL/SQL table type that is indexed by a VARCHAR2 string instead of a number. Normally, PL/SQL table elements are referenced by subscripts (numbers). This new type of PL/SQL table will have elements that are referenced by arbitrary strings. This will allow us to declare variables of type HASHTABLETYPE and GET and PUT values into it. We can have as many of these table types as we like. Here is the specification for our package:

```
tkyte@TKYTE816> create or replace type myScalarType
  2  as object
  3  ( key  varchar2(4000),
  4    val  varchar2(4000)
  5  );
  6  /

Type created.

tkyte@TKYTE816> create or replace type myArrayType
  2  as varray(10000) of myScalarType;
  3  /

Type created.

tkyte@TKYTE816> create or replace type hashTableType
  2  as object
  3  (
  4      g_hash_size     number,
  5      g_hash_table    myArrayType,
  6      g_collision_cnt number,
  7
  8      static function new( p_hash_size in number )
  9          return hashTableType,
 10
 11      member procedure put( p_key in varchar2,
 12                            p_val in varchar2 ),
 13
 14      member function get( p_key in varchar2 )
 15          return varchar2,
 16
 17      member procedure print_stats
 18  );
 19  /

Type created.
```

An interesting implementation detail here is the addition of the static member function NEW. This will allow us to create our own constructor. You should note that there is absolutely nothing special about the name NEW that I used. It is not a keyword or anything like that. What NEW will allow us to do is to declare a HASHTABLETYPE like this:

```
declare
    l_hashTable hashTableType := hashTableType.new( 1024 );
```

instead of like this:

```
declare
    l_hashTable hashTableType := hashTableType( 1024, myArrayType(), 0 );
```

It is my belief that the first syntax is in general, more readable and clearer than the second. The second syntax makes the end user aware of many of the implementation details (that we have an array type in there, that there is some variable G_COLLISION_CNT that must be set to zero, and so on). They neither need to know that nor do they really care.

So, now onto the type body itself:

```
scott@TKYTE816> create or replace type body hashTableType
  2  as
  3
  4  -- Our 'friendly' constructor.
  5
  6  static function new( p_hash_size in number )
  7  return hashTableType
  8  is
  9  begin
 10      return hashTableType( p_hash_size, myArrayType(), 0 );
 11  end;
 12
 13  member procedure put( p_key in varchar2, p_val in varchar2 )
 14  is
 15      l_hash  number :=
 16              dbms_utility.get_hash_value( p_key, 1, g_hash_size );
 17  begin
 18
 19      if ( p_key is null )
 20      then
 21          raise_application_error( -20001, 'Cannot have NULL key' );
 22      end if;
 23
```

This next piece of code looks to see if we need to 'grow' the table to hold this new, hashed value. If we do, we grow it out big enough to hold this index:

```
 27      if ( l_hash > nvl( g_hash_table.count, 0 ) )
 28      then
 29          g_hash_table.extend( l_hash-nvl(g_hash_table.count,0)+1 );
 30      end if;
 31
```

Now, there is no guarantee that the index entry our key hashed to is empty. What we do upon detecting a collision is to try and put it in the next collection element. We search forward for up to 1,000 times to put it into the table. If we hit 1,000 collisions, we will fail. This would indicate that the table is not sized properly, if this is the case:

```
35      for i in 0 .. 1000
36      loop
37          -- If we are going to go past the end of the
38          -- table, add another slot first.
39          if ( g_hash_table.count <= l_hash+i )
40          then
41              g_hash_table.extend;
42          end if;
43
```

The next bit of logic says 'if no one is using this slot *or* our key is in this slot already, use it and return.' It looks a tad strange to check if the G_HASH_TABLE element is Null, or if the G_HASH_TABLE(L_HASH+I).KEY is Null. This just shows that a collection element may be Null, or it may contain an object that has Null attributes:

```
46          if ( g_hash_table(l_hash+i) is null OR
47              nvl(g_hash_table(l_hash+i).key,p_key) = p_key )
48          then
49              g_hash_table(l_hash+i) := myScalarType(p_key,p_val);
50              return;
51          end if;
52
53          -- Else increment a collision count and continue
54          -- onto the next slot.
55          g_collision_cnt := g_collision_cnt+1;
56      end loop;
57
58      -- If we get here, the table was allocate too small.
59      -- Make it bigger.
60      raise_application_error( -20001, 'table overhashed' );
61  end;
62
63
64  member function get( p_key in varchar2 ) return varchar2
65  is
66      l_hash  number :=
67              dbms_utility.get_hash_value( p_key, 1, g_hash_size );
68  begin
```

When we go to retrieve a value, we look in the index element we think the value should be in, and then look ahead up to 1,000 entries in the event we had collisions. We short circuit this look-ahead search if we ever find an empty slot – we know our entry cannot be beyond that point:

```
71      for i in l_hash .. least(l_hash+1000, nvl(g_hash_table.count,0))
72      loop
73          -- If we hit an EMPTY slot, we KNOW our value cannot
74          -- be in the table. We would have put it there.
75          if ( g_hash_table(i) is NULL )
76          then
77              return NULL;
78          end if;
79
80          -- If we find our key, return the value.
```

```
 81              if ( g_hash_table(i).key = p_key )
 82              then
 83                  return g_hash_table(i).val;
 84              end if;
 85          end loop;
 86
 87          -- Key is not in the table. Quit.
 88          return null;
 89      end;
 90
```

The last routine is used to print out useful information, such as how many slots you've allocated versus used, and how many collisions we had. Note that collisions can be bigger than the table itself!

```
 97  member procedure print_stats
 98  is
 99      l_used number default 0;
100  begin
101      for i in 1 .. nvl(g_hash_table.count,0)
102      loop
103          if ( g_hash_table(i) is not null )
104          then
105              l_used := l_used + 1;
106          end if;
107      end loop;
108
109      dbms_output.put_line( 'Table Extended To.....' ||
110                              g_hash_table.count );
111      dbms_output.put_line( 'We are using..........' ||
112                              l_used );
113      dbms_output.put_line( 'Collision count put...' ||
114                              g_collision_cnt );
115  end;
116
117  end;
118  /

Type body created.
```

As you can see, we simply used the GET_HASH_VALUE to turn the string into some number we could use to index into our table type, to get the value. Now we are ready to see how this new type can be used:

```
tkyte@TKYTE816> declare
  2      l_hashTbl hashTableType := hashTableType.new(power(2,7));
  3  begin
  4      for x in ( select username, created from all_users )
  5      loop
  6          l_hashTbl.put( x.username, x.created );
  7      end loop;
  8
  9      for x in ( select username, to_char(created) created,
 10                        l_hashTbl.get(username) hash
 11                  from all_users )
```

```
12      loop
13          if ( nvl( x.created, 'x') <> nvl(x.hash,'x') )
14          then
15              raise program_error;
16          end if;
17      end loop;
18
19      l_hashTbl.print_stats;
20  end;
21  /
Table Extended To.....120
We are using.........17
Collision count put...1

PL/SQL procedure successfully completed.
```

And that's it. We've just extended the PL/SQL language again, giving it a hash table using the built-in packages.

Summary

This wraps up our overview of many of the procedures found in the DBMS_UTILITY package. Many, such as GET_TIME, GET_PARAMETER_VALUE, GET_HASH_VALUE, and FORMAT_CALL_STACK are in my list of 'frequently given answers'. This is to say, they are frequently the answer to many a question – people just weren't even aware they even existed.

UTL_FILE

UTL_FILE is a package that is supplied to allow PL/SQL to read and create text files in the file system of the server. The keywords here are:

- **Text Files** – UTL_FILE can only read and create clear text files. Specifically, it cannot be used to read or create binary files. Special characters contained within arbitrary binary data will cause UTL_FILE to do the wrong thing.

- **File System of the Server** – UTL_FILE can only read and write to the file system of the database server. It cannot read or write to the file system the client is executing on if that client is not logged onto the server itself.

UTL_FILE is an appropriate tool for creating reports and flat file dumps of data from the database or for reading files of data to be loaded. In fact, if you refer to Chapter 9 on *Data Loading* in this book, we have a full blown example of using UTL_FILE to create flat file dumps in a format suitable for easy reloading. UTL_FILE is also a good choice for doing 'debugging'. If you refer to the Chapter 21 on *Fine Grained Access Control* we introduced the DEBUG package. This package makes heavy use of UTL_FILE to record messages in the file system.

UTL_FILE is an extremely useful package as long as you are aware of its limits. If not, you may attempt to use UTL_FILE in a way in which it will not work correctly (it might work in testing but not in production) leading to frustration. Like all tools, knowing its limits and how it works will be useful.

We'll look at some issues frequently encountered when using UTL_FILE including:

❑ The UTL_FILE_DIR parameter in init.ora.

❑ Accessing mapped drives (network drives) in a Windows environment (there are no related issues in a Unix environment).

❑ Handling exceptions from UTL_FILE

❑ Using UTL_FILE to create static web pages on a recurring basis.

❑ The infamous 1023 byte limit.

❑ Getting a directory listing so you can process all files in a directory.

The UTL_FILE_DIR init.ora parameter

This is a key part to using UTL_FILE, which always runs as the Oracle software owner – it is your dedicated server or shared server that is performing the I/O and these are running as 'Oracle'. Given that they run as Oracle and Oracle can read and write to its datafiles, configuration files, and so on – it would be a very bad thing if UTL_FILE permitted access to just any directory. The fact that we must explicitly set the directories we want to be able to write to in the init.ora is a great safety feature – it is not an encumbrance. Consider if UTL_FILE allowed you to write to any directory Oracle could – any user could then use UTL_FILE.FOPEN to rewrite your system datafile. That, to put it mildly, would be a bad thing. Therefore, your DBA must open up access to specific directories – explicitly. You cannot even specify a root directory and allow access to it and all directories underneath – you must explicitly list out each and every directory you want to read and write to with UTL_FILE.

It should be noted that this init.ora parameter is not changeable while the database is up and running. You must restart the instance in order for a directory entry to be added or removed.

The UTL_FILE_DIR init.ora parameter takes one of two forms:

```
utl_file_dir = (c:\temp,c:\temp2)

or

utl_file_dir = c:\temp
utl_file_dir = c:\temp2
```

That is, you may either use a list of comma separated directories enclosed in parenthesis or you may list each directory on a line one after the other. The keywords here being 'one after the other'. If you have the following as the last lines in your init.ora file:

```
utl_file_dir = c:\temp
timed_statistics=true
utl_file_dir = c:\temp2
```

Only the **last** entry for UTL_FILE_DIR will be used. The first directory entry will effectively be ignored. This can be quite confusing as there will be no warning message or alert.log entries indicating the first UTL_FILE_DIR entry is ignored. All UTL_FILE_DIR entries must be contiguous in the init.ora file.

One word of warning on the Windows Platform with regards to this init.ora parameter. If you decide to add the trailing \ to the UTL_FILE_dir parameter like this:

```
utl_file_dir = c:\temp\
utl_file_dir = c:\temp2
```

You will receive the following error message upon startup:

```
SVRMGR> startup
LRM-00116: syntax error at 'c:\temputl_file_' following '='
LRM-00113: error when processing file 'C:\oracle\admin\tkyte816\pfile\init.ora'
ORA-01078: failure in processing system parameters
```

That is because the \ is considered an escape character at the end of the line in the init.ora file. It would allow you normally to continue long entries on 2 lines. You must simply use two slashes:

```
utl_file_dir = c:\temp\\
utl_file_dir = c:\oracle
```

in order to avoid this concatenation.

Another closing note on this init.ora parameter. If you use a trailing slash in the init.ora, you must use the trailing slash in your fopen calls. If you omit the trailing slash in the init.ora, you should omit it in your fopen calls as well. The directory parameter to fopen should match in case and contents the value you put into the init.ora file.

Accessing Mapped Windows Drives

This is a common area of confusion, especially to people used to working with Unix. On Unix, if you mount a device (for example, NFS mount a remote disk) – it is immediately visible to everyone on that machine – regardless of their session. Each user may have different access rights to it, but the mounted disk is an attribute of the system and not a specific session.

In Windows, this is very different. I may have many sessions executing on a given server and each will have its own set of 'disk drives' that it sees. It may very well be that when I log onto a machine – I see a network resource 'disk D:' that belongs physically to some other machine. That does not mean that every process running on that machine can see that disk. This is where the confusion comes in.

Many people log into the server and see 'disk D:'. They configure the init.ora to have UTL_FILE_dir = d:\reports in it ; a directory to write reports to using UTL_FILE. At runtime however they receive:

```
ERROR at line 1:
ORA-06510: PL/SQL: unhandled user-defined exception
ORA-06512: at "SYS.UTL_FILE", line 98
ORA-06512: at "SYS.UTL_FILE", line 157
```

Which if they used an exception handler (see below for the one I like to use) they would see something more informative like:

```
ERROR at line 1:
ORA-20001:  INVALID_PATH: File location or filename was invalid.
ORA-06512: at "TKYTE.CSV", line 51
ORA-06512: at line 2
```

Well, as far as they can tell – D:\reports is just fine. They use explorer and it is there. They use a DOS window and it is there. Only Oracle doesn't seem to be able to see it. This is because when the system started – D: drive didn't exist and furthermore, the account under which Oracle is running by default cannot see any network resources. Try as hard as you like, mounting that disk in any way possible, Oracle will not 'see' it.

When an Oracle instance is created the services that support it are setup to 'Log On As' the SYSTEM (or operating system) account, this account has very few privileges and no access to Windows NT Domains. To access another Windows NT machine the OracleServiceXXXX must be setup to logon to the appropriate Windows NT Domain as a user who has access to the required location for UTL_FILE.

To change the default logon for the Oracle services, go to (in Windows NT):

Control Panel | Services | OracleServiceXXXX | Startup | Log On As; (where XXXX is the instance name)

In Windows 2000, this would be:

Control Panel | Administrative Tools | Services | OracleServiceXXXX | Properties | Log On Tab; again XXXX is the instance name)

Choose the This Account radio button, and then complete the appropriate domain login information. Once the services have been setup as a user with the appropriate privileges, there are two options for setting UTL_FILE_DIR:

❑ Mapped Drive: To use a mapped drive, the user that the service starts as must have setup a drive to match UTL_FILE_DIR and be logged onto the server when UTL_FILE is in use.

❑ Universal Naming Convention: UNC is preferable to Mapped Drives because it does not require anyone to be logged on and UTL_FILE_DIR should be set to a name in the form \\<machine name>\<share name>\<path>.

You will of course need to stop and restart Oracle after changing the properties of the service.

Handling Exceptions

UTL_FILE throws exceptions when it encounters an error. Unfortunately, it uses user-defined exceptions – exceptions it has defined in its package specification. These exceptions, if not caught by name, produce the following less then useful error message:

```
ERROR at line 1:
ORA-06510: PL/SQL: unhandled user-defined exception
ORA-06512: at "SYS.UTL_FILE", line 98
ORA-06512: at "SYS.UTL_FILE", line 157
```

This tells you nothing about the error itself. In order to solve this issue, we have to surround our calls to UTL_FILE with an exception block that catches each of the exceptions by name. I prefer to then turn these exceptions into RAISE_APPLICATION_ERROR exceptions. This allows me to assign an ORA- error code and supply a more meaningful error message. We used this in the preceding example to turn the above error message into:

ORA-20001: **INVALID_PATH: File location or filename was invalid.**

Which is much more useful. The block I always use for this is:

```
exception
    when utl_file.invalid_path then
        raise_application_error(-20001,
        'INVALID_PATH: File location or filename was invalid.');
    when utl_file.invalid_mode then
        raise_application_error(-20002,
        'INVALID_MODE: The open_mode parameter in FOPEN was
        invalid.');
    when utl_file.invalid_filehandle then
        raise_application_error(-20002,
        'INVALID_FILEHANDLE: The file handle was invalid.');
    when utl_file.invalid_operation then
        raise_application_error(-20003,
        'INVALID_OPERATION: The file could not be opened or
        operated on as requested.');
    when utl_file.read_error then
        raise_application_error(-20004,
        'READ_ERROR: An operating system error occurred during
        the read operation.');
    when utl_file.write_error then
        raise_application_error(-20005,
            'WRITE_ERROR: An operating system error occurred
            during the write operation.');
    when utl_file.internal_error then
        raise_application_error(-20006,
            'INTERNAL_ERROR: An unspecified error in PL/SQL.');
end;
```

I actually keep this in a small file and read it into each routine that uses UTL_FILE to catch the exception and 'rename it' for me.

Dumping a Web Page to Disk

This is such a frequently asked question; I thought I would include it here. The scenario is that you are using Oracle WebDB, Oracle Portal, or have some procedures that use the Web Toolkit (the htp packages). You would like to take a report one of these tools is capable of displaying and instead of dynamically generating that report for each and every user – you would like to create a static file with this report every X minutes or hours. This is in fact how I myself generate the home page of the web site I manage at work. Every 5 minutes we regenerate the home page with dynamic data instead of generating each time for the thousands of hits we get during that period of time. Cuts way down on the resources needed to get the home page served up. I do this for frequently accessed, dynamic pages where the underlying data is relatively static (slow changing).

The following procedure is a generic procedure that I use for doing this:

```
create or replace procedure dump_page( p_dir      in varchar2,
                                        p_fname    in varchar2 )
is
    l_thePage         htp.htbuf_arr;
    l_output          utl_file.file_type;
    l_lines           number default 99999999;
begin
    l_output := utl_file.fopen( p_dir, p_fname, 'w', 32000 );

    owa.get_page( l_thePage, l_lines );

    for i in 1 .. l_lines loop
        utl_file.put( l_output, l_thePage(i) );
    end loop;

    utl_file.fclose( l_output );
end dump_page;
/
```

It is that simple. We only have to open a file, get the HTML page, print each line, and close the file. If I call this after calling a WebDB procedure – it will save the output of that WebDB procedure to the file I name.

The only caveat here is that we will be running the WebDB procedure not from the web but directly. If any of the code in the WebDB procedures uses the CGI environment, then that procedure will fail – since the environment was not set up. We can solve that simply by using a small block of code to setup an environment for our WebDB routine:

```
declare
    nm   owa.vc_arr;
    vl   owa.vc_arr;
begin
    nm(1) := 'SERVER_PORT';
    vl(1) := '80';
    owa.init_cgi_env( nm.count, nm, vl );
    -- run your webdb procedure here
    dump_page( 'directory', 'filename' );
end;
/
```

For example, if our WebDB code wanted to verify it was being run from the server on port 80 – we would need to provide the above environment for it. You would add any other environment variables that are relevant to your application in this block

Now all you need to do is refer to the DBMS_JOB section and schedule this block of code to be executed on whatever cycle you need.

1023 Byte Limit

Once upon a time, there was a 1023 byte limit to UTL_FILE. Each line written to a file could not exceed 1023 bytes. If it did, an exception was raised and UTL_FILE would fail. Fortunately, in Oracle 8.0.5, they introduced an overloaded version of FOPEN that allows us to specify the maximum line length up to 32 KB in size. 32 KB is the largest size a PL/SQL variable can ever be and is typically sufficient for most purposes.

Unfortunately, the documentation has this newly overloaded FOPEN function documented many pages *after* the original function. This leads to many people overlooking this ability. I still get many questions on this today with version 8.1.7. People did not see the overloaded version of FOPEN; they hit the limit and need to know how to get around it. The answer is simple – but you have to read through every UTL_FILE function to find it easily!

The solution to this particular problem is to use UTL_FILE in the way I did in the previous DUMP_PAGE routine above. The fourth parameter to UTL_FILE.FOPEN is the maximum length of the line of text you would like to produce. In my case above, I allow for up to 32,000 bytes per line.

Reading A Directory

This is a missing piece of functionality in the UTL_FILE package. Frequently people want to setup a recurring job that will scan a directory for new input files and process them, perhaps loading the data into the database. Unfortunately, out of the box there is no way for PL/SQL to read a directory listing. We can however use a tiny bit of Java to give us this ability. The following example demonstrates how you might accomplish this.

First I create a user with the minimum set of privileges needs to perform this operation and to be able to list files in the /tmp directory. If you wish to read other directories, you would need to make more calls to dbms_java.grant_permission (see Chapter 19 on *Java Stored Procedures* for more information) or change the /tmp into * to provide the ability to list all directories.

```
SQL> connect system/manager

system@DEV816> drop user dirlist cascade;
User dropped.

system@DEV816> grant create session, create table, create procedure
  2  to dirlist identified by dirlist;
Grant succeeded.

system@DEV816> begin
  2      dbms_java.grant_permission
  3      ('DIRLIST',
  4       'java.io.FilePermission',
  5          '/tmp',
  6          'read' );
  7  end;
  8  /
PL/SQL procedure successfully completed.
```

Next, after connecting as this new user DirList, we set up a global temporary table in this schema (to hold the directory listing). This is how we will get the results from the Java stored procedure back to the caller – in the temporary table. We could have used other means (strings, arrays and such) as well.

```
SQL> connect dirlist/dirlist
Connected.

dirlist@DEV816> create global temporary table DIR_LIST
  2  ( filename varchar2(255) )
  3  on commit delete rows
  4  /
Table created.
```

Now we create a Java stored procedure to do the directory listing. For ease of programming, I am using SQLJ to avoid having to code lots of JDBC calls:

```
dirlist@DEV816> create or replace
  2      and compile java source named "DirList"
  3  as
  4  import java.io.*;
  5  import java.sql.*;
  6
  7  public class DirList
  8  {
  9  public static void getList(String directory)
 10                  throws SQLException
 11  {
 12      File path = new File( directory );
 13      String[] list = path.list();
 14      String element;
 15
 16      for(int i = 0; i < list.length; i++)
 17      {
 18          element = list[i];
 19          #sql { INSERT INTO DIR_LIST (FILENAME)
 20                 VALUES (:element) };
 21      }
 22  }
 23
 24  }
 25  /
Java created.
```

The next step is to create a 'mapping' function, the PL/SQL binding to Java. This will simply be:

```
dirlist@DEV816> create or replace
  2  procedure get_dir_list( p_directory in varchar2 )
  3  as language java
  4  name 'DirList.getList( java.lang.String )';
  5  /
Procedure created.
```

Now we are ready to go:

```
dirlist@DEV816> exec get_dir_list( '\tmp' );
PL/SQL procedure successfully completed.
```

```
dirlist@DEV816> select * from dir_list where rownum < 5;

FILENAME
------------------
lost+found
.rpc_door
ps_data
.pcmcia
```

and that's it. Now we can list the contents of a directory into this temporary table. We can then apply filters to this easily using LIKE and sort the output if we like as well.

Summary

UTL_FILE is an excellent utility you will most likely find use for in many of your applications. In this section, we covered the setup necessary for using UTL_FILE and described how it works. We've looked at some of the most common issues I see people running into with UTL_FILE such as accessing network drives in a Windows environment, hitting the 1023 byte limit, and handling exceptions. For each we presented the solutions. We also explored some utilities you might develop with UTL_FILE such as the UNLOADER described in Chapter 9 on *Data Loading*, the ability to read a directory presented here, or dumping a web page to disk as described above.

UTL_HTTP

In this section, we'll look at UTL_HTTP and what it can be used for. Additionally, I would like to introduce a new and improved UTL_HTTP built on the SocketType implemented in the UTL_TCP section. It gives performance comparable to the native UTL_HTTP but provides many more features.

The UTL_HTTP package supplied with the database is relatively simplistic – it has two versions:

- **UTL_HTTP.REQUEST**: returns up to the first 2,000 bytes of the content of a URL as a function return value.

- **UTL_HTTP.REQUEST_PIECES**: returns a PL/SQL table of VARCHAR2(2000) elements. If you concatenated all of the pieces together – you would have the content of the page.

The UTL_HTTP package is missing the following functionality however:

- You cannot inspect the HTTP headers. This makes error reporting impossible. You cannot tell the difference between a Not Found and Unauthorized for example.

- You cannot POST information to a web server that requires POSTing data. You can only use the GET syntax. Additionally HEAD is not supported in the protocol.

- You cannot retrieve binary information using UTL_HTTP.

- The request pieces API is non intuitive, the use of CLOBs and BLOBs to return the data as a 'stream' would be much more intuitive (and give us access to binary data).

- It does not support cookies.

- It does not support basic authentication.

- It has no methods for URL encoding data.

One thing that `UTL_HTTP` does support that we will not in our re-implementation is SSL. Using the Oracle Wallet manager, it is possible to perform a HTTPS request (HTTPS is using SSL with HTTP). We will demonstrate using `UTL_HTTP` over SSL, but will not implement it in our own `HTTP_PKG`. Due to its size, the source code of the `HTTP_PKG` body will be omitted from this chapter – it is available in its entirety on the Apress website at http://www.apress.com.

UTL_HTTP Functionality

We will look at the `UTL_HTTP` functionality first as we will support its syntax on our own `HTTP_PKG`. The simplest form of `UTL_HTTP` is as follows. In this example, `myserver` is the name I have given to the web server. Of course, you should try this example using a web server to which you have access:

```
ops$tkyte@DEV816> select utl_http.request( 'http://myserver/' ) from dual;

UTL_HTTP.REQUEST('HTTP://MYSERVER/')
------------------------------------------------------------
<HTML>
<HEAD>
<TITLE>Oracle Service Industries</TITLE>
</HEAD>
<FRAMESET COLS="130,*" border=0>
<FRAME SRC="navtest.html" NAME="sidebar" frameborder=0>
<FRAME SRC="folder_home.html" NAME="body" frameborder="0" marginheight="0"
marginwidth="0">
</FRAMESET>
</BODY>
</HTML>
```

I can simply run `UTL_HTTP.REQUEST` and send it a URL. `UTL_HTTP` will connect to that web server and `GET` the requested page and then return the first 2,000 characters of it. As mentioned above, don't try to use the URL I have given above, it is for my web server inside of Oracle. You won't be able to get to it, the request will time out with an error message.

Most networks today are protected by firewalls. If the page I wanted was only available via a firewall proxy server; I can request that as well. A discussion of firewalls and proxy servers is beyond the scope of this book. However, if you know the hostname of your proxy server, you can retrieve a page from the internet via this method:

```
ops$tkyte@DEV816> select utl_http.request( 'http://www.yahoo.com', 'www-proxy')
from dual;

UTL_HTTP.REQUEST('HTTP://WWW.YAHOO.COM','WWW-PROXY')
------------------------------------------------------------
<html><head><title>Yahoo!</title><base href=http://www.yahoo.com/><meta http-
equiv="PICS-Label" content='(PICS-1.1 http://www.rsac.org/ratingsv01.html" l gen
true for "http://www.yahoo.com" r (n 0 s 0 v 0 l 0))'></head><body><center><form
action=http://search.yahoo.com/bin/search><map name=m><area coords="0,0,52,52"
href=r/a1><area coords="53,0,121,52" href=r/p1><area coords="122,0,191,52" href=r
```

The second parameter to `UTL_HTTP.REQUEST` and `REQUEST_PIECES` is the name of a proxy server. If your proxy server is not running on the standard port 80, we can add the port as follows (In the code this is `myserver` on port 8000):

```
ops$tkyte@DEV816> select utl_http.request( 'http://www.yahoo.com',
  2  'myserver:8000' ) from dual
  3  /

UTL_HTTP.REQUEST('HTTP://WWW.YAHOO.COM','MYSERVER:8000')
-------------------------------------------------------
<html><head><title>Yahoo!</title><base href=http://www.yahoo.com/
```

So, by simply adding the :8000 to the proxy server name, we are able to connect to that proxy server. Now, let's look at the REQUEST_PIECES interface:

```
ops$tkyte@DEV816> declare
  2      pieces  utl_http.html_pieces;
  3      n       number default 0;
  4      l_start number default dbms_utility.get_time;
  5  begin
  6      pieces :=
  7          utl_http.request_pieces( url => 'http://www.oracle.com/',
  8                                   max_pieces => 99999,
  9                                   proxy => 'www-proxy' );
 10      for i in 1 .. pieces.count
 11      loop
 12          loop
 13              exit when pieces(i) is null;
 14              dbms_output.put_line( substr(pieces(i),1,255) );
 15              pieces(i) := substr( pieces(i), 256 );
 16          end loop;
 17      end loop;
 18  end;
 19  /

<head>
<title>Oracle Corporation</title>
<meta http-equiv="Content-Type" content="text/html;
charset=iso-8859-1">
<meta name="description" content="Oracle Corporation provides the
software that
powers the Internet. For more information about Oracle, pleas
e call 650/506-7000.">
```

The request pieces API cannot be called from SQL since it does not return a SQL type but rather a PL/SQL table type. So, REQUEST_PIECES is only useful inside of a PL/SQL block itself. In the above, we are requesting the web page http://www.oracle.com/ and we are requesting the first 99,999 chunks, which are each of the size 2,000 bytes. We are using the proxy server www-proxy. We must tell REQUEST_PIECES how many 2,000 byte chunks we are willing to accept, typically I set this to a very large number as I want the entire page back. If the information that you want from the page is always in the first 5000 bytes, you could request just 3 chunks to get it.

Adding SSL to UTL_HTTP

UTL_HTTP also supports using SSL (Secure Sockets Layer). If you are not familiar with SSL and what it is used for, you can find a brief description at http://www.rsasecurity.com/rsalabs/faq/5-1-2.html. Both the REQUEST and REQUEST_PIECES functions in UTL_HTTP support the retrieval of URLs that are protected by SSL. However, the available documentation on doing so can be described as sparse at best. SSL support is provided by using the last two parameters in the UTL_HTTP.REQUEST and UTL_HTTP.REQUEST_PIECES procedures. These parameters are the WALLET_PATH and WALLET_PASSWORD.

Oracle uses the wallet as a metaphor for how a person stores their security credentials; just like you would keep your driver's license and credit cards in your wallet for identification purposes, the Oracle wallet stores the credentials needed by the SSL protocol. The WALLET_PATH is the directory where your wallet is stored on the database server machine. This wallet is password protected to prevent someone from using your credentials. This is the purpose of the WALLET_PASSWORD parameter, it is used to access the wallet. The password prevents people from copying the wallet directory and trying to impersonate you, as they will be unable to open and access the wallet. This is analogous to using a PIN for using an ATM machine. If someone steals your bank card, they need to have your PIN to get to your accounts.

The wallet, or the concept of a wallet is used not only by the Oracle database, but also in Web browsers. The important aspect is that when you connect to a site, e.g., http://www.amazon.com, how do you know that it is really Amazon.com? You have to get their certificate, which is digitally signed by someone. That someone is called a Certificate Authority or CA. How does my browser or database know to trust the CA that signed that certificate? For example, I could create a certificate for Amazon.com and sign it from hackerAttackers.com. My browser and database should not accept this certificate even though it is a legitimate X.509 certificate.

The answer to this trust issue is the wallet stores a set of trusted certificates. A trusted certificate is a certificate from a CA that you trust. The Oracle wallet comes with some common trusted certificates. You also have the ability to add certificates as necessary. Your browser does the same thing. If you ever connect to a site where your browser does not have the CA in its wallet, you will get a pop-up window that notifies you of this as well as a wizard that allows you to proceed or abort your connection.

Let's see some examples of how to use SSL. First, we need to create a new wallet. You can invoke the OWM (Oracle Wallet Manager) program on UNIX, or launch it from the Windows START menu on Windows(it is in ORACLE HOME|NETWORK ADMINISTRATION). The screen you receive to do this will look like this:

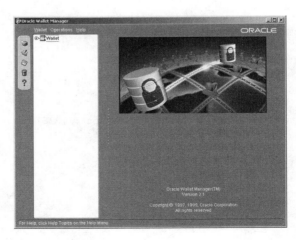

All you need to do is click on the NEW icon (the green 'cube') located on the left hand side of the display. It will prompt you for a password for this wallet, you are making up the password at this point so enter whatever password you would like. You may get a warning about a directory not existing, if you do, you should simply ignore it. It is the expected behavior if you have never created a wallet before. OWM at will then ask you to create a certificate request:

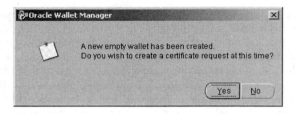

you do not need to this. The certificate request is so you can get a certificate for yourself. This would be used in SSL v.3 where the server needs the identification of the client. Most Web sites do not authenticate users via certificates, but rather by using a username and password. This is because an e - commerce site doesn't care who is buying from them as long as they get the money. But you do care that you are sending the money (and credit card information) to the correct entity, so we use SSL v.2 to identify the server for example, Amazon.com, and to provide all the encryption of data. So, click NO in response to this and save the wallet by clicking on the SAVE WALLET (the yellow floppy disk) icon and we are ready to go.

Let's go to Amazon.com first. Amazon's certificate was signed by Secure Server Certificate Authority, RSA Data Security, Inc. This is one of the defaults in the Oracle wallet.

```
tkyte@TKYTE816> declare
  2      l_output long;
  3
  4      l_url varchar2(255) default
  5             'https://www.amazon.com/exec/obidos/flex-sign-in/';
  6
  7      l_wallet_path varchar2(255) default
  8             'file:C:\Documents and Settings\Thomas Kyte\ORACLE\WALLETS';
  9
 10
 11  begin
 12     l_output := utl_http.request
 13                   ( url              => l_url,
 14                     proxy            => 'www-proxy.us.oracle.com',
 15                     wallet_path      => l_wallet_path,
 16                     wallet_password  => 'oracle'
 17                   );
 18     dbms_output.put_line(trim(substr(l_output,1,255)));
 19  end;
 20  /
```

```
<html>
<head>
<title>Amazon.com Error Page</title>
</head>
<body bgcolor="#FFFFFF"
link="#003399" alink="#FF9933" vlink="#996633" text="#000000">
```

```
<a name="top"><!--Top of
Page--></a>
<table border=0 width=100% cellspacing=0 cellpadding=0>
<tr

PL/SQL procedure successfully completed.
```

Don't worry about getting this error page; this is accurate. The reason for receiving this error page is that there is no session information being passed. We are just testing that the connection worked here; we retrieved an SSL protected document.

Let's try another site. How about E*Trade?

```
tkyte@TKYTE816> declare
  2     l_output long;
  3
  4     l_url varchar2(255) default
  5          'https://trading.etrade.com/';
  6
  7     l_wallet_path varchar2(255) default
  8          'file:C:\Documents and Settings\Thomas Kyte\ORACLE\WALLETS';
  9
 10
 11  begin
 12     l_output := utl_http.request
 13             ( url              => l_url,
 14               proxy            => 'www-proxy.us.oracle.com',
 15               wallet_path      => l_wallet_path,
 16               wallet_password  => 'oracle'
 17             );
 18     dbms_output.put_line(trim(substr(l_output,1,255)));
 19  end;
 20  /
declare
*
ERROR at line 1:
ORA-06510: PL/SQL: unhandled user-defined exception
ORA-06512: at "SYS.UTL_HTTP", line 174
ORA-06512: at line 12
```

That apparently does not work. E*Trade has a certificate signed by. www.verisign com/CPS Incorp.by Ref, which is not a default trusted certificate. In order to access this page, we'll have to add that certificate to our Oracle wallet – assuming of course that we trust Verisign! Here is the trick. Go to the site (https://trading.etrade.com). Double-click the PADLOCK icon on the bottom right corner of the window (in Microsoft Internet Explorer). This will pop-up a window that looks similar to this one:

Select the Certification Path tab on the top of this screen. This lists the certificate you are viewing here it is the one for E*Trade (trading.etrade.com), as well as who issued the certificate. We need to add the person who signed the certificate (the issuer) to our trusted certificates in the Oracle wallet. The issuer is www.verisign.com/CPS Incorp.by Ref. LIABILITY LTD as depicted by the tree-like hierarchy.

Click the View Certificate button while www.verisign.com/CPS Incorp. by Ref. is highlighted. This shows information for the issuer's certificate. Click the Details tab and you should see:

Now we need to Click the Copy to File button. Save the file locally as a Base-64 encoded X.509 (CER) file. The following screen shows the selection you should make, you can name the file anything you choose and save it anywhere. We'll be importing it in a moment, just remember where you save it to:

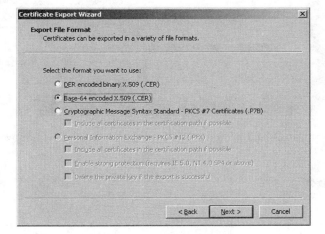

Now we can import this into our Oracle Wallet. Open the wallet in OWM and right click on the Trusted Certificates – this will present you with a popup menu that has Import Trusted Certificate:

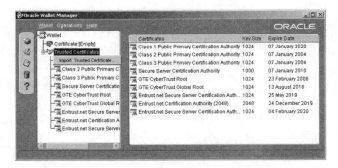

You will select that option and in the next dialog that comes up, choose Select a file that contains the certificate

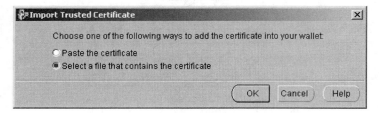

Use the standard 'file open' dialog that comes up to choose the certificate you just saved. Your screen should now look something like this:

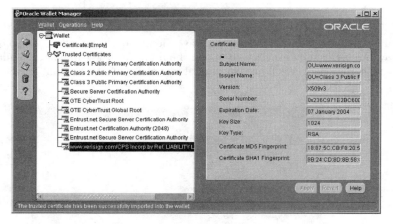

Now, save the wallet using clicking on the SAVE WALLET (the yellow floppy disk) icon and let's try our example again:

```
tkyte@TKYTE816> declare
  2      l_output long;
  3
  4      l_url varchar2(255) default
  5           'https://trading.etrade.com/cgi-bin/gx.cgi/AppLogic%2bHome';
  6
  7      l_wallet_path varchar2(255) default
  8           'file:C:\Documents and Settings\Thomas Kyte\ORACLE\WALLETS';
  9
 10
 11  begin
 12      l_output := utl_http.request
 13                   ( url               => l_url,
 14                     proxy             => 'www-proxy.us.oracle.com',
 15                     wallet_path       => l_wallet_path,
 16                     wallet_password   => 'oracle'
 17                   );
 18      dbms_output.put_line(trim(substr(l_output,1,255)));
 19  end;
 20  /
```

```
<HTML>
<HEAD>
<META http-equiv="Content-Type" content="text/html;
charset=ISO-8859-1">
<TITLE>E*TRADE</TITLE>
<SCRIPT LANGUAGE="Javascript"
TYPE="text/javascript">
        <!--

        function mac_comment(){
                var
agt=navigator.userAgent.toLowerCase();
                var is_mac

PL/SQL procedure successfully completed.
```

This time we are successful. Now we know how to use and extend the Oracle wallet to do secure HTTPS.

Really Using UTL_HTTP

Well, besides getting the content of a web page which is extremely useful – what else can we do with UTL_HTTP? Well, a common use for it is an easy way to make it so that PL/SQL can run a program – sort of like a HOST command. Since almost every web server can run cgi-bin programs and UTL_HTTP can send URLs, we can in effect have PL/SQL execute host commands by configuring the commands we wanted to execute as cgi-bin programs under the webserver.

What I like to do in this case is setup a web server running on IP address 127.0.0.1 – which is the TCP/IP loop back. This IP address is only accessible if you are physically logged onto the machine the web server is running on. In that fashion, I can set up cgi-bin programs for my PL/SQL programs to run that no one else can – unless they break in to my server machine in which case I have much larger problems to deal with.

One use I've made of this facility in the past is to send e-mail from PL/SQL. Let's say you have the Oracle 8i database without Java in it. Without Java you cannot use either UTL_TCP or UTL_SMTP – they both rely on the Java option in the database. So, without UTL_SMTP and/or UTL_TCP, how could we send an email? With UTL_HTTP and UTL_FILE – I can set up a cgi-bin program that receives a single input in the QUERY_STRING environment variable. The single input would be a file name. We will use /usr/lib/sendmail to send that file (on Windows I could use the public domain utility 'blat' to send mail, available from http://www.interlog.com/~tcharron/blat.html). Once I have that set up, I can simply run my host command via:

```
    …
    results := utl_http.request(
                'http://127.0.0.1/cgi-bin/smail?filename.text' );
    …
```

The cgi-bin program I set up, smail, would return a 'web page' that indicated success or failure, I would look at the result's variable to see if the mail was sent successfully or not. The full fledged implementation of this on Unix could be:

```
scott@ORA8I.WORLD> create sequence sm_seq
  2  /
Sequence created.

scott@ORA8I.WORLD> create or replace procedure sm( p_to in varchar2,
  2                                  p_from in varchar2,
  3                                  p_subject in varchar2,
  4                                  p_body in varchar2 )
  5  is
  6      l_output          utl_file.file_type;
  7      l_filename        varchar2(255);
  8      l_request         varchar2(2000);
  9  begin
 10      select 'm' || sm_seq.nextval || '.EMAIL.' || p_to
 11        into l_filename
 12        from dual;
 13
 14      l_output := utl_file.fopen
 15                      ( '/tmp', l_filename, 'w', 32000 );
 16
 17      utl_file.put_line( l_output, 'From: ' || p_from );
 18      utl_file.put_line( l_output, 'Subject: ' || p_subject );
 19      utl_file.new_line( l_output );
 20      utl_file.put_line( l_output, p_body );
 21      utl_file.new_line( l_output );
 22      utl_file.put_line( l_output, '.' );
 23
 24      utl_file.fclose( l_output );
 25
 26      l_request := utl_http.request
 27                      ( 'http://127.0.0.1/cgi-bin/smail?' || l_filename );
 28
 29      dbms_output.put_line( l_request );
 30  end sm;
 31  /

Procedure created.
```

You should refer to the section on UTL_SMTP to understand why I formatted the email as I did here with the From: and To: header records. In this routine we are using a sequence to generate a unique filename. We encode the recipient in the name of the file itself. Then, we write the email to an OS file. Lastly, we use UTL_HTTP to run our host command and pass it the name of the file. We simply print out the result of this in this test case – we would really be inspecting the value of l_result to ensure the e-mail was sent successfully.

The simple cgi-bin program could be:

```
#!/bin/sh

echo "Content-type: text/plain"
echo ""

echo $QUERY_STRING
to=`echo $QUERY_STRING|sed 's/.*EMAIL\.//'`
echo $to

(/usr/lib/sendmail $to < /tmp/$QUERY_STRING) 1>> /tmp/$$.log 2>&1
cat /tmp/$$.log
rm /tmp/$$.log
rm /tmp/$QUERY_STRING
```

The shell script starts by printing out the HTTP headers that we need in order to return a document; that is what the first two echoes are doing. Then, we are simply printing out the value of the QUERY_STRING (this is where the web server puts our inputs – the portion after the ? in the URL). We then extract the email address from the QUERY_STRING by using the sed (Stream EDitor) to remove everything in front of the word EMAIL/ in the filename. We then run sendmail in a subshell so as to be able to capture both its stdout and stderr output streams. I cat (type to stdout) the contents of the log we captured from sendmail. In this case I wanted both stdout and stderr to be returned as the contents of the web page, so the PL/SQL code could get any error messages and such. The easiest way to do that was to redirect both output streams to a temporary file and then type that file to stdout. We then clean up our temp files and return.

I can now test this via:

```
scott@ORA8I.WORLD> begin
  2      sm( 'tkyte@us.oracle.com',
  3          'tkyte@us.oracle.com',
  4          'testing',
  5          'hello world!' );
  6   end;
  7   /
m1.EMAIL.tkyte@us.oracle.com
tkyte@us.oracle.com
```

This shows us the QUERY_STRING and the To: environment variables, and since there is no other test (no error messages) we know the e-mail was sent.

So, this small example shows how UTL_HTTP can be used indirectly for something it was not really designed for; to allow PL/SQL to run HOST commands. You would set up a special purpose web server on IP Address 127.0.0.1, configure a cgi-bin type directory within it and place the commands you want PL/SQL developers to run in there. Then you have a secure way to allow PL/SQL to run the equivalent of SQL*PLUS's host command.

A Better UTL_HTTP

Given that we have the SocketType class developed in the UTL_TCP section (or just access to UTL_TCP alone) and knowledge of the HTTP protocol, we can make an improved UTL_HTTP package. We will call our implementation HTTP_PKG. It will support the "old fashioned" UTL_HTTP interface of REQUEST and REQUEST_PIECES but will also add support for:

❑ Getting the HTTP headers back with each request – These headers contain useful information such as the status of the request (e.g. **200 OK**, 404 Not Found, and so on), the name of the server that executed the URL, the content type of the returned content, cookies and so on.

❑ Getting the content back as either a CLOB or a BLOB – This allows your PL/SQL to retrieve a large PDF file to be inserted into a table indexed by interMedia as well as retrieve plain text from another page or just to access any binary data returned by a web server.

❑ Perform a HEAD of a document – This is useful to check and see if the document you retrieved last week has been updated for example.

❑ URL-encoded strings – for example, if you have a space or a tilde (~) in a URL request, they must be 'escaped'. This function escapes all characters that need to be.

❑ Sending Cookies with requests – If you are using this HTTP_PKG to get access to a web site that uses a cookie based authentication scheme, this is crucial. You would have to GET the login page, sending the username and password in the GET request. You would then look at the HTTP headers returned by that page and extract their cookie. This cookie value is what you need to send on all subsequent requests to prove who you are.

❑ POST data instead of just GET – The GET protocol has limits that vary by web server on the size of the request. Typically, a URL should not exceed 1 to 2 KB in length. If it does, you should POST the data. POSTed data can be of unlimited size.

We can implement all of this in PL/SQL using our SocketType from the UTL_TCP section and we can do it with a fairly small amount of code. The specification for our new HTTP_PKG package follows. We'll look at the specification and some examples that use it. What will not be in this book is the code that implements the body of the HTTP_PKG. This code is available and documented on the Apress website, (http://www.apress.com), it is about 15 printed pages long hence it is not included here. The package specification is as follows. The first two functions, REQUEST and REQUEST_PIECES, are functionally equivalent (minus SSL support) to functions found in the UTL_HTTP package in versions 7.3.x, 8.0.x, and 8.1.5, we even will raise the same sort of named exceptions they would:

```
tkyte@TKYTE816> create or replace package http_pkg
  2  as
  3      function request( url in varchar2,
  4                        proxy in varchar2 default NULL )
  5      return varchar2;
  6
  7      type html_pieces is table of varchar2(2000)
  8          index by binary_integer;
  9
 10      function request_pieces(url in varchar2,
 11                        max_pieces natural default 32767,
 12                        proxy in varchar2 default NULL)
 13      return html_pieces;
 14
 15      init_failed exception;
 16      request_failed exception;
```

The next procedure is GET_URL. It invokes the standard HTTP GET command on a web server. The inputs are:

❑ p_url is the URL to retrieve.

❑ p_proxy is the name:<port> of the proxy server to use. Null indicates you need not use a proxy server. Examples: p_proxy => 'www-proxy' or p_proxy => 'www-proxy:80'.

❑ p_status is returned to you. it will be the HTTP status code returned by the web server. 200 indicates normal, successful completion. 401 indicates unauthorized, and so on.

❑ p_status_txt is returned to you. It contains the full text of the HTTP status record. For example it might contain: HTTP/1.0 200 OK.

❑ `p_httpHeaders` may be set by you and upon return will contain the http headers from the requested URL. On input, any values you have set will be transmitted to the web server as part of the request. On output, the headers generated by the web server will be returned to you. You can use this to set and send cookies or basic authentication or any other http header record you wish.

❑ `p_content` is a *temporary* CLOB or BLOB (depending on which overloaded procedure you call) that will be allocated for you in this package (you need not allocate it). It is a session temporary LOB. You may use `dbms_lob.freetemporary` to deallocate it whenever you want, or just let it disappear when you log out.

```
19      procedure get_url( p_url          in varchar2,
20                         p_proxy        in varchar2 default NULL,
21                         p_status            out number,
22                         p_status_txt        out varchar2,
23                         p_httpHeaders   in out CorrelatedArray,
24                         p_content    in out clob );
25
26
27      procedure get_url( p_url        in    varchar2,
28                         p_proxy      in    varchar2 default NULL,
29                         p_status          out number,
30                         p_status_txt      out varchar2,
31                         p_httpHeaders in out CorrelatedArray,
32                         p_content  in out blob );
```

The next procedure is HEAD_URL. Invokes the standard HTTP HEAD syntax on a web server. The inputs and outputs are identical to `get_url` above (except *no* content is retrieved). This function is useful to see if a document exists, what its mime-type is, or if it has been recently changed, without actually retrieving the document itself:

```
34      procedure head_url( p_url       in varchar2,
35                          p_proxy     in varchar2 default NULL,
36                          p_status        out number,
37                          p_status_txt     out varchar2,
38                          p_httpHeaders    out CorrelatedArray );
```

The next function URL encode is used when building GET parameter lists or building POST CLOBs. It is used to escape special characters in URLs (for example, a URL may not contain a whitespace, a % sign, and so on). Given input such as `Hello World`, then urlencode will return **Hello%20World**'

```
40      function urlencode( p_str in varchar2 ) return varchar2;
```

Procedure Add_A_Cookie allows you to easily set a cookie value to be sent to a web server. You need only know the name and value of the cookie. The formatting of the HTTP header record is performed by this routine. The `p_httpHeaders` variable you send in/out of this routine would be sent in/out of the `<Get|Head|Post>_url` routines:

```
42      procedure add_a_cookie
43              ( p_name in varchar2,
44                p_value in varchar2,
45                p_httpHeaders in out CorrelatedArray );
```

The next procedure `Set_Basic_Auth` allows you to enter a username/password to access a protected page. The formatting of the HTTP header record is performed by this routine. The `p_httpHeaders` variable you send in/out of this routine would be sent in/out of the `<Get|Head|Post>_url` routines as well:

```
47      procedure set_basic_auth
48          ( p_username in varchar2,
49            p_password in varchar2,
50            p_httpHeaders in out CorrelatedArray );
```

The procedure `set_post_parameter` is used when retrieving a URL that needs a large (greater than 2,000 or so bytes) set of inputs. It is recommended that the POST method be used for large requests. This routine allows you to add parameter after parameter to a POST request. This post request is built into a CLOB which you supply:

```
52      procedure set_post_parameter
53          ( p_name in varchar2,
54            p_value in varchar2,
55            p_post_data in out clob,
56            p_urlencode in boolean default FALSE );
```

The next two routines are identical to GET_URL above with the addition of the `p_post_data` input `p_post_data` is a CLOB built by repeated calls to `set_post_parameter` above. The remaining inputs/outputs are defined the same as they were for GET_URL:

```
58      procedure post_url
59          (p_url          in      varchar2,
60           p_post_data    in      clob,
61           p_proxy        in      varchar2 default NULL,
62           p_status               out number,
63           p_status_txt           out varchar2,
64           p_httpHeaders   in out CorrelatedArray,
65           p_content       in out clob );
66
67      procedure post_url
68          (p_url          in      varchar2,
69           p_post_data    in      clob,
70           p_proxy        in      varchar2 default NULL,
71           p_status               out number,
72           p_status_txt           out varchar2,
73           p_httpHeaders   in out CorrelatedArray,
74           p_content       in out blob );
75
76
77  end;
78  /

Package created.
```

So, the specification of the package is done; the procedures defined within it are rather straightforward. I can do things like GET_URL to get a URL. This will use the HTTP GET syntax to retrieve the contents of a web page into a temporary BLOB or CLOB. I can HEAD_URL to get the headers for a URL. Using this I could look at the mime type for example to decide if I wanted to use a CLOB (text/html) to get the

URL or a BLOB (image/gif). I can even POST_URL to post large amounts of data to a URL. There are the other helper functions to set cookies in the header, to base 64 encode the username and password for basic authentication and so on.

Now, assuming you have downloaded the implementation of HTTP_PKG (the package body consists of about 500 lines of PL/SQL code) we are ready to try it out. We'll introduce a pair of utility routines that will be useful to test with first. Print_clob below simply prints out the entire contents of a CLOB using DBMS_OUTPUT. Print_Headers does the same for the HTTP headers we retrieve above in our CorrelatedArray type (an object type that is part of the HTTP_PKG implementation). In the following, the procedure P is the P procedure I introduced in the DBMS_OUTPUT section to print long lines:

```
ops$tkyte@DEV816> create or replace procedure print_clob( p_clob in clob )
  2  as
  3      l_offset number default 1;
  4  begin
  5     loop
  6        exit when l_offset > dbms_lob.getlength(p_clob);
  7        dbms_output.put_line( dbms_lob.substr( p_clob, 255, l_offset ) );
  8        l_offset := l_offset + 255;
  9     end loop;
 10  end;
 11  /

ops$tkyte@DEV816> create or replace
  2  procedure print_headers( p_httpHeaders correlatedArray )
  3  as
  4  begin
  5      for i in 1 .. p_httpHeaders.vals.count loop
  6          p( initcap( p_httpHeaders.vals(i).name ) || ': ' ||
  7                      p_httpHeaders.vals(i).value );
  8      end loop;
  9      p( chr(9) );
 10  end;
 11  /
```

Now onto the test:

```
ops$tkyte@DEV816> begin
  2          p( http_pkg.request( 'http://myserver/' ) );
  3  end;
  4  /
<HTML>
<HEAD>
<TITLE>Oracle Service Industries</TITLE>
</HEAD>
<FRAMESET COLS="130,*"
border=0>
<FRAME SRC="navtest.html" NAME="sidebar" frameborder=0>
<FRAME SRC="folder_home.html"
NAME="body" frameborder="0" marginheight="0" marginwidth="0">
</FRAMESET>

</BODY>
</HTML>
```

```
ops$tkyte@DEV816> declare
  2          pieces      http_pkg.html_pieces;
  3  begin
  4          pieces :=
  5              http_pkg.request_pieces( 'http://www.oracle.com',
  6                                      proxy=>'www-proxy1');
  7
  8          for i in 1 .. pieces.count loop
  9              p( pieces(i) );
 10          end loop;
 11  end;
 12  /
<head>
<title>Oracle Corporation</title>
<meta http-equiv="Content-Type" content="text/html;
...
```

The above two routines simply show that the UTL_HTTP methods of REQUEST and REQUEST_PIECES function as expected with our new package. Their functionality is identical. Now we will invoke our URLENCODE function that translates 'bad characters into escape sequences in URLs and POST data:

```
ops$tkyte@DEV816> select
  2  http_pkg.urlencode( 'A>C%{hello}\fadfasdfads~`[abc]:=$+''"' )
  3  from dual;

HTTP_PKG.URLENCODE('A>C%{HELLO}\FADFASDFADS~`[ABC]:=$+''"')
----------------------------------------------------------------
A%3EC%25%7Bhello%7D%5Cfadfasdfads%7E%60%5Babc%5D%3A%3D%24%2B%27%22
```

That shows that characters like > and % are escaped into %3E and %25 respectively and other sequences such as the word hello are not escaped. This allows us to use any of these special characters in our HTTP requests safely.

Now we will see the first of the new HTTP URL procedures. This procedure call will return Yahoo's home page via a proxy server, www-proxy1, (you'll need to replace this with your own proxy server of course). Additionally, we get to see the HTTP status returned – 200 indicates success. We also see the HTTP headers Yahoo returned to us. The mime-type will always be in there and that tells us what type of content we can expect. Lastly, the content is returned and printed out:

```
ops$tkyte@DEV816> declare
  2          l_httpHeaders       correlatedArray;
  3          l_status        number;
  4          l_status_txt     varchar2(255);
  5          l_content       clob;
  6  begin
  7          http_pkg.get_url( 'http://www.yahoo.com/',
  8                          'www-proxy1',
  9                          l_status,
 10                          l_status_txt,
 11                          l_httpHeaders,
 12                          l_content );
 13
 14          p( 'The status was ' || l_status );
```

```
15        p( 'The status text was ' || l_status_txt );
16        print_headers( l_httpHeaders );
17        print_clob( l_content );
18   end;
19   /
The status was 200
The status text was HTTP/1.0 200 OK

Date: Fri, 02 Feb 2001 19:13:26 GMT
Connection: close
Content-Type: text/html

<html><head><title>Yahoo!</title><base href=http://www.yahoo.com/><meta http-
equiv="PICS-Label"
```

Next, we will try the HEAD request against the home page of a sample site, let's call it, Sample.com, and see what we can discover:

```
ops$tkyte@DEV816> declare
2        l_httpHeaders          correlatedArray;
3        l_status       number;
4        l_status_txt      varchar2(255);
5   begin
6        http_pkg.head_url( 'http://www.sample.com/',
7                            'www-proxy1',
8                             l_status,
9                             l_status_txt,
10                            l_httpHeaders );
11
12        p( 'The status was ' || l_status );
13        p( 'The status text was ' || l_status_txt );
14        print_headers( l_httpHeaders );
15   end;
16   /
The status was 200
The status text was HTTP/1.1 200 OK

Server: Microsoft-IIS/5.0
Date: Fri, 02 Feb 2001 19:13:26 GMT
Connection: Keep-Alive
Content-Length: 1270
Content-Type: text/html
Set-Cookie: ASPSESSIONIDQQQGGNQU=PNMNCIBACGKFLHGKLLBPEPMD; path=/
Cache-Control: private
```

From the headers, it is obvious that Sample.com is running Windows with Microsoft IIS. Further, they are using ASP's as indicated by the cookie they sent back to us. If we were to have retrieved that page, it would have had 1,270 bytes of content.

Now we would like to see how cookies might work. Here I am using a standard procedure that is used with OAS (the Oracle Application Server) and iAS (Oracle's Internet Application Server); the cookiejar sample that shows how to use cookies in a PL/SQL web procedure. The routine cookiejar looks at the cookie value and if set, increments it by one and returns it to the client. We'll see what how that would work using our package. We are going to send the value 55 to the server and we are expecting it to send us 56 back:

```
ops$tkyte@DEV816> declare
  2      l_httpHeaders      correlatedArray;
  3      l_status      number;
  4      l_status_txt      varchar2(255);
  5      l_content      clob;
  6  begin
  7      http_pkg.add_a_cookie( 'COUNT', 55, l_httpHeaders );
  8      http_pkg.get_url
  9      ( 'http://myserver.acme.com/wa/webdemo/owa/cookiejar',
 10        null,
 11        l_status,
 12        l_status_txt,
 13        l_httpHeaders,
 14        l_content );
 15
 16      p( 'The status was ' || l_status );
 17      p( 'The status text was ' || l_status_txt );
 18      print_headers( l_httpHeaders );
 19      print_clob( l_content );
 20  end;
 21  /
The status was 200
The status text was HTTP/1.0 200 OK


Content-Type: text/html
Date: Fri, 02 Feb 2001 19:14:48 GMT
Allow: GET, HEAD
Server: Oracle_Web_listener2.1/1.20in2
Set-Cookie: COUNT=56; expires=Saturday, 03-Feb-2001 22:14:48 GMT


<HTML>
<HEAD>
<TITLE>C is for Cookie</TITLE>
</HEAD>
<BODY>
<HR>
<IMG SRC="/ows-img/ows.gif">
<H1>C
is for Cookie</H1>
<HR>
You have visited this page <STRONG>56</STRONG> times in the last 24
hours.
…
```

As you can see, the cookie value of 55 was transmitted and the server incremented it to 56. It then sent us back the modified value along with an expiration date.

Next, we would like to see how to access a page that requires a username and password. This is done via the following:

```
ops$tkyte@DEV816> declare
  2       l_httpHeaders    correlatedArray;
  3       l_status         number;
  4       l_status_txt     varchar2(255);
  5       l_content        clob;
  6  begin
  7       http_pkg.set_basic_auth( 'tkyte', 'tiger', l_httpheaders );
  8       http_pkg.get_url
  9       ( 'http://myserver.acme.com:80/wa/intranets/owa/print_user',
 10         null,
 11         l_status,
 12         l_status_txt,
 13         l_httpHeaders,
 14         l_content );
 15
 16       p( 'The status was ' || l_status );
 17       p( 'The status text was ' || l_status_txt );
 18       print_headers( l_httpHeaders );
 19       print_clob(l_content);
 20  end;
 21  /
The status was 200
The status text was HTTP/1.0 200 OK

Content-Type: text/html
Date: Fri, 02 Feb 2001 19:49:17 GMT
Allow: GET, HEAD
Server: Oracle_Web_listener2.1/1.20in2

remote user = tkyte
```

Here, I just set up a DAD (Database Access Descriptor) that did not store the username/password with the DAD. This means the web server is expecting the request to contain the username/password to use. Here I passed my credentials to a routine that simply printed out the REMOTE_USER cgi-environment variable in PL/SQL (the name of the remotely connected user).

Lastly, we would like to demonstrate the POST'ing of data. Here I am using a URL from Yahoo again. Yahoo makes it easy to get stock quotes in a spreadsheet format. Since the list of stock symbols you might be interested in could get quite large, I would suggest POSTing this data. Here is an example that gets a couple of stock quotes from Yahoo using HTTP. The data will be returned in CSV (Comma Separated Values) for easy parsing and loading into a table for example:

```
ops$tkyte@DEV816> declare
  2       l_httpHeaders    correlatedArray;
  3       l_status         number;
  4       l_status_txt     varchar2(255);
  5       l_content        clob;
  6       l_post           clob;
  7  begin
  8       http_pkg.set_post_parameter( 'symbols','orcl ^IXID ^DJI ^SPC',
  9                                     l_post, TRUE );
 10       http_pkg.set_post_parameter( 'format', 'sl1d1t1c1ohgv',
 11                                     l_post, TRUE );
 12       http_pkg.set_post_parameter( 'ext', '.csv',
```

```
13                                 l_post, TRUE );
14           http_pkg.post_url( 'http://quote.yahoo.com/download/quotes.csv',
15                               l_post,
16                               'www-proxy',
17                               l_status,
18                               l_status_txt,
19                               l_httpHeaders,
20                               l_content );
21
22           p( 'The status was ' || l_status );
23           p( 'The status text was ' || l_status_txt );
24           print_headers( l_httpHeaders );
25           print_clob( l_content );
26   end;
27   /
The status was 200
The status text was HTTP/1.0 200 OK

Date: Fri, 02 Feb 2001 19:49:18 GMT
Cache-Control: private
Connection: close
Content-Type: application/octet-stream

"ORCL",28.1875,"2/2/2001","2:34PM",-1.875,29.9375,30.0625,28.0625,26479100
"^IXID",1620.60,"2/2/2001","2:49PM",-45.21,1664.55,1667.46,1620.40,N/A
"^DJI",10899.33,"2/2/2001","2:49PM",-84.30,10982.71,11022.78,10888.01,N/A
"^SPC",1355.17,"2/2/2001","2:49PM",-18.30,1373.53,1376.16,1354.21,N/A
```

Summary

In this section, we have seen how to use the built-in UTL_HTTP package. We have seen how through a little creative thinking, we can use UTL_HTTP not only to grab data from the web, but to enable PL/SQL to have the equivalent of a HOST command. With just a couple of lines of code, we made it possible that any release of Oracle from 7.3 on up can easily send mail using UTL_FILE and UTL_HTTP.

We then investigated how to use UTL_HTTP over SSL – a concept not well documented in the *Oracle Supplied Packages Guide* (or any other document for that matter). We learned how to make any SSL enabled website available to our PL/SQL routines using the Oracle Wallet Manager.

Additionally, we've seen how we can take a good idea and make it better. In comparison to the section on DBMS_OBFUSCATION_TOOLKIT where we 'wrapped' the functionality of that package to make it easier and more flexible to use, here we totally re-implemented a package giving it *additional* functionality it never had. This came at a certain price, we do not support SSL in our implementation, but it is useful in many cases nonetheless.

We could easily take this a step further and user either Java or a C based External Procedure to add full support for SSL as well. There are also various third party and public domain classes and libraries out there to do just that.

UTL_RAW

UTL_RAW is a package supplied with Oracle since version 7.1.6. It is a utility package developed by the Procedural Gateway development team initially for accessing and converting mainframe data into ASCII, and then later by the replication development team. It contains four functions I use frequently, and you've seen these scattered throughout the book. I am going to cover these four functions only, as they are the ones I find to be of most use. There are other functions contained in the package (thirteen more to be exact), but I won't be covering them here. Check the *Supplied PL/SQL Packages Reference* for more details on these.

The four functions I will cover are:

- ❑ CAST_TO_VARCHAR2 – Converts a RAW to a VARCHAR2
- ❑ CAST_TO_RAW – Converts a VARCHAR2 to a RAW
- ❑ LENGTH – Returns the length of a RAW variable
- ❑ SUBSTR – Returns a substring of a RAW variable

We use these functions heavily when dealing with binary data. This can be seen in the CRYPT_PKG we use in the sections on DBMS_OBFUSCATION_TOOLKIT, DBMS_LOB, and UTL_TCP .

We'll start with the CAST_ functions. These simply change the type field of a RAW variable to be VARCHAR2, and vice-versa. They do this without any translation of the data contained in the variable whatsoever. Normally, if I assign a RAW to a VARCHAR2, the VARCHAR2 would be twice as long as the RAW was, and would contain hexadecimal digits. Each byte of the RAW would be converted to hexadecimal (we took advantage of this translation in the DBMS_OBFUSCATION_TOOLKIT routine for example, to display encrypted data in hexadecimal on screen). In the cases where we do not desire this translation to take place, the CAST_TO_VARCHAR2 function comes in handy. To see what it does, we can use the DUMP SQL function as follows:

```
tkyte@TKYTE816> create table t ( r raw(10) );
Table created.

tkyte@TKYTE816> insert into t values ( utl_raw.cast_to_raw('helloWorld' ) );
1 row created.

tkyte@TKYTE816> select dump(r) r1, dump(utl_raw.cast_to_varchar2(r)) r1
  2                    from t;

R1                                  R1
----------------------------------  ----------------------------------
Typ=23 Len=10:                      Typ=1 Len=10:
104,101,108,108,111,87,111,114      104,101,108,108,111,87,111,114
,108,100                            ,108,100
```

As you can see from the DUMP, the only thing that changed about the data was the TYP of it. It changed from 23 to 1. If you go to the *Oracle Call Interface Programmer's Guide* and look at the *Internal Datatypes* chart, you will find that type 23 is a RAW up to 2000 bytes in length, and type 1 is a VARCHAR2 up to 4000 bytes. The only thing CAST_TO_VARCHAR2 does is to change the data type flag in the variable – it does not touch the data at all. This is exactly what we need in the case where we use DBMS_LOB.SUBSTR on a BFILE, and this BFILE happens to contain 'clear text'. We need to convert this RAW into a VARCHAR2 without it being converted into hexadecimal – we only need change the data type.

UTL_RAW.CAST_TO_RAW goes the other way. If you have a VARCHAR2 that you need treated as a RAW, this will convert it by changing the type, and nothing else. We use this in our SIMPLE_TCP_CLIENT implementation, in the section on the UTL_SMTP supplied package. Externally, the PL/SQL client is sending us VARCHAR2 data, but the Java layer needs byte arrays (RAWs). PL/SQL does this conversion easily for us.

The last two functions of note are UTL_RAW.LENGTH and UTL_RAW.SUBSTR. When we have a RAW and send it to the built-in routines LENGTH and SUBSTR, the RAW will be implicitly converted to a VARCHAR2 (into hexadecimal) first. Unfortunately, the built-in functions are not overloaded to accept and receive RAW types, but rather they convert them into VARCHAR2. This means the return from LENGTH would always be twice the size, SUBSTR would always return a hexadecimal string, and we would have to fix the offset and length parameters as well. The UTL_RAW functions supply this missing functionality for us. They are equivalent to the following SQL:

```
tkyte@TKYTE816> select utl_raw.length(r), length(r)/2 from t;

UTL_RAW.LENGTH(R) LENGTH(R)/2
----------------- -----------
               10          10

tkyte@TKYTE816> select utl_raw.substr(r,2,3) r1,
  2             hextoraw(substr(r,3,6)) r2
  3     from t
  4  /

R1         R2
---------- ----------
656C6C     656C6C
```

Using the UTL_RAW functions is not mandatory, but it certainly makes life easier. Figuring out the byte offsets for a SUBSTR would be more complex, and remembering to divide by two is just something we don't need to do.

UTL_SMTP and Sending Mail

UTL_SMTP, introduced for the first time in Oracle 8.1.6, is an interface to the Simple Mail Transfer Protocol. It requires that you have an SMTP server in your network somewhere – most sites I have been to have at least one SMTP server running as it is the most popular method for sending mail.

The UTL_SMTP package is best suited for sending small, text only e-mails from the database. While its API supports the sending of attachments and everything else – it is left to you to actually encode the multi-part document – for example turning binary attachments into mime-encoded documents.

In this section we'll visit the example introduced in the DBMS_JOB section, which used UTL_SMTP, build upon it by adding additional functionality. We will also look at an alternative to UTL_SMTP that provides somewhat much more functionality – including the ability to easily send attachments with the e-mail. Since SMTP is a very low level protocol, we'll reuse existing public domain code to get an SMTP interface at much higher level – and we'll get it with very little code.

UTL_SMTP – a larger example

In the DBMS_JOB section, we explore how to send an e-mail using UTL_SMTP and 'apparently' making it execute faster by doing it asynchronously. We also made e-mail transactional in nature in that section; if you rollback, the e-mail does not get sent, if you commit – out it goes. I highly recommend the use of DBMS_JOB as a layer on your e-mail's routines for these reasons. In that section, the example UTL_SMTP routine we used was:

```
tkyte@TKYTE816> create or replace
  2    PROCEDURE send_mail (p_sender      IN VARCHAR2,
  3                         p_recipient IN VARCHAR2,
  4                         p_message   IN VARCHAR2)
  5    as
  6        l_mailhost VARCHAR2(255) := 'yourserver.acme.com';
  7        l_mail_conn utl_smtp.connection;
  8    BEGIN
  9        l_mail_conn := utl_smtp.open_connection(l_mailhost, 25);
 10        utl_smtp.helo(l_mail_conn, l_mailhost);
 11        utl_smtp.mail(l_mail_conn, p_sender);
 12        utl_smtp.rcpt(l_mail_conn, p_recipient);
 13        utl_smtp.open_data(l_mail_conn );
 14        utl_smtp.write_data(l_mail_conn, p_message);
 15        utl_smtp.close_data(l_mail_conn );
 16        utl_smtp.quit(l_mail_conn);
 17    end;
 18    /
Procedure created.

tkyte@TKYTE816> begin
  2           send_mail( 'me@acme.com',
  3                      'you@acme.com',
  4                      'Hello Tom' );
  5    end;
  6    /

PL/SQL procedure successfully completed.
```

This works OK but is very limited in nature. It sends e-mail to exactly one recipient, you cannot CC (Carbon Copy) or BCC (Blind Carbon Copy) anyone, you cannot setup a subject; the e-mail always arrives with a 'blank' subject line. We would like to support more options with this package.

A full discussion of all of the possibilities with UTL_SMTP would require in depth knowledge of the SMTP protocol itself – something that is outside the scope of this book. Readers interested in all of the opportunities available with SMTP should review RFC812 – which is the description of SMTP. This is available online at http://www.faqs.org/rfcs/rfc821.html. Below, I will simply present how to send an e-mail using UTL_SMTP that supports:

❑ Multiple 'To' recipients.

❑ Multiple 'CC' recipients.

❑ Multiple 'BCC' recipients.

❑ A single body of up to 32 KB in size.

❑ A subject line.

❑ A descriptive 'from' line (instead of showing just the e-mail address as the 'from' in the e-mail client).

A specification for a PL/SQL package that supports this might look like the following. Here, we define an array type to allow a caller to easily send a list of recipients as well as provide the external specification of the PL/SQL routine we will be implementing:

```
tkyte@TKYTE816> create or replace package mail_pkg
  2  as
  3          type array is table of varchar2(255);
  4
  5          procedure send( p_sender_e-mail in varchar2,
  6                          p_from          in varchar2,
  7                          p_to            in array default array(),
  8                          p_cc            in array default array(),
  9                          p_bcc           in array default array(),
 10                          p_subject       in varchar2,
 11                          p_body          in long );
 12  end;
 13  /
Package created.
```

The package body for this implementation is relatively straightforward – if understand just enough of the SMTP protocol and what an e-mail looks like (how e-mail clients get the From, To, CC and so on). Before we look at the code, we'll look at what an e-mail might actually look like. Consider the following ASCII text:

```
From: Oracle Database Account <me@acme.com>
Subject: This is a subject
To: you@acme.com, us@acme.com
Cc: them@acme.com

Hello Tom, this is the mail you need
```

That is what you would transmit as the *body* of the e-mail using UTL_SMTP to have the e-mail client set the From, Subject, and so on. There are no SMTP commands to do this piece of 'magic', rather, this header information is placed right in the body of the e-mail itself; separated from the text of the e-mail by a blank line. Once we understand this, sending an e-mail with all of the options that we need is pretty easy. The only thing we need to understand beyond that is that in order to send the e-mail to more then one recipient, we simply call UTL_SMTP.RCPT more then once – with different names. That's all of the information we need to know then to send an e-mail.

So, here is the package body. We start with a couple of constants and global variables. You will of course need to change the g_mailhost to be the name of a server you have access to, in this code I have given it a generic name; yourserver.acme.com:

```
tkyte@TKYTE816> create or replace package body mail_pkg
  2  as
  3
  4  g_crlf      char(2) default chr(13)||chr(10);
  5  g_mail_conn utl_smtp.connection;
  6  g_mailhost  varchar2(255) := 'yourserver.acme.com';
  7
```

Next, we have an internal (unpublished) function to send an e-mail to many recipients – it in effect addresses the e-mail. At the same time, it builds the To: or CC: lines that we will eventually send as part of the e-mail itself and returns that formatted string. It was implemented as a separate function since we need to do this separately for the To, CC, and BCC lists:

```
 8   function address_email( p_string in varchar2,
 9                            p_recipients in array ) return varchar2
10   is
11       l_recipients long;
12   begin
13       for i in 1 .. p_recipients.count
14       loop
15           utl_smtp.rcpt(g_mail_conn, p_recipients(i) );
16           if ( l_recipients is null )
17           then
18               l_recipients := p_string || p_recipients(i) ;
19           else
20               l_recipients := l_recipients || ', ' || p_recipients(i);
21           end if;
22       end loop;
23       return l_recipients;
24   end;
25
26
```

Now we have the implementation of our published function, the one that people will actually call to send mail. It starts with an internal procedure `writeData` that is used to simplify the sending of the e-mail headers (the `To:`, `From:`, `Subject:` records). If the header record is *not* Null, this routine will use the appropriate `UTL_SMTP` call to send it – along with the necessary end of line marker (the carriage return/line feed):

```
27   procedure send( p_sender_email in varchar2,
28                   p_from         in varchar2 default NULL,
29                   p_to           in array default array(),
30                   p_cc           in array default array(),
31                   p_bcc          in array default array(),
32                   p_subject      in varchar2 default NULL,
33                   p_body         in long  default NULL )
34   is
35       l_to_list    long;
36       l_cc_list    long;
37       l_bcc_list   long;
38       l_date       varchar2(255) default
39                    to_char( SYSDATE, 'dd Mon yy hh24:mi:ss' );
40
41       procedure writeData( p_text in varchar2 )
42       as
43       begin
44           if ( p_text is not null )
45           then
46               utl_smtp.write_data( g_mail_conn, p_text || g_crlf );
47           end if;
48       end;
```

Now we are ready to actually send the mail. This part is not very different from the very simple routine we started with. It begins in exactly the same fashion, by connecting to the SMTP server and starting a session:

```
49    begin
50        g_mail_conn := utl_smtp.open_connection(g_mailhost, 25);
51
52        utl_smtp.helo(g_mail_conn, g_mailhost);
53        utl_smtp.mail(g_mail_conn, p_sender_email);
54
```

Here is where it differs, instead of calling UTL_SMTP.RCPT once; it uses the address_email function to call it (potentially) many times, building the To: and CC: list for us as well. It builds the BCC: list but we won't actually send that (we don't want the recipients to see that list!)

```
55        l_to_list  := address_email( 'To: ', p_to );
56        l_cc_list  := address_email( 'Cc: ', p_cc );
57        l_bcc_list := address_email( 'Bcc: ', p_bcc );
58
```

Now, we use the OPEN_DATA call to start sending the body of the e-mail. The code on lines 61 through to 68 generates the header section of data. Line 69 sends the body of the e-mail (the contents of the e-mail) and line 70 terminates the e-mail for us.

```
59        utl_smtp.open_data(g_mail_conn );
60
61        writeData( 'Date: ' || l_date );
62        writeData( 'From: ' || nvl( p_from, p_sender_email ) );
63        writeData( 'Subject: ' || nvl( p_subject, '(no subject)' ) );
64
65        writeData( l_to_list );
66        writeData( l_cc_list );
67
68        utl_smtp.write_data( g_mail_conn, '' || g_crlf );
69        utl_smtp.write_data(g_mail_conn, p_body );
70        utl_smtp.close_data(g_mail_conn );
71        utl_smtp.quit(g_mail_conn);
72    end;
73
74
75  end;
76  /
Package body created.
```

Now I can test this API like this:

```
tkyte@TKYTE816> begin
  2        mail_pkg.send
  3        ( p_sender_email => 'me@acme.com',
  4          p_from => 'Oracle Database Account <me@acme.com>',
  5          p_to => mail_pkg.array( 'you@acme.com',' us@acme.com ' ),
  6          p_cc => mail_pkg.array( ' them@acme.com ' ),
  7          p_bcc => mail_pkg.array( 'noone@dev.null' ),
  8          p_subject => 'This is a subject',
  9          p_body => 'Hello Tom, this is the mail you need' );
 10  end;
 11  /

PL/SQL procedure successfully completed.
```

And that call is exactly what generated the ASCII text:

```
Date: 13 May 01 12:33:22
From: Oracle Database Account <me@acme.com>
Subject: This is a subject
To: you@acme.com, us@acme.com
Cc: them@acme.com

Hello Tom, this is the mail you need
```

We saw above, this is what gets sent to all of these recipients, including `noone@dev.null`, although we cannot see that recipient since it was on the BCC: line.

This covers most of the typical uses of the `UTL_SMTP` supplied package. Earlier I did say it is capable of sending e-mail with attachments and such but this would require an inordinate amount of effort on our part. We would have to:

❑   Learn how to format a multi-part mime encoded document, no small feat!

❑   Encode binary data using Base-64 (or use some equivalent encoding technique such as `uuencoding`, `binhex`, and so on).

That would be (conservatively) a couple of hundred, if not thousands of lines of PL/SQL code. Rather then do this; I will suggest that you use the already written and very robust `JavaMail` API as described below.

Loading and using the JavaMail API

In order to use the `UTL_SMTP` package, you must already have a Java enabled database in Oracle 8i. This is because `UTL_SMTP` relies on `UTL_TCP` and `UTL_TCP` which in turn are built on Java functions. (Remember, if you don't have a Java enabled database you can use `UTL_HTTP` (see that section) to send simple e-mails). So, if you are able to use `UTL_SMTP`, we can go to the Sun website and download their `JavaMail` API. This will give us the ability to send much more complicated e-mails from the database; including attachments. The following is based on work performed by a co-worker of mine, Mark Piermarini who helps me out with lots of my Java issues.

If you go to http://java.sun.com/products/javamail/index.html, you'll be able to download their `JavaMail` API. The download you get will consist of a couple of hundred files; only one of which we are interested in. After you download the `JavaMail` API – make sure also to get their the `JavaBeansTM Activation Framework` extension or JAF (`javax.activation`). This is needed to run the `JavaMail` API package.

After you have downloaded these two sets of files – you will need to extract `mail.jar` from the `JavaMail` APIdownload and `activation.jar` from the JAF download. This is all you will need from this – feel free to read through the documentation, there is a lot of functionality in there we are not using, we are just using the 'send an e-mail' part of the API. The API includes functions for receiving mail as well from IMAP, POP, and other sources.

We will need to load the `mail.jar` and `activation.jar` into the database using `loadjava` but before we can do that we must repackage them. These jar files are compressed in a format that is not understood by the database byte code interpreter. You need to 'unjar' and 'rejar' them without compression *or* use a tool such as WinZip to 'rejar' them into a zip file. What I did on Windows 2000 was:

1. Used WinZip to extract the contents of `mail.jar` into my c:\temp\mail directory

2. Used WinZip to create a new archive c:\temp\mail8i.zip

3. Put the contents of c:\temp\mail*.* including subdirectories into this new archive

I did the same thing for `activation.jar` – only replacing mail with activation in the above steps. Now we are ready to load these zip (or jar files, whatever you named them) into the database. These files need to be loaded into the database using the `SYS` user since they have 'protected' Java packages that regular users cannot upload. We will use the `loadjava` commands:

```
loadjava -u sys/manager -o -r -v -f -noverify -synonym -g public activation8i.zip
loadjava -u sys/manager -o -r -v -f -noverify -synonym -g public mail8i.zip
```

Where:

❑ **-u sys/manager** – is the user ID and password for your `SYS` account. Some of the packages are protected and must be loaded as `SYS`.

❑ **-o** – is shorthand for `-oci8`, I am using the `oci8` driver. You could use the `thin` driver as well but you'll need to modify the command to do so

❑ **-r** – is short for `-resolve`. This will resolve all external references in the loaded classes helping to verify that the loaded java classes will be able to function after we load them

❑ **-v** – is short for `-verbose`. This gives us something to do while `loadjava` is running. We can see it work through each step of its process.

❑ **-f** – is short for `-force`. This isn't necessary on the first load but is OK to use. If you try a `loadjava` and hit an error, you can correct it, and reload – then you would either need to use the `dropjava` command to drop the jar file from the database or use `-force`. Using `-force` just makes it easier for us.

❑ **-noverify** – does not attempt to verify the bytecode. You must be granted `oracle.aurora.security.JServerPermission`(Verifier) to execute this option. In addition, this option must be used in conjunction with `-r`. `SYS` has this privilege. This is needed because the bytecode verifier will flag some issues with the `mail.jar` file and this works around that issue.

❑ **-synonym** – creates public synonyms for these classes. Since we will *not* install the mail java code we write as `SYS`, this allows us to 'see' the `SYS` loaded java classes.

❑ **-g public** – grants execute on these loaded classes to `PUBLIC`. If this is not desirable, change the `-g` to be just the user you want to create the 'send mail' routines in, for example `-g UTILITY_ACCT`.

You can find out more about `loadjava` and the above options in the *Oracle8i Java Developers Guide*.

After these packages are loaded, we are ready to create a Java stored procedure to actually send the mail. This procedure will act as a thin layer on top of the `JavaMail` API and will let us ultimately write a PL/SQL binding layer with the following spec:

```
tkyte@TKYTE816> desc send
FUNCTION send RETURNS NUMBER
 Argument Name                        Type                     In/Out Default?
 ------------------------------       --------------------     ------ --------
 P_FROM                               VARCHAR2                 IN
 P_TO                                 VARCHAR2                 IN
 P_CC                                 VARCHAR2                 IN
 P_BCC                                VARCHAR2                 IN
 P_SUBJECT                            VARCHAR2                 IN
 P_BODY                               VARCHAR2                 IN
 P_SMTP_HOST                          VARCHAR2                 IN
 P_ATTACHMENT_DATA                    BLOB                     IN
 P_ATTACHMENT_TYPE                    VARCHAR2                 IN
 P_ATTACHMENT_FILE_NAME               VARCHAR2                 IN
```

This function will give us the ability to use CC's and BCC's and send an attachment. It is left as an exercise for the reader to implement passing arrays of BLOBs or overloading this to support CLOB or BFILE types for attachments as well.

The Java stored procedure we will create follows. It uses the basic functionality of the JavaMail API class and is relatively straightforward. Again, we are not going into all of the uses of the JavaMail API (that could be a book in itself), just the basics here. The mail class below has a single method; send. This is the method we will use to send a message. As it is implemented, it returns the number 1 if it is successful in sending the mail and a 0 otherwise. This implementation is very basic – it could be much more sophisticated, providing support for many attachment types (CLOBs, BFILEs, LONGs, and so on). It could also be modified to report back to the caller the exact error received from SMTP such as invalid recipient, no transport.

```
tkyte@TKYTE816> create or replace and compile
  2  java source named "mail"
  3  as
  4  import java.io.*;
  5  import java.sql.*;
  6  import java.util.Properties;
  7  import java.util.Date;
  8  import javax.activation.*;
  9  import javax.mail.*;
 10  import javax.mail.internet.*;
 11  import oracle.jdbc.driver.*;
 12  import oracle.sql.*;
 13
 14  public class mail
 15  {
 16    static String dftMime = "application/octet-stream";
 17    static String dftName = "filename.dat";
 18
 19    public static oracle.sql.NUMBER
 20                     send(String from,
 21                          String to,
 22                          String cc,
 23                          String bcc,
 24                          String subject,
 25                          String body,
 26                          String SMTPHost,
 27                          oracle.sql.BLOB attachmentData,
 28                          String attachmentType,
 29                          String attachmentFileName)
```

The above argument list matches up with the SQL call specification we outlined above – the arguments are mostly self-explanatory. The two that need some clarification are the `attachmentType` and the `attachmentFileName`. The `attachmentType` should be a MIME (Multi-purpose Internet Mail Extensions) type – as you may be familiar with, from HTML documents. The MIME type of a GIF image for example is `image/gif`, the mime type of a plain text document would be `text/plain`, and a HTML attachment would be `text/html`. The `attachmentFileName` in this example is *not* the name of an existing OS file that would be attached but rather the filename of the attachment in the e-mail itself – what the recipient of this e-mail will see the name of the attachment as. The actual attachment is the `oracle.sql.BLOB` that is sent to this routine. Now, onto the body of the code. We begin by setting the session property `mail.smtp.host` to the name of the SMTP host the caller sent to us – the `JavaMail` API reads this value when deciding what SMTP server to connect to:

```
30    {
31      int rc = 0;
32
33      try
34      {
35        Properties props = System.getProperties();
36        props.put("mail.smtp.host", SMTPHost);
37        Message msg =
38          new MimeMessage(Session.getDefaultInstance(props, null));
39
```

Next, we set up the e-mail headers. This part tells the `JavaMail` API who the message is from, who to send it to, who to send a carbon copy (CC) or blind carbon copy (BCC), what the subject of the e-mail is and what date should be associated with the e-mail:

```
40        msg.setFrom(new InternetAddress(from));
41
42        if (to != null && to.length() > 0)
43          msg.setRecipients(Message.RecipientType.TO,
44                            InternetAddress.parse(to, false));
45
46        if (cc != null && cc.length() > 0)
47          msg.setRecipients(Message.RecipientType.CC,
48                            InternetAddress.parse(cc, false));
49
50        if (bcc != null && bcc.length() > 0)
51          msg.setRecipients(Message.RecipientType.BCC,
52                            InternetAddress.parse(bcc, false));
53
54        if ( subject != null && subject.length() > 0 )
55            msg.setSubject(subject);
56        else msg.setSubject("(no subject)");
57
58        msg.setSentDate(new Date());
59
```

Next, we use one of two methods to send an e-mail. If the `attachmentData` argument is not Null, then we will MIME encode the e-mail – a standard that supports the sending of attachments and other multi-part documents. We do this by setting up multiple MIME body parts – in this case two of them, one for the body of the e-mail (the text) and the other for the attachment itself. Lines 76 through 78 need a little additional explanation. They are how we can send an e-mail via a BLOB. The `JavaMail` API doesn't understand the `oracle.sql.BLOB` type natively (it is after all a generic API). In order to send the BLOB attachment, we must provide a method for the JavaMail API to get at the BLOB data. We accomplish that by creating our own `DataHandler` – a class with an interface that the `JavaMail` API understands how to call in order to get data to populate the attachment. This class (`BLOBDataHandler`) is implemented by us as a nested class below.

1239

```
60          if (attachmentData != null)
61          {
62            MimeBodyPart mbp1 = new MimeBodyPart();
63            mbp1.setText((body != null ? body : ""));
64            mbp1.setDisposition(Part.INLINE);
65
66            MimeBodyPart mbp2 = new MimeBodyPart();
67            String type =
68                (attachmentType != null ? attachmentType : dftMime);
69
70            String fileName = (attachmentFileName != null ?
71                            attachmentFileName : dftName);
72
73            mbp2.setDisposition(Part.ATTACHMENT);
74            mbp2.setFileName(fileName);
75
76            mbp2.setDataHandler(new
77                DataHandler(new BLOBDataSource(attachmentData, type))
78            );
79
80            MimeMultipart mp = new MimeMultipart();
81            mp.addBodyPart(mbp1);
82            mp.addBodyPart(mbp2);
83            msg.setContent(mp);
84          }
```

If the e-mail does not have an attachment – setting the body of the e-mail is accomplished very simply via the single call to `setText`:

```
85          else
86          {
87            msg.setText((body != null ? body : ""));
88          }
89          Transport.send(msg);
90          rc = 1;
91       } catch (Exception e)
92       {
93          e.printStackTrace();
94          rc = 0;
95       } finally
96       {
97          return new oracle.sql.NUMBER(rc);
98       }
99    }
100
```

Now for our nested class `BLOBDataSource`. It simply provides a generic interface for the `JavaMail` API to access our `oracle.sql.BLOB` type. It is very straightforward in its implementation:

```
101    // Nested class that implements a DataSource.
102    static class BLOBDataSource implements DataSource
103    {
104      private BLOB   data;
105      private String type;
106
107    BLOBDataSource(BLOB data, String type)
```

```
108      {
109          this.type = type;
110          this.data = data;
111      }
112
113      public InputStream getInputStream() throws IOException
114      {
115        try
116        {
117          if(data == null)
118            throw new IOException("No data.");
119
120          return data.getBinaryStream();
121        } catch(SQLException e)
122        {
123          throw new
124          IOException("Cannot get binary input stream from BLOB.");
125        }
126      }
127
128      public OutputStream getOutputStream() throws IOException
129      {
130        throw new IOException("Cannot do this.");
131      }
132
133      public String getContentType()
134      {
135        return type;
136      }
137
138      public String getName()
139      {
140        return "BLOBDataSource";
141      }
142    }
143  }
144  /

Java created.
```

Now that we have the Java class created for PL/SQL to bind to, we need to create that binding routine to map the PL/SQL types to their Java types and to bind the PL/SQL routine to this Java class. This is simply done by the following:

```
tkyte@TKYTE816> create or replace function send(
  2      p_from                 in varchar2,
  3      p_to                   in varchar2,
  4      p_cc                   in varchar2,
  5      p_bcc                  in varchar2,
  6      p_subject              in varchar2,
  7      p_body                 in varchar2,
  8      p_smtp_host            in varchar2,
  9      p_attachment_data      in blob,
 10      p_attachment_type      in varchar2,
```

```
11        p_attachment_file_name  in varchar2) return number
12   as
13   language java name 'mail.send( java.lang.String,
14                                  java.lang.String,
15                                  java.lang.String,
16                                  java.lang.String,
17                                  java.lang.String,
18                                  java.lang.String,
19                                  java.lang.String,
20                                  oracle.sql.BLOB,
21                                  java.lang.String,
22                                  java.lang.String
23                                ) return oracle.sql.NUMBER';
24   /

Function created.
```

Now, the very last thing we must do before using this is to ensure our user (the owner of the above `mail` class and `send` stored procedure) has sufficient privileges to execute the routine. These would be the following:

```
sys@TKYTE816> begin
 2      dbms_java.grant_permission(
 3          grantee => 'USER',
 4          permission_type => 'java.util.PropertyPermission',
 5          permission_name => '*',
 6          permission_action => 'read,write'
 7      );
 8      dbms_java.grant_permission(
 9          grantee => 'USER',
10          permission_type => 'java.net.SocketPermission',
11          permission_name => '*',
12          permission_action => 'connect,resolve'
13      );
14   end;
15   /

PL/SQL procedure successfully completed.
```

Note that in the grant on `java.net.SocketPermission`, I used a wildcard in the `permission_name`. This allows USER to connect to and resolve *any* host. Technically, we could put in there just the name of the SMTP server we will be using. This would be the minimal grant we need. It is needed in order to resolve the hostname of our SMTP host and then connect to it. The other permission, `java.util.PropertyPermission`, is needed in order to set the `mail.smtp.host` in our sessions properties.

Now we are ready to test. I reused some code from the DBMS_LOB section where we had a routine `load_a_file`. I modified that and the DEMO table to have a BLOB column instead of a CLOB and loaded the `mail8i.zip` file we loaded in as a class into this demo table. Now I can use the following PL/SQL block to send it to myself as an attachment in an e-mail from the database:

```
tkyte@TKYTE816> set serveroutput on size 1000000
tkyte@TKYTE816> exec dbms_java.set_output( 1000000 )

tkyte@TKYTE816> declare
  2      ret_code number;
  3   begin
  4      for i in (select theBlob from demo )
  5      loop
  6        ret_code := send(
  7                         p_from => 'me@acme.com',
  8                         p_to => 'you@acme.com',
  9                         p_cc => NULL,
 10                         p_bcc => NULL,
 11                         p_subject => 'Use the attached Zip file',
 12                         p_body => 'to send email with attachments....',
 13                         p_smtp_host => 'yourserver.acme.com',
 14                         p_attachment_data => i.theBlob,
 15                         p_attachment_type => 'application/winzip',
 16                         p_attachment_file_name => 'mail8i.zip');
 17         if ret_code = 1 then
 18            dbms_output.put_line ('Successfully sent message...');
 19         else
 20            dbms_output.put_line ('Failed to send message...');
 21         end if;
 22      end loop;
 23   end;
 24   /
Successfully sent message...

PL/SQL procedure successfully completed.
```

You definitely want to set `serverouput on` and call the `DBMS_JAVA.SET_OUTPUT` routine when testing this. This is because the exception is being printed by the Java stored procedure to `System.out` and by default that will go into a trace file on the server. If you want to see any errors in your SQL*PLUS session, you need to make these two settings. It will be very useful for debugging purposes!

Summary

In this section, we briefly reviewed the existing UTL_SMTP package. Here we have seen how to send e-mails to multiple recipients with a custom `From:` and `Subject:` header. This should satisfy most people's needs for sending e-mail from the database. UTL_SMTP is good for sending simple text only e-mails but sending attachments or complex e-mails is beyond its capabilities (unless you want to encode the entire e-mail yourself). In the cases where you need this additional sophistication, we looked at how to use the JavaMail API. Since Sun has graciously supplied us with all of the logic we would need to do this – we'll just reuse their code. This section has demonstrated not only how to send mail but a powerful side effect of having Java as an alternative stored procedure language. Now you can use the entire set of public domain code and class libraries that are available. We can enable the database to do many things that were not previously possible. In fact, the PL/SQL developers at Oracle used the same technique themselves. UTL_TCP is built on Java itself in Oracle 8i.

UTL_TCP

Oracle 8.1.6 introduced for the first time, the UTL_TCP package. This package allows PL/SQL to open a network socket connection over TCP/IP to any server accepting connections. Assuming you know the protocol of a server, you can now 'talk' to it from PL/SQL. For example, given that I know HTTP (**H**yper **T**ext **T**ransfer **P**rotocol), I can code in UTL_TCP the following:

```
test_jsock@DEV816> DECLARE
    2     c utl_tcp.connection; -- TCP/IP connection to the web server
    3     n number;
    4     buffer varchar2(255);
    5  BEGIN
    6     c := utl_tcp.open_connection('proxy-server', 80);
    7     n := utl_tcp.write_line(c, 'GET http://www.apress.com/ HTTP/1.0');
    8     n := utl_tcp.write_line(c);
    9     BEGIN
   10       LOOP
   11           n:=utl_tcp.read_text( c, buffer, 255 );
   12           dbms_output.put_line( buffer );
   13       END LOOP;
   14     EXCEPTION
   15       WHEN utl_tcp.end_of_input THEN
   16         NULL; -- end of input
   17     end;
   18     utl_tcp.close_connection(c);
   19  END;
   20  /
HTTP/1.1 200 OK
Date: Tue, 30 Jan 2001 11:33:50 GMT
Server: Apache/1.3.9 (Unix) mod_perl/1.21
ApacheJServ/1.1
Content-Type: text/html

<head>
<title>Oracle
Corporation</title>
```

This lets me open a connection to a server, in this case a proxy server named `proxy-server`. It lets me get through our firewall to the outside Internet. This happens on line 6. I then request a web page on lines 7 and 8. On lines 10 through to 13, we receive the contents of the web page, including the all-important HTTP headers (something `UTL_HTTP`, another supplied package, won't share with us) and print it. When `UTL_TCP` throws the `UTL_TCP.END_OF_INPUT` exception, we are done, and we break out of the loop. We then close our connection and that's it.

This simple example demonstrates a majority of the functionality found in the `UTL_TCP` package. We didn't see functions such as `AVAILABLE`, which tells us if any data is ready to be received. We skipped `FLUSH`, which causes any buffered output to be transmitted (we didn't use buffering, hence did not need this call). Likewise, we did not use every variation of `READ`, `WRITE`, and `GET` to put and get data on the socket, but the example above shows how to use `UTL_TCP` fairly completely.

The one thing I don't necessarily like about the above is the speed at which it runs. It is in my experience that `UTL_TCP`, while functional, is not as high performing as it could be in this release (Oracle 8i). In Oracle 8.1.7.1, this performance issue is fixed (bug #1570972 corrects this issue).

So, how slow is slow? The above code, to retrieve a 16 KB document, takes anywhere from four to ten seconds, depending on platform. This is especially bad considering the native `UTL_HTTP` function can do the same operation with a sub-second response time. Unfortunately, `UTL_HTTP` doesn't permit access to cookies, HTTP headers, binary data, basic authentication, and the like, so using an alternative is many times useful. I think we can do better. To this end, we will implement our own `UTL_TCP` package. However, we will use the Object Type metaphor we discussed in Chapter 20 on *Using Object Relational Features*. What we will do is to implement a `SocketType` in PL/SQL with some of the underlying 'guts' in Java. In the `UTL_HTTP` section, we put this `SocketType` we created to use in building a better `UTL_HTTP` package for ourselves as well. Since our functionality will be modeled after the functionality available in the `UTL_TCP` package, when Oracle9i is released with native and faster `UTL_TCP` support, we can easily re-implement our type body using the real `UTL_TCP` package, and stop using our Java-supported one.

The SocketType

Our `SocketType` Object Type will use the following specification:

```
tkyte@TKYTE816> create or replace type SocketType
  2  as object
  3  (
  4      -- 'Private data', rather than you
  5      -- passing a context to each procedure, like you
  6      -- do with UTL_FILE.
  7      g_sock          number,
  8
  9      -- A function to return a CRLF. Just a convenience.
 10      static function crlf return varchar2,
 11
 12      -- Procedures to send data over a socket.
 13      member procedure send( p_data in varchar2 ),
 14      member procedure send( p_data in clob ),
 15
 16      member procedure send_raw( p_data in raw ),
 17      member procedure send_raw( p_data in blob ),
```

```
18
19        -- Functions to receive data from a socket. These return
20        -- Null on eof. They will block waiting for data. If
21        -- this is not desirable, use PEEK below to see if there
22        -- is any data to read.
23        member function recv return varchar2,
24        member function recv_raw return raw,
25
26        -- Convienence function. Reads data until a CRLF is found.
27        -- Can strip the CRLF if you like (or not, by default).
28        member function getline( p_remove_crlf in boolean default FALSE )
29              return varchar2,
30
31        -- Procedures to connect to a host and disconnect from a host.
32        -- It is important to disconnect, else you will leak resources
33        -- and eventually will not be able to connect.
34        member procedure initiate_connection( p_hostname in varchar2,
35                                              p_portno   in number ),
36        member procedure close_connection,
37
38        -- Function to tell you how many bytes (at least) might be
39        -- ready to be read.
40        member function peek return number
41    );
42    /

Type created.
```

This set of functionality is pretty much modeled after the UTL_TCP package, and provides much of the same interface. In fact, it could be implemented on top of that package if you wanted. We are going to implement it on top of a different package however, one which I call the SIMPLE_TCP_CLIENT. This is a ordinary PL/SQL package that the SocketType will be built on. This is really our specification of a UTL_TCP package:

```
tkyte@TKYTE816> CREATE OR REPLACE PACKAGE simple_tcp_client
 2    as
 3        -- A function to connect to a host. Returns a 'socket',
 4        -- which is really just a number.
 5        function connect_to( p_hostname in  varchar2,
 6                             p_portno   in  number ) return number;
 7
 8        -- Send data. We only know how to send RAW data here. Callers
 9        -- must cast VARCHAR2 data to RAW. At the lowest level, all
10        -- data on a socket is really just 'bytes'.
11
12        procedure send( p_sock    in  number,
13                        p_data    in  raw );
14
15        -- recv will receive data.
16        -- If maxlength is -1, we try for 4k of data. If maxlength
17        -- is set to anything OTHER than -1, we attempt to
18        -- read up to the length of p_data bytes. In other words,
19        -- I restrict the receives to 4k unless otherwise told not to.
20        procedure recv( p_sock    in  number,
21                        p_data    out raw,
```

```
22                      p_maxlength in     number default -1 );
23
24        -- Gets a line of data from the input socket. That is, data
25        -- up to a \n.
26        procedure getline( p_sock          in number,
27                           p_data          out raw );
28
29
30        -- Disconnects from a server you have connected to.
31        procedure disconnect( p_sock      in number );
32
33        -- Gets the server time in GMT in the format yyyyMMdd HHmmss z
34        procedure get_gmt( p_gmt out varchar2 );
35
36        -- Gets the server's timezone. Useful for some Internet protocols.
37        procedure get_timezone( p_timezone   out varchar2 );
38
39        -- Gets the hostname of the server you are running on. Again,
40        -- useful for some Internet protocols.
41        procedure get_hostname( p_hostname   out varchar2 );
42
43        -- Returns the number of bytes available to be read.
44        function peek( p_sock in number ) return number;
45
46        -- base64 encodes a RAW. Useful for sending e-mail
47        -- attachments or doing HTTP which needs the user/password
48        -- to be obscured using base64 encoding.
49        procedure b64encode( p_data in raw, p_result out varchar2 );
50   end;
51   /

Package created.
```

Now, as none of these functions can actually be written in PL/SQL, we will implement them in Java instead. The Java for doing this is surprisingly small. The entire script is only 94 lines long. We are using the native `Socket` class for Java, and will maintain a small array of them, allowing PL/SQL to have up to ten connections open simultaneously. If you would like more than ten, just make the `socketUsed` array larger in the code below. I've tried to keep this as simple, and as small as possible, preferring to do the bulk of any work in PL/SQL. I'll present the small class we need, and then comment on it:

```
tkyte@TKYTE816> set define off

tkyte@TKYTE816> CREATE or replace and compile JAVA SOURCE
  2   NAMED "jsock"
  3   AS
  4   import java.net.*;
  5   import java.io.*;
  6   import java.util.*;
  7   import java.text.*;
  8   import sun.misc.*;
  9
 10   public class jsock
 11   {
 12   static int             socketUsed[] = { 0,0,0,0,0,0,0,0,0,0 };
 13   static Socket          sockets[] = new Socket[socketUsed.length];
 14   static DateFormat      tzDateFormat = new SimpleDateFormat( "z" );
 15   static DateFormat      gmtDateFormat =
 16                          new SimpleDateFormat( "yyyyMMdd HHmmss z" );
 17   static BASE64Encoder encoder = new BASE64Encoder();
 18
```

This class has some static variables – the two arrays, socketUsed and sockets are the main ones. When returns are called from PL/SQL, we must return to it something it can send to us on subsequent calls, to identify the socket connection it wants to use. We cannot return the Java Socket class to PL/SQL, so I am using an array in which to store them, and will return to PL/SQL an index into that array. If you look at the java_connect_to method, it looks in the socketsUsed array for an empty slot, and allocates this to the connection. That index into socketsUsed is what PL/SQL will see. We use this in the remaining sockets routines to access the actual Java class that represents a socket.

The other static variables are there for reasons of performance. I needed some date format objects, and rather than NEW them each time you call java_get_gmt or java_get_timezone, I allocate them once, and just reuse them. Lastly is the base 64 encoder object. For the same reason I allocate the date formatter objects, I allocate the encoder.

Now for the routine that connects over TCP/IP, to a server. This logic loops over the socketUsed array looking for an empty slot (where socketUsed[I] is not set to 1). If it finds one, it uses the Java Socket class to create a connection to the host/port combination that was passed in, and sets the socketUsed flag for the array slot to 1. It then returns a -1 on error (no empty slots), or a non-negative number upon success:

```
19   static public int java_connect_to( String p_hostname, int p_portno )
20   throws java.io.IOException
21   {
22   int     i;
23
24       for( i = 0; i < socketUsed.length && socketUsed[i] == 1; i++ );
25       if ( i < socketUsed.length )
26       {
27           sockets[i] = new Socket( p_hostname, p_portno );
28           socketUsed[i] = 1;
29       }
30       return i<socketUsed.length?i:-1;
31   }
32
33
```

The next routines are the two most frequently called Java routines. They are responsible for sending and receiving data on a connected TCP/IP socket. The java_send_data routine is straightforward – it simply gets the output stream associated with the socket, and writes the data. The java_recv_data is slightly more complex. It uses OUT parameters, hence the use of int[] p_length for example, in order to return data. This routine inspects the length that was sent in by the caller, and if the length was -1, it will allocate a 4 KB buffer to read into, else it will allocate a buffer of the size specified. It will then try to read that much data from the socket. The actual amount of data read (which will be less than or equal to the amount requested) is placed in p_length as a return value:

```
34   static public void java_send_data( int p_sock, byte[] p_data )
35   throws java.io.IOException
36   {
37       (sockets[p_sock].getOutputStream()).write( p_data );
38   }
39
40   static public void java_recv_data( int p_sock,
```

```
41                                              byte[][] p_data, int[] p_length)
42   throws java.io.IOException
43   {
44       p_data[0] = new byte[p_length[0] == -1 ? 4096:p_length[0] ];
45       p_length[0] = (sockets[p_sock].getInputStream()).read( p_data[0] );
46   }
47
```

java_getline is a convenience function. Many Internet protocols respond to operations 'a line at a time', and being able to get a simple line of text is very handy. For example, the headers sent back in the HTTP protocol are simply lines of ASCII text. This routine works by using the DataInputStream.readLine method, and if a line of text is read in, it will return it (putting the new line, which readLine strips off, back on). Otherwise, the data will be returned as Null:

```
48   static public void java_getline( int p_sock, String[] p_data )
49   throws java.io.IOException
50   {
51       DataInputStream d =
52           new DataInputStream((sockets[p_sock].getInputStream()));
53       p_data[0] = d.readLine();
54       if ( p_data[0] != null ) p_data[0] += "\n";
55   }
56
```

java_disconnect is very straightforward as well. It simply sets the socketUsed array flag back to zero, indicating we can reuse this slot in the array, and closes the socket down for us:

```
57   static public void java_disconnect( int p_sock )
58   throws java.io.IOException
59   {
60       socketUsed[p_sock] = 0;
61       (sockets[p_sock]).close();
62   }
63
```

The java_peek_sock routine is used to see if data on a socket is available to be read. This is useful for times when the client does not want to block on a receive of data. If you look to see if anything is available, you can tell if a receive will block, or return right away:

```
64   static public int java_peek_sock( int p_sock )
65   throws java.io.IOException
66   {
67       return (sockets[p_sock].getInputStream()).available();
68   }
69
```

Now we have our two time functions. java_get_timezone is used to return the time zone of the database server. This is particularly useful if you need to convert an Oracle DATE from one time zone to another using the NEW_TIME built-in function, or if you just need know the time zone in which the server is operating. The second function, java_get_gmt, is useful for getting the server's current date and time in GMT (Greenwich Mean Time):

```
70   static public void java_get_timezone( String[] p_timezone )
71   {
72        tzDateFormat.setTimeZone( TimeZone.getDefault() );
73        p_timezone[0] = tzDateFormat.format(new Date());
74   }
75
76
77   static public void java_get_gmt( String[] p_gmt )
78   {
79        gmtDateFormat.setTimeZone( TimeZone.getTimeZone("GMT") );
80        p_gmt[0] = gmtDateFormat.format(new Date());
81   }
82
```

The `b64encode` routine will base 64 encode a string of data. Base 64 encoding is an Internet-standard method of encoding arbitrary data into a 7bit ASCII format, suitable for transmission. We will use this function in particular when implementing our HTTP package, as it will support basic authentication (used by many web sites that require you to log in via a username and password).

```
83   static public void b64encode( byte[] p_data, String[] p_b64data )
84   {
85        p_b64data[0] = encoder.encode( p_data );
86   }
87
```

The last routine in this class simply returns the hostname of the database server. Some Internet protocols request that you transmit this information (for example, SMTP – simple mail transfer protocol):

```
88   static public void java_get_hostname( String[] p_hostname )
89   throws java.net.UnknownHostException
90   {
91        p_hostname[0] = (InetAddress.getLocalHost()).getHostName();
92   }
93
94   }
95   /
```

```
Java created.
```

The Java methods themselves are rather straightforward. If you recall from Chapter 19 on *Java Stored Procedures*, in order to get OUT parameters, we must send, what appears to be an array, to Java. Hence, most of the procedures above take the form of:

```
40   static public void java_recv_data( int p_sock,
41                                       byte[][] p_data, int[] p_length)
```

This allows me to return a value in `p_data`, and return a value in `p_length`. Now that we have our Java class, we are ready to build our package body for the `SIMPLE_TCP_CLIENT` package. It consists almost entirely of bindings to Java:

```
tkyte@TKYTE816> CREATE OR REPLACE PACKAGE BODY simple_tcp_client
  2  as
  3
  4      function connect_to( p_hostname in  varchar2,
  5                           p_portno   in  number ) return number
  6      as language java
  7      name 'jsock.java_connect_to( java.lang.String, int ) return int';
  8
  9
 10      procedure send( p_sock in number, p_data in raw )
 11      as language java
 12      name 'jsock.java_send_data( int, byte[] )';
 13
 14      procedure recv_i ( p_sock      in number,
 15                         p_data          out raw,
 16                         p_maxlength in out number )
 17      as language java
 18      name 'jsock.java_recv_data( int, byte[][], int[] )';
 19
 20      procedure recv( p_sock       in   number,
 21                      p_data           out  raw,
 22                      p_maxlength in   number default -1 )
 23      is
 24          l_maxlength    number default p_maxlength;
 25      begin
 26          recv_i( p_sock, p_data, l_maxlength );
 27          if ( l_maxlength <> -1 )
 28          then
 29              p_data := utl_raw.substr( p_data, 1, l_maxlength );
 30          else
 31              p_data := NULL;
 32          end if;
 33      end;
```

Here, I have a RECV_I and a RECV procedure. RECV_I is a private procedure (the _I stands for internal), not directly callable out of this package. It is called by RECV. RECV provides a 'friendly' internal on top of RECV_I – it checks to see if any data was read from the socket and if so, it sets the length correctly. If you recall from the Java code above, we allocated a fixed size buffer in the RECV routine, and read *up to* that many bytes from the socket. We need to resize our buffer to be exactly that size here, and this is the purpose of the UTL_RAW.SUBSTR function. Otherwise, if no data was read, we simply return Null.

```
 34
 35      procedure getline_i( p_sock      in number,
 36                           p_data          out varchar2 )
 37      as language java
 38      name 'jsock.java_getline( int, java.lang.String[] )';
 39
 40      procedure getline( p_sock      in number,
 41                         p_data          out raw )
 42      as
 43          l_data     long;
 44      begin
 45          getline_i( p_sock, l_data );
 46          p_data := utl_raw.cast_to_raw( l_data );
 47      end getline;
```

Again, much like RECV_I/RECV above, GETLINE_I is an internal function called only by GETLINE. The external PL/SQL interface exposes all data as the RAW type, and the GETLINE function here simply converts the VARCHAR2 data into a RAW for us.

```
48
49      procedure disconnect( p_sock      in number )
50      as language java
51      name 'jsock.java_disconnect( int )';
52
53      procedure get_gmt( p_gmt    out varchar2 )
54      as language java
55      name 'jsock.java_get_gmt( java.lang.String[] )';
56
57      procedure get_timezone( p_timezone    out varchar2 )
58      as language java
59      name 'jsock.java_get_timezone( java.lang.String[] )';
60
61      procedure get_hostname( p_hostname    out varchar2 )
62      as language java
63      name 'jsock.java_get_hostname( java.lang.String[] )';
64
65      function peek( p_sock   in  number ) return number
66      as language java
67      name 'jsock.java_peek_sock( int ) return int';
68
69      procedure b64encode( p_data in raw, p_result out varchar2 )
70      as language java
71      name 'jsock.b64encode( byte[], java.lang.String[] )';
72   end;
73   /

Package body created.
```

We are now ready to test some of our functions to see that they are installed, and actually work:

```
tkyte@TKYTE816> declare
  2      l_hostname varchar2(255);
  3      l_gmt      varchar2(255);
  4      l_tz       varchar2(255);
  5  begin
  6      simple_tcp_client.get_hostname( l_hostname );
  7      simple_tcp_client.get_gmt( l_gmt );
  8      simple_tcp_client.get_timezone( l_tz );
  9
 10      dbms_output.put_line( 'hostname ' || l_hostname );
 11      dbms_output.put_line( 'gmt time ' || l_gmt );
 12      dbms_output.put_line( 'timezone ' || l_tz );
 13  end;
 14  /
hostname tkyte-dell
gmt time 20010131 213415 GMT
timezone EST

PL/SQL procedure successfully completed.
```

An important point for running the TCP/IP components of this package is that we need special permission to use TCP/IP in the database. For more information on the DBMS_JAVA package and privileges associated with Java, please see the DBMS_JAVA section in this appendix. In this case, we specifically we need to execute:

```
sys@TKYTE816> begin
  2    dbms_java.grant_permission(
  3    grantee => 'TKYTE',
  4    permission_type => 'java.net.SocketPermission',
  5    permission_name => '*',
  6    permission_action => 'connect,resolve' );
  7    end;
  8    /

PL/SQL procedure successfully completed.
```

Refer to the section on DBMS_JAVA for more details on what, and how, this procedure works. In a nutshell, it allows the user TKYTE to create connections and resolve hostnames to IP addresses to any host (that's the '*' above). If you are using Oracle 8.1.5, you will not have the DBMS_JAVA package. Rather, in this version you would grant the JAVASYSPRIV to the owner of jsock. You should be aware that the JAVASYSPRIV is a very 'broad' privilege. Whereas DBMS_JAVA.GRANT_PERMISSION is very granular, JAVASYSPRIV is very broad, and conveys a lot of privileges at once. Now that I have this permission, we are ready to implement and test our SocketType, similar to the way we tested in which we tested UTL_TCP initially. Here is the body of SocketType. The type body contains very little actual code, and is mostly a layer on the SIMPLE_TCP_CLIENT package we just created. It hides the 'socket' from the caller:

```
tkyte@TKYTE816> create or replace type body SocketType
  2    as
  3
  4    static function crlf return varchar2
  5    is
  6    begin
  7        return chr(13)||chr(10);
  8    end;
  9
 10    member function peek return number
 11    is
 12    begin
 13        return simple_tcp_client.peek( g_sock );
 14    end;
 15
 16
 17    member procedure send( p_data in varchar2 )
 18    is
 19    begin
 20        simple_tcp_client.send( g_sock, utl_raw.cast_to_raw(p_data) );
 21    end;
 22
 23    member procedure send_raw( p_data in raw )
 24    is
 25    begin
 26        simple_tcp_client.send( g_sock, p_data );
 27    end;
 28
 29    member procedure send( p_data in clob )
```

```
30  is
31      l_offset number default 1;
32      l_length number default dbms_lob.getlength(p_data);
33      l_amt    number default 4096;
34  begin
35      loop
36          exit when l_offset > l_length;
37          simple_tcp_client.send( g_sock,
38                  utl_raw.cast_to_raw(
39                      dbms_lob.substr(p_data,l_amt,l_offset) ) );
40          l_offset := l_offset + l_amt;
41      end loop;
42  end;
```

The SEND routine is overloaded for various data types, and takes a CLOB of arbitrary length. It will break the CLOB into 4 KB chunks for transmission. The SEND_RAW routine below is similar, but performs the operation for a BLOB:

```
43
44  member procedure send_raw( p_data in blob )
45  is
46      l_offset number default 1;
47      l_length number default dbms_lob.getlength(p_data);
48      l_amt    number default 4096;
49  begin
50      loop
51          exit when l_offset > l_length;
52          simple_tcp_client.send( g_sock,
53                  dbms_lob.substr(p_data,l_amt,l_offset) );
54          l_offset := l_offset + l_amt;
55      end loop;
56  end;
57
58  member function recv return varchar2
59  is
60      l_raw_data    raw(4096);
61  begin
62      simple_tcp_client.recv( g_sock, l_raw_data );
63      return utl_raw.cast_to_varchar2(l_raw_data);
64  end;
65
66
67  member function recv_raw return raw
68  is
69      l_raw_data    raw(4096);
70  begin
71      simple_tcp_client.recv( g_sock, l_raw_data );
72      return l_raw_data;
73  end;
74
75  member function getline( p_remove_crlf in boolean default FALSE )
76  return varchar2
77  is
78      l_raw_data    raw(4096);
79  begin
```

```
80          simple_tcp_client.getline( g_sock, l_raw_data );
81
82       if ( p_remove_crlf ) then
83           return rtrim(
84               utl_raw.cast_to_varchar2(l_raw_data), SocketType.crlf );
85       else
86           return utl_raw.cast_to_varchar2(l_raw_data);
87       end if;
88    end;
89
90    member procedure initiate_connection( p_hostname in varchar2,
91                                  p_portno    in number )
92    is
93       l_data     varchar2(4069);
94    begin
95       -- we try to connect 10 times and if the tenth time
96       -- fails, we reraise the exception to the caller
97       for i in 1 .. 10 loop
98       begin
99           g_sock := simple_tcp_client.connect_to( p_hostname, p_portno );
100          exit;
101      exception
102          when others then
103              if ( i = 10 ) then raise; end if;
104      end;
105      end loop;
106   end;
```

We try the connection ten times in order to avoid issues with 'server busy' type messages. It is not entirely necessary, but makes it so the caller doesn't get errors as often as it otherwise might on a busy web server, or some other service.

```
107
108   member procedure close_connection
109   is
110   begin
111      simple_tcp_client.disconnect( g_sock );
112      g_sock := NULL;
113   end;
114
115   end;
116   /

Type body created.
```

As you can see, these are mostly convenience routines layered on top of SIMPLE_TCP_CLIENT to make this package easier to use. It also serves as a nice way to encapsulate the functionality of the SIMPLE_TCP_CLIENT in an object type. Using SocketType instead of UTL_TCP, our simple 'get a web page via a proxy' routine looks like this:

```
tkyte@TKYTE816> declare
  2      s         SocketType := SocketType(null);
  3      buffer varchar2(4096);
  4  BEGIN
  5      s.initiate_connection( 'proxy-server', 80 );
  6      s.send( 'GET http://www.oracle.com/ HTTP/1.0'||SocketType.CRLF);
  7      s.send( SocketType.CRLF);
  8
  9      loop
 10          buffer := s.recv;
 11          exit when buffer is null;
 12          dbms_output.put_line( substr( buffer,1,255 ) );
 13      end loop;
 14      s.close_connection;
 15  END;
 16  /
HTTP/1.1 200 OK
Date: Thu, 01 Feb 2001 00:16:05 GMT
Server: Apache/1.3.9 (Unix) mod_perl/1.21
ApacheJServ/1.1
yyyyyyyyy: close
Content-Type: text/html


<head>
<title>Oracle Corporation</title>
```

This code is not radically different from using UTL_TCP directly, but it does show how encapsulating your packages with an Object Type can add a nice feeling of object-oriented programming to your PL/SQL. If you are a Java or C++ programmer, you feel very comfortable with the above code, declaring a variable of type SocketType and then calling methods against that type. This is as opposed to declaring a variable of some record type that you pass down to each routine as UTL_TCP does. The above is more object-oriented than the procedural method first shown.

Summary

In this section we looked at the new functionality provided by the UTL_TCP package. We also investigated an alternative implementation in Java. Additionally, we packaged this functionality into a new Object Type for PL/SQL, fully encapsulating the capabilities of the TCP/IP socket nicely. We saw how easy it is to integrate networking functionality into our PL/SQL applications using this facility, and in an earlier section on UTL_HTTP, we saw how we can make use of this to provide full access to the HTTP protocol.

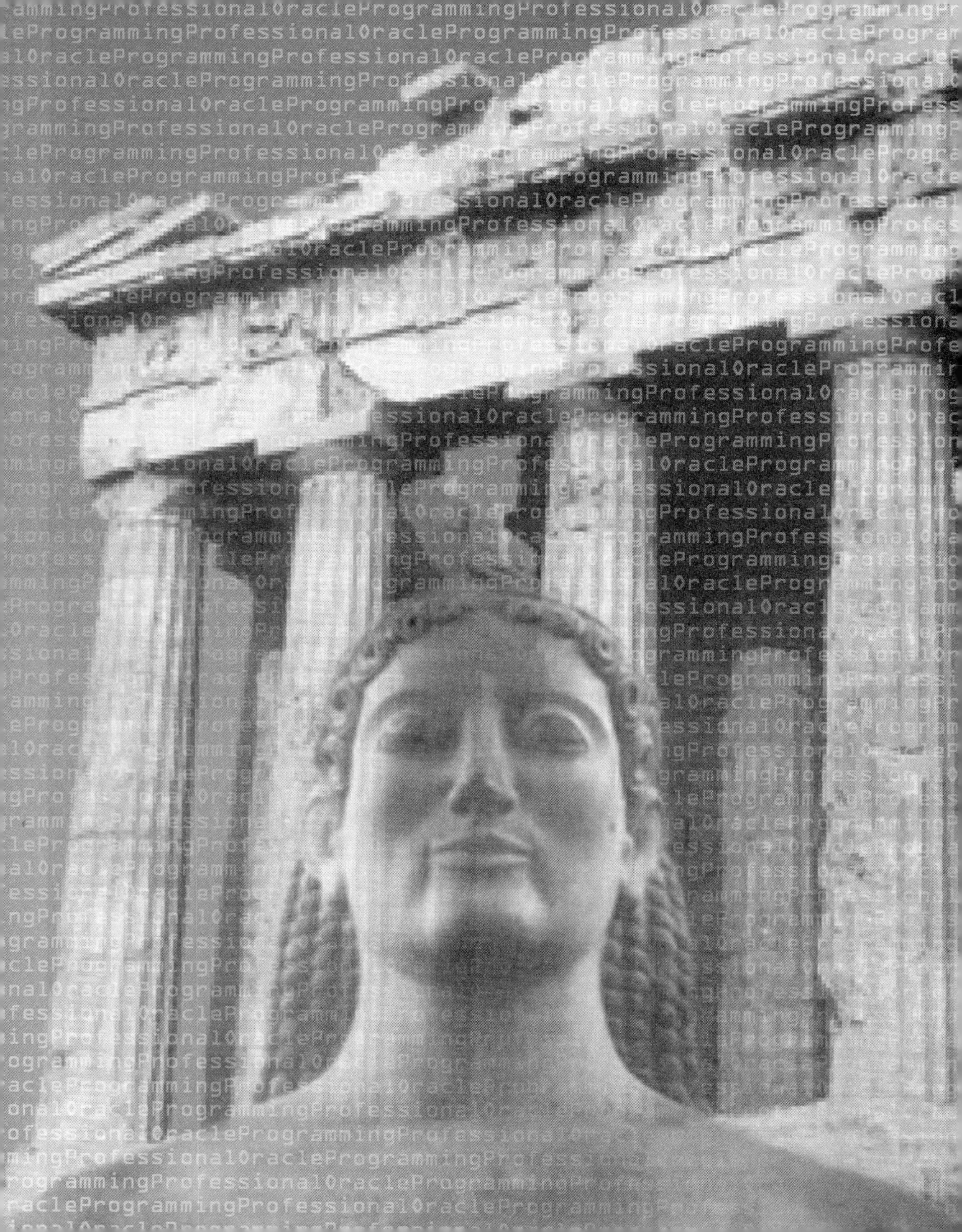

Index

A Guide to the Index

The index is arranged hierarchically, in alphabetical order, with symbols preceding the letter A. Most second-level entries and many third-level entries also occur as first-level entries. This is to ensure that users will find the information they require however they choose to search for it.

S

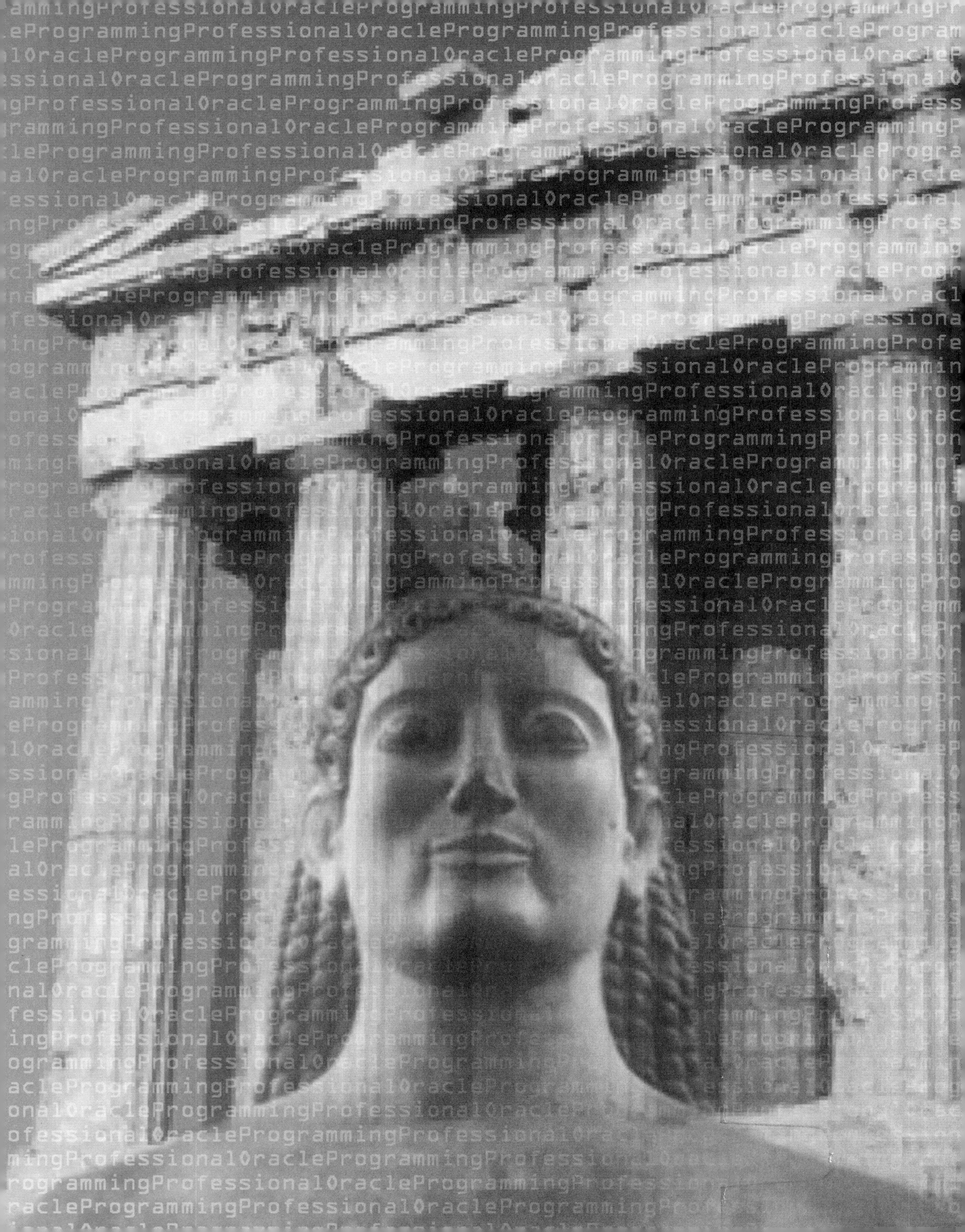